THE SYRIAC WORLD

'*The Syriac World* represents the most marvellous resource, not just for specialists in Syriac studies but also for scholars and students of global history and religion. Covering the broadest possible range of relevant topics, it brings together cutting-edge research by acknowledged experts, and succeeds in being both immensely learned and accessible. There is generous provision of maps, illustrations, and appendices, and the detailed bibliographies allow readers to pursue topics still further. A considerable achievement on the part of the editor, this volume will be an invaluable addition to private libraries as well as a must for institutions.'

– Alison G. Salvesen, *University of Oxford, UK*

This volume surveys the 'Syriac world', the culture that grew up among the Syriac-speaking communities from the second century CE and which continues to exist and flourish today, both in its original homeland of Syria and Mesopotamia, and in the worldwide diaspora of Syriac-speaking communities. The five sections examine the religion; the material, visual, and literary cultures; the history and social structures of this diverse community; and Syriac interactions with their neighbours ancient and modern. There are also appendices detailing the patriarchs of the different Syriac denominations, and another appendix listing useful online resources for students.

The Syriac World offers the first complete survey of Syriac culture and fills a significant gap in modern scholarship. This volume will be an invaluable resource to undergraduate and postgraduate students of Syriac and Middle Eastern culture from antiquity to the modern era.

Daniel King (Research Fellow, Cardiff University, UK) is a scholar of Syriac who specialises in the history of Syriac philosophy and its contribution to the progress of knowledge. His research is principally concerned with examining how the Syriac tradition adopted and adapted to its own environment the heritage of Greek Christian thought and ideas, and how it was able to translate large numbers of Greek texts into a new and distinctive idiom. He has a special interest in all aspects of the history of translation and currently works in East Africa advising and consulting on the translation of the Bible into the vernacular languages of the region.

THE ROUTLEDGE WORLDS

THE ISLAMIC WORLD
Edited by Andrew Rippin

THE WORLD OF POMPEII
Edited by Pedar W. Foss and John J. Dobbins

THE RENAISSANCE WORLD
Edited by John Jeffries Martin

THE GREEK WORLD
Edited by Anton Powell

THE ROMAN WORLD
Edited by John Wacher

THE HINDU WORLD
Edited by Sushil Mittal and Gene Thursby

THE WORLD OF THE AMERICAN WEST
Edited by Gordon Morris Bakken

THE ELIZABETHAN WORLD
Edited by Susan Doran and Norman Jones

THE OTTOMAN WORLD
Edited by Christine Woodhead

THE VICTORIAN WORLD
Edited by Marin Hewitt

THE ORTHODOX CHRISTIAN WORLD
Edited by Augustine Casiday

THE BUDDHIST WORLD
Edited by John Powers

THE ETRUSCAN WORLD
Edited by Jean MacIntosh Turfa

THE GOTHIC WORLD
Edited by Glennis Byron and Dale Townshend

THE ATLANTIC WORLD
Edited by D'Maris Coffman, Adrian Leonard, and William O'Reilly

THE POSTCOLONIAL WORLD
Edited by Jyotsna G. Singh and David D. Kim

THE SUMERIAN WORLD
Edited by Harriet Crawford

THE OCCULT WORLD
Edited by Christopher Partridge

THE WORLD OF INDIGENOUS NORTH AMERICA
Edited by Robert Warrior

THE WORLD OF THE REVOLUTIONARY AMERICAN REPUBLIC
Edited by Andrew Shankman

THE SHAKESPEAREAN WORLD
Edited by Jill L. Levenson and Robert Ormsby

THE WORLD OF COLONIAL AMERICA
Edited by Ignacio Gallup-Diaz

THE MODERNIST WORLD
Edited by Allana Lindgren and Stephen Ross

THE EARLY CHRISTIAN WORLD, SECOND EDITION
Edited by Philip F. Esler

THE SWAHILI WORLD
Edited by Stephanie Wynne-Jones and Adria LaViolette

THE SYRIAC WORLD
Edited by Daniel King

THE MEDIEVAL WORLD, SECOND EDITION
Edited by Peter Linehan, Janet L. Nelson, and Marios Costambeys

THE ELAMITE WORLD
Edited by Javier Álvarez-Mon, Gian Pietro Basello, Yasmina Wicks

For more information about this series, please visit: www.routledge.com/Routledge-Worlds/book-series/WORLDS

THE SYRIAC WORLD

Edited by

Daniel King

Routledge
Taylor & Francis Group
LONDON AND NEW YORK

First published 2019 by Routledge

2 Park Square, Milton Park, Abingdon, Oxon, OX14 4RN
605 Third Avenue, New York, NY 10017

Routledge is an imprint of the Taylor & Francis Group, an informa business

First issued in paperback 2020

British Library Cataloguing-in-Publication Data
A catalogue record for this book is available from the British Library

Library of Congress Cataloging-in-Publication Data
Names: King, Daniel, 1977– editor.
Title: The Syriac world / edited by Daniel King.
Description: First [edition]. | New York: Routledge, 2018. |
Series: Routledge worlds | Includes bibliographical references and index.
Identifiers: LCCN 2017060387 (print) | LCCN 2018019801 (ebook) |
ISBN 9781315708195 (ebook) | ISBN 9781317482123 (web pdf) |
ISBN 9781317482116 (epub) | ISBN 9781317482109 (mobi/kindle) |
ISBN 9781138899018 (hardback: alk. paper)
Subjects: LCSH: Syrians – Asia – History. | Syrians – Civilization. | Syriac Christians – History. | Syrian language – History. |
Syriac literature – History and criticism.
Classification: LCC DS28.S97 (ebook) | LCC DS28.S97 S97 2018 (print) |
DDC 950/.04923 – dc23
LC record available at https://lccn.loc.gov/2017060387

ISBN: 978-1-138-89901-8 (hbk)
ISBN: 978-0-367-73236-3 (pbk)

Typeset in Sabon
by Apex CoVantage, LLC

For Rachel

CONTENTS

List of figures xi
List of contributors xvii
Abbreviations xxv
Diachronic maps of Syriac cultures and their geographic contexts xxvii

Introduction 1
Daniel King

PART I: BACKGROUNDS 9

1 The eastern provinces of the Roman Empire in Late Antiquity 11
Muriel Debié

2 The Sasanian Empire 33
Touraj Daryaee

PART II: THE SYRIAC WORLD IN LATE ANTIQUITY 45

3 The pre-Christian religions of the Syriac-speaking regions 47
John F. Healey

4 The coming of Christianity to Mesopotamia 68
David G. K. Taylor

5 Forms of the religious life and Syriac monasticism 88
Florence Jullien

6 The establishment of the Syriac Churches 105
Volker Menze

7 The Syriac Church denominations: an overview 119
Dietmar W. Winkler

8 The Syriac world in the Persian Empire 134
Geoffrey Herman

9 Judaism and Syriac Christianity 146
Michal Bar-Asher Siegal

10 Syriac and Syrians in the later Roman Empire: questions of identity 157
Nathanael Andrade

11 Early Syriac reactions to the rise of Islam 175
Michael Penn

12 The Church of the East in the ʿAbbasid Era 189
David Wilmshurst

PART III: THE SYRIAC LANGUAGE 203

13 The Syriac language in the context of the Semitic languages 205
Holger Gzella

14 The Classical Syriac language 222
Aaron Michael Butts

15 Writing Syriac: manuscripts and inscriptions 243
Françoise Briquel-Chatonnet

16 The Neo-Aramaic dialects and their historical background 266
Geoffrey Khan

PART IV: SYRIAC LITERARY, ARTISTIC, AND MATERIAL CULTURE IN LATE ANTIQUITY 291

17 The Syriac Bible and its interpretation 293
Jonathan Loopstra

18 The emergence of Syriac literature to AD 400 309
Ute Possekel

19 Later Syriac poetry 327
Sebastian P. Brock

20 Syriac hagiographic literature 339
Jeanne-Nicole Mellon Saint-Laurent

21 The mysticism of the Church of the East 355
Adrian Pirtea

22 Theological doctrines and debates within Syriac Christianity 377
Theresia Hainthaler

23 The liturgies of the Syriac Churches 391
Fr Baby Varghese

24 Historiography in the Syriac-speaking world, 300–1000 405
Philip Wood

25 Syriac philosophy 422
John W. Watt

26 Syriac medicine 438
Grigory Kessel

27 The material culture of the Syrian peoples in Late Antiquity and the evidence for Syrian wall paintings 460
Emma Loosley

28 Churches in Syriac space: architectural and liturgical context and development 476
Widad Khoury

29 Women and children in Syriac Christianity: sounding voices 554
Susan Ashbrook Harvey

30 Syriac agriculture 350–1250 567
Michael J. Decker

PART V: SYRIAC CHRISTIANITY BEYOND THE ANCIENT WORLD 581

31 Syriac Christianity in Central Asia 583
Mark Dickens

32 Syriac Christianity in China 625
Hidemi Takahashi

33 Syriac Christianity in India 653
István Perczel

34 The renaissance of Syriac literature in the twelfth–thirteenth centuries 698
Dorothea Weltecke and Helen Younansardaroud

35 Syriac in a diverse Middle East: from the Mongol Ilkhanate to Ottoman dominance, 1286–1517 718
Thomas A. Carlson

36 The Maronite Church 731
Shafiq Abouzayd

37 The early study of Syriac in Europe 751
Robert J. Wilkinson

38 Syriac identity in the modern era 770
Heleen Murre-van den Berg

39 Changing demography: Christians in Iraq since 1991 783
Erica C. D. Hunter

Appendices 797

I The patriarchs of the Church of the East 799

II West Syrian patriarchs and maphrians 806

III Online resources for the study of the Syriac world 814

Index of Maps 824

Subject Index 835

FIGURES

1.1	Family Portrait Mosaic from Edessa	13
1.2	The Funerary Couch Mosaic, Edessa	14
1.3	The Tripod Mosaic, Edessa	15
1.4	P. Euphr. 19 (AD 242)	16
1.5	Triumph of Shapur over Valerian, Bishapur, Iran	18
1.6	Remains of the baptistery of Jacob of Nisibis	20
1.7	Map of the Diocese of the East ca. 400	23
1.8	Fresco depicting the Nativity, Deir al-Suryan, Egypt	25
2.1	Psalter Pahlavi Text on the Cross from Herat	34
2.2	Byzantine copper coin	36
2.3	Seal depicting a man before an altar and cross	38
3.1	Inscription between two figures in Pognon's Cave, Sumatar	55
3.2	Inscription from Sumatar mentioning the god Sīn	56
3.3	Funerary inscription for the governor of Birecik	60
3.4	Orpheus taming the wild animals	61
13.1	Shalman tomb inscription	214
14.1	P. Euphr. 6r	226
14.2	BL Add 12150, f.4r (dated AD 411)	228
14.3	BL Add 12150, f.53r	229
15.1	Mosaic inscription from church floor, Nabgha (AD 406–7)	246
15.2	Basufan inscription (Jabal Semʿan, Syria)	247
15.3	Mulanthuruthy inscription (Kerala, India)	250
15.4	Serto script (Ms Charfet Raḥmani 38)	256
15.5	Oriental script (DFM 44)	257
15.6	Keralese script (SEERI, Kottayam, Kerala 18)	258
15.7	Serto manuscript in Charfet with Greek vowels	259
15.8	Script as ornament at Mar Behnam Monastery, Mosul	262
16.1	Map of North-Eastern Neo-Aramaic and Central Neo-Aramaic dialect areas	267
17.1	Sample texts from Numbers 8:16–11:27 in the West Syrian 'Masora' (BL Add. MS 17162, fol. 10v)	305

26.1	The beginning of the Syriac and Arabic versions of Hippocrates's Aphorisms (BNF arabe 6734, fol. 29v., dated 1205)	443
26.2	Ḥunayn, *Questions on Medicine for Students* (Vat. sir. 192, f.129v)	445
26.3	Galen, *On Simple Drugs* (BL Add. 14661, f.32v–33r)	450
26.4	*Book on the Characteristics of Animals* (BL Or. 2784, f.2v)	454
27.1	Edessene funerary mosaic, Şanliurfa Museum, Turkey	463
27.2	Crucifixion from the Rabbula gospels	464
27.3	Amazonian Queen, Villa of the Amazons, Şanliurfa, Turkey	465
27.4	The Last Judgement, west wall, Deir Mar Musa al-Habashi, Nebek, Syria	469
27.5	Jonah and the Whale, Church of St Sergius, Sadad, Syria	472
28.1	Main routes of Byzantine Syria, and location of the Limestone Massif	477
28.2a	Church of Maʾramaya, southern façade and baptistery at the eastern extremity of the portico	480
28.2b	Lintel with three cross motifs	480
28.2c	Detail of the Greek cross of the central motif showing Greek characters	480
28.3a	Church of Maʾramaya, eastern façade	481
28.3b	Syriac inscription from the sixth century carved on a block of the facade	481
28.4a	Church of Maʾramaya, Arabic Christian inscription carved on the lintel of the baptistery	482
28.4b	Arabic Christian inscription 'In the Name of the Father and the Son and the Holy Spirit'	482
28.4c	Chrism motif carved in the centre of the baptistery lintel	482
28.5a	Plan of the Domus Ecclesiae	485
28.5b	Isometric view of the Domus Ecclesiae	485
28.6	Distribution of painted scenes inside the Domus Ecclesiae	486
28.7a	Baptismal font against the western wall of the Domus Ecclesiae	486
28.7b	The good Pastor and, below, Adam and Eve after the fall	486
28.8a	The healing of the paralytic	487
28.8b	Christ walking on the water	487
28.8c	The holy women at the tomb holding torches	488
28.8d	Samaritan woman near the well	488
28.9a	Plan of the Church of the Holy Sepulchre, Jerusalem	490
28.9b	Plan of the Church of the Nativity, Bethlehem	490
28.9c	Hypothetical reconstruction of the octagon of the 'Domus Aurea' in Antioch	490
28.10a	Archaeological regions of Syria	492
28.10b	Toponymy of the Limestone Massif	493
28.10c	Distribution of inhabited locations in the Limestone Massif in Late Antiquity	494
28.11	The church of Julianos established in a Roman temple	495
28.12a	Hūarte church	496
28.12b	Detail of the Mithraeum fresco beneath the church of Phocas	496
28.13a	Ecclesial complex of Banassara	497

28.13b Ecclesial complex of Fassūq 497
28.14a Fourth-century single-nave church, Bānaqfūr 498
28.14b Ma'aramāyā 499
28.14c Qirkbīze 499
28.15a Single-nave chapel, Sūrqānya (sixth century), southern façade 500
28.15b Single-nave chapel, Deiruné 500
28.16a Darqita, St Paul and Moses Church of Markianos 501
28.16b Ksēğbe, Church of Markianos 501
28.16c Babisqa, Church of Markianos 502
28.17a, b, c Decorated capitals from Markianos's church of Ksēğbe 502
28.18a Western façade and narthex of the western church at Baqirḥa 504
28.18b Eastern façade of the western church at Baqirḥa 505
28.18c Lintel with Syriac and Greek inscriptions on the western door of the western church at Baqirḥa 505
28.19 General plan of the monastery complex of Qalʿat Semʿān 506
28.20 Ṭurīn, western church II with T-shaped pillars 507
28.21 Partially enclosed apse of the southern church of Bānqūsa 507
28.22a, b Projecting apse, Qalblōze 508
28.22c Interior of projecting apse, Qalblōze 509
28.23 Three prominent apses of the eastern basilica, Qalʿat Semʿān 510
28.24 Ecclesial ensemble with three basilicas, al-Ruhaiyah 511
28.25a Tripartite eastern church, Ḥalabiyye 512
28.25b Tripartite central church, Palmyra 512
28.26a Lateral buttresses carrying the nave of the Holy Cross Basilica, Reṣafa 513
28.26b Rectilinear chevet in al-Rouhbane church, Ḥawarīn 514
28.27 Different forms of chevet in southern Syria 515
28.28 Aerial view of the northern church, Ḥīt 515
28.29 The cross-shaped church of Saint Babylas, Antioch-Qausiye 516
28.30a The cross-shaped church of the Martyrium, Qalʿat Semʿān 517
28.30b Eastern basilica of the Martyrium, Qalʿat Semʿān 517
28.31a South-western façade of the Martyrium, Deir Seta 518
28.31b South-eastern façade of the Martyrium, Deir Seta 518
28.32a Archangels's Church, Fa'lūl 519
28.32b Apamea Cathedral 519
28.32c Martyrium of Seleuceia Pieri 520
28.33a Bosra Cathedral 521
28.33b Church of St George, Ezra' 521
28.34a Bêma facing the apse at Kafr Daret Azzeh church 522
28.34b The bêma of Kirkbisé church 523
28.34c Throne of the bêma at Kirkbisé 524
28.34d Axonometric view of the church at Kalota 524
28.34e Reconstruction of the bêma of the Holy Cross Church, Reṣafa 525
28.34f Schematic presentation of three variants of the bêma 525
28.35a Tell Hassake church with shqaqonā and ambon 526
28.35b Detail of the circular ambon 527
28.35c, d, e, f Decorated capitals of Tell Hassake church 527

28.36 Parallels between the spatial organisation and the liturgy of mediaeval Mesopotamian churches and the ancient churches of northern Syria 530
28.37a Church of Mar Yaqub, western façade 531
28.37b Mar Yaqub, details of a lintel 531
28.38a Mor ʿAzozoyel, Keferzi 532
28.38b Mor Yaʿqub, Ṣalaḥ 532
28.38c Mor Aloho, Hab 532
28.39a Plan of the church of Bazian 533
28.39b General view of Bazian church 534
28.39c Shqaqona Tell Hassakeh church 534
28.39d Shqaqona of central church at Palmyra 535
28.40a The Chaldaean scheme of the Syriac Church 536
28.40b The Orthodox and Catholic scheme of the Syriac Church 536
28.41a Monastery of Mar Behnam near Mosul 537
28.41b Martyrion of Mar Behnam near Mosul 537
28.41c Church of El-Ḥira XI 538
28.41d Church of El-Tahira, Mosul 538
28.42a Church of Kilwa 539
28.42b Church of Kilwa plan 540
28.43 View of the hermitage of Centum Putea near Bir Jazal 541
28.44 The church of al-Qoussour 542
28.45a Church of Mar Touma of Beloulan 543
28.45b Church of Mart Maryam 543
28.46a Schematic plan of the Syriac Church in Kerala 544
28.46b Church of Kudamaloor 545
28.47 Ensemble of Ak Beshim (8th to 11th centuries) 546
31.1 Inscriptions from Urgut, showing two occurrences of the name Sargis 592
31.2 Inscription and cross from Urgut 592
31.3 Inscriptions with crosses from Urgut 593
31.4 Persian inscription in Syriac script from Urgut 593
31.5 Sogdian translation of Nicene Creed from Turfan, with Syriac rubric 595
31.6 Syriac liturgical text from Turfan 595
31.7 Bilingual Syriac-Sogdian lectionary from Turfan 596
31.8 Middle Persian psalter from Turfan 596
31.9 Syriac Legend of Mar Barshabba from Turfan 597
31.10 Syriac baptismal service, with instructions to the priest in Sogdian from Turfan 598
31.11 Graffiti in Syriac and Uyghur on blank side of folio from Syriac Hudra from Turfan 598
31.12 Bilingual Syriac-Persian psalter from Turfan 599
31.13 Psalm 148:1–3, with verses written in reverse order from Turfan 599
31.14 Christian wedding blessing, Uyghur in Syriac script, from Turfan 600

31.15	Wall painting from a ruined church building in Qocho, Turfan, probably showing a Christian priest and three female worshippers (now located in the Museum für Asiatische Kunst, Berlin)	600
31.16	Silk painting from Dunhuang of a possible Christian figure wearing a pectoral cross and a crown/headdress with a cross	601
31.17	Gravestone from Kyrgyzstan	611
32.1	Xi'an Stele	627
32.2	Xi'an Stele donor statement	628
32.3	Luoyang Pillar	630
32.4	Luoyang Pillar detail	631
32.5	Luoyang Pillar detail	631
32.6	Rubbing of the inscription from the Luoyang Pillar	632
32.7	Newly-Discovered Inscription in the White Pagoda near Hohhot	639
32.8	Syriac inscription with the words of Psalm 125 (124):2 at Ulaan Tolgoi	642
33.1	Pilgrimage to the Mount of Malayathur, for venerating the footsteps of Saint Thomas imprinted in a rock	657
33.2	Pilgrimage to the Mount of Malayathur	658
33.3	An early statue of Christ, probably from the second half of the sixteenth-first decades of the seventeenth century	659
33.4	Participants in the feast of Mor Baselios Yaldo in Kothamangalam, 2 October 2007	662
33.5a, b, c	Plate 2/2, 5/1 and 5/2 of the Kollam copper plates	668
33.6	One of the Persian crosses in Kottayam	672
33.7	The Muttuchira Persian cross	673
33.8	The Persian cross of Kadamattam	674
33.9	The Kumari-muṭṭam inscription, currently kept in the Padmanabhapuram Palace Museum in Tamil Nadu	676
33.10	Traditional decorative motifs: monkeys holding a baptismal font, Kanjoor	677
33.11	Traditional decorative motifs: worshipping angel from the pedestal of a cross, Koratthy	678
33.12	The tombs of the Pakalomaṭṭam archdeacons in Kuravilangad	679
33.13	St George Jacobite Church, Kadamattam, where Mar Denḥā resided in his last years	681
33.14	A granite plaque inscribed in Syriac and Malayalam, commemorating the finding of Mār Denḥā's bones in 1990, in the southern wall of the church	682
33.15	Ruins of the Portuguese fort at Kodungallur/Cranganore	683
33.16	Ruins of the Jesuit seminary at Vaipicotta/Chennamangalam	684
33.17	First pages of Mar Abraham's personal copy of the Nomocanon of Abdisho	685
33.18	First page of the extant copy of the Church Statutes of Francisco Roz, written in Malayalam, in Garshuni Malayalam characters, in 1607	686
33.19	St Mary's Orthodox Church in Thiruvithamcode, Tamil Nadu. View from the South	687

33.20 Bas-relief in granite above the entry of the Thiruvithamcode church. It represents the adoration of the Holy Sacrament, a Roman Catholic devotional practice introduced by the Portuguese 687
33.21 Upper part of the open-air cross in Korathy, with Syriac inscriptions 688
36.1 Deir Mar Elisha, Qadisha Valley 732
37.1 Editio Princeps of the Syriac New Testament 1555 752
37.2 Page from the Editio Princeps showing Hebrews Chapter 1 753
37.3 Guillaume Postel 754
37.4 The Sephirotic Tree 755
37.5 Amira's Grammar 757
37.6 Tremellius's Grammar 761
39.1 Easter Sunday breakfast at St George's Church, Dora, Baghdad 785
39.2 Thirteenth century doorway, Mar Behnam monastery 792
39.3 Enthronement of Mar Giwargis III, patriarch of the Assyrian Church of the East, 2015 793
39.4 Easter celebrations at Qaraqoche 794

CONTRIBUTORS

Shafiq Abouzayd of The Oriental Institute, University of Oxford, UK, is Chairman of the ARAM Society for Syro-Mesopotamian Studies and editor of the *ARAM Periodical*. He is also a priest in the Maronite Church.

Nathanael Andrade is an associate professor of ancient history in the Department of History at Binghamton University (SUNY), USA. His books include *Syrian Identity in the Greco-Roman World* (2013) and *The Journey of Christianity to India in Late Antiquity: Networks and the Movement of Culture* (2018). He has also published numerous articles and chapters on the Roman Near East, the city of Palmyra, Late Antique Christianity, and Roman contact with central, south, and east Asia.

Françoise Briquel-Chatonnet is Senior Researcher in Centre national de la Recherche Scientifique, France. She is a specialist of the Levant in the first millennium BC as well as of Syriac culture and texts. Her main focus is on script and writing, inscriptions, and manuscripts. Her main publications are *Manuscrits syriaques. Bibliothèque nationale de France (manuscrits entrés depuis 1911, nos 356–435). Aix-en-Provence, bibliothèque Méjanes. Lyon, bibliothèque municipale. Strasbourg, Bibliothèque nationale et universitaire. Catalogue* (1997); *Recueil des inscriptions syriaques*. Vol. 1. *Kérala* (with A. Desreumaux and J. Thekeparampil, 2008); and (with M. Debié), *Le monde syriaque. Sur les routes d'un christianisme ignoré* (2017).

Sebastian P. Brock is Emeritus Reader in Syriac Studies and Emeritus Fellow of Wolfson College, Oxford, UK. His main research interests lie in Syriac literature, including translations from Greek, in the pre-Islamic period. Publications include *The Luminous Eye: The Spiritual World Vision of St Ephrem*; *A Brief Outline of Syriac Literature*; and four volumes in the Variorum Reprints; he is the editor and main author of *The Hidden Pearl: The Syrian Orthodox Church and Its Ancient Aramaic Heritage*.

Aaron Michael Butts is Assistant Professor in the Department of Semitic and Egyptian Languages and Literatures at the Catholic University of America, USA. He specialises in the languages, literatures, and histories of Christianity in the Near East, including Arabic, Ethiopic, and especially Syriac. He recently published *Language Change in the Wake of Empire: Syriac in Its Greco-Roman Context*

(2016) and (with Simcha Gross) *The History of the 'Slave of Christ': From Jewish Child to Christian Martyr* (2016). He is also associate editor of *Aramaic Studies.*

Thomas A. Carlson is Assistant Professor of Middle Eastern History at Oklahoma State University, USA. He researches the social and cultural dynamics of religious diversity and change in the pre-modern Middle East. His *Christianity in Fifteenth-Century Iraq* (2018) explores what it meant to be Christian in a late mediaeval 'Islamic' society, including social relationships across religious boundaries, and the theological, ritual, hierarchical, and historical dimensions of belonging. His next book will explore Islamisation over the period 1000–1500 CE.

Touraj Daryaee is the Maseeh Chair in Persian Studies and the Director of the Dr. Samuel M. Jordan Center for Persian Studies at the University of California, Irvine, USA. He works on the history of ancient Iran and Zoroastrianism. His latest book is the *King of Seven Climes* (2017). He is also the editor of the *Oxford Handbook of Iranian History*, 2012, as well as *Sasanian Persia: The Rise and Fall of an Empire* (2009).

Muriel Debié is Professor of Eastern Christianities at the École Pratique des Hautes Études in Paris (EPHE-Sorbonne, Paris Sciences et Lettres), France, and was in residence in the United States as a Fellow at the Institute for Advanced Studies in Princeton while writing this chapter. She is a specialist of Late Antique Studies, especially Syriac, more particularly Syriac historiography. She is author (with F. Briquel-Chatonnet) of *Le monde syriaque. Sur les routes d'un christianisme ignoré* (2017).

Michael J. Decker is Maroulis Professor of Byzantine History and Orthodox Religion at the University of South Florida, USA. He writes on the economy and society of the Late Antique and mediaeval Near East. Major publications include *The Byzantine Dark Ages* (2016), *The Byzantine Art of War* (2013), and *Life and Society in Byzantine Cappadocia* (with J. E. Cooper, 2012).

Mark Dickens is a cultural historian of Central Asia and the Middle East who specialises in the interaction between Syriac Christianity and the inhabitants of Central Eurasia (particularly the Turkic peoples) in Late Antiquity and the Middle Ages. He has co-authored a catalogue of Syriac manuscripts from Turfan and published articles on the Church of the East, Syriac gravestones and other inscriptions from Central Asia, various Christian texts from Turfan, and extracts from Syriac Chronicles on interactions with Turkic peoples.

Holger Gzella is Professor of Hebrew and Aramaic at Leiden University, the Netherlands. He focuses on the historical-comparative study of Hebrew and Aramaic in its linguistic and cultural environment, especially the evolution of Aramaic as a scribal language from the Ancient Near East to Late Antiquity. Most recently, he wrote *A Cultural History of Aramaic* (2015) and edited the Aramaic volume of the *Theological Dictionary of the Old Testament* (2016).

Theresia Hainthaler is Honorary Professor for Christology of the Early Church and theology of the Christian East, Philosophisch-Theologische Hochschule Sankt Georgen, Frankfurt, Germany. Since 1994, she has led the project 'Christ in Christian Tradition' founded by the late Aloys Grillmeier SJ (1910–1998), a collaborator and co-author since 1986. She was editor and reviser of the *Christ in Christian Tradition* volumes and of their English, French, and Italian translations. She has been involved in many ecumenical dialogues with the Syriac Churches, with the Assyrian Church of the East, and with Eastern Orthodoxy. Her numerous publications, besides the *Christ in Christian Tradition* volumes, include *Christliche Araber vor dem Islam* (2007); *Wiener Patristische Tagungen* IV–VII; *Einheit und Katholizität der Kirche* (2009); *Heiligkeit und Apostolizität der Kirche* (2010); *Für uns und für unser Heil. Soteriologie in Ost und West* (2014); and *Sophia. The Wisdom of God – Die Weisheit Gottes* (2017).

Susan Ashbrook Harvey is Willard Prescott and Annie McClelland Smith Professor of Religion and History at Brown University, USA. She specialises in Syriac and Byzantine Christianity, and her scholarship has ranged widely across issues of women, embodiment, and lay piety, studied in contexts of asceticism, monasticism, hagiography, liturgy, hymnography, and domestic and civic religion. Most recently she co-edited with Margaret Mullett *Knowing Bodies, Passionate Souls: Sense Perception in Byzantium* (2017). Her major monograph, *Scenting Salvation: Ancient Christianity and the Olfactory Imagination*, was reissued in paperback in 2015.

John F. Healey is Professor Emeritus at the University of Manchester, UK. His research has focused upon Aramaic and Syriac Epigraphy; the history of the alphabet; and religion in the Roman-Period Near East. His numerous publications include *The Nabataean Tomb Inscriptions of Mada'in Salih* (1993), *The Religion of the Nabataeans* (2001), *Aramaic Inscriptions and Documents of the Roman Period* (2009), and, with H.J.W. Drijvers, *The Old Syriac Inscriptions of Edessa and Osrhoene* (1999).

Geoffrey Herman is a researcher at the Scholion Mandel Interdisciplinary Research Center in the Humanities and Jewish Studies, Hebrew University of Jerusalem, Israel. His research focuses on the interaction between Jews, Christians, and Zoroastrians in the Sasanian Empire. He has published extensively on the history of religious life in the Sasanian era. Among his recent publications are *A Prince without a Kingdom: The Exilarch in the Sasanian Era* (2012); *Jews, Christians and Zoroastrians: Religious Dynamics in a Sasanian Context* (2014); and *Persian Martyr Acts under King Yazdgird I* (2016).

Erica C. D. Hunter is Head and Senior Lecturer in Eastern Christianity, and also co-chair of the Centre of World Christianity, at the School of Oriental and African Studies, UK. She has a particular interest in the heritage of Christianity in Iraq. Between 2004 and 2013 she convened the highly successful annual Christianity in Iraq Seminar Day series. She is the editor of *The Christian Heritage of Iraq: Collected Papers from the Christianity of Iraq I-V Seminar Days.*

Florence Jullien is a researcher at the CNRS, France. She specialises in the study of Syriac Christianity and monasticism in the East. She has notably published *Apôtres des confins. Processus missionnaires chrétiens dans l'empire iranien* (*Res Orientales* 15) in 2002, as well as the following volumes in the CSCO: *Les Actes de Mâr Mâri. Aux origines de l'Eglise de Perse* (2003), *Le monachisme en Perse. La réforme d'Abraham le Grand, père des moines de l'Orient* (2008), and *L'Histoire de Mār Abba, catholicos de l'Orient. Martyres de Mār Grigor et de Mār Yazd-panāh* (2015).

She has also edited *Les Monachismes d'Orient* (2011) and *Eastern Christianity: a Crossroads of Cultures* (2012), as well as many articles on these problems.

Grigory Kessel is Research Fellow at the Division of Byzantine Research of the Institute for Medieval Research, Austrian Academy of Sciences, Austria, and Research Fellow at the School of Arts, Languages and Cultures, University of Manchester, UK. He specialises in the study of the literary heritage of Syriac Christianity with particular attention to its manuscript tradition. Besides manuscripts, his publications deal with Syriac medical and monastic texts, as well as bibliographic research. He is a participant in a number of cataloguing projects, including the Sinai Palimpsest Project and those of the Hill Museum and Manuscript Library. At present he is a principal investigator on the European Research Council Starting Grant Project, Transmission of Classical Scientific and Philosophical Literature from Greek into Syriac and Arabic, and holds a Wellcome Trust Research Fellowship in Humanities for an editorial project, The 'Syriac Epidemics' – Reception and Transmission of Classical Medicine in the East.

Geoffrey Khan is Regius Professor of Hebrew at the University of Cambridge, UK. His research interests include various fields of Semitic philology. His book publications include studies of Neo-Aramaic dialects, mediaeval traditions of Biblical Hebrew, and Arabic papyrology. He is conducting a major project that aims to document the endangered North-Eastern Neo-Aramaic dialects, some outcomes of which include his books *A Grammar of Neo-Aramaic. The Dialect of the Jews of Arbel* (Brill, Leiden, 1999), *The Neo-Aramaic Dialect of Qaraqosh* (2002), *The Jewish Neo-Aramaic Dialect of Sulemaniyya and Ḥalabja* (2004), *The Neo-Aramaic Dialect of Barwar. 3 vols. Vol. 1 Grammar. Vol. 2 Lexicon. Vol. 3 Texts.* (2008), *The Jewish Neo-Aramaic Dialect of Urmi* (Gorgias, Piscataway, 2008), *The Jewish Neo-Aramaic Dialect of Sanandaj* (2009), and *The Neo-Aramaic Dialect of the Assyrian Christians of Urmi. 4 vols. Vol. 1 Grammar: Phonology and Morphology. Vol. 2 Grammar: Syntax. Vol. 3 Lexical Studies and Dictionary. Vol. 4 Texts.* (2016).

Widad Khoury is Scientific Director of Archaeological Missions, DGAM, Damascus, Syria. She holds a degree in architectural engineering from the Faculty of Civil Engineering, Damascus. She has worked at the Aga Khan Foundation and has taught at the Department of Architecture as well as conducting Syrian archaeological missions at the Department of Excavations and Archaeological Studies, DGAM, Damascus. She has published a variety of articles on the ecclesiastical architecture of Late Antique Syria.

Daniel King is formerly Lecturer, now Research Fellow, in Syriac Studies and Semitic Languages, Cardiff University, UK. His research is principally concerned with examining how the Syriac tradition adopted and adapted to its own environment the heritage of Greek Christian thought and ideas, and how it was able to translate large numbers of Greek texts into a new and distinctive idiom. He has published an edition of *The Earliest Syriac Translation of Aristotle's Categories* (2010). He has a special interest in all aspects of the history of translation and currently works in East Africa.

Jonathan Loopstra teaches and researches in the fields of Early Christianity and the religious culture of the Near East, with a particular focus on Syriac-speaking

Christianity. His publications include *Job: The Syriac Peshitta Bible with English Translation* (2016) and *An East Syrian Manuscript of the Syriac 'Masora' Dated to 899 CE* (2014–2015). He received a PhD from The Catholic University of America, a Master of Studies from Oxford University in Syriac Studies, and a Master of Arts in Church History from Trinity Evangelical Divinity School.

Emma Loosley is Associate Professor of Theology and Religion at the University of Exeter, UK. She researches the relationship between early Middle Eastern, particularly Syrian, Christianity and its material culture, with a special interest in how early ritual shaped ecclesiastical architecture. She is currently exploring the relationship between Syria and Georgia in Late Antiquity in order to understand the diffusion of Syrian culture northwards into the Caucasus. Her works on later and contemporary Christian issues and publications include *The Architecture and Liturgy of the Bema in Fourth- to Sixth-Century Syrian Churches* (2012), *Messiah and Mahdi: Caucasian Christians and the Construction of Safavid Isfahan* (2009), and (edited with Anthony O'Mahony) *Christian Responses to Islam and Muslim-Christian Relations in the Modern World* (2008), *Eastern Christianity in the Modern Middle East* (Routledge, 2009).

Volker Menze is Director of the Center for Eastern Mediterranean Studies and Associate Professor in the Department of Medieval Studies at Central European University, Hungary. He works on Late Antique ecclesiastical, political, and religious history, and has published *Justinian and the Making of the Syrian Orthodox Church* (Oxford University Press, 2008) and, together with Kutlu Akalın, *John of Tella's Profession of Faith: The Legacy of a Sixth-Century Syrian Orthodox Bishop* (2009).

David A. Michelson is Associate Professor of the History of Christianity at Vanderbilt University, USA. He is the author of *The Practical Christology of Philoxenos of Mabbug* (2015) and is currently preparing a monograph on the theology of reading in Syriac asceticism. He is the general editor of *Syriaca.org: The Syriac Reference Portal* and co-editor, with Thomas A. Carlson, of *The Syriac Gazetteer*, an online geographical dictionary of Syriac places.

Heleen Murre-van den Berg is Professor of Eastern Christian Studies and Director of the Institute of Eastern Christian Studies, Radboud University Nijmegen, and Director of NOSTER (Netherlands School for Advanced Studies in Theology and Religion). She teaches and publishes in the field of Eastern Christian Studies, with a special interest in the Syriac tradition from 1500 onwards. Among her recent publications are a monograph, *Scribes and Scriptures: The Church of the East in the Eastern Ottoman Provinces (1500–1850)* (2015), and an edited volume (with S. R. Goldstein-Sabbah), *Modernity, Minority, and the Public Sphere: Jews and Christians in the Middle East* (2016).

Michael Penn is Teresa Hihn Moore Professor of Religious Studies and Classics at Stanford University. He researches Syriac Christian reactions to Islam, computer-assisted paleography, and Syriac manuscript culture. Penn's first book, *Kissing Christians: Ritual and Community in the Late Ancient Church*, was published in 2005 by the University of Pennsylvania Press. In 2015 he published two books on Christian-Muslim relations: *Envisioning Islam: Syriac Christians in the Early Muslim World* and *When Christians First Met Muslims: A Source Book of the Earliest Syriac Writings on Islam*.

István Perczel is professor of Byzantine and Eastern Christian studies in the Department of Medieval Studies at Central European University, Hungary. He has researched extensively on Neoplatonist and Patristic philosophy (especially the pseudo-Dionysian corpus) and on Malayalam texts. In 2000 he initiated the digitisation and cataloguing of the manuscript collections of the Saint Thomas Christians of Kerala, finally allowing scholars to write the history of these Indian communities. His publications include a co-edited volume, *The Eucharist in Theology and Philosophy* (2005); *The Nomocanon of Metropolitan Abdisho of Nisibis: A Facsimile Edition of MS 64 from the Collection of the Church of the East in Thrissur* (2009); *The Hymns of Divine Loves of Symeon the New Theologian* (in Hungarian: 2010); a co-edited volume, *Christianity in Asia: Sacred Art and Visual Splendour* (2016); a series of studies on the pseudo-Dionysian corpus, Origenism, and Neoplatonism and also on Indian Christianity and the Indian manuscript collections, including 'Classical Syriac as a Modern *lingua franca* in South India between 1600 and 2006' (2009); and 'Garshuni Malayalam: A Witness to an Early Stage of Indian Christian Literature' (2014). The material digitised in India will be published online by Hill Museum and Manuscript Library, Collegeville, USA, and the catalogues are forthcoming.

Adrian Pirtea has recently completed his PhD in Byzantine Studies at the Freie Universität Berlin, Germany, with a thesis on the 'spiritual senses' in Greek and Syriac Christian mysticism. His main research interests include Classical Byzantine and Syriac literature, Oriental Christian mysticism, philosophy and science in Late Antiquity, Gnosis, and Manichaeism. He has held research fellowships at the Warburg Institute (London) and the École des hautes études en sciences sociales (Paris), and has published several articles in the field of Patristic Studies.

Ute Possekel is Lecturer in Syriac at Harvard Divinity School, USA. She is author of *Evidence of Greek Philosophical Concepts in the Writings of Ephrem the Syrian* (1999) and has published articles on diverse topics in Syriac Christianity, especially on Ephrem and Bardaiṣan. She is currently editing the treatises of Thomas of Edessa.

Jeanne-Nicole Mellon Saint-Laurent is Assistant Professor of Historical Theology at Marquette University, USA. She is the author of *Missionary Stories and the Formation of the Syriac Churches* (2015) and, with Kyle Smith, of *The History of Mar Behnam and Sarah: Martyrdom and Monasticism in Medieval Iraq* (2018). She is also a co-editor of *Qadishe* and the *Bibliotheca Hagiographica Syriaca Electronica*, two databases on Syriac saints and their lives (www.syriaca.org/q/index.html; www.syriaca.org/bhse/index.html).

Michal Bar-Asher Siegal holds the Rosen Family Career Development Chair in Judaic Studies at The Goldstein-Goren Department of Jewish Thought, Ben-Gurion University of the Negev, Israel. A scholar of rabbinic Judaism, her work focuses on aspects of Jewish-Christian interactions in the ancient world. Her book *Early Christian Monastic Literature and the Babylonian Talmud* (2013) compared Christian monastic and rabbinic sources. She has also published on topics such as the Syriac version of Ben Sira, the Mishnah, and tannaitic Midrashim. Her forthcoming book will focus on narratives of heretics in the Babylonian Talmud.

Hidemi Takahashi is Professor at the Graduate School of Arts and Sciences, University of Tokyo, Japan. He is a researcher in Syriac Studies. His publications include

Aristotelian Meteorology in Syriac: Barhebraeus, Butyrum sapientiae, Books of Mineralogy and Meteorology (2003), and *Barhebraeus: A Bio-Bibliography* (2005), in addition to papers on the history of Christianity in China.

David G. K. Taylor is Associate Professor of Aramaic and Syriac in the Oriental Institute at the University of Oxford and a fellow of Wolfson College, UK. His primary research interests are in Syriac language, history, and literature; Aramaic dialects; and multilingualism and diglossia in the Late Antique Near East. He is currently working on new editions of the Old Syriac Gospels, and is completing the first two volumes of an edition of the sixth-century Syriac psalm commentary of Daniel of Ṣalaḥ.

Fr Baby Varghese is Professor of Syriac and Liturgical Studies at the Orthodox Theological Seminary, Kottayam, India, and Saint Ephrem's Ecumenical Research Institute (SEERI). He is also Priest of the Malankara Orthodox Syrian Church, Kottayam. He researches in the fields of the History and Theology of Syriac Liturgy and the History and Christology of the Syriac Churches. His publications include *Les onctions baptismales dans la tradition syrienne* (1989), *West Syrian Liturgical Theology* (2004), *The Anaphora of St James: History and Theology* (2016), together with numerous translations of Syriac liturgical commentaries by Moses Bar Kepha, Dionysius Bar Salibi, John of Dara, patriarch John I, George Bishop of the Arabs, and the Nomocanon of Bar Hebraeus.

John W. Watt is Honorary Research Fellow at Cardiff University, UK. His research interests in Syriac literature cover both its Late Antique and later phases, with a particular focus on the impact of Greek culture in the Syriac sphere. Among his publications are the commentary on Aristotle's Rhetoric by Bar Hebraeus, published as *Aristotelian Rhetoric in Syriac: Bar Hebraeus, Butyrum Sapientiae, Book of Rhetoric* (2005), and, with Frank Trombley, *The Chronicle of Pseudo-Joshua the Stylite* (2000). Several of his articles are collected in his *Rhetoric and Philosophy from Greek into Syriac* (2010).

Dorothea Weltecke is Professor of Mediaeval History II, Goethe-Universität Frankfurt, Germany, having previously held the Chair in Mediaeval History at the University of Konstanz. She specialises in the comparative history of religious diversity, the history of the Latin and Oriental churches, and the history of religious deviance. Her main publications include *Die «Beschreibung der Zeiten» von Mōr Michael dem Großen (1126–1199)* (Peeters, 2003), *«Der Narr spricht: Es ist kein Gott». Atheismus, Unglauben und Glaubenszweifel vom 12. Jahrhundert bis zur Neuzeit* (Campus-Verlag 2010), *Geschichte, Theologie, Liturgie und Gegenwartslage der syrischen Kirchen* (ed., Harrassowitz, 2012), and (with Johannes Pahlitzsch and Michael Marx) *Östliches Christentum in Geschichte und Gegenwart* (ed., special issue of *Der Islam*, 2011).

Robert J. Wilkinson was formerly Research Fellow of Wesley College, Bristol, and visiting Fellow in Theology at Bristol University, both UK. He specialises in early European Syriac studies. In addition to several articles, in 2007 he published a pair of monographs in this field: *Orientalism, Aramaic and Kabbalah in the Catholic Reformation* and *The Kabbalistic Scholars of the Antwerp Polyglot Bible*. His most recent monograph, *Tetragrammaton: Western Christians and the Hebrew Name of God*, was published in 2015.

David Wilmshurst was Academic Editor at the Chinese University of Hong Kong from 2008 until his retirement in July 2016. He is an ecclesiastical historian, with a particular interest in the history of the Church of the East. His main publications include *The Ecclesiastical Organisation of the Church of the East, 1318–1913* (2000), *The Martyred Church: A History of the Church of the East* (2011), and *Bar Hebraeus, The Ecclesiastical History: An English Translation* (2016).

Dietmar W. Winkler is Professor of Patristic Studies and Ecclesiastical History and the Director of the Center for the Study of the Christian East at the University of Salzburg, Austria. He specialises in the heritage of the Christian East which includes the Greek, Syriac, Coptic, and Armenian traditions and combines knowledge of patristic texts with a close familiarity with current ecumenical thinking and developments in dialogue. Among others, he is the editor of the Pro Oriente Studies in Syriac Tradition. His latest books include *Winds of Jingjiao. Studies in Syriac Christianity in China and Central Asia* (ed. with Li Tang, 2016) and (ed.) *Syrische Studien* (2016).

Philip Wood is Associate Professor at the Institute for the Study of Muslim Civilisations, Aga Khan University, UK, where he teaches History. He researches Christians in the Middle East c. 400–900. He has written two monographs: *We Have No King but Christ. Christian political thought on the eve of the Arab conquests (c. 400–585)* (2010) and *The Chronicle of Seert. Christian Historical Imagination in Late Antique Iraq* (2013). He is currently working on a third monograph on the Jazira in the first Abbasid century (c. 750–850).

Helen Younansardaroud (PhD Semitic and Arabic Studies, Freie Universität Berlin), was formerly Lecturer in Classical Syriac, and has authored (with Albrecht Berger) *Die griechische Vita des Hlg. Mamas von Kaisereia und ihre syrischen Versionen* (2003) and *Der neuostaramäische Dialekt von Särdä:rïd* (2001).

ABBREVIATIONS

ACO	*Acta Conciliorum Oecumenicorum*
AION	*Annali. Istituto Orientale di Napoli*
AMS	Bedjan, Paul. 1890–97. *Acta martyrum et sanctorum*. 7 vols. Paris and Leipzig: Harrassowitz
ANRW	*Aufstieg und Niedergang der Römischen Welt*
AS	*Aramaic Studies*
BASOR	*Bulletin of the American Schools of Oriental Research*
BEThL	*Bibliotheca Ephemeridum Theologicarum Lovaniensium*
BHO	Peeters, Paul. 1910. *Bibliotheca hagiographica orientalis*. Subsidia Hagiographica 10. Brussels: Société des Bollandistes
BJRL	*Bulletin of the John Rylands Library*
BSOAS	*Bulletin of the School of Oriental and African Studies*
CPG	Geerard, M. 1974–. *Clavis Patrum Graecorum*. Turnhout: Brepols.
CSCO	*Corpus Scriptorum Christianorum Orientalium*
DM	*Damaszener Mitteilungen*
DOP	*Dumbarton Oaks Papers*
GCS	*Die griechischen christlichen Schriftsteller der ersten Jahrhunderte*
GEDSH	Brock, S. P., A. M. Butts, G. A. Kiraz, and L. Van Rompay. 2011. *Gorgias Encyclopedic Dictionary of the Syriac Heritage*. Piscataway: Gorgias Press.
HE	*Historia Ecclesiastica*
HMML	*Hill Monastic Manuscript Library* [www.hmml.org]
HoS	*Handbuch der Orientalistik*
IGLS	Jalabert, L. et al. 1929–. *Inscriptions grecques et latines de la Syrie*. Paris: Paul Geuthner
JAOS	*Journal of the American Oriental Society*
JCSSS	*Journal of the Canadian Society of Syriac Studies*
JECS	*Journal of Early Christian Studies*
JEH	*Journal of Ecclesiastical History*
JJS	*Journal of Jewish Studies*

JLARC	*Journal for Late Antique Religion and Culture*
JRS	*Journal of Roman Studies*
JSJ	*Journal for the Study of Judaism*
JSOT	*Journal for the Study of the Old Testament*
JSQ	*Jewish Studies Quarterly*
JSS	*Journal of Semitic Studies*
JThS	*Journal of Theological Studies*
KAI	Donner, H., and W. Röllig. 1969–1973. *Kanaanäische und aramäische Inschriften mit einem Beitrag von O. Rössler*. Wiesbaden: Harrassowitz
LCL	*Loeb Classical Library*
LM	*Le Muséon*
MPIL	*Monographs of the Peshitta Institute Leiden*
MUSJ	*Mélanges de l'Université Saint Joseph*
OC	*Oriens Christianus*
OCA	*Orientalia Christiana Analecta*
OCP	*Orientalia Christiana Periodica*
OIRSI	*Oriental Institute of Religious Studies India*
OLA	*Orientalia Lovaniensia Analecta*
OLP	*Orientalia Lovaniensia Periodica*
OS	*L'Orient Syrien*
PdO	*Parole de l'Orient*
PO	*Patrologia Orientalis*
PS	*Patrologia Syriaca*
ROC	*Revue de l'Orient chrétien*
RHR	*Revue de l'histoire des religions*
RSO	*Rivista degli Studi Orientali*
RTL	*Revue théologique de Louvain*
SC	*Sources chrétiennes*
TTH	*Translated Texts for Historians*
VChr	*Vigiliae Christianae*
ZAC	*Zeitschift für Antikes Christentum*
ZDMG	*Zeitschrift der Deutsche Morgenländische Gesellschaft*
ZPE	*Zeitschrift für Papyrologie und Epigraphik*

DIACHRONIC MAPS OF SYRIAC CULTURES AND THEIR GEOGRAPHIC CONTEXTS

David A. Michelson, maps editor
Ian Mladjov, cartographer

MAPS

Map 1	Near East before the Islamic Conquest	xxxiv
Map 2	Near East following the Islamic Conquest	xxxvi
Map 3	Northern Syria, Cilicia, and Cyprus	xxxviii
Map 4	Lebanon and southern Syria	xxxix
Map 5	Egypt and Palestine	xl
Map 6	Arabia and the Red Sea	xli
Map 7	Northern Mesopotamia	xlii
Map 8	Southern Mesopotamia	xliv
Map 9	Iranian Plateau	xlvi
Map 10	Central Asia	xlvii
Map 11	East Asia	xlviii
Map 12	Southern India and Sri Lanka	l
Map 13	Central Kerala	li
Map 14	Map of Neo-Aramaic Usage	lii

INTRODUCTION

From its origins in Mesopotamia to its continuing development among a worldwide diaspora, the history of Syriac cultures and literature stretches widely across time and space. Conveying a range of nearly two millennia with its diversity of cultural contact from Asia to Africa to Europe and beyond is an inescapable challenge for geographers of Syriac cultures. It is impossible for traditional printed maps to exhaustively represent this extent. At the very least, one would need an entire atlas. Accordingly, the aim of these maps is more modest. Their primary purpose is to illustrate geographically the themes of this book, reflecting in a small way the current state of research on the historical geography of Syriac cultures. By extension, these maps offer a general, but abbreviated, cartography of Syriac cultures and their geographic contexts. As an aid for readers, this introduction explains the design principles of these maps and offers references for additional resources. The study of Syriac cultural geography is only in its beginning stages. It is hoped that the maps will spur further research. In particular, they are being released under an open license that will allow them to be widely used and re-published.

Selections of sites for inclusion in these maps has been guided foremost by the visualisation needs of individual chapters rather than by an attempt to be comprehensive or representative of the most important locations. The editor, David Michelson, and the cartographer, Ian Mladjov, solicited suggestions from all chapter authors and prepared a series of maps to collectively illustrate the themes of the volume as a whole.

The majority of the maps are diachronic. Not all of the places listed together on any single map were in existence or of historical significance at the same time. The decision to reflect multiple eras on the same map was necessitated by the wide chronological coverage of the chapters in this book and the space constraints of the printed volume. For reasons of simplicity, all of the maps depict modern topography including the present courses of rivers and deltas rather than historically changing river beds and coastlines. This diachronic design helps the reader to situate historical locations relative to modern geography.

Students and researchers in search of greater detail than these maps can provide are referred to a number of resources for historical geography which have been used in preparing the maps. The most recent and comprehensive source for Syriac geography is *The Syriac Gazetteer* (Carlson and Michelson 2014). *The Syriac Gazetteer* is an online reference work continually updated by Syriaca.org and a part of the burgeoning scholarly field of digitally 'enriched gazetteers' (Berman, Mostern, and Southall 2016: 5). The editor and cartographer are especially grateful to Thomas A. Carlson, co-editor of *The Syriac Gazetteer*, for his essential and varied assistance in the production of the maps. A number of other digital gazetteers were also indispensable in the creation of the maps. Whenever possible, coordinates for plotting locations were derived from *Pleiades: A Gazetteer of Past Places* (Bagnall et al. 2017), the *iDAI.gazetteer* (Deutsches Archäologisches Institut 2017), and the *Digital Atlas of the Roman Empire* (Åhlfeldt 2015–17). The combined 'linked open geodata' of these gazetteers are accessible through the Pelagios Commons project's *Peripleo* search tool (Pelagios Commons 2017; Simon, Isaksen, Barker, and de Soto Cañamares 2016). These online resources represent the rebirth or resurgence of the genre of 'gazetteer' as an essential geographic research tool for ancient and mediaeval historians in the digital age (Berman et al. 2016, 23).

The print maps published here have been prepared following the emerging standards for digital scholarship in historical geography. In particular, all place labels on the maps have been keyed to the unique identification numbers assigned to individual places in *The Syriac Gazetteer*. A place name index is provided on pages 824 ff. This index also contains cross-references to the corresponding numeric identifiers (e.g. Edessa is identified as 'http://syriaca.org/place/78'). These identifiers not only allow for disambiguation of homonyms but also direct the reader to further information online through *The Syriac Gazetteer* and *Peripleo*. In technical terms, these unique identifiers are formatted as URIs (Uniform Resource Identifiers). Following best practice for publishing linked data on the internet, the URIs of *The Syriac Gazetteer* also function as URLs (Uniform Resource Locators), or in common parlance 'web addresses'. By following these URLs, readers may find coordinates, additional name forms (including in Syriac script), and further bibliography related to each place. In short, readers are encouraged to use the maps published in this book in close conjunction with the index since the URIs link to a number of other relevant scholarly publications.

The design and compilation of these maps has also relied heavily on the materials which served as the basis of *The Syriac Gazetteer*, especially the *Gorgias Encyclopedic Dictionary of the Syriac Heritage* (GEDSH) and the maps created for it by the Ancient World Mapping Center at the University of North Carolina (Brock, Butts, Kiraz, and Van Rompay 2011: 471–80). The sources used for the GEDSH maps have also been consulted, especially the *Barrington Atlas of the Greek and Roman World* (Talbert 2000) and the relevant volumes of the *Tübinger Atlas des Vorderen Orients (TAVO)* (Sonderforschungsbereich 19 "Tübinger Atlas des Vorderen Orients" 1977–94). These resources were compared with the recently published volume on Syria of the *Tabula Imperii Byzantini* (TIB) (Todt and Vest 2015). In constructing new maps, several other regionally focused geographic and cultural reference works were consulted including the work of T. A. Sinclair on Eastern Turkey (1987), the *Encyclopaedia Iranica*, the *Encyclopedia of Islam* (EI2 and EI3), and the *Digital Dictionary of Buddhism* (Kotyk 2017).

A number of classic publications in Syriac studies also provided essential material for the maps, especially the works of the Syrian Orthodox patriarch I. A. Barsoum (2003), Ernst Honigmann (1951), and J. M. Fiey (see most notably 1965, 1993). These works remain invaluable for the study of Syriac cultural geography, but the exponential growth of Syriac studies in the last two decades now necessitates that they be used only in tandem with more recent literature (Brock 1995). For the Church of the East in Mesopotamia and the Iranian plateau, the maps published here rely heavily on the work of David Wilmshurst (2000, 2016) and Florence Jullien (2008, 2015) and also benefitted from brief personal communications with those same scholars. The map of Neo-Aramaic dialects (see also page 267) was based on the personal direction of Geoffrey Khan and drew in part upon the dialect database he has prepared (Khan 2017).

The above resources notwithstanding, it should be noted that the study of Syriac historical geography is very much in its infancy. For some regions (such as the Arabian peninsula and Central Asia), the maps published here are among only a handful of maps ever printed which focus on the history of Syriac cultures and literature in those areas. Because the historical geography of Syriac Christianity in Arabia and the Gulf has only begun to receive scholarly attention, the summary scholarship of R. A. Carter offered a useful starting point (Carter 2008; see the literature review in Bonnéric 2015). Because of the lack of previous scholarship and the number of languages involved, the maps of Central Asia, East Asia, and India would not have been possible without the extensive suggestions, revisions, and editorial assistance of Thomas A. Carlson, Mark Dickens, Daniel King, István Perczel, and Hidemi Takahashi (all errors of course remain the responsibility of the editor). In addition, recent publications by Li Tang and D. W. Winkler (Tang 2002; Tang and Winkler 2009, 2013),

Takahashi (2013), William Tabbernee (2014), T. H. F. Halbertsma (2015), Dickens (2015), P. G. Borbone and P. Marsone (2015) were consulted as well as the administrative atlas of Kerala published as a result of the 2011 census of India (Gopala Menon, Singh, Rastogi, and Chandramouli 2012).

Many of these Asian historical locations remain poorly documented in the archaeological literature. When coordinates could not be found in scholarly sources, preliminary data was collected from 'crowd-sourced' databases such as Geonames, Wikimapia, and Wikipedia. In all of these cases, however, the coordinates were also visually verified or corrected by the editor or the cartographer based on satellite imagery. For these difficult-to-plot locations, the editor is particularly grateful to the cartographer, Ian Mladjov, for his skill and determination in ensuring accuracy of the locations.

As noted above, the history of Syriac cultures is marked by the breadth of its contact with other cultures and languages, e.g. Arabic, Chinese, Greek, Latin, Malayalam, Mongol, Persian, Turkic, and more. One challenge in the preparation of these maps has been to achieve some limited uniformity in labels across so many languages. In general, the transliteration guidelines of the *Gorgias Encyclopedic Dictionary* have been used (GEDSH 2011: x). These guidelines were also adopted by *The Syriac Gazetteer* and thus are now the prevailing standard for Syriac place names. To facilitate usage, names with widely accepted English spellings, or having a form commonly used in Syriac scholarship, have been retained as exceptions to the rules (e.g. Edessa, Dailam, or Navekath). Otherwise, labels derived from Syriac have been Romanised according to the transliteration system of GEDSH, which for proper nouns requires representing *š* with *sh* and not marking long vowels. Gemination is generally not marked. In labelling places, preference has been given to Syriac transliteration rather than Arabic or Persian (thus Dinawar not Dīnavar). For Romanisation of other Middle Eastern languages, the transliterations system of the *International Journal of Middle East Studies* has largely been followed. Here again, deference has been shown to English usage and common forms, hence some names have been vocalised with Persian rather than Arabic vocalisation (e.g. Hormuz). Chinese names have been rendered using the pinyin system but without tone marks. Modern place names in India are listed as they appear in the official atlas of the 2011 census (Gopala Menon et al. 2012). In some cases, deference to popular spelling in the Romanisation of Malayalam has meant varying usage of u/oo, y/j, etc. In several cases, exceptions or inconsistencies may also be found on account of the particular needs of the chapter concerned or requests made by authors in this volume. In particular, the Neo-Aramaic labels on the 'Map of Neo-Aramaic Usage' reflect the transliteration style found in the corresponding chapter rather than following the above systems.

Labels for physical features are marked in italics (e.g. *Tigris R.*). Labels for regions have been set in capital letters (e.g. in full capitalisation: BETH QAṬRAYE). These labels include provinces, states, and ecclesiastical jurisdictions, such as dioceses where boundaries may have fluctuated over time. When a diocese shares a name with a city, however, only the city and not the region is listed (e.g. Beth Lapaṭ). For simplicity, types of settlements are not differentiated (e.g. villages, cities, monasteries). Uncertain places are indicated either by a hollow point (for uncertain coordinates) or by a question mark appended to the label (for uncertain names). When a place has been known by widely varying names, alternate names may be listed separated by '/' (e.g. Martyropolis/Maipherqaṭ). The '/' is also used in a few cases to attach the name of a containing region in order to clarify homonymous settlements (e.g. Yinchuan/ Xingqing/Ningxia).

To conclude, it should be noted that monographs and articles on Syriac topics have often lacked maps due to the scarcity of available maps. While the maps published here are only a first step towards correcting this scholarly gap, these maps have been expressly designed to address this problem through the use of open-access licenses. All of the maps published in this volume are licensed under the Creative Commons Attribution 4.0 International license. They may be freely re-used, reproduced, and re-published with proper attribution to the map editor (David Michelson) and the cartographer (Ian Mladjov) along with the publication details of this volume. In addition, high-resolution digital files of the maps will be permanently available for reuse through the digital repository of the Jean and Alexander Heard Library at Vanderbilt University.

Finally, the editor would like to note that credit for the creation of these maps is shared with the cartographer, Ian Mladjov of Bowling Green State University, who not only plotted the locations and labels but also researched unidentified locations and suggested the inclusion of many relevant places. His cartography was accomplished using Global Mapper software to plot the raw data and projection, and using CorelDraw for the final design. Once the maps were completed, additional proofreading was undertaken by Stephanie Fulbright, Julia Liden, Elizabeth LeFavour, Will Potter, and Charlotte Lew of Vanderbilt University, to whom the editor is also extremely grateful.

BIBLIOGRAPHY

Åhlfeldt, Johan, ed. 2015–17. *Digital Atlas of the Roman Empire*. http://dare.ht.lu.se/.

Bagnall, Roger, Richard Talbert, Tom Elliott, Lindsay Holman, Jeffrey Becker, Sarah Bond, Sean Gillies, et al., ed. 2017. *Pleiades: A Gazetteer of Past Places*. http://pleiades.stoa.org/.

Barsoum, A. I. 2003. *The Scattered Pearls: A History of Syriac Literature and Sciences*. Translated by Matti Moosa. 2nd Revised Edition. Piscataway, NJ: Gorgias Press.

Berman, Merrick Lex, Ruth Mostern, and Humphrey Southall, ed. 2016. *Placing Names: Enriching and Integrating Gazetteers*. Bloomington, IN: Indiana University Press.

Bonnéric, Julie. 2015. "Christianity in the Arab-Persian Gulf: An Ancient but still Obscure History." *Le Carnet de La MAFKF*. December 23, 2015. https://mafkf.hypotheses.org/1286.

Borbone, Pier Giorgio, and Pierre Marsone, ed. 2015. *Le christianisme syriaque en Asie centrale et Chine*. Paris: Geuthner.

Brock, Sebastian P. 1995. "Review of *Pour Un Oriens Christianus Novus: Répertoire Des Diocèses Syriaques Orientaux et Occidentaux*, by J.M. Fiey." *Journal of the Royal Asiatic Society* 5(2): 264–5.

Brock, Sebastian P., Aaron Butts, George A. Kiraz, and Lucas Van Rompay, ed. 2011. *Gorgias Encyclopedic Dictionary of the Syriac Heritage*. Piscataway, NJ: Beth Mardutho, The Syriac Institute/Gorgias Press.

Carlson, Thomas A., and David A. Michelson, ed. 2014. *The Syriac Gazetteer*. http://syriaca.org/geo.

Carter, R. A. 2008. "Christianity in the Gulf during the First Centuries of Islam." *Arabian Archaeology and Epigraphy* 19(1): 71–108.

Deutsches Archäologisches Institut. 2017. *IDAI Gazetteer*. https://gazetteer.dainst.org.

Dickens, Mark. 2015. "Le christianisme syriaque en Asie centrale." *In*: Pier Giorgio Borbone and Pierre Marsone, ed., *Le christianisme syriaque en Asie centrale et en Chine*. Paris: Geuthner, 5–40.

Fiey, J. M. 1965–68. *Assyrie chrétienne, Contribution á l'étude de l'histoire et de la géographiee ecclésiastiques et monastiques du nord de l'Iraq*. 3 vols. Beyrouth: Impr. catholique.

Fiey, J. M. 1993. *Pour un oriens christianus novus: Répertoire des diocèses syriaques orientaux et occidentaux*. Beirut: Orient-Institut.

Gopala Menon, V. M., A. P. Singh, Deepak Rastogi, and C. Chandramouli, ed. 2012. *Census of India 2011: Administrative Atlas Kerala*. New Delhi, India: Office of the Registrar General & Census Commissioner, Government of India. www.censusindia.gov.in/2011census/maps/atlas/Kerala.html.

Halbertsma, Tjalling H. F. 2015. *Early Christian Remains of Inner Mongolia: Discovery, Reconstruction and Appropriation*. Second Edition, revised, updated and expanded. Leiden: Brill.

Honigmann, Ernst. 1951. *Évêques et évêchés monophysites d'Asie antérieure au VIe siècle*. CSCO 127 Subsidia 2. Louvain: L. Durbecq.

Jullien, Florence. 2008. *Le monachisme en Perse: La réforme d'Abraham le Grand, père des moines de l'Orient*. Lovanii: Peeters.

———. 2015. "East Syrian Monasteries in Sasanian Iran." *Encyclopaedia Iranica*. www.iranicaonline.org/articles/east-syrian-monasteries.

Khan, Geoffrey. 2017. *The North Eastern Neo-Aramaic Database Project*. https://nena.ames.cam.ac.uk/index-new.php.

Kotyk, Jeffrey. 2017. "Nestorian Christianity." *Digital Dictionary of Buddhism*. www.buddhism-dict.net/cgi-bin/xpr-ddb.pl?q=%E6%99%AF%E6%95%99.

Pelagios Commons. 2017. *Peripleo, an Initiative of Pelagios Commons*. http://peripleo.pelagios.org/.

Simon, Rainer, Leif Isaksen, Elton Barker, and Pau de Soto Cañamares. 2016. "Peripleo: A Tool for Exploring Heterogeneous Data through the Dimensions of Space and Time." *The Code4Lib Journal* 31 (January). http://journal.code4lib.org/articles/11144.

Sinclair, T. A. 1987–90. *Eastern Turkey: An Architectural and Archaeological Survey*. 4 vols. London: Pindar Press.

Sonderforschungsbereich 19 "Tübinger Atlas des Vorderen Orients." 1977–1994. "Tübinger Atlas des Vorderen Orients (TAVO)." Wiesbaden: Reichert.

Tabbernee, William. 2014. *Early Christianity in Contexts: An Exploration Across Cultures and Continents*. Grand Rapids, MI: Baker Academic.

Takahashi, Hidemi. 2013. "Transcription of Syriac Names in Chinese-Language Jingjiao Documents." *In*: Li Tang and Dietmar W. Winkler, 13–24.

Talbert, Richard. 2000. *Barrington Atlas of the Greek and Roman World*. Princeton, NJ: Princeton University Press.

Tang, Li. 2002. *A Study of the History of Nestorian Christianity in China and Its Literature in Chinese: Together With a New English Translation of the Dunhuang Nestorian Documents*. Frankfurt: P. Lang.

Tang, Li, and Dietmar W. Winkler. 2009. *Hidden Treasures and Intercultural Encounters. 2. Auflage: Studies on East Syriac Christianity in China and Central Asia*. Münster: LIT Verlag.

Tang, Li, and Dietmar W. Winkler. 2013. *From the Oxus River to the Chinese Shores: Studies on East Syriac Christianity in China and Central Asia*. Münster: LIT Verlag.

Todt, Klaus-Peter, and Bernd Andreas Vest, ed. 2015. *Tabula Imperii Byzantini: Syria (Syria Prōtē, Syria Deutera, Syria Euphratēsia)*. Vol. 15:1–3. Vienna: Verlag der Österreichischen Akademie der Wissenschaften.
Wilmshurst, David. 2000. *The Ecclesiastical Organisation of the Church of the East, 1318–1913*. Lovanii: Peeters.
Wilmshurst, David., trans. 2016. *The Ecclesiastical Chronicle: An English Translation*. Piscataway, NJ: Gorgias Press.

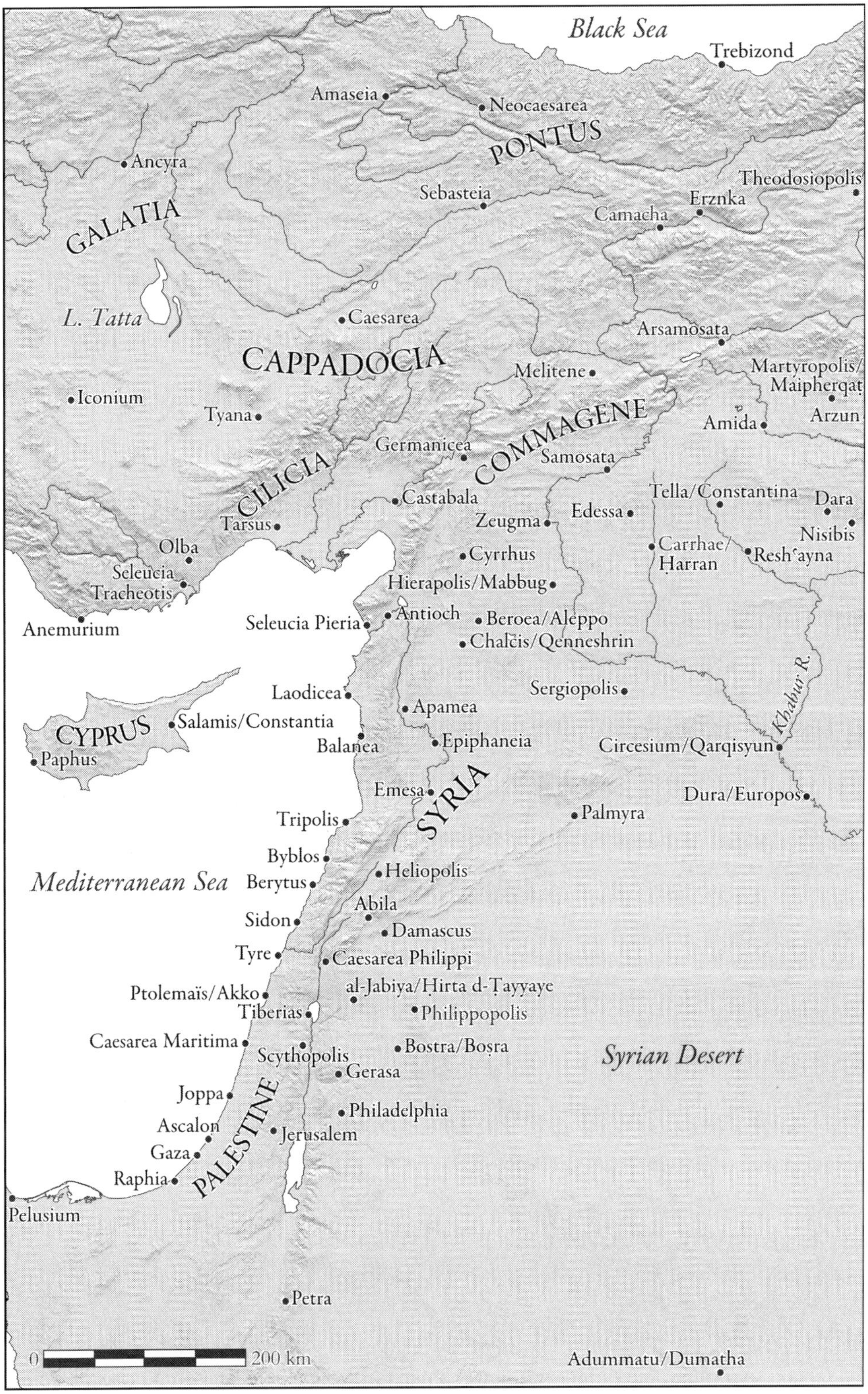

Map 1 Near East before the Islamic Conquest

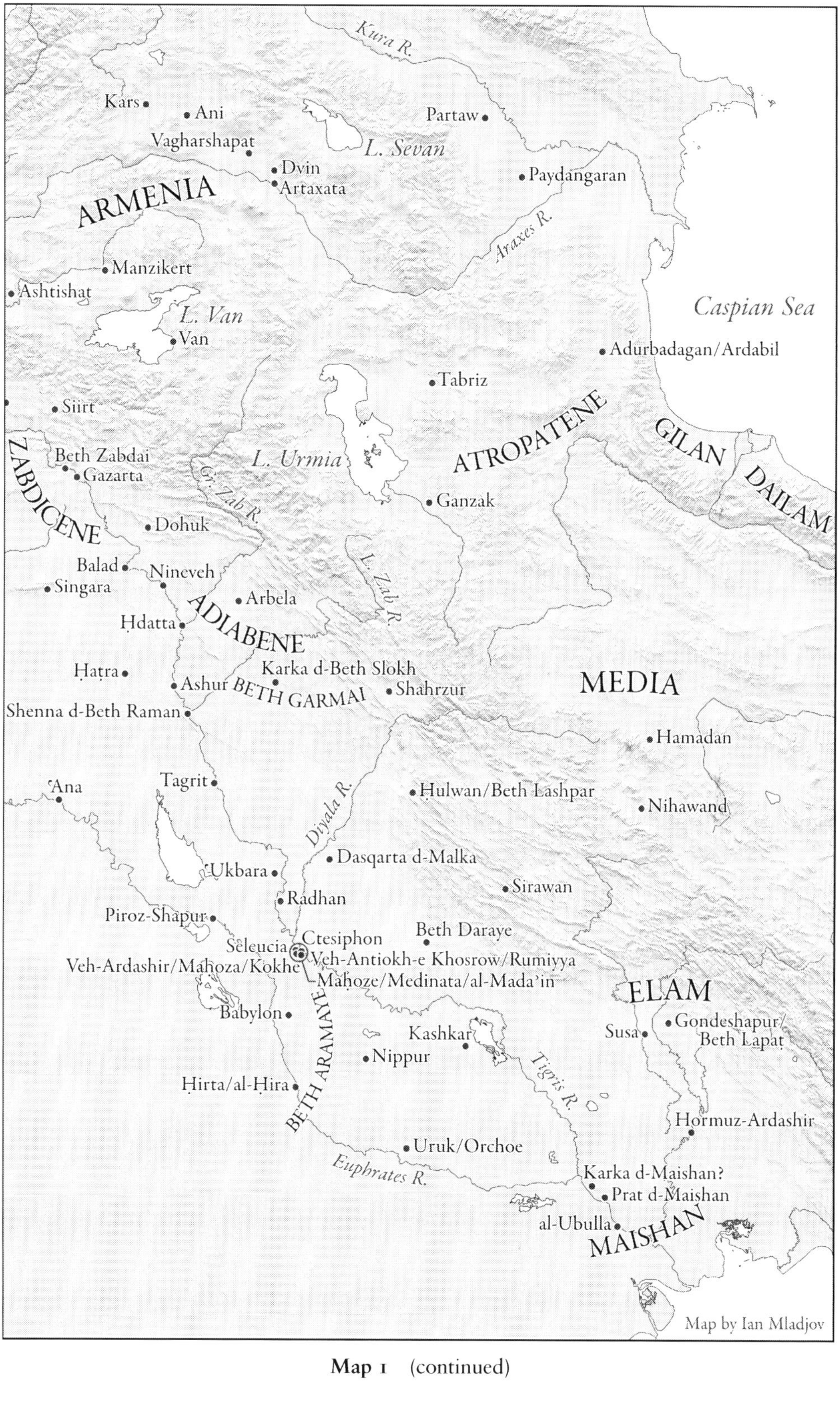

Map 1 (continued)

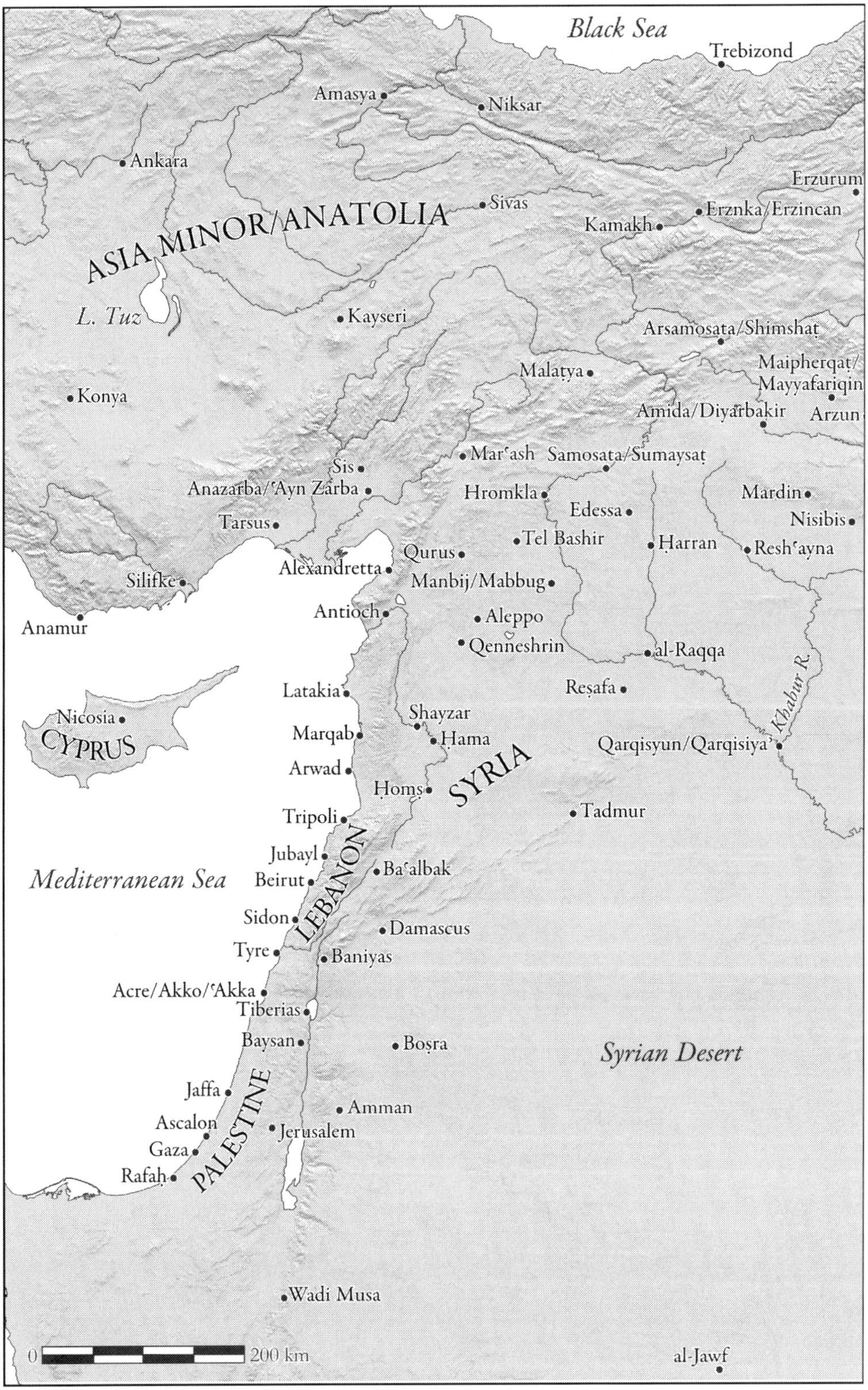

Map 2 Near East following the Islamic Conquest

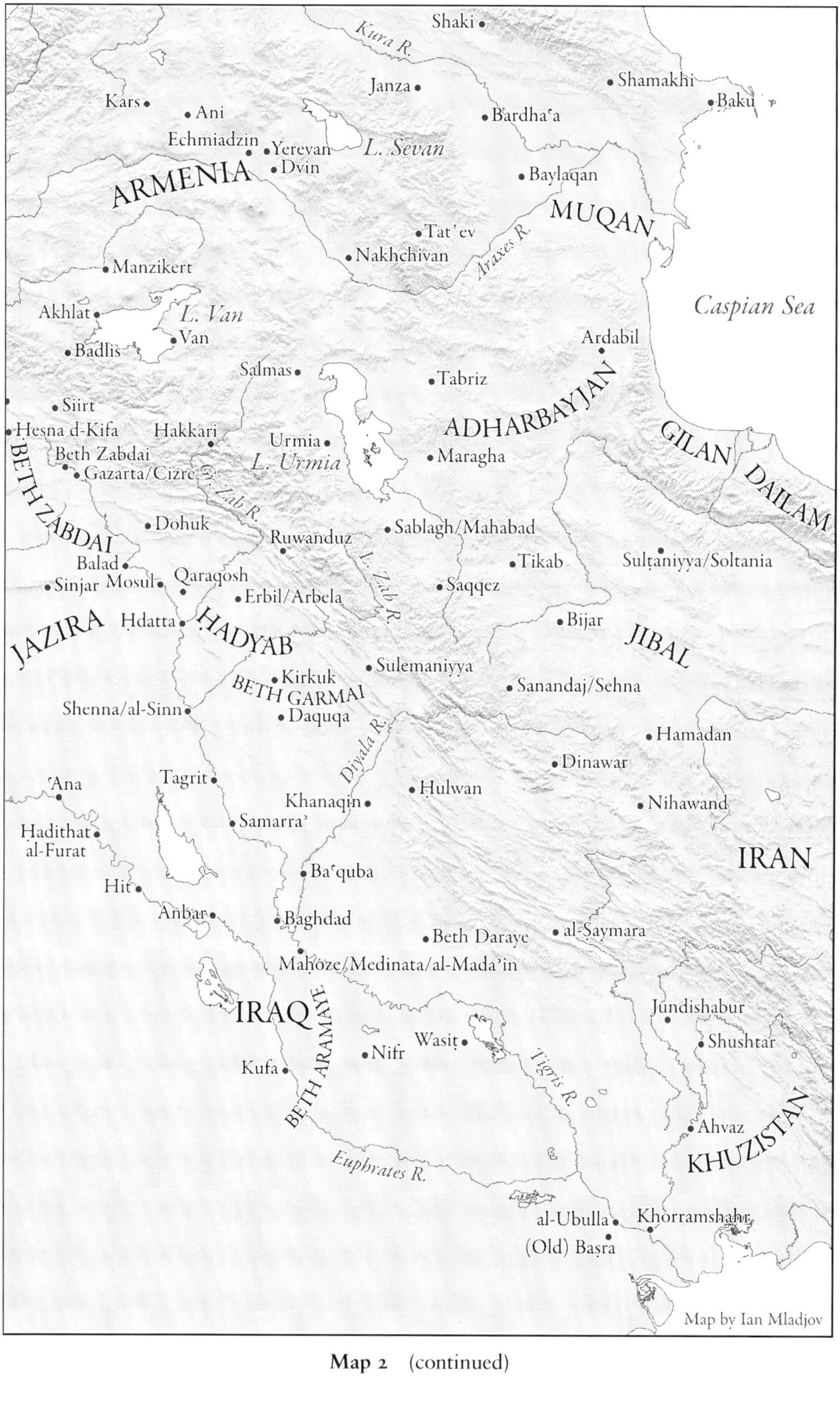

Map 2 (continued)

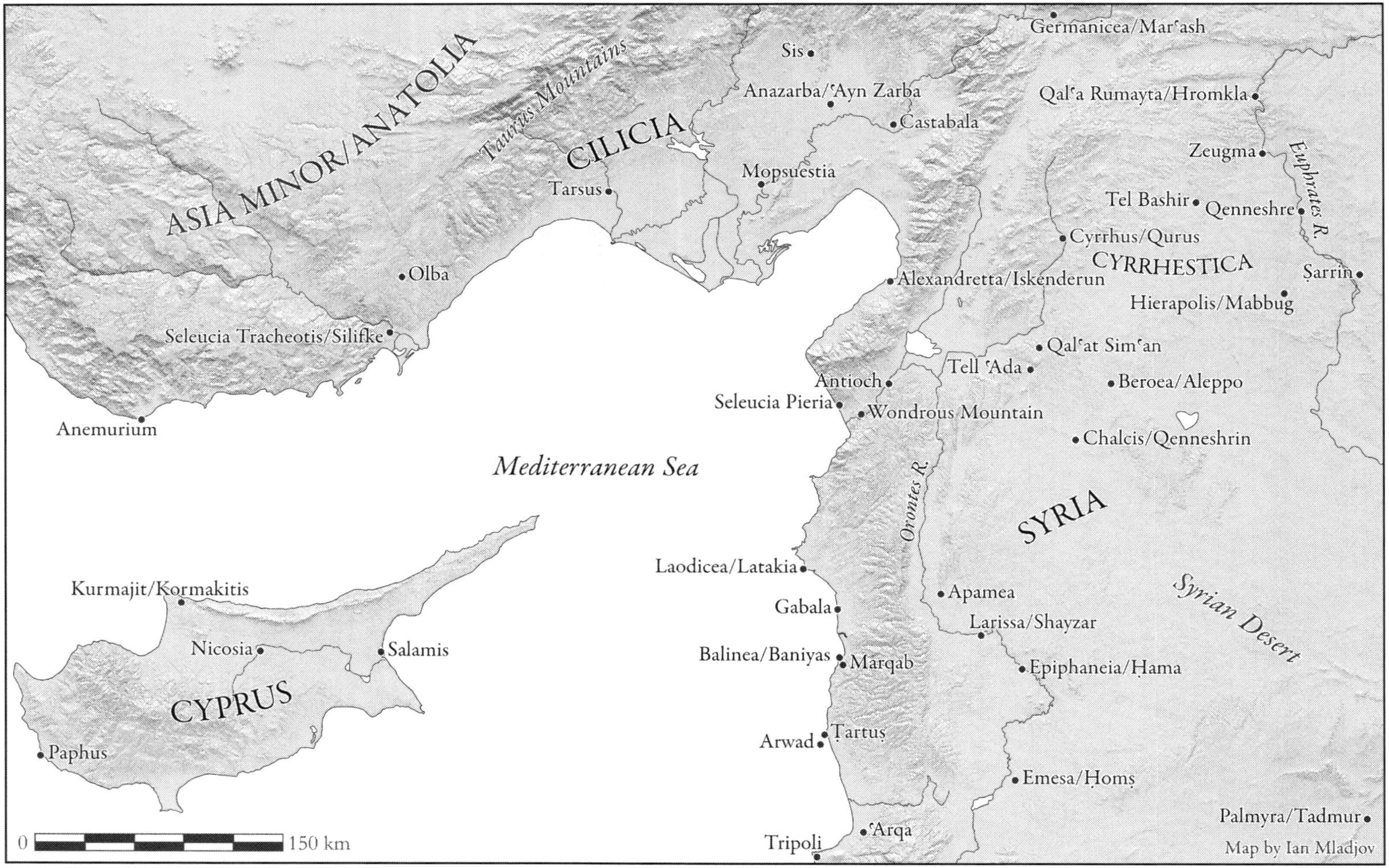

Map 3 Northern Syria, Cilicia, and Cyprus

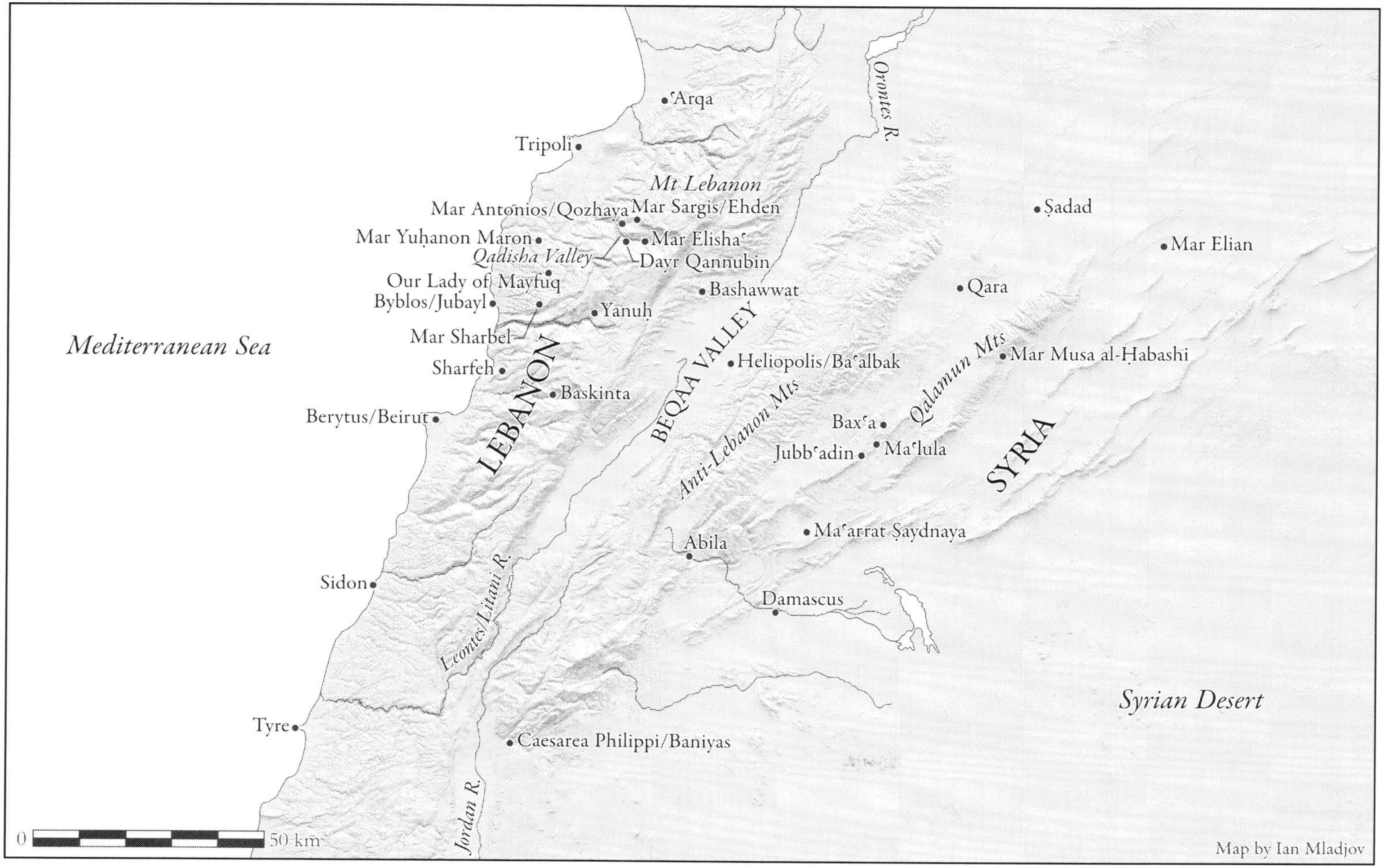

Map 4 Lebanon and southern Syria

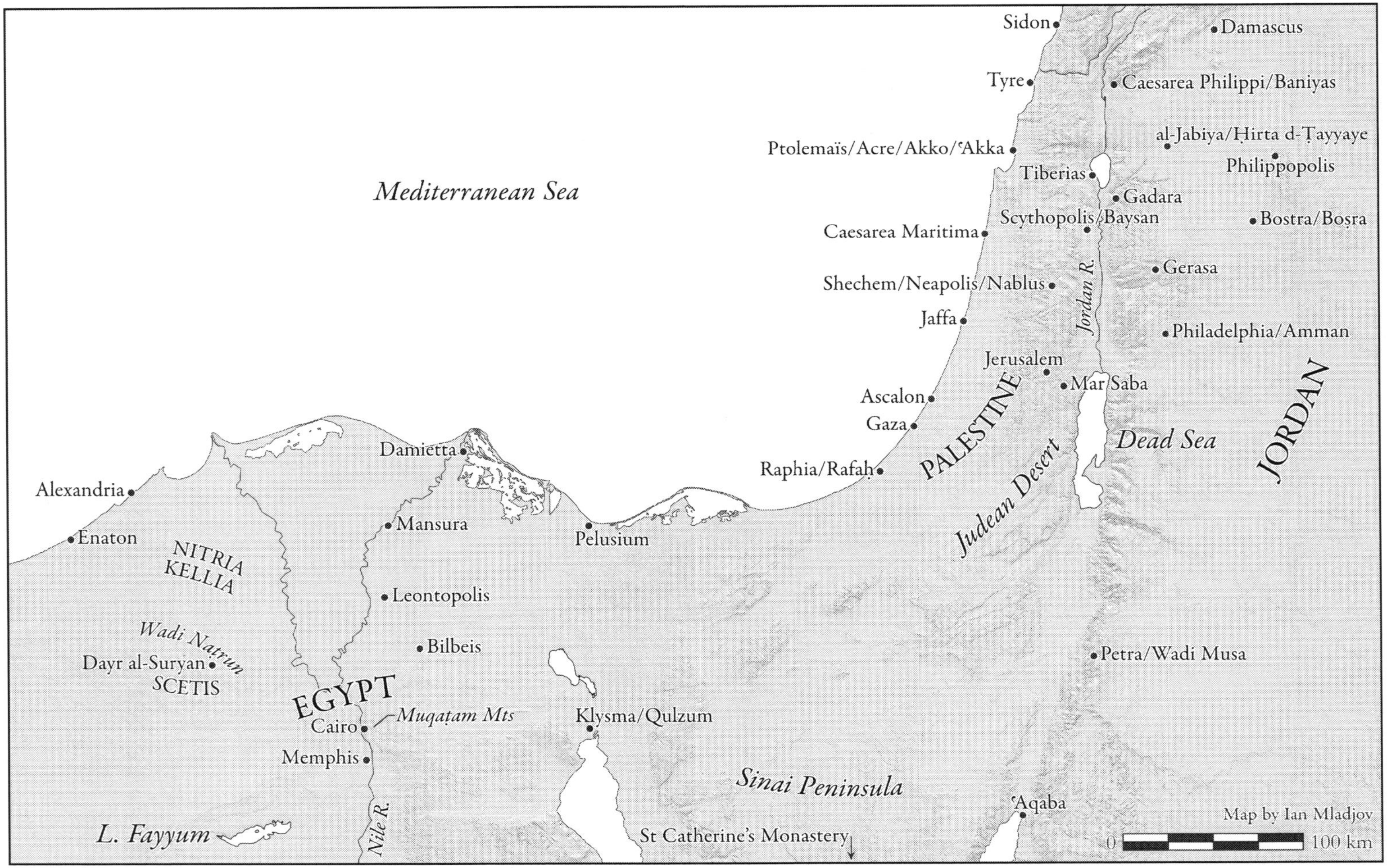

Map 5 Egypt and Palestine

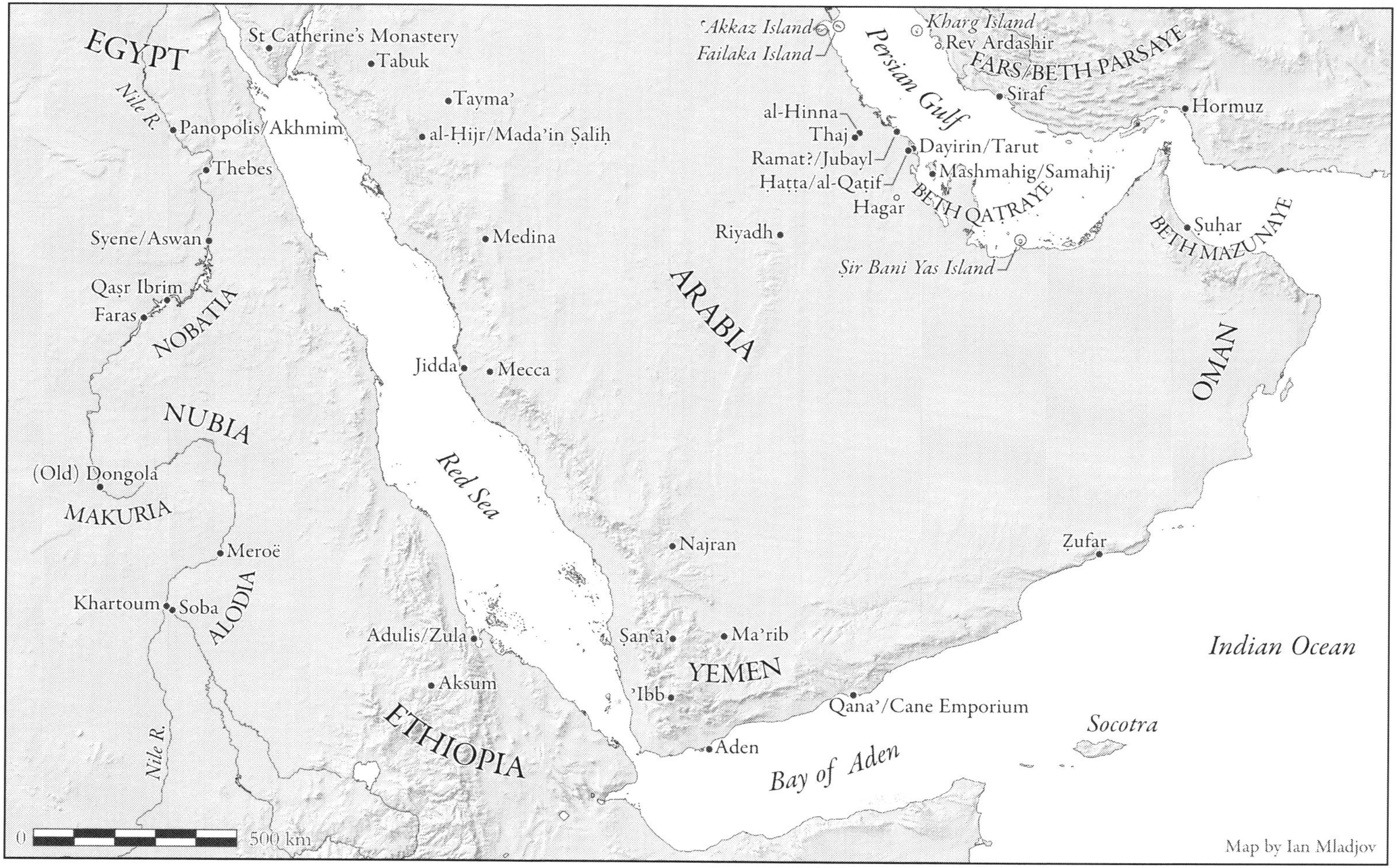

Map 6 Arabia and the Red Sea

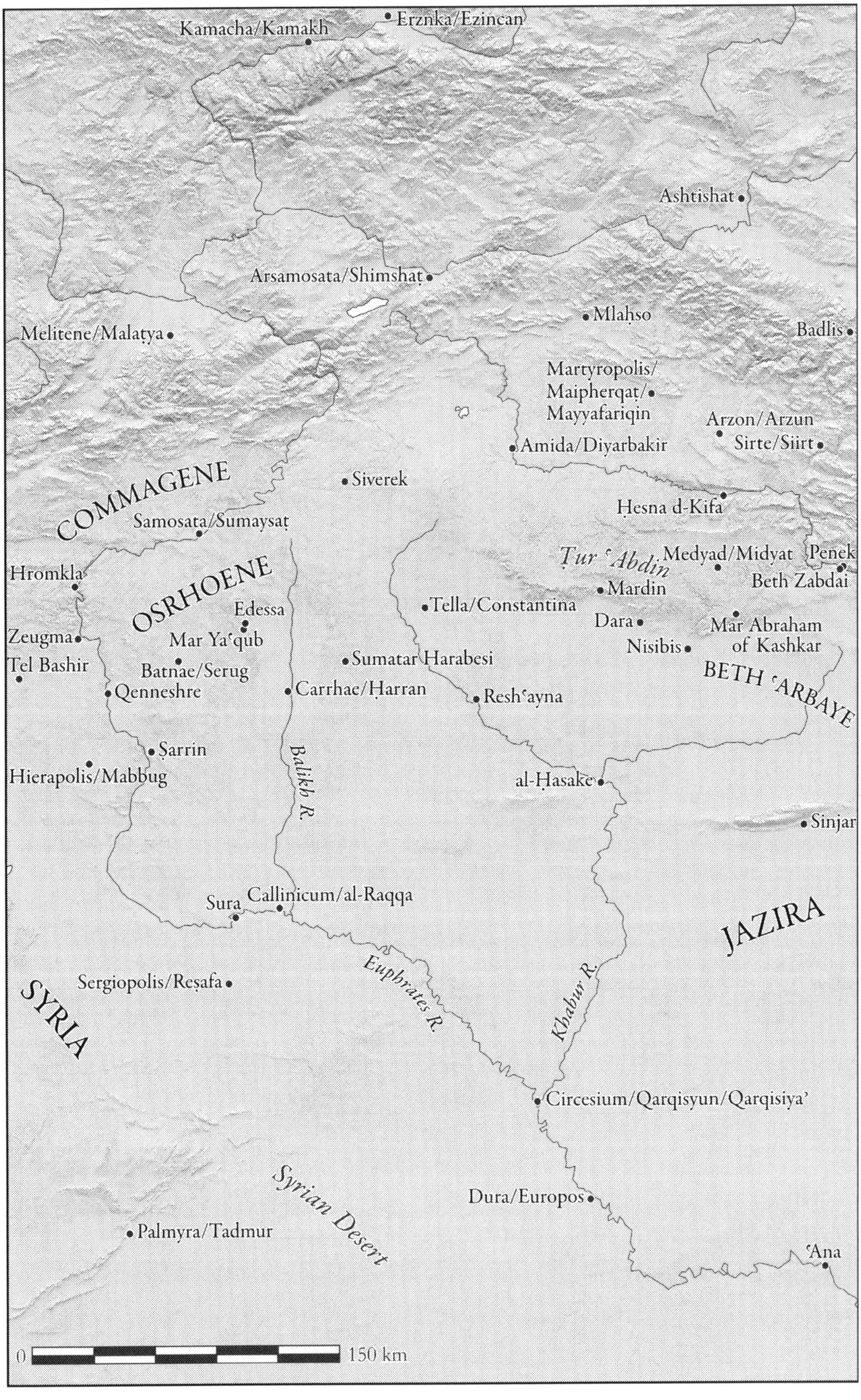

Map 7 Northern Mesopotamia

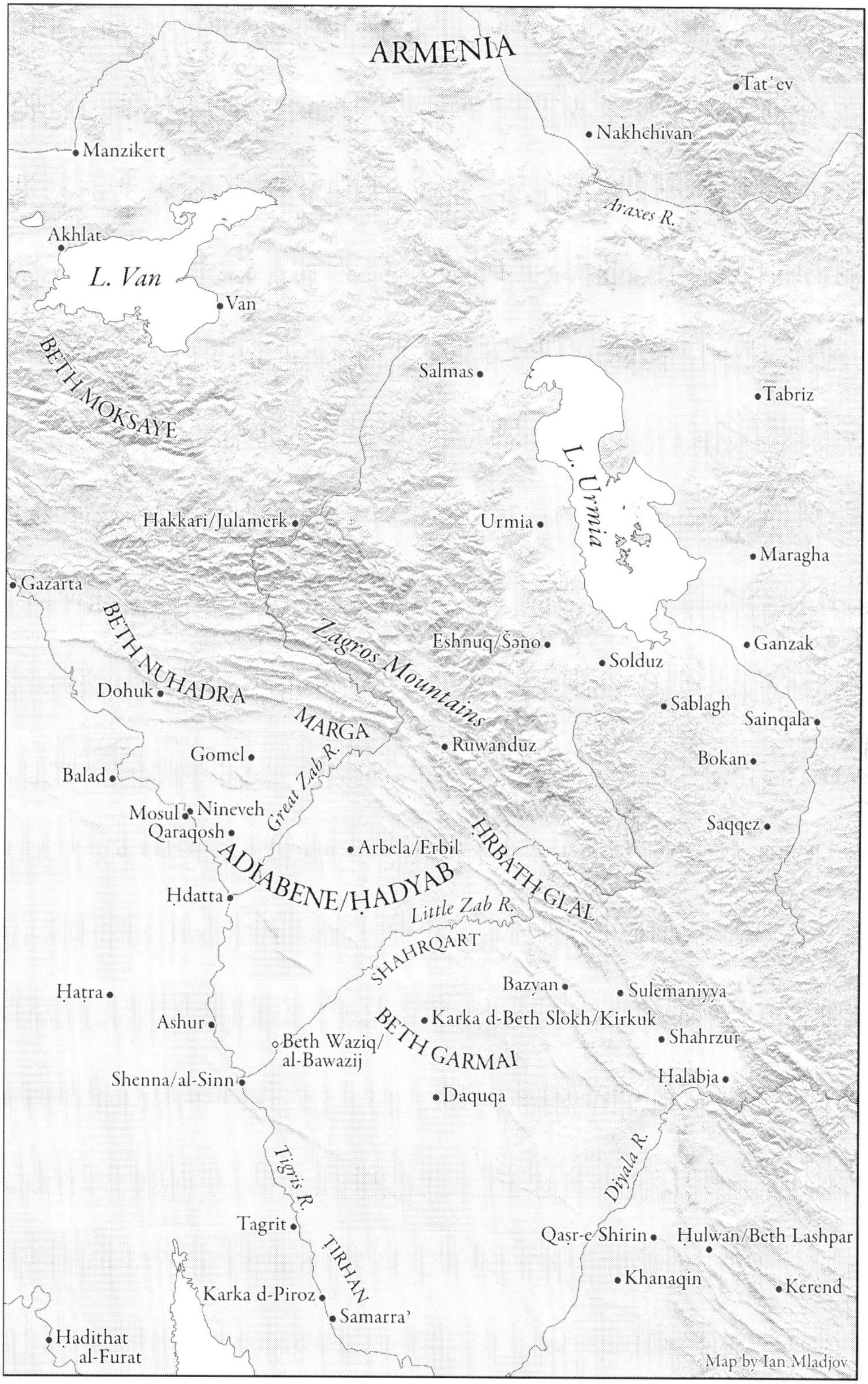

Map 7 (continued)

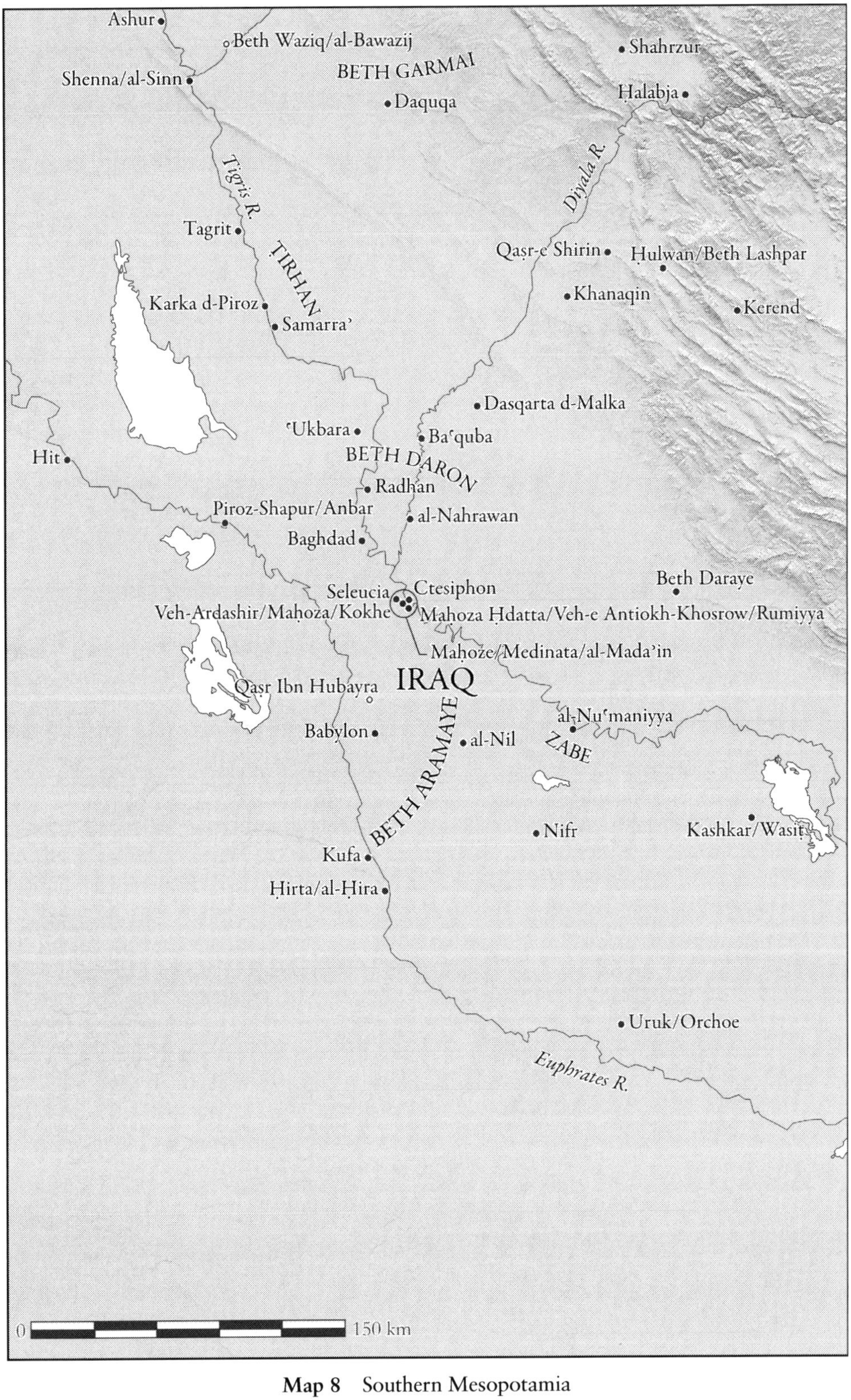

Map 8 Southern Mesopotamia

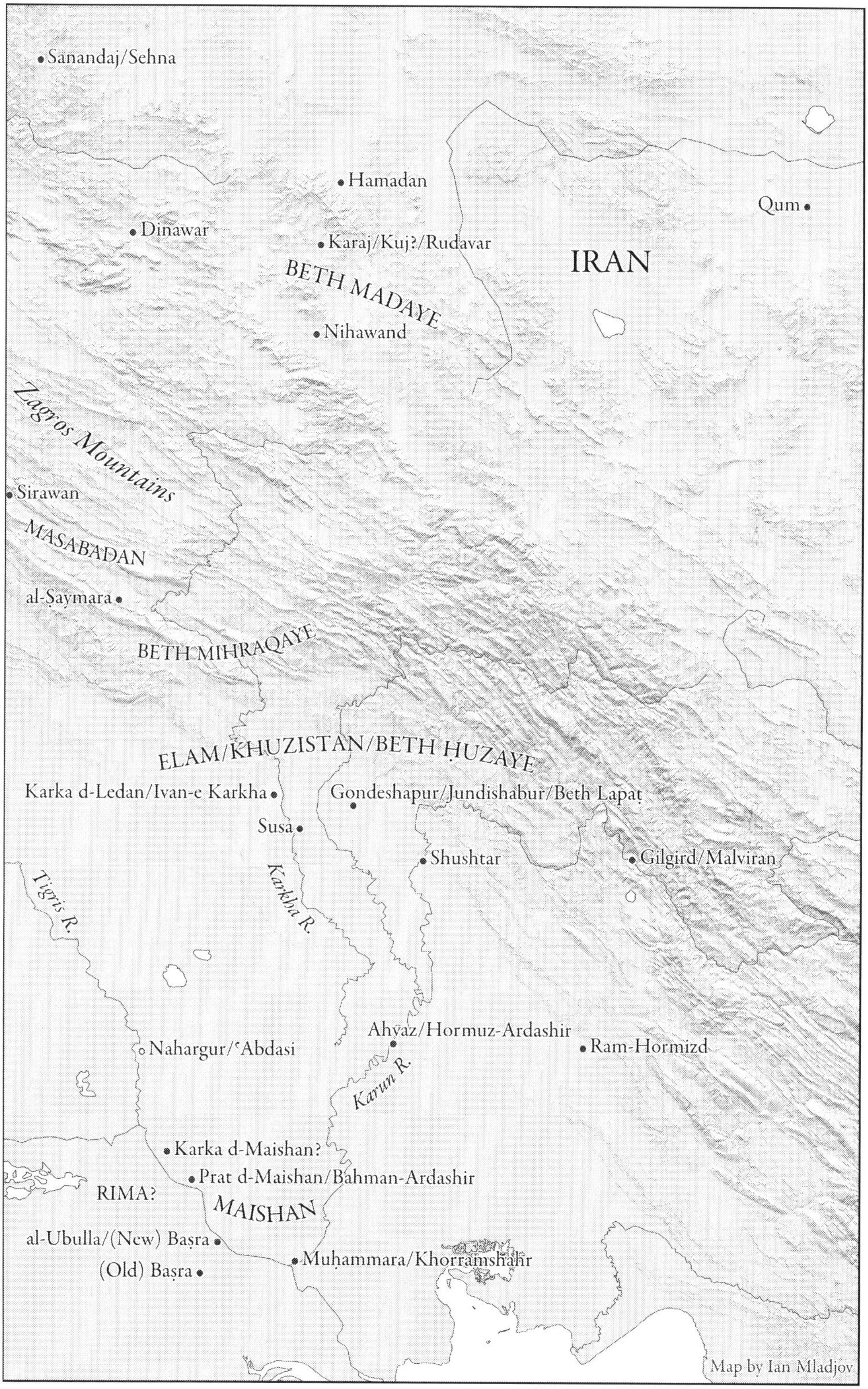

Map 8 (continued)

Map 9 Iranian Plateau

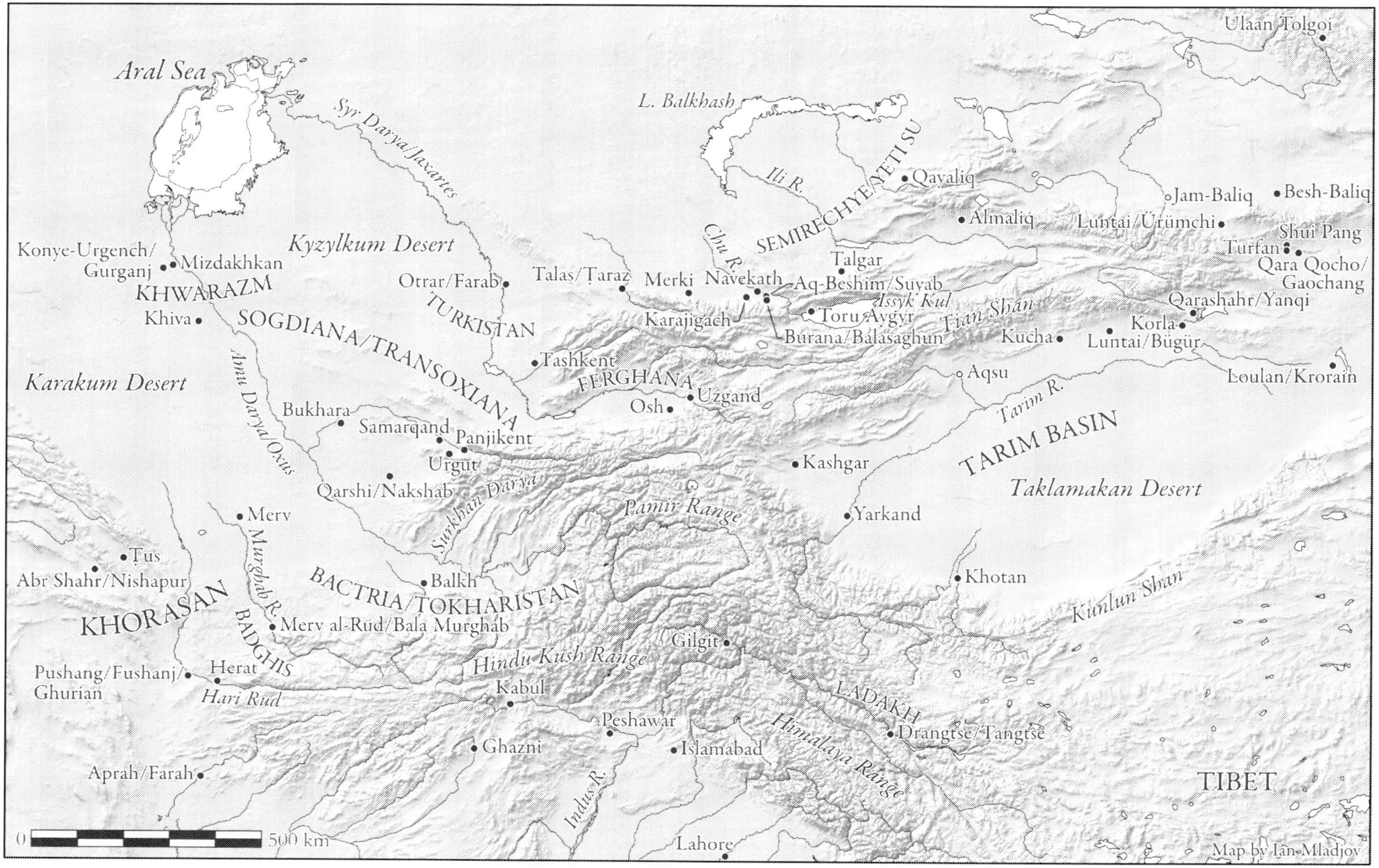

Map 10 Central Asia

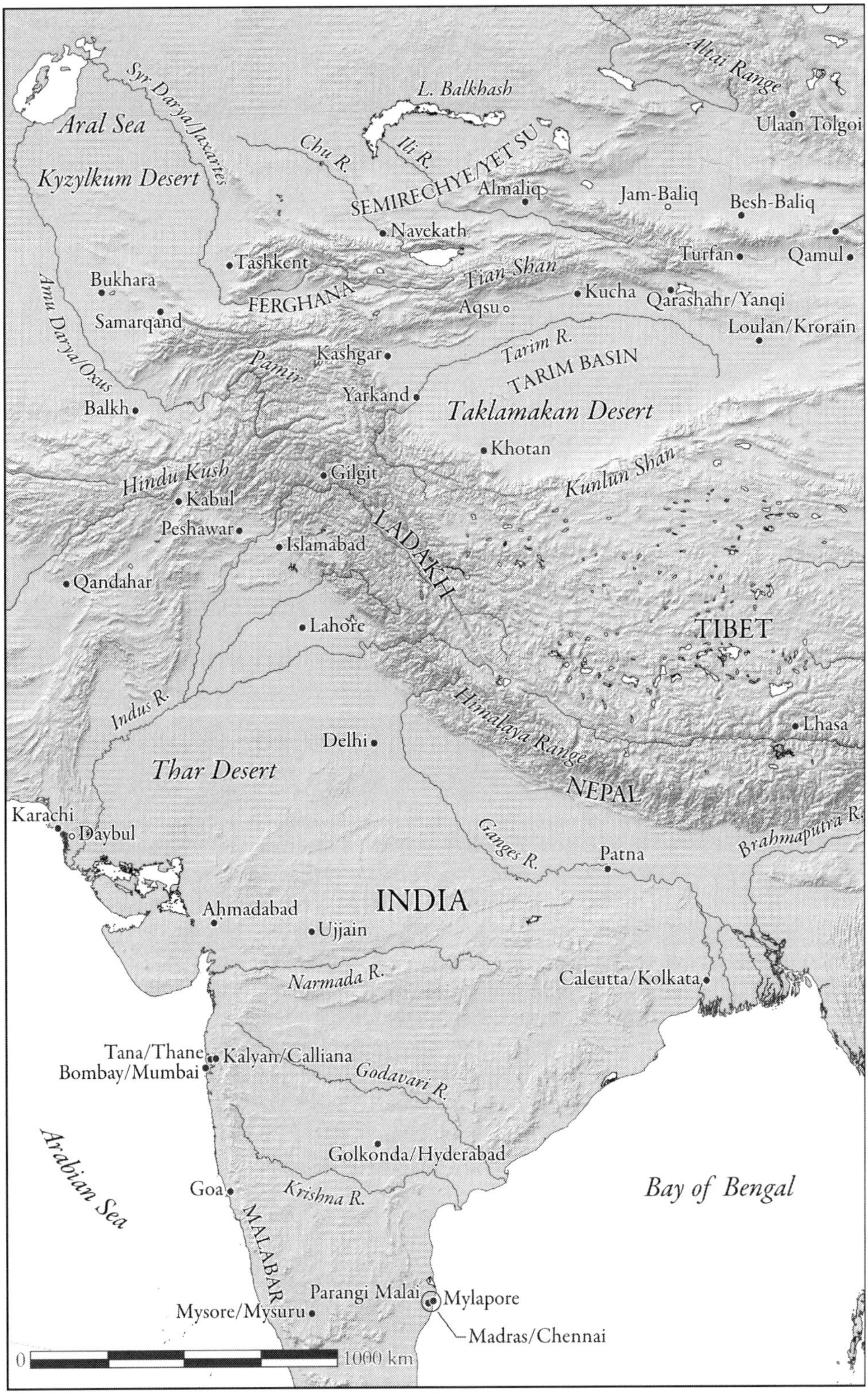

Map 11 East Asia

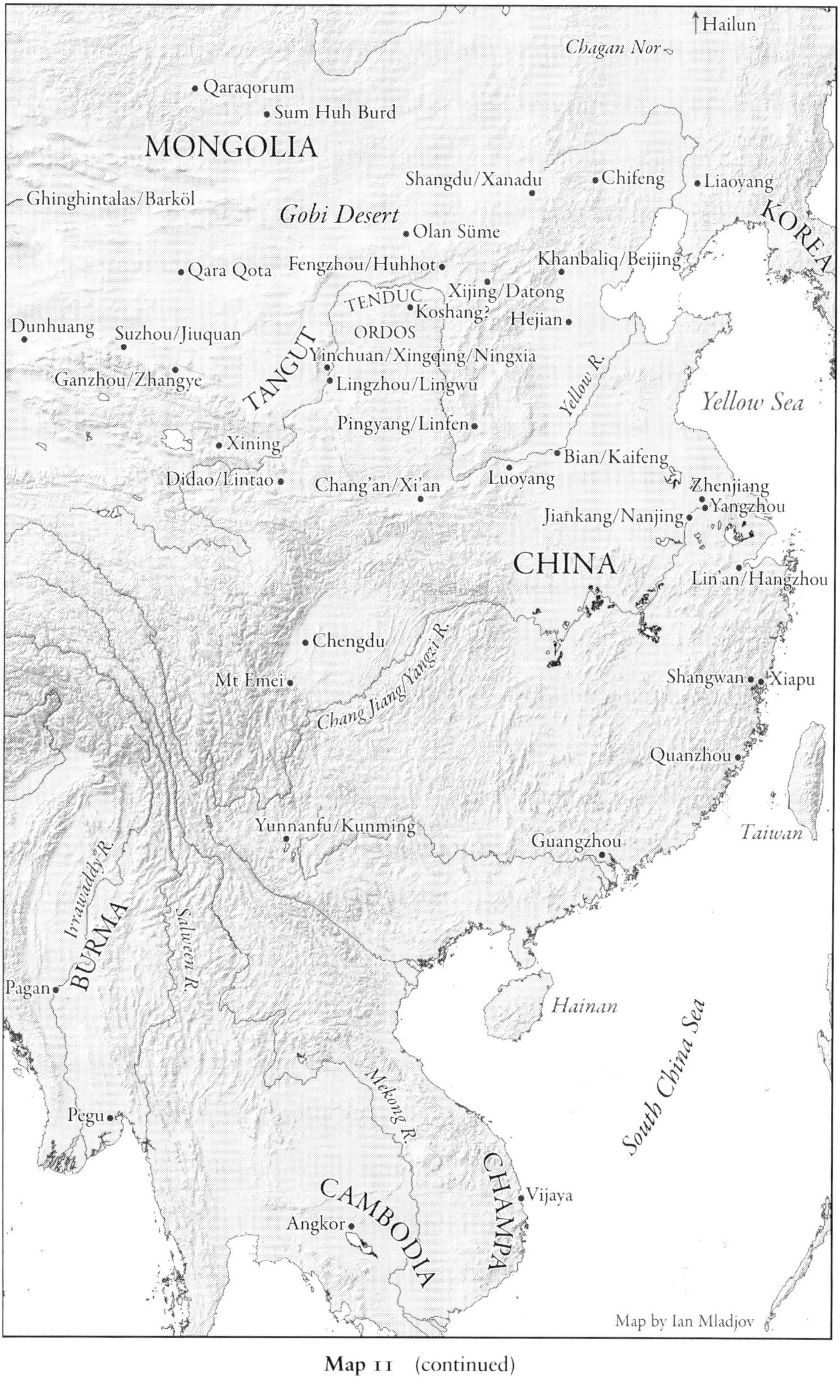

Map 11 (continued)

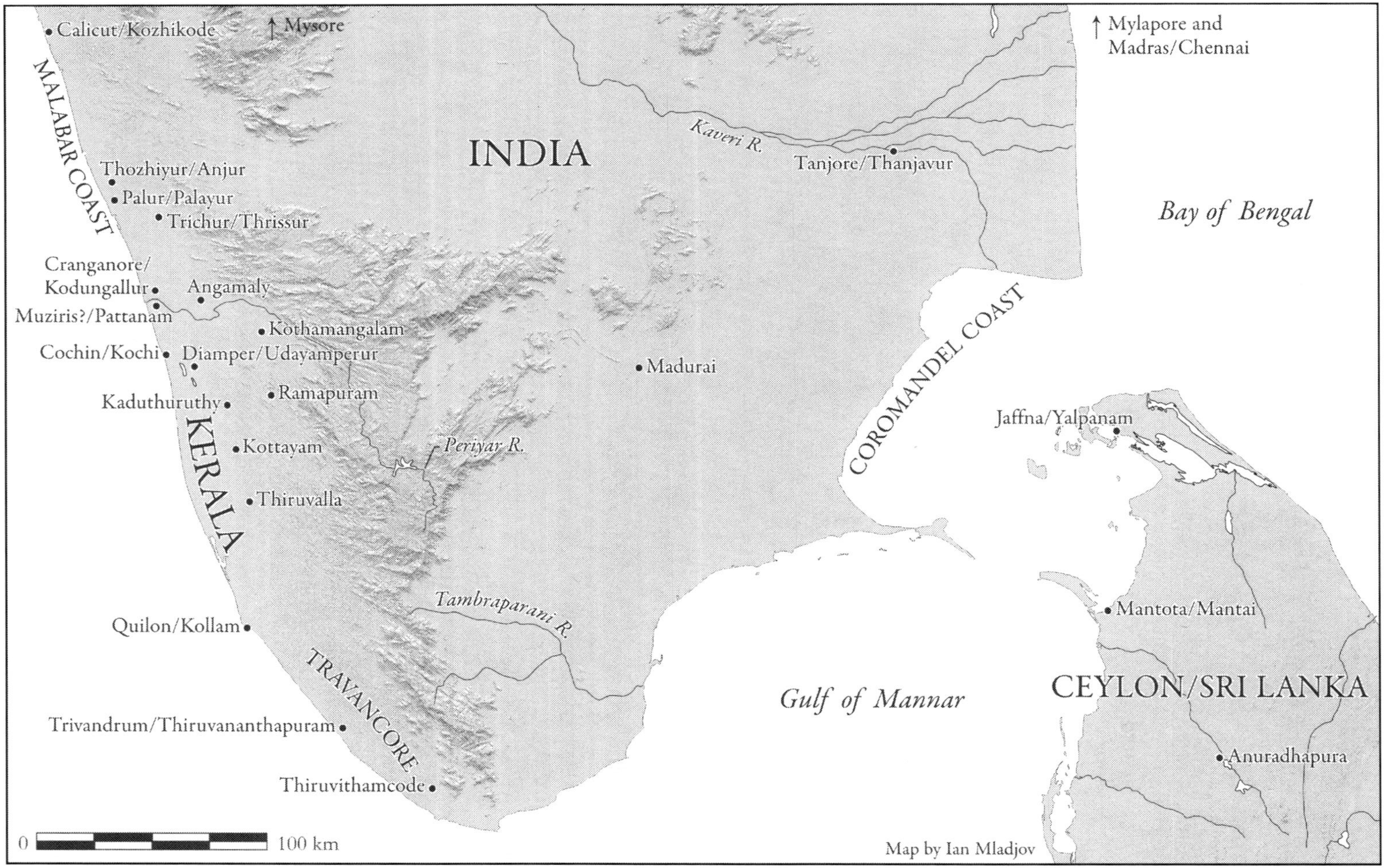

Map 12 Southern India and Sri Lanka

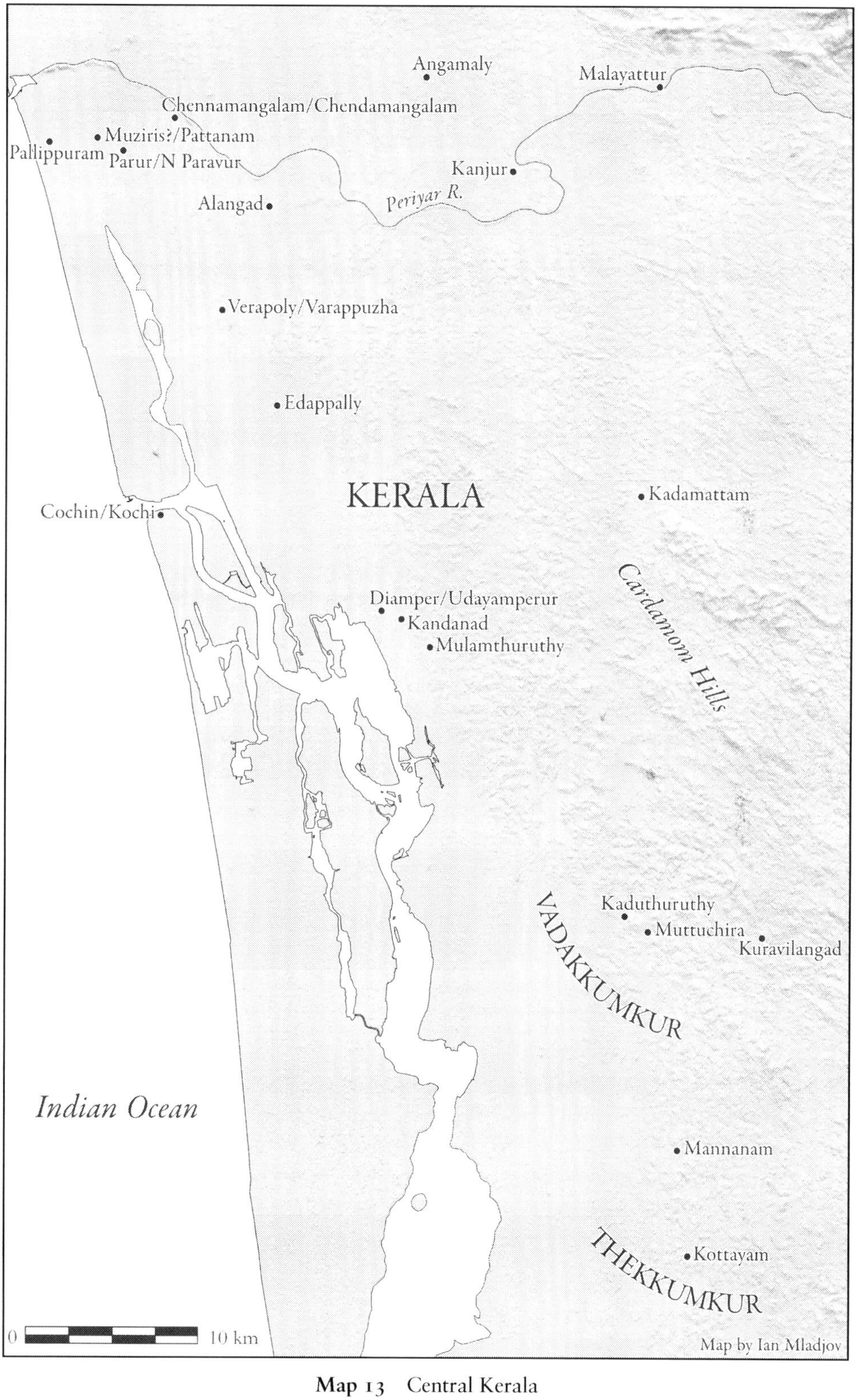

Map 13 Central Kerala

Map 14 Map of Neo-Aramaic Usage also found on p. 267

INTRODUCTION

Daniel King

The ancient Christian communities of the Near East, which have entered more firmly into the consciousness of the rest of the world in recent years as a result of conflicts in Iraq and Syria, share a rich heritage which predates even the earliest days of Christianity in the Middle East. It is the Syriac language that gives this heritage its focus and unity despite the vicissitudes of the long and diverse experiences of the various Syriac-speaking communities.

Aramaic was in its origins only the language of a small group of people dwelling in northern Mesopotamia at a time when historical sources begin to enter the historian's field of vision, coming gradually into focus through our meagre sources from the ninth/eighth century BC. Yet before it lay a significant future that belies its insubstantial roots. Having become an important language in the last years of the Late Assyrian Empire, by the fifth century Aramaic had been adopted as the administrative *lingua franca* of the Persian Empire and by the turn of the era a good proportion of the inhabitants of the Fertile Crescent and south-east Asia Minor were speakers of one or another of its increasingly various dialectal forms. Syriac was one of those dialects. Initially the dialect of Osrhoene, a small client kingdom of the Roman Empire, Syriac in time became a widely accepted literary standard and a fundamental marker of identity for communities throughout the Aramaic-speaking regions. It is with the life and character of those communities, insofar as they saw themselves as representatives of the Syriac language, that the chapters of this book are concerned.

If there ever was such a discrete entity as is at first suggested by the term 'The Syriac World', it certainly never possessed clear or immutable boundaries. In Late Antiquity, village- and town-based Syriophone communities could be found dispersed over a substantial geographical area – located equally in both the Roman and the Persian polities until the seventh century and thereafter subsumed under different provinces within the succession of caliphates. Their religious identities could be similarly diverse. Many Syriac-speaking localities clung to traditional forms of pre-Christian religious observance that partook of the wider religious phenomena of the Near East. Some communities in Edessa and elsewhere identified themselves as Jews, and continued to do so for a long time even while the rabbinic literature of Mesopotamia was being produced in different Aramaic dialects. Although in time the majority of Syriac-speaking communities gradually came to identify as Christians, it is again the variety of subgroups that remains a distinctive feature of the regional landscape. Until the fourth century and beyond, Marcionites, Manichaeans, and others competed with (proto) Nicene Christian groups to become the predominant form of Christian expression in Edessa. As the imperially sanctioned church hierarchy gradually pushed now-proscribed groups into the margins, it itself broke up into Persian and Western (Roman) forms, and then later into pro- and anti-Chalcedonian branches. Hence neither unity nor uniformity were ever a marked feature of Syriac religious life, while (as so much recent research shows) this same diversity and conflict was rarely a significant barrier to communications and relationships.

Hence while the Syriac communities never formed any political entity of their own, the churches themselves with their strong hierarchies led by patriarchs and metropolitan bishops won for themselves a status almost equal to that of secular governments. Classical Syriac of the Edessene variety was the official language of expression within those churches, and it is the Syriac language that above all defines and designates 'The Syriac World'. Lucas van Rompay has recently expressed the primary place in Syriac Studies held by studies of the language and its literature:

> To whatever new research questions and new methodologies recent developments will lead, the core of Syriac scholarship will remain the study of the language – our only means of communication with Syriac Christians of earlier days – and the interpretation of texts. . . . The disclosure and the first interpretation of texts seem to me to be the noblest task of Syriac scholars, a task we should cherish above anything else.[1]

Defined above all by its historical continuities and by its language, the study of the Syriac World has become a large and complex field in its own right, encompassing the study of its language and its literature, its social, religious, and economic histories, its art and architecture, its interactions with neighbouring language communities and other religions, and its ongoing contribution to world culture and the commonwealth of nations. Syriac Studies understood in this way does not have, nor could it be monopolised by, any single approach or research method; rather it fruitfully intersects with, and at the same time fundamentally influences, a wide variety of other fields of research, each with their own methodologies and trajectories.

The chapters of this volume thus emerge from and interact with a wide variety of academic disciplines as each seeks to illuminate its own specific sphere of interest. The two chapters of Part I offer a broad backdrop against which to interpret and measure all these different spheres by offering overviews respectively of the Roman and Persian empires of Late Antiquity, whose histories are so closely bound up with the trajectories followed by the Syriac peoples. The rest of the chapters cover an enormous range of subjects and issues that emerge from a number of different academic disciplines. The paragraphs that follow will survey in brief a selection of those fields of academic research that underlie Syriac Studies as covered by the chapters in this volume.

LATE ANTIQUITY

Late Antiquity, as a historiographical field that has been revolutionised since the 1970s, has always taken the Syriac World seriously and provides today probably the most frequently trod path into the hidden pearl that is Syriac literature and history. Older accounts of 'The Early Church' tended to find in the Syriac forms of Christianity merely a marginal expression of the core phenomena under investigation. Those ancient accounts of the first Church historians Eusebius, Jerome, and Theodoret of Cyrrhus, in which wild Syriac hermits followed divergent and deeply suspect forms of asceticism beyond the bounds of decent society, were often uncritically accepted by modern Church historians who thus privileged 'orthodox' and 'mainstream' expressions of Christianity and expounded a narrative in which the victory of Nicene Christianity came to seem inevitable. Walter Bauer's thesis (*Rechtgläubigkeit und Ketzerei im ältesten Christentum* 1934), by suggesting that in Edessa non-Nicene forms of Christian religion may in reality have been normative and even dominant even deep into Late Antiquity, paved the way for substantially more sympathetic and evidence-based accounts of early Syriac Christianity. The history and development of religious traditions in the East Roman and Persian political spheres in Late Antiquity, being thus central to the concerns of the wider field, naturally form the subject of a number of chapters in this volume, especially David Taylor's wide-ranging and novel exploration of the problem of the origins of Syriac Christianity (Chapter 4), which questions received wisdom about the dominant place of Edessa in the story.

In Chapter 5, Florence Jullien summarises research into the vital questions relating to early monasticism and asceticism, outlining the multiple forms of religious life that developed in the early centuries and prioritising the anthropological approach to the study of asceticism that has been pursued in late ancient studies in recent decades.

Going back now in time, John F. Healey in Chapter 3 explores the surviving evidence regarding the forms of religious life that preceded the coming of the multiform Christianities of the third century and after. Here we are firmly embedded in the discipline of the history of religions of ancient Mesopotamia. Taking this chapter together with the two that follow, what emerges forms the basis of an inquiry into the religious phenomena of the region in the third–fifth centuries that is based on readings of continuity and persistence through change rather than one that is lodged wholly in a framework of the comings and goings of different religions and their beliefs.

Chapters 6 and 7 offer assistance to those confused by the complexities of Church politics in Late Antiquity, tracing how the diverse forms of Christianity developed over time into a number of mutually competing hierarchically organised 'churches' (see also Chapter 22). Chapters 8 and 9 further explore late ancient Syriac Christianity's interaction with Zoroastrianism and Judaism: in the former of these, Geoffrey Herman shows how the not insignificant presence of Christians within the Persian Empire introduced challenges to both communities, challenges that resulted in new forms of accommodation and the emergence of a distinctive 'Persian' Christianity whose written medium nonetheless remained Syriac. Michal Bar-Asher Siegal (Chapter 9) bridges the rarely crossed boundary between Jewish Rabbinics and Syriac Christianity and shows how the two subjects, by being studied together in this way, can throw into sharper relief the contours of religious history.

ISLAMIC STUDIES

The field of Early Arabic and Islamic Studies has always recognised the importance of the interactions and mutual influences that took place in the early centuries of Islam between Syriac and Arabic language communities all over the Middle East. This touches on a number of fields. Students of Arabic philosophy and medicine, albeit from the opposite end from that of the classicists (see below), continue to debate the place that the Syriac traditions should hold within the history of the Arabic traditions (see Chapters 25–26). On the religious side, the significance of Syriac Studies within Islamic Studies is rather extensive, as may be appreciated from the material covered in Chapters 11, 31, 35, 38, and 39.

Indeed, regional histories and history of religion must be allowed their proper and substantial contribution here – the methodological separation of disciplines such as Church History, Late Antiquity, Islamic Studies, and Rabbinics (to name just some of those concerned) can only serve to veil rather than illuminate our understanding of a past that continues to have an enormous impact upon the present. This is a growing and productive field replete with studies of the interactions of Christian and Muslim communities. Chapters 11 and 12, by focusing on the early relations between Syriac Christians and Arab Muslims in the seventh–eighth centuries, contribute to the wider picture in just this way. The impact of the growth of Islam is also a major theme of Chapter 10, which explores how it came about that Syrians developed their own sense of 'ethnic' or even 'national' identity, initially only *in nuce* under the Roman and Persian empires and then increasingly under Islamic rule. Studies of identity formation and perceived ethnicities have been prominent within late ancient studies for some time now, and yet their application to the Syriac sphere is still at an early stage.

SEMITICS

Part III of the present volume explores key features of the Syriac language itself, the study of which constitutes the very heart of Syriac Studies. As Holger Gzella explains (Chapter 13), Syriac emerged out of the complex of Aramaic dialects on account of its adoption by the government of the Edessan kingdom in the late second century, and it is at that moment that we can begin to speak with some moment of a 'Syriac World'. Following this thread we may say that this Syriac World was able to establish itself as a vital historical phenomenon precisely because the Edessene dialect became 'a deregionalised and supradialectal written idiom' that even 'outlived the spread of Arabic in the wake of Islam in the seventh century' (p. 207). In time, this regional dialect broadened out into a standardised literary form and evolved to the point where it could support a high literary culture capable of profound theological expression in poetry and prose and of translating some of the most complex scientific and philosophical productions of the Hellenic tradition. In Chapter 14, Aaron Butts offers a typology of the language and its chronolects, explores features of its contacts with neighbouring languages, and introduces readers to the modern scholarly study of the language. Two other chapters offer overviews of important aspects of the linguistic study of Syriac: Chapter 15 summarises the writing systems and processes that resulted in all those beautiful manuscripts and inscriptions which have so often been the initial draw for young scholars entering the field of Syriac Studies; finally, lest we ever forget that Aramaic is far from a dead language, Geoffrey Khan (Chapter 16) offers a window into the complex variety of the modern Aramaic dialects via a comparative phonological and morphological description. Professor Khan has done an incalculable service to the Aramaic communities and to historical linguistics generally by his tireless quest to preserve and document these dialects and to highlight thereby the plight of language groups that have in modern times become increasingly marginalised, a situation that all those who study the Syriac World at any level and from any direction ought to be keenly aware of (see also Chapters 38–39).

BIBLICAL STUDIES

Biblical Studies has long been a common route into Syriac, as scholars traced the traditions of the Biblical manuscripts into their early translations. This was once an exercise purely in finding and assessing ancient variants for the textual criticism of the Hebrew Bible and New Testament, but has more recently become a whole field in its own right, exploring the reception of the Bible and its interpretation and influence with the Syriac World. Through such research, students of the Bible are able to be challenged by hermeneutical traditions very different from those of the Greek and Latin Churches, and the diversity of ancient Christianities can find its voice. Jonathan Loopstra (Chapter 17) offers an overview of how to engage with the deep and rich tradition of Syriac Biblical translation and interpretation. Another very fruitful area of recent research has been uncovering the previously under-appreciated networks that existed between Christian and Jewish communities, with each having an impact upon the other's hermeneutical traditions (Chapter 9).

CLASSICS

Classicists have at least since the middle of the nineteenth century been aware of the extent to which Syriac preceded Arabic as the language into which the Greek scientific and philosophical tradition was adopted. Although early hopes of finding numerous works lost since Antiquity did not in the end materialise, research carried out over recent decades has tended towards a richer appreciation that the ancient world and its heritage was kept alive as much on the far as on the near side of the Euphrates. Three areas are especially worthy of attention: historiography, philosophy, and medicine, which are treated respectively in Chapters 24–26. In all three areas, the reader is struck by the strong sense of continuity that pertains between Greek and Syriac traditions. Philip Wood (Chapter 24) shows how Syriac historiography developed out of the Greek genres of Late Antiquity and moreover that the Syriac historians, far from developing their own 'ethnic' or 'regional' histories, rather partook of the Eusebian 'universalistic' style of history writing. The chapters on philosophy (Chapter 25) and medicine (Chapter 26) evidence similar trajectories. What these chapters illustrate above all is the extent to which Syriac literary and intellectual culture in Late Antiquity was a regional and yet distinctive extension of the Greek intellectual culture of the period. The language barrier was not to such a great extent also a barrier of culture and intellectual endeavour. The Syriac World before the coming of Islam could be conceptually united with the Greek (and to some extent Persian) worlds of which it formed a part, while its own distinctive and individual genius only becomes apparent on its gradual isolation from those traditions.

THE WRITTEN AND VISUAL ARTS IN SOCIETY

In other fields of endeavour, however, the Syriac World seems to be all on its own. The poetry of Ephrem, although not entirely without antecedents in Near Eastern literature or relations with Greek literary forms, nonetheless causes his contemporary readers to feel that they have entered a world quite different from that of classical literature, a distinctive field of 'Syriac' literature whose beginnings are explored by Ute Possekel (Chapter 18) and whose later flowerings are expounded by Sebastian Brock (Chapter 19) right up to the present day. The particular impetuses within Syriac literature were themselves somewhat *sui generis* – the high status of ascetic practice in the church spawned a broad literature of hagiography (Chapter 20) and mysticism (Chapter 21), the Christological controversies that rent the church from the sixth century gave rise to whole genres of dispute literature which bore only a degree of resemblance to their Greek cousins (Chapter 22), while the church liturgies also gave rise to a whole swathe of writings (Chapter 23), which even today account for a large proportion of extant Syriac manuscripts.

These characteristic features of the Syriac written and oral traditions extend also to the visual sphere, and in Chapters 27 and 28 we may once again perceive the multiple ways in which the Syriac world was forging its own distinctive styles out of the raw materials provided by Greek or older indigenous models. In Chapter 27, Emma Loosley explores especially the history of Syriac wall painting, alongside other visual art forms, while Widad Khoury (Chapter 28) provides us with a richly illustrated overview of the church building traditions that grew initially out of the Antiochene styles, finally to yield a distinctive architecture that both drew on local traditions and yet was also held together at the regional level by frequent contact and pilgrimage routes.

This physical backdrop of church architecture and paintings offers the perfect context for Susan Ashbrook Harvey's search for the voice of women and children in Syriac society (Chapter 29), which she finds above all in the multiple roles that both women and children could fulfil in the performance of the liturgy; she hears their voices still echoing back to us in the sound of song. Indeed, music has ever been a significant feature of Syriac social and church life, as Chapters 23 and 36 attest. Its modern descendants are still readily available, although its history cannot easily or satisfactorily be encompassed in book form.

These explorations (Part IV) into the cultural features of the late ancient Syriac World, which interlock in so many ways with other fields of expertise, is rounded off with Michael J. Decker's outline of how the agricultural economy functioned in late ancient Mesopotamia (Chapter 30). Historians' outlooks are often skewed by the unrepresentative nature of the sources – the Syriac sources' preferences for matters ecclesiastical and spiritual can easily cause us to forget that most people are more concerned on a daily basis for their crops and the weather than for more transcendent or arcane questions, and the latter may only be properly appreciated in the context of the former. Decker might be speaking for almost any aspect of Syriac life and culture when he says of the Syriac farmers,

> theirs was not a timeless story akin to fable, but rather a series of successes and failures, of expansion and retraction, a mingling of ancient technique and structures with, in certain times and spaces, new methods developed locally or imported from half a world away.
>
> (p. 577)

THE HISTORIES OF CENTRAL ASIA, CHINA, AND INDIA

Whenever Syriac Christianity has impinged upon the consciousness of the West, it has often been on account of the astonishing extent of its eastward reach at certain periods of its history. Wallis Budge's publication in 1928 of the memoirs of Barṣauma, the monk who travelled from Beijing to Paris via Baghdad a generation before Marco Polo, did much to popularise and romanticise this corner of history. The impact of Syriac Christianity on the people groups of Central Asia is a vast and complex topic that is still being elucidated by publications of the finds from Turfan and Dunhuang and which is expertly summarised by Mark Dickens (Chapter 31). The study of the Syrians in China goes back to the 1625 discovery of the Xi'an Stele, an astonishing monument of religious interaction that takes early Christianity as far away from Western concerns as can be conceived. Hidemi Takahashi (Chapter 32) steers us expertly through the unfamiliar sources and cautiously explains what may be usefully extracted from them. It has been the fate of Syriac Christianity that the societies and cultures with which it has come into contact have often been themselves strong, well-embedded traditions (Chinese, Indian, Arab), not easily transformed by the appearance of a few Christian missionaries from distant lands, and the results are instructive. The Indian experience is the subject of Chapter 33, in which István Perczel offers new perspectives and judgements on the sources as traditionally understood. His chapter will serve as a starting point for future work on the Syriac traditions in India.

With these subjects, and especially the last, we move beyond the histories of the Syriac churches in the ancient world and into more recent eras. Although Late Antiquity was the period in which the Syriac communities arose and established themselves on the pages of human history and in which they flourished in their religion and their arts, nonetheless their experiences over the succeeding centuries cannot be passed over, and their sufferings ought not to be forgotten. In a fascinating take on the era of the so-called Syriac renaissance of the twelfth and thirteenth centuries (Chapter 34) Dorothea Weltecke and Helen Younansardaroud analyse the work of Barhebraeus and others who 'within a world of potentially disadvantageous power structures . . . wanted to develop spaces of autonomy as well as of participation and thus had to balance out separation and interaction, tradition, and innovation' (p. 711).

The story of the experiences of the Syriac communities over the next centuries is taken up by Thomas Carlson (Chapter 35), interaction and adaptation again being the outstanding features of the thirteenth to sixteenth centuries during which these communities and their churches were compelled to find novel ways of surviving in increasingly unforgiving conditions. That narrative is brought down into the contemporary era in

Chapters 38 and 39. The former (Heleen Murre-van den Berg) demonstrates how an understanding of the experience of the Syriac minorities in the Near East is crucial for our broader understanding of the history of the region over the last few centuries. Syrians, as much as any other language group around the world, were caught up in the mania for establishing national identities on cultural and historical grounds in the nineteenth and early twentieth centuries. Hopes that this renewed sense of identity might strengthen the status of minority communities in the Near East were shattered first by the genocide of 1915–1918 and then by the treatment of these communities after the Great War. Erica C. D. Hunter (Chapter 39) takes the story up into recent years and the trauma of Islamic State in Iraq.

To round off this survey of the academic disciplines that intersect in one or another manner with the Syriac World, mention must be made of the hold that Syriac matters held upon the minds of many renaissance scholars in Western Europe. Robert Wilkinson's publications have cast much light on how Western scholars' knowledge of Syriac grew out of Rome's contacts with the Maronites of Lebanon (see also Chapter 36), how these were influenced by characteristically sixteenth-century interests in mystical writings and Kabbalah, and how the Catholic and the Protestant efforts to publish Syriac-related material followed very different and conflicting paths. Yet out of these self-interested projects of the early modern era there grew, albeit through many and slow stages, the modern academy of Syriac Studies, as much influenced by Syriac-speakers themselves as by European antiquarians. Members of the Syriac communities are increasingly involved with the progress of Syriac Studies and the discipline is in turn progressively more involved with the survival and flourishing of the Syriac communities of today. It is to them that this book is dedicated, together with the prayer that by contributing to the wider knowledge and appreciation of Syriac history and culture, it may in some small way contribute also to the perseverance of those communities scattered around the world.

All the chapters here presented were written by experts in their respective fields and represent an up-to-date account of the state of research. In many cases they also break new ground. They aim to be as accessible as possible to all who seek a general overview of the state of Syriac studies at the time of writing. Within the narrow limitations of a single book, the accounts are necessarily succinct; hence extensive further reading lists are offered at the end of each chapter, that the reader may easily follow up further on any matter of interest. A path into the riches of Syriac life and literature having been once uncovered, there is almost no end to where it may lead; so 'let the Hidden Pearl be revealed to anyone who is interested in discovering it and learning from it'.[2] Much of its treasure lies open and available to all who wish to partake. Much remains to be discovered from within a thousand ancient manuscripts that are still waiting to tell the full story of an extraordinary group of communities who have preserved their heritage for many centuries yet and who, if they are better understood and appreciated by the rest of the world, may still for many more to come.

NOTES

1 Lucas van Rompay, 'Syriac Studies: The Challenges of the Coming Decade,' *Hugoye: Journal of Syriac Studies* 10:1, 23–35 (2007), cited from p. 27, 33.

2 Ibid., p. 34.

PART I

BACKGROUNDS

CHAPTER ONE

THE EASTERN PROVINCES OF THE ROMAN EMPIRE IN LATE ANTIQUITY

Muriel Debié

Syriac as such never was the official language of a state or the language of an ethnically defined 'people'. It might be precisely for that reason that it became so successful and spread ultimately beyond politically defined entities, as a cultural and religious language, never as an official one. This is a rare enough phenomenon that is worth highlighting. It was only during the short-lived kingdom of Osrhoene that Old Syriac or Edessan Aramaic was an official language, as inscriptions, coins, and documents exemplify. Syriac was the spoken language in Edessa, hence its name as 'urḥaya' from Urḥay, the Aramaic name of the city. We do not know, however, the extension of the zone where it was spoken, since other forms of Aramaic were in use in the region.

THE HELLENISTIC MELTING POT

Syriac is a major piece in the mosaic of spoken and written languages in Late Antiquity and the Middle Ages and goes back to the Hellenistic period. The ancient caravan city, known as Adme or Admun in Old-Assyrian or Babylonian, was (re)founded in 304 BC by Seleucos I Nicator as a Hellenistic city under the name of Edessa, a Macedonian city from which stemmed the new Macedonian-Greek settlers. Edessa became a Greek *polis* with its civic institutions and buildings (porticoes, theatre). Greek was the official as well as cultural and colloquial language, in addition to local Aramaic, and it took the place of the 'Standard Aramaic' that had been the official written medium of communication throughout the Middle East during the Achaemenid period. Hellenisation took place at a wide variety of levels (political, religious, artistic, as well as linguistic) on an Aramaic and Arabic substrate, thus creating a mixed culture in this 'Syrian' kingdom (the Seleucids are called 'Syrian kings') as it did further east, as far as Central Asia. This was not just a superficial process: what we call the 'Seleucid era', or *Anno Graecorum*, the inception of which celebrated the entrance of Seleucus I Nicator into Babylonia and was fixed as 1 October 312/311 BC, remained the preferred method of dating in Syriac almost until the nineteenth century. It was conceived as a Syrian way of dating, a local identity marker that remained in use well after the Christianisation of Edessa/Urḥay, as opposed to the Christian era that was also used in the Middle Ages but never replaced the 'Era of Alexander the Great', or 'Era of the Greeks' as it is called in Syriac. Time was thus recorded in Syriac in a Greek-Syrian mode.

While Greek became prominent, Aramaic did not disappear. Since it was no longer an official language, standardised in scribes' schools for the administration, local dialectic differences came to the fore. Aramaic that had remained mainly a spoken language during the Seleucid era re-emerged at the end of the period in a variety of local written forms. The decline of the Seleucid kingdom gave way to the emergence of the Parthian Empire and more or less independent city-states. The local level was prominent. The Nabataean kingdom as well as the city-states of Dura, Ḥatra, Palmyra, and Edessa thus promoted their independence and their own script, derived from the script used in the Persian period, in order to write the local forms of Aramaic they used. It is thus already in a multilingual as well as multiscript context that we must situate Edessan Aramaic.

ROMANISATION

Edessa became part of the Arsacid Empire slightly later than the middle of the second century BC. Its rulers adopted the title of 'mlk', king, instead of 'mry', lord, used until then. Osrhoene, with Urḥay/Edessa as its capital, became ca. 133 BC a kingdom ruled by a local dynasty until the middle of the third century AD. Its name is thought to derive from their tribe the Osrhoeni or their capital Urḥay/Orhay. Many in this line of kings were named Abgar and Maʿnu, which are North-Arabian onomastic forms. In 83 BC, Syria was integrated into the Armenian kingdom of Tigranes II, with the kingdom of Osrhoene as its vassal. In 63 BC, Pompey made Syria into a Roman province and recognised Abgar II as client king. The 'Romanisation' of the East took place in the second century AD during Septimius Severus's campaigns against the Parthian empire (capturing Ctesiphon in 197). In the 190s, Severus (r. 193–211) separated the provinces of *Syria Coele* (the region of Laodicea and Antioch) and *Syria Phoenice* (Tyre). In 193, when civil war broke out, the Parthian kingdoms of Osrhoene and Adiabene supported the bid of the governor of Syria, Pescennius Niger, against Septimius Severus.

Abgar VIII first sided with the Romans, but later turned against them. In 195, Septimius Severus liberated Nisibis from a siege by Adiabenenes and Osrhoenians. He then returned to Edessa and captured it. These events are depicted on the triumphal arch he erected in the Roman forum. The lower register depicts the siege engines against Edessa; in the central scene Abgar surrenders, and in the upper register, Septimius Severus announces the annexation of Osrhoene and Nisibis. Circa 197, he created the province of *Osrhoene*. The new province of *Mesopotamia* bordered Osrhoene to the east. Abgar VIII, also called 'The Great' (r. 177–212), remained the ruler of Edessa until 212 and took the Persian title of 'king of kings', yet he was only a client king since his kingdom was now a Roman province. A procurator supervised him and he had to hand over his children as hostages. He assisted Severus's expedition by providing archers and cataphracts. As we know from the writer Julius Africanus, Abgar's court cultivated a Parthian style, and Bardaiṣan (154–222), the Edessan philosopher, was renowned as an archer. Lush garments depicted on mosaics also attest the Parthian cultural influence. In 212/213, Edessa lost its independence and became a Roman *colonia*. The dynasty was briefly restored in 238 or 239 under Abgar X, son of Maʿnu. However, by 242 it had reverted to the status of *colonia* (P. Euphr. 20). With a *strategos* at its head and civic tribes, it became a typical Greek city-state and Roman colony. A new network of roads integrated Nisibis and Singara more firmly into Rome's eastern defences, and gave it access to the Tigris.

The mixed culture of Edessa shows up in the rich mosaics that adorned palaces (Haleplibahçe at the bottom of Edessa's citadel) and tombs (Figures 1.1–1.3; also Fig 27.1). Scenes from Homer's Iliad (Achilles cycle), of the Amazons or Orpheus (see Figure 3.4), showcase a shared cultural Hellenism among the elites, but in Aramaic dress since the legends identifying the characters are in Edessan script. Mosaics in tombs depict aristocratic families with their slaves, dressed in Parthian garb.

Figure 1.1 Family Portrait Mosaic from Edessa, probably second or early third century

Figure 1.2 The Funerary Couch Mosaic, Edessa dated 278

Reliefs have Parthian priests with Greek inscriptions. Roman polity, Greek culture, and Aramaic administrative practices tinted with Parthian and Arabic influence thus constitute the mixed background from which Syriac emerged as a cultural language.

The coins minted by the Abgarids bear Edessan inscriptions, whereas the silver tetradrachm struck in Edessa by Macrinus in 217–218 is in Latin. They show how Edessan Aramaic stopped being used as an official language when Edessa became Roman.

Figure 1.3 The Tripod Mosaic, Edessa, probably second or third century

In other places, the local forms of Aramaic more or less disappeared with the end of local independence: Nabatean survived for some time the end of the kingdom (annexed by the Roman Empire in 106), but the dialects of Dura Europos (Shapur I stormed it ca. 256) or Ḥatra (captured by the Sasanians in 240) were not used anymore after their destruction. Edessan Aramaic might have been erased the same way had it not become the cultural language of Aramaic-speaking converts to Christianity.

A LITERARY AND PUBLIC LIFE IDIOM

It is interesting to note, however, that Edessan Aramaic was still in use in the 240s for writing private legal documents such as bills of sale or property leases (Figure 1.4, also see Figure 14.1, p. 226). Among parchments and papyri in Greek, Latin (for the army), Parthian, and Aramaic, one parchment entirely in Syriac was found in Dura Europos and two others probably came from the Euphrates (Cotton, Cockle, and Millar 1995).

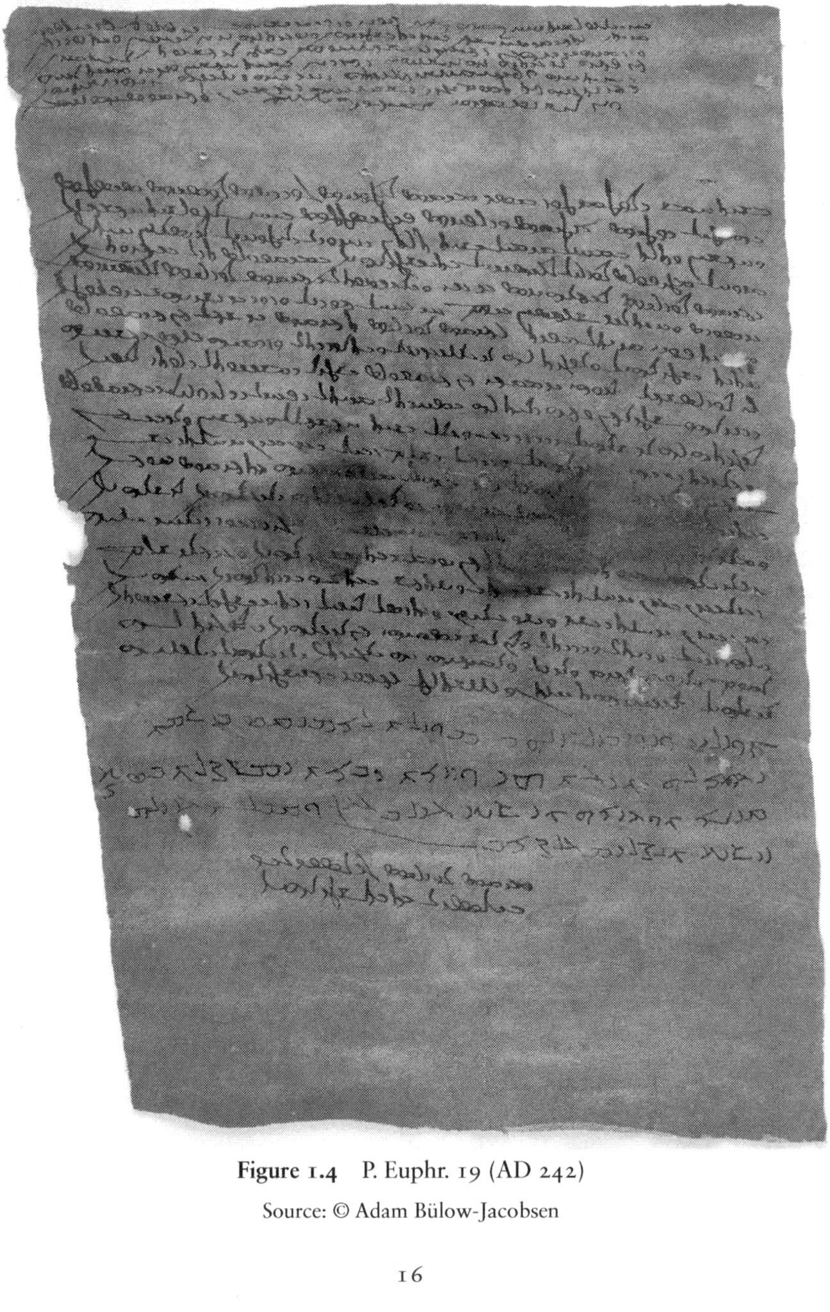

Figure 1.4 P. Euphr. 19 (AD 242)

Source: © Adam Bülow-Jacobsen

Greek documents on parchment or papyrus from the same archive also have a few lines or subscriptions in Syriac as well as names of witnesses. The officials mentioned have Roman titles (*bouleutes*, *strategos*, *praefectus*). Three of these documents were written in the province of Coele Syria, the others in Mesopotamia (Marcoupolis in the territory of Edessa). They attest a wide use of Edessan Aramaic beyond the borders of Osrhoene. These documents are interesting at different levels. They show how Edessan Aramaic was a language of the Roman Empire as much as Latin and Greek were. From a linguistic point of view, they display a form of Aramaic slightly different from Classical Syriac (Healey 2009: 252–75; see chs. 13, 14), meaning that an evolution in the written language was at play. Differences in the oral forms were most probably the norm as we can observe in modern contexts with spoken dialects that vary from one village to the next. Standardisation takes place in the writing process when orthographic and grammatical rules are transmitted in schools: here schools for the scribes in the administration, later on in the schools in Edessa and in monasteries where copyists (*katoba* in Syriac) learned the art of calligraphy or book writing.

Called *sephre* in Syriac, the scribes who wrote down these documents of the third century used a cursive script that would ultimately re-appear in the eighth century when *serṭo* started to be used for writing manuscripts in place of the more formal *esṭrangela* that was until then the only Syriac script in use for books (see Chapter 15). These documents exemplify a dual tradition of writing, parallel to what we find in manuscripts. The documents also attest links between scribes and the civic and religious archives in Edessa where P. Dura 28 was purportedly copied and deposited. Greek vocabulary and Aramaic archival practices are here combined in a unique way.

These archival traditions, which had a longstanding existence, were to have a deep influence on Syriac literature. The report of a dramatic flooding in Edessa in 201, as it is preserved in an anonymous chronicle of the city written ca. 530, was written down on king Abgar's orders by a royal scribe who deposited it in the city's archive. The historian Eusebius of Caesarea, who wrote in Greek, as well as the Armenian historian Movses Khorenatsi, also mention the archives in Edessa. Whatever the ongoing existence or not of the archives in the fourth century, hagiographic and apocryphal texts in Syriac use them as a literary device, in order to authenticate their tales, just as novels in the seventeenth or eighteenth centuries pretended to be documents found in an attic or a trunk, not a work of fiction. Acts of the Edessan martyrs or the *Doctrina Addai* thus pretend that they were written as documents by civic scribes and deposited in the archives. From reality to fictional process, the Mesopotamian archival tradition proved to have long-lasting effects all the way through Syriac literature.

THE EAST ROMAN PROVINCES IN THE THIRD–FOURTH CENTURIES

The standardisation of Edessan or Old Syriac attested in inscriptions and documents into Classical Syriac took place gradually. It is likely that the translation of the Peshiṭta of the Old Testament from Hebrew and the first literary texts written in Syriac or soon translated from Greek (Diatessaron, Acts of Thomas, etc.) in the second–third centuries contributed to creating a standard literary language. We do not have any clue about this process, very little being known about the evolution of the language. The oldest Syriac manuscripts, BL Add. 12 150, dated 411 (see fig 14.2–3), and St Petersburg 1, dated 462 and copied in Edessa, are interesting in that they show an already well formed *esṭrangela* script and page layout as well as a relatively standardised form of Syriac. The Christianisation of Nisibis and Edessa and the surrounding regions continued contemporaneously with translations of the Bible and the composition of Syriac Christian texts that ensured the transformation of Old Syriac into a cultural language that was adopted as the religious and cultural medium of Aramaic-speaking populations well beyond Osrhoene, Syria, and Mesopotamia, whatever the local forms of spoken Aramaic. By 238/9, the Sasanians attacked Roman Syria and Mesopotamia and captured a number of cities. In 240, the crown-prince Shapur subdued the kingdom of Ḥatra.

The year 224 marks the coming to power of the Sasanian Dynasty in Iran and the beginning of a new hegemony in the region, which disrupted the former status quo between Rome and the Parthian kingdom. Roman-Persian wars remained a major threat for local security until the end of both empires. The populations of the borders were recurrently subjected to massacres, plunders, sieges, captivity, and deportations to the Sasanian Empire. Treaties and wartimes alternated constantly. Gordian III led an expedition which liberated some of the captured cities but suffered a major defeat near the Sasanian twin royal city of Seleucia-Ctesiphon. Shapur (r. 242–272) directed a series of raids from 252 onwards against Syria, Commagene, and Cappadocia: he captured Antioch (253 and 256), marched into Lesser Armenia, and destroyed Dura Europos and Circesium (256). During his third campaign, Shapur I marched into Osrhoene. Valerian (r. 253–60) was defeated near Edessa in his attempt to oppose the invasion and led into captivity in Persia (Figure 1.5).

Figure 1.5 Triumph of Shapur over Valerian, Bishapur, Iran

The victorious Persians plundered Syria, Cilicia, and Cappadocia. Local resistance by Valerian's officers at Pompeiopolis and by Odaenathus, the prince of Palmyra who raided deep into Sasanian-held Mesopotamia (Asorestan), finally halted Shapur. Rome had effectively lost control of territories south of the Anti-Taurus. The year 272 was a turning point: Rome regained control over her Near Eastern possessions from the Palmyrenes and *shahanshah* ('king of kings') Shapur died. The Roman emperor Carus took advantage of this and made a successful raid against Asorestan in 283, penetrating as far as Seleucia-Ctesiphon (Dodgeon and Lieu 1991: 2).

Diocletian's reign (r. 284–305) stabilised the empire after the crisis of the third century. With a co-emperor and two Caesars he instituted the 'tetrarchy', or 'rule of four', each emperor ruling over a quarter-division of the empire. He reorganised the empire's provincial divisions, establishing new administrative centres in Nicomedia and Antioch. He overhauled the defence of the eastern provinces. He constructed a line of communication, the so-called *Strata Diocletiana*, across the Syrian Desert from Sura on the Euphrates to Damascus via Palmyra, interspersed with fortresses along the *limes* (borders). He fortified the city of Circesium (Buseire, Syria) on the Euphrates, and during his reign a legion was stationed at Edessa, Legio IIII Parthica. In 296, the *shahanshah* Narses defeated Diocletian and the Cesar Galerius near Carrhae (Ḥarran), but in 297/8, he was forced to hand over the Transtigritanian regions. In 299, Galerius sacked his capital, Seleucia-Ctesiphon. The Peace of Nisibis ensued. Nisibis officially became the only place for trade exchange between the two countries. It became known in Syriac as 'the city of the borders'. This had long-lasting consequences since trade routes thus moved from the Euphrates to the Tigris and the city became disputed and preyed upon by both empires. Rome would exercise control over the five satrapies between the Tigris and Armenia: Ingilene, Sophanene, Arzanene, Corduene, and Zabdicene (near modern Hakkâri, Turkey). These regions included the passage of the Tigris. The cities of northern Mesopotamia like Amida, Nisibis, Singara, and Bezabde thus gained a new defensive role in the frontier zone (Dodgeon and Lieu 1991: 3).

In 286, Nicomedia (modern Izmit in Turkey) became the eastern capital city of the Roman Empire as well as the interim capital city for Constantine until in 330 he declared the nearby Byzantium (renamed Constantinople) as his new capital. As the capital city of the empire, its fate was no stranger to the authors writing in Syriac: Ephrem the Syrian (ca. 306–373) wrote 16 *memre* on Nicomedia lamenting the destruction of the city (that he still calls 'the royal city') in a devastating earthquake on 24 August 358. These *memre* that vividly depict everyday life in a Late Antique city are today preserved only fragmentarily in Syriac and in an Armenian translation made in the fifth century (Ephrem, *Hymns on Nicomedia*; on Ephrem, see Chapter 18).

The last and bloodiest persecution took place at that time (the Diocletianic persecution, 303–11), and local martyrs are known from later texts. Diocletian also turned against Manichaeans and ordered that the leading followers of Mani be sent to forced labour camps, killed, or burnt alive along with their scriptures and their properties seized. The Edict of Milan (Feb. 313) gave Christianity legal status, and under emperor Theodosius I in 380 Christianity was proclaimed the official religion of the Roman empire. As a result, *Osrhoene* became the civil and ecclesiastical province of the diocese of Oriens from the fourth to the seventh century, extending east from the Euphrates River as far as the province of Mesopotamia. In addition to Edessa it contained 18 cities (Constantina, Kallinikos, Kirkesion, Batnae/Sarug, and Carrhae/Ḥarran, to cite only the main ones). Osrhoene remained under Roman rule until the Persian occupation of the Middle East and the Arab-Islamic conquests in the seventh century (Millar 2006).

Hostilities were resumed between the Roman and Sasanian empires in 337. Shapur II (309–79) made repeated but unsuccessful attacks on Nisibis (in 337, 346, and 350). Latin, Greek, and Syriac histories and chronicles minutely describe the sieges and their aftermath, while history was slowly twisted into legend in order to explain miraculous escapes (Debié 2006).

Ephrem the Syrian composed *madrashe* on Nisibis that interpreted the success as the result of the protection endowed by the presence of the tomb of bishop Jacob of Nisibis inside the city walls (Figure 1.6) and by the prayers of the inhabitants, which are described as the true walls and defences against the pagan (Zoroastrian) enemies (Ephrem, *Hymns on Nisibis*). Mass persecutions of Christians took place in the Sasanian kingdom, as Christians were suspected of sympathising with Rome (see Chapter 8).

Some cities were lost to the Persians in 359/60, but the Sasanians could not follow up. However, the premature death of Constantius's successor Julian, in the course of his Persian campaign (363), led to the loss of three of the five Transtigritanian regions, which they had gained through the victory of Galerius, as well as of Nisibis and a number of key fortresses, including Singara and Castra Maurorum (Dodgeon and Lieu 1991: 3). Ephrem authored a vivid description of the walls of Nisibis draped in black, the Sasanian banner fluttering in the wind above the fortress and Julian's coffin exposed outside the city walls after the surrounding of the city (Ephrem of Nisibis, *Hymns against Julian*). Like most of his Christian co-religionists, Ephrem

Figure 1.6 Remains of the baptistery of Jacob of Nisibis

moved to Edessa under the truce negotiated between Shapur II and Julian's successor Jovian. In Amida, a new district was incorporated into the defensive walls for the exiles who had fled Nisibis.

Ephrem's *Hymns against Julian* echo the discourses *Against Julian* written in Greek by Gregory of Nazianzus and Cyril of Alexandria as an answer to Julian's own writing *Against the Galileans* and in Latin by Augustine. These vindictive exchanges mark the end of the process of transformation of Christianity into a state religion. The promise made by Julian to the Jews to authorise the reconstruction of the temple in Jerusalem caused a negative reaction in the region of Edessa (Brock 1976, 1977). The so-called *Julian Romance* was subsequently written in Syriac as a re-imagination of Julian as an Anti-Constantine and Edessa in contrast as a pious Christian city confided to Christ by Constantine, a city that resisted Julian's and his Jewish allies' attempts to corrupt it. A competing tale of the Christian history of Edessa is at play here, in contrast to the better known one told in Eusebius's *Ecclesiastical History* and the *Doctrina Addai* (see chapter 4).

The fourth century marks the triumph of the 'Great Church' and its claim to represent Christianity within the Roman Empire. Ephrem (and Aphrahaṭ in the Persian Empire), as had his Greek and Latin counterparts, contributed to creating an 'orthodox' dogmatic position against the heretics whom he incriminated in his compositions. Liturgical poems were the chosen means for catechising. Ephrem presents his own *madrashe* as barriers protecting the faithful against the attacks of the wolves, as he calls the heretics. In Syriac Christianity, the sense of hearing was especially targeted, as a means of reaching the intellect through the ear. The liturgical performance was thus a sensorial experience ultimately aiming at striking the mind of the audience. Images are encompassed in poetry more than on painted walls or illuminated manuscripts. Writing is the favoured media of Syriac culture. *The Doctrina Addai* vividly pictures how at the last judgement each human being will have his/her deeds written on the skin (as living manuscripts written by God's finger) and how each one will be able to read them (although literacy was not common in Late Antique society). It might not be by accident then that Mani in contrast was a painter, not a poet like Bardaiṣan or Ephrem. Manichaeism expressed its cosmology in beautiful frescoes, illuminated manuscripts, and painted textiles all the way from the Mediterranean to China as a way of converting and luring people from different cultures and languages.

Holy men and bishops rose up as intermediaries between God and their contemporaries (Brown 1982). The social changes induced by Christianisation became more visible. The social as well as the natural landscape was affected by new forms of living (Brown 1995). Sons and Daughters of the Covenant in the Syrian-Mesopotamian regions were consecrated for the service of the churches, the poor, and women (see Chapters 5, 29). Hermits and ascetics of all kinds lived in the desert steppe, in caves, in trees, or on top of pillars, praying, living on herbs and bread, and practicing ascetic mortifications. The holy poor (such as the Man of God in Edessa) and holy fools roamed the cities' streets. Married or widowed women and men chose to live a consecrated life as Members of the Covenant or as nuns and monks. Monasteries similar to the ones in Egypt and Palestine (*laurae* or *coenobia*, with varied degrees of common life) were founded in cities, villages, or remote places. Powerful bishops and churches' stewards managed the city's buildings and amenities (canals, bridges, baths, inns, mills, and walls in addition to hospices and churches).

Schools were an important feature of Syriac culture, based on an Antiochene theology that presented God as the first and foremost teacher of both angels and human beings. Conversion is described as a philosophical attitude; converts are presented as enlightened by the Christian doctrine and as disciples. They do not 'turn' towards Christianity in Syriac texts, but rather become students of the divine doctrine (hence the title of the *Doctrina Addai* that tells the story of Addai's teaching that converted king Abgar, his courtiers, and the whole city). Parallel to the School of Nisibis, three schools existed in Edessa: the School of the Persians (closed by emperor Zeno in 489 because of its dyophysite stance), the School of the Armenians, and the School of the Syrians (nothing is known, however, of a school of the Greeks). In Amida, a School of the Urtaye (region of Anzitene, in Roman Armenia, north of Amida) associated with the namesake monastery is known from the *Lives of the Eastern Saints* written by John of Ephesus.

THE FIFTH–SIXTH CENTURIES

In Syriac manuscripts of the fifth–sixth centuries, Edessa is called the 'capital of Bet Nahrin', i.e. Mesopotamia (Brock 2012b: 102) even though it was not part of the Roman province of Mesopotamia (Amida was its capital). Interestingly, they attest a different view of the hierarchy of cities and regions than the official divisions of the Roman Empire, Edessa/Urḥay being considered here as the main city in the region between the Tigris and Euphrates rivers. It is during these centuries that Syriac as a language of Christian literature and public life spread westwards, across the Euphrates, into the Late Roman provinces of Euphratensis and of Syria I and II (Millar 2006: 16). It was used in the area between the Euphrates and Antioch, in the Syrian steppe, in the Limestone Massif, and as far south as the region of Apamea.

A NEW GEO-ECCLESIOLOGY

The Council of Ephesus (431) that condemned Nestorius, the patriarch of Constantinople, and his followers estranged the Church of the East from the Church of the Roman Empire. The Council of Chalcedon in 451 that condemned Eutyches and his partisans and the Christological formulation of Cyril of Alexandria ushered in new divisions over faith and institutional partitions (see Chapters 6, 22). At first, Chalcedonian and non-Chalcedonian bishops alternated on the main seats of the patriarchates of Antioch (Jerusalem chose the side of Constantinople) and Alexandria.

Syriac was not an official language of the Roman Church, unlike Latin and Greek, which were the official languages of the empire. Yet official documents such as the acts of the councils were translated into Syriac. We thus have the acts of the Second Council of Ephesus in 449, which was not recognised as ecumenical and was named *Latrocinium*, the 'Robber' council by the pope, only in the Syriac translation of the second session, the Greek original being lost. Participants in the councils sometimes signed in Syriac and we find mentions of ecclesiastics who expressed themselves in Syriac and whose words were translated (or the other way around). The famous letter of Ibas, bishop of Edessa, to 'Mari the Persian' in the 430s that analysed the Council of Ephesus of 431 was translated into Greek and read at the Council of Constantinople. Syriac was thus one of the three languages of the East

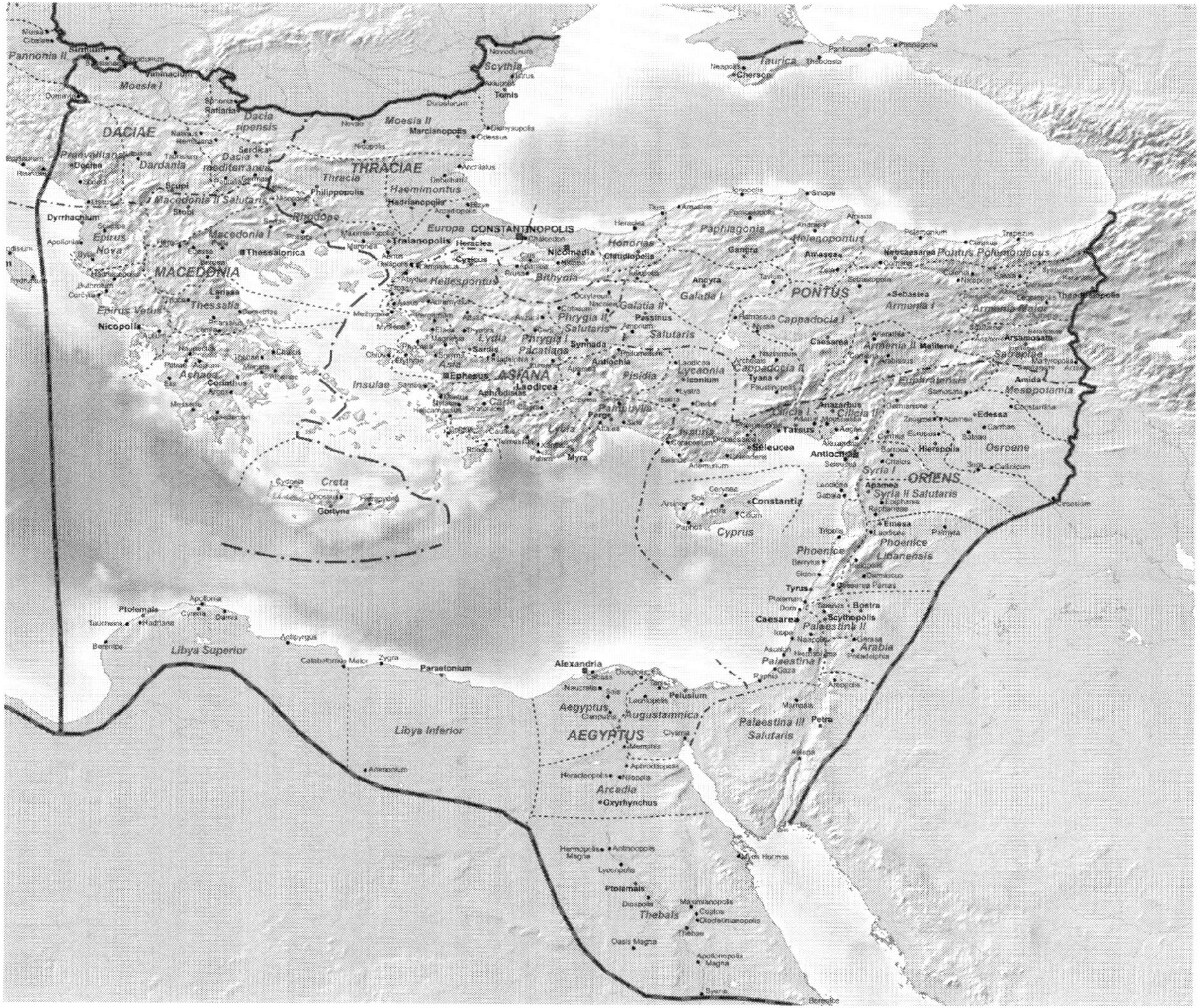

Figure 1.7 Map of the Diocese of the East ca. 400

Roman Church although not an official one (and no other language of the Christian Orient is mentioned as being used in any official circumstances). Petitions, cries of the crowds, were also in Syriac as the everyday language of the faithful to the local or imperial authorities.

At a time of religious contention, Bishop Rabbula of Edessa (411–435) is a noteworthy figure of a powerful bishop and opponent of Antiochene theology: he fiercely opposed the views of Theodore of Mopsuestia and Nestorius, even on one occasion in Constantinople where he preached before Theodosius II. He corresponded with Cyril of Alexandria and translated into Syriac treatises on the nature of Christ, notably 'Concerning the Right Faith', advocating the Alexandrian position. His strong opinions are also visible in his condemnation of the use of Tatian's *Diatessaron* or *Gospel Harmony*: he ordered it to be replaced in all churches by a four Gospels version and promoted the use of the Peshiṭta New Testament (see Chapter 17). A fierce reformer of the Church, he wrote still extant rules for clerics and monks. As a Greek-educated civil servant, he was an effective administrator. He built civic and ecclesiastical buildings in line with a general tendency in the first half of the fifth century in West and East alike. At the order of the emperor, he converted a Jewish synagogue into a Christian church dedicated to St Stephen, the first martyr killed by the Jews; he worked at the *xenodocheion* or hospice/hospital, and created one reserved for women. His Syriac biography presents him panegyrically as living an ascetical life even during his time as bishop and taking care of the poor (*The History of Rabbula*).

When the emperor Justin I (518–527) chose to back up the decisions of Chalcedon and started to enforce acceptance of the council, miaphysite bishops and monks were sent into exile, first and foremost Severus the patriarch of Antioch, exiled to Egypt in 518. This had long-lasting consequences, since Egypt became a place of refuge for Syrian miaphysites in the monasteries of the Enaton, nine miles from Alexandria, and in the Nitrian desert. Deir al-Suryan in Nitria is still today a monastery where paintings (Figure 1.8) and Syriac manuscripts attest the long-term presence of Syrian Orthodox monks and has been a major conservatory of Syriac written culture (Brock and van Rompay 2014; Brock 2004 and 2012a; Hunt 2003). This massive exile more broadly created a geo-ecclesial network between the Syrian Orthodox and Egyptian miaphysite churches.

In Syria and Mesopotamia, the strongholds of the resistance to the council's creed, a geo-ecclesial displacement took place. The imperial, often violent, attempts to re-establish Church unity under official orthodoxy proved unsuccessful. Jacob Burdʿana or Baradeus (bishop of Edessa 543/544–578), nicknamed 'the man in ragged clothes', roamed Mesopotamia, Anatolia, Syria, Palestine, and Egypt under the cover of a beggar to escape the imperial agents that pursued non-Chalcedonians. He ordained patriarchs, bishops, and priests, thus re-creating a miaphysite hierarchy after the persecutions and exile. It would become an independent Church called 'Jacobite', from his name 'Jacob', as its opponents called it, or Syrian Orthodox since it claimed that it was the only warrant of orthodoxy against the Greeks who had strayed from it. Forbidden to enter their ecclesiastical capital of Antioch, the Syrian Orthodox patriarchs stayed in monasteries, thus creating the unique model of a mobile ecclesiastical power. Patriarchs have governed the Church from different monasteries over time, each travelling from one place to another in order to enforce his authority on a Church with a geography displaced from the imperial one. Although the patriarch

Figure 1.8 Fresco depicting the Nativity, Deir al-Suryan, Egypt

is 'Patriarch of Antioch and all the East', his seat has been, since Severus's exile until today, a mobile one, outside of Antioch. The anti-Chalcedonians thus occupied decentred places of authority, most prominently monasteries, which hence became a constant factor in the history of the Syrian Orthodox Church and more broadly for Syriac literary and cultural history.

The Persian Empire became, in addition to Egypt, another place of exile for miaphysites as well as a place for conversion and competition with the Church of the East. The monastery of Mar Mattai, near Mosul, and the city of Tikrit (today in Iraq) became the strongholds of the Syrian Orthodox Church with a *maphrian* (as he would later be called) at its head in the East.

The Arab tribes also played a role in the contemporary geo-ecclesiology: whereas the Arabs of the Persian Empire remained largely polytheists (although individuals and families became Christian), the Arabs of the Roman Empire more substantially converted to Christianity. Some of them were connected to monks in the Palestinian area and joined the official church. Those, however, in the Syrian and northern Mesopotamian regions and in the Arabian Peninsula adopted the miaphysite position and rejected the Council of Chalcedon (451), following the lead of the local ascetics and monks who converted them and had the stronger influence. Al-Ḥarith ibn Jabalah (ca. 528–569) who received from Justinian I (r. 527–565) the title of king (in addition to 'patrician and phylarch of the Saracens') urged Empress Theodora to let them have a bishop of their faith. Pope Theodosius I of Alexandria then consecrated bishops Jacob Baradeus for Edessa and Theodore for the Arabs.

Under Justinian I, the organisation of the Church as a Pentarchy (still the model in the Eastern Orthodox Church but rejected in the West as well as in the Church of the East) was first legally expressed in legislation and the Quinisext Council of 692 gave it formal recognition. For the first time, the term 'patriarch' was used for the bishops of the five major episcopal sees of the Roman Empire: Rome, Constantinople, Alexandria, Antioch, and Jerusalem, in that order of precedence.

GEOPOLITICS OF EMPIRES

Diplomacy temporarily prevailed between Romans and Sasanians. In 417/18, catholicos Yahballaha went to Constantinople as ambassador, and in 419/20 bishop Acacius of Amida visited Seleucia-Ctesiphon as Roman ambassador. Church representatives played a diplomatic role between the Roman and Sasanian empires and would still be considered as 'ambassadors' of the Christians during the Islamic period. The threat posed by the Hephthalites (a Hunnic tribe) led to closer relations between Rome and Iran. However, a military conflict broke out shortly after the accession of Vahram V Gor (421–438) in the reign of Theodosius II (408–450): Theodosius failed to take Nisibis in 421, and Yazdgerd II (439–457) strived to obtain financial aid from the Roman emperor. In 422, the Roman emperor consented to covering the costs of defence against the Hephthalites, and both parties pledged to discontinue erection of new strongholds along the border. Huns and more generally Central Asian Turkic tribes were a major element in the Roman-Persian equation.

The Arab tribes under their 'phylarchs' or chieftain kings, who were in charge of the defence of the borderlands for the Roman and the Sasanians, were called in Syriac sources 'The Arabs of the Romans' and 'The Arabs of the Persians'. They were in the fifth and sixth centuries a powerful element in the geopolitics of the borderlands (which were the centre of western Asia) of the Roman and Sasanian empires, as were the South Arabian and Ethiopic kingdoms (Fisher 2011).

At the turn of the century, Kawad I (488–497/499–531) attacked Roman territory. His Arab ally Nuʿman II (500–504) ravaged the surroundings of Carrhae and Constantina. Kawad took Martyropolis (502) and seized Amida in 503. He deported the inhabitants to Iran and Sasanian forces occupied the city for three years. They evacuated it for a large sum of money paid by the Romans, and the city was then rebuilt thanks to imperial patronage. Greek and Syriac chronicles describe the causes of the war, the siege and its aftermath as well as the reconstruction. The great poet and theologian Jacob of Sarug (ca. 450–521) who was an ecclesiastical visitor at that time wrote a letter and two *memre* on the event, as an attempt to comfort the Christian populations in the neighbourhood who were fearful and were tempted to flee and abandon the defence of their cities. The Roman army took Theodosiopolis, plundered Bet ʿArabaye, and carried out a penal expedition to Ḥirta/al-Ḥira, the capital of the Arabs who allied to the Persians (503). King Nuʿman II, who operated mainly in Osrhoene, died of his injuries in 504. Emperor Anastasius I (r. 491–518) resolved to strengthen the Roman defence system in Mesopotamia and had the fortress of Dara built. Bishop Thomas of Amida was the linchpin of this process, as we can see in Syriac chronicles: he is the one who handled finances and workers. The Arabian allies of both sides, the Naṣrids and the Jafnids, played a growing part in the warfare. Military operations in the years 527–531 were due to the activities of the Arab allies of both states in the borderlands but did not bring about any territorial alterations. Taking the opportunity of the death of the Iranian king, the Huns allied with him reached Cilicia (531/532). In 532, Khosrow I Anushirwan (531–579) signed with Justinian I (527–565) a treaty of 'Eternal Peace'. For financial reasons, in 540, taking advantage of Justinian's engagement in the west, Khosrow I was able to go as far as Antioch which he sacked and whose inhabitants he took into captivity.

In the past twenty years, the place of the Arabic peninsula in the economic and geopolitical game between Late Antique empires has been re-evaluated. Himyarite rulers converted to a local Judaism, or some form of a Judaic monotheism as early as the fourth century. Christians belonging to the Church of the East as well as the Syrian Orthodox Church and the Ethiopian Orthodox Church had also been present since the fourth century in South and Eastern Arabia alongside polytheists. The Syrian theologian and writer Philoxenus of Mabbug (d. 523), champion of the miaphysites, had ordained a bishop for Najran in South Arabia. He also wrote to the 'statelets' of Ḥirta/al-Ḥira (where the Church of the East was well established) about Christological issues, which had created a schism inside the miaphysite movement. In the sixth century, Yusuf As'ar Dhu Nuwas, who had converted to Judaism, seized power and became king. He massacred an Ethiopian garrison, destroyed churches, killed the local Christian community, sent punitive expeditions to a number of regions, and attempted to convert communities to Judaism. News of the events immediately spread as far as Syria, Constantinople, and Ethiopia through the miaphysite networks of bishops and monasteries. They were interpreted in religious terms, as the martyrdom of Christians at the hands of a Jewish king and as a geo-religious conflict between Christianity and Judaism that required a counteroffensive by Christian rulers. For economic (Najran controlled the Red Sea trade route) as much as for religious reasons, Justin I asked for help from the patriarch of Alexandria and at the latter's request the Ethiopian Negus Ella-Asbeha of Aksum sent an army and restored Christianity. Aksum occupied Ḥimyar until the Persians regained control of the region in the early 570s. Rome and Ctesiphon competed in order to gain the alliance of the Hujrides, a third group of Arab tribes that dominated the Arabic peninsula. These episodes show how economics, politics, and religion were entangled and how Arabia was fully integrated into the Late Antique geopolitics of empires. It attests also the links between Syriac Christianity and the Arabic Peninsula in the wake of Islam (Beaucamp et al. 2010; Robin 2012; Bowersock 2013).

The historians Procopius in Greek and John of Ephesus in Syriac wrote about Justinian's time and described the Roman-Persian wars as well as the outbreak of the plague in 541 that decimated the inhabitants of Constantinople, the Eastern Roman Empire, and the Sasanian Empire. The pandemic put a halt to the war. It also had a significant social and cultural impact and weakened the Byzantine Empire in the long-term.

In 543, Edessa was besieged but not captured, an event that signalled the end of the war. A 'Fifty-Year Peace' treaty was signed in 562. Justin II (565–578) undertook military operations against Iran simultaneously in Armenia and northern Mesopotamia. Khosrow attacked Syria, captured Dara (573), went into Lesser Armenia, and later attacked Amida and Martyropolis while Justin II twice failed to capture Nisibis. New military operations took place in the years 580–582 under Hormizd IV (579–590) and Tiberius II (578–582). In the years 582–589 again, a war erupted between emperor Maurice (582–602) and Hormizd IV.

THE SEVENTH CENTURY

The murder by Phokas of the emperor Maurice (602), who had helped Khusrow II (591–628) regain his throne, served as a pretext for the Sasanians to launch military actions against the Roman Empire. Khusrow II reached the Euphrates, conquering within several years the following strongholds in Mesopotamia: Dara (604), Amida (606), Edessa (609), and Circesium (610). Then the Iranian army devastated Asia Minor, marching as far as Chalcedon (610), but failed to reach Constantinople. They conquered Damascus (613), Caesarea (614), besieged Jerusalem after a revolt led to the massacre of the Sasanian garrison (614) – booty, including the palladium of Roman Christianity, the True Cross, was sent with prisoners to Seleucia-Ctesiphon – then Egypt and Alexandria (619). Avars menaced Constantinople and Heraclius had to fight on two fronts. Passing through Cappadocia, he moved towards Armenia and in 623–625 had successes in the Sasanian Empire. He destroyed a royal fire allegedly in retaliation for the destruction by the Sasanians of the Holy Places in Jerusalem. In June 626 a huge army of Avars, Slavs, Bulgars, and Gepids laid siege to Constantinople by land and sea while Sharhrbaraz, one of the principal Persian generals, encamped on the Bosphorus. The failure of the Avar siege, however, put an end to the Persian invasion. In 627, the final Byzantine offensive began and Heraclius marched south inside Iranian territory, and in 628 Khosrow was deposed and murdered.

During the first phase of the conquest, the Roman provinces had been pillaged and large portions of the population, especially skilled workers, sent as a slave labour force to the Persian Empire each time the Persians captured a city (a practice going back to the Assyrians). Battles, sieges, and the capture of cities provoked enormous massacres and losses. Those who could fled to Cyprus, North Africa, Italy, and Constantinople. The Syrian Orthodox clerics, being heretics from the imperial point of view, withdrew to Alexandria and Cyprus since they were not *personae gratae* in most places. The cities that opened their doors after negotiations were treated leniently. Troops of occupation remained in the cities: they levied taxes and were in charge of the administration with the help of the local elites. Fire cult was practiced by the occupants, but Jews and Christians were allowed to proceed with their own practices. Churches were not attacked but were sometimes victim of acts of war when they were located on or near the city walls. The destruction described in Greek texts does not seem to be confirmed by archaeology, according to recent revaluations of excavations (Avni 2010).

Benevolent towards the Jews to begin with, the Sasanians however forbade them to enter Jerusalem, reconnecting with the Roman tradition, if we are to believe the Christian sources. The Jews were presented in Christian sources as the objective allies of the Sasanians and persecutors of the Christians so long as they had the support of the king of kings. The Syrian Orthodox had gained influence at the court of Khosrow thanks to their co-religionists, the famous physician Gabriel of Sinjar, and the

Queen Shirin. Khosrow trusted Syrian Orthodox bishops coming from the Sasanian Empire to oversee the Christians in the Eastern Roman Empire: he was suspicious of the loyalty of the Roman imperial Christians but favoured the Syrian Orthodox, whom the Byzantines considered heretics and enemies. He had himself resided earlier in Edessa and enjoyed the hospitality of the aristocratic Syrian Orthodox families. A change in the balance between the different religious communities thus took place at that time.

After the re-conquest, Heraclius decreed forced baptism for the Jews (enforced only in North Africa) and attempted again to bring back miaphysites to imperial orthodoxy through the monoenergist controversy in a desperate attempt to re-unite the empire religiously in order to strengthen it against its enemies. When the Council of Constantinople in 680 condemned monotheletism, its decisions ignored the oriental provinces now under Muslim rule that had largely adopted monoenergism and monotheletism as outcomes of Neo-Chalcedonianism. The Maronite Church would emerge as a separate entity from these controversies (see Chapter 36).

The Byzantine recovery that Heraclius achieved proved to be short-lived. What happened over the next decades marked the end of the Eastern Roman Empire: the Arab conquests cut off the imperial provinces from Constantinople. The empire retrenched on the remaining provinces and in a way really became Byzantine only at that time. For the first time since Alexander the Great, the regions west and east of the Tigris were part of the same polity. Although a disaster for the Byzantine Empire that never won back its oriental provinces, the change was not very different from the previous occupation by the Sasanians. No one at the time could imagine that it would be permanent. Yet, in less than a century (ca. 634–750), a gigantic empire stretched from the Pyrenees to as far as India and China.

In 632–633, after the *ridda* wars, the whole of Arabia was under political control of the Believers' movement – as Muhammad's followers are designated (Donner 2010: 101). From 632 on, campaigns took place under the rule of Abu Bakr (11–13/632–634), 'Umar ibn al-Khattab (13–23/634–644) and 'Uthman ibn 'Affan (23–35/644–656). The battles of the Yarmuk (south of the Golan), in 636, and Qadisiyya in Iraq came to symbolise the victory of the Arabs. The most vigorous resistance was in the cities of the Syrian and Palestinian coasts that the Byzantines could supply and reinforce from sea. From Damascus to Ḥoms (ca. 636/7), Apamea and Antioch, the Syrian cities were taken into obedience. In 638, Edessa itself surrendered to the Muslims after negotiations. Again, those who could fled to the West, but they were a minority. Past the five first years when the local populations experienced disruptions due to military operations and global instability, life soon resumed, as it had already under the Sasanians. The new situation did not entail major changes. Islamic identity was itself in the making. There were no forced conversions. Material culture did not change and social changes were gradual. A tribute was levied, but life and religious practices went on much the same. It was not until the ninth century, for instance, that the status of *dhimmi* (protected but discriminated religious groups) was legally defined.

The balance between religions once again changed but not in a dramatic way. No Christian denomination or church was favoured over the others. Rather, the Chalcedonians, considered as loyal to the emperor (*Malka*, in Syriac 'king,' hence their name 'Melkites') were henceforth viewed with some suspicion. Conversely, the

Syrian Orthodox Church and miaphysite communities were better considered by the Caliphs than they had been by the Roman emperors, no dogmatic difference applying anymore. Each church tried to demonstrate its difference from its counterparts and assert its position to the new rulers. Hence, ecclesiastical identities were redefined one over the other, 'in the shadow of the mosque' to borrow the title of a book on Christians in the first centuries of Islam (Griffith 2007). Caliph ʿUmar I (634–644) once again allowed the Jews to enter Jerusalem and the Temple Mount. He received therefore the nickname *al-farûq*, the redeemer.

Military and political history thus retain the collision and collapse of empires. Social, economic, and above all cultural history emphasise continuity (although the production of Greek texts shrunk dramatically). The successive defeats and occupations, by the Sasanians and then the Arabs (the last one proving definitive) did not impair Syriac culture, since education and culture had already been privatised by the Syrian Orthodox Church (the same is true for the Church of the East in the Sasanian Empire) because of the official condemnation of miaphysite theology, liturgy, and literary production. It is precisely in the seventh century that a vast number of Greek texts were translated into Syriac and commented on. The scholars in Qenneshre monastery ('The Eagles' nest' on the bank of the Euphrates), Severus Sebokht, Athanasius of Balad, Thomas of Ḥarqel, Jacob of Edessa, and George of the Arabs, acculturated Greek medicine, astronomy, geography, mathematics, logic and – in a somewhat more expected way – the Bible and Patristics into Syriac (see Chapters 25, 26). The steady translation and commentary movement from Greek into Syriac attest the continuity of Hellenism, yet in another language than Greek, in the Roman and the Iranian Empire likewise. It made possible the so-called 'translation movement' in Baghdad in the ninth century. Political, religious, and cultural history do not have the same periodisation and chronology, the changes occurring decades and even centuries apart. Christians remained a majority for several centuries and were fully part of the Islamicate world. Syriac sources are thus as pivotal as other Christian, Jewish, or Zoroastrian sources for the study of the Syrian-Mesopotamian regions in the Islamic period. Syriac literary and religious texts were produced until the fourteenth century, Arabisation taking place at different paces in the various churches and communities. Use of vernacular Aramaic also slowly took over Classical Syriac.

Although the seventh century marks the end of Roman hegemony in Syria, Mesopotamia, Palestine, and Egypt, a clear-cut transformation in our modern perspective, it did not entail a dramatic change for the local populations once acts of war ended. Populations of the borders, the Syriac communities were sadly used to regular wars between empires: sieges, destructions, massacres, rapes, deportations, and plundering had occurred throughout the Roman period (indeed from Mesopotamian antiquity until nowadays). They had also been rejected by official orthodoxy since the sixth century, thus becoming non-imperial Christian communities albeit still part of the Roman Empire. Their perception of contemporary events were thus different from their Chalcedonian and Byzantine counterparts. The end of Roman hegemony did not ring the same way for the different Christian denominations and certainly did not mark the end of Syriac culture, and churches are still alive today in spite of the latest recent blows against them in the Middle East.

BIBLIOGRAPHY

Primary sources

Ephrem of Nisibis, *Hymns against Julian*: E. Beck (ed. with German trans.), *Des heiligen Ephraem des Syrers Hymnen de Paradiso und Contra Julianum*. CSCO 174/175. Louvain: Sécretariat du CorpusSCO, 1957; English Trans.: S. N. C. Lieu, *The Emperor Julian: Panegyric and Polemic/Claudius Mamertinus, John Chrysostom, Ephrem the Syrian*. Translated texts for historians 2. Liverpool: Liverpool University Press, 1989².

Ephrem of Nisibis, *Hymns on Nicomedia*: C. Renoux (ed. with French trans.), *Memre sur Nicomédie, Éphrem de Nisibe: édition des fragments de l'original syriaque et de la version arménienne, traduction française, introduction et notes*. PO 37. Turnhout: Brepols, 1975.

The History of Rabbula: Robert R. Phenix, Jr., and Cornelia B. Horn (ed. with English trans.), *The Rabbula Corpus*. Writings from the Greco-Roman World 17. Atlanta: SBL Press, 2017. Another English trans.: Robert Doran, *Stewards of the Poor: The Man of God, Rabbula, and Hiba in Fifth-Century Edessa*. Cistercian Studies Series 208. Kalamazoo, MI: Cistercian Publications, 2006.

John of Ephesus, *Lives of the Eastern Saints*: E. W. Brooks, *John of Ephesus: Lives of the Eastern Saints*. PO 17.1, 18.4, 19.2. Paris: Firmin-Didot, 1923–25.

The Julian Romance: M. Sokoloff, *The Julian Romance: A New English Translation*. Texts from Christian Late Antiquity 49. Piscataway, NJ: Gorgias Press, 2016.

Secondary Literature

Avni, G. 2010. The Persian Conquest of Jerusalem (614 c.e.): An Archaeological Assessment. *BASOR* 357, 35–48.

Beaucamp, Joëlle, Françoise Briquel-Chatonnet, and Christian Julien Robin. 2010. *Juifs et Chrétiens en Arabie aux Ve et VIe siècles. Regards croisés sur les sources*. Monographies (Centre de recherche d'histoire et civilisation de Byzance 32). Le massacre de Najrân 2. Paris: Association des amis du Centre d'histoire et civilisation de Byzance.

Bowersock, G. W. 2013. *The Throne of Adulis: Red Sea Wars on the Eve of Islam*. Oxford: Oxford University Press.

Brock, Sebastian P. 1976. The Rebuilding of the Temple Under Julian: A New Source. *Palestine Exploration Quarterly* 108, 103–7.

———. 1977. A Letter Attributed to Cyril of Jerusalem on the Rebuilding of the Temple. *BSOAS* 40:2, 267–86.

———. 1991 [1993]. Some New Syriac Documents from the Third Century AD. *ARAM* 3, 259–67.

———. 2004. Without Mushê of Nisibis, Where Would We Be? Some Reflections on the Transmission of Syriac Literature. *Journal of Eastern Christian Studies* 56, 15–24.

———. 2012a. Abbot Mushe of Nisibis, Collector of Syriac Manuscripts. *In*: C. Baffioni et al., ed., *Gli studi orientalistici in Ambrosiana nella cornice del IV centenario, 1609–2009*. Orientalia Ambrosiana 1. Roma: Bulzoni/Milano: Biblioteca Ambrosiana, 15–32.

——— 2012b. Dating Formulae in Syriac Inscriptions and Manuscripts of the 5th and 6th Centuries. *In*: G. A. Kiraz and Zeyad Al-Salameen, ed., *From Ugarit to Nabataea: Studies in Honor of John F. Healey*. Gorgias Ugaritic Studies 6. Piscataway, NJ: Gorgias Press, 85–106.

Brock, Sebastian P. and L. van Rompay. 2014. *Catalogue of the Syriac Manuscripts and Fragments in the Library of Deir al-Surian, Wadi al-Natrun (Egypt)*. OLA 227. Leuven: Peeters.

Brown, P. 1982. *Society and the Holy in Late Antiquity*. Berkeley, CA: University of California Press.

———. 1995. *Authority and the Sacred: Aspects of the Christianisation of the Roman World*. Cambridge and New York, NY: Cambridge University Press.
———. 2002. *Poverty and Leadership in the Later Roman Empire*. Menahem Stern Jerusalem Lectures. Brandeis University Press.
Cotton, H. M., W. E. H. Cockle, and F. G. B. Millar. 1995. The Papyrology of the Roman Near East. *JRS* 85, 214–35.
Debié, Muriel. 2006. Nisibe sauvée des eaux: les sources de Théodoret et la place des versions syriaques. *In* B. Caseau, J.-Cl. Cheynet, and V. Déroche, ed., *Pèlerinages et lieux saints dans l'Antiquité et le Moyen-Âge. Mélanges offerts à Pierre Maraval*. Monographies (Centre de recherche d'Histoire et Civilisation de Byzance 23). Paris: Association des amis du Centre d'histoire et civilisation de Byzance, 135–51.
Dodgeon, Michael H. and S. N. C. Lieu, ed., 1991. *The Roman Eastern Frontier and the Persian Wars (AD 226–363): A Documentary History*. London and New York, NY: Routledge.
Donner, F. 2010. *Muhammad and the Believers: At the Origins of Islam*. Cambridge, MA: Belknap.
Fisher, Greg. 2011. *Between Empires: Arabes, Romans, and Sasanians in Late Antiquity*. Oxford Classical Monographs. Oxford: Oxford University Press.
Griffith, S. 2007. *The Church in the Shadow of the Mosque: Christians and Muslims in the World of Islam*. Princeton, NJ: Princeton University Press.
Healey, John F., 2009. *Aramaic Inscriptions and Documents of the Roman Period*. Textbook of Syrian Semitic Inscriptions, Volume IV. Oxford: Oxford University Press.
Hunt, Lucy-Anne. 2003. Stuccowork at the Monastery of the Syrians in the Wādī Natrūn: Iraqi-Egyptian Artistic Contact in the 'Abbasid Period'. *In*: David Thomas, ed., *Christians at the Heart of Islamic Rule: Church Life and Scholarship in 'Abbasid Iraq'*. The History of Christian-Muslim Relations 1. Leiden: Brill, 93–128.
Millar, Fergus. 2006. *A Greek Roman Empire: Power and Belief Under Theodosius II (408–450)*. Sather Classical Lectures, Volume 64. Berkeley, CA: University of California Press.
Robin, Christian Julien. 2012. Arabia and Ethiopia. *In*: Scott Johnson, ed., *The Oxford Handbook of Late Antiquity*. Oxford: Oxford University Press, 247–332.

CHAPTER TWO

THE SASANIAN EMPIRE

Touraj Daryaee

The Sasanian Empire was founded in 224 by Ardašīr I (224–41) after defeating the last Arsacid monarch, Ardawan V (213–24). Ardašīr assumed the royal title of *Šāhān Šāh*, 'king of kings', which was already used by the Arsacids, and proceeded to bring a territory roughly equivalent to modern Iran, Iraq, and Afghanistan under his control (Daryaee 2009: 3–5). The Sasanian campaign to establish *Ērānšahr*, 'Empire of the Iranians', had begun in 205/6 with Ardašīr's father, Pābag, whose father Sāsān in turn was a priest of the goddess Anāhīd in the city of Istakhr, the capital of the province of Persis/Fars (Tabari and Bosworth 1999: 4). The temple of Anāhīd seems to have become the rallying point for Persian warriors who united to dethrone the local governor of Istakhr. Thus the dynasty that claimed descent from a semi-legendary eponymous ancestor, Sāsān, was able to expand religious authority into secular power and remain on the throne from the third to the seventh century.

It appears that Pābag intended to make his eldest son, Shapur, the first Sasanian ruler (Tabari and Bosworth 1999: 8), but that prince died under mysterious circumstances and another son, Ardašīr, was the one to complete the conquest of Persis/Pārs and beyond. The emergence of this new power naturally alarmed the Arsacids, but they were unable to stop the Sasanian advancements. Ardawan V, and eventually his rival and temporary successor Walakhsh VI (229), soon fell victim to Ardašīr at the Battle of Hormozgan. Conquests in the east, particularly the conquest of the important town of Marv in north-eastern Khorasan, as well as the subjugation of the territory of the Indo-Parthians in Sīstān were the final achievement of Ardašīr I.

After some conflict with the Roman Empire in Syria, Ardašīr appointed his son Shapur I (241–70) as co-regent and eventually retired to his home province. During the reign of Shapur I, Sasanian conquests continued. There appears to have been a significant increase in the size of the administrative apparatus, based on the inscription of Shapur at Ka'be-ī Zardošt, consistent with imperial centralisation. The inscriptions suggests that early Sasanian rule was made possible by co-opting local kings, as well as Sasanian princes ruling a number of provinces, while the king of kings sat at Ctesiphon. New coins were minted with the image of the king of kings on the obverse with the slogan 'Mazda-worshipping King of Kings of the Iranians, whose lineage is

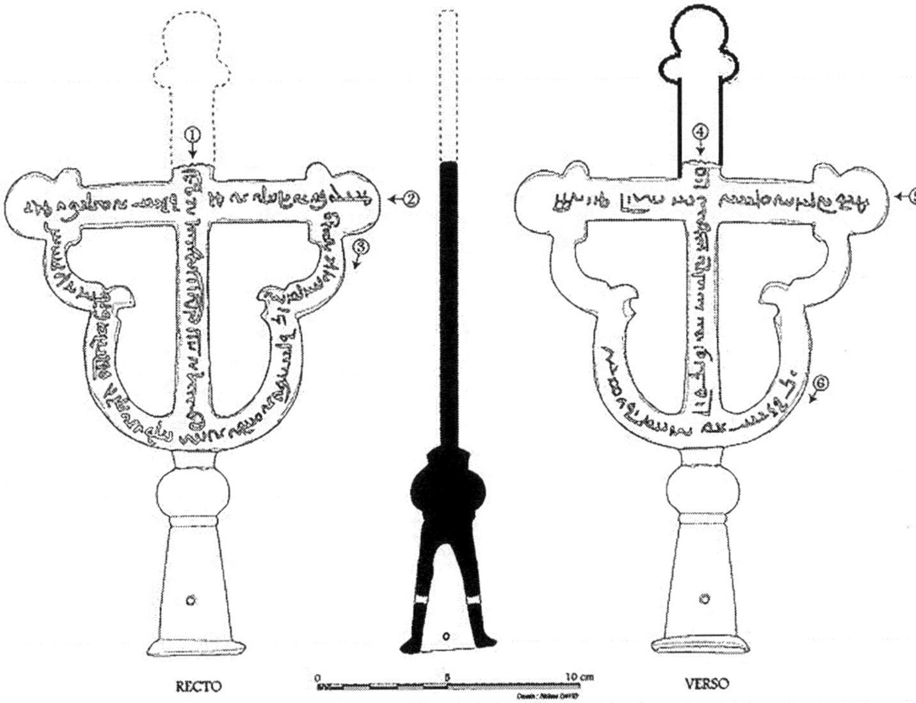

Figure 2.1 Psalter Pahlavi Text on the Cross from Herat

Source: Gignoux 2001

from the gods'. On the reverse the king's fire was placed, attesting to their devotion to the Zoroastrian religion.

At this time, Armenia became the major point of contention between the Sasanians and the Romans, and it remained so until it was partitioned between the two empires in the fifth century. Shapur famously defeated Gordian III, captured emperor Valerian, and forced Philip the Arab to a humiliating treaty, a set of events reflected in both his inscription at Ka'aba-ī Zardošt in Pārs (Honigmann and Maricq 1953), as well as a major relief in the vicinity of the same inscription. Militarily, the reign of Shapur marked the return of the military to form after a relatively long slump in the second and early third centuries that had allowed Roman incursions into the Near East and Mesopotamia in the terminal Arsacid period (Gyselen 2010).

The next kings, Hormizd I (270–1) and Wahram I (r. 271–4), had relatively short rules and very little is known about them. Both were chosen over the heir apparent Narseh (293–302), the third son of Shapur I. Wahram I's eldest son, Wahram II (r. 274–93), also bypassed Narseh, probably with the backing of the Zoroastrian establishment and its powerful head, Kerdīr. During his reign, Wahram II had to deal with hostile Romans and his own rebellious brother, Hormizd (Daryaee 2008: 34–5). It is in the third century CE that we first come across the mention of Christianity in the Sasanian Empire. Christians fleeing the Roman Empire had already been moving to the Iranian Plateau and especially Mesopotamia. However, the first hint of persecution comes from the inscription of the Zoroastrian priest, Kerdīr, who states (KNRm 11):

> And Jews and Buddhists and Hindus and Nazarenes (*nāsrā*) and Christians (*kristiyān*) and Baptists and demons disrupted and made into thrones and seats of the gods.
>
> (MacKenzie 1989: 58)

It has been said that in the third century the situation of Christians vis-à-vis the Sasanian Empire was unclear and unsure (Brock 1982). This may be so, but we must remember that the king and as the state apparatus was coming into its own, and it had to figure out how to deal with the many religious communities. This tacit acknowledgment of non-Zoroastrians may be seen in the Middle Persian *an-ērān* (non-Iranian), which we first encounter with Shapur I. Furthermore, Shapur I was responsible for the movement of Christians from Syria and the eastern Mediterranean into the Sasanian Empire (Chaumont 1988: 74–83). It may be that because of the influx of Christians into the empire, during the reign of Wahram II, the Zoroastrian priest Kerdīr recognised the importance and numbers of the Christians, and if we are to accept the *Chronicle of Se'ert*, the king was complicit in their persecution (Chaumont 1988: 105–8).

Wahram III, known as the *King of the Sakās*, a title indicating his dominance over the Iranian-speaking peoples to the east of the Sasanian Empire, was brought to the throne through a conspiracy in the imperial administration. His grand-uncle Narseh, at the time functioning as king of Armenia, managed to depose him through a major campaign which has been detailed in his inscription of Paikuli (Humbach and Skjærvø 1978: pt. 1). The rule of Narseh (293–302) coincided with the popularisation of Christianity in Armenia, and its eventual adoption, and bitter wars over that kingdom with the Roman Empire. A defeat at the hands of the Roman general Galerius resulted in the treaty of Nisibis in 298 which allowed Tīrīdātes III back on the Armenian throne and brought Iberia (Kingdom of Georgia) into the Roman sphere of influence (Daryaee 2009: 13). Narseh appears to have ended the persecutions instigated by Kerdīr and Wahram II and brought a period of peace vis-à-vis the Christians and other religious minorities (Asmussen 1983: 936).

Narseh's death in 302 brought his son, Hormizd II, to the throne (Daryaee 2008: 43–4). The new king also mainly presided over the conflict with Rome on the issue of Armenia, whose king Tīrīdātes III reputedly converted to Christianity in 301 (Agathangelos and Thomson: 243–4). Hormizd was initially succeeded by a son called Ādūr-Narseh who ruled only for a short while in 309 (Taffazoli 1983). There are, however, no notices of him from the numismatic evidence or in the later Islamic sources, while Byzantine sources only mention his existence as the elder son of Hormizd II.

The circumstances of the birth and reign of Shapur II (r. 309–379), the longest reigning Sasanian monarch, are quite legendary and include him being crowned while still in his mother's womb and forty days after the death of his father, Hormizd II (*Mojmal ol-Tavarikh*: 34). When he came of age, he set off curbing the Arab incursions in the south and punishing the perpetrators (Tabari and Bosworth 1999: 50–6), thus being known by the epithet 'Lord of Shoulders' (Arabic *Dhu-l-Aktaf*). In the east, Shapur II was faced with a major invasion by the Huns (Chionites) who only

Figure 2.2 Byzantine copper coin

Source: © K. Gholami

agreed to form an alliance after fierce battles. This resulted in the termination of the rule of the Sasanian cadet branch, known as the Kushano-Sasanians, over the Bactrian, and the establishment of autonomous Hunnic rule in Transoxiana and Bactria (Ammianus Marcellinus 17.5.1; Nikitin 1999). In the west, Shapur had to face the Romans under Julian the Apostate in 363, although that campaign was soon abandoned following the assassination of Julian by his own troops. The resulting peace treaty with Jovian put the important border town of Nisibis under Sasanian control and created a long-lasting point of contention between the two empires (Blockley 1988). The long and relatively calm rule of Shapur helped bring stability to the Sasanian Empire, as well as establishing Sasanian control over both the eastern provinces, as well as the Persian Gulf region.

It is again during the reign of Shapur II that Christianity came under suspicion as Constantine the Great proclaimed to be the leader of all Christians. We have some detailed information from the Syriac literary tradition, known as the Acts of Martyrs, which attest to the persecution of the Christians by mainly the Zoroastrian priests. Bishop Maruta of Maiferqat provides us a great amount of data through the *Chronicle of Se'ert*. Major accusations against the Christians included the defiling of sacred elements in Zoroastrianism, i.e. sun (*šemšā*), fire (*nūrā*), and water (*mayyā*) (Asmussen 1962: 11; Asmussen 1983: 937–8), which prompted retaliations by the Zoroastrian priests. There are many martyrologies attesting to the persecutions of Christians between 340 and 379 CE, but it has been noted that they were written centuries after the event and embellished (Payne 2015: 38). Furthermore, the persecutions may have to do less with Rome than with domestic matters and the relations between the king and his subjects. One reason put forth is that such Christians subjects as Simeon (Martyrdom of Simeon) was killed due to the fact that he refused to collect taxes from the Christians for the king (Payne 2015: 40). Also, Shapur II appears to have allowed Mar Awgin, the founder of the Christian Monasticism in the East, to establish a monastery in Susa (Jullien 2006: 150–1). This means that the relations between the Sasanian and the Christian subjects were more complicated.

Ardašīr II (379–83) succeeded his brother Shapur II, probably as result of an agreement with the latter. The relief at Taq-ī Bustan (Tanabe 1985; Kaim 2009) shows an exchange of diadems between the brothers, possibly a reward for Ardašīr's bravery in the wars against Rome (Shahbazi 1986). Tabari associated Ardašīr II with a great purge in the Sasanian nobility in order to control their increasing power, an act that resulted in his removal from the throne (Tabari and Bosworth 1999: 67–8). The agreement between Shapur II and Ardašīr II probably guaranteed the succession of Shapur III (383–388), the son of Shapur II (Shahbazi 1986). The reign of Shapur III may be considered the start of a temporary weakening of Sasanian royal power, as reported by the chroniclers. Like Ardašīr II, his nobles were successful in removing him, this time through causing his death under the collapsing weight of his own tent (Tabari and Bosworth 1999: 68; al-Yaghubi, I/183). Wahram IV (388–399), another son of Shapur II, seems to have had a similarly short reign. His most significant action was to be the replacement of his brother *Wahrām-Shapur* (Arm. *Vramšāpuh*) on the Armenian throne. Like his brother (or perhaps father?) Shapur III, Wahram IV also fell victim to the conspiracy of the court nobles and was removed in favour of his son (or perhaps brother), Yazdgerd I (Klíma 1988).

The reign of Yazdgerd I (399–420) marks the beginning of a restoration in Sasanian history. The king, occasionally called 'the Sinful One' (Tabari and Bosworth 1999: 70), was more strong-willed than his immediate predecessors. The less than complimentary title given to him in the Islamic sources, presumably based on Iranian ones, has also been interpreted as a comment on his famous religious tolerance and accommodation of Christians. Indeed, Christian sources from Rome (Procopius, 1.2, 8) consider him a noble soul and even a second Cyrus (McDonough 2008; Shahbazi 2003). His strong-handed treatment of the Sasanian nobility and priesthood made him many enemies among his courtiers (Socrates Scholasticus, *History* 7.8), although he seems to have survived their wrath, finally being killed by a kick from his horse (Shahbazi 2003)! On his coins, he calls himself *Rāmšahr* (he who brings peace) which might indeed be a reflection of his rule as a whole (Daryaee 2002/3), and in the Syriac sources he is given a similar benevolent title (*malkā zkāyā wenasīhā*) (Asmussen 1962: 3).

Wahram V (420–38), a son of Yazdgerd I who was sent to the Arab court at al-Hira, had to wrestle his crown from a usurper named Khosrow (Tabari and Bosworth 1999: 90–3). Wahram's reign is highly romanticised in the Classical Persian literature, particularly in a great compendium of interrelated stories called *Haft Peykar* by the poet Nezami (twelfth century), whose fanciful stories might have drawn on actual Sasanian period romances. These stories include the coming of Indian minstrels known as *lur* (Gypsies?) and the pleasure the king took in drinking and hunting. Wahram is commonly known by the epithet *Gur/Gōr* (*Jur* in Arabic sources: Tabari and Bosworth 1999: 82), meaning 'onager', presumably because of his love of hunting. The story of his death is equally colourful, for it was said that while hunting in Mah (Media), Wahram fell into a marsh and disappeared (Daryaee 2008: 60–1). We also hear of a new title in the sources which suggest the firm establishment of Christianity in the Sasanian Empire, the 'Katholicos of the East' (*qatolīqā demadnhā*) (Asmussen 1962: 5).

Yazdgerd II (438–57), unlike his namesake and grandfather, does not appear to have been very tolerant towards Christianity, at least in Armenia. The tale of the great rebellion of Vardan Mamikonian and its suppression at the battle of Avarayr by Mehr-Narseh, Yazdgerd's vizier (Tabari and Bosworth1999: 104–5; Daryaee 2012), is recorded in the work of Armenian historian Elishe (Elishē and Thomson 1982: 178ff.). It seems that for Yazdgerd II and Mehr-Narseh, the control of Armenia meant a re-conversion of Armenians from Christianity to Zoroastrianism, making them part

Figure 2.3 Seal depicting a man before an altar and cross

Source: The Pahlavi text reads, *I, Sadag, true to the God.* © R. Gyselen

of a Zoroastrian *oecumene* designed to create a centralised Sasanian state. Persarmenia, the majority of the Armenian territory under the Sasanian rule, was from this point on managed directly by the Sasanian court through a *Marzpan* (margrave) and was effectively incorporated into the Sasanian realm (Blockley 1987). Yazdgerd II is also significant because he is the first Sasanian monarch who uses the title of *Kay* (Phl. *Kdy*) on his coins, a reference to the shifting Sasanian ideology and incorporation of a Kayanid political identity (Daryaee 1995).

According to al-Tabari, the two sons of Yazdgerd II, Hormizd III (r. 457–9) and Peroz (459–84) ruled consecutively, although the latter deposed the former in a power struggle (Tabari and Bosworth 1999: 107–9). During the rule of Peroz, Nestorianism's position became even stronger in the Sasanian Empire because of Bar Sauma with the support of the king of kings (Asmussen 1983: 942–4). The Synod of Bet Lapaṭ in 484 and the Synod of 'Aqaq in 486 had important consequences for Christianity in the Sasanian Empire (Asmussen 1983: 944).

During this confusion, Georgia gained independence and the eastern borders of the Sasanian Empire were laid open to attacks from the Hephthalites. Peroz pacified Caucasian Albania and made an agreement with the Eastern Roman Empire to cooperate in defending the Caucasus from invaders (Pseudo-Joshua the Stylite, 9–10). He was, however, captured by the Hephthalites in 469, and the Sasanians were forced to cede territory in the east and pay tribute to the invaders. In an attempt to avenge his losses, Peroz was killed and his army destroyed in 484, and his rule is remembered as a low point for the Sasanian dynasty (Daryaee 2009: 25). Peroz was followed briefly by his son Walakhsh (484–8), who was deposed in favour of Kawad I (488–97, 499–531), the second son of Peroz.

Kawad I was faced with the economic and political problems of a Sasanian Empire in flux. It seems that as part of the weakness of the previous rulers and/or their engagement in extra-territorial wars, the nobility and the Zoroastrian priests attained new levels of influence. In this atmosphere, a radical cleric named Mazdak was able to form an alliance with Kawad I and instigate extreme religious reforms (for a different assessment, see Crone 1991). It is likely that Kawad I was using Mazdak's movement in an attempt to weaken the more orthodox factions of the government and the priestly establishment. The latter, in turn, removed and imprisoned the king and installed his brother Zāmāsp (497–9) in his place (Tabari and Bosworth 1999: 136).

Kawad was able to escape, however, and later regained the Sasanian throne with Hephthalite assistance (Litvinsky 1996: 140). His second reign, characterised by a prolonged war with the Eastern Roman Empire, mostly under Anastasius and Justin, was also marked by a series of reforms, this time implemented more carefully (Schindel 2013). Upon his death, his eldest son Kawus, supported by the Mazdakites, made a bid for the throne, but was defeated and removed in favour of his younger brother Khosrow I Anūšīrwān (531–79), who then had Mazdak and many of his followers killed.

Khosrow's reign was a high point in Sasanian history. He is remembered as a wise and just ruler in both Persian and Arabic histories (Tabari and Bosworth 1999: 146ff.). Kawad I and Khosrow I together reorganised the Sasanian Empire and made it one of the strongest in the world in the sixth century. The reforms initiated by Kawad were continued and strengthened by Khosrow, and in fact are mostly credited to the latter (Rubin 1995). Khosrow is also known for continuing the war with the Eastern Roman Empire of Justinian I, the details of which can be found in the famous work of Procopius (Dignas and Winter 2007: 100–9). While this was a period of peace for Christianity vis-à-vis the state, the internal dispute between the Nestorian and Monophysite became manifest (Asmussen 1983: 947). By the sixth century CE the Sasanian Empire was divided into six metropolitan provinces, suggesting a well-organised Christian church (Walker 2006: 99).

Hormizd IV (579–90), however, did not live up to the example set by his father and grandfather and managed to earn the enmity of the nobility and priesthood who deposed him in favour of his own son Khosrow II Abarwēz (590–628) (Tabari and Bosworth 1999: 298–303). However, the plot to remove Hormizd IV and to replace him with Khosrow II ran into trouble when Wahram Chūbīn, the hero of the war with the Hephthalites, rose in rebellion, under the pretext of avenging Hormizd, against Khosrow and the conspirators (Tabari and Bosworth 1999: 303–14).

Forced to flee from the rebellious general Wahram, Khosrow went to the Eastern Roman Empire and sought the aid of emperor Maurice (Tabari and Bosworth 1999: 310–14). Wahram in turn declared himself the new king, Wahram VI, marking the first time someone outside the Sasanian royal house had reached that position since the accession of Ardašīr I. Emperor Maurice supplied mainly Armenian forces to Khosrow II, with whose help he managed to defeat Wahram and recapture his crown (Dignas and Winter 2007: 236–40). Khosrow then took revenge on those who had contributed to the murder of his father, although it is possible that he himself had a hand in that crime. A second rebellion by Wīstahm, a maternal uncle of Khosrow and a conspirator in the removal of Hormizd, was soon put down, allowing the new king to establish his rule (Daryaee 2008: 85). Khosrow II consolidated his power around the Persian Gulf and sent envoys to Arabia, as far as Mecca, to inquire about the situation there. He appears to have given favour to the Monophysite church, largely due to the influence of his wife Šērīn who was Aramaean in origin (Syriac *šyryn ʾrmytʾ*) (Asmussen 1962: 8). Furthermore, Khosrow II appears to have presided over the Synod of 605 CE in person, suggesting his interest and support of the Persian Christian church (Walker 2006: 87).

Starting in 602, Khosrow II undertook a series of campaigns against the Eastern Roman Empire and succeeded in making significant territorial gains. The campaigns started under the pretext of avenging the murder of Maurice, Khosrow's ally, at the hand of Phocas, an usurper who was now elevated to the position of the emperor (Dignas and Winter 2007: 240–1). These campaigns resulted in the fall of Syria, Palestine, and Egypt, as well as significant portions of Anatolia, into the hands of the Sasanians (Dignas and Winter 2007: 115). The Sasanian general Šāhīn also managed to lay siege to Constantinople itself, a venture that proved ultimately unsuccessful. These gains in many senses marked the height of Sasanian power and the culmination of the dynasty's efforts at consolidating power and initiating socio-economic reforms. A successful counteroffensive by Heraclius, who by this time had managed to remove Phocas and re-organise the defences of the empire, resulted in a quick reversal of fortunes in the mid-620s. By 628, not only were the territories in the Mediterranean realm restored to the Romans/Byzantines, but with the help of elements in the Sasanian court, the Roman emperor had routed the Sasanian armies inside their own territories (Howard-Johnston 1999). Khosrow was removed in a palace coup and his eldest son Šīrūye was installed as Kawad II (628) (Dignas and Winter 2007: 148–51). The very short reign of Kawad II was marked by internal chaos, as well as a major plague known by his name, the Plague of Šīrūye, which had devastating demographic effects (Morony 2007).

The final phase of Sasanian rule was a period of factionalism and division within the empire, during which a number of kings came to power and were challenged by other distant members of the family of Sāsān. Ardašīr III (Sept. 628 – April 629), the son of Kawad II, was a child who was soon removed from the throne by one of the commanders of the war with Byzantium, Šahrbarāz. He in turn was toppled by the nobility who then installed Būrān (628–630/31?), a daughter of Khosrow II (Emrani 2009). Her rule was a period of consolidating imperial power and rebuilding the empire. She was probably brought to the throne because she was the only legitimate heir. Another daughter of Khosrow II, Azarmīgduxt (630–631?), replaced her sister. Būrān and Azarmīgduxt were deposed by another Sasanian general, and here we see that the military commanders were assuming more and more power in the face of the shaken monarchy, the competing nobility, and the Zoroastrian priests. Claimants such as Khosrow III or IV are also speculated mainly through numismatic evidence, before finally in 632, Yazdgerd III (632–651), grandson of Khosrow II, was installed on the throne (Shahbazi 2005).

Yazdgerd III's rule coincided with the conquest of the Sasanian Empire by the Muslims (Tyler-Smith 2000). Starting in 637, the Muslim armies quickly managed to defeat the Sasanians in Qadisiyya, in south-western Iraq, and soon in their capital at Ctesiphon. The last Sasanian king was forced to retreat to the east, from province to province, demanding loyalty and support from local populations. Finally, his dwindling forces were defeated by a coalition of local Persian and Hephthalite governors of Bactria. Tradition has it that Yazdgerd III was killed in 651 in Marv by a miller who did not recognise the king of kings.

The sons of Yazdgerd III fled further east, asking the Chinese emperor Gaozong to aid them in their battle against the Muslims. For a time Sasanian descendants continued to be recognised by the Chinese as legitimate holder of the Persian throne-in-exile and as governors of a 'Persian Area Command' (*Bosi dudufu*) in Sīstān. In the early eighth century, a Sasanian named Khosrow made a final, failed attempt to retake Iran from the Muslims, and this is the last time we hear of the family of Sāsān (Compareti 2009). The world of ancient Persia had come to an end and a new chapter in the history of the nation had begun. The grandeur of the kings, their wisdom and opulence, was emulated by the Muslim caliphs and the name Khosrow, given as *Kisra*, became the general designation for a great ruler. The Sasanians also passed on the idea of *Ērānšahr*, 'Iran', which held as a form of idealised territorial designation by dynasties from the Buyids to the Mongols and was utilised effectively in the pre-modern and modern periods in order to form the modern nation-state.

BIBLIOGRAPHY

Primary Sources

Agathangełos, *History of the Armenians*. Tr. with commentary R. W. Thomson. Albany: State University of New York Press, 1976.

Ammianus Marcellinus, *The Surviving Books of the History*. Ed. and tr. J. C. Rolfe. Cambridge, MA: Loeb, 1937–1939.

Ełishē, *History of Vardan and the Armenian War*. Tr. with commentary R. W. Thomson. Cambridge, MA: Harvard University Press, 1982.

Joshua the Stylite, *Chronicle*. Ed. and tr. W. Wright, *The Chronicle of Joshua the Stylite, Composed in Syriac A.D. 507*. London, 1882. Tr. F. Trombley and J. Watt, *The Chronicle of Pseudo-Joshua the Stylite*. TTH 15. Liverpool: Liverpool University Press, 2000.

Socrates, *Ecclesiastical History*. Ed. G. Hansen, *Sokrates. Kirchengeschichte*. GCS n.f. 1. Berlin, 1995: Berlin-Brandenburgische Akademie der Wissenschaft. Tr. A. C. Zenos, *In*: P. Schaff, *A Select Library of Nicene and Post-Nicene Fathers*. Second Series, Vol. 2, 1890.

Tabari, *The History of al-Tabarī, Vol. V*. Tr. C. E. Bosworth, *The Sāsānids, the Byzantines, the Lakhmids, and Yemen*. Albany: State University of New York Press, 1999.

Secondary Literature

Asmussen, J. P. 1962. Das Christentum in Iran und sein Verhältnis zum Zoroastrismus. *Studia Theologica* xvi, 1–24.

———. 1983. Christians in Iran. *In*: E. Yarshater, ed., *The Cambridge History of Iran*. Cambridge: Cambridge University Press, 924–48.

Blockley, R. C. 1987. The Division of Armenia Between the Romans and the Persians at the End of the Fourth Century A.D. *Historia* 36, 2, 222–34.

———. 1988. Ammianus Marcellinus on the Persian Invasion of A.D. 359. *Phoenix* 42, 3, 244–60.

Brock, S. P. 1982. Christians in the Sasanian Empire: A Case of Divided Loyalties. *In*: S. Mews, ed., *Religion and National Identity. Papers read at the Nineteenth Summer Meeting and the Twentieth Winter Meeting of the Ecclesiastical History Society*. Oxford: Blackwell, 1–19.

Chaumont, M.-L. 1988. *La Christianisation de l'Empire Iranien: des origines aux grandes persécutions du iv siècle*. Louvain: Peeters.

Compareti, M. 2009. Chinese-Iranian Relations xv. The Last Sasanians in China. *Encyclopaedia Iranica*. Online edition available at www.iranicaonline.org/articles/china-xv-the-last-sasanians-in-china (accessed Sept. 2017).

Crone, P. 1991. Kavād's Heresy and Mazdak's Revolt. *Iran* 29/1, 21–42.

Daryaee, T. 1995. National History or Keyanid History? The Nature of Sasanid Zoroastrian Historiography. *Iranian Studies* 28, 3–4, 129–41.

———. 2002/3. History, Epic, and Numismatics: On the Title of Yazdgerd I (Rāmšahr). *Journal of the American Numismatic Society* 14, 89–95.

———. 2008. *Sasanian Iran (224–651 CE): Portrait of a Late Antique Empire*. Costa Mesa: Mazda Publishers.

———. 2009. *Sasanian Persia: The Rise & Fall of an Empire*. London: IB Tauris.

———. 2012. Mehr Narseh. *Encyclopaedia Iranica*. Online edition available at www.iranicaonline.org/articles/mehr-narseh (accessed Sept. 2017).

Dignas, B. and E. Winter. 2007. *Rome and Persia in Late Antiquity: Neighbours and Rivals*. Cambridge: Cambridge University Press.

Emrani, H. 2009. Like Father, Like Daughter: Late Sasanian Imperial Ideology and the Rise of Boran to Power. *Nāme-ye Iran-e Bastan* 13, 3–18.

Gignoux, Ph. 2001. Une croix de procession de Hérat inscrite en pehlevi. *Le Muséon* 114, 291–304.

Gyselen, R. 2006. Les témoignages sigillographiques sur la présence chrétienne dans l'empire sassanide. *In*: R. Gyselen, ed., *Implantation et Acculturation*. Studia Iranica Cahier 33, Chrétiens en terre d'Iran 1. Paris: Bures-sur-Yvette, 17–78.

———. 2010. Romans and Sasanians in IIIth Century: Propaganda War and Ambiguity of the Images. *In*: H. Börm and J. Wiesehöfer, ed., *Commutatio et Contentio. Studies in the Late Roman, Sasanian, and Early Islamic Near East in Memory of Zeev Rubin*. Düsseldorf: Wellem, 71–87.

Honigmann, E. and A. Maricq. 1953. *Recherches sur les Res Gestae divi Saporis*. Bruxelles: Palais des Académies.

Howard-Johnston, J. 1999. Heraclius' Persian Campaigns and the Revival of the Eastern Roman Empire, 622–630. *War in History* 6, 1–44.

Humbach, H. and O. P. Skjærvø. 1978. *The Sassanian Inscription of Paikuli*. Part 1. Wiesbaden: Reichert.

Jullien, F. 2006. Le monachisme chretien dans l'empire iranien (IVe-XIVe siecles). *In*: R. Gyselen, ed., *Implantation et Acculturation*. Studia Iranica Cahier 33, Chrétiens en terre d'Iran 1. Paris: Bures-sur-Yvette, 143–84.

Kaim, B. 2009. Investiture or Mithra. Towards a New Interpretation of So Called Investiture Scenes in Parthian and Sasanian Art. *Iranica Antiqua* XLIV, 403–15.

Klíma, O. 1988. Bahrām V Gōr. *Encyclopaedia Iranica* III/5, 514–22. Online edition available at www.iranicaonline.org/articles/bahram-05 (accessed Sept. 2017).

Litvinsky, B. A. 1996. The Hephthalite Empire. *In*: B. A. Litvinsky, ed., *History of the Civilizations of Central Asia, Vol. III: The Crossroads of Civilizations, A.D. 250 to 750*. Paris: UNESCO, 135–62.

MacKenzie, D. N. 1989. Kerdir's Inscription. *In*: G. Herrmann, ed., *The Sasanian Rock Releifs at Naqsh-i-Rustam*. Iranische Denklmäler, Lideferung 13, Iranische Felsreliefs I. Berlin: Dietrich Reimer Verlag, 35–72.

McDonough, S. 2008. A Second Constantine? The Sasanian King Yazdgard in Christian History and Historiography. *Journal of Late Antiquity* 1, 1, 128–41.

Morony, M. G. 2007. '*For Whom Does the Writer Write?*' The First Bubonic Plague Pandemic According to Syriac Sources. *In*: L. K. Little, ed., *Plague and the End of Antiquity*. Cambridge: Cambridge University Press 59–86.

Nikitin, A. B. 1999. Notes On the Chronology of the Kushano-Sasanian Kingdom. *In*: M. Alram and D. E. Klimburg-Salter, ed., *Coins, Art and Chronology: Essays on the Pre-Islamic*

History of the Indo-Iranian Borderlands. Wien: Osterreichischen Akademie Der Wissenschaften, 1999, 259–63.
Payne, R. E. 2015. *A State of Mixture: Christians, Zoroastrians, and Iranian Political Culture in Late Antiquity*. Oakland: Universiy of California Press.
Rubin, Z. 1995. The Reforms of Khusrō Anūshirwān. *In*: A. Cameron, ed., *The Byzantine and Early Islamic Near East, States, Resources and Armies, Vol. III: States, Resources and Armies*. Princeton: Darwin Press, 227–96.
Schindel, N. 2013. Kawād I: i. Reign. *Encyclopaedia Iranica* XVI/2, 136–41. Online edition available at www.iranicaonline.org/articles/kawad-i-reign (accessed Sept. 2017).
Shahbazi, A. Sh. 1986. Ardašīr II. *Encyclopaedia Iranica* II/4, 380–1. Online edition available at www.iranicaonline.org/articles/ardasir-ii-sasanian-king-of-kings-a (accessed Sept 2017).
———. 2003. Yazdgerd I. *Encyclopaedia Iranica*. Online edition available at www.iranicaonline.org/articles/yazdegerd-i (accessed Sept. 2017).
———. 2005. Sasanian Dynasty. *Encyclopaedia Iranica*. Online edition available at www.iranicaonline.org/articles/sasanian-dynasty (accessed Sept. 2017).
Tanabe, K. 1985. Date and Significance of the So-Called Investiture of Ardašīr II and the Images of Shapur II and III at Taq-i Bostan. *Orient* 21, 102–21.
Taffazoli, A. 1983. Ādur Narseh. *Encyclopaedia Iranica* I/5, 477. Online edition available at www.iranicaonline.org/articles/adur-narseh-son-of-the-sasanian-king-hormizd-ii-a (accessed Sept. 2017).
Tyler-Smith, S. 2000. Coinage in the Name of Yazdgerd III (AD 632–651) and the Arab Conquest of Iran. *The Numismatic Chronicle* 160, 135–70.
Walker, J. T. 2006. *The Legend of Mar Qardagh: Narrative and Christian Heroism in Late Antique Iraq*. Berekeley: University of California Press.

PART II

THE SYRIAC WORLD IN LATE ANTIQUITY

CHAPTER THREE

THE PRE-CHRISTIAN RELIGIONS OF THE SYRIAC-SPEAKING REGIONS

John F. Healey

Syriac is thought of as a 'Christian' language which became predominantly, so far as surviving records are concerned, a theological and liturgical tongue. We are fortunate, however, in having sources of information on the *pre*-Christian Syriac-speaking communities of Edessa and its surroundings, though, as we will see, these sources provide us with an incomplete picture of the society and linguistic situation in which Christian Syriac emerged.

There is an additional difficulty in defining precisely the geographical boundaries of the Syriac linguistic region in the first centuries CE, and they did not remain fixed over time. Our approach here will be to concentrate on pre-Christian Edessa and its immediate region, while referring also briefly to comparable evidence of pre-Christian paganism more widely in northern Mesopotamia and Syria (especially Ḥaṭra and Palmyra).

SOURCES

Very few scholarly treatments of religion in pre-Christian Edessa exist (Segal 1970: 42–61; Drijvers 1980; Ross 2001: 85–101). All have to cope with the limitations of the sources, which can be considered under the following headings.

Literary sources

Literary accounts of pre-Christian religion in Syriac date from the Christian period and these obviously have to be treated with caution, since the inherent Christian bias of such writings is hardly likely to give either an accurate or fair picture of pre-Christian paganism. A few appear to contain genuine information reported in contexts in which it is unlikely that basic details have been falsified. Thus, *The Book of the Laws of Countries* of Bardaiṣan (ca. 154–222), a dialogue written down by one of his followers, contains useable details. Bardaiṣan was a Christian, if barely recognised as such by later writers, who tend to treat him as a pagan and a heretic. This circumstance gives more credence to the book as a source of information. A similar trustworthiness attaches to Julian the Apostate's comments on Edessan religion in his *Oration IV*: it is hard to imagine why it would contain false information.

In some other sources, the context in which information is provided is polemical and a judgement has to be made as to whether the information is likely to be correct. Frequently cited in the present context are *The Teaching of Addai* (dated perhaps to the fifth century) and the *Homily on the Fall of Idols* by Jacob of Sarug (late-fifth century). To these we will return. Reference will also be made to the *Oration of Pseudo-Meliton* (of uncertain date), though the author's approach is euhemeristic and the details given are hard to corroborate.

Archaeology[1]

Archaeological evidence in the strict sense is extremely meagre: Edessa itself has grown into the sprawling modern city of Şanlıurfa and there has been little scientific archaeological excavation of relevance, except in one area to the west of the city centre. There are, however, the important sites of Dayr Yaqub on the southern edge of the modern city and Sumatar Harabesi further to the south, both of which have yielded relevant inscriptions. The former of these sites has been subjected to close study (Deichmann and Peschlow 1977; inscription As62) and the latter was surveyed superficially by J. B. Segal (1953, see also 1954), to whom we owe what is still the most important work on Edessa itself (Segal 1970). And from Edessa there have also been sporadic but revealing finds, often uncovered by modern building works. Sadly even the most elementary recording of such finds is neglected, and the local museum is rarely called in to deal with finds before they disappear, either completely or onto the antiquities market.

The Haleplibahçe area to the west of the city centre is a rare exception. Recent discoveries there include a series of mosaics probably of fifth/sixth century date. Though pagan in their themes, these mosaics (Karabulut et al. 2011) are of Byzantine date and are paralleled elsewhere in the Edessa region (e.g. in the sixth century at Serrīn in Syria: Balty 1990).

Among the surviving mosaics and fragments of mosaics of *earlier* date, some are from tomb chambers (such as the mosaics containing inscriptions Am4 and Am5), but several probably come from villas or similar buildings. Broadly these mosaics belong to the tradition of mosaic-making well known to us from western Syria (see Balty 1995). They reveal decorative themes derived from Greco-Roman mythology, reflecting the interests of a westward-looking elite which was imitating Roman fashion, but containing Syriac inscriptions which, apart from helping us to identify the persons depicted, also show a high degree of integration between Syriac and Greco-Roman traditions. Figures depicted (and named in Syriac script) include Māralāhē/Zeus, Hera, Chronos, Prometheus, Achilles, Patroclus, Priam, Hecuba, Briseis, Troilus, and the River Euphrates. The mosaics are numerous enough to give us a rather full picture of the local Edessan tradition of mosaic-making, its artistic conventions and its iconography (Colledge 1994; Parlasca 1983, 1984; Balty and Briquel-Chatonnet 2000).

To the south of Edessa there are two tomb-towers incorporating inscriptions, the one at Dayr Yaqub (As62, above) and another at Serrīn in Syria. Both have been studied archaeologically (for Serrīn, see Gogräfe 1995; Bs1).

Inscriptions

The pre-Christian Syriac inscriptions (on stone, in mosaics, and also on parchments) are our most important source of information on pre-Christian Edessan religion and society. Called 'Old Syriac' because of minor linguistic differences from Classical Syriac (Healey 2008), they extend in date from a probable 6 CE to about 250 CE. By the latter date Christianity was already established in Edessa, though it was more than another fifty years before Bishop Qona began to build the city's cathedral around the time the Edict of Constantine made Christianity licit. Whatever about the size of the earlier Christian community and its date of origin, it is noteworthy that the Old Syriac inscriptions reflect a *pagan* culture which was predominant at least among the elite: there is no reason to believe that any of these inscriptions was written by a Christian.[2]

The evidence of the inscriptions is most important, however, because of what they tell us about the pagan religious practices of the region in the pre-Christian period. The vast majority of the pagan Syriac inscriptions (and the three long legal parchments from the 240s CE which are of no religious interest apart from providing some theophoric personal names) are gathered in the corpus published in Drijvers and Healey (1999) (DH). Depending on the way of counting, the total number of inscriptions in stone and mosaic in 1999 was about ninety-five (excluding coins and the parchments). This database has been expanded since 1999 by the addition of approximately forty further epigraphic items of varying lengths and places of origin, many of which are not yet published. We are thus dealing with a (meagre) total corpus of about 150 items.

Apart from personal names (on which see below), relatively few of these inscriptions have direct religious content – the number increases if we assume that the funerary mosaics have some bearing on religious beliefs, but, as we will see, the literary sources remain vitally important.

Theophoric personal names

There are in the inscriptions and parchments a number of transparent theophoric personal names, i.e. names incorporating the name of an identifiable deity. The list which follows is selective and references are not given, but most can be traced easily through DH:

Allāhā:	*brlhʾ*, *brtlhʾ* (is 'the god' one of those named below?)
Allāt:	*ʿbdlt*, *ʿwydlt*, *ʿwydlt*, *zydlt*
Atargatis:	*ʾbdʿtʾ*, *mtrʿtʾ*, *brʿtʾ*, *šlmʿtʾ*, *zbdʿtʾ*
Baʿalšamīn:	*brbʿšʾ*, *brbʿšmyn*
Bēl:	*blbnʾ*, *blšw*, *ʿlbl*, *bly*, *mrʾbylhʾ* (?)
Hadad:	*brhdd*
Naḥay:	*ʾbdnḥy*, *ʿbdnḥy*, *ʾmtnḥy*, *šrdwnḥʾ* (?)
Nanaya:	*btnny*
Nebō:	*brnbw*, *brnbs*, *brny*
Nešrā:	*nšryhb*
Šamaš:	*ʾmšmš*, *bršmš*, *ʿbdšmš*, *šmšgrm*, *šmšyhb*, *šmšʿqb*, *lšmš*
Sēmēion/a:	*brsmyʾ*, *btsmyʾ*, *ʿbsmyʾ*, *bsmyʾ*
Sīn:	*ʾmtsyn*, *wrdsyn*, *šlmsyn*, *blsyn*
al-ʿUzzā:	*mtʿzt*

(Some theophoric names are harder to analyse: *brklbʾ* [Kalbā = Nergal?; see comment on As48 in DH; it also appears in *The Teaching of Addai* in Howard 1981: 67,

Syr. 33, l. 12]; *bršlm'*, *btšlm'* and *'bšlm'* [a deity called Šalmā related to Šalman, as at Ḥaṭra (Beyer 1998: 150; Drijvers 1977: 834)], and *'bdšwk*. A number of the 'pagan' names above, and others, occur in the early *Christian* literature in Syriac, names such as Šarbēl, 'Abdnebō, 'Absamyā, Barsamyā, 'Abšalmā and 'Abdšamaš [see Preissler 1989; Harrak 1992].)

Of the more than forty names in the list above, the god Šamaš appears in seven (names of about fifteen separate individuals), but he is not explicitly mentioned in any inscription, though there is other evidence of his cult (below). Bēl appears in five, as does Atargatis, but neither is explicitly mentioned in any inscription, though Atargatis's importance is clear from a passage in Bardaiṣan (below). Sīn (four) and Naḥay (four) are both explicitly mentioned in inscriptions, but Nebō (three times) does not appear in the inscriptions. He and Bēl do appear, however, in the literary sources (below). Ba'alšamīn, the great pan-Syrian deity, appears in two names, but there is no other direct evidence of his cult at Edessa or its immediate region.

It will be clear from the above that the amount of information available to us from Syriac-language sources and from the immediate area of Edessa is meagre. There is a temptation to look to other, better-evidenced centres in the general region of Edessa for further light on its religion. Palmyra is not far away and has a number of points of cultural contact with Edessa: because of the number of inscriptions and the extent of archaeological works there, it is much better known than Edessa. And Ḥaṭra, to the east, is similar, though with a smaller number of inscriptions. Hierapolis is a special case because of the survival of Lucian's *Dea Syra*.

The temptation to refer constantly to these to fill out information lacking at Edessa should, however, be avoided. Apart from the obvious fact that the gaps to be filled are so enormous that a high degree of speculation would be involved, recent scholarship has made us more aware of the *variety* of religious expression in this region (see e.g. Kaizer 2008). Each cultural centre had its own religious construct with its own rituals and styles, as we can see from the immense differences between Palmyra, Ḥaṭra, and Hierapolis themselves. (For a fuller account drawing in evidence from outside Edessa and its environs, see Drijvers 1980.)

EVIDENCE OF JUDAISM

Before turning to the detailed evidence of pagan deities, we should note that Judaism was well established in the city of Edessa and its region in the pre-Christian period (Drijvers 1985; Segal 1970: 41–2). Hints of this are provided by literary evidence. Firstly, according to legend, the first steps towards Christianity involved Jews. In *The Teaching of Addai*, it is to the Jewish household of Tobiah that the evangelist Addai first comes for lodging (Howard 1981: 11). It is hardly likely that this would have been introduced at a late stage into the tradition, since all the evidence suggests that antisemitism was strong in the area in the later Christian period and is already evident in the Addai story. Secondly, it is established that much of the Syriac Old Testament of the Peshiṭta translation had a Jewish origin, i.e. the Hebrew Bible was translated into the local Aramaic dialect, Syriac, by Jews, before 300 CE (Weizmann 1999; Brock 2006: 23–7). This suggests that the local Jewish community must have been of significant size and sophistication. And finally we have the direct evidence of inscriptions: several Jewish inscriptions of very early date have been found in and around Edessa and they too are written in the local Aramaic of the region, though using a Jewish form of the Aramaic script (Noy and Bloedhorn 2004: 128–32).

THE PAGAN DEITIES IN EDESSA

The evidence of the literary sources does not fit easily with that of the personal names and of the inscriptions themselves, mainly because deities proclaimed in the literary sources as having been prominent at Edessa appear only in personal names. This may be because of the unevenness of the epigraphic record. Thus there are several explicit references to the god Sīn, though these are concentrated at rural Sumatar, while there are no religious inscriptions as such at all from the immediate area of Edessa itself, so that we only have personal names from the city as a guide. This may explain why, for example, the deities Bēl, Nebō, and Atargatis appear epigraphically only in personal names, despite the fact that they were prominent in the city according to the literary sources.

Bēl and Nebō

In fact there is strong literary evidence that Nebō, Bēl (possibly identified with Hadad, who appears in a single theophoric name: Ross 2001: 90), and Atargatis (below) were major deities of pagan Edessa, despite their limited appearance in direct evidence. Drijvers (1980: 40–75) adduces a number of later Christian polemical texts which accuse the Edessans of having followed these cults. Addai's sermon at Edessa in *The Teaching of Addai* (probably fifth century) includes the following passage:

> Who is this man-made idol Nebō whom you worship and Bēl whom you honour? Behold, there are some of you who worship Bat-Nikkal, like the inhabitants of Ḥarran your neighbours, and Tarʿatā, like the inhabitants of Mabbōg, and Nešrā (the Eagle), like the Arabs, and the sun and the moon, like the rest of the inhabitants of Ḥarran.
>
> (Howard 1981: 49, Syr. 24, ll. 15–20)

This implies that there were some Edessans who worshipped deities not regarded as being fully native to the city, such as Tarʿatā and the sun and moon deities (see below). As far as Bat-Nikkal is concerned, she is clearly a moon-goddess, daughter of Ningal, who was worshipped at Ḥarran (where an as yet unpublished Syriac dedication to *nykl* has been found: to be published by M. Önal and A. Desreumaux). Nešrā, here associated with the Arab element of the population (probably the 'Arabs' of the area called 'Arab' to the south-east of Edessa), cannot be clearly identified, though his name means 'the Eagle' and 'Our Lord the Eagle' figures in Hatran religion (Drijvers 1980: 41; Beyer 1998: 149). The god Nasr was worshipped in pre-Islamic north Arabia (Höfner 1965: 457).

There are other passages in *The Teaching of Addai* which mention the worship of Bēl and Nebō. In one place they are specified as being the gods of the city ('their gods') (Howard 1981: 69, Sy. 34, l. 6) and in Addai's final address he warns his followers:

> Again, beware of pagans who worship the sun and the moon, Bēl and Nebō, and the rest of those they call gods.
>
> (Howard 1981: 87, Syr. 43, ll. 22–3)

While not specifying Edessa, these texts further reinforce the evidence of the earlier passage quoted above.

There is also a section of the *Homily on the Fall of Idols* by Jacob of Sarug (ca. 451–521) referring to Satan's activity:

> in Edessa he set Nebō and Bēl together with many others, he led astray Ḥarran by Sīn, Baʿalshamīn and Bar Nemrā and by my Lord with his Dogs . . . and the goddesses Tarʿatā and Gadlat.
>
> (Martin 1876: 110, ll. 52–4; Bedjan 1907: 797–8)

The allocation of different deities to particular places or peoples is noteworthy, though some of the identifications are unclear (see e.g. Dirven 2009). These texts cannot be regarded as the last word on these issues, nor do they imply water-tight boundaries marking the geographical spheres of each of the deities. Sīn and the moon-goddess Bat-Nikkal are not *restricted* to Ḥarran or Atargatis to Hierapolis/Mabbōg. But the texts do suggest a strong association between Edessa and the pair Bēl and Nebō. It is notable also that both deities have a long history going back to ancient Mesopotamia (Bēl-Marduk of Babylon, Nebō or Nabū of Borsippa), but they are equally prominent in Palmyra and Ḥaṭra (Gawlikowski 1990: 2608–25, 2644–6; Kaizer 2002: 67–79, 89–99; Beyer 1998: 149). We should not assume that the deity behind each name was identical with the ancient Mesopotamian version. Local deities probably adopted the name and some features from Mesopotamian tradition, Bēl representing some local divinity in a kind of *interpretatio babyloniaca* (so Drijvers 1980: 53, 73, also identifying Nebō as Mercury, 62–3).

Atargatis (Tarʿata or ʿAtā/eh), Hadad, and the Sēmēion (smyʾ)

There is another important literary source referring to the religion of Edessa in *The Book of the Laws of Countries* of Bardaiṣan (154–222):

> In Syria and Edessa there was the custom of self-emasculation in honour of Tarʿata, but when king Abgar had come to the faith, he ordered that every man who emasculated himself should have his hand chopped off.
>
> (Drijvers 1965: 58–9, ll. 20–1)

Given the date and nature of this work, it is strong testimony to the importance of Atargatis at Edessa. We have seen that her name appears relatively often in theophoric names and other, iconographic evidence has been adduced (Drijvers 1980: 76–121, especially 80–3). The fish-pools which still exist in modern Şanlıurfa may go back to the pools observed by the pilgrim Egeria (Wilkinson 1999: 133, §19. 7) and to fish-pools sacred to Atargatis, a feature of her cult reflected in Lucian's *Dea Syra*. Hierapolis is, of course, very close to Edessa.

Hadad, who is associated with Atargatis at Hierapolis, appears only in a personal name at Edessa, *brhdd*, while the *sēmēion* appears to have a role at Edessa associated with that of Atargatis and Hadad as a pairing: thus in a relief from Edessa interpreted as representing Atargatis and Hadad with the *sēmēion* (Drijvers 1980: 80–2, pl. xxii). It figured also in the cults at Hierapolis and Ḥaṭra, but is not directly known in

Edessa except through personal names like *'bsmy'* and *brsmy'* (see Lightfoot 2003: 446–8 [inc. fig. 36], 540–7; Beyer 1998: 152–3; Drijvers 1977: 828–36). The name Barsamyā appears in *The Teaching of Addai* (Howard 1981: 71, Syr. 45:6).

Šamaš, Azizos, and Monimos

Apart from personal names we may note that the south gate of the city of Edessa was called the 'Gate of Beth Šamaš', with reference, one assumes, to a temple dedicated to that deity (see the *Chronicle of Edessa*, § lxviii). Christian martyrs met their fate when they refused to worship the sun (*Martyrdom of Shmōnā and Gūryā*: Burkitt 1913: §§ 42–3, where the sun-god is called *šamšā māran*, 'the Sun our Lord'). We may note also the fact that the emperor Julian (r. 361–63) regarded Edessa as a centre of the worship of the sun-god. In his *Oration IV* on King Helios (Lacombrade 1964: 128, §34), he makes reference to the cult of Helios at Edessa:

> The inhabitants of Edessa, a place sacred to Helios from of old, have Monimos and Azizos seated alongside him. And Iambilichus . . . takes this to mean that Monimos is Hermes and Azizos Ares, associates of Helios, dispensing many benefits on the earth.

Both Emesa (which some prefer to read instead of Edessa here, though without justification) and Ḥaṭra are known for the special role that the sun-god played in each (Tubach 1986, specifically 63–125 on Edessa; on Ḥaṭra Sommer 2005: 383–8). Only the Julian passage attests to it explicitly at Edessa. Azizos and Monimos appear to represent Semitic *'Azīz* and *Mun'im* ('Mighty' and 'Kindly': Drijvers 1980: 159–61 notes that both appear as divine names in Palmyra), probably morning and evening stars, perhaps manifestations of the planet Venus, traditionally conceived as connected with sunrise and sunset (Drijvers 1980: 149–52, though Tubach 1986: 63–71 prefers to associate Monimos with Nebō/Mercury, who was associated with the sun-god in Mesopotamia). Nabataean al-'Uzzā, 'the Mighty Goddess', is another manifestation (Healey 2001: 114–19; note Syriac *'wzy* in Isaac of Antioch as worshipped by the Arabs: Bickell 1873: 210, l. 101; the same text in Isaac calls the moon-god *syn'*: 214: l. 214). Al-'Uzzā's name appears in a single Syriac personal name, *mt'zt*.

Naḥay

The only deity mentioned explicitly in the inscriptions apart from Sīn (below) is Naḥay (Bs1 at Serrīn and also on a coin-type, Co2). The Serrīn inscription is funerary and only mentions in passing the function of the builder of the monument, Ma'nū, as '*bdr* of Naḥay'. He is also called *qaššīša*, which in Classical Syriac is used for 'priest' (the equivalent of *prebytêros*), though in the Serrīn inscription it probably simply means 'the elder'.

Naḥay is known also in the personal names (above) and in Palmyrene personal names (Stark 1971: 99). Drijvers (1980: 155–6) and others refer to the gods of Adummatu (al-Jawf/Dūmat al-Jandal in Saudi Arabia) taken away by Sennacherib (704–681 BCE) in one of his campaigns in north Arabia: 'Atar-samayin, Dāya, Nuḫāya, Ruldāwu, Abirillu and Atar-qurumâ, the gods of these Arabs' (Leichty 2011: 1–26, no. 1, specifically p. 19, ll. 10–12 [p. 49]; similarly no. 6, iii′, 5′–7′; no. 97, ll. 10–11 [p. 180]). The divine name *nhy* appears commonly in Thamudic B inscriptions (Höfner 1965: 456–7) and there is no doubt that the deity Nuḫaya (in cuneiform *Nu-ḫa-a-a*) of Adummatu is the same as the *nhy* who appears in a Dumaitic inscription from Sakāka, where a similar list of local gods appears: 'Ruḍā and Nuhay (*nhy*) and ʿAttarsam' (Winnett and Reed 1970: 80–1, no. 23: the suggestion there, repeated in Drijvers 1980: 156 [earlier in Drijvers 1972b: 360], that NHY might be a sun-deity is based on a single inscription of doubtful reading and interpretation). To judge from the spelling (with {ḥ}), Old Syriac NḤY appears to be borrowed from a Mesopotamian source.[3]

So far as Syriac evidence is concerned, it is likely that Naḥay is a deity worshipped in the Euphrates and Palmyrene areas, of male gender if the coin evidence is reliable (Cs2: *ʾlh ʾnḥy*, read as *ʾlhʾ nḥy*). The author of the Serrīn inscription seems to be a local ruler of the east bank of the Euphrates. There is no indication in the inscription of a direct connection with Edessa, though the language and script suggest it, as do the personal name Maʿnū and the religious details (*bdr* [on which seen below at Sumatar], *qšyšʾ*, Naḥay).

Kutbay

There are other sources which allude to Edessan deities, but they are often euhemeristic and fanciful. One which is worthy of mention is the *Oration of Pseudo-Meliton of Sardis*, which tells us of the worship in Edessa of the goddess Kutbay (*kwtby*), who might be related to the Arab/Nabataean al-Kutbā (Cureton 1855: 44, ll. 31–3, Syr. 25, ll. 12–14; Lightfoot 2007; Healey 2001: 123), though the evidence is inconclusive.

Baʿalšamīn

Baʿalšamīn, the great pan-Syrian deity, appears in two names, but, surprisingly perhaps, there is no other direct evidence of his cult at Edessa or its region. This may just be an accident of discovery, since he is well known in Palmyra and at Ḥaṭra.

THE GOD SĪN AT SUMATAR HARABESI

The moon-god, Sīn, played the central role at least at the site of Sumatar (or Soğmatar) Harabesi about 60 km south-east of Edessa in the Tektek mountains (in general Drijvers 1980: 122–45). It is closer to Ḥarran than to Edessa itself. The Syriac-related monuments at the site were first noted by Pognon, who visited the area in 1901 and 1905 and published the inscriptions he found in 1907 (Pognon 1907). He found the cave on the site which came to be known as 'Pognon's cave', but remained unaware of the importance of the central hill at the site and did not mention its many inscriptions. The discovery of the latter was left to J. B. Segal in 1952, with subsequent publication of the inscriptions and a general assessment of the site published in Segal 1953 (Figure 3.1).

Sīn is named explicitly in three texts from Sumatar, and the presence there of his cult is one of the few firmly established facts on religion in the Edessa region in this period.

Figure 3.1 Inscription between two figures in Pognon's Cave, Sumatar

Source: Author

The texts mentioning Sīn explicitly read as follows:

As27, to the left of a relief on the central hill:

> Šīlā [son of Šīl]ā made the image in honour of the god Sīn, for the life of Tiridates son of Adōnā and for the life of his brothers.

As28, to the left of As27:

> I, the god, see him. . . . . . I see him and behold, I, Sīn (?), the g[od . . .]

As60, on a statue from Sumatar (Figure 3.2):

> Image of Lišamaš son of Šamašyahb, which Barnay, his brother, made for him. Whoever destroys it, Sīn will be his judge.

Figure 3.2 Inscription from Sumatar mentioning the god Sīn

Source: Author

Sīn also appears in a Greek and Syriac legal parchment from the Middle Euphrates witnessed by *ʾwrls brsmyʾ mksʾ dsyn*, 'Aurelius Barsamyā, tax-collector of [the god] Sīn' (P. Euphr. 10:24; the text is a sale executed in Ḥarran and the reference appears to be to the Ḥarran temple of Sīn: Feissel et al. 1997: 45–53, specifically 52). Sīn may also be alluded to through the relief pillars surmounted by a crescent shape in 'Pognon's cave' (Pognon 1907: 25).

Sīn is, of course, in origin an ancient deity of southern Mesopotamia, with his main temple at Ur. We do not need, however, to look so far away for a context for the appearance of Sīn at Sumatar, since Ḥarran, which in the Assyrian and Neo-Babylonian periods became a major centre of the Sīn cult, is close by (Green 1992). It is not surprising that Sīn worship should have spilled over from Ḥarran, and indeed it had been well known in the area of Upper Mesopotamia and Syria in older Aramaic evidence: thus the priest Si'-gabbar and various moon deities in the Neirab inscriptions, possibly of the early seventh century BCE (Gibson 1975: 93–8, nos 18–19). That this association of the area with the moon-god continued into Late Antiquity is reflected in Julian the Apostate's praying there to the moon-goddess (Ammianus Marcellinus XXIII.3.2).

Beyond the mere occurrence of the name of Sīn as that of the deity worshipped at least at Sumatar, there is a little more we can add.

Sumatar was a religious site connected with significant funerary monuments and memorials. The former (initially identified by Segal as planetary temples like the temples at Ḥarran described by tenth-century author al-Masʿūdī: Segal 1953: 113–14) are located on hills which surround the central hill. The funerary memorials are located near the centre of the site in Pognon's Cave, which has its walls lined with full-sized carvings of human figures (in the 'Parthian' style typical of the region) and, importantly, inscriptions identifying the individuals as local rulers who probably exercised power under the ultimate authority of the king in Edessa. The cave is best interpreted as a focus of a funerary ritual, though it was not, apparently, the place of burial of the officials involved.

At the centre of the site is a high limestone outcrop, on which the inscriptions referring to Sīn and other religious details are found. Some are on natural steps in the limestone which provide suitable vertical surfaces. Much more remarkable are the dozen or so inscriptions which are carved horizontally (facing the sky) on the top surface of the hill.

That this hill had religious significance cannot be in any doubt. One of the horizontal inscriptions actually refers to 'this blessed mountain' (As37):

> In Šebaṭ of the year 476 (= 165 CE), in that month, I, Maniš son of Adōnā and Maʿnā, and Alkūr and Bēlbena and Alkūr, his brother, we set up (*śmn*) this pillar (*nṣbtʾ*) on this blessed mountain (*ṭwrʾ brykʾ*) and erected a seat (*ʾqymn krsʾ*) for the one who maintains it. The governor will be *budar* (*bwdr*) after Tiridates, the governor, and he will give the seat to the one who is going to maintain it. His recompense will be from Māralāhē. But if he withholds the seat or the pillar is ruined, he, the god, will be the judge.

The other major inscription, As36, refers to an altar set up at the site:

> In the month of Šebaṭ of the year 476, I, Tiridates son of Adōnā, governor of ʿArab, built (*bnyt*) this altar (*ʾlt*ʾ) and set up a pillar (*śmt nṣbt*ʾ) for Māralāhē, for the life of my lord the king and his children and for the life of Adōnā, my father, and for my own life and that of my brothers and of our children.

There is some dispute about the precise nature of the *nṣbt*ʾ here said in each inscription to have been located on top of the hill. Segal and those following him took the term to refer to a 'pillar'. Palmer (2015) has argued that a better translation would be 'sapling', understanding this as a poetic term for a wooden cultic sculpture or monument. There is nothing in the inscriptions, of course, to help us decide between a wooden and a stone monument: one can only decide on the basis of comparison with other monuments and with contemporary and later dialects of Aramaic. In favour of 'sapling' would be especially the later Classical Syriac usage of the word *nṣbt*ʾ, though the verb *śym* for the action involved suggests 'to place' rather than 'to plant (a sapling)' or 'to build (a wooden structure described as a sapling)'. Earlier translators of the text (DH: 106; Segal 1954: 25–6) gave more weight to contemporary usage in Palmyrene Aramaic and in other languages, while bearing in mind the common Classical Syriac use of NṢB for the 'founding' of monasteries. The near-contemporary Palmyrene evidence is that of an inscription referring to the 'making' (*ʿbd*) of 'this *nṣbt*ʾ and altar' (Hillers and Cussini 1996: no. 1546: 3–4: *nṣbt*ʾ *dh wʾlt*ʾ).

The precise nature of what was erected remains uncertain, but there were two of them, erected by different persons at more or less the same time. We may note also that there was an altar of some sort on the hill. Indeed, Segal clearly thought that there was a substantial building there, in which case the above inscriptions may have been located *inside* this temple building (and then would not have been open to the elements). As37 refers to the establishing of a 'chair', and Segal drew attention to coins on which there appear a pillar and a throne (Segal 1970: 58).

Maintenance is one of the concerns of As37, and here we are given a hint that the person responsible for this was called *bwdr*. This term is obscure. It occurs elsewhere only once, in the Serrīn inscription (above), where there is reference to the *bdr* (note the difference of spelling and hence more uncertainty) of the deity Naḥay. It is assumed that one of these is a variant spelling of the other: the implication would be that the vocalisation was something like *budar* or *būdar*. The root BDR in Syriac means 'to sprinkle', and one might imagine a term describing a ritual function. There is, however, no evidence to support such an interpretation and Segal (1954: 27) looked (improbably) to a mediæval Arabic term of unknown meaning connected with the cult at Ḥarran according to Ibn al-Nadīm.

Other inscriptions on the top of the hill are less momentous. They mostly belong to the 'Remembered be . . .' category and would be secondary to the main religious function of the hill (e.g. As31; on such inscriptions see Healey 1996).

One other detail that can be derived from the inscriptions at the site is the fact that the main god at Sumatar was given the epithet Māralāhē, 'lord of the gods' (Ross 2001: 91; As36: 3; As37: 8 and As31: 3).

We know from the Syriac New Testament that this title, in the form *māre 'alāhē*, was regarded by the translators as a suitable substitute for the name of Zeus (Acts 14: 12–13). In one of the mosaics containing Syriac text, the god Zeus (alongside Hera) is called Māralāhē (*mrlh'*) (Cm11: 1). It is clear, therefore, that this epithet could be applied to Zeus. But at Sumatar it appears to refer to Sīn, as the ultimate divine title of the highest deity worshipped there. The title has its historical roots in Akkadian *bēl ilāni*, 'Lord of the Gods', a title used of Sīn and of other deities in Mesopotamian tradition. In As20: 6 from Edessa itself Māralāhē is the god who might curse anyone who disturbs a tomb, and As31 is a call for remembrance 'before Māralāhē'. There is also evidence of the title from Ḥaṭra (*syn mrlh'* on coins, Vattioni 1981: 107), Ashur (Aggoula 1985: 38, no. 15b: 2 = Bēl), Sa'adiyyah (Vattioni 1981: 106), and Tille (Lightfoot and Healey 1991: line 6 = Zeus), as well as Palmyra (Gawlikowski 1974: 78–9, no. 154; Hillers and Cussini 1996: no. 1939). At Sumatar it is virtually certain that 'Māralāhē' refers to Sīn.

The only direct evidence of a cult of Sīn at Edessa itself is the statement in *The Teaching of Addai* cited earlier to the effect that some Edessans worshipped him, just as the Ḥarranians did, though Sīn-based theophoric names suggest that the deity was widely venerated. It is possible that Māralāhē in As20 from a cave-tomb on the edge of Edessa also refers to Sīn, which seems more likely in this context than Zeus. Bēl or Ba'alšamīn are other possibilities.

Sumatar, Serrīn, and politics

While it is impossible on the basis of the above evidence to reach any far-reaching conclusions, there does emerge from the Sumatar inscriptions and from the Serrīn inscription a common theme: the connection between religious practice at these sites and regional politics.

Sumatar inscriptions frequently refer to the Adōnā family and to the *šlyṭ' d'rb*, 'the ruler of the 'Arab region' (As36: 2; As47: 3; As49: 2–3; As51: 4–5; As52: 4–5). The reference is to the area south-east of Edessa stretching towards Ḥaṭra. At the same time As36: 4 implies loyalty to the king, probably the king of Edessa (though the dated inscriptions at Sumatar appear to come from the period of Parthian control of the city, when Parthian puppet rulers were imposed). The funerary cult of Pognon's cave thus appears to be connected with the kingship in Edessa and with control of the local region by officials of the king, members of the Adōnā family. It is almost certain that the same officials were the custodians of the cult of Sīn at Sumatar, responsible for its maintenance and possibly holding the office of *budar*.

The information in the Serrīn inscription is thinner, but it seems to imply a similar situation of a local ruler who was ultimately under the authority of the Edessan

Figure 3.3 Funerary inscription for the governor of Birecik

king. The inscription is funerary, not religious, but the title *budar* again appears on the inscription and the implication is that this was an important religious office in the locality. Thus the Serrīn inscription too can be regarded as reflecting the power structures of the Edessan kingdom.

We may even be able to add the Birecik inscription, not so far mentioned, to this picture (As55) (Figure 3.3). This funerary inscription, probably dated to 6 CE (though the date is damaged and 106 cannot be ruled out completely), also has a semi-official character, since it was erected by 'Zarbiyan, son of Abgar, governor of Birtā (= Birecik), tutor (*mrbyn*ʾ, on which note the *mrbyn*ʾ of the king at Ḥaṭra: Vattioni 1981: 74–5, no. 203: 2) of ʿAwīdallāt son of Maʿnū son of Maʿnū'. On the date of the inscription, see Luther (2009: 20–2) and Kiraz (2012: 245).

EVIDENCE FOR THE SPREAD OF GRECO-ROMAN RELIGIOUS IDEAS

Already in the first centuries CE Edessa was subject to strong cultural and to some extent religious influence from the Greco-Roman world. In artistic terms this is exemplified by the prominence of mosaics. Many relate to tombs and conceptions of the afterlife (below), but some show striking reflections of Greco-Roman mythology and legend.

Figure 3.4 Orpheus taming the wild animals (mosaic from Edessa, AD 194)

Source: Author

The 'mythological' mosaics include one which depicts the creation of man by Zeus in the guise of Māralāhē and includes depictions of Hera, Chronos, and Prometheus (Cm11; Balty and Briquel Chatonnet 2000: 32–51), two which have Orpheus as the central figure (Am7; Segal 1970: pl. 44; Healey 2006) (Figure 3.4) and fragments which depict Achilles, Patroclus, Priam and Briseis, Hecuba, and Troilus (Cm5, Cm4; Balty and Briquel Chatonnet 2000: 51–71) and the mythologised River Euphrates (Bm1 from Tell Maʿsūdiyyah, south-east of Aleppo). In all of these cases the mosaic figures are accompanied by Syriac text indicating who is depicted, which shows very concretely the integration of Hellenic ideas into the local culture of the Edessa region. Some of these mosaics appear to have originated in villas (the creation, the Euphrates, and probably the Trojan War series). It seems probable that the mosaics containing Syriac were commissioned by patrons who wanted to assert their Syrian identity as well as their integration into Western culture.

Ross argued (2001: 96) that there is an absence of evidence of *interpretatio graeca* of the local deities of Edessa (by contrast with, e.g., Palmyra). It is fair to say that there is no wholesale conversion of the Edessan deities into Greek versions of themselves, again suggesting an independence of spirit in the religious sphere. We have noted, however, the equating of Māralāhē with Zeus.

This local character is evident also in most of the funerary mosaics, of which there are several well-preserved examples incorporating inscriptions which at least vaguely hint at conceptions of death and the afterlife, though they are inevitably hard to interpret (Am2, Am3, Am4, Am5, Am8, Am10, etc.). These funerary mosaics display a very different spirit from the 'classical' ones mentioned earlier. They contain only Syriac inscriptions, sometimes using typical dating and memorial formulae which are well known from places like Palmyra, and reflect the local artistic traditions, with so-called 'Parthian' elements (in frontality and clothing) which are again paralleled at Palmyra (and also at Ḥaṭra) (Colledge 1977: 80–121; 1994; Parlasca 1984).

It is hard to pin down attitudes to death and afterlife from this slight evidence, but the inscriptions in these mosaics typically describe the tomb itself as a *byt ʿlmʾ*, a 'house of eternity' or 'eternal dwelling' (As7: 3, etc.; appearing also in Palmyrene, Nabataean, etc. and known also from Egypt and in Greek funerary inscriptions). There are a few variations on this terminology: 'house of rest' (*byt mškbʾ* [or *mšknʾ*]: Healey 2006: 316, line 4), 'dwelling-place' (*byt mšryʾ*: As5: 2). Perhaps a reflection of this notion of permanent dwelling at ease are the several depictions in mosaic of whole families, wife and children surrounding a principal male figure (e.g. Am8, Am5). These scenes have their closest parallels in Palmyrene funerary sculpture depicting the central figure reclining as at a family meal or a banquet.

A phoenix is central in one mosaic (Am6), standing on a funerary stele beside a sarcophagus and identified explicitly by the Syriac writing beside its head. We cannot be sure of what the phoenix meant to the people of Edessa, but in the wider context we know that it became a symbol of post-mortal revival in the Roman world (and thence in Christianity). It is thus part of the repertoire of symbols used at Edessa, even if not native to it, sitting alongside the paradisiacal Orpheus theme, also found in tombs (Am7; for the second mosaic, now in Urfa Museum, see Healey 2006 and Possekel 2008; Colledge 1994: 191). It is very likely that such mosaics were intended to proclaim the local identity of the tombs' owners: they were, like Bardaiṣan, committed adherents of the new culture which came from the West, but that did not swamp local identity (and again there is a parallel at Palmyra).

Going beyond the prosaic are two funerary inscriptions which give us a glimpse of the sophistication of pre-Christian Edessa. One contains at the end of its inscriptions the following (slightly uncertain and obscure) epigram: 'Whoever removes the sorrow of his offspring and mourns for his forefathers will have a happy afterlife' (Am5: 13–16). Segal (1970: 34, 44–5), translating slightly differently, finds the influence, here and in other evidence, of Gnosticism. In another funerary text we appear to have a rather poetic reflection on the life of the deceased, who was, perhaps, an astrologer: 'And you saw the height and the depth and the distant and the near and the hidden and the manifest' (As5: 11–13).

PAGAN RELIGION AND THE DEVELOPMENT OF SYRIAC CHRISTIANITY

The Syriac New Testament attests at a very early stage to a certain degree of assimilation of the most important local deity (Bēl/Māralāhē) to Zeus (Acts 14: 12–13), as in the creation mosaic referred to above (Cm11), and on that basis we may speculate on a certain local readiness for such syncretisms. There is no doubt, however, that Syriac Christianity became ferociously anti-pagan, and writers like those cited above mocked the pagan gods as powerless.

There may, on the other hand, be themes in Syriac Christianity which have a pre-Christian parallel. I am thinking here especially of the importance of asceticism and specifically celibacy. We know that in pre-Christian Hierapolis, Edessa's near neighbour, the cult of Atargatis included a tradition of self-emasculation as an act of devotion to the goddess (Lightfoot 2003: § 50 on the *galli*). The Atargatis cult seems to have been strong also in Edessa, as we have seen. In the fifth century the Bishop of Edessa, Rabbula (d. 435/6), issued regulations forbidding the practice of self-emasculation by monks and *bnay qyāmā* (Vööbus 1960: 40 §55; Drijvers 1980: 77).

It is remarkable also that there grew up a Christian transformation of the cult of the *galli*, who climbed the pillars at Hierapolis in a phallic cult (Lightfoot 2003: 418–21, discussing §§ 28–9), into the central figure of the ascetic stylite. Simeon Stylites (ca. 389–459) is the best known of these, and the habit of asceticism associated with pillar-hermitages spread widely. It remains the fact, however, that the pre-Christian cult is attested principally at Hierapolis, some way from Edessa itself, and there is no attestation of it in Syriac epigraphy.

Perhaps the most important thing to say about the inheritance from the pre-Christian environment is not so much concerned with the local ('Semitic'?) religious tradition, but with the Edessa region's being deeply imbued with Hellenism already in the pre-Christian period. Edessa itself was a Seleucid foundation (or perhaps re-foundation), and when it gained its independence under the Abgarids (c. 140 BCE) it retained a Hellenistic style of kingship and society. Mosaics became popular, incorporating Hellenistic themes (above), but also intellectual life was deeply affected by Hellenistic influences. This is exemplified especially by what we know of the philosophical ideas and method of argument of the earliest named Syriac author, Bardaiṣan.

Bardaiṣan's whole mode of life is a reflection of a Greek model. He was a court philosopher and poet, part of the entourage of Abgar VIII of Edessa. His mode of philosophical debate, as reflected in *The Book of the Laws of Countries* (Drijvers 1965), was Socratic: the book is essentially a report of a dialogue between Bardaiṣan and his pupils, written up as a report by Philippos, one of those pupils. The whole subject of the dialogue is the role of fate in the life of men, and it shows an awareness of and use of Greek philosophical notions and terms, though transformed into Syriac dress (see Drijvers 1966; Segal 1970: 35–8).

All the indications are that Edessa was thoroughly Hellenised long before it became part of a Roman province in 212/13 CE. Its elite was well prepared, therefore, for engagement with the debates in the Greek-speaking church as they emerged in the third and fourth centuries CE. Greek was widely known among elites at least, and its role was reinforced in the area after the Roman liberation of the territory, as can be seen from the Middle Euphrates papyri (Feissel et al. 1995, 2000, 1997).

Paganism did not disappear quickly from Edessa and its region. The polemics of the religious authorities testify to this, as do occasional references to pagan practices, as, for example, in *The Chronicle of Pseudo-Dionysius*, where we find reference to orgiastic pagan festivals taking place in Edessa in the late-fifth century (Trombley and Watt 2000: 28, 32; Syr. in Chabot 1927: 256–7, 259; see also Segal 1970: 105–8; Drijvers 1982). Pagan personal names too were retained by converts to Christianity, as in *The Teaching of Addai*. It is perhaps more surprising that in subsequent centuries pagan names were still in use (Harrak 1992).

NOTES

1 Both mosaics and inscriptions are identified here through the *sigla* found in Drijvers and Healey 1999 (otherwise abbreviated as DH). Other items are cited in the usual way.

2 There is one inscription in DH, As10, which is probably Christian. It is of unknown date and was only included because it had appeared in Drijvers 1972a, which was being updated.

3 I thank Michael Macdonald and Dr. Ahmad al-Jallad for their advice on matters Safaitic and Thamudic.

BIBLIOGRAPHY

Aggoula, B. 1985. *Inscriptions et graffites araméens d'Assour*. AION 43. Naples: Istituto Universitario Orientale di Napoli.

Balty, J. 1990. *La mosaïque de Sarrîn (Osrhoène)*. Paris: Geuthner.

———. 1995. *Mosaïques antiques du Proche-Orient*. Centre de Recherches d'Histoire Ancienne 140. Paris: Les Belles Lettres.

Balty, J. and F. Briquel-Chatonnet. 2000. Nouvelles mosaïques inscrites d'Osrhoène. *Monuments et Mémoires publiés par l'Académie des Inscriptions et Belles-Lettres* 79, 31–72.

Bedjan, P. 1907. *Homiliae Selectae Mar-Jacobi Sarugensis III*. Paris and Leipzig: Harrassowitz.

Beyer, K. 1998. *Die aramäischen Inschriften aus Assur, Hatra und dem übrigen Ostmesopotamien*. Göttingen: Vandenhoeck & Ruprecht.

Bickell, G. 1873. *S. Isaaci Antiocheni, doctoris syrorum, opera omnia. Vol. I*. Giessen: J. Ricker.

Brock, S. P. 2006. *The Bible in the Syriac Tradition*. Gorgias Handbooks 7. Piscataway, NJ: Gorgias Press.

Burkitt, F. C. 1913. *Euphemia and the Goth*. Text and Translation Society 2. London and Oxford: Williams and Norgate. (Reprint 1981).

Chabot, J.-B. 1927. *Incerti auctoris Chronicon Anonymum Pseudo-Dionysianum vulgo dictum I*. CSCO 91, scriptores syri 43. Paris: E Typographeo Reipublicae.

Colledge, M. A. R. 1977. *Parthian Art*. London: Paul Elek.

———. 1994. Some Remarks on the Edessa Funerary Mosaics. *In*: J.-P. Darmon and A. Rebourg, ed., *La mosaïque gréco-romaine IV. Actes du IVe Colloque International pour l'Étude de la Mosïque Antique, Trèves, 8–14 Août 1994*. Paris: Association Internationale pour l'Étude de la Mosaïque Antique, 189–97.

Cureton, W. 1855. *Spicilegium Syriacum: Containing Remains of Bardesan, Meliton, Ambrose and Mara bar Serapion*. London: Rivingtons.

Deichmann, F. W. and U. Peschlow. 1977. *Zwei spätantike Ruinenstätten in Nordmesopotamien*. Bayerische Akademie der Wissenschaften, Philosphisch-historische Klasse. Sitzungsberichte. Munich: Verlag der Bayerischen Akademie der Wissenschaften.

Dirven, L. 2009. My Lord With His Dogs. Continuity and Change in the Cult of Nergal in Parthian Mesopotamia. *In*: L. Greisiger, C. Rammelt and J. Tübach, ed., *Edessa in hellenistisch-römischer Zeit: Religion, Kultur und Politik zwischen Ost und West*. Beiruter Texte und Studien 116. Beirut: In Kommission Ergon Verlag Würzburg [f-68].

Drijvers, H. J. W. 1965. *The Book of the Laws of Countries: Dialogue on Fate of Bardaiṣan of Edessa*. Assen: van Gorcum.

———. 1966. *Bardaiṣan of Edessa*. Assen: van Gorcum.

———. 1972a. *Old-Syriac (Edessean) Inscriptions*. Semitic Study Series 3. Leiden: Brill.

———. 1972b. The Cult of Azizos and Monimos at Edessa. *In*: C. J. Bleeker, S. G. F. Brandon and M. Simon, ed., *Ex Orbe Religionum. Studia Geo Widengren . . . oblata I*. Leiden: Brill, 355–71.

———. 1977. Hatra, Palmyra und Edessa. Die Städte der syrisch-mesopotamischen Wüste in politischer, kulturgeschichtlicher und religionsgeschichtlicher Beleuchtung. *In*: H. Temporini and W. Haase, ed., *Aufstieg und Niedergang der römischen Welt: II Principate* 8. Berlin: de Gruyter, 799–906.

———. 1980. *Cults and Beliefs of Edessa*. Études préliminaires aux religions orientales dans l'empire romain 82. Leiden: Brill.

———. 1982. The Persistence of Pagan Cults and Practices in Christian Syria. *In*: N. G. Garsoïan, T. F. Mathews and R. W. Thomson, ed., *East of Byzantium: Syria and Armenia in the Formative Period*. Dumbarton Oaks Symposium 1980. Washington, DC: Dumbarton Oaks, Center for Byzantine Studies, 35–43.

———. 1985. Jews and Christians at Edessa. *Journal of Jewish Studies* 36, 88–102.

Drijvers, H. J. W. and J. F. Healey. 1999. *The Old Syriac Inscriptions of Edessa and Osrhoene: Texts, Translations and Commentary*. Handbuch der Orientalistik I/42. Leiden, Boston MA and Cologne: Brill.

Feissel, D. and J. Gascou. 1995. Documents d'archives romains inédits du moyen euphrate (IIIe s. après J.-C.), I. Les pétitions (P. Euphr. 1 à 5). *Journal des Savants*, 65–119.

———. 2000. Documents d'archives romains inédits du moyen euphrate (IIIe s. après J.-C.), III. Actes diverses et lettres (P. Euphr. 11 à 17). *Journal des Savants*, 157–208.

Feissel, D., J. Gascou and J. Teixidor. 1997. Documents d'archives romains inédits du moyen euphrate (IIe s. après J.-C.), II. Les actes de vente-achat (P. Euphr. 6 à 10). *Journal des Savants*, 3–57.

Gawlikowski, M. 1974. *Receuil des inscriptions palmyréniennes provenant de fouilles syriennes et polonaises récentes à Palmyre*. Extrait des mémoires présentés par divers savants à l'Académie des Inscriptions et Belles-Lettres 16. Paris: Imprimerie Nationale/Librairie Klincksieck.

———. 1990. Les dieux de Palmyre. *In*: W. Haase and H. Temporini, ed., *Aufstieg und Niedergang der römishcen Welt: II Principate* 18.4. Berlin and New York: de Gruyter, 2605–58.

Gibson, J. C. L. 1975. *Textbook of Syrian Semitic Inscriptions II. Aramaic Inscriptions*. Oxford: Clarendon Press.

Gogräfe, R. 1995. Die Grabtürme von Sirrin (Osroëne). *Damaszener Mitteilungen* 8, 165–201.

Green, T. M. 1992. *The City of the Moon God: Religious Traditions of Harran*. Religions in the Graeco-Roman World 114. Leiden, New York, NY and Cologne: Brill.

Harrak, A. 1992. Pagan Traces in Syriac Christian Onomastica. *In*: A. Harrak, ed., *Contacts Between Cultures: West Asia and North Africa: Selected Papers From the 33rd International Congress of Asian and North African Studies, Toronto, August 15–25, 1990*. Lewiston, NY: Mellen, 318–23.

Healey, J. F. 1996. "May He Be Remembered for Good": An Aramaic Formula. *In*: K. J. Cathcart and M. Maher, ed., *Targumic and Cognate Studies. Essays in Honour of Martin McNamara*. JSOT Supplement Series 230. Sheffield: Sheffield Academic Press, 177–86.

———. 2001. *The Religion of the Nabataeans: a Conspectus*. Religions in the Graeco-Roman World 136. Leiden: Brill.

———. 2006. A New Syriac Mosaic Inscription. *Journal of Semitic Studies* 51, 313–27.

———. 2008. Variety in Early Syriac: the context in contemporary Aramaic. *In*: H. Gzella and M. L. Folmer, ed., *Aramaic in its Historical and Linguistic Setting*. Akademie der Wissenschaften und der Literatur, Mainz; Veröffentlichungen der Orientalischen Kommission 50. Wiesbaden: Harrassowitz Verlag, 221–29.

Hillers, D. R. and E. Cussini. 1996. *Palmyrene Aramaic Texts*. Baltimore, MD: John Hopkins University Press.

Höfner, M. 1965. Die Stammesgruppen Nord- und Zentralarabiens in vorislamischer Zeit. *In*: H. W. Haussig, ed., *Wörterbuch der Mythologie I. Götter und Mythen im vorderen Orient*. Stuttgart: Ernst Klett, 407–81.

Howard, G. 1981. *The Teaching of Addai* [Syriac text of G. Phillips]. Texts and Translations 16/Early Christian Literature 4. Chico, CA: Scholars Press.

Kaizer, T. 2002. *The Religious Life of Palmyra*. Oriens et Occidens 4. Stuttgart: Franz Steiner.

———. (ed.). 2008. *The Variety of Local Religious Life in the Near East in the Hellenistic and Roman Periods*. Religions in the Graeco-Roman World 164. Leiden and Boston, MA: Brill.

Karabulut, H., M. Önal and N. Dervişoğlu. 2011. *Haleplibahçe Mozaikler, Şanlıurfa/Edessa*. Istanbul: Arkeoloji ve Sanat Yayınları.

Kiraz, G. 2012. Old Syriac Graphotactics. *Journal of Semitic Studies* 57, 231–64.

Lacombrade, Ch. 1964. *L'empereur Julien: oeuvres complètes* II, 2. Paris: Société d'Édition "Les Belles-Lettres".

Leichty, E. 2011. *The Royal Inscriptions of Esarhaddon, King of Assyria (680–669 BC)*. The Royal Inscriptions of the Neo-Assyrian Period 4. Winona Lake, IN: Eisenbrauns.

Lightfoot, J. L. 2003. *Lucian. On the Syrian Goddess*. Oxford: University Press.

———. 2007. The Apology of Ps.-Meliton. *Studi Epigrafici e Linguistici* 24, 59–110.

Lightfoot, C. S. and J. F. Healey. 1991. A Roman Veteran on the Tigris. *Epigraphica Anatolica* 17, 1–7.

Luther, A. 2009. Osrohener am Niederrhein. Drei altsyrische Graffiti aus Krefeld-Gellep (und andere frühe altsyrische Schriftzeugnisse). *Marburger Beiträge zur antiken Handels-, Wirtschafts- und Sozialgeschichte* 27, 11–30.

Martin, P. 1876. Discours de Jacques de Saroug sur la chute des idoles. *ZDMG* 29, 107–47.

Noy, D. and H. Bloedhorn. 2004. *Inscriptiones Judaicae Orientis* III. Texts and Studies in Ancient Judaism 102. Tübingen: Mohr Siebeck.

Palmer, A. 2015. Sumatar Revisited: The Long Inscription of 165 CE. *Journal of Semitic Studies* 60, 63–92.

Parlasca, K. 1983. Das Mosaik von Masʿudije aus dem Jahre 228/9 n.Chr. *DM* 1, 263–7.

———. 1984. Neues zu den Mosaiken von Edessa und Seleukeia am Euphrat. *In*: R. Fariola Campanati, ed., *III Colloquio internazionale sul mosaico antico, Ravenna 6–10 Settembre 1980*. Ravenna: Edizioni del Girasole, 227–34.

Pognon, H. 1907. *Inscriptions sémitiques de la Syrie, de la Mésopotamie et de la région de Mossoul*. Paris: Imprimerie Nationale.

Possekel, U. 2008. Orpheus among the Animals: A New Dated Mosaic From Osrhoene. *Oriens Christianus* 92, 1–35.

Preissler, H. 1989. Altsyrische heidnische Namen in der frühen syrischen Literatur. *Klio* 71, 503–7.

Ross, S. K. 2001. *Roman Edessa: Politics and Culture on the Eastern Fringes of the Roman Empire, 114–242 C. E.* London: Routledge.

Segal, J. B. 1953. Pagan Syriac Monuments in the Vilayet of Urfa. *Anatolian Studies* 3, 97–119.

———. 1954. Some Syriac Inscriptions of the 2nd–3rd Century A.D. *BSOAS* 16, 13–36.

———. 1970. *Edessa, the Blessed City*. Oxford: University Press.

Sommer, M. 2005. *Roms orientalische Steppengrenze: Palmyra – Edessa – Dura-Europos – Hatra: ein Kulturgeschichte von Pompeius bis Diocletian*. Oriens et Occidens 9. Stuttgart: Franz Steiner Verlag.

Stark, J. K. 1971. *Personal Names in Palmyrene Inscriptions*. Oxford: Clarendon Press.

Trombley, F. R. and J. W. Watt. 2000. *The Chronicle of Pseudo-Dionysius the Stylite*. Translated Texts for Historians 32. Liverpool: Liverpool University Press.

Tubach, J. 1986. *Im Schatten des Sonnengottes. Der Sonnenkult in Edessa, Ḥarrān und Ḥaṭrā am Vorabend der christlichen Mission*. Wiesbaden: Harrassowitz.

Vattioni, F. 1981. *Le Iscrizioni di Hatra*. AION Supplement 28. Naples: Istituto Orientale di Napoli.

Vööbus, A. 1960. *Syriac and Arabic Documents Regarding Legislation Related to Syrian Asceticism*. Papers of the Estonian Theological Society in Exile 11. Stockholm: Estonian Theological Society in Exile.

Weizmann, M. P. 1999. *The Syriac Version of the Old Testament*. Cambridge: Cambridge University Press.

Wilkinson, J. 1999. *Egeria's Travels: Newly Translated With Supporting Documents and Notes*. Warminster: Aris and Pillips.

Winnett, F. V. and W. L. Reed. 1970. *Ancient Records from North Arabia*. Near and Middle East Series 6. Toronto: University of Toronto Press.

CHAPTER FOUR

THE COMING OF CHRISTIANITY TO MESOPOTAMIA

David G. K. Taylor

We know frustratingly little about the early expansion of Christianity in the eastern Mediterranean world before the fourth century. The New Testament texts provide us with valuable information about how their authors in the second half of the first century understood the beginnings of their movement, and how early disciples began to travel away from Jerusalem in order to proclaim their beliefs to others. In the sources for the second and third centuries, we occasionally hear of prominent bishops, of persecutions and martyrs, of notable heresies, and, occasionally, we are lucky enough to possess the surviving writings of isolated authors. But we hear little or nothing of the means or agency by which Christianity was spread in cities, towns, and villages, we have no statistics for the numbers of converts, and we know little about contemporary church organisation. Only in the fourth-century sources do we start to receive a clearer picture, and even then it is far less than we would like.

Take for example the city of Antioch, one of the three greatest cities of the Roman Empire, whose emerging church is better documented than most (Downey 1961: ch. 11–12). The Acts of the Apostles tell us that early followers of Jesus fled there from Jerusalem (Acts 11:19), that Barnabas (Acts 4:36), later joined by Paul (Acts 11:22–26), taught there for more than a year, and that it was in Antioch that the followers of Jesus were first called Christians (Acts 11:26), presumably in the early 40s. Simon Peter (Kephas) was the first of the twelve apostles to visit Antioch (Gal 2:11), though it is only later tradition that describes him as the first bishop of Antioch (at a time when Peter and Paul had been claimed for Rome, Mark for Alexandria, and James for Jerusalem). After the end of the apostolic age, we have the seven letters written by bishop Ignatius during his journey to Rome, where he was martyred during the reign of Trajan, perhaps in December 116, and we have the apology *Ad Autolycum* of bishop Theophilus (d. pre 188), and we know of the martyrdom of bishop Babylas (ca. 250), preserved in a highly legendary form. In 256, Antioch was captured by the Persians and bishop Demetrianus was taken into exile along with numerous skilled craftsmen (Peeters 1924). In 260, when Antioch was again taken by the Persians, Paul of Samosata was made bishop, and was soon accused of financial and moral corruption, and heterodox theology, which led to his expulsion in 270. There is then little to report until the outbreak of the Diocletianic persecution of the

Christians in 303 and the subsequent martyrdoms of Antiochene citizens, including the biblical scholar Lucian in 312. Constantine's victory at the Milvian bridge outside Rome in October 312 marked the beginning of a process that led to official toleration of Christian worship and practice and the start of an imperially sanctioned and financed programme of church building, including the Great Church in Antioch, which was begun in 327 and completed in 341.

At first glance this might look like abundant evidence for the early development and organisation of Christianity in Antioch, but we know nothing about the actual size of the Christian community in the city, or its relative membership in comparison to the local Jewish community or to the various gnostic and other sects said to have thrived there. There is only evidence for one church building (the Old Church) prior to Constantine (Mayer and Allen 2012: 100), although others may have existed, and there is so little reliable archaeology for the city that the location of Constantine's Great Church remains unknown (Mayer and Allen 2012: 73). There is good reason, then, that most histories of Christianity in Antioch begin with Constantine and focus on fourth-century writers such as Libanius and John Chrysostom (Devreesse 1945; Festugière 1959).

When we turn inland from Antioch to the villages and small towns of the city's hinterland, we have a profusion of epigraphic evidence from the fourth century onward that can be drawn upon to illuminate the progress of the expansion of Christianity. It reveals that 'the new religion spread through northern Syria at rates that differed from massif to massif and from village to village' (Trombley 1993: 2.311), with sites on the main road network providing evidence of conversion from the late fourth century (usually by individuals, rather than entire communities together). The clergy of Antioch appear to have increased their efforts in the countryside between 365 and 425, a period described as 'the crucible of religious transformation for the Syrian peasantry' (Trombley 1993: 2.134), starting with preaching and then moving towards the construction of village churches. Following the imperial edict of Thessalonica issued in February 380 which promulgated Christianity, Christian radicals from Antioch began to destroy pagan temples, and yet it is clear that in many areas of Syria polytheism survived into the fifth and even the sixth centuries.

A similar pattern of Christian missionary activity can be seen in Asia Minor. Paul, who came from Tarsus in Cilicia, preached in Ephesus on the Aegean coast (Acts 19.1, Eph), and in Antioch of Pisidia (Acts 13:14), and in Iconium, Lystra, and Derbe in Lycaonia (Acts 14:1, 6, 16:1), and in Phrygia and Galatia (Acts 16:6, Col, Gal, 1 Pet 1.1). The Book of Revelation attributed to John (late first century) addresses letters to seven churches in Asia Minor (Rev 1:11), three on the Aegean, three in Lydia, and one in Phrygia. By the late second century, there were Christian communities in many of the towns of Asia Minor, as far east as Cappadocia, and these grew rapidly from the mid-third century on, as the epigraphic evidence shows (Trombley 1993: ch. 7). By the time of the Council of Nicaea in 325, most of the cities had bishops (Harnack 1908: 2.182–229). The villages and countryside, however, only provide evidence of conversion from the mid-fourth century on, intensifying during the fifth century. And John of Ephesus can still plausibly claim to have converted 80,000 pagans in western Asia Minor during his campaign of ca. 538–566 (Trombley 1985).

Turning now to Mesopotamia (used here as a geographical rather than a provincial term, to indicate the lands from the Euphrates in the west to the lands on either side of the Tigris in the east, on both sides of the shifting Roman and Iranian frontier), we will see a very similar pattern of Christianisation emerge. Local epigraphic evidence only begins to appear from the mid-fourth century on, and prior to that we are heavily reliant on extracting data from the surviving writings of a few early writers, from brief entries in histories and chronicles, and from hagiographical accounts and legends.

ROMAN MESOPOTAMIA

From the records of synods and councils, it is clear that during the fourth century an extensive church hierarchy was being established in the region. For the Roman territories we have lists of the signatories of bishops at the councils of Nicaea in 325 and Constantinople in 381 (Gelzer et al. 1898; Kaufhold 1993), which can be compared with the fully developed structure outlined in the *Notitia Antiochena* of the 580s (Rahmani 1920):

Nicaea 325	*Constantinople 381*	*Notitia Antiochena 580s*	
Mesopotamia:	Osrhoene:		
Edessa	Edessa	Edessa, and her sees:	Antioch, and her sees:
Nisibis	Carrhae	Birta	Beroea / Aleppo
Reshaina	Batnan	Mʿarta	Chalkis / Qenneshrin
Makedonopolis/Birta		Harran / Carrhae	Gabala
Fars		Tella / Constantina	Seleucia
	Mesopotamia:	Marcopolis	Anazartha
	Amida	Batnan of Sarug	Platon
	Constantina	Telmahrin	Gabbula
	Amaria	Amorin	(Salamia)
		Circession	(Barcuson)
Syria:	Coele Syria:	Daushar	Autocephalous:
Antioch	Antioch	Callinicium	Beirut
Seleucia	Laodicea	Neo-Valentia	Emessa
Laodicea	Beroea		Laodicea
Apamea	Apamea	Amid, and her sees:	Cyrrhus
Hierapolis/Mabbug	Seleucia	Martyropolis	
Germanikaia	Epiphaneia	Iggilon	Apamea, and her sees:
Samosata	Seleukobelos	Bolebtina	Epiphaneia / Hamath
Doliche	Larissa	Aršamišat	Seleukobelos
Balanaion	Paltos	Beth Sophanaia	Larissa
Gabala	Chalkis	Qidarizon	Balaneos
Zeugma	Gabala	Hesen Kepha	Mariames
Raphane	Raphane	Zugmatos	Raphaneas
Larissa			Arista
Arethusa	Augusto-Euphratesia:	Dara, and her sees:	
Neo-Caesarea	Hierapolis	Reshaina	Hierapolis, and her sees:
Cyrrhus	Samosata	Tur Abdin	Zeugma

Nicaea 325	*Constantinople 381*	*Notitia Antiochena 580s*	
Gindaron	Cyrrhus	Menasobion	Šura Romaeorum
Arboukadamon	Perre		Beth Balash
Gaboulon	Doliche		Neo-Caesarea
Epiphaneia			Perrin
Ibalas			Orim
			Doliche
			Germanicia
			Europos
			Lragiz
			Samosata

These lists should be understood as snapshots of church hierarchies in Roman Mesopotamia and surrounding regions in the fourth century, rather than as complete listings of all bishoprics – Ammianus Marcellinus, for example, in his account of the wars in 360 (XX.7.7; Rolfe 1940), mentions the bishop of Bet Zabdai, then a fortified Roman town on the Tigris. The lists are not easy reading because so many of the place names are unfamiliar, and because of the changing designations of civic and ecclesiastical provinces. But they remind us that while our sources may drive us to focus on a small number of missionary centres, usually within the Roman Empire, Christianity was actually spreading out from numerous cities simultaneously (many of which are hardly mentioned in our sources), including cities on the edges of Mesopotamia (for example, Samosata and Zeugma). It should also be noted that Christian expansion in the Iranian world was not a later development, totally dependent upon that in the eastern Roman provinces, but, as will be shown below, it was a contemporary and largely independent movement that had extraordinary success. Both east and west of the Iranian-Roman frontier, however, our sources for the earliest centuries are disappointingly few, and poor in reliable information.

Although it is an easy fact to overlook, it needs to be noted that no apostle or early disciple is recorded in the New Testament as having visited or written to a Mesopotamian city (Harnack 1908: 2.91–4), and no contemporary city or town of Mesopotamia is mentioned, with the exception of the 'church in Babylon' in 1 Peter 5:13, which is usually thought to be a coded reference to Rome. In the Acts of the Apostles 2:8, Jews from Mesopotamia, along with 'Parthians, Medes, and Elamites' are included among those who are said to have witnessed the first post-ascension Pentecost in Jerusalem. So early Christians in Mesopotamia who wished to establish local links with biblical episodes had a limited set of options. They could link their community to the 'Magi from the East' (Mt 2:1), who numbered twelve in the Syriac tradition (Jullien and Jullien 2002b: 111–17) and could be seen as the very earliest confessors of Christ (Monneret de Villard 1952; Briquel-Chatonnet et al. 2000), or could even be claimed as founders of churches, as at Ḥaḥ in the Ṭur ʿAbdin (Anschütz 1984: 98). Another option was to emphasise the links with Old Testament events and prophets, such as the landing of Noah's ark on mount Qardu (mount Judi, near Cizre, rather than Ararat, according to the Syriac Old Testament), Abraham's origin in Harran (see below), or Jonah and the fast of the Ninevites (an annual Christian fast in the Syriac tradition).

An even more radical solution was adopted by unknown Christians in Edessa (modern Urfa) prior to the early fourth century. They produced a legend that not only provided the missing apostolic link for their city, but actually put one of their ancient kings, called Abgar V Ukāmā ('the black', r. 4 BC–AD 7 and AD 13–50), in contact with Jesus. The earliest version of this tradition is to be found in Eusebius of Caesarea's *Ecclesiastical History* (HE I.xiii), in a section thought to have been written in 311, but which is only preserved in a final edition issued by Eusebius in 325. (A Syriac translation of the *Ecclesiastical History* was produced by the late fourth or early fifth century.) Eusebius twice notes that his source was originally written in Syriac (HE I.xiii.5, 11), and states that the original documents were taken from the archives at Edessa and found in public documents there (Eusebius, HE I.xiii.5). It is unlikely that Eusebius has simply invented this tradition, but since he appears never to have travelled to Mesopotamia (Bauer 1934:14), he cannot have personally searched the archives for this document. A reference he makes to 'a narrative which has reached us' (Eusebius, HE I.xii.3) makes it more plausible to suppose that he was sent a Greek translation of documents which he was told were preserved in the archives.

Eusebius reports that 'the toparch Abgar Ukāmā', who was very sick, heard of Jesus and of the miraculous healings he was performing in the region of Jerusalem, and so wrote to him, via the courier Ananias, to proclaim that Jesus must either be God who 'came down from heaven to do these things', or a son of God, and to request that he come to Edessa to heal him. Jesus wrote a reply, blessing Abgar for his faith (alluding to John 20:29), but stating that he had first to complete his mission and be taken up to him who sent him, but that after that he would send one of his disciples to heal Abgar. Eusebius says that his source text went on to state that after the ascension of Jesus, Judas Thomas sent Thaddaeus, one of the seventy disciples (although not named as such in the New Testament) to Edessa, where he stayed with Tobias son of Tobias. When the king heard of his arrival he summoned him to court, and then bowed down to Thaddaeus, having seen his face transformed, and confessed his faith in Jesus and in his Father. Thaddaeus healed Abgar, and other notables, and the following day preached the incarnation of Jesus, and his crucifixion, his descent to Hades, his raising of the dead, and his ascension to heaven with them.

A heavily expanded form of this narrative (for a textual comparison see Brock 1992a; Mirkovic 2004) is to be found in *The Teaching of Addai* (Howard 1981; Illert 2007), a Syriac text usually thought to have reached its present form by the early fifth century, and preserved (at least in part) in several manuscripts, the earliest of which (BL Add. 14654, 14644) date to the fifth or sixth centuries. This text explains how king Abgar had heard about Jesus from ambassadors sent to a Roman procurator of Syria named Sabinus (a name perhaps derived from the procurator of Syria, fl. 4 BC, named by Josephus *Jewish War* 2.2.2, *Antiquities* 17.9.3), and states that the letter reached Jesus on the Wednesday before his crucifixion. Jesus's reply includes the addition of a blessing on Edessa: 'May your city be blessed, and may an enemy (or "the enemy", Satan) never again rule over it'. It then introduces a brief account of Ananias (in Syriac Ḥanan) painting a portrait of Jesus. In this text the disciple who is sent to Edessa is named Addai rather than Thaddaeus, the name used by Eusebius (and by the Syriac translation of Eusebius). Addai tells Abgar a long story about how the wife of Claudius Caesar (r. 41–54), said to be called Protonike ('first victory'), was converted by Simon Peter in Rome and travelled to Jerusalem, and while there forced the Jews to reveal the hiding place of Christ's cross. There is then a much longer form of Addai's preaching, said to have been delivered not only to the nobles of Edessa, but also to the craftsmen, both pagans and Jews, and to people from Nisibis, Ḥarran, and the whole region of Mesopotamia. The multitudes converted to Christ, including even the pagan high priests (who tore down all their shrines except the main temple) and the Jews. Abgar promised to pay for a church and for the teachers of the Gospel, and so at the time of prayer the converts read the Old and New Testaments, the Prophets and the Acts of the Apostles, and the Diatessaron (the Gospel harmony of Tatian, produced around 170) – later the Law, and the epistles of Paul are also mentioned. More churches were built, which attracted easterners from across the Iranian frontier who were in turn converted and ordained priests, before returning to the 'country of the Assyrians' where they built their own churches. The king of the Assyrians, Narsai (based on shah Narseh, r. 293–302, or maybe just a good Iranian name), wrote to Abgar requesting either that Addai be sent to him or that Abgar relate the whole story, which is what he did. This royal correspondence is followed by an exchange of letters between Abgar and Tiberius Caesar (r. 14–37), both of whom criticise the Jews for their rejection and treatment of Jesus. Before he died, Addai is said to have built churches in other (unnamed) towns 'both near and far' and to have appointed Aggai as his successor and Paluṭ as a priest. Aggai is later killed by an anonymous son of Abgar, and so Paluṭ went to Antioch to 'receive priesthood' (i.e. consecration as bishop) from Serapion, bishop of Antioch (r. 190–211), who was himself said to have been consecrated by Zephyrinus, bishop of Rome (r. 198–217), in succession to Simon Peter.

This is a delightfully detailed story that appears to answer many of our questions about the coming of Christianity to Mesopotamia, and so it is not a surprise that many historians have been reluctant to exclude it from their accounts of the Christianisation of the region. But it needs to be emphasised once again that this story is entirely legendary, in both its short and long forms, with no basis in historical fact. It tells us nothing about the earliest origins of Syriac Christianity, but it is of course a witness to the beliefs and ambitions of its authors in the early fourth century and those of its later redactors in the following century.

Only some of the legendary and anachronistic features of these texts can be detailed here (the minor chronological problems should be obvious from the dates given above), if space is to be left for discussion of genuine historical sources. To start with, no contemporary source independently records the conversion of a local Edessan king to messianic Judaism/Christianity (it is not even mentioned in the *Chronicle of Edessa*, which genuinely used the city archives; Guidi 1903; Hallier 1892), and neither is there any archaeological evidence of the Christian faith of Abgar V Ukāmā or of any of his successors (who reigned, with breaks, until 242). By contrast, the conversion to Judaism of Abgar's younger contemporary king Izates (r. AD 31–55) of Adiabene (centred on Arbela), and of his mother Helen, was recorded, and there is also supporting epigraphic evidence (Marciak 2014). Since the late nineteenth century (Lipsius 1880; Burkitt 1904), scholars have attempted to retrieve historical value from the legend by arguing that it was not Abgar V Ukāmā who converted, but Abgar VIII the Great (r. 177–212), wrongly labelled Abgar IX in earlier scholarship, at whose court the early Christian philosopher Bardaiṣan flourished. While this is a more plausible historical context, there is again no evidence to support the idea. It is not what our legends actually say; there are no Christian inscriptions from Edessa at this date; and a mosaic portrait of Abgar VIII (Drijvers 1981, 1982a; Drijvers and Healey 1999) discovered in 1979 has no Christian symbols. Indeed, none of the dozen or so third-century mosaics from Edessa contain any Christian imagery, although produced by local nobles said to have converted with the king.

No local coin of Edessa (where the mint operated until 251) has any Christian symbolism, which is perhaps unsurprising since the first Roman coin with such a symbol, a (tiny) Chi-Rho labarum on Constantine's helmet, was minted in 315, and only from the 320s did Christian symbols start to become more common (Bruck 1955). On some small coins produced in Edessa during the reign of Commodus (r. 180–192), Abgar VIII is portrayed on the reverse wearing the distinctive Parthian domed tiara of the Abgarids (Hill 1922: 94, pl.XIII.14) with a pattern that some have identified as a cross. This claim ignores the fact that Parthian kings also wore tiaras with a similar pattern (Olbrycht 1997: pl. IV.J; Sellwood 1980), and that the larger coins portraying Abgar VIII during the reign of Septimius Severus (r. 193–211) have him wearing a tiara with a crescent moon and stars (Hill 1922: 94, pl.XIII.16). In contrast to the coins of many Syrian cities, there are no obvious Graeco-Roman deities portrayed on Roman Edessan coins, if one excludes (a) a brief run of silver denarii produced by the Antonines in 167–169, modelled on Roman denarii with images of Mars, Juno, and Ceres (Hill 1922: 92–3), and (b) the local Tyche, modelled on the Tyche of Antioch (Christof 2001), who was regularly portrayed on Edessan coins from the reign of Caracalla (r. 211–217). But each city in Syria and Mesopotamia had a distinctive identifying emblem added to its silver and (on occasion) bronze coins (Prieur and Prieur 2000); for Hierapolis (Mabbug) the lion (associated with Atargatis); for Ḥarran (Carrhae) a bucranium (ox skull) or crescent moon; for Nisibis (on bronze coins only) a ram. The symbol for Edessa was a depiction of a temple containing a baetyl, or sacred stone, which made its first appearance (Hill 1922: 91, pl.XIII.7, 8) on coins of king Wael bar Sahru (r. 163–165), more than fifty years earlier than the reign of the emperor Elagabalus (r. 218–222) who brought notoriety to the cult of the baetyls, and it continued to be used until the end of the reign of Gordian III (r. 238–244). The presence of non-Christian religious symbols on Edessan coins does not mean that there were no Christians in Edessa, but it does not seem compatible with the mass conversion to Christianity of the king and nobles.

No early Syriac author (Bardaiṣan, Aphrahaṭ, Ephrem, Liber Graduum) refers to Addai, or to king Abgar becoming a Christian. The early third-century Syriac text of the *Book of the Laws of the Countries* (§45), composed by a disciple of Bardaiṣan, states that king Abgar outlawed self-emasculation in honour of the goddess Atargatis 'when he believed', but since these words are not found in the Greek quotation of the passage by Eusebius (PE 6.10.44), they are likely to be a later Syriac addition (Brock 1992a: 223).

By the time the pilgrim Egeria visited Edessa in 384 (Wilkinson 1981), it is clear that the legend of Abgar's correspondence with Christ was well known (she already had a copy at home in Western Europe, and was given another copy as a souvenir, §19). However, no mention is made of Addai, and indeed she states (§17) that the apostle sent to Edessa was Thomas (Devos 1967). Given her praise (§19) for the splendour of the Edessan martyr shrine newly built for the bones of Thomas (the return of which from India is mentioned by Ephrem, Nisibene Hymns 42.1–2; Beck 1963), her reference to Thomas might be considered an obvious confusion. But a fourth- or fifth-century Greek inscription found in Edessa, which repeats Christ's letter to Abgar, includes a statement that the disciple to be sent will be 'Thaddaeus, also called Thomas' (von Oppenheim 1914; Canali de Rossi 2004: 19; Illert 2007: 180). This possibly exploits an ambiguity in the wording of Eusebius's mention of Judas, also called Thomas, sending Thaddaeus (HE I.xiii.11), but it does raise the question of whether the legend of Addai had failed to supplant an earlier tradition of Thomas as the local apostle, or whether the arrival of Thomas's relics led some to assert for the first time that the great apostle of the east had in fact been their apostle.

Turning to *The Teaching of Addai* itself, it is obvious that the original legend has become a vehicle for many later narrative elements. The story of the painting of an icon of Christ by Abgar's emissary is clearly anachronistic in any account of art history. No such icon existed in 384 when Egeria visited, since she was shown only marble images of Abgar and his son. The first clear references to an actual icon of Christ in Edessa, which became the object of great devotion, date from the mid-sixth century (Cameron 1983), a period when various miraculous icons began to appear in Syria (Kitzinger 1954). Again, the legend of Protonike's discovery of the Cross is clearly dependent upon the legend of the empress Helena's finding of the Cross, which itself probably came into being in the late fourth century (Drijvers 1992). The Protonike legend later forced Syriac writers to explain just how, having been found, the Cross so quickly managed to get lost again (Brock 1992b).

The editor of *The Teaching of Addai* also included references to Christian practices and institutions that were normal in his age, but which were quite unknown in the early years of Christianity. Examples of this include the biblical canon, mentioned above, which he takes for granted, but which took years to be written and collected together; and the institution of a Christian priesthood, with the associated practice of ordination. Less obviously problematic at first glance are his references to Addai building churches in Edessa and in other cities. And yet the archaeological evidence makes it clear that Christians before the fourth century rarely worshipped in buildings whose only function was to be a church, but instead met in a variety of temporary worship spaces (Adams 2016). In fact, the only certain archaeological example in the entire Mediterranean world, including Rome, of a building in the pre-Constantinian era whose sole use was as a Christian place of prayer is the church at Dura Europos on the Euphrates, which was converted from prior domestic use between 232 and 256 (Adams 2016: 95, 111; Kraeling 1967). A building in Megiddo has also been identified as a Christian prayer hall, but its dating (and much else) is controversial, ranging from 230 to the fourth century (Adams 2016: 96–9). The late sixth-century *Chronicle of Edessa*, in the account of a catastrophic flood that damaged Edessa in November 201, famously refers to the destruction of 'the building of the church of the Christians' (Guidi 1903: 2.4). Scholars have often suspected this reference of being a later interpolation since it is not included in the repetition of the flood account in the *Chronicle of Zuqnin* of 775 (Chabot 1927; Harrak 2017: anno 2232), and for 313 the *Chronicle of Edessa* says that Bishop Qune laid the foundations of 'the church' in Edessa, which was completed by his successor. In any case, the references to church building in *The Teaching of Addai* cannot be based on historical fact.

So, if both the early fourth-century Eusebian account of the conversion of Abgar V and the later *The Teaching of Addai* are legends, why were they produced when they were, and what do they tell us about Christianity in Mesopotamia at these dates? Some have attempted to link the account found in Eusebius to the news of the emperor Constantine's conversion to Christianity, or to the accounts of the conversion of king Tiridates III of Armenia (r. ca. 287–330) between 301 and 314, and of king Mirian of Georgia during the reign of Constantine, among other notable conversions (Mirkovic 2004: 120–2). Each of these accounts has its own historical problems, however, and the exact chronology of their production and circulation is debateable. Given that it is also not known exactly when the Abgar materials were incorporated into Eusebius's history (Mirkovic 2004: 105), which provides the earliest date for the legend, the dangers of circular argument are evident. Clearly the early fourth century was a time when such stories could flourish and when there must have been a degree of regional rivalry about whose ruler was the first to acknowledge Christ, but this does not establish the original motive for writing.

One of the distinctive features of *The Teaching of Addai*, with traces also in the Eusebian account, is the central role played by the noble families of Edessa. It is two nobles, Maryahb and Shmeshgram, along with Hanan, who first saw Christ in Jerusalem, and celebrated with the crowds, before bringing the news to Abgar. Addai appeared before Abgar and his nobles at the court in Edessa and healed the king and a noble named Abdu bar Abdu, 'the second of his kingdom'. It is the royal family (including Abgar's mother, and Shalmath the queen) and the nobles (Howard 1981: 35, 65, 67) who first believe in Christ, and it is only nobles (and priests) who are named in the text. This is also a feature of the spurious martyr acts of Sharbel the high priest and the confession of Barsamya the bishop (Cureton 1864: 45, 63), which depend upon *The Teaching of Addai* and are set in 104 but were probably written in the fifth century (Millar 1993: 464; Brock 1992a: 223). Some of the same noble names appear in both texts, and several also appear in Syriac inscriptions of the second and third centuries (Brock 1992a: 228; Drijvers and Healey 1999; Camplani 2009). By contrast, the acts of the genuine martyrs Shmona and Gurya (AD 297), and Habib the deacon (AD 309), reveal a quite different social world (Burkitt 1913; von Gebhardt and von Dobschütz 1911). The martyrs are attested by Ephrem (d. 373; Nisibene Hymns 33.13; Beck 1961) and the Syriac martyrology of 411 (Nau 1912), although, as Millar dryly notes, the acts 'are certainly not documentary records of events' (Millar 1993: 486–8). Nevertheless, all of these martyrs are villagers from outlying regions, taken to Edessa to be tried, (interestingly, Habib was said to be away working with Christians in villages around Zeugma when his family was arrested), and while little else is said of their origins, they are clearly not noble or, apparently, wealthy. This suggests that by the early fourth century the noble families of Edessa, including the former royal family, were attempting to give their ancestors central roles in the Christianisation of their city, whereas in reality it may well have been villagers and ordinary citizens who were preaching the Gospel (Brock 1992a: 228).

Another notable feature of *The Teaching of Addai* is precisely the change of the apostle's name from Thaddaeus, as in Eusebius's Greek text and in the Syriac translation of this, to Addai. This is not a scribal slip, but a deliberate change, and it is tempting to see a link with the famous Manichaean missionary called Addai/Adda who was active in Parthian Mesopotamia, and who also preached in Roman Syria and Mesopotamia in the 260s as part of a long mission in the west (Lieu 1994: ch. II). Edessa was an early centre of Manichaeism, and according to the Cologne Mani Codex (64.7; Gnoli 2003: 74), some of Mani's (ca. 216–274) own writings were addressed to his followers there. The followers of Marcion (d. ca. 160) also flourished in Mesopotamia (Bundy 1988; Lieu 2015), as also small gnostic groups such as the Quqites (Drijvers 1967), and of course the followers of Bardaiṣan (154–222), a highly educated heterodox Christian philosopher at the court of Abgar VIII whose followers fragmented into rival groups, some with strongly gnostic tendencies (Drijvers 1966). When Ephrem moved from Nisibis to Edessa after 363, he was horrified to discover the strength of these rival religious movements in the city (Hymns against Heresies 22.5–6; Beck 1957), where his fellow Christians were ignominiously named Palutians, after the early bishop, rather than 'Christians', and so engaged in polemical writings against his rivals in both poetry (Beck 1957) and prose (Overbeck 1865; Mitchell 1912, 1921). Ephrem may well have played a key role in boosting the confidence and numbers of the orthodox, but only during the episcopacy of the ruthless Rabbula (411–436) were many of the heretical groups suppressed, although never completely (Blum 1969; Phenix and Horn 2017).

In his influential book on 'orthodoxy and heresy', Bauer thus chose Edessa as the first test case for his thesis that in many regions the earliest Christians were 'heretics' rather than those who would eventually become the Nicene 'orthodox', and that only later did the orthodox manage to write the heretics out of history (Bauer 1934). In such a scenario it is obvious why local Edessan Christians might want to appropriate the name of a famous Manichaean missionary, Addai, and then turn the tables on their opponents by projecting their own hero back into the apostolic era (Drijvers 1982b: 161), and so assert the primacy of their own brand of Christianity, with its claimed links both to Christ and to the orthodox churches in Antioch and Rome (Brock 1992a: 227–8). Whatever one thinks of some of Bauer's particular arguments, he is clearly correct in his assertion that many of the early converts to 'Christianity' in Mesopotamia would not have been considered Christians by the later Nicene orthodox, and that from the late fourth and early fifth centuries there must have been many new Nicene Christians who had previously been 'heretics' or came from 'heretical' families. But his assertion (Bauer 1934: 26) that the 'orthodox' group only arrived in the region after the Marcionites and others cannot be affirmed without the discovery of new archaeological evidence, and the focus on heretical groups also tends to draw our attention away from the fact that the great majority of Mesopotamian converts to Christianity must previously have been of Graeco-Roman or Zoroastrian religious belief, with a leavening of converts from Judaism, at least some of whom must have had formal religious education, given the transmission of Jewish exegetical traditions to Syriac Christian writers (Brock 1979; cf. Segal 1964).

But perhaps the most important motivation for the production of the legend of king Abgar's correspondence with Christ and his conversion at the hands of Addai is so obvious that it is rarely commented upon, namely the legend's central claim that the source and centre of all Christianity in Mesopotamia is Edessa. This is a claim that has been internalised by all Syriac scholarship, so that even when the historicity of the Abgar legend is rejected, the central role of Edessa in the early spread of Christianity is rarely questioned, and Syriac texts of no known provenance are routinely assigned to Edessa. But this claimed role needs to be challenged and put in context.

Although the earliest dated Christian Syriac manuscript, containing translations of Greek texts, was produced in Edessa in AD 411 (see Figs 14.2, 14.3; Brock 2013), no major early Syriac writer came from Edessa, with the possible exception of Philip, the disciple of Bardaiṣan (himself brought up in Hierapolis), who wrote the *Book of the Laws of the Countries* (third century). Aphrahaṭ 'the Persian sage' (fl. 337–345) lived and worked in Iranian Mesopotamia; Ephrem (ca. 306–373) was born in the region of Nisibis and lived there until 363; the ascetic *Book of Steps* (late fourth century) was produced in Iranian Mesopotamia; Balai (early fifth century) came from the Aleppo region; Narsai (ca. 399–ca. 502) was born and brought up in Iranian Mesopotamia; Jacob of Sarug was born in Kurtam on the Euphrates; Philoxenus (d. 523) was born in Tahel in Iranian Mesopotamia. Literary genius, like sanctity, does not necessarily arise in centres of missionary activity or learning, but the lack of early Edessan authors and texts is striking.

The earliest inscription to refer to Christianity in Mesopotamia is the famous Greek funerary epitaph of Abercius (d. ca. 167), the bishop of Hierapolis in Phrygia, which was incorporated into his *Life* (Wischmeyer 1980; Thonemann 2012). After referring to a visit to Rome, he says: 'I saw, too, the plain of Syria and all its cities, even Nisibis, beyond the Euphrates. I found brothers everywhere' (Thonemann 2012). The reference to Christian brethren in Mesopotamia at such an early date is invaluable, but unquantifiable. Is Nisibis mentioned as the furthest east of his travels, as seems likely, or as a notable Christian centre? Given that the inscription mentions only Rome, Nisibis, and Hierapolis, the failure to mention Edessa is not significant. However, it is noteworthy that the earliest Christian inscription found in Mesopotamia, dated 359, also comes from Nisibis, from the still-standing baptistery of St James or Jacob (Sarre and Herzfeld 1920: 337–8; Canali de Rossi 2004: 39). This Greek inscription records that the baptistery was erected in the time of bishop Vologases, the successor of saint James of Nisibis, and so it would have been seen by Ephrem. Further Greek inscriptions were found during recent archaeological work on the baptistery, but have not yet been published (Keser-Kayaalp and Erdoğan 2013: 148). The earliest church we know of in Nisibis, the cathedral, was built between 313 and 320 (Brooks 1910: annus 624; Fiey 1977: 23), at the same time as that in Edessa (see above).

Further evidence of Nisibis's early role as a Christian centre is to be found in the Syriac martyrology of 411 (Nau 1912). This has a section devoted to the western martyrs listed calendrically, mostly from Nicomedia, Antioch, and Alexandria, which appears to have been translated from Greek. Also included are a handful of martyrs from Mesopotamia. Shmona, Gurya, and Habib from Edessa have already been mentioned, but there are as many saints from Nisibis: the famous bishop Jacob of Nisibis (d. 338), perhaps the most celebrated saint of Roman Mesopotamia (15 July; Peeters 1920); the martyr Hermes and his military companions (Friday after Easter), who are also mentioned in the Acts of Shmona and Gurya (Devos 1972); Adelphius and Gaius (30 July); and another individual or group whose name has been lost (23 May). Other martyrs associated with Nisibis, such as Febronia, have early cults, but their acts preserve no reliable data (Simon 1924; Halkin 1958).

In Edessa all the early Syriac inscriptions produced up to AD 259, numbering about 110, plus three documents on parchment, are pagan (Drijvers and Healey 1999). The earliest discovered Christian inscriptions from Edessa are funerary inscriptions of the late fourth or fifth century and, like the inscriptions in Nisibis, are also written in

Greek (Sachau 1882; Canali de Rossi 2004: 21; the third-century baptismal inscription published by Ramelli 2003 actually comes from Edessa in Macedonia). A series of interesting Greek Christian inscriptions dating from the late fourth to the sixth centuries were found in Tella/Constantina, to the east of Edessa (Canali de Rossi 2004: 23–6). The earliest Syriac Christian inscriptions, from 389 to the late fifth century, all come from North Syria, west of the Euphrates, whereas the earliest Syriac inscription in Edessa is dated 493 (Sachau 1882; Brock 2009 provides a chronological listing of all early Syriac inscriptions and manuscripts). Some Christian funerary mosaics with Syriac texts recently found in Edessa will be an important addition to this body of evidence, but they remain unpublished as yet (Arkeofili 2016). The relative lack of early Christian inscriptions from North Mesopotamia is notable, reflecting the fact that only in recent decades have archaeologists begun to undertake thorough investigation of regional late antique sites. Nevertheless, the fact that Christian inscriptions are far from confined to Edessa is striking, as also that the earliest Christian inscriptions from Edessa are in Greek.

Egeria's visit to Edessa in 384 has already been mentioned (Wilkinson 1981), but on her way there from Antioch she also stopped in Baṭnan (Sarug), where there was a godly monk-bishop, a church, and several martyria (§19). She also visited Carrhae (Ḥarran), which is interesting for two reasons. Despite having no Christian population (§20), it did have a monk-bishop who showed her the local sacral landscape, which was clearly well developed, including a church on the site of Abraham's house and a spring identified as Rebecca's well (Gen 24:15). She was told that Nahor's and Bethuel's tombs were a mile away, but Ur of the Chaldees was ten staging-posts away, in Iranian territory. She was then taken to Jacob's well (Gen 29.2), six miles from Carrhae (§21), where there was a large church. In nearby Fadana she was shown the tomb of Laban the Syrian. In addition to this Christian sacral landscape, Egeria also mentions the many ascetics living in cells whom she met at Jacob's well, and says that at Abraham's house in Carrhae there was a martyr shrine for a monk named Helpidius. She happened to be there for his feast day, 23 April, when all the ascetics came in from the surrounding desert. As Egeria makes clear, these ascetics were not living in monasteries, a practice introduced locally from the end of the fourth century (Vööbus 1960), but were living in caves and cells. These are the 'sons and daughters of the covenant' addressed by Aphrahaṭ in his 6th Demonstration, written in 337 (Vööbus 1958: 173; Brock 1973), and they were clearly spread throughout the region, not just in major cities. Ammianus Marcellinus (XVIII.10.4; Rolfe 1935) mentions a group of female ascetics who were captured (and well-treated) by Shapur II in 359 when he took two Roman fortresses in the region of Amida.

Edessa clearly played an important role in the spread of Christianity in Roman Mesopotamia, but the fragments of available evidence suggest that it was part of a larger movement, and not the source of that movement.

Iranian Mesopotamia

Just as we lack a detailed picture of the early development of Christianity in the eastern provinces of the Roman Empire, so too is it lacking in Iranian Mesopotamia (i.e. modern Iraq) and beyond. In 363, Nisibis and its region was ceded to Iran/Persia, but by this time Christianity had already spread widely, as will be seen. By the early fifth century it is clear that there was a strong church hierarchy in the Iranian empire, with at least six metropolitan sees and more than thirty bishoprics, as recorded by the signatures of the bishops who attended the first general synod of the empire in 410, and from the list of church provinces said to be subject to the catholicos of Seleucia-Ctesiphon in the acts of the synod of 420 (Chabot 1902: 274, 617, 276; Wiessner 1967a). Within two centuries these expanded to ten metropolitan sees and ninety-six bishoprics. An even earlier list of sees in Iranian Mesopotamia has often been cited from the *Chronicle of Arbela*, which has exercised great influence on the historiography of Christianity in Iran, but although this work is no longer considered to be a modern forgery (Jullien and Jullien 2001), it is still a totally unreliable historical source for the early centuries of Christianity (Peeters 1925).

Synod of 410 (sees of signatories)	*Synod of 420 (regions/provinces)*	*Mar Mari's legendary itinerary*
Seleucia and Ctesiphon	Bet Lapaṭ	Edessa
Kaškar	Nisibis	Nisibis
	Persia	Arzanene
Bet Huzaye province:	Armenia	(disciple sent to Qardu)
Bet Lapaṭ	Prat d-Maišan	Bet Zabdai
Karka d-Ledan	Adiabene	Bet ʿArabaye
Hormizd-Ardashir	Bet Garmai	Arbela/Assyria and Nineveh
Šušterin	Gurzan	Bet Garmai
Šuš	Bet Madaye	Šahrgard
	Aran	Darabad
Bet ʿArabaye province:	Abrašahr	Ḥarbatgelal
Nisibis	Adorbigan	'territory of the Persians'
Arzon	The Islands	Bet Aramaye
Arzon d-Bet Aoustan	Istaḥr	Radan
Qardu	Karka	Kaškar (§30)
Bet Zabdai	Arzon	Seleucia-Ctesiphon
Bet Rahimai	Šuš	Dura d-Qunni
Bet Moksaye	Šušter	Kokhe
	Belašpar	Maišan
Maišan province:	Dasqarta	Bet Huzaye
Prat d-Maišan	Zabe	Bet Parsaye
Karka d-Maišan	Peruz-Šapur	
Rima	Dargerd	
Nehargur	Bet Daraye	
	Šapur-Kuast	
Adiabene province:	Ardašir-Parihd	
Arbela	Bet Šapur	
Bet Nuhadra	Ṣaimarat	
Bet Bagaš		
Bet Dasen		
Ramonin		

Synod of 410 (sees of signatories)
Bet Mahqart
Dabarinos/Rabarinḥesn
Bet Garmai province:
Karka d-Bet Selok
Šahrgard
Lašom
Arewan
Radani
Ḥarbatgelal
'Distant sees' (not present):
Fars
The Islands (Qatar/Gulf)
Bet Madaye (Media)
Bet Raziqaye (S. of Caspian)
Abrašahr (Khorasan)

How did such a widespread church develop? We have seen that 'Parthians, Medes, and Elamites' were among those who were said to have witnessed Pentecost in Jerusalem (Acts 2:8), and that *The Teaching of Addai* claims that priests were ordained for the 'country of the Assyrians'. Another legendary source, the *Acts of Mar Mari*, builds upon *The Teaching of Addai* by claiming that one of Addai's disciples, Mari, was sent 'to the land of Babylonia' to preach the Gospel. The text in its present form was compiled by a monk in the monastery of Mar Qunni, 90 km south of Baghdad, between the sixth and early seventh centuries (Harrak 2005: xvii; Jullien and Jullien 2003: 111). Like the *Teaching of Addai*, it is not a reliable source for the earliest expansion of Christianity, but it does throw some light on its own period. Notably, the catholicos had controversially been based in Seleucia-Ctesiphon rather than in North Mesopotamia since around 300, and yet the *Acts* say that at first Mari found not one person to follow him in Seleucia, because all the people were evil drunken pagans (§19), and the people of Maishan were little better; and whereas the Synod of 410 established (or reaffirmed?) a strict hierarchy of church provinces, with Bet Huzaye in the south-east preceding Nisibis in the north-west, and then Maishan in the south preceding Adiabene and Bet Garmai in the north, the *Acts of Mar Mari* have the apostle working his way south through Mesopotamia (see Table above), which creates a hierarchy of conversion starting with Nisibis and its province, then Adiabene and Bet Garmai. In a sixth-century church that was intellectually dominated by Nisibis and its monasteries, while its leadership resided in Seleucia-Ctesiphon and the cities of Iran, this looks highly political.

So we need to turn to other sources for snapshots of the development of early Christianity in the Iranian empire. The *Book of the Laws of the Countries* (early third century), written by Philip, a pupil of Bardaiṣan (Drijvers 1965), refers in passing to Christian 'brothers and sisters' in Hatra, Parthia, Gilan, and Kushan (south of the Caspian), Fars (Persia), and Media. These Christians were presumably first converted by missionaries moving along the trade routes from Roman Mesopotamia. In 256 and 260 Shapur I, after his raids into Roman Syria, deported large numbers of people from Antioch and other cities and resettled them in various regions of his own empire, away from the frontiers, including the provinces of Fars and Bet Huzaye, and in the latter they rebuilt Bet Lapaṭ (Gundishapur), the capital (Morony 2004). These deportees included Christians (presumably a small proportion of the total), among whom was Demetrianus the bishop of Antioch (Peeters 1924), and they organised church communities which were independent of the Syriac-using communities deriving from Mesopotamia, and were sometimes in conflict with them (Jullien 2006). Shapur II (r. 309–379) also invaded Roman territory on several occasions and took captives back to Iran, where he founded Karka d-Ledan for them. So the seniority of Bet Huzaye in the hierarchy of the Synod of 410 starts to make sense, as also the hostility of the churches of Nisibis and North Mesopotamia.

No pre-Islamic Christian inscriptions have yet been found in Iranian territories (Harrak 2010). But in the late third century a senior Zoroastrian priest named Kartīr or Kirdīr (Skjærvø 2011) had an account of his career under seven kings carved as an inscription in three locations, laying emphasis on his reformation of Zoroastrianism and his persecution of foreign religions, including the conversion of their holy places ('the residence of demons') into Zoroastrian shrines (MacKenzie 1989: 58; Gignoux 1991: 69). Amongst the groups that he saw as foreign threats he mentions Jews, Shamans, Bramans, Manichaeans, and Makdags (baptists?), but also 'Christians' (*klstyd'n*) and 'Naṣraye' (*n'čl'y*). There has been much debate about the precise meaning of these two terms, but an emerging consensus seems to be that the former term designates the Christian deportees from Roman territories and the latter Christian converts among the native population of the Iranian empire (Jullien and Jullien 2002a, 2002b: 183).

Further periods of persecution arose during the reigns of Shapur II, especially after 340, Yazdgard I (ca. 420), Vahram V (ca. 421–422), and Yazdgard II (ca. 446–448; Brock 1982). In a limited number of cases, their acts and passions were given literary form (listed chronologically in Brock 2008), but a far longer list of names was preserved in the martyrology of 411 (Nau 1912; Brock and Van Rompay 2014: 389–92). Noble converts from Zoroastrianism were always vulnerable to prosecution and punishment, but at times of royal weakness and a corresponding growth in the influence of Zoroastrian priests, or in times of war with Rome, ordinary Christians became vulnerable and could be put to death in large numbers. A recent study argues that punishment of Christians was a tool of political strategy or an assertion of hierarchical dominance, rather than a consequence of blind religious hatred, and that as such it signalled the integration of Christians into imperial politics (Payne 2015). Such a nuanced historical view is needed now but may not have been obvious to contemporary Iranian Christians. The sources for the persecution under Shapur II still need a thorough geographical analysis, but among the martyrs listed are bishops, clergy, and lay people from each of the provinces recorded in 410 (excluding Nisibis, which still belonged to the Romans), with strong concentrations from Bet Huzaye and Bet Garmai (Wiessner 1967b). This is important, but rather neglected, evidence for the early spread of Christianity in the Iranian empire.

The available sources for the early spread of Christianity in Mesopotamia, on both sides of the frontier, are frustratingly limited, and many attractive accounts are quite without historical value. The Gospel was not spread through the region by apostles, nor by kings and nobles, but by countless anonymous Christians – lay people, deacons, priests, and ascetics – some by choice and some as captives of a foreign power. They were active not just in the religious centres of Edessa and Nisibis, nor only at royal courts as in Seleucia-Ctesiphon, but in countless small villages, towns, and cities, from Dura on the Euphrates to Khorasan in the east of Iran. It is a less memorable story than that of the *Teaching of Addai* or the *Acts of Mar Mari*, but no less remarkable, and more true.

BIBLIOGRAPHY

Adams, E. 2016. *The Earliest Christian Meeting Places: Almost Exclusively Houses?* 2nd ed. Library of New Testament Studies 450. London: Bloomsbury.

Anschütz, H. 1984. *Die syrischen Christen vom Tur 'Abdin. Eine altchristliche Bevölkerungsgruppe zwischen Beharrung, Stagnation und Auflösung.* Das Östliche Christentum 34. Würzburg: Augustinus-Verlag.

Arkeofili (website), anonymous, 30 October 2016. *Şanlıurfa'da Abgar Krallığı Dönemine Ait Taban Mozaiği Bulundu.* http://arkeofili.com/sanliurfada-abgar-kralligi-donemine-ait-taban-mozaigi-bulundu [New mosaics found in Urfa/Edessa.]

Bauer, W. 1934. *Rechtgläubigkeit und Ketzerei im ältesten Christentum.* Beiträge zur historischen Theologie 10. Tübingen: J. C. B. Mohr (Paul Siebeck). [ET: Bauer, W. 1971. *Orthodoxy and Heresy in Earliest Christianity.* Translated by Kraft, R. A. and Krodel, G. Philadelphia, PA: Fortress Press.]

Beck, E. 1957. *Des heiligen Ephraem des Syrers Hymnen contra Haereses.* CSCO 169–170. Louvain: L. Durbecq.

———. 1961. *Des heiligen Ephraem des Syrers Carmina Nisibena, I.* CSCO 218–219. Louvain: Secrétariat du CorpusSCO.

———. 1963. *Des heiligen Ephraem des Syrers Carmina Nisibena, II.* CSCO 240–241. Louvain: Secrétariat du CorpusSCO.

Blum, G. G. 1969. *Rabbula von Edessa. Der Christ, der Bischof, der Theologie.* CSCO 300. Louvain: Secrétariat du CorpusSCO.

Briquel-Chatonnet, F., F. Jullien, C. Jullien, C. Moulin Paliard, and M. Rashed. 2000. Lettre du patriarche Timothée à Maranzekhā, évêque de Nineve. *Journal asiatique* 288, 1–13.

Brock, S. P. 1973. Early Syrian Asceticism. *Numen* 20, 1–19.

———. 1979. Jewish Traditions in Syriac Sources. *JJS* 30, 212–32.

———. 1982. Christians in the Sasanian Empire: A Case of Divided Loyalties. *In*: S. Mews, ed., *Religious and National Identity.* Studies in Church History 18. Oxford: Basil Blackwell, 1–19.

———. 1992a. Eusebius and Syriac Christianity. *In*: H. W. Attridge and G. Hata, ed., *Eusebius, Christianity, and Judaism.* Studia Post-Biblica 42. Leiden: Brill, 212–34.

———. 1992b. Two Syriac Poems on the Invention of the Cross. *In*: N. el-Khoury, H. Crouzel, and R. Reinhardt, ed., *Lebendige Überlieferung: Prozesse der Annäherung und Auslegung. Festschrift für Hermann-Josef Vogt zum 60. Geburtstag.* Beirut/Ostfildern: Rückert, 55–82.

———. 2008. *The History of the Holy Mar Ma'in, With a Guide to the Persian Martyr Acts.* Persian Martyr Acts in Syriac: Text and Translation 1. Piscataway, NJ: Gorgias Press.

———. 2009. Edessene Syriac Inscriptions in Late Antique Syria. *In*: H. M. Cotton, R. G. Hoyland, J. J. Price, and D. J. Wasserstein, ed., *From Hellenism to Islam: Cultural and Linguistic Change in the Roman Near East.* Cambridge: Cambridge University Press, 289–302. [Includes an appendix with a chronological listing of Syriac inscriptions and manuscripts from the first to the mid-seventh century.]

———. 2013. Manuscripts Copied in Edessa. *In*: P. Bruns and H. O. Luthe, ed., *Orientalia Christiana: Festschrift für Hubert Kaufhold zum 70. Geburtstag*. Wiesbaden: Harrassowitz, 109–28.

Brock, S. P. and L. van Rompay. 2014. *Catalogue of the Syriac Manuscripts and Fragments in the Library of Deir al-Surian, Wadi al-Natrun (Egypt)*. OLA 227. Leuven: Peeters. [Fragment 27 has four additional fragments of the martyrology of BL Add. 12150 of AD 411, including the names of lay men and women.]

Brooks, E. W. (ed.). 1910. *Eliae metropolitae Nisibeni opus chronologicum I*. CSCO 62*–63*. Paris: E Typographeo Reipublicae; Rome: de Luigi.

Bruck, G. 1955. Die Verwendung christlicher Symbole auf Münzen von Constantin I. bis Magnentius. *Numismatische Zeitschrift* 76, 26–32.

Bundy, D. 1988. Marcion and the Marcionites in early Syriac apologetics. *LM* 101, 21–32.

Burkitt, F. C. 1904. *Early Eastern Christianity: St. Margaret's Lectures 1904 on the Syriac-Speaking Church*. London: John Murray.

———. 1913. *Euphemia and the Goth With the Acts of Martyrdom of the Confessors of Edessa*. London: Williams and Norgate.

Cameron, A. 1983. The History of the Image of Edessa: The Telling of a Story. *Harvard Ukrainian Studies* 7, 80–94.

Camplani, A. 2009. Traditions of Christian Foundation in Edessa: Between Myth and History. *Studi e materiali di storia delle religioni* 75, 251–78.

Canali De Rossi, F. 2004. *Iscrizioni dello estremo oriente greco: un repertorio*. Inschriften griechischer Städte aus Kleinasien 65. Bonn: Dr. Rudolf Habelt.

Chabot, J. B. 1902. *Synodicon orientale ou recueil de synodes nestoriens*. Paris: Imprimerie Nationale.

———. 1927. *Incerti auctoris Chronicon Pseudo-Dionysianum vulgo dictum* I. CSCO 91. Paris: E Typographeo Reipublicae. [Chronicle of Zuqnin, Syriac text.]

Christof, E. 2001. *Das Glück der Stadt: Die Tyche von Antiochia und andere Stadttychen*. Frankfurt am Main: Peter Lang.

Cureton, W. 1864. *Ancient Syriac Documents relative to the Earliest Establishment of Christianity in Edessa*. London: Williams and Norgate. (Martyr acts of Sharbil and Barsamya: 41–72).

Devos, P. 1967. Égérie à Édesse. S. Thomas l'apôtre. Le roi Abgar. *Analecta Bollandiana* 85, 381–400.

———. 1972. La liste martyrologique des Actes de Guriā et Shamōnā. *Analecta Bollandiana* 90, 15–26.

Devreesse, R. 1945. *Le Patriarcat d'Antioche depuis la paix de l'Eglise jusqu'à la conquête arabe*. Paris: Gabalda.

Downey, G. 1961. *A History of Antioch in Syria from Seleucus to the Arab Conquest*. Princeton, NJ: Princeton University Press.

Drijvers, H. J. W. 1965. *The Book of the Laws of Countries: Dialogue on Fate of Bardaisan of Edessa*. Semitic Texts with Translations 3. Assen: Van Gorcum.

———. 1966. *Bardaiṣan of Edessa*. Studia Semitica Neerlandica 6. Assen: Van Gorcum.

———. 1967. Quq and the Quqites: An Unknown Sect in Edessa in the Second Century A.D. *Numen* 14, 104–29.

———. 1980. *Cults and Beliefs at Edessa*. Études préliminaires aux religions orientales dans l'Empire Romain 82. Leiden: Brill.

———. 1981. Ein neuentdecktes edessenisches Grabmosaik. *Antike Welt* 12, 17–20.

———. 1982a. A Tomb for the Life of a King: A Recently Discovered Edessene Mosaic With a Portrait of King Abgar the Great. *LM* 95, 167–89.

———. 1982b. Facts and Problems in Early Syriac-Speaking Christianity. *The Second Century* 2, 157–75.

———. 1996. Early Syriac Christianity: Some Recent Publications. *VChr* 50, 159–77.
Drijvers, H. J. W., and J. F. Healey. 1999. *The Old Syriac Inscriptions of Edessa and Osrhoene: Texts, Translations, and Commentary*. Handbuch der Orientalistik. Erste Abteilung, Nahe und der Mittlere Osten 42. Leiden: Brill.
Drijvers, J. W. 1992. *Helena Augusta: The Mother of Constantine the Great and the Legend of her Finding of the True Cross*. Brill's Studies in Intellectual History 27. Leiden: Brill.
Festugière, A. J. 1959. *Antioche païenne et chrétienne. Libanius, Chrysostome et les moines de Syrie*. Bibliothèque des Écoles françaises d'Athènes et de Rome 194. Paris: Boccard.
Fiey, J.-M. 1977. *Nisibe, métropole syriaque orientale et ses suffragants des origines à nos jours*. CSCO 388. Louvain: Secrétariat du CorpusSCO.
Gebhardt, O. von, and E. von Dobschütz. 1911. *Die Akten der edessenischen Bekenner Gurjas, Samonas und Abibos*. Texte und Untersuchungen zur Geschichte der altchristlichen Literatur 37.2. Leipzig: J.C. Hinrichs.
Gelzer, H., H. Hilgenfeld, and O. Cuntz. 1898. *Patrum nicaenorum nomina latine, graece, coptice, syriace, arabice, armeniace*. Leipzig: B.G. Teubner.
Gignoux, P. 1991. *Les quatre inscriptions du Mage Kirdīr. Textes et concordances*. Collection des sources pour l'histoire de l'Asie centrale pré-islamique II.1. Studia Iranica 9. Paris: Association pour l'avancement des études iraniennes.
Gnoli, G. (ed.). 2003. *Il Manicheismo*. Volume 1. *Mani e il Manicheismo*. Milan: Fondazione Lorenzo Valla/A. Mondadori.
Griffith, S. 2003. The Doctrina Addai as a paradigm of Christian thought in Edessa in the fifth century. *Hugoye* 6, 2.
Guidi, I. 1903. *Chronica Minora*. CSCO 1. Paris: E Typographeo Reipublicae.
Halkin, F. 1958. La Passion grecque des saintes Libyè, Eutropie et Léonis martyres à Nisibe. *Analecta Bollandiana* 76, 293–315.
Hallier, L. 1892. *Untersuchungen über die edessenische Chronik mit dem syrischen Text und einer Übersetzung*. Texte und Untersuchungen zur Geschichte der altchristlichen Literatur 9.1. Leipzig: J. C. Hinrichs.
Harnack, A. 1908. *The Mission and Expansion of Christianity in the First Three Centuries*. tr. J. Moffatt. 2 vols. London: Williams and Norgate.
Harrak, A. 2005. *The Acts of Mār Mārī the Apostle*. SBL Writings From the Greco-Roman World 11. Atlanta, GA: Society of Biblical Literature.
———. 2010. *Syriac and Garshuni Inscriptions of Iraq*. Recueil des inscriptions syriaques 2. Paris: De Boccard.
———. 2017. *The Chronicle of Zuqnīn. Parts I and II: From the Creation to the Year 506/7 AD*. Gorgias Chronicles of Late Antiquity 2. Piscataway, NJ: Gorgias Press.
Hill, G. F. 1922. *Catalogue of the Greek Coins of Arabia, Mesopotamia, and Persia*. Catalogue of the Greek Coins in the British Museum 28; London: Longmans & Co.
Howard, G. 1981. *The Teaching of Addai*. SBL Texts and Translations 16. Chico, CA: Scholars Press.
Illert, M. 2007. *Doctrina Addai. De imagine Edessena/Die Abgarlegende. Das Christusbild von Edessa*. Fontes Christiani 45. Turnhout: Brepols.
Jullien, C., and F. Jullien. 2001. La Chronique d'Arbèles: propositions pour la fin d'une controverse. *OC* 85, 41–83.
———. 2002a. Aux frontières de l'iranité: "nāṣrāyē" et "krīstyonē" des inscriptions du *mobad* Kirdīr: enquête littéraire et historique. *Numen* 49, 282–335.
———. 2002b. *Apôtres des confins. Processus missionnaires chrétiens dans l'empire iranien*. Res Orientales 15. Bures-sur-Yvette/Leuven: Peeters.
———. 2003. *Aux origines de l'église de Perse: les Actes de Mār Māri*. CSCO 604; Leuven: Peeters.
Jullien, C. 2006. La minorité chrétienne "grecque" en terre d'Iran à l'époque sassanide. *In*: R. Gyselen, ed., *Chrétiens en terre d'Iran: Implantation et acculturation*. Cahiers de Studia

Iranica 33, Chrétiens en terre d'Iran 1. Paris: Association pour l'avancement des études iraniennes, 105–42.

Kaufhold, H. 1993. Griechisch-syrische Väterlisten der frühen griechischen Synoden. *OC* 77, 1–96.

Keser-Kayaalp, E., and N. Erdoğan. 2013. The cathedral complex at Nisibis. *Anatolian Studies* 63, 137–54.

Kitzinger, E. 1954. The Cult of Images in the Age before Iconoclasm. *DOP* 8, 83–150.

Kraeling, C. H. 1967. *The Christian Building*. The Excavations at Dura-Europos. Final Report 8.2. New Haven, CT: Dura-Europos Publications.

Lieu, J. M. 2015. *Marcion and the Making of a Heretic: God and Scripture in the Second Century*. Cambridge: Cambridge University Press.

Lieu, S. N. C. 1994. *Manichaeism in Mesopotamia and the Roman East*. Religions in the Graeco-Roman World 118. Leiden: Brill.

Lipsius, R. A. 1880. *Die edessenische Abgar-Sage kritisch untersucht*. Braunschweig: C.A. Schwetschke.

MacKenzie, D. N. 1989. Kerdir's inscription. *In*: G. Hermann, ed., *The Sasanian Rock Reliefs at Naqsh-i Rustam. Naqsh-i Rustam 6*. Iranische Denkmäler. Lief. 13. Reihe II: Iranische Felsreliefs I. Berlin: Dietrich Reimer, 35–72.

Marciak, M. 2014. *Izates, Helena, and Monobazos of Adiabene: A Study on Literary Traditions and History*. Philippika 66. Wiesbaden: Harrassowitz Verlag.

Mayer, W., and P. Allen. 2012. *The Churches of Syrian Antioch (300–638 CE)*. Late Antique History and Religion 5. Leuven: Peeters Press.

Millar, F. G. B. 1993. *The Roman Near East 31 BC–AD 337*. Cambridge, MA: Harvard University Press.

Mirkovic, A. 2004. *Prelude to Constantine: The Abgar Tradition in Early Christianity*. Arbeiten zur Religion und Geschichte des Urchristentums 15. Frankfurt am Main: Peter Lang.

Mitchell, C. W. 1912, 1921. *S. Ephraim's Prose Refutations of Mani, Marcion, and Bardaisan*. 2 vols. London: Williams and Norgate.

Monneret de Villard, U. 1952. *Le leggende orientali sui magi evangelici*. Studi e Testi 163. Vatican City: Biblioteca Apostolica Orientalia.

Morony, M. G. 2004. Population Transfers Between Sasanian Iran and the Byzantine Empire. *In*: *La Persia e Bisanzio. Atti del Convegno internazionale (Roma, 14–18 ottobre 2002)*. Atti dei Convegni Lincei 201. Rome: Accademia Nazionale dei Lincei, 161–79.

Nau, F. 1912. *Un martyrologe et douze ménologes syriaques*. PO 10.1. Paris: Firmin-Didot. (Martyrology of 411: 5–26).

Olbrycht, M. J. 1997. Parthian King's Tiara: Numismatic Evidence and Some Aspects of Arsacid Political Ideology. *Notae Numismaticae* 2, 27–61.

Oppenheim, M. von, and F. Hiller von Gaertingen. 1914. Höhleninschriften aus Edessa mit dem Briefe Jesu an Abgar. *Sitzungsberichte der Königlich preussischen Akademie der Wissenschaften zu Berlin, philosophisch-historische Klasse* 32, 817–28.

Overbeck, J. J. 1865. *S. Ephraemi Syri, Rabulae episcopi Edesseni, Balaei aliorumque Opera selecta e codicibus syriacis manuscriptis in museo Britannico et bibliotheca Bodleiana asservatis primus edidit*. Oxford: Clarendon Press. [Prose refutation, *Ad Hypatius* I: 21–58].

Payne, R. E. 2015. *A State of Mixture: Christians, Zoroastrians, and Iranian Political Culture in Late Antiquity*. Transformation of the Classical Heritage 56. Oakland, CA: University of California Press.

Peeters, P. 1920. La légende de saint Jacques de Nisibe. *Analecta Bollandiana* 38, 285–373.

———. 1924. S. Démétrianus évêque d'Antioche? *Analecta Bollandiana* 42, 288–314.

———. 1925. Le "passionnaire d'Adiabène". *Analecta Bollandiana* 43, 261–304.

Phenix, R. R., and C. B. Horn. 2017. *The Rabbula Corpus: Comprising the Life of Rabbula, His Correspondence, a Homily Delivered in Constantinople, Canons, and Hymns*. Writings from the Greco-Roman World 17. Atlanta, GA: SBL Press.

Prieur, M., and K. Prieur. 2000. *A Type Corpus of the Syro-Phoenician Tetradrachms and their Fractions from 57 BC to AD 253*. Lancaster, PA: Classical Numismatic Group.

Rahmani, I. E. 1920. *I fasti della chiesa patriarcale antiochena*. Rome: Accademia dei Lincei.

Ramelli, I. L. 2003. Un'iscrizione cristiana edessena del III sec. d.C.: contestualizzazione storica e tematiche. *'Ilu: revista de ciencias de las religiones* 8, 119–26 [From Edessa in Macedonia, not Edessa in Mesopotamia, as claimed in error].

Rolfe, J. C. 1935–1940. *Ammianus Marcellinus*. 3 vols. Loeb Classical Library 300, 315, 331. London: Heinemann.

Ruggieri, V. 1993. The IV Century Greek Episcopal Lists in the "Mardin Syriac. 7" (olim Mardin Orth. 309/9). *OCP* 59, 315–56.

Sachau, E. 1882. Edessenische Inschriften. *ZDMG* 36, 142–67.

Sarre, F., and E. Herzfeld. 1911–1920. *Archäologische reise im Euphrat- und Tigris-Gebiet*. Forschungen zur islamischen Kunst 1. 2 vols. Berlin: Dietrich Reimer.

Segal, J. B. 1964. The Jews of North Mesopotamia Before the Rise of Islam. *In*: J. M. Grintz and J. Liver, ed., *Studies in the Bible Presented to Professor M.H. Segal*. Publications of the Israel Society for Biblical Research 17. Jerusalem: Kiryat Sepher, 32*–63*.

Sellwood, D. 1980. *An Introduction to the Coinage of Parthia*, 2nd ed. London: Spink.

Simon, J. 1924. Note sur l'original de la Passion de Sainte Fébronie. *Analecta Bollandiana* 42, 69–76.

Skjærvø, P. O. 2011. Kartīr. *In*: E. Yarshater, ed., *Encyclopædia Iranica* XV.6. New York, NY: Encyclopædia Iranica Foundation, 608–28.

Thonemann, P. 2012. Abercius of Hierapolis: Christianization and Social Memory in Late Antique Asia Minor. *In*: B. Dignas and R. R. R. Smith, ed., *Historical and Religious Memory in the Ancient World*. Oxford: Oxford University Press.

Trombley, F. R. 1985. Paganism in the Greek World at the End of Antiquity: The Case of Rural Anatolia and Greece. *The Harvard Theological Review* 78, 327–52.

———. 1993. *Hellenic Religion and Christianization c.370–529*. Religion in the Graeco-Roman World 115. 2 vols. Leiden: Brill.

Vööbus, A. 1958. *History of Asceticism in the Syrian Orient: A Contribution to the History of Culture in the Near East*. I. *The Origin of Asceticism. Early Monasticism in Persia*. CSCO 184. Louvain: Secrétariat du CorpusSCO.

———. 1960. *History of Asceticism in the Syrian Orient: A Contribution to the History of Culture in the Near East*. II. *Early Monasticism in Mesopotamia and Syria*. CSCO 197. Louvain: Secrétariat du CorpusSCO.

Wiessner, G. 1967a. Zu den Subskriptionslisten der ältesten christlichen Synoden in Iran. *In*: G. Wiessner, ed., *Festschrift für Wilhelm Eilers. Ein Dokument der internationalen Forschung zum 27. September 1966*. Wiesbaden: Otto Harrassowitz, 288–98.

———. 1967b. *Zur Märtyrerüberlieferung aus der Christenverfolgung Schapurs II*. Abhandlungen der Akademie der Wissenschaften in Göttingen, Philologisch-historische Klasse III.67. Göttingen: Vandenhoeck & Ruprecht.

Wilkinson, J. 1981. *Egeria's Travels to the Holy Land*, 2nd ed. Jerusalem: Ariel.

Wischmeyer, W. 1980. Die Aberkiosinschrift als Grabepigramm. *Jahrbuch für Antike und Christentum* 23, 22–47.

CHAPTER FIVE

FORMS OF THE RELIGIOUS LIFE AND SYRIAC MONASTICISM

Florence Jullien

In the Syriac milieu, the practical ways that developed for living out the religious life came in several forms (thematic bibliography in Jullien 2010: 305–32). There are few traditions that can claim such a variety of forms. Some, such as stylitism, have become famous for their spectacular and exaggerated outward appearance and through its exemplary characters. Monastic stories, canonical regulations, historiography, or hagiographies all reflect this situation. If we attempt to form a typology, we may identify four major strands: the pre-monastic *q^eyama* movement that was specific to the Syriac community; the various forms of solitary life (anchoritism); semi-anchoritism; and cœnobitism. It should however be noted that these last two models, in every nuance in which they were expressed, developed synchronically rather than according to any strictly chronological evolution.

Over the last twenty years, interest in the history of monasticism has been on the increase, thanks especially to archaeological discoveries in the Arabo-Persian gulf region (Steve 2003; Calvet 1998; Salles 2011) and in Iraq (Déroche 2013). Up until this time, following the work of Paul Bedjan, Ernest A. W. Budge, Jean-Baptiste Chabot, and Alphonse Mingana, researchers had focused above all on editing texts. When studies as such were carried out, they tended to deal with the very earliest period of the monastic movement and the origins of asceticism, such as Arthur Vööbus's magisterial *History of Asceticism in the Syrian Orient*, published in three volumes (1958, 1960a, 1988). However, it ought to be noted that these studies almost always concerned themselves with certain specific regions of northern Mesopotamia (especially the areas around Nisibis and Mosul) and with certain individuals renowned for their holiness. Vööbus's approach is instructive because it takes into account the types of asceticism that characterise earliest Christianity in its context, making especial use of data from unedited manuscripts. But it must be admitted that within this approach the institutional dimension of monasticism does predominate, while little attention is directed towards the margins, towards inter-religious controversies, and towards daily life within the monasteries. His method further depends upon exclusive categorisations. Following the work of Antoine Guillaumont (1978, 1979), and also of Peter Brown on the figure of the holy man, more recent studies have placed an emphasis upon the importance of contextualisation, often of a comparativist type, and also upon the anthropological dimensions of monasticism, the economic conditions of its development, the place of monks within wider social life, and their investment in the theological debates and in the diffusion of knowledge (e.g. Villagomez 1998; Escolan 1999; Becker 2006; Jullien 2008a; Wood 2013).

TRADITIONS OF ORIGINS

The Syriac tradition itself attributes the first monastic foundations to two ascetic figures. The first is Mar Mari, who was considered to have been one of Christ's seventy disciples and was said to have built 365 churches and convents during his missionary journeys throughout the Partho-Sasanian Empire (Jullien and Jullien 2003). Thus, the institution of monasticism was projected back into the apostolic age. The second figure is Mar Awgin (Eugenius), who in fourth-century Syria and Mesopotamia was reckoned to have been the initiator of the monastic life. He gathered followers and imitators who in turn constructed monasteries across these territories. However, it must be stressed that the sources for the 'Eugenian cycle' are late (his biography has been transmitted to us in a hagiographic account dating to the very end of the ninth century, Bedjan 1892: 376–480) and imbued with historiographic reconstructions borrowed from the lives of other ascetics, in particular Abraham of Kashkar, founder of a wide-ranging reform of the monastic life and therefore known as 'the Father of the Eastern monks' (Chialà 2005; Jullien 2008a, 2008b).

The question of the initial institution of monasticism in the Syriac world and of its relationship with Egypt has long been raised on account of the direct connection, established by monastic historiographers, with the Mesopotamian anchoritic current that had developed in the deserts bordering the Nile valley: the pilgrimage to the sources of monasticism in Thebaid functioned as a rite of passage, a formative and character-building experience, and became a recurring theme in Syriac hagiographical literature. Beyond the anachronisms and the traditional constructions, we must question the mythographic aspects of this 'trip to Egypt' and the various topoi that are attached to it, in view of the fact that forms of the monastic life appeared contemporaneously in Syria, Mesopotamia, and Egypt (Jullien 2009).

THE PRE-MONASTIC *Q^{E}YAMA* MOVEMENT

The writings of Ephrem the Syrian give evidence for the existence of secular ascetics, distinct from monks, who lived a form of life which has been called 'pre-monastic' (Beck 1958; Vööbus 1959): the *b^{e}nay* and *b^{e}nat q^{e}yama*, 'sons and daughters of the Covenant', or 'members of the Order'. The Syriac term *q^{e}yama* evokes the idea of a close-knit group or fraternity;[1] etymologically it actually refers to 'a standing position' (which is the position, par excellence, for prayer), but also to the resurrection. Belonging to the *b^{e}nay q^{e}yama* does not imply at all the notion of a withdrawal to the desert (in the mountains or in caves) as would become the case a few years later within the monastic current properly so-called, especially under the influence of the ascetic literature of the Fathers of Egypt which spread across the Syriac world from the fourth century. Rather, these lay people were committed to a life of celibacy and were attached to a parish in which they ensured the continuity of the liturgy and in particular the recitation of the offices; but their main tasks consisted firstly in the instruction of the faithful, a training that was conducted under the close supervision of the hierarchical authority (Pierre 2010; Macina 1999), and secondly in providing assistance to the poor and sick and visiting prisoners. Their service was thus exercised right in the midst of the church community.

The Persian sage Aphrahaṭ, from northern Mesopotamia, was one of the first to describe the special status of the *b^e^nay* and *b^e^nat q^e^yama* in his *Demonstrations* dated to 337. The author distinguishes them from others whom he calls 'sons of our faith', i.e. the regular faithful.[2] They used to gather in small communities around the church they served. Aphrahaṭ mentions that in his day there were mixed groups of consecrated lay men and women, although his own preference was to have them separated into two communities (Pierre 1988: 385–6, 375). A century later in his canons, Rabbula bishop of Edessa prohibited *b^e^nay q^e^yama* from living with women, allowing visits only by close relatives (Vööbus 1960b: 36). The final commitment was marked by vows of voluntary renunciation, in particular of chastity. Asceticism and privation (especially fasting) remained a daily feature of their life: Rabbula recommends that members ought not to eat meat or drink wine, excepting the sick and infirm. Subsequently, these brothers were allowed to eat with the monks whenever they were staying in a monastery (Vööbus 1960b: 138, canon 3). Their conduct should always remain an example for the Christian community. It is possible to relate the *b^e^nay q^e^yama* to the institution, known in the Byzantine context, of clerics known as *kanonikos*: both groups consisted of minor staff in the Church, lay people committed to the service of the brothers (Macina 1999).

This movement was particularly well established in Babylonia and in areas to the east of the Tigris: the martyr narratives relate the lives of certain women who shared a common life and played the role of assistants to the deacons.[3] The system lasted until the end of the Sasanian era, since there are traces of it in Syriac texts of the sixth century such as the *Life of Catholicos Mar Abba* (Jullien 2015: 5–9; Fiey 1965b: 281–306).

IḤIDAYUTHA AND THE FORMS OF THE SOLITARY LIFE

In his *Treatise on the Solitude of the Weeks*, the ascetic author Dadishoʿ Qaṭraya (d. about 690) provides a catalogue of the various forms of religious life practised in his day, as well as those from the past. Besides the *b^e^nay q^e^yama*, he mentions monks (*dayraya*) and solitaries (*iḥidaya*), among whom he distinguishes, in order: beginners (*sharwaye*), who live in monasteries and are subject to the community life; solitaries of the cells (*iḥidaya qelaya*), who keep silence for one week; those who keep silence for seven weeks and who fast strictly for several periods of the year; and the lonely who live in the desert 'separated from all community'. He adds to these the gyrovagues or itinerants (*metkarkane*), who have no attachment to any monastery, and solitary anchorites (*nukrayata*, from the Greek *anachôrêtês*), whose conduct is qualified as 'superior, laboured and perfect' (Mingana 1934: 102, trans. 78; Fauchon 2010; Brock 1999–2000: 93–4). Each wears a tonsure according to his status, the smallest being carried by members of the Order (*q^e^yama*), the largest by the solitaries. For Dadishoʿ, what distinguished the monks from the solitaries was above all their lifestyle and their environment: the first had chosen the communal life, often worked outside the monasteries, and practiced hospitality, 'serving with zeal all who come by, men and women of every condition'; the second was more specifically isolated from the civilian world. Among Syriac authors, there were several terms for describing monks, well summarised by C. Fauchon (2010: 47–9). The most common is *qaddisha*, 'holy man/woman', which originally also signified 'continent', and *aḥa*, 'brother'; we also find *ʿamila*, for those who practised ascetic exercises; *makkika*, that is the 'humble ones', meaning those who carried out prostrations; the mourners, *abila*; and the people of the desert, *madbraya*. The Syriac term *iḥidaya* refers to the anchorite and to the solitary (etymologically *ḥad* – *monos* in Greek – refers to the concept of uniqueness). In our sources, the *iḥidaya* was first of all unified in his being and in his heart as was the Christ, and then by extension he is the one who lives alone, isolated, who has made the choice of celibacy. For Syriac authors until the fourth century, this ideal of detachment and purity of heart by means of asceticism is offered to every Christian. Such a choice for asceticism within a secular environment brings about behavioural transformations. Syriac hagiographic narratives often depict particularly committed Christians as prototypical figures, sometimes converted from paganism or Zoroastrianism (in the Sasanian Empire): after their baptism, they decide to adopt a new lifestyle, often a very harsh one, answering to the requirements of their zeal. Mar Abba, the future catholicos of the Eastern Church in the sixth century, while still yet a neophyte, was especially noted for his repeated vigils and fasts. At Karka d-Beth Slokh (modern Kirkuk), east of the Tigris, *Shirin* lived a form of religious life in her own home, imposing upon herself a regime that she regulated without the knowledge of her Zoroastrian parents, but also without specific commitment or special relationship with the local clergy. This emphasises above all the significance of individual initiative in this area. The earliest liturgical and canonical texts of Syrian Christianity reflect the importance of encratite influence (from the Greek *enkratês*, 'continent') in fervent Christian circles. This common early Christian tradition was connected with Tatian, a disciple of Justin (Eusebius, *Ecclesiastical History* 4, 28–9; Epiphanius of Salamis, *Panarion* 46), and was condemned repeatedly in the Byzantine Empire (in 382 and 428) due to its opposition to marriage. Throughout the Syriac regions, celibacy was from a very early stage regarded as a prerequisite for access to baptism (Brock 1973: 7–8). Several former hagiographic narratives depict the breaking off of conjugal relations when a new convert adopts a life of austerity. The *Acts of Thomas*, written in Osrhoene early in the third century, bears the mark of this: the apostle foils the wedding (§4–16) and breaks marriages (§82–170). Such encratite tendencies, together with Judeo-Christian baptist sects and Manichean communities, readily testify how these ideas spread and penetrated deep into the regions outside of Syria, especially Mesopotamia and Persia (Cirillo 1986: 133–7).

It was only later, thanks to the development of monasticism, that the term *iḥidaya* ended up being primarily associated with solitaries leading the life of a hermit or semi-anchorite (*yḥydyʾ*) and became equivalent to the Greek word *monachos*, 'monk' (Guillaumont 1969a: 35; Brock 1985: 114–5; AbouZayd 1993: 269–72; 318–9). Solitaries stand out as 'many different ladders for ascending to heaven', to use the words of the fifth-century ecclesiastical historian Theodoret of Cyrus, who mentions several such people within the Syro-Mesopotamian region: those who live in tents, huts, or caves or who just expose their bodies to the open air; those recluses (*ḥbysh'*) who refuse any contact with the people, and those who reveal themselves to the gaze of all (*Historia Philotheos* 27, 1, Canivet and Leroy-Molinghen 1979: 216–9). The great diversity of ascetic practices adopted by the solitaries testifies to the wealth of Syriac anchoritism. It is not here a question of monasticism properly so-called, but of particular forms of the religious life.

Voluntary confinement and its extreme manifestations

The most extreme of these ways of life was no doubt voluntary confinement, which could take on various different aspects. The lifestyle could be realised either inside a monastery or in close relation to one, in a nearby tower for example, and the remains of these buildings are still numerous in the mountains north of Nisibis. In the fourth century, Abraham of Qidoun lived as a recluse of this type in a small room in Edessa in Osrhoene; he had under his charge his niece Mary, an orphan he had welcomed and who lived in an adjoining room. He introduced her to the monastic life through the little window that separated their living quarters (Brock and Ashbrook Harvey 1987: 29; Jullien 2010: 83 n.105). Huts without any light are often mentioned in the sources; in this period, for example, there was Eusebius of Tell ʿAda (Teleda for Greek writers), who never went out, spoke to no one, but still managed by his influence to export his way of life throughout a whole network of people (*Historia Philotheos* 4, 3–4, Canivet and Leroy-Molinghen 1977: 294–7). 'Stationaries', who chose to remain in a standing position for years, also participated in this sort of reclusive lifestyle. Besides those who retreated into tombs (*Historia Philotheos* 9, 3; 12, 2, Canivet and Leroy-Molinghen 1977: 410–3; 462–3), we find cases of people walling themselves in but open to the sky, for example Eusebius of Asikha (in the north of the region of Cyrus) who lived in the centre of a small open-air enclosure (*hypaithros*), the door of which he sealed with a stone (18, 1–2, Canivet and Leroy-Molinghen 1979: 52–5). Among these forms of confinement, special mention should be made of the stylites, both men and women, and of dendrites (solitaries who chose to isolate themselves in the branches of a tree or the cavity of a hollow trunk), two aspects of a single form of life lived between heaven and earth and which developed specifically in northern Syria. The tree is seen as a symbol, that of the cross of Christ considered as the tree of life; this explains the well-developed literary motif of the peaceful martyrdom of these hermits who were attached to trees, as a form of bloodless crucifixion (Charalampidis 1997: 141; Smith 2009). The Syrian Orthodox Church historian John of Ephesus mentions the example of a hermit named Maron who lived eleven years in the trunk of a tree at the end of the fourth century (*Lives of the Eastern Saints*, Brooks 1923: 56–9).[4] The stylite's column, which could sometimes be occupied for periods of time by the brothers of the same monastery in turn, was primarily a place of isolation, and the ascetic practices of stylitism remained those of the recluse (Callot and Gatier 2004 574; on female stylites, Delehaye 1908; Vööbus 1960a: 273–5). The best known of them was undoubtedly Simeon the Elder, who gradually increased the drums of his column until reaching a height of 18 m, the better to escape the public. This spectacular form of life, which specifically developed in the Antiochene, paradoxically became representative of all solitary lifestyles, and the term 'stylite' came to designate, from the eighth century, any kind of hermit or recluse in Syria and Mesopotamia (Callot and Gatier 2004: 586). Exposed to outward view as the very model of monastic heroism, this kind of recluse could induce pilgrimages, as did Simeon the Younger in the sixth century: the construction of a large monastery around his column, and buildings to accommodate pilgrims on the Wondrous Mountain in the hinterland of Antioch, was accomplished within his lifetime.

Monastic wanderings

The continuous movements of wandering solitaries, known as gyrovagues and mendicants (*mtkrkn'*), may be considered in itself as a form of asceticism (Guillaumont 1969a, 1979). Among them, those that Greek texts call *boskoi* (shepherds) and that were found throughout the area from Egypt to Syria-Mesopotamia (Špidlik et al. 1999: 248), were characterised by their preference for the outdoor life and for their willingness to consume only plants and wild fruits in their natural state, so that they might commune with creation as if it was the garden of Eden. In the fourth century Ja'qub, before he became bishop of Nisibis, had adopted this form of rough life (Theodoret, *Historia religiosa*, 1, 2). On several occasions, Ephrem speaks highly of its merits. These mendicants practised *xeniteia* (being a stranger in the world), a complete detachment favoured by their continual wanderings, a sort of mental reclusion (Fauchon 2012). This lifestyle of wandering was nonetheless often condemned by church authorities because of its excesses. The control exercised by the authorities upon these practises may be explained on account of the strong influence that Messalianism exerted upon Syriac monasticism, whose initial current came from northern Syria and which was widely spread around Antioch and Upper Mesopotamia in the second half of the fourth century, according to the testimony of Ephrem and Epiphanius of Salamis. Condemned by imperial law in 428, and again in 431, and expelled from the Roman Empire, the Messalians reached the Sasanian Empire. Right up until the seventh century, the great success of this movement was a significant challenge for East Syrian monasticism. Those who called themselves *pneumatikoi* (spiritual ones) roamed towns and villages preaching and proclaiming contempt for the hierarchy and the sacraments (Caner 2002; Escolan 1999: 91–124; Guillaumont 1980). Renouncing all possessions, they lived by begging and devoted all their time, as they claimed, to prayer (whence the nickname that was given to them – the root *ṣly* meaning 'to pray') to the detriment of any work. The East Syrian synods challenged their spiritual mysticism and accused their followers of impersonating monks (they are 'clothed in a counterfeit habit of ascetics and members of religious orders') and of wandering with women, the cause of numerous scandals. For monks, to follow a mendicant life was forbidden without the authorisation of the local bishop (Chabot 1902: 301–3; 374–5). The decline of Messalianism within the Persian Empire may certainly be explained by the dynamism of the reformed monastic movement (Fiey 1977: 270–1; Jullien 2008a: 18–21). Several brothers came to establish themselves as anchorites in areas where these Messalian communities had previously been strongly established, especially in the Sinjar region south of Nisibis, with the aim of eradicating that movement. The model of a life perceived as heroic could also promote the influence of the holy man on local populations.

GROUPS OF ASCETICS

The anchorites often won followings and initiated disciples. This is not yet a matter of communities, strictly speaking, but of groups of ascetics sharing the same form of life. One of the great ascetic authors of sixth-century Persia, Abraham of Nethpar, spent his whole life in seclusion in a cave, welcoming disciples who came to him and who dug small cells (*qly'*, from the Greek *kellia*) around his cave (Scher and Griveau 1919: 174). Several of the places chosen by these cave-hermits (*speleots*) bear in the sources the name of *M'arre*, that is to say 'the caves'. A woman of the name of Shoshan, a Persian aristocrat from the region of Arzanene, attracted to her cave a crowd of lay men and women and monks to seek advice (John of Ephesus, *Lives of the Eastern Saints*, Brooks 1924: 554–5).

These sets of anchorites, gathered around a guide, could follow an eremitic lifestyle and sometimes be involved in evangelisation; these small monastic-like structures are attested very early in the Sasanian Empire, from the fourth century. The biography of Miles, later Bishop of Susa, reported that he divided his time between life in the desert and periods of preaching to the pagan or Zoroastrian populations, sometimes in the company of other monks who left their 'desert' to join up with him and assist (Bedjan 1891: 269–72). The precise location of this small community base is unknown, as also is the precise form of life that was followed there. Hagiographic literature mentions also the name of Barshibia, established in Fars, near whom ten brothers came to settle (around 342) and who were subsequently persecuted because of the success of their preaching (Bedjan 1891: 281–4). This evolution of the eremitic form of life from one lived in strict solitude towards one in which hermits lived in groups is something rather classic in Syria, Mesopotamia, Babylonia, and Persia. Nevertheless, there was no specific Syriac word for denoting this type of collegial eremitic life. It was similar to the model of lavras but without there being any enclosure.

THE SEMI-CŒNOBITIC MODEL

In Palestine, the lavriotic structure (*lwr'* from the Greek *laura*) is attested at the end of the fourth century and marks a stage in the organisation of a more communal way of life arranged around a small church building at the centre of a brotherhood surrounded by an enclosure. Cyril of Scythopolis was the first to use this terminology to describe this way of functioning, particularly for the lavra St Saba founded in the fifth century in the desert of Judea (Festugière 1962). There is no parallel specifically attested in Mesopotamia and Persia, except for what is hinted at in the *History of Karka d-Beth Slokh*: the author mentions some small constructions built in the countryside around Ḥaṣa in the fifth century by a group of anchorites who joined together for the dominical office (Bedjan 1891: 514; Vööbus 1958: 222–3).

The reform of Abraham of Kashkar: the rise of a semi-cœnobitic model

From the sixth century, semi-cœnobitism became common in the East Syrian church thanks to the reform carried out by Abraham of Kashkar (d. 588) who gave 'a new form to the monasteries and the cells'. His work brought about a profound renewal of monasticism east of the Euphrates, at the time when the monastic movement had been reduced to secondary practices since the end of the fifth century following a period of relaxation. Moreover, it was deeply challenged by the rise of the Syrian Orthodox movement which was spreading extensively throughout Persia following the persecutions of Justinian (Scher and Dib 1910: 172; Chialà 2005; Jullien 2008a). Abraham settled on Mount Izla in Ṭur ʿAbdin (the 'mountain of the servants' in allusion to the hundreds of monks there) and lived the eremitic life in caves, before founding the Great Monastery with those disciples who came to join him. The establishment was made up of several architectural units built around a central sanctuary, then further surrounded by communal buildings (infirmary, *xenodocheion*, libraries, refectory, etc.). It was only in the final period of his life, around 571, that Abraham agreed, at the request of his bishop, metropolitan Simeon of Nisibis, to draft a rule for governing their life. Abraham instituted a tonsure which was differentiated from that of the miaphysite monks; the choice of a specific habit was thus also an external sign of Christological identity.

This way of life nonetheless privileged an ideal of complete solitude within the community, as was expressed, for example, by catholicos Mar Sabrishoʿ in 598, himself a former monk: he refers to 'those who, being gathered together in a convent, no longer live on their own and separately in cells'. Sabrishoʿ describes everyday life in these mixed structures centred on the celebration of the Synaxis, as in the desert of Egypt, in Kellia or Scete:

> those who [are] in the convent . . . will complete the holy mysteries each day. . . . On Sundays and other holy days, we shall all gather together as one in the convent and fulfil the divine office and the reading of the holy scriptures . . ., we shall then return to our cells and our monasteries.
>
> (Chabot 1902: 464)

It is notable that during the Synaxis brothers were gathered from several monasteries, which therefore belonged to a single monastic network.

According to the reformed model, the monk is a hesychast (Syr. *shelya*, a term that signifies 'solitude, immobility, repose, silence' and which goes back to the Greek concept of *hesychia*, 'quiet'); he stays in his cell, sometimes within, but more often away from a monastery, either in a tiny shack or a dug-out cave (Vööbus 1960b: 161; Jullien 2008a: 130, 71, 102, 272). During the same period, Cosmas Indicopleustes underlines the diffusion of the hesychast ideal in the Persian Empire: 'Among the Bactrians, Huns, Persians, among other Indians, Persarmenians, Medes and Elamites . . . there are countless churches, bishops, numerous Christian populations, many martyrs, and hesychast monks' (*Christian Topography* III, §65, Wolska-Conus 1968: 504–5). Many monastic texts of the seventh and eighth centuries had a considerable influence on the development of hesychasm; especially noteworthy was Isaac of Nineveh, but also John of Dalyatha, who translated the *Paradise of the Western Monks* (probably Palladius's *Lausiac History*), and Simeon d'Ṭaybuteh and his *Exposition of the Mysteries of the Cell* (Duval 1907; Brock 1998; Brock 1999–2000; Chialà 2014, 2010). In his *Book of the Founders*, a kind of catalogue of the principal figures of East Syrian monasticism from the fourth to the seventh centuries, Ishoʿdenaḥ also mentions Babai the scribe who wrote books for anchorites and hermits, and Joseph Ḥazzaya who composed a collection of biographies of the eastern ascetics, now lost. Dadishoʿ

Qaṭraya, who lived in one of the reformed monasteries in Susiana, at Rabban-Shabuhr, underlines the importance of hesychasm in both his *Letter to Abkosh* and his *On Solitude*, wherein he reported one of the religious and ascetic practices that was in use: the confinement to one's cell for between one to seven consecutive weeks, a period referred to as a 'retreat of weeks' (Guillaumont and Albert 1984). During that time, the brothers were exempted from attending church on Sundays with the rest of the community, instead participating in the Synaxis in a purely spiritual manner. The originality of the way of life constituted at Izla is less evident with respect to what was practiced in Palestine or Syria, where the Egyptian semi-anchorite models were well known (Jullien 2009: 155–6), than against the background of the monastic regimes found within the Sasanian Empire.

The stages of the religious life

The steps taken by the young aspirant to the monastic life are known from canonical regulations and are generally the same as for a strictly cœnobitic context. The length of the apprenticeship and training varied according to different rules and locations; in general, it was fixed at three years. For the East Syrian monasteries, the *Life of Rabban Bar 'Edta* (first half of the seventh century) tells us that during this probationary period, the postulant lived 'like a cœnobite' (*qnwby'*) according to the custom concerned (Budge 1902: 172, 21; Vööbus 1960b: 191–204; Jullien 2008a: 149–51, 2006b). He also participated in the tasks of the community, in the preparation of meals, in serving seniors and guests, alongside those who were performing common services in turn on a weekly basis. In the West Syrian monasteries of Ṭur 'Abdin, the period of apprenticeship appears to have been more rigorous, according to John of Ephesus. About one of the great monasteries of Amida, he says that the postulant attained the novitiate by a series of very strict stages. After abandoning all his property, he stayed at the door of the monastery for thirty days before being allowed inside the enclosure. He was then assigned to minor daily tasks for a period of three months, and received a special mark as a sign of his renunciation of the world (an allusion to the tonsure?). At the end of this year, in which he was required to prove his aptitude for the ascetic life, he was clothed with a straw tunic tied with a rope and a hood. But it was only after three years that he was able to take the monastic habit itself (John of Ephesus, *Lives of the Eastern Saints*, Brooks 1923: 280–2). After this preparatory period of time, if he had performed well in accordance with the demands of the rule, the young monk was permitted to build a cell and was thereby definitively admitted to the monastery. The older monks could assist him in building his new habitation (Vööbus 1960b; Jullien 2008a: 157–76).

From master to disciples

Inside the monastery, some of the monks were considered as masters of the religious life, gathering around themselves those of their followers whom they were training during their probationary period. In this matter, the notice concerning Mar Yonan in the *Book of the Founders* informs us that as a young man he attached himself to an older monk named Sebokht and became one of his spiritual children (Chabot 1896: 27, §49). Sebokht himself had followed the teachings of Babai of Nisibis at the Great

Monastery, possibly as one among his group of followers (Chabot 1896: 17, §29). Such decentralisation of authority is probably an expression of the growing number of monks but did not in any way detract from the powers of the abbot and his council.

Scattered suggestions in the evidence indicate that some brothers from affluent social categories were allowed to keep a servant. Isho'denaḥ of Baṣra and the East Syrian *History of Seert* relate similar situations: thus Mar Gani entered the Great Monastery with a slave whom he had freed and who did not hesitate to follow him into a new foundation in Central Babylonia (Chabot 1896: 16, §28). Such a situation would necessarily have led to inequalities among the brethren. If we follow the narratives given us by certain church historians such as Theodoret, even a solitary could have staff: the Bishop of Cyrus mentions in this connection two female hermits around Beroea, each living in an roofless enclosure, who had arranged a small adjoining building for their maids; an opening in a wall allowed the hermits to train their servants in prayer and to receive food from them in turn (Canivet and Leroy-Molinghen 1977, I: 232–3).

The increasing strength of cœnobitism

Gradually, the rule that was revised by Abraham of Kashkar's successors manifested increasingly cœnobitic tendencies. It is no coincidence that around the middle of the seventh century, when this process had become very strong, the author of the *Life of Rabban Bar 'Edta* presents Abraham as the legitimate successor of Pachomius (Budge 1902: 182; Jullien 2008a: 107–13), a rather uncommon claim and one that allows us to see clearly that there had been some internal alteration in outlook. The monastic remains found on Kharg Island, off Bushir in the Persian Gulf, have been associated with this reform movement; they testify to a decidedly cœnobitic architectural plan that overlay semi-anchoritic forms that have also been found in the immediate environment of the monastery (seventh–ninth centuries): although it is difficult to detect outer cells on account of the lightweight materials used in their construction, the excavators have unearthed isolated dwellings with an enclosure and a garden. Within the precincts of the monastery, over sixty cells have been identified, as well as the communal buildings which make Kharg the largest monastic complex found in this region to date (Steve 2003; Jullien 2006a; Salles 2011; for discussion see also Carter 2008).

LIFE IN THE *CŒNOBIUM* AND ITS MANIFESTATIONS

In the *Book of the Founders*, two words are used to denote a monastery: *dayra*, which refers to a monastic structure in the wider sense, and *'umra*, used for the semi-cœnobitic type of monastery. In the Byzantine sphere, cœnobia are attested very early by Greek chroniclers and church historians, but also in the rules of the convents of Osrhoene and North Mesopotamia; those attributed to certain bishops such as Rabbula (d. 435) or Maruṭa of Maipherqaṭ (d. early fifth century) show that the environment of the monastic life consisted in a large network of dwellings with the church located in the centre; meals were eaten together. The brothers were not allowed to sleep in beds with the exception of the superior and the sick (canon 19). The Pseudo-canons of Maruṭa furnish a description of the tasks of the higher authorities, especially the *rishdayra* (the superior), and the *rabbaita* (a kind of sub-prior, or bursar appointed to deal with external affairs) (Vööbus 1960a: 154–8, 1960b: 130–1; Hendriks 1960). Cœnobia can be identified in Persian territory from the fourth century: the Persian Martyrs Acts describe how Badma built a small monastic establishment close to the town of Beth-Lapaṭ in Susiana for his seven disciples. His biographer relates interesting elements of his daily life: abstinence, weekly fasting, the raising of hands towards the sky at night in prayer, and wakefulness (Bedjan 1891: 347–51). It is certainly to this stage of development that we should also attribute the small fraternities established within sanctuaries and *martyria*. This type of establishment is attested in Mosul, for example, around the relics of Mar Behnam and his sister Sara (Bedjan 1891: 433). It eventually gave rise to genuine monasteries such as the one at Karka on the site of the martyrs executed under king Yazdgird II (Bedjan 1891: 530–1).

In general, Syriac historiographical and hagiographical sources attest to the deep integration of religious communities not only in the rural economy, but also in urban and suburban contexts, regardless of the particular form of life adopted. In his *Lives of the Eastern Saints*, John of Ephesus depicts important monastic dwellings located either within towns or close by such as at Amida where a convent was erected under the ramparts which counted fifty monks at the time of death of its founder, Mar Yoḥannan Urtaya (Brooks 1926: 207–9). The canonical legislative documentation that relates to the monastic reform movement of the sixth and seventh centuries reflects the importance of outlying buildings and land attached to monasteries, in some cases consisting of very large areas. Working in the fields was one of the activities imposed upon the monks (Budge 1902: 177–8; Vööbus 1960b: 161; Scher and Griveau 1919: 470). Foundations were often established near major routes and at crossroads in the vicinity of towns, and a monastery's economy was dependent upon its relations with these centres of population (Wipszycka 1994; Villagomez 1998).

Networks and international monasteries

In some cases, the mother-monastery and its affiliated offshoots shared a single controlling authority, such as at Tell ʿAda in the Antiochene, which was at the centre of a collection of convents managed by an overall superior; upon the monastery of Qarṭmin, founded at the opening of the fifth century in Ṭur ʿAbdin (Palmer 1990), there were several dependent monastic centres forming a vast and complex network. In his *Life of Theodosius*, Theodore of Petra 'the Cœnobiarch' mentioned, around 530, a community in Palestine organised into four divisions: the Greek brothers, the Bessi (a Romanised Balkan tribe), Armenians, and 'penitents' (Festugière 1963). Greek and Syriac were both used as liturgical languages and the responses could be alternated. This type of so-called 'international monastery', either bilingual or trilingual, is well attested in Mesopotamia, Syria, Palestine, and Persia (Hendriks 1958). In his *History of the Monks of Syria*, Theodoret describes one such founded by a certain Publius near Zeugma, in which the two communities, Greek and Syriac, each had their own abbot, again subject to a common superior who governed the whole monastery (Canivet and Leroy-Molinghen 1977: 335). Ishoʿdenaḥ mentions a similar foundation of Persian and Syriac monks by John of Daylam in the seventh century, between Beth-Huzaye and Fars (Chabot 1896: 50, §116; Scher and Périer 1908: 222; Brock 1981–1982).

The cœnobium and the apostolic life: the convent-schools

Some cœnobia stood out in particular for their missionary endeavours. In central Babylonia in the fourth century, the monk Mar ʿAbda had instituted a form of religious life that combined a cœnobitic setting with a scholastic life and a missionary apostolate to the outside world. In his canons, ʿAbda emphasises the education of students, who were following the monastic rule together with the brothers. The monks brought together three types of activity, arranged in three stages: rest, common service (including education), and prayer. The community was subdivided into three groups, which were to take turns every seven hours for chanting the psalms in church. One of the characteristic features of the rule relates in particular to the missionary aspect of the community: ʿAbda carried out missions of evangelisation and was involved in controversies throughout the territory of Beth-Aramaye (Babylonia) (Scher and Dib 1910: 307–9). This double vocation of teaching and mission ensured that Christianity became thoroughly anchored in the region of the monastery, and its influence was to last long thanks to the further foundations of its disciples. The *History of Seert* points to the significance of this monastic movement of Dura d-Qonie not far from the capital city Seleucia-Ctesiphon, noting that before the sixth century reform, 'the monasteries were like those of Mar ʿAbda and his companions' (Scher and Dib 1910: 172). The inclusion of schools in the monasteries is not so common, and it was initially the parish church that played the role of educating children. When patriarch Ishoʿyahb I (582–95) tried to impose a 'student residence' within the monastery of Beth-ʿAbe, the majority of monks firmly opposed it (Budge 1893: 132). Conversely, however, the monks did sometimes participate in education in village schools: after his training at the Great Monastery, Abimelech taught in the school of the Beth-Sahde (that is, of the *Martyrion*), near Nisibis, before founding in his turn another school attached to the convent he had built (Chabot 1896: 23). He was even buried in the 'monastery of the school'. The internal organisation of convent-schools, especially those which were permitted to teach higher-level courses, was based on a monastic regime; the students were tonsured, bound to celibacy, wore the religious habit (*eskima*), lived in cells, and participated in the religious offices (Vööbus 1960b; Chabot 1896: 43–93; Becker 2008). At Nisibis, the famous 'School of the Persians' (whose articles, written by one of its first directors, Narsai, have been preserved) was a renowned centre where the leadership of the Church of Persia was educated; hence this form of the monastic life was especially influential on the identity of the Church of the East. The bishops were required to observe the fast, to abstain continually from meat and wine, and to bear the religious habit as a sign of humility. In order to promote better integration of Christians in Persian territory at a time of persecution – the Persians being quite opposed to celibacy – the priestly commitment to chastity (an ancient characteristic of the Syriac communities) was challenged in the Church of the East following the action of Barṣauma of Nisibis in 484 and of former Zoroastrians converted to Christianity who had become catholicoi (Gerö 1983). The reform of clerical discipline undertaken by Mar Abba in the sixth century was to revive the primitive ascetic tradition. This tradition deeply influenced the miaphysite Church, which was particularly connected with the monastic institutions: the penetration of this Christological movement into Mesopotamia and Persia owed much to the monk Jacob Baradaeus (d. 578; Bundy 1978). The structure and constitution of the Syrian Orthodox Church were primarily the work of monks, ordained in droves for missionary purposes. The convent of Mor Mattai to the east of Mosul played a key role in this process. Among the miaphysite cœnobitic centres, John of Ephesus mentions the regions of Zeugma, Qenneshrin, Ṭur ʿAbdin, Amida, where some 1,000 monks lived, and Adiabene (*Lives of the Eastern Saints*, Brooks 1926: 206–27).

Supervision and centralisation

Justinian imposed the institution of the monastic enclosure across the entire Byzantine world in his 133rd Novella, which was concerned solely with monks and which was formulated between 535 and 556. These fences sometimes evolved into fortifications against the danger of external attack, as shown by the site of Bazyan in Beth-Garmai (Déroche and Amin 2013) in the context of the insecurity of the Romano-Persian wars. It is likely that economic stakes favoured the centralisation of monastic establishments and productions in times of political instability (Wipszycka 1986). The cœnobitic model certainly came to be reinforced by these contingencies. The reclusive aspect of monastic life is strongly emphasised in the regulations: the monk is held to his unchanging station and must not leave the perimeter of the monastery without permission, which was proffered only subject to specific criteria (family concerns, ministerial office in village churches). The canons of Rabbula of Edessa, for example, forbad monks from entering the town. When he was required to travel, with the permission of his superior, the monk had always to stay in monasteries (Vööbus 1975: 153). The doorman played an important mediating role in the monastery (Fauchon forthcoming); Maruṭa placed great insistence on this function of both monitoring the brothers and welcoming passing travellers, strangers, the poor, and pilgrims, who were housed in the collection of buildings that formed the *xenodocheion* (individual cells, parlours, the refectory). The desire to control those people who were spreading Christological ideas perceived as dangerous after the Council of Chalcedon also explains the willingness of ecclesiastical authorities to supervise and regulate the monks more strictly.

The arrival of Islam did not at first slow down the rapid pace of the expansion of Syriac monasticism, but the movement would gradually undergo a retreat to the margins. In the eleventh century, the chronographer Elias of Nisibis lamented the inexorable disappearance of cœnobia and monasteries in Mesopotamia (Brooks 1910: 36) before the final blow was administered by the last Mongols and Timurids.

NOTES

1 It is in this sense that Ephrem applied the term to Greek philosophical schools (Beck 1958: 280–1).

2 The anonymous fourth-century work known by the title *Book of Steps* equally distinguishes the 'righteous' from the 'perfect', which latter term refers to those who had made a commitment to a way of life, the *b*[e]*nay q*[e]*yama*. Edition in Kmosko (1926), Vööbus (1958: 178–84, 190–7), Guillaumont (1976), Kitchen & Parmentier 2004.

3 The Life of Martha (Bedjan 1891: 233–41); of Tarbo: 254–60; of Thecla and her companions: 308–13; of Anahid († 447): 583–603.
4 Another example is Adolas, from Mesopotamia, of whom John Moschos in his *Spiritual Meadow* tells us that he lived in a large hollow plane tree; he had made a small window through the bark by which he communicated with the outside world (Rouët de Journel 1946: 111–2, §70).

BIBLIOGRAPHY

AbouZayd, S. 1993. *Ihidayutha: A Study of the Life of Singleness in the Syrian Orient. From Ignatius of Antioch to Chalcedon 451 A.D.* Oxford: Aram Society for Syro-Mesopotamian Studies.
Beck, E. 1958. Ascétisme et monachisme chez saint Ephrem. *L'Orient syrien* 3, n°3: 273–98.
Becker, A. H. 2006. *Fear of God and the Beginning of Wisdom: The School of Nisibis and the Development of Scholastic Culture in Late Antique Mesopotamia.* Divinations: Rereading Late Ancient Religion. Philadelphia: University of Pennsylvania Press.
———. 2008. *Sources for the Study of the School of Nisibis.* Translated Texts for Historians 50. Liverpool: Liverpool University Press.
Bedjan, P. 1891. *Acta Martyrum et Sanctorum syriace*, vol. II. Paris, Leipzig: Harrassowitz.
———. 1892. *Acta Martyrum et Sanctorum syriace*, vol. III. Paris, Leipzig: Harrassowitz.
———. 1894. *Acta Martyrum et Sanctorum syriace*, vol. IV. Paris, Leipzig: Harrassowitz.
Brock, S. P. 1973. Early Syrian Asceticism. *Numen* 20, n°1: 7–8. Reprinted in id., *Syriac Perspectives on Late Antiquity* (Ashgate, 1984), ch. I.
———. 1981–1982. A Syriac Life of John of Dailam. *Parole de l'Orient* 10: 123–89.
———. 1985. *The Luminous Eye: The Spiritual World Vision of Saint Ephrem.* Cistercian Studies. Rome: Cistercian Publications c/o Liturgical Press.
———. 1998. Le monachisme syriaque: histoire et spiritualité. *In*: *Le monachisme syriaque aux premiers siècles de l'Église IIe-début VIIe siècles*, vol. I, 21–31. Patrimoine syriaque. Antelias, Liban: CERO.
———. 1999–2000. Syriac writers from Beth Qatraye. *ARAM* 11–12: 85–96.
Brock, S. P. and S. Ashbrook Harvey. 1987. *Holy Women of the Syrian Orient.* The Transformation of the Classical Heritage 13. Berkeley: University of California Press.
Brooks, E.-W. 1910. *Eliae metropolitae Nisibeni Opus chronologicum*, vol. I. CSCO 63*, scriptores syri 23. Louvain: Peeters.
———. 1923–1926. *John of Ephesus: Lives of the Eastern Saints.* 3 Vols. Patrologia orientalis 17–19. Paris: Firmin-Didot.
Budge, E. A. W. 1893. *The Book of Governors: The Historia Monastica of Thomas Bishop of Marga A.D. 840*, vol. II. London: Kegan Paul, Trench, Trübner & Co.
———. 1902. *The Histories of Rabban Hôrmîzd the Persian and Rabban Bar-'Idtâ*, vol. II. London: Luzac and Co.
Bundy, D. 1978. Jacob Baradaeus. The State of Research, a Review of Sources and a New Approach. *Le Muséon* 91: 45–86.
Callot, O. and P.-L. Gatier. 2004. Les stylites de l'Antiochène. *In*: B. Cabouret et al., ed., *Antioche de Syrie: histoire, images et traces de la ville antique.* Topoi Supplément 5. Lyon: Maison de l'Orient méditerranéen, 573–96.
Calvet, Y. 1998. Monuments paléo-chrétiens à Koweit et dans la région du Golfe. *In*: R. Lavenant, ed., *VIIe Symposium syriacum, Uppsala University, Department of Asian and African Languages, 11–14 August 1996.* OCA 256. Rome: Pontificio Istituto Orientale, 671–85.
Caner, D. 2002. *Wandering, Begging Monks: Spiritual Authority and the Promotion of Monasticism in Late Antiquity.* The Transformation of the Classical Heritage 33. Berkeley: University of California Press.

Canivet, P. and A. Leroy-Molinghen (eds.). 1977–1979. *Théodoret de Cyr. Histoire des moines de Syrie*. 2 vols. Sources chrétiennes 234, 257. Paris: Le Cerf.

Carter, R. A. 2008. Christianity in the Gulf during the first centuries of Islam. *Arabian Archaeology and Epigraphy* 19:1, 71–108.

Chabot, J.-B. 1896. *Le livre de la chasteté composé par Jésusdenah, évêque de Baçrah*. Mélanges d'archéologie et d'histoire 16, n°1. Rome: École Française.

———. 1902. *Synodicon orientale*. Paris: Imprimerie nationale.

Charalampidis, K. 1997. Dendrites "Martyrs of Peace". *Studi sull'Oriente cristiano* 1, n°1–2: 135–44.

Chialà, S. 2004. *Simone di Taibuteh. Abitare la solitudine; Discorso per la consacrazione della cella*. Testi dei Padri della Chiesa 72. Monastero di Bose: Qiqajon.

_____. 2005. *Abramo di Kashkar e la sua comunità. La rinascita del monachesimo siro-orientale*. Bose: Edizioni Qiqajon.

_____. 2010. Simeone di Taibuteh e il suo insegnamento sulla vita nella cella. *In*: E. Vergani and S. Chialà, ed. *La grande stagione della mistica siro-orientale (VI-VIII secolo)*. Ecumenismo e dialogo. Milano: Centro Ambrosiano, 121–38.

Cirillo, L. (ed.). 1986. Elchasaiti e Battisti di Mani: i limiti di un confronto delle fonti. *In*: L. Cirillo, ed., *Codex Manichaicus Coloniensis. Atti del Simposio Internazionale (Rende-Amantea 3–7 sett. 1984)*. Studi e ricerche 4. Cosenza: Università degli Studi della Calabria, 97–139.

Delehaye, H. 1908. Les femmes stylites. *Analecta bollandiana*, 27: 391–3.

Déroche, V. and N. A. Amin. 2013. La fouille de Bazyan (Kurdistan irakien): un monastère nestorien? *In*: F. Briquel-Chatonnet, ed., *Les églises en monde syriaque*. Études syriaques 10. Paris: Geuthner, 363–80.

Duval, R. 1907. *La littérature syriaque*. Paris: Lecoffre.

Escolan, P. 1999. *Monachisme et Église. Le monachisme syrien du IVe au VIIe siècle: un monachisme charismatique*. Théologie historique 109. Paris: Beauchesne.

Fauchon, C. 2010. Les formes de vie ascétique et monastique en milieu syriaque, V^e^–VIIe siècles. *In*: F. Jullien, ed., *Le monachisme syriaque*. Études syriaques 7. Paris: Geuthner, 37–63.

———. 2012. *De la xénia païenne à l'aksénia monastique: définition, représentations et pratiques de l'hospitalité dans les communautés grecques et syriaques de grande Syrie (IVe–VIe siècles)*. Thèse de doctorat. Université de Lyon 3.

———. Forthcoming. Accueil et surveillance des moines voyageurs, errants ou réfugiés en Orient (V^e^-VIe siècles): la figure du moine portier dans les sources grecques et syriaques. *In*: O. Delouis et al., ed., *Les moines autour de la Méditerranée. Mobilités et contacts à l'échelle locale et régionale*. Mélanges de l'École Française de Rome. Rome: ÉFR.

Festugière, A.-J. 1962–1963. *Les moines d'Orient*, vol. III, n°2–3. Paris: Le Cerf.

Fiey, J. M. 1965a. *Assyrie chrétienne*, vol. I–II. Beyrouth: Imprimerie catholique.

———. 1965b. Cénobitisme féminin dans les Églises syriennes orientales et occidentales. *L'Orient syrien* 10, n°3: 281–306.

———. 1977. *Nisibe, métropole syriaque orientale et ses suffragants des origines à nos jours*. CSCO 388, Subsidia 54. Louvain: Peeters.

Gerö, S. 1983. Die Antiasketische Bewegung im Persischen Christentum – Einfluss zoroastrischer Ethik? *In*: R. Lavenant, ed., *III Symposium Syriacum, Goslar 7–11 September 1980: Les contacts du monde syriaque avec les autres cultures*. OCA 221. Rome: Pontificium Institutum Studiorum Orientalium, 187–91.

Guidi, I. 1903. Chronicon anonymum. *In*: idem, ed., *Chronica minora*, vol. I. CSCO 1–2, scriptores syri 1–2. Paris: Harrassowitz.

Guillaumont, A. 1969a. Le dépaysement comme forme d'ascèse dans le monachisme ancien. *Annuaire de l'École pratique des hautes études, Section des sciences religieuses* 76: 31–58.

———. 1969b. Le nom des Agapètes. *Vigiliae Christinae* 23: 30–7.

———. 1976. Liber Graduum. *In*: *Dictionnaire de Spiritualité* 9, 749–54. Paris: Beauchesne.

———. 1978. Esquisse d'une phénoménologie du monachisme. *Numen* 25: 40–51.
———. 1979. *Aux origines du monachisme chrétien: pour une phénoménologie du monachisme*. Spiritualité orientale 30. Abbaye de Bellefontaine.
———. 1980. Messaliens. *In*: *Dictionnaire de spiritualité* 10, 1074–83. Paris: Beauchesne.
Guillaumont, A. and A. Albert. 1984. Lettre de Dadisho Qatraya à Abkosh, sur l'hésychia. *In*: F. Lucchesi and H.D. Saffrey, ed., *Mémorial André-Jean Festugière. Antiquité païenne et chrétienne*. Cahiers d'Orientalisme 10. Genève: Cramer, 235–45.
Hendriks, O. 1958. Les premiers monastères internationaux syriens. *L'Orient Syrien* 3, n°2: 165–84.
———. 1960. La vie quotidienne du moine syrien. *L'Orient Syrien* 5: 293–330, 401–31.
Jullien, C. and F. Jullien. 2003. *Les Actes de Mār Māri*. CSCO 602, scriptores syri 234. Louvain: Peeters.
Jullien, F. 2006a. La réforme d'Abraham de Kaškar dans le golfe Persique: le monastère de l'île de Khārg. *Parole de l'Orient* 31: 201–11.
———. 2006b. Le monachisme chrétien dans l'empire iranien (IVe–XIVe siècles). *In*: R. Gyselen, ed., *Chrétiens en terre d'Iran*. Cahiers de Studia Iranica 29. Chrétiens en terre d'Iran I. Paris: AAEI, 143–84.
———. 2008a. *Le monachisme en Perse. La réforme d'Abraham le Grand, père des moines de l'Orient*. CSCO 622, Subsidia 121. Louvain: Peeters.
———. 2008b. Aux sources du monachisme oriental. Abraham de Kashkar et le développement de la légende de Mar Awgin. *Revue de l'Histoire des Religions* 225, n°1: 37–52.
———. 2009. Types et topiques de l'Égypte: sur quelques moines syro-orientaux des VIe-VIIe siècles. *In*: F. Jullien and M.-J. Pierre, ed., *Les Monachismes d'Orient. Images – Échanges – Influences*. Bibliothèque de l'École des Hautes Études. Sciences religieuses 148. Turnhout: Brepols, 151–63.
———. (ed.) 2010. *Le monachisme syriaque*. Études syriaques 7, Paris: Geuthner. [See especially Bibliographie thématique sur le monachisme syriaque on pp. 305–32].
———. 2015. *Histoire de Mār Abba, catholicos de l'Orient, Martyres de Mār Grigor, général en chef du roi Khusro Ier et de Mār Yazd-panāh, juge et gouverneur*. CSCO 658–9, scriptores syri 254–5. Louvain: Peeters.
Kitchen, R. A. and M. F. G. Parmentier. 2004. *The Book of Steps: The Syriac Liber Graduum*. Translated with an Introduction and Notes. Cistercian Studies Series 196. Kalamazoo, Michigan: Cistercian Publications.
Kmosko, M. 1926. *Liber Graduum*. Patrologia Syriaca 3. Paris: Firmin-Didot.
Macina, M. 1999. Les bnay et bnat qyama de l'Église syriaque: une piste philologique sérieuse. *In*: *Le monachisme syriaque: du VIIe siècle à nos jours*, vol. II, 13–49. Patrimoine syriaque. Antélias, Liban: CERO.
Mingana, A. 1934. *Early Christian Mystics*. Woodbrooke Studies 7. Cambridge: W. Heffer and Sons.
Palmer, A. 1990. *Monk and Mason on the Tigris Frontier. The Early History of Ṭur Abdin*. University of Cambridge Oriental Publications 39. Cambridge: University Press.
Pierre, M.-J. 1988–1989. *Aphraate le sage persan*, vol. I–II. Sources chrétiennes 349–59. Paris: Le Cerf.
———. 2010. Les membres de l'Ordre, d'Aphraate au *Liber Graduum*. *In*: F. Jullien, ed., *Le monachisme syriaque*. Études syriaques 7. Paris: Geuthner, 11–35.
Rouët de Journel, M.-J. 1946. *Jean Moschos, Le Pré spirituel*. Sources chrétiennes 12. Paris: Le Cerf.
Salles, J.-F. 2011. Chronologies du monachisme dans le golfe arabopersique. *In*: F. Jullien and M.-J. Pierre, ed., *Les Monachismes d'Orient. Images – Échanges – Influences*. Bibliothèque de l'École des Hautes Études. Sciences religieuses 148. Turnhout: Brepols, 291–312.
Scher, A., and J. Périer. 1908. *Histoire nestorienne inédite (Chronique de Séert)*. PO 4.3. Paris: Firmin-Didot.

Scher, A., and P. Dib. 1910. *Histoire nestorienne inédite (Chronique de Séert)*. PO 5.2. Paris: Firmin-Didot.

Scher, A. 1911. *Histoire nestorienne inédite (Chronique de Séert)*. PO 7.2. Paris: Firmin-Didot.

Scher, A., and R. Griveau. 1919. *Histoire nestorienne inédite (Chronique de Séert)*. PO 13.4. Paris: Firmin-Didot.

Smith, K. 2009. Dendrites and Other Standers in the 'History of the Exploits of Bishop Paul of Qanetos and Priest John of Edessa'. *Hugoye: Journal of Syriac Studies* 12, n°1: 117–34.

Špidlik, T., M. Tenace, and R. Cemus. 1999. *Questions monastiques en Orient*. OCA 259. Rome: Pontificio istituto orientale.

Steve, M.-J. 2003. *L'île de Khārg. Une page de l'histoire du golfe Persique et du monachisme oriental*. Civilisations du Proche-Orient Série I. Archéologie et Environnement 1. Neuchâtel, Paris: Recherches et Publications.

van Esbroeck, M. 1999. Le monachisme syriaque. *In*: *Le monachisme syriaque: du VIIe siècle à nos jours*, vol. II, 71–80. Patrimoine syriaque. Antélias, Liban: CERO.

Villagomez, C. 1998. *The Fields, Flocks, and Finances of Monks: Economic Life at Nestorian Monasteries, 500–850*. Ph.D. dissertation. Los Angeles: University of California.

Vööbus, A. 1958. *History of Asceticism in the Syrian Orient*, vol. I. CSCO 184, Subsidia 14. Louvain: Peeters.

———. 1959. Le reflet du monachisme primitif dans les écrits d'Ephrem le Syrien. *L'Orient syrien* 4, n°3: 299–306.

———. 1960a. *History of Asceticism in the Syrian Orient*, vol. II. CSCO 197, Subsidia 17. Louvain: Peeters.

———. 1960b. *Syriac and Arabic Documents Regarding legislation Relative to Syrian Asceticism*. Papers of the Estonian Theological Society in Exile 11. Stockholm: ETSE.

———. 1961. The Institution of the *benay qeiama* and *benat qeiama* in the Ancient Syrian Church. *Church History* 30: 19–27.

———. 1975. *The Synodicon in the West Syrian Tradition*. CSCO 368, scriptores syri 162. Louvain: Peeters.

———. 1988. *History of Asceticism in the Syrian Orient*, vol. III. CSCO 500, Subsidia 81. Louvain: Peeters.

Wipszycka, E. 1986. Les aspects économiques de la vie de la communauté des Kellia. *In*: P. Bridel, ed., *Le site monastique des Kellia. Sources historiques et explorations archéologiques*. Genève: Mission Suisse d'archéologie copte, 337–62.

———. 1994. Le monachisme égyptien et les villes. *Travaux et Mémoires* 12: 1–44.

Wolska-Conus, W. 1968. *Cosmas Indicopleustes. Topographie chrétienne*, vol. I. Sources chrétiennes 141. Paris: Le Cerf.

Wood, P. 2013. *The Chronicle of Seert: Christian Historical Imagination in Late Antique Iraq*. Oxford Early Christian Studies. Oxford: University Press.

CHAPTER SIX

THE ESTABLISHMENT OF THE SYRIAC CHURCHES

Volker Menze

The holy man cried out into the tombs, saying:
'My Godloving fathers who have died in the Orthodox Faith,
do you command me to subscribe to the Tome of Leo? [. . .]'
and at once, as from a single mouth, the bones of the holy men
cried out saying: 'Anathema to the synod of Chalcedon!
Anathema to the one who would be in communion with them!
Anathema to the one who would say 'Hail' to them!
Anathema to the one who would divide Emmanuel into
two natures or two forms!'
Panegyric on Macarius, Bishop of Tkôw (Johnson 1980: 57–8)

INTRODUCTION

Eusebius of Caesarea's *Church History* and especially his *Life of Constantine* leaves the reader with the impression that once a Roman emperor had recognised Christianity as the only true religion, Church and State formed a natural alliance. Supported and guided by the bishops, the emperor ruled the Christian *oikoumenê* as God's tool on earth. Constantine I (306–337) built churches, financed the production of manuscripts, and admonished quarrelling parties when necessary. In other words, he acted as the good patron of the Church, while the bishops not only preached to their flock and baptised those willing to join the Church but also actively engaged in administrating the now supposedly Christian Roman Empire.

In reality, however, neither the bishops nor the emperors were prepared for this union when Christianity entered the highest social strata of the Roman Empire. While it took the emperors generations to realise that Christianity was not like previously favoured cults that could easily be exchanged or modified when a new emperor deemed it appropriate, it took Christianity even longer to establish structures that defined a *church*. At the beginning of the fourth century, when Christianity first became a licit and then a favoured religion, there was no ecclesiology in any institutional sense. Christianity was a universal religion that anyone could join independent of gender and status. But how was it to be universally organised?

What is called *church* today was actually only beginning to develop during Late Antiquity. While the claim to be the *Church* united Christians already since the first century, an institution that was able to govern itself and agree on doctrine, hierarchy, rituals etc. was a development of centuries up to the Arab Conquest in the seventh century and beyond. One important step in defining what 'orthodoxy', that is, 'correct belief', is, and *in extenso* therefore also what the *Church* believes, was the institutionalisation of church councils. Councils were not a new development since they appear already in the biblical Acts of the Apostles and were called on a regional level throughout the third century, but empire-wide councils that could retrospectively be labelled 'ecumenical' were a new phenomenon from the time of Constantine.

The first ecumenical council, convened by Constantine, took place in Nicaea (325), the second in the reign of emperor Theodosius I (379–395) in Constantinople (381). As no acts have survived, contemporaries may not have regarded the councils as important enough to record their minutes, and it remains difficult to detail the full involvement of the state in this ecclesiastical enterprise.

Considering how the Roman Empire functioned in pre-Christian times, however, there can be hardly any doubt that Constantine certainly considered himself personally responsible for the religious affairs of the empire. While Eusebius praised Constantine for his personal involvement in church affairs – after the Diocletianic persecutions an understandable attitude – this imperial involvement came under scrutiny already in the time of Constantine's son Constantius II, and remained a constant bone of contention throughout Late Antiquity: 'What has the church to do with the emperor?' (Edwards 1997: 62). Once Christianity had not only become a licit but even the dominant religion of the empire in the second half of the fourth century, the state attempted to enforce a unified Christian belief among its subjects. In combination with an ecclesiastical quest for orthodoxy, this led to manifold divisions and ultimately also to the establishment of independent churches.

While the councils of the fourth century caused various sects and divisions which did not survive the centuries of Late Antiquity, the councils of the fifth and sixth centuries led to the establishment of the Syriac churches which still exist today: (1) the first division in the wake of the Council of Ephesus in 431 led to the later establishment of the Church of the East (formerly referred to as 'Nestorians'); (2) the second followed twenty years later when those who resisted the Council of Chalcedon in 451 split away and formed what would later become known as the Syrian Orthodox Church (initially known as 'Jacobites' or 'West Syrians'); (3) those who supported the council, the Chalcedonians, who ultimately became the Church of the Empire (often referred to in Syriac sources as 'Melkites'). These splits can be regarded as such only retrospectively following fierce ecclesiastical struggles that lasted for generations.

The condemned pre-Ephesian theology did not disappear, but survived via mainly Syriac translations handed down by Christians in the eastern provinces of the Roman Empire, and especially in Sasanian Persia. Today this tradition is preserved and honoured by several 'Assyrian Churches' in the Near East and India. The Council of Chalcedon caused an even greater uproar in the eastern provinces, first in Palestine, but later especially in Egypt, which remained largely united against Chalcedon in the form of the later Coptic Church. In Syria and Mesopotamia, sixth-century bishops led the foundation of the later so-called Syrian Orthodox Church, but the Chalcedonian tradition also found its place among Christian communities in Syria.

As Richard Price (2009: 307) rightly noted, at the time of the Arab Conquest in the seventh century, 'three defined ecclesial blocks' had been established: Chalcedonian, non-Chalcedonian, and pre-Ephesian Christianity.

CAUSES OF THE ECCLESIASTICAL DIVISIONS OF THE FIFTH AND SIXTH CENTURIES

While the doctrinal controversy of the fourth century focused on the Trinitarian question of the relationship between God the Father and the Son, the fifth- and sixth-century quarrels were concerned with the Son: how can his divine nature as the second part of the Trinity be understood whilst still believing in his incarnation in the flesh and his suffering on the cross? The non-Chalcedonians emphasised the incarnation in the flesh and later accused their opponents of aligning themselves with the Jews: the Chalcedonians – who understood Christ to be *in* two natures also after the incarnation – allegedly would consider the suffering Christ on the cross merely as man (van Rompay 1981). Dividing the second entity of the Trinity into two would result in charges that the Chalcedonians would worship a Quaternity. The Chalcedonians on the other hand were not shy to call the non-Chalcedonians heretics for mixing up the natures in Christ and believing in *one* nature that is neither fully human nor fully divine. Because of their opposing Christological perceptions, scholars call the non-Chalcedonians 'miaphysites' (Gk *mia phusis*, 'one nature') and the Chalcedonians, as well as the pre-Ephesians (who even more strongly emphasise the two natures character), 'Dyophysites'.

However, the history of the divisions of the churches in the fifth and sixth centuries is more than the history of Christian dogma. Dogma is probably not even the most important ingredient in it, but only one among several factors that led over the next centuries to the establishment of independent churches. While the sincerity of the theological and Christological persuasions of the main protagonists cannot be doubted, politics (ecclesiastical and imperial), loyalties, communal ties and boundaries, and local or regional traditions, played equally important roles in the making of the ecclesiastical splits.

In the fifth century, the metropolitan order of the church was well established: within a Roman province, the bishop of the capital was the metropolitan bishop who oversaw the other bishoprics within the province. The metropolitan could convene provincial councils and ordain new bishops within the province but had no jurisdiction outside it. However, beyond that, on a universal ecclesiological level, the *Church* had not yet worked out how to rule itself.

Traditionally, in the west, once the competition with Carthage had been settled, the bishop of Rome held the most important see – although he could hardly claim that it was he who could convene ecumenical councils and preside over them as the papal legates claimed in 451. In the east, it was Alexandria that not only controlled unopposed every bishopric in Egypt, Libya, and Pentapolis, but held the absolute supremacy, as Eduard Schwartz once aptly phrased it (Schwartz 1927: 203). Already Athanasius of Alexandria (328–373) had been not only an influential theologian but also a most powerful bishop who shaped the doctrinal controversy of the fourth century. The power that the holder of the episcopal see of Alexandria had at his disposal, however, increased even further under the tenures of Theophilus (385–412) and his nephew Cyril (412–444), who ruled the see for over half a century in which they deposed two bishops of Constantinople, convened (ecumenical) councils, and condemned several opposing theologians as heretical.

Since at least the time of Eusebius, Alexandria was also regarded as the see of the evangelist Mark. The apostolicity of the major episcopal sees became an important issue in Late Antiquity but was not the origin of Alexandria's leading position. Canon 6 of the Council of Nicaea confirmed Alexandria's rule over Egypt as well as Libya and the Pentapolis because this had been the tradition, not because Alexandria supposedly had been founded by Mark. Nevertheless, it became the rule to regard Rome as the see of Peter, Alexandria as that of Mark. Antioch also inherited the see of Peter but in importance was regarded third in Christendom behind Rome and Alexandria (Leo the Great, *ep.* 119). The newcomers among these traditionally preeminent episcopal sees were Constantinople and Jerusalem. The latter reached its status solely on religious grounds as the cradle of Christianity, despite the fact that the city never gained any political importance. Only at the Council of Chalcedon in 451 was it established as the fifth patriarchate in addition to Rome, Alexandria, Antioch, and Constantinople. Constantinople on the other hand did not hold any traditional religious significance, but began to play a major political role after Constantine and his successors built it as new Roman capital in the 330s. Only in the early Middle Ages was it regarded as the see of an apostle (St Andrew), long after its ecclesiastical status as second to Rome had been confirmed by the Council of Chalcedon. The Church of the East in Sasanian Persia also regarded five patriarchs as the highest Christian authorities but included their own bishop of Seleucia-Ctesiphon among them instead of the bishop of Jerusalem.

For centuries, Alexandria and Rome enjoyed a special relationship (Klug 2014) and for a time the two cities became allies, during the Council of Ephesus in 431. In the long run, however, competing claims, combined with shrewd and power-conscious bishops such as Cyril of Alexandria or Pope Leo the Great (440–461), could only lead to a clash. This is not to say that the theological, and especially Christological, issues were not a considerable ingredient in the increasing division between Rome and Alexandria, as well as the language divide between east and west. New languages like Syriac and Coptic that appeared as literary languages of Christianity in the east, and the need for translations (or the lack of them) complicated the Christological quarrels. However, the geopolitical antagonisms between the leading ecclesiastical (the respective popes in Rome and patriarchs in Alexandria) and imperial (the emperor in Constantinople) protagonists and their ambitions can hardly be underestimated for the divisions that began in the fifth century and led to independent Syriac churches (Blaudeau 2006, 2012).

Politics is about humans, not Christ, and humans care about established traditions, loyalties, personal ties, and family bonds, and, analysing the quarrels of the fifth and sixth centuries, it should become obvious how much this human factor played a decisive role. Sixth-century Syriac ecclesiastical canons witness persons not fit for the clerical office being elected deacon or priest, and bishops may even have sold offices, as complaints of simony are not unheard of in fifth- and sixth-century Syria. Clerics may also have been chosen for office for their loyalty, and again not for their spiritual or pastoral qualities. Having been the archdeacon of a leading bishop often proved to be an important step for a future ecclesiastical career. Athanasius had been his predecessor's deacon and accompanied his bishop to the Council of Nicaea. Being deacon of a bishop usually meant to be his confidant – even more than the parish priest who theoretically should have been superior to the deacon. And who could be more trusted than a family member?

It may not be completely surprising, therefore, to find a good number of family members among the highest clergy in the Eastern Roman Empire: the see of Alexandria was inherited by relatives three times within just over a century, starting with Theophilus who bequeathed his office to his nephew Cyril in 412. Blood ties also played an important role among the theological opponents of the Alexandrians from the diocese of Oriens: patriarch John II of Antioch (429–442) was the uncle of his successor Domnus II (442–449), and Ibas of Edessa (435–449) had his nephew Daniel made bishop of Ḥarran and his cousin Sophronius bishop of Tella, according to the acts of the Second Council of Ephesus (449). This may have happened more often than is known today, as the lack of documentation often prevents scholars from verifying family relationships between bishops in those years.

What can be detected, however, is the zeal of patriarchs, metropolitans, and bishops to install loyal followers to vacant episcopal sees. In 449, in the year of the Second Council of Ephesus, patriarch Dioscorus (444–451/4) had reached the status of a quasi-ecumenical patriarch – Pope Leo scolded him a 'new pharaoh' – by having filled the most important ecclesiastical positions with his confidents or with people whom his confidents had ordained: Dioscorus himself had ordained Anatolius deacon before he was promoted patriarch of Constantinople (449–458) as the successor of Flavian (446–449) whom Dioscorus had deposed. Anatolius on the other hand ordained one of his clergy, Maximus, as patriarch of Antioch (449–455?) after Dioscorus had deposed patriarch Domnus.

Quite apart from any theological controversy, this must have caused resistance among the ecclesiastical ranks who were not favoured and could not hope to forge for themselves a high-flying ecclesiastical career. Maybe Dioscorus went too far in his ambition to oversee the churches – he further caused internal resistance in the Alexandrian church by having ousted Cyril's relatives immediately after his accession – and did not show the same level of diplomacy and shrewdness that his uncle Cyril was capable of. Among the many letters that have survived from Cyril, there is one (Cyril, *ep.* 96; written by Cyril's staff) that appears to be the largest bribe that was ever paid in antiquity. Large quantities of gold, thrones, textiles etc. were sent to persons of power and influence at the court, most likely following the Council of Ephesus in order to ensure that the court, that is, the emperor, would approve Cyril's council as the Third Ecumenical Council.

Cyril was unquestionably one of the most prominent and influential theologians of Late Antiquity, and his sincerity in theological matters should not be doubted. However, to understand the divisions of the churches in this period, it is important to take into account that more than theology and Christology was at stake, and Cyril – like Athanasius and Theophilus before him or Dioscorus and others after him – were also politicians who knew very well how to gather their forces in order to ensure that *their* theology would be accepted as orthodoxy in the Later Roman Empire.

FROM THE COUNCIL OF EPHESUS (431) TO THE ACCESSION OF JUSTIN I (518)

A lasting division within Syriac Christianity began at the Council of Ephesus in 431, although the scope of its impact was not visible to contemporaries. Nestorius, the new patriarch of Constantinople (428–31), inherited a controversy in the capital concerning the Virgin Mary: was it appropriate to call her *Theotokos*, that is, 'God bearer'? Nestorius tried to stay on the safe side and requested that Mary should only be called a *Christotokos*, the 'Christ bearer'. He probably did not foresee the repercussions of this controversy that in the end caused his downfall and condemnation (Wessel 2004).

Nestorius was from Germanicia in Syria and trained as theologian by the 'Antiochene School' that emphasised the full humanity of Christ and thereby also his dual nature. While the terminology of 'school' has been debated in this case, the differences between the theological teachings of Antioch and Alexandria, which latter focused upon the incarnate Christ and his suffering, is unquestionable. Whether Nestorius's Christology can in fact be regarded as 'orthodox' has been debated at length by Western scholars in the twentieth century, since a Syriac translation of Nestorius's apology, *The Bazaar of Heracleides*, written around 450, was discovered in 1895.

The controversy over the 'Mother of God', the title by which Mary had been venerated since the beginning of the fifth century, led to a Christological controversy that caused Theodosius II (408–450) to summon the Council of Ephesus in 431. However, not one but two councils were held, one by Cyril of Alexandria and his followers who condemned Nestorius, and one by John of Antioch who supported Nestorius, having been taught in the same theological tradition, but probably also because Cyril's increasing influence on ecclesiastical politics worried the Antiochenes. At this time, Theophilus of Alexandria's attack and condemnation of John Chrysostom, bishop of Constantinople (397–403) and another former cleric from Antioch, was still fresh in the memory.

Theodosius II opted to back Cyril's council, which also had the support of the papal legates, together with Cyril's condemnation of Nestorius. The emperor endorsed the condemnation by decree, Nestorius went into exile, and his books were to be burned throughout the Roman Empire (*CTh* 16.5.66). Beyond the borders of the Roman Empire it was a different manner: although Nestorius spoke and wrote Greek, his apology survives in Syriac only, and while hardly playing a role as theologian for the Church of the East, he is held in esteem by Eastern Syrians as a martyr of Antiochene theology (Baum and Winkler 2003: 30).

The beginnings of what came later to be the Church of the East or East Syrian Church can be traced back to the second-century Parthian, later (from 224 CE) Sasanian, Empire. Christianity had spread towards the East from early in its existence (see chapter 4). However, as a fully autonomous church, the Church of the East only established itself in the two centuries following the Council of Ephesus and the 'Nestorian controversy', although its growth was not directly caused by this doctrinal quarrel. By ignoring the theological developments within the Roman Empire and adhering to the dyophysite Antiochene theologians such as Nestorius, the Church separated itself from the ecclesiastical communities within the Roman Empire.

While it was Nestorius who was the focus of the controversy in Greek and Latin theology, the Church of the East rather venerated one of Nestorius's teachers, Theodore, bishop of Mopsuestia (392–428), as the cornerstone of their orthodoxy (also called the 'interpreter'; McLeod 2009). Theodore exemplifies the parting of the ways among Syrian Christians: within the Eastern Roman Empire, he was condemned at the Second Council of Constantinople in 553 as a heretic despite having died in peace with the 'Church' in 428. In Sasanian Persia, however, he was venerated by this time as the foremost theologian and church father of the Church of the East.

Within the Roman Empire, the Council of Ephesus did not lead to church unity. Initially, in 433, Alexandria and Antioch settled the Christological matter and agreed to be in communion with each other. Although the Council had been a complete success for Cyril, the patriarch had to make some theological compromises in 433 in order to pacify his opponents from the Antiochene faction. He even showed leniency when it was reported to him that theologians like Theodore of Mopsuestia were venerated (Cyril *ep.* 72).

However, political compromises did not help to clarify the doctrinal controversy of how to understand the nature(s) of Christ, since the Council had merely confirmed the Councils of Nicaea (325) and Constantinople (381) without issuing a definition of faith in light of the ongoing Christological discourse. Furthermore, theologians from the Antiochene theological tradition still occupied a good number of sees in Syria and strongly opposed both Cyril's miaphysite Christology and the Alexandrian's claim to ecclesiastical supremacy in the Eastern Roman Empire. The most prolific theologian at this time was certainly Theodoret of Cyrrhus (423–457), not only author of a church history and collection of hagiographies but also of a number of theological works and polemics. However, at first it seemed that Alexandria again got its way when at the Second Council of Ephesus in 449, Dioscorus of Alexandria condemned not only Theodoret but also Ibas of Edessa as well as the patriarch of Antioch Domnus together with further bishops within Antioch's jurisdictional territory. In 449/50, the eastern Roman Empire had almost completely shifted towards a miaphysite Christological understanding under the ecclesiastical leadership of Alexandria.

The death of Theodosius II in 450 and the call for an ecumenical council in order to issue a new formula of faith – a request initially strongly opposed by Pope Leo, dramatically changed the ecclesiastical map. Although certainly not intended this way, the Council of Chalcedon in 451 decided the fate of the churches in Egypt and the Near East. Neither the later Coptic nor the Syrian Orthodox Church ratified it as the Fourth Ecumenical Council but regarded the deposed Dioscorus (and his retinue of Egyptian bishops) orthodox, whereas the rest of Christendom fell into heresy, including the patriarchs of Constantinople and Antioch as well as the pope.

In the period following Chalcedon, many Christians resisted the new formula of faith, especially as it appeared in the East as a betrayal of Cyril's Christology. The *Tome of Leo*, a letter in which Pope Leo had laid out his own doctrine, written in 448 and accepted at Chalcedon as a cornerstone of orthodoxy, became a bone of contention (Gaddis and Price 2007, vol. 2: 14–24; see the quotation at the head of this chapter). A rebellion in Palestine in 452/3 was only the prelude to the upcoming struggles between Chalcedonians and non-Chalcedonians. Proterius, Dioscorus's Chalcedonian successor as patriarch of Alexandria, was killed by a non-Chalcedonian mob in 457. Eastern Roman emperors tried with little success in the following decades, right up until the accession of Justin I (518–527) to balance the opposing groups. Zeno (474–5 and 476–91) went so far as to publish a decree, the so-called *Henoticon* of 482, which tried to appease both sides by avoiding a stance on Chalcedon (Whitby 2000: 147–9). However, the decree merely caused the so-called Acacian schism – named after the Chalcedonian patriarch of Constantinople, Acacius (471–88) – between Rome and the East which lasted until 518.

Until the end of the fifth century, Palestine seems to have been largely non-Chalcedonian, but this clearly shifted in the sixth century in favour of Chalcedon. Egypt remained opposed to Chalcedon, and after the failure with Proterius to install a Chalcedonian patriarch, emperors stopped interfering with Alexandrian patriarchal appointments for the next eighty years. Syria, however, was divided – both opponents as well as supporters of the Council of Chalcedon quarrelled and attempted to get the upper hand through ordinations of bishops of their persuasion. In the last quarter of the fifth century, one of the key players of the non-Chalcedonian cause was the Syriophone Philoxenus, the metropolitan of Mabbug (485–519). Having being ordained by Peter the Fuller, the non-Chalcedonian patriarch of Antioch (471–88, himself the successor of a Chalcedonian patriarch), Philoxenus, also famous for having revised the Syriac Bible, actively advocated his non-Chalcedonian persuasion in ecclesiastical politics and created a network of bishops who supported further non-Chalcedonian appointments. It was certainly also not the least because of his efforts that in 512 the Greek-speaking Severus was appointed patriarch of Antioch (512–18). Severus was one of the greatest theologians of Late Antiquity, which he established in a number of polemics that he wrote against the Council of Chalcedon and its supporters (Alpi 2009).

At the beginning of the sixth century, the tide seemed to have turned in favour of the non-Chalcedonians in the Eastern Roman Empire. The emperor Anastasius (491–518) had to provide a Chalcedonian statement of faith when he came to power, but his later actions clearly leaned towards non-Chalcedonianism. This can partially be accredited to the Acacian schism – Constantinople's not being in communion with Rome gave the emperor more flexibility to reach out to his non-Chalcedonian subjects. Why agree to Roman demands which, in the form of the *Tome of Leo*, found hardly any popular support in the Eastern Roman Empire? The city of Rome was not part of the Eastern Roman Empire, and a Western Roman Empire no longer existed. The imperial priority not to lose the support of the large number of non-Chalcedonians within the empire is therefore easily understandable. The other reason for Anastasius's non-Chalcedonian leanings can probably be found in the towering figure of Severus, who influenced ecclesiastical and thereby also imperial politics after 508. Having become patriarch in 512, he may have expected to build up a permanent non-Chalcedonian Church of the Empire. Ecclesiastical politics, however, remained highly complicated, with the patriarchates of Alexandria and Antioch being non-Chalcedonian, Rome refusing communion with all patriarchs in the East, and Constantinople (and Jerusalem) negotiating somewhere in the middle. The patriarchs of Constantinople considered themselves to be Chalcedonian, yet while on the one hand they were not regarded as orthodox by Rome because they were in communion with Antioch and Alexandria, on the other hand they were placed under severe imperial pressure to accommodate the non-Chalcedonians in the East within the Church of the Empire.

FROM JUSTIN'S ACCESSION TO THE SECOND COUNCIL OF CONSTANTINOPLE (553)

This complicated nature of what constitutes the Church of the Empire ended with the accession of Justin I in 518, the uncle of his more famous successor Justinian I (527–565). This is not to say that Justin found a smooth solution, but he needed the ideological backing of Rome for ruling as Chalcedonian emperor and accepted Pope Hormisdas's (514–523) terms for a union to end the Acacian schism. The papal terms, however, were strict, and Hormisdas followed his fifth-century predecessors who had claimed ecclesiastical primacy for Rome. His *libellus* clearly regarded Rome as the only apostolic see that had remained immaculate since the beginning of Christianity, and all eastern bishops as well as lower clergy were supposed to sign the letter in order to subject themselves to papal primacy. Thereby, a union between east and west was established after more than 30 years of schism; but further unrest was hardly surprising.

This was first of all the case for all the non-Chalcedonian bishops who could not submit to the Council of Chalcedon and the *Tome of Leo*. More than fifty bishops went into exile, among them Severus, who fled to Egypt, and Philoxenus, who was banished to Thrace and then Paphlagonia where he died under suspicious circumstances in 523. However, Chalcedonian bishops also had difficulties in coming to terms with a union that requested them to submit to the jurisdiction of the papacy in Rome. There were still ecclesiastical battles to fight, but Justin managed to make the patriarch of Constantinople agree to the terms of the union. This leaves no doubt as to the extent of the emperor's influence on the patriarch and the church in the capital – in stark contrast to Alexandria and Egypt where Justin was unable or unwilling to install a Chalcedonian patriarch. Egypt became a safe haven for exiled non-Chalcedonian bishops from Syria for a time, including the former patriarch Severus.

Syria was divided between (a) the supporters of Chalcedon who later, after the Arab Conquest, would be considered the 'Melkite' Church, that is, the 'royal' church that sided with the imperial Byzantines; (b) opponents of the Council of Chalcedon, the later Syrian Orthodox Church; and (c) a smaller number of pre-Ephesian Eastern Syrians. Although Hormisdas's *libellus* was enforced and non-Chalcedonian bishops were exiled, Chalcedonian rule was not universally accepted. Especially east of the Euphrates, resistance seems to have been considerable.

Soon after the non-Chalcedonian bishops left for exile between 519 and 521, one of them, John of Tella (519–521), began to ordain deacons and priests and continued to do so throughout the 520s and early 530s. In doing this, he ensured that faithful non-Chalcedonians did not have to enter Chalcedonian Eucharist communities but could receive their Eucharist from a non-Chalcedonian clergy. This grassroots initiative ensured the survival of the non-Chalcedonians in Syria at the time of their greatest despair and laid the foundations of the later Syrian Orthodox Church. John did not ordain bishops, perhaps because he had an ecclesiastical model in mind that did not depend for its foundations upon sees with an apostolic lineage (Menze and Akalın 2009). A few decades later in the 550s, Jacob Baradaeus (543–578) started to use this pool of thousands of ordained deacons and priests to appoint new bishops, who may be regarded as the first episcopal hierarchy of an emerging Syrian Orthodox Church.

However, this was a development that occurred only after the Second Council of Constantinople in 553. The process up until that time was not linear – on the contrary, when Justinian succeeded his uncle in 527, he put a stop to the persecutions and initiated a policy of rapprochement towards the non-Chalcedonians. His reasoning for this was the same as it had been for emperors before him: any Christian emperor was embedded in the ideological construction of a united Christian Church. A fierce and stubborn opposition, such as the non-Chalcedonians were putting up in Egypt, Syria, and Mesopotamia, was a dangerous liability for any emperor – even more so as Justinian was about to reconquer parts of the former western empire and needed above all loyal subjects and stable provinces in the east.

During his long rule of almost forty years, Justinian invited theological debates at his court and convened councils. Whether this activity was due to his personal theological tastes may be a matter for debate, but he in any case certainly had a strategic goal in mind: to find common ground between the rival Christian parties. Although towards the end of his reign (in 561) he also invited an eastern Syrian delegation from Persia to his court, the main focus of the debates and councils was on the Chalcedonian controversy. The first debate took place in 532 between Chalcedonian and non-Chalcedonian bishops in Constantinople, but without Severus (Brock 1981). It was certainly a diplomatic success for Justinian to persuade Severus to leave his exile and travel to Constantinople a few years later (535/6). However, what might have been a promising conciliatory meeting ended with the condemnation of the non-Chalcedonians by a council in Constantinople in 536. This council was a turning point as the non-Chalcedonians, after eighty-five years of refusing the Council of Chalcedon, now became officially condemned heretics of the Roman Empire. The Council of Chalcedon could no longer be questioned as such, and the result was further widespread persecutions of non-Chalcedonians – especially harassment of non-Chalcedonian monasteries – in Syria and Mesopotamia.

While this clarified matters of what was regarded 'orthodoxy' and 'heresy', the problem had hardly changed at all for the emperor, who still needed to integrate the non-Chalcedonians into the empire. Until the death of his wife, Theodora, in 548, Justinian had a confidante who acted as patroness of the non-Chalcedonians and kept them at bay. It was a relationship that benefited both sides, as the non-Chalcedonians had an influential listener at court (and leading non-Chalcedonian bishops sent her letters and doctrinal treatises), while the empress ensured that the non-Chalcedonians would not be completely alienated from Constantinople (Menze 2008: 208–88). After Theodora's early death, Justinian forced upon the papacy and eastern Chalcedonians the Second Council of Constantinople (553) in order to modify the meaning of Chalcedon (Price 2009). However, the measures he enacted regarding the 'Three Chapters Controversy' – a controversy that had already started long before Theodora's death – and the condemnation of Theodore of Mopsuestia, some of the writings of Theodoret of Cyrrhus, and of the letter of Ibas of Edessa to Mari merely created tensions among the western Chalcedonians without persuading the non-Chalcedonians to accept Chalcedon as the fourth ecumenical council.

DIVISIONS AND THE MAKING OF SEPARATE CHURCHES

On the contrary, following the council, Jacob Baradaeus, titular bishop of Edessa, began ordaining a separate episcopal hierarchy (Mellon Saint-Laurent 2015). He ordained dozens of bishops and even two patriarchs all over the Near East. The future Syrian Orthodox Church did not stop at the imperial borders, but bishoprics existed also in Sasanian Persia and parts of Arabia that proved to be a non-Chalcedonian stronghold in the sixth century. One of the Arab tribes, the Ghassanids, acted as vassals of the Eastern Roman Empire but doctrinally remained adamant supporters of the non-Chalcedonian cause.

Attempts at reconciliation between Chalcedonians and non-Chalcedonians continued nonetheless, both under Justinian and also his successors Justin II (565–578) and Tiberius (578–582). The latter was for a short time successful by introducing a new edition of the *Henoticon*. Even a dedicated non-Chalcedonian bishop like John, titular bishop of Ephesus (ca. 558–588), fervent partisan of the non-Chalcedonian cause, who lived through the troubled times of Justinian and had himself been ordained deacon by John of Tella in 528 and bishop by Jacob Baradaeus in the 550s, agreed to the reunion. However, this was a very short-lived reconciliation and could not prevent the establishment of the Syrian Orthodox Church, although its true independence from Constantinople may have become obvious to a majority of Christians in the Near East only after the Arab Conquest.

Christianity did play a significant role in the sixth century in diplomatic relations with Persia. The Persian martyr acts provide evidence of the extent of Christianity in the Persian Empire, even among the ruling class. One of the most famous Christians was Shirin, wife of shah Khosrow II (590–628), who may also have influenced her husband to make offerings to Saint Sergius, one of the most venerated Christian saints in the Late Antique Near East, at Reṣafa south of the Euphrates (Key Fowden 1999). Martyr shrines were certainly places where Christians of different denominations met, even though ecclesiastical leaders were rather anxious not to have their flock interacting with and maybe even donating gifts to 'heretics'. Probably out of diplomatic considerations, a shared Eucharistic celebration took place in 587 between the Constantinopolitan Court and the catholicos of the Church of the East, Išoʿyahb of Arzun (582–95), when the latter visited the Eastern Roman Empire on a diplomatic mission.

Despite such short-lived ecumenical moments and some noticeable uncertainties concerning the canonisation of ecclesiastical traditions in fifth- and sixth-century Syria, communal boundaries became more and more stable. Historiographers and hagiographers noted 'their' history, tradition, and saints in opposition to the other Christian groups, and thereby established and confirmed distinct self-identities throughout the sixth century (Debié 2009). John of Ephesus's *Church History* as well as his *Lives of the Eastern Saints* became foundational texts for mediaeval Syrian Orthodox authors and for expressing Syrian Orthodox confessional identity. It was a partisan's view, written in Syriac for a Syrian audience, even though John spent a good part of his life in Constantinople, where he acted as the non-Chalcedonian contact person for the Justinianic court. The literary use of the Syriac language certainly also increased the extent of separation from the 'Byzantines', and the Syriac language became a common religious marker of the Syriac churches in the centuries to come. This separation of the *Suryāyē* had begun already during the time of the Chalcedonian controversy, when important theological works – such as the polemical treatises of Severus of Antioch – had been translated into Syriac within a few years of their composition. The development of such Syriac intellectual resources assisted the formation of ecclesiastical hierarchies, which in turn then ultimately caused the establishment of different Syriac churches.

In this sense, Late Antiquity also proves to be a coming of age for the Christian Church: the papacy in the West established itself as an institution independent from the Eastern Roman emperor as did the pre-Ephesian and non-Chalcedonian churches in the Near East. The Church of the East was the first to find its place within a state that did not support or favour it, while most Syrian Orthodox may still have hoped even under Justinian that imperial favour would return to them and that they would eventually become the Church of the Empire. The turbulent first half of the seventh century proved to be the last time that a Roman emperor, Heraclius (610–41), unsuccessfully attempted to unite the Christian communities into a single Church under his rule. After the Arab Conquest, only the Byzantine Church, and especially the patriarch of Constantinople, remained closely linked to the emperor. The Syriac churches became independent ecclesiastical institutions without any ideological links to the new Muslim state and its ruler.

However, already before the Arab Conquest, the natural integration of Church and State as proposed by Eusebius was no longer working for the Syriac communities within the Roman Empire as well as beyond its borders. This had proved to be a troublesome process lasting many generations and included the development of an independent priesthood, a doctrinal tradition, liturgy etc. on the side of the emerging Syriac churches. However, the making of these churches can only be understood in the context of late ancient ecclesiastical controversies. The fifth and the sixth centuries were the formative period for the Syriac traditions and for the churches that grew out of it, which still exist today.

BIBLIOGRAPHY

Primary Sources

The Acts of the Council of Chalcedon. 3 Vols. Trans. M. Gaddis and R. Price. Liverpool: Liverpool University Press. 2007.

The Acts of the Council of Constantinople of 553. Trans. R. Price. Liverpool: Liverpool University Press. 2009.

Evagrius, Ecclesiastical History. Trans. M. Whitby. Liverpool: Liverpool University Press. 2000.

John of Tella's Profession of Faith*: The Legacy of a Sixth-Century Syrian Orthodox Bishop*. Ed. and trans. V. Menze and K. Akalın. Piscataway, NJ: Gorgias Press. 2009.

Optatus: Against the Donatists. Trans. M. Edwards. Liverpool: Liverpool University Press. 1997.

A Panegyric on Macarius, Bishop of Tkôw, Attributed to Dioscorus of Alexandria. Ed. and trans. D. W. Johnson. CSCO 415–516. Louvain: Secrétariat du CorpusSCO. 1980.

Secondary Literature

Alpi, F. 2009. *La Route Royale. Sévère d'Antioche et les Églises d'Orient (512–518)*. 2 Vols. Beyrouth: Institut Français du Proche-Orient.

Amirav, H. 2015. *Authority and Performance: Sociological Perspectives on the Council of Chalcedon (AD 451)*. Göttingen: Vandenhoeck & Ruprecht.

Andresen, C. 1971. *Die Kirchen der alten Christenheit*. Stuttgart: Kohlhammer.

Ashbrook Harvey, S. 1990. *Asceticism and Society in Crisis: John of Ephesus and the Lives of the Eastern Saints*. Berkeley: University of California Press.

Baum, W. and D. Winkler. 2003. *The Church of the East: A Concise History*. London: Routledge Curzon.

Behr, J. 2011. *The Case Against Diodore and Theodore: Texts and their Contexts*. Oxford: Oxford University Press.

Blaudeau, P. 2006. Rome contre Alexandrie? L'interprétation pontificale de l'enjeu monophysite (de l'émergence de la controverse eutychienne au schism acacien 448–484). *Adamantius* 12, 140–216.

———. 2012. *Le Siège de Rome et l'Orient 448–536*. Rome: École française de Rome.

Brock, S. 1981. The Conversations with the Syrian Orthodox under Justinian (532). *OCP* 47, 87–121.

———. 1996. The 'Nestorian' Church: A Lamentable Misnomer. *Bulletin of the John Rylands Library* 78, 23–55.

Debié, M. 2009. Syriac Historiography and Identity Formation. *Church History and Religious Cultures* 89, 93–114.

Fisher, G. 2011. *Between Empires: Arabs, Romans, and Sasanians in Late Antiquity*. Oxford: Oxford University Press.

Fowden, G. 1993. *Empire to Commonwealth: Consequences of Monotheism in Late Antiquity*. Princeton: Princeton University Press.

Frend, W. H. C. 1970. *The Rise of the Monophysite Movement: Chapters in the History of the Church in the Fifth and Sixth Centuries*. Cambridge: Cambridge University Press.

Ginkel, J. van. 1995. *John of Ephesus: A Monophysite Historian in Sixth-Century Byzantium*. Dissertation. Rijksuniversiteit Groningen.

Greatrex, G. 2003. Khusro II and the Christians of His Empire. *JCSSS* 3, 78–88.

Grillmeier, A. 1979–1990. *Jesus der Christus im Glauben der Kirche*. 5 Vols. Freiburg: Herder [reprint with some revisions 2004].

Guillaumont, A. 1969/1970. Justinien et l'église de Perse. *DOP* 23/34, 39–66.

Haar Romeny, Bas ter. 2009. *Religious Origins of Nations? The Christian Communities of the Middle East*. Church History and Religious Cultures 89. Leiden: Brill.

Key Fowden, E. 1999. *The Barbarian Plain: Saint Sergius Between Rome and Iran*. Berkeley: University of California Press.

Klug, S. 2014. *Alexandria und Rom. Die Geschichte der Beziehungen zweier Kirchen in der Antike*. Jahrbuch für Antike und Christentum. Ergänzungsband. Kleine Reihe 11. Münster: Aschendorff.

Lange, C. 2012. *Mia Energeia. Untersuchungen zur Einigungspolitik des Kaisers Heraclius und des Patriarchen Sergius von Constantinopel*. Tübingen: Mohr Siebeck.

MacMullen, R. 2006. *Voting about God in Early Church Councils*. New Haven: Yale University Press.

McLeod, F. G. 2009. *Theodore of Mopsuestia*. London and New York: Routledge.

Mellon Saint-Laurent, J.-N. 2015. *Missionary Stories and the Formation of the Syriac Churches*. Oakland: University of California Press.

Menze, V. L. 2008. *Justinian and the Making of the Syrian Orthodox Church*. Oxford: Oxford University Press.

———. 2013. Chalcedonian Controversy. *In*: R. S. Bagnall, ed., *Encyclopedia of Ancient History*. Malden: Wiley-Blackwell, 3:1428–31.

Menze, V. L. and K. Akalın. 2013/14. '*Kann man Bücher verbrennen?* Severus of Antioch's Letter to Nonnus Scholasticus, a Heretical Codex and a Late Roman *Autodafé*. *OC* 97, 1–22.

Michelson, D. 2014. *The Practical Theology of Philoxenos of Mabbug*. Oxford: Oxford University Press.

Millar, F. 2006. *A Greek Roman Empire: Power and Belief Under Theodosius II (408–450)*. Berkeley: University of California Press.

Morony, M. 1984. *Iraq After the Muslim Conquest*. Princeton: Princeton University Press.
Palmer, A. 2014. A Tale of Two Synods. The Archimandrite Barsumas at Ephesus in 449 and at Chalcedon in 451. *Journal of Eastern Christian Studies* 66, 37–61.
Price, R. 2009. The Development of Chalcedonian Identity in Byzantium (451–553). *Church History and Religious Cultures* 89, 307–25.
Russell, N. 2000. *Cyril of Alexandria*. London and New York: Routledge.
Schor, A. 2011. *Theodoret's People: Social Networks and Religious Conflict in Late Roman Syria*. Berkeley: University of California Press.
Schwartz, E. 1927. Die Kaiserin Pulcheria auf der Synode von Chalkedon. *In*: Festgabe für A. Jülicher. Tübingen: J.C.B. Mohr (Paul Siebeck), 203–12.
van Rompay, L. 1981. A Letter of the Jews to the Emperor Marcian concerning the Council of Chalcedon. *OLP* 12, 215–24.
Vries, W. de. 1975. Das Konzil von Ephesus 449, eine Räubersynode? *OCP* 41, 357–98.
Walker, J. T. 2006. *The Legend of Mar Qardagh. Narrative and Christian Heroism in Late Antique Iraq*. Berkeley and Los Angeles: University of California Press.
Wessel, S. 2004. *Cyril of Alexandria and the Nestorian Controversy: The Making of a Saint and the Making of a Heretic*. Oxford: Oxford University Press.
Winkler, D. W. 1997. Miaphysitism. A New Term for the Use in the History of Dogma and in Ecumenical Theology. *The Harp* 10, 33–40.
Wood, P. 2010. *'We Have No King But Christ': Christian Political Thought in Greater Syria on the Eve of the Arab Conquest (c. 400–585)*. Oxford: Oxford University Press.
———. 2013. *The Chronicle of Seert: Christian Historical Imagination in Late Antique Iraq*. Oxford: Oxford University Press.

CHAPTER SEVEN

THE SYRIAC CHURCH DENOMINATIONS

An overview

Dietmar W. Winkler

Although rarely documented, already for the first century there seems to be good evidence that Christianity spread not only within the Roman Empire – i.e. Europe and the Mediterranean region – but also beyond the imperial boundaries. Christian communities are found not only in Greece, Italy, and Spain but also in Syria, Mesopotamia, Egypt, and Asia Minor. Christianity crossed the language barrier in the north-east and reached Osrhoëne and Pontus. In the fourth century – while standard textbooks to Ecclesiastical History are focused upon the imperial Church History of the Greco-Roman World – Syriac Christianity was already flourishing in Syria, Persia, the Arabian Peninsula, and the South Indian Malabar coast. It is Syriac Christianity which crosses the Oxus River as early as the fifth century and reaches Sogdians and Turks. Moreover, at a time when Europe had still not yet been completely re-evangelised following the period of the Germanic migrations, Syriac Christianity was expanding along the Silk Roads and in the seventh century reached the Chinese imperial court of the Tang Dynasty.

It is because of its vast geographical diversity, theological disputes, and complex history that the Syriac Christian tradition and cultural world became divided into several church denominations. It is helpful to distinguish between East and West Syriac liturgical traditions as well as denominational affiliation (Brock 2006: 72).

West Syriac Liturgical Tradition			*East Syriac Liturgical Tradition*	
Oriental Orthodox	*Reformed*	*Catholic*		*Church of the East*
Syrian Orthodox Church *Malankara Jacobite Syrian Orthodox Church*	Mar Thoma Syrian Church	Maronite Church	Chaldean Catholic Church	Assyrian Church of the East
Malankara Orthodox Syrian Church		Syrian Catholic Church	Syro-Malabar Church	Ancient Church of the East
Malabar Independent Syrian Church		Syro-Malankara Catholic Church		

The Syrian Orthodox Church of Antioch with its Indian branch, the Malankara Syrian Orthodox Church, together with the Malankara Orthodox Syrian Church, belong to the family of oriental orthodox churches which also comprises the Coptic Orthodox, the Armenian Apostolic, Ethiopian, and Eritrean Orthodox Churches. Their common point of reference is the rejection of the Council of Chalcedon (451) and a miaphysite Christology. They have been active in ecumenical dialogues together since the 1960s (Winkler 2016: 201–12).

The Malabar Independent Syrian Church is an independent church with oriental orthodox origins, while the Mar Thoma Syrian Church is the result of a reformation during the era of British colonial rule in India.

The Maronite, Syrian Catholic, Syro-Malankara, Chaldean, and Syro-Malabar Churches are in full communion with the Roman Catholic Church. The Assyrian Church of the East and the Ancient Church are independent churches sharing a single East Syriac heritage with the Chaldean Church. In the above table, the tinted items are those churches that are affiliated to larger organisations.

In what follows, I shall concentrate on offering some account of historical developments, so as better to explain the expansion of Syriac Christianity and the origins of its various denominations.

CHRISTOLOGICAL DISPUTES AND CHURCH DIVISIONS

As Edessa occupied a position where significant trade routes intersected, and Antioch on the Mediterranean was the most influential metropolis of the Roman province of Syria, the Gospel travelled a route from Jerusalem through Antioch and Edessa to Mesopotamia. Syriac Christianity was spread by soldiers, merchants, and travellers into Persia and India, as well as to Central Asia and China in later centuries.

Besides trade, an additional significant factor that contributed to the development of Christianity was the increasing movement of refugees and wartime deportations because of the constant conflict between the Roman and Persian empires.

The Church of the East

In the early third century, Christianity in Persia had already developed an episcopal structure (Baum and Winkler 2003: 7–41). In the synodical documents of Late Antiquity, this Persian Church was called the 'Church of the East'. Today, the Chaldean Catholic Church, the Assyrian Church of the East, and the Ancient Church of the East refer to this origin.

The Church of the East's traditional label of the 'Nestorian Church' has been called a 'lamentable misnomer' (Brock 1996: 23–36). Encyclopaedic information for East Syriac Christianity has generally been categorised under this entry. From a theological point of view, this term must be rejected today, because 'Nestorian' refers to a doctrine that regards as separate the humanity and divinity in the one Jesus Christ. This does not reflect the Christological teachings of this church. Moreover, it is a doctrine that the Church of the East itself has rejected as incorrect since at least the sixth century.

The major developments that occurred within the church in the Roman Empire following the Edict of Milan (313), such as the Arian controversy and the Council of

Nicea (325), had no impact whatsoever on the Persian Church. The Persian Church never was part of the Roman Imperial Church or of the ecclesiastical politics of the emperors of the Roman Empire.

In the early fifth century, the shah Yazdgird I (399–421) sought to ease political tensions with the Roman Empire and began to integrate Christians into imperial politics. Thus began the period of diplomatic exchanges between the two great empires of Late Antiquity, exchanges in which the Christian hierarchy of Persia played an essential role. It was at that time that the Church of the East began what may be called its 'synodical period'. At the first Synod of Seleucia-Ctesiphon (410), the Persian Church was not only reorganised following the persecutions, but was also brought into harmony with the faith of the West by receiving the faith of Nicea (325). Like the councils of the Roman Empire, the first synod of the Church of the East was called and supported by the state authorities. With further synods in the fifth century, the Persian Church established its ecclesial and theological independence. However, contact with the Roman Imperial Church was in no way broken off.

The church developed a strong Antiochene Christology centred on the School of Edessa (Winkler 2003: 42–80), which since about 430 had been under the influence of the doctrines and works of Theodore of Mopsuestia (d. 428). Even during his lifetime, virtually all of Theodore's works – as well as those of his teacher Diodore of Tarsus – were translated into Syriac. Through this translation, Antiochene theology became influential in Edessa. In this way graduates of the school, who during peaceful times returned to the Persian Empire, spread a dyophysite (two nature) theology in the Sasanian Empire even before the Council of Ephesus (431).

Since Theodore stands as the classic representative of Antiochene theology, opposed to Arianism and Apollinarianism, and since his work was studied intensively at the school of Edessa, it is hardly surprising that the delegates from Edessa opposed Cyril of Alexandria at the Council of Ephesus (431). Together with John of Antioch, Ibas of Edessa (d. 457) and his bishop Rabbula (d. 435) spoke up against Cyril.

As a result of the Christological disputes that followed the Councils of Ephesus and Chalcedon in the Roman Empire, emperor Zeno had the school closed and the teachers expelled in 489. The new centre of theological reflection became the school of Nisibis, a short distance across the Persian boarder. Nisibis developed into an intellectual centre and became the theological powerhouse of the East Syriac Church in the Sasanian Empire.

The Synods of Beth Lapaṭ (484) and Seleucia-Ctesiphon (486) have sometimes been considered to be the route by which the Church of the East officially adopted Nestorianism. However, the creeds of the synods of the fifth and sixth centuries can be identified only as a strict form of Antiochene Christology. While the teachings of Nestorius, who appears in the synodical records of the Church of the East for the first time only in 612, seem to have had no theological significance, Theodore of Mopsuestia became the most influential of all the Greek Fathers (Winkler 2012: 148–65).

At the court of the ʿAbbasid caliphs (750–1258) in Baghdad, one of the most spectacular and momentous movements in the history of thought took place. Almost all the secular Greek books in philosophy, science, and medicine that were available throughout the former Eastern Roman and Persian empires were translated into Arabic. East Syriac Christians played a fundamental role in this 'translation movement' (Gutas 1998) as translators came overwhelmingly from within their ranks and as they tended to know at least three languages: Syriac, Greek, and Arabic. In this way, much of the intellectual heritage of antiquity was transmitted to the blossoming world of Arabic scholarship and provided the basis for a philosophical terminology for Islam. This is of utmost cultural and historical significance also for the West, as works translated – via Syriac into Arabic – entered Europe through Spain and Sicily even before the Greek originals were known.

Although the politics of the ʿAbbasid caliphs brought about widespread conversions of Christians to Islam, the Church of the East maintained bishoprics in Damascus, Jerusalem, Alexandria, Cyprus, and the Gulf. Even more significant was the well-organised missionary enterprise towards the East. Monks, sent by catholicos-patriarch Timothy I along the Silk Road, spread Christianity, together with their own Aramaic culture and liturgy, among the peoples of Persia, Azerbaijan, Afghanistan, Turkey, Mongolia, China, Tibet, and India (Malek 2006; Winkler and Tang 2009; Tang and Winkler 2013, 2016). These missionary efforts came to an end in the middle of the ninth century when the Chinese emperor at that time opposed foreign religions. At about the same time, Christianity in Central Asia, especially in Tibet, declined because of strong Buddhist influence.

In further missionary endeavours, East Syrians succeeded in bringing Christianity to the Turco-Mongol people. In the eleventh century, the Kerait south of Lake Baykal were converted. When Genghis Khan established his power in this area in the thirteenth century, Christianity had already spread among other Mongolian tribes, e.g. Naiman, Uighurs, Tangut, and Ongut (Tang 2011). When the Mongols conquered China, Christianity returned, no longer as a 'foreign' religion but as part of the new ruling class of the empire. Their further conquests in the West strengthened Central Asian Christianity.

When the Mongols captured Baghdad in 1258, missions flourished along the Silk Road from the Oxus to the Yellow Sea. The thirteenth and fourteenth centuries were the heyday of the Church of the East. However, in 1368 the Mongol-Yuan dynasty was expelled by the Ming after a long period of foreign rulers. In the reaction that followed, the Turco-Mongol people and many other non-Chinese groups were expelled, and with them went also the Christian faith. This second decline was so complete that the Jesuits, who reached China more than two hundred years later, were regarded as the very first Christians there.

In addition, the Mongol Il-Khans eventually turned to Islam. In the last decades of the fourteenth century, the cruel campaigns of the armies of Timur Lenk (Tamerlane 1336–1405) nearly wiped out the East Syriac Church in the Middle East. It shrunk to become a small community in the Hakkari Mountains and northern Mesopotamia. In the fifteenth century, its contacts with the Roman Catholic Church intensified, leading eventually to a major church union (see below, Chaldean Church).

At the beginning of the twentieth century, the 'Assyrians' – as they were called by Anglican missionaries (Coakley 1992) – counted only 150,000 members. Then, during World War I, they lost a further third of their population through massacres and deportations at the hands of Kurds and Turks in the Ottoman Empire because of their suspected collaboration with the British. In 1933, after the end of the British mandate in Iraq, the Iraqi government expelled the East Syrian patriarch, Mar Eshai Shimun, who finally went into exile to the United States. The people have been scattered all over the world (Coakley 1996: 179–98; Winkler 2009: 321–34).

In the 1960s, a schism within the Assyrian Church over questions of liturgy, calendar, and church leadership brought about a situation in which there are today two official churches, the 'Assyrian Church of the East', with approximately 385,000 members, and the 'Ancient Church of the East', which numbers perhaps 50–70,000 faithful in total. Both church heads currently reside in Baghdad.

The Syrian Orthodox Church

The Christological conflicts of the fifth century caused a schism within the patriarchate of Antioch. A large body of Christians, mainly those who spoke Syriac, repudiated the Christological formula of the Council of Chalcedon (451). At the time when the anti-Chaledonian Severus was the patriarch of Antioch (512–518), the Chalcedonian opposition covered Egypt, together with the provinces of Arabia, Syria, Osrhoëne, Armenia, Cilicia, Cappadocia, Thracia, and communities in Mesopotamia (Sélis 1988).

In 519, a Chalcedonian restoration was initiated under emperor Justin (519–527) and the anti-Chalcedonian bishops were deposed and exiled. Only Egypt was strong enough that patriarch Timothy III of Alexandria (517–535) could publicly condemn the Council of Chalcedon, the Tome of Pope Leo (449), and the Henoticon of Emperor Zeno (482). As a result, the most eminent theologian of the miaphysites (anti-Chalcedonians), Severus of Antioch, operated out of Egypt following his deposition in 519.

With the support of Empress Theodora, the patriarchal sees of the eastern Roman Empire were reconciled again. However, in 536, Pope Agapetus of Rome (535–536) arrived in Constantinople. He was forced into diplomatic and political action by the king of the Goths because the eastern Roman forces of Justinian were already moving towards Rome. The pope refused communion with patriarch Anthimos of Constantinople because of his anti-Chalcedonian attitude. Emperor Justinian (527–565) soon realised that it was better for his political plans of reuniting the whole Roman Empire if he maintained good relations with the west. Therefore, at a synod in Constantinople (536), Severus of Antioch and patriarch Anthimos of Constantinople were condemned. A new wave of persecution overtook the Anti-Chalcedonians. This time it also reached Egypt.

During the persecutions, Severus of Antioch authorised his associate John of Tellâ to ordain deacons, priests, and bishops to strengthen the anti-Chalcedonian movement. However, in 537, practically all anti-Chalcedonian priests and bishops, including John of Tellâ, became victims of the persecution or were deposed. Severus died in 538; the Antiochene anti-Chalcedonian party was without leaders.

Even the powerful patriarch of Alexandria, Theodosios (535–566), was exiled to Derkos in Thrace during this Chalcedonian restoration. In 539, he found a safe refuge in one of the palaces of empress Theodora in Constantinople. From there he was able to guide all those of the anti-Chalcedonian movement who had lost their bishops (Winkler 2006: 73–89). In 542, the ruler of the Ghassanid Arabs, who formed a pro-Byzantine buffer state in Syria, had asked Theodora for bishops. Theodosios ordained Theodore of Arabia as Metropolitan of Bostra and Jacob Baradai (Syr. *bûrd'ânâ*, from Greek *baradaios*, 'the ragged') as Metropolitan of Edessa. Theodore concerned himself with the Arab tribes in the Syrian Desert and the Transjordanian territory, while Jacob Baradai, whose name signifies the ragged cloak he wore to disguise himself as a beggar, ordained bishops and priests on his adventurous journeys from Syria, Armenia, and Asia Minor to Isauria and Egypt. He thereby laid the groundwork for a West Syriac anti-Chalcedonian church organisation.

Jacob became a symbol for this resurrection of West Syriac Christianity, which has been called 'Jacobite' after him. In 558/59, Jacob Baradai succeeded in ordaining a bishop of Takrit in the Sasanian Empire. With this event, the basis of a Syrian Orthodox hierarchy was established in Persia, although the Church of the East with its catholicos-patriarch in Seleucia-Ctesiphon still represented the majority of Christians in the Sasanian Empire.

The Chalcedonian patriarch of Antioch remained within the communion of the Imperial Church. He still had his see in the city, but the church had lost its power and mainly served the Greek community and a Syriac-speaking minority. The larger group of Antiochene Christians opposed Chalcedon and formed the Syrian Orthodox Church. Their patriarchs had to reside in secret, frequently in monasteries in North Syria or Mesopotamia. A dialogue between the two parties was hardly possible, mainly because of the political events of the seventh century.

Following the high point of Sasanian power under Shah Khosrow II (590–628), who conquered most of the Middle East between 602 and 619, the third decade of the seventh century was marked by the advance of emperor Heraclius (610–641). Since his rise to power, he had strengthened the eastern provinces. From 622 to 628 he undertook a noteworthy campaign against Persia. His political efforts were ideologically supported by his otherwise unsuccessful ecclesiastical politics, the propagation of the theological compromises of Monotheletism/Monoenergism (Lange 2012).

In 630, a treaty brought the region a few more years of temporary peace. During this time, from 609 to 629, the Orthodox (Chalcedonian) See of Antioch was vacant, while the Syrian Orthodox patriarch succeeded in promoting the bishopric of Takrit to a metropolitanate, who took residence in the monastery of Mar Mattai, north of Mosul. Since the eleventh century, this metropolitan used the title 'maphrian' (Syr. *maphryânâ*, the one who fructifies).

When the Arabs began to advance from the south to conquer the Middle East, the traditional powers of the Roman and Sasanian empires were exhausted from their wars. In 636, the Arabs defeated the Byzantine Army at the battle of Yarmuk. In 637 Antioch fell; Alexandria in 642. The Syrian Orthodox Christians appear to have looked upon the Muslim conquests with a guarded hope of increased freedom that would liberate them from the persecutions, bonds, and duties of the Christian empire of Byzantium. All Christian denominations now had the same status as 'people of the book' (*ahl al-kitâb*) and were treated as minorities under the protection of Islam (*dhimmis*).

In the course of the eighth and ninth centuries, the Syrian Orthodox Church had also to overcome a period of discord. The bishops of northern Mesopotamia gained strength and opposed the homeless patriarch. This led to two internal schisms. When the Byzantines regained possession of Antioch and North Syria (969–1085), the Chalcedonian patriarchate prospered while the Syrian Orthodox Church was persecuted again.

In 1085, Antioch fell to the Seljuk Turks, and in 1098, the Crusaders took Antioch. It was at that time that the Syrian Orthodox Church recovered and relations with the Roman Catholic Church started.

The Syrian Orthodox Church reached its climax in the twelfth and thirteenth centuries. There were bishoprics from Cyprus and Anatolia to Syria, Persia, and today's Afghanistan; further communities could be found in the Far East, in Turkistan and Sinkiang. Syriac literature and scholarship had its renaissance although the language was gradually displaced as a colloquial language by Arabic. Relations with Muslims continued along constructive lines.

From 1292 to 1495, the Syrian Orthodox Church again suffered from severe schisms. The division of the Middle East among different political powers supported the intracommunal rivalries. Up to four patriarchs were simultaneously in office: one in Mardin under Mongol rule, one in the monastery of Barsauma under the Mamluks, a third one in Sis in Cilicia, and a fourth one in the Ṭur ʿAbdin. The consequence of these schisms was not only the constant decay of the church and conversions to Islam, but also that individual bishops or metropolitans started negotiations with the Roman Catholic Church (see The Syrian Catholic Church).

The politics of the ʿAbbasid caliphate had caused substantial conversions of Christians to Islam already since the late eighth century. The numbers declined further late in the Middle Ages. Finally, the invasion of of Timur Lenkh in the fourteenth century destroyed most monasteries and churches. World War I and the post-war politics caused further terrible losses. The Syrian Orthodox Church remained a minority in Iraq, Syria, and Lebanon. But most of them left their home countries, especially the important Ṭur ʿAbdin in south-east Turkey (Hollerweger 2000). They migrated to Western Europe, or to North and South America. The patriarch of the Syrian Orthodox Church, with about 250,000 faithful, resides in Maarad Sednaya (Syria) and Damascus.

The Maronite Church

From the sixth century, the patriarchate of Antioch was split into two, the mainly Greek (but also some Syriac-speaking) patriarchate within the Roman Imperial Church, and the anti-Chalcedonian miaphysite (Syrian Orthodox) patriarchate. As a consequence of imperial politics and the Arab Conquest in the seventh century, the Antiochene Church suffered another schism and a third patriarchate came into being: the Maronite Church (Suermann 1998).

The name Maronites derives from a fifth century Syriac-speaking monastic community, which found its orientation in the life of the ascetic hermit Maron (d. ca. 410). The monastery Beit Maron was established on the banks of the Orontes River under the patronage of emperor Marcian to defend the Christological doctrine of Chalcedon. Emperors like Justinian (527–565), who pushed forward the Chalcedonian Christological teachings in the context of their imperial politics, became generous supporters of the monastery.

The Maronite community was at times characterised as Monothelete. However, the subject seems to be more one of semantics than of doctrine. Monotheletism was condemned at the Council of Constantinople (680/81) where Maronites could not take part because of the Arab invasion. After the conquest of Antioch, only titular patriarchs were assigned by Constantinople until 702. Afterwards, until 742, the Chalcedonian see of Antioch remained vacant, and the Chalcedonians were without a leader. Therefore, the bishops and monks of the surrounding area elected a patriarch by themselves. Maronite sources place this election in 685. In 745, the caliph recognised them as a separate community.

Because of persecutions, the Maronite community sought refuge in the inaccessible mountains of Lebanon in the ninth and tenth centuries. The Arab Conquest and the separation from the Chalcedonian patriarchs as well as the rupture between Rome and Constantinople left the Maronites in isolation, which was only broken in the times of the Crusades. Jeremias Al Amshitti (1199–1230) was the first Maronite patriarch to visit Rome, where he participated in the fourth Lateran Council (1215). Since that time, relations and communion between the Maronites and Rome have been uninterrupted.

Today the Maronites and their patriarch, who has resided in Bkerke north of Beirut since 1790, play a considerable role within the Lebanese state. Because of the political situation and especially the Lebanese civil war, there has been a steady decline in the number of Maronites in Lebanon. Today there are flourishing communities abroad, mainly in Western Europe, the Americas, and Australia, with about 1.5 million faithful worldwide.

CHURCH UNIONS WITH ROME

The Chaldean Church

In 1340, a group of East Syriac Christians in Cyprus placed themselves under the Catholic Church. The Catholics referred to them as the 'Chaldeans'. This union was successfully renewed by the council of Ferrara-Florence in 1445. The East Syriac bishop received the title 'Archiepiscoporum Chaldeorum, qui in Cypro sunt'. However, little by little the Chaldeans of Cyprus dissolved into local Maronite and Latin communities already by 1489.

In the fourteenth century, Christian Mongol diplomats reached the West. The most famous of these was the Uighur monk Bar Ṣauma, who was sent by the Mongolian Il-Khan (Budge 1928; Toepel 2008). According to his account, Bar Ṣauma celebrated the East Syriac Liturgy in Rome and finally received the Eucharist from the hand of the pope. It was through Bar Ṣauma's journey that the Roman Curia became acquainted with the known Church of the East, which had reached its greatest extent under Yahballaha III (1291–1317), from Jerusalem to China and India, with its centre in Baghdad, but which had been little known until then.

However, following the political transformation of China, when the Ming dynasty took power, and after the military campaigns of Timur Lenkh in the Middle East, only a handful of churches in northern Mesopotamia and the remote Hakkari mountains of Kurdistan survived into the fifteenth century. The patriarchal office had become hereditary, which had the result that one family dominated the church. This led to schism, especially when untrained minors were being elected to the patriarchal throne. By 1552, the catholicos-patriarch Shemun Bar Mama had become so unpopular that numerous opponents, especially from the regions of Amid (Diyarbakir) and Seert, met in an anti-synod at Mosul. They elected as patriarch Yohannan Sulaqa, superior of the monastery of Rabban Hormizd. The dignitaries and clerics under the influence of western missionaries sent a delegation to Rome to explain the situation and there he was consecrated bishop and patriarch. His profession of faith was recognised. Believing that Shemun Bar Mama had died, Rome confirmed Sulaqa as 'Patriarch of Mosul' on April 28, 1553 (Habbi 1966: 199–230).

When Sulaqa returned to Mesopotamia, he established himself in Amid and ordained two metropolitans and three bishops. However, catholicos-patriarch Shemun Bar Mama won over the pasha (governor) of Amadiyia, who invited Sulaqa to visit him, but then had him imprisoned and tortured for four months, and finally put him death in January 1555. The Chaldean Church regards him as a martyr of union with Rome (de Vries 1952: 236–52).

The five bishops consecrated by Sulaqa elected a successor, who obtained recognition by Pope Pius IV in 1562. The succeeding patriarchs remained in communion with Rome until the seventeenth century. However, when patriarch Shemun XIII Dinkha (1662–1700) definitively moved his see to Qudshanis in the remote Hakkari mountains, this patriarchal line gradually returned to the traditional doctrine. The patriarchate remained relatively isolated and Rome lost contact with Qudshanis. It is unclear when the patriarchate became hereditary again, a principle that ended only in 1974. The present Assyrian Church of the East traces its descent from this line, and its patriarchate is a continuation of the Sulaqa line and of the Qudshanis patriarchate.

In 1667, Capuchin missionaries worked among the East Syrians in Amid and in 1672 convinced their metropolitan Joseph to become a Catholic. In 1677 he gained recognition by the civil authorities as an independent archbishop with jurisdiction over Amid and Mardin. Rome confirmed him in 1681 as Joseph I, 'Patriarch of the Chaldean nation deprived of its patriarch'. The successors in the patriarchal line of Amid had significant success in spreading the Catholic faith within their own jurisdiction and also in the territories of the Mosul patriarchate. But in the following decades, there were severe conflicts between those in favour of being united with Rome and those who were not.

In 1804, Augustine Hindi became bishop of Amid and patriarchal administrator. He was not given the title patriarch because at that time Rome saw the possibility of uniting the then various East Syriac patriarchates (Habbi 1971: 121–43, 305–27). Although never fully recognised by the pope, Hindi's service was rewarded with the pallium in 1818, which he interpreted as a confirmation of his patriarchal status. With his death in 1828, the patriarchate of Amid, which had existed in communion with Rome for 146 years, expired. There was always only one officially recognised Catholic patriarch, in contrast to the Assyrian lines, where there were patriarchates in Qudshanis, Amid, and Mosul.

The Mosul patriarchate had retained the influential monastery of Rabban Hormizd, and its patriarchs were descendants of the old patriarchal line. Rome therefore especially wanted to gain the line of the Mosul patriarchate and to bring it into communion with the Catholic Church. This was finally achieved early in the nineteenth century in the person of Yohannan Hormizd, who came from the old patriarchal family. After conflicts between various metropolitans and patriarchs, Pope Pius VIII finally confirmed Yohannan Hormizd as the only 'Patriarch of Babylon of the Chaldeans' on 5 July 1830. At that time, two East Syriac patriarchates, those of Amid and Mosul, were reunited and were in communion with Rome. Only the Qudshanis patriarchate remained isolated.

Since 1830, the old patriarchal line of the Church of the East has been in communion with the Roman Catholic Church. To block Yohannan Hormizd's attempt to preserve the patriarchal succession in his family, Rome appointed a coadjutor with the right of succession. In 1844, an Ottoman imperial firman recognised the patriarch of the 'Chaldeans'. Thus, the Chaldean Church was legally established as a nation (*millet*).

Today, the Chaldeans are the most important Christian community in Iraq, with its patriarch residing in Baghdad. Because of the wars and conflicts in the Middle East, most Chaldeans emigrated and developed communities all over the world, consisting of about 420,000 members.

The Syrian Catholic Church

While the deposition of the Greek Orthodox patriarchate of Antioch and the establishment of a Latin patriarchate by the Crusaders cut a deep wound into the Byzantine Orthodox community, the relations between the Crusaders and the Syrian Orthodox Church were friendly and cordial. The Syrian Orthodox patriarch Michael I the Great (1166–1199) praised the tolerance of the Crusaders and the relations between the two churches. The highly respected patriarch was even invited by Pope Alexander III to participate in the third Lateran Council (1179); he, however, refused to come. The friendly relations between the two churches led to a strong desire for union (de Vries 1956: 137–57). This pro-Roman sentiment allowed a rival of Michael's to bring the greater part of the community in Jerusalem over to the Catholic community (1183).

In 1237, patriarch Ignatius II David al-Haishûmi (1222–1252) visited Jerusalem and in the presence of the Dominican provincial, Philip, he made his submission to Rome. Nevertheless, the church did not follow its head, and only a small portion of the Syriac community, based in Tripoli, maintained the union. Ignatius resigned his office as patriarch after his submission and entered the Order of the Friars Preachers in the Holy Land. With the collapse of the Latin power in the Holy Land, even long before the ultimate surrender of Acre (1291), the rapprochement came to an end for the time being in this region.

From the thirteenth to the fifteenth centuries, individual bishops were seeking union with the Roman Church because of the various schisms that arose within the Syrian Orthodox Church, which at times had up to four patriarchs. However, all those remained personal unions. A more formal contact was made at the council of Florence (1438–1445), which also announced the union between the Catholic and the Syrian Orthodox churches. But the fall of Constantinople to the Ottomans (1453) and the complicated ecclesiastical divisions of the Syrian Orthodox Church led to the decree of union being repudiated by the vast majority of West Syriac Christians. There were constant but unsuccessful attempts at union in the course of the fifteenth and sixteenth centuries.

By the seventeenth century, Latin orders and missionaries had spread throughout the Middle East and were focused especially on Aleppo with its sizable Christian population. They were so successful that by the end of the century a majority of West Syriac Christians had been received into communion with Rome. The Syrian Orthodox patriarch Ignatius Shimun I had been convinced to install a Catholic as archbishop of the Syriac *millet* in Aleppo. The patriarch contacted the missionaries, who suggested Andrew Akhijan as a qualified candidate. Andrew was a

Syrian Orthodox Christian who, in 1643, had converted to the Catholic Church under the influence of Carmelite and Jesuit missionaries. When Andrew arrived in Aleppo, the Syrian Orthodox patriarch, who was originally willing to install him, was offended that the Catholic Maronite patriarch had been asked to consecrate his bishop and refused to accept Akhijan. It was not possible to reconcile the frequent succeeding conflicts between Catholic and Orthodox Syriac Christians and Andrew had to take refuge in Lebanon. However, Andrew was officially recognised by the pope as the legitimate archbishop of Aleppo. Consequently, the efforts of the archbishop, the missionary activity of the Latin orders, and the material help of the French consul together led to the enlargement of the Catholic Syriac community.

When in 1661 the Syrian Orthodox patriarch died in Mardin, Catholic missionaries and the French wanted to have Akhijan nominated as patriarch. By that, the Syriac *millet* should have entered the Catholic Church as a whole. There was no intention to double the hierarchy. With French diplomatic support, Andrew Akhijan was elected patriarch and the sultan confirmed him as the head of the Syriac nation with a firman.

After the death of patriarch Andrew Akhijan, severe conflicts over his succession shook the West Syriac community and finally led to a vacancy in the Syrian Catholic patriarchate which lasted until the eighteenth century. The majority of the Syriac Christians, who had followed Andrew Akhijan in Aleppo, returned to the Syrian Orthodox Church under its patriarch.

It was not until the second half of the eighteenth century that the Syriac Catholic Church was revitalised. In 1774, the Syrian Orthodox archbishop of Aleppo, Michael Jarweh, formally joined the Catholic Church. After the death of the Syrian Orthodox patriarch in 1781, Michael was invited by a group of orthodox bishops to accept the patriarchate of their church. Michael agreed to the invitation under the condition that the bishops had to promise to become Catholic. Early in 1782, four out of the six bishops convened in Deir al-Zaʾfarân (monastery), accepted Catholicism, and elected him patriarch. He was enthroned as Ignatius Michael III (1783–1800). Because Michael had started as the canonically elected head of the Syrian Church, he received papal confirmation in 1783 as 'patriarch of Antioch'. The Catholic Church considered continuing the ancient anti-Chalcedonian West Syriac Church renewed in communion with Rome.

Unfortunately for Michael and his followers, he did not receive the confirmation of the sultan. The two bishops who had not joined the Catholic Church ordained four other bishops and elected another patriarch, who received confirmation from the sultan. Immediately following this, Michael Jarweh was dispossessed and sought refuge in Lebanon. His reign became one of exile and imprisonment. In Lebanon, the Maronite Church helped him to obtain a see in the mountains at Sharfeh. However, with Michael Jarweh began an uninterrupted succession in communion with Rome. Finally in 1830, the Syrian Catholic Church was officially recognised as its own millet by the Ottoman Empire. Thus, the West Syriac millet was divided into two hierarchies.

Today, there are about 208,000 Syrian Catholics, mainly in Lebanon, Iraq, and Syria. Syriac is still spoken in some villages in northern Iraq and eastern Syria, but the common language today is Arabic.

SYRIAC CHURCHES IN INDIA: THE THOMAS CHRISTIANS

Since ancient times, a Christian community has existed at the Malabar Coast in southwest India, in contact with Christianity in Persia (Vellian 1970). According to tradition, it was the Apostle Thomas who landed on the Malabar coast in AD 52, where he founded seven churches. He is supposed to have travelled further to the Koromandel coast, where he suffered martyrdom in AD 68 at Mylapore near Madras. The very obscure and complex question of the historicity of Apostolic origin has been meticulously studied in modern scholarship, including some noteworthy evidence affirming the Indian mission of the Apostle Thomas (Nedungatt 2008; but see esp. ch.33 in this volume).

The Thomas Christians were in full communion with the Church of the East but not affected by the developments in the Middle East. They formed their own ecclesial reality while using an East Syriac liturgical rite.

The Church of the East had regularly sent bishops as metropolitans to the Malabar Coast to ordain priests and bishops. These Persian bishops were usually not able to speak the local language, and therefore the real civil and religious power over the entire Indian Christian community was in the hands of a local priest with the title 'Archdeacon of All India'. Until the arrival of the Portuguese in India, the Thomas Christians constituted a single and undivided church.

The colonisation of 1498 marks a turn in the history of Syriac Christianity in India. At first, the newcomers were received as fellow Christians, and Catholic priests could celebrate in the churches of the Thomas Christians while the oriental bishops were welcomed in Portuguese chapels. But the following history of encounter, clash, and Latinisation between European Christian colonial powers and genuine Indian Syriac Christianity led to lasting schisms (Pallath 2010).

The Malankara Jacobite Syrian Orthodox Church

At the so-called Synod of Diamper (1599), the local clergy was forced to reject the East Syriac patriarch 'of Babylon' – who in fact was in full communion with Rome at that time – as a Nestorian heretic and schismatic. Moreover, the 'Synod' started a comprehensive process of Latinisation in liturgy and discipline. Candidates to the priesthood were educated in the Latin rite, but were unable to celebrate their East Syriac rite after ordination. While modern observers have claimed that the Synod of Diamper was invalid (Nedungatt 2001), it nonetheless had its fatal impact on the history of Syriac Christianity in India.

The Thomas Christians resented these and succeeding humiliations. An assembly took place in a church at Mattancherry in 1653, which took a solemn oath – the so-called Coonan Cross Oath – no longer to obey the Latin Archbishop or any other Jesuits. Twelve priests placed their hands on the archdeacon and the first ecclesial division among the Thomas Christians was sealed.

The Coonan Cross Oath was not against the see of Rome, but against the Latin archbishop and the missionary work of the Jesuits. This situation led to investigations by Rome to pacify the members of the churches, but it was also intended subtly to eradicate the Syrian rite. The result was a hardening of the split into a party in communion with Rome and a party which joined the Syrian

Orthodox Church of Antioch in 1665 and thus changed its liturgical rite to West Syriac.

The 'Malankara Jacobite Syrian Orthodox Church', as it is called today, has its own catholicos and is an autonomous church of the Syrian Orthodox Church of Antioch. It has about 1.2 million members. This Indian West Syriac Church suffered further divisions in the nineteenth and twentieth centuries.

The Malankara Orthodox Syrian Church

Because of jurisdictional disputes, a part of this autonomous church declared itself completely independent (autocephalous) from the Syrian Orthodox patriarchate of Antioch in 1912.

The two factions – one loyal to Antioch, the other independent – were reconciled only in 1958, when the Indian Supreme court declared that only the autocephalous part had legal standing. In 1975, the Syrian Orthodox patriarch excommunicated the catholicos of the autocephalous Malankara Orthodox Syrian Church, which resulted in another schism. Attempts at reconciliation in the following decades were not fruitful. Severe quarrels over church property and court suits followed. In 1995, the supreme Indian court decided that the Syrian Orthodox patriarch of Antioch was the spiritual head of the universal Syrian Church, while the autocephalous catholicos had legal standing as the head of the entire church, and that he was custodian of its parishes and properties. This decision did not, however, result in peace and even up to the present day the two groups, referred to as 'patriarchal' and 'autocephalous', remain jurisdictionally separate, even though theologically they are in full communion.

Today the autocephalous Malankara Orthodox Syrian Church is said to have about 2.5 million members.

The Syro-Malankara Catholic Church

Since the eighteenth century there have been several attempts to reconcile the Catholic Church with those Thomas Christians who had become Syrian Orthodox. In the 1920s, the opposition to the jurisdiction of the Syrian Orthodox patriarch of Antioch resulted not only in the autocephalous Malankara Orthodox Syrian Church, but also in several bishops carrying out negotiations with Rome.

The highly erudite Mystic Mar Ivanios had founded the first monastic communities within the Malankara Orthodox Syrian Church. In 1930, he and his chorepiscopos Mar Theophilose became Catholic. Soon two more bishops from the Malankara Orthodox Syrian Church followed. They asked only that their liturgy should be preserved and that they should be allowed to keep their dioceses. A significant number of faithful followed them into the newly named Syro-Malankara Catholic Church. Pope John Paul II raised this church to the rank of a major archepiscopal church in 2005. It has about 420,000 members.

The Syro-Malabar Catholic Church

Catholic missionary efforts in the years following the Coonan Cross Oath were so successful that by 1662 the majority of Thomas Christians had re-entered communion with Rome. However, until the end of the nineteenth century, it was European Carmelites who served as bishops for the 'Syro-Malabar Catholic Church' – as it has been called since 1840 – and there was a constant danger of commotion. Gradually, Rome realised that granting true autonomy and self-government was the best solution, and cautiously changed its policy. In 1896, three vicariates apostolic for the Thomas Christians (Trichur, Ernakulam, and Changanacherry), under the guidance of indigenous Syro-Malabar bishops, were established by Rome. Another was founded for Kottayam in 1911. In 1923, a complete Syro-Malabar Catholic hierarchy was established. This autonomy led to a flourishing renewal of the church. While in 1876 there were approximately 200,000 Syro-Malabar Catholics, today they number almost four million.

Since 1934, there have been attempts to re-establish the genuine East Syriac rite, and in 1962 the Chaldean Pontifical was introduced. But Latin rite priests and bishops of the Syro-Malabar Church opposed those who wanted to preserve the old Syriac rite and identified them as 'traditionalists'. In 1986 Pope John Paul II reintroduced the revised Syriac liturgy personally in Kottayam, but the question of the liturgy is still not clarified (Karukaparambil 2008). In 1993, the Syro-Malabar Catholic Church was elevated to a major archbishopbric.

The Malabar Independent Syrian Church and the Mar Thoma Syrian Church of Malabar

In 1757, a Syrian orthodox bishop from Jerusalem ordained an opponent of the legitimate metropolitan. This bishop, Mar Cyril, had to flee to the north where he established the Malabar Independent Syrian Church in the village of Thozhiyur (Kerala) with about 10,000 faithful. Today it maintains relations with Lutheran and Anglican churches, such as the Mar Thoma Syrian Church of Malabar. The latter is the product of a reform under the patronage of Anglican missionaries among the Thomas Christians. Despite the western influence, this church of about 1.6 million members has preserved its Syriac and oriental heritage. The Mar Thoma Syrian Church is ecumenically oriented and has an episcopal character.

BIBLIOGRAPHY

Baum, Wilhelm and Dietmar W. Winkler. 2003. *The Church of the East: A Concise History*. London and New York: Routledge Curzon.

Brock, Sebastian P. 1996. The 'Nestorian' Church: A Lamentable Misnomer. *BJRL* 78(3), 23–36.

———. 2006. *An Introduction to Syriac Studies*. Piscataway, NJ: Gorgias Press.

Budge, Ernest A. Wallis. 1928. *The Monks of Ḳûblâi Khân, Emperor of China*. London: Religious Tract Society.

Coakley, J. F. 1992. *The Church of the East and the Church of England: A History of the Archbishop of Canterbury's Assyrian Mission*. Oxford: Oxford University Press.

———. 1996. The Church of the East Since 1914. *BJRL* 78, 179–98.

De Vries, Wilhelm. 1952. Nel quarto centenario della Chiesa cattolica caldea. *Civiltà Cattolica* 103, 236–52.

———. 1956. Dreihundert Jahre syrisch-katholische Hierarchie. *Ostkirchliche Studien* 5, 137–57.

Gutas, Dimtri. 1998. *Greek Thought, Arabic Culture: The Graeco-Arabic Translation Movement in Baghdad and Early Abbasid Society*. London and New York: Routledge.

Habbi, Joseph. 1966. Signification de l'union chaldéenne de Mar Sulaqa avec Rome en 1553. *OS* 11, 99–132; 199–230.

———. 1971. L'Unification de la hiérarchie chaldéenne dans la première moitié du XIXe siècle. *PdO* 2, 121–43; 305–27.

Hollerweger, Hans. 2000. *Lebendiges Kulturerbe Turabdin: Wo die Sprache Jesu gesprochen wird/Living Cultural Heritage Turabdin: Where Jesus' language is spoken*. Linz: Friends of Turabdin.

Karukaparambil, Cherian. 2008. *Identity – Restoration – Renewal: The Syro-Malabar Church Since Vatican II in the Context of Her Ecumenical Task as a Catholic Eastern Church*. Salzburg: Theol. Diss.

Lange, Christian. 2012. *Mia Energeia. Untersuchungen zur Einigungspolitik des Kaisers Heraclius und des Patriarchen Sergius von Constantinopel*. Studien und Texte zu Antike und Christentum 66. Tübingen: Mohr Siebeck.

Malek, Roman. 2006. *Jingjiao. The Church of the East in China and Central Asia*. Sankt Augustin: Institut Monumenta Serica.

Nedungatt, George. 2001. *The Synod of Diamper Revisited*. Kanonika 9. Rome: Pontifical Oriental Institute.

———. 2008. *Quest for the Historical Thomas, Apostle of India: A Re-reading of the Evidence*. Bangalore: Theological Publications in India.

Pallath, Paul. 2010. *The Catholic Church in India*. Completely revised, updated and elaborated Indian edition. Kottayam: OIRSI.

Sako, Louis R. 1986. *Le rôle de la hiérarchie syriaque orientale dans les rapports diplomatiques entre la Perse et Byzance aux Ve-VIIe siècles*. Paris.

Sélis, Claude. 1988. *Les Syriens orthodoxies et catholiques*. Fils d'Abraham. Turnhout: Brepols.

Suermann, Harald. 1998. *Die Gründungsgeschichte der Maroniten*. Orientalia biblica et christiana 10. Wiesbaden: Harrasowitz.

Tang, Li. 2011. *East Syriac Christianity in Mongol-Yuan China*. Orientalia biblica et christiana 18. Wiesbaden: Harrasowitz.

Tang, Li and Dietmar W. Winkler. 2013. *From the Oxus River to the Chinese Shores: Studies on East Syriac Christianity in China and Central Asia*. orientalia – patristica – oecumenica vol. 5. Berlin: LIT.

———. 2016. *Winds of Jingjiao. Studies on Syriac Christianity in China and Central Asia*. orientalia - patristica - oecumenica 9. Berlin: LIT.

Toepel, Alexander. 2008. *Die Mönche des Kublai Khan. Die Reise der Pilger Mar Yahballaha und Rabban Sauma nach Europa*. Darmstadt: Wissenschaftliche Buchgesellschaft.

Vellian, Jacob. 1970. *The Malabar Church*. OCA 186. Rome: Pontifical Oriental Institute.

Winkler, Dietmar W. 2003. *Ostsyrisches Christentum. Untersuchungen zu Christologie, Ekklesiologie und zu den ökumenischen Beziehungen der Assyrischen Kirche des Ostens*. Studien zur Orientalischen Kirchengeschichte 26. Berlin: LIT.

———. 2006. Theodosios of Alexandria and Some Theological Trends of His Time (535–566). *The Harp* 21, 73–89.

———. 2009. East Syriac Christianity in Iraq: A Glance at History From the First World War Until Today. *In*: Winkler and Tang 2009, 321–34.

———. 2012. Nestorius (um 381–451/453). *In*: Gregor M. Hoff and Ulrich H.J. Körtner, ed., *Arbeitsbuch Theologiegeschichte. Diskurse-Akteure-Wissensformen, Vol. 1: 2.–15. Jh.* Stuttgart: Kohlhammer, 148–65.

———. 2016. Les débuts de la collaboration entre les Églises orientales orthodoxes au XXe siècle. *Istina* 61, 201–12.

Winkler, Dietmar W., and Li Tang. 2009. *Hidden Treasures and Intercultural Encounters. Studies on East Syriac Christianity in China and Central Asia*. orientalia – patristica – oecumenical vol. 1. Berlin: LIT.

CHAPTER EIGHT

THE SYRIAC WORLD IN THE PERSIAN EMPIRE

Geoffrey Herman

INTRODUCTION

Gospel legend places the first encounter between Christianity and the Persian world with the very birth of Jesus and the visit of the Persian Magi to Judea (Matthew 2:1–12). The main period of intercourse between Christians and Persians occurred, however, with the introduction of Christianity into the Persian realm and its expansion there, particularly within the framework of the Sasanian Empire (224–651 CE). This chapter will therefore follow the experience of the Syriac Christians living in this Persian world.

THE SPREAD OF CHRISTIANITY TO PERSIA

The arrival of Christians in the Sasanian Empire and the establishment of the first Christian communities there is told in many different ways.[1] Contemporary historical evidence points to the existence of pockets of Christians in this region already in the second and third centuries. The literary trail reveals a steady trickle of Christians following the established trade routes through northern Mesopotamia, and they may have migrated through Osrhoene (Edessa), Adiabene (Arbela), and Armenia. Later, some Persian communities would trace their arrival to the period of Sasanian incursions into Roman territory by Shapur I (241–272 CE), and the subsequent deportations to Persia of the Roman population of the conquered areas. The proportion of Christians among the Roman population of the regions conquered and deported by the Sasanians in this early period can only be guessed.

There are other signs of a growing Christian presence in the third century. Archaeological remains place a Christian community on the Persian Gulf island of Khārg from the third century (Lerner 1991). A Christian place of worship is known in Dura Europas from 232 CE, which was then under Roman dominion (Kraeling 1967: 34–9, 140). One should, however, probably hesitate before accepting the entire testimony of the early third century *Book of the Laws of Countries*, which speaks broadly of Christians in the Persian realm in Parthia, Media, Kāshān, and Pārs. This statement is employed for the sake of his philosophical argument, but as an expression of precise ethnography it may be found wanting. The emergence of Manichaeism in the third century also presumes the existence of Christian sects within late Parthian and early Sasanian Babylonia. Further evidence is provided by the prominence given to Christians in the late-third-century inscription put up by the powerful court Magus, Kerdīr at Kaʿba-yi Zardušt (Back 1978: 384). It suggests that by then there may have been a significant Christian presence within the Sasanian realm.

Later sources and, in particular, church chronicles assert the establishment of Christianity and its hierarchical organisation on Persian soil much earlier than the third century. However, while the veracity of such claims cannot be verified, their polemical purpose is self-evident. Typically, these sources promote the prestige of particular regions or cities within the Sasanian Empire. This could be accomplished by asserting an unbroken apostolic link, whether through Addai, Mar Mari, or others.[2] The *Chronicle of Arbela* (Kawerau 1985) is one such source. For Edessa, it is the *Doctrine of Addai* that makes this claim.

ORGANISATION AND STRUCTURE

The hierarchical structure of the Christians of the Sasanian Empire is described in detail in the synod proceedings of the church, beginning in the early fifth century. It tended to reflect the imperial administrative geography (Gyselen 1989). If we follow the attendance records within the proceedings, we can plot a steady expansion of Christian communities eastwards in the course of time. At a synod held in Seleucia-Ctesiphon in 410 CE, representatives of six metropolitan sees and a few dozen bishoprics were in attendance, reaching a total of ten metropolitan sees and ninety-six bishoprics by the end of the Sasanian kingdom. How the disparate Christian communities of the empire were organised before this landmark synod is hard to determine with confidence. The testimony of Aphrahaṭ, a Christian author who flourished in the first half of the fourth century, suggests that in his time there was a centralised hierarchy of some kind, at least for Mesopotamia (Herman 2012: 123–32). He devoted one of his *demonstrations* to a passionate critique of the excessive powers acquired by the Christian authorities in Seleucia-Ctesiphon and their abuse (Parisot 1894: 573–726).

An issue of the foremost significance was the power relationship between the church in the Persian Empire and the ecclesiastical hierarchy of the West, that is, the Roman Empire. While the synod proceedings of the synod in 410 CE describes in detail Roman involvement in the person of Marutha, bishop of the Roman city of Martyropolis, the synod held by Dadīshōʿ in 424 CE emphasised the independence of the Persian Church from Rome. This independence, in theory and in practice, was an important development in maintaining the status of the Persian Church as autocephalous, not subordinate to the church authorities of the Roman sphere.

The bishop of Seleucia-Ctesiphon, the imperial capital, acquired first the title 'catholicos' and subsequently is referred to in the sources as a 'catholicos-patriarch'. The presence of the royal palace there was a vital component in the elevation of this city within the Christian hierarchical structure and its claims to pre-eminence. The bishop of Seleucia-Ctesiphon could rely upon the direct support of the king, but this contention of pre-eminence was not uncontested. Bet Lapaṭ, a city in a different province, Huzestan, also hosted a synod in 484 CE. Its ability to do so can be explained by the presence there of the summer royal residence. These same synod proceedings, and other sources such as the *Acts of Miles*, attest, then, to lively competition between the various provinces and cities over rank and hierarchy. They reveal, notwithstanding the declarations of denial in a few sources, the closely negotiated power dynamic in the relationship between the regions. The considerable politicisation of the church leadership is evidenced by the frequent involvement of the crown in the choice and endorsement of the new catholicoi.

ROME, PERSECUTION, MARTYRDOM, AND PERSIA

Notwithstanding the close connections between the leadership of the Persian Church and the royal crown, and, in particular, the church's dependence on the crown for its authority, more familiar to many is the vexation it underwent. The church of the Persian East has a reputation as long-suffering, having endured repeated persecutions, such that it would eventually acquire for itself the image of 'the church of the martyrs'. An early example of Persian antagonism towards the Christians, albeit alongside other non-Zoroastrian faiths, is found in Kerdīr's monumental inscriptions from the late third century in which he boasts of smiting Christians (Back 1978: 384). The main accounts of persecution, however, belong to a later period.

It was with the Christianisation of the Roman Empire in the early fourth century that the politicisation of the condition of the Christian inhabitants of the Sasanian Empire really began. The first source to bear witness to this change is a letter allegedly sent by Constantine to Shapur II (309–379 CE). This letter, recorded by Eusebius in his *Vita Constantini* (4, 8–13), expresses concern over the welfare of the Persian Christians. Soon after, it would seem, the Persian kings confirmed these fears and turned against the Christians of the empire.

The key evidence of persecution is found in the acts of the Persian martyrs, dozens of accounts of varying length recounting, often in sordid detail, the martyrdom of Christians in various locations throughout the Sasanian Empire. They are mostly written and preserved in Syriac, but some have reached us in translation in Greek, Arabic, and other languages.[3] The accounts tend to cluster in certain periods. The majority relate to the reign of Shapur II. Most of the other sources describe bouts of persecution occurring under the following Persian kings: Yazdgird I (399–420), Warahrān V (421–438), Yazdgird II (439–457), Khosrow I (531–579), and Khosrow II (591–628).

The true extent of the persecution is hard to determine, and the figures provided by various authors lack conviction. The total number of martyrs given by Sozomen, for instance, just for the reign of Shapur II is 16,000. In one Syriac account, *Mar Bassus and Suzanne*, we hear that Shapur massacred 9,000 Christians in one day (Bedjan 1894: 475). The figures provided in the Armenian *Life of Marutha of Maipherkat* are even more bombastic. This cleric, acting under the political reconciliation between Rome and Persia at the time of Yazdgird I, was said to have brought to his see an astonishing number of martyr relics. The number of martyrs was 20,000 from 'Asorestan' (Babylonia), 80,000 from 'the kingdom of the Persians', and 60,000 from Armenia (Marcus 1932: 68).

In an effort to reconcile the striking contrast between the evidence of a more serene state of coexistence for Christians, and that for persecution, it has been suggested by scholars that while the Christians were left in peace, there were heightened incidences of religious persecution at times of acute conflict between Rome and Persia. Persian Christianity was then viewed with suspicion by the authorities as a fifth column. This accusation of secretly supporting Rome is, in fact, explicit in a number of martyrdom sources (Brock 1982). Other explanations have been offered for this said Zoroastrian persecution of Christianity. Zoroastrians would have objected to the conversion of their brethren to Christianity, which was, in fact, forbidden by Persian law. The extent of Christian conversion of Zoroastrians, however, is hard to discern, lest we take the claims of the tendentious Christian sources at face value.

The way in which these martyrdom accounts are read by scholars has actually undergone a major change over the years. Earlier scholars explored the historical veracity of these accounts, distinguishing between the more credible and fictional accounts and identifying their legendary elements. More recent efforts, however, have been devoted to probing the function they serve in the social consolidation of the Christian communities that wrote and preserved them. Thus, far from seeing them as records of the historical events of the times they describe, scholars ask how they contributed towards the creation of communal values and the development of local Christian identity at the time they were put down in writing. Few of these martyrdom accounts are believed to be truly contemporary to the events they depict. One of the objectives of some of these compositions was to grapple with the conflicts facing Christians within the Persian world and its values. One encounters debate between the prospective martyrs and Zoroastrian priests or the king on various theological issues, and these give ear to the promotion of Christian values. Not only are scholars looking for different things in these martyrdom texts, however, but the assumption that their portrayal of the condition of Christians in the Sasanian Empire is fundamentally accurate in the big picture, even if not in the more legendary details, has been brought into question. For instance, the works of Ephrem, a native of Nisibis who lived in Edessa during the reign of Shapur, seem to be hardly touched by the image of Shapur II as the arch-persecutor of the Christians. Instead, Ephrem's focus remains on the Roman Empire, the events surrounding the rise and fall of the emperor Julian, and the change in the position of Christianity during Julian's reign. His hymns, many of which do mention Shapur in some detail, seem to suggest that Shapur's reputation as a persecutor of Christianity entirely passed him by (Griffith 1987; Smith 2016).

It is not clear, then, whether Persia really was the arch-persecutor of Christianity in Late Antiquity. What is clear, however, and is in evidence in so many of the texts and descriptions that we find, is the burning desire of Rome to depict Persia in this role. A long history of conflict between Rome and Persia had prepared them for this moment. With Persia and its Parthian forebears perceived as constituting the greatest and ultimate threat to Roman civilisation, there was a long tradition of imagining Persia playing the role of the barbarian threat, cruel, pernicious, and intimidating. This tradition was now inherited by the newly Christian empire. The only transformation that had occurred was the addition of the element of religion into this conflict. The existence of a Christian community in the Sasanian Empire was manipulated by the Romans from the very start, in the context of their political regional aspirations. Already Constantine had cynically treated the situation of the Persian Christians as a tool and pretext for Roman intervention in the affairs of the Sasanian Empire. This view of Persia was nurtured by the Romans on both local and imperial levels. Many of the martyrdom narratives were composed on the Roman side of the border, and Romans could be portrayed in these accounts as saviours for Persian Christian victims. Accounts would tell of the timely arrival of Roman envoys who would save the martyr from his peril. We see the dramatisation of this literature, the export of the genre and its adaptation to the Persian milieu, and the construction of *martyria* to house the relics of these martyrs.[4] All this sustained a demonised image of the Persian Empire, its king and religion, and served to polarise the opposition and to perpetuate a state of conflict.

Notwithstanding the allegations evident in many of the ancient sources, the extent to which Persian Christians actually endorsed Constantine and his successors' claims to represent their welfare, or put their trust in Rome in light of its conversion to Christianity, are hard to gauge. While at least one early Syriac author, Aphrahaṭ, *did* pin his hopes on a Roman conquest of Persia (*Demonstrations* 5:1, 24; Barnes 1985), the degree to which the Persians themselves perceived their Christian citizens as disloyal simply because they practiced the same religion as their Roman foe remains unclear. Persian Christianity itself certainly had every good reason to believe this and was at pains to distance itself from Rome on a political level. The synod of 424 CE, as already noted, had formally declared the independence of Persian Christianity from the ecclesiastical authorities found in the Roman Empire.

In some ways, it is actually the very same martyrdom literature that serves to nuance the image of persecution we have spoken of. Indeed, while a hostile attitude towards the Persian Christians is in evidence in many of the martyrdom sources, these contrast with the more subtle depictions of interaction with Persia found in some of the other martyrdom accounts, which may perhaps better reflect conditions within the Sasanian Empire. In these martyrdom acts, a far more complex relationship with Persia finds expression. We encounter Christian protagonists who declare their profound and uncompromising loyalty to the crown in spite of their predicament, expounding their conviction that there is no contradiction in their identity. It is possible to be both politically Persian and religiously Christian. An image of the Sasanian Empire, too, is created in these sources to confirm this thesis. The Persian king stands in contrast with the magi. He is portrayed as neutral and reluctant to punish the Christian martyr; whilst the Magi are presented as the instigators (Walker 2006: 54–5; Herman 2014: 78, 82; Herman 2016: 4). Cruelty and friction, then, are associated specifically with the Magi, whereas hesitation, regret, and concern belong to the king.

If the king is often portrayed as sympathetic to the martyrs, the mirror image of this occurs where the martyrs declare their absolute loyalty to the king and emphasise a distinction between loyalty to one's religion and loyalty to the kingdom. One of the more emphatic pronouncements to this effect is made by a martyr named Gushtazad, who features in Simeon bar Ṣabbaʿe's *History* and *Martyrdom* cycle. In these texts, the martyrs underline their loyalty to the king and a careful distinction emerges between the person and the religion of the king (Smith 2014: 44, 144). Such an approach is more in line with the kind of sentiment that *this* community would probably have wished to express for itself.

While we may be right to assume that the condition of the Persian Christians was less oppressive than earlier scholarly accounts assumed, there were, nevertheless, areas of friction between Zoroastrianism and Christianity, one of which concerned burial customs. Zoroastrians practiced exhumation rather than inhumation in this period. Sources of diverse kinds testify to Zoroastrian interference in Christian burial practice, taking the form of non-burial of the dead or exhumation – the digging up of the Christian dead. The ultimate purpose of this interference, to be sure, was not so much to afflict Christians than to preserve what was perceived by Zoroastrians to be the purity of the earth from the pollution of corpse impurity – they would have taken offence at the burial of any corpse in the earth (Herman 2010; Francisco 2016). Evidence for conflict over this issue begins roughly in the middle of the fourth century, but continues until the end of the Sasanian era. It was not confined to the Christians, but also affected Jews.

The likelihood that the Christians had a more positive experience under the Persians is intimated by other contemporary sources. Indeed, the self-image of Sasanian Christianity, as energetically projected in many autochthonous martyrdom accounts and quite a number of other sources, implies, in fact, a fairly successful symbiosis and political integration of Christians in the Persian kingdom. The account of the *Life of Mar Abba*, for instance, argues for the possibility of Christians of becoming fully fledged participants in the Iranian ethnos. Christians may even contribute to the political culture and are a significant element in the population, allowing for the king to overcome rebellion in a major province of his empire, Huzestan. In another source, the *Martyrdom of Narse*, we encounter the concession that the Sasanian legal system is reliably non-partisan and will honour the legal ownership of a Christian against Zoroastrians, when supported by legal documentation. The so-called *Huzestan Chronicle* has the Sasanian king see the catholicos in a vision leading him into battle, and it describes the conquest of Jerusalem as a coordinated affair with Yazdin, a Christian noble, alongside the Persian forces. There is evidence of royal support for the church through donations and the sponsorship of synods. A number of accounts even go so far as to imagine the conversion of the Sasanian monarchs to Christianity, or that some of the Persian kings were closet Christians, although the historical veracity of these assertions is very questionable (Schilling 2008).

CHRISTIANITY AND ZOROASTRIANISM: POLEMICS AND ACCOMMODATION

The experience of Christians living in an empire as a minority where the dominant religion was Zoroastrianism was not uniform. Having considered the evidence for anti-Christian persecution, in particular martyrdom, and how this literature has and can be read, we now turn to less violent and sometimes less hostile expressions of the interaction between Syriac Christianity and Zoroastrianism. Religious polemics was but one component of this relationship, but there were others that lacked the confrontational aspect and that reflect a more marked degree of accommodation between Christianity and Zoroastrianism.

Syriac literature, which is itself an extensive corpus, reveals a considerable degree of knowledge about Zoroastrianism. This ranges from accounts of Zoroastrian mythology, religious practices, and rituals to their aetiology, history, and law.[5] The religious festival in honour of the spirits of the dead, *Frawardīgān*, is described (*Grigor*, 3–6, at Jullien 2015: 48), there is awareness of the complex process of constituting a new fire temple (*Martyrdom of Narse*, 15, at Herman 2016: 14–15), while elsewhere the manner of oral study of their religious literature is outlined (Kiperwasser and Ruzer

2014). The physical proximity between Zoroastrians and Christians inevitably led to the sharing and incorporation of religious concepts or practices associated with one of the religions into the practice of the other. The Christian ouranological scheme described in the *Cave of Treasures*, for instance, would absorb from the Zoroastrian mythological religious system the term Rapithwin for the firmament (Minov 2014: 153–65). Much of this information appears in the course of polemical works, and yet since the audience of such literature was Christian, they reveal the broad familiarity among this Christian audience of the Zoroastrian religious practices and beliefs they mention.

Many works of polemical literature were composed by Christians specifically against Zoroastrianism from the fourth century onwards. They include works by authors such as Theodore of Mopsuestia, whose Greek composition was soon translated into Syriac; Theodoret of Cyrus; and a number of works composed in Syriac in the sixth century. None of these works, however, has survived (Minov 2013: 183–4). Criticism of certain aspects of Zoroastrianism, such as the close-kin marriage custom, is found in many early Christian works in Syriac, including the *Book of the Laws of Countries* attributed to Bardaiṣan.

Some Christian sources suggest that religious disputation between Christians and Zoroastrians was conducted in a formal setting (e.g. *Mar Abba*, Jullien 2015: XLVII–XIX). Such a setting is not, however, known from the Zoroastrian literature. Anti-Christian polemical literature is attested only in compositions belonging to the post-Sasanian era, such as the ninth-century Middle Persian *Škand Gumānīg wizār* – the 'doubt-dispelling exposition' (Cereti 2014), or the collection of responses to the Christian Bōxt-Mārē in the *Dēnkard*.

The martyrdom literature itself usually served a polemical function. While many martyrdom acts focus on the Zoroastrian veneration of the sun, fire, and water, others provide a more detailed and specific critique. The *Acts of Ādur-Hormizd, Pethiōn and Anāhīd*, for instance, evoke numerous terms that belong to the Zoroastrian religious lexicon. Some of the accounts reveal a particularly close familiarity with Zoroastrian beliefs and practices, and include disputation on matters of belief.

More generally, Syriac literature reveals in its polemical discourses knowledge of much of the Zoroastrian religious lexicon, including terms such as *barsom*, the bunch of twigs used in the Yasna ceremony; *dēn* and *dēnīg*, terms for 'religion' and 'religious'; *drōn*, the consecrated bread and the ceremony in which it is used; *yazd*, 'god'; *xwadāy*, 'lord'; *xwēdōdah*, 'kin marriage'; *maguš*, 'Magian'; *mowbed*, 'chief of the Magians'; *Abestāg*, Avesta; *nask*, a section of Avesta; and *kustīg*, the sacred girdle (Bruns 2014).

In addition to overt religious polemics, we find also more subtle varieties of anti-Zoroastrian motifs. The sixth-century *Cave of Treasures* intriguingly attributes to Ardašīr, the founder of the Sasanian dynasty, the invention of astrology (Minov 2013: 234–47). By associating a reprehensible tradition such as astrology to Ardašīr, it was undoubtedly striking a contrast to what would most probably have been the rich current tradition attributing to Ardašīr positive accomplishments.

Syriac works reveal the same tendency known from other Christian (and Jewish) works of antiquity in integrating the biblical legacy with other current historiographical or mythological traditions. The legend of the adoration of the Magi acted as an early example of the direct contact between Christianity and Zoroastrianism, capable of inspiring a precedent for positive interaction and exchange between the two religions. It is true that the original sense of this legend may not have had the Zoroastrian priests in mind, and the distinction between Chaldeans and Persians was blurred in the west, it being primarily the former who had a reputation for astrology. This is, however, beside the point, as this legend would be picked up and understood by many in the period being considered as speaking of Zoroastrians (Frenschkowski 2015: 457–8). In the Persian Empire, there was a particular interest in the local biblical scene, and it was related to Zoroastrian tradition. The Magi were descendants of Bile'am (Minov 2013: 261). One key character was Nimrod. Perhaps continuing a western tradition of confounding Chaldeans with Persians, and perhaps aided by his association with the hunt, a pursuit closely associated with the Persians, Nimrod is portrayed as the founder of fire worship, and establishing Ādurbādagān, a city and region of particular significance for Zoroastrianism (Minov 2013: 200–8).

The efforts of the Christian religious authorities to suppress expressions of Zoroastrianism among its adherents could actually be understood as a sign that such expressions of religious symbiosis prevailed among their adherents. As the legislation of the official wielders of religious power, whether Zoroastrian priests or Christian clergy, strived to ensure a clear separation between the members of their own faiths and their respective religious lifestyles,[6] reality appears, on occasion, to have defied their best efforts. Repeated synodical legislation aimed at distancing Christians from their pagan neighbours suggests the persistence of such relations. The catholicos Mar Abba, for instance, sought to anathemise Christians who took *wāz* – the Zoroastrian prayer recited particularly at meals, or who practiced *xwēdōdā* – close-kin marriage, a religious practice customary among the Zoroastrians (Chabot 1902: 624). These cases attest to the existence of Christian adherents who *also* observed Zoroastrian practices. Whether they were recent converts to Christianity from Zoroastrianism who were retaining their former religious practices, recent converts from Christianity to Zoroastrianism who continued to maintain a connection with Christianity, or whether some other constellation was at play here is beyond our ability to discern. Many of the Persian martyr acts also thematise characters referred to as 'so-called Christians'. They seem to cross, with remarkable ease, the barrier between Christianity and Zoroastrianism. All this suggests that there were people inhabiting the space between the two religions, somehow with access to both camps, notwithstanding the efforts of the Christian clergy to force a clearer division between the religions. Another kind of evidence, incantation bowls, also attest to the crossing of religious boundaries and imply a degree of interaction in this realm, if not actual syncretism. These ancient artefacts contain spells for protection from demonic attack, and many were written in Syriac by Christian scribes for clients with unambiguously Zoroastrian names, but evoking supernatural forces of diverse sorts (Moriggi 2014).

PERSIAN ACCULTURATION

Within the Sasanian orbit as a whole, the Persian language had pride of place as the foremost medium for communication. As the language of the rulers of the kingdom, it also enjoyed a distinct prestige. Persian literature, too, shared this prestige and made an impression upon all the inhabitants of the Sasanian Empire, and also beyond.

This elite status of Persian culture and language left its mark on the Christians, even in the parts of the empire where the ethnic Persian element of the population was probably in the minority, such as Mesopotamia, and not only through the acceptance of ethnic Persian converts to Christianity. For the Christians living in the more Persian regions of the empire, the effect was certainly greater.

Evidence of Persian acculturation can be found in the fields of language, onomastics, and culture. A large number of Persian loanwords are employed in Syriac literature, testifying to the absorption of the Christians within the Persian linguistic milieu (Ciancaglini 2008). Persian loanwords are attested in a number of semantic fields, including state administration, military terms, religion, the law and justice system, medicine, botany, and pharmacopoeia. Numerous Christians, including some of the highest ecclesiastical leaders, bore Iranian names.[7] Quite a number of Christians even had Persian names with a Zoroastrian theophoric element in place, but some conversion accounts feature a scene whereby the convert trades his or her former Persian Zoroastrian name for a new Christian alternative.

The Christian leadership would have been expected to function in the Persian language in their political dealings with the palace and its officials. A number of church leaders are associated with translation between Persian and Syriac. Isaac, the catholicos under Yazdgird I (399–420 CE), for instance, is said to have translated for the king an official letter from the Roman clerical envoy, Marutha, from Greek to Persian (Chabot 1902: 19), and the fifth-century catholicos, Aqaq, to have translated a summary of Christian doctrine by Elisha bar Quzbaye from Syriac into Persian for Kawād I (488–531 CE). Khosrow I apparently preferred the appointment of Ezekiel as catholicos on account of his knowledge of Persian (*Chron. Seert*, 178). It has also been observed that Christians tended to use Middle Persian on their official seals (Lerner 1977).

Persian also entered the church. In fact, even though Persian Christianity as a whole is generally perceived as employing Syriac in its literature and liturgy, there is a large body of evidence demonstrating the considerable use of Persian by Christians for their own use in Christian literature, particularly those Christians inhabiting Iran proper and the eastern reaches of the empire. Some of the evidence even points to the use of Persian in formal liturgical settings. Thus, Ma'na of Shiraz, the metropolitan of Rēw Ardašīr, is reputed to have composed various works in Persian including hymns (*madrashe*), discourses (*memre*), and responses (*ʿonyata*) for liturgical use. Fragments of a Middle Persian psalter uncovered in Turfan clearly attest to the Christian liturgical use of this language. This psalter was translated from the Syriac Peshiṭta version already in the Sasanian period. Also discovered at Turfan were fragments of various Christian works, such as martyrologies and other texts in a different Middle Iranian language, Sogdian, which were translated from Syriac or based on Syriac models (Sims Williams 2009). The Christian *Corpus Iuris* that has survived in an eighth-century Syriac translation of a Middle Persian original written in Fārs by Īšōʿbōxt is a particularly illustrative example of the penetration of Persian among Christians. This work offers testimony not only to the use of the Persian language, but also to the adoption of Persian legal usages and terminology by the church (Macuch 2018). For instance, it would appear that some Christians practiced a form of substitute successorship customary among Zoroastrians and encoded in Zoroastrian law. Īšōʿbōxt is quite explicit when condemning the practice, saying that it has spread among Christians because they 'were settled among the Magians' (Sachau 1914: 100, 5–10).

Another indication of Persian acculturation among Christians may be noted in their employment of literary styles and their choice of motifs. Literary tropes typical of the Persian ambience emerge in various Christian works from the Sasanian era. Thus, the *Life of Mar Qardagh*, a martyrdom text, deliberately echoes the flavour of the Persian epic account of the rise of the founder of the Sasanian dynasty, Ardašīr I (224–240 CE), *Kār-nāmag ī Ardašīr*, with its evocative references to archery, horsemanship, the hunt, and polo (Walker 2006: 121–63; Wiessner 1969). It consciously evokes and then contrasts the warrior image familiar from Sasanian epic tradition with a devoted monastic ethos. In another text, *The Martyrdom of Jacob the Notary*, when the saint warns King Warahrān V that his father, Yazdgird I, had died a wondrous death with his corpse lost and never brought to burial, he discloses familiarity with the Persian traditions about the death of Warahrān, legends which were inspired by Zoroastrian mythology (Herman 2014: 82–3).

Whether through language, law, literature, or liturgy, the impact of Persian on the Syriac church of the east in Late Antiquity, and the degree of its Persian acculturation, was considerable.

NOTES

1 The most detailed discussion on this subject is Chaumont (1988).

2 One can safely set aside the evidence of Acts 2:9 as testimony for the spread of Christianity in Parthia, Media, and Elam.

3 For a summary of the sources, see Brock (2008).

4 For other martyrs' shrines in Persia and the eastern Roman Empire, see Fowden (1999) and Payne (2011).

5 For Syriac literature on Zoroaster and the adoration of the Magi, see already Bidez and Cumont (1938: 93–135).

6 See the examples provided in Williams (1996: 41–4).

7 The evidence for all the names is provided in *Iranisches Personennamenbuch*, Bd. VII, Iranische Namen in semitischen Nebenüberlieferungen, f. 5, Noms propres syriaques d'origine iranienne. Many of the bishops listed in the synod proceedings (Chabot 1902) bore Iranian names.

BIBLIOGRAPHY

Asmussen, J. P. 1983. Christians in Iran. *In*: E. Yarshater, ed., *Cambridge History of Iran* 3(2). Cambridge: Cambridge University Press, 924–48.

Back, M. 1978. Die Sassanidischen Staatinschriften. *Acta Iranica 18*. Leiden-Téhéran-Liège.

Barnes, T. D. 1985. Constantine and the Christians of Persia. *JRS* 75, 126–36.

Bedjan, P. 1894. *Acta Martyrum et Sanctorum IV*. Parisiis: Lipsiae.

Bidez, J. and F. Cumont, 1938. *Les mages hellenisés. Zoroastre, Ostanès et Hystaspe d'après la tradition grecque*, vol. 2. Paris: Société d'éditions "Les Belles lettres".

Brock, S. P. 1982. Christians in the Sasanian Empire: A Case of Divided Loyalties. *In*: S. Mews, ed., *Religion and National Identity*. Studies in Church History 18. Oxford: Blackwell, 1–19. Reprinted in S. P. Brock, *Syriac Perspectives on Late Antiquity*, 1984, ch. VI.

———. 2008. *The History of the Holy Mar Ma'in, With a Guide to the Persian Martyr Acts*. Piscataway, NJ: Gorgias Press.

Bruns, P. 2014. Antizoroastrische Polemik in den Syro-Persischen Märtyrakten. *In*: G. Herman, ed., *Jews, Christians and Zoroastrians, Religious Dynamics in a Sasanian Context*. Piscataway, NJ: Gorgias Press, 47–65.

Cereti, C. G. 2014. ŠKAND GUMĀNĪG WIZĀR. *Encyclopædia Iranica*, online edition. Available at www.iranicaonline.org/articles/shkand-gumanig-wizar (accessed on 03 February 2017).

Chabot, J.-B. 1902. *Synodicon orientale ou Recueil des synods nestoriens*. Paris: Imprimerie nationale.

Chaumont, M.-L. 1988. *La christianisation de l'empire iranien: des origines aux grandes persécutions du IVe siècle*. Louvain: Peeters.

Ciancaglini, C. A. 2008. *Iranian Loanwords in Syriac*. Beiträge zu Iranistik 28. Wiesbaden: Ludwig Reichert.

Fiey, J. M. 1970. *Jalons pour une histoire de l'église en Iraq*. CSCO 310. Louvain: Peeters.

Fowden, E. 1999. *The Barbarian Plain: Saint Sergius between Rome and Iran*. Berkeley, CA: University of California Press.

Francisco, H. R. 2016. Corpse Exposure in the Acts of the Persian Martyrs and Its Literary Models. *Hugoye: Journal of Syriac Studies* 19:1, 192–235.

Frenschkowski, M. 2012. Frühe Christen in der Begegnung mit dem Zoroastrismus: Eine Orientierung. *In*: P. Wick and M. Zehnder, ed., *The Parthian Empire and Its Religions, Studies in the Dynamics of Religious Diversity*. Gutenberg: Computus Druck Satz & Verlag, 163–94.

———. 2015. Christianity. *In*: M. Stausberg and Y. Sohrab-Dinshaw Vevaina, ed., *The Wiley Blackwell Companion to Zoroastrianism*. Chichester: Wiley-Blackwell, 457–75.

Gignoux, P. 1999. Sur quelques relations entre chrétiens et mazdens d'après les sources syriaques. *Studia Iranica* 28, 83–94.

Griffith, Sidney G. 1987. Ephraem the Syrian's Hymns against Julian: Meditations on History and Imperial Power. *VChr* 41, 238–66.

Gyselen, R. 1989. La géographie administrative de l'Empire Sassanide: Les témoignages sigillographiques. Res Orientales I. Bures-sur Yvette, GECMO.

Herman, G. 2010. "Bury My Coffin Deep!": Zoroastrian Exhumation in Jewish and Christian Sources. *In*: J. Roth, M. Schmeltzer and Y. Francus, ed., *Tiferet leYisrael: Jubilee Volume in Honor of Israel Francus*. New York, NY: The Jewish Theological Seminary, 31–59.

———. 2012. *A Prince Without a Kingdom, The Exilarch in the Sasanian Era*. Tübingen: Mohr Siebeck.

———. 2014. The Last Years of Yazdgird I and the Christians. *In*: G. Herman, ed., *Jews, Christians and Zoroastrians, Religious Dynamics in a Sasanian Context*. Piscataway, NJ: Gorgias Press, 67–90.

———. 2016. *Persian Martyr Acts under King Yazdgird I*. Piscataway, NJ: Gorgias Press.

Hutter, M. 2003. Mār Abā and the Impact of Zoroastrianism on Christianity in the 6th Century. *In*: C. G. Cereti, M. Maggi and E. Provasi, ed., *Religious Themes and Texts of pre-Islamic Iran and Central Asia: Studies in Honour of Professor Gherardo Gnoli on the Occasion of his 65th Birthday*. Wiesbaden: Reichert Verlag, 167–73.

Jullien, F. 2015. *Histoire de Mār Abba, Cathlicos de l'Orient, Martyres de Mār Grigor, Général en chef du roi Khusoro Ier et de Mār Yazd-Panāh, Juge et Gouverneur*. Louvain: Peeters.

Kawerau, P. 1985. *Die Chronik von Arbela*. CSCO 467–8. Louvain: Peeters.

Kiperwasser, R. and S. Ruzer. 2014. To Convert a Persian and Teach Him the Holy Scriptures: A Zoroastrian Proselyte in Rabbinic and Syriac Christian Narratives. *In*: G. Herman, ed., *Jews, Christians and Zoroastrian: Religious Dynamics in a Sasanian Context*. Piscataway, NJ: Gorgias Press, 91–127.

Kraeling, C. H. 1967. *The Christian Building*. The Excavations at Dura-Europos, Final Report 8/2. New Haven, CT.

Labourt, J. 1904. *Le Christianisme dans l'empire perse sous la dynastie Sassanide*. Paris: Victor Lecoffre.

Lerner, J. 1977. *Christian Seals of the Sasanian Period*. Nederlands: Historisch-Archaeologisch Instituut te Istanbul.

———. 1991. Christianity II. In Pre-Islamic Persia: Material Remains. *Encyclopedia Iranica* vol. V, fasc. 5. Costa Mesa, 328–30. Available at www.iranicaonline.org/articles/christianity-ii

Macuch, M. 2018. A Pahlavi Legal Term in Jesubōxt's Corpus Iuris. *In*: G. Herman, J. Rubanovich and S. Shaked, ed., *Irano-Judaica VII*. Ben-Zvi Institute. Forthcoming.

Marcus, R. 1932. The Armenian Life of Marutha. *Harvard Theological Review* 25, 47–71.

Minov, S. 2013. *Syriac Christian Identity in Late Sasanian Mesopotamia: The Cave of Treasures in Context*. Dissertation, Hebrew University of Jerusalem.

———. 2014. Dynamics of Christian Acculturation in the Sasanian Empire. *In*: G. Herman, ed., *Jews, Christians and Zoroastrians: Religious Dynamics in a Sasanian Context*. Piscataway, NJ: Gorgias Press, 149–201.

Moriggi, M. 2014. *A Corpus of Syriac Incantation Bowls, Syriac Magical Texts From Late Antique Mesopotamia*. Leiden: Brill.

Parisot, J. 1894/1907. *Aphraatis Sapientis Persae Demonstrationes*. Patrologia Syriaca 1–2. Paris: Firmin-Didot.

Payne, R. E. 2011. The Emergence of Martyrs' Shrines in Late Antique Iran: Conflict, Consensus, and Communal Institutions. *In*: P. Sarris, M. Dal Santo and P. Booth, ed., *An Age of Saints? Power, Conflict and Dissent in Early Medieval Christianity*. Leiden: Brill, 89–113.

———. 2015. *A State of Mixture: Christians, Zoroastrians and Iranian Political Culture in Late Antiquity*. Oakland, CA: University of California Press.

Sachau, E. 1914. *Syrische Rechtsbücher*. 3 Band. Berlin: Georg Reimer Verlag.

Schilling, A. M. 2008. *Die Anbetung der Magier und die Taufe der Sasaniden. Zur geistesgeschichte des iranischen Christentums in der Spätantike*. CSCO 621. Louvain: Peeters.

Sims-Williams, N. 2009. Christian Literature in Middle Iranian Languages. *In*: R. E. Emmerick and M. Macuch, ed., *The Literature of Pre-Islamic Iran, Companion Volume I to A History of Persian Literature*. London and New York, NY: I.B. Tauris, 266–87.

Smith, K. 2014. *The Martyrdom and the History of Blessed Simeon bar Ṣabba'e*. Persian Martyr Acts in Syriac: Text and Translation 3. Piscataway, NJ: Gorgias Press.

———. 2016. *Constantine and the Captive Christians of Persia: Martyrdom and Religious Identity in Late Antiquity*. Berkeley, CA: University of California Press.

Walker, J. 2006. *The Legend of Mar Qardagh the Assyrian: Narrative and Christian Heroism in Late Antique Iraq*. Berkeley, CA: University of California Press.

Wiessner, G. 1969. Zur Auseinandersetzung zwischen Christentum und Zoroastrismus in Iran. *ZDMG*, Supplement I, 2. Wiesbaden: Franz Steiner Verlg, 411–17.

Williams, A. V. 1996. Zoroastrians and Christians in Sasanian Iran. *BJRL* 78, 37–53.

CHAPTER NINE

JUDAISM AND SYRIAC CHRISTIANITY

Michal Bar-Asher Siegal

In a 2008 article, Sebastian Brock laments the fact that Syriac literature is underused by historians in reconstructing the history and theology of Late Antiquity (Brock 2008). Brock specifically notes the disregard for Eastern material in the curricula of Western educational institutions. In Brock's opinion, this disdain for non-classical languages stems largely from a tendency to associate Christianity with the Roman Empire and the writings of Western church fathers, a tendency greatly abetted by the representation of the history of the Christian church in Eusebius's *Life of Constantine* and the works of subsequent historians (Brock 1982: 9). Brock identifies a strong Protestant bias against Eastern Christianity, which is viewed as 'degenerate and heretical'. As a result of these underlying prejudices, the study of Eastern Christianity has been acutely neglected in modern scholarship. Furthermore, when Eastern texts have been examined, their readers' negative preconceptions have often influenced their analysis.

Brock's observations have important ramifications for the study of rabbinic literature produced in the East in light of its non-Jewish background. In this young emerging field, they explain the objective and subjective reasons for its relative smaller size. Indeed, a survey of the academic literature dealing with Jewish-Christian interactions reveals many of the same biases: the association of Christianity with the Roman Empire and with the writing of Western church fathers has led scholars to assume a more natural connection between Christian materials and Palestinian Jewish literature than with the Babylonian literature – namely, the Babylonian Talmud. Therefore, scholarly work on the connection between Christianity and rabbinic texts is often preoccupied with Western patristic writings, neglecting Eastern Christian texts. Indeed, as most academics in the field of Jewish Studies rely heavily on the findings of scholars of Christianity as a basis for comparative analysis, these general tendencies in the study of Christianity have influenced which Christian materials are used in rabbinic scholarship. Further, scholars of rabbinic Judaism have often not paid careful attention to Eastern Christianity, despite the significant centres of Jewish population that existed in the Persian Empire,[1] and rabbinic students are more often required to study Greek and Latin than Syriac.

The Jewish community of Talmudic Babylonia was the largest concentration of Jews in the diaspora from the third to seventh centuries CE (Gafni 2006: 805). It was located in the area surrounding the narrow meeting of the Tigris and Euphrates rivers, in close proximity to Ctesiphon, and southward to the Persian Gulf. There were also Jewish settlements in northern Mesopotamia, most notably in Nisibis, probably dating back to the late Second Temple period (Segal 1964; especially map on p. 806). In these areas, as well as in Babylonia itself, Christians and Jews were living in close proximity (Fiey 1967). The two communities also shared a language, Aramaic, but spoke different dialects, Syriac for the Christians, Jewish Babylonian Aramaic for the Jews, both traditionally categorised (together with Mandaic) within the same eastern dialect branch of Late Aramaic. This group of dialects shared a number of features that set them apart from other contemporary dialects (the western branch) (Bar-Asher Siegal 2013: 21–3, 2015). Among these features are: (1) *l/n* as the 3m marker of the prefix conjugation, (2) the suffix *-e* as a masculine plural marker, (3) lack of a formal marker for definiteness, (4) apocopation of final open syllables, (5) the *qtil li* pattern, and (6) the development of a new tense formed from the participle with nominative pronominal suffixes (i.e. the participial conjugation) (Bar-Asher Siegal 2013: 22). These differences of dialect and script marked out the different communities, but the close proximity of the dialects still permitted the language to serve as an important vehicle of communication between the two communities (Millar 2011; Taylor 2002).

Since the interactions between Syriac literature and Palestinian rabbinic sources are much less well researched than those with Babylonian sources, this chapter will focus on the interactions between the Syriac world and rabbinic Judaism specifically within the region of Talmudic Babyonia and the Persian Empire. The reason for the lack of attention to Palestinian sources is largely chronological: Palestinian sources such as the Mishnah, Tosefta, and legal midrashim were all edited before or around the third century CE and thus less likely to reflect direct connections with Christian materials (Schremer 2010). On the other hand, while the Palestinian Talmud and later Palestinian midrashim may very well offer evidence of a literary relationship to Syriac sources, these parallels still need to be examined more closely in relation to both Greek and Syriac Christian sources. Unfortunately, very little work has been done on this topic (Rubenstein 2017; Siegal 2016).

A passage from the Babylonian Talmud itself has often been cited as proof that Christianity is irrelevant to a full understanding of the Talmud's background. In *b. Avodah Zarah* 4a, we find a story in which *minim* (literally, 'heretics') pose a question about a biblical verse to the Babylonian sage Rav Safra, which he is incapable of answering. R. Abbahu, a Palestinian sage of the late third to early fourth century CE, explains his colleague's incompetence: 'We, who are located among you, set ourselves the task of studying the verses [thoroughly], but they, who are not among you, do not study it'.[2] According to this passage, R. Abbahu explains that his colleague, Rav Safra, is not learned in the polemical use of scripture because he comes from Babylonia. The Talmud itself thus appears to proclaim that Babylonian Jews did not encounter Christians to the extent that Palestinian Jews did. Indeed, the famed rabbinic scholar Ephraim E. Urbach relied on this Talmudic passage when he argued that the Babylonian rabbinic exegesis of the book of Jonah lacked a strong polemical character because of the relative unimportance of Christianity in the Babylonian context (Urbach 1949).

Nevertheless, recent scholarship has made clear that the significance of Christian religious groups in the Persian Empire can no longer be ignored (Payne 2015). As a result, scholars of rabbinic Judaism have begun to reconsider the assumption that Jews and Christians had minimal social, cultural, and literary contact in Late Antique Babylonia, during the last decades of the Talmud's composition (as shall be discussed below). In light of this shift, a number of new readings have been proposed for the story of Rav Safra cited above. Rather than minimising the role of Christianity in the lives of Jews in the Persian Empire, this story has been reread variously as a rhetorical device, fiercely denying connections that actually existed between the two communities (Boyarin 2007: 358); a warning and a call to vigilance against heretical polemics (Schremer 2009: 365–6, n66; Schremer 2005: 223–4); and even as a reference to a specific group of Christians, less prevalent in the Persian Empire, who were concerned with scriptural polemics (Siegal 2013: 17–18, n63).

However, even as we increasingly recognise the prevalence of Christian Syriac literature in Late Antique Persia and its importance for a full understanding of contemporary rabbinic literature, there remain major obstacles to a comparative study of Jewish and Christian texts (for more on comparative methodology, see Smith 1990). First, as noted above, most scholars have access to limited research tools. In addition to the constraints on language study (Syriac and Babylonian Aramaic) during graduate training, rabbinic and Christian scholars often have very little exposure to the other tradition's texts. This has led scholars in both fields to feel uneasy attempting to answer questions related to the interactions between the two textual traditions based solely on their own expertise. In addition, only recently have translations (or even printed editions) of Syriac texts and critical editions of rabbinic texts become more widely available. Given the relative lack of archaeological evidence and historical accounts, claims of actual interaction between the two religious communities often rely solely on the ability of scholars to demonstrate literary contacts between Christian and rabbinic traditions.

Still, even when literary analogies between Christian and rabbinic sources are found, one cannot always easily draw a direct historical conclusion, for several reasons. First, analogy does not necessarily indicate a genealogical connection between two sets of texts. Similarities may arise for a variety of reasons, such as for the sake of a polemical argument or satire, but at other times may just be the result of coincidental resemblance or a parallel, non-dependent, thought process, and the interpretation of such similarities often depends upon the point of view of the beholder (further discussion in Siegal 2013: 25–34). Therefore, even when a relationship is identified, the historical and textual meaning of this relationship between two sources is often contested. Second, the nature and evolution of the relationship between two texts is not always easy to identify. When one recovers a rabbinic tradition in a Syriac text, it does not necessarily indicate the author's familiarity with the rabbinic source. It might, for example, result from a similar reading of scripture, born of either a shared background or independent – but parallel – readings. Conversely, when a Christian tradition can be identified in the Babylonian Talmud, how are we to know, in certain cases, whether it was known to the rabbis via Western sources transmitted to the East or via local, Syriac sources and translations?

Nevertheless, it is now beginning to be acknowledged that the linguistic, temporal, and geographic literary relationships between the Babylonian Talmud and Syriac literature demand that scholars of rabbinics pay closer attention to Eastern Christian texts. Though the nature of the connections between the corpora is not fully understood, a side-by-side reading at the very least deepens our understanding of the *sitz im leben* of the Babylonian Talmud and its readers.

It is important to consider the question of genre as we attempt to illustrate the nature of the interactions between Babylonian Jewry and Eastern Christianity. Different types of texts – including church canons, incantation bowls, hagiography, and others – provide different perspectives on the relationship between the two communities, and each deserves scholarly attention. As will be shown in the survey below, the various sources examined thus far, when considered all together, have already produced a more nuanced and complex picture than any single source would. Scriptural disputes showcase polemical interactions between the two religious communities, while incantation bowls often reveal a mélange of religious elements, suggesting shared magical traditions. Even the strong anti-Jewish polemical arguments in the writings of the Eastern church fathers show striking familiarity with Jewish midrash. These sources might be evidence for a type of Jewish-Christian interaction that served to define differences and boundaries, while at the same time offering proof of shared knowledge.

While I construct this survey using a variety of literary genres, these should not be taken as a unified corpus. The *sitzen im leben* of the different texts are crucial for understanding the weight that is given to each such source in the grand picture that is the relationship between the two religious communities. Incantation bowls used to evoke magic will obviously represent something different than a scholarly and subtly ironic, polemical story recorded in the Babylonian Talmud. The supposed contexts in which the texts were created, their function and purpose at the time of their creation, as well as the history of their transmission, all have ramifications for how they should be understood. I shall not attempt to draw these lines myself, as current research has learned to avoid facile categorisations such as 'popular' (magic bowls?) and elite literature (Talmud?), which do not withstand careful examination. But this methodological issue should stand nonetheless at the background of this survey.

Through what follows, I shall attempt to show that a careful examination of various types of rabbinic and Syriac sources reveals a remarkably diverse picture of the interactions between the two textual traditions. I will also argue that these types of studies have great potential to add to our understanding of historical interactions between the two communities in the Late Antique East. It is clear that work in this area has only begun. The number of studies on this topic is still relatively small, but recent advances by scholars of Christianity and the regular publication of Syriac manuscripts in accessible critical editions will make possible much more important work on these questions.

I begin my survey with legal documents. Even as late as the sixth century, we find legal texts that attest to close ties between Jews and Christians in the East. Canons issued by the Church of the East's Synod of 585 deal with social relations between Christians and non-Christians in eastern Syria. For example, Canon 15 states:

> We have learned that some Christians, either through ignorance or through imprudence, are going to see people of other religions and taking part in their festivals, that is to say, going to celebrate festivals with Jews, heretics, or pagans, or accepting something sent to them from the festivals of other religions. We thus order, by heavenly authority, that no Christian is allowed to go to the festivals

> of those who are not Christians, nor accept anything sent to the Christians from their festivals, for it [the gift] is part of the oblation made in their sacrifice.
> (Chabot 1902: 157.31–158.8, trans. 417–8; Walker 2012)

Canon 27 further shows that Christians in the Sasanian Empire intermarried, exchanged blessings, and even shared altars with 'heretics' (Chabot 1902: 158.20–159.2, trans. 418). These rules are meant to enforce the separation of Christians from other religious groups, among them Jews, and to delineate the social lines between them. By the same token, they clearly reflect a situation on the ground in which Christians and Jews were taking part in each others' festivals as late as the sixth century.

Evidence from incantation bowls is even more suggestive of close ties. These bowls, which contain textual formulae or graphical depictions that were believed to offer protective magic, have been found placed upside-down under thresholds, in walls, and in cemeteries (Morony 2003: 83–107). For example, an incantation bowl has been discovered containing an explicit reference to Jesus written in Jewish Babylonian Aramaic:

> By the name of I-am-that-I-am *yhwh ṣb'wt*, and by the name of Jesus, who conquered the height and the depth by his cross, and by the name of his exalted father, and by the name of the holy spirits for ever and eternity. *Amen amen selah.*
> (Levene 1999: 290)

This text, alongside other synchronistic elements in the bowls, demonstrates a mixture of Jewish, Babylonian, Hellenistic, Mandaean, Iranian, and Christian traditions. This diversity of influences has led Shaul Shaked to describe a 'cultural koine' in this region of Sasanian Mesopotamia reflected in the bowl texts. In this cultural context, a Jewish composer of an incantation bowl could use Christian theological elements to achieve his magical goals. As this and other bowls suggest, 'themes and ideas, and sometimes even whole textual passages, were taken over by each group of practitioners in Mesopotamia from the neighbouring communities' (Shaked 1999: 315–6).

Jean Maurice Fiey, discussing Jewish-Christian interactions in the East, has concluded that the non-textual nature of the liturgical, homiletic, and exegetical domains of contemporary Judaism and Christianity made them natural loci for such 'unprejudiced openness' (Fiey 1988: 936). This shared pool of 'popular religion' in Mesopotamia linked Christians and Jews and was strongly denounced by the Christian bishops as a result (Shaked 1997).

We should add that these synchronistic elements are characteristic of Jewish and Mandean bowls, in particular. Tapani Harviainen has noted that this is not the case for Syriac bowls which, for example, differ in their use of specific formulae and lack references to Christianity, Judaism, and Zoroastrianism. Harviainen argues that the Syriac bowls have a 'pagan origin' (Harviainen 1995).

An examination of liturgical traditions in early Syriac Christian communities also provides evidence for Jewish-Christian interactions. Gerard Rouwhorst's work in this area focuses on the Jewish antecedents of the East Syrian liturgy. He cites, for example, church floor plans containing a *bêma* (see also ch. 28, pp. 522–6); the uncommon liturgical practice of reading selections from both the Torah and the Prophets; similarities between the Jewish grace after meals and the fourth-century Syriac *Anaphora of Addai and Mari*;

the *Apostolic Constitutions*' call to observe the Sabbath on Saturday in addition to Sunday; and the date and content of the Easter celebration, its emphasis on the passion and the death of Christ rather than his resurrection (Rouwhorst 1997).

Connections have also been noted between Jewish traditions and the writings of contemporary Syriac church fathers, particularly Ephrem and Aphrahaṭ. Naomi Koltun-Fromm's work on Aphrahaṭ has concentrated on the Jewish-Christian polemical confrontations particular to Persian Mesopotamia. She argues that these texts demonstrate familiarity with rabbinic arguments and concludes that we should take seriously Aphrahaṭ's claims that his interpretations are based on conversations with 'a Jew' (Koltun-Fromm 1996). She posits an exchange of ideas, biblical exegesis, and theology in this fourth-century context and 'an ongoing conversation between Jews and Christians in Mesopotamia at the height of the Persian persecutions on the subject of true faith' (Koltun-Fromm 1996: 51). In her most recent book, Koltun-Fromm (2010) examined Aphrahaṭ's writings on the concepts of holiness and asceticism and presented a more nuanced approach. Here she makes the subtler argument that both Jewish and Christian sources demonstrate a need to deal with the tension between one's spiritual and daily life, and that the two traditions' attempts to resolve this tension are based on similar and shared traditions of biblical exegesis. Most importantly, Koltun-Fromm uses her findings to venture into social history and concludes that contemporary Christian and Jewish communities were both using these exegetical traditions to define their communal boundaries and their relations to one another.

Adam Becker (2003) has argued we should read Aphrahaṭ's literary production in light of a context in which 'the local Jewish and Christian communities were not fully distinct and separate from one another'. He points out references in Christian texts to Christians who flee to local synagogues in times of persecution and who are circumcised or refuse to eat blood; the use of the Jewish calendar in martyrs' accounts; and the use of terms such as 'priests' and 'Levites' to describe Christian clergy. Moreover, Christine Shepardson (2008) has argued that we must read Ephrem's anti-Jewish rhetoric in light of fourth-century intra-Christian debates. Elena Narinskaya (2010) has detected in Ephrem's exegetical writings some dependence on Jewish traditions,[3] while other scholars still contend that these Jewish traditions in Ephrem could have reached his writings orally and indirectly (Brock 1985: 20).

Outlining polemical arguments in Jewish and Christian texts offers another angle on the interactions between Eastern Jewish and Christian communities. Scholars have identified a number of Talmudic passages as possible satires or parodies of New Testament traditions: *b. Shabbat* 116a–b has been read as a parody on the Sermon on the Mount (Zellentin 2007); *b. 'Avodah Zarah* 18a–b as a parody of Jesus's cry from the cross (Boyarin 2012: 246–66); and a complex parody of the metaphor of Jesus as a fountain of living water has been identified in *b. Sukkah* 48b (Halbertal and Naeh 2006); among others (Siegal 2013: 34n46). The Christian traditions referred to in these polemical passages and satirical puns usually derive from the New Testament and could have been known to the rabbinic authors through Western sources. However, they could just as easily have been circulated in the East through Syriac sources, whether oral or written. The fact that some of these examples are only found in the Babylonian Talmud may point to the Babylonian rabbis' familiarity with local Christian traditions.

Peter Schäfer discusses the possibility that the Talmudic authors had knowledge of these New Testament, Jesus traditions through Tatian's *Diatessaron*, a Syriac work of the second century CE. This would explain why certain details of the Jesus traditions are found only in the Babylonian Talmud and nowhere in Palestinian rabbinic sources (Schäfer 2007: 129). These include, among others, the story of Jesus's virgin birth; his association with the name of Mary Magdalene; the notion of Jesus as a teacher of Torah; healings performed in the name of Jesus; and the dating of his execution to the fourteenth of Nisan.

Some studies have focused on lexical overlap, examining Syriac sources in order better to understand key passages in rabbinic literature. So, for example, Shlomo Naeh recognised a loanword from Syriac Christian literature, *ḥeruta*, in a Talmudic story in *b. Qiddushin* 82b, referring to abstinence from sexual relations (Naeh 1997). This study sheds new light on the Talmudic story about an ascetic rabbi and reveals it to be a mockery of the Christian view of abstinence. However, using Syriac literature as a kind of dictionary, only to enrich our understanding of the rabbinic lexicon, is not the optimal use for this rich literature and should only be the first step in exploring the value it can bring to our study of both corpora. Adam Becker (2010) has recently suggested that we must undertake a broader comparative examination of the ancient sources produced by these two religious minorities in the Persian Empire, rather than looking only for Christian texts that illuminate specific rabbinic passages. In the case of Naeh's article, his argument may have benefited from a broader survey of monastic texts in which women are viewed as incarnations of the holy man's illicit desires and his struggles against this temptation. Such a reading could illuminate the Talmudic story of R Ḥiyya as a unique portrayal of an ascetic rabbi fighting his urges, in the mould of the monastic holy man (Siegal, forthcoming).

It is clear that there is much to be gained from a comparison of Christian hagiographic writings, which describe the lives of the holy men and women of the Eastern landscape, with Talmudic stories about the lives and thoughts of rabbinic figures.[4] Differences in literary genre and chronology present methodological difficulties, but even given these difficulties a comparative analysis yields interesting parallels and analogies. One key problem is whether these Christian traditions reached the composers of the Talmudic passages via local Syriac sources or via Palestinian traditions more closely connected to Western sources. As noted above, this question is relevant to other examples of literary interactions as well, but it is particularly acute in the case of analogous stories that share literary motifs, where it is much harder to discern the 'smoking gun' that proves textual interaction. Nevertheless, a growing number of studies suggest a degree of Talmudic engagement with Christian literary traditions. Given the importance of Syriac Christianity in the region, it is very likely that Babylonian rabbis were exposed to Christian traditions via Syriac sources.

Let us take as an example Jeffrey Rubenstein's comparative work on the story of the death and burial of R. Eleazar the son of R. Shimon bar Yoḥai (Rubenstein 2017). This story appears in *b. Baba Metsi'a* 84b and in the Palestinian midrash *Pesiqta Derav Kahana* 11. Rubenstein suggests reading the rabbinic traditions regarding the post-mortem treatment of the rabbi's body in light of the Late Antique, Christian cult of the relics of holy men. As in stories of Christian holy men, and unlike in prevailing rabbinic attitudes, R. Eleazar's body does not decay after his death, and the townsfolk refuse to allow its burial because of its protective qualities. In this case, there are parallels between Babylonian and Syriac sources and between the Palestinian midrash and Western Christian sources, but the development of the story as it appears in the Babylonian Talmud is particularly suggestive of shared literary motifs.

My own work finds literary connections between the Babylonian Talmud and the monastic traditions circulating in Syriac in the Persian Empire (Siegal 2013). The portrayal of key rabbinic figures resembles that of monastic descriptions of Christian holy men. In addition, identifying literary connections between Jewish and Christian corpora invites us to consider the historical relations between the two religious communities in the Persian Empire. The parallels between the sources are even more suggestive, since most cases I discuss are found only in the Babylonian Talmud and not in Palestinian sources. Even in cases such as these, it is still possible that the Christian source material came to the rabbis via Western traditions that did not leave a trace in Palestinian rabbinic sources. This possibility is less likely, however, than the simpler explanation that local, Syriac sources interacted with rabbinic traditions that were included in the Babylonian Talmud.

For example, a comparison of Christian monastic sources with parallel passages in the two Talmuds on the figure of R. Shimon bar Yoḥai reveals that only the Babylonian tradition makes use of monastic motifs (Siegal 2011, 2013, ch. 5). The Babylonian passage draws on popular Christian literary themes to reshape the Palestinian story of R. Shimon into a quasi-monastic tale, portraying R. Shimon as a monastic holy man whose sojourn in a cave brings about a spiritual transformation. Since only the Babylonian version of the story includes these Christian literary analogies, it is most likely that local Christian traditions, circulating in Syriac, are at the basis of this literary reworking.

The literary genre of martyrdom stories is an interesting test case for a comparative analysis of rabbinic and Syriac material. Daniel Boyarin (1999) has suggested viewing martyrdom stories in rabbinic sources as a reflection of a shared, Late Antique rabbinic and Christian discourse. Jeffrey Rubenstein notes in response (Rubenstein 2018) that Boyarin's analysis relies exclusively on Christian sources from the Greco-Roman world, written in Greek and Latin. Rubenstein himself suggests examining martyrdom accounts in the Babylonian Talmud in comparison with the *Persian Martyr Acts*, a 'corpus' of about seventy stories of Christian martyrs, primarily from the Sasanian Empire. Rubenstein finds numerous parallels, attesting to a common cultural context, but he gives special emphasis to the differences between the two corpora, including the enthusiasm they express at the idea of a martyr's death, and their treatment of the themes of tricksterism and conversion. Ultimately, Rubenstein finds the differences between the Jewish and Christian narratives to be much deeper than their commonalities.

The bread and butter of comparative historical analysis is the examination of contemporary works dealing with the same topic. From the perspective of rabbinic texts, we are very fortunate to have two sets of sources, from the West and the East, deriving from overlapping time periods. The existence of the two Talmuds has supplied rabbinics scholars with a large amount of material to research and compare, whether they are studying passages within one Talmud or parallels between the two. However, a study of the rabbinic period that is confined only to rabbinic literature will a priori produce limited results. Syriac literature can serve, alongside Persian and Hellenistic materials and, of course, archaeological evidence, as an Archimedean point, a hypothetical vantage point from which an observer can objectively perceive the subject of inquiry. The same can be said of the study of Syriac sources in isolation from contemporary rabbinic texts. A long enough lever, combined with this remote Archimedean point, is able to unveil the grand picture, hidden from the occupants of the earth itself.

Identifying parallels between rabbinic and Christian traditions can help us re-address some of the most important research questions facing scholars of both literatures. This comparative approach will allow us better to understand the nature of Jewish-Christian relations in the first centuries CE and the so-called parting of the ways. It will provide a better understanding of specific passages in both literatures. It may even afford us further insights into larger questions relating to the redaction of the texts themselves. Through the examination of a shared motif, which suggests possible literary interaction, we can more easily map the chronology and literary redaction of parallel passages. We are then in a better position to ask questions about how these two texts came to be and about their creators, audiences, and tradents. Including the vast Syriac literature circulating in the East in our comparative framework and not only those circulating in the West is crucial to advancing the scholarly understanding of both corpora of texts and the religious communities in which they were produced and preserved.

NOTES

1 The small number of Syriac scholars in academic posts, or even Syriac language classes offered at leading universities, is itself an indication of this state of affairs. See Brock's second observation in his article, regarding the separation of the teaching of Oriental languages and literatures from the field of Classics in the Western educational system.

2 All translations from the Talmud are the author's.

3 But see reviews of this book by Walters in Hugoye: *Journal of Syriac Studies* 16.1 (2013), 195–8; and that of Morrison in *JThS* 62.2 (2011), 748–51, and others besides.

4 Brock (2008: 182): 'Hagiography was a literary genre in late antiquity where texts were particularly apt to cross, and sometimes, re-cross linguistic boundaries, and so an awareness of the existence of the hagiographical literature in Armenian, Coptic, Ethiopic, Georgian, and Syriac is likely to be of importance at some stage or other for anyone who is concerned with hagiographical texts in Greek and Latin'. I will add to Brock's list that it is of importance for those interested in similar passages in the Talmudic corpora, not just in the Persian Empire, due to the nature of this literary genre.

BIBLIOGRAPHY

Bar-Asher Siegal, Elitzur A. 2013. *Introduction to the Grammar of Jewish-Babylonian Aramaic.* Münster: Ugarit-Verlag.

———. 2015. From a Non-Argument-Dative to an Argument-Dative: The Character and Origin of the qṭīl lī Construction in Syriac and Jewish Babylonian Aramaic. *Folia Orientalia* 51: 59–111.

Becker, Adam H. 2003. Beyond the Spatial and Temporal Limes: Questioning the 'Parting of the Ways' Outside the Roman Empire. *In*: Adam H. Becker et al., ed., *The Ways that Never Parted: Jews and Christians in Late Antiquity and the Early Middle Ages.* Tübingen: Mohr Siebeck, 373–92.

———. 2010. The Comparative Study of 'Scholasticism' in Late Antique Mesopotamia: Rabbis and East Syrians. *AJS Review* 34: 91–113.

Boyarin, Daniel. 1999. *Dying for God: Martyrdom and the Making of Christianity and Judaism*. Stanford, CA: Stanford University Press.

———. 2007. Hellenism in Jewish Babylonia. *In*: Charlotte E. Fonrobert and Martin S. Jaffee, ed., *The Cambridge Companion to the Talmud and Rabbinic Literature*. Cambridge: Cambridge University Press, 336–63.

———. 2012. *Socrates and the Fat Rabbis*. Chicago, IL: University of Chicago Press.

Brock, Sebastian P. 1982. Christians in the Sasanian Empire: A Case of Divided Loyalties. *In*: Stuart Mews, ed., *Religion and National Identity*. Studies in Church History XVIII. Oxford: Basil Blackwell, 2–19.

———. 1985. *The Luminous Eye: The Spiritual World Vision of St. Ephrem the Syrian*. Placid Lectures 6. Rome: Center for Indian and Inter-Religious Studies.

———. 2008. Saints in Syriac: A Little-Tapped Resource. *JECS* 16.2: 181–96.

Chabot, J.-B. 1902. *Synodicon orientale ou recueil de synodes nestoriens*. Paris: Imprimerie Nationale.

Fiey, Jean-Maurice. 1967. Topographie Chrétienne de Mahozé. *OS* 12: 397–420.

———. 1988. Juifs et chrétiens dans l'Orient Syriaque. *Hispania Sacra* 40: 933–53.

Gafni, Isaiah M. 2006. The Political, Social, and Economic History of Babylonian Jewry, 224–638 CE. *In*: Steven T. Katz, ed., *The Cambridge History of Judaism, Vol. 4: The Late Roman-Rabbinic Period*. Cambridge: Cambridge University Press, 792–820.

Halbertal, Moshe, and Shlomo Naeh. 2006. Springs of Salvation: Interpretive Satire and the Refutation of Heretics. *In*: J. Levinson, ed., *Higayon Leyonah: New Aspects in the Study of Midrash, Aggadah and Piyyut in Honor of Yonah Fraenkel*. Jerusalem: Magnes Press, 179–98 [in Hebrew].

Harviainen, Tapani. 1995. Pagan Incantations in Aramaic Magic Bowls. *In*: M. J. Geller, J. C. Greenfield, and M. P. Weitzman, ed., *Studia Aramaica: New Sources and New Approaches*. Oxford: Oxford University Press, 53–60.

Koltun-Fromm, Naomi. 1996. A Jewish-Christian Conversation in Fourth-Century Persian Mesopotamia. *JJS* 47: 45–63.

———. 2010. *Hermeneutics of Holiness: Ancient Jewish and Christian Notions of Sexuality and Religious Community*. New York: Oxford University Press.

Levene, Dan. 1999. '. . . And by the Name of Jesus . . .': An Unpublished Magic Bowl in Jewish Aramaic. *JSQ* 6: 283–308.

Millar, Fergus. 2011. A Rural Jewish Community in Late Roman Mesopotamia, and the Question of a 'Split' Jewish Diaspora. *JSJ* 42: 351–74.

Morony, Michael G. 2003. Magic and Society in Late Sasanian Iraq. *In*: Scott Noegel, Joel Walker, and Brannon Wheeler, ed., *Prayer, Magic, and the Stars in the Ancient and Late Antique World*. University Park, PA: Pennsylvania State Press, 83–107.

Naeh, Shlomo. 1997. Freedom and Celibacy: A Talmudic Variation on Tales of Temptation and Fall in Genesis and Its Syrian Background. *In*: Judith Frishman and Lucas Van Rompay, ed., *The Book of Genesis in Jewish and Oriental Christian Interpretation*. Louvain: Peeters, 73–90.

Narinskaya, Elena Ephrem. *A "Jewish" Sage: A Comparison of the Exegetical Writings of St. Ephrem the Syrian and Jewish Traditions*. Turnhout: Brepols, 2010.

Payne, Richard E. 2015. *A State of Mixture: Christians, Zoroastrians, and Iranian political culture in Late Antiquity*. Oakland, CA: University of California Press.

Rouwhorst, Gerard A. M. 1997. Jewish Liturgical Traditions in Early Syriac Christianity," *VChr* 51: 72–93.

Rubenstein, Jeffrey L. 2016. A Rabbinic Translation of Relics. *In*: Kimberly Stratton and Andrea Lieber, ed., *Crossing Boundaries in Early Judaism and Christianity: Ambiguities,*

Complexities, and Half-Forgotten Adversaries. Essays in Honor of Alan F. Segal. Leiden: Brill, 314–32.

———. 2017. Hero, Saint, and Sage: The Life of R. Elazar b. R. Shimon in Pesiqta de Rab Kahana 11. *In*: Michal Bar-Asher Siegal, Christine Hayes, and Tzvi Novick, ed., From Text to Context in Ancient Judaism: Studies in Honor of Steven Fraade. *Journal of Ancient Judaism Supplements* 22. 509–28.

———. 2018. Martyrdom in the Persian Martyr Acts and in the Bavli. *In*: Geoffrey Herman and Jeffrey L. Rubenstein, ed., *The Aggada of the Bavli and Its Cultural World*. Brown Judaic Studies. Providence, RI: Society of Biblical Literature.

Schäfer, Peter. 2007. *Jesus in the Talmud*. Princeton, NJ: Princeton University Press.

Schremer, Adiel. 2005. Stammaitic Historiography. *In*: Jeffrey L. Rubenstein, ed. *Creation and Composition: The Contribution of the Bavli Redactors (Stammaim) to the Aggadah*. Tübingen: Mohr Siebeck, 219–36.

———. 2009. The Christianization of the Roman Empire and Rabbinic Literature. *In*: Lee Levine and Daniel Schwartz, ed., *Jewish Identities in Antiquity: Studies in Memory of Menahem Stern*. Tübingen: Mohr Siebeck, 349–66.

———. 2010. *Brothers Estranged: Heresy, Christianity, and Jewish Identity in Late Antiquity*. Oxford/New York: Oxford University Press.

Segal, Benjamin J. 1964.The Jews of North Mesopotamia before the Rise of Islam. *In*: Jehoshua M. Grintz et al., ed., *Studies in the Bible Presented to Professor M. H. Segal*. Jerusalem: Qiryat Sefer, 32–63.

Shaked, Shaul. 1997. Popular Religion in Sasanian Babylonia. *Jerusalem Studies in Arabic and Islam* 21: 103–17.

———. 1999. Jesus in the Magic Bowls. Apropos Dan Levene's '. . . and by the Name of Jesus . . .'. *JSQ* 6: 309–19.

Shepardson, Christine. 2008. *Anti-Judaism and Christian Orthodoxy: Ephrem's Hymns in Fourth-Century Syria*. North American Patristics Society Patristic Monograph Series 20. Washington, DC: The Catholic University of America Press.

Siegal, Michal Bar-Asher. 2011. The Making of a Monk-Rabbi: The Background for the Creation of the Stories of R. Shimon bar Yohai in the Cave. *Zion* 76.3: 279–304 [in Hebrew].

———. 2013. *Early Christian Monastic Literature and the Babylonian Talmud*. Cambridge: Cambridge University Press.

———. 2016. Saying of the Desert Fathers, Sayings of the Rabbinic Fathers: Avot Derabbi Nattan and the Apophthegmata Patrum. *ZAC* 20.2: 243–59.

———. Forthcoming. Syriac monastic sources in the Babylonian Talmud: Heruta story reconsidered. *In:* Aaron Butts and Simcha Gross, ed., *Judaism and Syriac Christianity: Identities and Intersections*. Texts and Studies in Ancient Judaism. Tübingen: Mohr Siebeck.

Smith, Jonathan Z. 1990. *Drudgery Divine: On the Comparison of Early Christianities and the Religions of Late Antiquity*. Chicago, IL: University of Chicago Press.

Taylor, David. 2002. Bilingualism and Diglossia in Late Antique Syria and Mesopotamia. *In*: James N. Adams et al., ed., *Bilingualism and Ancient Society: Language Contact and the Written Text*. Oxford: Oxford University Press, 298–331.

Urbach, Efraim E. 1949. The Repentance of the People of Nineveh and the Discussions Between Jews and Christians. *Tarbiz* 20: 118–22 [in Hebrew].

Walker, Joel Thomas. 2012. From Nisibis to Xi'an: The Church of the East in Late Antique Eurasia. *In*: Scott F. Johnson, ed., *The Oxford Handbook of Late Antiquity*. Oxford University Press, 994–1052.

Zellentin, Holger M. 2007. Margin of Error: Women, Law, and Christianity in Bavli Shabbat 116a-b. *In*: Eduard Iricinschi and Holger M. Zellentin, ed., *Heresy and Identity in Late Antiquity*. Tübingen: Mohr Siebeck, 339–63.

CHAPTER TEN

SYRIAC AND SYRIANS IN THE LATER ROMAN EMPIRE

Questions of identity

Nathanael Andrade

Around the year 700 CE, Jacob of Edessa wrote a critique of scholars who had rendered the name of God as '*pipi*' while he was engaged in the work of translating Severus of Antioch's homilies. The error had originated from a tendency for Greek copyists to misunderstand the Hebrew tetragrammaton as consisting of Greek letters (pi-iota-pi-iota) that resembled its lexical form. But Jacob's concerns elicited his broader contemplation of how writers of Syriac had translated Greek texts (Brière 1960: 190–207; on Jacob and Hebrew, see Salvesen 2010). Jacob thus described how people had translated biblical works from Greek into 'the Syrian (*Suryaya*) language', and he referred to such people as 'Greeks' (*Yawnaye*). But he then noted that 'other Syrians (*Suryaye*)' had received and transmitted their works (Brière 1960: 192–3). Here Jacob hinted that speakers of both Greek and Syriac could be reckoned Syrian due to their regional origins. After all, since he described speakers of Syriac as 'other Syrians', he was implying that speakers of Greek in Syria were Syrian too (Andrade 2010–2011: 1–2).

But later in his discussion, Jacob specified that people who spoke Syriac could be called either Aramaeans (*Aramaye*) or Syrians (*Suryaye*), with these being roughly synonymous names (Brière 1960: 196–7; for more on 'Aramaean', see Nöldeke 1871). This means that Jacob had at least two different definitions of who Syrians were. According to one, Syrians (or Aramaeans) were speakers of Aramaic or of Syriac ('Syrian') specifically, which in its more literary form Jacob sometimes qualified as 'Edessene' or 'Mesopotamian' (Phillips 1869: 11 of Syriac; Van Rompay 2000: 78). But according to the other definition, speakers of Greek ('Greeks') who had lived in the Roman Syrian provinces were Syrians too. This is why Jacob distinguished 'Greek' Syrians who translated Scripture into Syriac from 'other Syrians', or Aramaeans, who spoke Aramaic or Syriac and who benefited from their work (Andrade 2010–2011: 1–2).

Jacob, of course, was active during the early phases of Islamic rule. The Roman Empire no longer controlled its former Syrian and Mesopotamian territories. But the numerous meanings with which Jacob endowed the word 'Syrian' were not new. By his day, writers of Greek had been labelling Aramaeans and other Aramaic-speaking populations as 'Syrians' (*Suroi*) for nearly one thousand years. During Late Antiquity, if not before, the word *Suros* had entered the Syriac language as *Suryaya*, and Jacob's discussion thus represents how the term 'Syrian' as a synonym for 'Aramaean' had penetrated Syriac discourse. Likewise, for centuries of Roman rule, 'Syrian' had been the identifying label used for and by all inhabitants of the Syrian provinces, regardless of whether they spoke Greek or an Aramaic dialect. This is why Jacob implicitly treated speakers of Greek from Syria as Syrians. In the Roman Near East, many people who did not speak Syriac or other Aramaic dialects identified themselves as Syrian.

But one can specify yet another meaning that the term 'Syrian' bore in Jacob's corpus. 'Syrian' and its synonym 'Aramaean' could specifically denote the putative descendants of the biblical figure Shem or his son Aram who spoke Syriac (or Aramaic) as their ancestral language. In his *Commentary on the Octateuch* (Vat. Syr. 103, f.36r), a related scholion (BL Add. 17193, f.64v–65r), and in a letter (Wright 1876: g), Jacob conceived of Noah's son Shem as having been allotted the territory between the Euphrates and the Mediterranean. According to a later commentary that is indebted to Jacob's work (Vat. Syr. 103, f.17v), Shem's son Aram settled the Syrian territories west of the Euphrates (Haar Romeny et al. 2010: 16; Haar Romeny 2008a: 146–7; Debié 2010; see Kruisheer 1997, 1998; Haar Romeny 2008b: 540–2 on the texts). Michael the Syrian's arguments that ancient Aramaeans or Syrians spoke Syriac and were descended from Aram were probably much indebted to Jacob's learnedness too (Chabot 1899–1910: 4.748–51/3.442–7, esp. 750–1/3.447 and Ibrahim 2009: 751–4, esp. 753–4; see Debié 2010: 96 and 104 and Conclusion). Clearly, by Jacob's lifetime, certain Syrian Orthodox Christians were crafting ethnic identities as Syrians who shared both a common language (Syriac, or at least Aramaic) and a common descent (from Aram).

Jacob's varying usages for the identifying label 'Syrian' invites us to explore the link between Syriac and Syrian identity in the later Roman Empire. It also inspires us to define when exactly certain self-named *Suryaye* (or *Aramaye*) formed an ethnic consciousness based on shared language. These questions are complicated ones, and they have inspired debate among scholars of later Roman Syria. The complications in part spring from the diverse forms that Syrian identity assumed in preceding periods. When the Romans ruled the Near East and upper Mesopotamia, many inhabitants of the region conceived of themselves as Syrians. Even so, they spoke Greek, Latin, or any dialect of Aramaic. But during the Islamic period, centuries later, Syrian Orthodox Christians deemed membership in their Syrian community to be defined by shared religious allegiance and Syriac language. Much had clearly changed between Rome's annexation of Syria (64–63 BCE) and the erudition of Jacob of Edessa. But how and when the social category of 'Syrian' transformed in the intervening period of Roman rule are topics of debate.

This chapter therefore explores the formation of Syrian ethnicity and its links to religious community and Syriac language in the later Roman Empire. It begins by providing a general overview of how polyvalent Syrian identities were under Roman rule. It then proceeds to explore two issues raised by recent scholarly debates. One is whether speakers of Syriac or kindred Aramaic dialects formulated concepts of Syrian ethnicity before the rise of Islam. The other is whether they defined religious affiliation and Syriac speech as its key cultural markers. The article concludes with some observations regarding whether we can conceive of certain speakers of Syriac as cultivating Syrian ethnicity or nationhood in the later Roman Empire and by the time of the Islamic conquests.

SYRIANS AND ARAMAIC IN THE ROMAN EMPIRE

The Romans, like the Greeks before them, conceived of Syrians in numerous different ways. In its most expansive sense, 'Syrian' referred to all the populations in the Levant and Mesopotamia in which Aramaic was spoken. Romans thus often deemed Syrians and Assyrians to be the same people (Strabo, 16.1.1–2), and they believed that Syrians typically called themselves Aramaeans in their own language (Strabo, 1.2.34 and 16.4.27; Josephus, *Antiquities of the Jews* 1.142–44; Andrade 2013, 2014). But after the Romans conquered the Levant in the mid-first century BCE, they labelled all the populations west of the Euphrates Syrians. The descendants of Greek settlers and indigenous Syrians thus became 'Syrian' subjects of the Roman Empire, whatever their ancestries and languages were. Roman authors writing in Greek and Latin often described Syrians in such terms (Strabo, 16.2.1–3; Josephus, *AJ* 18.1–2; *Digest* 48.22.7.14–15, 50.15.1, and 50.15.3, in Mommsen and Watson 1985; Ammianus, 14.8.7–11). For them, everyone in Syria or its provinces was Syrian, and as the Romans parcelled Osrhoene and other upper Mesopotamian territories into provinces during the second and third centuries, they classified the resident population as 'Syrian' too (Andrade 2013: esp. 109–10; Andrade 2014: 304–5).

How Greeks and Romans understood Syrians is evident. But what has inspired debate is whether Syrians cultivated any ethnic self-definition as Syrians before Late Antiquity. After all, the people that Romans called Syrians may not have defined themselves as such. Even if they had, they could simply be using geographic labels. Likewise, Aramaic dialects assumed various diverse forms throughout Syria (Gzella 2015: 212–80). One can similarly describe cultural and religious practices of Near Eastern origin as regionally variable too, with Canaanite, Hittite, Aramaean, and Arabian influences (just to name a few) having greater bearing in different parts of Roman Syria. Since Greek language and culture were key languages of civic activity throughout the region, the variations in Aramaic language and Near Eastern cultural life have been invoked as evidence for the absence of a Syrian or analogous 'Near Eastern' identity (seminal is Millar 1993, 2013a: 106–50, with many articles now found in 2006b, 2015). Some scholars have responded to this premise by emphasising continuities in material culture, especially that of a religious nature, that could suggest that such forms of identity existed (Ball 2000/2016). The problem is that this perspective often assumes that any material form that putatively originates from the Near East expresses a Syrian, Near Eastern, or even a 'Semitic' identity without demonstrating it (Butcher 2013).

Some recent scholarship has aimed to reconcile these perspectives by claiming that Syrian, Greek, and Roman categories were culturally negotiable. Different people had different ways to be Syrian, Greek, and Roman, and they expressed these identities through somewhat variable cultural forms (Butcher 2003: 270–334; Sartre 2008; Andrade 2013, 2014). Some have even advanced the premise that 'Syrian' was primarily a regional category in the Roman Empire. Not all social identities are necessarily ethnic in formulation, and Syrians who spoke Greek, Latin, or Aramaic, in keeping with Roman imperial ideology, saw themselves as part of a Syrian regional collective that aligned with how Roman imperial authorities had defined it (Andrade 2013). Syrians throughout the Roman Empire thus identified themselves by their provincial origin (Solin 1983; Noy 2000: 318–21). Under this rubric, Phoenicians and Palestinians too were Syrians (Mark 7:26; Lucian, *Assembly of the Gods* 4; Ammianus, 14.8.7–11; John of Ephesus, *Lives of the Eastern Saints*, in Brooks 1923–25: 18.527–9, 18.658–9, 18.694–5, 19.154–5). The regional category also accommodated local and regional cultural variations. According to this premise, people in different parts of Syria expressed Syrian identities through cultural symbols that varied in origin, with some being customary and others new.

Alongside 'Syrian' as a meaningful regional identity, recent scholarship has also maintained that a distinctly ethnic articulation of 'Syrian' circulated in the Roman Empire (Andrade 2014). Among writers of Greek, the label Syrian could refer to any Aramaic dialect or speakers of it (Plutarch, *Antony* 46.2–3; Lucian, *Alexander* 52 and *Salaried Positions* 10; *Historia Augusta*, *Aurelian* 27.6). Moreover, speakers of Greek could conceive of Aramaic-speakers, or people descended from them, as Syrians by ethnicity. But this ethnic construct was mostly a Greek and Roman invention. In this formulation, the putative ancestors of ethnic Syrians were the Assyrians and Babylonians, whose largely mythical kings (like Belus, Ninus, Semiramis, and Sardanapalus) circulated in Greek narratives (Diodorus Siculus, 2.1–29, 6.1.10; Strabo, 16.1.1–2; Isidore of Charax, *Parthian Stopping Points*, 1 and 5, now *Brill's New Jacoby* 781, Fr. 2). But to a certain degree, Syrians themselves adopted this formulation and understood their past through it. As such, they arguably conceived of themselves as Syrian by ethnicity even if they often expressed the concept in Greek or with pasts of Greek invention. In *On the Syrian Goddess*, Lucian of Samosata thus illustrates in Greek how Syrians ('Assyrians') at Hierapolis-Mabbug created narratives of their sacred site's history by embracing Greek myths and Greek versions of Near Eastern myths (Lucian, *Dea Syria* 10–28 and 39–40, in Lightfoot 2003, who provides a learned commentary; Andrade 2013: 288–313, 2014: 307–11).

The work of the Byzantine author Photius yields another intriguing example of this phenomenon. According to one of his scholiasts, the second-century novelist Iamblichus, who wrote in Greek but was a native speaker of Aramaic, conceived of himself as the descendent of 'autochthonous' Syrians. This scholion on Iamblichus is worth quoting:

> Iamblichus was a Syrian (*Suros*) by both paternal and maternal genealogy, but he was not a Syrian of the Greeks who had inhabited Syria, but of the autochthonous. He knew the Syrian language and lived according to their customs.
>
> (Henry 2003: 2.40, n. 1, in Photius, *Bibl.* 94.75b; see Millar 1993: 491)

The scholiast's testimony was obviously rendered much later than Iamblichus's Roman context. But it seems to be commenting accurately on the definitions of 'Syrian' that were in play in Iamblichus's lifetime. One was the conception of 'Syrian' as a regional category to which all inhabitants of Syrians could lay claim, including the descendants of Greek settlers. The other was an ethnic definition classifying 'Syrians' as people for whom Aramaic ('Syrian') was an ancestral language. But even so, we have reason to suspect that Iamblichus understood his ancestry through a lens crafted at least in part by the Greek and Roman literary tradition (Millar 1993: 489–92; Sartre 2008: 28–9).

A key premise of the scholarly perspectives on Syrian identity described so far is that not all ethnic or national identities are expressed through a single language of 'indigenous' origin. Although the 'imagined communities' of modern European nation-states have often conceived of their members as having shared ethnic backgrounds and national languages (Anderson 2006), this does not mean that people in antiquity thought of themselves in the same manner (Andrade 2013, 2014). If ethnicity is principally deemed a mode of cognition (see Conclusion and the works of Brubaker in the Bibliography), then speakers of Greek or Aramaic conceivably thought of themselves as ethnic Syrians through perceived descent from Aramaic-speaking ancestors, including (in their view) Assyrians and Babylonians.

In summary, despite the scholarly debates, we know that writers of Greek, including self-identifying Syrians or 'Assyrians', conceived of Syrians in various ways during the Roman imperial period. Sometimes they defined Syrians exclusively as indigenous Aramaic-speakers or their descendants (who could speak Greek). We also know that by the Islamic period, some Syrian Orthodox Christians had appropriated for themselves the Greek term 'Syrian' and charged it with explicitly ethnic implications (Haar Romeny et al. 2010; Haar Romeny 2012). But whether later Roman speakers of Syriac or Aramaic deemed themselves to be Syrians by ethnicity and language is still a debated issue. To this debate we now turn.

SYRIANS AND SYRIAC IN LATER ROMAN SYRIA

In the early phases of Roman imperialism, Syriac was the Aramaic dialect of Edessa and nearby upper Mesopotamian locations (Healey 2007; Gzella 2015: 256–60 and 366–78). During the later Roman period, it notably became a key religious and liturgical language of Christianity. Its significance was most conspicuous in areas of upper Mesopotamia, whose inhabitants principally spoke it and shared many other cultural or religious traditions. But as codices, inscriptions, and literary texts bear witness, its usage came to extend throughout Roman upper Mesopotamia, lowland territories of Sasanian Persia, and Roman Syrian provinces west of the Euphrates (Millar 2009a, 2009b, 2011a, 2011b, 2012, 2013a: 106–38, 2013b, many of which are in Millar 2015; Brock 1997, 1998, 2001, 2005, 2009, 2012; Johnson 2015). Of course, works of Syriac literature were produced in earlier periods. For example, already in the first to third centuries were written the *Letter of Mara bar Sarapion* (perhaps first century; see Merz and Tieleman 2012), the Syriac version of the *Odes of Solomon*, and the texts composed by Bardaiṣan's literary circle (the collected articles of Drijvers 1984, 1994; Ramelli 2009a,b; Johnson 2015: 18–19). But in subsequent centuries, if not earlier, a body of literature often associated with 'Syriac Christianity' took shape alongside distinctive religious beliefs and practices. Syriac translations of the Hebrew Bible and Christian New Testament and the poetry of Ephrem are just some notable examples of this phenomenon (the collected articles of Brock 1984, 1992b, 1999, 2006; Weitzman 1999; Haar Romeny 2005; Van Rompay 2008b; Shepardson 2009; Wood 2012; Griffith 2013; Johnson 2015: 11–12, 17–27).

Despite the increased usage and circulation of Syriac, it is debatable whether Syrian ethnicity or identity was coherently expressed in the later Roman East. As with earlier phases, a fundamental problem is that people who called themselves Syrians were diverse in language and cultural practices (see Millar's works in the Bibliography). The languages of Near Eastern origin that Syrians spoke, including Aramaic and Arabic, were regionally different (see Gzella 2015: 281–381; Taylor 2002). A unique Aramaic dialect, for example, was used among Christians in Palestine (Hoyland 2004, 2010; Griffith 1997; Gzella 2015: 317–26). In the fifth century, Theodoret of Cyrrhus grasped such regional variation. As he states:

> For just as the Osrhoenians, Syrians, Euphratesians, Palestinians, and Phoenicians speak the language of the Syrians, but their manner of speaking nonetheless bears considerable difference.
>
> (*Quaest. in Iud.* 19, in Petruccione and Hill 2007; see Millar 2007a: 118, 2013a: 118)

For such reasons, Aramaic and Syriac do not appear to have marked any self-ascribed ethnic or national identity. As had occurred in previous periods, the 'indigenous' dialects and cultural practices of Syrians varied from region to region.

By contrast, Greek cultural practices were fairly uniform and pervasive throughout Roman Syria, and they facilitated a cultural *koine* in the Near East (Bowersock 1990: esp. 7–9; Millar 1993: esp. 489–534, and his subsequent work in the Bibliography; Butcher 2003: 270–334; Sartre 2001, 2005, 2008). They certainly had an impact on the cultures of people who spoke Syriac (see Brock 1989, 1994, 1996, 1999; Griffith 2013; Johnson 2015). Greek language and culture penetrated most urban and rural areas and played key roles in civic and ecclesiastical institutions. Bilingualism was therefore common among people of authority, and many native speakers of Aramaic adopted Greek (see the seminal works of Brock and Millar in the Bibliography; Taylor 2002). The regional pre-eminence and uniformity of Greek, combined with the absence of a uniform Aramaic counterpart, thus poses challenges to scholarly premises that 'Syrian' was an ethnic identity.

Another problem is that arguably no distinctly ethnic 'Syrian' church took shape until the Islamic period, even as Syriac became increasingly prominent among the non-Chalcedonian miaphysite Christians that would eventually form the Syrian Orthodox church (Millar 2013b; Haar Romeny 2010). The grounds for this objection are easy to find. Non-Chalcedonians often spoke or wrote in Greek, and Syriac was not exclusive to them (on the non-Chalcedonian church, see Menze 2008). Some Chalcedonians of the Roman empire spoke or wrote Syriac or other Aramaic dialects (Hoyland 2004; Griffith 1997; Gzella 2015: 317–26; Debié 2015: 447–50; Johnson 2015: 29–35, 88–92), and Syriac was undoubtedly a key language of the Persian Church of the East (see, for example, Walker 2006; Becker 2008; Brock 2008a,b; Payne 2015: 148–9; Smith 2016). Moreover, non-Chalcedonian miaphysite dissension extended beyond Roman Syria (Fowden 1993; Wood 2010: 209–56; Hoyland 2009). It is thus hard to identify an ecclesiastical community of the later Roman Empire that claimed an exclusive ethnic Syrian identity and embraced Syriac (or Aramaic) language as one of its central markers.

But despite such serious issues, some scholars posit that Syrians did create coherent expressions of Syrian identity in the later Roman Empire. They have also made such claims from varying perspectives and vantage points. What some have emphasised is that expressions of Syrian identity were regionally variable and could be anchored in the Greek or Aramaic languages. As had been the case in previous periods, different Syrians had different ways of being Syrian, and being Syrian could variously occupy regional, linguistic, or ethnic registers. For example, many self-identifying Syrians, including speakers of Syriac, Greek, and Latin, conceived of themselves as part of a 'Syrian people' defined by regional origins, not linguistic or ethnic ones (Andrade 2010–2011). Writers ranging from Ammianus to John of Ephesus understood 'Syrians' to be all the inhabitants of the Roman territories of the Levantine and upper Mesopotamia that traditionally housed speakers of Aramaic. By the sixth century, these had been parcelled into the many provinces that bore the names of either Syria, Phoenice, Palaestina, Euphratensis, Osrhoene, or Mesopotamia (Ammianus, 14.8.7–11; John of Ephesus, *Lives of the Eastern Saints*, in Brooks 1923–1925: 18.527–9, 18.658–9, 18.694–5, 19.154–5; *Life of Alexander the Sleepless* 22, in de Stoop 1911; Theodoret, *Ecclesiastical History* 2.24.25, with perhaps 1.7.4 and 2.30.1, in Parmentier and Hansen 1998). In short, all the provinces in which populations traditionally spoke Aramaic ('Syrian') were understood to be inhabited by Syrians, and speakers of Greek with no command of Aramaic thus conceived of themselves as Syrians by regional affiliation.

At the same time, 'Syrian' could also refer specifically to Aramaic dialects or the people who spoke them. A figure from Sophanene named Zoara is accordingly described by John of Ephesus (favourably) and the Greek records from the Council of Constantinople in 536 (less favourably) as a troublesome 'Syrian' (Brooks 1923–1925: 17.26–7, 34–5; *ACO* III, 5, 12; Millar 2008a: 72–4). 'Syrian' seems to highlight Zoara's primary language in these instances, and textual references for this type of usage are abundant. Just a few of the authors or texts that employ it are Libanius (*Or.* 42.31), Eusebius (*Ecclesiastical History* 1.13.11, in Schwartz and Mommsen 1999), Theodoret (*Ecclesiastical History* 1.7.4, 2.30.11, 3.24.1, 4.10.1, 4.29.1, in Parmentier and Hansen 1998; *Historia Religiosa* 5.6, 10.9, 13.2,7, 14.2, 21.15, in Canivet and Leroy-Molinghen 1977–1979), the *Life of Hypatius* (Bartelink 1971: Ded. 6), the *Life of Daniel the Stylite* (Delehaye 1923: §3, 14), Leontios's *Life of Symeon the Holy Fool* (Festugière 1974: 58), the *Life of Alexander the Sleepless* (de Stoop 1911: §22), the *Life of Rabula* (Overbeck 1865: 172), Mark the Deacon's *Life of Porphyry* (Grégoire and Kugener 1930: §68–9), the chronicle composed by ps.-Zachariah (§7.12, Brooks 1919–1924: 2.55), Philoxenus of Mabbug (de Halleux 1962: 38, 1963: 51–5), the *Life of John of Tella* (Brooks 1907: 43), the records of the Council of Constantinople (in *ACO* III, 5, 68–9), and the *Itinerary of Egeria* (Maraval 1982: §47.3–4).

Yet, the use of 'Syrian' was arguably not limited to expressions of regional or linguistic identity. We can perhaps conceive of 'Syrian' as an ethnic categorisation cultivated by speakers of Aramaic or Greek who traced their 'Syrian' origins to Aramaic-speaking ancestors. This formulation was rooted in Jewish and Christian traditions that conceived of Syrians (or Aramaeans) as the descendants of Aram, a son of Noah's son Shem. Josephus is exemplary. According to his *Jewish Antiquities*, Aram was the common ancestor of all Aramaeans, but the Greeks called them Syrians. His brother Ashur was the ancestor of the Assyrians (*AJ* 1.142–4). Josephus's viewpoint was repeated by some Christian Syrians of Late Antiquity. For example, the surviving Armenian translation of the *Chronicle* of Eusebius indicates that Ashur and Aram were sons of Shem and that Ashur's descendants, who included the mythical figure of Ninus mentioned so prominently in Greeks texts, were the Assyrians. But it also claims that the Aramaeans, who were called Syrians and came to inhabit the empire of the ancient Assyrians, were descended from Aram (Karst 1911: 35). Eusebius's *Chronicle* and its sources had a substantial impact on subsequent Syriac historiography (Debié 2006, 2015: 303–13) and formulations of ethnicity, certainly by the Islamic period.

As part of these formulations, Late Antique Syrian Christians began to distinguish Syrians (or Aramaeans) from Assyrians (or Babylonians/'Chaldaeans') in ways that challenged prior Greek conceptions of Syrians as the descendants of the ancient Assyrians and their mythical monarchs like Semiramis, Ninus, and Belus. We have just noted how Eusebius draws this distinction in his *Chronicle* (Karst 1911: 1–35 generally). So, it seems, does John Malalas (*Chron.*1.8–13, in Thurn 2000), who treats the legendary rulers of the ancient Assyrians as descended from Shem but makes no mention of Aram or Aramaeans. The impact of works like those of Eusebius and John Malalas can be detected in subsequent Syriac historiography (Debié 2004, 2006). During the Islamic period, Syrian Orthodox authors would distinguish Syrians, as the Aramaean descendants of Aram, from Assyrians (see Conclusion). Likewise, Syriac-writing authors in the classical Assyrian territories of the Sasanian Persian empire noticeably traced their 'Assyrian' pasts to ancient figures derived from Greek traditions but did not necessarily associate themselves with Aramaean lineages (Bedjan 1890–1897: 2.507–11; Becker 2008: 398–402; Walker 2006; Payne 2015: 140–52; still relevant is Fiey 1965).

Significantly, as recent scholarship has argued, the Syriac-speaking inhabitants of Edessa and neighbouring places in upper Mesopotamia were fashioning kindred formulations of 'Syrian' ethnicity during the fifth and sixth centuries too (Wood 2010: 83–162 most prominently). Among them circulated the belief that Syrians were descended from the biblical figure Shem or his son Aram, spoke Syriac (or Aramaic), or inhabited cities established by the biblical figure Nemrud. As we have seen, these formulations had their roots in Judaeo-Christian literature of the Roman imperial period, especially Eusebius's *Chronicle*. In tandem with them, Syriac literature produced at this time also shows how Edessenes and other Syriac-speakers of upper Mesopotamia were conceiving of themselves as cultivating a unique Christian culture, as possessing a prominent stature among the Christian communities of the Middle East, and as distinct from Jews and, more generally, Romans (including Greek-speaking Syrians). Some key works cited to this effect are the *Teaching of Addai*, *Euphemia and the Goth*, the *Julian Romance*, and various martyr acts (Wood 2010: esp. 83–162, Wood 2012). Among these, the *Teaching of Addai* and its legend of king Abgar are particularly important. A tradition with roots to the third century, Eusebius describes it in his *Ecclesiastical History* and claims that it circulated at Edessa in the 'Syrian' language (Eusebius, *HE* 1.13 and 2.1.6–8 in Schwartz and Mommsen 1999; Brock 1992a). The surviving Syriac text of the *Teaching of Addai* dates to the fifth century or so. It narrates how king Abgar the Black engaged in correspondence with Jesus of Nazareth and how the apostle Addai brought the gospel to Edessa after Jesus's death (Griffith 2003; Wood 2010: 82–100, 2012: 175–81). The Syriac text thus claims that Edessenes played a key role in the history of Christianity in the Near East. In Persian territory, the *Acts of Mar Mari* engaged with this tradition too (Jullien and Jullien 2002: esp. 77–8, 2003; Wood 2010: 110–16).

But more explicit testimony for the formulation of Syrian ethnicity in Edessene or related Syriac texts comes from the *Book of the Cave of Treasures* (Wood 2010: 117–26; Minov 2013, who talks of a 'Syriac Christian' identity). Probably composed in Sasanian Assyria ('the land of Nod'), its precise dating between the fifth and seventh centuries is hard to fix. But it can be squarely situated in a religious and literary culture that spanned Roman and Sasanian Mesopotamia and in which the traditions of Edessa played vital roles (Wood 2010: 117–20). In fact, the writer, whom early commenters apparently believed to be Ephrem himself (Minov 2013: 157–65), was perhaps a non-Chalcedonian miaphysite in orientation. In various respects, the work reflects and helps promote the belief that the Syrians were a Syriac- or Aramaic-speaking ethnicity. First, the work significantly defines Syriac ('the Syrian language'), which it also calls Aramaic (*Aramaya*), as the world's oldest language and as 'the king of all the languages'; before the tower of Babel, it was the only language that people spoke (24.10 in Ri 1987). The text was thus enmeshed in a broader debate regarding whether Hebrew or Syriac was the oldest language (Ri 2000: 293; Minov 2013: 166–75), and it indicates that Syriac could be referred to as either 'Aramaean' or 'Syrian'.

Likewise, in an echo of Ephrem's *Commentary on Genesis and Exodus* (Tonneau 1955: 65), the *Book* subsequently portrays the biblical king Nemrud as founding many of the cities of Mesopotamia that Syrians came to inhabit. These included Babel, Nineveh, Resen, Seleucia-Ctesiphon, Adorbigan (27.23 in Ri 1987), and Nisibis, Edessa, and Ḥarran (30.19 in Ri 1987). The text however does not explicitly mention Aram, even if the descendants of his father Shem are allotted the territory between Persia and the Mediterranean (and even the Adriatic) (24.21 in Ri 1987; Ri 2000: 295–302). Intriguingly, the *Book* also claims that at Jesus's crucifixion, Pilate fixed the names of Jesus's murderers to the cross. These were Herod 'the Greek', Pilate the Roman, and Caiaphas the Hebrew. But since king Abgar of Edessa and the Syrians (*Suryaye*) had no part in his death, there was no mention of them (53.21–2 and 25, in Ri 1987). In this way, the *Book* refers to the Abgar legend and links it to the pre-eminence of Syrians as people who spoke the world's oldest language and who did not kill the Messiah (Wood 2010: 120–6; Minov 2013: 175–84).

The *Book of the Cave of Treasures* is significant in many respects. The text shows that writers of Syriac texts in Roman and Sasanian Mesopotamia and nearby areas conceived of Syriac-speakers of the region as *Suryaye*. They also deemed Syrians to be the descendants of Shem and to inhabit the cities founded in Mesopotamia by the mythical Nemrud. One can thus posit that the foundations for concepts of Syrian ethnicity for which Syriac speech was a key marker had taken shape at Edessa and nearby locations by the sixth century. Unfortunately, it is presently unclear to what extent Syrians living west of the Euphrates, whether Greek- or Aramaic-speaking, conceived of Syrian ethnicity in such terms. But as we have seen, the Armenian recension of Eusebius's *Chronicle* treats Syrians as descended from Shem and Aram, and it is certainly possible that Syrian Christians, whatever language they spoke, construed Aramaic-speaking Syrians as having such ethnic roots. A text attributed to John of Apamea (but without certainty), which stresses the superiority of a 'pure' Syriac over one influenced by Greek, even seems to endow the language with explicit connotations of ethnic difference, much like the *Book of the Cave of Treasures* (A.58–60 in Strothmann 1988: 4; Minov 2013: 180–1).

Moreover, when later Roman Syrians discussed the Syriac poet Ephrem, they apparently conceived of him not merely as a poet who wrote in Syriac but as one who served a Syrian people. One can cite Greek-writing authors to this effect. Theodoret of Cyrrhus thus describes Ephrem as a poet who 'daily waters the *ethnos* of Syrians (*to Surôn ethnos*) with streams of grace' (in *Ep.* 146, Azéma 1955–1998: 3.190, with *HE* 2.30.11 and 4.29.1 in Parmentier and Hansen 1998; Millar 2008b: 86–90). Sozomen makes a kindred statement (*HE* 3.16 in Bidez and Hansen 1995). He claims that Ephrem, who wrote in the language of the Syrians, surpassed the Greeks in wisdom. He also notes that Ephrem's works had been translated from Syriac to Greek by his lifetime (Andrade 2010–2011: 18). In such ways, Greek-speaking Christians in Syria seem to have attributed an ethnic consciousness to Aramaic-speaking ones, even if they did not always comment on descent.

Significantly, similar concepts circulated among writers of Syriac, who eventually deemed Ephrem to be the exemplary poet of an 'Aramaean' or 'Syrian' people. As early as the writer Posidonius (first century BCE), whose testimony is cited by Strabo, Greek-writing authors from Syria were noting that 'Aramaean' was a name that Syrians called themselves in Aramaic (Strabo, 1.2.34 and 16.4.27). It is perhaps possible that some Aramaic-speakers continually called themselves Aramaeans throughout the Roman period, with the Greek term 'Syrians' (*Suroi*) being adopted in Late Antiquity as its synonym (*Suryaye*). But the usage of 'Aramaean' among Syriac-writing authors in the later Roman empire also placed an emphasis upon the descent of Syrians from Aram, a tradition that they inherited from Josephus's *Jewish Antiquities* and Eusebius's *Chronicle* (now surviving in Armenian). In the fourth century, Ephrem thus describes Bardaiṣan as an 'Aramaean' (*Aramaya*) philosopher (Mitchell 1912–1921: 2.225; Griffith 2002: 12). In turn, over a century later, Jacob of Sarug explicitly vaunted Ephrem as the poet of a Syrian people, and he seems to have framed this Syrian people as descended from Aram. In a hymn about Ephrem, Jacob described him as a wondrous 'rhetor' who 'triumphed over the Greeks (*Yawnaye*)' (verse 32 in Amar 1995). But intriguingly, he later in the hymn asserted that Ephrem was the 'crown of all the Aramaean people (*Armayuta*)' and the great rhetor 'among the Syrians (*Suryaye*)' (verse 155–6 in Amar 1995; Andrade 2010–2011: 20; Sokoloff 2009: 102). His sentiment is echoed by his contemporary Philoxenus of Mabbug, who described Ephrem as 'the teacher of us *Suryaye*' (de Halleux 1962: 38; Minov 2013: 160). While engaging with the legends of king Abgar and the early Edessene martyrs, Jacob even defined Abgar as a 'son of the Aramaeans' (*bar Aramaye*, in Bedjan 1890–1897: 1.131; Wood 2012: 187). These statements suggest that Jacob and Philoxenus understood Syrians to be speakers of Syriac who constituted an 'Aramaean people', in part due to their shared descent from Aram. Even if it is not clear whether speakers of Syriac or Aramaic throughout Roman Syria were conceiving of Syrian ethnicity in such terms, those in upper Mesopotamia and immediately west of the Euphrates apparently were.

The formation of a non-Chalcedonian miaphysite church and identity in Syria during the mid-sixth century occurred independently of the rise of a Syrian ethnic consciousness in which Syriac played a prominent role (Menze 2008; Millar 2013b; Taylor 2009). But the two processes would become intimately linked and mutually informing (Wood 2010: 163–209 and 2012: 189–90). Over time, the church's formation in areas of widespread Syriac speech and bilingualism encouraged compositions in Syriac by churchmen and monks like Philoxenus, Jacob of Sarug, Daniel of Ṣalaḥ, John of Tella and his main hagiographer, the author of the chronicle of ps.-Zachariah, and John of Ephesus, to name some later Roman examples (Millar 2013a: 131–8, 2013b; Menze 2008; Andrade 2009). After the collapse of Roman rule in the East and the slow decline of Greek, the principal language of literary output and copying was Syriac, and many texts of non-Chalcedonian authors originally composed in Greek have only survived in the language (Haar Romeny et al. 2010: 48–9; Millar 2013b). Thus when Jacob of Edessa criticised how Syrians of various stripes had misunderstood the name of the Christian divinity, he did so while translating the homilies of Severus of Antioch from the now-lost Greek originals into a Syriac version that has survived (Van Rompay 2008a; Debié 2015: 440–7). Moreover, by Jacob's lifetime, the study of Greek was apparently disparaged in some Syrian Orthodox circles (Michael the Syrian, in Chabot 1899–1910: 4.446/2.472; Ibrahim 2009: 449).

As the preceding discussion suggests, some Syriac-writing Syrians of the later Roman period did formulate beliefs that speakers of Syriac or Aramaic were descended from Aram. Others specified that Syrians were the Syriac-speaking inhabitants of regions governed by the biblical king Nemrud and subsequently by ancient Assyrian/ Babylonian figures. Their views were largely informed by Judaeo-Christian narratives of the biblical past, but they were also variable to a certain degree. Moreover, Syrians had not yet established exclusively 'Syrian' political or ecclesiastical institutions or engaged in coordinated group action at the regional level, even if the rise of the non-Chalcedonian miaphysite movement would catalyse this. Whether speakers of Syriac fashioned Syrian ethnic identities in the later Roman Empire thus depends on how 'ethnicity' is defined. In our concluding thoughts, we comment on this issue.

CONCLUSION

As Syrian Orthodox Christians from the Islamic period increasingly viewed their past through the lens of the Hebrew Bible, the belief that Syrians were Syriac-speakers descended from Aram or the ancient Aramaeans gained momentum. We have seen how Jacob of Edessa, writing ca. 700, and subsequent commentators conceived of the descendants of Shem and his son Aram as inhabiting the territories in which Syrians dwelled. The *Zuqnin Chronicle* variously describes Syrian Orthodox Christians as Syrians, Aramaeans, and 'sons of Aram' (Chabot 1927–1933: 2.154 and 256, with Harrak 1999: 225–6). Michael the Syrian (twelfth century) also traced the lineage of the Aramaeans (Syrians) to Aram while discussing the use of Aramaic among the inhabitants of the empires of the ancient Assyrians and Babylonians/Chaldaeans (Chabot 1899–1910: 4.748–51/3.442–7, esp. 749–50/3.445–6, with 4.522–4/3.76–8 and Ibrahim 2009: 751–4, esp. 752–3, with 525–7; Debié 2010: 103–5, 2015: 464–7). His main sources were Josephus, Eusebius, Jacob of Edessa, and Dionysius of Tel-Maḥre (ninth century). In keeping with Greek antecedents, Michael acknowledged that the term Syrian could describe people east of the Euphrates who spoke the language of the Aramaeans and were putatively descended from Assyrians and Babylonians ('Chaldaeans'), who had spoken their language too. But despite the prominence of Edessa, he also maintained that 'Syrian' referred most specifically to Aramaic-speakers ('Aramaeans') west of the Euphrates who traced descent from Aram (Chabot 1899–1910: 4.749–50/3.445–6 and Ibrahim 2009: 752–3).

In the Islamic period, Syrian Orthodox Christians had thus created their own unique Syriac-speaking ecclesiastical community, even if many adopted Arabic too (Griffith 2008). They generally traced their ancestral roots to Shem and Aram (Debié 2010). But as we have discussed, whether they or other self-identifying Syrians had formulated similar ethnic self-perceptions under later Roman rule is more debatable. One must account for the fact that people who cultivated premises of Syrian descent did not always speak or write the Aramaic language of their putative ancestors or cultivate uniform cultural markers. In fact, Syrians often expressed their regional or ancestral identities through Greek culture and language (Bowersock 1990: esp. 7–9; Andrade 2010–2011, 2013, 2014). We would also have to accept that perceptions of Syrian ethnicity and ancestry assumed a certain measure of variety. As we have witnessed, later Roman Syrians conceived of their ethnic lineages in different ways. Syrians could express how they, as Syrians, were generally descended from speakers of Aramaic ruled by Assyrian (or Babylonian/Chaldaean) dynasts or by the biblical king Nemrud. But they could also claim, more specifically, that Syrians were descended from Aram or his father Shem. Some Syrians combined these various traditions.

But at a certain level, the debate on Syrian ethnicity and identity hinges on how 'ethnicity' is defined and to what extent it is meaningfully distinguished from 'nation'. If one defines it as a belief in common descent that is expressed through shared language and cultural practices and that constitutes the basis for political movements, regional mass actions, or national states, then it is difficult to establish the existence of Syrian ethnicity in the later Roman Empire. But it is perhaps better to reserve such a definition for a 'nation' (for definitions of 'nation', see Brubaker 1996, 2004d; Smith 2004, 2008), to be distinguished from 'ethnicity'. If ethnicity is defined by cognition of shared descent and certain identity markers, as some scholars argue (Brubaker 2004a, 2004b, 2004c; Brubaker et al. 2004; see Smith 2004: esp. 17–23, 2008: 28–47; Wood 2010: 9–16 and 71–81 on 'ethnie'), then it can be posited that certain Syrians conceived of themselves as members of a Syrian ethnicity. But such formulations did not become the basis of exclusively 'Syrian' (or 'non-Greek') political institutions, regional mass movements, and thus a 'nation' in the later Roman Empire.

One can perhaps then conceive of later Roman Syrians, both Greek- and Aramaic-speaking, as having formed an ethnic consciousness based on premises of shared descent and a language that their ancestors had spoken (but which they did not necessarily speak in the present). It is also reasonable to claim that certain speakers of Syriac, especially those living in upper Mesopotamia, maintained an ethnic consciousness rooted in the use of Syriac language and beliefs of shared descent. Altogether, the fact that various Syrians had different ways to formulate 'Syrian' ethnic genealogies does not mean that Syrian ethnicity did not exist. It means that their beliefs had not yet materialised in shared political aims, group actions, and institutions through which they could form a 'nation' and express a single unanimous formulation of ethnicity. The creation of an autonomous Syriac Orthodox Church in the sixth and seventh centuries may have enabled its members to attain to such a near-unanimous formulation. But this would only have come to fruition in the Islamic period. For such reasons, we can discuss how some speakers of Syriac cultivated Syrian ethnic identities, but not national ones, during the later Roman Empire.

BIBLIOGRAPHY

Amar, Joseph. 1995. *A Metrical Homily on Holy Mar Ephrem by Mar Jacob of Sarug: A Critical Edition of the Syriac Text, Translation and Introduction.* PO 47.1. Brepols: Turnhout.
Anderson, Benedict. 2006. *Imagined Communities: Reflections on the Origin and Spread of Nationalism*, Rev. ed. London: Verso.
Andrade, Nathanael. 2009. The Syriac Life of John of Tella and the Frontier *Politeia. Hugoye* 12.2, 199–234.
———. 2010–2011. Framing the 'Syrian' of Late Antiquity: Engagements With Hellenism. *Journal of Modern Hellenism* 28, 1–41.
———. 2013. *Syrian Identity in the Greco-Roman World.* Cambridge: Cambridge University Press.
———. 2014. Assyrians, Syrians, and the Greek Language in the Late Hellenistic and Roman Imperial Periods. *JNES* 73.2, 299–317.
Azéma, Yvan. 1955–1998: *Theodoret de Cyr: Correspondance*, 4 vols. SC 40, 98, 111, and 429. Paris: Les Belles Lettres.
Ball, Warwick. 2000/2016. *Rome and the Distant East: Transformation of an Empire*, 2nd ed. London: Routledge.
Bartelink, G. J. M. 1971. *Vie d'Hypatios.* SC 177. Paris: Cerf.
Becker, Adam. 2008. The Ancient Near East in the Late Antique Near East: Syriac Appropriation of the Biblical East. *In*: Gregg Gardner and Kevin Osterloh, ed., *Antiquity in Antiquity: Jewish and Christian Pasts in the Greco-Roman World.* Tübingen: Mohr Siebeck, 394–415.
Bedjan, Paul. 1890–1897. *Acta martyrum et sanctorum syriace.* 7 vols. Leipzig: Harrassowitz.
Bidez, Joseph and G. H. Hansen. 1995. *Kirchengeschichte: Sozomenus*, 2nd ed. GCS NF 4. Berlin: Akademie Verlag.
Brill's New Jacoby. 2007–. Ed. Ian Worthington. Leiden: Brill.
Bowersock, Glen. 1990. *Hellenism in Late Antiquity.* Ann Arbor: University of Michigan Press.
Brière, Maurice. 1960. *Les homiliae cathedrales de Sévère d'Antioche: traduction syriaque de Jacques d'Édesse.* PO 29. Paris: Firmin-Didot, 29.1–262.
Brock, S. P. 1984. *Syriac Perspectives on Late Antiquity.* London: Variorum.
———. 1989. From Ephrem to Romanos. *Studia Patristica* 20, 139–51.
———. 1992a. Eusebius and Syriac Christianity. *In*: Harold Attridge and Gohei Hata, ed., *Eusebius, Christianity, and Judaism.* Leiden: Brill, 212–34.
———. 1992b. *Studies in Syriac Christianity.* Aldershot: Variorum.
———. 1994. Greek and Syriac in Late Antique Syria. *In*: Alan Bowman and Greg Woolf, ed., Cambridge: Cambridge University Press, 149–60.
———. 1996. Greek Words in Syriac: Some General Features. *Scripta Classica Israelica* 15, 251–62.
———. 1997. *A Brief Outline of Syriac Literature.* Kottayam: St. Ephrem Ecumenical Research Institute.
———. 1998. Syriac Culture. *In*: Averil Cameron and Peter Garnsey, ed., *The Cambridge Ancient History, Vol. 13: The Late Empire, AD 337–425.* Cambridge: Cambridge University Press, 708–19.
———. 1999. *From Ephrem to Romanos: Interactions Between Syriac and Greek in Late Antiquity.* Aldershot: Ashgate.
———. 2001. *The Hidden Pearl: The Syrian Orthodox Heritage and Its Ancient Aramaic Heritage*, vols. 1–2. Rome: Trans World Film Italia.
———. 2005. The Syriac Orient: A Third 'Lung' for the Church? *OCP* 71, 5–20.
———. 2006. *Fire From Heaven: Studies in Syriac Theology and Liturgy.* Aldershot: Ashgate.
———. 2008a. Saints in Syriac: A Little-Tapped Resource. *JECS* 16.2, 181–96.
———. 2008b. *The History of Holy Mar Ma'in With a Guide to the Persian Martyr Acts.* Piscataway, NJ: Gorgias.

———. 2009. Edessene Syriac Inscriptions in Late Antique Syria. *In*: Hannah Cotton *et al.*, ed., *From Hellenism to Islam: Cultural and Linguistic Change in the Roma Near East*. Cambridge: Cambridge University Press, 289–302.
———. 2012. A Tentative Check List of Dated Syriac Inscriptions up to 1300. *Hugoye* 15.1, 21–48.
Brooks, E. W. 1907. *Vitae virorum apud Monophysitas celeberrimorum*. CSCO 7–8. Paris: Typographeus Reipublicae.
———. 1919–1924. *Historia ecclesiastica Zachariae rhetori vulgo adscripta*, 4 vols. CSCO 83–4 and 87–8. Paris: Typographeus Reipublicae.
———. 1923–1925. *John of Ephesus: Lives of the Eastern Saints*. PO 17–19. Paris: Firmin-Didot, 17.1–304, 18.513–697, and 19.153–227.
Brubaker, Rogers. 1996. *Nationalism Reframed: Nationhood and the National Question in the New Europe*. Cambridge: Cambridge University Press.
———. 2004a. Ethnicity Without Groups. *In*: Brubaker 2004b, 7–27.
———, ed. 2004b. *Ethnicity Without Groups*. Cambridge, MA: Harvard University Press.
———. 2004c. 'Civic' and 'Ethnic' Nationalism. *In*: Brubaker 2004b, 132–47.
———. 2004d. In the Name of the Nation: Reflections on Nationalism and Patriotism. *Citizenship Studies* 8.2, 115–27.
———, Mara Loveman and Peter Stamatov. 2004. Ethnicity as Cognition. *In*: Brubaker, ed., 64–87.
Butcher, Kevin. 2003. *Roman Syria and the Near East*. London: British Museum Press.
———. 2013. Continuity and Change in Lebanese Temples. *In*: Andrew Gardner, Edward Herring and Kathryn Lomas, ed., *Creating Ethnicities and Identities in the Roman World*. London: Institute of Classical Studies, 195–212.
Canivet, Pierre and Alice Leroy-Molinghen. 1977–1979. *Histoire des moines de Syrie; Histoire Philothée, Théodoret de Cyr*, 2 vols. SC 234, 257. Paris: Cerf.
Chabot, J.-B. 1899–1910. *Chronique de Michel le Syrien: Patriarche Jacobite d'Antioche (1166–1199)*. Paris: Leroux.
———. 1927–1933. *Chronicon anonymum pseudo-Dionysianum vulgo dictum*, 2 vols. CSCO 91, 104. Paris: Typographeus Reipublicae.
Debié, Muriel. 2004. Jean Malalas et la tradition chronographique de langue syriaque. *In*: Joëlle Beaucamp, ed., *Recherches sur la chronique de Jean Malalas*, 2 vols. Paris: Association des amis du centre d'histoire et civilization de Byzance, 1.147–64.
———. 2006. L'héritage de la *Chronique* d'Eusèbe dans l'historiographie syriaque. *JCSSS* 6, 18–29.
———. 2010. Syriac Historiography and Identity Formation. *In*: Haar Romeny 2010, 93–114.
———. 2015. *L'Écriture de l'histoire en syriaque: transmissions interculturelles et constructions identitaires entre hellénisme et islam*. Leuven: Peeters.
Delehaye, Hippolyte. 1923. *Les saints stylites*. Brussels: Bollandistes.
Drijvers, Han J. W. 1984. *East of Antioch: Studies in Early Syriac Christianity*. London: Variorum.
———. 1994. *History and Religion in Late Antique Syria*. Aldershot: Variorum.
Festugière, A. J. 1974. *Vie de Syméon le Fou et Vie de Jean de Chypre*. Paris: Geuthner.
Fiey, J.-M. 1965. 'Assyriens' ou Araméens. *OS* 10, 141–60.
Fowden, Garth. 1993. *Empire to Commonwealth: Consequences of Monotheism in Late Antiquity*. Princeton, NJ: Princeton University Press.
Grégoire, Henri and M.-A. Kugener. 1930. *Vie de Porphyre, évêque de Gaza*. Paris: Les Belles Lettres.
Griffith, Sidney. 1997. From Aramaic to Arabic: The Languages of Palestine in the Byzantine and Early Islamic Periods. *DOP* 51, 11–31.
———. 2002. Christianity in Edessa and the Syriac-Speaking World: Mani, Bar Daysan, and Ephraem: the Struggle for Allegiance on the Aramaean Frontier. *JCSSS* 2, 5–20.
———. 2003. The *Doctrina Addai* as a Paradigm of Christian Thought in Edessa in the Fifth Century. *Hugoye* 6.2, 269–92.

———. 2008. *The Church in the Shadow of the Mosque: Christians and Muslims in the World of Islam*. Princeton, NJ: Princeton University Press.
———. 2013. Christianity in Syria. *In*: Michele Salzman and William Adler, ed., *The Cambridge History of Religions in the Ancient World, Vol. 2: From the Hellenistic Age to Late Antiquity*. Cambridge: Cambridge University Press, 138–64.
Gzella, Holger. 2015. *A Cultural History of Aramaic: From the Beginnings to the Advent of Islam*. Leiden: Brill.
Haar Romeny, Bas ter. 2005. The Syriac Versions of the Old Testament. *In*: P. P. Khoury and P. G. Rahme, ed., *Nos sources: Art et littérature syriaques*. Beirut: CERO, 58–83.
———. 2008a. Jacob of Edessa on Genesis: His Quotations of the Peshitta and His Revision of the Text. *In*: Bas ter Haar Romeny, ed., *Jacob of Edessa and the Syriac Culture of His Day*. Leiden: Brill, 145–57.
———. 2008b. Ephrem and Jacob of Edessa in the Commentary of the Monk Severus. *In*: George Anton Kiraz, ed., *Malphono w-Rabo d-Malphone: Studies in Honor of Sebastian P. Brock*. Piscataway, NJ: Gorgias, 535–58.
———, ed. 2010. *Religious Origins of Nations? The Christian Communities of the Middle East*. Leiden: Brill.
———. 2012. Ethnicity, Ethnogenesis, and the Identity of Syrian Orthodox Christians. *In*: Walter Pohl, Clemens Gantner and Richard Payne, ed., *Visions of Community in the Post-Roman World: The West, Byzantium, and the Islamic World, 300–1100*. Farnham, UK: Ashgate, 183–204.
———. *et al*. 2010. The Formation of a Communal Identity Among West Syrian Christians: Results and Conclusions of the Leiden Project. *In*: Haar Romeny, ed., 1–51.
Halleux, A de. 1962. Nouveaux textes inédits de Philoxène de Mabbog. *Le Museon* 75, 31–62.
Harrak, Amir. 1999. *The Chronicle of Zuqnīn, Parts III and IV: A.D. 488–775*. Toronto: PIMS.
———. 1963. *Lettre aux moines de Senoun*. CSCO 231–2, SS 98–9. Louvain: CorpusSCO.
Healey, J. F. 2007. The Edessene Milieu and the Birth of Syriac. *Hugoye* 10.2, 1–34.
Henry, René. 2003. *Bibliothèque: Photius*, 2nd ed. 9 vols., Paris: Belles Lettres.
Hoyland, Robert. 2004. Language and Identity: The Twin Histories of Arabic and Aramaic (and: Why Did Aramaic Succeed Where Greek Failed?). *Scripta Classica Israelica* 23, 183–99.
———. 2009. Late Roman Provincia Arabia, Monophysite Monks, and Arab Tribes: A Problem of Center and Periphery. *Semitica et Classica* 2, 117–39.
———. 2010. Mount Nebo, Jabal Ramm, and the Status of Christian Palestinian Aramaic and Old Arabic in Palestine and Arabia. *In*: M.C.A. MacDonald, ed., *The Development of Arabic as a Written Language*. Oxford: Archaeopress, 29–46.
Ibrahim, Gregorios Yuhanna. 2009. *The Edessa-Aleppo Syriac Codex of the Chronicle of Michael the Great*. Piscataway, NJ: Gorgias.
Johnson, Scott Fitzgerald. 2015. Introduction: Languages and Cultures of Eastern Christianity: Greek. In: S. F. Johnson, ed., *Languages and Cultures of Eastern Christianity: Greek*. Ashgate: Variorum, 1–122.
Jullien, Christelle and Florence Jullien. 2002. *Apôtres des confins: processus missionnaires chrétiens dans l'empire iranien*. Bures-sur-Yvette: GECMO.
———. 2003. *Aux origines de l'église de Perse: les Actes de Mār Māri*. Leuven: Peeters.
Karst, Josef. 1911. *Eusebius: Werke, Vol. 5: Die Chronik aus dem armenischen Übersetzt*. Leipzig: Hinrichs.
Kruisheer, Dirk. 1997. Reconstructing Jacob of Edessa's *Scholia*. *In*: J. Frishman and L. Van Rompay, ed., *The Book of Genesis in Jewish and Oriental Christian Interpretation: a Collection of Essays*. Leuven: Peeters, 187–96.
———. 1998. Ephrem, Jacob of Edessa, and the Monk Severus: An Analysis of Ms. Vat. Syr. 103, ff. 1–72. *In*: René Lavenant, ed., *Symposium Syriacum VII*. Rome: Pontificio Istituto Orientale, 599–603.

Lightfoot, J. L. 2003. *On the Syrian Goddess*. Oxford: Oxford University Press.

Maraval, P. 1982. *Journal de voyage: Itinéraire, Égérie*. SC 296. Paris: Cerf.

Menze, Volker. 2008. *Justinian and the Making of the Syrian Orthodox Church*. Oxford: Oxford University Press.

Merz, Annette and Teun Tieleman, ed. 2012. *The Letter of Mara bar Sarapion in Context*. Leiden: Brill.

Millar, Fergus. 1993. *The Roman Near East, 31 BC-AD 337*. Cambridge, MA: Harvard University Press.

———. 1998a. Ethnic Identity in the Roman Near East, AD 325–450: Language, Religion, and Culture. *Mediterranean Archaeology* 11, 159–76.

———. 1998b. Il ruolo delle lingue semitiche nel Vicino Oriente tardo-romano (v-vi secolo). *Mediterraneo antico* 1, 71–93.

———. 2006a. *A Greek Roman Empire: Power and Belief under Theodosius II (408–450)*. Berkeley, CA: University of California Press.

———. 2006b. *Rome, the Greek World, and the East, Vol. 3: The Greek World, the Jews, and the East*. Ed. Hannah Cotton and Guy Rogers. Chapel Hill, NC: University of Carolina Press.

———. 2007a. Theodoret of Cyrrhus: A Syrian in Greek Dress? *In*: Hagit Amirav and Bas ter Haar Romeny, ed., *From Rome to Constantinople: Studies in Honor of Averil Cameron*. Leuven: Peeters, 105–25.

———. 2007b. Libanius and the Near East. *Scripta Classica Israelica* 26, 155–80.

———. 2008a. Rome, Constantinople, and the Near Eastern Church Under Justinian: Two Synods of CE 536. *JRS* 98, 62–82.

———. 2008b. Community, Religion, and Language in the Middle-Euphrates Zone in Late Antiquity. *Scripta Classica Israelica* 27, 67–93.

———. 2009a. The Syriac Acts of the Second Council of Ephesus. *In*: Richard Price and Mary Whitby, ed., *Chalcedon in Context: Church Councils 400–700*. Liverpool: Liverpool University Press, 45–69.

———2009b. Christian Monasticism in Roman Arabia at the Birth of Muhammad. *Semitica et Classica* 2, 71–115.

———. 2010. Jerome and Palestine. *Scripta Classica Israelica* 29, 59–79.

———. 2011a. Greek and Syriac in Edessa and Osrhoene, CE 213 to 363. *Scripta Classica Israelica* 30, 93–111.

———. 2011b. Greek and Syriac in Edessa: From Ephrem to Rabbula (CE 363–465). *Semitica et Classica* 4, 99–113.

———. 2012. Greek and Syriac in Fifth-Century Edessa: The Case of the Bishop Hiba. *Semitica et Classica* 5, 151–65.

———. 2013a. *Religion, Language, and Community in the Roman Near East: Constantine to Muhammad*. Oxford: Oxford University Press.

———. 2013b. The Evolution of the Syrian Orthodox Church in the Pre-Islamic Period: From Greek to Syriac? *JECS* 21.1, 43–92.

———. 2013c. A Syriac *Codex* from Near Palmyra and the Ghassanid Abokarib. *Hugoye* 16.1, 15–35.

———. 2015. *Empire, Church, and Society in the Late Roman Near East: Greeks, Jews, Syrians, and Saracens (Collected Studies 2004–2014)*. Leuven: Peeters.

Minov, Sergey. 2013. The *Cave of Treasures* and the Formation of Syriac Christian Identity in Late Antique Mesopotamia: Between Tradition and Innovation. *In*: B. Bitton-Ashkelony and L. Perrone, ed., *Between Personal and Institutional Religion: Self, Doctrine, and Practice in Late Eastern Christianity*. Turnhout: Brepols, 155–94.

Mitchell, C. W. 1912–1921. *S. Ephraim's Prose Refutations of Mani, Marcion, and Bardaiṣan*, 2 vols. London: Williams and Norgate.

Mommsen, Theodor and Alan Watson. 1985. *The Digest of Justinian*, 4 vols. Philadelphia, PA: University of Pennsylvania Press.

Nöldeke, Theodor. 1871. Die Namer der aramäischen Nation und Sprache. *ZDMG* 25.1–2, 113–31.

Noy, David. 2000. *Foreigners at Rome: Citizens and Strangers*. London: Duckworth.

Overbeck, J. J. 1865. *S. Ephraemi Syri, Rabulae episcopi Edesseni, Balaei aliorumque opera selecta*. Oxford: Clarendon.

Parmentier, Léon and G. C. Hansen. 1998. *Theodoret: Kirchengeschichte*, 3rd ed. GCS 5. Berlin: Akademie Verlag.

Payne, Richard. 2015. *A State of Mixture: Christians, Zoroastrians, and Iranian Political Culture in Late Antiquity*. Berkeley, CA: University of California Press.

Petruccione, John and Robert Hill. 2007. *Theodoret of Cyrus: The Questions on the Octateuch, Vol. 2: On Leviticus, Numbers, Deuteronomy, Joshua, Judges, and Ruth*. Washington, DC: Catholic University of America Press.

Phillips, George. 1869. *A Letter by Mar Jacob, Bishop of Edessa, on Syriac Orthography*. London: William and Norgate.

Ramelli, Ilaria. 2009a. *Bardesane di Edessa: Contro il fato*. Bologna: Studio Domenicano.

———. 2009b. *Bardaiṣan of Edessa: A Reassessment of the Evidence and a New Interpretation*. Piscataway, NJ: Gorgias Press.

Ri, Su-Min. 1987. *La Caverne des Trésors: les deux recensions syriaques*, 2 vols. CSCO 486–7, SS 207–8. Louvain: Peeters.

———. 2000. *Commentaire de la Caverne des Trésors: étude sur l'histoire du texte et de ses sources*. Louvain: Peeters.

Salvesen, Alison. 2010. Was Jacob Trilingual? Jacob of Edessa's Knowledge of Hebrew Revisited. *In*: Gregorios Ibrahim and George Anton Kiraz, ed., *Studies on Jacob of Edessa*. Piscataway, NJ: Gorgias Press, 93–105.

Sartre, Maurice. 2001. *D'Alexandre à Zénobie: histoire du Levant antique, IVe siècle avant J.-C.-IIIe siècle après J.-C.* Paris: Fayard.

———. 2005. *The Middle East under Rome*. Cambridge, MA: Belknap Press of Harvard University Press.

———. 2008. The Nature of Syrian Hellenism in the Late Roman and Early Byzantine Periods. *In*: Yaron Eliav, Elise Friedland and Sharon Herbert, ed., *The Sculptural Environment of the Near East: Reflections on Culture, Ideology, and Power*. Leuven: Peeters, 25–49.

Schwartz, Eduard and Theodor Mommsen. 1999. *Die Kirchengeschichte*, 3 vols., 2nd ed. GSC NF 2. Berlin: Akademie Verlag.

Shepardson, Christine. 2009. Syria, Syriac, Syrian: Negotiating East and West. *In*: Philip Rousseau, ed., *A Companion to Late Antiquity*. Chichester, UK: Wiley-Blackwell, 455–66.

Smith, Anthony. 2004. *The Antiquity of Nations*. Cambridge: Polity.

———. 2008. *The Cultural Foundations of Nations: Hierarchy, Covenant, Republic*. Malden, MA: Blackwell.

Smith, Kyle. 2016. *Constantine and the Captive Christians of Persia: Martyrdom and Religious Identity in Late Antiquity*. Oakland, CA: University of California Press.

Sokoloff, Michael. 2009. *A Syriac Lexicon: A Translation from the Latin, Correction, Expansion, and Update of C. Brockelmann's Lexicon Syriacum*. Winona Lake, IN: Eisenbrauns.

Solin, Heikki. 1983. Juden und Syrer im westlichen Teil der römischen Welt: eine ethnisch-demographische Studie mit besonderer Berücksichtigung der sprachlichen Zustände. *Aufstieg und Niedergang der römischen Welt* 2.29.2, 587–789 and 1222–49.

Stoop, E. de. 1911. *Vie d'Alexandre l'Acémète*. PO 6. Paris: Firmin-Didot, 641–705.

Strothmann, Werner. 1988. *Kohelet-Kommentar des Johannes von Apamea: syrischer Text mit vollständigem Wörterverzeichnis*. Wiesbaden: Harrassowitz.

Taylor, David G. K. 2002. Bilingualism and Diglossia in Late Antique Syria and Mesopotamia. *In*: J. N. Adams, Mark Janse and Simon Swain, ed., *Bilingualism in Ancient Society: Language Contact and the Written Text*. Oxford: Oxford University Press, 293–331.

———. 2009. The Psalm Commentary of Daniel of Salah and the Formation of Sixth-Century Syrian Orthodox Identity. *Church History and Religious Culture* 89.1–3, 65–92.

Thurn, Johannes. 2000. *Ioannis Malalae Chronographia*. Berlin: de Gruyter.

Tonneau, R.-M. 1955. *Sancti Ephraem Syri in Genesim et in Exodum commentarii*. CSCO 152–3, SS 71–2. Louvain: Durbecq.

Van Rompay, Lukas. 2000. Past and Present Perceptions of Syriac Literary Tradition. *Hugoye* 3.1, 71–103.

———. 2008a. Jacob of Edessa and the Sixth Century Translator of Severus of Antioch's Cathedral Homilies. *In*: Bas ter Haar Romeny, ed., *Jacob of Edessa and the Syriac Culture of His Day*. Leiden: Brill, 189–204.

———. 2008b. The East (3): Syria and Mesopotamia. *In*: Susan Ashbrook Harvey and David Hunter, ed., *The Oxford Handbook of Early Christian Studies*. Oxford: Oxford University Press, 365–86.

Walker, Joel. 2006. *The Legend of Mar Qardagh: Narrative and Christian Heroism in Late Antique Iraq*. Berkeley, CA: University of California Press.

Weitzman, Michael. 1999. *The Syriac Version of the Old Testament: An Introduction*. Cambridge: Cambridge University Press.

Wood, Philip. 2010. *'We Have No King But Christ': Christian Political Thought in Greater Syria on the Eve of the Arab Conquest (c. 400–585)*. Oxford: Oxford University Press.

———. 2012. Syriac and the 'Syrians'. *In*: Scott Fitzgerald Johnson, ed., *The Oxford Handbook of Late Antiquity*. Oxford: Oxford University Press, 170–94.

Wright, W. 1876. Two Epistles of Mar Jacob, Bishop of Edessa. *Journal of Sacred Literature and Biblical Record* 10, 430–3 and a-kz.

CHAPTER ELEVEN

EARLY SYRIAC REACTIONS TO THE RISE OF ISLAM

Michael Penn

It is hard to overstate the importance of Syriac sources for the history of Christian-Muslim relations and for our understanding of earliest Islam. Syriac authors of the seventh through ninth centuries discussed Muslims in theological tractates, inscriptions, apocalypses, manuscript colophons, ecclesiastical letters, canon collections, universal chronicles, scriptural exegesis, hagiographies, pseudepigrapha, martyrologies, local histories, prayers, and scientific treatises. Their texts constitute the largest surviving corpus of early Christian writings on Islam.

Even more important than the sheer number and antiquity of these sources, however, is the variety of experiences that they represent. Although Western authors were far from uniform in their discussions of Islam, they were frequently writing from the context of military conflict or had very little direct contact with Muslims. In contrast, just a few years after Muḥammad's death, almost all Syriac Christians were under Muslim rule. By the 640s, Muslims were no longer military opponents, nor was Islam a distant phenomenon for Syriac Christians. Rather, emergent Islam was an aspect of daily life. In the Islamic Empire, Syriac Christians held key government positions, attended the caliph's court in Baghdad, collaborated with Muslim scholars to translate Greek science and philosophy into Arabic, accompanied Muslim leaders on their campaigns against the Byzantines, and helped fund monasteries through donations from Muslims – including money from the caliph himself. Syriac Christians ate with Muslims, married Muslims, bequeathed estates to Muslim heirs, taught Muslim children, and were soldiers in Muslim armies. Members of the Syriac churches had a very different experience of Islam than did most Greek and Latin Christians.

Such encounters did not, however, result in a unified Syriac view of Islam. Instead, what makes these sources so valuable is the incredible diversity of their responses to Muslims. Ranging from overtly antagonistic to downright friendly, Syriac sources belie the notion of any monolithic Christian reaction to Islam and serve as an important corrective to the reductionist views that characterise many modern depictions of the history of Christian-Muslim relations.

In addition to their value in providing a more nuanced understanding of early Christian-Muslim relations, these sources often contain essential data for better understanding early Islamic history. Coming as they do from an external perspective, early Syriac sources often contained eyewitness accounts to the events that they described. Such texts include the first manuscript to mention Muḥammad by name, most likely an autograph written only five years after Muḥammad's death and which spoke of the most important battle of the Islamic conquests. The earliest surviving lists of Muslim rulers were all in Syriac, and the only extant first-hand account of the second *fitna* (civil war, 683–692 CE) was written by an East Syrian monk. Likewise, most of the earliest accounts of conversion to (and from) Islam come from Syriac texts, as do many of the earliest discussions of the Qur'an, including some of the first extant quotations of Qur'anic suras. Every early Syriac text on Islam had its own bias and must be used critically. Nevertheless, these works provide a treasure trove of information enabling scholars better to understand the first Islamic centuries.

Despite the significance of Syriac writings on Islam, their perspectives have rarely been fully utilised in modern studies of Islam in the seventh through ninth centuries. In large part this has been due to the general neglect of Syriac materials by Western scholarship. To some extent this reflected a trend in much twentieth-century Syriac studies that prioritised earlier sources, such as the fourth-century writers Ephrem and Aphrahaṭ, at the expense of later texts. This was in part due to the existence of a fundamental division between scholars of classical Islam, who focused on Arabic and Persian sources, and scholars of Eastern Christianity who studied Syriac. As a result, until quite recently, Syriac writings on Islam were relegated to the margins of modern scholarship.

Nevertheless, in the late nineteenth and in the first half of the twentieth century, many of the most renowned scholars of Syriac such as Jean-Baptiste Chabot, Alphonse Mingana, François Nau, Theodor Nöldeke, and William Wright spent at least some time with this material. Their editions and translations remain foundational to the field. But efforts to synthesise their work essentially had to wait until 1977 with the publication of Patricia Crone and Michael Cook's *Hagarism: The Making of the Islamic World*. Crone and Cook built *Hagarism*'s controversial reassessment of Islamic origins primarily on early Christian sources, including a number of documents previously known only to a few specialists. Although its conclusions regarding the formation of early Islam were mostly rejected, Crone and Cook's citation and analysis of so many early Christian references to Muslims motivated others to investigate further Syriac texts that spoke of Islam.

Crone and Cook's work also helped spur a long-term shift in the chronological focus of Syriac studies. Previously, most scholarship in the field concentrated on the so-called 'Golden Age' of Syriac literature, with the bulk of scholarship examining fourth-, fifth-, and early sixth-century authors such as Aphrahaṭ, Ephrem, and Jacob of Sarug. After *Hagarism*, many scholars began to shift their attention towards later material; they produced editions of ancient Syriac references to Islam and tackled some of the thorniest source-critical issues surrounding these documents' composition. Of particular note were the numerous publications of Sydney Griffith, Andrew Palmer, Gerrit Reinink, and Barbara Roggema. Equally ground-breaking were Robert Hoyland's *Seeing Islam as Others Saw It* and *Christian-Muslim Relations: A Bibliographic History, Volume 1 (600–900)*, edited by David Thomas and Barbara Roggema, which provided a synopsis and extensive bibliography of most early Christian writings on Islam.

Since the 1977 publication of *Hagarism*, the sources themselves have also become increasingly accessible to non-specialists. English translations of almost all of the pre-750 texts can now be found in a single volume (Penn 2015a). So, too, modern translations of key ʿAbbasid-era works such as Timothy's *Apology*, the *Chronicle of Zuqnin*, and the *Syriac Bahira Legend* have recently been published. While earlier scholars generally concentrated on a single Syriac text or small collection of texts, recent scholarship has begun to look at this corpus more synthetically (Penn 2015b). So, too, these Syriac texts are starting to have some influence within the discipline of Islamic studies itself, in which analyses of early Islamic history are beginning to use them more systematically (e.g. Howard-Johnston 2010; Shoemaker 2012; Hoyland 2014). Thanks to this bourgeoning scholarship one can now produce a much more comprehensive narrative of Syriac Christian reactions to Islam, albeit one that, by necessity, remains tentative, as work on these sources and their context continues to expand.

REACTIONS FROM THE MID-SEVENTH CENTURY: THE EARLIEST SYRIAC SOURCES

The earliest surviving witness to Islam is extremely fragmentary and, in this sense, emblematic of mid-seventh-century Syriac sources. In 637 an anonymous author used the guard leaf of a biblical manuscript to compose an eyewitness report of the conquests. Now called the *Account of 637*, this one-page note is poorly preserved and, due to numerous lacunae, remains frustratingly incomplete. Nevertheless, as the earliest surviving manuscript to ever mention Muḥammad, it deserves quoting in full.

> Muḥammad . . . priest, Mār Elijah . . . and they came . . . and . . . and from . . . strong . . . month . . . and the Romans [fled] . . . And in January [the people] of Emesa received assurances for their lives. Many villages were destroyed through the killing by [the Arabs of] Muḥammad and many people were killed. And captives [were taken] from the Galilee to Bēt . . . Those Arabs camped by [Damascus]. We saw . . . everywhere . . . and the [olive oil] that they [had brought] and . . . them. On the twenty-sixth of May, [the *sacellarius*] went . . . from Emesa. The Romans pursued them . . . On the tenth [of August] . . . the Romans fled from Damascus . . . many, about ten thousand. The following year, the Romans came. On the twentieth of August in the year nine hundred and forty-seven [636 C.E.] there assembled in Gabitha . . . the Romans and many people were killed, from the Romans about fifty thousand . . . In the year nine hundred and forty-[eight].
> (Ed. Nöldeke 1875: 77–8; transl. Penn 2015a: 23–4)

Even in its present state, the extant text clearly refers to Arabs (Syriac: *ṭayyāyē*). Originally a designation for a specific tribe, prior to the conquests *ṭayyāyē* was the term usually used to speak of people living in Arabia, especially those seen as nomadic (Segal 1984: 89–124). Over time the term *ṭayyāyē* began to bear an increasingly religious valence and came closer to the modern usage of the term *Muslim*. But written just a few years after Muḥammad's death, the *Account of 637* still used this term as a tribal name just as its predecessors had. It shows no sign of attributing specific religious beliefs to the *ṭayyāyē*. In addition to speaking of Arabs in general, the *Account of 637* also spoke of Muḥammad, of what is most likely the Battle of Yarmuk, of towns surrendering, and of substantial Byzantine casualties. Over the next decades, similar annalistic accounts of the Islamic conquests appeared in Syriac sources, such as the *Chronicle ad 640* or, in more extended form, the *Khuzistan Chronicle*, thereby providing important information for the military history of early Islam (*Chronicle ad 640*, Penn 2015a: 25–9; *Khuzistan Chronicle*, Penn 2015a: 47–53).

Mid-seventh-century Syriac sources also witnessed the emergence of a Syriac theology of defeat. That is, contrary to the claims of some modern scholars, early Syriac writers universally depicted the conquests as a disaster and they constantly wrestled with the question of how God could have allowed them to happen. For example, an author probably dating to the mid-seventh century, but who claimed to be the fourth-century poet Ephrem, wrote over a hundred lines of verse depicting the conquests in the most horrific terms and proclaiming them as the first of several harbingers of the world's imminent end (*Apocalypse of Pseudo-Ephrem*, Penn 2015a: 37–46). So, too, the author of the *Syriac Life of Maximus* considered the conquests to be both the catalyst and the punishment for Christian heresy (ed. Brock 1973: 299–346, transl. Penn 2015a: 62–8). Similar views would be much further expanded in apocalyptic texts written towards the century's end.

This earliest stratum of post-conquest Syriac sources also provides essential information about early Christian knowledge and impressions of Islam. While the author of the *Account of 637* spoke of Arabs (*ṭayyāyē*), other mid-century sources used a variety of additional terms such as Ishmaelites, Sons of Ishmael, and in one case, a newly coined term Hagarene (*mhaggrāyē*, most likely derived from the name Hagar). These sources also very slowly began to attribute some religious characteristics to their conquerors. Perhaps the most important of such references occurred in a letter from the East Syrian catholicos Išoʿyahb III (d. 659). When writing to a bishop rebelling against his authority, Išoʿyahb stated:

> For also these Arabs [*ṭayyāyē*] to whom at this time God has given rule over the world, behold [how] they are toward us. Not only, as you know, do they not oppose Christianity. Rather, they are givers of praise to our faith, givers of honor to our Lord's priests and holy ones, and givers of aid to churches and monasteries. Indeed how did your inhabitants of *Mzwn* forsake their [own] faith on pretext of theirs? And this when, as even the *Mzwnāye* say, the Arabs did not force them to forsake their faith. To keep their faith they only asked them to forsake half of their possessions.
>
> (*Epistle* 14C, Duval 1904: 251; transl. Penn 2015a: 36)

Modern scholars usually emphasise either (1) the passage's beginning, to illustrate Muslim authorities' general benevolence towards Christianity or (2) the conclusion, to illustrate Muslim discrimination against Christians, in this case a fifty percent poll tax (otherwise unattested) on non-Muslims. The often unacknowledged difficulty with either interpretation is Išoʿyahb's own agenda. The goal of his letter was not an accurate description of Christianity in *Mzwn* (which scholars place in either Turkmenistan or the Persian Gulf), a topic about which Išoʿyahb had at best indirect knowledge. Rather, Išoʿyahb wanted to portray his subordinate bishop and personal nemesis in as negative a light as possible. But, regardless of the historical veracity of this particular depiction, Išoʿyahb's letter remains an important witness to how Syriac Christians were beginning to distinguish between their own religion and that of their conquerors. According to Išoʿyahb, on the one hand the Arabs supported Christian institutions and praised Christianity (though he never explained why or how they did this), while on the other, they seemed to have their own faith (though he gives no details as to what this entailed) and imposed financial disincentives on those who desired to stay Christian.

Other contemporary authors similarly spoke of their conquerors as having some distinctive religious attributes. But they did so extremely rarely and without offering much detail. Were one to combine information from all mid-seventh century sources, the sum total essentially would be: these people, most often called *ṭayyāyē*, were relatively benevolent towards Christianity and could be helpful allies in battles against Christian 'heretics'. According to Išoʿyahb, they had a faith whose content remained unspecified, and they may have provided financial disincentives for people to remain Christian. According to the *Khuzistan Chronicle*, they kept the 'covenant of Abraham'. According to the *Maronite Chronicle*, one of their rulers once prayed at Christian holy sites but nevertheless minted coins without the sign of the cross (Penn 2015a: 41–61). In other words, just as the *Account of 637* was full of physical lacunae, so too mid-seventh-century Syriac sources were often as remarkable for what they did not say about Islam as for what they did.

REACTIONS FROM THE LATE SEVENTH AND EARLY EIGHTH CENTURIES: THE SECOND *FITNA* AND ITS AFTERMATH

Such absences become particularly noteworthy when compared to Syriac sources written just a few years later. Towards the end of the seventh century, the circumstances of Syriac Christians under Muslim rule quickly changed. In 683, the death of the caliph Muʿawiya II initiated a devastating nine years of civil war as the Umayyad caliphs Marwan (d. 685) and his son ʿAbd al-Malik (d. 705) fought against a rival caliph, ʿAbd Allah ibn al-Zubayr (d. 692). Emerging as the sole caliph, ʿAbd al-Malik then began to institute a programme of Islamisation that publically proclaimed Islam as a supercessionary religion to Judaism and Christianity. ʿAbd al-Malik's building the Dome of the Rock in Jerusalem and a series of coinage reforms that replaced Christian iconography with anti-Trinitarian verses from the Qurʾan made it abundantly clear to late-seventh-century Syriac Christians that they were living in a very different environment than their predecessors had.

The initial Syriac reaction to these events was a spate of apocalyptic works including what became one of the most widely read texts in Syriac history, the *Apocalypse of Pseudo-Methodius*. Although this apocalypse claims for its author the early-fourth-century bishop Methodius (d. 311), it most likely was written towards the end of the second *fitna* (Penn 2015a: 108–29). *Pseudo-Methodius* then became immensely popular. Multiple Syriac recensions appear in both West and East Syrian manuscripts. The text was also soon translated into Greek and is now preserved in fifteen Greek manuscripts. It was later translated into Latin and became popular throughout Christendom. Today there remain almost 200 Latin manuscripts that include *Pseudo-Methodius*, one dated to 727. Additional translations were made in Armenian, Church Slavonic, and Middle English. Excerpts were even printed in Vienna during the Turkish siege of 1683.

Stubbornly proclaiming the invincibility of the Byzantine Empire and the Sons of Ishmael's imminent demise, this surprisingly popular author was unrelenting in his harsh depiction of Muslims. They were 'barbarian tyrants', 'rebels, murderers, blood shedders, and annihilators' who were 'not men but children of devastation'. Set in the fourth century, *Pseudo-Methodius* 'predicted' that these Sons of Ishmael would 'later' wage war against the Byzantines, destroy the Persians, decimate the Christian population, and cause many to deny their faith. But *Pseudo-Methodius* emphasised that, despite all evidence to the contrary, the Sons of Ishmael would not remain for long. They were merely God's tool to chastise Christians and separate the truly faithful from the faithless. God would soon raise up the last king of the Greeks, defeat the Sons of Ishmael, and usher in a brief period of unparalleled peace before the world's imminent end. Similar apocalyptic scenarios appeared in other late-seventh- and early-eighth-century Syriac texts such as John bar Penkaye's *Book of Main Points* (ed. Mingana 1907, transl. Penn 2015a: 85–107), the *Edessene Apocalypse* (ed. Martinez 1985: 222–8), and the *Apocalypse of John the Little* (ed. Harris 1900, transl. Penn 2015a: 146–55).

Such predictions turned out to be misguided. As the Umayyad dynasty solidified under ʿAbd al-Malik and his successors, Christian hopes for a quick end to Arab rule faded away and Syriac authors developed alternative responses to Islam's rise. Of particular import for understanding everyday life in the late seventh and early eighth centuries are a series of Syriac legal writings that deal with Christian-Muslim interactions. These discussions appear in both East Syrian sources, such as the *Canons* of George I (ed. Chabot 1902: 333–48, transl. Penn 2015a: 69–76), and West Syrian works such as the letter of Athanasius of Balad (ed. Ebied 2013: 169–74; transl. Penn 2015a: 79–84). The most extensive early treatment of this subject, however, came from Jacob, the miaphysite Bishop of Edessa (d. 708).

Jacob became renowned for his church regulations and many wrote to him regarding legal questions, several of which directly related to Islam. Their questions, along with Jacob's responses, provide a very different perspective on Christian-Muslim interactions than do contemporary apocalyptic texts. In particular, Jacob's correspondence depicts a world of fuzzy religious boundaries where the entities we call Christianity and Islam were not as cleanly separated as we would expect (or as Jacob would have liked). For example, Jacob's friend the priest Addai once asked him:

> Concerning a Christian woman who willingly marries a Hagarene, [I want to learn] if priests should give her the Eucharist and if one knows of a canon concerning this. [I want to learn]: if her husband were threatening to kill a priest if he should not give her the Eucharist, is it right for [the priest] to temporarily consent because [otherwise the husband] would seek his death? Or would it be a sin for him to consent? Or, because her husband is compassionate toward Christians, is it better to give her the Eucharist and she not become a Hagarene?
>
> (*Letter to Addai #75*, *Harvard Syr.* 93, f. 26b–27a; transl. Penn 2015a: 164–5)

As if a Hagarene husband demanding that his Christian wife receive the Eucharist was not confusing enough, Jacob went on to discuss even more perplexing situations. In another letter, Jacob stated that when in Byzantine territory, some Muslims had stolen the Eucharistic elements. Once they returned to Edessa, they felt so bad about their theft that they brought the pilfered elements to Jacob, who in turn sent them to the nearest Chalcedonian Christian. Other of Jacob's decisions were also significant, such as closing church doors prior to the Eucharist so that Muslims 'might not enter and mingle with believers', discussions about whether a Christian abbot could accept a dinner invitation from a Muslim ruler, Jacob's encouragement of priests to accept hire as teachers to Muslim children, a ruling that clergy could exorcise demon-possessed Muslims, and even use a mixture of holy water and relics to perform such healings. These interminglings had become so prevalent that Jacob had to remind a congregation that a cloth embroidered with the 'Hagarene confession of faith' could not be re-used as a Christian altar covering (Penn 2015a: 160–74).

In the late seventh century, the Umayyad government certainly did not demand that most Christians become Muslims, and its policies often made it particularly difficult for non-Arabs to do so. For a non-Arab to become Muslim, that individual first had to gain membership in an Arab tribe by becoming the *mawlâ* (client) of an Arab sponsor (Bernards and Nawas 2005: ix–x; Bulliet 1979: 41; Crone 1989: 874–83; Fowden 1993: 181; Hawting 2000: 4–5; Robinson 2005: 76). So, too, throughout most of the Umayyad era, conversion to Islam provided converts little economic benefit (Choksy 1997: 114; Hoyland 2004: xxiv–v; Hoyland 1997: 340; Reinink 2006: 130). Nevertheless, like the anecdote of the benevolent (yet potentially homicidal) Hagarene husband, Jacob's letters contained several additional discussions of conversion and re-conversion. These spoke of circumstances in which the boundaries between Christianity and Islam were easily and not infrequently traversed. Christians intermarried with Muslims and were at a particularly high risk of becoming Muslim. Overly harsh penance might further precipitate their apostasy. Other Christians had already become Muslim, and some later wanted to return to Christianity. In an emergency, these double converts could quickly be pardoned. Otherwise they should undergo a ritual for readmission into the Christian community, even if their eventual fate remained indeterminate. Like most legal texts, Jacob's letters were not direct witnesses to life as actually experienced among late seventh-century Syriac Christians and Muslims. Nevertheless, their constant references to cross-confessional interactions hinted at these communities' permeability. Although often more insistent of clear religious boundaries than even Jacob was, eighth- and ninth-century Syriac legal texts would continue to wrestle with the same questions, evidence that these issues persisted long after Jacob's day.

Jacob's correspondence represented a very different trajectory than did the *Apocalypse of Pseudo-Methodius* and its ilk. Instead of proclaiming the world's imminent end, Jacob was trying to negotiate how Christians could navigate everyday life under ʿAbd al-Malik and his successors. In many cases, the questions posed to Jacob were practical and quotidian: who could eat, marry, teach, and worship with whom. In other cases, Jacob's writings were concerned with more explicitly theological issues that arose in interactions with Muslims: Why did Christians venerate images? Why did Christians face east when they prayed? Was Jesus's mother Mary really from the line of David? In his discussion of these later topics, Jacob showed a theological knowledge of early Islam unseen among his Syriac predecessors, and he more clearly categorised Islam as a religion than did any previous Christian author.

Jacob only sporadically addressed theological questions brought up by Muslims. In contrast, these became the focus of two of the most important Syriac texts written in the early eighth century, the West Syriac (miaphysite) *Disputation of John and the Emir* (ed. Penn 2008: 83–109; transl. Penn 2015a: 200–8) and the East Syrian *Bēt Ḥālē Disputation* (Taylor 2015: 187–242). Both works alleged to be verbatim accounts of debates between Christian and Muslim interlocutors. Despite such claims, it remains extremely unlikely that either reflected an actual, historical encounter. Nevertheless, these authors' decision to write in this genre reveals much about Syriac Christians' changing views of their conquerors. Such disputations, both in real life and in literature, almost always occurred between proponents of competing religious traditions. By discussing Muslim beliefs and practices in the framework of a disputation, the authors of *John and the Emir* and the *Bēt Ḥālē Disputation* implicitly gave them the categorical status of a religion – specifically, a religion that threatened Christian orthodoxy.

The content of these works also illustrated the vast differences between Syriac Christians before and after the second *fitna*, particularly regarding what they knew (or at least cared to share) about Islam. In part this was due to the Syriac Christians' greater exposure to Islamic beliefs and practices. Such differences also likely reflected developments within Islam itself as specific traditions developed and were more widely disseminated. In the case of *John and the Emir*, the emir's questions highlighted the issues that Syriac Christians found most pressing in their theological debates, real and imagined, with Muslims. The emir began by asking if the Gospel was one. He then inquired how one could account for the diversity of Christian beliefs, whether Christ was God and, if Christ were God, who governed the world when Christ was in Mary's womb? The emir then shifted to a discussion of the religious affiliation of Abraham, Moses, and other Old Testament notables and finally issues of inheritance law. So, too, the *Bēt Ḥālē Disputation* illustrated the theological fault lines between early Christianity and Islam. But unlike *John and the Emir*, it provided a much more give-and-take dialogue between the Christian and the Muslim characters, resulting in a more extensive discussion of Muḥammad and of the Qurʾan. By debating such issues as the meaning behind the Islamic conquests, circumcision, proper scriptural exegesis, Christology, Christian veneration of relics, proper prayer, and soteriology, the *Bēt Ḥālē Disputation* marked what it saw as essential differences between Christian and Muslim doctrine and practice.

A comparison between the fragmentary fly-leaf note now known as the *Account of 637* and the extensive theological discussions of the *Bēt Ḥālē Disputation* reminds us of how much had changed within a single century. Towards the end of the Umayyad era, Syriac Christians had become relatively well versed in Islam. With the initial conquests and the second *fitna* well behind them, Syriac Christians no longer considered their conquerors simply one of a series of late ancient military invaders nor as the harbingers of the end times. Rather, by the later part of the Umayyad era, Syriac authors began to designate their conquerors as having a religion, albeit one whose boundaries, especially in daily life, remained porous and hard to define.

REACTIONS FROM THE LATE EIGHTH AND NINTH CENTURIES: SYRIAC CHRISTIANS UNDER ʿABBASID RULE

In 747, the ʿAbbasid family led a revolt against Umayyad rule and three years later took control of the Islamic empire. In the subsequent early ʿAbbasid period, there was even greater contact between Syriac Christians and Muslims than in the Umayyad era. As a result of the process of Arabicisation that started a century earlier, many Syriac Christians were now bilingual, allowing for more direct interactions with Muslims and a greater knowledge of Islam. Early ʿAbbasid society also began a widespread translation project in which government authorities and private elites sought to translate texts of Greek science and philosophy into Arabic. Because many of these works had already been translated from Greek into Syriac, Syriac scholars were active participants in the ʿAbbasid translation movement. The translation movement also popularised Aristotelian logic, which became a common intellectual currency shared by Christians and Muslims. At the same time, cities and towns had increasingly mixed populations that, combined with the ongoing effects of Arabicisation, facilitated everyday contact between Christians and Muslims.

This does not mean that the eighth and ninth centuries were an age of universal tolerance. During the ʿAbbasid period, conversion to Islam became more prevalent. Several ʿAbbasid caliphs also became increasingly aggressive in the ongoing project of Islamisation, and a set of legal traditions designed to differentiate non-Muslims from Muslims began to reach its classical form, the so-called *Pact of ʿUmar*. Scholars continue to debate how often such regulations were actually enforced. Nevertheless, it remains clear that over time these rules became increasingly discriminatory and more frequently implemented.

Syriac texts written during the first 150 years of the ʿAbbasid caliphate reflect these authors' more frequent interactions with Muslims and their greater exposure to Islam. Syriac writings on Islam spread to almost every imaginable genre and often were of substantial length, in some cases devoting almost a hundred folia to life under Islamic rule. In addition to fully extant sources, modern scholars can often reconstruct other ʿAbbasid-era works from later mediaeval writings that frequently quoted them. For example, the two most important chronicles of this period, the so-called *Syriac Common Source*, most often attributed to the mid-eighth-century writer Theophilus, and the mid-ninth-century *Chronicle* of the West Syrian patriarch Dionysius, no longer survive, but later authors cited them so extensively that we still have an extremely good idea of their content even if the exact wording of any given passage remains uncertain (Hoyland 2011). The result is a plethora of Syriac sources representing a myriad of perspectives on Muslims, on Islam, and on Islamic rule.

This extensive corpus includes some of the world's most positive depictions of Muslim rule, for example prayers for a newly appointed emir whose governance was compared to that of king David and through whom the 'entire empire sees all the glory of [your] rule, understands its advantages, and glorifies God, its author' (*To the Rulers of the World*, Penn 2009: 71–84). So, too, ʿAbbasid-era texts often incorporated more extended narratives of benevolent Muslim rulers. For example, the *Life of John of Dailam* told of its protagonist having successfully exorcised demons from the daughter of the seventh-century caliph ʿAbd al-Malik. According to this *vita*, ʿAbd al-Malik subsequently subsidised John's construction of churches and monasteries, granted all Christian clergy tax exemption, and commanded his governors to honour Christian laws (Brock 1981–1982: 139). Needless to say, it seems unlikely that the historical ʿAbd al-Malik, who erected the Dome of the Rock with its anti-Trinitarian inscriptions and initiated a programme of Islamisation, would have encouraged – to say the least, would have directly funded – an empire-wide church-building project. Such depictions often were a combination of revisionist history, wishful thinking, and *Realpolitik*.

On the other hand, ʿAbbasid-era authors also wrote descriptions of Muslim leaders that would have made the late-seventh-century author of *Pseudo-Methodius* proud. For example, around the year 775 the anonymous author of the *Chronicle of Zuqnin* stated, 'all the sheets and papers of the world are not enough to write on them about the evils which were applied to people in our days' (*Chronicle of Zuqnin*, Book 4, *CSCO* 104: 317; transl. Harrak 1999: 274). Nevertheless, he gave it his best try, dedicating more than 170 pages to ten years' worth of afflictions under a caliph who 'enjoyed the sword more than peace' and his governor, who could rightly be called the anti-Christ (*CSCO* 104: 263, 253; transl. Harrak 1999: 232, 223). Although one suspects a degree of hyperbole, there is little doubt that such reports reflected a wide range of suffering experienced by Syriac Christians in the seventh through ninth centuries.

What most distinguished ʿAbbasid-era writers from their Umayyad counterparts, however, was the degree of their familiarity with Islam and Islamic sources. Syriac authors, now often bilingual, had access to the Qurʾan, which they frequently quoted, and assumed that their audience would also be knowledgeable about Islamic beliefs and practices. As a result, eighth- and ninth-century Syriac texts directly addressed key theological issues ranging from Muslim perspectives on Christ's incarnation to the scriptural status of the Qurʾan.

The most famous of such exchanges was written by the late-eighth-century catholicos, Timothy I. As the head of the East Syrian church from 780 to 823, Timothy attended the courts of four ʿAbbasid caliphs and, with their support and sometimes with their funding, expanded the East Syrian church throughout the Middle East, and into India, Afghanistan, Tibet, and China. Timothy was also personally commissioned by the caliph al-Mahdi to translate Aristotle's *Topics* into Arabic and even accompanied the caliph on a military campaign against the Byzantines. In a lengthy letter recounting an audience he had with al-Mahdi, the catholicos reportedly told his occasional patron:

> Muḥammad is worthy of all praise from all rational people. For he walked on the road of the prophets and he journeyed on the path of the lovers of God. For if all the prophets taught about one God and Muḥammad taught about one God, then it is evident that Muḥammad also walked on the path of the prophets. . . . And if Muḥammad taught about God and His Word and His Spirit and all the prophets prophesied about God, His Word, and His Spirit, then Muḥammad also walked on the path of all the prophets. . . . I as well as all lovers of God say these and similar things concerning Muḥammad.
>
> (*Apology* 15, Heimgartner 2011: 99–102)

Timothy's presentation of Muḥammad as a righteous, commendable monotheist comes across as accommodating. Nevertheless, Timothy insisted that Muḥammad was not himself a prophet because, according to Timothy, Muḥammad never performed any miracles nor had scripture foretold his coming.

Later in the same letter, Timothy went a step further and stated that Muḥammad actually had been a secret supporter of Christian Trinitarianism. He substantiated this claim by citing the Qurʾan's use of the first-person plural for God and the appearance of untranslatable letters preceding several Qurʾanic suras:

> [Muḥammad] openly taught about one God. But as for the Trinity, he professed it with symbols and with signs by [expressions] such as 'His word,' and 'His spirit,' and 'We have sent our spirit,' and 'We have formed a completed man.' Thus he did not teach openly about [the Trinity] lest [the Arabs] be scandalised by it as by polytheism. But also he did not completely hide it lest he stray from the way of Moses and of Isaiah and of all the prophets. But he professed [the Trinity] with symbols, with the three letters at the beginning of the suras.
>
> (*Apology* 16, Heimgartner 2011: 114)

Regardless of how persuasive one might find Timothy's logic, these and similar passages reflected a familiarity with Islamic traditions rarely found among Western authors.

Syriac Christians also used their newly acquired knowledge in more overtly polemical texts. For example, the early-ninth-century *Syriac Bahira Legend* took an earlier Islamic narrative in which the Christian monk Bahira was one of the first to recognise Muḥammad's prophethood, and turned it on its head (Roggema 2009). In this Christian re-telling of the story, the same monk (along with a malicious Jewish scribe) actually wrote the Qurʾan and invented the religion of Islam. Bahira then taught Muḥammad about monotheism, the Trinity, and Islamic rituals. To make the content more palatable, he instructed Muḥammad to tell his followers of a materialistic heaven filled with wine, milk, honey, and virgins. To authenticate this deception, Bahira stuck the book he wrote on a horn of a cow (hence the Qurʾan's first sura became known as the Sura of the Cow) and sent it to Muḥammad one Friday (hence Friday became a Muslim holy day). Similar etymologies were developed to account for a variety of Muslim traditions, ranging from Muslim claims of Muḥammad's illiteracy to the timing of the Ramadan fast. All betray the author's intricate knowledge of contemporary Islam. In order to appreciate the jokes, his ninth-century audience must also have been familiar with these details.

Syriac apologetic and literary texts, such as the *Syriac Bahira Legend*, often depicted and reflected a high level of religious interchange between Christians and Muslims. Throughout the early ʿAbbasid period, one comes across narratives of Muslims attending Christian services, seeking healings from Christian holy men, funding Christian monasteries, and praying to Christian saints. There are also narratives in which Christians proclaim a Muslim-like Christology. Nevertheless, as in the Umayyad period, ʿAbbasid-era legal texts provide perhaps the best evidence that on-the-ground interactions were particularly challenging for those who wanted to draw strict lines of religious demarcation. Canonical rulings witness to the continuing phenomena of intermarriage, laity and clergy seeking out rulings in Islamic (as opposed to Christian) courts, Christian attendance at Muslim festivals, and congregation members wanting to be circumcised like Muslims (Penn 2015b: 142–82).

* * *

During the Syriac renaissance of the twelfth and thirteenth centuries, several important descriptions of Muslim rule such as the *Chronicle* of Michael the Syrian (d. 1199) (Ibrahim 2009, transl. Moosa 2014) and the *Chronicle ad 1234* (Chabot 1920, 1937; Abouna and Fiey 1974) were written in Syriac, as were the anti-Islamic polemics of Dionysius bar Ṣalibī (d. 1171) (Amar 2005). But by the end of the ninth century, the majority of Syriac Christian texts on Islam were no longer composed in Syriac. By then most Eastern Christian discussions of Islam had already switched to Arabic (Griffith 2008). Nevertheless, the first 250 years of Syriac writings on Islam were foundational for these later works that often quoted from them. So, too, even a brief survey of a small selection of these sources indicates that they can substantially affect our understanding of the first encounters of what eventually became the world's two largest religions.

Syriac discussions of Islam were more multivariate than those found among most Western Christian texts and reflected a world of direct, often everyday interactions. The task of integrating this largest corpus of early Christian writings on Islam into Islamic history and the history of Christian-Muslim relations is now well overdue. The incredible diversity of Syriac writings about Muslims makes it very difficult to construct a simple-to-summarise Syriac perspective. But, at the same time, these sources make it very easy to contest any depiction of a monolithic Christian reaction to Islam, whether a paradigm of inevitably clashing civilisations or a paradigm of universally tolerant *convivencia*. Even more challenging to reductionist models of inter-religious encounters is the amorphous nature of what we call 'Islam'. Syriac texts constantly suggested that in the first centuries after Muḥammad's death there was much greater hybridity and overlap between the categories 'Christian' and 'Muslim' than has commonly been acknowledged. Even beneath the surface of the most polemical writings lies evidence of connected cultures, shared histories, and religious interdependence.

FURTHER READING

Griffith, Sidney H. 2008. *The Church in the Shadow of the Mosque: Christians and Muslims in the World of Islam*. Princeton: Princeton University Press.

Grypeou, Emmanouela, Mark N. Swanson and David Thomas. 2006. *The Encounter of Eastern Christianity With Early Islam*. Leiden: Brill.

Hoyland, Robert G. 1997. *Seeing Islam as Others Saw It: A Survey and Evaluation of Christian, Jewish and Zoroastrian Writings on Early Islam*. Princeton: Darwin Press.

Penn, Michael Philip. 2015. *Envisioning Islam: Syriac Christians and the Early Muslim World*. Philadelphia: University of Pennsylvania Press.

———. 2015. *When Christians First Met Muslims: A Sourcebook of the Earliest Syriac Writings on Islam*. Berkeley: University of California Press.

Roggema, Barbara and David Thomas. 2009. *Christian-Muslim Relations: A Bibliographic History, Volume 1 (600–900)*. Leiden: Brill.

Van Ginkel, J.J., H. L. Murre-Van den Berg, T. M. Van Lint. 2005. *Redefining Christian Identity: Cultural Interaction in the Middle East Since the Rise of Islam*. Leuven: Peeters.

BIBLIOGRAPHY

Abouna, A. and J. M. Fiey. 1974. *Chronicon ad A.C. 1234 pertinens*. Translation. CSCO 354. Leuven: Peeters.

Amar, J. P. 2005. *Dionysius bar Salibi: A Response to the Arabs*. CSCO 614–5. Leuven: Peeters.

Bernards, Monique and John Nawas. 2005. Introduction. *In*: Monique Bernards and John Nawas, ed., *Patronate and Patronage in Early and Classical Islam*. Leiden: Brill, ix–xiv.

Brock, S. P. 1973. An Early Syriac Life of Maximus the Confessor. *Analecta Bollandiana* 91, 299–346.

———. 1981/2. A Syriac Life of John of Dailam. *PdO* 10, 123–89.

Bulliet, Richard W. 1979. *Conversion to Islam in the Medieval Period: An Essay in Quantitative History*. Cambridge, MA: Harvard University Press.

Chabot, J. B. 1899–1910. *Chronique de Michel le Syrien, patriarche jacobite d'Antioche (1166–1199)*. Paris: E. Leroux.

———. 1902. *Synodicon orientale ou recueil de synodes nestoriens*. Paris: Imprimerie Nationale.

———. 1920. *Chronicon ad A.C. 1234 pertinens*. Text. CSCO 81–82. Leuven: Peeters.

———. 1937. *Chronicon ad A.C. 1234 pertinens*. Translation. CSCO 109. Leuven: Peeters.

Choksy, Jamsheed K. 1997. *Conflict and Cooperation: Zoroastrian Subalterns and Muslim Elites in Medieval Iranian Society*. New York: Columbia University Press.

Crone, P. 1989. Mawlā. *In*: E. van Donzel et al., ed., *Encyclopaedia of Islam*, 2nd ed. Leiden: Brill, 874–82.

Crone, Patricia and Michael Cook. 1977. *Hagarism: The Making of the Islamic World*. Cambridge: Cambridge University Press.

Duval, R. 1904. *Išoʿyahb III, Patriarch of the Church of the East. Liber Epistularum*. CSCO 11. Paris: e Typographeo Reipublicae.

Ebied, Rifaat Y. 2013. The Syriac Encyclical Letter of Athanasius II, Patriarch of Antioch, which Forbids the Partaking of the Sacrifices of the Muslims. *In*: Peter Bruns and Heinz Otto Luthe, ed., *Orientalia Christiana: Festschrift für Hubert Kaufhold zum 70. Geburtstag*. Wiesbaden: Harrassowitz Verlag, 169–74.

Fowden, Garth. 1993. *Empire to Commonwealth: Consequences of Monotheism in Late Antiquity*. Princeton: Princeton University Press.

Griffith, Sidney H. 2008. *The Church in the Shadow of the Mosque: Christians and Muslims in the World of Islam*. Princeton: Princeton University Press.

Harrak, Amir. 1999. *The Chronicle of Zuqnin, Parts III and IV*. Toronto: Pontifical Institute of Mediaeval Studies.

Harris, J. Rendel. 1900. *The Gospel of the Twelve Apostles Together With the Apocalypses of Each One of Them*. Cambridge: Cambridge University Press.

Hawting, Gerald R. 2000. *The First Dynasty of Islam: The Umayyad Caliphate AD 661–750*, 2nd ed. New York: Routledge.

Heimgartner, M. 2011. *Timotheos I, ostsyrischer Patriarch: Disputation mit dem Kalifen Al-Mahdi*. CSCO 631. Peeters: Leuven.

Howard-Johnston, James. 2010. *Witnesses to a World Crisis: Historians and Histories of the Middle East in the Seventh Century*. Oxford: Oxford University Press.

Hoyland, Robert. 1997. *Seeing Islam as Others Saw It: A Survey and Evaluation of Christian, Jewish and Zoroastrian Writings on Early Islam*. Princeton: Darwin Press.

———. 2004. Introduction: Muslims and Others. *In*: Robert Hoyland, ed., *Muslims and Others in Early Islamic Society*. Aldershot: Ashgate, xiii–xxx.

———. 2011. *Theophilus of Edessa's Chronicle and the Circulation of Historical Knowldge in Late Antiquity and Early Islam*. Liverpool: Liverpool University Press.

———. 2014. *In God's Path: The Arab Conquests and the Creation of an Islamic Empire*. Oxford: Oxford University Press.

Ibrahim, Gregorios Yuhanna. 2009. *The Edessa-Aleppo Syriac Codex of the Chronicle of Michael the Great*. Piscataway, NJ: Gorgias Press.
Martinez, Francisco Javier. 1985. *Eastern Christian Apocalyptic in the Early Muslim Period: Pseudo-Methodius and Pseudo-Athanasius*. Ph.D. Dissertation, The Catholic University of America.
Mingana, Alphonse. 1907. *Sources syriaques I*. Leipzig: Dominican Press.
———. 1928. The Apology of Timothy the Patriarch before the Caliph Mahdi. *In*: idem, ed., *Christian Documents in Syriac, Arabic and Garshuni, Edited and Translated with a Critical Apparatus*. Cambridge: Heffer and Sons, 1–162.
Moosa, Matti. 2014. *A Syriac Chronicle of Michael Rabo (The Great): A Universal History From the Creation*. Teaneck: Beth Antioch Press.
Newman, N. A. 1993. *The Early Christian-Muslim Dialogue: A Collection of Documents from the First Three Islamic Centuries (632–900 A.D.) Translation With Commentary*. Hatfield: Interdisciplinary Biblical Research Institute.
Nöldeke, Theodor. 1875. Zur Geschichte der Araber im 1. Jahrh. d.H. aus syrischen Quellen. *ZDMG* 29, 76–98.
Penn, Michael. 2009. Addressing Muslim Rulers and Muslim Rule. *OC* 93, 71–84.
———. 2008. John and the Emir: A New Introduction, Edition and Translation. *LM* 121, 83–109.
———. 2015a. *When Christians First Met Muslims: A Sourcebook of the Earliest Syriac Writings on Islam*. Berkeley: University of California Press.
———. 2015b. *Envisioning Islam: Syriac Christians and the Early Muslim World*. Philadelphia: University of Pennsylvania Press.
Reinink, Gerrit J. 2006. Following the Doctrine of the Demons: Early Christian Fear of Conversion to Islam. *In*: Jan N. Bremmer, Wout J. van Bekkum, and Arie L. Molendijk, ed., *Cultures of Conversions*. Leuven: Peeters, 127–38.
Robinson, Chase F. 2005. *'Abd al-Malik*. Oxford: Oneworld.
Roggema, Barbara. 2009. *The Legend of Sergius Baḥīrā: Eastern Christian Apologetics and Apocalyptic in Response to Islam*. Leiden: Brill.
Roggema, Barbara and David Thomas. 2009. *Christian-Muslim Relations: A Bibliographic History, Volume 1 (600–900)*. Leiden: Brill.
Segal, J. B. 1984. Arabs in Syriac Literature before the Rise of Islam. *Jerusalem Studies in Arabic and Islam* 4, 89–124.
Shoemaker, Stephen J. 2012. *The Death of a Prophet: The End of Muhammad's Life and the Beginnings of Islam*. Philadelphia: University of Pennsylvania Press.
Taylor, David G. K. 2015. The Disputation between a Muslim and a Monk of Bēt Ḥālē: Syriac Text and Annotated English Translation. *In*: Sidney H. Griffith and Sven Grebenstein, ed., *Christsein in der islamischen Welt: Festschrift für Martin Tamcke zum 60. Geburtstag*. Wiesbaden: Harrassowitz Verlag, 187–242.

CHAPTER TWELVE

THE CHURCH OF THE EAST IN THE ʿABBASID ERA

David Wilmshurst

OVERVIEW

During the seventh century, the Arab Conquest brought over half of the world's Christians under Muslim rule. Because the tide of Arab expansion was eventually stemmed before it could reach the heartland of Europe, modern Europeans often forget the scale of this catastrophe for Christianity in the lands which gave it birth. Even at the most conservative estimate, without taking into account the losses of the patriarchates of Rome and Constantinople, the Arab Conquest of Egypt placed under Muslim rule the nine metropolitan provinces of the patriarchate of Alexandria, and the conquest of Mesopotamia and Syria added a further three metropolitan provinces in the patriarchate of Jerusalem and twelve metropolitan provinces in the patriarchate of Antioch. The Arab Conquest also netted the vast majority of Syriac-speaking Christians. The ten metropolitan provinces of the Church of the East in Iraq, Iran, and northern Arabia, containing around 80 dioceses, were engulfed by the invaders.

Some Christians reacted by fleeing from their homes and taking refuge in Byzantine territory. Others converted to Islam, but their numbers were probably not large, except in Arabia itself. The conquerors were relatively few in number, kept themselves to themselves in military camps, and at first actively discouraged conversion by Jews and Christians because they needed their tax revenue. Most Christians remained where they were, paid the oppressive poll tax (*jizyah*), and adapted to life under the Muslims. Because they were 'people of the book', whose prophet Jesus had been a forerunner of Muhammad, they were treated by the conquerors as a 'protected community' (*dhimmi*). For the East Syrians, this condition was in many respects akin to their tolerated status under the Sasanians. The caliphs, like the Persian kings before them, dealt directly with the East Syrian patriarchs, and most internal affairs were dealt with by the Christians' own representatives. Christians were forbidden to preach their faith to Muslims, just as they had been forbidden to preach to Zoroastrians; and apostasy from Islam to Christianity was in theory punishable by death, just as apostasy from Zoroastrianism had been (McAuliffe 1991).

Over time, Muslim discrimination first slowed, then halted, then reversed the growth that the East and West Syrian Churches had experienced under the Sasanians.

The process of decline was slow and undramatic, and it continues to this day. The Christian population of the caliphate began to fall, partly through conversions to Islam and partly through emigration. The decline could not be stopped, because there were few new Christian recruits in the lands of Islam. Conversions to Christianity, frequent enough during the Sasanian period when its main competition came from fire-worshipping Zoroastrians and idolatrous pagans, dried up after the Arab Conquest. In the contest for hearts, minds, and souls, the Muslims were far more redoubtable opponents than were the Zoroastrians. Some new East Syrian dioceses were created during the Umayyad period, because the Muslims were at first so thin on the ground that the eclipse of the Zoroastrians gave the Church of the East a brief window of opportunity; but the number of East Syrian Christians living in the caliphate peaked at the end of the Umayyad period and thereafter began to fall. Significantly, some of the new dioceses were established not to serve a growing Christian population but to confront the threat of defection to the West Syrian, miaphysite, Church (Wilmshurst 2011: 116–21).

Under the Sasanians the main threat to Persia's Christians had come from the state religion of Zoroastrianism. After the Arab Conquest, this threat rapidly diminished. Persia's Arab conquerors treated Zoroastrians with great harshness, partly because, as the dominant religion in Persia, Zoroastrianism represented a challenge to Islam which could not be ignored, and partly because they were repelled by its beliefs and practices which, unlike those of Judaism and Christianity, were alien to the spirit of Islam. Muslim persecution broke the power of the Zoroastrian religion in Persia, and within a few decades Zoroastrians probably accounted for a smaller proportion of Persia's population than did Christians. Muslim attitudes towards Jews and Christians in the conquered territories were rather more complex. Unlike Zoroastrianism and other pagan religions, the teachings of Judaism and Christianity were regarded as successive revelations from God, which prefigured the final, authentic revelation entrusted to the prophet Muhammad. Although superseded by Islam, these earlier revelations deserved respect as the fullest expression of God's will available at the time they were made, and Jews and Christians enjoyed in Muslim eyes a special status as *ahl al-kitab*, 'people of the book'. Just as Christians continued to hold the Jewish scriptures of the Old Testament in respect, while insisting that God's relationship with humankind had been transformed by the life, death, and resurrection of Christ, Muslims did not deny the value of the earlier revelations of God's will, but also insisted that Christian teachings had been superseded by the message given to Muhammad (McAuliffe 1991). The construction of the Dome of the Rock in Jerusalem in 692 by the caliph ʿAbd al-Malik (685–705) starkly demonstrated the limits of Muslim tolerance. The Qur'anic texts that decorated the Dome asserted the superiority of Islam in the most uncompromising terms, rebuking the Christians for 'claiming too much' for their religion.

From the earliest days of the Arab Conquest, Christians were subjected to a battery of repressive measures designed to harass and humiliate them. They were required to wear a distinctive belt and turban, to proclaim their inferior faith. They were allowed to keep existing churches in good repair, but not to build new ones. They were forbidden to disturb Muslims with the clanging of church bells, the singing of hymns, or the sound of prayer and were not allowed to try to convert Muslims to Christianity. They were forbidden to carry weapons or ride horses. Mixed marriages were possible, but the rules on inheritance of property were weighted in favour of the Muslim partner. The testimony of a Christian in a law court was worth less than that of a Muslim. These spiteful measures were often not enforced, or could often be evaded by bribery, but their mere existence was dispiriting. The honour of Islam required Muslims to exert constant pressure upon the misguided 'people of the book', and ultimately this insidious and unrelenting attrition did more to weaken Christianity than the violent but sporadic persecutions of the Zoroastrians.

Although Muslim discrimination against Christians impinged to a greater or lesser degree upon all Christians living in the caliphate, contacts between Christians and Muslims during the Umayyad period were relatively infrequent. Indeed, many of the Christians who lived in the rural districts of northern Iraq probably never saw a Muslim in their life, unless business affairs happened to take them to Mosul or Nisibis. This was because the administration of the Christians, including the collection of taxes, was in the hands of village headmen (*dihqans*) and country squires (*shaharija*), and these local magnates were themselves Christians. This system went back to Sasanian times, and persisted into the 'Abbasid period. The ninth-century East Syrian author Thomas of Marga disapproved of these local gentry, and claimed that they were Christians in name only (Wallis Budge 1893: 309–10). Their rank and consequence brought them frequently into social contact with Muslim officials, and in the presence of influential Muslims, who had the power to advance their careers, they referred to Christ as 'Jesus, son of Mary', as the Muslims did. Christians were doing the same thing elsewhere in the Umayyad realms, notably in Palestine: not exactly denying their faith, but rather choosing not to make an issue of it in everyday life.

Such temptations were bound to occur, as there were some very attractive jobs available for educated Christians under the Umayyad caliphs. The East Syrian medical school of Jundishapur had long been admired, and this school continued to produce high-calibre graduates after the Arab Conquest, whose skills were much in demand. Like the Persian kings before them, the Umayyad caliphs surrounded themselves with Christian doctors, because they knew that they were far better than their Muslim counterparts. These Christian doctors, trading on their irreplaceable expertise, enjoyed much the same influence at the court of the caliphs as they had done at the Sasanian court. Christians also served as administrators, sometimes rising to high rank, and as teachers, scribes, and accountants. They were also respected for their high level of general culture. During the Umayyad period, the limited Islamic education available to an Arab Muslim could not compare with the breadth of a Christian education. A well-educated East or West Syrian monk would have been familiar with the riches of the Christian literary tradition, may have had a limited knowledge of the Greek classics, and would also have read a number of Greek medical and philosophical works, although in most cases only in Syriac translation.

The collapse of the Umayyad dynasty in the middle of the eighth century was welcomed by the Christians of the caliphate. The new 'Abbasid rulers, according to Barhebraeus, were better disposed towards the Christians than their predecessors had been (Abbeloos and Lamy 1877: 153), and there can be little doubt that, from the point of view of the captive Christian churches, they were a distinct improvement on the Umayyads. Under the relatively enlightened patronage of the 'Abbasid caliphs, Jewish and Christian intellectuals found themselves valued more highly than they had been by their Umayyad predecessors. The East Syrians benefited more than their West Syrian or Melkite rivals did from the change of dynasty, as their patriarch was once again close to the seat of power, as he had not been since the fall of the Sasanian Empire. The later Umayyad caliphs had governed the caliphate from remote Damascus, but the ʿAbbasid caliphs resided in Iraq. Baghdad, the ʿAbbasid capital, became one of the world's foremost centres of learning and a vibrant site of debate among Muslim, Christian, and Jewish intellectuals. The East Syrian patriarchs, who frequented the caliph's court and were members of his council of state, enjoyed considerable consequence under the more reasonable Muslim rulers.

At the same time, Muslim pressure on the 'people of the book' gradually increased. Whereas the Umayyad caliphs had preferred to tax the Christians than to convert them, the ʿAbbasids, in a calmer and more prosperous age, wanted to spread Islam. Christians were now subjected to pressure to convert. In high society, such pressure was normally applied politely. An educated Muslim would write a courteous letter to a Christian friend, demonstrating the intellectual attractions of Islam and also pointing out the practical advantages of becoming a Muslim. These suave representations spurred the growth of a popular species of Christian apologetic in which Christians invariably had the better of epistolary exchanges with their Muslim correspondents, best exemplified by the (possibly fictitious) correspondence between a Muslim named ʿAbd Allah ibn Ismaʿil al-Hashimi and his Christian friend ʿAbd al-Masiḥ ibn Isḥaq al-Kindi (Griffith 2008: 86–8). Lower down the social scale, however, Christians were made to feel their inferiority. Like the Jews in mediaeval Europe, the Christians of the caliphate were subjected to sumptuary laws and other restrictions which publicly marked them as a tolerated species. They were also hit in their pockets. The poll tax (*jizyah*) which they had to pay was far more onerous than the charitable contribution (*zakat*) levied on Muslims. Finally, they were under intense social pressure to conform to the prejudices of their Muslim neighbours. Faced with this kind of financial and social pressure, it is hardly surprising that some Christians simply gave up the struggle to maintain their faith and went over to Islam.

During the ʿAbbasid period, the Christian churches of the caliphate began their long, unspectacular decline into insignificance. It is sometimes asserted that the Church of the East reached the height of its power during the reign of Timothy I (780–823), the most flamboyant East Syrian patriarch of the ʿAbbasid period. In fact, it was considerably weaker in Timothy's day than it had been under Ishoʿyahb III (649–59). East Syrian Christian doctors still had the ear of the caliphs and were occasionally able to sway their policy. Timothy was denounced by his enemies to the caliph al-Rashid (786–809) as a traitor, but was able to convince the caliph that his Greek enemies hated the 'Nestorians', whom they viewed as heretics, just as much as they hated the Muslims (Abbeloos and Lamy 1877: 171–5). The East Syrian patriarchs were also accorded a slightly higher status by the Muslim authorities than their West Syrian and Melkite counterparts. But beyond Baghdad, the picture was rather different. An analysis of the distribution of the dioceses of the Church of the East makes it clear that the East Syrians were losing ground in Maishan, Beth Huzaye, Beth Garmai, Fars, Khorasan, and Segestan (Wilmshurst 2011: 159–72).

Although the ʿAbbasid caliphs continued nominally to rule in Baghdad until 1258, for the last three centuries before the Mongol conquest power lay in the hands of two warrior dynasties, the Buyids of Dailam and the Turkish Seljuqs. The world of Islam fragmented, and although the caliphs still sat at Baghdad and were accorded a degree of respect as guardians of the faith, true power lay in the hands of the Buyid and Seljuq sultans. The number of Christians living in the caliphate fell significantly during the Seljuq period. Many Christians simply abandoned their faith and converted to Islam. Analysis of tax records suggests that there was a decisive shift of religion in the territories under Arab rule during the tenth century. Before 850, Muslims were still a minority, accounting on average for less than twenty percent of the population. After 950, they were in a majority, accounting for more than sixty percent. Christians continued to leave the caliphate and resettle in the Byzantine territories. Those who continued to live under Muslim rule began to band together in search of greater security. There was a gradual exodus of East Syrian Christians from southern Mesopotamia and Fars, where the Muslims were now a majority of the population, to the towns and villages of northern Mesopotamia, where Christians could still be found in substantial numbers.

Conversions to Islam during the Seljuq period, as in previous centuries, were driven partly by its appeal as a religion and partly by the social and financial advantages conversion brought. They were also now driven by fear. The Crusades embittered Muslim attitudes towards Christians, and the Muslims were portrayed as oppressors in Christian sources far more frequently than in earlier centuries. The fortunes of Christians living under Muslim rule depended almost entirely on the disposition of individual caliphs. Mari and Barhebraeus portrayed the ʿAbbasid caliph al-Qadir (991–1031) as a fair and reasonable ruler, who personally intervened in 1002 after an outbreak of mob violence in Baghdad to ensure that his Christian subjects received justice (Gismondi 1899: 111–2; Abbeloos and Lamy 1877: 261–9). But at the same time, further to the west, the despotic Fatimid caliph al-Hakim (996–1021) launched a decade-long persecution against the Jews and Christians of Egypt, Palestine, and Syria which was only ended after thousands of Christians had either converted to Islam or fled for their lives into Byzantine territory.

The Church of the East stood at bay during the Seljuq period. It was an age of worldly accommodation with the Muslim authorities, in which corruption was commonplace and high ideals were in short supply. The East Syrian patriarchs during the three final centuries of the ʿAbbasid caliphate were probably richer than they had ever been, and their institutional relationship with the caliphs was now defined by letters of appointment which spelled out the privileges theoretically enjoyed by the Christians. At the same time, disputes between Christians and Muslims became more frequent, and references in the historical sources to the destruction, pillage, confiscation, or ransom of churches and monasteries increased. Despite increasing Muslim pressure, the East Syrians continued to squabble with the West Syrians and the Melkites, and their patriarchs spent much time, money, and effort in asserting their dignity against their Christian rivals. The monastic ideals of the Sasanian period were also now a thing of the past. Few solitaries now probed the limits of self-mortification. Instead, Christian monasteries became proverbial among Muslims for the agreeable lifestyle of their monks. Not all East Syrian patriarchs, bishops, and abbots were corrupt or self-indulgent, of course, but the worldliness of the Church of the East at this period was admitted even by its own members. In fact, this development was merely part of a wider Christian trend. In both the Latin West and the Greek East, prelates were assuming the airs of princes and shamelessly exploiting their privileged positions to enrich themselves. Christian practice has often fallen short of Christian theory during the long and eventful history of the Church, but rarely has the gap between the two been wider than in the tenth to thirteenth centuries.

In the second half of the thirteenth century, the Mongols succeeded in imposing a precarious period of stability in Asia, and the Syriac-speaking churches briefly flourished under their protection. The East Syrians, indeed, were able to return to China during the Mongol period and revive a presence which had disappeared centuries earlier. The destruction of the ʿAbbasid caliphate by the Mongols in 1258 encouraged many Christians to believe that the Muslim world had been fatally weakened, and during the period of Mongol ascendancy the Church of the East worked to encourage a Mongol-Christian alliance against Islam that would restore Christianity to its old primacy. The Mamluk victory at ʿAin Jalut in 1261, which halted the Mongol advance to the Mediterranean, and the subsequent expulsion of the Crusaders from their last footholds in Palestine, put an end to these hopes. By the end of the century, the Muslims were back in control throughout the Middle East. Meanwhile, the excesses committed by some Christians during the exhilarating years after the fall of Baghdad in 1258 had embittered Muslim opinion against the Christian minority.

Nevertheless, the Mongols still ruled much of the Muslim world, including Iraq and Persia, and during the last four decades of the thirteenth century some of the Mongol il-khans were Christians, and Christian governors ruled in many Muslim cities. They naturally did their best for their fellow Christians, but they had a hard task. The Muslims were restive under Mongol rule, and if they were no longer allowed to persecute the Christians officially, they were still able to do so in more subtle ways. Muslims outnumbered Christians substantially in the major cities, and came out onto the streets in force if they felt that the Christians were getting above themselves. Relations between the two faiths were very tense, and the slightest suspicion of an insult could trigger a major riot. There were scenes of unrest not only in Baghdad, long a flashpoint for violence between Christians and Muslims, but also in the Mongol garrison town of Erbil. In 1274 the Christians of Erbil, determined to celebrate Palm Sunday with a public procession to the citadel, persuaded a number of Christian soldiers from the Mongol garrison to act as an escort. A large crowd of disgruntled Muslims assembled near the citadel. As the procession made its way towards them, the Muslims pelted the Christians and their cavalry escort with stones. The Mongol soldiers scattered, the procession disintegrated, and for several days afterwards Christians did not dare show themselves in the streets of Erbil (Wallis Budge 1932: 451).

Ultimately, this contest could only have one ending. It took time for the Muslims to prise the Christian governors from their positions of power, but the accession of the Muslim il-khan Ghazan in 1295 was an important turning point. The histories of the East and West Syrian Churches during the second half of the thirteenth century gave enormous space to the fortunes of individual Christian governors and the narrative of small-scale clashes between Christians and Muslims, because such events dramatised the gradual revival of Muslim power. The tensions generated at this period culminated in a massacre of East Syrian Christians in and around Erbil in 1310 by a Muslim military commander who defied the orders he had received from his Mongol superiors (Wallis Budge 1928: 261–302). No redress was offered to the Christians for this gross injustice, and the author of the massacre was hailed by fellow Muslims as a hero of Islam.

ECCLESIASTICAL ORGANISATION

The size and influence of the Church of the East before the fourteenth century has often been exaggerated. Too many writers have been dazzled by the fact that, at various points in its history, the Church of the East maintained a couple of dozen dioceses in Central Asia, India, and China alongside the seventy or eighty dioceses it possessed in Iraq and Persia. Some scholars have estimated that there were as many as twenty-seven metropolitan provinces and 230 dioceses. Both figures need to be reduced by about half. The number of metropolitan provinces was exaggerated by mediaeval historians who were incapable of distinguishing between doublets and who listed functioning provinces alongside lapsed provinces, and the number of dioceses was inflated for the same reasons. The number of East Syrian dioceses probably reached a peak at the beginning of the tenth century. In 893, according to the historian Eliya of Damascus, the Church of the East had around eighty dioceses, most of which were in Mesopotamia and Persia. Eliya was clearly working from good information, and if there were several dioceses in Central Asia and India that he was not aware of, the total number of East Syrian dioceses is unlikely to have exceeded 100. To put this figure into perspective, the Roman Empire on the eve of the Arab Conquest had just under 2,000 dioceses.

There was eager competition for the position of patriarch, as it brought its holder considerable wealth and patronage. Most patriarchal elections during the 'Abbasid period were vigorously contested, and the contenders nearly always resorted to bribery to square the powerful Christian officials at the court of the caliph and to sway the votes of the metropolitans of the electoral college. Most patriarchs, having incurred enormous debts to get elected, recouped their losses by taking bribes for the appointment of metropolitans. Simony, the selling of ecclesiastical posts, was so commonplace that the twelfth-century historian Mari singled out for praise the very few patriarchs who remained honest. The metropolitans, in their turn, sold on the dioceses of their province. Patriarchs, metropolitans, and bishops all made money from the contributions of the faithful. At least in Mesopotamia, there was no such thing as a poor bishop, and some of the East Syrian patriarchs and metropolitans flaunted their wealth scandalously.

The patriarchs occasionally held synods, attended by the Mesopotamian metropolitans, whose decisions became the basis of the canon law of the Church. Judging from the surviving corpus of East Syrian canon law, these synods normally dealt with mundane matters of church discipline. Most patriarchs were not interested in administration, though there were occasional bouts of unfocused activism. There was little planning for the long-term interests of the Church. Dioceses were often allowed to lapse on the death of their bishops, particularly in the mission field, and it normally took a delegation from the bereaved diocesans to prod the patriarch into action. In theory, the patriarch could overrule his bishops, provided he covered himself by consulting first, but in practice attempts to intervene in a particular diocese tended to provoke the entertaining 'dissensions' that feature so largely in the contemporary chronicles of the Church of the East.

The patriarch Timothy I (780–823), who took an unusual interest in the missionary role of the Church of the East, reformed the metropolitan system. Before Timothy's time, all metropolitans were eligible to vote in a patriarchal election.

Timothy recognised the geographical realities of the eighth century by creating two classes of metropolitan province: the provinces of 'the interior', which from then on would form the electoral college, and the provinces of 'the exterior', which were given greater autonomy than the interior provinces to compensate them for losing their vote. The provinces of the interior comprised the five traditional Mesopotamian provinces (Elam, Nisibis, Maishan, Adiabene, and Beth Garmai) and neighbouring Hulwan. The long-established provinces of Fars, Merv, and Herat became exterior provinces, as did all the other provinces created since the sixth century. Henceforth, the metropolitans 'of the exterior' were allowed to consecrate suffragan bishops without reference to the patriarch. The patriarch Theodosius (853–58) took these reforms a step further. The metropolitans of the 'interior provinces' were obliged to attend the election of a patriarch, and were also required to report in person to the patriarch every four years. The metropolitans of the ten 'exterior' provinces (Fars, Merv, Herat, Rai, Armenia, Bardaʿa, Samarqand, India, China, and Damascus) were merely required to submit a written report from their province every six years. These reforms simplified the administration of the metropolitan system and were doubtless also intended to provide the exterior provinces with more vigorous leadership. But however justifiable on practical grounds, the new system distanced congregations from their bishops. Greeks, Armenians, Persians, Turks, Mongols, Tibetans, Chinese, and Indians attended church services conducted in Syriac. Their priest may have been trained locally, but their bishop, if they ever saw him, was nearly always a Syriac-speaking monk educated in one of the Mesopotamian monasteries. The failure of the Church of the East to root the churches of the mission field more firmly in native soil was one of the main reasons why their ultimate collapse in the fourteenth century was so complete.

The bishops, metropolitans, and patriarchs of the Church of the East after the Arab Conquest were nearly all celibate monks. Bishops tended to fall into two main categories: unworldly ascetics and social climbers. Good administrators were not in high demand, and the best that can be said for the quality of the East Syrian episcopate is that the holy men probably outnumbered the fixers. Given the choice, the villagers of the average East Syrian diocese preferred to be governed by a nonagenarian ascetic, gaunt and withered from decades of mortification and abstinence but overflowing with spiritual power. Some of these holy men did their best to evade such unwelcome appointments by going into hiding, and had to be rooted out, conducted to their dioceses, and consecrated forcibly. The social climbers, on the other hand, made the most of the opportunities for patronage afforded by episcopal rank. The metropolitan Yoḥannan bar Bokhtishoʿ of Mosul, who flourished at the end of the ninth century, scandalised and delighted the faithful of his province with his retinue of silk-clad Greek and Nubian servants and his flamboyant baggage train of laden camels and mules (Abbeloos and Lamy 1877: 233–5). He may have been exceptional in the lengths to which he took his extravagance, but he was certainly not the only bishop who believed that modest understatement was not a requirement for the post. Some bishops, particularly those from the lawless Hakkari mountains, were not of impeccable social standing. The bishop Narsai of Shenna d-Beth Ramman, who flourished in the early years of the ninth century, was a native of the village of Zereni in the Jilu district. Narsai himself was a gentle soul, but his brother Shalman was a ruthless fighter. According to Thomas of Marga, he took no prisoners when he led raids against the

Kurds of the neighbouring villages, used for his nightly pillow the skulls of robbers and brigands he had personally beheaded, and lost his appetite whenever the supply of victims dried up (Wallis Budge 1893: 523–4).

MONASTICISM

During the final decades of Sasanian rule, scores of new East Syrian monasteries had been established in the hills of northern Iraq. Some of them were deliberately planned, while others were founded as the result of quarrels over discipline or doctrine. Such quarrels were distressingly frequent, and when they occurred the aggrieved losers often left the scene of their defeat and built a new monastery somewhere else. This process of creative fission continued into the Umayyad period. For several decades, the Muslims were so thin on the ground that Christian life in Iraq continued much as though the Arab Conquest had never happened. The extremism of the early Christian centuries had by now somewhat faded, and in most of these monasteries the monks lived the conventional communal life envisaged by the sixth-century reformer Abraham of Kashkar. Many monasteries were located just off the main roads and often provided accommodation for travellers. Their monks lived a blameless existence tilling the fields, studying scripture and treatises on the monastic life, and copying manuscripts. The monastery of Beth Ḥale near Ḥdatta, a typical example of such worthy 'faith-based' community institutions, was exempted from tax by the caliph al-Mansur because it offered hospitality to Muslim travellers (Gismondi 1899: 61).

In theory, monasticism should have provided the perfect opportunity for a display of all the Christian virtues. In practice, monastic life throughout the Umayyad period was embittered by partisan clashes between the East and West Syrian Churches. East Syrian monks probably lived quietly and soberly enough in districts where there was no provocative West Syrian presence; but in the Mosul plain and the hill country around ʿAmadiya and ʿAqra, where members of the two rival Churches lived cheek by jowl, their monks spent much of their energies fighting among themselves. Law and order in northern Iraq largely broke down during the decades of the Arab Conquest, and warring bands of East and West Syrian monks terrorised the villages and monasteries of Adiabene and Beth Nuhadra almost with impunity. This power vacuum was only gradually filled by the Muslim conquerors. Large-scale violence was only suppressed at the end of the seventh century, when the Umayyad caliphs finally mastered the chaos created by the collapse of the Sasanian Empire. Several East Syrian monastic histories mention strife and violence in the countryside beyond Mosul during the Umayyad period, and one text, the *History of Rabban Hormizd the Persian*, glorified these unedifying clashes.

The most important East Syrian monastery during the Umayyad period was Beth ʿEbe near ʿAqra, which supplied two patriarchs, Ishoʿyahb III (649–59) and Giwargis I (660–80). Giwargis, an enthusiastic patron of literature, entrusted one of its monks, ʿEnanishoʿ, with the task of making a redaction of the *Paradise* of Palladius for use in the monasteries of the Church of the East. The monastery's prosperity continued into the ninth century, and its proud history was described by the bishop Thomas of Marga in the *Book of Governors*, one of the liveliest East Syrian texts from that period. According to Thomas, the eighth-century superior Quriaqos predicted that forty-two of the monks under his care would later become bishops, metropolitans, or even patriarchs, and Thomas diligently tracked most of them down. One of them, Peter, was bishop of Sana'a in Yemen around 840. In a striking testimony to the geographical extension of the Church of the East in the 'Abbasid period, Thomas mentioned that Peter had earlier accompanied the metropolitan David of Beth Ṣinaye to remote China (Wallis Budge 1893: 448).

The *Book of Chastity*, a celebration of monastic founders written by the ninth-century metropolitan Ishoʿdnaḥ of Basra, mentioned well over 100 East Syrian monasteries. Most of them were in northern Mesopotamia and the metropolitan provinces of Mosul and Nisibis, but several monasteries could still be found in southern Mesopotamia, particularly around Kashkar, and Ishoʿdnaḥ also mentioned three or four monasteries in Khorasan and Segestan. In the Seljuq period, however, a sense of decline is evident. Several East Syrian monasteries were confiscated by the Muslims, and many of the smaller monasteries in the hills around ʿAqra and ʿAmadiya closed down. The monastery of Beth 'Abe remained an important seminary for the Church's higher clergy but is rarely mentioned in other contexts. It was eclipsed by the monastery of Mar Gabriel near Mosul, which played an important role in stabilising the liturgy of the Church of the East, and by the monastery of Mar Abraham the Penitent near ʿAmadiya, described in a tenth-century text as 'exalted above all monasteries'.

Valuable light is thrown on the decline of monasticism in Mesopotamia in the biography of the patriarch Yahballaha III (1281–1317), who was educated in a monastery in northern China. When the future patriarch and his friend Rabban Ṣawma arrived in Mesopotamia in the late 1270s on an abortive pilgrimage to Jerusalem, they visited most of the surviving East Syrian monasteries. Apart from the monastery of Dorqoni in Beth Aramaye, supposedly founded by the first-century Apostle Mari, all the sites on their itinerary were well to the north of Baghdad. After visiting the monastery of Mar Ezekiel near Daquqa, the two Ongut monks went on to the monastery of Beth Qoqa near Erbil, the monasteries of Mar Mikhaʾil, Mar Eliya, and Rabban Hormizd near Mosul, the monasteries of Mar Yoḥannan the Egyptian and Mar Aḥḥa the Egyptian near Gazarta, and the monastery of Mar Awgin near Nisibis (Wallis Budge 1928: 142–3). This passage is an eloquent testimony to the decline of East Syrian Christianity in its Mesopotamian heartland. It is doubtful whether there were more than half a dozen monasteries left in Beth Huzaye, Maishan, or Fars at this period.

LITERATURE AND SCHOLARSHIP

Baghdad under the ʿAbbasid caliphs boasted some of the world's finest and most eminent scholars. Many of the caliphs were determined patrons of literature and scholarship, and Muslims, Christians, and Jews alike contributed to the intellectual life of the caliphate. Such was the lure of the salons of Baghdad that Syriac-speaking authors began increasingly to write in Arabic instead of Syriac. Most East Syrian authors of the Umayyad period had written in Syriac, but under the ʿAbbasids the prestige of Arabic rose sharply. Although Syriac literature continued to flourish for several centuries more, ordinary Christians increasingly communicated with their Muslim neighbours in Arabic. Many East Syrian authors could switch effortlessly between Syriac and Arabic, and composed works in both languages. On the whole, however, their output stood more chance of reaching a wide audience if it was written in Arabic. The ninth-century *Chronicle of Seert*, a wide-ranging history of the eastern Mediterranean and the Middle East before and after the Arab Conquest, was written in Arabic to attract a Muslim as well as a Christian readership. Its secular content, particularly its account of Muhammad and the early caliphs, was of obvious interest to Muslim readers, and they could always skip the chapters that dealt with ecclesiastical history. Syriac tended to be used increasingly in the Church of the East for books written for internal consumption by its members. Thomas of Marga's *Book of Governors*, a monastic history that no Muslim was ever likely to read, was written in Syriac (Wallis Budge 1893).

As the ʿAbbasid caliphs consolidated their hold on Palestine, Syria, and Mesopotamia, Muslim scholars began to explore the intellectual heritage of the classical world. Philosophy was particularly congenial to their tastes, though their exposure tended to be limited to a prescribed selection of the works of Aristotle. Above all, they were interested in acquiring practical knowledge. They were gradually made aware by their Jewish and Christian subjects that Hebrew and Greek literature contained books on medicine, astronomy, physics, and mathematics, which could be immediately exploited if they were translated into Arabic. A demand for accurate Arabic translations established itself, which only the caliphate's Jews and Christians could satisfy. The task of translating the heritage of the Roman Empire into Arabic therefore fell on bilingual Jewish and Christian scholars, who were familiar with this heritage and who enjoyed access to the superb book collections of Pumbeditha, Nisibis, and Jundishapur and to smaller collections in their synagogues and monasteries. Their work helped to make mediaeval Baghdad one of the world's most important centres of learning. It is sometimes claimed that, during the ʿAbbasid period, 'the torch of classical learning burned most brightly beyond the frontiers of Christendom', before it was finally passed back to benighted Europe during the Renaissance. This is an exaggeration. The bulk of the classical heritage, including nearly all texts of general interest, was preserved in the monasteries of the Latin West and the Greek East. But it is certainly true that the Arabs helped to preserve the texts of a fair number of philosophical and technical works that would otherwise have been lost, and scholars can only regret that their literary interests were not wider. Most of the credit for the preservation of these texts should be given to the Jewish and Christian scribes who translated them into Arabic at the behest of their patrons.

The vogue for translating useful classical Greek works into Arabic, both directly and through the medium of Syriac, reached its peak in the ninth century, and an outstanding contribution in this field in both quantity and quality was made by the East Syrian doctor Ḥunain ibn Isḥaq (808–73), a native of Hirta in Beth Aramaye. Fluent in both Syriac and Arabic, he became chief physician to the caliph al-Mutawakkil, and over a number of years at court put his linguistic talents to use in translating much of the extensive corpus of the Greek physician Galen into Arabic. A conscientious and dedicated scholar with a natural feel for language, his translations set far higher standards of linguistic accuracy and critical acumen than any of his more literal-minded predecessors had achieved. Ḥunain's achievement placed at the service of Arab doctors the most practical, comprehensive, and organised medical treatise yet compiled, and helped the mediaeval Arab world to build up a medical expertise which Western Christendom could only envy. Except in the field of mathematics, where he lacked the specialist knowledge for a mastery of the discipline, his translations became immediate classics, and were read by Arab scholars with both pleasure and confidence.

Many of the Christians who took part in the translation movement were motivated not just by the money they could make. They were also concerned, particularly through their translations of philosophical works, to defend the Christian faith to an elite group of Muslims who shared their admiration for the truths of philosophy. The works of Aristotle enjoyed great prestige in ninth-century Baghdad, and he was praised as 'the master of all who know' by both Christian and Muslim intellectuals. This shared reverence for Aristotle's teachings offered a rare opportunity for dialogue between the two faiths. Muslim rationalists, excited by the possibilities of a way of life grounded in 'common humanity' (*al-insaniyyah*) and dismayed by the rhetorical tricks employed by many Muslim theologians, debated eagerly with educated Christians who accepted the same Aristotelian premises. One of the most absorbing works of the patriarch Timothy I (780–823) is an apology for the Christian faith he supposedly made before the caliph al-Mahdi (774–85). Timothy corrected a number of common Muslim misconceptions, and while he stoutly upheld the truth of Christianity, he also praised Muhammad for leading the Arabs away from their pagan past and into monotheism. Timothy's *Defence of the Faith*, translated into English in 1928 (Mingana 1928), is a gripping book on a theme of the first importance. Ḥunain ibn Isḥaq also exploited his prestige as the *doyen* of the translation movement to write a number of works of Christian apologetic, one of which bore the title *On the Fear of God*. Some scholars have hailed this courteous and well-informed exchange of ideas between leading Christian and Muslim philosophers in ʿAbbasid Baghdad as a model for modern interfaith dialogue (Griffith 2008). It is doubtful, however, whether the mutual esteem of a coterie of cultivated academics did much to change attitudes beyond the ivory tower. The ʿAbbasid caliphs did not stop pulling down Christian churches because they discovered a respect for 'common humanity'.

During the tenth century, East Syrian scholars began to assemble, arrange, and codify their knowledge. The writing of expository literature – dictionaries, lexicons and encyclopaedias, and historical, geographical, ecclesiastical, biblical, and linguistic treatises – is not always indicative of a culture that has lost faith in its own future, but it often can be. It certainly seems to have been so in the case of the East Syrians. It can hardly be coincidental that the work of codifying the language, literature, and history of the Church of the East began during a period when conversions to Islam were frequent and Christianity was visibly fading out in southern Mesopotamia and Persia. These indications of decline could not be gainsaid, and East Syrian scholars in Baghdad surely sensed that the best days of the Church of the East were already behind it. The tenth century saw the beginning of an 'encyclopaedic' trend that continued unabated into the fourteenth century, when Syriac literature almost dried up during the disorders of the age.

BIBLIOGRAPHY

Abbeloos, J. B., and T. J. Lamy. 1877. *Gregorii Barhebraei Chronicon Ecclesiasticum*. Paris: Maisonneuve / Louvain, Peeters.

Gismondi, H. 1896. *Maris, Amri, et Salibae: De Patriarchis Nestorianorum Commentaria I: Amri et Salibae textus et versio latina*. Rome: Excudebat De Luigi.

———. 1899. *Maris, Amri, et Salibae: De Patriarchis Nestorianorum Commentaria I: Maris textus arabicus et versio latina*. Rome: Excudebat De Luigi.
Griffith, S. H. 2008. *The Church in the Shadow of the Mosque: Christians and Muslims in the World of Islam*. Princeton: Princeton University Press.
McAuliffe, J. D. 1991. *Qur'anic Christians: An Analysis of Classical and Modern Exegesis*. Cambridge: Cambridge University Press..
Mingana, A. 1928. The Apology of Timothy the Patriarch Before the Caliph Mahdi. *BJRL* 12, 137–298. Repr. in *Woodbrooke Studies*, Vol. 2. Cambridge: Heffer & Sons.
Wallis Budge, E. A. 1893. *The Book of Governors: The Historia Monastica of Thomas, Bishop of Marga, AD 840*, Vol. 2. London: Kegan Paul.
———. 1928. *The Monks of Kublai Khan*. London: The Religious Tract Society.
———. 1932. *The Chronography of Gregory Abû'l Faraj*. London: Oxford University Press.
Wilmshurst, D. 2011. *The Martyred Church: A History of the Church of the East*. London: East & West Publishing.

PART III

THE SYRIAC LANGUAGE

CHAPTER THIRTEEN

THE SYRIAC LANGUAGE IN THE CONTEXT OF THE SEMITIC LANGUAGES

Holger Gzella

SYRIAC AND ARAMAIC: INTRODUCTORY AND TERMINOLOGICAL MATTERS

Syriac is Aramaic, but Aramaic is more than Syriac. Forms of Aramaic – the term is derived from the ancient toponym Aram, which basically meant the Syrian Desert as far as the Euphrates River in original usage (Nöldeke 1871) – have been employed by many different ethnic and religious communities in the Fertile Crescent for some three thousand years as spoken, administrative, or literary idioms (see now Gzella 2015a, with a brief synopsis on pages 382–90). As a consequence, Aramaic first and foremost refers to a cluster of numerous linguistic varieties,[1] many of which were and are mutually unintelligible. It has to be distinguished from the ethnic (in a general sense) designation Aramaean, which by and large ceased to denote any specific group sometime after the erstwhile independent Aramaean polities of Syria had been incorporated into the Assyrian empire by the end of the eighth century BCE.[2]

The essential unity of all these distinct varieties lies in a common historical origin, as can still be seen in some shared phonetic, morphological, and lexical features that have developed in Aramaic only and are at variance with the situation in other Semitic languages.[3] Yet change over time, geographic spread, and distinct communicative situations have produced a greatly diversified language sub-family (Gzella 2015a: 16–45). Together with its 'Canaanite' sister branch on the one hand, which chiefly comprises Hebrew and Phoenician, and Ugaritic, the local idiom of a Syrian Bronze Age city-state, on the other, Aramaic constitutes, according to current majority opinion, the 'North-west Semitic' group (which proves difficult to define) and is thus deeply rooted in the linguistic matrix of ancient Syria-Palestine (Gzella 2011).[4] Among its more distant relatives are the indigenous Semitic idioms of northern and southern Arabia, Ethiopia, and Mesopotamia.

The history of Aramaic, however, is unique. It evolved from a set of regional vernaculars of tribal societies with unknown origins that grew into small polities in the ninth and eighth centuries BCE (early Old Aramaic), then later into an international means of expression under the empires of the Assyrians, the Babylonians, and the Persians between the seventh and the fourth centuries BCE (late Old Aramaic and Official Aramaic); it then gave rise to various regional bureaucratic and literary traditions with an increasing sense of local autonomy during the Hellenistic and Roman periods (third century BCE to third century CE); and eventually came to act as the carrier of religious lore of Jews, Christians, Samaritans, and Mandaeans in Late Antiquity, when a consolidation of religious identity replaced political affinity (since about the fourth century CE). In addition, many unwritten Aramaic dialects whose roots disappear in the mist of time have been spoken uninterruptedly as native languages until today: originally throughout Syria and Mesopotamia, now also in expatriate communities all over the world.

It is the perennial interaction of linguistic evolution and regional variation, both of which promote diversity, with the stabilising influence of periodical standardisation and codification that characterises the manifold uses of Aramaic in its Near Eastern setting with all its continuity and disruptions. As a result, phases of great linguistic homogeneity in the written record, as in early Old Aramaic (eighth to ninth century BCE), Official Aramaic (fifth century BCE), or Classical Syriac (after about the fifth century CE), precede or follow situations of intriguing variety due to the absence of a common literary language.[5] Aramaic's tenacity over the millennia, during which it subsequently resisted Akkadian, Greek, and, to some extent, even Arabic, is presumably the result of its rapid and wide spread – for reasons not yet well understood – as a means of communication; a firmly entrenched bureaucratic tradition buttressed by imperial policy and consolidated in scribal practice; and its prestige as a language of law, religion, and literature maintained by close-knit classes of professionals (Healey forthcoming).

Since the closing decades of the nineteenth century, a considerable number of epigraphic witnesses to Aramaic have come to light and, together with the surviving spoken forms, now document the complicated history of the language more fully than did the canonical religious literatures of Jews, Christians, and others that have been handed down in manuscripts since antiquity. Hence the outdated binary distinction, according to cultural affiliation, between 'Jewish Aramaic' (or 'Chaldaean') and 'Christian Aramaic' (or 'Syriac'), that was common until the early twentieth century, has been replaced by more sophisticated schemes chiefly based on chronological and geographical factors. Although the exact internal subclassification of Aramaic and the corresponding terminology remains a matter of debate (Gzella 2015a: 45–52), it is clear that Syriac – in its modern scholarly sense as the literary language of Syrian Christianity[6] – ultimately goes back to the local Aramaic dialect of Edessa and its surroundings in the Hellenistic and early Roman periods.

This dialect evidently belongs to the Eastern branch of Aramaic (Gzella 2015a: 256–61), which also comprises later Jewish Babylonian Aramaic and Mandaic and is distinguished by certain pervasive phonological, morphological, and lexical traits from its Western counterpart, which consists of Jewish Palestinian, Christian Palestinian (the older designation 'Palestinian Syriac' is contradictory), and Samaritan Palestinian Aramaic (Gzella 2015a: 265–8 and 334–42).[7] More specifically, it is part of a north-western, Syrian, subgroup of Eastern Aramaic and differs slightly from the eastern, Mesopotamian, dialects to which the language of the roughly contemporaneous inscriptions from Hatra and Assur belongs (Gzella 2015a: 271–6). It may be akin to the Eastern Aramaic dialect component in Palmyrene, but the regional element there is often eclipsed by the strong presence of an older literary tradition and defies exact dialectal classification (Gzella 2015a: 250–3).

Aramaic vernaculars were in all likelihood spoken in the region of Edessa from time immemorial and evolved naturally in the course of native acquisition or second language learning. A continuous network of dialects shading into each other made it possible for changes in pronunciation – the normal by-product of language transmission over time – to spread like waves caused by pebbles in a pond across the entire Aramaic speech area (for the period in question, see Gzella 2015a: 40–3). Similar to other Aramaic varieties of the Hellenistic and Roman eras, such as those from Palmyra and Hatra, the Edessan dialect only became visible when a local government promoted its written use, in part patterned after earlier written traditions of Aramaic, for administration and representation, and also coined a script specifically for that purpose. The basis of Syriac is thus a standardised form of the Eastern Aramaic dialect of Edessa from around the late second century BCE. It participates in both the regional context of Aramaic and the time-honoured official, global, use of the language.

With the ensuing rapid spread of Christianity in Syria and Mesopotamia from the second and third centuries CE, 'Edessan Aramaic', or 'Old Syriac', eventually turned into 'Classical Syriac', a deregionalised and supradialectal written idiom chiefly employed for religious, scientific, and edifying literature and, presumably, learned discourse. In this classical form, Syriac outlived the spread of Arabic in the wake of Islam in the seventh century and the concomitant interruption of the former network of Aramaic vernaculars by about the ninth or tenth century. It still acts as a strong unifying token of cultural affinity among Christian speakers of the many and diverse modern Aramaic dialects and also underlies the formal spoken idiom of learned Syrian Orthodox since the early twentieth century (Kiraz 2007). However, the wider prestige of Aramaic in present-day Christian communities that belong to the Syriac tradition also rests on the use of different forms of Aramaic by Jesus, in parts of the Old Testament, and under the great Near Eastern empires of the first millennium BCE. By way of back-projection, the name 'Aramaean' has even assumed strong cultural and ethnic notions among the present-day Syrian Orthodox and thus acts as a counterpart to 'Assyrian' for the Church of the East (Fiey 1965).[8] Not only in terms of the linguistic background against which it emerged, but also from the point of view of later reception history, Syriac is intimately connected to its broader Aramaic context. While its role in scholarship is generally that of an important source language for biblical textual criticism, Eastern Christian Studies, and the history of Late Antiquity, a more holistic Aramaic approach to Syriac brings to light wider-ranging socio-linguistic aspects. They will be the focus of this chapter.

THE HISTORICAL LANGUAGE SITUATION IN OSRHOENE IN CONTEXT

In the absence of written documentation before the first century CE and because of the fragmentary nature of the data thereafter (due to accident of transmission and the use of perishable writing materials), the linguistic map of Osrhoene and thus the origins of Syriac remain conjectural. Multilingual situations are by definition complex, and one must carefully distinguish between different functional contexts, especially between written and oral use, for a reliable assessment. Indirect evidence and common sense suggest, at any rate, that the entire area was Aramaic speaking before the Hellenistic period, and that Aramaic subsequently continued to be used as a – or perhaps even the – normal means of communication of at least a sizeable part of the population.

This conclusion can be supported by a series of arguments. First, the vast majority of the ninth- and eighth-century inscriptions discovered throughout Syria, as well as personal and place names, are Aramaic. Moreover, regional variation between the scribal language of central Syria and that of the Gozan inscription from Eastern Syria makes it clear that these chancellery idioms are based on standardised local vernaculars and arose in the context of urbanisation and early state formation, that is, they presuppose spoken dialects (Gzella 2015a: 53–72). Second, Aramaic was unrivalled among the Syro-Palestinian languages in its spread throughout the mainland far into Mesopotamia (and perhaps also into parts of northern Palestine) during the ensuing centuries (Gzella 2015a: 104–24). So there is every reason to believe that its use throughout the whole of Syria also continued, even if only a handful of texts from the seventh and sixth centuries and none from the fifth to second centuries have yet been found there. Third, Old Syriac and the roughly contemporaneous Aramaic varieties from Palmyra in the Syrian Desert and from Hatra, Assur, and other places in Eastern Mesopotamia all exhibit regional peculiarities that cannot simply be derived from a common written ancestor. This implies that they, too, have evolved from firmly entrenched vernaculars as a result of a new phase of codification in the late Hellenistic or early Roman period (Gzella 2015a: 212–25). Fourth, Syriac and its Eastern Aramaic sister languages share a number of non-trivial later developments in phonology and morphology. Such instances of wide-ranging areal change were only possible in a region covered by a network of Aramaic dialects, employed in many situations of daily life, whose speakers were in regular contact with each other (Gzella 2015a: 330–48).

While there cannot be any reasonable doubt that Aramaic acted as the historically dominant spoken language in Osrhoene as it did in other parts of Syria and remained in widespread use throughout the Hellenistic and Roman periods, the broader linguistic matrix was further complicated by the changing imperial contexts. Political developments had an obvious impact on official language policy but may in part also have affected day-to-day communication. Syria was successively a province of the Assyrian, the Babylonian, and the Persian empires, which implies that the local written registers of Aramaic first underwent at least some influence from the Aramaic varieties employed, though not yet rigorously standardised, in imperial administration and international correspondence under Assyrian and Babylonian rule.[9] Judging from the situation in other parts of the Persian Empire, such as Egypt, Palestine, and Bactria, the new overlords will subsequently have introduced Achaemenid Official Aramaic as the standard language for provincial administration also in Syria.

Achaemenid Official Aramaic is a highly unified variety that was apparently codified in the context of a wide-ranging bureaucratic reform in the early years of Achaemenid rule (Gzella 2015a: 157–82). It is immediately recognisable by certain orthographic peculiarities, above all the distinctive spelling of 'long' consonants ('geminates') with a preceding *n* in many cases. Remnants of this orthographic practice still survive in certain high-frequency words in Syriac such as *ʾnt* 'you', *ʾntt* 'woman', or *mdyntʾ* 'city' (later pointed texts mark this *n* as 'mute' by adding a *linea occultans*; Drijvers and Healey 1999: 25); likewise, *hw* 'he' and *hy* 'she' replaced older *hʾ*. The Persian chancellery language was a truly international written code that connected the Syrian scribal schools and the provincial administrators trained in them with the wider imperial backdrop. Hence it acted as a vehicle for exchanging legal practice (Healey 2005), literary traditions (in particular court novels: Gzella 2017), and presumably also science across the vast territory under Achaemenid sway. Technical terms, such as the juridical and administrative expressions that permeate Syriac texts from the beginning, were borrowed from Achaemenid Official Aramaic (Beyer 1966). As a prestigious and widely used register for formal prose, it would function as an obvious model for the later creation of regional written forms of the language.[10]

The language situation became even more diversified when Alexander the Great conquered the Persian Empire around 333 BCE and the dynasty of his general Seleukos ruled over Syria and Mesopotamia for the next two hundred years. During this period, the Seleucids founded a number of Hellenistic cities, such as Antioch, Nisibis, Seleucia-Ctesiphon, and indeed re-founded the ancient site of Orhay as the Greek polis Edessa in 303/2 BCE. After earlier sporadic contacts, Greek would now have been used as the official language of provincial administration, international trade with the West, and, at least in urban centres, as a token of culture. Yet the ongoing development of Aramaic vernaculars that is reflected in the many phonetic, morphological, and syntactic innovations of the new scribal idioms such as Syriac, Palmyrene, and Hatran Aramaic, to which these same vernaculars subsequently gave rise, proves that Greek did not supplant but complemented the use of the indigenous dialects to varying degrees. Otherwise one could not explain why the Aramaic varieties from Syria and Mesopotamia all exhibit several post-Achaemenid developments that can still be observed even in consonantal writing: they expanded the demonstrative pronouns by /hā-/, replaced the 'short imperfect' (or 'jussive') for wishes and commands by the 'long' form, extended the use of the predicative participle as a present-tense verbal category, and gradually lost short unstressed vowels in open syllables as well as word-final long vowels (Gzella 2015a: 217–25).

Nonetheless, Greek remained the official administrative means of communication under Roman rule, which began in 64 BCE in Syria, and Latin was mostly confined to the inner circle of Roman administrators and the army. Greek eventually became the main theological language of Christianity in the Eastern Roman Empire, just as Latin was in the West. The precise distribution of Aramaic and Greek across communicative situations and social layers of the population is still unknown, but the semantic fields covered by the Greek loans in early Syriac and contemporaneous Aramaic from Syria and Mesopotamia offer some clues as to the domains in which Greek was especially prominent during the Hellenistic and Roman periods: terms of offices, measures, currencies, other bureaucratic vocabulary, political institutions, and architecture, yet not items of basic vocabulary (Drijvers and Healey 1999: 30–2; Gzella 2006: 26–7; 34). The highest proportion occurs in the dating formulae of parchments geared towards a Roman legal context (Healey 2007: 120–1). Greek and

Aramaic inscriptions from Syria and Mesopotamia also contain a share of personal names that are linguistically Arabian (e.g. Abgar 'the big-bellied'; Waʾel 'refugee') or Iranian (such as Tiridates) as well as some Iranian lexemes (e.g. *nwhdr* 'commander'; *ʾwzn* 'hollowed out stone'), but the extent to which either language may have been spoken in this region is completely unclear.[11]

A new chapter in the linguistic history of Osrhoene and Syria began when a gradual weakening of Seleucid rule after the mid-second century BCE led to increasing disintegration (Healey 2009: 2–18). Local dynasties such as the Abgarids at Edessa after 132 BCE rose to power and enjoyed greater local autonomy, which, together with economic welfare and trading opportunities during the relatively stable early Roman period that followed, apparently triggered a wave of new political and cultural self-consciousness. As a result of waning loyalty to Seleucid rule, several novel Aramaic written languages appeared in the region and are directly attested since the first century BCE: Old Syriac at Edessa and Osrhoene, Palmyrene at Palmyra in the Syrian Desert and in Palmyrenean expatriate communities, and Hatran Aramaic at various sites in Eastern Mesopotamia. They were employed for representational and funerary epigraphs, public edicts and declarations of burial rights chiselled in stone, and private contracts on parchment (Healey 2009 has a selection with translations and notes).

All these languages are transmitted in proper, local, script varieties that descend from the former Achaemenid chancellery ductus, belong to distinct parts of the Aramaic dialect continuum between Western Syria and Eastern Mesopotamia, reflect different degrees of interaction between the older Achaemenid scribal tradition and influences of the regional vernacular (be it local peculiarities or common phonetic and morphological innovations), and underlie somewhat divergent 'epigraphic habits', such as a more extensive form of civic public display at Palmyra versus the predominantly private *memoria* at Edessa or Hatra (Healey 2009: 26–51; Gzella 2015a: 217–21; 246–76). Similar developments occurred in the wider periphery of the old homeland of Aramaic: the unbroken continuation of Achaemenid Official Aramaic into Nabataean in North Arabia, whose inhabitants presumably spoke Arabian dialects and only used Aramaic as a written code for law and representation; the emergence of a Jewish literary language in Hasmonaean Palestine, where Aramaic was installed as the standard administrative idiom by the Achaemenid government and which, in the form of a spoken dialect that presumably spread from Syria, also increasingly replaced Hebrew as the dominant vernacular (see Gzella 2015a: 225–46); and the persistence of 'Arsacid' Aramaic as a fossilised medium of bureaucracy and representation in parts of Iran (Gzella 2015a: 276–8).[12]

The relative inner uniformity of the respective Aramaic corpora shows that the underlying standards were all controlled by regional chancelleries and implemented by means of formal scribal training. Parallels in the structure of funerary and honorific inscriptions as well as in the rendering of Greek epithets indicate that this process of local codification of Aramaic across the Fertile Crescent did not take place in isolation. Micro-variation in, e.g., dating formulae and other fixed expressions nonetheless points to local autonomy (see Gzella 2006 for a survey of the evidence). Since writing in the Ancient Near East was never simply a matter of representing sounds by graphic symbols alone but often intimately connected with the whole 'package' of a literate education (including mastery of certain document patterns, a formal prose style, and various clerical tasks), the creation of a written tradition for a language that was previously confined to spoken use presupposes rather strong political or cultural driving forces. It is thus unlikely that these new written forms of Aramaic appeared by chance or due to purely pragmatic factors; they must have resulted from the conscious decision of the respective local government and illustrate, in a highly visible fashion, a process of identity formation and changes of political alliance.

As one might expect, orthographic conventions and phraseology were to some extent patterned after Achaemenid Official Aramaic. It is unclear how exactly knowledge of Achaemenid standards was transmitted between the fourth and the first centuries BCE. The cursive nature of the new scripts may point to an origin in local commerce and bookkeeping, where Aramaic presumably continued to be used in writing as well, and not only in speech. Mutual contact between emerging and more established scribal traditions in the area could result in knowledge transfer and a wider regional dissemination of certain bureaucratic practices. Yet the absence of any documentation from this period (in all likelihood owing to the use of perishable materials like papyrus and parchment, which have survived only in exceptional circumstances, such as the Syriac slave sale contracts from Dura Europos), precludes any definite conclusions. By the same token, the appearance of Greek inscriptions outside urban centres does not establish the status of Greek as a vernacular in the countryside; it could simply indicate the absence of an Aramaic writing tradition. The consolidation of Edessan, Palmyrene, Hatran, and other Aramaic varieties in chancelleries and their use for elite representation, public edicts, and private law in any case mark them as languages of prestige.[13]

FROM A REGIONAL VERNACULAR TO A STANDARDISED LITERARY LANGUAGE

Owing to the subsequent exposure of the Aramaic-speaking population of Syria first to Achaemenid Official Aramaic and then to Greek, and to the coexistence of various new written forms of Aramaic in the area, Syriac took on its shape against a richly textured linguistic and cultural background. It enters onto the stage of history in the form of some hundred brief pre-Christian texts mostly from Edessa and Osrhoene, composed in a local script and dated between the early first and the mid-third centuries CE, a few also from further afield. These are by and large funerary, memorial, and building inscriptions; some epigraphs on mosaics, coins, and pottery fragments; and a handful of extensive private contracts as well as Syriac additions to Greek texts from Dura Europos from the mid-third century (Drijvers and Healey 1999 plus a new mosaic epigraph conveniently accessible in Healey 2009: 245–7).

The earliest-known inscription was produced in the year 6 CE and discovered at Birecik, ancient Birtha, at the border of Osrhoene, a little less than fifty kilometres west of Edessa (see fig 3.3). However, the regular script and spelling found already in the oldest witnesses and their geographical distribution, as well as the unified pattern of the various epigraphic genres, indicate that by that time the underlying scribal conventions must to some extent have become formalised and established throughout the region. Excepting the Dura findings and a few short graffiti from Krefeld (Germany) of all places, both presumably reflecting mercantile activities of expatriates, Syriac epigraphic material is confined to Osrhoene proper until the late fourth century CE (Gzella 2015a: 260). The creation of a new and relatively stable writing tradition requires a suitable infrastructure and thus presupposes a political will. Hence, this seems to have taken place only after the Abgarid dynasty had consolidated its power at Edessa at the expense of the Seleucids and increasingly exercised its political and cultural influence between the Euphrates and the River Khabur from the late second century BCE onwards. Their rule as client kings lasted until the Romans claimed full control over the city and its surroundings during the third century CE (Healey 2009: 13–16).

The exact social and political history of Edessa during this early period is shrouded in darkness, and it remains uncertain how far its cultural influence extended into the neighbouring territories of Commagene in the west and Adiabene in the east.[14] Yet the linguistic evidence still reflects a process of standardisation and codification of a regional Eastern Aramaic vernacular (belonging to the north-western subgroup, see the first section above) that eventually produced Syriac, or, more precisely, Old Syriac. Since Greek must have been the official language of Edessa when it was re-founded as a Seleucid city – early Syriac mosaics executed in a local style even reveal a knowledge of Greek mythology (see Healey 2009: 238–9 for a Phoenix, and 245–7 for Orpheus taming the wild beasts [Figure 3.4 in this volume]; cf. Healey 2007: 118–19) – the return to Aramaic no doubt results from a conscious decision of the ruling elite to promote the local idiom to a scribal language. Greek was thus purposefully downgraded (Drijvers and Healey 1999: 33; Healey 2008: 225; Gzella 2015a: 257–8; similarly already Beyer 1966: 245–6). The presence of mythical themes in art, conversely, does not presuppose familiarity with Greek literature but was presumably transmitted by means of theatrical performances, against which Christian authors polemicised vehemently. Specific Eastern Aramaic dialect traits found already in Old Syriac, especially the emphatic-state ending /-ē/ of the masculine plural, and other post-Achaemenid features, e.g. the early expansion of demonstrative pronouns by /hā-/, loss of the 'short imperfect', increasing verbalisation of the active participle as a present-tense form (as a consequence of which the 'imperfect' became more and more confined to modal and future uses),[15] and a few lexical innovations like the shift from *ntn* 'to give' to *ntl*,[16] prove beyond doubt that the Achaemenid chancellery tradition did not continue unbroken, but that written Aramaic at Edessa resulted from a linguistic, or rather a scribal, revival.

Nonetheless, orthographic conventions were to some extent inspired by Achaemenid norms: such a specific model would greatly facilitate the ambitious project of creating a new written code of Aramaic and the Achaemenid standard would constitute the model most readily at hand. Historical spellings in particular, i.e. graphic renderings at variance with what can reasonably be assumed about the actual pronunciation, such as the use of a silent *n* for formerly long consonants in certain words (e.g. *ʾnt* 'you', see the previous section) and the distinction of etymological */ś/ (written with *š*, as in *šmt* 'I placed' or *ʿšryn* 'twenty') from */s/ (spelled *s*), although both were presumably identical in pronunciation by then, as well as the generally high degree of consistency, all suggest that the agents of this codification were literate, perhaps even learned, administrators. Hence, some knowledge of Aramaic formal writing must have survived under Seleucid rule. The script, too, derives from the Achaemenid cursive; its monumental variant used for public display subsequently gave rise to the Christian Syriac bookhand ('Estrangela'), while the cursive style of the documentary parchments encroached on literary texts from the eighth century CE and evolved into the normal script of the West Syriac tradition ('Serto'; see Healey 2000; Table 15.1, and ch. 15).

On account of a fairly stable scribal tradition that continued into the Christian period, supposedly following the conversion of the literate elite, Old Syriac is very closely related to Classical Syriac.[17] It does, however, exhibit some minor divergences that were lost in the later evolution of Syriac and the second phase of codification during the Christian period (for a nuanced assessment of the data, see Drijvers and Healey 1999: 21–34). The graphic difference between */ś/ and */s/ in Old Syriac was subsequently abolished in favour of *s* for both sounds and the originally sparing use of vowel letters somewhat expanded, in particular by employing *w* also for short /o/. In both respects, Old Syriac is closer to Achaemenid Official Aramaic than Classical Syriac. The pre-Christian inscriptions also contain a few lexemes that were no longer in regular use in the classical period but are known from contemporaneous Aramaic varieties, such as *ṭmʾ* 'bones' or *kpr* 'tomb'. Conversely, the later ubiquitous function words *dēn*, *gēr*, and *man*, whose particular behaviour in Classical Syriac was affected by Greek (see below), do not yet crop up here (cf. Gzella 2015b: 4). That is, Old Syriac borrowed from Greek some specialised terms but did not, as far as one can tell, undergo structural influence. This may be related to a limited degree of advanced Greek-Aramaic bilingualism (as presumably in Hatra; cf. Healey 2007) or to conscious language maintenance (as in Palmyra).

Despite this early attempt at codification, there is some variation in Old Syriac. It offers glimpses into the more dynamic linguistic situation that lurks behind the largely homogeneous profile already found in the first textual witnesses. A few phonetic spellings with assimilation especially of dentals and weakening of /ʾ/ and /ʿ/ (Drijvers and Healey 1999: 24–5) may reflect an occasional influence from the colloquial. The most important feature, however, is the oscillation between the third-person 'imperfect' preformative /y-/, the original form in Aramaic that was also preserved in the Western dialect group, which is found in the oldest inscriptions, and /n-/, as regularly in Classical Syriac, increasingly after about 200 CE. Since there is no functional difference, both forms presumably reflect distinct registers or styles, e.g. a more literary versus a more colloquial one (Healey 2008). The /n-/ preformative can be phonetically connected with its variant /l-/ in Eastern Aramaic dialects from Eastern Mesopotamia and Babylonia (Gzella 2015a: 266–7). Hence it may be a feature of the vernacular that spread westwards from Assyria or Babylonia, where it is first attested, then triggered the shift from /y-/ to /n-/ in Osrhoene (even though hypothetical intermediate forms in /l-/ are not yet attested here), and, after a brief period of coexistence, eventually encroached on the written language. This latter development could possibly be related to an increase in literary activity, if indeed the greater number of dated inscriptions from the second and third centuries is representative (e.g. fig 13.1). However that may be, it shows that Aramaic continued to be spoken, and hence to evolve, in Roman Osrhoene. Other changes were presumably also underway but remained invisible in the largely consonantal writing system and only surface in the pointing of Classical Syriac.

Figure 13.1 Shalman tomb inscription (Drijvers and Healey 1999: 53–6)

THE LINGUISTIC EVOLUTION OF SYRIAC IN THE CHRISTIAN PERIOD

The consolidation of Christianity in Edessa during the second century CE and the conversion of the elite, romanticised in stories about the apostle Addai's missionary activities and a legendary exchange of letters between king Abgar and Jesus, had a lasting impact on the local literary culture that henceforth accompanied the further spread of Christian belief and practice throughout Syria and Mesopotamia. Right from the outset, Bible translations were produced, followed by exegetical works and a rich tradition of religious poetry (the main contribution of Syriac Christianity to world literature). They triggered the rise of novel discursive, narrative, and hymnic styles with their respective innovations vis-à-vis older Aramaic: technical theological terminology, means for sophisticated storytelling, colourful imagery, and fixed quantitative metric patterns (see Morrison 2008 on the new narrative conjugations in Syriac, and Brock 2008 on native metre and other poetic devices). Moreover, a growing infrastructural apparatus with bishoprics and clergy soon presupposed formal training in monasteries and scribal schools as well as new administrative procedures. And steady contacts with the wider Christian orbit in a period of increasingly precise definition of the tenets that were meant to constitute the common basis of faith resulted in regular exposure of at least parts of Syrian Christianity to Greek language and theology, and even brought about translations from Greek into Syriac. These different factors thus shaped the subsequent evolution of Old Syriac, the indigenous written language of Edessa, into Classical Syriac and its advance to a *koiné* of Christian Syria and Mesopotamia (Gzella 2015a: 366–79). By contrast, the established Aramaic chancellery languages of Palmyra and Hatra, which were formerly current in wider parts of Syria and Eastern Mesopotamia, disappeared with the sack of their cultural and administrative centres during the third century CE. The lack of possible competitors also facilitated the advance of Syriac as a transregional Christian literary code among Aramaic-speakers.

The Old Syriac inscriptions are exclusively pagan, or at most indifferent as to the religious affiliation of the people who commissioned them, since they do not contain any specifically Christian symbols, names, or expressions (even if Orpheus and the Phoenix were also popular themes in early Christian iconography, where they symbolised Paradise and the Resurrection), and Christian Syriac ones only appear from the late fourth century onwards. Nevertheless, the early epigraphic material overlaps in time with the earliest Christian literary compositions in Syriac. Judging from the language or the general contents, the anonymous 'Odes of Solomon', Bardaiṣan's 'Book of the Laws of the Countries', and some poetic pieces like the 'Hymn of the Pearl' that were incorporated into later prose writings all belong to the second half of the second or the early third century CE. This is also the commonly accepted date of the earliest Syriac translations of at least the Pentateuch (from the Hebrew) and the Gospels (from the Greek). Produced in a variegated cultural and religious milieu, early Syriac literature absorbed Hellenistic, Jewish, Gnostic, and presumably other influences. The remarkably sudden appearance of diverse literary genres from this melting pot, each with their own registers and conventions as well as increasingly intricate sentence patterns (as opposed to the terse and schematic style of the inscriptions on the one hand[18] and the technical legalese of the parchments on the other) must count as a major cultural achievement that emerged from an exceptionally creative 'buzz'. Although even in earlier periods Aramaic did not act as a mere bureaucratic idiom, having already long given rise to non-documentary forms of expression (Gzella 2017), the more complex styles that surface already in the earliest Classical Syriac compositions, and which were so quickly consolidated, bear witness to a boom of literary activity. Only few individuals are known until the fourth century, but the amount and quality of production are remarkable.

Enduring contact with Greek, which had been continuously present in the region since the Hellenistic period and persisted among West Syrians in the Roman Empire, reached its climax in Syriac in the sixth and seventh centuries CE. It resulted not only in the borrowing of ecclesiastical and philosophical terms, but also in the replication of a few syntactic patterns already in the earliest literature (Butts 2016, with Gzella 2016a). The most obvious case are the discourse particles *dēn* and *gēr*, which go back to native Aramaic words but came to behave like Greek *de* and *gar*, and Greek *men*, which was borrowed as *man*. Degrees of proficiency in Greek will have varied among Syriac writers, however. While syntactic replication generally implies a higher degree of bilingualism than lexical borrowing, an advanced command of Greek may initially have been confined to small circles, such as learned translators (probably including pagan and Hellenistic Jewish converts) and intellectuals such as the author of the *Book of the Laws of the Countries* (Healey 2007: 124–5); borrowings could then have spread via the new literary and theological style these people coined. Persian lexical loans (Ciancaglini 2008) were partly inherited from Achaemenid Official Aramaic, partly absorbed from the Parthian sphere of influence, and partly borrowed by the later East Syriac tradition under Sassanid rule. Several Akkadian words pertaining to popular religion and lore that, among the Aramaic languages, are first attested in Classical Syriac will long have been integrated into the lexical stock.

Despite its new styles, the Classical Syriac literary language by and large continued the Old Syriac scribal tradition, and the early Christian bookhand directly emerged from the monumental script of the first epigraphic witnesses. The earliest surviving dated manuscript (British Library, Add. 12150), a collection of translations from Greek theological literature, was written in Edessa in 411 CE and confirms this smooth transition (see Figures 14.2–3). By that time, however, the graphic representation of */ś/ and */s/ was universally *s*, and /n-/ as the third-person 'imperfect' preformative had been generalised. A second phase of standardisation became operative during the fifth century CE, presumably as a result of an infrastructural consolidation of Christian administrative practice and literary culture. The principal aim was to further normalise orthographic conventions, in particular a more extensive use of vowel letters (including *w* for short /o/) and greater consistency in the spelling of ʾ and assimilated consonants, and to modernise a few idiomatic expressions and abandon archaic forms.[19] Some fourth- or fifth-century manuscripts, notably *Sinaiticus* and *Curetonianus* (of the Old Syriac Gospels) and *Codex Syriacus* 1 of the St. Petersburg Public Library (containing Eusebius's *Ecclesiastical History*), still reflect traces of the situation preceding this linguistic reform (Beyer 1966; Van Rompay 1994; Brock 2003; van Peursen 2008; Gzella 2015a: 370–1). Classical Syriac thereby turned into an even more codified and deregionalised literary language with a high degree of maintenance, comparable to Classical Latin. It therefore still provides the obvious point of departure for studying the older Aramaic languages. As the most widespread and prestigious Aramaic literary language among Christians, it also exercised some influence on the less far-reaching attempts of Palestinian Christians to develop a written tradition for their Western Aramaic dialect, which is best termed 'Christian Palestinian Aramaic' (Gzella 2015a: 317–26).

For centuries, texts in the estrangela bookhand were transmitted without overt vocalisation. Syriac pointing systems, which were first developed soon after the beginning of Arab rule as means for ensuring the correct liturgical pronunciation, but which were based on already established recitation traditions, also attest to a number of phonetic developments that had taken place in the meantime. In particular, the loss of word-final long vowels (which gradually spread across the Aramaic dialects after the end of the second century BCE but were preserved in Syriac historical consonantal spelling) and of unstressed vowels in open syllables (completed in the mid-third century CE), together with the emergence of fricative allophones of plosive stops in post-vocalic position (by the end of the third century BCE), give Syriac and the other Aramaic literary languages of Late Antiquity their distinctive sound (Gzella 2015a: 41–3, based on Beyer's chronology of the phonetic laws in Aramaic). There are a few morphological peculiarities, too. Innovative forms occur with roots ending in /-ī/ in Classical Syriac (Gzella 2015a: 369–70), and the long /ā/ in the suffixes /-āk/ 'your' and /-āh/ 'her' are presumably derived from analogy with verbal forms (Denz 1962: 39), but comparative information for other older Aramaic varieties is ambiguous. Some of these changes may already have been underway in Old Syriac but cannot be traced due to the small size of the corpus, the limitations of the consonantal writing (especially the local tradition in Osrhoene with its more sparing use of vowel letters), and the absence of Greek transcriptions.

Two distinct vocalisation traditions emerged around the eighth century CE, sometime after persisting disagreements over the exact relationship between the human and the divine in the person of Christ during the fifth century CE had cemented a split within Syrian Christianity. From that time on, a Western denominational branch in the Roman territory with close ties to Greek ecclesiastical language and culture coexisted with an Eastern one in Sassanid Persia. The latter remained a minority in a largely Zoroastrian society and was less directly affected by developments in the Christianised Roman Empire. Both adopted proper letterforms and vowels signs: 'Serto' (an offshoot of the older cursive script) with vocalisation marks inspired by Greek letters in the West, and the newly created 'Nestorian' alphabet with vowel dots in the East. The respective reading conventions also differed and were affected by regional pronunciation: in the West Syriac tradition, among other, mostly minute, differences, original /ā/ was consistently realised as [ō], /ē/ and /ō/ as [ī] and [ū] respectively and /o/ as [u], and long consonants were simplified; none of this applies to East Syriac, where, however, /ḥ/ was realised as [x] (instead of [ħ]). Consequently, the original pronunciation of unpointed estrangela texts before the cleavage must be reconstructed with the help of comparative philology (cf. Gzella 2015a: 372). West Syriac scribes also introduced some innovative spellings (Brock 2003: 99–101).

Besides the two different scribal and reading traditions, Syriac after the fifth century was so coherently standardised that no consistent regional, and very little diachronic, variation has yet been established. It is nonetheless likely that the spoken language at Edessa and its surroundings developed further and that Classical Syriac as a literary idiom existed side by side with other, evolving, local dialects of Aramaic throughout Syria and Mesopotamia. The formal spoken discourse of fourth-century Edessan authors may have been comparatively similar to the way they wrote, as was the case with the Latin of the educated Roman elite in the Republic; even so, diglossic situations presumably appeared at later periods and in regions further afield. More research may bring to light occasional substrate influences on Syriac from spoken forms of Aramaic, in particular in the syntax and lexicon (Talay 2009; Gzella 2015a: 340–1), but the overall linguistic core remained stable. At least some non-standard features in the sub-literary register of the Syriac magic bowls may derive from Aramaic vernaculars as well; however, the discussion is still ongoing (see Moriggi 2014: 5–9).

AFTERMATH

As a literary idiom, Classical Syriac was so well entrenched that its use, contrary to Christian Palestinian Aramaic and even Greek, survived the gradual shift to Arabic that occurred with the spread of Islam after the seventh century CE. The general similarity between Arabic and Syriac in their linguistic structures and shared lexical resources buttressed the role of Syriac scholars as transmitters of Greek philosophy and science to the Islamic elites in the early caliphate; yet the language maintained its grammatical and lexical shape as it had been established in the preceding centuries. Subsequently, Christian missionaries brought Syriac language and culture to Central Asia and as far as China, and literary production continued unbroken during phases of greater and lesser originality. With the advance of Arabic as the new language of prestige and also as the dominant medium of communication in the Middle East by about the ninth century CE or even earlier, however, the continuum of Aramaic vernaculars in Syria was interrupted and spoken forms of Aramaic were eventually reduced to minority languages. They nonetheless continued to develop further within their respective speech communities. Some of them eventually gave rise to proper literary traditions in the modern period that drew on the Classical Syriac heritage but did not directly derive from Syriac (Murre-van den Berg 2008).

NOTES

1 The term 'variety' is more neutral than '(local/regional) dialect', which usually refers to a spoken vernacular, or 'language', which often presupposes formal recognition by a political or cultural entity.

2 It could subsequently mean 'gentile', as already in the Peshiṭta New Testament (e.g. Acts 21:28; Rom 1:16). Later Syriac writings occasionally differentiate between *ʾārāmāyā* 'Aramaic'/'Aramaean' and *ʾārmāyā* 'pagan' (see Sokoloff 2009: 101–2), but the origin of this distinction remains unclear.

3 The most stable of these include a reflex of */ṣ/ that was first graphically represented with *q* and later merged with /ʿ/, the feminine absolute-state plural ending /-ān/, the emphatic-state ending /-ā/ (from */-āʾ/), and several typical words like /bar/ 'son' or *ʾzl* 'to go'. Some other traits occur in the earlier phases of the language but were then subject to change again, cf. Gzella 2015a: 21.

4 The only really uncontested common hallmarks of North-west Semitic are the shift of word-initial /w-/ to /y-/ (excepting the conjunction /wa-/ 'and') and bisyllabic bases together with external plural markers in the plural of nouns according to the patterns /qaṭl,qiṭl,quṭl/ > /qaṭal,qiṭal,quṭal/ (later simplified again in Aramaic with the loss of short unstressed vowels in open syllables); assimilation of /n/ to the following consonant is also pervasive but may have happened independently. Other structural innovations in the languages of Syria-Palestine presumably emerged by way of contact-induced convergence after 1000 BCE, especially the rise of definiteness and differential object marking and a restructuring of the verbal system.

5 Hence a simple classificatory scheme such as the five phases (Old, Official, Middle, Late, Modern), though popular in North American scholarship since the mid-twentieth century, is hardly sufficient.

6 In the Syrian-Christian tradition, by contrast, 'Aramaic' (*ʾārāmāyā*) and 'Syriac' (*suryāyā*) are often used interchangeably, which has a pedigree in the Septuagint translation of the Hebrew word 'Aramaic' with 'Syriac' in the Greek of Dan 2:4a. See Nöldeke (1871); cf. Gzella (2015a: 367 n. 1242).

7 In particular, the secondary masculine plural emphatic-state ending in /-ē/ (replacing older common Aramaic /-ayyā/) and the direct object marker *l-* (instead of the Western Aramaic innovation /yāt/) are two important regular traits of all Eastern Aramaic languages: the former, as a linguistic innovation, positively defines Eastern Aramaic, the latter distinguishes it from Western Aramaic. Likewise, Syriac partakes in the expansion of the demonstrative pronouns by /hā-/ already in the first known sources, the later loss of the determinative function of the emphatic state, which is also common in Eastern Aramaic, the shift of the third-person 'imperfect' preformative from /y-/ to /n-/ after ca. 200 CE (presumably via /l-/, as in some other Eastern Aramaic varieties), and the emergence of compound present-tense forms based on the active participle and a phonetically reduced personal pronoun. This confirms that Syriac originated and continued to be embedded in an Eastern Aramaic dialect matrix. By contrast, a few alleged Western Aramaic elements (i.e. a handful of instances of the Western object marker /yāt/ in early Syriac texts, which were no doubt borrowed, and the spelling of certain feminine forms with *-y*, which may be a purely orthographic device that arose independently by way of analogy) are of insufficient independent classificatory value, and thus cannot support occasional claims that Syriac had greater affinity with the Western dialect branch than other Eastern Aramaic languages. See van Peursen (2008: 240 n. 44); Gzella (2015a: 288 with n. 962) (cf. also Brock 2003: 99–100); 369 with n. 1245.

8 It is less easy to assess whether the occasional synonymy between 'Aramaic' and 'Syriac' in earlier Syriac historiography also reflects an ethnic sense of belonging that goes beyond the ordinary meaning 'Aramaic-/Syriac-speaking'.

9 A few texts document the use of written Aramaic for official purposes such as representation, and private as well as public law in seventh- (i.e. Assyrian) and sixth-century (i.e. Babylonian) Syria, but their regional affiliation remains inconclusive. See the references in Gzella (2015a: 109).

10 This adstrate of formal language use is sometimes associated with 'Standard Literary Aramaic', but there is no reason to postulate such an elusive and ill-defined category. It is clear that Achaemenid Official Aramaic also acted as a literary, and not only as an administrative, idiom: there are no linguistic differences between Achaemenid documentary and fictional texts, since both would have been produced by the same group of professional scribes and clerks. Consequently, the term 'Standard Literary Aramaic' should be abandoned (see Gzella 2015a: 165 with n. 523).

11 Pliny calls the inhabitants of Osrhoene 'Arabs' (*Natural History* 6, 9, 25; 31, 129), yet this was a vague term in Antiquity without overt ethnic connotations (Drijvers and Healey 1999: 105). On Arabian names, see Gzella (2015a: 224). Arabian loans are rare in Syriac, but cf. Drijvers and Healey (1999: 196–7) on *kpr* meaning 'tomb'. Vicinity to the Parthian cultural orbit explains the Iranian influence.

12 They are often subsumed under the notion 'Middle Aramaic', but since they do not represent the same developmental stage (Nabataean and Arsacid Aramaic are purely written offshoots of Official Aramaic), such a category has but limited explanatory power (Moriggi 2012; Gzella 2015a: 217–18).

13 The latter two points are not sufficiently taken into account in older scholarship, especially in studies on the language situation described by Greek and Roman historians (see Gzella 2015a: 221–5).

14 An alleged presence of Syriac in first century CE Commagene, as suggested in some recent scholarship, rests exclusively on the implausible early dating of the so-called letter of Mara bar Sarapion (on historical and linguistic grounds rather a third- or fourth-century document, see Gzella 2015b). By contrast, another local Aramaic writing tradition may indeed surface in the somewhat idiosyncratic script of the tomb inscription of Queen Helena of Adiabene in Jerusalem, the letterforms of which resemble Palmyrene and Syriac ones (Gzella 2015a: 264).

15 For an illustration of this crucial development in the history of Aramaic at large, see an undated tomb inscription from Kırk Mağara (Drijvers and Healey 1999: 78–81; the /n/-preformative suggests a date after 200 CE, see below): the combination of the active participle with an enclitic form of the personal pronoun *bʿynʾ* 'I am asking' in line 3, here perhaps with the performative nuance 'I hereby ask' (for which older Aramaic varieties would have the 'perfect'), corresponds to the widespread use of this new present-tense form in Syriac and indeed other Eastern Aramaic literary languages, whereas the generalising relative clause in line 5 *wmn dnzyʿ* 'and whoever removes' employs the 'imperfect', as is customary in Old and Official Aramaic. Cf. Gzella (2015a: 44; 338).

16 See Gzella (ed.) 2016b: 514. The secondary form *ntl* is already attested in the Old Syriac inscriptions (Drijvers and Healey 1999: 271, *s.v.*). Classical Syriac also evidences the general post-Achaemenid loss of *hūk* 'to go', *yṭb* in the basic stem 'to be good', and *khl* (in addition to *ykl*; instead, the causative stem of *škḥ* 'to find' is used as a modal verb 'can' in Syriac) 'to be able to' (Gzella [ed.] 2016b: 229; 319–20; 351–2), but the situation in Old Syriac is inconclusive due to the lack of attestations.

17 Old Syriac inscriptions show that members of the local elite were connected to the royal family by bonds of patronage (As1; As47; Am10 in Drijvers and Healey 1999; cf. As36). After a patron had adopted Christianity, their clients may soon have done likewise since they would have viewed conversion as a token of loyalty. That would explain the unbroken transition from pagan to Christian scribal culture at Edessa.

18 But note a quasi-poetic eulogy of an astrologer with rhythmic antithetic parallelism in a (third-century CE?) epitaph (Drijvers and Healey 1999: 53–6) that recalls the hymn in Dan 2:20–3 and a wisdom maxim in a mosaic (ibid. 172–5). See Fig 13.1.

19 Jacob of Edessa's later plea for a correct spelling in his *Letter on Orthography* gives an idea of what the underlying discussion may have been like. It is also indicative of a highly developed book culture.

BIBLIOGRAPHY

Beyer, K. 1966. Der reichsaramäische Einschlag in der ältesten syrischen Literatur. *ZDMG* 116, 242–54.

Brock, S. P. 2003. Some Diachronic Features of Classical Syriac. *In*: M. F. J. Baasten and W. Th. van Peursen, ed., *Hamlet on a Hill: Semitic and Greek Studies Presented to Professor T. Muraoka on the Occasion of his Sixty-Fifth Birthday*. OLA 118. Louvain: Peeters, 95–111.

———. 2008. Poetry and Hymnography (3): Syriac. *In*: S. A. Harvey and D. Hunter, ed., *The Oxford Handbook of Early Christian Studies*. Oxford: Oxford University Press, 657–71.

Butts, A. M. 2016. *Language Change in the Wake of Empire: Syriac in Its Greco-Roman Context*. Linguistic Studies in Ancient West Semitic 11. Winona Lake, IN: Eisenbrauns.

Ciancaglini, C. 2008. *Iranian Loanwords in Syriac*. Wiesbaden: Reichert.

Denz, A. 1962. *Strukturanalyse der pronominalen Objektsuffixe im Altsyrischen und klassischen Arabisch*. Ph.D. diss., Munich.

Drijvers, H. J. W., and J. F. Healey. 1999. *The Old Syriac Inscriptions of Edessa & Osrhoene: Texts, Translations & Commentary*. Handbuch der Orientalistik I/42. Leiden: Brill.

Fiey, J.-M. 1965. "Assyriens" ou "Araméens"? *OS* 10, 141–60.

Gzella, H. 2006. Das Aramäische in den römischen Ostprovinzen: Sprachsituationen in Arabien, Syrien und Mesopotamien zur Kaiserzeit. *Bibliotheca Orientalis* 63, 15–39.

———. 2011. Northwest Semitic in General. *In*: S. Weninger, ed., *The Semitic Languages: An International Handbook*. Handbücher zur Sprach- und Kommunikationswissenschaft 36. Berlin and Boston: Mouton De Gruyter, 425–51.

———. 2015a. *A Cultural History of Aramaic: From the Beginnings to the Advent of Islam*. Handbuch der Orientalistik I/111. Leiden: Brill.

———. 2015b. Review of Merz, A. and Tieleman, T., ed., The Letter of Mara bar Sarapion in Context. *Orientalistische Literaturzeitung* 110, 1–5.
———. 2016a. Review of Butts 2016. *Bibliotheca Orientalis* 73, 759–73.
———. ed. 2016b. *Aramäisches Wörterbuch*. Theologisches Wörterbuch zum Alten Testament, vol. IX. Stuttgart: Kohlhammer. English tr: *Aramaic Dictionary. Theological Dictionary of the Old Testament*, vol. XVI. Grand Rapids, MI 2018: Eerdmans.
———. 2017. Von der Kanzlei- zur Kultursprache: Die Anfänge der aramäischen Weltliteratur. *Theologische Quartalschrift* 197, 107–32.
Gzella, H., and M. L. Folmer, ed. 2008. *Aramaic in its Historical and Linguistic Setting*. Veröffentlichungen der Orientalischen Kommission 50. Wiesbaden: Harrassowitz.
Healey, J. F. 2000. The Early History of the Syriac Script: A Reassessment. *JSS* 45, 55–67.
———. 2005. New Evidence for the Aramaic Legal Tradition: From Elephantine to Edessa. *In*: P. S. Alexander et al., ed., *Studia Semitica. The Journal of Semitic Studies Jubilee Volume*. Journal of Semitic Studies Supplement 16. Oxford: Oxford University Press, 115–27.
———. 2007. The Edessan Milieu and the Birth of Syriac. *Hugoye* 10.2, 115–27.
———. 2008. Variety in Early Syriac: The Context of Contemporary Aramaic. *In*: Gzella and Folmer 2008, 221–9.
———. 2009. *Aramaic Inscriptions & Documents of the Roman Period: Textbook of Syrian Semitic Inscriptions, Volume IV*. Oxford: Oxford University Press.
———. Forthcoming. Aramaic, Jewish and Syriac *koinaí*. *In*: K. Vlassopoulos, ed., *A Companion to Early Globalisation*. Routledge.
Kiraz, G. A. 2007. Kthobonoyo Syriac: Some Observations and Remarks. *Hugoye* 10.2, 129–42.
Moriggi, M. 2012. Middle Aramaic: Outlines for a Definition. *In*: L. Bettini and P. La Spisa, ed., *Au-delà de l'arabe standard: Moyen arabe et arabe mixte dans les sources médievales, modernes et contemporaines. Atti del III Convegno AIMA/Proceedings of the 3rd AIMA Symposium*. Quaderni di Semitistica 28. Florence: Università di Firenze, 279–89.
———. 2014. *A Corpus of Syriac Incantation Bowls: Syriac Magical Texts From Late-Antique Mesopotamia*. Magical and Religious Literature of Late Antiquity 3. Leiden: Brill.
Morrison, C. E. 2008. The Function of *qṭal hwā* in the Acts of Judas Thomas. *In*: Gzella and Folmer 2008, 257–85.
Murre-van den Berg, H. L. 2008. Classical Syriac, Neo-Aramaic, and Arabic in the Church of the East and the Chaldean Church between 1500 and 1800. *In*: Gzella and Folmer 2008, 335–51.
Nöldeke, Th. 1871. Die Namen der aramäischen Nation und Sprache. *ZDMG* 25, 113–38.
Peursen, W. Th. van. 2008. Language Variation, Language Development, and the Textual History of the Peshitta. *In*: Gzella and Folmer, 231–56.
Sokoloff, M. 2009. *A Syriac Lexicon: A Translation from the Latin, Correction, Expansion, and Update of C. Brockelmann's* Lexicon Syriacum. Winona Lake, IN and Piscataway, NJ: Eisenbrauns and Gorgias Press.
Talay, S. 2009. Spuren des Neuaramäischen in syrischen Inschriften aus dem Tur Abdin und Umgebung. *In*: W. Arnold et al., ed., *Philologisches und Historisches zwischen Anatolien und Sokotra: Analecta Semitica in Memoriam Alexandri*. Wiesbaden: Harrassowitz, 378–86.
Van Rompay, L. 1994. Some Preliminary Remarks on the Origins of Classical Syriac as a Standard Language: The Syriac Version of Eusebius of Caesarea's Ecclesiastical History. *In*: G. Goldenberg and S. Raz, ed., *Semitic and Cushitic Studies*. Wiesbaden: Harrassowitz, 70–89.

CHAPTER FOURTEEN

THE CLASSICAL SYRIAC LANGUAGE

Aaron Michael Butts

Syriac, the principal self-designation of which is *suryāyā*, refers to a language, known predominantly in written form, that flourished among Christian communities located primarily in Syria and Mesopotamia during Late Antiquity. Linguistically, Syriac is a dialect of the Aramaic language branch of the Semitic language family, as is reflected in another of its self-designations, *ʾārāmāyā* 'Aramaic'. Syriac is attested by a written corpus of tens of millions of words, making it by far the best-documented Aramaic dialect. Geographically, Syriac originated in or around Edessa (Syriac *ʾurhāy*), present-day Urfa in south-eastern Turkey, which is reflected in yet another self-designation, *ʾurhāyā* 'that belonging to Edessa'. From Edessa, it spread, as a language of Christianity, over most of Syria and Mesopotamia – reflected in one final self-designation, *nahrāyā* 'that belonging to (Meso)potamia' – reaching as far as Ethiopia, India, and Central Asia. Syriac is first attested in the early centuries of the Common Era. Its classical period spans from approximately the fourth through seventh centuries, ending with the rise of Arabic at the end of the seventh century. Syriac, however, continued to be spoken and written from this time up until the present day.

SYRIAC WITHIN ITS ARAMAIC (AND SEMITIC) SETTING

Syriac is a dialect of Aramaic, which is a member of the Semitic language family, which in turn belongs to the larger Afroasiatic language phylum.[1] The Semitic family also includes, *inter alia*, the ancient languages of Akkadian, Gəʿəz (Classical Ethiopic), Hebrew, Old South Arabian, Phoenician, and Ugaritic as well as modern ones, such as the languages/dialects belonging to the Modern Arabic, Modern South Arabian, and Neo-Ethiopian branches. In general, the Semitic languages exhibit more similarity to one another and so form a more uniform family than, for instance, the Indo-European family (a comparison with Romance would be more apt). Semitic phonology is characterised by a number of consonantal triads that consist of a voiceless, voiced, and 'emphatic' member. The latter, which is traditionally marked with an under-dot in Semitic studies, was most likely ejective in the proto-language but is realised as pharyngeal in many of the daughter languages, including most traditional pronunciations of Syriac. The most well-known feature of Semitic morphology is its nonconcatenative root-and-pattern system. That is, consonantal roots are intercalated with vowels and various consonantal prefixes, infixes, and suffixes. In Syriac, for instance, the root *k-t-b* can produce such diverse words as *ktab̲* 'he wrote', *kt̲āb̲ā* 'book', *kāt̲ob̲ā* 'writer, scribe', *mak̲tb̲ānā* 'author, scribe', etc. Proto-Semitic word order is reconstructed as verb-subject-object (VSO) with modifiers following the head. One of the many interesting syntactic features attested in the Semitic family is the use of an infinitive in coordination with a finite verbal form of the same root to focalise the verb – the Syriac reflex of this construction is discussed below.

The classification of the Semitic family is summarised in the following stemma:[2]

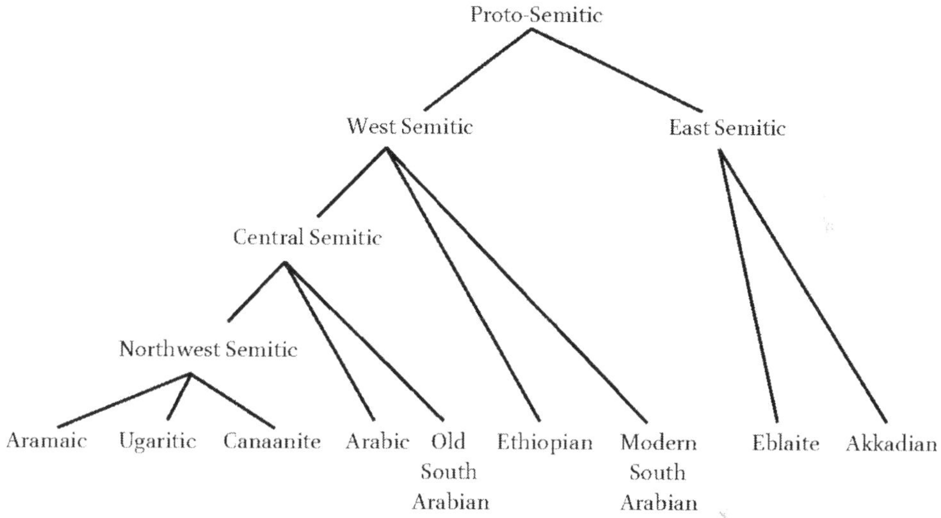

As outlined in this stemma, Aramaic is grouped as a member of the Northwest Semitic branch and is most closely related to Ugaritic, which is attested in about 2,000 alphabetic cuneiform texts from the end of the Late Bronze Age (ca. 1250–1190 BCE), and the Canaanite subgroup, which includes Hebrew, Phoenician, and a number of sparsely attested languages, such as Ammonite, Edomite, and Moabite.

The Aramaic language branch comprises a diverse group of dialects that span from early in the first millennium BCE until the present day.[3] Some dialects are attested in a single inscription, such as the recently discovered inscription of KTMW from Zincirli (Pardee 2009), whereas others have a huge literary corpus, such as Syriac. Some dialects show significant difference from others, such as the various Neo-Aramaic dialects, whereas others are much more similar, such as the dialects in use around the turn of the Common Era, though there are still differences. The dialects of Aramaic are fragmented both geographically and chronologically. In fact, in the vast majority of cases, a given dialect will appear for a specific period of time in a specific place and then disappear without a trace. There are very few, if any, cases in which a dialect from an earlier period can be connected genetically to a dialect of a later period.[4]

Given the fragmented nature of the dialects, it perhaps comes as no surprise that there continues to be no agreed-upon genetic classification for the Aramaic branch of Semitic. Instead of a genetic classification, most scholars resort to the following five-fold chronological division that was first proposed by Fitzmyer (1979), which is based almost exclusively on written texts:[5]

1 Old Aramaic (tenth century BCE–538 BCE) consists of a relatively small number of royal and funerary inscriptions from Syria, Palestine, and Mesopotamia.[6] The language of this period is characterised by dialect diversity, with several different dialect clusters represented, not to mention two groups of texts for which there is no scholarly consensus about whether they even belong to Aramaic: the Sam'alian inscriptions (KAI 214, 215) and the Deir ʿAllā plaster inscription (ed. Hoftijzer and van der Kooij 1976).
2 Achaemenid Aramaic (583 BCE–333 BCE) consists of a small number of inscriptions as well as a larger number of papyri, parchments, and ostraca, the majority of which were recovered in Egypt.[7] A variety of genres are attested among the perishable texts, including legal documents, letters, literature, historical texts, and administrative texts. Texts from this period reflect the adoption of Aramaic as the 'official' language by the Achaemenid Empire – note that this period is also termed 'Official Aramaic' (from *Reichsaramäisch*). All of the texts from this period strive for a standardised linguistic form; features of the individual dialects can, however, often still be seen hiding beneath this standard (Folmer 1995).
3 Middle Aramaic (ca. 333 BCE–ca. 200 CE) is attested in two broad categories of texts: epigraphic texts from Edessa, Ḥaṭra, and Palmyra, as well as from the Nabataean Empire, with its capital in Petra, and the literary texts of the book of Daniel, Targum Onqelos and Jonathan, and the Dead Sea Scrolls. Though some dialects, such as Nabataean, hold closely to the standard of the previous Achaemenid Aramaic, the language of this period is marked by a clearer view of distinct dialects.[8]
4 Late Aramaic (ca. 200 CE–ca. 1200 CE) traditionally consisted of six dialects: Christian Palestinian Aramaic, Jewish Palestinian Aramaic, and Samaritan Aramaic in the Levant, Mandaic and Jewish Babylonian Aramaic in Mesopotamia, and Syriac geographically in between.[9] To these can be added Late Jewish Literary Aramaic, which is witnessed in Targum Pseudo-Jonathan as well as a number of Targumim to the writings (Kaufman 2013). Late Aramaic witnesses the explosion of literary texts and represents by far the largest written body of Aramaic, well surpassing that of all of the other periods combined. The internal classification of Late Aramaic remains disputed. Traditionally, Syriac was classified as a Late East Aramaic dialect along with Mandaic and Jewish Babylonian Aramaic. This was challenged by Boyarin (1981), who argued that Syriac shares several innovations with the late West Aramaic dialects of Christian Palestinian Aramaic, Jewish Palestinian Aramaic, and Samaritan Aramaic. Some scholars have rejected Boyarin's argument – or ignored it – and maintain the traditional classification that divides Late Aramaic into two branches, East and West (see e.g. Creason 2004: 392; Muraoka 2005: 1). Many scholars, however, have accepted Boyarin's proposal, at least to some degree. Most of these opt to create a new branch of Late Aramaic, often called Central or Syrian Late Aramaic, to which Syriac and Late Jewish Literary Aramaic belong (see e.g. Kaufman 1997: 117–8). In contrast, but still following Boyarin's argument, I prefer a convergence model for the Late Aramaic dialects, according to which common features that are shared by groups of dialects, such as the traditional West and East Late Aramaic, are

explained as the result of contact due to geographic proximity, not shared innovations in a putative proto-language.

5 Neo-Aramaic (primarily modern) does not denote a single, homogeneous language, but rather is a cover term for the many contemporary (or near contemporary) daughter languages of earlier Aramaic. Geographically, they span from Lake Van and Lake Urmia in the north to Damascus and Ahvāz in the south. Within this area, they are clustered in small groups. Four different dialect groups of Neo-Aramaic are currently distinguished: West Neo-Aramaic, Central Neo-Aramaic, North-Eastern Neo-Aramaic (NENA), and Neo-Mandaic. Neo-Aramaic is primarily attested in the modern period; earlier written records, however, do survive for both Christian and Jewish dialects of NENA. The Neo-Aramaic dialects are discussed in detail in chapter 16 of the present volume.

Syriac is first attested in the early decades of the Common Era and continues to be written and even spoken today. Thus, it presents a challenge for this chronological classification of Aramaic, since it spans three periods: Middle, Late, and Neo-Aramaic. This can best be addressed by looking at the periodisation of the Syriac language, to which we now turn.

PERIODISATION OF SYRIAC

The Syriac corpus can be divided into four chronological periods: Old Syriac, Early Syriac, Classical Syriac, and Post-Classical Syriac.

Old Syriac

Old Syriac refers to the inscriptions and documents written in the Syriac language that date from the first to the third centuries CE (Butts Forthcoming). Well over 100 Old Syriac inscriptions are known, the earliest of which is (probably) dated to 6 CE.[10] The inscriptions stem primarily from Edessa and the surrounding area of Osrhoene. A few were also found at Dura Europos. A vast majority of the Old Syriac inscriptions belong to funerary contexts and are either inscribed in stone or tiled in mosaic (see Figures 3.3, 3.4). In contrast to the Old Syriac inscriptions, the Old Syriac documents are written on perishable material, and thus the number that are extant is much more limited.[11] In fact, only a few Old Syriac documents have been found to date. One document, P. Dura 28, was discovered at Dura Europos, though it was likely written in Edessa, since the text specifically states that, 'one copy of it, kept as a record, would enter into the archive of Antonia Edessa' (ln. 19). The other two Old Syriac documents, known as P. Euph. 19 and 20, probably originate from Appadana (Neapolis), just north of Dura Europos on the Euphrates. These two Old Syriac documents were found in a cache that also includes 19 Greek papyri and parchments (ed. Feissel and Gascou 1989, 1995, 2000; Feissel, Gascou, and Teixidor 1997). On several of these Greek texts, there is additional writing in Syriac. P. Euph. 6 (with its duplicate P. Euph. 7), for instance, contains a bill of sale for a slave in Greek, which is followed by seven lines of Syriac summarising the sale as well as a list of witnesses and guarantors (verso), both in Syriac (see Figure 14.1).

The Old Syriac corpus, both inscriptions and documents, provides an important witness to an early stage of the Syriac language. Old Syriac belongs to the Middle Aramaic

Figure 14.1 P. Euphr. 6r

Source: © Adam Bülow-Jacobsen

period (ca. 333 BCE–ca. 200 CE) and shares a number of similarities with dialects of this period, at times against later Classical Syriac. This includes several orthographic features, such as the writing of the etymological voiceless lateral fricative *ɬ (= traditional *ś*) with <*š*>, e.g. <*ʿšryn*> 'twenty', against <*s*> in Classical Syriac, e.g. <*ʿsryn*>, and the defective writing of the historic short **u*, e.g. <*ḥšbn*> 'reckoning', against the plene writing with a *mater lectionis* in Classical Syriac, e.g. <*ḥwšbn*>. Old Syriac shares both of these orthographic features with other dialects of Middle Aramaic. In addition to regular differences such as these, the orthography of Old Syriac is not as standardised as would develop later in Classical Syriac. The morphology of Old Syriac also shares some similarities with that of Middle Aramaic against that of Classical Syriac. This is most striking with the person prefix forms of the third-person masculine prefix conjugation. In Classical Syriac this is <*n*>, e.g., *neḵtoḇ* 'let him write', whereas in earlier forms of Aramaic it is <*y*>, e.g., *yeḵtoḇ* 'let him write, he will write'. Old Syriac represents a transitional stage between these two. In the earlier inscriptions, the person marker is <*y*>, while in the later inscriptions it is <*n*>; the innovative form <*n*> is first attested in the recently discovered mosaic dated to 194 CE (ed. Healey 2006; see Figure 3.4). The Old Syriac documents, all of which stem from the mid-third century, uniformly attest <*n*> as in Classical Syriac. Not only does the prefix <*y*> in the earlier inscriptions link Old Syriac with Middle Aramaic, but the occurrence of both <*y*> and <*n*> shows that Old Syriac was in a state of change and not (yet) linguistically standardised (Healey 2008).

Early Syriac

Early Syriac refers to the traces of the pre-standardised form(s) of Classical Syriac that can occasionally be found in the earliest compositions and earliest manuscripts. Some early Syriac manuscripts, such as ms. St. Petersburg, Public Library, Cod. Syr. 1 (461/462), which contains a Syriac translation of Eusebius of Caesarea's *Ecclesiastical History*, attest a language that is less uniform than that of the later manuscripts and that differs in places from later, standardised Classical Syriac (Van Rompay 1994). In contrast, other early Syriac manuscripts, including the earliest dated one, ms. London, Brit. Libr. Add. 12,150, which was written in Edessa in 411 (Figures 14.2–3), preserve very few, if any, such traces. Thus, early Syriac manuscripts may occasionally – though not necessarily – provide glimpses of the diversity and variety of the pre-standardised form(s) of Classical Syriac; this Early Syriac is, however, always mediated through the later standardised Classical Syriac, which even the earliest manuscripts primarily reflect. Early Syriac can also occasionally be seen in later Syriac manuscripts that preserve early compositions. Consider, for instance, the Old Testament Peshiṭta (see van Peursen 2008: 173). The Pentateuch was translated probably by ca. 150 (Weitzman 1999: 248–58); the earliest manuscript, however, stems from the fifth century (5b1 = ms. London, Brit. Libr. Add. 14,425, dated to 463/464). This manuscript, as well as others after it, does not preserve the Syriac language from the time of composition, but rather it witnesses a text that has been updated towards the standardised literary language of Classical Syriac. At the same time, however, the Old Testament Peshiṭta as we now have it, especially in certain manuscripts like 5b1 and the later 9a1 (= ms. Florence, Biblioteca Medicea Laurenziana, Or. Ms. 58), preserves some early linguistic features that were lost in the later standardised language.[12] The same is true of other early Syriac compositions that are preserved in later manuscripts, including the

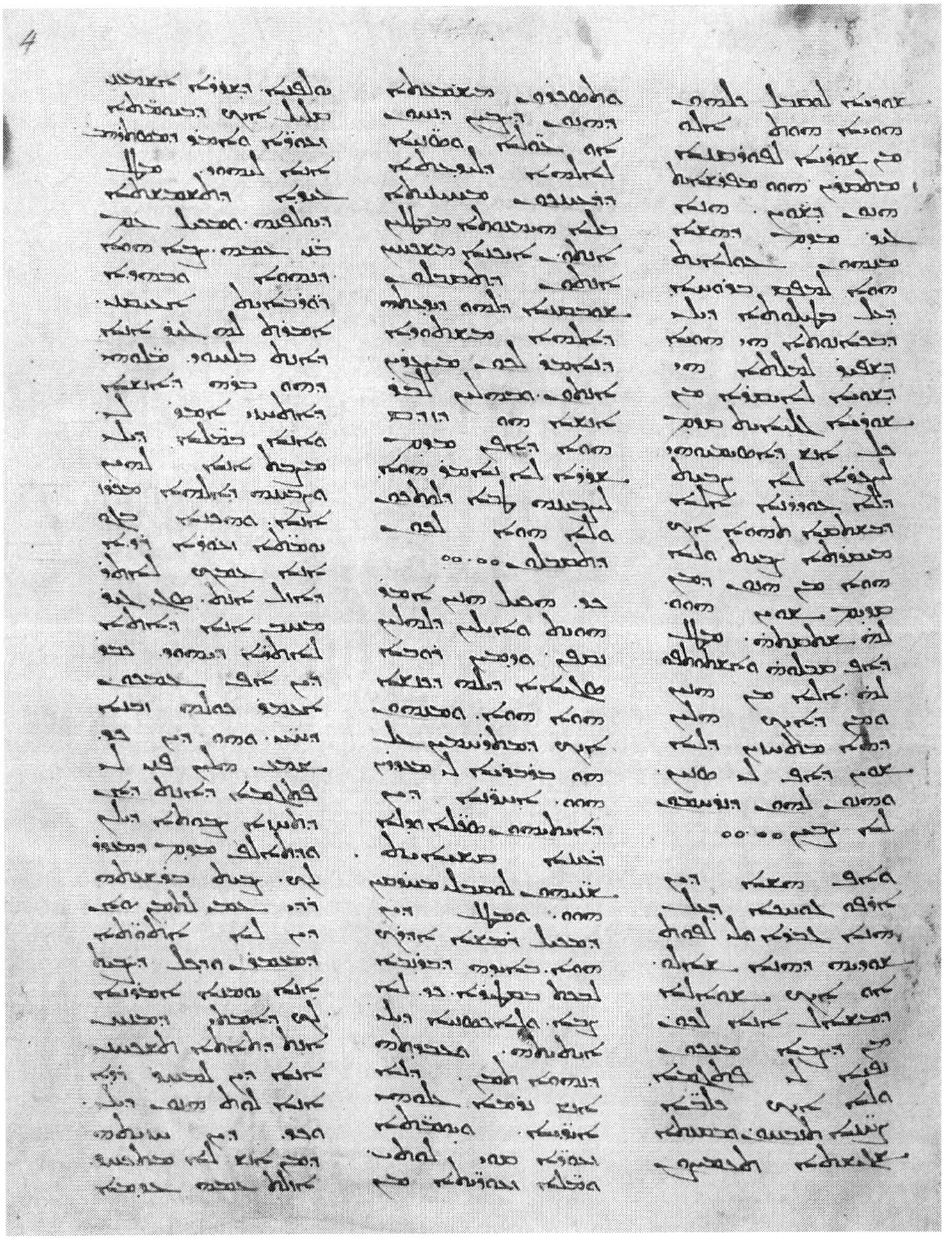

Figure 14.2 BL Add 12150, f.4r (dated AD 411)

Source: © The British Library Board

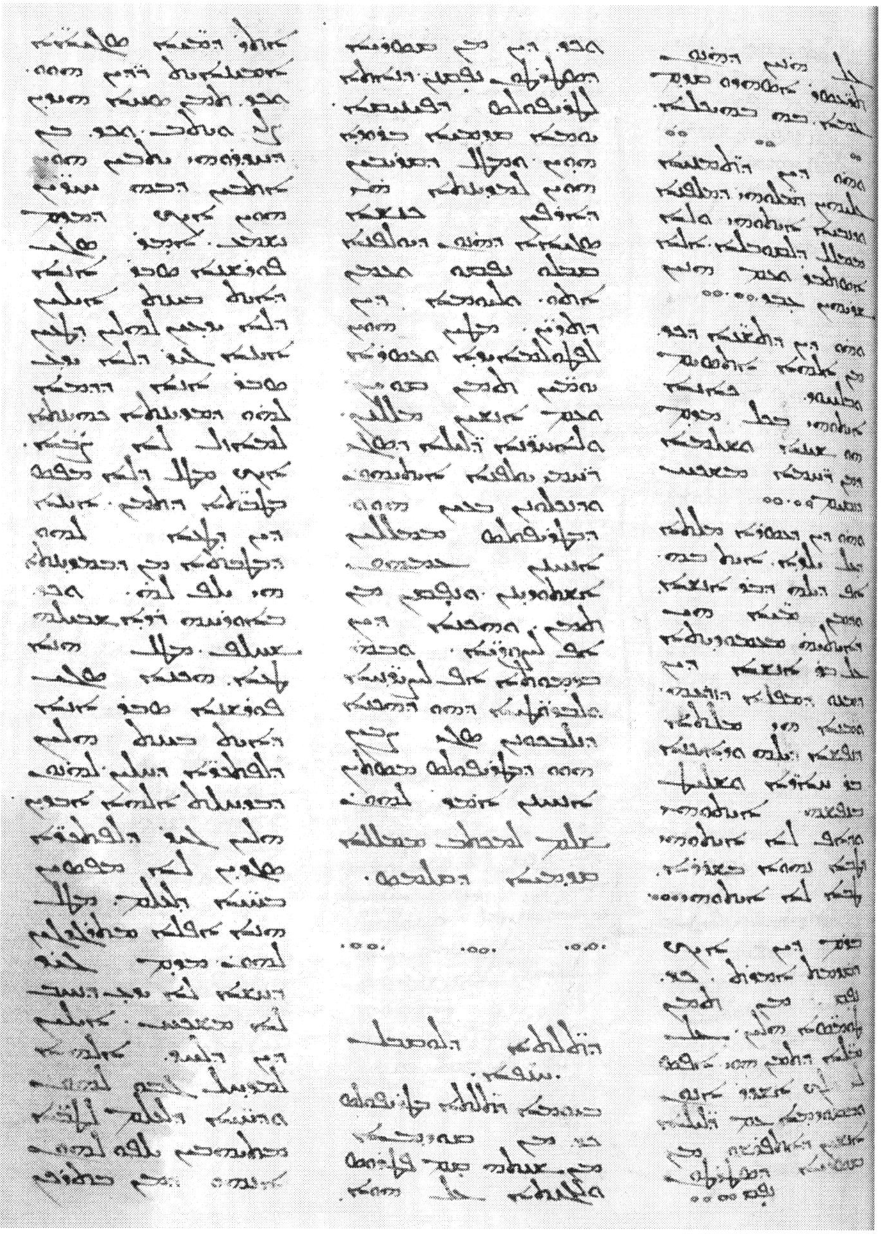

Figure 14.3 BL Add 12150, f.53r

Old Syriac Gospels (ed. Kiraz 1996), the *Odes of Solomon* (ed. Charlesworth 1973), the *Acts of Thomas* (ed. Wright 1871a: 2.171–333), the *Books of the Laws of the Countries* (ed. Drijvers 1965), as well as perhaps the *Letter of Mara bar Serapion* (ed. Cureton 1855: 43–8, 70–6, 101–2), unless it is a later rhetorical exercise or the like (see McVey 1990; Chin 2006). Thus, while we do not have direct, unmediated access to the pre-standardised form of Classical Syriac, we can occasionally find traces of it in the earliest manuscripts and the earliest compositions.

Classical Syriac

Classical Syriac refers to the standardised literary language that emerges most clearly in the works of the fourth-century authors Aphrahaṭ (fl. 337–345) and Ephrem (d. 373), as preserved in manuscripts from as early as the fifth and sixth centuries. Jacob of Edessa (d. 708) often serves as a convenient endpoint for Classical Syriac, since he is thought to have been among the last generation of individuals who learned Syriac as a first language before the advent of an Arabic-speaking political context.[13] Classical Syriac is a remarkably uniform and homogeneous language. It is difficult, for instance, in the current state of research to identify more than a few geographic and even diachronic differences within Classical Syriac. This is at least partly due to the lack of grammatical studies that address these topics – a point to which I return below.[14] It is, however, also in large part a result of the standardisation of the language. Still, there are occasional hints at variation and diversity even in the Classical Syriac corpus. For instance, the earliest Syriac translation of *Kalila and Dimna*, which was made from Middle Persian in the sixth century, preserves a number of non-standard features (ed. Schulthess 1911). Texts such as this, however, represent outliers to the highly standardised language of Classical Syriac. One interesting feature of this standardisation is the orthography of Classical Syriac: not only is it extremely stable, especially with native Syriac words, but it is also conservative, resembling the Aramaic of centuries earlier more than its late Aramaic sister dialects (Beyer 1966). As a standardised, literary language, Classical Syriac, as we know it, does not reflect exactly the spoken variety (or better, varieties) of the language in Late Antiquity. Questions remain, however, as to the degree of difference between the written and spoken varieties. One can imagine a hypothetical continuum from, say, present-day English, where the spoken and written varieties are very similar though not exactly the same, to present-day Arabic, where a diglossic situation exists with the written (*fuṣḥā*) and spoken (*ʿāmmiyya*) being mutually incomprehensible (the classic statement on diglossia is Ferguson 1959). The distance between the written form of Classical Syriac, which we know, and the spoken varieties, to which we have little to no access, will have varied diachronically and geographically. Thus, it is entirely possible – and perhaps even likely – that there was minimal distance between the written and spoken varieties, comparable, say, to modern English, for someone like Ephrem, who was active in the fourth century in Nisibis and then Edessa. This may well even be reflected in how far Ephrem can push his written Syriac, not only in poetry but also in prose. More distance between the written and spoken varieties, perhaps even comparable to the diglossic situation of modern Arabic, may, however, have been the case for people such as Aḥob Qaṭrāyā and Gabriel Qaṭrāyā, who lived in the sixth and seventh centuries in Beth Qaṭrāyē, where we have some evidence for the presence of a different variety of Aramaic, which existed alongside

Persian and Arabic (Contini 2003).[15] Finally, we should not draw too sharp of lines between Classical Syriac and what comes before and after it, since all of the witnesses to Early Syriac have been thoroughly revised towards Classical Syriac during the transmission process and since Post-Classical Syriac – to which we now turn – often, if not always, looks to Classical Syriac as its literary and linguistic model.

Post-Classical Syriac

Post-Classical Syriac refers to the language beginning from around the eighth century and extending to the present day. The Arab Conquests in the seventh century (Seleucia-Ctesiphon fell in 637) did not lead to the death of Syriac, whether as a spoken or a written language. Rather, Post-Classical Syriac was written – and probably also spoken – throughout the mediaeval period. Written Syriac even witnessed what has been termed a renaissance beginning in the eleventh century and climaxing in the thirteenth (Teule and Tauwinkl 2010). This renaissance culminated with the polymath Bar Hebraeus (d. 1286), who wrote over forty works on a wide range of topics, including exegesis, theology, philosophy, history, grammar, and science, mostly in Syriac, but also in Arabic (Takahashi 2005). Post-Classical Syriac continues to be in use today among Syriac Christians both in the Middle East and the worldwide diasporas (Brock 1989a; Kiraz 2007). Notwithstanding this uninterrupted use, a key socio-linguistic difference exists with Post-Classical Syriac compared to the earlier periods of Syriac: Post-Classical Syriac was never a primary spoken language and perhaps not a native language either. For many users of Post-Classical Syriac, especially in the earlier part of this period, Arabic served as the primary spoken language and often the native language. In addition, for the pockets of the population that continued to speak a variety of Aramaic as their native language, there must have been an ever-growing distance between the written and spoken forms of Aramaic. An important piece of evidence for this diglossic situation comes from the early written attestations of Neo-Aramaic beginning in the sixteenth century. These consist of a body of religious poetry written in a NENA *koine* based on the dialect of Alqosh (and possibly also of Telkepe) (see the texts in Mengozzi 2002, 2011). These texts witness a fully developed Neo-Aramaic, the incipient form(s) of which must stretch back centuries earlier, given the amount of time necessary for the witnessed changes, such as the restructuring of the verbal system, to take place. What is more, the NENA dialects do not derive directly from Syriac but rather find their ancestors in different dialects of Aramaic. This all points to a diglossic situation for native-Aramaic speakers of this period, in which their spoken varieties of Aramaic increasingly became mutually unintelligible with Post-Classical Syriac. Given that Post-Classical Syriac was not a primary spoken language, most of its attestation, especially as one moves later in time, represents literary compositions. Still many texts in Post-Classical Syriac, such as those by Isho'dad of Merv (fl. ca. 850), Mushe bar Kipho (d. 903), or even the aforementioned Bar Hebraeus (d. 1286), are of a very high-quality literary Syriac often very similar to the Classical Syriac of the previous period. Other texts, in contrast, witness some artificiality, as can be illustrated by the poetry of two fifteenth-century authors, Isḥaq Shbadnaya of the Church of the East (Carlson 2011) and Dawid Puniqoyo of the Syriac Orthodox Church (Butts 2009b).

SYRIAC AS A CONTACT LANGUAGE

Throughout its long history, Syriac has been in contact with a variety of different languages. Due to its earlier Aramaic history, Syriac inherited a number of words ultimately from Akkadian (Kaufman 1974). This is, for instance, the case with Syriac *šṭārā* 'deed, document', which derives ultimately from Akkadian *šaṭāru* via an earlier dialect of Aramaic (Kaufman 1974: 101). Akkadian also served as a bridge for Sumerian loanwords in Syriac, such as Sumerian É.GAL 'big house', which is found in Akkadian as *ekallu* 'royal palace' and which eventually made its way into Syriac as *hayklā* 'palace, temple' (Kaufman 1974: 27). Syriac also includes a large number of loanwords from various Iranian languages (Ciancaglini 2008). Some of these Iranian words were inherited in Syriac, like the Akkadian (and Sumerian) words in Syriac, and so they find their ultimate source in earlier Iranian languages, such as Syriac *gazzā* 'treasure', which derives ultimately from Old Persian **ganza-* via an earlier dialect of Aramaic (Ciancaglini 2008: 142). Others, in contrast, were transferred from an Iranian dialect contemporaneous with Syriac, such as Syriac *byspn*ʾ 'messenger' from an Iranian dialect such as Pahlavi *bayaspān* (Ciancaglini 2008: 126–7). The Iranian loanwords in Syriac remind us that throughout Late Antiquity a large number of Syriac-speaking Christians were located outside of the (Eastern) Roman Empire in Sasanian Persia. In its later history, Syriac borrowed a number of words from Arabic. Some of these are connected directly to Islamic rule, such as Syriac *ʾamirā* 'prefect, commander' from Arabic *ʾamīr*. Others, however, are not, such as Syriac *baḡlā* 'mule' from Arabic *baḡl*. These Arabic loanwords reinforce the point that Post-Classical Syriac was a minority language among an Arabic-speaking majority.

Out of all of the languages with which Syriac was in contact, one language had by far the greatest impact: Greek.[16] Syriac contains numerous Greek loanwords. There are in fact more than 800 Greek loanwords attested in Classical Syriac texts from before the eighth century that were not translated from Greek. Some of these are already found in the earliest Syriac texts, such as the Old Testament Peshiṭta, which was translated from Hebrew (not Greek), and they increase in number throughout the history of Classical Syriac (Brock 1999–2000; Butts 2016: 205). In addition to the transfer of lexical items (loanwords), there are also cases involving the transfer of semantic-conceptual material from Greek to Syriac.[17] Contact with Greek, for instance, led to the development of the ubiquitous discourse particle *dēn* 'then, but' from the earlier Aramaic temporal adverb * *ʾiδayn* 'then, at that time' as well as to the creation of a fully functioning copula from the earlier existential particle *ʾiṯ* 'there is' (Butts 2016: 174–91 and 153–73, respectively). These changes in the Syriac language, which are the result of contact with Greek, provide important evidence for the pervasive impact that the Greco-Roman world had on Syriac Christianity beginning already in the early centuries of the Common Era and extending throughout Late Antiquity.

A NICETY OF SYRIAC: FOCUS-MARKING

It is impossible to discuss in this contribution the many wonderful features of the Syriac language. It would, however, be remiss to skip over this topic entirely. So, I briefly want to look at one particular nicety from the realm of syntax: focus-marking. Syriac has the ability to mark any element of a sentence as focalised. This is perhaps best illustrated through a series of examples. I begin with an example in which a substantive, in this case the logical subject of a sentence, is marked as focalised:

Acts of Thomas (Wright 1871a: 2.187.7)

birtā	banyā	(h)y	wṯaṭlilā	(h)w	ḥassir	lāh
palace	she.is.built	she	and+roof	he	he.is.lacking	to+her

'the palace is built, and it is (only) the roof that is missing'

To understand the focus-marking here, we first need some context. In the previous narrative, the king has asked Thomas for an update on the status of the palace that Thomas is building for him. The text continues with the sentences directly above. The structure of the first sentence is unmarked: the subject is *birtā* 'palace', and the predicate is the passive participle *banyā* 'built', which is followed by an optional enclitic pronoun agreeing in gender (feminine) and number (singular) with the subject. The next sentence has a similar structure: the logical subject is *taṭlilā* 'roof', and the logical predicate is the adjective *ḥassir* 'lacking' (but this time without the optional enclitic pronoun), which is followed by a prepositional phrase referring back to the previously mentioned 'palace'. There is, however, one additional element in this second sentence: the third-person singular enclitic personal pronoun *(h)w* 'he' (the non-enclitic form is *hu*). The pronoun in this sentence forms what can be called an imperfectly transformed cleft-sentence, following Goldenberg (1977=1998: 116–22; 1990=1998: 569–78). This imperfectly transformed cleft-sentence focalises the logical subject *taṭlilā* 'roof'. That is, according to the predication structure of the sentence, it is a given that something is missing, but the question is what is missing. This can be contrasted with the unmarked sentence, *wṯaṭlilā ḥassir lāh* 'and the roof is missing', which would answer a question such as, 'What can one say about the roof?' The semantic import of the imperfectly transformed cleft-sentence is difficult to capture in idiomatic English translation, as can be seen in my translation above with the English cleft-sentence ('It is X that Y'), which is more pronounced – and clumsy – than the Syriac construction.[18] Hopefully, however, the focus of the sentence is not entirely lost in the English translation: there is something that is not yet built for the palace, and that is the roof!

Another example, this time involving a different part of speech, will help to clarify further the Syriac imperfectly transformed cleft-sentence:

Acts of Thomas (Wright 1871a: 2.186.10–11)

hākannā	(h)w	meškḥā	birtā	dṯeṯbnē
thus	he	she.is.able	palace	that+she.can.be.built

'it is in this way that a palace can be built'

Judas is here explaining to the king the manner in which a palace can be built, namely, in the winter and not in the summer, as is usual for other buildings. In this sentence, the adverb *hākannā* 'thus, in this way' is marked as focalised. Thus, the discourse semantics of this sentence is not simply that a palace can be built in answer to the question, 'What can one say about a palace?' This would be simply *hākannā meškḥā birtā dṯeṯbnē* 'Thus (or: in this way), a palace can be built', without *(h)w*. Rather, the sentence above with the imperfectly transformed cleft-sentence focalises the manner in which the palace can be built, in answer to the question, 'How can a palace be built?' This focus is again marked in Syriac by the enclitic third-person singular personal pronoun 'he', which is realised as *(h)w* here.

The imperfectly transformed cleft-sentence is quite a powerful structure in Syriac. It allows any element in a sentence apart from the verb – to which we turn shortly – to be focalised.[19] The imperfectly transformed cleft-sentence is also quite common in Syriac. The two examples cited above, for instance, occur in the span of just three pages in Wright's edition of the Syriac text of the *Acts of Thomas*, and there are at least a couple of others over these same pages as well (see 185.13 and 186.9–10). Imperfectly transformed cleft- sentences are found in other languages, whether Semitic or not (Goldenberg 1977: 129 = 1998: 118), but Syriac seems to have developed this construction to a much higher degree than most other languages, especially other Semitic languages. An interesting comparison can be made on the semantic level with the so-called second-tenses in Coptic (the classic study of these is Polotsky 1944=1971: 102–207), a language that shares a number of socio-linguistic features with Syriac. The Coptic second-tenses, however, differ in several key ways from the Syriac imperfectly transformed cleft-sentence, including that the former is synthetic and not analytic like the latter (i.e. the Coptic second-tenses are encoded in verbal morphology and not syntax) and that the former indicates generally that there is focalisation but does not mark the exact element that is focalised.[20] The frequency, versatility, and specificity of its focus-marking with imperfectly transformed cleft-sentences sets Syriac apart from many other languages, Semitic and non-Semitic.

As already noted, the imperfectly transformed cleft-sentence cannot by itself mark the focalisation of the verb. The verb is after all the default new information (Arabic *ḫabar*) of any sentence (Goldenberg 1971: 51 = 1998: 181). The verb, however, can be focalised with a different construction in Syriac, as illustrated in the following example:

Acts of Thomas (Wright 1871a: 2.173.15)

mzabbānū	zabbnāḵ	li
to.sell	he.sold+you	to+me
'He sold you to me'		

This sentence comes from the most well-known story in the *Acts of Thomas*: Thomas refuses to go to India, and so Jesus sells him to a merchant headed there. The merchant then goes to Thomas and asks him if Jesus is his master. Thomas responds in the affirmative, to which the merchant retorts with the sentence above. The force of this sentence is more than simply 'he sold you to me', which would be *zabbnāk li* in Syriac, without the infinitive *mzabbānū* 'to sell'. Rather, the sentence above with the infinitive has a different focus: sell you to me, that's what your master did! This construction, which is best called a tautological infinitive, following Goldenberg (1971 = 1998: 66–115) or, less accurately, an infinitive absolute, focalises the action of the verb. Unlike the imperfectly transformed cleft-sentence, the tautological infinitive is found in a number of the Semitic languages.

Far from exhausting the topic, the few examples given here illustrate just some of the complexity of focus-marking in Syriac. It is important to note that the basic outline of these focus-marking structures has only become clear in the last several decades, primarily thanks to the work of G. Goldenberg, whose article 'On Some Niceties of Syriac Syntax' (1990 = 1998: 569–78) inspired the title of this section. There is no doubt that our understanding of focus-marking in Syriac will be further refined by additional grammatical studies of Syriac, a topic to which we now turn.

THE STUDY OF SYRIAC GRAMMAR AND LEXICON

The grammar of the Syriac language has long been an object of study.[21] Already in the sixth century, the Greek *Art of Grammar* (*technē grammatikē*) attributed to Dionysius Thrax was translated into Syriac and supplemented with a comparative analysis of Greek and Syriac grammar (Contini 1998). This Syriac adaptation seems to have been the work of Joseph Huzaya (ca. 500), who wrote other works on Syriac grammar as well (see Van Rompay 2011c with further references). The first known systematic grammar of the Syriac language was written by Jacob of Edessa (d. 708) (for Jacob as a grammarian, see Talmon 2008). Unfortunately, however, it survives only in fragments (ed. Wright 1871b). In addition, two grammatical works by Jacob were incorporated into the so-called West Syriac Masora (*mašlmānutā*): his *Letter on Syriac Orthography* (ed. Martin 1869; Phillips 1869) and *Treatise on Persons and Tenses*, which is often entitled simply *On Points* (ed. Phillips 1869). The West Syriac Masora also contains vocalised texts of the Old Testament, New Testament, and patristic authors, which serve as a rich source of philological and grammatical material (see Juckel 2006; Loopstra 2009). The East Syriac Masora similarly contains vocalised and annotated texts of the Bible, both Old and New Testament, but without many of the additional patristic writings and the grammatical treatises (Weiss 1933; a facsimile edition is available in Loopstra 2014–2015). A number of grammarians of Syriac are known starting in the eleventh century, including Elias of Ṣoba (d. 1049), Elias of Ṭirhan (d. 1049), Joseph bar Malkon (thirteenth century), John bar Zoʿbi (thirteenth century), and Severus/Jacob bar Šakko (d. 1241). Many of their grammatical works, such as the influential one by Elias of Ṭirhan (ed. Baethgen 1880), are indebted to contemporary Arabic models of grammar. As is the case with so many of the sciences, the grammatical tradition of Syriac was codified by Bar Hebraeus (d. 1286), who wrote both a shorter metrical grammar (ed. Martin 1872) and a much larger opus entitled *The Book of Splendors* (*kṯāḇā dṣemḥē*) (ed. Moberg 1922 with a German translation in Moberg 1907–1913).[22]

The study of the Syriac language in the West began in the sixteenth century.[23] The first Syriac grammar outside of the Syriac-speaking world was written by Andreas Masius (1514–1573), who learned Syriac from Mushe of Mardin (Contini 1994).[24] The study of the Syriac language culminated at the turn of the twentieth century with the publication of a grammar by Th. Nöldeke (1880, 1898 [2nd ed.]; English translation in 1904). Nöldeke's grammar, with an occasional clarification from the works of Duval (1881), Brockelmann (1951), and Muraoka (2005), remains the state of the art for the description of the phonology and morphology of Classical Syriac. In contrast and as already noted, the past several decades have witnessed a number of studies on Syriac syntax that have not so much refined Nöldeke's description as entirely replaced it.[25] It is not, however, only the syntax portion of Nöldeke's grammar that needs updating. Lest we forget, Nöldeke himself entitled his grammar 'compendious, concise' (*kurzgefasste*), insisting that it was not 'in any respect a *complete* Syriac Grammar' (1904: vii; emphasis in the original). An updated grammar of the Syriac language will need to include a thorough presentation of diachronic changes in Syriac as well as dialectical differences, including East versus West Syriac. A comparative approach to Syriac, which locates Syriac within its broader Aramaic (and Semitic) context, will also undoubtedly clarify a number of features (see similarly Goshen-Gottstein 1989: 239).

The study of the Syriac lexicon also begins with the Syriac communities themselves. Though there are earlier antecedents, the earliest works that can be called lexica stem from the ʿAbbasid translation movement. The well-known translator Ḥunayn b. Isḥāq (d. 873) wrote several treatises on Syriac lexicography, including a *Compendious Lexicon* (*lhksyqwn bp̄āsiqāṯā*), which unfortunately does not survive. Ḥunayn's lexicographic work was incorporated into a number of later lexica. This includes the *Lexicon* of his student Ishoʿ bar ʿAli, who lived in the second half of the ninth century (ed. Hoffmann 1874; Gottheil 1910–1928).[26] In the introduction to his *Lexicon*, Bar ʿAli states that he employed the *Lexicon* of Ḥunayn as well as that of another ninth-century lexicographer, Ishoʿ of Merv, when compiling his own *Lexicon*. In the mid-tenth century, another lexicographer Ḥasan bar Bahlul composed a large *Lexicon* (ed. Duval 1888–1901), which relied on Ḥunayn as well as a number of other sources, including especially Ḥenanishoʿ bar Seroshway (ninth century). The lexica of Bar ʿAli and especially of Bar Bahlul represent extensive treatments of Syriac lexicography within the Syriac tradition itself.

The lexica of Bar ʿAli and Bar Bahlul were incorporated into the two large Syriac lexica that were published at the end of the nineteenth century: the *Thesaurus Syriacus* by R. Payne Smith (1879–1901), which appeared in an English abridgment as *A Compendious Syriac Dictionary* by his daughter Jessie Payne Smith (1903), and, to a lesser extent, the *Lexicon Syriacum* by C. Brockelmann (1895, 1928 [2nd ed.]), which was recently translated into English, with substantial updates and corrections, as *A Syriac Lexicon* by M. Sokoloff (2009). These two Latin lexica, along with their English versions, represent the state of the art of Syriac lexicography. There is, however, much room for improvement. One of the many *desiderata* is fuller coverage, especially in terms of attestation, of each individual lexeme. To take just one example, not a single attestation is provided for the Syriac word *man* 'indeed' (< Greek *men*) in Brockelmann's *Lexicon Syriacum* (1928: 393) or in its English update (Sokoloff 2009: 778). Payne Smith (1879–1901: 2151) provides a number of citations, but primarily from Greek translations and later authors, especially Bar Hebraeus. These incomplete treatments inevitably invite problems. Thus, even Brock (1996: 259; see also 1975: 89 fn. 55a) has incorrectly stated that this Greek loanword is not attested in Syriac before the fifth century, even though it is found already in the *Prose Refutations* by Ephrem (d. 373) as well as arguably in the even earlier *Odes of Solomon* (Butts 2013). The lack of adequate lexica not only leads to problems in our understanding of individual passages, as may well be the case with the passage from the *Odes of Solomon* (18.7), but it limits us in broader ways as well: in this particular instance, the appearance of Greek particles in the earliest layer of Syriac suggests significant contact between Greek and Syriac already in the early centuries of the Common Era (Butts 2016: 120). A twenty-first-century lexicon of Syriac will need to be based on a much larger corpus of Syriac texts with a copious – perhaps even exhaustive – listing of attestations. This daunting task can be aided by the development of digital tools, which will hopefully one day enable a Syriac equivalent to the monumental *Thesaurus Linguae Graecae* (TLG).[27]

NOTES

* I would like to thank Lucas Van Rompay for reading a draft of this paper as well as for discussing, over the years, a number of topics presented here.

1 For Afroasiatic, see Frajzyngier and Shay (2012). For Semitic, see Hetzron (1997); Weninger (2011); as well as the relevant chapters in Woodard (2004) on the ancient Semitic languages.

2 The main divisions of this classification, especially the branch of Central Semitic, were first proposed in a series of articles by Hetzron from the 1970s (see especially Hetzron 1976) and subsequently developed by others (see especially Huehnergard 1995, 2005, 2006, 2017; Huehnergard and Rubin 2011; Porkhomovsky 1997; Rubin 2008; Voigt 1987).

3 For brief overviews of Aramaic, see Brock (1989b); Kaufman (1992, 1997); Van Rompay (2011a). For a more wide-ranging discussion, see Gzella (2015). The Comprehensive Aramaic Lexicon (CAL) is also an invaluable resource (see http://cal1.cn.huc.edu/).

4 This was traditionally thought to be the case with Neo-Mandaic and Classical Mandaic, but see now Morgenstern (2010).

5 An idiosyncratic alterative was proposed in Beyer (1986), who adopts what might be called a political classification.

6 Fitzmyer (1979) ended the period at ca. 700 BCE. I, however, follow Folmer (1995: 1–5) here in pushing the end to 538 when the Babylonian Empire fell to the Achaemenid king Cyrus. This is, however, to be understood as a fuzzy boundary with the texts from the seventh and sixth centuries marking a transition from Old Aramaic to Achaemenid Aramaic.

7 Fitzmyer (1979) ended the period in ca. 200. I, however, again follow Folmer (1995) in giving dates that coincide with those of the Achaemenid Empire.

8 For the dialectology of Middle Aramaic, see Cook (1992, 1994).

9 Fitzmyer (1979: 62) ended this period at ca. 700 based on the Arab conquests. He, however, noted that Late Aramaic did not die out at this time but continued to live on for centuries, as is shown, for instance, by Jewish literature from the Gaonic period (589–1038 CE) and Syriac literature from even later. Given the continued use of Late Aramaic well beyond the Arab conquests, I adopt an endpoint of ca. 1200, though this is not itself without problems for Syriac: after all, one of the most prolific Syriac authors, Bar Hebraeus (d. 1286), lived entirely after this time (see 'Post-Classical Syriac' below).

10 Most are edited in Drijvers and Healey (1999).

11 These are currently being re-edited by J. F. Healey and the present author.

12 Interestingly, manuscripts that preserve early linguistic features also often attest variant readings some of which seem to reflect the earliest stage of the Peshiṭta pre-dating that found, for instance, in the base text of the Leiden Peshiṭta edition (7a1); for 5b1, see van der Kooij (1988); Haar Romeny (1995); for 9a1, see Weitzman (1988); van der Kooij (2006).

13 There is another, more practical reason that linguistic studies often end the Classical Syriac period with Jacob of Edessa: a majority of the Syriac texts from this period have been edited, whereas many from the eighth century and afterwards have not (see Brock 2010: 124; Butts 2016: 3 fn. 9).

14 See, however, Brock (2003), as a representative of one of several exceptions.

15 For Syriac authors from Beth Qaṭrāyē, see Kozah, Abdulrahim Abu-Husayn, Saif Shaheen Al-Murikhi, and Haya Al Thani (2014, 2015).
16 For a broad overview, see Butts (2014) and, with more detail, Butts (2016).
17 These are termed *grammatical replication* in Butts (2016), following the work of Heine and Kuteva (see e.g. Heine and Kuteva 2005).
18 The translation with a cleft-sentence is more idiomatic in French: *C'est un toit qui manque.*
19 The imperfectly transformed cleft-sentence can, however, be combined with other constructions to focalise the verb (see Goldenberg 1971: 50–8 = 1998: 80–8).
20 This at least seems to be the case for Coptic (Layton 2004: §444–60, especially §445), though perhaps not for earlier phases of Egyptian.
21 In general, see still Merx (1889), with editions of many of the relevant texts.
22 For more details, see Takahashi (2005: 355–84).
23 For the beginning of Syriac studies more broadly, see chapter 37 in this volume, and Strothmann (1971).
24 For more information on Masius, see Van Rompay (2011b) with further references.
25 It is for this reason that the present author is currently preparing a new syntax of Classical Syriac to be published with Ugarit-Verlag in the series Lehrbücher orientalischer Sprachen (LOS).
26 There has been a good deal of confusion in the secondary literature concerning the biography and identity of the lexicographer Bar ʿAli; for which, now see Butts (2009a).
27 In this regard, mention should be made of the Digital Syriac Corpus Project, which aims to prepare a large corpus of annotated Syriac texts linked to one or more dynamic lexica (see https://syriaccorpus.org).

BIBLIOGRAPHY

Baethgen, F. W. A. 1880. *Turrāṣ mamllā suryāyā, oder Syrische Grammatik des Mar Elias von Tirhan*. Leipzig: J. C. Hinrichs.

Beyer, K. 1966. Der reichsaramäische Einschlag in der ältesten syrischen Literatur. *ZDMG* 116, 242–54.

———. 1986. *The Aramaic Language. Its Distribution and Subdivisions*. Trans. J. F. Healey. Göttingen: Vandenhoeck & Ruprecht.

Boyarin, D. 1981. An Inquiry Into the Formation of the Middle Aramaic Dialects. *In*: Y. L. Arbeitman and A. R. Bomhard, ed., *Bono Homini Donum. Essays in Historical Linguistics in Memory of J. Alexander Kerns*. Amsterdam: John Benjamins, 2:613–49.

Brock, S. P. 1975. Some Aspects of Greek Words in Syriac. *In*: A. Dietrich, ed., *Synkretismus im syrisch-persischen Kulturgebiet*. Göttingen: Vandenhoeck & Ruprecht, 80–108. (= Brock 1984: IV).

———. 1984. *Syriac Perspectives on Late Antiquity*. London: Variorum Reprints.

———. 1989a. Some Observations on the Use of Classical Syriac in the Late Twentieth Century. *JSS* 34, 363–75.

———. 1989b. Three Thousand Years of Aramaic Literature. *ARAM* 1, 11–23.

———. 1996. Greek Words in Syriac: Some General Features. *Scripta classica Israelica* 15, 251–62. (= Brock 1999: XV).

———. 1999. *From Ephrem to Romanos. Interactions Between Syriac and Greek in Late Antiquity*. Aldershot: Ashgate.

———. 1999–2000. Greek Words in Ephrem and Narsai: A Comparative Sampling. *ARAM* 11–12, 439–49.

———. 2003. Some Diachronic Features of Classical Syriac. *In*: M. F. J. Baasten and W. Th. van Peursen, ed., *Hamlet on a Hill: Semitic and Greek Studies Presented to Professor T. Muraoka on the Occasion of His Sixty-fifth Birthday*. OLA 118. Louvain: Peeters, 95–111.

———. 2010. A Criterion for Dating Undated Syriac Texts: The Evidence From Adjectival Forms in *-aya*. *PdO* 35, 111–24.
Brockelmann, C. 1895. *Lexicon Syriacum*. Berlin: Reuther & Reichard.
———. 1928. *Lexicon Syriacum*. 2nd ed. Halis Saxonum: Sumptibus M. Niemeyer.
———. 1951. *Syrische Grammatik*. 6th ed. Leipzig: Harrassowitz.
Butts, A. M. 2009a. The Biography of the Lexicographer Ishoʿ bar ʿAli (ʿĪsā b. ʿAlī). *OC* 93, 60–71.
———. 2009b. The Afflictions of Exile. A Syriac *Memrā* By David Puniqāyā. *Le Muséon* 122, 53–80.
———. 2013. Greek μέν in Early Syriac. *Hugoye* 16, 211–23.
———. 2014. Greek and Syriac. *In*: G. Giannakis, ed., *Encyclopedia of Ancient Greek Language and Linguistics*. Leiden: Brill, 80–3.
———. 2016. *Language Change in the Wake of Empire: Syriac in its Greco-Roman Context*. Linguistic Studies in Ancient West Semitic 11. Winona Lake: Eisenbrauns.
———. Forthcoming. Old Syriac. *In*: P. J. J. van Geest and B. J. L. Peerbolte, ed., *Brill Encyclopedia of Early Christianity*. Leiden: Brill.
Carlson, T. 2011. A Light From 'The Dark Centuries': Isḥaq Shbadnaya's Life and Works. *Hugoye* 14, 191–214.
Charlesworth, J. H. 1973. *The Odes of Solomon*. Oxford: Clarendon Press.
Chin, C. 2006. Rhetorical Practice in the Chreia Elaboration of Mara bar Serapion. *Hugoye* 9, 145–71.
Ciancaglini, C. A. 2008. *Iranian Loanwords in Syriac*. Wiesbaden: Ludwig Reichert Verlag.
Contini, R. 1994. Gli inizi della linguistica siriaca nell' 'Europa rinascimentale'. *Rivista di Studi Orientali* 68, 15–30.
———. 1998. Considerazioni interlinguistiche sull'adattamento siriaco della Τέχνη γραμματική di Dionisio Trace. *In*: R. B. Finazzi and A. Valvo, ed., *La diffusione dell'eredità classica nell'età tardoantica e medioevale*. L'eredità classica nel mondo orientale 2. Alessandria: Edizioni dell'Orso, 95–111.
———. 2003. La lingua del Bēt Qaṭrāyē. *In*: J. Lentin and A. Lonnet, ed., *Mélanges David Cohen: Études sur le langage, les langues, les dialectes, les littératures, offertes par ses élèves, ses collègues, ses amis, présentées à l'occasion de son quatre-vingtième anniversaire*. Paris: Maisonneuve & Larose, 173–81.
Cook, E. M. 1992. Qumran Aramaic and Aramaic Dialectology. *Abr-Nahrain Supplement* 3, 1–21.
———. 1994. A New Perspective on the Language of Onqelos and Jonathan. *In*: D. R. G. Beattie and M. J. McNamara, ed., *The Aramaic Bible: Targums in Their Historical Context*. Journal of the Study of the Old Testament Supplement Series 166. Sheffield: Sheffield Academic Press, 142–56.
Creason, S. 2004. Aramaic. *In:* Woodard 2004: 391–426.
Cureton, W. 1855. *Spicilegium Syriacum Containing Remains of Bardesan, Meliton, Ambrose and Mara Bar Serapion*. London: F. & J. Rivington.
Drijvers, H. J. W. 1965. *The Book of the Laws of the Countries*. Semitic Texts with Translations 3. Assen: Van Gorcum.
Drijvers, H. J. W. and J. F. Healey. 1999. *The Old Syriac Inscriptions of Edessa and Osrhoene*. HoS 42. Leiden: Brill.
Duval, R. 1881. *Traité de grammaire syriaque*. Paris: F. Vieweg.
———. 1888–1901. *Lexicon Syriacum auctore Hassano bar Bahlule*, 1–3. Collection orientale 15–17. Paris: Typographeo Reipublicae.
Feissel, D. and J. Gascou. 1989. Documents d'archives romains inédits du Moyen-Euphrate (IIIe siècle après J.-C.). *CRAIBL* 1989, 535–61.
———. 1995. Documents d'archives romains inédits du moyen Euphrate (IIIe s. après J.-C.). I. Les pétitions (P. Euphr. 1 à 5). *Journal des Savants* 1995, 65–119.

———. 2000. Documents d'archives romains inédits du moyen Euphrate (IIIe s. après J.-C.). III. Actes diverses et lettres (P. Euphr. 11 à 17). *Journal des Savants* 2000, 157–208.

Feissel, D., J. Gascou, and J. Teixidor. 1997. Documents d'archives romains inédits du moyen Euphrate (IIIe s. après J.-C.). II. Les actes de vente-achat (P. Euphr. 6 à 10). *Journal des Savants* 1997, 3–57.

Ferguson, C. 1959. Diglossia. *Word* 15, 325–40.

Fitzmyer, J. A. 1979. The Phases of the Aramaic Language. *In*: idem, *Wandering Aramean. Collected Aramaic Essays*. Missoula: Scholars Press, 57–84.

Folmer, M. 1995. *The Aramaic Language in the Achaemenid Period: A Study in Linguistic Variation*. OLA 68. Louvain: Peeters.

Frajzyngier, Z. and E. Shay. 2012. *The Afroasiatic Languages*. Cambridge: Cambridge University Press.

Goldenberg, G. 1971. Tautological Infinitive. *IOS* 1, 36–85. (= Goldenberg 1998: 66–115).

———. 1977. Imperfectly-Transformed Cleft Sentences. *In*: *Proceedings of the Sixth World Congress of Jewish Studies*. Jerusalem: ha-Igud ha-ʿolami le-madaʿe ha-Yahadut, 1:127–33. (= Goldenberg 1998: 116–122).

———. 1990. On Some Niceties of Syriac Syntax. *In*: R. Lavenant, ed., *V Symposium Syriacum 1988*. OCA 236. Rome: Pontificium Institutum Studiorum Orientalium, 335–44. (= Goldenberg 1998: 579–590).

———. 1998. *Studies in Semitic Linguistics. Selected Writings*. Jerusalem: Magnes Press.

Goshen-Gottstein, M. H. 1989. Exercises in Semitic Linguistics 1 – Classical Syriac. *Jerusalem Studies in Arabic and Islam* 12, 233–42.

Gottheil, R. J. H. 1910–1928. *Bar ʿAli (Ishoʿ). The Syriac-Arabic Glosses*, 1–2. Atti della R. Accademia dei Lincei. Classe di Scienzi morali, storiche e filologiche Ser. 5, vol. 13. Rome: Tipografia della R. Accademia nazionale dei Lincei.

Gzella, H. 2015. *A Cultural History ofAramaic: From the Beginnings to the Advent of Islam*. HoS 111. Leiden: Brill.

Haar Romeny, R. B. ter. 1995. Techniques of Translation and Transmission in the Earliest Text Forms of the Syriac Version of Genesis. *In*: P. B. Dirksen and A. van der Kooij, ed., *The Peshitta as a Translation*. MPIL 8. Leiden: Brill, 177–85.

Healey, J. F. 2006. A New Syriac Mosaic Inscription. *JSS* 51, 313–27.

———. 2008. Variety in Early Syriac: The Context in Contemporary Aramaic. *In*: H. Gzella and M. L. Folmer, ed., *Aramaic in Its Historical and Linguistic Setting*. Veröffentlichungen der Orientalischen Kommission 50. Wiesbaden: Harrassowitz, 221–9.

Heine, B. and T. Kuteva. 2005. *Language Contact and Grammatical Change*. Cambridge: Cambridge University Press.

Hetzron, R. 1976. Two Principles of Genetic Reconstruction. *Lingua* 38, 89–108.

———. 1997. *The Semitic Languages*. New York: Routledge.

Hoffmann, G. 1874. *Syrisch-Arabische Glossen. Autographie einer gothaischen Handschrift enthaltend Bar Ali's Lexikon von Alaf bis Mim*. Kiel: Schwers'sche Buchhandlung.

Hoftijzer, J. and G. van der Kooij. 1976. *Aramaic texts from Deir ʿAlla*. Documenta et monumenta Orientis antiqui 19. Leiden: Brill.

Huehnergard, J. 1995. What Is Aramaic? *ARAM* 7, 261–82.

———. 2005. Features of Central Semitic. *In*: A. Gianto, ed., *Biblical and Oriental Essays in Memory of William L. Moran*. Biblica et Orientalia 48. Rome: Pontificio Istituto biblico, 155–203.

———. 2006. Proto-Semitic and Proto-Akkadian. *In*: G. Deutscher and N. J. C. Kouwenberg, ed., *The Akkadian Language in Its Semitic Context. Studies in the Akkadian of the Third and Second Millennium BC*. Leiden: Nederlands Instituut voor het Nabije Oosten, 1–18.

———. 2017. Arabic in Its Semitic Context. *In*: A. Al-Jallad, ed., *Arabic in Context, Celebrating 400 Years of Arabic at Leiden*. Leiden: Brill, 3–34.

Huehnergard, J. and A. D. Rubin. 2011. Phyla and Waves: Models of Classification of the Semitic Languages. *In:* Weninger 2011: 259–78.

Juckel, A. K. 2006. The 'Syriac Masora' and the New Testament Peshitta. *In*: R. B. ter Haar Romeny, ed., *The Peshitta: Its Use in Literature and Liturgy. Papers Read at the Third Peshitta Symposium*. MPIL 15. Leiden: Brill, 107–21.

Kaufman, S. A. 1974. *Akkadian Influences on Aramaic*. Assyriological Studies 19. Chicago: University of Chicago Press.

———. 1992. Aramaic. *In:* D. N. Freedman, ed., *The Anchor Bible Dictionary*. New York: Doubleday, 4:173–8.

———. 1997. Aramaic. *In:* Hetzron 1997: 114–30.

———. 2013. The Dialectology of Late Jewish Literary Aramaic. *Aramaic Studies* 11, 145–8.

Kiraz, G. A. 1996. *Comparative Edition of the Syriac Gospels*. Leiden: Brill.

———. 2007. Kthobonoyo Syriac. Some Observations and Remarks. *Hugoye* 10, 129–42.

Kooij, A. van der. 1988. On the Significance of MS 5b1 for Peshitta Genesis. *In*: P. B. Dirksen and M. J. Mulder, ed., *The Peshitta: Its Early Text and History*. MPIL 4. Leiden: Brill, 183–99.

———. 2006. MS 9a1 of the Peshitta of Isaiah: Some Comments. *In*: R. B. ter Haar Romeny and W. T. van Peursen, ed., *Text, Transmission and Tradition*. MPIL 14. Leiden: Brill, 71–6.

Kozah, M., Abdulrahim Abu-Husayn, Saif Shaheen Al-Murikhi, and Haya Al Thani. 2014. *The Syriac Writers of Qatar in the Seventh Century*. Gorgias Eastern Christian Studies 38. Piscataway, NJ: Gorgias Press.

———. 2015. *An Anthology of Syriac Writers From Qatar in the Seventh Century*. Gorgias Eastern Christian Studies 39. Piscataway, NJ: Gorgias Press.

Layton, B. 2004. *A Coptic Grammar With Chrestomathy and Glossary. Sahidic Dialect*. 2nd ed. Porta linguarum orientalium ns 20. Wiesbaden: Harrassowitz.

Loopstra, J. A. 2009. *Patristic Selections in the "Masoretic" Handbooks of the Qarqaptā Tradition*. Ph.D. Diss., The Catholic University of America.

———. 2014–2015. *An East Syrian manuscript of the Syriac 'Masora' Dated to 899 CE: Introduction, List of Sample Texts, and Indices to Marginal Notes in British Library, Additional MS 12138*, 1–2. Piscataway, NJ: Gorgias Press.

Martin, J.-P. P. 1869. La tradition karkaphienne ou la massore chez les Syriens. *Journal asiatique* VI, 14, 245–379.

———. 1872. *Œuvres grammaticales d'Abou'lfaradj dit Bar Hebreus*. Paris: Maisonneuve.

McVey, K. E. 1990. A Fresh Look at the Letter of Mara Bar Sarapion to His Son. *In*: R. Lavenant, ed., *V Symposium Syriacum, 1988: Katholieke Universiteit, Leuven, 29–31 août 1988*. OCA 236. Rome: Pontificium Institutum Studiorum Orientalium, 257–72.

Mengozzi, A. 2002. *Israel of Alqosh and Joseph of Telkepe. A Story in a Truthful Language. Religious Poems in Vernacular Syriac (North Iraq, 17th century)*. CSCO 589–590/230–231. Leuven: Peeters.

———. 2011. *Religious Poetry in Vernacular Syriac From Northern Iraq (17th–20th Centuries). An Anthology*. CSCO 627–628/240–241. Leuven: Peeters.

Merx, A. 1889. *Historia Artis Grammaticae Apud Syros*. Leipzig: F. A. Brockhaus. English Translation available at: www.academia.edu/18999813/Merx_History_of_the_Syriac_Grammatical_Tradition

Moberg, A. 1907–1913. *Buch der Strahlen. Die grössere Grammatik des Barhebräus*. Leipzig: Otto Harrassowitz.

———. 1922. *Le Livre des Splendeurs: La grande grammaire de Grégoire Barhebraeus*. Acta Regiae Societatis Humaniorum Litterarum Lundensis 4. Lund: C. W. K. Gleerup.

Morgenstern, M. 2010. Diachronic Studies in Mandaic. *Orientalia* 79, 505–25.

Muraoka, T. 2005. *Classical Syriac. A Basic Grammar With a Chrestomathy*. 2nd ed. Porta linguarum orientalium ns 19. Wiesbaden: Harrassowitz.

Nöldeke, Th. 1880. *Kurzgefasste syrische Grammatik*. Leipzig: T.O. Weigel.
———. 1898. *Kurzgefasste syrische Grammatik*. 2nd ed. Leipzig: C. H. Tauchnitz.
———. 1904. *Compendious Syriac Grammar. Translated From the Second and Improved German Edition By James A. Crichton*. London: Williams & Norgate.
Pardee, D. 2009. A New Aramaic Inscription From Zincirli. *BASOR* 356, 51–71.
Payne Smith, J. 1903. *A Compendious Syriac Dictionary*. Oxford: Clarendon Press.
Payne Smith, R. 1879–1901. *Thesaurus Syriacus*. Oxford: Clarendon Press.
Peursen, W. van. 2008. Language Variation, Language Development, and the Textual History of the Peshitta. *In*: H. Gzella and M. L. Folmer, ed., *Aramaic in Its Historical and Linguistic Setting*. Veröffentlichungen der Orientalischen Kommission 50. Wiesbaden: Harrassowitz, 153–78.
Phillips, G. 1869. *A Letter By Mār Jacob, Bishop of Edessa on Syriac Orthography*. London: Williams and Norgate.
Polotsky, H. J. 1944. *Études de syntaxe copte*. Cairo: L'Institut français d'archéologie orientale. (= Polotsky 1971: 102–207).
———. 1971. *Collected Papers*. Jerusalem: Magnes Press.
Porkhomovsky, V. 1997. Modern South Arabian Languages From a Semitic and Hamito-Semitic Perspective. *Proceedings of the Seminar for Arabian Studies* 27, 219–23.
Rubin, A. D. 2008. The Subgrouping of the Semitic Languages. *Languages and Linguistics Compass* 2, 61–84.
Schulthess, F. 1911. *Kalīla und Dimna: Die altsyrische Version des indischen Fürstenspiegels, Pantschatantra, oder, Bidpai's Fabeln*. Berlin: G. Reimer.
Sokoloff, M. 2009. *A Syriac Lexicon. A Translation From the Latin, Correction, Expansion, and Update of C. Brockelmann's Lexicon Syriacum*. Winona Lake: Eisenbrauns and Piscataway, NJ: Gorgias Press.
Strothmann, W. 1971. *Die Anfänge der syrischen Studien in Europa*. Göttinger Orientforschungen, I. Reihe: Syriaca 1. Wiesbaden: Otto Harrassowitz.
Takahashi, H. 2005. *Barhebraeus: A Bio-Bibliography*. Piscataway, NJ: Gorgias Press.
Talmon, R. 2008. Jacob of Edessa the Grammarian. *In*: R. B. ter Haar Romeny, ed., *Jacob of Edessa and the Syriac Culture of His Day*. MPIL 18. Leiden: Brill, 159–87.
Teule, H. and C. F. Tauwinkl (with B. ter Haar Romeny and J. van Ginkel). 2010. *The Syriac Renaissance*. Leuven: Peeters.
Van Rompay, L. 1994. Some Preliminary Remarks on the Origins of Classical Syriac as a Standard Language. *In*: G. Goldenberg and Sh. Raz, ed., *Semitic and Cushitic Studies*. Wiesbaden: Harrassowitz, 70–89.
———. 2011a. Aramaic. *In*: *GEDSH*, 28–33.
———. 2011b. Masius, Andreas. *In*: *GEDSH*, 275–6.
———. 2011c. Yawsep Huzaya. *In*: *GEDSH*, 437–8.
Voigt, R. 1987. The Classification of Central Semitic. *JSS* 32, 1–21.
Weiss, Th. 1933. *Zur ostsyrischen Laut- und Akzentlehre*. Bonner orientalistische Studien 5. Stuttgart: W. Kohlhammer.
Weitzman, M. P. 1988. The Originality of Unique Readings in Peshitta MS 9a1. *In*: P. B. Dirksen and M. J. Mulder, ed., *The Peshitta: Its Early Text and History*. MPIL 4. Leiden: Brill, 225–58.
———. 1999. *The Syriac Version of the Old Testament*. Cambridge: Cambridge University Press.
Weninger, S. 2011. *The Semitic Languages: An International Handbook*. Berlin: De Gruyter Mouton.
Woodard, R. D. 2004. *The Cambridge Encyclopedia of the World's Ancient Languages*. Cambridge: Cambridge University Press.
Wright, W. 1871a. *Apocryphal Acts of the Apostles*. London: Williams and Norgate.
———. 1871b. *Fragments of the Turrāṣ mamllā nahrāyā or Syriac Grammar of Jacob of Edessa*. Clerkenwell: Gilbert and Rivington. Printed also as an appendix in Merx 1889.

CHAPTER FIFTEEN

WRITING SYRIAC
Manuscripts and inscriptions

Françoise Briquel-Chatonnet

Syriac script is an Aramaic script comprising twenty-two alphabetical consonantal symbols. It developed based on the script that had been used at Edessa (Syr. Urhay, today called Sanlı Urfa) in modern-day Turkey, which was the birthplace of Syriac culture and the centre from whence it spread eastwards together with Christianity.

Aramaic script (Naveh 1987) is attested from the ninth century BC and was used in the small Aramaic kingdoms of Syria, which were confronted with the advance of the Neo-Assyrian empire. At that period, the West Semitic linear alphabet was just the same in the Phoenician, Aramaic, Hebrew, or Moabite inscriptions. The Assyrian conquest and the deportations of Aramaic-speaking populations that followed gave an opportunity for the Aramaic script to spread across the Near East. The Aramaic alphabet gradually became different from the others and the Aramaic script developed a specific form, which is especially identifiable in the Achaemenid era of the Persian Empire (539–333 BC), where it manifests a high degree of uniformity from southern Egypt to Central Asia and from Anatolia to Arabia and northern India. The Graeco-Macedonian conquest swept away the official use of Aramaic and from then on there are barely any Aramaic inscriptions except in marginal areas. It is at the very end of the period of the Seleucid kingdom, in the last century BC, that Aramaic made a reappearance of some significance for writing in the Near East. Between those periods, it had evolved in different ways in different localities, and at the beginning of the Roman period we can distinguish a variety of scripts, including those of the Nabataeans and the Judaeans and of Palmyra, Hatra, and Edessa.

EDESSAN SCRIPT

In the first three centuries of the Christian era, Edessa was the capital of a small kingdom, Osrhoene, which extended into the bend of the Euphrates and was annexed by the Roman Empire in 216. The inscriptions written in Aramaic and the first literary texts in Christian Aramaic (Syriac), which were composed in the second century, evidence a city suffused with Greek culture and enriched by Arabic and Persian influences.

Pre-Christian Edessan script (Drijvers and Healey 1999) is attested in inscriptions on stone, stelae, or construction blocks: these inscriptions were for the most part, as was the case all over the Near East, funerary or votive. Original to Edessa also was the practice of writing in mosaic around figurative scenes, following a Greek model most likely imported from Antioch. In the territory of Edessa, we find funerary mosaics representing an entire family surrounding the head of the family. The name of each person is written vertically near their head, while a horizontal inscription in the centre of the lower register of the panel celebrates the foundation of the tomb by the father of the family. A mosaic of this type, but bearing a Christian cross, was recently exhumed in the autumn of 2016. Other mosaics from tombs or rich houses are adorned with Greek mythological scenes with a legend in Edessan script (Balty and Briquel Chatonnet 2000; Lavagne 2011). The coins of the kingdom of Edessa also have legends in Aramaic. All these inscriptions are in a formal script close to what will later become estrangela, the Classical Syriac script, although the mosaic inscriptions at times already present more cursive characters (see Table 15.1).

At the same time, there was also another script being used in the Edessan world for writing in the context of everyday life. An Aramaic contract on parchment dated AD 243 was found during the excavations at Dura Europos on the Euphrates in Syria. Two further such contracts have since been brought to light, in amongst a hoard of Greek documents some of which also carry subscriptions in the Edessan script (Drijvers and Healey 1999). They revealed a form of cursive writing quite different from the monumental writing of the inscriptions. The letters are almost all ligatured and are in many cases closer to those of what will later be called *Serto* script, or even to Arabic script.

Although the earliest Edessan inscriptions date back to the end of the first century AD (Serrin's inscription on the Euphrates is dated 73), they mostly date from the third century. There is then a documentary vacuum until the appearance of the first documents written in Syriac, i.e. in Christian Aramaic at the end of the fourth century.

SYRIAC INSCRIPTIONS

Although most of the Syriac documents we have are manuscripts, Syriac has also been used as a monumental script inscribed on stone or other hard surfaces (metal, wood), or painted on frescoes. Long neglected, these inscriptions are now the subject of a programme of systematic publication in the series *Recueil des inscriptions syriaques* published by the Académie des inscriptions et Belles-Lettres in Paris.

The oldest Syriac inscriptions

The very oldest Syriac writings found on parchment and those found on stone both date from approximately the same period, namely the turn of the fifth century. The earliest dated inscription may be a three-letter word (ʾSB) on a lintel inscribed in Greek, found at Babisqa in the Syrian Limestone Massif, in the hinterland of Antioch, bearing the date 389 (Jalabert and Mouterde 1939, no. 555c, p. 303), if indeed we suppose that these three characters are contemporaneous with the dedication of the lintel. But the earliest true dated Syriac inscription is on a mosaic discovered in 2007 decorating the floor of a church in Nabgha, in the Jerablus region north of Aleppo in Syria (Figure 15.1). It is dated to AD 406–7. On both sides of the steps leading to the sanctuary, an inscription of twenty-two lines evokes the work and recalls the memory of those who were involved (Briquel Chatonnet and Desreumaux 2011). It revealed a script-form that is still very close to certain aspects of the Edessene script, and which is less standardised than the script of the oldest manuscripts. Another inscription dating from a few years later presents a similar script: it is carved on stone and memorialises Bishop Rabbula, probably the famous Rabbula who was bishop of Edessa (Briquel Chatonnet, Desreumaux and Moukarzel 2008).

Value	Edessean script on stone	Edessean script on mosaic	Edessean script in contracts	Nabgha inscription (406-407 AD)	Rabbula inscription (425-426 AD)	Ms BL Add 12150 (411 AD)
ʾ						
B						
G						
D						
H						
W						
Z						
Ḥ						
Ṭ						
Y						
K						
L						
M						
N						
S						
ʿ						
P						
Ṣ						
Q						
R						
Š						
T						

Figure 15.1 Mosaic inscription from church floor, Nabgha (AD 406–7)

Source: © Syrian-French Expedition "Syriac Inscriptions of Syria"

The Syriac inscriptions of the fifth and sixth centuries come for the most part from the Antiochene and the region to the north of Aleppo, notably the Jebel Semʿan and the area even further north. Most of these, however, are found west of the Euphrates and are hence outside the borders of Osrhoene. This suggests that Syriac Christianity, coming from an Edessene culture, had from the end of the fourth century acquired enough prestige to break out of its province of origin. In a region where Aramaic was still widely spoken, as witnessed by Severus of Antioch (*Cathedral Homily* 19: 34–35; *PO* 37/1 [1975], 38), the first Christian Aramaic literary culture, from Edessa (i.e. translation of the Bible, Bardaiṣan's *Book of the Laws of the Countries*, *Acts of Thomas* etc.), has no doubt served as model for the new beginning of Aramaic writing in a Christian context. It is also possible that the arrival of Christians retreating westwards when confronted to the advance of the Sassanid Empire also played a role in the spread of the Eastern Aramaic language and writing.

Different types of inscriptions

The Syriac language was never the language of a state or power: the Syriac populations lived in the Greek/Byzantine Roman Empire, in the Persian-speaking Sasanian Empire, and later in various Muslim empires, initially Arabic and later Turkish or Persian, not to mention communities in India, Central Asia, and China. There was therefore never any inscription emanating from a civil power, even though some of them set up by private individuals may have no religious connotations. Yet the majority of inscriptions are of a religious nature and were inscribed on Christian

Figure 15.2 Basufan inscription (Jabal Semʿan, Syria)

Source: © Syrian-French Expedition "Syriac Inscriptions of Syria"

monuments. Even small testimonials, such as ostraca or graffiti, appear to proceed generally from the religious sphere.

Among the various genres of Syriac inscriptions, the most typical are surely those that are engraved on churches or other religious monuments such as monastic buildings. They are found especially on lintels or door jambs, but can also be on interior or exterior walls. They are sometimes dedications or invocations (e.g. an invocation to the Holy Trinity at Dar Qita, Syria; Briquel Chatonnet, Desreumaux and Khoury 2004–2005), more often the commemoration of the completion of building works, perpetuating the memory of those who carried them out or financed them (Figure 15.2). The inscription of Khirbet Hassan, which mentions the cost of the construction and the extra expenses that were incurred, is rather unusual; more often it is a matter of commemorating the one who sponsored and paid for the monument and requests prayers for him. Such is already the case in the oldest inscription, that of Nabgha in Syria. Interior elements of churches and furnishings also carry inscriptions: altars, especially wooden ones, seats, or episcopal thrones. The churches served as a base for formal, official inscriptions, but also for graffiti. These consist principally of proper names of individuals wishing to leave their names on religious buildings and to perpetuate the benefits to be gained in their passing by memorialising it.

The most common genre of inscriptions at any period is that of the funeral inscriptions, whether within the churches or in adjoining cemeteries. They most often relate to dignitaries of the Church or members of the clergy, or at least this constitutes the most developed type, but there are also some relating to simple believers. Their form ranges from the simplest ('on [date], passed away X, son of Y, and possibly a function is added') to rather long inscriptions, containing details about the life of the deceased or his character, together with invocations to the divine mercy. The text might even be composed as a poem in a particular metre.

Some inscriptions bear real historical texts: thus the text engraved on the wall of the Church of St Sergius at Ehnesh on the Euphrates in Turkey, dating from the beginning of the ʿAbbasid period, presents itself in the form of a genuine chronicle and refers in parallel to both the Messiah and the Mahdi (Palmer 1993). Thus also in quite another genre is the inscription of Kothamangalam in Kerala, which relates the mission to India in 1685 of two Syrian Orthodox bishops from Ṭur ʿAbdin, (Briquel Chatonnet, Desreumaux and Thekeparampil 2008: 89–93).

Inscriptions found on moveable objects are mainly to be found on metallic cult objects such as the pair of fans or flabella, of which one is now preserved at the Louvre (Paris) and the other at the Musée Royal de Mariemont (Belgium) (Van Rompay 2004b), or like the chalice and paten, of Frankish origin but with a Syriac inscription added, which were excavated at Reṣafa in Syria and which are now in the Damascus Museum.

One very occasionally finds purely civil inscriptions, mainly among the old inscriptions of Syria, but these are private inscriptions, very short, consisting of a proper name on a house (Briquel Chatonnet 2010), or 'signboard' on a building (Briquel Chatonnet, Desreumaux and Khoury 2004–2005).

Diffusion from Cyprus and Egypt to India and China

The places where Syriac inscriptions have been discovered offer an excellent image of the extent of expansion of Syriac culture, even if they are curiously absent in certain regions where the Church of the East was nevertheless present. The heart of the Syriac world, in which the majority of inscriptions are naturally found, lies between modern-day Turkey, Syria, and Iraq. In Turkey they are mostly found in Osrhoene, in the case of the very oldest, but also west of the Euphrates bend. They later developed further east to the Ṭur ʿAbdin (Palmer 1987) and up to the region of Van. In Syria, where a team and I were conducting annual missions until 2010 to catalogue inscriptions, the Antiochene and the Jebel Semʿan region contain the oldest, pre-Islamic, inscriptions. They continue until the eight or even the ninth century. In the ʾUmayyad and ʿAbbasid periods, they are distributed partly along the Euphrates, partly in sites at the edge of the steppe, including Andarin, or in the monasteries of Qaryatayn, Qara, and Mar Musa on the slopes of the Anti-Lebanon. This is the most southern evidence found in Syria. These inscriptions are engraved in stone, but also often in mosaics or painted on frescoes. In Iraq (Harrak 2010), they began to develop in the ʿAbbasid era and continued to be engraved until very recently. The great majority of them come from Mosul and the villages of the Nineveh plain. They are also found in Iraqi Kurdistan, that is, in the regions of Duhok, Erbil, Sulaymaniah, and Kirkuk. But the oldest dated inscriptions, though much less numerous, have been found further south in Tagrit, Ctesiphon, Qusayr, and in the vicinity or very near Najaf, in Al-Hira and its surroundings. In Iraq, inscriptions with magical or prophylactic character were also written on bowls (Moriggi 2014), in Syriac as well as in other varieties of Aramaic.

Lebanon also furnishes a number of inscriptions (Kassis, Badwi and Yon 2004). Apart from a very ancient one, which is found close to Syria and belongs to the Syrian corpus, the oldest inscriptions are found near Kamid el-Loz and were made by quarrymen from Mesopotamia who belonged to the Church of the East. These go back as far as the eighth century. The other inscriptions, which relate to building constructions, or else are dedicatory or funerary, originate for the most part in Mount Lebanon and date from the thirteenth century until modern times (Moukarzel, Yon and Dergham 2010). We ought also to note a great number of painted inscriptions associated with church decoration.

To the west, some inscriptions are found in Cyprus, in the town of Famagusta: one set consists of legends on fresco in the apse of the so-called 'Nestorian' church of Mart Mariam which dates from the middle of the fourteenth century (Vaivre and Plagnieux 2012), while the other set consists of two stone inscriptions of Syrian Orthodox origin that have since disappeared after being re-used in an Ottoman-era building (Mouterde 1939). In Egypt, the inscriptions that are found in the monastery of Dayr as-Suryan in the desert of Scete are linked to the presence of a Syrian Orthodox community. In the same location there are also inscriptions on frescoes that are linked to individuals represented in the church, as well as inscriptions on wood or other objects which date mostly to between the ninth and the thirteenth centuries (Van Rompay 2004a). In Sinaï, in the holy places of Jerusalem (Brock, Goldfus and Kofsky 2007) and Bethlehem, and in other locations in Palestine and Sinaï, the presence of graffiti indicates the passage of pilgrims (Desreumaux 2004a), although inscriptions relating to building constructions and memorials do testify to the presence of a Syrian Orthodox community in the monastery of St Mark in Jerusalem (Palmer and van Gelder 1994).

Although the Iranian plateau was an area into which Syrian Christianity did expand at a very early date, nonetheless no inscriptions have been found testifying to it. The only epigraphic evidence is that of the Christian cemeteries of the Urmia region that date from between the seventeenth and the nineteenth centuries (Hellot-Bellier 2004; Al Jeloo 2010). Similarly, no inscriptions have ever been found in Christian sites excavated along the shores of the Arabian-Persian Gulf, notably in the region known as Beth Qatraye which covered much of the western shore of the Gulf. In Kerala, India (Briquel Chatonnet, Desreumaux and Thekeparampil 2008), there is no inscription that can be securely attributed to the period before the arrival of the Portuguese, although this question remains open with respect to the symbols engraved on the step under the altar of Palai. The epigraphy develops in the sixteenth century in displaying signs of Latin influence (e.g. the use of *qadiš(t)a* in place of *mar(t)* to designate a church dedicatee) (Figure 15.3). In the seventeenth and nineteenth centuries, the inscriptions bear the mark of relations with the Syrian Orthodox Church in the Near East and particularly with Ṭur ʿAbdin.

In Central Asia, Mongolia, and China, Syriac inscriptions are old and well attested. The oldest is also the most remote: the bilingual inscription in Syriac and Chinese that was found in Xi'an, the capital of the Tang dynasty (see Figures 32.1–2), which dates back to 781 (Pelliot and Forte 1996). It relates to the settlement with imperial authorisation of a community of Sogdian origin in the seventh century and gives an exposition of the Christian faith in Chinese. More recently, a pillar was found in

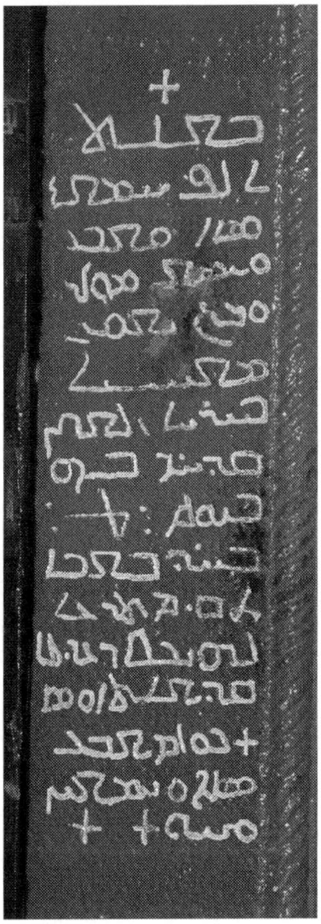

Figure 15.3 Mulanthuruthy inscription (Kerala, India)

Source: Author

Luo-Yang, of a Chinese model, bearing a private inscription. It is especially from the Mongol period that inscriptions are known, almost all of them funerary. In Kyrgyzstan, the Semirechye region has offered up hundreds of uncut stones bearing epitaphs engraved around a cross, dating from the middle of the thirteenth to the middle of the fourteenth century (Klein 2000), the remains of a dynamic community. In Mongolia and China, inscriptions are spread over an arc from the Kyrgyz border to Yangzhou and Quangzhou on the south-eastern coast of China, through inland Mongolia and the Beijing region (Niu 2010), and up to the Republic of Mongolia (Osawa and Takahashi 2015).

The tradition of engraving Syriac inscriptions has survived to the present time especially in traditional areas where Syriac communities still survive, such as Ṭur ʿAbdin, Iraqi Kurdistan, Lebanon, important cities of Iraq and Syria, and Kerala, where they are found on new constructions or restorations of churches. But they may also be found everywhere in the diaspora of Europe, America, or Australia, where people readily engrave inscriptions on religious buildings that are founded for the faithful in the lands to which they have immigrated.

SYRIAC MANUSCRIPTS

The corpus of extant Syriac manuscripts extends from the early fifth century to the beginning of the twentieth. We can estimate the number of extant manuscripts at around 20,000, but it is a very rough estimate since catalogues are not available for all collections and some are barely known at all.

The oldest Syriac dated manuscript, according to the present state of knowledge, dates back to the year AD 411 and was copied in Edessa. It is preserved at the British Library in London (BL Add. 12150) (see Figures 14.2–3) but came there from the monastery of Dayr as-Suryan in the desert of Scete in Egypt (Wright 1870–1871, II, 633). It was here above all, as well as in the monastery of St Catherine on Sinai, also in Egypt, that the most ancient manuscripts were preserved. This is due both to drier climate of Egypt and also to the fact that these areas remained isolated from the invasions and destruction that ruined Syria and Mesopotamia in the Middle Ages and into the modern era. The Sinai manuscripts belong to the Chalcedonian (Melkite) tradition, whereas those of Dayr as-Suryan are of the Syrian Orthodox Church (miaphysite). Many were written in Mesopotamia and were brought to Egypt in the tenth century by Moses of Mardin (Brock 2004; Brock and van Rompay 2014).

The iconic manuscript BL Add 12150 already displays all the characteristics of Syriac manuscripts throughout their history (Borbone and Briquel Chatonnet 2015). It is truly remarkable that the method of manuscript production evolved very little over fifteen centuries, as if the scribes had been concerned all along history to perpetuate a tradition that had been fixed early.

The method of manuscript production

All Syriac manuscripts that have been preserved have the form of a codex, that is to say the form of a modern book. The only exceptions are a few magical scrolls, not very old, which were unrolled vertically and read from top to bottom (*rotulus*). There is no known example of a *volumen*, the model used in antiquity and which was unrolled horizontally and written in columns, an image particularly well known from the examples at Qumran. Although there are a small number of fragments of papyrus manuscripts from Egypt, where it was the standard material, the oldest manuscripts are all on parchment, which was progressively supplanted from the tenth century onwards by paper (Briquel Chatonnet 2015). Initially, this paper was of oriental manufacture, without any visible weft; later, paper was imported from Italy which was characterised by a net of laid-lines and chaine-lines and by watermarks; finally, there were late imitations of Italian papers made in the Ottoman Empire.

Most of the manuscripts are composed of quires each of ten folios, i.e. five bifolios, all of which are superimposed in the same direction before being written and sewn together: thus, for manuscripts on parchment, the flesh side is always turned towards the inside of the quire, and the hair side towards the outside. This model differs from that of Greek or Latin manuscripts; for example, the Latin manuscripts were often copied on a large skin, in a very precise order, which then allowed for folding and cutting; this procedure thus automatically creates quires of two, four, eight, or sixteen folios, but never quires of ten folios. As early as the fifth century,

Syriac manuscripts follow a specific model, which is to be found later in Arab-Muslim manuscripts. It should be noted that Melkite Syriac manuscripts, made by copyists of a church which remained in the Chalcedonian confession and in communion with the Byzantine empire, are usually made in eight-folio quires under the influence of the Greek model.

The oldest manuscripts are frequently written on two, three, or even exceptionally four columns per page. This is related to the format of the manuscripts. Since there was no use of a system of ruling for marking lines to guide the copying process, copyists preferred to write in short lines, which were easier to keep horizontal on the page. They first used a system of pricking, tiny holes made with a needle marking the corners of the columns, and later also at the beginning and end of each line. A system of ruling, that is the drawing of lines, generally with a dry nib, developed only secondarily. These lines trace the first line and the lateral margins. It is only in the most recent manuscripts that all lines are ruled.

The older manuscripts are never paginated. Fairly early the custom emerged of numbering the quires, with a number placed in the lower margin of the first and last pages of each quire, first along the inner margin and then in the centre of the lower margin. The use of pagination, as well as of catch words, did not really develop until after the seventeenth century, following the model of printed books from Western Europe.

Syriac bookmakers also developed a special type of binding, different from that of Greek, Armenian, or Arabic manuscripts. It has been observed and described for the moment mainly based on manuscripts of the Syrian Orthodox tradition found in the collection of the Syro-Catholic patriarchate at Charfet in Lebanon (Dergham and Vinourd 2015, upon whose observations I here depend). The wooden boards, rather thin, do not have grooves on the edges; the text-block is sewn without a couser or support, in one piece, directly on the upper board; the board and the book itself are attached by one or more canvases; the headbands begin and end on the boards and include a passage in the middle of each quire; the whole is covered either by tanned goat or sheep leather, or by canvas.

Colophons

Syriac manuscripts very often contain colophons (Briquel Chatonnet 1998), sometimes quite long (consisting of several pages), and marked out as distinct either by a script or a layout different from that of the main text, or else by a framework in red ink. They may include the date and place of the copy, the name of the copyist and his genealogy, the sponsor and the recipient of the manuscript, which are not always the same, and sometimes the circumstances in which the work was performed, such as particular events that mark the period (invasions, epidemics, natural disasters, the ceremonial arrival or visit of an important individual). It is therefore an important source for the local history of the Near East. An abstract of the colophon, perhaps the name of the copyist or the date, may also be written elsewhere in the manuscript, for example at the end of the various texts copied in the manuscript or in the decoration of the title. These additional notes are particularly important because the colophons being written on the last pages of the manuscript are thereby the more likely to be lost if a manuscript is in poor condition or incomplete.

Manuscripts were most often copied in monasteries. But even for those most often mentioned as places of copying, there is no evidence that they had any real scriptoria such as those found in the monasteries of Europe. Some, mostly liturgical manuscripts, were copied in churches. The context is therefore always religious.

As already mentioned, the oldest extant dated manuscript comes from the beginning of the fifth century. There are about fifty such dated manuscripts from before the arrival of Islam. This situation contrasts markedly from that of Greek or Hebrew manuscripts, for example, among which there are none that are explicitly dated before the ninth century. The contrast is all the more striking as the Greek or Hebrew manuscripts that have been preserved are much more numerous, and as the regions in which Syriac was written were much more adversely affected by invasions, the destruction of libraries, and the removal of books from one place to another. When a manuscript deteriorates, the first and last pages are the first to be lost, and the colophons are particularly threatened. We may therefore assume that many colophons have been lost in manuscripts that are currently incomplete, from which we may infer that copyists in the Syriac world had a very particular concern to note down information about the copies they were making.

The style of these colophons is very uniform, full of praise for the scribe's superiors or for his brothers of the monastery, but of depreciation towards himself. The scribe describes himself as a miserable sinner, unworthy for his name to be written on the manuscript, and he justifies his signing of his work by asking his readers to pray for him. He sometimes mentions those who paid for the materials of the book, but always adds that he did his work for free, for the remission of his sins. Sometimes, at the end of the volume, we find the phrase, 'As the sailor rejoices when he arrives in port, so the scribe rejoices at the end of his work'. These colophons contain a wealth of information, not only for locating the origins of manuscripts, but also for all the data they provide about the lives of local communities.

Dating systems

The most widely used system of calculating dates in Syriac manuscripts is that of the Seleucid era, which begins on 1 October 312 BC, which was in official use in the Near East during the Hellenistic, Roman, and Proto-Byzantine eras. The scribes call it the 'era of Alexander' or the 'era of the [blessed] Greeks'. It has been in use throughout the history of Syriac manuscripts and is peculiar to the Syriac churches. But since the Syrians have throughout their history lived within different states and cultures, so Syriac culture is typically a culture of contact, and scribes have also made use of systems from the environments in which they lived. The oldest manuscripts copied in the cities of the Levant sometimes use the era of the city (Antioch, Apamea, or Bostra, the latter being in fact the era of the Roman province of Arabia). In the Sasanian Empire, the copyists used the year of the sovereign's rule, which was the standard method there in use. The scribes of the Melkite manuscripts, under Byzantine influence, used the year of the Byzantine world, sometimes called 'the era of Adam', or else they calculated the date of the indiction. From the time of the Arab-Muslim conquest, they often refer to the Hegira. In Central Asia, the Sino-Mongol calendar (a twelve-year cycle using animal names) is sometimes found; in Kerala, the local era called *kullam* is used, while in Egypt we find the Coptic era of the martyrs, which was actually a regnal year of Diocletian. A Christian era was used from time to time in the East Syrian Church, but it is an era based on the Ascension which corresponds to a different calculation than that used in the West calculated by Dionysius Exiguus. It was only later that the latter system was introduced into the Syriac world, following relations with the Latins: the use of this dating system in the Ṭur ʿAbdin in 1190 (BnF syr 39, Zotenberg 1874: 14) testifies perhaps to an influence from the Latin county of Edessa earlier in the century. Colophons are commonly found which combine two, three, and even up to six different dating eras, not without occasional mistakes in the synchronisations. Finally, mentioning the dignitaries of the Church at the time of copying (e.g. 'at the time of the Patriarch Mar . . ., at the time of the bishop of . . . mar . . ., in the time of the superior of the monastery mar') can situate manuscripts in time. It indicates that the religious community related to its head in the same way as a civil community does to its sovereign.

The scribe also often dates the end of the copying process by mentioning the actual month, day, and sometimes even hour of finishing the work. This time-reference may also be made by reference to liturgical time, e.g. 'the 20th day of the fast of Elijah' (BnF Syr 393), or to the liturgy itself, e.g. 'the day whose *onita* is *šubhoro d-lo*' (BnF 405–406).

SCRIPTS

The development of scripts

Syriac script, in all its forms and whatever the medium, is a script with pronounced cursive features (for various dated examples of manuscript hands, see Hatch 1946). It is also a script that is full of ligatures and which sometimes even when inscribed on stone can present a full and precise imitation of script written in ink. It was written vertically, from top to bottom, the lines being added from left to right, as evidenced by certain inscriptions on lintels which are made in small vertical lines (see Figure 15.2), but also by the vocabulary of the grammarians who refer to points being to the left or right of the writing line, when we see them under or above the line. It was then read horizontally, however. The reason for this system is probably that since the lines are written from right to left, horizontal writing was difficult for right-handers (Desreumaux 2009).

We have seen that, from the time of the kingdom of Edessa, scripts may appear in different forms depending on whether the letters were engraved on stone or traced in ink on a more supple medium. The script we find on the mosaics is somewhat intermediate between the two types. From the very beginning of writing in Syriac, therefore, there was both a formal hand used for special display, as well as another hand for everyday use.

The oldest preserved manuscripts are copied in a beautiful elegant estrangela script that reproduces the one engraved on stone (see the images of BL Add 12150 in Figures 14.2–3). This is still a script of a formal type. From the seventh century onwards, some letters take on a less calligraphic appearance, with a more rounded form, which did not require the scribe to lift the *calamus* as often. Some letters which have an open form in formal estrangela (*he*, *waw*, and *mim*) adopt closed loops. This is still very much an estrangela script, albeit a less formal one.

Table of Aramaic Scripts, © H. Gzella, De eerste wereldtaal. Athenaeum, 2017.

Value	Estrangela Ms BnF syr. 33 (6th cent.)	Late Estrangela Ms. Lyon Bib. Mun.01 (1138 AD)	Serto Ms Charfet Raḥmani 38 (1466 AD)	Syriac-Melkite Ms Oxford. Bod Dawkins 5 (1418 AD)	Oriental Syriac Ms BL Add 7177 (1484 AD)	Keralese Syriac Ms Kottayam SEERI 18 (19-20th cent.)
ʾ	ܐ	ܐ	ܐ	ܐ ܐ	ܐ	ܐ
B	ܒ	ܒ	ܒ	ܒ	ܒ	ܒ
G	ܓ	ܓ	ܓ	ܓ	ܓ	ܓ
D	ܕ	ܕ	ܕ	ܕ	ܕ	ܕ
H	ܗ	ܗ	ܗ	ܗ	ܗ	ܗ
W	ܘ	ܘ	ܘ	ܘ	ܘ	ܘ
Z	ܙ	ܙ	ܙ	ܙ	ܙ	ܙ
Ḥ	ܚ	ܚ	ܚ	ܚ	ܚ	ܚ
Ṭ	ܛ	ܛ	ܛ	ܛ	ܛ	ܛ
Y	ܝ	ܝ	ܝ	ܝ	ܝ	ܝ
K	ܟ	ܟ ܟ	ܟ	ܟ	ܟ ܟ	ܟ ܟ
L	ܠ	ܠ	ܠ ܠ	ܠ ܠ	ܠ	ܠ ܠ
M	ܡ	ܡ	ܡ ܡ	ܡ	ܡ	ܡ
N	ܢ ܢ	ܢ ܢ	ܢ ܢ	ܢ ܢ	ܢ	ܢ
S	ܣ	ܣ	ܣ	ܣ	ܣ	ܣ
ʿ	ܥ	ܥ	ܥ	ܥ	ܥ	ܥ
P	ܦ	ܦ	ܦ	ܦ	ܦ	ܦ
Ṣ	ܨ	ܨ	ܨ	ܨ	ܨ	ܨ
Q	ܩ	ܩ	ܩ	ܩ	ܩ	ܩ
R	ܪ	ܪ	ܪ	ܪ	ܪ	ܪ
Š	ܫ	ܫ	ܫ	ܫ	ܫ	ܫ
T	ܬ	ܬ	ܬ	ܬ	ܬ ܬ ܬ	ܬ ܬ ܬ

Serto script had long been regarded as a development of estrangela, only simplified and quicker to write. The discovery of the Euphrates parchments (see Figures 1.4 and 14.1), documents of every day life (contracts) written in the third century, upset this pattern, because it revealed that traits that were considered typically Serto, such as the vertical alaph and the rounded rish and dalath, already existed in the Edessan practical script. However, it was still not well understood how to bridge the gap between everyday Edessan script of this type and the Serto that appears in manuscripts only from the eighth century onwards. Observation of the colophons and concluding notes of some ancient manuscripts showed that, in parallel with the formal bookhand, a more common type of script had also been maintained which was used outside the copying of texts (e.g. BL Add. 14542, f. 94r). In the appearance of Serto we are not, therefore, witnessing the birth of an entirely new script but rather the accession of an already existing script to a status of being sufficiently prestigious to be used in the copying of biblical and theological manuscripts (Healey 2000; Briquel Chatonnet 2001). This explains why Serto writing developed only in the West Syriac milieu, for it was here, in Edessa and west of the Euphrates, that the Edessan cursive that was its origin was used in everyday life. Serto became the regular script of the Syriac Orthodox and Maronite Churches (Figure 15.4).

In the West Syriac region, a particular form of Syriac script was developed in the monasteries of the Black Mountain above Antioch. This is known as the Syriac Melkite script (Desreumaux 2004b) and was used by the members of the Chalcedonian Church. Derived from the estrangela in its less formal ductus, it was also influenced by the Aramaic Melkite writing of Palestine (Christian-Palestinian). It has long been closely associated with East Syrian script, with which it has in fact no historical connection, since both are related to estrangela in its already evolved and less formal form.

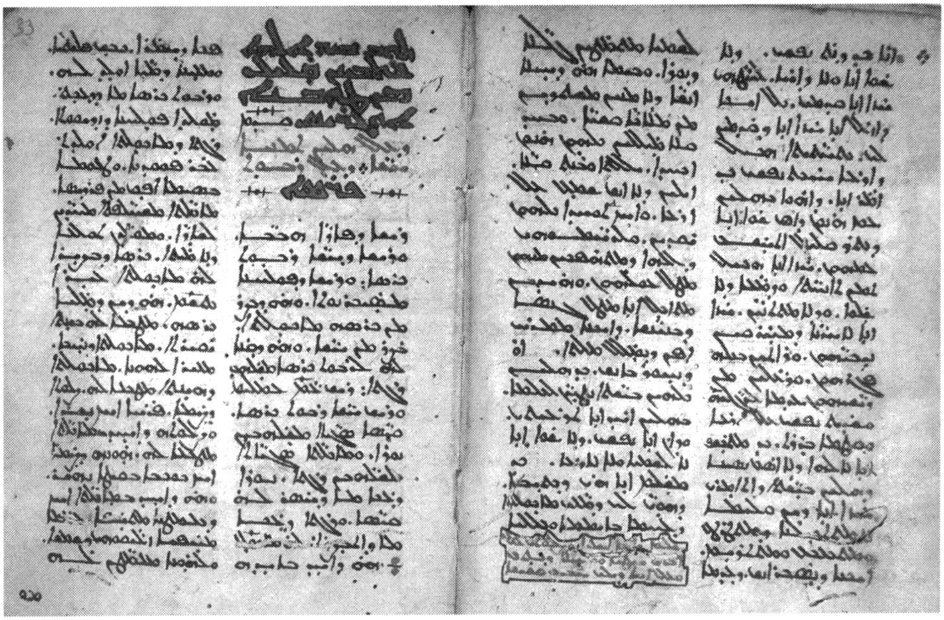

Figure 15.4 Serto script (Ms Charfet Raḥmani 38)

Source: Syriac Catholic Patriarchate, Charfet, Lebanon

In the East, outside the Roman Empire, Syriac remained only the language for the communication of culture and for use within the Church. For everyday use, other Aramaic dialects and other forms of script were practiced, for which, in the first centuries of our era, the inscriptions of Hatra and the graffiti of Assur, as well as the inscription of the Upper Tigris, are good examples (Beyer 1998). In the Church of the East, therefore, estrangela merely followed an internal evolution which resulted in the East Syriac script, and this has remained closer to its estrangela origin than the western Serto (Figure 15.5).

In the regions into which the East Syriac church expanded, the East Syriac script took on specific forms. In Central Asia, especially in the Turkish milieu, the script is often irregular, but also evidences early forms that are later found in East Syriac script (Klein 2002; for a description of certain signs, Desreumaux 2015). Rather than positing an influence from the Syrian-Turkish script of Central Asia upon the more recent East Syriac script, we ought once more to assume that these inscriptions reflect an informal script that was already in use in the centre of East Syriac world but was not yet used there for manuscripts or inscriptions. A supplementary letter was even

Figure 15.5 Oriental script (DFM 44)

Source: CNMO (Centre de numérisation des manuscrits orientaux)

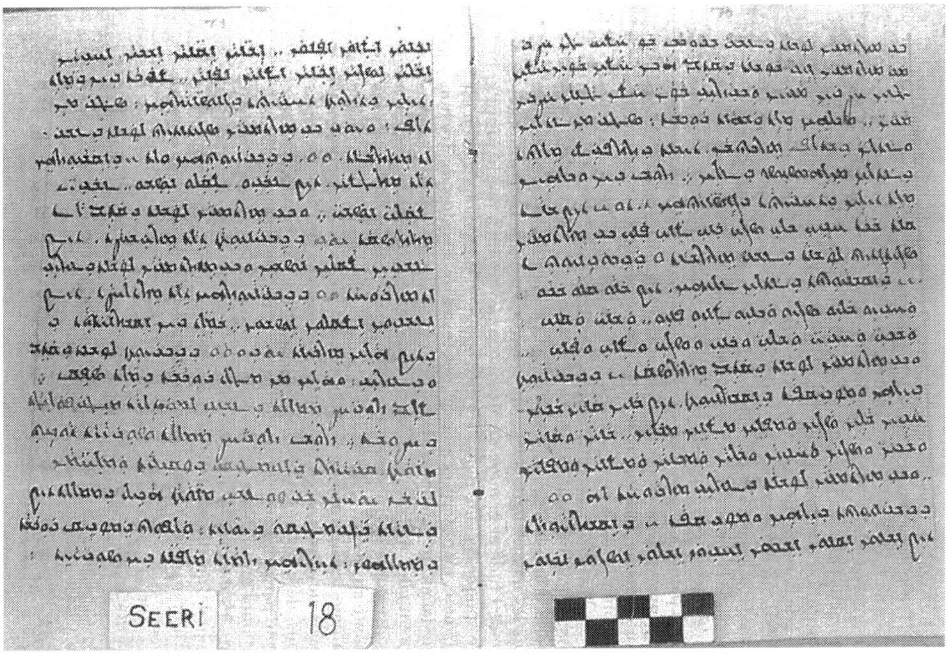

Figure 15.6 Keralese script (SEERI, Kottayam, Kerala 18)

Source: SEERI

created based on a kaph, to which was added an extra oblique line in order to express a phoneme specific to old Turkish and used in proper names.

In a much more recent period (eighteenth–twentieth centuries), there has also been a rather specific evolution of the East Syriac script in Kerala, India (Briquel Chatonnet and Desreumaux 2010), which is attested both in manuscripts and inscriptions and the reading of which is sometimes difficult. In a very broken way, this script actually pushes to the extreme features already present in East Syriac script (Figure 15.6).

Finally, although Arabic script appears in Arabia on stone inscriptions in a form derived from Aramaic Nabatean writing, it seems likely that it was also influenced during its development by the ductus of Syriac script, in a way that made possible the appearance of a regular and formal bookhand in manuscripts.

Systems of vocalisation

As with all Semitic alphabets, the Syriac script is consonantal. As early as the eighth century BC, Aramaic writing made use of *matres lectionis*, that is to say semi-consonants or certain laryngeals to indicate long vowels (*alaph* or *he* for /a/, *waw* for /u/, *yudh* for /i/). Their usage, however, was to assist reading and was not applied systematically. The practice was systematised by Syriac even sometimes outside the context of long vowels: the *waw* for /u/ is always marked, even when the vowel is short, save in the words *mṭl* and *kl*. These *matres lectionis* were also frequently used to transcribe words of foreign origin: *mṭrwplys* for metropolis.

Another system that was in use, particularly in unvocalised manuscripts, was that of the diacritic point, which is but one of the many points used in the script for a wide variety of different functions. The vocalising point does not specifically note the quality of the vowel, but makes it possible to distinguish homographic words by indicating their vocalisation. One point above a word indicates /a/ or /o/, while a point below a word indicates either /i/, /e/ or else the absence of a vowel. This makes it possible, by writing a point above the first consonant of a word to mark the form *qoṭel* (in Western Syriac) of the active participle, and to distinguish it from the form *qəṭal*, for which the /q/ carries a point below; or again to distinguish *šanto* (year) from *šento* (sleep). Another diacritical point distinguishes in the perfect tense between the third-person feminine singular and the second-person masculine singular.

Attempts were made to indicate vowels more precisely by specific signs. The oldest such system is that invented by Jacob of Edessa (seventh century), as transmitted by Bar Hebraeus, in which each vowel is noted by a specific sign (Talmon 2008: 164–6). This system never came into general use, however.

In the West Syriac world, a system was developed, probably in the tenth century when it is first attested, by monks from the region of Melitene which was at that time once again under Byzantine rule, for the purpose of compiling the Syriac Massora (Coakley 2011; see chapter 17). It consists in indicating the five vowels of the West Syriac phonological system by means of five signs derived from the Greek vowels, which can be placed optionally either above or below the consonants to which they belong (Figure 15.7). In the East Syriac world, where the vocalic system is richer,

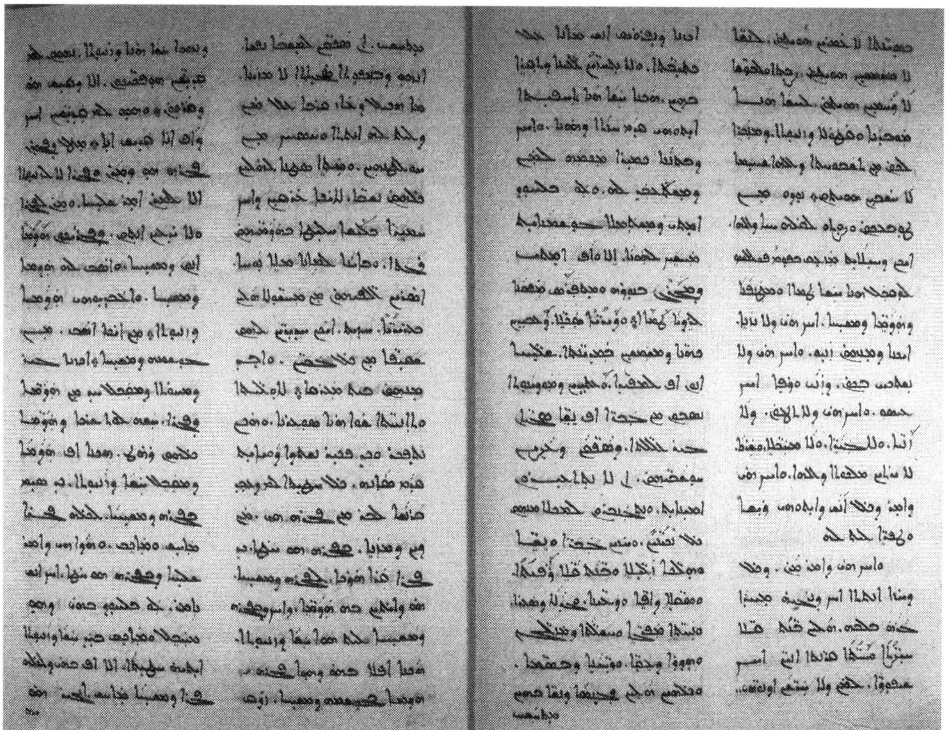

Figure 15.7 Serto manuscript in Charfet with Greek vowels

Source: Syriac Catholic Patriarchate, Charfet, Lebanon

vowels could be noted by a system of seven signs formed out of points and written either above or below the consonants: this system of vowel notation is present in manuscripts from the twelfth century on (see Figure 15.5). Neither of these systems was ever adopted systematically, but they were used rather to remove ambiguities in reading. Their use did become both more frequent and more abundant in later manuscripts, a sign that the Syriac language was becoming less familiar as the use of Arabic and other vernaculars spread and that vocalising an unvocalised script was beginning to pose a problem. In the manuscripts of the Syrian Orthodox Church copied in Mesopotamia, in the territory of the maphrianate of the East, and under the influence of the east Syriac script, there are also Serto manuscripts vocalised with the East Syrian system or else that combine the two types of vocalisation.

The points

Points are also used to note plural forms (double point above, or *seyame*), the spirantised and unspirantised pronunciations of the letters /b,g,d,k,p,t/ (*qušaya* and *rukaka*), certain grammatical distinctions and phrasal punctuation. The sheer abundance of points on a manuscript page, varying in size, thickness, and sometimes colour if a manuscript uses red ink, together with the breadth of functions that they could cover, is such that a treatise on grammar could be entitled 'Treatise on the points', such as was that of Joseph bar Malkon from the twelfth–thirteenth century (on the meaning of the various systems of punctuation, see Duval 1881; Segal 1953, and especially now Kiraz 2015).

Other small signs, such as a line above a word, may be used to indicate that the writing of the word has been abbreviated, or that one of the consonants should not be pronounced.

Phrasal punctuation, which marks the articulations of the sentence, is particularly rich. The signs differ by the number and position of the points between the parts of the sentence, either alone or in pairs, in vertical or oblique columns, or following each other on the line (Segal 1953). Since indentation for marking paragraphs is not used in Syriac; the most important breaks are often marked by a combination of points in the shape of a diamond, which can also mix red and black dots.

Garshuni

Occasionally from the ninth/tenth century, more systematically from the fourteenth, and then very abundantly between the seventeenth and nineteenth centuries, a writing system was used for recording the Arabic language by the use of Syriac script. This was known as Garshuni (or, Karshuni in Arabic), a word whose origin remains unknown. It has the disadvantage of having only the twenty-two signs of the Syriac alphabet in order to mark the twenty-eight consonant phonemes of Arabic, and it therefore included signs with several equivalents, sometimes distinguished by points. The aim of using such a script was to assert a Christian identity and to retain the use of Syriac writing, while the Syriac language was in process of going out of use. Many manuscripts combine texts in Syriac and others in Garshuni; one can even find liturgical manuscripts in which the prayers are in Syriac, with indications for the priest or server are in Arabic written in Garshuni (Moukarzel 2014).

This system was developed especially in the Syrian Orthodox and the Syrian Catholic Churches, and well as the Maronite Church. Hence, it is almost exclusively Serto script that is to be found in Garshuni manuscripts. This hybrid system originally developed for the notation of Arabic came to be used also to record Turkish, Kurdish, Armenian, Uighur, Old Turkish, and Malayalam in Syriac script (Kiraz 2014 and various examples studied in the same volume: den Heijer, Schmidt and Pataridze 2014).

Printing and manuscripts

The first book printed in Syriac was a Gospel book. The initiative came from the Syrian Orthodox patriarch, already aware of the significance presented by this new technology, who sent the monk Moses of Mardin to Europe with a Gospel book to be printed. The latter did not find the help that he sought in Rome, but succeeded in convincing the chancellor of the Austrian Empire, Widmanstetter. It was, therefore, thanks to the latter and under his auspices that the book was printed in 1555, with its circulation divided between a diffusion in the West and a batch of books that were taken back to the East by Moses (Strothmann 1971; Le livre et le Liban 1982: 123–7; and see chapter 37).

The first book to be published in the Asian part of the Ottoman Empire was the Syriac-Garshuni Bilingual psalter printed at the Monastery of St Anthony of Qozḥayyā in the Qadisha Valley in the Lebanese Mountains in 1610 (Moukarzel 2010–2011).

In the West, especially at Rome and Florence, but also at Paris, Syriac publications continued to develop: tools such as grammars and dictionaries, the polyglot Bibles of Antwerp, Paris, and London, various psalters, ecclesiastical works published in Rome by the Maronite College and the Congregation for the Propagation of the Faith, and the catalogues and publications of texts by members of the Assemani family.

In the nineteenth century, publications in Europe multiplied: there were catalogues of manuscripts, and then at the end of the century the founding of the two major collections of edited texts with translations, *Patrologia Orientalis* and *Corpus Scriptorum Christianorum Orientalium*. In the East, there were also the presses of the American mission at Ourmiah, the Dominican press in Mosul, the Catholic printing press at Saint Joseph University in Beirut, the Saint Joseph press in Mannanam, and the Mar Narsai press at Trichur in Kerala, to name just a few.

All these editions and publications led to the creation of fonts for the various forms of Syriac script, together with a very wide creativity (see the fundamental study of Coakley 2006, with a catalogue of font types). This was all the more difficult since Syriac writing is fundamentally cursive and it was necessary to reproduce the specific forms of letters according to their place in the word, to allow for ligatures, to create types for combined characters (*lamad-alaph in Serto, taw-alaph* in eastern), and to manage the combinations of letters with vowel signs and points. Syriac printing has thus also for a long time been accustomed to merely reproducing pages written by calligraphers: for example, the first publications of the Saint-Ephrem presses in the Netherlands, whose books were handwritten by Bishop Julius Čiček. These days, Syriac printing presses benefits from the advantages of computer science and in particular the unicode fonts offered by Beth Mardutho at the initiative of George Kiraz.

The copying of manuscripts continued in the East until the beginning of the twentieth century and in Kerala well into the century. Western scholars had manuscripts copied at a time when they could not yet microfilm them. Many manuscripts were thus copied at Alqosh at the request of Henri Pognon, who provided texts to Mgr Graffin for the *Patrologia Orientalis*. It was no longer monks who performed the role of copyists, but lay copyists who handed on their professions within their families. These manuscripts often imitated printed books in their layout.

CONCLUSION

Syriac culture is a culture of writing. Syriac never developed a cult of images as the Greeks did and gave a particular importance to written documents (as the supposed letter of Jesus Christ to Abgar) and to the copying of manuscripts. A theology of writing even developed, illustrated in the *Cause of the Foundation of the Schools*, in which God himself teaches the letters to Adam in form of creation.

As Syriac communities were always living in political contexts where other cultures were dominant, the Syriac language, script, and texts became an essential element of their common heritage and identity. This is why they spread this script throughout Asia along with the Christian mission. It was even used as a form of decoration, as in the ornamentation of the monastery of Mar Behnam near Mosul (Figure 15.8): a testimony to the value of script in the Syriac world.

Figure 15.8 Script as ornament at Mar Behnam Monastery, Mosul

BIBLIOGRAPHY

Al-Jeloo, Nicholas. 2010. Evidence in Stone and Wood: The Assyrian/Syriac History and Heritage of the Urmia Region in Iran, as Reconstructed From Epigraphic Evidence. *PdO* 35, 39–63.

Balty, Janine, and Françoise Briquel Chatonnet. 2000. Mosaïques édesséniennes inscrites. *Fondation Eugène Piot. Monuments et mémoires* 79, 31–72.

Beyer, Klaus. 1998. *Die aramäischen Inschriften aus Assur, Hatra und dem übrigen Ostmesopotamien (datiert 44v. Chr. bis 238 n. Chr.)*. Göttingen: Vandenhoeck & Ruprecht.

Borbone, Pier-Giorgio and Briquel Chatonnet, Françoise. 2015. Codicology of Syriac Manuscripts. *In*: *Comparative Oriental Manuscript Studies. An Introduction*. Hamburg: Tredition, 252–66.

Briquel Chatonnet, Françoise. 1998. Le temps du copiste. Notations chronologiques dans les colophons de manuscrits syriaques. *In*: F. Briquel Chatonnet and H. Lozachmeur, ed., *Proche-Orient ancien temps pensé, temps vécu. Actes de la table-ronde du 15 novembre 1997*. Paris: Maisonneuve, 197–210.

———. 2001. De l'écriture édessénienne à l'estrangelâ et au sertô. *Semitica* 50, 81–90.

———. 2010. L'inscription de Bamuqqa et la question du bilinguisme gréco-syriaque dans le massif Calcaire de Syrie du Nord. *In*: F. Briquel Chatonnet and M. Debié, ed., *Sur les pas des Araméens chrétiens. Mélanges offerts à Alain Desreumaux*. Cahiers d'études syriaques 1. Paris: Geuthner, 269–77.

———. 2015. De l'usage du parchemin à celui du papier dans les manuscrits syriaques. *In*: Briquel Chatonnet and Debié, 141–60.

———, and M. Debié, ed. 2015. *Manuscripta Syriaca. Des sources de première main*. Cahiers d'études syriaques 4. Paris: Geuthner.

———, M. Debié, and A. Desreumaux, ed. 2004. *Les inscriptions syriaques*. Études syriaques 1. Paris: Geuthner.

———, and Alain Desreumaux. 2010. A Study and Characterization of the Syro-Malabar Script. *JSS* LV/2, 407–21.

———, and Alain Desreumaux. 2011. Oldest Syriac Christian Inscription Discovered in North Syria. *Hugoye* 14, 45–61.

———, Alain Desreumaux, and Widad Khoury. 2004–2005. Inscriptions syriaques de Syrie. Premiers résultats. *Annales archéologiques arabes syriennes* XLVII–XLVIII [2008], 187–95.

———, Alain Desreumaux, and Joseph Moukarzel. 2008. Découverte d'une inscription syriaque mentionnant l'évêque Rabbula. *In*: G. Kiraz, ed., *Malphono w-Rabo d-Malphone, Festschrift for Sebastian P. Brock*. Piscataway, NJ: Gorgias Press, 21–9.

———, Alain Desreumaux, and Jacob Thekeparampil. 2008. *Recueil des inscriptions syriaques. 1. Kérala*. Paris: Académie des inscriptions et Belles-Lettres.

Brock, Sebastian P. 2004. Without Mushe of Nisibis, Where Would We Be? Some Reflections on the Transmission of Syriac Literature. *Journal of Eastern Christian Studies* 56, 15–24.

———, Haim Goldfus, and Aryeh Kofsky. 2006–2007. The Syriac Inscriptions at the Entrance to Holy Sepulchre, Jerusalem. *Aram* 18–19, 415–38.

———, and Lucas Van Rompay. 2014. *Catalogue of the Syriac Manuscripts and Fragments in the Library of Deir al-Surian, Wadi al-Natrun (Egypt)*. OLA 227. Leuven: Peeters.

Coakley, James F. 2006. *The Typography of Syriac: A Historical Catalogue of Printing Types, 1537–1958*. New Castle, Del.-London: Oak Knoll Press-British Library.

———. 2011. When Were the Five Greek Vowel-Signs Introduced Into Syriac Writing? *JSS* LVI (2), 307–26.

Den Heijer, J., A. Schmidt and T. Pataridze, ed. 2014. *Scripts Beyond Borders: A Survey of Allographic Tradition in the Euro-Mediterranean World*. Publications de l'Institut orientaliste de Louvain. Louvain, Peeters.

Dergham, Youssef, and François Vinourd. 2015. Les reliures syriaques: essai de caractérisation par comparaison avec les reliures byzantines et arméniennes. *In*: Briquel Chatonnet and Debié, 271–304.

Desreumaux, Alain. 2004a. Des inscriptions syriaques de voyageurs et d'émigrés. *In*: Briquel Chatonnet, Debié and Desreumaux, 45–53.

———. 2004b. La paléographie des manuscrits syriaques et araméens melkites. Le rôle d'Antioche. *In*: B. Cabouret, P.-L. Gatier and C. Saliou, ed., *Antioche de Syrie. Histoire, images et traces de la ville antique.* Topoi. Orient-Occident Suppl. 5. Lyon, 555–71.

———. 2009. Comment peut-on écrire en syriaque? ou Des problèmes du scribes devant sa page blanche. *In*: Chr. Batsch et Mârtejanu-Joubert, ed., *Manières de penser dans l'Antiquité méditerranéenne et orientale. Mélanges offerts à Francis Schmidt.* Supplements to the Journal for the Study of Judaism. Leiden-Boston: Brill, 105–26.

———. 2015. La collection des pierres tombales syro-orientales du Turkestan conservées à Paris et à Lyon. *In*: P.-G. Borbone and P. Marsone, ed., *Le christianisme syriaque en Asie centrale et en Chine.* Études syriaques 12. Paris: Geuthner, 237–56.

Drijvers, Han J. W., and John F. Healey. 1999. *The Old Syriac Inscriptions of Edessa and Osrhoene. Texts, Translations and Commentary.* Handbuch der Orientalistik I, 42. Leiden, NewYork and Köln: Brill.

Duval, Paul Rubens. 1881. *Traité de grammaire syriaque.* Paris: F. Vieweg.

Harrak, Amir. 2010. *Recueil des inscriptions syriaques. Tome 2, Syriac and Garshuni inscriptions of Iraq.* 2 vols. Paris: Académie des Inscriptions et Belles-Lettres.

Hatch, W. H. P. 1946. *An Album of Syriac Dated Manuscripts.* Boston: American Academy of Arts and Sciences. [Reprint: Gorgias Press, 2012].

Healey, John F. 2000. The Early History of the Syriac Script. A Reassessment. *JSS* 45, 55–67.

Hellot-Bellier, Florence. 2004. L'apport des inscriptions syriaques à la connaissance de l'histoire des chrétiens d'Ourmia. *In*: Briquel Chatonnet, Debié and Desreumaux, 117–23.

Jalabert, Louis and René Mouterde. 1939. *Inscriptions grecques et latines de la Syrie II. Chalcidique et Antiochène.* Bibliothèque archéologique et historique 32. Paris: Geuthner.

Kassis, Antoine, Abdo Badwi, and Jean-Baptiste Yon. 2004. Les inscriptions syriaques du Liban. Bilan archéologique et historique. *In*: Briquel Chatonnet, Debié and Desreumaux, 29–43.

Kiraz, George Anton. 2014. Garshunography: Terminology and Some Formal Properties of Writing One Language in the Script of Another. *In*: Den Heijer et al., 65–74.

———. 2015. *The Syriac Dot: A Short History.* Piscataway, NJ: Gorgias Press.

Klein, Wassilios. 2000. *Das nestorianische Christentum an den Handelswegen durch Kyrgyzstan bis zum 14. Jh.* Silk Road Studies 3. Turnhout: Brepols.

———. 2002. Syriac Writings and Turkic Language According to Central Asian Tombstone Inscriptions. *Hugoye* 5/2, 213–23.

Lavagne, Henri. 2011. Une Andromède chrétienne (?) sur une mosaïque avec inscriptions en syriaque provenant de la région d'Édesse. *In*: O. Brandt and P. Pergola, ed., *Marmoribus vestita. Miscellanea in honore di Federico Guidobaldi.* Città del Vaticano: Pontificio Istituto di archeologia cristiana, 821–33.

Le livre et le Liban jusqu'à 1900. 1982. Catalogue d'exposition publié sous la direction de S Exc. l'ambassadeur Camille Aboussouan. Paris: UNESCO.

Moriggi, Marco. 2014. *A Corpus of Syriac Incantation Bowls. Syriac Magical Texts From Late-Antique Mesopotamia.* Leiden: Brill.

Moukarzel, Joseph. 2010–2011. Le Psautier syriaque-garchouni édité à Qozhaya en 1610. Enjeux historiques et présentation du livre. *Mélanges de l'Université Saint-Joseph* 63, 511–66.

———. 2014. Le Garshuni: remarques sur son histoire et son évolution. *In*: Den Heijer et al., 107–37.

———, Jean-Baptiste Yon, and Youssef Dergham. 2010. Le site de Ḥraš (Liban). *In*: F. Briquel Chatonnet and M. Debié, ed., *Sur les pas des Araméens chrétiens. Mélanges offerts à Alain Desreumaux*. Cahiers d'études syriaques 1. Paris: Geuthner, 279–86.

Mouterde, Paul. 1939. Deux inscriptions Jacobites. *Mélanges de l'Université Saint-Joseph* 22.2, 49–56, pl. 21.

Naveh, Joseph. 1987. *Early History of the Alphabet*. 2nd ed. (1st ed. 1982). Jerusalem: The Magness Press, Hebrew University.

Niu, Ruji. 2010. *La croix-lotus: inscriptions et manuscrits nestoriens en écriture syriaque découverts en Chine (xiii*e*-xiv*e *siècles)*. Shanghai: Shanghai gu ji chu ban she.

Osawa, Takashi, and Hidemi Takahashi. 2015. Le prince Georges des Önggüt dans les montagnes de l'Altaï de Mongolie: les inscriptions d'Ulaan Tolgoi de Doloon Nuur. *In*: P.-G. Borbone and P. Marsone, ed., *Le christianisme en Asie centrale et en Chine*. Études syriaques 12. Paris: Geuthner, 257–90.

Palmer, Andrew. 1987. A Corpus of Inscriptions From Tur ʿAbdin and Environs. *OC* 71, 53–139.

———. 1993. The Messiah and the Mahdi. History Presented as the Writing on the Wall. *In*: H. Hokwerda, E. R. Smits, and M. M. Woesthuis, ed., *Polyphonia Byzantina. Studies in Honour of Willem J. Aerts*. Groningen: Egbert Forsten, 45–84.

———, and Geert Jan Van Gelder. 1994. Syriac and Arabic Inscriptions at the Monastery of St Mark's in Jerusalem. *OC* 78, 33–63.

Pelliot, Paul, and Antonino Forte. 1996. *L'inscription nestorienne de Si-Ngan-Fou. Edited with Supplements By A. Forte*. Paris: Collège de France. Institut des Hautes études chinoises.

Segal, Jean-Baptiste. 1953. *The Diacritical Point and the Accents in Syriac*. Oxford: Clarendon Press.

Strothmann, W. 1971. *Die Anfange der syrischen Studien in Europa*. Göttinger Orientforschungen I.1. Wiesbaden: Harrassowitz.

Talmon, Rafael. 2008. Jacob of Edessa the Grammarian. *In*: Bas ter Haar Romeny, ed., *Jacob of Edessa and the Syriac Culture of His Day*. Monographs of the Peshitta Institute Leiden 18. Leiden-Boston: Brill, 159–87.

Vaivre, Jean-Bernard de, and Philippe Plagnieux. 2012. *Monuments médiévaux de Chypre. Photographies de la mission de Camille Enlart en 1896*. Paris, Association des Amis du Centre d'Histoire et Civilisation de Byzance.

Van Rompay, Lucas. 2004a. Les inscriptions syriaques du couvent des Syriens (Wadi al-Natrun, Égypte). *In*: Briquel Chatonnet and Debié, 55–73.

———. 2004b. The Syriac Texts of the Flabellum. Appendice p. 134–137 in Bas Snelders and Mat Immerzeel. The Thirteenth-Century Flabellum From Deir al-Surian in the Musée Royal de Mariemont (Morlanwelz, Belgium). *Eastern Christian Art* 1, 113–39.

Wright, William. 1870–1871. *Catalogue of the Syriac Manuscripts in the British Museum*. 3 vols. London.

Zotenberg, Hermann. 1874. *Catalogue des manuscrits syriaques et sabéens (mandaïtes) de la la Bibliothèque nationale*. Paris: Imprimerie nationale.

CHAPTER SIXTEEN

THE NEO-ARAMAIC DIALECTS AND THEIR HISTORICAL BACKGROUND

Geoffrey Khan

THE CLASSIFICATION OF NEO-ARAMAIC

Spoken vernacular dialects of Aramaic, generally known as Neo-Aramaic dialects, have survived down to modern times in four subgroups:

1 Central Neo-Aramaic
2 North-Eastern Neo-Aramaic
3 Neo-Mandaic
4 Western Neo-Aramaic

The dialect geography of Neo-Aramaic has undergone radical changes over the last one hundred years, as a result of which a large number of the speakers of the dialects have been displaced from the places where they have lived for many centuries. The following geographical description, therefore, relates to the situation that existed at the beginning of the twentieth century, before these major upheavals.

Central Neo-Aramaic

The Central Neo-Aramaic subgroup of dialects were spoken by Christian communities in south-eastern Turkey in the region of Ṭūr ʿAbdīn, which extends from the town of Mardin in the west up to the boundary of the Tigris river in the east and north. The main component of this subgroup is the cluster of dialects of the Neo-Aramaic variety generally known in the academic literature as Ṭuroyo. Native speakers of the language generally refer to it by the term Ṣurāyt. The main dialect split in Ṭuroyo is between the dialect of the town of Midyat and the dialects of the surrounding villages. The differences between the Ṭuroyo dialects are small and they are mutually comprehensible (Jastrow 1985; Ritter 1990; Waltisberg 2014). In addition to the Ṭuroyo cluster, one other dialect is known to have existed in the Central Neo-Aramaic subgroup. This is the dialect of the Christians of the village of Mlaḥso (now Yünlüce), situated near Lice in northern Diyarbakir province, which is related to Ṭuroyo but exhibits a number of significant differences (Jastrow 1994a, 2011).

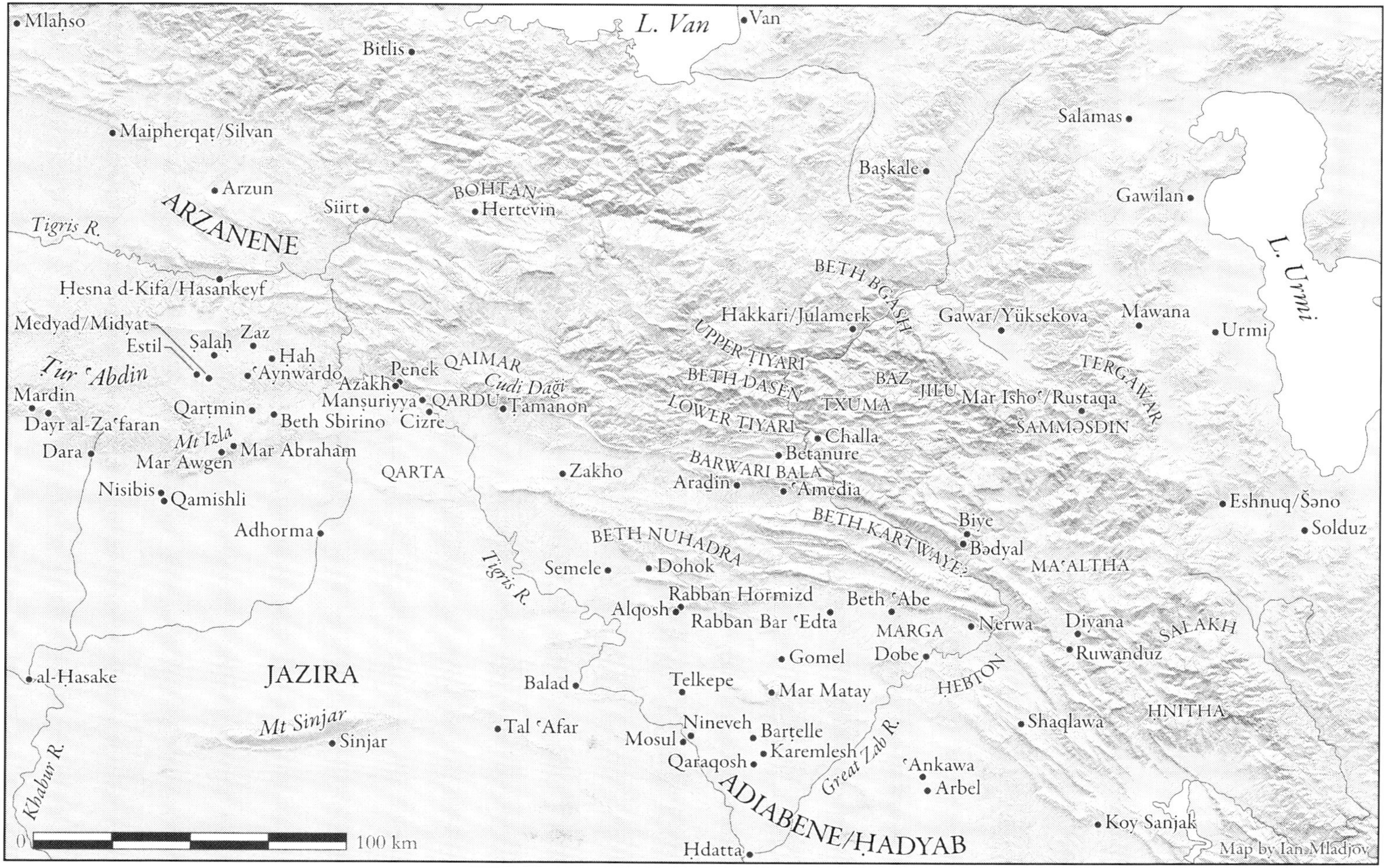

Figure 16.1 Map of North-Eastern Neo-Aramaic and Central Neo-Aramaic dialect areas

North-Eastern Neo-Aramaic

North-Eastern Neo-Aramaic (NENA)[1] is a highly diverse subgroup of over 150 dialects spoken by Christians and Jews originating from towns and villages east of the Tigris river in northern Iraq, south-eastern Turkey, and western Iran. Within NENA itself, one may identify a number of subgroups based on linguistic structure and lexicon.

There is a fundamental split between the dialects spoken by the Christians and those spoken by the Jews. This applies even to cases where Jewish and Christian communities lived in the same town, such as Koy Sanjak, Sulemaniyya (both in northern Iraq), Urmi (north-western Iran), and Sanandaj (western Iran). In these towns, the dialect of the Christians differed radically from the dialect of the Jews in all levels of grammar (phonology, morphology, syntax) and lexicon.[2]

Within Jewish NENA dialects, two main subgroups are clearly identifiable:

One of these was spoken in the north-west of Iraq, mainly in Dohuk province in locations to the west of the Great Zab river, such as Zakho (Avinery 1988; Sabar 2002; Cohen 2012), Dohuk, Amedia (J. Greenblatt 2011), Betanure (Mutzafi 2008a), and also across the Zab in Iraq near the Turkish border in villages such as Nerwa and in small communities in what is now south-eastern Turkey in, for example, Challa (Fassberg 2010) in Hakkâri province and Cizre (Nakano 1969, 1973) in Şırnak province. This subgroup is generally referred as *lišana deni* ('our language'), the native term used by speakers of the dialects, which contains the form of the 1pl. genitive pronoun that is distinctive of the group.

The dialects of the other Jewish subgroup were spoken in locations east of the Great Zab river in Iraq, north-western Iran and western Iran. This subgroup is generally referred to as trans-Zab (following Mutzafi 2008c). In Iraq this included the dialects of locations in the Erbil (Arbel) and Sulemaniyya provinces, e.g. Rustaqa (Khan 2002b), Ruwanduz, Koy Sanjak (Mutzafi 2004a), villages of the plain of Arbel (Khan 1999),[3] the village of Dobe which is on the western bank of the Great Zab, Ḥalabja and Sulemaniyya to the east (Khan 2004b), and as far south as Khanaqin on the Iranian border. In north-western Iran, it includes the Jewish dialects of the towns of Urmi, Šəno (official name Ushnuye), Solduz (official name Naqadeh) and Sablagh (now Mahabad) (Garbell 1965; Khan 2008a), the district of Salamas north of the Urmi plain (Duval 1883; Mutzafi 2015), and in adjacent towns that are now situated in the east of Turkey, such as Başkale and Gawar (official name Yüksekova). In western Iran, the trans-Zab subgroup includes a cluster of dialects spoken by Jewish communities in various localities in the Kordestan and Kermanshah provinces in an area that includes Sainqala, Bokan, Saqqez on its northern border, Sanandaj in the centre, Bijar on the eastern border, and in the south Kerend and Qasr-e Širin (Hopkins 1999; Khan 2009; Israeli 1998). Various native names of the language are used by the trans-Zab Jewish communities, e.g. *lišanət nošan* (north-eastern Iraq), *lišana nošan* (western Iran), and *lišana didan* (north-west Iran), all of which mean 'our language', also *hulaula* (western Iran), which is an abstract noun meaning 'Jewishness/Judaism' (< **hūḏāyūṯā*).

In addition, there was a small cluster of Jewish dialects in the region of Barzan, located in Iraq between the areas of the *lišana deni* and trans-Zab dialects, which exhibit a linguistic profile that is transitional between the two main subgroups (Mutzafi 2002, 2004b). The native term for the language in this cluster is *lišān dideni* 'our language'.

The divisions among the Christian NENA dialects on structural and lexical grounds are not so clear-cut. One may, nevertheless, identify clusters of dialects with distinctive features.

In Iraq, the following clusters of Christian dialects are found:

- The dialects of the Mosul plain in Nineveh province, e.g. Qaraqosh (Khan 2002a), Alqosh (Coghill 2003), Telkepe, Barṭelle, Karəmlesh.
- The dialects in the far north close to the Turkish border in Dohuk province mainly west of the Zab, e.g. Ara<u>d</u>in (Krotkoff 1982), Barwar [= Barwari Bala] (Khan 2008b), Nerwa (Talay 2001), Derigne.
- The dialects east of the Zab in Erbil (Arbel) and Sulemaniyya provinces, e.g. Ankawa (Borghero 2015), Shaqlawa, Bədyal, Koy Sanjak (Mutzafi 2004c), Sulemaniyya.

As can be seen, the second two clusters correspond broadly to the Jewish *lišana deni* and trans-Zab subgroups respectively.

The Christian NENA dialects of south-eastern Turkey and Iran may be classified into several clusters. These include the following (Talay 2008a: 47–8; Hopkins 1999):

- The Bohtan cluster, spoken in villages in the area that is now the Şırnak and Siirt provinces of Turkey, such as Hertevin (Jastrow 1988), Ruma, Shwata, Borb (Fox 2009), Umra (Hobrack 2000), and Jənnēt (Jastrow 1994b; Talay 2008a: 44–5).
- The Cudi cluster, spoken in villages in the area of the Cudi mountain (Cudi Daği) that is now in the Şırnak province of Turkey (Sinha 2000).
- The Ṭiyare cluster, divided into Upper Ṭiyare and Lower Ṭiyare, spoken in villages on the western side of what is now the Hakkari province of Turkey (Talay 2008a; Talay 2008b; Borghero 2005).
- The Txuma cluster, spoken in villages lying to the east of the Lower Ṭiyare area (Jacobi 1973; Talay 2008a).
- The Hakkari cluster, spoken in a variety of villages in the Hakkari mountains east and north-east of Ṭiyare, including villages of the Jilu (Fox 1997) and Baz (Mutzafi 2000; Talay 2008a) tribes, Sat (Mutzafi 2008b), the villages in the area of lake Van, and Salamas (Mutzafi 2015) in north-western Iran.
- The cluster of dialects spoken in the far east of Turkey in the areas of Šamməsdin, Gawar (Talay 2008a), and, over the border in north-western Iran, in the mountains of Tergawar (Khan 2016).
- The Urmi cluster, which includes varieties of a dialect spoken by Christians in villages situated on the plain of Urmi in north-western Iran and within the town of Urmi (Khan 2016).
- The dialect of Sanandaj in western Iran (Panoussi 1990; Panoussi 1991; Heinrichs 2002).

Native names of the language among Christian NENA-speakers include those designating the religious community, such as *surət̲* (northern Iraq) and *lišanət surayə* (Urmi), and those such as *ḥadit̲an* 'our speech' (Qaraqosh, Iraq).

Neo-Mandaic

Neo-Mandaic is spoken by Mandaeans in south-western Iran. This exists in two known varieties originally spoken in the towns of Ahvāz and Khorramshahr respectively (Macuch 1965, 1989, 1993; Häberl 2009, 2011; Mutzafi 2014a). The native name of this spoken language is *raṭnā*, derived from a verbal root meaning 'to whisper or mutter'.

Western Neo-Aramaic

Western Neo-Aramaic is spoken in three mountain villages in the Anti-Lebanon of Syria north of Damascus, namely Maʿlula, Baxʿa, and Jubbʿadin. The population of Maʿlula is Christian with a small minority of Muslims. The inhabitants of Baxʿa (official name Ṣarxa) and Jubbʿadin are all Muslim (Arnold 1989–1991, 2011). There are no significant differences in the dialect of Maʿlula between the speech of Christians and Muslims. The native name is *siryōn* or *arōmay*.

HISTORY OF THE SPEECH COMMUNITIES

Central Neo-Aramaic and NENA speech communities

The geographical division between the Central Neo-Aramaic subgroup and the NENA subgroup coincides with the ancient border between the Romans and Parthians, and later between the Byzantines and the Sasanians (Kim 2008). The linguistic boundary between the two subgroups also coincides with an early Christian ecclesiastical division between the Jacobite (Syrian Orthodox) denomination of the communities west of the Tigris and the Nestorian (Church of the East) denomination of the communities to the east of the Tigris. The Christianity of the NENA-speaking communities has become more diverse in recent centuries, especially after the formation of the Chaldean Church, which is in communion with Rome, and the activities of Protestant missionaries in the nineteenth century.

There are only sparse historical records relating to the settlements of speakers of Central Neo-Aramaic and NENA in the region. Some linguistic aspects of the dialects, however, give us insights into the history of the communities. The diversity of the NENA dialects in northern Iraq and south-eastern Turkey, for example, can be interpreted as a reflection of the antiquity of settlement of the communities in these regions, which must have constituted the ancient heartland of NENA. The lack of diversity in the Jewish cluster of dialects in western Iran south of the Urmi region suggests that the communities who spoke these dialects migrated in a single wave into the region in relatively recent centuries. The close relationship of the Jewish dialects of western Iran with the J. Sulemaniyya dialect points to north-eastern Iraq as the origin of the migration. The isolated Christian dialect spoken in Sanandaj must, likewise, have been the result of migration from the region of Sulemaniyya, due to great similarity between the Christian dialects of the two towns.

As remarked, the Jewish NENA dialects exhibit major differences in their structure from the neighbouring Christian NENA dialects. This reflects the differing migration histories of the communities. The Jews of Urmi, for example, had settled in the town at an early period, whereas the Christians of the area were almost exclusively agriculturalists living in the surrounding villages and only began to settle in the town in large numbers in the late nineteenth century.

The Neo-Aramaic-speaking communities underwent a major upheaval during the First World War in 1915, when they suffered massacres and mass displacement from their homes in an Ottoman-led campaign in south-eastern Turkey. No accurate statistics are available for the total death toll, but it is estimated that as much as half of the Neo-Aramaic-speaking population perished, through either violence, disease, or starvation, possibly amounting to around 250,000. Some of the survivors of the Christian communities subsequently returned to their homes in the Ṭūr ʿAbdīn area and the villages in the vicinity of the Cudi mountain. The NENA-speaking communities in the remainder of south-eastern Turkey, however, became permanently displaced. The majority settled initially in refugee camps in Iraq, then subsequently in Iraqi towns, in particular Baghdad and Kirkuk. Some of the Christians from the Bohtan region fled northwards and found safety in the Russian empire, eventually settling in the village of Gardabani in Georgia or in Krosnodar in Russia. From 1933 to 1935, about 10,000 refugees from south-eastern Turkey were settled in refugee camps in north-eastern Syria, then subsequently in villages on both sides of the Khabur River. During the Kurdish uprisings in the second half of the twentieth century, there were further upheavals. The villages in the Cudi region of south-eastern Turkey and the villages in northern Iraq close to the Turkish border were destroyed in the 1980s and early 1990s, and the NENA-speaking population were forced to settle elsewhere, many outside the Middle East. Many of the speakers of Ṭuroyo left the region, settling in Turkish cities, especially Istanbul, or emigrating, mainly to Germany, Sweden, and the United States.

During the upheavals of the First World War, the Jews of south-eastern Turkey and the adjacent region of north-western Iran underwent considerable hardship and, like the Neo-Aramaic-speaking Christian communities of the region, permanent displacement from their original homes. Some Jews, notably those from the region of Salmas (Salamas) in the far north-western tip of Iran, fled into the Caucasus and settled in Tbilisi (Mutzafi 2015). They suffered further under the regime of Stalin, who moved virtually the entire community in 1950 to Almaty in Kazakhstan, where a large proportion of the Jews speaking the Salmas dialect can be found to this day. Other dialects of Jewish communities who were displaced during the First World War have become extinct, such as those from the region of Gawar. Since the nineteenth century, several Jews of the region immigrated to Palestine for religious motives. This emigration increased after the First World War, in the first half the twentieth century, due to the activities of the Zionist movement. In the early 1950s, after the foundation of the State of Israel, this migration turned into a mass exodus. As a result, the vast majority of surviving NENA-speaking Jews are now resident in Israel. In western Iran, some remained during the time of the Shah but left after the Iranian Revolution in 1979 (Ben-Yaʿqov 1980, 2nd:149; Khan 2009: 1).

Neo-Mandaic speech community

Neo-Mandaic is spoken by the Mandaeans, who follow a religion that is a descendant of a pre-Islamic Gnostic sect. The traditional homeland of the Mandaean community is the south of Iraq and the adjacent Khuzestān province of south-western Iran.

They are known in Iraq and Iran as 'Sabians' (Arabic *ṣābiʾūn*, colloquial *ṣubba*), who are one of the 'peoples of the book' (*ʾahl al-kitāb*) recognised in Islam.

Neo-Mandaic appears to have ceased to be the spoken language of the Mandaeans of Iraq by the beginning of the nineteenth century. There are references to a few speakers in Iraq in the twentieth century, but these seem to be of Iranian origin (Häberl 2009: 36–7). After the first Gulf War in 1991, the Iraqi Mandaean community was displaced from their homes in southern Iraq by the army of Saddam Hussein.

Up until the nineteenth century, Neo-Mandaic was spoken in a variety of localities in the Khuzestān region. The Mandaeans subsequently came to be concentrated in Khorramshahr and Ahvāz, where two distinct varieties of the language survived until modern times. During the Iranian revolution in 1979 and in subsequent conflicts with Iraq, Khorramshahr was largely destroyed and abandoned by its inhabitants, including the Mandaean community. Within Iran, the language seems now to be spoken only in Ahvāz (Mutzafi 2014a: 1–5).

Western Neo-Aramaic speech community

The Western Neo-Aramaic that is now spoken in three villages in the Qalamūn mountain of the Anti-Lebanon range is a vestige of the western branch of Middle Aramaic, which was originally spoken throughout the Levant. There are reports that in the seventeenth century, Neo-Aramaic was still spoken more widely in the area, including in mountain villages in Lebanon. Traces of this have survived in various features of the current Arabic dialects of the area, which must be attributed to a Neo-Aramaic substrate and also in Aramaic place names (Parisot 1898: 244–6).

The Christians of Maʿlula belong to the Greek Orthodox and Greek Catholic churches. The conversion of the inhabitants of the villages of Jubbʿadīn and Baxʿa to Islam seems to have taken place in recent centuries. A few Christian families still lived in Baxʿa at the end of the nineteenth century (Parisot 1898: 256), and a church building remained in the village until modern times (Arnold 1990: 9).

CURRENT STATUS OF THE SPEECH COMMUNITY

Central Neo-Aramaic

The Ṭuroyo-speaking community of the Ṭūr ʿAbdīn region is now considerably depleted. Currently only about 2,500 still live in their original homeland, mainly in the town of Midyat. The dialect of Mlaḥso, which was documented by Jastrow (1994a) is now, apparently, extinct.

NENA speech communities

There are now no NENA-speaking communities in south-eastern Turkey. There are still some Christians living in the Urmi region, almost exclusively now in the town of Urmi rather than the villages. A large proportion of the Christian community, however, has left the region. Some have settled in the large Iranian cities, mainly Tehran. In the nineteenth and early twentieth centuries, many Christian speakers of the dialect of Urmi and other dialects of north-western Iran and the adjacent region moved to the Caucasus. These dialects, especially the Urmi dialect, are still spoken by communities in Georgia and Armenia, and elsewhere in the former Soviet Union (Tsereteli 1970). A large proportion of speakers have now settled in the United States, in particular in California, and Australia.

In recent times, the communities who settled in the Khabur region have been under considerable pressure, in particular during the current military conflict in Syria.

As remarked, now virtually all Jewish NENA-speakers have left their original places of residence and have settled in the State of Israel.

The size of the surviving speech community of individual NENA dialects varies considerably. Some dialects are now reduced to a handful of final speakers. This applies in particular to the Jewish dialects, all of which are highly endangered and will not survive much beyond the next two decades. Several Jewish dialects have recently become extinct, e.g. J. Nerwa in 2012, J. Sandu in 2010, J. Challa in 2007, J. Shahe in 2000, J. Bədyal in 1998 (Mutzafi 2014b). Some dialects of small Christian communities in Iraq are also highly endangered, e.g. C. Bədyal. In general, however, Christian dialects are generally less endangered than Jewish ones. It is not possible to give precise statistics for individual dialects, but some of the larger ones have several thousand speakers, taking into account speakers in migrant communities. Among Christian NENA-speakers from Iraq, a particularly widely spoken dialect is a *koine* that developed in the towns after the merging of various refugee communities after the First World War (Odisho 1988: 19–38).

Neo-Mandaic

There are numerous Mandaeans living in the urban centres of Iraq and in communities that have settled outside of the Middle East, especially in Sweden, Australia, and the United States. The vast majority, however, do not speak neo-Mandaic. The number of competent speakers of the language is rapidly dwindling. Häberl (2009: 8) estimated there to be around 100–200 elderly speakers, most of whom are living in Iran. Neo-Mandaic, therefore, will inevitably become extinct within the next few years.

Western Neo-Aramaic

According to the latest estimate of Arnold (2011), the Western Neo-Aramaic dialects are spoken by a maximum of 15,000 people. In the last few years, however, there have been major upheavals in the villages as a consequence of the war in Syria, which has led to their destruction and the evacuation of their inhabitants. This, inevitably, will have a major impact on the dialects, due to the dispersal of the speakers.

SOCIOLINGUISTIC SITUATION

Central Neo-Aramaic speech communities

In the Ṭūr ʿAbdīn area, speakers of Ṭuroyo often speak also vernacular Arabic (of the town of Mardin or the Mḥallamī bedouin), Kurdish, and Turkish, the latter being the official state and school language. In addition, Classical Syriac is used as a liturgical language and also, by some learned members of the community, as a written language. In Sweden in the 1980s, an official written form of Ṭuroyo in the Roman alphabet was created by Yusuf Ishaq and his collaborators (Ishaq 1990; Heinrichs 1990).

NENA speech communities

In the NENA-speaking area of south-eastern Turkey at the beginning of the twentieth century before the upheavals, there was general bilingualism in Neo-Aramaic and Kurdish. The communities from south-eastern Turkey who settled in the Khabur area of Syria in the 1930s speak Arabic in addition to their native NENA dialects. In north-western Iran, speakers of the NENA dialects had contact with Kurdish and Azeri Turkish. Nowadays most Christian speakers of NENA who still live in the area also speak Azeri, the vernacular of the Muslim population in this area, and also Persian, the official language of Iran, but not Kurdish. There are, however, numerous Kurdish loanwords in the NENA dialects of this area, and their morphology indicates that they form an older historical layer of the lexicon than the many Azeri words. This indicates that there must have been a more widespread knowledge of Kurdish in the NENA communities at an earlier period (Khan 2016, vol. 3: 1–3). Western missionaries who were active among the Christian communities of the area in the middle of the nineteenth century developed a literary form of the Christian Urmi dialect written in Syriac script. This form of literary language became widely used by learned native speakers and is still used to this day (Murre-van den Berg 1999).

In Iraq, the Christians of the Mosul plain region speak Arabic in addition to their local Aramaic dialects. Aramaic-speakers elsewhere are generally fluent in Kurdish, the language of the majority of the surrounding Muslim population, and those who have been through the Iraqi education system know Arabic. In some areas, Aramaic-speakers spoke Turkoman, especially Turkoman converts to Christianity.

The NENA-speakers who live in the Caucasus speak also Russian, Armenian, or Georgian. In Armenia, the Christian NENA-speakers live in villages together with Armenians and there are many intermarriages. Many of the native Armenian-speakers in these villages also speak NENA.

The surviving Jewish speakers of NENA who settled in Israel are fluent in Modern Hebrew, which is now their primary language. The communities who have survived in Almaty now generally prefer to speak in Russian, especially the young generations.

Neo-Mandaic speech community

The Mandaeans in the Iranian province of Khuzestān are trilingual. In addition to neo-Mandaic, they speak the local dialects of Arabic, which constitute the vernacular of much of the Muslim population of the area, and also Persian, which is the official language and language of education. Some of the speakers use an adapted form of the Classical Mandaic script to write down the vernacular language.

Western-Neo-Aramaic speech community

All speakers of Western Neo-Aramaic also speak the local vernacular Arabic with people from outside the villages and are familiar with Modern Standard Arabic, which is the language of education. Arabic has had a major impact on some aspects of the structure of the language, in particular its syntax (Correll 1978). The influence on the lexicon is reflected by many Arabic borrowings, with verbs in many cases retaining the morphology of Arabic derivative stems (Arnold 1990: 53–66).

SELECTED FEATURES OF THE DIALECTS

As can be seen in the foregoing introductory sections, there is considerable diversity across the Neo-Aramaic dialects. Here we shall focus on a few features that reflect this diversity. These include two features of phonology, viz. the reflexes of the *bgdkpt* consonants and the pharyngeal consonants, and the developments in the core structure of the verbal system.

bgdkpt consonants

In earlier Aramaic, the stop consonants *bgdkpt* developed fricative allophones after vowels, which can be represented *[ḇ], *[ḡ], *[ḏ], *[ḵ], *[p̄], *[ṯ]. In the Neo-Aramaic dialects, these fricative allophones became phonemicised, with the result that minimal pairs are found with stops and fricatives, e.g. NENA C. Qaraqosh:[4] *šata* 'year' – *šaθa* 'fever'; *guda* 'wall' – *guða* 'churn'.

Central Neo-Aramaic dialects

Ṭuroyo in the Central Neo-Aramaic subgroup is the most conservative dialect with regard to this feature, since it is the only dialect that has preserved all the original fricative forms of the *bgdkpt* consonants (Jastrow 1985: 6–10), e.g.

táwno	'straw'	< *taḇnā*
ráġlo	'foot'	< *raḡlā*
bóxe	'he weeps'	< **bāxē*
ʾíðo	'hand'	< *ʾīḏā*
káfno	'hunger'	< **kap̄nā*
tlóθo	'three'	< **tlāṯā*

Mlaḥso is less conservative in that the interdental fricatives *ḏ and *ṯ have merged with /s/ and /z/ respectively (Jastrow 1994a):

tevnó	'straw'	< **taḇnā*
reġló	'foot'	< **raḡlā*
ʾizó	'hand'	< *ʾīḏā*
boxé	'he weeps'	< **bāxē*
nofél	'he falls'	< **nāp̄el*
tlosó	'three'	< **tlāṯā*

Mlaḥso differs from Ṭuroyo also in the reflex of fricative *ḇ. In Ṭuroyo this reflex is /w/, which coincides with the reflex of historical **w*. In Mlaḥso the reflex of *ḇ is the labio-dental /v/, which is distinct from the reflex of historical **w*:

Ṭuroyo: *táwno* 'straw' (< **taḇnā*); *gáwzo* 'nut' (< **gawzā*)
Mlaḥso: *tevnó* 'straw' (< **taḇnā*); *gawzó* 'nut' (< **gawzā*)

Central Neo-Aramaic, both Ṭuroyo and Mlaḥso, is distinguished from the adjacent NENA dialects (see below) in the preservation of the fricatives /ġ/ and /f/ in the *bgdkpt* series of consonants, probably due to contact with Arabic, which has these sounds in its phoneme inventory (Jastrow 2015).

NENA dialects

The reflexes of the fricative allophones *ḇ, *p̄, and *ḡ are broadly uniform across the NENA dialects.

The reflex of the fricative allophone *ḇ is generally /*w*/, e.g. C. Barwar:

sawa 'grandfather' < **sāḇā*

The usual reflex of **p* is, as a general rule, the stop /*p*/, irrespective of whether this was realised as a stop or fricative in earlier forms of Aramaic, e.g. C. Barwar:

kepa 'stone' < **kēp̄ā*

In most dialects the fricative allophone of the unvoiced velar **k* has been preserved, e.g. C. Barwar:

baxe 'he weeps' < **bāḵē*

In a few dialects on the north-western periphery of the NENA area, the unvoiced velar fricative has shifted to an unvoiced pharyngeal fricative, e.g. C. Hertevin:

baḥe 'he weeps' < **bāḵē*

A distinctive feature of NENA is its loss of the original fricative allophone of the voiced velar **g*. The voiced velar fricative underwent a historical development, the first stage of which was the shift to a voiced pharyngeal fricative /ʿ/ (Tsereteli 1990). The pharyngeal has survived in some isolated words in a few dialects, generally in the environment of sonorant consonants that at some point became pharyngealised, e.g. J. Amedia

ṛaʿola 'valley' < **rāḡōlā*

In most dialects, the pharyngeal has become weakened to a laryngeal /ʾ/ or to zero, e.g. C. Qaraqosh:

raʾola 'valley' < **rāḡōlā*

C. Barwar:

năra 'axe' < **nārḡā*
rawola 'valley' < **rāḡōlā*

In dialects on the north-eastern periphery of the NENA area where the historical pharyngeal has been weakened to zero, the trace of the pharyngeal remains in the form of a suprasegmental pharyngealisation of the whole word (represented here by ⁺), e.g. C. Urmi:

⁺lina 'jar' < **lḡīnā*

The historically fricative allophones of **d* and **t* exhibit the most diversity of all the *bgdkpt* consonants across the NENA area. These are illustrated here by the reflexes of *ʾīḏā 'hand', *māṯā 'village' and *bayṯā 'house' across a selection of dialects:

C. Barwar	*ʾiða*	*maθa*	*bɛθa*
C. Mne Maθa	*ʾiða*	*maθa*	*bɛša*
J. Zakho	*ʾiza*	*masa*	*besa*
C. Urmi	*ʾida*	*mata*	*beta*
C. Baz (Mahaye)	*ʾida*	*ma*	*beya*
J. Sanandaj	*ʾila*	*mala*	*bela*

The lateral reflex /l/ is a distinctive feature of the Jewish trans-Zab dialects. Most of the reflexes presented above are consistent within each of the dialects. The /š/ reflex of *ṯ in C. Mne Maθa and other Upper Ṭiyare dialects, however, does not occur after low vowels, as in *maθa*.

The dorsal stops *k and *g of the *bgdkpt* series undergo palatalisation in some NENA dialects, in some cases resulting in the affricates /č/ and /j/. The process is most advanced in the varieties of the C Urmi dialect that were spoken on the southern Urmi plain, in which affrication of *k and *g is regular in all contexts. A similar palatalisation of dorsals is found in the Kurdish and Azeri dialects of this area (Khan 2016, vol. 1: 109–12), e.g.

Gulpašan (C. NENA Urmi) *malča* 'king' (< *malkā), *jəšra* 'bridge' (< *gəšra).

Neo-Mandaic

Neo-Mandaic has preserved all of the fricative *bgdkpt* consonants except fricative *ḏ, which has shifted to a stop /d/ (Macuch 1965: 32–40; Häberl 2009: 48–65). The examples below are taken from Häberl's description of the Khorramshahr dialect (the traditional orthography is transcribed in italics and the pronunciation is represented in square brackets):

*ḇ	[v], e.g. *gaḇrā* [ˈgævrɔ] 'man', [w] in the environment of back rounded vowels, e.g. *əḇod* [əˈwod] 'do! (ms.)'
*ḡ	[ɣ], e.g. *palḡā* [ˈpalɣɒ] 'split', *loḡrā* [ˈloɣərɔ] 'leg'
*ḏ	[d], e.g. *idā* [ˈiːdɔ] 'hand'
*ḵ	[χ], e.g. *əḵal* [aˈχɑl] 'he ate'
*p̄	[f], e.g. *nəp̄aq* [nəˈfɑq] 'he went out'
*ṯ	[θ], e.g. *bieṯā* [ˈbiĕθɔ] 'house', *hāṯā* [hɔːθɔ] 'sister'

The shift of the original *ḏ to the stop *d* in Neo-Mandaic seems to be a relatively recent development. A glossary of the spoken language written in Mandaic script in the seventeenth century indicates the existence of the fricative pronunciation of the letter in many native Aramaic words by a diacritcal dot (Borghero 2004: 70–1).

Western Neo-Aramaic

In Western Neo-Aramaic, the fricative reflexes of the *bgdkpt* consonants have been preserved. One of the features that distinguishes Western Neo-Aramaic from other Neo-Aramaic subgroups is the occurrence of the fricative reflexes in word-initial position, e.g.

ṯaʿla	'fox'	< **taʿlā*
xarma	'vineyard'	< **karmā*
ġerma	'bone'	< **garmā*

This can be correlated with a difference in the marking of diacritical points on word-initial *bgdkpt* letters between West and East Syriac manuscripts. In the West, a *rukkāḵā* was marked on an initial *bgdkpt* letter after a word ending in a vowel, whereas in the East Syriac manuscripts a *quššāyā* point was marked in this context (Segal 1989: 487–8).

The original voiced stops **b*, **g*, and **d* were devoiced and the original unvoiced stops **t* and **k* were palatalised. There is a greater degree of palatalisation in the dialects of Baxʿa and Jubbʿadīn than in Maʿlūla. The original stop **p* shifted to /*f*/ and the fricative **ḇ* [v] shifted to the stop /*b*/. The full range of reflexes are represented in the following, with the distinctive reflexes of Baxʿa and Jubbʿadīn indicated in brackets (Arnold 1990: 12–14; Arnold 2008):

Middle Aramaic	Maʿlūla	Example	
**p*	*f*	*affeḵ* 'to bring out'	< **ʾappeq*
**p̄*	*f*	*xēfa* 'stone'	< **kēp̄ā*
**b*	*p*	*xalpa* 'dog'	< **kalbā*
**ḇ*	*b*	*ḏēba* 'wolf'	< **debbā*
**t*	*č* (Baxʿa *ć* [ts])	*berča (berća)* 'daughter'	< **bertā*
**ṯ*	*ṯ*	*ḥōṯa* 'sister'	< **ḥāṯā*
**d*	*t*	*ġelta* 'skin'	< **geldā*
**ḏ*	*ḏ*	*ḏōḏa* 'uncle'	< **dōḏā*
**k*	*k* (Jubbʿadīn *č*)	*ḏokkṯa (ḏoččṯa)* 'place'	< **dokṯā*
**ḵ*	*x*	*bōx* 'he weeps'	< **bāxē*
**g*	*k* (Jubbʿadīn *č*)	*ṯelka (ṯelča)* 'snow'	< **talgā*
**ḡ*	*ġ*	*foġla* 'radish'	< **poḡlā*

The phenomenon of fricativising *bgdkpt* consonants in word-initial position was extended to Arabic words that were borrowed at an early period into the dialects, e.g.

xaffa	< *kafā*	'enough!'
ḏīka	< *dīk*	'cock'

PHARYNGEAL CONSONANTS

Central Neo-Aramaic

The pharyngeal consonants **ḥ* (unvoiced pharyngeal fricative) and *ʿ (voiced pharyngeal fricative) have been preserved in CNA, most likely facilitated by the fact that many Ṭuroyo speakers also speak Arabic (Jastrow 2015):

Ṭuroyo: *ḥamro* 'wine' (< **ḥamrā*), *ʿafro* 'dust' (< **ʿap̄rā*)

NENA

In most NENA dialects, *ḥ has shifted to /x/, e.g.

C Urmi: *xmara* 'donkey' (< **ḥmārā*)

In a small group of NENA dialects in the Bohtan cluster on the western periphery of the region, the reflex of *ḥ is /ḥ/ (Jastrow 1994b; Talay 2008a: 44–5). In such dialects a velar fricative *ḵ has shifted to the pharyngeal /ḥ/, so the pharyngeal reflex of *ḥ may have resulted in the development *ḥ > *x > *ḥ:

Hertevin (C NENA Bohtan): *ḥmara* 'donkey' (< **ḥmārā*)

In all NENA dialects the voiced pharyngeal *ʿ has been weakened to the laryngeal /ʾ/ (occasionally /h/) or to ∅

C. Qaraqosh: *zraʾa* (< **zrāʿā*) 'cultivation', *daʾər* (< **dāʿer*) 'he returns', *bəʾta* (< **bēʿtā*) 'egg', *šaməʾ* (< **šāmeʿ*) 'he hears', *tarʾa* (< *tarʿā*) 'door'
C. Barwar: *zraya*, *dayər̥*, *bita*, *šăme*, *tăra*

Neo-Mandaic

The original Aramaic pharyngeals have been lost in Neo-Mandaic. The normal reflex of *ḥ is /h/ and that of *ʿ is zero.

hamšā	[ˈhæmʃɔ] 'five'	< **ḥamšā*
ālmā	[ˈɒlmɔ] 'world'	< *ʿ*ālmā*
ārbin	[ɔɹˈbin] 'forty'	< *ʾ*arbʿīn*

The speakers of Neo-Mandaic from Khuzestān are today all bilingual in Arabic and their Neo-Mandaic contains loanwords from Arabic containing the Arabic pharyngeal consonants that are not weakened. The loss of the Aramaic pharyngeals therefore must have taken place at an early period, before the speakers came into contact with Arabic.

Western Neo-Aramaic

In Western Neo-Aramaic the original pharyngeals have been preserved, e.g.

ḥōṯa	'sister'	< **ḥāṯā*
ṯarʿa	'door'	< **tarʿā*

VERBAL SYSTEM

In this section, we shall examine briefly how the basic perfective and imperfective forms of earlier Aramaic developed in the various branches of Neo-Aramaic. The starting point of the various developments can be assumed to be the predominant system of verbal forms that is attested in the various literary Middle Aramaic dialects of the first millennium CE. This may be represented as follows

Perfective past	*qṭal*	suffix conjugation
Imperfective realis	*qāṭel*	active participle
Imperfective irrealis	*yiqṭul*	prefix conjugation

NENA and Central Neo-Aramaic

The verbal systems of NENA and Central Neo-Aramaic underwent radical reorganisations of the system of Middle Aramaic due to convergence with the model of Iranian languages (Pennacchietti 1988; Kapeliuk 1996, 2011). The original suffix conjugation (*qṭal*) and prefix conjugation (*yiqṭul*) of Middle Aramaic were replaced by various constructions deriving historically from nominal forms, including participles and verbal adjectives.

	Middle Aramaic	NENA	Central NA
Perfective past	*qṭal*	*qṭil*	*qṭil* *damix*
Imperfective realis	*qāṭel*	*ʾi-qaṭəl* *bəqṭala*	*ko-qoṭəl*
Imperfective irrealis	*yiqṭul*	*qaṭəl*	*qoṭəl*

The form *qṭil* in NENA and Central Neo-Aramaic is derived historically from the passive/resultative participle **qṭīl* of Middle Aramaic. The forms *qaṭəl* (NENA) and *qoṭəl* (Central Neo-Aramaic) are derived from the active participle **qāṭel*. The form *damix* of Central Neo-Aramaic derives from the verbal adjective **dammīx*.

These historically nominal forms now function as the bases of verbal forms. They correspond to the past base and present base of Iranian languages. The distinction between realis and the irrealis of the imperfective forms of most NENA and Central Neo-Aramaic dialects is expressed by further innovations in the form of the imperfective realis. This involves the prefixing of particles (e.g. Ṭuroyo *ko-qoṭəl*, NENA C. Barwar *ʾi-qaṭəl*, NENA C. Urmi *ci-⁺k̭aṭəl*,) or, in the case of many NENA dialects, the replacement of the *qaṭəl* form by a form based on the infinitive (e.g. C. Urmi *⁺bək̭ṭala*).

The historical participles and verbal adjective in NENA and Central Neo-Aramaic are inflected by two sets of suffixes, referred to here as D-suffixes and L-suffixes, which indicate the grammatical relations of verbal arguments in the clause. D-suffixes (i.e. 'direct' suffixes) are historically clitic pronouns agreeing in number, gender, and person with the nominative subject of a clause in the original nominative–accusative alignment system of Aramaic. L-suffixes are historically prepositional phrases consisting of the dative preposition *l-* and a pronominal suffix.

The forms of the suffixes in NENA C. Urmi are as follows:

	D-suffixes	L-suffixes
3ms	-Ø	*-lə*
3fs	*-a*	*-la*

3pl	*-i*	*-lun*
2ms	*-ət*	*-lux*
2fs	*-at*	*-lax*
2pl	*-itun*	*-loxun*
1ms	*-ən*	*-li*
1fs	*-an*	*-li*
1pl	*-ax*	*-lan*

In NENA dialects, the D-suffixes are used to express the pronominal subject of the imperfective form, whereas the L-suffixes express the pronominal object:

C. Urmi

patəx-Ø-lun	'he opens them'
patx-a-lun	'she opens them'
patx-i-lun	'they open them'

In the inflection of the perfective, this is reversed in that the L-suffixes express the pronominal subject and the D-suffixes express the pronominal object:

C. Urmi

ptix-i-lə	'he opened them'
ptix-i-la	'she opened them'
ptix-i-lun	'they opened them'

These are derived historically from passive constructions (*ptix-i-lə* 'they were opened by him'), but now the constructions have active voice. This innovation in the verbal system was induced by convergence with Iranian languages, many of which exhibit parallel types of constructions with a historical passive participle and an agentive subject with oblique case-marking. This results in ergative alignment, whereby intransitive subjects and transitive objects are coded in the same way, and this contrasts with the oblique coding of the transitive subject (Khan 2004a; Khan 2017; Haig 2004).

In most NENA dialects, the L-suffixes are used to express the subject of both transitive and intransitive verbs:

C. Urmi

ptəx-lə	'he opened (transitive)'[5]
dməx-lə	'he slept' (intransitive)

This is likely to be the original configuration in NENA, although Iranian languages have oblique marking of the subject only in the transitive. The NENA configuration developed by partial, not full, convergence with Iranian. This came about by a process of development whereby the original pattern of occurrence of identical subject suffixes on the transitive and intransitive verbs in the suffix conjugation of earlier

Aramaic was continued by replicating it with the placement of L-suffixes on both types of verb (Khan 2017):

Syriac	*graš-t*	*dmex-t*
	pull $_{\text{PST}}$- 2MS	sleep$_{\text{PST}}$-2MS
NENA	*grəš-lux*	*dməx-lux*
	pull $_{\text{PERF}}$-L.2MS	sleep$_{\text{PERF}}$-L.2MS
	'you pulled'	'you slept'

Some NENA dialects, however, use D-suffixes to mark the subject of intransitive verbs. This is likely to have been a later developed resulting from a greater degree of convergence with the alignment of Iranian languages. It seems this originally emerged in forms expressing a stative perfect, which existed alongside perfective verbs. This configuration is found in a few dialects, such J. Urmi:

J. Urmi

grəš-la	'she pulled' (transitive perfective)
$^{+}$*sməx-la*	'she stood' (intransitive perfective)
$^{+}$*smix-a*	'she has stood' (intransitive stative perfect)

In the cluster of Jewish dialects in western Iran, the form with the D-suffixes developed into a perfective and took the place of the intransitive perfective with L-suffixes:

J. Sanandaj

grəš-la	'she pulled' (transitive perfective)
$^{+}$*smix-a*	'she stood' (intransitive perfective)

In some dialects on the north-western periphery of NENA, there is a different type of development of the stative perfect forms with D-suffixes whereby their distribution is extended to express the stative perfect also of transitive verbs, the transitive and intransitive perfective retaining the inflection with L-suffixes. This is found, for example, in some dialects in the Bohtan cluster:

C. Ruma (Fox 2009)

grəš-la	'she pulled' (transitive perfective)
dməx-la	'she slept' (intransitive perfective)
griš-a	'she has pulled' (transitive stative perfect)
dmix-a	'she has slept' (intransitive stative perfect)

In the Central Neo-Aramaic dialects, developments similar to those that are found in NENA J. Sanandaj and C. Ruma are found. In Ṭuroyo, the L-suffixes are restricted to the transitive perfective, whereas intranstive perfectives are inflected with D-suffixes. The intransitives, moreover, have a different base from that of transitive verbs:

Ṭuroyo (Jastrow 1985):

grəš-la	'she pulled' (transitive perfective)
damix-o	'she slept' (intransitive perfective)

The origin of the intransitive perfective base is a verbal adjective corresponding to the Syriac pattern *dammīx* 'asleep'. This reflects the origin of the intransitive form as a stative perfect. The Ṭuroyo configuration of past verbal forms can be assumed, therefore, to have developed from a configuration similar to that of J. Urmi, which ultimately derived from one corresponding to that of C. Urmi. Mlaḥso preserves L-suffixes on both transitive and intransitive past forms and uses D-suffixes on verbal adjectives to express the stative perfect, which is extended to cover both intransitive and transitive, as in the configuration of C. Ruma:

Mlaḥso (Jastrow 1994a)

grəš-la	'she pulled' (transitive perfective)
dməx-la	'she slept' (intransitive perfective)
gariš-a	'she has pulled' (transitive stative perfect)[6]
damix-a	'she has slept' (intransitive stative perfect)

With regard to the system of derivative verbal stems, the Central Neo-Aramaic dialects have preserved a wider range of the inventory of stems than NENA. The verbal systems of Central Neo-Aramaic contain, in addition to forms deriving historically from the simplex *peʿal* stem (exemplified in the forms given above), also stems corresponding to the *paʿʿel*, *ʾap̄ʿel*, *ʾeṯpeʿel*, *ʾeṯpaʿʿal*, and *ʾettap̄ʿal* stems of Syriac. In the NENA dialects, by contrast, the T-stems (*ʾeṯpeʿel*, *ʾeṯpaʿʿal*, and *ʾettap̄ʿal*) have been lost and only the stems deriving from the *peʿal*, *paʿʿel*, and *ʾap̄ʿel* have been preserved. Moreover, several dialects in the eastern sector of the NENA area have lost the *paʿʿel* and have only two stems (Mutzafi 2004c).

Neo-Mandaic

Neo-Mandaic has preserved the suffix conjugation of Middle Aramaic to express the perfective past. The use of the historical active particle is extended to express both the imperfective realis and irrealis. The realis is distinguished from the irrealis by a prefixed indicative particle *qə-*:

	Middle Aramaic	Neo-Mandaic
Perfective past	*qṭal*	*gəṭal*
Imperfective realis	*qāṭel*	*qə-gāṭel*
Imperfective irrealis	*yiqṭul*	*gāṭel*

The perfective and imperfective forms are inflected with suffixes as follows:

	Perfective	Imperfective
3ms	*gəṭal-Ø*	*qə-gāṭel*

3fs	*gəṭl -at*	*qə-ġaṭl-ā*
3pl	*gəṭal-yon*	*qə-ġaṭl-en*
2s	*gəṭal-t*	*qə-ġaṭl-et*
2pl	*gəṭal-ton*	*qə-ġaṭl-etton*
1ms	*gəṭl-it*	*qə-ġaṭel-nā*
1pl	*gəṭal-ni*	*qə-ġaṭl-enni*

Macuch (1965, 1989, 1993) cites distinct suffixes of the perfective for the 2fs, 3fpl, and 2fpl, but these do not occur in the material gathered by Häberl (2009: 180), who gives the paradigm above.

The derivative verbal stems include the historical *pe'al*, *pa''el*, *'ap̄'el* forms as well as the T-stems *'eṯpe'el*, *'eṯpa''al*, and *'ettap̄'al.*

Western Neo-Aramaic

Western Neo-Aramaic has preserved both the suffix conjugation and the prefix conjugation of Middle Aramaic:

	Middle Aramaic	Western Neo-Aramaic
Perfective past	*qṭal*	*iḳṭal*
Imperfective realis	*qāṭel*	*ḳōṭel*
Imperfective irrealis	*yiqṭul*	*yiḳṭul*

The subject inflections of these are shown in the following table. The initial *i-* in the perfective forms with a zero suffix is a prosthetic vowel. The gender and number of the imperfective realis is indicated by suffixes, which are the historical gender and number inflections of the active participle. Unlike other Neo-Aramaic subgroups, however, the inflection for first and second person is expressed by prefixing rather than suffixing pronominal elements (Arnold 1990: 67–78):

Ma'lūla			
Perfective		Imperf. irrealis	Imperf. realis
3ms	*iḳṭal -∅*	*yi-ḳṭul*	*ḳōṭel*
3fs	*ḳaṭl-aṯ*	*či-ḳṭul*	*ḳōṭl-a*
3mpl	*iḳṭal -∅*	*y-ḳuṭl-un*	*ḳōṭl-in*
3fpl	*iḳṭal -∅*	*y-ḳuṭl-an*	*ḳōṭl-an*
2ms	*ḳaṭl-ič*	*či-ḳṭul*	*č- ḳōṭel*
2fs	*ḳaṭl-iš*	*či-ḳṭul*	*č- ḳōṭl-a*
2mpl	*ḳaṭl-ičxun*	*č-ḳuṭl-un*	*č-ḳōṭl-in*
2fpl	*ḳaṭl-ičxen*	*č-ḳuṭl-an*	*č- ḳōṭl-an*
1ms	*ḳaṭl-iṯ*	*ni-ḳṭul*	*n-ḳōṭel*
1fs	*ḳaṭl-iṯ*	*ni-ḳṭul*	*n-ḳōṭl-a*
1mpl	*ḳaṭl-innaḥ*	*ni-ḳṭul*	*n-ḳōṭl-in*
1fpl	*ḳaṭl-innaḥ*	*ni-ḳṭul*	*n-ḳōṭl-an*

The inventory of the derivative verbal stems in Western Neo-Aramaic include the original Aramaic *pe'al*, *pa''el*, *'ap̄'el*, and *'eṯpa''al* stems. This has been supplemented by Arabic stems, including the Arabic stem III (*fāʿal*), VI (*tafāʿal*), VII (*infaʿal*), VIII (*iftaʿal*), and X (*istafʿal*), which are integrated into the inflectional morphology of the verbal system.

RELATIONSHIP OF NEO-ARAMAIC TO EARLIER FORMS OF LITERARY ARAMAIC

The Neo-Aramaic dialects are clearly closely related to the written forms of Aramaic of earlier periods. The Neo-Aramaic subgroups can be correlated broadly with dialectal divisions that are reflected in written Aramaic sources from the Middle Aramaic period. Central Neo-Aramaic, NENA, and Neo-Mandaic are related to the eastern branch of Middle Aramaic, whereas Western Neo-Aramaic is related to the western branch. Neo-Mandaic appears to be the direct descendent of Classical written Mandaic (Macuch 1965: lv; Häberl 2009: 13). The other subgroups of Neo-Aramaic, however, do not have such a direct relationship with any of the attested forms of the literary Middle Aramaic varieties. This applies in particular to NENA. Although the NENA dialects have some affinities to Syriac and Babylonian Aramaic, they have their roots in an ancient vernacular form of Aramaic spoken in the region of northern Mesopotamia that differed from the vernacular underlying the literary languages of Syriac to the west and Jewish Babylonian Aramaic to the south. This is shown by the fact that, although exhibiting numerous innovations, they are more conservative than Syriac and Jewish Babylonian Aramaic in some features (Khan 2007; Fox 2008). Some of the dialects, moreover, have preserved lexical items of apparently Akkadian origin that do not appear in dictionaries of the earlier forms of literary Aramaic (Krotkoff 1985; Khan 2002a: 515; Sabar 2002: 12).

NOTES

1 The term was coined by Hoberman (1988: 557).
2 In this article, Christian dialects are distinguished from Jewish dialects by the abbreviation C. and J. respectively before the name of the location of the dialect.
3 The Jews in the town of Arbel itself spoke Arabic (Jastrow 1990).
4 Unless otherwise indicated, the data in this chapter are taken from the published descriptions of NENA dialects. These include Khan 2002a (C. Qaraqosh), Khan 2008b (C. Barwar), Khan 1999 (J. Arbel), Khan 2004b (J. Sulemaniyya), Coghill 2003 (C. Alqosh), Greenblatt 2011 (J. Amedia), Mutzafi 2004a (J. Koy Sanjak), Mutzafi 2008a (J. Betanure), Napiorkowska 2015 (C. Diyana-Zariwaw). Some material is taken from the data of the NENA database project gathered by G. Khan, E. Coghill, and R. Borghero.
5 In C. Urmi and many other dialects, the vowel /i/ of the perfective base *ptix-* is shortened to /ə/ in a closed syllable.
6 In the corpus of material from Mlaḥsō documented by Jastrow, transitive stative perfect forms are attested only from verbal roots containing weak radicals, but this form can nevertheless be inferred to have existed.

BIBLIOGRAPHY

Arnold, Werner. 1989. *Das Neuwestaramäische*. Vol. 1–5. Semitica Viva 4. Wiesbaden: Harrassowitz.

———. 1990. *Das Neuwestaramäische: V. Grammatik*. Semitica Viva 4/5. Wiesbaden: Harrassowitz.

———. 2008. The Begadkephat in Western Neo-Aramaic. *In*: Geoffrey Khan, ed., *Neo-Aramaic Dialect Studies*. Piscataway, NJ: Gorgias Press, 171–6.

———. 2011. Western Neo-Aramaic. *In*: Stefan Weninger, Geoffrey Khan, Michael Streck, and Janet Watson, ed., *The Semitic Languages: An International Handbook*. Berlin-Boston: de Gruyter Mouton, 685–96.

Avinery, Iddo. 1988. *Ha-Niv Ha-Arami Shel Yehude Zakho: Ṭeḳsṭim Be-Tseruf Targum 'Ivri, Mavo U-Milon*. Kitve Ha-Aḳademyah Ha-Le'umit Ha-Yiśre'elit Le-Mada'im, Ha-Ḥativah Le-Mada'e-Ha-Ruaḥ. Yerushalayim: ha-Aḳademyah ha-le'umit ha-Yiśre'elit le-mada'im.

Ben-Ya'qov, Avraham. 1980. *Qehillot Yehude Kurdistan*. Vol. 2. Jerusalem: Kiryat Sepher.

Borghero, Roberta. 2004. Some Linguistic Features of a Mandaean Manuscript From the Seventeenth Century. *Aram* 16, 61–83.

———. 2005. *The Neo-Aramaic Dialect of Ashitha*. Ph.D. Thesis, Cambridge: University of Cambridge.

———. 2015. The Present Continuous in the Neo-Aramaic Dialect of 'Ankawa and Its Areal and Typological Parallels. *In*: Geoffrey Khan and Lidia Napiorkowska, ed., *Neo-Aramaic and Its Linguistic Context*. Piscataway, NJ: Gorgias Press, 187–206.

Coghill, Eleanor. 2003. *The Neo-Aramaic Dialect of Alqosh*. Ph.D. Thesis, University of Cambridge.

Cohen, Eran. 2012. *The Syntax of Neo-Aramaic: The Jewish Dialect of Zakho*. Piscataway, NJ: Gorgias Press.

Correll, Christoph. 1978. *Untersuchungen zur Syntax der neuwestaramäischen Dialekte des Antilibanon*. Abhandlungen für die Kunde des Morgenlandes 44/4. Mainz: Deutsche Morgenländische Gesellschaft.

Duval, Rubens. 1883. *Les dialectes néo-Araméens de Salamâs: Textes sur L'état actuel de la Perse et contes populaires publiés avec une traduction française*. Paris: F. Vieweg.

Fassberg, Steven. 2010. *The Jewish Neo-Aramaic Dialect of Challa*. Leiden-Boston: Brill.

Fox, Samuel E. 1997. *The Neo-Aramaic Dialect of Jilu*. Semitica Viva 16. Wiesbaden: Harrassowitz.

———. 2008. North-Eastern Neo-Aramaic and the Middle Aramaic Dialects. *In*: Geoffrey Khan, ed., *Neo-Aramaic Dialect Studies*. Piscataway, NJ: Gorgias Press, 1–18.

———. 2009. *The Neo-Aramaic Dialect of Bohtan*. Piscataway, NJ: Gorgias Press.

Garbell, Irene. 1965. *The Jewish Neo-Aramaic Dialect of Persian Azerbaijan; Linguistic Analysis and Folkloristic Texts*. Janua Linguarum. Series Practica 3. London: Mouton.

Greenblatt, Jared R. 2011. *The Jewish Neo-Aramaic Dialect of Amadiya*. Studies in Semitic Languages and Linguistics 61. Leiden: Brill.

Häberl, Charles. 2009. *The Neo-Mandaic Dialect of Khorramshahr*. Semitica Viva 45. Wiesbaden: Harrassowitz.

———. 2011. Neo-Mandaic. *In*: Stefan Weninger, Geoffrey Khan, Michael Streck, and Janet Watson, ed., *The Semitic Languages: An International Handbook*. Berlin-Boston: de Gruyter Mouton, 725–37.

Haig, Geoffrey. 2004. *Alignment in Kurdish: A Diachronic Perspective*. Habilitationsschrift. Kiel: Christian-Albrechts-Universität zu Kiel.

Heinrichs, Wolfhart. 1990. Written Turoyo. *In*: Wolfhart Heinrichs, ed., *Studies in Neo-Aramaic*. Harvard Semitic Studies 36. Atlanta: Scholars Press, 181–8.

———. 2002. Peculiarities of the Verbal System of Senaya Within the Framework of North Eastern Neo-Aramaic (NENA). *In*: Werner Arnold and Hartmut Bobzin, ed., *Sprich doch mit deinen Knechten Aramäisch, wir verstehen es! 60 Beiträge zur Semitistik. Festschrift für Otto Jastrow zum 60. Geburtsag*. Wiesbaden: Harrassowitz, 238–68.

Hoberman, Robert. 1988. The History of the Modern Aramaic Pronouns and Pronominal Suffixes. *JAOS* 108, 557–75.

Hobrack, Sebastian. 2000. *Der Neuaramäische Dialekt von Umra (Dere-Köyü). Laut- und Formenlehre. Texte. Glossar.* MA Thesis, Ünivérsität Erlangen-Nürnberg.

Hopkins, Simon. 1999. The Neo-Aramaic Dialects of Iran. *In*: Shaul Shaked and Amnon Netzer, ed., *Irano-Judaica IV*. Jerusalem: Magnes, 311–27.

Ishaq, Yusuf M. 1990. Turoyo – From Spoken to Written Language. *In*: Wolfhart Heinrichs, ed., *Studies in Neo-Aramaic*. Harvard Semitic Studies 36. Atlanta: Scholars Press, 189–99.

Israeli, Yaffa. 1998. *Ha-Aramit Ha-Ḥadashah Shebe-Fi Yehude Saḳiz (Derom Kurdisṭan).* Ph.D. thesis, Hebrew University of Jerusalem.

Jacobi, Heidi. 1973. *Grammatik des Thumischen Neuaramäisch (Nordostsyrien).* Mainz: Deutsche Morgenländische Gesellschaft.

Jastrow, Otto. 1985. *Laut- und Formenlehre des neuaramäischen Dialekts Von Mīdin im Ṭūr 'Abdīn.* Wiesbaden: Harrassowitz.

———. 1988. *Der Neuaramäische Dialekt von Hertevin (Provinz Siirt).* Semitica Viva 3. Wiesbaden: Harrassowitz.

———. 1990. *Der Arabische Dialekt der Juden von 'Aqra und Arbīl.* Semitica Viva 5. Wiesbaden: Harrassowitz.

———. 1994a. *Der Neuaramäische Dialekt von Mlaḥsô.* Semitica Viva 14. Wiesbaden: Harrassowitz.

———. 1994b. Neuentdeckte Aramäische Dialekte in der Türkei. *In*: C. Wunsch, ed., *XXV. Deutscher Orientalistentag. Vorträge, München, 1991.* Deutsche Morgenländische Gesellschaft: ZDMG Supplement 10. Stuttgart: Franz Steiner Verlag, 69–74.

———. 2011. Ṭuroyo and Mlaḥsô. *In*: Stefan Weninger, Geoffrey Khan, Michael Streck, and Janet Watson, ed., *The Semitic Languages: An International Handbook.* Berlin: de Gruyter Mouton, 697–707.

———. 2015. Language Contact as Reflected in the Consonant System of Ṭuroyo. *In*: Aaron M. Butts, ed., *Semitic Languages in Contact.* Leiden-Boston: Brill, 234–50.

Kapeliuk, Olga. 1996. Is Modern Hebrew the Only 'Indo-Europeanized' Semitic Language? And What About Neo-Aramaic? *Israel Oriental Studies* 16, 59–70.

———. 2011. Language Contact Between Aramaic Dialects and Iranian. *In*: Stefan Weninger, Geoffrey Khan, Michael Streck, and Janet Watson, ed., *The Semitic Languages: An International Handbook.* Berlin-Boston: de Gruyter Mouton, 738–46.

Khan, Geoffrey. 1999. *A Grammar of Neo-Aramaic: The Dialect of the Jews of Arbel.* Boston: Brill.

———. 2002a. *The Neo-Aramaic Dialect of Qaraqosh.* Studies in Semitic Languages and Linguistics 36. Boston: Brill.

———. 2002b. The Neo-Aramaic Dialect of the Jews of Rustaqa. *In*: Werner Arnold and Hartmut Bobzin, ed., *Sprich doch mit deinen Knechten Aramäisch, wir verstehen es! 60 Beiträge zur Semitistik. Festschrift für Otto Jastrow zum 60. Geburtstag.* Wiesbaden: Harrassowitz, 395–410.

———. 2004a. Aramaic and the Impact of Languages in Contact with it through the Ages. *In*: Pedro Bádenas de la Peña et al., ed., *Lenguas en contacto: el Testimonio escrito.* Manuales y Anejos de Emerita 46. Madrid: Consejo Superior de Investigaciones Científicas, 87–108.

———. 2004b. *The Jewish Neo-Aramaic Dialect of Sulemaniyya and Ḥalabja.* Studies in Semitic Languages and Linguistics 44. Leiden: Brill.

———. 2007. The North-Eastern Neo-Aramaic Dialects. *Journal of Semitic Studies* 52 (1), 1–20.

———. 2008a. *The Jewish Neo-Aramaic Dialect of Urmi.* Piscataway, NJ: Gorgias Press.

———. 2008b. *The Neo-Aramaic Dialect of Barwar*. Leiden: Brill.
———. 2009. *The Jewish Neo-Aramaic Dialect of Sanandaj*. Piscataway, NJ: Gorgias Press.
———. 2016. *The Neo-Aramaic Dialect of the Assyrian Christians of Urmi*. 4 vols. Leiden-Boston: Brill.
———. 2017. Ergativity in Neo-Aramaic. *In*: Jessica Coon et al., ed., *Oxford Handbook of Ergativity*. Oxford: Oxford University Press, 873–99.
Kim, Ronald. 2008. The Subgrouping of Modern Aramaic Dialects Reconsidered. *JAOS* 128 (3), 505–31.
Krotkoff, Georg. 1982. *A Neo-Aramaic Dialect of Kurdistan: Texts, Grammar, and Vocabulary*. American Oriental Series 64. New Haven: American Oriental Society.
———. 1985. Studies in Neo-Aramaic Lexicology. *In*: Ann Kort and Scott Morschauer, ed., *Biblical and Related Studies Presented to Samuel Iwry*. Winona Lake: Eisenbrauns, 123–34.
Macuch, Rudolf. 1965. *Handbook of Classical and Modern Mandaic*. Berlin: de Gruyter.
———. 1989. *Neumandäische Chrestomathie: mit grammatischer Skizze, Kommentierter Übersetzung und Glossar*. Porta Linguarum Orientalium, neue Serie, 18. Wiesbaden: Harrassowitz.
———. 1993. *Neumandäische Texte im Dialekt von Ahwāz*. Semitica Viva 12. Wiesbaden: Harrassowitz.
Murre-van den Berg, Heleen L. 1999. *From a Spoken to a Written Language: The Introduction and Development of Literary Urmia Aramaic in the Nineteenth Century*. Leiden: Nederlands Instituut voor het Nabije Oosten.
Mutzafi, Hezy. 2000. The Neo-Aramaic Dialect of Maha Khtaya d-Baz. Phonology, Morphology and Texts. *JSS* 45 (2), 293–322.
———. 2002. Barzani Jewish Neo-Aramaic and its Dialects. *Mediterranean Language Review* 14, 41–70.
———. 2004a. *The Jewish Neo-Aramaic Dialect of Koy Sanjaq (Iraqi Kurdistan)*. Semitica Viva 32. Wiesbaden: Harrassowitz Verlag.
———. 2004b. Two Texts in Barzani Jewish Neo-Aramaic. *Bulletin of the School of Oriental and African Studies* 67 (1), 1–13.
———. 2004c. Features of the Verbal System in the Christian Neo-Aramaic Dialect of Koy Sanjaq and their Areal Parallels. *JAOS* 124 (2), 249–64.
———. 2008a. *The Jewish Neo-Aramaic Dialect of Betanure (Province of Dihok)*. Semitica Viva 43. Wiesbaden: Harrassowitz.
———. 2008b. The Neo-Aramaic Dialect of Sat (Hakkâri, Turkey). *In*: Geoffrey Khan, ed., *Neo-Aramaic Dialect Studies*. Piscataway, NJ: Gorgias Press, 19–38.
———. 2008c. Trans-Zab Jewish Neo-Aramaic. *Bulletin of the School of Oriental and African Studies* 71 (3), 409–31.
———. 2014a. *Comparative Lexical Studies in Neo-Mandaic*. Studies in Semitic Languages and Linguistics 73. Leiden-Boston: Brill.
———. 2014b. Jewish Neo-Aramaic. *In*: *Encyclopedia of Jews in the Islamic World*. Leiden: Brill.
———. 2015. Christian Salamas and Jewish Salmas: Two Separate Types of Neo-Aramaic. *In*: Geoffrey Khan and Lidia Napiorkowska, ed., *Neo-Aramaic and Its Linguistic Context*. Piscataway, NJ: Gorgias Press, 289–304.
Nakano, Aki 'o. 1969. Preliminary Reports on the Zaxo Dialect of Neo- Aramaic. *Journal of Asian and African Studies, Tokyo* 2, 126–42.
———. 1973. *Conversational Texts in Eastern Neo-Aramaic (Gzira Dialect)*. Study of Languages and Cultures of Asia and Africa, A Series, no. 4. Tokyo: Institute for the Study of Languages and Cultures of Asia and Africa.

Napiorkowska, Lidia. 2015. *A Grammar of the Christian Neo-Aramaic Dialect of Diyana-Zariwaw*. Leiden-Boston: Brill.
Odisho, Edward Y. 1988. *The Sound System of Modern Assyrian (Neo-Aramaic)*. Semitica Viva 2. Wiesbaden: Harrassowitz.
Panoussi, Estiphan. 1990. On the Senaya Dialect. *In*: Wolfhart Heinrichs, ed., *Studies in Neo-Aramaic*. Atlanta: Scholars Press, 107–29.
———. 1991. Ein Vorläufiges Verbglossar zum aussterbenden neuaramäischen Senaya-Dialekt. *Rivista Degli Studi Orientali* 65 (3/4), 165–83.
Parisot, Jean. 1898. *Le Dialecte de Malula: Grammaire, vocabulaire et textes*. Journal Asiatique. Reprint. Paris: Imprimerie Nationale.
Pennacchietti, Fabrizio. 1988. Verbo Neo-Aramaico e Verbo Neo-Iranico. *In*: Vincenzo Orioles, ed., *Tipologie della Convergenza Linguistica: Atti del Convegno della Società Italiana di Glottologia, Bergamo, 17–19 Dicembre 1987*. Biblioteca della Società Italiana di Glottologia 12. Pisa: Giardini, 93–110.
Ritter, Helmut. 1990. *Ṭūrōyō: Die Volkssprache der Syrischen Christen des Ṭūr ʿAbdīn. C: Grammatik*. Stuttgart: Franz Steiner.
Sabar, Yona. 2002. *A Jewish Neo-Aramaic Dictionary*. Semitica Viva 28. Wiesbaden: Harrassowitz.
Segal, J. Benzion. 1989. Quššaya and Rukkaḵa: A Historical Introduction. *JSS* 34 (2), 483–91.
Sinha, Jasmin. 2000. *Der Neuostaramäische Dialekt von Bēṣpən (Provinz Mardin, Südosttürkei). Ein Grammatische Darstellung*. Semitica Viva 24. Wiesbaden: Harrassowitz.
Talay, Shabo. 2001. Grammatikalische Anmerkungen und Texte zum neuaramäischen Dialekt von Nerwa (Nordirak). *Mediterranean Language Review* 13, 1–37.
———. 2008a. *Die Neuaramäischen Dialekte der Khabur-Assyrer in Nordostsyrien: Einführung, Phonologie und Morphologie*. Semitica Viva 40. Wiesbaden: Harrassowitz.
———. 2008b. The Neo-Aramaic Dialects of the Tiyari Assyrians in Syria: With Special Consideration of their Phonological Characteristics. *In*: Geoffrey Khan, ed., *Neo-Aramaic Dialect Studies*. Piscataway, NJ: Gorgias Press, 39–63.
Tsereteli, Konstantin. 1970. Die Assyrer in der USSR. *In:* Ruth Stiehl and Hans Erich Stier, ed., *Beiträge zur alten Geschichte und deren Nachleben. Festschrift für Franz Altheim*. Berlin: de Gruyter, 2:375–85.
———. 1990. The Velar Spirant ġ in Modern East Aramaic Dialects. In: Wolfhart P. Heinrichs, ed., *Studies in Neo-Aramaic*. Harvard Semitic Studies 36. Atlanta, Georgia: Scholars Press, 35–42.
Waltisberg, Michael. 2016. *Syntax Des Ṭuroyo*. Semitica Viva 55. Wiesbaden: Harrassowitz.

PART IV

SYRIAC LITERARY, ARTISTIC, AND MATERIAL CULTURE IN LATE ANTIQUITY

CHAPTER SEVENTEEN

THE SYRIAC BIBLE AND ITS INTERPRETATION

Jonathan Loopstra

Much of Syriac literature was shaped by the Bible, and the Bible, in turn, helped shape the ways Syriac-heritage communities viewed themselves, others, and the world around them. Though proud that their Bible was written in a dialect of Aramaic, the language Jesus spoke, Syriac-speaking Christians also understood that their geographic and cultural situation meant that they frequently had a foot in two worlds: the Graeco-Roman world of the West and the Mesopotamian-Persian-Islamic world of the East. The story of the Syriac Bible and its interpretation, therefore, is a story of how this branch of Middle Eastern Christians sought to read the Scriptures faithfully in the midst of constantly shifting political, cultural, and religious landscapes.

THE SYRIAC BIBLE

There is a remarkably wide range of biblical translations in Syriac. Compiled across seven centuries and influenced by shifting translation techniques and methodologies, some translations gained wide acceptance; others did not. Although the Peshiṭta, or 'simple', translation of the Old and New Testaments eventually became the dominant version used in Syriac-speaking Christianity, the rich tapestry of distinct biblical translations remained a memorable part of the Syriac heritage.

The oldest translations of the Bible into Syriac are the books that constitute the Peshiṭta Old Testament, thought to have been translated mostly from the Hebrew between the first to third centuries CE. Some parts of the Bible, such as the Pentateuch and Chronicles, were rendered earlier than others; as a result, the Peshiṭta Old Testament comprises a variety of different translation techniques. One noticeable feature, particularly in earlier books, is the presence of interpretations similar to those found in the Jewish Targumim (Brock 1979). While most scholars agree that the early translators of the Peshiṭta would have required some Jewish background to render the Hebrew correctly (Weitzman 1996), there is little overall consensus regarding the religious identity of many of these translators. The Peshiṭta version of the Old

Testament was widely recognised as the standard version in Syriac even before the break between East and West Syrian Churches in the fifth century. Only by the ninth century, however, can we truly speak of the development of a standardised text of the Peshiṭta Old Testament, a *Textus Receptus*.

The earliest Syriac translation of New Testament scripture is the Diatessaron (or *ewangeliyon da-mḥallṭe*, 'The Mixed Gospel', in Syriac), a harmony of the four Gospels written in the second half of the second century. Later tradition would ascribe authorship of this harmony to Tatian, a native of 'Assyria' who studied with Justin Martyr in Rome, though his name does not occur in our earliest manuscripts (Koltun-Fromm 2008). The Diatessaron is of particular importance because it preserves second-century readings that do not appear in later Greek manuscripts. Regrettably, we do not have full manuscripts of this version in Syriac. Instead, portions of the text survive in quotations by later writers and in an important commentary by the fourth-century writer Ephrem (McCarthy 1993; Petersen 1994). As was true of some books in the Peshiṭta Old Testament, passages in the Diatessaron also bear similarities to Jewish biblical interpretation. In addition, the text has been influenced by ascetic tendencies present in early Syriac Christianity. In Matthew 3:4, for example, the Diatessaron recounts that John the Baptist ate 'milk and honey', instead of the traditional reading, 'locusts and wild honey'. This new menu was doubly significant: it was a vegetarian meal, true to ascetic tastes; and it was also the food of the Promised Land, as mentioned in Deuteronomy 6:3.

Between the third and early fourth centuries, the four separate Gospels were translated into Syriac, a version now known as the 'Old Syriac' (or *ewangeliyon damparrshe*, 'The Separated Gospel'). This earliest-known Syriac translation of the four separate Gospels survives in two manuscripts – Codex Curetonianus (fifth century) (Burkitt 1904) and Codex Sinaiticus (4th–5th c.) (Smith Lewis 1910). Although both of these manuscripts contain only the text of the Gospels, it is likely that this translation originally extended to other New Testament books as well. This 'Old Syriac' was based on Greek manuscripts that differ in many ways from the Greek text underlying the later Peshiṭta New Testament. Curiously, rather than translating the Old Testament citations in these manuscripts directly into Syriac, the translators inserted quotes from the Peshiṭta Old Testament, an indication of the prominence the Peshiṭta had already achieved (Brock 2006: 33).

Elements common to this 'Old Syriac' heritage, perhaps more accurately thought of as the 'Pre-Peshiṭta' (Juckel 2009), were revised, eventually taking the form of the Peshiṭta New Testament. On the whole, this New Testament version preserves readings close to those found in Western Greek manuscripts such as the fifth-century Codex Bezae. By the time of Rabbula Bishop of Edessa (d. 435), the replacement of the Diatessaron and Old Syriac by the Peshiṭta New Testament was a *fait accompli*, though this change may have been encouraged, or even enforced, by local authorities.

Between the sixth and seventh centuries, increasing interest in word-for-word, literal translations from the Greek stimulated the development of newer biblical versions. This movement was motivated in part by the increasing availability of Syriac translations of Greek texts, in part by the perceived need for more literal translations in light of the doctrinal controversies that were dividing the Syriac churches at the time.

One of the first of these re-translations of the Syriac New Testament was commissioned by the West Syrian bishop Philoxenus of Mabbug, hence it is known as the 'Philoxenian' (though, in truth, this version appears to have been translated by the Chorepiscopus Polycarp around the year 508). In his *Commentary on the Prologue on John*, Philoxenus presents an apology for his new translation.

> those who originally translated the Scriptures into Syriac erred in many things – whether intentionally or through ignorance. . . . It was for this reason that we have now taken the trouble to have the holy books of the New Testament interpreted anew from Greek into Syriac.
>
> (Brock 2008: 198)

Although quite an undertaking, no full manuscript of this version is known to exist, and much of this work survives only in later quotations. It appears that the Minor Catholic Epistles were also included – a first in Syriac – and it is also possible that some books of the Old Testament, such as Psalms and Isaiah, were re-translated at this time as well. Though more literal than the Peshiṭta, the Philoxenian version was not as exceedingly literal as the Ḥarqlean that would come a century later.

It is now widely understood that the Philoxenian version served as a basis for the Ḥarqlean recension (Brock 1981), so named because it was completed by Thomas of Ḥarqel in 615/616. Writing from the monastery of the Enaton near Alexandria, Thomas strove to achieve extreme formal equivalence. In other words, he sought to copy every detail of the Greek in a 'mirror-like' Syriac translation; he even went so far as to include Greek variants in the margins. This translation enjoyed wide circulation in West Syrian circles and is found in New Testament manuscripts, 'masoretic' handbooks, and, at times, in lectionaries.

As part of the same translation movement, the West Syrian Paul of Tella completed a Syriac translation of the Septuagint column of Origen's Hexapla between 614 and 617. This translation is known to modern scholars as the Syro-Hexapla, although the Syriac title is appropriately rendered *Shab'in* ('Seventy'). The complete text of this translation no longer exists, though extracts can be found in mainly West Syrian biblical manuscripts and commentaries. Because the Syro-Hexapla incorporated features from Origen's Hexapla, such as critical signs and selections from older Jewish translations of the Greek, surviving fragments are especially valuable for the text-critical study of the Old Testament (Juckel 2011: 395).

About a century later, another highly skilled West Syrian linguist named Jacob of Edessa revised several books of the Old Testament based on manuscripts of the Greek Septuagint and the Peshiṭta. Unfortunately, very little of Jacob's translation survives apart from individual manuscripts of the Pentateuch, 1–2 Kingdoms/1–2 Samuel, Isaiah, Ezekiel, and Daniel. Recent studies of this material have shed new light on Jacob's remarkable linguistic abilities, his methodologies, and his goals in attempting such an innovative translation (Saley 1998; Salvesen 1999). It has been suggested that Jacob aimed not so much to provide a better translation of the Peshiṭta as to provide readers with greater detail about the texts of the Septuagint and Peshiṭta – a 'maximalist approach' (Salvesen 2008: 135). Despite Jacob's expertise, however, his new translation appears never to have gained a wide following for a variety of possible reasons (Haar Romeny 2008: 157–8).

Today, therefore, we know of at least seven versions of the Bible in Syriac, ranging from very dynamic translations to exceedingly literal, 'mirror-like' renditions.

Old Testament	*New Testament*
Peshiṭta (1st–3rd c.)	
Diatessaron (2nd c.)	
	Old Syriac (3rd c.)
	Peshiṭta (4th–5th c.)
Philoxenian (6th c.)	Philoxenian (508)
Syro-Hexapla (616)	Ḥarqlean (616)
Jacob of Edessa (8th c.)	

SYRIAC BIBLICAL INTERPRETATION

Over the centuries, Syriac biblical interpreters have used a wide variety of genres to interpret these translations, including the media of poetic homilies, prose commentaries, liturgical commentaries, and even dramatic 'dialogue poems'. In providing an overview of Syriac biblical interpretation, it is helpful to divide this history into three broad periods: (1) the second–fourth centuries, (2) the fifth–seventh centuries, and (3) the eighth–thirteenth centuries.

The second to fourth centuries

Because translation is, at least to some degree, interpretation, our earliest sources for Syriac biblical interpretation are these translations of the Bible. As previously mentioned, many of our earliest Syriac translations contain themes in common with contemporary Jewish interpretations. For example, in Genesis 4:8, the Syriac Peshiṭta adds an exhortation by Cain to Abel: 'let us go out to the *valley*'. This addition is unique to the Syriac; the Hebrew omits it entirely, and other ancient versions read instead 'let us go into the *field*'. But it is this interpretation, that Cain went downward into the *valley* to kill Abel, which is also found in Jewish Talmudic writings and was used by early Syriac writers to conceive of Paradise as a mountain. In addition, because the books of the Peshiṭta Old Testament were translated over such a long period of time, there are indications that later translators borrowed vocabulary, phraseology, and other themes from books that had been translated earlier (Weitzman 1997: 393–6).

Although some early non-biblical texts such as the *Book of the Laws of the Countries*, the *Didascalia*, the *Odes of Solomon*, and the *Acts of Thomas* contain references to the Syriac Bible, it is only in the fourth century that Syriac biblical interpretation truly takes on a definitive character. Two authors in particular stand out: Aphrahaṭ, writing from within the Sasanian Empire, and Ephrem, writing from the edge of the Roman frontier. Both writers were deeply immersed in the scriptures, and both interpreted the Bible in light of the political, theological, and cultural issues facing their Christian communities.

Between the years 337 and 345, a writer known as 'The Persian Sage' set down a series of twenty-three 'demonstrations', whose primary purpose was to remind his Christian community of the practical basics of the Christian life. Later, post-ninth-century manuscripts will identify the author as Aphrahaṭ ('Farhad' in Persian). These *Demonstrations* incorporate hundreds of biblical quotations and allusions of which, it has been suggested, many were written down from memory (Lehto 2010). A key element of Aphrahaṭ's biblical interpretation was to counter Jewish claims on the Old Testament. Unlike many other early Christian apologists, Aphrahaṭ's Jewish opponents are thought to have been real, not just fictional.

One of Aphrahaṭ's key principles of biblical interpretation is that the New Testament fulfils the Old Testament scriptures and the Gentiles have replaced the Jews as inheritors of the earlier promises of God. Aphrahaṭ cites the Old Testament extensively to this effect, demonstrating a surprisingly sophisticated use of typology. In addition, the *Demonstrations* are important for what they tell us about the development of Christian biblical interpretation outside Roman-controlled territories. Of particular interest is Aphrahaṭ's interpretation of the vision of the ram and the goat in Daniel 8: the ram is the Sassanid emperor Shapur II, and the goat is the Roman Christian emperor who will overturn the ram. Throughout his writings, Aphrahaṭ makes use of two key terms, *raza* ('mystery') and *ṭupsa* ('type'), both of which will be further developed and expounded by his younger contemporary, a poet-theologian by the name of Ephrem.

Raised in Nisibis, Ephrem moved to Edessa in 363 when his hometown became part of the Sassanid realm following emperor Julian's failed war in the East. As with Aphrahaṭ, Ephrem's writings similarly reveal an extensive familiarity with the Bible. Indeed, it has been suggested that one of Ephrem's most enduring characteristics is his 'close adherence to the Bible' (Florovsky 1987). Unlike Aphrahaṭ, however, Ephrem interprets the Bible through a wide variety of literary genres, including exegetical commentaries (*turgama* and *pushaqa*), poetic homilies (*memre*), and teaching songs (*madrashe*).

Although later tradition will suggest that Ephrem wrote commentaries on most books of the Bible, only his commentaries on Genesis and Exodus have been preserved today in Syriac. In addition, part of a commentary on the *Diatessaron* is ascribed to him, although it now appears that this work may have been written in part by Ephrem's disciples (Lange 2005). Other commentaries attributed to Ephrem are preserved only in Armenian, including one on the Acts of the Apostles and the Pauline epistles, although there are questions about the genuineness of these texts. Throughout his prose commentaries, Ephrem is primarily concerned with the 'factual' sense of the biblical text, though what today constitutes 'factual' interpretation often fails to do justice to the ways Ephrem dramatically retells the scriptural narrative (Wickes 2008). Some have compared Ephrem's method in his commentaries with Jewish *midrash* or *haggadah* (Murray 2004: 281–8).

Apart from Ephrem's prose commentaries, over four hundred of his *madrashe* and several *memre* are extant. While Ephrem appears to have held to one 'factual' interpretation of a verse, he also believed that an interpreter whose eye is 'luminous' would be able to discern multiple 'spiritual' interpretations in the same verse (Brock

2012: 27). A key interpretive strategy in Ephrem's poetry is his use of *raze* (pl.) to expound these spiritual meanings in the Bible. Seely Beggiani has suggested that Ephrem uses these *raze* in four ways: as private 'messages', as incomprehensible 'mysteries', as 'signs', or as 'symbol-mysteries' that reflect the realities of the New Testament church in the Old Testament (Beggiani 2014: 31–2). For example, in his *Hymns against Heresies* XXV:3, Ephrem writes,

> In the Torah Moses trod
> the Way of the 'mystic symbols' [*raze*] before that People
> who used to wander every which way.
> But our Lord, in his testaments,
> definitively established the path of Truth
> for the Peoples who came to the Way of Life.
> All the 'mystic symbols' [*raze*] thus travelled
> on that Way which Moses trod
> and were brought to fulfillment in the Way of the Son.
> (Griffith 1997: 20)

This use of symbology and typology to interpret the Bible through the medium of poetry is one unique characteristic of early Syriac Christianity. As Sebastian Brock has suggested, this type of poetic theology, so refined by Ephrem, may well constitute a 'third lung' of biblical interpretation in the ancient church, alongside the Greek and Latin branches of the Christian faith (Brock 2005). Still, although Ephrem's worldview was largely formed in a Semitic and Syriac-speaking environment, it appears that he could not entirely escape the ideologies and exegetical language emerging from Greek-speaking regions to the West (Possekel 1999; Monnickendam 2015).

Another unique form of early Syriac biblical interpretation can be found in a poetic genre known in Syriac as *soghitha* (pl. *soghyatha*), though better known in Western scholarship as 'dialogue poems' (Brock 1987). Following an ancient Mesopotamian tradition, the authors of these dialogue poems sought to interpret scripture by means of precedence disputes between two (or more) characters. Quite often, these creative poems clarify what is left unstated – or understated – in the biblical narrative. One poem, for example, expounds on an imaginative, lively repartee between Joseph and Potiphar's wife in Genesis 39 (Brock 2012: 104); while another, attributed to Ephrem, follows the penitent woman in Luke 7 as she prepares to pour fragrant perfume over the feet of the saviour (Brock 2012: 185). Many of these dialogue poems were chanted antiphonally, and their continued popularity has ensured their presence in the Syriac-speaking churches until today.

The late fourth- or early fifth-century *Book of Steps* (*Liber Graduum*) provides yet another example of how the Bible was interpreted in early Syriac Christianity. This anonymous work consists of a series of thirty discourses (*memre*) on topics of interest to a pre-monastic community of the 'Perfect' (*gmire*) and 'Upright' (*kene*) living within the Sasanian Empire (Kitchen and Parmentier 2004). In his biblical exposition, the author of the *Book of Steps* incorporates a variety of genres, including sermons, treatises, and biblical exegesis.

The fifth to seventh centuries in the East Syrian tradition

Though not as well known as Aphrahaṭ and Ephrem, Syriac writers in the fifth–seventh centuries demonstrate a notable degree of ingenuity in the face of rapidly changing cultural, theological, and political pressures. One significant influence on biblical interpretation throughout this period was the increasing number of Greek writings that were translated into Syriac. Many of these Syriac translations either predate our earliest extant Greek texts or preserve a Greek text that no longer exists (as with many of Severus of Antioch's *Cathedral Homilies*). During this time, the interpretive methods of the Greek schools made more decisive inroads into Syriac-speaking Christianity.

In particular, it was the translation of the works of Theodore of Mopsuestia (d. 428) that had a decisive impact on the direction of East Syrian biblical interpretation throughout this period. A strong advocate of the Antiochene exegetical tradition, Theodore was an outspoken opponent of the allegorism of the Alexandrian school as exemplified in the work of Origin and, later, Cyril. Many of Theodore's works were translated in the so-called School of the Persians at Edessa. Several complete texts of his writings survive in Syriac, such as his *Commentary on the Gospel of John* (Vosté 1940) and his *Catechetical Homilies* (Mingana 1932; also Schwartz 2013). These commentaries, along with excerpts in Syriac of his other works, reveal an interpreter with a strong emphasis on the historical background of the text, often dismissing (or just ignoring) the traditional messianic interpretations of Old Testament passages.

Theodore's works were eventually incorporated into the Eastern, dyophysite branch of Syriac Christianity, but not without controversy. Debates over the two-nature doctrine of the Council of Chalcedon and the death in 457 of the pro-Theodorian bishop Hiba of Nisibis left the School of the Persians vulnerable to the controversies raging in the Eastern Roman Empire. In 498, emperor Zeno closed the school. As a result, a group of teachers and students from Edessa crossed the border into the Sasanian-controlled city of Nisibis and re-established the school there. The later condemnation of Theodore during the so-called Three-Chapter Controversy and the Second Council of Constantinople in 553 only further alienated this East Syrian community.

As head of the school during this period of transition, the poet and exegete Narsai (d. 500) directed the community along a path that would further aggravate the split in East and West Syrian biblical interpretation. Narsai would have been one of the first to study Theodore's works in Edessa, and he became one of Theodore's most effective interpreters in Syriac. Well versed in the Bible, Narsai's genre of choice was the poetic *memra*, to which he effectively applied Theodore's interpretive method. Narsai's biblical interpretation, therefore, represents a mixture between the earlier Syriac tradition and Theodore's Antiochene approach. Following Ephrem, Narsai retains the *raza* and *ṭupsa*, though slightly altered. Following Theodore, he views human history through a pedagogical lens: from creation, through humankind's developing maturity, to the coming of Christ and the fulfilment of history. As does Theodore, Narsai rejects much of the messianic typology in the Old Testament.

Even before this rift between East and West Syrian communities, scribes had begun to develop a system of dots used to help the reader punctuate, read, and interpret the Bible (Kiraz 2015: 108–19). One such mark from this early period was the two-dotted *zawga ʿelaya*, used to indicate that a passage should be taken as a 'yes-or-no' question and not as a rhetorical statement, an important distinction in biblical interpretation (Coakley 2012). Yet sometime in the late sixth century, a teacher of reading (or *maqryana*) in the School of Nisibis named Joseph Huzaya is said to have altered this system to reflect increasingly distinct East Syrian reading traditions. While it is still unclear how much Huzaya is responsible for this change, East Syrian biblical manuscripts from 600 and 615 onwards provide evidence of just such a shift (BL Add. MS 14460 / BL Add. MS 7157). Although these reading dots were dutifully passed down by East Syrian scribes, and entire treatises were written about them, these marks fell out of use centuries later. Through close examination of biblical manuscripts, however, we can still glimpse ways these marks were used in East Syrian biblical interpretation, though their manner of intonation remains unclear. Some of these marks include the *metkashpana*, indicating 'beseeching' (e.g. Matthew 6:9; Luke 11:2); the *mshalana*, designating the 'interrogative' (e.g. Job 6:5); and the *taḥtaya da-tlata*, signifying the vocative – often with a sense of exclamation (e.g. Acts 17:22; John 1:51).

Although East Syrian biblical interpretation was heavily influenced by Theodore of Mopsuestia, who became known as the 'Interpreter', some within this community sought to include a wider range of authorities. Between 572 and 610, the director of the School of Nisibis, Ḥenana of Adiabene, attempted to broaden this interpretive framework (Reinink 2009). For reasons that are still unclear, Ḥenana was condemned by the East Syrian Council of 587; as a result, we have only excerpts from his writings. Yet his efforts, whatever they truly were, resulted in a schism within the School of Nisibis, triggering an exodus of students and teachers to other schools.

East Syrian monastic leaders at this time were coming increasingly under the influence of the writings of Evagrius of Pontus (4th c.) and other writers on the monastic life, and this impacted views of biblical interpretation in monastic circles. In his *Commentary on Abba Isaiah's Asceticon*, Dadishoʿ of Qaṭraya (7th c.) discusses the need for monks to look beyond the 'outward aspects' of biblical interpretation.

> Thus in all the outward aspects of Scripture and the entire natural world there lies hidden a spiritual understanding which teaches us concerning godliness and virtue. . . . It is clear that all these outward actions, which took place by providence in connection with these holy men of old, convey a hint of hidden spiritual actions carried out by solitaries and holy people in the spiritual way of life.
> (Brock 2008: 225)

Dadishoʿ suggests, in fact, that Theodore would approve of this type of 'spiritual' interpretation. Yet, as is so often the case, it is difficult for us to determine whether Theodore would have agreed with Dadishoʿ, given the limited number of the Interpreter's writings on the spiritual life that have been preserved. Elsewhere, Dadishoʿ proposes a three-tier approach to biblical interpretation. In this model, Theodore's approach represents the tier of 'historical' interpretation, while 'homiletic' and 'spiritual' interpretation make up the additional tiers (Van Rompay 2000: 565); in other words, each interpreter – scholar, preacher, or monk – would bring his or her own unique insights to bear on a biblical text.

The fifth to seventh centuries in the West Syrian tradition

Throughout this period, West Syrian interpreters moved along a different, though parallel trajectory. While still anxious to preserve the heritage of Ephrem and other elements of early Syriac Christianity, they were increasingly influenced by methods of biblical interpretation found in the writings of Cyril of Alexandria, Severus of Antioch, John Chrysostom, and the Cappadocians, among others.

A contemporary of Narsai in the School of Edessa, the West Syrian poet Jacob of Sarug (d. 521) rejected the interpretation of Theodore of Mopsuestia to which he was exposed as a student. Instead, Jacob embraced the use of typology and symbology in his preferred genre – the poetic *memra*. Known as the 'Flute of the Holy Spirit' and the 'Harp of the Church', Jacob's overall number of *memre* is said to have been more than 700, although approximately 380 of these are known to exist today. Jacob's biblical interpretation tends to be expansive, including wide-ranging exposition around a single *raza*, before moving on to the next (Coakley 2013: 710–12). Although he was opposed to Theodore's methods of biblical interpretation, there are signs of the Interpreter's influence in Jacob's writings.

Another well-known interpreter, Daniel of Ṣalaḥ (6th c.), is best known for his commentary on the Psalms. In this massive work, which is preserved in its entirety, Daniel makes use of both historical and spiritual interpretation to expound the scriptures, bringing together excerpts from a variety of writers, including Ephrem and Aphrahaṭ. Because the Psalms was the basic teaching book for Syriac Christians, this commentary offers valuable insights into Syriac biblical exegesis as well as the miaphysite worldview in the aftermath of the fifth-century Christological divisions (Taylor 2009).

Jacob of Edessa (d. 708) is a figure of seminal importance for the development of West Syrian biblical interpretation in this period. A linguist comfortable in both Syriac and Greek (with some Hebrew, as well), Jacob undertook a major revision of the Syriac Bible towards the end of his life. His methods of biblical interpretation are expressed in a number of different genres. These works include letters, scholia, and at least two commentaries: one on the *Octateuch* and another on the *Hexaemeron* (Brock 2006: 76). Excerpts from these commentaries have been preserved in later collections of catenae, indicating the popularity of Jacob's writings among West Syrian scribes.

The eighth to thirteenth centuries in the East Syrian tradition

The period between the eighth and thirteenth centuries can best be described as one of consolidation. Authors compiled commentaries on the entire Bible in increasing detail and complexity, culminating in the encyclopaedic work of the West Syrian Bar ʿEbroyo (13th c.) and the East Syrian Isḥaq Shbadnaya (15th c.). Towards the end of this period, commentators would increasingly cross confessional lines, borrowing from authors of the opposing confession with more and more frequency.

As early as the sixth century, East Syrian interpreters began developing a type of commentary based on the question-and-answer format (Haar Romeny 2004), a genre similarly used by Greek-speaking authors such as Theodoret (5th c.) and by the later Arabic-speaking writer Ḥunayn ibn Ishḥaq (9th c.). Regrettably, some of the earliest

East Syrian writings in this genre have been lost, such as the commentary of John of Beth Rabban (6th c.) and that of Michael Badoqa (6th–7th c.) (Clarke 1962: 10–11).

The earliest East Syrian interpreter whose commentary in this format still survives is Theodore bar Koni; his *Book of the Scholion* can be dated to 792/3. How much Bar Koni borrowed from earlier works is yet unclear. Yet the *Book of the Scholion* is more than just an exegetical commentary; it may have also functioned as a handbook to the theology of the Church of the East, a type of *Summa* for a Christian community that was learning how to adjust to life in the emerging ʿAbbasid world (Griffith 1981). In his biblical interpretation, Bar Koni closely follows Theodore of Mopsuestia, an indication that, as a teacher at Kashkar, he must have had first-hand access to many of the Interpreter's writings. Bar Koni follows even some of Theodore's more unconventional conclusions, such as his rejection of the canonical status of the Song of Songs (Scher 1910: 324).

A few decades later, between 823 and 828, Ishoʿ bar Nun, the East Syrian catholicos, composed his own commentary on the entire Bible in this question-and-answer format. As the title, *Select Questions*, indicates, Bar Nun appears to have selected his material from some sort of common exegetical tradition – whether in part oral or written – that was available to the East Syrian community at that time. Bar Nun's way of organising this exegetical material differs substantially from that of Bar Koni, and it is still unclear how far they would have had access to the same background material (Clarke 1962). Although he is familiar with Theodore's writings, Ishoʿ bar Nun often freely diverges from the opinions of the Interpreter.

Another important source for our knowledge of East Syrian biblical interpretation in this period is the anonymous Commentary Diyarbakir 22 (8th c.), which includes selections from Genesis to Exodus 9:32 (Van Rompay 1986). The excerpts in this commentary are based largely on Theodore's corpus, with additional material from other Greek and Syriac exegetes. It is thought that much of this material may be representative of the type of common exegetical collections that Bar Koni, and later Ishoʿdad, would have used in their own compilations.

Ishoʿdad of Merv (9th c.), the bishop of Ḥdatta, is well known for his commentary on the entire Bible (Van den Eynde and Vosté 1950–1981; Gibson 1911–1913). In this work, Ishoʿdad incorporated material from Theodore, but he also apparently tapped into common East Syrian exegetical traditions that were shared by Bar Nun, the anonymous Diyarbakir Commentary, and other East Syrian commentaries. His work is especially valuable because it includes many excerpts from earlier commentators whose works are now lost, such as Ḥenana of Adiabene. Though an East Syriac, Ishoʿdad incorporates quotes from Severus of Antioch and other West Syrian authors. Also, Ishoʿdad does not always agree with the interpretations of Theodore. For example, Ishoʿdad discusses the Song of Songs at length, a book Theodore considered questionable; he even quotes the West Syrian Syro-Hexapla in his exposition of this controversial book.

The type of collection and consolidation we see in East Syrian commentaries from this period is also evident in our only surviving handbook of the so-called East Syrian 'Masora' (fig 17.1) dated to 899 CE (Loopstra 2014–2015), slightly postdating Ishoʿdad. This handbook, apparently meant for students and teachers, chiefly consists of excerpts of 'difficult' sample texts from the Syriac Peshiṭta. According to the compiler, these texts were vocalised, diacritically marked, and provided with reading dots to help the student learn to read the Bible after the manner of the teachers of the School of Nisibis. This 'masoretic' primer is valuable not only for the evidence it provides for how the Bible was read in this period, but also for many of the marginal notes that correspond well with the collected exegetical traditions we find in the work of East Syrian commentators such as Ishoʿdad.

Another type of commentary is based on the liturgical year, and this is well represented by the tenth-century *Gannat Bussāme* (the 'Garden of Delights') (Reinink 1988). The anonymous compiler of this work elaborated on elements of the East Syrian liturgy using material similar to the Diyarbakir Commentary and other early works. The *Gannat Bussāme* is of particular importance to scholars because it preserves excerpts from many works which are now lost, such as the writings of Mar Aba II (ca. 400) and Ṣharbokht bar Msargis (9th c.).

Finally, it is worth noting that vibrant traditions of East Syrian biblical interpretation persisted even during the tumultuous events of the fourteenth and fifteenth centuries. One of the most well known of these later East Syrian interpreters was George Warda, whose popular, biblically based hymns have been preserved. As Martin Tamcke (2008) has recently shown, Warda creatively adapted East Syrian biblical interpretation for his community in light of the Mongol conquests. Similarly, Isḥaq Shbadnaya (d. 1439/40) provided a systematic overview of biblical history within a Christian framework in his celebrated 'Poem of the Divine Economy' (Carlson 2011). As a testament to his extensive learning, Shbadnaya amassed excerpts from a spectrum of Syriac and Greek biblical interpreters in the form of a running commentary on his own poem.

The eighth to thirteenth centuries in the West Syrian tradition

West Syrian biblical interpretation likewise underwent a period of consolidation after the seventh century. Towards the end of this period, West Syrian writers also demonstrate an increasing openness to East Syrian exegesis.

One of the lesser-known commentators from this period is Loʿozar of Beth Qandasa (8th c.?) who is thought to have authored a commentary on the Pauline epistles, partially preserved in BL Add. MS 14683. In this manuscript, Loʿozar is said to have been responsible for the *buḥono d-dogma* ('examination of dogma') in Edessa (fol. 138v), evidently a position of great esteem, though we still know little about this post. Much of Loʿozar's commentary appears to be based on the work of the fourth-century Greek writer John Chrysostom. Both his title and his commentary raise questions about how West Syrian networks of disciples or schools collected and transmitted material related to the interpretation of the Bible.

Also from this period are two valuable catenae manuscripts containing collections of extracts from a number of earlier writers. In one of these manuscripts, Vat. syr. MS 103, a monk named Severus collected extensive excerpts from Jacob of Edessa and Ephrem for the Old Testament and from John Chrysostom for the New Testament (Kruisheer 1998; Haar Romeny 2006). While the original compilation may date to 861, a later scribe expanded this manuscript with additional marginal notes from other Greek and Syriac writers, including a particularly important witness to Jacob of Edessa's *Commentary on the Octateuch*. Another catena manuscript from this period, BL Add. MS 12168, includes a wide selection of extracts primarily by Greek writers, making it an important source for our knowledge of many of these Greek texts in Syriac translation (Wright 2004: 904–8).

A West Syrian author from the north of Tikrit, Moshe bar Kepha (d. 903), is credited with an assortment of writings, including works on liturgy, theology, and biblical interpretation. His works include a *Commentary on the Hexaemeron*, a *Commentary on the Psalms*, and commentaries on Matthew, John, Luke, and Acts. In these works, he shows a willingness to include East Syrian exegesis, which may reflect his close proximity to these communities in northern Iraq and his desire to look beyond confessional divisions. As was true in the West Syrian catenae mentioned above, Bar Kepha includes a large number of excerpts from both Greek and Syriac writers.

West Syrian biblical interpretation in this later period reached a climax in the so-called 'Syriac renaissance' of the eleventh–thirteenth centuries, though much exegesis continued to be characterised by consolidation rather than innovation (Haar Romeny 2010). This period is named after a 'renewal' of learning brought about, in part, from a confluence of Arabic, Syriac, and Greek linguistic, scientific, and cultural ideas centred around Melitene following the Byzantine re-conquest of the mid-tenth century.

One noteworthy development, beginning in the earliest days of this 'renaissance', was the formation of distinctly West Syrian 'masoretic' handbooks. These large manuscripts are different from the earlier East Syrian 'masora' in that most volumes include sample texts from works of particular significance for the West Syrian heritage: including selections from the Peshiṭta, the Ḥarqlean, and from 255 Greek homilies in Syriac translation (Loopstra 2009). A series of tracts towards the end of each volume bring together the grammatical and exegetical opinions of various authorities, ranging from Epiphanius of Salamis to Jacob of Edessa. Many of these handbooks include exegetical notes in the margins attributed to Ephrem, Jacob of Sarug, or others; additional notes detail how to read the biblical text in accordance with the tradition (*mašlmonutho*) of prominent West Syrian scribes. At least a dozen of these larger 'masoretic' readers have been preserved, perhaps a testimony to the high scholastic culture of the Syriac 'renaissance'.

It is also possible to link Dionysius bar Ṣalibi (d. 1171) with this period of revitalisation. Though greatly influenced by Moshe bar Kepha, Dionysius does not shy away from using East Syrian sources in his extensive commentary; in fact, he appears to have relied heavily upon Ishoʿdad's works. One major characteristic of Dionysius's writing is his extensive use of the Syro-Hexapla. He uses the Syro-Hexapla, for example, rather than the Peshiṭta, for his commentary on Qohelet (Strothmann 1988) and also for much of his commentary on Job (Jacobsen 1929). Another characteristic of Dionysius's commentary is his division of biblical books into 'factual' (*suʿrono'it*) and 'spiritual' (*ruḥono'it*) sections. In his 'spiritual' commentary on the book of Job, for example, Dionysius portrays Job as a type (*ṭupsa*) of both Christ and Adam; likewise, Job's wife is a type of Eve, who tempts Job as Eve did Adam.

Lastly, the polymath Gregory Bar ʿEbroyo (d. 1286) represents the height of the West Syrian commentary tradition during the late Syriac renaissance. Among his many writings (Takahashi 2005), his commentary on the entire Bible, the *Storehouse of Mysteries*, is a wide-ranging collection of excerpts taken from earlier biblical exegetes, which brought together insights from a variety of disciplines (including lexicography, phonology, and grammar). In his commentary, Bar ʿEbroyo is especially drawn to differences between East and West Syrian biblical readings, and he

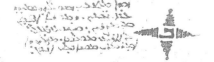

Figure 17.1 Sample texts from Numbers 8:16–11:27 in the West Syrian 'Masora' (BL Add. MS 17162, fol. 10v)

Source: © The British Library Board

is fond of quoting the Armenian and Coptic biblical versions as well. Many of his exegetical comments seem to be drawn from the works of Dionysius bar Ṣalibi, and possibly from Isho'dad of Merv. Though West Syrian biblical interpretation would continue after Bar 'Ebroyo, none would attempt again a commentary on such a massive scale.

EPILOGUE

In this chapter, we have briefly surveyed the development of the Syriac Bible and biblical interpretation over a period of roughly 1,400 years. As we have seen, Syriac-speaking interpreters use a remarkably varied number of genres and literary styles to expound the scriptures. The Bible and its interpretation deeply influenced most aspects of Syriac literature, especially liturgical and mystical treatises. In addition, Syriac exegetes and commentators had a substantial impact on literature in Armenian, Georgian, Ethiopic, and Christian Arabic. Though the period after Isḥaq Shbadnaya and Bar 'Ebroyo saw fewer novel developments, the previous millennium and a half of energetic, often creative, biblical exposition is still a celebrated and essential part of the heritage of the Syriac world.

BIBLIOGRAPHY

Beggiani, S. 2014. *Early Syriac Theology With Special Reference to the Maronite Tradition*, 2nd rev. ed. Washington, DC: The Catholic University of America Press.

Brock, S. 1979. Jewish Traditions in Syriac Sources. *JJS* 30, 212–32.

———. 1981. The Resolution of the Philoxenian/Harclean Problem. *In*: E. J. Epp and G. D. Fee, ed., *New Testament Textual Criticism: Its Significance for Exegesis. Essays in Honour of Bruce M. Metzger*. Oxford: Clarendon Press, 325–43.

———. 1987. Dramatic Dialogue Poems. *In*: H. J. W. Drijvers et al., ed., *IV Symposium Syriacum, 1984: Literary Genres in Syriac Literature (Groningen – Oosterhesselen 10–12 September)*. OCA 229. Rome: Pontificium Institutum Studiorum Orientalium, 135–47.

———. 2005. The Syriac Orient: A Third 'Lung' for the Church? *OCP* 71, 6–20.

———. 2006. *The Bible in the Syriac Tradition*, 2nd rev. ed. Piscataway, NJ: Gorgias Press.

———. 2008. *A Brief Outline of Syriac Literature*, 2nd rev. ed. Moran Etho 9. Kottayam: St. Ephrem Ecumenical Research Institute.

———. 2012. *Treasure-House of Mysteries*. New York: St. Vladimir's Seminary Press.

Brock, S. and L. Van Rompay. 2014. *Catalogue of the Syriac Manuscript and Fragments in the Library of Deir Al-Surian, Wadi al-Natrun (Egypt)*. OLA 227. Leuven: Peeters.

Burkitt, F. C. 1904. *Evangelion da-Mepharreshe: The Curetonian Version of the Four Gospels, With the Readings of the Sinai Palimpsest and the Early Syriac Patristic Evidence*, 2 vols. Cambridge: University Press.

Carlson, T. 2011. A Light From "the Dark Centuries": Isḥaq Shbadnaya's Life and Works. *Hugoye: Journal of Syriac Studies* 14.2, 191–214.

Clarke, E. 1962. *The Selected Questions of Ishō bar Nūn on the Pentateuch*. Leiden: Brill.

Coakley, C. 2012. An Early Syriac Question Mark. *AS* 10, 193–213.

———. 2013. Syriac Exegesis. *In*: J. Paget and J. Schaper, ed., *The New Cambridge History of the Bible. Volume 1: From the Beginnings to 600*. Cambridge: Cambridge University Press, 697–713.

Florovsky, G. 1987. *The Eastern Fathers of the Fourth Century. Volume 7: The Collected Works of Georges Florovsky*. C. Edmunds (tr.). Vaduz: Büchervertriebsanstalt.

Gibson, M.D. 1911–1913. *The Commentaries of Isho'dad of Merv, Bishop of Madatha (c. 850 A.D.) in Syriac and English*, 5 vol. Horae Semiticae 5–7, 10–11. Cambridge: Cambridge University Press.

Griffith, S. 1981. Chapter Ten of the Scholion: Theodore bar Kônî's Apology for Christianity *OCP* 47, 158–88.

———. 1997. *'Faith Adoring the Mystery': Reading the Bible With St. Ephrem the Syrian*. Milwaukee, WI: Marquette University Press.

Haar Romeny, B. ter. 2004. Question-and-Answer Collections in Syriac Literature. *In*: A. Volgers and C. Zamagni, ed., *Erotapokriseis: Early Christian Question-and-Answer Literature in Context*. Leuven: Peeters, 143–63.

———. 2006. Ephrem and Jacob of Edessa in the Commentary of the Monk Severus. *In*: G. Kiraz, ed., *Malphono w-Rabo d-Malphone*. Piscataway, NJ: Gorgias Press, 535–57.

———. 2008. Jacob of Edessa on Genesis: His Quotations of the Peshitta and His Revision of the Text. *In*: B. ter Haar Romeny, ed., *Jacob of Edessa and the Syriac Culture of His Day*. MPIL 18. Leiden: Brill, 145–58.

———. 2010. The Contribution of Biblical Interpretation to the Syriac Renaissance *In*: H. G. B. Teule et al., ed., *The Syriac Renaissance*. Leuven: Peeters, 205–22.

Jacobsen, T. 1929. *The Commentary of Dionysios bar Salibi on the Book of Job*. Unpublished Ph.D. Dissertation, University of Chicago.

Juckel, A. 2009. Research on the Old Syriac Heritage of the PeshiṭtaGospels: A Collation of MS Bibl. Nationale Syr. 30 (Paris). *Hugoye: Journal of Syriac Studies* 12.1, 41–115.

———. 2011. The Ḥarqlean Version. *In*: S. P. Brock et al., ed., *Gorgias Encyclopedic Dictionary of the Syriac Heritage*. Piscataway, NJ: Gorgias Press, 188–91.

Kiraz, G. 2015. *The Syriac Dot: A Short History*. Piscataway, NJ: Gorgias Press.

Kitchen, R. and Parmentier, M. 2004. *The Book of Steps: The Syriac Liber Graduum*. Kalamazoo, MI: Cistercian Publications.

Koltun-Fromm, N. 2008. Re-Imagining Tatian: The Damaging Effects of Polemical Rhetoric. *JECS* 16, 1–30.

Kruisheer, D. 1998. Ephrem, Jacob of Edessa, and the Monk Severus: An Analysis of ms. Vat. Syr. 103, ff. 1–72. *In*: R. Lavenant, ed., *Symposium Syriacum VII: Uppsala University, Department of Asian and African Languages, 11–14 August 1996*. OCA 256. Rome: Pontificio Istituto Orientale, 599–605.

Lange, C. 2005. *The Portrayal of Christ in the Syriac Commentary on the Diatessaron*. CSCO 616. Leuven: Peeters.

Lehto, A. 2010. *The Demonstrations of Aphrahaṭ, the Persian Sage*. Piscataway, NJ: Gorgias Press.

Loopstra, J. 2009. *Patristic Collections in the 'Masoretic' Manuscripts of the Qarqaptha Tradition*. Unpublished Ph.D. Dissertation, 2 vol. Washington, DC: The Catholic University of America.

———. 2014/15. *An East Syrian Manuscript of the Syriac 'Masora' Dated to 899 CE*, 2 vol. Piscataway, NJ: Gorgias Press.

McCarthy, C. 1993. *Saint Ephrem's Commentary on Tatian's Diatessaron: An English Translation of Chester Beatty Syriac MS 709 With Introduction and Notes*. JSS Supplement 2. Oxford: University Press.

Mingana, A. 1932. *Catechetical Homilies*. Woodbrook Studies, Vol. 5. Cambridge: Heffer & Sons.

Monnickendam, Y. 2015. How Greek is Ephrem's Syriac?: Ephrem's *Commentary on Genesis* as a Case Study. *JECS* 23, 213–44.

Murray, R. 2004. *Symbols of Church and Kingdom*, Rev. ed. Piscataway, NJ: Gorgias Press.

Petersen, W.L. 1994. *Tatian's Diatessaron. Its Creation, Dissemination, Significance, and History in Scholarship*. Leiden: Brill.

Possekel, U. 1999. *Evidence of Greek Philosophical Concepts in the Writings of Ephrem the Syrian*. CSCO 580. Leuven: Peeters.

Reinink, G. 1988. *Gannat Bussame. Volume 1: Die Adventssontage*. CSCO 501, 502. Leuven: Peeters.

———. 2009. Tradition and the Formation of the 'Nestorian' Identity in Sixth- to Seventh-Century Iraq. *Church History and Religious Culture* 89.1–3, 217–50.

Saley, R. 1998. *The Samuel Manuscript of Jacob of Edessa: A Study in Its Underlying Textual Traditions*. MPIL 9. Leiden: Brill.

Salvesen, A. 1999. *The Books of Samuel in the Syriac Version of Jacob of Edessa*. MPIL 10. Leiden: Brill.

———. 2008. Jacob of Edessa's Version of 1–2 Samuel: Its Method and Text-Critical Value. *In*: B. ter Haar Romeny, ed., *Jacob of Edessa and the Syriac Culture of His Day*. MPIL 18. Leiden: Brill, 127–44.

Scher, A. 1910. *Theodorus bar Kōnī. Liber Scholiorum*. CSCO 55. Leuven: Peeters.

Schwartz, D. 2013. *Paideia and Cult: Christian Initiation in Theodore of Mopsuestia*. Hellenic Studies 57. Washington, DC: Center for Hellenic Studies, Trustees for Harvard University.

Smith Lewis, A. 1910. *The Old Syriac Gospels or Evangelion da Mepharreshê*. London: Williams and Norgate.

Strothmann, W. 1988. *Kohelet-Kommentar des Dionysius bar Salibi: Auslegung des Septuaginta-Textes*. Göttinger Orientforschungen I. Reihe, Syriaca, 31. Wiesbaden: Otto Harrassowitz.

Takahashi, H. 2005. *Barhebraeus: A Bio-Bibliography*. Piscataway, NJ: Gorgias Press.

Tamcke, M. 2008. How Giwargis Warda Retells Biblical Texts: Some Remarks. *In*: A. Laato and J. van Ruiten, ed, *Rewritten Bible Reconsidered: Proceedings of the Conference in Karkku, Finland August 24–26 2006*. Winona Lake, IN: Eisenbrauns, 249–69.

Taylor, D. 2009. The Psalm Commentary of Daniel of Salah and the Formation of Sixth-Century Syrian Orthodox Identity. *Church History and Religious Culture* 89.1–3, 65–92.

Van den Eynde, C. and J. M. Vosté. 1950–1981. *Išoʿdad de Merv. Commentaire de l'Ancien Testament*. CSCO 156, 179, 230, 304, 329, 434. Leuven: Peeters.

Van Rompay, L. 1986. *Le commentaire sur Genèse – Exode 9,32 du manuscript (olim) Diyarbakir 22*. CSCO 483, 484. Leuven: Peeters.

———. 2000. Development of Biblical Interpretation in the Syrian Churches of the Middle Ages. *In*: M. Sæbø, ed., *Hebrew Bible/Old Testament: The History of Its Interpretation, Volume 1.2: The Middle Ages*. Göttingen: Vandenhoeck & Ruprecht, 559–77.

Vosté, J. 1940. *Theodori Mopsuesteni Commentarius in Evangelium Iohannis Apostoli*. CSCO 115, 116, Syr. 62–63. Louvain: Secrétariat du CorpusSCO.

Weitzman, M. 1996. The Interpretive Character of the Syriac Old Testament. *In*: M. Saebø, ed., *Hebrew Bible/Old Testament: The History of Its Interpretation. Volume 1.1: From the Beginnings to the Middle Ages (Until 1300)*. Göttingen: Vandenhoeck & Ruprecht, 587–611.

——— 1997. Hebrew and Syriac Texts of the Book of Job. *In*: J. Emerton, ed., *International Organization for the Study of the Old Testament Congress Volume, Cambridge 1995*. Vetus Testamentum Supplement 66. Leiden: Brill, 381–99.

Wickes, J. 2008. Ephrem's Interpretation of Genesis. *St. Vladimir's Theological Quarterly* 52.1, 45–65.

Wright, W. 2004. *Catalogue of the Syriac Manuscripts in the British Museum*, vols. 1–2, Rev. ed. Piscataway, NJ: Gorgias Press.

CHAPTER EIGHTEEN

THE EMERGENCE OF SYRIAC LITERATURE TO AD 400

Ute Possekel

INTRODUCTION

Over the course of the first few centuries of the Common Era, a rich and diverse body of Syriac literature emerged, ranging from compelling poetry to scholarly commentaries on the Bible, from lively sermons to profound reflections on theological and philosophical questions, and from imaginative re-tellings of biblical stories to insightful spiritual discourses. In the period under consideration, the Syriac language was employed both in Roman Mesopotamia and in Sasanian Persia, so that from the very outset Syriac literature transcended political and cultural boundaries.

The earliest Christianity in northern Mesopotamia evolved in a religiously and intellectually diverse milieu. The main urban centres, Edessa and Nisibis, were home to important Jewish communities with which Syriac Christians would have close affinities, and to a variety of pagan cults. The latter by no means ceased to exist with the advent of Christianity, for the main pagan altar in Edessa still stood in the fifth century. Graeco-Roman traditions exerted influence over the northern Mesopotamian regions, as did currents originating from Parthia or Armenia. Out of their own native heritage and these diverse influences, the local elites forged idiosyncratic cultural expressions, of which the richly decorated polychrome mosaics – often furnished with inscriptions and depicting intimate family banquets, wild hunting scenes, or mythological motifs such as Orpheus or Phoenix – offer tangible evidence (see Figures 1.1, 1.2, 3.4). The early Syriac Christianity that arose in this multifaceted world was itself not a homogeneous entity but rather consisted of several fiercely competing groups, prominent among whom in the second century were the Marcionites (see Chapter 4).

Among the oldest Syriac literary texts are the *Odes of Solomon*, the *Acts of Thomas*, and the *Book of the Laws of the Countries*, three disparate literary entities that are difficult to date and situate, yet that reveal in different ways, already at this initial stage, some central features of the Syriac literary tradition. The *Odes* exemplify the central role that poetry has always occupied in Syriac literature; the *Acts of Thomas* highlight the preeminent concern with asceticism, monasticism, and Christian life; and the *Book of the Laws* adumbrates the later profound interest in philosophical subjects. And all of them engage with the biblical tradition.

From the mid-third century onwards, Manichaeism began to spread, and it gained numerous converts in northern Mesopotamia. In fact, Mani even dispatched a personal letter to the people of Edessa in which he affirmed the divine origin of his proclamation (Koenen 1988: 42–5). Not surprisingly, this situation of fierce religious competition occasioned polemical discourses and apologetic treatises, though what survives largely represents the view of the victorious group, the 'orthodox'.

In the fourth century, sometimes called the 'Golden Age' of Syriac literature, the most prominent and best-loved of Syriac authors flourished, the poet-theologian Ephrem (d. 373). His timeless hymns are still deeply appreciated today among Syriac Christians, his biblical commentaries were valued and referenced for generations, and his theological and apologetic treatises helped shape the identity of the Syriac-speaking communities. Whereas Ephrem lived in the Roman Empire and self-confidently regarded himself and his church as an integral part of imperial Christianity, further to the east, somewhere in Sasanian Persia, dwelt his older contemporary Aphrahaṭ (d. 345) who dedicated a series of twenty-three discourses to central aspects of Christian faith and life. Aphrahaṭ's prose is, like that of Ephrem, highly artistic, although he composed as it were in a different key. Aphrahaṭ was somewhat further removed from Graeco-Roman thought than were Christians in Roman northern Mesopotamia, and – though he and his community were distinctly Christian – he evidently shared much exegetical lore with his Jewish neighbours. Perhaps also from the Persian realm – though this has been subject to debate – comes an anonymous collection of thirty spiritual essays known as the *Book of Steps*.

The fourth century also saw the persecution of Christians in both the Roman and Persian empires, albeit at different times in each realm, and several martyrdom accounts have come down to us. In the city Edessa, under Roman imperial control in the fourth century, the martyrs Shmuna, Guria, and Habbib died in the Diocletianic persecution. In Sasanian Persia, by contrast, violent persecution of Christians on a larger scale occurred only after the Constantinian peace in the West and took the lives of numerous Christians under Shapur II (r. 325–379), including Simeon bar Ṣabbaʿe (d. ca. 340), bishop of Seleucia-Ctesiphon (see Smith 2016).

As this essay will highlight, early Syriac literature has a number of distinctive features, but this should not be understood to imply that Syriac authors were isolated within their linguistic milieu. On the contrary, they avidly engaged with their surrounding cultures, a process facilitated by the presence of bilingual writers. Syriac texts were rendered into Greek at a surprisingly early stage, and a vibrant translation activity from Greek into Syriac over time produced an impressive array of translated biblical, theological, philosophical, and medical literature. In addition, Syriac authors profoundly interacted with other neighbouring languages and traditions, notably Armenian (see Van Rompay 2011) and, later, Arabic. A complex web of mutual influences can be traced. With this brief overview in place, let us turn in more detail to several of the works mentioned above.

THE ODES OF SOLOMON

The *Odes of Solomon* are a collection of forty-two hymns that, until the astonishing rediscovery of the Syriac original, were known only from a few citations in patristic works. Finding himself with 'a little leisure time' one day in January 1909, the scholar J. R. Harris decided to clean up his files. To his amazement – and that of the scholarly world – his efforts at 'identifying a heap of torn and stained paper leaves written in the Syriac language' resulted in the staggering realisation that this was not, as initially surmised, a copy of the psalter, but rather an entirely different hymnbook: the *Odes of Solomon* (Harris 1909). The *Odes* were soon published, but despite an ongoing robust academic debate, questions of original language, date, and provenance have not been satisfactorily settled even a century later (see Harris and Mingana 1920: 138–75 for an early exposition of the arguments). A Syriac original now appears likely (Charlesworth 1985: 726; Drijvers 1998), although one prominent scholar of the *Odes*, M. Lattke, has consistently argued in favour of a Greek original. The hymns presumably date from the late second century, although other dates have been proposed.

The overwhelming sentiment of the *Odes* is one of exuberant joy, praise, and thanksgiving. The odist exalts the Lord and is grateful for the grace and salvation received.

> My joy is the Lord and my course is towards him.
> This way of mine is beautiful.
>
> (*Ode* 7,2)

Occasionally, however, the odist also reflects on his fear of being persecuted, and he articulates his trust in the Lord in times of trouble (5,4.10–11).

Although the name of Jesus is not mentioned, a Christian authorship or redactorship ought to be supposed, as there are many allusions to both the Hebrew Bible and the New Testament, especially the Gospel of John. The *Odes* hint at central episodes from the life of Jesus, such as the nativity (28,2), the baptism by John (24,1), miracles (39,10), crucifixion, and ultimate victory (28,8–19). These allusions, however, remain vague and alternative interpretations have been put forth (see Lattke 2009 for comprehensive overview). Christian provenance is further indicated by the odist's linking the usual prayer posture, namely standing upright with outstretched arms, to the shape of the cross.

> I stretched out my hands and hallowed my Lord,
> Because the extension of my hands is his sign,
> And my straight posture, the wood that is upright. Hallelujah.
>
> (*Ode* 27)

The hymns affirm that the Lord, the Most High, is the creator (16,10–19) and that 'the world came into existence by his Word' (16,19). The Saviour is also called Son or Christ. 'The Son of the Most High appeared in the perfection of his Father' (41,13). Several poems are interspersed with passages in which the Redeemer speaks in the first person and affirms his own pre-existence (8,13) and divine sonship (36,3). In one segment, he recalls aspects of his earthly existence (28,9–19). The odist repeatedly references the Spirit (construed as feminine as dictated by Syriac grammar), often by echoing biblical phrases. Alluding to Romans 8:26, the odist extols the Spirit as the agent of prayer or, perhaps, hymnic praise.

> I will open my mouth
> and his Spirit will speak in me
> the praise of the Lord and his beauty.
> (*Ode* 16,5; cf. 6,1–2)

Frequent references to being crowned with a 'living crown' (17,1), water metaphors (6,18; 30,1–3), the reception of milk and honey (8,14; 40,1), being robed (11,11), the ritual kiss (28,7), and the transformative and salvific effect of these rites on the individual (17,4) – all of which constitute integral aspects of ancient baptismal liturgies – make it highly likely that these hymns, or at least a large portion thereof, originally were sung in the context of the baptismal ceremony. The *Odes* movingly reflect the experience of being saved and renewed.

In some ancient baptismal rites, and presumably so in the liturgy of the community whence the *Odes* originated, the newly baptised received a cup of milk, and this custom probably informed passages such as the following in which Christ speaks:

> I constructed their limbs
> and prepared my breasts for them,
> so that they might drink my holy milk and be saved by it.
> (*Ode* 8,14)

This usage of milk metaphors in the *Odes* may strike the modern reader as unusual, but it must be remembered that according to ancient medical understanding, milk was blood transformed, so that milk images within a theological context would immediately resonate with Eucharistic practice. While such imagery of being fed by Christ with milk is particularly developed in the *Odes*, similar metaphors occur already in the Pauline epistles (1 Cor 3:2) and were popular among other early Christian writers, including Clement of Alexandria, Irenaeus of Lyons, and Ephrem (Harvey 1993; Penniman 2017).

The *Odes* celebrate the renewal of life, a sharing in the (divine) sonship, and the anticipatory experience of paradise. Echoing both the *Song of Songs* and Pauline theology, the author expresses his love for the Son which, in turn, allows him to participate in the relation of sonship.

> I was united because the lover found the beloved;
> because I will love the Son, I shall become a son.
> (*Ode* 3,7)

> And he lifted his voice towards the Most High
> and offered him the sons that had come to be through him.
> (*Ode* 31,4)

In embracing this new way of life, the believer 'puts on incorruption' (15,8) and already now tastes the sweet delights of paradise (11,16–24).

THE ACTS OF THOMAS

The *Acts of Thomas* relate the missionary journeys and adventures of Thomas the apostle, named Judas Thomas in the narrative, to whom fell the lot of travelling to India and there spreading the Gospel message. Setting sail with a merchant ship, Thomas subsequently takes up the task and successfully preaches a message of conversion and asceticism in distant lands. The name Thomas means 'twin', and the story employs this motif to great effect (Stang 2016). Evidently, Thomas is the 'twin' of Jesus, who appears in Thomas's likeness in support of the missionary effort (*ATh* 11). Cast in the popular genre of an ancient novel, the text engages the reader by vivid descriptions of Thomas's miraculous deeds and persuasive sermons, and by inserting enigmatic hymns and liturgical episodes. The thirteen *Acts* fall into two main parts: whereas *Acts* 1–6 recount several loosely connected adventures, *Acts* 7–13 constitute a more cohesive narrative with recurring characters. The *Acts* conclude with a moving description of Thomas's martyrdom in India and the subsequent translation of his bones 'to the West'. In the event they were taken to Edessa, where by the later fourth century a splendid martyr's shrine attracted pilgrims from near and far (Egeria, *Pilgrimage*, 17.1; 19.2; Ephrem, *Hymns on Nisibis* 42).

The *Acts of Thomas* were composed in Syriac in the early third century and soon circulated in Greek as well. Their textual history is complex, for the great popularity of the narrative resulted in repeated revisions in order to meet the changing theological standards of later generations. Although Syriac is thought to have been the original language, the extant Syriac text is more heavily revised than the Greek version. The existence of translations into Coptic, Armenian, Arabic, Ethiopic, and Latin testifies to the enormous popularity of the Thomas narrative among Christian audiences. Manichaeans also valued the *Acts of Thomas*, in part surely because of the shared interest in asceticism and the theme of the divine twin (Poirier 1998).

The captivating opening scenes of the *Acts* may serve to illustrate several integral features of the narrative and its theological agenda. Thomas's first adventure occurs *en route* to India. Anchoring overnight in a 'royal city' named Andrapolis (or, as in the Syriac text, Sandaruk), Thomas happens upon a wedding banquet. Solitarily sitting apart from the festivities, he nevertheless garners attention when he accurately predicts the dismal end of a servant who had violently slapped him for no good reason. The king then bids Thomas pray for his daughter, about to be married; the apostle consents and in a long discourse calls upon the 'physician of souls' to bless the young couple. Similar prayers are interspersed throughout the *Acts*, and as here they often include creedal statements. After Thomas has departed from the bridal chamber, Jesus – confusingly in the likeness of Thomas – appears to the betrothed couple and urges them to embrace a celibate life, superior to the marriage they were about to enter. Several persuasive arguments are set forth. First, Jesus points out the looming practical problems: children, the nuptial couple are informed, will in all probability only cause them grief, for most 'become unprofitable, possessed by demons, . . . for they become lunatic or . . . paralytic or stupid', and even healthy offspring may afflict their parents by criminal deeds. Jesus-looking-like-Thomas then invites the betrothed to keep their souls pure in anticipation of an 'incorruptible and true marriage' with which they will enter into the bridal chamber of immortality and light; here they will have 'living children' and remain free of care and anxiety (*ATh* 12).

Thus persuaded, the young people profess their conversion. Upon discovering these astonishing developments next morning, the king, father of the bride, wants no part of his daughter's talk of being 'bound in another marriage' and angrily dispatches servants to seize Judas Thomas. But the apostle has already embarked and set sail for his next adventure.

The prominent theme of ascesis, especially chastity, is apparent in this episode and permeates the entire *Acts of Thomas*. But the apostle's preaching of abstinence is rooted not in a disparaging view of the body or a disdain for the material world, as might be surmised, but in the recognition of its contingent and transient nature. Thomas's gospel message continuously highlights the eschatological orientation of the Christian life. While on the one hand this leads the converted to eschew mundane things, especially marriage, on the other hand the *Acts* display a strong and persistent concern for the poor and socially marginalised of *this* world. This is particularly well illustrated in the encounter between Thomas and the Indian king Gundaphoros.

Thomas, a skilled carpenter like his 'divine twin', presents himself to Gundaphoros as a versatile craftsman and is entrusted with constructing a splendid and elaborate royal palace. Yet the generous building funds he regularly receives from the royal treasury he spends on the poor, the widows and orphans, and those who suffer. While Thomas's personal asceticism, his miraculous deeds, and social welfare programme endear him to the locals, Gundaphoros reacts with rage once he becomes cognizant of the scheme. Thomas is cast into prison, but released when the king's brother in a near-death experience discovers that the apostle was indeed constructing a heavenly palace. The king ruefully converts and, after an anointing ceremony, Thomas addresses the populace with a persuasive sermon, interwoven with citations from the Gospels not to worry about the morrow, in which he extols the virtues of a 'right ordering of the body' and invites his audience to believe so that they 'may live and not die' (*ATh* 28–29).

BARDAIṢAN AND THE *BOOK OF THE LAWS OF COUNTRIES*

With the figure of Bardaiṣan, Syriac literature comes into clearer historical light. Bardaiṣan (154–222) belonged to the aristocratic elite of Edessa, at the time the capital city of a small, independent kingdom. Bardaiṣan's intellectual interests ranged broadly from astronomy and science to theology and philosophy. The visiting Roman dignitary Julius Africanus met him in person during his stay at the royal court of king Abgar VIII (177–212) and commented on Bardaiṣan's skilled archery, scientifically minded thinking, and social wit (*Kestoi* I 20). Nothing is known of Bardaiṣan's upbringing and education, except that – as he casually remarks in the *Book of the Laws of Countries* – he once belonged to the 'Chaldeans' (that is, astrologers). But upon his conversion to Christianity he left behind his commitment to astral determinism and took up its confutation. Bardaiṣan is said to have written refutations of Marcionism (a group with a strong presence in Late Antique Edessa); a philosophical treatise 'To Domnus' in which he challenged certain positions of the Platonists; a 'Book of Mysteries', perhaps on the soul; astronomical works; a book on India; and hymns (*madrashe*) that were still wildly popular in the days of Ephrem. But only the

Book of the Laws survives, a dialogue penned by his disciple Philip and in which Bardaiṣan is the main interlocutor.

Although Bardaiṣan was appreciated and admired in his own day, he was not fondly remembered by posterity. His novel ways of reasoning, his speculative approach to theology, his catchy songs – whereas all this endeared him to his contemporaries, it acquired an objectionable taste of heresy among later generations who in consequence opted to destroy rather than to transmit his writings.

The *Book of the Laws* offers fine insight into the thought-world and discursive strategies of one of the earliest Syriac authors. It was much appreciated by Greek readers as well, who could access it in an early translation that circulated under the title 'On Fate' (*Peri heimarmenēs*) of which Eusebius cites substantial portions in his *Praeparatio evangelica*. The *Book of the Laws* purports to record a conversation between Bardaiṣan and several of his students, convening more or less by chance in the private home of one disciple. As was common in philosophical study-circles and other ancient settings (Rapp 2016), they address each other with the familial epithets of 'father', 'son', and 'brother'. And while the opening scene is reminiscent of the first lines of Plato's *Republic*, the master's pedagogy is not at all that of a Socratic teacher: rather, Bardaiṣan gives long discursive speeches in which he lays out his position in response to the students' inquiries and even chides one of the newcomers for surreptitiously inquiring about a subject among his fellow students rather than turning to the teacher:

> If you wish to learn, it is better for you to learn the subject from someone who is older than they. And if you wish to teach, it is not necessary that you should ask them, but you should instruct them to ask whatever they wish. For the teachers are questioned, they do not ask.
>
> (*BLC* 3, ed. Nau: 539)

In the first half of the dialogue, the conversation ranges freely and touches on a variety of subjects such as epistemology, human freedom and fate, and the divine ordering of the universe. In the second half, whence it acquired its name, Bardaiṣan adduces a long list of regional customs and traditions in order to defy the notion that human behaviour is determined by the astral constellation at the time of one's birth. To the contrary, he maintains that the plurality of customs and norms across the globe proves that matters of behaviour are subject to human freedom and not determined by fate. This section of the dialogue reveals Bardaiṣan's deep familiarity with astral science, ethnographic traditions, and forms of religious behaviour typically expected from Jews (see Cohen 2016) and Christians.

Bardaiṣan asserts that the one God is creator of the world and humankind, thus refuting Marcionite notions of a creator god different from the God proclaimed by Jesus in the Gospels. The question of one interlocutor, 'Why did God not make us such that we would not sin and become guilty?' gives the master occasion to articulate his thoughts on human freedom. Bardaiṣan affirms that God did not wish to make humankind entirely subject to laws – in the way that nature is governed by laws – but wanted human beings, created in the *imago Dei*, to be free and able to choose the good. God gave to humankind two laws, Bardaiṣan explains, and proceeds to cite a form of the Golden Rule (cf. Matt. 7:12); these commandments, he encouragingly notes, are easy to keep. No advanced skills, no wealth or great strength are required to do good, help the sick and disabled, or be charitable. He emphasises that acting rightly will inevitably generate feelings of joy and gladness, whereas sinful deeds will arouse sentiments of gloom, anger, and despair. But such an anticipation of the Ignatian 'discernment of spirits' was not unique to Bardaiṣan, as similar ideas were propagated in the Graeco-Roman philosophical schools (Hadot 2002).

Human beings, then, are free in their actions and subject to none. But as experience shows, not all aspects of human life can be thus willed. The laws of nature do govern human bodies, and undesirable, uncontrollable events happen. Sickness, poverty, or disaster seemingly strike at random. It is these last kinds of events that Bardaiṣan attributes to the power of fate. Fate, for him, is the influence of astral bodies over life on earth, that is, the impact of the constellations as they appear at the nativity of each person on this individual's destiny. This, he emphasises, is not to undermine God's sole dominion over everything: the astral bodies, while being subject to some laws, are granted a certain power by God for a time only, but at the end of days their influence will cease. In the 'new world', he trusts, 'the foolish will be persuaded, the needs will be fulfilled, and tranquillity and peace will be by a gift of the Lord of all natures' (*BLC* 46, ed. Nau: 611).

Bardaiṣan developed this tripartite scheme of a balance of power between human freedom, natural law, and fate – all of which are subject to God's superior governance – so as to give a satisfactory response to profound theological and philosophical questions. Comparable efforts were undertaken by a contemporary, the Greek philosopher Alexander of Aphrodisias in his treatise 'On Fate' (cf. Frede 2017; Dihle 1979), though fundamental differences remain between him and the Syrian. In taking a speculative approach to challenging subjects, Bardaiṣan showed himself a keen and bold religious thinker, exhibiting the same confidence with which the apologists, and his younger contemporary Origen, embarked upon the venture to formulate an intellectually satisfactory, *theological* response to the deep questions of human existence and Christian faith – and to answer challenges raised by opponents.

Bardaiṣan's thought overall was less deeply rooted in Scripture that that of other early Christian authors, but operated rather more within the parameters of Greek philosophy. Yet a careful analysis of the cursory biblical references in the *Book of the Laws* and of the allusions to Bardaiṣan's teachings by other authors shows that Bardaiṣan indeed attempted to formulate a Christian theology and that he strove to base his arguments on the Bible, which he evidently interpreted in rather a literal fashion. For instance, Bardaiṣan took at face value the words of Jesus in John 8:51 that promise that none of those who kept his word should experience death, observing that even the disciples had died a bodily death, and concluding that Jesus's promise of immortality must needs relate to the soul alone.

The limited role Bardaiṣan granted to fate, the belief that only the soul will be resurrected, and certain other ideas were no longer palatable to later generations of Christians, and Bardaiṣan's thought was declared heretical. Notwithstanding this negative judgement, he exerted quite a remarkable influence: his clever arguments against Marcionism were tacitly absorbed by Ephrem; his anti-deterministic reasoning was appreciated and adapted by Eusebius of Caesarea, Diodore of Tarsus, and the anonymous author of the Pseudo-Clementines; and his hymns were chanted still in the fourth century – prompting Ephrem to furnish the old tunes with new texts.

These three instances of early Syriac literary activity – the *Odes of Solomon*, the *Acts of Thomas*, and the *Book of the Laws* – vividly illustrate the pluriformity of early Syriac Christianity. Poetic contemplation, ascetic commitment, engagement with the Bible, and philosophical reflection mark these earliest treatises, and would continue to be hallmarks of Syriac literature.

APHRAHAṬ

Aphrahaṭ, the 'Persian Sage', flourished in the Sasanian Empire in the first half of the fourth century and composed twenty-three treatises, commonly known as *Demonstrations* (*taḥwyata*), purportedly in response to a friend's inquiry, that address subjects of religious life, asceticism, and Christian devotion. Their most notable feature is their profoundly biblical character. Curiously, no one knows who Aphrahaṭ was and where exactly he lived, nor whether it was 'Aphrahaṭ' at all who penned these tractates. The Armenian tradition, for example, (erroneously) attributed them to the fourth-century bishop Jacob of Nisibis. Yet happily, the *Demonstrations* can be dated securely from internal references. *Demonstrations* 1–10 were written in AD 336/7, whereas *Demonstrations* 11–22 date from AD 343/4 (*Dem.* 22.25). *Demonstration* 23 was added to the collection in August of 345. That they were meant to constitute a literary unit can be deduced from the fact that the beginning letters of *Demonstrations* 1–22 form an alphabetic acrostic, whereas *Demonstration* 23 begins anew with the letter *alaph*. In terms of content, the *Demonstrations* clearly fall into two groups. *Demonstrations* 1–10 primarily address fundamental themes of Christian devotion, such as faith, love, fasting, prayer, the resurrection, and humility, and they convey exhortations to various constituents of the community, such as the ascetics, the penitents, and the clergy. In the later discourses, the focus shifts towards a range of subjects contentious between Jews and Christians, including circumcision, the Pasch, the Sabbath, and dietary laws. Aphrahaṭ formulates a response to arguments and allegations with which Jews are said to challenge Christians, but which in fact may reflect inner-Christian debates. Much scholarly effort has been expended on determining Aphrahaṭ's precise relation to Judaism, ranging from asserting his dependence upon Jewish literature, to positing that his remarks are based on conversations and contact with actual Jews, to more cautious evaluations highlighting the shared religious and cultural milieu (Koltun-Fromm 2010; Walters 2016).

Aphrahaṭ's thought is steeped in Scripture, and he often intersperses his line of reasoning with long lists of supporting biblical examples. Citations and allusions come from virtually all the books of the Syriac Bible, and he expressly notes that both Testaments are normative (22.26; cf. 18.7). For the New Testament, the Persian Sage relies primarily upon Tatian's *Diatessaron*, but appears to have been familiar with the four canonical Gospels as well (Baarda 1975). Aphrahaṭ locates his exegesis and theology within the ecclesiastical tradition and considers his writings as representative of this tradition; yet at the same time he concedes room to alternative viewpoints.

> If a person reads these discourses and finds words that do not agree with his opinion, he should not scoff at them, because what is written in these chapters is not written according to the thinking of one person or for the persuasion of

> one reader, but it is the thinking of the whole church and it is according to the persuasion of the entire faith.
>
> (*Dem.* 22.26)

This received ecclesiastical tradition to which he alludes would have included particular exegetical patterns, certain ethical imperatives, and the liturgy, for he regularly intersperses his tractates with hymnic passages, prayers, and a creed (1.19, 14.14–15, 23.53–56).

In the first treatise, titled 'On Faith', Aphrahaṭ responds to his friend's petition for instruction and at the outset likens faith to a building, underscoring the vital role of fasting, prayer, love, charity, humility, and celibacy – subjects developed in subsequent *Demonstrations* – in constructing a suitable dwelling-place for Christ. He then explains how Christ can both be the foundation (1 Cor 3:11) and inhabit the dwelling, that is, the devout human person. Disputed exegetical questions of a similar nature recur throughout the corpus, illuminating the profound engagement with Scripture of Aphrahaṭ's community, as well as the frictions and diversity of opinions within it.

Prior to the creation of the world, God conceived (*bṭen*) of Adam within his mind; and once the world was made and adorned, God fashioned (*gbal*) with his hands the human being and breathed his spirit into him: Adam became a temple of God (17.7; cf. 6.14). Yet human sin aggrieved this divine Spirit (18.2) and subsequently it was lost (cf. Bruns 1991, vol. 1: 67–71). But in baptism a person receives the Holy Spirit: 'In the second birth, that of baptism, they receive the Holy Spirit from a particle of the Godhead (*beṣra d-alahuta*)' (6.14). The Christian now is called upon to protect and preserve this gift, and it is in support of this effort that Aphrahaṭ principally writes.

Demonstration 6, 'On the Covenanters', admonishes in particular the so-called Sons and Daughters of the Covenant, that is men and women dedicated to a life of simplicity, celibacy, and service within the larger community. This treatise commences with an exhortation on how to prepare for the eschatological return of the Lord. Aphrahaṭ encourages his audience to purify the heart, visit the sick, become alien to this world, and imitate Christ (6.1). Both the eschatological expectation and the *imitatio Christi* are motivations underlying the life of the ascetic (*iḥidaya*) who single-mindedly follows Christ the only-begotten (*iḥidaya*; John 1:14). By recourse to bridal imagery, the author encourages the Covenanters to adhere to their chosen life in humility and wakefulness.

EPHREM

In the poet-theologian Ephrem (d. 373), the Syriac Christian tradition found what may well be its most creative and subtle exponent, whose writings exerted influence for centuries and are cherished to this day. Ephrem's poetry exemplifies the Syriac tradition at its best: profoundly rooted in the biblical narrative, appreciative of nature and its wonders, engaged in theological debate, and deeply pastoral in intent.

The poet was born around the year 300 in Nisibis, an important bastion of defence on the Roman eastern frontier. He grew up in a Christian family (*Hymns against Heresies* 26.10; *Hymns on Virginity* 37.10) and was tutored by Bishop Jacob of Nisibis, a participant at the Council of Nicaea in 325, who may well have instilled in him appreciation of Nicene trinitarian doctrine. Ephrem was not a monk (as later legend will have it) but more likely belonged to the 'Sons of the Covenant'; he served his church as a deacon. Nisibis in the fourth century suffered from three prolonged sieges by Sasanian forces, dramatic events that Ephrem recalls in haunting detail in his *Hymns on Nisibis*. During the last siege in 350, Shapur II even dammed up the river, intending to crumble the city walls with the force of the amassed water – a scenario that for Ephrem evokes images of Noah and the Ark. The Nisibenes successfully withstood all three sieges, but to their dismay were forced in 363 to abandon their city when it was ceded to Shapur as part of the peace treaty negotiated after Julian's disastrous defeat. These political events, too, Ephrem features in a cycle of *madrashe* (see below) in which he maligns the 'Apostate' emperor and recollects his complex emotions as he suddenly chanced upon Julian's corpse being paraded in the city (*Hymns against Julian* 3.1). The Christian population was forced to emigrate, and Ephrem spent the last decade of his life in Edessa, where he took up his pen to write a commentary on Genesis and to refute Marcionites, Bardaiṣanites, and Manichaeans.

Ephrem's literary output consists of both poetry and prose. His preferred mode of expression were the *madrashe* ('hymns' or 'teaching songs'), and his fame rightly rests principally upon these. *Madrashe* are stanzaic poems in which each strophe follows an identical metrical pattern based on syllable count, and a refrain is chanted after each stanza. The patterns of his many *madrashe* vary greatly and can be quite complex. The ancient manuscripts identify for each teaching-song the name of its tune, but regrettably the melodies themselves are not preserved.

The *madrashe* come down to us in thematic collections, some of which may go back to Ephrem himself or to his early disciples. Several of these hymn cycles focus on particular liturgical feasts, such as the Nativity, Epiphany,[1] Crucifixion, and Resurrection, whereas others develop theological and pastoral themes (*On Paradise*, *On Virginity*, *On the Church*); still others concentrate on historical topics (*On Nisibis* Part I, *Against Julian*) or aim at refuting theological opponents of various sorts (*Against Heresies*, *Hymns on Faith*). These *madrashe* captivate the reader by their astonishing poetic quality, their acute theological insight, and their vivid and often surprising imagery. Yet notwithstanding their lyrical nature, Ephrem's *madrashe* pursue a profoundly intellectual project, and the occasional stab against those who unduly inquire into things divine is to be understood not as an indication of an anti-intellectual attitude but rather as a critique of the excessive ratiocination of which he accuses the so-called 'Neo-Arian' party of the later fourth century.

Ephrem approaches theological topics in language that primarily relies upon symbol, type, and paradox, qualities that convey to his poetry a nuanced texture of meaning and an emotive immediacy. Even in translation these features remain, as already the fifth-century historian Sozomen observed (*Eccl. hist.* III 16). At the basis of this theological method stands the conviction that humankind is ontologically separated from God, as it were by a deep abyss, and that only by God's self-revelation can this chasm be bridged. God, as the poet puts it, 'clothed himself in names'. Such names can come in the form of the anthropomorphisms of the Hebrew Bible; that is, passing names that do not really convey information about God's true nature. Other names, by contrast, Ephrem regards as 'true names', such as the epithets Merciful one, Just one, Father, Son, or Spirit, which reveal certain aspects of God's essence. A surprisingly imaginative illustration for the divine accommodation to human weakness meets the reader in the *Hymns on Faith*, where the poet compares the divine self-revelation to how one would train a parrot to speak by hiding behind a mirror so that the bird only sees its own image.

> This bird is a fellow creature with the man,
> but although this relationship exists, the man beguiles and teaches
> the parrot something alien to itself by means of itself;
> in this way he speaks with it.
> The Divine Being that in all things is exalted above all things
> in his love bent down from on high and acquired from us our own habits:
> he labored by every means so as to turn all to himself.
> (*Hymns on Faith* 31.7, tr. Brock 1992: 62)

The tool of paradoxical language serves Ephrem especially well in the *Nativity Hymns* to circumscribe the mystery of the incarnation. Christ is the ruler of all and without limit even when he finds himself constricted in Mary's womb. The *Nativity Hymns*, like other *madrashe*, occasionally include direct speech by biblical characters. Mary and Joseph, for instance, sing lullabies to their new-born son, and the mother chants in wonderment, 'How shall I open the fount of milk to you, the Fount?' (*Nat* 5.24, tr. McVey).

Ephrem's *memre* are metrical compositions consisting of couplets of seven-plus-seven syllables that, unlike the *madrashe*, were not meant to be sung. Best known are his *Memre on Faith* (also titled *Sermons on Faith*) that most likely date from his Nisibene period and that may have originated in a teaching context. Ephrem here contemplates God's transcendence and self-revelation towards humankind, the relation between Father and Son, God as creator, and the limits of human ability to know God. He also extols the value of learning:

> Although learning is older
> than teachers and students,
> it becomes companion of the youth,
> so that it also may become all for all.
> It is teacher with the masters
> and student with the disciples,
> that is, it teaches and learns,
> for it is striving on both sides.
> (*Memre on Faith* 5,1–8, ed. Beck)

These *memre* have a distinct polemical edge, and although Ephrem rarely employs the names of his opponents, these treatises clearly target the theology of fourth-century Arians and Neo-Arians in ways quite comparable to refutations by the Cappadocian fathers (see Russell 1994). The *Memre on Nicomedia*, extant only in an Armenian version, reflect on God's justice and mercy in light of the destructive earthquake that ruined that city in 358. Besides these *memre*, a substantial corpus of further Syriac metrical homilies survives under Ephrem's name, much of which, however, is not genuine.

Ephrem expressed himself in prose as well. Like his hymns, the prose writings frequently employ paradox, parallel, and symbol. Some treatises are characterised by a particularly high lyrical quality and artfully crafted language and are hence singled out as 'artistic prose' (*Kunstprosa*). In the *Letter to Publius*, attributed to Ephrem in the manuscripts, the author compares the Gospel to a mirror that reflects each person's moral state and calls for improvement. The theme of judgement and penance developed here is one that features prominently in the later Syriac and Greek Ps.-Ephremic writings.

Certainly authentic is the *Sermon on Our Lord*, a treatise replete with genuinely Ephremic images and ideas that unfolds in highly lyrical fashion the mystery of the incarnation and the drama of salvation history. Hymnic elements in praise of the incarnation abound: 'Glory to you who clothed yourself with the body of mortal Adam, and made it a fountain of life for all mortals!' (*Sermon on Our Lord* 9.1, tr. Amar: 284). The first part of the discourse highlights the salvific effect for humankind of Christ's birth, death, and resurrection. The one 'begotten of Divinity underwent a second birth in order to bring us to birth again' (*Sermon* 2.2; tr. Amar: 276). Christ's death and descent into Sheol tricked the deceiver and brought life to humankind. 'Since death was unable to devour him without a body, or Sheol swallow him without flesh, he came to a virgin to provide himself with a means to Sheol' (*Sermon* 3.2, tr. Amar: 278). Ephrem calls Christ by a wide variety of titles, some drawn from Scripture but others flowing freely from his poetic imagination (see Murray 2004). Particularly noteworthy are healing metaphors, for Christ is both 'medicine of life' and 'physician'. Here, the poet emphasises these titles as he interprets with theological insight and nuanced feeling the pericope of the woman who anoints Jesus in the house of Simon the Pharisee (Luke 7:36–50). The woman's tears, he observes, are the remedy that procures her healing. 'This is the physician who heals a person with the medicine that that person brings to him!' (*Sermon* 44.1, tr. Amar: 319).

Lastly, Ephrem's prose works include biblical commentaries and a collection of treatises known as the *Prose Refutations*. Of his biblical commentaries, those on Genesis, Exodus, and the Diatessaron survive in Syriac; in Armenian translation we have commentaries on Acts and the Pauline epistles. The lengthy *Commentary on Genesis* often merely paraphrases the biblical narrative, but at other times dwells on central episodes of the Genesis account, such as the creation, fall, flood, Abraham and Sarah, Jacob, or the Joseph cycle. The commentary largely avoids allegory and generally does not, as do the *Hymns on Paradise*, offer a typological reading of the text, although occasionally Ephrem includes a spiritual interpretation (*ruḥana'it*) alongside the passage's literal or factual sense (*su'rana'it*) (*CGen* 43.1, ed. Tonneau: 118). It has repeatedly been observed that Ephrem's exegesis, and in particular his *Commentary on Genesis*, displays extensive intertextuality with Jewish modes of biblical interpretation (Kronholm 1978; Hidal 1974; Kremer 2012), and while it is difficult to document literary dependency in one direction or another, these shared exegetical motifs reveal that Ephrem and Jewish exegetes flourished within the same intellectual and religious milieu and shared much religious lore.

The *Commentary on the Diatessaron*, the final redaction of which was undertaken not by Ephrem himself but rather by one of his students, constitutes one of our principal sources for this no longer extant Syriac Gospel harmony. Whereas Ephrem knew and used the four canonical Gospels alongside the harmony, the Syriac Diatessaron enjoyed great popularity and liturgical usage – hence inviting commentary – until Bishop Rabbula of Edessa in the early fifth century undertook a concerted effort to collect and destroy hundreds of copies of what he considered an inferior gospel book. The *Commentary* commences with a long reflection on the incarnation, occasioned by the first verses of John with which the Diatessaron began. At times, this commentary appears as little more than notes, but in other sections the author offers nuanced and elaborate exegetical remarks, such as on the episode of the woman with a haemorrhage whom Jesus healed (*CDiat* 7; cf. Luke 8).

The title *Prose Refutations* summarily refers to a collection of Ephrem's treatises that target theological opinions attributed – albeit sometimes erroneously – to Marcion, Mani, and Bardaiṣan. These essays reflect on the one hand the very real diversity within fourth-century Syriac Christianity, and on the other hand Ephrem's ongoing effort to impose theological normativity upon his community. He here employs a variety of rhetorical and argumentative strategies and uses concepts originating from Greek philosophy to undermine, for instance, Bardaiṣan's theory of primordial elements or Marcion's understanding of God.

Ephrem's literary fame soon reached beyond the Syriac-speaking regions, and some of his works were rendered into Greek. Yet surprisingly, whereas little of this genuine Ephraem Graecus survives, an enormous (and as of yet little-studied) corpus of Pseudo-Ephremic treatises (*CPG* 3905–4165) has come down to us that for the most part will have originated in Byzantine monastic circles (Hemmerdinger-Iliadou 1961). Ephrem's writings also filtered down into Latin Christendom where his poetic imagination came to take on new life, for instance, in the mediaeval mystery plays (Schmidt 1973).

CONCLUSION

After the year 400, the trajectories perceptible in the earlier centuries persisted. Poetry continued to be a favoured genre, as exemplified by the fifth-century authors Balai and Cyrillona (Griffin 2016). Philosophy remained a subject of great interest, and from the sixth century onwards Syriac authors would dedicate themselves to rendering Aristotle's works into Syriac (chapter 25). The spiritual treatises by John the Solitary of Apamea (early fifth century) signal the ongoing vitality of ascetic and spiritual literature, as does the *Book of Steps* that exhorts its readers to an upright and virtuous life (chapter 21). Biblical exegesis, whether in sermons, commentaries, or dogmatic treatises, remained a prime concern of Syriac authors (chapter 17).

Yet at the same time new impulses arose, different themes emerged, and novel challenges elicited a theological response. In particular, the Christological controversies began to cause a deep rift within the Syriac-speaking churches – developments for which the fierce disputes in Edessa between the uncompromising Rabbula (d. 435) and the flamboyant Ibas constitute but one example – and called for a nuanced response. In a more positive vein, homiletic literature flourished, as did hagiography that commemorated the Edessan martyrs (ca. 306), the Sinai-bound ascetic Julian Saba (d. 377), the nun Febronia, and numerous others. Education became more formalised, and engagement with Greek patristic literature considerably deepened. A vast movement of translating Greek theology and philosophy began to take shape, for which the earliest tangible evidence comes from a manuscript copied in AD 411 (in fact, the oldest extant dated Syriac manuscript) that contains Syriac translations of the Pseudo-Clementines, Eusebius's *Theophany* (lost in Greek), and Titus of Bostra's *Against the Manichaeans*. And the creative genius of the Syriac poetic spirit, drawing upon ancient Sumerian literary precedents as well as Scripture, forged the novel and hugely popular genre of dialogue poem, imaginary conversations in which biblical characters such as Abraham and Sarah, Cain and Abel, or the Angel and Mary engage in thoughtful and humorous dispute.

Syriac literature of the first few centuries of the Common Era thus exhibits a remarkable depth and breadth, giving it a rightful claim to be considered among the principal expressions of early Christianity. Syriac authors shaped an idiosyncratic Christian tradition in which imaginative poetry and ascetic exhortation, philosophical reflection, and biblical interpretation constitute the key features of the literary corpus.

NOTE

1 Not all the *Hymns on Epiphany* can claim genuine Ephremic authorship.

BIBLIOGRAPHY

General Literature

Baumstark, A. 1922. *Geschichte der syrischen Literatur mit Ausschluß der christlich-palästinensischen Texte*. Bonn: A. Marcus und E. Weber.

Brock, S. P. 1997. *A Brief Outline of Syriac Literature*. Moran Etho 9. Baker Hill, Kottayam, India: SEERI.

Brock, S. P., A. M. Butts, G. A. Kiraz, and L. Van Rompay, ed. 2011. *The Gorgias Encyclopedic Dictionary of the Syriac Heritage*. Piscataway, NJ: Gorgias Press.

Primary Sources

Aphrahaṭ. *Demonstrations* 2010. Ed. and trans. A. Lehto. *The Demonstrations of Aphrahat, the Persian Sage*. Piscataway, NJ: Gorgias Press.

Bardaiṣan 1907. Ed. F. Nau. *Bardesanes: Liber Legum Regionum*, Patrologia Syriaca 1.2. Paris: Didot.

Bardaiṣan 1965. Ed. and trans. H. J. W. Drijvers. *The Book of the Laws of Countries: Dialogue on Fate of Bardaiṣan of Edessa*. Semitic Texts with Translations 3. Assen: Van Gorcum.

Book of Steps 2004. Trans. R. A. Kitchen and M. F. G. Parmentier. CSS 196. Kalamazoo: Cistercian.

Cyrillona 2016. Ed. and trans. C. W. Griffin. *The Works of Cyrillona*. Piscataway, NJ: Gorgias Press.

Doctrina Addai 1981. Ed. and trans. G. Howard. *The Teaching of Addai*. Ann Arbor: Scholars Press.

Egeria. *Pilgrimage* 1970. Trans. G. E. Gingras. *Egeria: Diary of a Pilgrimage*. ACW 38. New York: Newman Press.

Ephrem. *Commentary on the Diatessaron* 1963. Ed. L. Leloir. *Saint Éphrem: Commentaire de l'Évangile concordant: texte syriaque (Manuscrit Chester Beatty 709)*. Chester Beatty Monographs 8. Dublin: Hodges Figgis.

Ephrem. *Commentary on the Diatessaron* 1993. Trans. C. McCarthy. *Saint Ephrem's Commentary on Tatian's Diatessaron: An English Translation of Chester Beatty Syriac MS 709*. Journal of Semitic Studies Supplement 2. Oxford: University Press.
Ephrem. *Commentary on the Diatessaron* 1990. Ed. L. Leloir. *Saint Éphrem: Commentaire de l'Évangile Concordant: texte syriaque (Manuscript Chester Beatty 709). Folios additionnels*. Chester Beatty Monographs 8. Louvain: Peeters, 1990.
Ephrem. *Commentary on Genesis* 1955. Ed. with Latin trans. R. M. Tonneau. *Sancti Ephraem Syri In Genesim et in Exodum commentarii*. CSCO 152–153 / Subsidia 71–72. Louvain: Durbecq.
Ephrem. *Commentary on Genesis* 1994. Trans. E. G. Mathews and J. P. Amar. *St. Ephrem the Syrian: Selected Prose Works*. FC 91. Washington, D.C.: Catholic University of America Press.
Ephrem. *Hymns* 1989. Trans. K. E. McVey. *Ephrem the Syrian: Hymns*. CWS. New York: Paulist Press. (includes Hymns on the Nativity, Hymns on Virginity, Hymns against Julian).
Ephrem. *Hymns against Heresies* 1957. Ed. with German translation E. Beck. *Des heiligen Ephraem des Syrers Hymnen contra haereses*. CSCO 169–170 / Syr. 76–77. Louvain: Peeters.
Ephrem. *Hymns on Paradise* 1990. Trans. S. P. Brock. *Saint Ephrem: Hymns on Paradise*. Crestwood: St. Vladimir's Seminary Press.
Ephrem. *Letter to Publius* 1976. Ed. with English translation S. P. Brock. "Ephrem's Letter to Publius." *Muséon* 89, 261–305.
Ephrem. *Memre on Faith* 1961. Ed. with German trans. E. Beck. *Des heiligen Ephraem des Syrers Sermones de Fide*. CSCO 212–213 / Syr. 88–89. Louvain: Secrétariat du CorpusSCO.
Ephrem. *Prose Refutations* 1912–1921. Ed. with English trans. C. W. Mitchell, A. A. Bevan, and F. C. Burkitt. *S. Ephraim's Prose Refutations of Mani, Marcion, and Bardaisan*. 2 vols. London: Williams and Norgate.
Ephrem. *Sermon on Our Lord* 1966. Ed. with German translation E. Beck. *Des heiligen Ephraem des Syrers Sermo de Domino Nostro*. CSCO 270–271 / Subsidia 116–117. Louvain: Secrétariat du CorpusSCO. Trans. E. G. Mathews and J. P. Amar. *St. Ephrem the Syrian: Selected Prose Works*. FC 91. Washington, DC: Catholic University of America Press, 1994.
Odes of Solomon 1977. Ed. and trans. J. H. Charlesworth. *The Odes of Solomon. The Syriac Texts, Edited With Translation and Notes*. Chico: Scholars Press.

Secondary Literature and Further Reading

Baarda, T. 1975. *The Gospel Quotations of Aphrahat, the Persian Sage: Aphrahat's Text of the Fourth Gospel*. Amsterdam: Vrije Universiteit.
Biesen, K. den 2006. *Simple and Bold: Ephrem's Art of Symbolic Thought*. Piscataway, NJ: Gorgias Press.
Bremmer, J. N., ed. 2001. *The Apocryphal Acts of Thomas*. Louvain: Peeters.
Brock, S. P. 1992. *The Luminous Eye: The Spiritual World Vision of Saint Ephrem*. CSS 124. Kalamazoo: Cistercian Publications.
Bruns, P. 1991. *Aphrahat: Unterweisungen. Aus dem Syrischen übersetzt und eingeleitet*, 2 vols. Fontes Christiani 5. Freiburg: Herder.
Charlesworth, J. H. 1985. Odes of Solomon. *In:* Charlesworth, ed., *The Old Testament Pseudepigrapha*. Vol. 2. New York: Doubleday.
Coakley, J. F. 2013. "Syriac Exegesis." *In*: J. Carleton Paget and J. Schaper, ed., *The New Cambridge History of the Bible*. Cambridge: Cambridge University Press, 697–713.
Cohen, Sh. 2016. "Sabbath Labor Prohibitions in 'The Book of the Laws of Countries' by Bardaisan the Syrian" (in Hebrew). *In*: M. Ben Shaḥar, G. Herman and A. Oppenheimer, ed., *Between Babylonia and the Land of Israel: Studies in Honor of Isaiah M. Gafni*. Jerusalem: Merkaz Zalman Shazar, 169–82.
Cosgrove, Ch. H. 2015. "Singing Thomas: Anatomy of a Sympotic Scene in *Acts of Thomas*." *VigChr* 69, 256–75.

Dihle, A. 1979. "Zur Schicksalslehre des Bardesanes." *In:* A. M. Ritter, ed., *Kerygma und Logos. Beiträge zu den geistesgeschichtlichen Beziehungen zwischen Antike und Christentum. Festschrift für Carl Andresen zum 70. Geburtstag.* Göttingen: Vandenhoeck & Ruprecht, 123–35.

Drijvers, H. J. W. 1998. Syriac Culture in Late Antiquity: Hellenism and Local Traditions. *Mediterraneo Antico* 1:1, 95–113.

Emérean, C. 1918. *Saint Ephrem le Syrien: son œuvre littéraire grecque.* Études critiques de littérature et de philologie byzantines. Paris: Maison de la Bonne Presse.

Frede, D. 2017. "Alexander of Aphrodisias." *In*: E. N. Zalta, ed., *The Stanford Encyclopedia of Philosophy* (Spring 2017 Edition https://plato.stanford.edu/archives/spr2017/entries/alexander-aphrodisias/).

Griffin, C. W. 2016. *Cyrillona: A Critical Study and Commentary.* Piscataway, NJ: Gorgias Press.

Griffith, S. H. 1997. *Faith Adoring the Mystery: Reading the Bible with St. Ephraem the Syrian.* Milwaukee: Marquette University Press.

———. 2003. "The *Doctrina Addai* as a Paradigm of Christian Thought in Edessa in the Fifth Century." *Hugoye* 6.2, 269–92.

Grypeou, E. 2013. "Ephraem Graecus, 'Sermo In Adventum Domini': A Contribution to the Study of the Transmission of Apocalyptic Motifs in Greek, Latin and Syriac Traditions in Late Antiquity." *In:* S. K. Samir and J. P. Monferrer-Sala, ed., *Graeco-Latina et Orientalia: Studia in honorem Angeli Urbani heptagenarii.* Series Syro-Arabica 2. Cordoba: CNERU, 165–79.

Hadot, P. 2002. *What is Ancient Philosophy?* Cambridge, MA: Belknap Press.

Harris, J. R. 1909. *The Odes and Psalms of Solomon.* Cambridge: University Press.

Harris, J. R. and A. Mingana 1916–1920. *The Odes and Psalms of Solomon.* 2 vols. Manchester: Manchester University Press.

Harvey, S. A. 1993. "Feminine Imagery for the Divine: The Holy Spirit, the Odes of Solomon, and Early Syriac Tradition." *St. Vladimir's Theological Journal* 37, 111–39.

Heal, K. S. and R. A. Kitchen. 2014. *Breaking the Mind: New Studies in the Syriac Book of Steps.* Washington, DC: Catholic University of America Press.

Hemmerdinger-Iliadou, D. 1961. "Vers une nouvelle édition de l'Éphrem grec." *Studia Patristica* 3, 72–80.

Hidal, S. 1974. *Interpretatio Syriaca. Die Kommentare des heiligen Ephräm des Syrers zu Genesis und Exodus mit besonderer Berücksichtigung ihrer auslegungsgeschichtlichen Stellung.* Lund: Gleerup.

Koenen, L., ed. 1988. *Der Kölner Mani-Kodex: Über das Werden seines Leibes.* Opladen: Westdeutscher Verlag.

Koltun-Fromm, N. 2010. *Hermeneutics of Holiness: Ancient Jewish and Christian Notions of Sexuality and Religious Community.* Oxford: Oxford University Press.

Kremer, Th. 2012. *Mundus Primus: Die Geschichte der Welt und des Menschen von Adam bis Noach im Genesiskommentar Ephräms des Syrers.* CSCO 641 / Subsidia 128. Lovain: Peeters.

Kronholm, T. 1978. *Motifs from Genesis 1–11 in the Genuine Hymns of Ephrem the Syrian with Particular Reference to the Influence of Jewish Exegetical Tradition.* Lund: Gleerup.

Lattke, M. 2009. *Odes of Solomon: A Commentary.* Minneapolis: Fortress Press.

Murray, R. 2004. *Symbols of Church and Kingdom: A Study in Early Syriac Tradition.* 2nd ed. Piscataway, NJ: Gorgias Press.

Penniman, J. D. 2017. *Raised on Christian Milk – Food and the Formation of the Soul in Early Christianity.* New Haven: Yale University Press.

Poirier, P.-H. 1998. Les *Actes de Thomas* et le manichéisme. *Apocrypha* 9, 263–90.

Possekel, U. 2006. "Bardaisan of Edessa. Philosopher or Theologian?" *ZAC* 10, 442–61.

———. 1999. *Evidence of Greek Philosophical Concepts in the Writings of Ephrem the Syrian.* CSCO 580 / Subsidia 102. Louvain: Peeters.

Rapp, C. 2016. *Brother-Making in Late Antiquity and Byzantium: Monks, Laymen, and Christian Ritual*. Oxford: Oxford University Press.
Russell, P. S. 1994. *St. Ephraem the Syrian and St. Gregory the Theologian Confront the Arians*. Moran Etho 5. Kottayam, India: SEERI.
Schmidt, M. 1973. Influence de Saint Éphrem sur la littérature latine et allemande du début du Moyen-Age. *PdO* 4, 325–341.
Shepardson, Ch. 2008. *Anti-Judaism and Christian Orthodoxy: Ephrem's Hymns in Fourth-Century Syria*. Washington, DC: Catholic University of America Press.
Smith, K. 2016. *Constantine and the Captive Christians of Persia: Martyrdom and Religious Identity in Late Antiquity*. Oakland: University of California Press.
Stang, Ch. M. 2016. *Our Divine Double*. Cambridge, MA: Harvard University Press.
Van Rompay, L. 1996. "The Christian Syriac Tradition of Interpretation." *In*: M. Sæbo, ed., *Hebrew Bible/Old Testament: The History of Its Interpretation*. Göttingen: Vandenhoeck & Ruprecht, 612–41.
———. 2011. "Armenian Christianity, Syriac contacts with." *In*: GEDSH, 33–7.
Walters, J. 2016. *Aphrahat and the Construction of Christian Identity in Fourth-Century Persia*. Ph.D. Dissertation, Princeton Theological Seminary.

CHAPTER NINETEEN

LATER SYRIAC POETRY

Sebastian P. Brock

INTRODUCTION

Throughout the history of Syriac literature, right up to and including the present day, writing in verse of one form or another has always been a very popular undertaking. In his history of (West) Syriac literature entitled *The Scattered Pearls*, the learned Syrian Orthodox patriarch Ephrem Barsoum (d. 1957) divided Syriac poets into four categories (Barsoum 2003: 36–7), and of those in the first we find (besides, of course, Ephrem): from the fifth/sixth century, two Isaacs, Simeon the Potter, Jacob of Sarug; then come Jacob of Edessa (d. 708) and George of the Arabs (d. 725), followed by Bar Sobto (d. 829), Bar Qiqi (d. 1016), Bar Sabuni (d. 1095), Bar Andrew (d. 1156), Bar Ma'dani (d. 1263) and Barhebraeus (d. 1286). The eleven names in the second category range in date from the ninth to the eighteenth centuries, while the thirty or so names in the third and fourth categories span from the twelfth to the twentieth centuries. Barsoum of course excludes poets from the Church of the East, among whom several should certainly find their place in his first category, notably Narsai, 'Abdisho' of Soba, Gewargis Warda, and Khamis, the last three all from the thirteenth/fourteenth century.

POETIC FORM

Before turning to the poets themselves, however, a brief outline of the nature of Syriac poetry is needed. Syriac metre is essentially based on syllable count; this applies both to stanzaic verse (*madrashe*) and to couplets (*memre*); the former were normally sung (often with a refrain after each verse), the latter recited or chanted. *Memre* take on a small number of regular forms, of which two remain popular over the centuries; the first consists of couplets each of 7+7 syllables and is known as the metre of Ephrem (d. 373), while the other is associated with the name of Jacob of Sarug (d. 521) and consists of couplets of 12+12 syllables (where each unit of twelve syllables is made up of 4+4+4 syllables). Three other metres are sometimes found, 5+5 syllables (associated with the name of Balai [fourth/fifth century]), 6+6 syllables, which features in some of the earliest Syriac poetry, but evidently largely fell out of favour later, and

8+8 syllables. *Madrashe* have a very large number of possible syllabic structures, known as *qale/qole* (singular *qala/qolo*), a term that in fact refers to the name of the melody that fits the particular syllabic structure. Ephrem already employed over fifty different *qale*, and many further ones later came to be used (modern liturgical collections list some 150, most of which are probably not, or only rarely, used); in the Middle Ages repertories of these were put together, giving a small number of model stanzas for each *qala/qolo*; such a collection was known as a *Beth Gazo*. Classifications of Maronite *qole* can be found in Breydy 1979 and Hage 1987 (a list of those already used by Ephrem is given in Brock 2013, 68–77). Since the eight tones came to be adopted in the Melkite and Syrian Orthodox traditions over the course of the ninth to eleventh centuries (Cody 1982; Jeffrey 2001), in the Syrian Orthodox *Beth Gazo* the most frequently used *qole* were provided with a model stanza for each of the eight tones. At about the same time or somewhat later, a new genre came into widespread use in the East Syriac tradition, namely the *ʿonitha* (literally 'response'); this was a long stanzaic poem with a simple regular metre, apart from a short introduction and conclusion, employing a different and sometimes more complex metre. Finally, it is important to note that in the manuscripts, poetry is written out as continuous text (and not line by line, as in modern editions); the metrical structure being indicated solely by the punctuation and (if a stanzaic poem) the indication of a *qala*.

MAIN AUTHORS

Seeing that the works of many later poets remain unpublished, the following chronological survey is largely confined to authors of works in verse that happen to have been published, in some cases only in anthologies.

Best known to modern scholars are, of course, the great poets of the fifth and sixth centuries, beginning with Balai, who is probably the author (rather than Ephrem; Phenix 2008) of the twelve-book epic poem on the patriarch Joseph, as well as of a group of *madrashe*, one on the dedication of a church in Qenneshrin (Calchis) and five on Akakios (d.436), bishop of Beroea. Although the *memra* on Joseph uses the seven-syllable metre, the name of Balai is associated with the five-syllable metre found in many short liturgical *baʿawatha* ('Supplications') attributed to him. Roughly contemporary with Balai was Qurillona (Cyrillona), to whom two poems are specifically attributed, and a further four may belong, in a single manuscript; his only anchor in time is provided by the single non-religious topic of one of the poems, on an invasion of the Huns (thus ca. 396). A large number of *memre* in seven-syllable couplets were published under the name of Isaac of Antioch (Bedjan 1903; Mathews 2002), although (as Jacob of Edessa already knew) at least three different Isaacs were involved, Isaac of Edessa, Isaac of Antioch, and Isaac of Amid, all belonging to the fifth/sixth centuries; since many more *memre* than the sixty-five published by Bedjan are to be found in manuscripts, the task of allocating poems to one or other Isaac probably needs to wait until all (or at least those in early manuscripts) are published, although in a few cases the content provides some guidance (Bou Mansour 2003, 2007).

Whereas only a few of the *memre* in Bedjan's edition of 'Isaac of Antioch' are exegetical, this is not the case with the two other major poets of the fifth and early sixth centuries, the East Syriac Narsai (d. ca. 500) and the West Syriac Jacob of Sarug

(d. 521), both of whose verse homilies have remained extremely popular over the centuries in their respective traditions (Brock 1987, 2009). With both men, exegetical topics feature prominently in their extensive oeuvres (the editions of Mingana 1905 for Narsai, and Bedjan 1905–1910 for Jacob, are far from complete). Since both had connections with the famous School of Edessa, Narsai as a teacher, and Jacob as a student, it is not surprising that Jacob's exegesis should quite often follow in the tradition of Theodore of Mopsuestia, the exegete par excellence for the Church of the East. Of the two, Narsai is the more didactic (especially in his *memre* on the dominical Feasts: McLeod 1979), and Jacob the more pastoral. Besides *memre* on biblical lections and on the main feasts, Jacob has several devoted to particular saints, including Symeon the Stylite. More unusual is a group of six *memre* 'against the Jews' (Albert 1976), where one takes the form of a dialogue between a Jew and a Christian. Jacob was also the author of several *madrashe* and *soghyatha*, most of which still remain to be published.

Narsai employs both the seven- and the twelve-syllable metres, whereas the latter is regularly used by Jacob (and hence came to be associated with his name, for there is no good reason to suppose that he actually invented it).

Simeon the Potter (*quqoyo*), allocated by Barsoum to his first category, is said to have been a 'discovery' of Jacob's while he was travelling around villages in his duties as a chorepiscopos. A group of nine short stanzaic poems on Mary survive and gave rise to a genre of liturgical poems known as *quqoye*.

A vast amount of verse, especially liturgical verse, in Syriac is anonymous. A distinctive category here is provided by the many dialogue *soghyatha*, the majority of which seem likely to belong to the fifth and sixth centuries (list in Brock 1991). Whether or not they originated in a liturgical context is unclear, but it is almost exclusively in liturgical manuscripts, normally featuring the night office, that they come down to us. These poems belong to the genre of the 'precedence dispute' which has a long ancestry in Mesopotamia, going back to Sumerian literature by way of Akkadian and (very probably) earlier Aramaic literature. It first appears in Syriac in three poems by Ephrem where Death and Satan dispute in alternating short verses over which of the two has greater control over human beings. The majority of the later poems, however, take as their starting point a moment of tension in the biblical text, and then explore that tension by means of a dialogue between the two characters involved. *Soghyatha* with biblical topics which were transmitted in both East and West Syriac traditions (and so quite likely belonging to the fifth century) concern Cain and Abel, Joseph and Potiphar's wife, Joseph and Benjamin, the Angel and Mary, Mary and the Magi, John the Baptist and Christ, and the Cherub and the Thief (Genesis 3:24, Luke 23:43). An alphabetic acrostic features regularly. Certain topics gave rise to multiple poems; thus, there are four different dialogue poems between Body and Soul where, prior to the Judgement, they argue who is more to blame for sins committed. Among the small number of non-biblical topics is a dispute of the months, preserved in two manuscripts a thousand years apart in date; this has the added interest that it has a close analogue in Jewish Aramaic poetry preserved in the Palestinian Targum tradition (where it features at Passover). In both cases, it is Nisan who is the winner. The Syriac poem also nicely combines the ancient Mesopotamian precedence dispute with the Greek *ekphrasis* tradition.

Sometimes wrongly attributed to Ephrem in view of their metre, a smaller group of *memre* whose true authors are unknown contain imaginative re-tellings of episodes in the biblical text. In many ways, these resemble in character *memre* on similar topics by Jacob of Sarug, but they differ in that they have no specifically homiletic content. Several concern episodes in the life of Joseph (Heal 2006); other topics include the Binding of Isaac (Gen. 22), the prophet Elijah, and Joseph and Mary (whose narrative draws on the Protogospel of James). Considerable use is made of direct speech and dialogue; imagined speeches ('what N might have said . . . but did not') are sometimes present (Brock 2010), a feature also found in certain Greek homilies of a similar date. It is likely that Syriac poets of this period were aware of, and sometimes made use of, certain features characteristic of the tradition of Greek rhetorical education (McVey 1983).

Although authors are only rarely named in liturgical texts, the East Syriac liturgical tradition does give names for authors of a number of short *tešbḥatha* ('Praises') used on particular occasions; the names include Barsauma of Nisibis, Išoʿyahb II, Babai the Great, Babai of Nisibis, Sabrišoʿ, and Yazdin, all belonging to the period from the late fifth to the seventh centuries. Very surprisingly, fifteen of these poems were at some point taken over into the Maronite liturgy where they feature in the weekday office; there, however, they are left anonymous and are designated as *soghyatha* (Brock 2004); for the most part they are composed in couplets of 4+4 syllables, sometimes with an alphabetic acrostic.

The only Syrian Orthodox poet from the seventh century mentioned by Barsoum is the learned Jacob of Edessa, but even his inclusion is surprising, since his well-known works are all in prose. As examples of his verse, Barsoum mentions some *madrashe* for Holy Week (but without identifying them further) and a few *memre* (unpublished). His inclusion of George, bishop of the Arab tribes, however, was only to be expected, for he composed a number of *memre* in the twelve-syllable metre on a variety of topics, including the life of Severus (largely based on that attributed to John of Beth Aphtonia). No name of any further poet of note until the ninth century seems to be known, and from the first half of that century there is only David of Beth Rabban, who conducted most of his correspondence in verse; he is also author of a poem which sets out to list the trees of Paradise, a topic typical of the encyclopaedic bent of much literature (and not just Syriac) of the seventh and following centuries. Belonging to some time in the ninth century there is Anton of Tagrit who, besides leaving some poems of his own, was the author of a work on rhetoric in five books, of which the fifth is specifically on poetry (Watt 1986). This important work not only preserves illustrative excerpts from a large number of sometimes lost works, but is a valuable guide to the aesthetic sensibilities of contemporary readers of Syriac poetry. As a poet himself, Anton is said to have made two innovations; first, introducing the eight-syllable metre (though in fact it appears earlier), and second, introducing rhyme as a regular feature.

Writing in verse seems to have picked up again in the tenth century, and by now it had acquired an essentially educational purpose. Thus the East Syriac author, Elia, bishop of Anbar, has left an extensive poem in ten *memre* entitled 'The Book of Instruction', of which only the first three *memre* have been published so far (Juckel 1996). Each *memra* is divided into a series of 'Centuries', each unit of which consists of four or six lines of 7+7 syllables, with end rhyme (always *-a*). The content has a gnomic character and is strongly influenced by the Pseudo-Dionysian corpus. Another East Syriac writer, from somewhat later in the tenth century, was Emmanuel d-Beth Šahhare, who was associated with the School of the famous 'Upper Monastery' near Mosul; his main work was a verse commentary on the six days of Creation; unlike Narsai's and Jacob's homiletic treatments of the subject, Emmanuel has a greater scientific interest, drawing on the prose commentaries of Basil and later writers. Similarly pedagogic in approach is his verse commentary on the East Syriac baptismal rite. The same subject, along with other liturgical rites, was taken up, again in verse, by Yoḥannan bar Zoʿbi, who belongs to the late twelfth/early thirteenth century; Yoḥannan, who belonged to another famous East Syriac monastery, Beth Qoqa, was one of the most learned monks of his time. For all these East Syriac poets, both the seven- and twelve-syllable metres were favoured.

Among the West Syriac poets of the tenth to twelfth centuries whom Barsoum placed in his first category were three whose works, with very few exceptions, have still to be published: bar Qiqi (d. 1016), author of a lament written after he had returned to Christianity after having apostatised, bar Sabuni, metropolitan of Melitene (d. 1095), author of verse *ḥusoye* and of *qonune*, and bar Andrew, metropolitan of Mabbug (d. 1156), known for his funeral *madrashe* and a long verse epistle to a friend, Michael. An East Syriac writer who seems to belong to the eleventh century is Abraham of Zabe, author of a long biographical poem, in the seven-syllable metre, on Rabban bar ʿEdta (edited and translated in Budge 1902).

It is especially from the thirteenth and fourteenth centuries, the end of the time of the 'Syriac renaissance', that we encounter a more marked revival in composition in verse, and often the influence of Arabic poetic form and choice of topics can be observed. On the West Syriac side there is a sizable collection of poems by Yuḥanon bar Maʿdani, who became maphrian in 1252 (along with a rival), and is best known for a poem where the soul is symbolised by a bird. A younger contemporary of Yuḥanon was the polymath Bar ʿEbroyo (Barhebraeus, d. 1286) who, besides his massive body of prose works, also left a great deal of poetry (Takahashi 2013); particularly popular – to judge by the number of manuscripts – was his small verse grammar, which evidently served as an educational text book. Essentially theological in character is a long verse letter, in the seven-syllable metre, addressed to Denḥa, catholicos of the Church of the East. Other poems dealt with (from a Western point of view) more poetic topics such as Divine Wisdom. Bar ʿEbroyo most frequently employed the twelve-syllable metre, sometimes organised in rhyming quatrains. The twelve-syllable metre was also the vehicle for the verse biography of Bar ʿEbroyo by Dioscoros, bishop of Gozarto, following a long tradition of biographical and hagiographical compositions in verse; in this verse, rhyme only features intermittently.

Best known, however, of the poets of the thirteenth and fourteenth centuries is ʿAbdišoʿ bar Brikha, East Syriac metropolitan of Soba (the biblical city with which Nisibis was identified), who died in 1318. Besides composing two major works of canon law which remain authoritative, ʿAbdišoʿ sought to demonstrate that the Syriac language was just as able as Arabic to serve as the vehicle for the latest fashions in poetic form. To prove this, he composed the 'Paradise of Eden', in fifty *memre*, making use of both the seven- and the twelve-syllable metres, but distinguished by very complex rhyme patterns. Thus, for example, the second *memra* consists of ten-line verses, providing an alphabetic acrostic where each line of a verse both begins and ends with the same letter of the alphabet. The sixth *memra* is written in two metres simultaneously, depending on whether one includes or excludes a monosyllable (usually a particle) which is written in red. Even more of a tour de force are *memra* fifteen, which totally avoids the use of *alaph*, but has every line ending in nun, and *memra* forty-two, where every word contains a *semkath*. In places the vocabulary is so recherché that ʿAbdišoʿ himself later provided a commentary. The topics of each *memra* vary considerably, though they normally have a moralising tone. Rather surprisingly, *memra* eleven belongs to the genre of the dispute poem and consists in a dialogue between Body and Soul, each accusing the other of being the cause of sinning. Despite its frequent obscurity, the Paradise of Eden has enjoyed huge popularity throughout the centuries. Much more appreciated, however, by Western scholars is ʿAbdišoʿ's long poem on Syriac authors, arranged chronologically. In many ways, this constitutes the first history of Syriac literature and was used as a framework for the first part of the third volume of J.S. Assemani's magisterial *Bibliotheca Orientalis* (Assemani 1725).

A great deal of uncertainty surrounds the identity and date of Gewargis Warda; he has usually been dated to the thirteenth century, although he is absent from ʿAbdišoʿ's list of writers, and an *ʿonitha* attributed to him on the catholicoi of the Church of the East includes mention of Timothy II (1318–32). His name Warda ('Rose') derives from his association with 'The Book of Warda' which collects together the poetic compositions known as *ʿonyatha* for the East Syriac liturgical year (Pritula 2015). The collection grew over time and the work of other authors came to be incorporated, although the core seems to belong to a single author, namely Gewargis. The topics vary considerably according to the particular commemoration; disastrous events such as raids and famines are also sometimes commemorated. Gewargis evidently had access to many different sources, of which he makes considerable use at times; thus his seven-syllable *memra* on 'Man as a microcosm', said to be used on the fourth Sunday of Lent, draws on a much earlier prose work on the same subject by Aḥudemmeh.

Another prolific East Syriac poet, dating from perhaps slightly later than Gewargis, is Khamis bar Qardaḥe, who seems to have been a priest active in the region of Arbela. A number of liturgical *ʿonyatha* are transmitted under his name, but it is as the author of poems on profane subjects that he is better known; in particular he took up the fashion of writing *khamriyyat*, or 'wine poems' (Taylor 2010), though he was not the first Syriac poet to do so. These poems, like their Arabic counterparts, quite often carried an allegorical or even mystical sense. The metre used for these poems is normally quatrains of 7+4 (occasionally 4+7) syllables.

Though consultation of standard histories of Syriac literature (Baumstark 1922; Macuch 1976; Barsoum 2003) will provide the names of numerous poets of subsequent centuries, very little of their work has been published; one notable exception, however, is the long biographical poem by Sargis bar Wahle on Rabban Hormizd (Budge 1902), which employs a complex pattern of end rhyme. Sargis may date from the sixteenth century. Extracts of other poets of the fourteenth to twentieth centuries sometimes feature in anthologies, such as those of Cardahi 1875 and the more recent collections edited by Çiçek (1981, 1987). In all of these, both the seven- and the twelve-syllable metres feature prominently, very often with end rhyme, and in the case of *soghyatha* sometimes with an alphabetic acrostic. Verse writing in Classical

Syriac ('Modern literary Syriac') still remains very much alive in the twenty-first century in certain circles.

Although Syriac Christianity goes back a very long way in southern India, there is hardly any evidence of an indigenous literary tradition in Syriac, though recently a seventeenth-century poet named Alexander has come to light (Perczel 2014), and in modern times several examples of creative writing in Syriac verse are to be found. One published example is a versification, in the twelve-syllable metre, of the Gospel of Mathew (Kaniamparampil 1999).

TRANSLATIONS OF GREEK POETRY

Rather surprisingly, there were three major undertakings of translating Greek poetic texts; in two cases these were liturgical, and so less surprising. The earliest was an early seventh-century translation, by Paul bishop of Edessa, of responsorial hymns to psalm verses composed by Severus, patriarch of Antioch (d. 538), and others; in Syriac these were entitled *maʿnyatha*, 'responsorial (hymns)'; in a few cases the Greek original has been identified, usually on a papyrus fragment. Paul seems to have aimed to keep approximately to the syllabic structure of the Greek, but later in the seventh century his translation was carefully revised, from a philological perspective, by Jacob of Edessa, and it is this form that comes down to us (Brooks 1909, 1911). The liturgical genre of *maʿnyatha* enjoyed considerable popularity for several centuries, to judge by the large number of manuscripts up to about the thirteenth century.

Much more unexpected is the translation, made in the mid-seventh century by Candidatus of Amid, of a considerable number of Gregory of Nazianzus's learned iambic poems – further indication of the high regard in which Gregory 'the Theologian' was held, especially in the Syrian Orthodox tradition. Though no attempt seems to have been made to fit these to a Syriac metre, their verse origin is hinted at by the careful recording of the number of stichoi (*esṭukse*) at the end of each poem. There is evidence that at least some poems were translated twice.

The origins of the Greek liturgical genre of the *kanōn* belong to Syria/Palestine of the seventh and eighth centuries, two famous names being John of Damascus and Kosmas of Jerusalem. Very early on, many of the canons composed by these two, and other authors, were translated into Syriac, sometimes in more than one version. Probably representing an intermediary stage are the small number of cases where Greek *troparia* (stanzas) were written out in Syriac script (Géhin 2014). No doubt the translations were first made in Melkite circles (where Syriac remained an important liturgical language, alongside Greek and Arabic, until the seventeenth century), and then soon taken over in Syrian Orthodox circles. The translations are quite free since there was evidently an attempt to achieve approximately the same number of syllables in each stanza as in the Greek. In due course Syriac imitations of canons came to be made, and so one finds a distinction in liturgical manuscripts between 'Greek' (*yawnoye*) and 'Syriac' *qonune* (Husmann 1975, 1978). Remarkably, some translations (usually somewhat abbreviated) of Greek canons feature both in the seven-volume printed Syrian Catholic edition of the West Syriac Festal Hymnary (*Fenqitho*) and in the three-volume Syrian Orthodox edition published in Kerala (Brock forthcoming).

TRANSLATIONS OF POETRY IN OTHER LANGUAGES

In certain intellectual lay circles in the early twentieth century, a need was felt to provide Classical Syriac with some examples of European secular literature, including poetry. Some more recent examples of such verse translations from French can be found in Ghattas Maqdasi Elias (2007).

TERMINOLOGY

The poetic terminology can be rather flexible; thus the term *memra* is also used to denote a prose discourse (corresponding to Greek *logos*), while *madrashe* consisting of short stanzas (*tar'e*) with simple syllabic patterns came to be termed *soghyatha*. A refrain for a *madrasha* could be termed variously as *'onitha*, *'unaya*, or *'enyana*. The term *qala*, in particular, took on a variety of different senses, and could simply replace *madrasha* and refer to any stanzaic poem (Husmann 1979). In liturgical texts, numerous new and specialised terms came into use; these primarily depended on the liturgical function of the verse text in one or other of the liturgical traditions, rather than on its specific form; examples of such terms are *quqoyo*, *'enyono, turgama*, *ḥuttama*, etc.

When the eight-tone system (*oktoechos*) came into use in the Melkite and Syrian Orthodox traditions, a variety of different terms are to be found employed in the liturgical manuscripts to designate 'tone': *'ikos* (from the Greek term *echos*), *rekna*, *qala*, *qinta*.

SOME SPECIFIC FEATURES

1 Rhyme. In earlier poetry rhyme is normally absent, apart from the occasional brief use for special effect; it was only introduced in a consistent way in the ninth century under the influence of Arabic poetry (Barsoum 2003, 29), after which it was to become a common feature in much subsequent verse composition, again under Arabic influence. End rhyme normally covers just the final syllable, but occasionally it may include the last two syllables.

2 Acrostics, both alphabetical and spelling out the author's name, already feature in Ephrem's *madrashe*. The use of authorial acrostics seems subsequently to have been dropped, but alphabetic ones remain popular, especially in *soghyatha*. On rare occasions the alphabetic acrostic is to be found in the last letter of the end rhyme (thus in a poem by Khamis: Shleymon 2002, 151), rather than in the initial letter of the stanza (sometimes extended to each stichos of the stanza).

3 In verse of the thirteenth/fourteenth century and later, certain exotic features are occasionally found, such as lipograms, where throughout a poem the use of a particular letter is strictly excluded: in the case of the letters *alaph* and *tau* in particular, this was actually achieved by 'Abdišo', as noted above, in his Pearl. A further exotic feature, the picture poem, was employed in 1616 by Gabriel, metropolitan of Ḥesno d-Kifo for a poem in honour of Pope Paul V; the idea goes back to Hellenistic times for Greek, but Gabriel will have had Arabic picture poems as his models.

SYRIAC WRITERS ON SYRIAC POETRY

An early attempt to provide a classification of *qale* and the *madrashe* of Ephrem which employ them is to be found in an eighth-century manuscript (de Halleux 1972). Much more serious and important is Anton of Tagrit's five-book work on rhetoric, mentioned above, whose fifth book is specifically on poetry, where he deals with two main topics, metres (*mušḥatha*) and figures (*gbulye*), in the course of which he provides numerous examples, quite often taken from lost works. Poetry is also covered, in the pedagogic form of questions and answers, by Jacob bar Šakko (d. 1241) in book three of the first half of his *Book of Dialogues* (Martin 1879). Many centuries later, the learned Maronite patriarch Stephen Douayhi (d. 1704) provided a systematic study of the syllabic structure of the different *qale* (Hage 1987). In modern times it has again been Maronite scholars who have been most active in the study of the various metres: Michel Breydy (d. 1994) and Louis Hage (d. 2010), who was primarily a musicologist. The third volume of the former's *Kult, Dichtung und Musik* provides a valuable analysis of the *qale* in use in Maronite tradition. Hage's *magnum opus* was a multi-volume work entitled *Musique maronite*, of which volumes V–VII, on *Les strophes-types syriaques*, constitute a very rich resource. Finally, mention should be made of an interesting short work entitled *pu'iṭutho*, 'Poetry', by Philoxenos Yuḥanon Dawlabani, metropolitan of Mardin (d. 1969), published posthumously in both Syriac and Arabic (Dawlabani 1970).

POETRY IN MODERN SYRIAC

In the past, most Western scholars interested in the various Modern Syriac dialects have paid more attention to the language than to the literature produced; in recent years, however, this imbalance is beginning to be remedied. Verse texts in vernacular Syriac began to be written down in northern Iraq in the seventeenth century; many of the earliest authors, such as Hormizd and Israel, were associated with Alqosh. Thanks to the work of Mengozzi and others, several works of these and later authors have now been published (Mengozzi 2002, 2011); among these writers is an isolated woman, Anne of Telkepe, living at the beginning of the twentieth century, who was the author of a long stanzaic poem on the famine of 1898. Most of these poems employ Classical Syriac metres, predominantly the seven-syllable, with end rhyme. Contemporary poems in a slightly different Modern Syriac dialect can be found in most numbers of the *Journal of Assyrian Academic Studies*. An unpublished study of versification in modern Syriac (Sureth) was made ca.1913 by the Dominican Jacques Rhetoré, himself an accomplished poet in Sureth. In modern times a few collections of poems that have an oral background, known as *zmiratha d-rawe*, 'songs of *Rawe*' (a term of uncertain origin) have been published; these consist of rhyming triplets of seven-syllable lines. Short seven-syllable verses also feature in the folk epic of *Qatina gabbara* ('Qatina the hero'). Some examples of more experimental verse forms were to be found in the now defunct periodical *Qala Suryaya*, published in Baghdad in the late 1970s and 1980s. As with contemporary Classical Syriac, verse translations of poems in other languages are also to be found, some notable examples being by the versatile poet Hannibal Alkhas (1930–2010), from Iran, who translated *ghazals* by the famous Persian poet Hafiz (d. 1390) and Pushkin's poem on the fisherman and the gold fish (samples in Josephson 2010).

NOTE

For Syriac terms, the East Syriac transcription is used except for those terms which are specifically West Syriac.

BIBLIOGRAPHY

Albert, M. 1976. *Jacques de Saroug. Homélies contre les Juifs*. Patrologia Orientalis 38.1. Turnhout: Brepols.

Assemani, J. S. 1725. *Bibliotheca Orientalis Clementino-Vaticana*, III.1. Rome: Congregatio de Propaganda Fidei.

Barsoum, I. A. 2003. *The Scattered Pearls: A History of Syriac Literature and Sciences*, 2nd ed. Piscataway, NJ: Gorgias.

Baumstark, A. 1922. *Geschichte der syrischen Literatur*. Bonn: A. Marcus und E. Webers Verlag.

Bedjan, P. 1903. *Homiliae S. Isaaci Syri Antiocheni*. Paris/Leipzig: Harrasowitz.

———. 1905–1910. *Homiliae Selectae Mar-Jacobi Sarugensis*. Paris/Leipzig: Harrasowitz; repr. with extra vol. VI, Piscataway, NJ: Gorgias, 2006.

Bou Mansour, T. 2003. Une clé pour la distinction des écrits des Isaac d'Antioche. *Ephemerides Theologicae Lovanienses* 79, 365–402.

———. 2007. Les écrits ascétiques ou monastiques d'Isaac, dit d'Antioche. *Journal of Eastern Christian Studies* 59, 49–84.

Breydy, M. 1979. *Kult, Dichtung und Musik im Wochenbrevier der Maroniten*, III, *Rishaiqole Kobayath*. Lebanon: Kobayath.

Brock, S. P. 1987. The published verse homilies of Isaac of Antioch, Jacob of Serugh, and Narsai: Index of incipits. *JSS* 32, 279–313.

———. 1991. Syriac dispute poems, the various types. *In*: G. J. Reinink and H. L. J. Vanstiphout, ed., *Dispute Poems and Dialogues*. OLA 42. Leuven: Peeters, 109–19. Reprinted in *From Ephrem to Romanos*. Aldershot: Ashgate, 1999. ch. VII, with Addenda, 4–5.

———. 2004. Some early witnesses to the East Syriac liturgical tradition. *Journal of Assyrian Academic Studies* 18:1, 9–45.

———. 2008. Poetry and hymnography 3: Syriac. *In*: S. A. Harvey and D. G. Hunter, ed., *Oxford Handbook of Early Christian Studies*. Oxford: Oxford University Press, 657–71.

———. 2009. A guide to Narsai's homilies. *Hugoye: Journal of Syriac Studies* 12:1, 21–40.

———. 2010. Dramatic narrative poems on Biblical topics in Syriac. *Studia Patristica* 45, 183–96.

———. 2011. Poetry. *In*: S. P. Brock, A. Butts, G. A. Kiraz, L. Van Rompay, ed., *The Gorgias Encyclopedic Dictionary of the Syriac Heritage*. Piscataway, NJ: Gorgias, 334–6.

———. 2013. In search of St Ephrem. *Khristianskii Vostok* NS 6XII, 13–77.

———. 2016. Poësie, syrische. *In*: *Realenzyklopädie für Antike und Christentum* 27, cols. 1124–1135.

———. forthcoming. Interactions between Syriac and Greek hymnography. *In*: A. Avdokhin, ed., *Hymns of the First Christian Millennium*.

Brooks, E. W. 1909, 1911. The Hymns [Maʿnyatha] of Severus and others in the Syriac version of Paul of Edessa revised by Jacob of Edessa. *Patrologia Orientalis* 6, 1–179; 7, 593–802.

Budge, E. A. W. 1902. *The Histories of Rabban Hormizd the Persian and Rabban Bar ʿIdta*, 2 vols. London: Luzac & Co.

Cardahi, G. 1875. *Liber thesauri de arte poetica Syrorum necnon de eorum poetarum vitis et carminibus*. Rome: de propaganda fidei.

Cassingena-Trevédy, F. 2006. L'hymnographie syriaque. *In:* F. Cassingena-Trevédy and I. Jurasz, ed., *Les liturgies syriaques*. Études syriaques 3. Paris: Geuthner, 183–219.

Çiçek, Mor Julius Yeshu'. 1981. *Mimre d-'al Sayfe da-sbalw mšiḥoye b-Turkiya men šnat 1714–1914*. Glane: Monastery of St Ephrem.

———. 1987. *Tenḥoto d-Ṭur 'Abdin*. Glane: Barhebraeus Verlag.

———. 1992. *Beth Gazo Rabo*. Glane: Barhebraeus Verlag.

Cody, A. 1982. The early history of the Octoechos in Syria. *In:* N. Garsoian et al., ed., *East of Byzantium: Syria and Armenia in the Formative Period*. Washington, DC: Dumbarton Oaks Center for Byzantine Studies, 89–114.

Dawlabani, Ph. Y. 1970. *Pu'itutho*. Aleppo.

de Halleux, A. 1972. Un clé pour les hymnes d'Éphrem d'après le ms. Sinaï syr. 10. *Le Muséon* 85, 171–99.

Géhin, P. 2014. Écrire le grec en lettres syriaques: les hymnes du Sinaï syriaque 27. *In:* A. Schmidt and T. Pataridze, ed., *Scripts beyond Borders*. Louvain la Neuve: Institut Orientaliste, 155–85.

Ghattas Maqdasi Elias. 2007. *Pi're lqišoye*. Aleppo: Mardin Publishing House.

Hage, L. 1987. *The Syriac Model Strophes and their Poetic Metres by the Maronite Patriarch Stephan Douayhi*. Kaslik: Université Saint-Esprit.

———. 2001. *Musique Maronite, V–VII, Les strophes-types syriaques*. Kaslik: Université Saint Esprit.

Heal, K. 2006. Reworking the Biblical text in the dramatic dialogue poems on the Old Testament Patriarch Joseph. *In:* B. Ter Haar Romeny, ed., *The Peshitta: Its Use in Literature and Liturgy*. Monographs of the Peshitta Institute 15. Leiden: Brill, 87–98.

Husmann, H. 1975. Die melkitische Liturgie als Quelle der syrischen Qanune iaonaie. *OCP* 41, 5–56.

———. 1976. Madrasche und Seblatha: Repertorienuntersuchungen. *Acta Musicologica* 48, 113–50.

———. 1978. Syrischer und byzantinischer Oktoechos. Kanones und Qanune. *OCP* 44, 65–73.

———. 1979. Zur Geschichte des Qala. *OCP* 45, 99–113.

Jeffrey, P. 2001. The earliest Oktoechoi. *In:* P. Jeffrey, ed., *The Study of Medieval Chant*. Cambridge: Cambridge University Press, 147–209 [esp. 178–81].

Josephson, M. E. 2010. Hannibal Alkhas 1930–2010: A painter with a passionate love for his mother tongue. *Journal of Assyrian Academic Studies* 24:2, 17–42.

Juckel, A. 1996. *Der Ktaba d-Durraša des Elija Al-Anbari, Memra I–III*. CSCO 559–560, scriptores syri 226–7. Leuven: Peeters.

Kaniamparampil, C. 1999. *The Gospel of Matthew*. Moran Etho 11. Kottayam: SEERI.

Macuch, R. 1976. *Geschichte der spät- und neusyrischen Literatur*. Berlin: de Gruyter.

Martin, J-P. P. 1879. *De la métrique chez les Syriens*. Abhandlungen für die Kunde des Morgenlandes 7.2. Leipzig: F.A. Brockhaus.

Mathews, E. G. 2002. A bibliographical Clavis to the corpus of works attributed to Isaac of Antioch. *Hugoye* 5:1, 3–14; cf. also 6:1, 51–76.

McLeod, F. G. 1979. *Narsai's Metrical Homilies on the Nativity, Epiphany, Passion, Resurrection and Ascension: Critical Edition of Syriac Text*. Patrologia Orientalis 40.1. Turnhout: Brepols.

McVey, K. 1983. The Memra of Narsai on the Three Nestorian Doctors as an example of forensic rhetoric. *In:* R. Lavenant, ed., *IIIe Symposium Syriacum: Les contacts du monde syriaque avec les autres cultures (Goslar 7–11 Septembre 1980)*. OCA 221. Rome: Pontificium Institutum Studiorum Orientalium, 87–96.

Mengozzi, A. 2002. *Israel of Alqosh and Joseph of Telkepe: Religious Poems in Vernacular Syriac*. CSCO 589–590. Leuven: Peeters.

———. 2011. *Religious Poetry in Vernacular Syriac From Northern Iraq 17th–20th Centuries*. CSCO 627–628. Leuven: Peeters.

Mingana, A. 1905. *Narsai Doctoris Syri Homiliae et Carmina*, 2 vols. Mosul: Typis Fratrum Praedicatorum.

Perczel, I. 2014. Alexander of the Port/Kadavil Chandy Kattanar. A Syriac poet and disciple of the Jesuits in seventeenth-century India. *JCSSS* 14, 30–49.

Phenix, R. R. 2008. *The Sermons on Joseph of Balai of Qenneshrin*. Tübingen: Mohr Siebeck.

Pritula, A. 2015. *The Wardā:An East Syriac Hymnological Collection. Study and Critical Edition*. Göttinger Orientforschungen, I. Reihe: Syriaca 47. Wiesbaden: Harrassowitz Verlag.

Shleymon Isho' Hadbshabba. 2002. *Khamis bar Qardahe*. Nuhadra: Nisibin.

Takahashi, H. 2013. The poems of Barhebraeus: A preliminary concordance. *Khristianskii Vostok* 6:XII, 78–139.

Taylor, D. G. K. 2010. Drink, desire and devotion in the Syriac wine songs of Khamis bar Qardahe. *In:* H. Teule et al., ed., *The Syriac Renaissance*. Eastern Christian Studies 9. Leuven: Peeters, 31–52.

Watt, J. W. 1986. *The Fifth Book of Rhetoric of Antony of Tagrit*. CSCO 480–481. Leuven: Peeters.

CHAPTER TWENTY

SYRIAC HAGIOGRAPHIC LITERATURE

Jeanne-Nicole Mellon Saint-Laurent

INTRODUCTION

Hagiography denotes the genre of the lives of the saints (Hinterberger in Efthymiadis 2014; Harvey 2008; Insley and Saint-Laurent 2018). The production of saints' lives blossomed in Late Antiquity alongside the growth of the cult of the saints. It emerged as a literary form to commemorate Christians whose lives were promoted as models of sanctity. Hagiography contains elements of myth, history, biblical exegesis, romance, and theology.[1]

Hagiographic corpora exist in all the linguistic traditions of the ancient Church. In this article, we examine the features and idiosyncrasies of Syriac hagiographic texts. We address questions of method and mention tools for the study of these texts. We will then study a few stories in more detail that demonstrate the variety of texts that Syriac hagiographic literature comprises. We will discuss not only extended saints' *Lives*, but also other forms of hagiographic literature, including apocryphal *Acts* narratives, metrical homilies and liturgical hymns on saints, shorter stories about saints contained in larger collections, and martyr romances or passions, including the Persian Martyr Acts.

SYRIAC HAGIOGRAPHY

Syriac-speaking Christians from the Roman and Sasanian empires composed a wide array of hagiographic texts to commemorate the saints (*qaddiše*), from stories (*taš'iyata*) to poetic homilies and hymns on saints (*memre* and *madraše*). Over 1,200 works of hagiographic literature are extant in the Syriac language, when one includes stories and hagiographic poetry on Mary and biblical figures from the Hebrew Bible (Peeters 1910; Fiey 2004; Saint-Laurent and Michelson 2015). The corpus of Syriac hagiography comprises texts that were composed originally in Syriac as well as translations from other languages of the Late Antique world like Greek (Brock 2008b; Brakke 1994; Draguet 1980).

Syriac-speaking communities flourished within the Roman and Sasanian empires, and we can distinguish between two large corpora that comprise the body of Syriac hagiographic literature: those written within the Roman Empire and those written in the Sasanian Empire. A further sub-category within Sasanian Christian hagiography includes what scholars call the Persian Martyr Acts. This large collection comprises texts that describe and mythologise the persecution and martyrdom of Christians living in the Sasanian Empire (Becker forthcoming; Brock 2009; Walker 2006; Smith 2016; Payne 2015; Jullien 2012).

METHOD OF ANALYSIS: BETWEEN LITERARY AND HISTORICAL QUESTIONS

Hagiographies teach us a great deal not just about the persons whom they honour but also about the communities who wrote them. The study of Syriac hagiography offers scholars an important window onto the cultural and religious history of the Middle East. Yet, because of the unique characteristics of the hagiographic genre, both literary and historical questions of analysis are required to interpret these entertaining and edifying texts.

Hagiography portrays persons and events in exaggerated language meant to engage the memory and imagination of the reader or listener: the language of wonder (*tahiruta*, *tedmurta*, *dumara*) pervades its rhetoric. It can be didactic, romantic, homiletic, poetic, and even humorous. The hagiographer's chief intent, however, is to show how the saint becomes a vehicle of divine power through his or her way of life (*dubara*).

Hagiographers adhere to literary conventions in their portrayal of the saints, which make the similarities among the saints quite obvious. Hagiographers weave references to the Bible and other hagiographies into their texts, clothing their saints in the symbols of holiness represented in the stories of the prophets, apostles, and biblical heroes. Hagiographers imitate the motifs, themes, and narrative structure found in biblical stories, other hagiographies, and even stories and myths from non-Christian precedents (Greek, Latin, Mesopotamian, or Iranian). Literary conventions for depicting different types of saints and motifs for demonstrating their divine authority were transmitted and canonised. Hagiographers take these patterns and reshape them according to their individual interests, impressing their stories with the marks of their own culture, community, and ideological or theological agendas. In this way, they craft new stories adorned with literary relics or *spolia* from earlier texts (Insley and Saint-Laurent 2018). Yet behind tropes and stock hagiographic themes is a hagiographer or a community with a unique agenda to promote through the composition, transmission, or translation of the story. Using hagiography to understand the past means asking specific questions of the story to unveil its ideologies:

Whom does the text commemorate? What details of the saint's life does the text include, and what is absent? Who wrote the text, and for whom? What are the locations or communities commemorated in the text? Whom does the text identify as the saints' friends and rivals? If this person existed, how do historical or historiographical sources contrast with the portrait contained in hagiographic texts? Which tradition or traditions seek to identify with this saint?

RESEARCH TOOLS

The critical study of Syriac hagiography began when S. E. Assemani published a work in two volumes, the *Acta Sanctorum Martyrum orientalium et occidentalium* in 1748, a collection of Syriac hagiographic texts from the Vatican library (Binggeli 2012a; Brock 2011a: 44). Paul Bedjan (d. 1920), a Chaldean Catholic from Iran, later published a seven-volume series of saints' lives in the Syriac language: the *Acta Martyrum et sanctorum syriace* (*AMS*). Through the efforts of orientalists François Nau and E. W. Brooks, many Syriac saints' lives were published in *Patrologia Orientalis* and *Revue de l'Orient chrétien*. The Bollandist Paul Peeters produced the *Bibliotheca hagiographica orientalis* (*BHO*), which contained an annotated index of saints' lives and manuscripts from the oriental linguistic traditions.

J.-M. Fiey wrote an important guide to the Syriac saints, *Saints syriaques*, published posthumously in 2004, listing over 400 saints from the West and East Syriac traditions, including modern saints. *Saints syriaques* is organised according to holy person rather than hagiographic text. Fiey provides a brief description of each saint along with pertinent primary and secondary material. It is a natural starting point for scholars interested in Syriac hagiography. Sebastian Brock and Susan Ashbrook Harvey's *Holy Women of the Syrian Orient* is a collection of translated Syriac hagiographies on women which brought the distinctive features of Syriac hagiography to the attention of scholars of Late Antiquity in the English-speaking scholarly world (Brock and Harvey 1987, updated 1998).

In the past twenty years, many Syriac hagiographies have been translated into modern languages. Syriac hagiography has been increasingly integrated into broader historical and theological studies of the Late Antique period, as demonstrated in a number of monographs (Brock and Harvey 1998; Harvey 1990; Walker 2006; Saint-Laurent 2015; Payne 2015; Smith 2016). The series of the Persian Martyr Acts (see Brock 2009) has made a vital contribution in bringing East Syrian hagiographies into English translation, with helpful commentary on the Sasanian context and milieu of these stories.

MANUSCRIPTS AND LITURGICAL CONTEXT

Syriac hagiography has a rich manuscript tradition with major collections now in Berlin, London, Paris, and the Vatican (Binggeli 2012b). Some Syriac manuscripts with hagiographic collections are quite early, dating from the fifth century (London BL Add. 12150 which dates to 411; London BL Add. 17204; Saint Petersburg, National Library of Russia, N.S. 4) (Binggeli 2012b).

In an important article on Syriac hagiographic manuscripts, André Binggeli notes that it is difficult to find any sense of order to these hagiographic collections of saints' lives (Binggeli 2012b: 49). Not one compilation is identical to another. Syriac hagiographic literature is often collated with other saints' lives, homilies, or ascetic literature. Examining the collation of hagiography sheds light on the text's interpretation and the development of a saint's cult (Becker forthcoming; Binggeli 2012b).

One large Syriac twelfth-century manuscript (separated today into two volumes) is contained in the library of the Syrian Orthodox patriarch (Dolabani et al. 1994). This venerable manuscript contains 125 saints' lives (Binggeli 2012b). The beginning of the volume is missing, and thus we cannot study the prologue to understand the scribe's project. But, as Binggeli has shown, it seems that the collation and editing of these lives was done in the entourage of the Syrian Orthodox patriarch Michael the Syrian (d. 1199), under whom another important Syriac manuscript with numerous hagiographies, BL Add. MS 12,174 (1196 CE), was also produced. Rather than collating the lives according to their order in the liturgical calendar, hagiographies in these manuscripts were organised according to type: monk, bishop, women, etc. This is significant, because it suggests that hagiographic literature was meant to be understood as a corpus, with chapters of different types of holy people, who, when seen as a grand community of the friends of God, were idealisations of the church as a whole. The transmission and collation of hagiographic corpora helped the leaders of the church to idealise their sacred history, trace their tradition to biblical heroes, and prove their community to be the descendants of the earliest followers of Jesus (Binggeli 2012b). Thus, as we approach these stories as individual works, extracted from their place within a larger compilation of *Lives*, we are perhaps losing some of the meaning attributed to the hagiography when it was seen as one component of a greater corpus.

The oldest extant Christian manuscript, BL Add. 12150, is dated to 411 CE and was produced in Edessa (Wright 1871, II; Binggeli 2012b: 62–3). Although its contents are primarily theological, it ends with a hagiographical section where one finds the oldest martyrological collection in Syriac, Eusebius's *History of the Martyrs of Palestine* (Cureton 1861). This manuscript also contains the most ancient Syriac calendar (Taylor 2012). It has a list of names and dates for the commemoration of Western martyrs, together with a list of Persian martyrs and their feast days.

The cult of the saints flourished in the Syriac-speaking milieu, and Christian communities celebrated the memory of saints on their feast days. The faithful attended to the stories of the saints as they were proclaimed in the liturgy (Taylor 2012: 77–8). In order to keep track of these feast days, they created calendars or menalogia that listed the names, together with a short description of the saint of the day. Through examining Syriac menalogia, we understand more clearly which saints were venerated in different locations and at different times (Taylor 2012: 79; Nau 1912: 3). The Syrian Orthodox and Maronite traditions use a *Fenqitho* in their liturgies, a collection of hymns for Sundays and feast days, and this provides important information about which saints were commemorated and when.

TYPES OF SYRIAC HAGIOGRAPHIC LITERATURE

In this second section, we discuss specific examples of Syriac hagiographic literature. Not all of the stories described below would be considered 'hagiography', when one understands that as the genre of 'saints' lives'. Rather, I am considering any Syriac texts that commemorate the saints to be hagiographic literature, whether short or long, poetic or narrative.

Apostolic acts and extended narratives

We begin with a discussion of the apostolic *Acts* narratives: apocryphal legends about the first followers of Jesus. These texts were mirrored on the form of the canonical Acts of the Apostles. The themes and patterns for depicting holy people that are found in these 'Christian novels' re-appear in hagiography. Fundamental stories belonging to this category include the *Acts of Thomas* and the *Teaching of Addai*.

The *Acts of Thomas* describes the conversion of kingdoms in northern India through the preaching and miracle working of the apostle Thomas (Klijn 1962; Bremmer 2001; Saint-Laurent 2015). In the story Thomas, who travels with merchants, becomes an apostle not only for the Christians of India but also for many of the Syriac-speaking communities east of the Euphrates. He is commissioned to travel and convert the kingdoms of India. Although the *Acts of Thomas* was probably originally written in Greek (Drijvers 1963), it was immediately translated into Syriac and became a popular text among many of the Syriac Christian communities. The story elevates the role of ascetic practice (sexual renunciation, fasting, prayer, almsgiving, care of the poor), healing miracles, imprisonment, and martyrdom; these motifs become symbols of holiness in many later Syriac hagiographies (Saint-Laurent 2015).

Many of these apocryphal narratives tell of the saints' interactions with kings and emperors, queens, and empresses, both Christian and non-Christian, and the introduction of these characters allowed hagiographers to rethink and rewrite their community's posture vis-à-vis the ruler of the land (Debié 2012; Wood 2010; Saint-Laurent 2015). Conversion of cities began with the conversion of the monarch. The apostolic narrative that describes the conversion of Edessa, the *Teaching of Addai*, was compiled in the fifth century to demonstrate the purity of their city's Christian lineage, which stretched back to the time of Jesus through the apostle Addai, missionary to Edessa (Howard 1981). Addai, in turn, sent the apostle Mari to convert Persia, and Sasanian Christians crafted a story about Mar Mari, the *Acts of Mari*, to prove their own orthodox heritage (Harrak 2005; Saint-Laurent 2015). Later Sasanian Christian and Manichean traditions even imagined that the Zoroastrian shah himself converted to Christianity (Schilling 2008) or Manichaeism (Gardner et al. 2014).

Hagiographic poetry

Syrians wrote not just prose but also verse to commemorate saints. There are two main categories of verse in Syriac literature: metrical verse homilies called *memre* and liturgical hymns known as *madrashe*. *Memre* and *madrashe* on saints show how stories about saints were retold in new literary forms for liturgical purposes.

Brock (2012) details the various types of hagiographic *memre* in Syriac literature. The genre of Syriac hagiographic *memre* comprises several forms, ranging from verse homilies rich in narrative details to those that are largely panegyric. They are important sources for the creation and diffusion of saints' portraits in Syriac religious memory.

Different stories and hymns on the saints can offer a variety of images of the same person, as the author or community exaggerates and embellishes his hagiographic portrait according to their agenda. Jacob of Sarug, an important Syriac theologian-poet from the sixth century, wrote numerous hagiographic *memre*. In his *memra* on St Ephrem the Syrian (Amar 1995), the celebrated theologian-poet of the Syriac tradition, Jacob praises his subject for his ministry in leading women's choirs. The portrait of Ephrem that Jacob presents in this homily contrasts with the one presented in the hagiographic *Life* or *Vita* of Ephrem. In his *Vita* tradition, Ephrem is clothed in the garb of a Byzantine monk, although he was a Syriac-speaking homilist and hymnist in the service of the urban church (Amar 2011).

Memre also provide imaginative expansions or exegeses of earlier hagiographic texts. Jacob of Sarug, for example, composed a verse homily on the forty martyrs of Sebaste (*AMS* VI: 663–73), and it is clear that he used a Syriac translation of the Greek hagiography on these saints to compose his verse (Brock 2012). Jacob also wrote hagiographic *memre* with the characteristics of panegyric, as exemplified in his *memra* on Sts. Sergius and Bacchus (*AMS* VI 650–61). In these, the narrative element is not as strong. Instead, the homily contains general praise for the virtues of the saints. Other panegyric *memre* in Syriac borrow rhetorical elements and schema from the Greek encomium.

Madrashe, in contrast to *memre*, are poetic hymns sung antiphonally in the context of the Syriac liturgy. Hagiographic *madrashe* are found in the West Syrian (Syrian Orthodox or Maronite) *Fenqitho* (Brock 2012). Ephrem the Syrian perfected the Syriac *madrasha*. Many of his *madrashe* commemorate saints, as demonstrated in his cycle of hymns known as the *Hymns on Nisibis*, which contains *madrashe* on Sts. Abraham Qidunaya and Julian Saba (Griffith 1994; Brock 2012).

Syriac poets also composed a type of *madrasha* called the dialogue poem or *sogita*, which features disputes between characters, sometimes saints, who antiphonally debate matters with each other. These debate poems show the intersection of hagiography and exegesis. For example, there is a *sogita* that features a debate between Saint Marina, an ascetic who lived in a monastery disguised as a male monk, and Satan (Brock 2008a). Many other such hagiographic dialogue poems have yet to be published.

Hagiographic narratives

The majority of hagiographic materials, however, are extended lives and short episodic vignettes contained within larger hagiographic collections. We turn to describe a few of the chief types of stories found in Syriac hagiography.

Ascetic heroes and monastic hagiographers

In 360, Athanasius of Alexandria composed the first extended hagiographic narrative in Greek, *The Life of Antony of Egypt*. This text was canonised as the literary exemplar for describing the life of a saint. It was translated into several ancient languages including Syriac (Draguet 1980). Subsequent Late Antique hagiographers imitated Athanasius's narrative structure that depicted the saint's childhood, conversion, asceticism, miracles, extraordinary death, and communal commemoration (Insley and Saint-Laurent 2018).

The Greek-speaking world learned of the accomplishments of the Syrian monks through the work of Theodoret of Cyrrhus, *The History of the Monks of Syria* (Price 1988). His tales were short and episodic, with sayings material and miracle stories within a larger collection. Theodoret compares the theatrical Syrian monastic practices to athletic training camps for wrestlers, and he depicts Syrian monks according to the patterns of Greek hagiography. One of the monks whom Theodoret describes is Simeon the Stylite (d. 451), and stories about Simeon circulated in Greek and Syriac (AMS 4:507–644; Doran 1992). Simeon stands on a pillar with arms outstretched as a symbol of his devotion to God. He mediates in both heavenly and temporal affairs, an incarnation of the joining of heaven and earth (Brown 1971). The Syriac version of Simeon's life is much longer than the Greek version, and it contains more extensive miracle stories, sensory language, liturgical imagery, and vivid descriptions of Simeon's feats and interactions with pilgrims (Insley and Saint-Laurent 2018).

One of the most important collections of short Syriac hagiographic texts is John of Ephesus's *Lives of the Eastern Saints* (Brooks 1923–25; Harvey 1990; Saint-Laurent 2015). His stories commemorate ascetics who lived in northern Mesopotamia, in monasteries near the city of Amida, modern-day Diyarbakir in south-east Turkey. His hagiography is an important source for shedding light on the Christological controversies of the fifth and sixth centuries (Harvey 1990; Wood 2010; Saint-Laurent 2015). Because of aggression from Chalcedonian bishops, miaphysite monks and bishops had to ordain new leaders for their communities throughout Mesopotamia and Syria. John commemorates these ascetic heroes and heroines in his collection, with noteworthy *Lives* of John of Tella, Jacob Baradaeus, Simeon of Beth Arsham, and John of Hephaestopolis. The Empress Theodora championed the cause of the miaphysites, and Syrian Orthodox hagiographic traditions remember her as a saint and daughter of a Syrian Orthodox priest (Harvey 2001), a stark contrast to Procopius portrayal of Theodora in his *Anecdota* or *Secret History* (Dewing 1935).

John of Ephesus also presents some distinctive examples of holy women. Harvey wrote a notable article in which she examines the presentation of the mother-daughter bond in Syriac hagiography (Harvey 1996). She draws attention to two important models of holiness that are featured in John of Ephesus, Mary and Euphemia (Brooks 1923: 166–86; Brock and Harvey 1998: 122–33). These sisters represent distinct models of piety available to women: one contemplative and the other active. Mary practices a life of prayer, fasting, and asceticism. Her sister Euphemia, a widow with a daughter, collects alms for the poor. The sanctity and religious authority of these women's lives were not immediately linked to men of their family or social structure (Saint-Laurent 2012).

The Greek hagiographic sketches of Palladius's *Lausiac History*, which describes the Egyptian ascetic fathers and mothers, was translated into Syriac and became influential for future Syriac hagiographies (*AMS* 7: 1–192; Brock 2008b; Brock 2011c). The collection contains a large compilation of short lives of ascetic men and women; some have names, others are anonymous. There are several Syriac recensions of this important text. The earliest two may be translations of an earlier Greek version which was later lost. The popularity of Palladius was further extended in the Syriac world in the seventh century through ʿEnanišoʿ of Beth ʿAbhe, who translated Palladius into Syriac in the first part of his *Paradise of the Fathers* (Budge 1904; Brock 2008b; Brock 2011c).

A ninth-century bishop from the Church of the East, Thomas of Marga, wrote a collection of stories about abbots, catholicoi, and metropolitans from the Church of the East entitled *The Book of Governors* (ktābā d-rešāne) (Budge 1893), modelled on Palladius's *Paradise of the Fathers*. This collection is also an important source for understanding the development of East Syrian monasticism (Witakowski 2011: 417).

Many hagiographic texts were produced, translated, and transmitted by Syrian monks. Accordingly, an interest in monasticism and asceticism is an outstanding feature of Syriac hagiography. Numerous Syriac hagiographies honour monastic saints and connect theses heroes to the foundations of particular monasteries (Debié 2012). The monasteries of Ṭur ʿAbdin (a region in south-east Turkey and centre of the Syrian Orthodox world) produced important hagiographic cycles on their founders, like the trilogy of hagiographies on the founding monks of the monastery of Qartmin, Sts. Gabriel, Simeon, and Samuel (Palmer 1990). Later hagiography that comes from this region also gives us important evidence about the encounters of Christians and

Muslims in the early days of Islam. For example, the *Life* of Theodotus of Amida (d. 698), a seventh-century miaphysite bishop, vividly portrays the saint's interactions with Muslims and Muslim authorities (Tannous 2012; Penn 2015). In this story, the saint has the special gift of spiritual discernment to identify hidden Muslims in his midst.

Syrian monks also wrote hagiography to affiliate their monasteries with others in both the Syriac-speaking world and Egypt. Syriac hagiographic traditions, for example, attribute the founding of many monasteries in Mesopotamia to disciples of the legendary ascetic, Mar (Saint) Awgin (*AMS* III: 376–480). Awgin is a pearl diver from Clysma (in Egypt) who becomes a monk in the monastery of Pachomius. Awgin and some disciples leave Egypt and build monasteries throughout Mesopotamia. This imagined link between the monks of Egypt and Mesopotamia is mythologised in hagiographies describing founders who traced their roots to Awgin (Insley and Saint-Laurent 2018), including those of Aaron of Sarug, Abraham of Beth Ṣayyare the Penitent, Dodo, Daniel the Doctor, Mar Eulogius, Mar Ezekiel, Isaiah of Aleppo, and John the Arab (Fiey 2004; Nau 1913, 1914, 1917).

The stories of the penitent harlots (Ward 1987) comprise another hagiographic narrative type of ascetic hero. These tales feature women of 'loose' sexual mores who undergo radical changes of heart to follow Christ. In the story of Pelagia of Antioch (*AMS* VI: 616–49; Brock and Harvey 1998: 40–62) we meet an actress and prostitute who adorns herself in jewels, provocative clothing, and perfumes as she parades the streets of Antioch with her entourage of fellow performers. She is struck with a desire to cast off her way of life, however, and converts to Christianity. She becomes a transvestite monk, 'Pelagion'. She gains many disciples, and only at her death do people realise her sex. These narratives idealise the possibility of sanctification for any person with a changed heart (Insley and Saint-Laurent 2018).

In Syriac narrative imagination, the ideal bishop was formed by the disciplines of monasticism. We see this in the hagiography of Rabbula, a fifth-century bishop of Edessa (*AMS* 4:396–450). He combines monastic training with pastoral tenderness and concern for the poor and sick of his city (Doran 2006). The stories of Rabbula are part of a larger cycle of texts associated with the city of Edessa. The story of 'the man of God', for instance, celebrates an anonymous Roman man (although he acquired the name 'Alexius' in later tradition) who gives up his wealth and fame to live the life of a beggar in the streets of Edessa, praying each night in the church. Bishop Rabbula, who identifies this man's holiness, promotes his example of a 'holy fool' and model of Christ (Doran 2006).

MARTYR ACTS

As in Greek and Latin hagiography, the Syriac hagiographic corpus contains a large number of stories about martyrs and their deaths. These stories characteristically include a description of the saint's virtue, arrest, dialogue with a judge, torture, death, burial, and the distribution or enshrining of relics. They also tend to distinguish martyrdom as betrothal to Christ (Brock and Harvey 1998: 9). Syriac martyr stories that took place within the boundaries of the Roman Empire were typically set in the time of the persecution of the emperor Diocletian at the beginning of the fourth century (Insley and Saint-Laurent 2018).

One of the most important martyrdom stories in Syriac was originally written in Greek: Eusebius of Caesarea's *History of the Martyrs of Palestine*. This collection portrays the martyrdom of about forty men and women whom Eusebius claims were killed during the Diocletianic Persecution at the beginning of the fourth century in Palestine (Cureton 1861). This collection of short martyr acts is contained in the oldest extant Christian manuscript, London BL Add. 12150, mentioned above (Binggeli 2012b: 62). There are two versions of these stories, one in Greek and one in Syriac. The Greek version is an appendix to Eusebius's *Ecclesiastical History;* the longer complete version of this text is extant only in Syriac translation (Binggeli 2012b: 62–3; Brock 2011b: 271).

The city of Edessa was home to local martyr traditions around which cultic devotions grew. Edessan martyr stories include the *Martyrdom of Shmona, Guria, and Ḥabib* (Burkitt 1913; *BHO* 363) and the *Acts of Sharbel, Babai, and Barsamya* (*BHO* 1049). The passion of *Shmona, Guria, and Ḥabib* describes the martyrdom of two lay men and a deacon, and it circulated shortly after their death (during the Diocletianic persecution); their shrine became a centre of pilgrimage.

The *Acts of Sharbel, Babai,* and *Barsamya*, an imagined story retrojected into the reign of emperor Trajan, portrays the martyrdom of a former pagan priest, his sister, and an early bishop of Edessa (Brock 2011b: 271; Insley and Saint-Laurent 2018). This cycle belongs to a collection of fifth-century texts that includes the *Teaching of Addai*, and these sacred fictions were compiled to add eminence to Edessa's Christian lineage (Brock 2011b: 271). To this group of texts we can add the story of *Euphemia and the Goth*, an important romance that elevated the local martyr cult of Shmona, Guria, and Ḥabib (Burkitt 1913). It tells the story of the widow Sophia and her daughter Euphemia, who quarter a Goth in the Roman army in Edessa. The Goth forces Sophia to give Euphemia to him in marriage, but he then enslaves her. The intercession of Sts. Shmona, Guria, and Ḥabib saves Euphemia and returns her to Edessa (Saint-Laurent 2012).

The *Life of Febronia* (*AMS* V, 573–615; Brock and Harvey 1998; Saint-Laurent 2012; *BHO*: 302) is a martyr hagiography that describes a monastic scholar, Febronia. She lives in community with her fellow nuns in the city of Nisibis. Her beauty attracts the attention of Roman guards, who have come to persecute Christians and convince them to sacrifice to the Roman gods. Febronia refuses the sexual advances of the Roman senators, and she is tortured and killed. A cult to Febronia developed and spread from Nisibis to Constantinople, and even to Sicily.

Persian Martyr acts

The *Acts* of the Persian martyrs is a large body of hagiographic texts that come from the East Syriac heritage, a tradition that flourished in modern-day Iran and Iraq (Brock 2009; Smith 2014, 2016; Payne 2015; Becker forthcoming). The corpus portrays stories of Christians in the (largely Zoroastrian) Persian Empire who were persecuted and martyred for their Christian faith. There are approximately sixty extant *Acts* of the Persian martyrs, and most were composed in the fifth through seventh centuries (Becker forthcoming). The heroes are idealised as virtuous, courageous, eloquent imitators of Christ who withstand brutal torture at the hands of their Sasanian Zoroastrian accusers. The narratives show knowledge of Zoroastrian religious practices and ideologies (Payne 2015; Walker 2006) and are important literary artefacts from Christians living under Sasanian rule. We should not treat these sources as 'reflections of their ultimate historical environments', but rather 'take deeper interest in the kind of textual, imaginative landscapes they establish' (Becker forthcoming).

Many of the Persian martyr texts, although set in the fourth century, were written several centuries later. The story of the *Martyrs of Mount Berʿain*, for example, was written in the seventh century, but situated 318/9, at the start of Shapur II's reign (Smith 2014; Brock and Dilley 2014). More than two-thirds of the Persian martyr acts were set in the reign of Shah Shapur II (d. 379), remembered as a time of great trial and conflict (Smith 2014). One of them, the account of the martyrdom of Simeon bar Shabba, is one of the longest Late Antique Christian narratives in any language.

Some of the stories, although vital to East Syrian Christian memory, might have been purely fictive (Smith 2012; Smith 2016; Becker forthcoming), as is true of hagiographical literature from other linguistic traditions. It is difficult to extract historical claims about Christians living in the Sasanian Empire based on these texts, but they do teach us about how Christians living in Sasanian rule saw themselves and used narrative to elevate their local communities and the prestige of Persian Christianity. Many of them are gruesome in their descriptions of martyrdoms, one of the most popular ones depicting the dismemberment of Jacob Intercisus, 'the Cut-up' (*AMS* 2: 539–558). It is a text that may have been more didactic or catechetic in purpose, and thus cannot be interpreted as a description of Christian life in the Sasanian milieu (Becker forthcoming).

The story of the *Martyrdom of Martha*, who is described in the subtitle as 'a daughter of the covenant and daughter of Posi', (*AMS* II: 231–241; Brock and Harvey 1998: 67–73) portrays the martyrdom of a woman who belonged to a type of ascetic community unique to the Syriac-speaking world known as 'the sons and daughters of the covenant', the *Bnay* and *Bnat Qyama* (see Chapter 5). The 'sons and daughters of the covenant' were groups of men and women living in community in a proto-monastic structure. They took vows of moderate asceticism and dedicated their lives to single-hearted devotion to Christ: *iḥidayutha*. They were involved in the administration of churches, hospitals, and charitable organisations and sung in the choirs of the Christian churches. Martha's father Posi was a man who worked for the Sasanian shah, and he converted to Christianity. His wife and daughter converted as well, with Martha going on to consecrate her virginity to Christ as a 'daughter of the covenant'. In this narrative cycle, both father and daughter are martyred, and the heroine, Martha, equates true daughterhood to following her father's example of Christian martyrdom.

While Martha's story exemplifies a Sasanian Christian family whose Christian conversion united them, many stories of the Persian martyrs, such as the *Legend of Mar Qardagh*, *Behnam and Sara*, and the *Martyrs of Ṭur Berʿain*, feature high-born converts who are punished by members of their families for renouncing their Zoroastrian identity (Walker 2006; Brock 2014; Becker forthcoming). *Behnam and Sarah*, for instance, is a twelfth-century Syriac hagiography about a brother-sister pair of martyrs who are the children of King Sennacherib (*AMS* II: 397–441; Saint-Laurent and Smith 2018). They convert to Christianity through their relationship with the monk Mattai, who heals Sara of her leprosy. Their father has them killed for abandoning their Zoroastrian religion, and a shrine is built to commemorate them.

Many of these stories can be linked to specific sites where cults developed to particular saints. The story of *Behnam and Sarah* comes from the monastery of Mar Behnam, a site which lies 36 km south-east of the modern Iraqi city of Mosul on the plain of Nineveh (Younansardaroud 2002: 185–94) between the Tigris and the Upper Zab rivers. A few kilometres north-west of the monastery of Mar Behnam is a small stream, ʿAin Sārā, named after the female heroine of the hagiography. ISIS attacked the monastery of Mar Behnam in March 2015, thus destroying one of the region's most sacred Christian centres (Jones 2015).

CONCLUDING REMARKS

Syrian Christians identified the saints as their models of holiness, and they claimed them for their tradition through the composition, translation, performance, and transmission of hagiographic literature. The saints are a vital component of Syriac Christian theology, and hagiographic literature expresses this theology in vivid colour, with narrative and poetic texts that engage the imagination and memory.

The large corpus of Syriac hagiographic literature remains a 'little tapped' resource (Brock 2008b). Research *desiderata* range from historical investigations to raw philological and text-critical work on unpublished or unedited texts. With new digital tools available to students and scholars that illustrate the links between saints, their stories, and their hagiographers, more attention can be given to this important genre. We still have much to learn not just about saints of the Syrian Orient, but also about the communities who cherished and mythologised their memories.

APPENDIX: DIGITAL RESOURCES FOR HAGIOGRAPHY

There are a growing number of electronic and digital resources for the study of Syriac hagiography. Sergey Minov of Oxford/Hebrew University has built *A Comprehensive Bibliography on Syriac Christianity*, an important online bibliography for Syriac studies with essential information on hagiography (www.csc.huji.ac.il) (Minov 2015). The Syriac Reference Portal (www.syriaca.org) has created a two-volume database entitled the *Gateway to the Syriac Saints*. One of these concerns Syriac hagiographic works, the *Bibliotheca Hagiographica Syriaca Electronica* (*BHSE*) (Saint-Laurent and Michelson 2015a); the other deals specifically with Syriac holy persons, and is entitled *Qadishe* (Saint-Laurent and Michelson 2015b). The *BHSE* is a project that Syriaca.org inherited from Fr. Ugo Zanetti and Claude Detienne, who created an electronic version of the *Bibliotheca Hagiographica Syriaca* in the scholarly tradition of the Bollandists mentioned above (Zanetti 1993). *Qadishe*, on Syriac saints, is a database built on Fiey's volume, *Saints syriaques*. For all the names mentioned in this chapter, further bibliographical references and information may be found in these two resources, including data about manuscript witnesses and descriptions of the saints.

Scholars at Oxford, including Drs. Bryan Ward-Perkins, David Taylor, and Sergy Minov, have created a database with information on the cult of the saints in Late Antiquity, including an important section on Syriac traditions (http://cultofsaints.history.ox.ac.uk/). Another project at Ghent University on *Novel Saints* is also doing digital scholarship on saints' lives from a literary point of view, and Drs. Flavia Ruani and Annunziata di Rienzo are leading the section on Syriac hagiographic literature (www.novelsaints.ugent.be/).

Much data on Syriac manuscripts has been digitised through the scholarship of André Binggeli, Muriel Debié, François Briquel-Chatonnet, and Alain Desreumaux of the Centre national de la recherche scientifique (www.mss-syriaques.org/index.php). In addition, a large number of Syriac manuscripts have been catalogued and digitised at the HMML library in Collegeville, Minnesota, under the leadership of Columba Stewart, OSB, and Adam McCollum (www.hmml.org/). Kristian Heal has directed a team at Brigham Young University's Center for the Preservation of Ancient Religious Texts that has also digitised Syriac manuscripts, including collections from the Vatican Library (http://cpart.mi.byu.edu/home/vs/).

NOTE

1 Some of the material in this article is replicated in other articles that I wrote on this subject: see Saint-Laurent (2012, 2016) 'The Gateway to the Syriac Saints: a database project' in the *Journal of Religion, Media & Digital Culture*, the introductions to Syriac hagiography that I wrote for Syriaca.org's volumes on Syriac hagiographic works (*BHSE*) and persons (*Qadishe*), as well as a section on Syriac hagiography in an article that I co-authored with Dr. Sarah Insley, 'Biography, Autobiography, and Hagiography'. I have tried to note all those places in the article where there is overlap. I thank my student Fr. Nathaniel Kidd for proofreading and editing this article for me.

BIBLIOGRAPHY

Primary Sources

Amar, Joseph. 1995. *A Metrical Homily on Holy Mar Ephrem*. PO 47. Turnhout: Brepols.

———. 2011. *The Syriac Vita Tradition of Ephrem the Syrian*. CSCO 629–30. Louvain: Peeters.

Assemani, Stephen. 1748. *Acta sanctorum martyrum orientalium et occidentalium*. 2 Vols. Rome: J. Collini.

Bedjan, Paul. 1890–97. *Acta martyrum et sanctorum* [*AMS*]. 7 Vols. Paris and Leipzig: Harrassowitz. Reprinted 1968, Hildesheim: G. Olms. Reprinted 2009, Piscataway, NJ: Gorgias Press.

Brock, Sebastian P. 2008a. St Marina and Satan: A Syriac Dialogue Poem. *Collectanea Christianana Orientalia* 5, 35–57.

———. 2009. *History of the Holy Mar Maʿin*. Persian Martyr Acts in Syriac: Text and Translation 1. Piscataway, NJ: Gorgias Press.

Brock, Sebastian P. and Paul C. Dilley. 2014. *The Martyrs of Mount Berʿain*. Persian Martyr Acts in Syriac: Text and Translation 4. Piscataway, NJ: Gorgias Press.

Brock, Sebastian P. and Susan Ashbrook Harvey. 1987 (2nd ed. 1998). *Holy Women of the Syrian Orient*. Berkeley: University of California Press.

Brooks, Ernest W. 1923–5. *John of Ephesus' Lives of the Eastern Saints*. PO 17, 1–304; PO 18, 513–698; PO 19, 153–282 . Paris: Firmin-Didot.

Budge, Ernest A. W. 1893. *The Book of Governors: The Historia Monastica of Thomas Bishop of Margâ, A.D. 840*. 2 Vols. London: Kegan Paul, Trench, Trübner & co. Reprinted 2003, Piscataway, NJ: Gorgias Press.

———. 1904. *Book of Paradise, Being the Histories and Sayings of the Monks and Ascetics of the Egyptian Desert By Palladius, Hieronymus and Others: The Syriac Texts, According to the Recension of ʿAnân-Îshôʿ of Bêth ʿÂbhê*. London: W. Drugulin.

Burkitt, Francis C. 1913. *Euphemia and the Goth With the Acts of Martyrdom of the Confessors of Edessa*. London and Oxford: Williams and Norgate. Reprinted, 2007. Piscataway, NJ: Gorgias Press.

Canivet, Pierre and Alice Leroy-Molinghen (1977–79) *Théodoret de Cyr, Histoire des moines de syrie*. SC 234, 257. Paris: Éditions de Cerf.

Cureton, William. 1861. *History of the Martyrs in Palestine By Eusebius, Bishop of Caesarea*. London: Williams and Norgate.

Dewing, Henry B. 1935. *Procopius, The Anecdota or Secret History*. LCL 290. Cambridge: Harvard University Press.

Doran, Robert. 1992. *Lives of Simeon Stylites*. Kalamazoo: Cistercian Publications.

———. 2006. *Stewards of the Poor: The Man of God, Rabbula, and Hiba in Fifth-Century Edessa*. Kalamazoo: Cistercian Publications.

Draguet, René. 1980. *La vie primitive de S. Antoine conservée en Syriaque*. CSCO 417–418/ Scr. Syr. 183–184. Louvain: Secrétariat du CorpusSCO.

Drijvers, Han. J. 1963. Acts of Thomas. *In*: W. Schneemelcher, ed., *New Testament Apocrypha, Vol.* 2. Philadelphia: Westminster Press, 322–411.

Gregg, Robert. 1980. *The Life of Antony and the Letter to Marcellinus*. New York: Paulist Press.

Harrak, Amir. 2005. *The Acts of Mār Māri*. Writings from the Greco-Roman World 11. Atlanta: Society of Biblical Literature.

Howard, George. 1981. *The Teaching of Addai*. SBL Texts and Translations 16. Chico: Scholars Press.

Klijn, Albertus. F. J. 1962. *Acts of Thomas*. Novum Testamentum Supplement 5. Rev ed. 2003. Leiden: Brill.

Nau, François. 1912. *Un martyrloge et douze ménologes syriaques*. PO 10/1. Paris: Firmin-Didot.

———. 1913–14, 1917. Résumé de monographies syriaques. *ROC* 1, 270–6, 379–89; 19, 113–34, 278–89, 414–40; 20, 3–32.

Penn, Michael. 2015. *When Christians First Met Muslims: A Sourcebook of the Earliest Writings on Islam*. Berkeley: University of California Press.

Phillips, George. 1876. *The Doctrine of Addai, the Apostle*. London: Trübner and Co.

Price, Richard M. 1988. *A History of the Monks of Syria*. Kalamazoo: Cistercian Publications.

Saint-Laurent, Jeanne-Nicole Mellon, and Kyle Smith. 2018. *History of Mar Behnam and Sarah: Martyrdom and Monasticism in Medieval Iraq*. Persian Martyr Acts in Syriac: Text and Translation 7. Piscataway, NJ: Gorgias Press.

Smith, Kyle. 2014. *Martyrdom and History of Blessed Simeon Bar Sabba'e*. Persian Martyr Acts in Syriac: Text and Translation 3. Piscataway, NJ: Gorgias Press.

Secondary Literature

Becker, Adam. Forthcoming. The Invention of the Persian Martyr Acts. *In:* Aaron Butts and Robin D. Young, ed., *Proceedings of the VII North American Syriac Symposium*. Washington, DC: Catholic University of America Press.

Binggeli, André. 2012a. Introduction. *In:* André Binggeli, ed., *L'hagiographie syriaque*. Études Syriaques 9. Paris: Geuthner, 3–8.

———. 2012b. Les Collections de Vies de Saints dans les Manuscrits Syriaques. *In:* André Binggeli, ed., *L'hagiographie syriaque*. Études Syriaques 9. Paris: Geuthner, 49–75.

Brakke, David. 1994. The Greek and Syriac Versions of the Life of Antony. *Le Muséon* 107, 29–53.

Bremmer, Jan. 2001. *Apocryphal Acts of Thomas*. Louvain: Peeters.

Brock, Sebastian P. 2008b. Saints in Syriac: A Little Tapped Resource. *JECS* 16, no. 8, 181–96.

———. 2011a. Assemani, Stephanus Evodius. *In:* S. P. Brock, A. M. Butts, G. A. Kiraz, and L. van Rompay, ed., *Gorgias Encyclopedic Dictionary of the Syriac Heritage*. Pisctaway: Gorgias Press, 44.

———. 2011b. Martyrs and Persecutions. *In:* S. P. Brock, A. M. Butts, G. A. Kiraz, and L. van Rompay, ed., *Gorgias Encyclopedic Dictionary of the Syriac Heritage*. Pisctaway: Gorgias Press, 272–3.

———. 2011c. Palladius. *In:* S. P. Brock, A. M. Butts, G. A. Kiraz, and L. van Rompay, ed., *Gorgias Encyclopedic Dictionary of the Syriac Heritage*. Pisctaway: Gorgias Press, 319–20.

———. 2012. L'hagiographie Versifiée. *In:* André Binggeli, ed., *L'hagiographie syriaque*. Études Syriaques 9. Paris: Geuthner, 113–26.

Brown, Peter. 1971. The Rise and Function of the Holy Man in Late Antiquity. *JRS* 61, 80–101.

Butts, Aaron. M. 2011. Syriac Language. *In:* S. P. Brock, A. M. Butts, G. A. Kiraz, and L. van Rompay, ed., *Gorgias Encyclopedia of the Syriac Heritage*. Piscataway, NJ: Gorgias Press, 390–1.

Debié, Muriel. 2012. "Marcher dans leurs Traces": Les Discours de L'Hagiographie et de L'Histoire. *In:* André Binggeli, ed., *L'hagiographie syriaque*. Études Syriaques 9. Paris: Geuthner, 9–48.

Dolabani, Yuhanna, René Levenant, S. P. Brock and S. K. Samir. 1994. Catalogue des manuscrits de la bibliothèque du Patriarchat syrien orthodoxe à Ḥomṣ. *Parole de l'Orient* 19, 555–661.

Efthymiadis, Stephanos. 2011/14. *The Ashgate Research Companion to Byzantine Hagiography*. 2 Vols. Farnham and Burlington: Ashgate.

Fiey, J-.M. 2004. *Saints syriaques*. Edited by L. Conrad. Studies in Late Antiquity and Early Islam 6. Princeton: Darwin Press.

Gardner, Iain, Paul Dilley and Jason BeDuhn. 2014. *Mani's Wisdom at the Court of the Persian Kings: Studies on the Chester Beatty Kephalaia Codex*. Leiden: Brill.

Griffith, Sidney. 1993. "Monks, 'Singles', and the 'Sons of the Covenant'": Reflections on Syriac Ascetic Terminology. *In:* E. Carr et al., ed., *ΕΥΛΟΓΗΜΑ: Studies in Honor of Robert Taft, S.J.* Studia Anselmiana 110, Analecta Liturgica 17. Rome: Pontificio Ateneo S. Anselmo, 141–60.

———. 1994. Julian Saba, "Father of the Monks" of Syria. *JECS* 2, 185–216.

Harvey, Susan Ashbrook. 1990. *Asceticism and Society in Crisis: John of Ephesus and the Lives of the Eastern Saints*. Berkeley: University of California Press.

———. 1996. Mothers and Daughters in Early Syriac Hagiography. *JECS* 4, no. 1, 27–56.

———. 2001. "Theodora the Believing Queen:" A Study in Syriac Historiographical Tradition. *Hugoye: Journal of Syriac Studies* 4, no. 2, 209–34.

———. 2005. Revisiting the Daughters of the Covenant: Women's Choirs and Sacred Song in Ancient Syriac Christianity. *Hugoye: Journal of Syriac Studies* 8, no. 2, 125–49.

———. 2008. Martyr Passions and Hagiography. *In:* Susan A. Harvey and David G. Hunter, ed., *The Oxford Handbook of Early Christian Studies*. Oxford: Oxford University Press, 603–27.

Insley, Sarah and Jeanne-Nicole Mellon Saint-Laurent. 2018. Biography, Autobiography, and Hagiography. *In:* Edward Watts and Scott McGill, ed., *A Companion to Late Antique Literature*. Blackwell Companions to the Ancient World. Hoboken: John Wiley and Sons, 373–88.

Jones, Christopher. 2015. *What We've Lost: Mar Behnam Monastery*. https://gatesofnineveh.wordpress.com/2015/05/12/what-weve-lost-mar-behnam-monastery/, accessed March 22, 2016.

Jullien, Christelle. 2012. Les *Actes des martyrs perses*. Transmettre l'histoire. In: André Binggeli, ed., *L'hagiographie syriaque*. Études Syriaques 9. Paris: Geuthner, 127–40.

Palmer, Andrew. 1990. *Monk and Mason on the Tigris Frontier: The Early History of Tur Abdin*. Cambridge: University of Cambridge Press.
Payne, Richard. 2015. *A State of Mixture: Christians, Zoroastrians, and Iranian Political Culture in Late Antiquity*. Berkeley: University of California Press.
Peeters, Paul. 1910. *Bibliotheca Hagiographica Orientalis*. Subsidia Hagiographica 10. Brussels: Société des Bollandistes.
Saint-Laurent, Jeanne-Nicole Mellon. 2012. Images de Femmes dans L'Hagiographie Syriaque. *In:* André Binggeli, ed., *L'hagiographie syriaque*. Études Syriaques 9. Paris: Geuthner, 201–24.
———. 2015. *Missionary Stories and the Formation of the Syriac Churches*. Berkeley: University of California Press.
———. 2016. The Gateway to the Syriac Saints: A Database Project. *Journal of Religion, Media & Digital Culture* 5, no. 1, 183–204.
Schilling, Alexander M. 2008. *Die Anbetung der Magier und die Taufe der Sāsāaniden: Zur Geistesgeschichte des iranischen Christentums in der Spätantike*. CSCO 621. Louvain: Peeters.
Smith, Kyle. 2012. Constantine and Judah the Maccabee: History and Memory in the Acts of the Persian Martyrs. *JCSSS* 12, 16–33.
———. 2016. *Constantine and the Captive Christians of Persia: Martyrdom Religious Identity in Late Antiquity*. Berkeley: University of California Press.
Tannous, Jack. 2012. L'hagiographie Syro-Occidentale à la Période Islamique. *In:* André Binggeli, ed., *L'hagiographie syriaque*. Études Syriaques 9. Paris: Geuthner, 225–45.
Taylor, David G. K. 2012. Hagiographie et Liturgie Syriaque. *In:* André Binggeli, ed., *L'hagiographie syriaque*. Études Syriaques 9. Paris: Geuthner, 77–112.
Walker, Joel. 2006. *Legend of Mar Qardagh: Narrative and Christian Heroism in Late Ancient Iraq*. Berkeley: University of California Press.
Ward, Benedicta. 1987. *Harlots of the Desert: A Study of Repentance in Early Monastic Sources*. Cistercian Studies Series 106. Kalamazoo: Cistercian Publications.
Witakowski, W. 2011. Toma of Marga. *In:* S. P. Brock, A. M. Butts, G. A. Kiraz, and L. van Rompay, ed., *Gorgias Encyclopedic Dictionary of the Syriac Heritage*. Pisctaway: Gorgias Press, 417.
Wood, Philip. 2010. *'We Have No King But Christ': Christian Political Thought in Greater Syria on the Eve of the Arab Conquest c.400–585*. Oxford: Oxford University Press.
Wright, William. 1870–1872. *A Catalogue of the Syriac Manuscripts in the British Museum Acquired Since the Year 1838, I-III*. London: British Museum, Department of Oriental Printed Books and Manuscripts.
Younansardaroud, Helen. 2002. Die Legende von Mar Behnam. *In:* Martin Tamke, ed., *Syriaca: Zur Geschichte, Theologie, Liturgie und Gegegswartlage der syrischen Kirchen*. Studien zur orientalischen Kirchengeschichte 17. Münster: Lit, 185–96.
Zanetti, Ugo. 1993. Projet d'une Bibliotheca Hagiographica Syriaca. *Aram* 5, 657–70.

Digital Resources

Binggeli, André. et al. 2015. *E-ktobe, Manuscrits Syriaques*. www.mss-syriaques.org/
Carlson, Thomas A. and David A. Michelson, eds. 2014. *The Syriac Gazetteer*. Part of *The Syriac Reference Portal*. www.syriaca.org
Heal, Kristian and Carl W. Griffin. *Center for the Preservation of Ancient Texts*. http://cpart.mi.byu.edu/
Minov, Sergey, 2015. *A Comprehensive Bibliography on Syriac Christianity*. www.csc.org.il/
Minov, Sergey and David G. Taylor. *The Syriac World*. Part of *The Cult of the Saints: A Research Project on the Cult of the Saints From Its Origins to Circa AD 700, Across the Entire Christian World*. http://cultofsaints.history.ox.ac.uk/
Novel Saints: Studies in Ancient Fiction and Hagiography. www.novelsaints.ugent.be/

Saint-Laurent, Jeanne-Nicole Mellon and David A. Michelson. 2015a. *Qadishe: A Guide to the Syriac Saints*. Part of *The Syriac Reference Portal.* www.syriaca.org
———. 2015b. *Bibliotheca Hagiographica Syriaca Electronica: A Guide to the Syriac Saints.* Part of *The Syriac Reference Portal.* www.syriaca.org
Stewart, Columba. *The Hill Manuscript Library.* www.hmml.org/ [See also Adam McCollum's blog on the contents of the HMML collection of oriental hagiography https://hmmlorientalia.wordpress.com/].

CHAPTER TWENTY-ONE

THE MYSTICISM OF THE CHURCH OF THE EAST

Adrian Pirtea

INTRODUCTION

Along with its thriving scholastic culture at the School of Nisibis and its intense missionary activity in Central Asia and China, the Church of the East is perhaps best known for the rich and highly influential mystical tradition it has fostered. Isaac of Nineveh, the great seventh-century ascetic from Beth Qaṭraye, is perhaps the first name that comes to mind (Brock 1999–2000, Chialà 2002: 283–321). But there were also others, such as John of Dalyatha (8th c.) who became an uncontested authority even among miaphysite Christians as the anonymous 'Spiritual Elder', or Isaac's contemporary Dadishoʿ, whose works were studied in places as far apart as the Ethiopian highlands and the foothills of the Tian Shan mountains (Sims-Williams 1985: 78–86, 1989; Witakowski 2006).

What follows is a very brief introduction to the most important authors, texts, and ideas that shaped Syro-oriental mysticism in the first Christian millennium. I will first give an overview of the major periods and trends in Syriac Christian mysticism, including a survey of the most representative authors for each period. Since there is still much editorial work to be done in this field, it will further prove helpful to address the question of sources. I have included a short account of the manuscript evidence, the ancient translations, and the different genres of mystical literature preferred by Eastern Syriac authors. Next, I will succinctly present some of the fundamental concepts of Syriac mysticism: the stages of ascent, knowledge, wonder, contemplation, etc. Finally, I will discuss the influence exerted by Eastern Syriac mystics on the spirituality of other Christian groups (miaphysites, Chalcedonians) and the possible links with Early Islamic mysticism.

SOME DEFINITIONS AND A HISTORICAL OUTLINE

Mysticism and mystical literature

Instead of searching for all-encompassing definitions of *mysticism* as such, scholars of religion appeal more and more to provisional or 'working definitions' of mystical phenomena, tailored to specific areas, periods, or religious traditions. In the case of

Syriac Christianity a good starting point is still Robert Beulay's basic but adequate observation that mysticism ('mystique') refers 'not to that which indicates, indirectly, [. . .], the personal experience of union with God, *but the description of this experience or the reflection of which it is the object*' (Beulay 1987: 242–3, my emphasis). On this account, mystical literature only emerges when ascetical authors and theologians begin to reflect upon and extensively discuss the very acts of perceiving/knowing/uniting with God, as well as the 'conditions of possibility' for such acts.

Closely connected with this type of reflection is an increasingly systematic use of technical terms in mystical texts and even a certain formalism in literary expression. This can perhaps best be explained by the 'esoteric' nature of most mystical treatises: they were usually written by elders for their inner circle of disciples, who were in turn already acquainted with the ascetical jargon of their masters. This has led some researchers to differentiate between *mystography*, i.e. mere descriptions of personal mystical experiences, and *mystology/mystagogy*, i.e. writings with either a strong theoretical focus or with the pedagogical aim to guide *others* towards the contemplation of God (Blum 2001, 2009). In fact, most Syriac mystical writings belong to the two latter types, insofar as they served as handbooks for entire generations of coenobites and solitaries. Furthermore, Syriac mystical authors typically avoid reporting personal experiences in any significant detail: references to oneself as the recipient of mystical visions are veiled and often echo Saint Paul's deflective phrase, 'I know a man in Christ, who . . .' (2Cor 12:2, cf. Wensinck 1923: xix–xx). In other words, in the Late Antique Christian context, mysticism is not so much about what the individual 'subject' (in the modern sense of the term) feels and experiences, but rather about the fulfilment of the highest potential to which *all* human beings are called: transcending the fallen state of sin, restoring the image of God in oneself, and being granted the vision of God through the workings of Divine grace.

The fourth century Syriac Christian texts documenting ascetical practices and/or describing the different stages of spiritual life (the *Book of Steps*, Aphrahaṭ, Ephrem) would not qualify, strictly speaking, as mystical (on this early period, see Vööbus 1958–88). To be sure, these early writings are foundational for the subsequent mystical tradition and need to be taken into account when researching later authors. For example, the anonymous author of the *Book of Steps*, a collection of thirty discourses dated to the late fourth/early fifth century (see Heal/Kitchen 2014), likens spiritual perfection (*gmīrūtā*) to the prelapsarian state of Adam and Eve, and extolls the virtue of humility (*makkīkūtā*) in a way similar to later Syriac mystics. However, most of the defining features listed above (the theoretical approach, an advanced technical terminology, etc.), are notably absent in these early texts. Although they sometimes speak about spiritual perception, or the indwelling of the Holy Spirit in the present life, early Syriac ascetical authors generally allow for a *visio Dei* only in the Hereafter. The late fourth century was nevertheless a crucial period in the history of Syriac mysticism insofar as it witnessed the emergence of Messalianism (from *mṣallyānē*, 'the ones who pray') around Edessa and in Asia Minor (Stewart 1991; Fitschen 1998). Among their many controversial teachings, the Messalians held that the Holy Spirit could be perceived by our bodily senses, a claim for which they were criticised by both Greek and Syriac church fathers. Against the Messalian position, theologians such as the miaphysite Philoxenus of Mabbug (d. 523) had to insist on the *noetic* and *incorporeal* nature of mystical contemplation (*theōria*). Although later Eastern

Syriac mystics endorsed the same view of contemplation as Philoxenus, they were often tendentiously described as 'Messalians' because they argued for the possibility of seeing God in this life. The persisting tensions between monks and clergy on this subject eventually led to the condemnation of three major mystical authors by the Eastern Syriac catholicos Timothy I (r. 780–823), an event to be described in greater detail below.

The early period: fifth–sixth centuries

The most prolific Syriac ascetical author of the fifth century was John the Solitary, a monk whose exact identity is still a matter of debate (Beulay 1987: 95–7). Writing in a period of intense Christological debates (ca. 430–450), John the Solitary's confessional allegiance is not entirely clear: his theology has sometimes been described as miaphysite (Strothmann 1972: 68–80), while others have pointed out similarities between John's teachings and those of the dyophysite Theodore of Mopsuestia (ca. 350–428) (Hansbury 2013: xviii–xxiii). Regardless of his theological viewpoints, however, John the Solitary was recognised by both Western and Eastern Syriac writers as a major authority on spiritual life and can be considered one of the first Syriac mystics in his own right. John is the principal advocate of the threefold division of ascetic life into the corporeal, psychic, and spiritual orders (*ṭaksē*), which was embraced by the large majority of later Syriac mystics (Beulay 1987: 97–125). With many of John the Solitary's writings still unpublished (Strothmann 1972: 12–35), other significant aspects of his thought and his role in the broader development of Syriac mysticism still remain to be fully determined.

During the fifth and early sixth centuries, Syriac translations of Greek ascetical authors began to awaken the interest of Western Syriac theologians. This was a turning point in the history of Syriac literature, as it introduced a series of new concepts and models of asceticism to Syria and Mesopotamia. The most influential authors to be translated were Evagrius of Pontus, Pseudo-Macarius, Gregory of Nyssa, Basil of Caesarea, Mark the Solitary, Abba Isaiah, and Pseudo-Dionysius. The case of Evagrius is particularly instructive: by the sixth century, there existed already three different Syriac translations of Evagrius's treatises *Praktikos* and *Gnostikos*, as well as two translations of his *Kephalaia Gnostika*. Some of these translations underwent a process of doctrinal revision: while one version of the *Kephalaia* (S2) remained true to the original Greek, the 'common version' S1 supressed some of Evagrius's more controversial ideas (Guillaumont 1962, cf. Casiday 2013: 64–71). Via these early translations, Evagrius rapidly became a central figure of Syriac spirituality: salient Evagrian ideas pertaining to ascetical practice and to divine contemplation can be found throughout Philoxenus's letters and ascetical treatises, but also in the treatise on the spiritual life (Sherwood 1960–1961) composed by Sergius of Resh'ayna (d. 536), the first Syriac translator of the Dionysian corpus. Sergius takes over from Evagrius the two-fold division of spiritual life into *praktikē* and *theōria* and describes the latter, in Pseudo-Dionysian terms, as culminating with the 'hidden vision that stretches out towards the inaccessible ray of Divine Essence' (Sherwood 1960–1961: 124, cf. 134).

With the resurgence of Origenism in early sixth century Palestine (Hombergen 2001), more daring approaches to mystical theology developed. In the Western Syriac milieu, the 'extremist' branch of Origenism is best represented by the *Book of Hierotheos* (Marsh 1927), purportedly written by the teacher of (Pseudo-)Dionysius. The real author was probably Stephen bar Sudaili (early 6th c.), who was notorious for claiming that all creatures will become coessential with God. This pantheistic-monistic standpoint is indeed central to the *Book of Hierotheos* as well (Marsh 1927: 120*–21*). As Widengren (1961) already pointed out, the *Book*'s peculiar teachings on the mind's ascent, its crucifixion, and its commingling with the Divine Essence (which foreshadows the future mixture of all creatures with God) are claimed by 'Hierotheos' to be rooted in his personal mystical experiences. Despite these potentially heretical claims, the *Book of Hierotheos* was not dismissed entirely, and even inspired theological-mystical commentaries, first by Theodosius of Antioch (d. 895/6) and later by Bar Hebraeus (Pinggéra 2002).

In general, the wide reception of Greek ascetical texts in the Eastern Syriac church occurred at a somewhat later stage than in the Syro-Orthodox communities. In fact, only in the wake of Abraham of Kashkar momentous monastic reforms (after ca. 550) can one observe the emergence of a distinctive monastic culture and of a truly mystical literature within the Church of the East (Jullien 2006a; Jullien 2008; Chialà 2005). Abraham's establishment of the Great Monastery on Mt. Izla, together with a clear set of monastic rules, provided the essential guidelines for all the major monastic foundations in the following centuries and a favourable institutional setting for mysticism to flourish.

The classical period: the seventh and eighth centuries

A number of ascetics in the first generation after Abraham of Kashkar (d. ca. 588) still followed traditional Syriac models. Authors like Abraham of Nathpar, Bābai of Nisibis, and Shubḥalmaran (early 7th c.) relied heavily on the Holy Scriptures and rather insisted on the fundamentals of monastic life (fasting, repentance, humility, etc.) than on the advanced stages of mystical contemplation. At the same time, Abraham of Kashkar turn towards Egypt as the ideal model of monasticism generated new tendencies within Eastern Syriac asceticism. A prominent representative of this new movement was Babai the Great, who acted as the *de facto* leader of the Church during the vacancy of the catholicosate (608/9–628). Through his commentary on Evagrius's *Kephalaia Gnostika* (Frankenberg 1912), in which the vision of God's glory is repeatedly discussed, Babai facilitated the full acceptance of Evagrian mysticism within the Church of the East (Engelmann 2013: 34–107). Another mystic in close contact with the Great Monastery, and a contemporary of Babai, was Gregory of Cyprus. Born in Ahwaz in the sixth century, Gregory apparently spent several years as an exile (*ʾaksnāyā*) in Cyprus, where he worked as a gardener in a Greek monastery. Reputed for receiving multiple visions and revelations,[1] Gregory concurrently adopted an Evagrian approach to contemplation and took a special interest in Evagrius's complex demonology.

As Sabino Chialà (2011a) rightly observes, a few other monastic settlements in Mesopotamia and Persia were almost as instrumental in the propagation of mystical literature as the Great Monastery. The monastery of *Beth ʿAbe* (est. 595/6) rapidly became an important spiritual centre in northern Mesopotamia and was home to several major figures: Sahdona (Martyrios), Aphnimaran, and ʿEnanishoʿ, among others. Criticised on account of perceived Chalcedonian leanings in his Christology, Sahdona is a telling example of how closely interrelated mysticism and dogmatic theology can be (Ioan 2011). The mysticism of Sahdona's main work, *The Book of Perfection*, appears to be centred on the heart, the spiritual organ which can contain God and behold His glory (Brock 1987: 200). Criticism was also levelled against Sahdona's contemporary Aphnimāran, another monk of Beth ʿAbe, who was one of the first Eastern Syriac mystics of this period to be openly accused of Messalianism. Finally, ʿEnanishoʿ compiled his comprehensive anthology of Greek monastic histories (*The Paradise of the Fathers*) in the same monastery around 645. This popular anthology not only established the continuity between Abraham's reformed monasticism and its Egyptian role models, but it also proved the originality of the Eastern Syriac adaptation of these sources.

The most significant monastic centre in the southern dioceses of the Church of the East was the monastery of *Rabban Shapur* in Khuzestan (Jullien 2006b), where at least three great ascetics resided in roughly the same period (second half of 7th c.): Isaac of Nineveh, Dadishoʿ Qaṭraya, and Shemʿon d-Ṭaybuteh.[2] Perhaps more than any of their contemporaries, these prolific and highly complex writers gave Syriac mysticism its finest expression, its distinctiveness, and its subtlety. A native of Qatar, Isaac was ordained bishop of Nineveh in the late 670s, but soon abdicated and retreated to the vicinity of Rabban Shapur. Isaac presents a balanced synthesis of Theodore of Mopsuestia's theology, John the Solitary's asceticism, and Evagrius's teachings on contemplation, but he also develops a deeply personal approach to spiritual experience. In his work, Isaac often approaches fundamental topics which go beyond mystical theology in the narrow sense defined here: God's compassion and mercy towards creation, the hope of universal salvation, human sinfulness, etc. (Chialà 2002: 143–278). It is precisely within this broader theological worldview that Isaac develops a theory of natural and supernatural forms of knowledge (*īdaʿtā*) which closely correspond to different forms of mystical prayer.

A remarkable similarity to Isaac's teachings can be observed in the works of Shemʿon d-Ṭaybuteh. Shemʿon's writings indicate the author's solid medical and theological training, as he tries to combine elements of anthropology and physiology with mystical teachings. Shemʿon is most renowned for his *Book of Grace*, which consists of seven hundred short but theologically complex *kephalaia* on the activity of Divine Grace, the intellect's luminous essence, the vision of Christ's glory, etc. Dadishoʿ of Qatar chose to convey his doctrines primarily via learned commentaries to ascetical classics, such as the *Logoi* of Abba Isaiah and ʿEnanishoʿs *Paradise of the Fathers*. These commentaries highlight Dadishoʿs admiration for the heyday of Egyptian monasticism, but also reveal his critical attitude towards what he believed to be the laxness in the monasteries of his own time (Abramowski 1991). Two other writings by Dadishoʿ (*Treatise on Solitude*, *Letter to Abkosh*) revolve around the concept of *stillness* (*šelyā*). Much like the *hesychia* of later Byzantine mysticism, stillness for Dadishoʿ is the fruit of ascetical labour and the state in which the light of Christ's glory can illumine the purified mind of the solitary (del Río Sánchez 2011).

Another monastic centre mentioned by Chialà (2011a) was located on Mt. Judi (near Cizre, SE Turkey): the monastery of *John of Kamul*. Two lesser-known authors of gnostic *kephalaia* resided here in the seventh and eighth centuries: the chronicler and ascetic John bar Penkaye and Beh Ishoʿ. The monastery is also known for a providential event that involved Joseph Ḥazzaya, one of the greatest Eastern Syriac mystics of the eighth century. Born around 710 in a Zoroastrian family and forcibly converted to Islam as a young slave, Joseph once visited the monastery of Kamul and, upon seeing the piety of the monks there, received baptism and decided to embrace solitary life. Joseph wrote extensively throughout his monastic career. His widely read letter on the three stages is a comprehensive exposition of ascetic life (Graffin/Harb 1992). Equally important are the long *Memra on Divine Providence* (Kavvadas 2016) and the *Book of Questions and Answers*, which cover a broad array of topics and have only recently caught the attention of scholars. Joseph also composed about 3,000 gnostic chapters, a few hundred of which still survive in manuscripts. Generally faithful to Evagrius, Isaac, and Shemʿon, Joseph in many instances develops the mystical doctrines of his predecessors in new directions.

Despite a discernible influence on later Syriac mysticism, Joseph's ideas and writings were soon overshadowed by those of his contemporary, John of Dalyatha (John Saba). John became a monk at the monastery of Mar Yozadaq and eventually retreated to solitary life on a mountain called Beth Dalyatha ('house of vine-branches'). John's writings include fifty letters, twenty-nine homilies, and a series of gnostic *kephalaia* (Beulay 1972). John stands out as a master of apophaticism and is closer to Gregory of Nyssa and Pseudo-Dionysius in his theological outlook than to Evagrius or even John the Solitary (Beulay 1987: 214). One key element of John's mysticism is his careful distinction between God's eternal glory and God's essence: while denying the possibility of seeing the latter, John did stress the full experiential reality of the former, which was a controversial position to hold (see below).

The acuteness of the theological problems that the *visio Dei* entailed (Beulay 1990: 423–64) eventually brought about a crisis that proved devastating for the later history of Eastern Syriac mysticism. Alarmed by some of the claims made by Joseph Ḥazzaya and John of Dalyatha, the energetic catholicos Timothy I convened a council in 786/7 in order to condemn the two authors, together with the works of John of Apamea (Treiger 2009). Among the accusations, the council claimed that the mystics supported 'Messalian' ideas on the possibility of seeing God. Although the accusations were based on a biased reading of the authors in question, Timothy's concerns were partially legitimate, at least from the point of view of official church doctrine (Berti 2011). As an immediate result of the council, newly elected bishops like Joseph's disciple Nestorius of Beth Nuhadra had to publicly denounce Messalianism (see Berti 2005).

The later periods: the ninth to fourteenth centuries and the modern era

Despite the revocation of Timothy's anathema by his successor Ishoʿ bar Nun (d. 828), the mystical movement within the Church of the East had already lost its momentum. From the ninth century onwards we may observe a rapid process of 'canonising' the great names of the past. The monastic histories of both Ishoʿdnaḥ of Baṣra and Thomas of Marga seem to display an awareness that the golden period of asceticism had already passed. Nevertheless, it would be wrong to affirm that interest in mysticism faded away entirely within the Church of the East. During the tenth and early eleventh centuries there are at least a few authors worthy of mention: John bar Khaldun composed a detailed biographic account of his master Joseph Busnaya, in which he combined hagiography, history, and mystical theology. Not long afterwards,

ʿAbdmshiḥa wrote a considerable number of mystical homilies and sermons, which remain unedited and unstudied. In even later times, only a few names can be associated with mystical theology in the Syro-oriental church: Shemʿon the Persecuted composed an anti-Origenistic treatise and a series of gnostic chapters in the thirteenth century (Reinink 2010), John of Mosul rendered at least one of John of Dalyatha's homilies into verse (13th c.), and an otherwise unknown Ephrem of Qirqephion (13th/14th c.) commented on Joseph Ḥazzaya's *Kephalaia Gnostika*.

Even as the Eastern Syriac mystical tradition ebbed during the later Middle Ages, Syro-Orthodox authors began to show a renewed interest in this type of literature. Notable examples include Dionysius bar Ṣalibi's commentary on Evagrius's *Kephalaia Gnostika* and the ascetic-mystical writings of Athanasius Abu Ghalib (Fotescu-Tauwinkl 2010), both from the twelfth century. A century later, Western Syriac mystical literature reached its zenith with the great philosopher and theologian Gregory Bar Hebraeus (d. 1286). Gregory's disillusion with confessional debates and with the worldly sciences, famously described in his *Book of the Dove*, led him to search for the teachings of the 'true Gnostics'. Inspired by the writings of Evagrius, John of Dalyatha, 'Hierotheos', and even al-Ġhazali, Bar Hebraeus composed a few mystical treatises which contributed decisively to the revival of asceticism and spirituality in the Syro-Orthodox church. This revival continued at least until the fifteenth century and was especially strong in the region of Ṭur ʿAbdin. Not only were numerous monastic anthologies copied and compiled there in this period, but at least two of the patriarchs of Ṭur ʿAbdin, Abu al-Maʿani (d. 1481), and Masʿud (d. 1512), wrote mystical compendia of their own.

The modern period (sixteenth to twentieth centuries) is in many respects a *terra incognita* with regard to both Eastern and Western Syriac mystical literature. A census of the works written in this period indicates that although copies of classical authors continued to be made, original treatises on mysticism were very seldom written. Moreover, after parts of the Eastern Syriac church entered full communion with Rome, there was a conscious turn towards Western (Roman Catholic) spiritual literature. The works of the Chaldean patriarch Joseph II (1696–1713) are a case in point: Joseph's *Book of the Magnet* is a devotional handbook and contains examples of piety and moral maxims based almost exclusively upon Latin sources in Arabic translation (Teule 2004).

THE SOURCES

The manuscripts

Syriac manuscripts with ascetical and mystical content can be divided into two large groups: volumes dedicated to a single author, and anthologies (miscellanies, etc.). In many cases, early Syriac editors and compilers created complete volumes comprising the works of one major writer. Isaac of Nineveh's writings are a good example: the earliest complete manuscript of Isaac's *Second Part* (*Bodleian, syr. e. 7*, 11th c.), famously discovered by Sebastian Brock in 1983 (see Brock 1990), is exclusively dedicated to Isaac. On the Western Syriac side, we often find manuscripts containing only the writings of John of Dalyatha and simply entitled 'The Book of the Spiritual Elder'. Unfortunately, countless such volumes are now lost, e.g. an early complete(?) copy of Gregory of Cyprus in Mosul (ms. *syr. 96*), or a large manuscript with Joseph Ḥazzaya's works in Siirt (ms. *syr. 78*). However, this type of 'dedicated' volumes are the exception. Scholars have to rely mostly on monastic anthologies, many of which are of much later date than the original writings. These anthologies and miscellanies clearly reflect previous models, such as the Late Antique compendia of Greek ascetical authors in Syriac translation.[3] Although many texts constantly recur in various miscellaneous manuscripts over the centuries, the creation of Syriac monastic florilegia remained bound to specific monasteries and never became 'standardised', as opposed to some widely diffused collections in Greek or Armenian (Teule 1998: 261).

Perhaps the single most important monastic anthology of Eastern Syriac mysticism preserved today is the manuscript Baghdad, *Dawra syr. 680* (olim Alqoš, *N.-D. des Semences* 237), dated to 1289 (Vosté 1929; Teule 1998: 254–5). The manuscript contains an impressive number of works by almost all the mystics of the classical period discussed above, but also by other minor authors such as Ḥnanisho' (7th c.) or Abraham bar Dashandad (8th c.). With some of its texts still unedited, this codex is one of the very few anthologies of Syro-oriental provenance to survive. The very opposite is the case for Western Syriac manuscripts, where Herman Teule (1998: 263–4) could identify over seventy ascetic-mystical florilegia in European libraries alone. The more or less equal distribution of these collections between the ninth and the fifteenth centuries point to a sustained and continuous interest in mystical literature among the Syro-Orthodox. The composition and structure of some of these anthologies have been studied in detail (Colless 1966; Vööbus 1978; Brock 1998).

It should also be emphasised that the monastic anthologies are much more than a gateway to the original texts. Syriac manuscripts with ascetical and mystical contents also deserve to be studied as witnesses to the social, historical, and economic circumstances of their production and distribution (including scribes, editors, patrons, buyers, readers, etc.). They can further shed light on the changing interests, concerns, tastes, and preferences of their respective audiences. Given the recent advances in Syriac manuscript studies (see Briquel Chatonnet/Debié 2015) and the large-scale digitisation projects currently underway (*Hill Museum & Manuscript Library*, *Bibliotheca Apostolica Vaticana*, *Bibliothèque Nationale*, etc., for which see Appendix 2), more comprehensive and interdisciplinary studies are to be expected in the future.

Ancient translations

Already towards the end of the eighth century, the works of Eastern Syriac mystics began to be translated into various languages. Because in some cases the Syriac originals are either lost or reflect much later strata of the text, these ancient translations can be important witnesses and require careful examination. The greatest corpus of such translations from Syriac are found in *Arabic*: the Christian Arabic versions of Isaac of Nineveh and John of Dalyatha were particularly popular, but others including 'Enanisho', Dadisho', or Shem'on were translated as well. A unique aspect of the later *Ethiopic* translations, which derive exclusively from the Arabic, is that Isaac, John, and Dadisho' were integrated into the traditional monastic curriculum as the three greatest authorities on spiritual life. In Byzantine *Greek*, the only extensive corpus to be translated was that of Isaac, but this translation inadvertently transmitted works by John of Dalyatha and Philoxenus of Mabbug as well (Pirard 2012). The *Sogdian* translations discovered at Bulayïq (Xinjiang province, NW China), dated to the ninth–tenth centuries, include two highly remarkable but fragmentary monastic anthologies: they comprise the Greek authors Evagrius, Pseudo-Macarius, and Abba Isaiah, but also the Eastern Syriac mystics Dadishoʿ, Shemʿon, Babai of Nisibis, and Isaac of Nineveh (Sims-Williams 1985, 2017).[4] Smaller, but significant corpora were passed down in the Caucasian languages: a number of *Armenian* manuscripts preserve fragments from John of Dalyatha and Joseph Ḥazzaya, while large parts of Isaac and selections from John of Dalyatha, Sahdona, and John the Solitary are found in *Georgian* codices (Outtier 2011; Pataridze 2011).

The main genres of mystical literature in Syriac

A survey of the extant Syriac ascetic literature allows for a rough categorisation into the following genres: (a) letters, (b) homilies and sermons, (c) questions and answers (*erotapokriseis*), (d) gnostic chapters (*kephalaia*), (e) commentaries, and (f) prayers. The *epistolary* and the *homiletic genres* were probably the earliest and most widespread means of communicating ascetical and mystical doctrines. The great Egyptian ascetics had already set an important precedent: collections of letters and/or homilies were (sometimes falsely) attributed to Anthony the Great, Pachomius, Ammonius, or Macarius and integrated into the earliest Syriac anthologies. Among the Eastern Syriac mystics of the classical period, the most extensive and original epistolary corpus belongs to John of Dalyatha (Beulay 1978; Khayyat 2007), while the largest collection of homilies by far is that of Isaac of Nineveh. Suitable for educational purposes, the *Questions and Answers* were often addressed by anonymous 'brothers' to a collective of 'elders', but in some cases mystics such as Joseph Ḥazzaya chose to respond with lengthy treatises to the questions of a specific inquirer.

The signature genre of mystical literature in Syriac is undoubtedly the *gnostic chapters* (*kephalaia gnostika, rīšē d-īdaʿtā*). These are short enigmatic sentences, usually organised in groups of one hundred individual chapters ('centuries'), but sometimes also arranged alphabetically. There are notable parallels in pagan Greek writers (the sentences of Sextus, Pythagoras, Porphyry) and in the wisdom literature of the Ancient Near East (Aḥiqar, Proverbs of Solomon), but the distinctive style of *kephalaia* in Syriac Christian literature is directly dependent on Evagrius of Pontus (Guillaumont 1962). Following the Evagrian model, several Syriac mystics (Aphnimaran, Isaac, Shemʿon, Joseph Ḥazzaya, Bar Hebraeus) composed their own series of gnostic chapters. Interestingly, for some of these authors the actual composition of *kephalaia* was intrinsically related to the mystical experience. Thus, when Joseph testifies that his *kephalaia* were directly communicated by the Holy Spirit, or when Bar Hebraeus calls his chapters 'revelations' imparted by 'a flash of lightning in the nightly darkness' (Wensinck 1919: 62), their words are perhaps not to be taken figuratively. Several collections of gnostic chapters were accompanied by extensive *commentaries*: at least three commentaries were written on Evagrius's *Kephalaia Gnostika* (Babai the Great, Joseph Ḥazzaya, Dionysius bar Ṣalībī), and explanations were later composed on Aphnimaran's and Joseph Ḥazzaya's own chapters. Unlike the Greek fathers, who often delineated their mystical theology in exegetical works on the Bible (e.g. Gregory of Nyssa's *Commentary on the Song of Songs*), Syriac mystical authors generally preferred to write commentaries on the classics of asceticism, such as on the works of Abba Isaiah or of Mark the Solitary.

The last genre that needs to be mentioned here are *mystical prayers*. Together with theological reflections *on* prayer, as exemplified by Evagrius's treatise on the subject and by other texts of the Syriac fathers (Brock 1987), Syro-oriental ascetics also authored original prayers for liturgical use and personal devotion. These prayers, which were often collected into florilegia and books of hours, represent rare tokens of Syriac mystical theology *in practice*. Sadly, with a few exceptions (Sanders 1977; Bunge 1982: 27–33), these theologically challenging and inspiring prayers have been almost entirely neglected in scholarship.

MAJOR THEMES IN EASTERN SYRIAC MYSTICISM

The structure and stages of spiritual life

Syriac Christian authors usually divide spiritual life into different stages or degrees. Although there were early examples, such as the well-known distinction between the 'righteous' and the 'perfect' in the *Book of Steps*, the two models that soon became dominant were those of John the Solitary and Evagrius. On the one hand, John the Solitary adapted a tripartite anthropological model (body – soul – spirit) to his mystical teachings, by devising three corresponding orders: the corporeal (*pagrānūtā*), the psychic (*napšānūtā*), and the spiritual (*rūḥānūtā*). The first stage is characterised by subservience to passions and vices, the second by ascetic struggle and the attainment of virtue, the third by mystical insight, participation in Divine love, and the contemplation of God (to be fully reached in the Hereafter). Evagrius on the other hand followed the Platonic division of the soul into three parts: two lower parts, *appetite* and *anger*, both subject to passions and in need of purification, and a higher part, *reason*. Accordingly, Evagrius proposed a somewhat different scheme of spiritual ascent: (a) *practice* (*praktikē*), i.e. the purification of the lower soul; (b) first and second natural *contemplation* (*theōria*); and (c) theology, i.e. the contemplation of God (Guillaumont 2004). It should be noted that the Evagrian outline of spiritual life is not incompatible with John's model and that some Syriac authors successfully harmonised the two. Both John the Solitary and Evagrius further argued that the different stages are intimately connected with specific states or dispositions of the soul, which function as 'indicators' of one's progress. Thus, in Evagrius's view, the aim of *practice* is to reach freedom from passions (*apatheia*), while the aim of natural contemplation is to raise the intellect to its primordial, or 'naked' condition, in which the mind becomes translucent or sapphire and can receive the light of God (Harmless/Fitzgerald 2001; Stewart 2001). Similarly, John distinguishes two different states of inner immaculacy: *purity* (*dakyūtā*) and *limpidity* (*šapyūtā*), with the latter being the fulfilment of the first (Nin 2005). Consistent with the baptismal imagery of rebirth and childhood in the Bible, ascetic progress can also be described as a 'coming of age': in Isaac, Bābai, Joseph, and others, to reach spiritual *maturity* is equivalent to the realisation of the full potential of human beings *qua* creatures.

Knowledge, discernment, and the spiritual senses

The centrality of *gnōsis* (*īdaʿtā*) and *theōria* in the ascetical doctrines of all the major Eastern Syriac authors is another clear sign of Evagrian influence. In Evagrius's view, knowledge and contemplation differ according to each stage of spiritual life, but ultimately point towards God. For instance, natural contemplation (*theōria physikē*) does not consist in having scientific insights about the world, but rather in discerning 'the manifold wisdom of God' (Eph 3:10) expressed in creation. The essential truth of things can only be grasped by the intellect (*haunā*) through its inherent powers of understanding and discernment (*pārūšūtā*). Although these natural powers must be transcended upon reaching the highest form of contemplation (i.e. of God), most mystics (Evagrius, Babai, Isaac, Joseph) regard the intellect as the only 'organ' receptive of this knowledge. Even if others (Pseudo-Macarius, Sahdona, Shemʿon) seem to attribute the same role to the heart (*lebbā*), there need not be a direct opposition between the two views. According to both the 'Evagrian' and the 'Macarian' position, there is a fundamental analogy between the ways in which the intellect and the heart operate, since both contemplate and are receptive of the light of God. Moreover, the virtue of discerning good and evil thoughts, the importance of which had been already established by the Desert Fathers (Rich 2007), is also attributed to both the heart and the mind.

Another way in which mystical knowledge is said to be conveyed is via the *five spiritual senses*. This theory of 'spiritual perception' originated in Alexandrian philosophy and theology (Plotinus, Origen) and rapidly became influential in Western and Eastern Christian mysticism (Coakley/Gavrilyuk 2012). The same can be firmly said about Eastern Syriac authors: Bābai, Gregory of Cyprus, Isaac, Joseph, and John of Dalyāthā all adopt the Evagrian version of the theory and attribute a central role to the pentad of spiritual senses, although sometimes with different accents: Bābai and Isaac focus more on spiritual sight, while Joseph attributes a special role to spiritual hearing (Pirtea 2017). However, as Susan Harvey (2006) has demonstrated in the case of scent/smell, the sensorial aspect of religious experience was already highly relevant in early Syriac spirituality, i.e. before the reception of Evagrius.

Mystical states: drunkenness, wonder, ignorance

Syriac writers often reflect on the conditions and states ascetics undergo when attaining mystical insights. One preferred way of describing these states is to appeal to analogies: for example, the metaphor of *drunkenness/inebriation* (*rawāyūtā*), already used by Philo of Alexandria, is found in Sahdonā, Isaac, and ʿEnanishoʿ. This image has evident Eucharistic overtones and is meant to express the intoxicating experience of divine love (Brock 2005). Perhaps the most characteristic Syriac term for describing mystical states is *amazement* or *wonder* (*tehrā, temhā*), which refers to the stillness of the mind in front of an overwhelming experience of divine grace: the intellect finds itself numbed not only by God's unfathomable mercy and love, but also by the limitlessness of Divine wisdom and majesty. The foretaste of eternal life and of the New World can also render the contemplative's mind 'speechless'. Isaac of Nineveh fittingly designates that which *causes* this state of wonder by another technical term: *maggnānūtā*, the overshadowing presence of the Holy Spirit that rests upon the saints and raises the mind to the contemplation of God's mysteries (Brock 1988). Even though divine contemplation is in a real sense a mediation of supernatural *knowledge* (see Kavvadas 2015), Syriac mystics also refer to the highest form of *theōria* as a form of *ignorance* (*lā īda'tā*) which is above knowledge. Adumbrated in the writings of Evagrius and Gregory of Nyssa and central in the Dionysian corpus, this type of apophaticism is intimately connected to the vision of the 'luminous darkness' (*'amṭānā nhīrā*), simultaneously revealing and obscuring God's essence, which John of Dalyatha describes in his letters (Beulay 1990: 395–404).

Divine essence and Divine glory

Ever since the Messalian heresy, claims of 'seeing God' were met with suspicion by Syriac theologians. As the reticence of Early Syriac ascetics to address these matters gradually gave way to more explicit and detailed discussions in seventh–eighth century mysticism, church authorities began to express their concerns regarding the dogmatic implications of these ideas. The Christological problems that were entailed by the claim that human nature could behold divine nature, whether in the special case of Jesus Christ, or in general, struck at the very heart of the clear-cut Dyophysitism defended by the Church of the East and prompted Timothy's anathemas discussed above. There was, however, an even more severe issue at stake: the safeguarding of Divine transcendence. How could one uphold, at the same time, the transcendence of God *and* the reality of mystical union with that very same transcendent reality? An extreme stance in either direction could easily compromise both tenets: a monistic position like that of Stephen bar Sudaili effectively made created intellects equal to God, but a resolute affirmation of Divine incomprehensibility undermined the Evangelic promise that 'the pure in heart shall see God' (Matth 5:8). As Beulay (1990: 447–64) has shown, the solution proposed by some Eastern Syriac mystics (Joseph Ḥazzaya, John of Dalyatha, Nestorius of Beth Nuhadra) was to introduce a fine distinction between God's hidden essence and His manifested glory: while the first remains for ever beyond grasp, sanctified individuals can become truly united with the Divine Light and thus have direct knowledge of God Himself.

THE LASTING INFLUENCE OF EASTERN SYRIAC SPIRITUALITY

As I have pointed out, the works of many Eastern Syriac ascetics soon became popular outside the Church of the East. A number of early manuscripts of Syro-Orthodox and Melkite provenance (9th–10th c.) already attest to a lively interest in Syro-oriental spirituality among the monastic communities of Palestine, Sinai, and Egypt. Throughout the Middle Ages this interest was sustained by numerous copies, translations, and adaptations (e.g. Ibn aṣ-Ṣalt's Arabic epitome of Isaac). Bar Hebraeus's deep admiration for John of Dalyatha further encouraged the reception and dissemination of mystical ideas within the Syro-Orthodox church during the fourteenth and fifteenth centuries. In Ethiopia, the project of the emperor Lebna Dengel (r. 1501–1540) to translate the works of Isaac, John, and Dadisho' had a comparable effect on the development of Ethiopic monasticism. Similarly, the Greek translation of Isaac's *First Part*, preserved in over 300 manuscripts, had a significant impact on the Hesychastic movement in Byzantium and was one of the driving forces behind the nineteenth-century Philokalic renaissance in the Eastern Orthodox world.

Finally, the emergence of Sufism in the first centuries of Islam can be taken as an indication that the legacy of Eastern Syriac mysticism extended beyond Christianity. Even though it is difficult to uphold Alphonse Mingana's simplifying claim (1934: v) that 'Islamic mysticism . . . is wholly based on the teaching and practices of the Christian monks and ascetics', the profound similarities between Syriac and Islamic mysticism are indeed striking. Early attempts to study these parallels were made by Arent J. Wensinck (1919) and Margaret Smith (1931). Tor Andrae (1931) stressed the importance of the Syriac monastic tradition for explaining *zuhd*, the earliest expression of Islamic asceticism, which predated and influenced Sufism. Conversely, Louis Massignon (1954) argued that despite an evident Syriac influence Sufi terminology mainly derived from the Qur'an itself. More recent studies have focused on selective analogies and similarities between Eastern Syriac and Sufi concepts: e.g. remembrance (*dhikr*) of God (Teule 2010), the love of God (Khayyat 2011), the pre-existence of souls (Gobillot 2011). Of the few synthetic studies available, one could mention here Georg Günter Blum's comprehensive survey (2009) and Serafim Seppälä's comparative study of ecstasy, mystical language, and religious discourse (2003).

A BRIEF GUIDE TO SYRIAC MYSTICAL LITERATURE

This short overview is meant to be a *beginner's guide* to the most important Syriac mystics, their works, and the main critical editions (if available). I rely here primarily on Kessel and Pinggéra 2011, with a few additions. For a complete bibliography on each individual author, readers may also consult the *GEDSH* and the online 'Comprehensive Bibliography of Syriac Christianity' (www.csc.org.il), maintained by Dr. Sergey Minov. For a list of editions of Syriac texts in progress, see syri.ac/editions (maintained by Dr. Grigory Kessel).

I. Greek Ascetical and Mystical Authors in Syriac Translation

Abba Isaiah (5th c.)	
Asketikon	Draguet 1968
Ammonius (4th c.)	
Letters	Kmoskó 1915
Antony the Great (4th c.)	
First Letter	Nau 1909
Evagrius of Pontus (d. 399)	
Antirrheticus	Frankenberg 1912
Chapters on Prayer	unedited (ed. Géhin, in prep.)
De octo spiritibus malitiae	unedited
Gnostikos	Frankenberg 1912; (ed. Taylor/Duca, in prep.)
Kephalaia Gnostika	Guillaumont 1958
Letters	Frankenberg 1912; (ed. Géhin, in prep.)

On Thoughts	unedited
Praktikos	unedited (ed. Taylor/Duca, in prep.)
Shorter Treatises	Muyldermans 1952
Mark the Solitary (5th c.)	
Ascetical Works	unedited (ed. Taylor/Duca, in prep.)
Palladius (d. ca. 430)	
Lausiac History	Draguet 1978
Pseudo-Dionysius (early 6th c.)	
Celestial Hierarchy	unedited (ed. Perczel, in prep.)
Divine Names	Fiori 2013
Ecclesiastical Hierarchy	unedited (ed. Perczel, in prep.)
Letters	Fiori 2013
Mystical Theology	Fiori 2013
Pseudo-Macarius (late 4th c.)	
Homilies and *Letters*	Strothmann 1981

II. Early Syriac Spirituality

Anonymous (4th/early 5th c.)	
Book of Steps	Kmoskó 1926
Aphrahaṭ (4th c.)	
Demonstrations	Parisot 1894–1907
Ephrem the Syrian (d. 373)	
Ascetical Sermons	Beck 1973
Letter to the Solitaries	Beck 1973
John the Solitary (5th c.)	
Four Discourses on the Soul	Dedering 1936
Letter on Stillness	Rignell 1960
Letters to Eutropius and Eusebius	Rignell 1941
Letter to Hesychius	unedited (ed. Brock, in prep.)
Letters to Theodoulos	Rignell 1941, 1960
Letters to Thomasius	Strothmann 1972
Six Dialogues with Thomasius	Strothmann 1972
Other Letters, Treatises, and Sentences	unedited

III. Eastern Syriac Mystics

Anonymous (8th c.)	
Commentary on Abba Isaiah's Asketikon	Draguet 1973

Babai the Great (d. 628)

Commentary on Evagrius's Kephalaia Gnostika	Frankenberg 1912

Dadisho' Qaṭraya (7th c.)

Commentary on Abba Isaiah's Asketikon	Draguet 1972
Commentary on the Paradise of the Fathers	Bedjan 1897; (ed. Phillips, in prep.)
Letter to Abkosh	Guillaumont/Albert 1984
On Solitude	del Río Sánchez 2001

'Enanisho' (7th c.)

Paradise of the Fathers	Bedjan 1897, Budge 1904

Gregory of Cyprus (7th c.)

Chapters on Prayer	unedited (ed. Pirtea, in prep.)
Eight Memre	unedited
Letters	unedited
On Divine Contemplation(= Memra 7)	Hausherr 1937

Isaac of Nineveh (7th c.)

First Part	Bedjan 1909
Second Part	Brock 1995
Third Part	Chialà 2011b

John of Dalyatha (8th c.)

Homilies	Colless 1969, Khayyat 2007
Kephalaia Gnostika	unedited
Letters	Beulay 1978

Joseph Ḥazzaya (8th c.)

Book of Questions and Answers	unedited (ed. Fiori, in prep.)
Fifth Letter to a Friend	Mingana 1934; Khalifé-Hachem 1969
Kephalaia Gnostika	unedited (ed. Kalinin et al., in prep.)
Letter on the Three Stages	Graffin/Harb 1992
On Providence	Kavvadas 2016
Two Letters on the Workings of Grace	Beulay 1978
Shorter Treatises	Mingana 1934

Nestorius of Beth Nuhadra (8th c.)

Letter on the Movement of Divine Grace	Berti 2005

Sahdona/Martyrius (7th c.)

Book of Perfection	De Halleux 1960–5
Letters and *Maxims*	De Halleux 1965

Shemʿon d-Ṭaybuteh

Book of Grace	unedited (ed. Kessel, in prep.)
Book of Medicine/Excerpts	Mingana 1934; (ed. Kessel, in prep.)
Homily on the Consecration of the Cell	unedited (ed. Kessel, in prep.)
Profitable Counsels	Kessel/Sims-Williams 2011

Shubḥalmaran (early 7th c.)

Book of Gifts	Lane 2004
Other Chapters, Excerpts	Lane 2004

IV. Western Syriac Mystics

Abu al-Maʿani (d. 1481)

Ascent of the Mind	unedited (ed. Fiori, in prep.)

Athanasius Abu Ghalib (12th c.)

Treatises	unedited (ed. Fotescu-Tauwinkl, in prep.)

Dionysius bar Ṣalibi (12th c.)

Commentary on Evagrius's Kephalaia Gnostika	unedited

Gregory Bar Hebraeus (d. 1286)

Book of the Dove	Bedjan 1898
Commentary on the Book of Hierotheus	Marsh 1927, Pinggéra 2002 (partial)
Ethicon	Bedjan 1898

Jacob of Sarug (d. 521)

Memre on Ascetic Topics	Bedjan 1905–1910
Letters	Olinder 1937 (partial)

Masʿud of Ṭur ʿAbdin (d. 1512)

Spiritual Ship	unedited

Philoxenus of Mabbug (d. 523)

Ascetical Homilies	Budge 1894
Letter to Patrikios	Lavenant 1963

Stephen bar Sudaili (6th c.)

Book of Hierotheos	Marsh 1927

Theodosius of Antioch (9th c.)

Commentary on the Book of Hierotheus	Marsh 1927, Pinggéra 2002 (partial)

NOTES

1 The 'Revelation of Saint Gregory', a text preserved in Arabic and sometimes attributed to Gregory of Cyprus, most likely belongs to a later author (cf. Perczel 2013).

2 The anonymous eighth-century commentator on Abba Isaiah's *Logoi* (ed. Draguet 1973), who describes himself as a 'disciple of Mar Isaac', must probably be linked to the same monastery.

3 For instance, the large sixth-century manuscript *Add 12,175* in the British Library contains numerous works by Evagrius, Mark the Solitary, various apophthegmata, the letters of Pseudo-Macarius, the letters of Ammonius, etc.

4 The 'unidentified homily on the solitary life' published by Sims-Williams (1985: 69–77) is in fact a fragment from Isaac of Nineveh's unedited *Kephalaia Gnostika* (see Pirtea, forthcoming). A new edition of this Sogdian text is in preparation. Following this identification, Nicholas Sims-Williams and I were able to identify further fragments from Isaac's First and Second Parts in the Sogdian manuscript E28 (Sims-Williams 2017).

BIBLIOGRAPHY

Abramowski, L. 1991. Dadisho Qatraya and His Commentary on the Book of Abbas Isaiah. *The Harp* 4, 67–83.

Andrae, T. 1931. Zuhd und Mönchtum. *Le Monde Oriental* 25, 296–327.

Beck, E., ed. 1973. *Des heiligen Ephraem des Syrers Sermones IV*. CSCO 334/5. Leuven: Peeters.

Bedjan, P., ed. 1897. *Acta martyrum et sanctorum VII*. Paris/Leipzig: Harrassowitz.

———., ed. 1898. *Ethicon, seu Moralia Gregorii Barhebraei*. Paris/Leipzig: Harrassowitz.

______., ed. 1905–1910. *Homiliae selectae Mar-Jacobi Sarugensis*. Paris/ Leipzig: Harrassowitz.

———., ed. 1909. *Mar Isaacus Ninivita. De Perfectione Religiosa*. Paris/Leipzig: Harrassowitz.

Berti, V. 2005. Grazia, visione e natura divina in Nestorio di Nuhadra, solitario e vescovo siro-orientale (d. 800 ca.). *Annali di scienze religiose* 10, 219–57.

———. 2011. Le débat sur la vision de Dieu et la condamnation des mystiques par Timothée Ier: la perspective du patriarche. *In:* A. Desreumaux, ed., *Les mystiques syriaques*. Études syriaques 8. Paris: Geuthner, 151–76.

Beulay, R. 1972. Des centuries de Joseph Ḥazzaya retrouvées? *Parole d'Orient* 3, 5–44.

———., ed. 1978. *La collection des lettres de Jean de Dalyatha*. PO 39, 3. Turnhout: Brepols.

———. 1987. *La Lumière sans forme. Introduction à l'étude de la mystique chrétienne syro-orientale*. Chevetogne: Éditions de Chevetogne.

———. 1990. *L'enseignement spirituel de Jean de Dalyatha, mystique syro-oriental du VIII*^{e} *siècle*. Théologie historique 83. Paris: Beauchesne.

Blum, G. G. 2001. *'In der Wolke des Lichtes': Gesammelte Aufsätze zu Spiritualität und Mystik des Christlichen Ostens*. Edited by Karl Pinggéra. Oikonomia – Quellen und Studien zur orthodoxen Theologie. Erlangen: Lehrstuhl für Geschichte und Theologie des Christlichen Ostens.

———. 2009. *Die Geschichte der Begegnung christlich-orientalischer Mystik mit der Mystik des Islams*. Orientalia Biblica et Christiana 17. Wiesbaden: Harrassowitz Verlag.

Briquel Chatonnet, F., Debié, M., ed. 2015. *Manuscripta Syriaca: des sources de première main*. Cahiers d'études syriaques 4. Paris: Geuthner.

Brock, S. P. 1987. *The Syriac Fathers on Prayer and the Spiritual Life*. Cistercian Studies Series 101. Kalamazoo: Cistercian Publications.

———. 1988. *Maggnānūtā*. A Technical Term in East Syrian Spirituality and its Background. *In:* R. Coquin, ed., *Mélanges Antoine Guillaumont. Contributions à l'étude des christianismes orientaux*. Cahiers d'orientalisme, 20. Genève: Cramer, 121–9.

———. 1990. Lost and Found: Part II of the Works of St Isaac of Nineveh. *Studia Patristica* 18/4, 230–3.

———., ed. 1995. *Isaac of Nineveh (Isaac the Syrian). 'The Second Part', Chapters IV–XLI*. CSCO 554/5. Leuven: Peeters.

———. 1998. A Monastic Anthology From twelfth-century Edessa. *In:* R. Lavenant, ed., *Symposium Syriacum VII: Uppsala University, Department of Asian and African Languages, 11–14 August 1996*. Orientalia Christiana Analecta 256. Rome: Pontificio Istituto Orientale, 221–31.

———. 1999–2000. From Qatar to Tokyo, By Way of Mar Saba. The Translations of Isaac of Beth Qatraye (Isaac the Syrian). *Aram* 11–12, 475–84.

———. 2005. Sobria Ebrietas According to Some Syriac Texts. *ARAM* 17, 181–95.

Budge, E. A. W., ed. 1894. *The Discourses of Philoxenus, Bishop of Mabbôgh, A.D. 485–419*. London: Asher.

———., ed. 1904. *The Book of Paradise: The Syriac Text According to the Recension of 'Anân-Îsho' of Bêth Âbhê*. London: W. Drugulin.

Bunge, G. 1982. *Rabban Jausep Hazzaya. Briefe über das geistliche Leben und verwandte Schriften: Ostsyrische Mystik des 8. Jahrhunderts*. Sophia: Quellen östlicher Theologie 21. Trier: Paulinus-Verlag.

Casiday, A. 2013. *Reconstructing the Theology of Evagrius Ponticus: Beyond Heresy*. Cambridge: Cambridge University Press.

Chialà, S. 2002. *Dall' ascesi eremitica alla misericordia infinita. Ricerche su Isacco di Ninive e la sua fortuna*. Biblioteca della Rivista di Storia e Letteratura Religiosa, Studi 14. Firenze: Leo S. Olschki.

———. 2005. *Abramo di Kashkar e la sua comunità. La rinascita del monachesimo siro-orientale*. Comunità di Bose. Magnano: Edizioni Qiqajon.

———. 2011a. Les mystiques syro-orientaux: une école ou une époque? *In*: A. Desreumaux, ed., *Les mystiques syriaques*. Études syriaques 8. Paris: Geuthner, 63–78.

———., ed. 2011b. *Isacco di Ninive: Terza Collezione*. CSCO 637/8. Leuven: Peeters.

Coakley, S., Gavrilyuk, P., ed. 2012. *The Spiritual Senses: Perceiving God in Western Christianity*. Cambridge: Cambridge University Press.

Colless, B. 1966. A Pot-Pourri of Eastern Mysticism: Mingana Syriac Ms. no. 86. *Milla wa-Milla. The Australian Bulletin of Comparative Religion* 6, 34–43.

———. 1969. *The Mysticism of John Saba*. Ph.D. Thesis. University of Melbourne.

Dedering, S., ed. 1936. *Johannes von Lykopolis. Ein Dialog über die Seele und die Affekte des Menschen*. Arbeten utgivna med understöd av Vilhelm Ekmans Universitetsfond 43. Leipzig: Harrassowitz.

De Halleux, A., ed. 1960–1965. *Martyrius (Sahdona). Œuvres spirituelles*. CSCO 200/1, 214/5, 252/3. Leuven: Peeters.

———., ed. 1965. *Martyrius (Sahdona). Œuvres spirituelles IV. Lettres à des amis solitaires. Maximes sapientiales*. CSCO 254/5. Leuven: Peeters.

del Río Sánchez, F., ed. 2001. *Los cinco tratados sobre la quietud (šelyā) de Dādīšō' Qaṭrāyā*. Aula Orientalis Supplementa 18. Barcelona: Editorial Ausa.

———. 2011. Dadišo' du Qatar et la quiétude. *In*: A. Desreumaux, ed., *Les mystiques syriaques*. Études syriaques 8. Paris: Geuthner, 87–98.

Desreumaux, A., ed. 2011. *Les mystiques syriaques*. Études syriaques, 8. Paris: Geuthner.

Draguet, R., ed. 1968. *Les cinq recensions de l'Ascéticon syriaque d'Abba Isaïe*. CSCO 289/90, 293/4. Leuven: Peeters.

———., ed. 1972. *Commentaire du livre d'Abba Isaïe par Dadišo Qatraya (VIIe siècle)*. CSCO 326/7. Leuven: Peeters.

———., ed. 1973. *Commentaire anonyme du Livre d'abba Isaïe*. CSCO 336/7. Leuven: Peeters.

———., ed. 1978. *Les formes syriaques de la matière de l'Histoire lausiaque*. CSCO 389/90, 398/9. Leuven: Sécretariat du CorpusSCO.

Engelmann, T. 2013. *Annahme Christi und Gottesschau: Die Theologie Babais des Großen*. Göttinger Orientforschungen, I. Reihe: Syriaca 42. Wiesbaden: Harrassowitz.

Fiori, E., ed. 2013. *Dionigi Areopagita. Nomi divini, teologia mistica, epistole: La versione siriaca di Sergio di Rēš'aynā (VI secolo)*. CSCO 656/7. Leuven: Peeters.

Fitschen, K. 1998. *Messalianismus und Antimessalianismus: Ein Beispiel ostkirchlicher Ketzergeschichte*. Forschungen zur Kirchen- und Dogmengeschichte 71. Göttingen: Vandenhoeck & Ruprecht.

Fotescu-Tauwinkl, C. 2010. A Spiritual Author in 12th Century Upper Mesopotamia: Abū Ghālib and His Treatise on Monastic Life. *In:* H. Teule et al., ed., *The Syriac Renaissance*. Eastern Christian Studies 9. Leuven: Peeters.

Frankenberg, W., ed. 1912. *Euagrius Ponticus*. Abhandlungen der Akademie der Wissenschaften in Göttingen, Philologisch-Historische Klasse, NF 13,2. Berlin: Weidmannsche Buchhandlung.

Gobillot, G. 2011. La première mystique musulmane a-t-elle eu des liens avec les mystiques syriaques?. *In:* A. Desreumaux, ed., *Les mystiques syriaques*. Études syriaques 8. Paris: Geuthner, 189–234.

Graffin, F., Harb, P., ed. 1992. *Joseph Ḥazzāyā. Lettre sur les trois étapes de la vie monastique*. PO 45/2. Turnhout: Brepols.

Guillaumont, A., ed. 1958. *Les six centuries des "Képhalaia Gnostika" d'Évagre le Pontique*. PO 28/1. Paris: Firmin-Didot.

———. 1962. *Les "Kephalaia Gnostica" d'Évagre le Pontique et l'histoire de l'origénisme chez les Grecs et chez les Syriens*. Patristica Sorbonensia 5. Paris: Éditions du Seuil.

———. 2004. *Un philosophe au désert, Évagre le Pontique*. Paris: J. Vrin.

Guillaumont, A., Albert, M. 1984. Lettre de Dadisho Qatraya à Abkosh sur l'hésychia. *In:* E. Lucchesi, H. D. Saffrey, ed., *Mémorial André-Jean Festugière. Antiquité païenne et chrétienne*. Cahiers d'Orientalisme 10. Genève: Cramer.

Hansbury, M. T., ed. 2013. *John the Solitary on the Soul*. Texts from Christian Late Antiquity 32. Piscataway, NJ: Gorgias Press.

Harmless, W., Fitzgerald, R. R. 2001. The Sapphire Light of the Mind: The *Skemmata* of Evagrius Ponticus. *Theological Studies* 62, 493–529.

Harvey, S. 2006. *Scenting Salvation: Ancient Christianity and the Olfactory Imagination*. Berkeley: University of California Press.

Hausherr, I., ed. 1937. *Gregorii Monachi Cyprii De Theoria Sancta quae syriace interpretata dicitur visio divina*. Orientalia Christiana Analecta 110. Rome: Pont. Institutum Orientalium Studiorum.

Heal, K. S., Kitchen, R. A., ed. 2014. *Breaking the Mind. New Studies in the Syriac "Book of Steps"*. Washington, DC: The Catholic University of America Press.

Hombergen, D. 2001. *The Second Origenist Controversy: A New Perspective on Cyril of Scythopolis' Monastic Biographies as Historical Sources for Sixth-century Origenism*. Studia Anselmiana 132. Rome: Pontificio ateneo S. Anselmo.

Ioan, O. 2011. Martyrius-Sahdona: La pensée christologique, clé de la théologie mystique. *In*: A. Desreumaux, ed., *Les mystiques syriaques*. Études syriaques 8. Paris: Geuthner, 45–61.

Jullien, F. 2006a. Le monachisme chrétien dans l'empire iranien (IVe-XIVe siècles) en terre d'Iran. *In*: R. Gyselen, ed., *Chrétiens en terre d'Iran: Implantation et acculturation*. Studia Iranica, 33. Paris: Association pour l'avancement des études iraniennes, 143–84.

———. 2006b. Rabban-Šāpūr: un monastère au rayonnement exceptionnel. La réforme d'Abraham de Kaškar dans le Bēth-Hūzāyē. *Orientalia Christiana Periodica* 72/2, 333–48.

———. 2008. *Le monachisme en Perse. La réforme d'Abraham le Grand, père des moines de l'Orient*. CSCO 622, Subsidia 121. Leuven: Peeters.

Kavvadas, N. 2015. *Isaak von Ninive und seine Kephalaia Gnostika. Die Pneumatologie und ihr Kontext*. Supplements to Vigiliae Christianae 128. Leiden: Brill.

———., ed. 2016. *Joseph Hazzaya, on Providence.* Texts and Studies in Eastern Christianity 8. Leiden: Brill.
Kessel, G., Pinggéra, K. 2011. *A Bibliography of Syriac Ascetic and Mystical Literature.* Eastern Christian Studies 11. Leuven: Peeters.
Kessel, G., Sims-Williams, N. 2011. The Profitable Counsels of Šemʿōn d-Ṭaibūtēh. The Syriac Original and Its Sogdian version. *Le Muséon* 124/3–4, 279–302.
Khalifé-Hachem, É. 1969. Deux textes du Pseudo-Nil identifiés. *Melto* 5, 17–59.
Khayyat, N., ed. 2007. *Jean de Dalyatha. Les Homélies I-XV.* Sources syriaques 2. Antélias: Centre d'Études et de Recherches Orientales.
———. 2011. L'amour gratuit chez Rabiʿa al-ʿAdawiya et Jean de Dalyata. *In:* A. Desreumaux, ed., *Les mystiques syriaques.* Études syriaques 8. Paris: Geuthner, 79–86.
Kmoskó, M., ed. 1915. *Ammonii Eremitae Epistolae.* PO 10/6. Paris: Firmin-Didot.
———., ed. 1926. *Liber Graduum.* Patrologia Syriaca 3. Paris: Firmin-Didot.
Lane, D., ed. 2004. *Šubḥalmaran: The Book of Gifts.* CSCO 612/3. Leuven: Peeters.
Lavenant, R., ed. 1963. *La lettre à Patricius de Philoxène de Mabboug.* PO 30/5. Paris: Firmin-Didot.
Marsh, F. S., ed. 1927. *The Book of Holy Hierotheos Ascribed to Stephen bar Sudhaile (c500 A.D.).* London: Williams & Norgate.
Massignon, L. 1954. *Essai sur les origines du lexique technique de la mystique musulmane.* Études musulmans 2. Paris: Vrin.
Mingana, A., ed. 1934. *Early Christian Mystics.* Woodbrooke Studies 7. Cambridge: Heffer & Sons.
Muyldermans, J. 1952. *Evagriana Syriaca. Textes inédits du British Museum et de la Vaticane.* Bibliothèque du Muséon 31. Louvain: Publications universitaires/Institut Orientaliste.
Nau, F. 1909. La version syriaque de la première lettre de Saint Antoine. *Revue de l'Orient chrétien* 14, 282–97.
Nin, M. 2005. La sintesi monastica di Giovanni il Solitario. *In:* E. Vergani, S. Chialà, ed., *Le Chiese sire tra IV e VI secolo: dibattito dottrinale e ricerca spirituale. Atti del 20 Incontro sull'Oriente Cristiano di tradizione siriaca (Milano, Biblioteca Ambrosiana, 28 marzo 2003).* Milano: Centro Ambrosiano, 95–117.
Olinder, G. 1937. *Iacobi Sarugensi Epistulae quotquot supersunt.* CSCO 110. Leuven: Peeters.
Outtier, B. 2011. La mystique syriaque en Géorgie. *In:* A. Desreumaux, ed., *Les mystiques syriaques.* Études syriaques 8. Paris: Geuthner, 177–88.
Parisot, I., ed. 1894–1907. *Aphraatis Sapientis Persae Demonstrationes.* Patrologia Syriaca I/II. Paris: Firmin-Didot.
Pataridze, T. 2011. Les discours ascétiques d'Isaac de Ninive: Étude de la tradition géorgienne et de ses rapports avec les autres versions. *Le Muséon* 124/1–2, 27–58.
Perczel, I. 2013. The Revelation of the Seraphic Gregory Found in Two Indian Manuscripts. *Adamantius* 19, 337–58.
Pinggéra, K. 2002. *All-Erlösung und All-Einheit. Studien zum 'Buch des Heiligen Hierotheos' und seiner Rezeption in der Syrisch-Orthodoxen Kirche.* Sprachen und Kulturen des Christlichen Orients 10. Wiesbaden: Reichert.
Pirard, M., ed. 2012. *Abba Isaak tou Syrou: Logoi Askētikoi.* Agion Oros: Iera Monē Ibēron.
Pirtea, A. 2017. *Die 'geistigen Sinne' in der ostsyrischen christlichen Mystik. Untersuchungen zum Wahrnehmungsbegriff und zur Gotteserkenntnis in der griechischen und syro-orientalischen asketischen Literatur der Spätantike.* Ph.D. Thesis, Freie Universität Berlin.
———. forthcoming. St. Isaac of Nineveh's Gnostic Chapters in Sogdian: The Identification of an Anonymous Text from Bulayïq. Studia Patristica.

Reinink, G. 2010. The East Syriac Monk Simeon the Persecuted and His Book of Chapters. *In:* M. Tamcke, ed., *Gotteserlebnis und Gotteslehre. Christliche und islamische Mystik im Orient*. Göttinger Orientforschungen, I. Reihe: Syriaca 38. Wiesbaden: Harrassowitz, 61–70.

Rich, A. 2007. *Discernment in the Desert Fathers. Διάκρισις in the Life and Thought of Early Egyptian Monasticism*. Milton Keynes/Colorado Springs/Hyderabad: Paternoster.

Rignell, L. G., ed. 1941. *Briefe von Johannes dem Einsiedler*. Lund: H. Ohlssons Boktryckeri.

———., ed. 1960. *Drei Traktate von Johannes dem Einsiedler (Johannes von Apamea)*. Lunds Universitets Årsskrift 54,4. Lund: Gleerup.

Sanders, J. 1977. Un manuel de prières populaire de l'Église syrienne. *Le Muséon* 90/1–2, 81–102.

Seppälä, S. 2003. *"In Speechless Ecstasy": Expression and Interpretation of Mystical Experience in Classical Syriac and Sufi Literature*. Studia Orientalia 98. Helsinki: Finnish Oriental Society.

Sherwood, P., ed. 1960–1961. Mimro de Serge de Rešayna sur la vie spirituelle. *L'Orient syrien* 5, 433–57; 6, 95–115, 121–56.

Sims-Williams, N., ed. 1985. *The Christian Sogdian Manuscript C2*. Berliner Turfantexte 12. Berlin: Akademie-Verlag.

———. 1989. Bulayïq. *Encyclopædia Iranica* IV/5, 545. www.iranicaonline.org/articles/bulayq-town-in-eastern-turkestan (accessed 15.12.2016).

———. 2017. *An Ascetic Miscellany: The Christian Sogdian Manuscript E28*. Berliner Turfantexte 42. Turnhout: Brepols.

Smith, M. 1931. *Studies in Early Mysticism in the Near and Middle East*. London: Sheldon Press.

Stewart, C. 1991. *"Working the Earth of the Heart". The Messalian Controversy in History, Texts, and Language to AD 431*. Oxford: Oxford University Press.

———. 2001. Imageless Prayer and the Theological Vision of Evagrius Ponticus. *Journal of Early Christian Studies* 9, 179–210.

Strothmann, W. 1972. *Johannes von Apamea*. Patristische Texte und Studien 11. Berlin: De Gruyter.

———., ed. 1981. *Die syrische Überlieferung der Schriften des Makarios*. Göttinger Orientforschungen, Syriaca 21. Wiesbaden: Harrassowitz.

Teule, H. 1998. Les compilations monastiques syriaques. *In:* R. Lavenant, ed., *Symposium Syriacum VII: Uppsala University, Department of Asian and African Languages, 11–14 August 1996*. Orientalia Christiana Analecta 256. Rome: Pontificio Istituto Orientale, 249–64.

———. 2004. Joseph II, Patriarch of the Chaldeans (1696–1713/4), and the *Book of the Magnet*. First Soundings. *In:* H. Teule, R. Ebied, ed., *Studies on the Christian Arabic Heritage in Honour of Father Prof. Dr. Samir Khalil Samir S.I. at the Occasion of His Sixty-Fifth Birthday*. Eastern Christian Studies, 5. Leuven: Peeters.

———. 2010. An Important Concept in Muslim and Christian Mysticism: The Remembrance of God – *dhikr Allah – ʿuhdōnō d-Alōhō*. *In*: M. Tamcke, ed., *Gotteserlebnis und Gotteslehre. Christliche und islamische Mystik im Orient*. Göttinger Orientforschungen, I. Reihe: Syriaca 38. Wiesbaden: Harrassowitz, 11–24.

Treiger, A. 2009. Could Christ's Humanity See His Divinity? An Eighth-Century Controversy Between John of Dalyatha and Timothy I, Catholicos of the Church of the East. *Journal of the Canadian Society for Syriac Studies* 9, 9–27.

Vööbus, A. 1958–1988. *History of Asceticism in the Syrian Orient. A Contribution to the History of Culture in the Near East*. 3 volumes. CSCO 184, 197, 500. Leuven: Sécretariat du CorpusSCO/Peeters.

———. 1978. Die Entdeckung eines Florilegiums der asketischen und mystischen Schriften im Syrischen. *In:* G. Wiessner, ed., *Erkenntnisse und Meinungen*. Göttinger Orientforschungen, I. Reihe: Syriaca 17. Wiesbaden: Harrassowitz, 263–71.

Vosté, J.-M. 1929. Receuil d'auteurs ascétiques nestoriens du VIIe et VIIIe siècle. *Angelicum* 6, 143–206.

Wensinck, A. J. 1919. *Bar Hebraeus's Book of the Dove, Together With Some Chapters From His Ethikon*. De Goeje Fund 4. Leiden: Brill.

———. 1923. *Mystic Treatises By Isaac of Nineveh*. Verhandelingen der Koninklijke Akademie van Wetenschappen te Amsterdam, Afdeeling Letterkunde 23,1. Amsterdam: Koninklijke Akademie van Wetenschappen.

Widengren, G. 1961. Researches in Syrian Mystical Experiences and Spiritual Exercises. *Numen* 8, 161–98.

Witakowski, W. 2006. Filekseyus, the Ethiopic Version of the Syriac Dadisho Qatraya's Commentary on the Paradise of the Fathers. *Rocznik orientalistyczny* 59, 281–96.

CHAPTER TWENTY-TWO

THEOLOGICAL DOCTRINES AND DEBATES WITHIN SYRIAC CHRISTIANITY

Theresia Hainthaler

INTRODUCTION

The differences that existed between the various Christian communities presented to later Muslims a confusing picture, and at the same time reduced the credibility of the Christian faith, being inferior (in the eyes of Muslims) compared to the clear statements of their faith. Already the famous author al-Ğāḥiẓ (777–869) from Baṣra, whose family originated in Abyssinia, i.e. Ethiopia, wrote in his refutation against the Christians, one of the first Muslim writings of this kind:

> Even if one were to exert all his zeal, and summon all his intellectual resources with a view to learn the Christian teachings about Jesus, he would still fail to comprehend the nature of Christianity, especially its doctrine concerning the Divinity. How in the world can one succeed in grasping this doctrine, for were you to question concerning it two Nestorians, individually, sons of the same father and mother, the answer of one brother would be the reverse of that of the other. This holds true also of all Melchites and Jacobites. As a result, we cannot comprehend the essence of Christianity to the extent that we know the other faiths.
>
> (Finkel 1927: 333–4)

Thus, Ğāḥiẓ knew the three main Christian communities: Nestorians, Jacobites, and Melkites, perhaps from Baṣra or Baghdad where he lived. These three names are derived respectively from archbishop Nestorius of Constantinople (428–431), Jacob Baradaeus (Episcopal consecration in 542, d. 578), and from the Syriac word *malkā*, king (Arabic *malik)*.

The Melkites accepted the doctrine of the two natures of Chalcedon (451) and therefore held the same confession as the Byzantine emperor. Nestorians meant the members of the 'Church of the East' as they called themselves, who were Syriac-speaking Christians, East Syrians. Their Christological formula (since the first half of seventh century) is: Christ is one person (Syr. *parṣopa)* with two hypostases *(qnome)* and two natures *(kyane)*. In polemics, they have been accused of confessing a doctrine of two persons which, in fact, they reject. Nestorius himself, who was no Syrian and never a hierarch of the Persian church, rejected such a doctrine. Jacobites are West Syrians and anti-Chalcedonians. Their Christological formula is: Christ is one nature (or *hypostasis*) of the incarnate God Logos (μία φύσις τοῦ Θεοῦ λόγου σεσαρκωμένη, the so-called *mia physis* formula). In polemics, they have been accused of introducing a commixtion of natures and thus they were called monophysites, which suggested the doctrine of a single nature in Christ. The present-day Oriental Orthodox Churches justly reject this name for themselves, since in their profession of one nature in Christ they understand 'by *nature* not purely a simple nature, but rather one single composed nature, in which divinity and humanity are united without division and without confusion' (cf. Declaration of the Joint Commission of the Catholic Church and the Coptic Orthodox Church in Vienna, 16–29 August 1976; Grillmeier 1987: 335, n. 48). Since the *mia physis* formula and their rejection of the two natures' doctrine of the fourth ecumenical Council of Chalcedon (451) are constitutive for these churches, they should be called 'miaphysites'[1] or 'anti-Chalcedonians' instead of 'monophysites'.

In a similar way, some sensitiveness is needed with regard to the name 'Nestorian', if it refers to the heretical doctrine of two sons. Instead of using such a misnomer (Brock 1996), it is often preferable to speak of 'strict Antiochene' or 'Theodorian', meaning from Theodore of Mopsuestia, whose theology put a decisive mark on the Church of the East from the middle of the fifth century onwards.

SOME PRELIMINARY REMARKS ON SYRIAC CHRISTOLOGY

Here we concentrate on the Christological disputes which led to lasting divisions. We shall not be dealing with the early discussions against the followers of Bardaiṣan, fought by Ephrem and others, or against Marcian or the Arians (Fiano 2015).

While there is hardly any reflection on the constitution of the Son in the early sources of Syriac theology (such as Odes of Solomon, Syriac Didascalia, Acts of Thomas, or Tatian and Bardaiṣan), and while even also Aphrahaṭ apparently did not speculate about the kind of union that was in Christ, Ephrem developed ideas which could become a starting point for further development. In a certain manner, Ephrem is able to speak of a human 'nature', even if this concept is still ambiguous in his writing. The union in Christ has an ontological significance; Christ has mixed his natures, he became human, a body, visible.

The teaching of one nature in Christ and the two natures doctrine (dyophysitism), which can be seen as the main point of conflict in Christology, did not originate in the Syriac world. But there were Syriac-speaking partisans of the one nature formula from a very early stage in the Christological dispute, such as Rabbula of Edessa, and on the other hand there was Ibas of Edessa, his successor, and Narsai, the leader of the school of the Persians in Edessa (and later, after the transfer of the school, in Nisibis), who held a marked two natures doctrine.

The Christological debate between Cyril of Alexandria and Nestorius of Constantinople which led to the Council of Ephesus (431) was a dispute in Greek, not in Syriac. But it had a lasting effect, especially in the Syriac churches, and had its aftermath in the later West Syrian Church and the East Syrian Church in Persia. Also, the Council of Chalcedon (451) received as the fourth ecumenical Council by the Western Churches (Catholics and Protestant) and Orthodoxy as a whole, was conducted in Greek, with very few Syriac participants. Similarly, this holds true for the later ecumenical councils of 553 and 680/1 in Constantinople (the fifth and sixth ecumenical councils). But there were reactions to these doctrinal developments in the Syriac churches.

Some other theological debates which had been held in Greek have survived only in Syriac translations which indicate that there was, at least, some interest in the Syriac world. This holds true, for instance, for the Agnoetes, the Tritheists, and the doctrine of John Philoponus on the Resurrection. Authors such as Theodore of Mopsuestia, Cyril of Alexandria, Nestorius of Constantinople, Severus of Antioch etc. wrote in Greek, but their legacy is partly or, with the exception of Cyril, mostly preserved in Syriac. Therefore, their teaching cannot be neglected in order to get an understanding of the religious debates in the Syriac world.

The beginnings of the lasting antagonism between the later East Syrian and West Syrian churches may be seen in the years following the Nestorian controversy, when Rabbula of Edessa took sides with Cyril of Alexandria and later started his campaign against Theodore of Mopsuestia, and then against Ibas and the School of the Persians in Edessa. Among the main debates in the Syriac world, we can list:

- Philoxenus against Ḥabib (representing Edessene Theodorians)
- Jacob of Sarug against two natures doctrine
- Simeon of Beth Aršam, the so-called Persian debater, against the East Syrian theology
- Severus of Antioch against Chalcedon and two natures in Christ
- Severus and Julian of Halicarnassus
- Severus and Sergius Grammaticus
- Agnoetic debate
- Tritheist controversy
- Debate on the Resurrection body (Philoponus)
- Proba and John Barbur and the Severans
- Controversy in the school of Nisibis, debate on Ḥenana's approach
- Išoyahb III against Sahdona.

THE DOCTRINAL DEVELOPMENT

Through the clear statement of the council of Nicaea of 325 about Jesus Christ as the consubstantial *(homoousios)* son of God, the question regarding the union of divinity and humanity in Christ became even more acute. The faith of Nicaea, the faith of the 318 fathers, as it was called, which was further reflected in the symbol of the second ecumenical Council of Constantinople in 381, became the norm of orthodoxy from the fifth century onwards. This can be seen for the first time at the Council of Ephesus in 431, when both parties, the Synod of Cyril of Alexandria, as well as the synod around John of Antioch, took the faith of Nicaea as the criterion of orthodoxy.

Theodore of Mopsuestia, who died in 428 in peace with the Church and as a theological authority especially on account of his fight against Apollinarius (and also against Arianism), described the unity of the two natures in Christ by using the term *prosopon*, not *hypostasis*. The Logos dwelt in the human nature of Jesus from the first moment of its existence and never left it. But Theodore also knows about a liturgically defined concept of *prosopon*, not to be misunderstood in an ontological manner. The common worship is the most important consequence of the participation in the divine nature which the human nature of Christ attained to (Abramowski 1992; Grillmeier 1975: 431–4). In an ontological manner, Theodore speaks of the two natures of Christ and their differences, while the unity of Christ's person is for him presumed. But to describe this unity, or even to define it ontologically, was impossible for Theodore with the concepts available at that time (Abramowski 1992: 4; Grillmeier 1975: 436–7). It is the merit of Theodore to have fought against the concept of a union according to nature, as understood by Arians and Apollinarians. He succeeds in giving theological weight to Christ's human soul. Characteristic is Theodore's distinction of two ages, before Christ and after Christ, the two catastases. In recent research, a more holistic approach to Theodore's theology and piety is favoured in order to do justice to his specific positions on Christology and on the theology of grace (Bruns 1995; Davids 1998: 38–52, esp. 43; Grillmeier 1975: 421–5).

The FIRST CHRISTOLOGICAL CRISIS took place in the controversy between the newly appointed archbishop Nestorius of Constantinople and Cyril of Alexandria. The starting point was a conflict with which Nestorius was confronted in Constantinople, namely whether the Virgin Mary, the mother of Christ, can be called *theotokos* (bearer-of-God); some rejected this title and instead spoke of *anthropotokos* (bearer-of-Man). Nestorius suggested the title *christotokos* (bearer-of-Christ), thereby indicating what he later also wrote to Cyril in his letter (429), that *Christ* is the name used in Holy Scripture whenever both his natures are involved. This conflict, however, could not be solved and was exacerbated by a certain antagonism between Constantinople and Alexandria after the decision in Constantinople 381 to give the second place in the order of the seats to Constantinople instead of Alexandria (see already the deposition of John Chrysostom at the instigation of Theophilus of Alexandria, Cyril's uncle). In the conflict, two theological schools with different accents opposed one another: in Alexandria emphasis was placed upon the unity in Christ, and they took John 1:14 (the Logos became flesh) as the starting point. In the controversy with Nestorius, Cyril adopted the *mia physis* formula of Apollinarius of Laodicaea as a summary of orthodox Christology, without however recognising its true origin in Apollinarius. After the condemnation of Apollinarius in Constantinople 381, his followers propagated the writings of their master under the name of Orthodox fathers such as Athanasius, Julius, and Felix of Rome, or Gregory the Wonderworker, a very successful and efficacious fraud that was uncovered only in the sixth century. In fact, the *mia physis* formula was coined by Apollinarius in his work addressed to Jovian (Lietzmann 1904: 250, 1–251, 6) and was quoted by Cyril in his letter to Arcadia and Marina (430) as being a quotation from the 'thrice blessed' and 'famous in piety' Athanasius, Cyril's predecessor as archbishop of Alexandria (*ACO* I,1,5: 65, 22–30; also *ACO* I,1,7: 48, 28–33). The early Cyril, however, until the Nestorian controversy, did not use this formula (van Loon 2009: 518–31). The distinction between *ousia* or *physis* and *hypostasis*, reached by the Cappadocian fathers at the end of the fourth century in Trinitarian doctrine (God is one *ousia* and three *hypostases*), was not followed in Christology by the Alexandrians.

NESTORIUS, on the other hand, started with a traditional Antiochene structure (Abramowski 1963: 228–9): the ontological unity in Christ is presumed as self-evident and is somehow viewed from the outside, both in the liturgy and in Christ's activity, in the one *prosopon*. For God's absolute transcendent nature, no physical union with a created nature is allowed or possible, according to the Antiochene system. Therefore, they strive to avoid any confusion of the divine and the human natures. No passion can be ascribed to the divinity. The Antiochians emphasised the discernibility of the divine and of the human natures in Christ. Especially for soteriological reasons it is necessary, according to Antiochene understanding, that Christ's human nature is complete. Otherwise, how would it be possible for Christ to heal Adam's disobedience and to make a new beginning in salvation history?

Starting from his unitarian christology, CYRIL OF ALEXANDRIA presented his own concept of a union in Christ that was *kath' hypostasin* (or *kata physin*), a solution more by intuition. The concepts *hypostasis* and *physis* in Christology, however, are for him largely taken synonymously. The result is ambiguous statements of his Christological position such that later Chalcedonians as well as anti-Chalcedonians were able to take them both as confirmation for their respective convictions. For the Antiochians, and for Nestorius, the formula of the hypostatic or physical union sounds like a confusion of natures, a physical union indicated a union out of natural necessity, while the incarnation was purely 'of grace'.

The COUNCIL OF EPHESUS, that is, the synod opened and led by Cyril (22 June 431) condemned Nestorius, and canonically approved the second letter of Cyril to Nestorius as being an authentic interpretation of Nicaea. In the following years, in the dispute between Alexandria and Antioch, the third letter of Cyril to Nestorius with its twelve anathemas (written in 430 and read, but not canonised, in 431) became increasingly controversial. On the Antiochian side, Theodoret of Cyrus and Andrew of Samosata tried to refute it, while Proclus and Flavian of Constantinople tried to mediate. In 433, on the initiative of the emperor Theodosius II, a union between Cyril and the Antiochians was reached: Cyril acknowledged in his so-called *Laetentur* letter to John of Antioch the symbol of the Antiochians (drafted first in 431, then reworked) as orthodox, rephrasing it with some minor but theologically important changes. In this 'cyrilline' version, the symbol of the Antiochians later formed the first part of the Definition of Chalcedon. The Union of 433, however, met with resistance on the part of the strict Alexandrians as well as on that of the strict Antiochians. The latter gathered in the school of the Persians in Edessa or took refuge in the Persian Empire, beyond the imperial borders. In the school of the Persians, the majority belonged to the Antiochene party (for which Theodore of Mopsuestia increasingly became the norm in exegesis as well as in theology), a minority, however, joined the Alexandrian party, like Philoxenus (later bishop of Mabbug) and Jacob of Sarug.

Soon after Ephesus, Rabbula (bishop of Edessa 412–435) initiated a campaign against Theodore of Mopsuestia. Rabbula knew Greek from his youth onwards, but spoke Syriac throughout his life (Blum 1969: 15, n7). He fought against heretics, first Arians, then Marcionites, Manichaeans, Borborians, Audians, Messalians, and Jews. Around 431/2 he anathematised Theodore and confessed one nature in Christ in what was a unilateral action, unsupported by the other bishops in the diocese of Antioch. Andrew of Samosata replied and Rabbula's arguments may be seen in Andrew's reply. In the writings of Andrew of Samosata we find the one *prosopon*, the distinction of two natures, especially in their properties (*idiômata*). For Andrew, Cyril and his union according to *hypostasis* follows the tradition of Apollinarius. The essential points for Andrew were the confession of two natures and the impassibility of the divinity (Blum 1969: 182). Rabbula's battle against the writings of Theodore continued after the Union of 433. He intervened in the Armenian Church and called the writings of Theodore a corrupt faith. Cyril also made an intervention at Rabbula's request with some writings of his own. Proclus of Constantinople had been asked for advice by Armenians who had some writings of Theodore (Proclus's *Tomus ad Armenios* in 435 was the reply). But no condemnations resulted. This was the first phase of what later came to be called the Three Chapters Controversy. After the death of Rabbula, Ibas, a strict Antiochene, became his successor.

In 448, a SECOND CHRISTOLOGICAL CRISIS began, when at the home synod under archbishop Flavian of Constantinople the archimandrite Eutyches was accused of heresy and condemned. He confessed one nature of Christ after the union of the two natures but not Christ's consubstantiality with us. At the Second Council of Ephesus (449) under the leadership of archbishop Dioscorus I of Alexandria (444–451; d. 454), Eutyches was rehabilitated while Flavian was condemned and deposed together with Theodoret of Cyrus and Ibas of Edessa. The Tome of Pope Leo to Flavian, composed as a stand against Eutyches, was not allowed to be read in Ephesus. After the emperor Theodosius II, who favoured Dioscorus, died in 450, the COUNCIL OF CHALCEDON was convened by the new emperor Marcian.

The Christological definition of the council was, according to its own understanding, an interpretation of the teaching of the fathers and of Nicaea, and a compromise in the spirit of Cyril, according to more recent research (de Halleux 1976; Hainthaler 2006). The definition of Chalcedon took the step of distinguishing *physis* and *hypostasis* in Christology: Christ is one *prosopon* (resp. *persona*) or one *hypostasis* in two natures *(en dyo physesin)*. The characterisation of Christ's unity by the four-fold expression, 'without confusion, without change, without division, without separation' belongs to traditions in East and West. Further, the continuing distinction between the properties of divinity and humanity in Christ, expressed by the Tome of Leo but also by Cyril, is stated in the definition. For the Alexandrian school the main scandal was (a) the composition of a new formula of faith, which was seen as contradicting the prohibition of Ephesus 431, besides the deposition of Dioscorus; and (b) the acceptance of the formula 'one hypostasis *in* two natures' and the rejection of the Cyrillian-Alexandrian expression 'from two natures'. The statement of two natures was interpreted by the opponents of the council as a division of Christ into two subjects and two persons. A hidden Nestorianism was thus insinuated.

AFTER CHALCEDON

For the first twenty years, the hierarchy in the church of Antioch followed Chalcedon. Serious disorders surfaced from 470 to 488 with Peter the Fuller's fight against Chalcedonian archbishops and on behalf of the so-called theopaschite addition to the Trisagion in the liturgy. The opponents of Chalcedon prevailed. After Peter the Fuller, the struggle for the Trisagion turned into a general struggle under the leadership of Philoxenus of Mabbug against the two natures teaching.

In the anti-Chalcedonian party the leading theologians were, besides the Alexandrian archbishop Timothy Aelurus (deposed in 458 because of uncanonical installation) who wrote treatises against Chalcedon and the Tome of Leo (translated also into Armenian), the Persian Philoxenus, or Aksenaia (ordained as bishop of Mabbug by Peter the Fuller), and Jacob of Sarug (who wrote in a more irenic spirit while Philoxenus fought without compromise against the council).

The school of the Persians in Edessa was a centre of strict Antiochene theology and principles, albeit outside the bounds of the Roman Empire after its enforced closure in 489 when a new foundation was made by Narsai in Nisibis. Among representatives of the Antiochene line of thinking in Edessa, besides Narsai, another important figure was the Persian monk Ḥabib, the opponent of Philoxenus. Recent research (Abramowski 2005, 2013) has shown that Narsai as well as Ḥabib did not yet speak about two hypostases (Syriac: *qnome*) in Christ (statements of Philoxenus in this regard are polemics). Philoxenus placed his concept of the 'becoming without change' of the God Logos up against the Antiochene notion of an 'assumption'.

In the second half of the fifth century, imperial policy initially supported Chalcedon, but tried to calm the opponents of the council by the HENOTICON, an edict of emperor Zeno, pronounced in autumn 482, which prescribed the first three councils (Nicaea 325, Constantinople 381, and Ephesus 431), together with Cyril's letter of anathemas against Nestorius, while condemning whoever 'thinks anything else . . . either in Chalcedon or in any synod whatever'. This policy of silencing the content of Chalcedon satisfied neither the strict Chalcedonians (people such as the *akoimêtoi*, or *Sleepless Monks*) nor the strict anti-Chalcedonians (Peter the Iberian, Philoxenus), and was the cause of the so-called Acacian schism between Rome and Constantinople (482–519). Reconciliation became increasingly unlikely due to the agitation of Philoxenus and later of Severus at the beginning of the sixth century. In 512 Philoxenus was successful: bishop Flavian of Antioch, who refused to anathematise Chalcedon, was deposed, and Severus was installed as head of the Church of Antioch (512–518).

NARSAI (d. 502/3) wrote his poetry in the Antiochene spirit while the predominant authority for him was Theodore of Mopsuestia, as he himself stated (Homily 11). The unity of Christ is seen by Narsai in the fact that the eternal Son, hidden in the Father, wore the perfect man and made him one with himself in power and rule. The unity is in existence from the very moment of conception. The Son carried a man in order to hide his splendour, and he elevated us in clothing himself with our (despicable) nature and bringing it up to the heavens. God does not change, he is not subject to passion, but the passions are those of the human nature. Several times Narsai rejects a teaching of two *prosopa* in a physical distance, but held there to be a single *prosopon* of the Logos and his temple, one son and two natures. Again and again he rejects the accusation of teaching two sons.

JACOB OF SARUG (d. 521) represents a marked Christology of unity, which is Alexandrian in inspiration, mixed with elements of the Syriac tradition such as the *docta ignorantia* of Ephrem, or the formula 'to become of the same kind'. The formula that he favours using in his letters is: 'the one nature which is embodied'. Again and again he polemicises against a unity of *prosopon* of the 'Nestorians', which he presents as a unification of the Logos with the man Jesus, and against the conception of an indwelling of the Logos in the man. In this context, he rejects also the concept of a conjunction, or of 'clothing', and also of the distribution of the properties among the two natures (this against both 'Nestorians' and Chalcedonians). 'To divide' and 'to distinguish' are here synonymous for Jacob. Since Christ the mediator is 'out of two', no further distinction is allowed, just as the mystery of the unity of the son is also inscrutable.

The polemic against Nestorianism (and Chalcedonians were seen as closet Nestorians) pervades the whole opus of PHILOXENUS OF MABBUG (d. 523). Against a teaching of two sons he underlines the unity of the incarnating subject. The incarnation is performed by the divine will in the person of the God Logos. Divine nature and will are not contradictory since there is no opposition in God. How both of them relate to one another remains inscrutable. The formula of 'one of the Trinity who was embodied' was chosen by Philoxenus against Nestorianism and Eutychianism. It is directed above all against Nestorianism and is designed to ensure that there is no addition to the Trinity.

His specific conception of 'becoming without change', Philoxenus explains by comparing it with the sacrament of baptism by which Christians remain human and corporeal although they become sons of God filled with the spirit. Nevertheless, God's becoming without change remains an absolutely new mystery. The Logos came out from his fullness, while we are filled in baptism. God's becoming is a movement of descent, while there is an ascending one in baptism. Against the dyophysite conception of assumption, Philoxenus set his tireless polemics. In his ten-book work against Ḥabib (known as the Memre against Ḥabib or the *De uno e sancta trinitate incorporato et passo*), written during his exile (under Calendion of Antioch, till 482–84), Philoxenus defended his theology and argued that in his conception the reality of incarnation, the body and soul of Christ, is fully preserved.

The Syriac-speaking monk ḤABIB, from the Sasanian Persian Empire, composed an important counter-project among the East Syrian 'Theodorians', the *Mamlela*, or *Tractatus*, reconstructable only from Philoxenus's refutation of it (Abramowski 2013). He confessed two natures but not two hypostases nor two *prosopa* (nor two sons). For Ḥabib the concept of *hypostasis* is strictly rooted in Trinitarian doctrine, and he refuses a Christological usage – this seems to have been a peculiarity of the Theodorians in Edessa of that time. The unity in Christ is inexpressible for Ḥabib. He rejects one nature and one *hypostasis* for the one Christ; his expression for the unity in Christ probably was the one *prosopon* but in this regard Philoxenus is silent as he also left out the soteriological context of Ḥabib's statements. According to Ḥabib, God has taken a body but he did not embody. For him, the 'becoming of God' is a pagan expression, God remained what he was, he took a body from Mary.

While for Philoxenus the creedal phrase, 'descended from heaven', is a reference to the *hypostasis* of the Logos, in Ḥabib's understanding this statement can be said of the *hypostasis* only in metaphorical sense, since it is not possible to make statements of location about the *hypostasis* of the Logos. Statements on the divine *hypostasis* must keep strictly to what is proper to the divine nature. Classifications of 'metaphorical' statements seem to be a tradition of the Edessene School.

According to Ḥabib, passion and death was suffered by the man, while God can be said to have suffered only in a metaphorical sense. To speak of God's death in a theologically correct manner would be thus: Christ – not God nor the man – died, in order that death happened not only in the order of his nature but in both the dispensation of salvation (*oikonomia*) and in nature. Death was realised for us in nature, and in *oikonomia*, and in will, by the one Jesus Christ, the son of God.

One further figure of the fifth century was Simeon of Beth Aršam, also known as the Persian debater, who successfully had a discussion with the East Syrian catholicos Babai (497–502/3) before the Persian king and was made bishop afterwards. In

Armenia he gained the support of the church for his party (505/6 in Dvin) against the 'Nestorians'.

THE SIXTH CENTURY

Severus of Antioch fought his whole life as a theologian against the Council of Chalcedon and worked at the imperial court under emperor Anastasius I for an anti-Chalcedonian interpretation of the Henoticon (that is, as a condemnation of Chalcedon). He fought against Chalcedonians (such as Nephalius, John the Grammarian of Caesarea) and fellow anti-Chalcedonians (Sergius Grammaticus, Julian of Halicarnassus). For Severus, the 'teacher of orthodox faith' was Cyril of Alexandria, the 'king of explaining dogma', and his *mia physis* Christology is the common point of reference in all his controversies.

Against the monk Nephalius from Alexandria, who converted to Chalcedon, and his apology of the Synod of Chalcedon, Severus composed two *Orationes* (*CPG* 7022), probably around 509 in Constantinople.

The Florilegium Cyrillianum, a collection of 244 quotations from the work of Cyril of Alexandria in favour of the two natures, brought by John Talaia of Alexandria in 482 to Rome, was attacked and refuted by Severus in the *Philalethes* (*CPG* 7023), a masterpiece of anti-Chalcedonian Christology; the 'friend of truth' (*philalethes*) was a reference to Cyril. Severus became acquainted with this florilegium during his stay in Constantinople (508–511) and he characterised the intention of its composers as wishing to 'show that the teacher of the orthodox faith thought and spoke the same as those who wish to divide our one Lord and God Jesus Christ in two natures after the inexplicable union'. Throughout his life, Severus always understood the teaching of two natures to mean a division into two. The florilegium and its refutation by Severus show that Cyril could be used as an arsenal for arguing in favour of *dyo physeis* and also in favour of the *mia physis*. Consequently, Severus deleted any terminology of two natures from his theological vocabulary in order to eradicate the Nestorian 'disease of separation' (Grillmeier 1995: 72). Therefore, terms and concepts such as 'conjunction' (*synapheia*) and 'the assumed man' (*homo assumptus*), which had been accepted by Cyril in his earlier writings, now also had to be deleted. With this purification of language (Grillmeier 1995: 72–9), Severus presents a pure type of the *mia physis* Christology.

A heavy challenge for Severus from the Chalcedonian side came from the grammarian John of Caesarea. His *Apologia concilii Chalcedonensis* (*CPG* 6855), written before 519, is not preserved and has to be reconstructed from its refutation, Severus's *Liber contra impium Grammaticum* (*CPG* 7024, preserved only in Syriac), completed only after the end of his patriarchate (518). John the Grammarian is considered as the first great representative of so-called Neo-Chalcedonianism. He tried to mediate between Cyril of Alexandria and Chalcedon, partly by analysing concepts (the distinction between *physis* and *ousia*, the concept of *hypostasis*, and *enhypostaton*) and partly by a dialectic use of formulas (*mia physis* against Nestorianism, and 'two natures' against Eutychianism). However, this solution brought further terminological difficulty in that the Old Nicene equation of *physis* and *hypostasis* was again introduced into the *mia physis* terminology and was connected with the Neo-Nicene, Chalcedonian distinction of the two concepts. Severus concluded that the only way forward was a purification of language. According to Grillmeier (1995: 61–7), the term *enhypostaton* in John's formula 'two enhypostatically united natures' still retains its basic meaning of existence or reality. John also made a criticism of Severus's first oration against Nephalius.

A controversy within the anti-Chalcedonian party arose around 515 with the ideas of SERGIUS GRAMMATICUS, who developed his own conception of the union in Christ. Starting from a word of Cyril's, he took the idea of a *henosis* of the *ousia* and developed the new concept of the one *ousia* Christ with new properties. This kind of an ontological monophysitism was strongly rejected by Severus, when Sergius presented his work to him. Severus also refused the concept of a 'mixture without confusion', which Sergius had invented; instead, Severus introduced the concept of *synthesis*, here going beyond Cyril. The correspondence of three letters of Sergius and the energetic reprimands of Severus are preserved (Torrance 1988).

The most important controversy was that which involved JULIAN OF HALICARNASSUS. For Julian, corruption (*phtharsia*) arises from the necessity of passions within the fallen human being and which originates with sin; Christ, however, was not subject to this necessity, but suffered the passions totally voluntarily in true humanity (consubstantial with us). Therefore, Julian declared the body of Christ to be incorrupt *(aphthartos)*, even from conception. When Julian published his ideas in a *Tomus* (and thought to be sure of Severus's consent), a controversy started which lasted for the main part from 520 to 527, while both parties were in exile in Egypt. Julian later published a supplement to his *Tomus* (*Additiones*); then he wrote an *Apology* as confirmation and finally a kind of treatise entitled *Against the Blasphemies of Severus*. Against Julian's thesis that Christ's body was incorruptible already before the resurrection, Severus wrote three letters (*CPG* 7026) and five other treatises (*CPG* 7027–7031). Of particular importance is his work *Censura tomi Iuliani*, a critique of Julian's *Tomus*. Julian composed a large writing of ten logoi in defence of his *Tomus*, which is known through the *Apologia Philalethis* (*CPG* 7031) of Severus (few of the writings of Julian are preserved; besides three letters to Severus, there are only fragments (*CPG* 7126)). Already in 528 a Syriac translation of Severus's anti-Julianist writings, made by Paul of Callinicum, was available. The accusation of docetism (which became common since Severus) does not hold true for Julian himself. The dispute led finally to a schism of the anti-Chalcedonians between Severans and Julianists which lasted for centuries. Followers of Julian's teaching can be found, besides in Egypt (Gaianus), in Mesopotamia, South Arabia, and Armenia (mid-sixth century).

The texts of all these controversies of Severus are preserved almost exclusively in Syriac and his argumentation was used in the debates and discussions that followed, such as the controversy of Proba and John Barbur with Severan monks at the end of the sixth century (see below).

THE THREE CHAPTERS CONTROVERSY

The Council of Constantinople II condemned, in its canons 12–14, the 'Three Chapters' (namely, Theodore of Mopsuestia as a person together with his work; Theodoret of Cyrus with his anti-Cyrillian writings; and the letter of Ibas of Edessa to the Persian Mari). Justinian did not succeed in winning back the anti-Chalcedonians by these actions. Rather, a deep gap was opened up with the Persian Church, since for them Theodore of Mopsuestia had become the norm for faith, doctrine, and exegesis, the interpreter par excellence, since the middle of the fifth century, and even more completely in the sixth (cf. the synodical decisions of the years 544, 585, 596, 605 in the Synodicon Orientale, Chabot 1902). The work of Nestorius, brought to Persia in the first half of the sixth century by the later catholicos Mar Aba and also translated into Syriac, then achieved a certain, albeit limited, influence. Mar Aba represented a typically strict Antiochene position, based on Holy Scripture. Nestorius was seen as a martyr of the faith, while the theological authority was Theodore.

ANTI-CHALCEDONIANS AFTER 553

The anti-Chalcedonian party in the second half of the sixth century was split into many groupings, often in exile. The schisms originated around the question of Christ's knowledge (Agnoetes), of Tritheism, and the teaching of John Philoponus concerning the Resurrection. A lasting schism between the Alexandrians (patriarch Damian) and the Antiochenes (patriarch Peter of Callinicum) originated in differences of Trinitarian doctrine, although both of them wrote against Tritheism. As a theologian, Theodosius of Alexandria acted as the head of the anti-Chalcedonians even in exile (Van Roey and Allen 1994; Grillmeier 1996: 53–9). Tritheism, propagated by John Ascoutzanges and theoretically expounded by the philosopher John Philoponus, was fought by Theodosius in his writing *De trinitate*. John Philoponus, who commented on Aristotle in Alexandria, offered already before 553, in his *Diaetetes*, a philosophical grounding for the *mia physis* formula (as *mia physis synthetos*, one composite nature).

The second half of the sixth century was marked by analyses of concepts and struggles between Chalcedonians and anti-Chalcedonians following the establishment of separate ecclesiastical hierarchies. Cyril of Alexandria and Severus are the fathers for the anti-Chalcedonian monks in the controversy surrounding Proba and John Barbur in 596 – under the presidency of Anastasius of Antioch who had won the confidence of Severans because of his struggle against the Tritheists (against the concept of *ousia idikê* or *physis idikê*, the individual substance or nature). The debate was held on the question of whether the remaining distinction of the two natures in Christ, a teaching which was worked out by Severus of Antioch for the anti-Chalcedonians, entails a confession of two natures. This controversy is preserved only in Syriac, but A. Van Roey presumed the original to have been Greek (Hainthaler 2004; 2013: 386–418).

TRITHEIST CONTROVERSY

From 556/7 in Constantinople, John Ascoutzanges from Apamea started to propagate his ideas. When *physis* and *hypostasis* become nearly synonymous in Christology, it has some repercussions in Trinitarian doctrine: if one confesses three hypostases in God, then as a consequence the question arises whether to confess also three *physeis* and three *ousiai*. Tritheism has a philosophical starting point, as was clearly explained by John Philoponus. For Philoponus, *hypostasis* is the individual nature, that is, the individual exemplar. As a consequence, the one divinity in the Trinity has existence only in abstraction.

In 563/4, Theodosius of Alexandria intervened, after the death of Sergius of Antioch. The *Oratio Theologica* of Theodosius is preserved in Syriac in three versions. The controversy continued among the Severans even after his death in 566, the texts again being preserved only in Syriac (original in Greek). The teaching of the Tritheists found followers in the monasteries in the eastern part of Syria (Hainthaler 2013: 268–80, esp.273–4). Around 568, there was a clear division into two parts in the Severan Church, not only at Constantinople but in Syria and Egypt as well, and Mundhir the Ghassanid king tried to mediate. After Justin II's second edict failed (571), a persecution of the anti-Chalcedonians began and therefore the Tritheists also were expelled and spread abroad.

Another schism between Peter of Callinicum and Damian of Alexandria arose which lasted for twenty years, although both were struggling against the Tritheists, a family feud between two anti-Tritheist patriarchs (Grillmeier 2013: 275–6). This was a heavy burden for the Syriac Church. There was, however, no proper hierarchy among the Tritheists.

THE AGNOETIC DEBATE

Originally, this was a debate among anti-Chalcedonians in Alexandria, which started with the Severan deacon Themistius (in the time of Timothy of Alexandria, 517–535) and was transferred from Alexandria to Constantinople, when Theodosius was brought there in exile. However, the debate spread to other parts of the empire, including Syria, though there not so acutely (Van Roey and Allen 1994: 3–22, esp. 7–8); besides, later also the Chalcedonians were involved. Themistius ascribed ignorance to Christ in his humanity. He started from an anti-Julianist position: since Christ's humanity was consubstantial to us and subject to natural needs and passions, consequently it is subject also to human ignorance. In this, Themistius remained within the *mia physis* doctrine. Theodosius refuted Themistius and stated that it is not possible after the union in Christ to speak of ignorance in Christ. The texts of the controversy are from the period after Severus. Many of them were written in Greek, but preserved only in Syriac. The texts of the Agnoetic debate and the Tritheist controversy all date from the period 530–580 (Van Roey and Allen 1994: IX; Grillmeier 1995: 362–82).

CONTROVERSIES WITHIN THE EAST SYRIAC CHURCH

At the end of the sixth century in the Persian Church, Ḥenana of Adiabene, the head of the school of Nisibis, introduced other theological authorities besides Theodore, and he seems to have propagated the teaching of a *hypostasis synthetos*, as is found in Neo-Chalcedonianism, in place of the former teaching of two natures and one *prosopon*. This caused an exodus of disciples from the school of Nisibis, and Ḥenana's teaching was condemned in the Persian Church. These developments happened while miaphysite communities were growing within the Persian Empire.

In the Persian Church, Babai the Great, challenged by the concept of the one composite *hypostasis* of Neo-Chalcedonianism, laid out his own Christology in his *Liber de unione* (Vaschalde 1915), which became the leading theology for the Church of the East. The simple formula 'two natures and one *prosopon*' was developed into the formula 'two natures, two hypostases, one *prosopon*', already at the Colloquy of 612.

Babai fought against Philoxenus and against Justinian and Neo-Chalcedonianism (Ḥenana?), and also attacked Origen. A *prosopon* (Syr. *parṣopa*) is 'that property of whatsoever *qnoma*, by which it is distinct from others, since the *qnoma* of Paul is not that of Peter, although they are equal regarding *kyana* [nature] and *qnoma*, since both have body and soul, and are living and rational and bodily, but one is distinct from another through the *parsopa* because of the indivisible singularity which each one possesses', (meaning age, figure, temperament, wisdom, authority, paternity, filiation etc.). *Parṣopa*, the total sum of the properties, is fixed but it could be communicated and assumed by another *qnoma* (*De unione* 17; Chediath 1982: 90).

Christ's becoming flesh and human is, according to Babai, the assumption of a complete human being, formed by the Holy Spirit from Mary. The God Logos assumed it in the union, and this union lasts forever (*De unione* 8) (already from the very moment of conception, at the annunciation, before the human flesh was ensouled, the Logos took the human nature as his temple and habitation and created the soul in it). This was a process without mixture of the natures and the hypostases with their properties (*De unione* 8, Vaschalde 1915: 48, 33–49, 5). For Babai, the union in Christ is not loose and insufficient, but of singular firmness, valid forever, and is actually even 'more' than a hypostatic union (because the hypostatic union of soul and body is dissolvable), since the unity of the two natures in Christ endures passion, death, and resurrection; this is due to the divine Logos. With his concept of *prosopon/parṣopa*, Babai nevertheless takes an approach from outside, one based upon appearance; yet it is obvious that behind this he stands before the miracle of the union of the two natures (Abramowski 1974: 243–4), which in itself is unfathomable, inscrutable, ineffable; how infinite and finite united is beyond human thinking (*De unione* 6, Vaschalde 1915: p. 30,12; *De unione* 17, p. 134; Abramowski 1975: 341).

The principal controversies in the East Syrian Church in the seventh century were with the miaphysites, who were gaining in influence, and with dissidents such as Sahdona, who seems to have returned to the older formula of two natures and one *prosopon*, and who was suspected of Chalcedonian or monophysite leanings.

NOTE

1 'Miaphysite' is the term accepted by the Oriental Orthodox themselves. See the recent 'Agreed Statement Revised on Christology' of 15 October 2014 in Cairo of the Anglican–Oriental Orthodox International Commission, § 7. The term is criticised in Luisier (2013), and defended in Brock (2016).

BIBLIOGRAPHY

Abramowski, L. 1963. *Untersuchungen zum "Liber Heraclidis" des Nestorius*. CSCO 242, Subsidia 22. Louvain: Secrétariat du CorpusSCO.

———. 1974. Die Christologie Babais des Grossen. *OCA* 197, 219–44.

———. 1975. Babai der Große: Christologische Probleme und ihre Lösungen. *OCP* 41, 289–343.

———. 1992. The Theology of Theodore of Mopsuestia. *In: Formula and Context: Studies in Early Christian Thought*. Ashgate. No.II, 1–36 (= English version, trans.L. Wickham, of 'Zur Theologie Theodors von Mopsuestia'. *Zeitschrift für Kirchengeschichte* 72 [1961], 263–93).

———. 2005. Die nachephesinische Christologie der edessenischen Theodorianer. *In:* L. Greisiger, C. Rammelt and J. Tubach, ed., *Edessa in hellenistisch-römischer Zeit: Religion, Kultur und Politik zwischen Ost und West.* Beiruter Texte und Studien 116. Würzburg: Ergon in Kommission, 1–9.

———. 2013. From the Controversy on 'Unus ex Trinitate passus est': The Protest of Habib Against Philoxenus' Epistula Dogmatica to the Monks. *In:* T. Hainthaler, ed., *Christ in Christian Tradition*, vol. 2/3. Oxford: Oxford University Press, 545–620.

Blum, G. G. 1969. *Rabbula von Edessa. Der Christ, der Bischof, der Theologe.* CSCO 300, Subs. 34. Louvain: Secrétariat du CorpusSCO.

Brock, S. P. 1996. The Nestorian Church, a Lamentable Misnomer. *BJRL* 78, 23–35.

———. 2016. Miaphysite, Not Monophysite! *Cristianesimo nella storia* 37, 45–54.

Bruns, P. 1995. *Den Menschen mit dem Himmel verbinden. Eine Studie zu den katechetischen Homilien des Theodor von Mopsuestia.* CSCO 549, Subs. 89. Leuven: Peeters.

Chabot, J. B. 1902. *Synodicon orientale ou Recueil de synodes nestoriens.* Paris: Imprimerie Nationale.

Chediath, G. 1982. *The Christology of Mar Babai the Great.* Kottayam/Paderborn: Oriental Institute of Religious Studies.

Davids, A. 1998. The Person and Teachings of Theodore of Mopsuestia and the Relationship Between Him, His Teachings and the Church of the East With a Special Reference to the Three Chapters Controversy. *In:* A. Stirnemann and G. Wilflinger, ed., *Non-Official Consultation on Dialogue Within the Syriac Tradition* 3. Vienna: Pro Oriente, 38–52.

Fiano, E. 2015. The Trinitarian Controversy in Fourth Century Edessa. *Le Muséon* 128, 85–125.

Finkel, J. 1927. A Risāla of al-Jāḥiẓ. *JAOS* 47, 311–34.

Grillmeier, A. 1975. *Christ in Christian Tradition, Volume 1: From the Apostolic Age to Chalcedon (451).* London: Mowbray.

———. 1987. *Christ in Christian Tradition, Volume 2: From the Council of Chalcedon (451) to Gregory the Great (590–604), Part 1: Reception and Contradiction, the Development of Discussion About Chalcedon.* London: Mowbray.

——— and T. Hainthaler. 1995. *Christ in Christian Tradition, Volume 2: From the Council of Chalcedon (451) to Gregory the Great (590–604), Part* 2. London: Mowbray.

——— and T. Hainthaler. 1996. *Christ in Christian Tradition, Volume 2: From the Council of Chalcedon (451) to Gregory the Great (590–604), Part 4: Church of Alexandria With Nubia and Ethiopia after 451.* London: Mowbray.

Hainthaler, T. 2004. The Christological Controversy on Proba and John Barbur. *Journal of Eastern Christian Studies* 56, 155–70.

———. 2006. A Short Analysis of the Definition of Chalcedon and Some Reflections. *The Harp* 20, 317–31.

———. 2013. *Christ in Christian Tradition, Volume 2: From the Council of Chalcedon (451) to Gregory the Great (590–604), Part 3: The Churches of Jerusalem and Antioch from 451 to 600.* Oxford: Oxford University Press.

Halleux, A. de. 1976. La définition christologique à Chalcédoine. *RTL* 7, 3–23; 155–70; reprinted in de Halleux, *Patrologie et Oecuménisme.* BEThL 93. Leuven: Peeters, 1990, 445–80.

Lietzmann, H. 1904. *Apollinaris von Laodicea und seine Schule.* Tübingen: Mohr Siebeck.

Loon, H. van. 2009. *The Dyophysite Christology of Cyril of Alexandria.* Leiden: Brill.

Luisier, Ph. 2013. Il miafisismo, un termine discutibile della storiografia recente. Problemi teologici ed ecumenici. *Cristianesimo nella Storia* 35, 297–307.

Torrance, I. R. 1988. *Christology After Chalcedon. Severus of Antioch and Sergius the Monophysite.* Norwich: Canterbury Press.

Van Roey, A. and P. Allen. 1994. *Monophysite Texts of the Sixth Century.* OLA 56. Leuven: Peeters.

Vaschalde, A. A, ed. 1915. *Babai Magni, Liber de unione.* CSCO 79, 80, Syr. 34, 35. Paris; e Typographeo Reipublicae.

CHAPTER TWENTY-THREE

THE LITURGIES OF THE SYRIAC CHURCHES

Fr Baby Varghese

Syriac liturgy belongs to the Antiochene family of liturgies of which Byzantine and Armenian are the other members. Following the fifth-century Christological controversies, Syriac Christianity split into two branches: East Syriac followed the 'Nestorian' Christology, and West Syriac, 'miaphysite' or anti-Chalcedonian Christology. East Syriac tradition had its origin in and around the city of Edessa, the cultural capital of Syriac-speaking Mesopotamia. However, a considerable section of the population spoke Greek as well. Among the modern descendants of the first of these two branches, the Church of the East and the Chaldean Catholics, follow the East Syriac liturgy. There are also in South India two churches belonging the East Syriac tradition: the Church of the East and the Syro-Malabar Catholics. The latter use a highly Latinised version of the East Syriac liturgy. The other original branch which followed the West Syriac liturgy, more Antiochene in its origin and affinity, is represented today by the Syrian Orthodox, Syrian Catholic, and Maronite Churches. In India there are four churches belonging to the West Syriac tradition: the Malankara Orthodox Church, the Syro-Malankara Catholic Church, the Independent Syrian Church of Malabar or Thozhiyoor Church (since 1772), and the Reformed Syrian Church, also known as the Mar Thoma Church, which uses a reformed version inspired by Low Church Anglican missionaries.

The liturgical texts of both traditions in their present forms are many layered, with archaic and much more recent elements side by side. Both share several elements in common (e.g. poetry), which go back to the period before the division. The Syrian Orthodox and the Maronites have a common liturgical heritage, and the separation between these two traditions must have taken place in about the seventh century. The former have retained archaic elements, lost in the latter (e.g. liturgical texts in baptism and the weekday office). There are close parallels between the Maronite and the East Syriac traditions: the Maronite *Anaphora* (i.e. liturgy) *of Peter Sharar* has many prayers in common with the East Syrian *Anaphora of Addai and Mari*, and the Maronite weekday office includes several hymns (*sugyotho*) of East Syrian origin, in which they have named authors of the sixth and seventh centuries.

EAST SYRIAC LITURGY

After the Council of Ephesus (431) which condemned Nestorius, the adherents of the Antiochene Christology in Mesopotamia broke communion with the Church in the Roman Empire and became known as 'the Church of the East'. They are also variously called Nestorians, Assyrians, Persians, Babylonians, or Chaldeans (a name now used by the Catholic faction). A very vibrant monastic tradition kept their spiritual and intellectual life alive with a remarkable literary activity until the end of the Middle Ages. By the end of the first millennium, the monks travelling along the Silk Road brought Christianity to Central Asia, China, and Mongolia. Although there were attempts at enculturation in these areas, Syriac remained the liturgical language. Even though the Church of the East has not been in communion with the Byzantine and oriental Orthodox Churches since the fifth century, it shares in almost every element of the Eastern spiritual and liturgical traditions.

The first major reform of the East Syriac liturgy is attested in the canons of the Synod of Seleucia-Ctesiphon (410), organised by Mar Isaac and Marutha of Maipherqat (Martyropolis, near Amid, SE Turkey). Canon 13 decreed:

> Now and henceforward, we will with one accord celebrate the liturgy according to the western rite, which the bishops Isaac and Marutha taught us and which we have seen them celebrate here in the church of Seleucia. In each city the deacons shall make the proclamation as they ought to. Similarly the scripture shall be read. The pure and holy oblation shall be offered on a single altar. Henceforward the custom of ancient memory shall no longer exist among us, and sacrifice shall no longer be offered in houses. We shall celebrate uniformly the feast of the Epiphany of Our Saviour and the great day of His Resurrection, just as the Metropolitan, Archbishop, and catholicos of Seleucia-Ctesiphon has indicated to us. He who dares to celebrate in his church and among his people the feast of the Nativity, Lent, or the great day of the Azymes [= Passover] on his own and out of harmony with the Church of the West and of the East, should be rejected from all ecclesiastical ministries without mercy as a corrupting individual, and there shall be no remedy for him.
>
> (Chabot 1902: 266–7)

Canon 13 directs the churches to follow uniform liturgical practices and forces them to conform to the 'western rite'. The exact nature of this rite is open to discussion. It could be the liturgical practices of either Edessa or of Antioch (Varghese 2007: 272–4). In fact, Edessa and its famous school were always open to Antiochene influence. In the fourth century, the Christians of Antioch were even called 'Palutians' following Palut, the bishop consecrated by Serapion of Antioch. In the course of time, several elements of Antiochene origin were incorporated into the East Syrian liturgy. These include the suppression of the Diatessaron, which was the official Gospel book of the Syriac Church until the beginning of the fifth century, and the introduction of the four separate Gospels. The custom of the proclamation and the reading of the Gospel by a deacon is also probably of Antiochene origin.

Another development took place during the patriarchate of Mar Aba (540–552), who is credited with translating the *Anaphora of Nestorius* and possibly that of

Theodore of Mopsuestia from Greek into Syriac. Mar Aba may have been responsible for introducing the two litanies (*koruzwoto*) that follow the Gospel, which have much in common with those of the Byzantines (Maccomber 1977: 111).

The most important liturgical reforms were introduced by the patriarch Išoʿyahb III (580–659), who revised the *Hudra* or service book for the Sundays of the whole year. He re-arranged the liturgical cycles and the seasons and fixed their length, and assigned the anaphoras to each festival and reduced their number to the three presently used: apostles Addai and Mari, Theodore of Mopsuestia, and Nestorius. He composed a *Taksa*, or the euchology for priests, which contains both rubrics and the texts of the three anaphoras besides other ceremonies such as baptism. Išoʿyahb was responsible for the fixed forms of these ceremonies.

Išoʿyahb's reforms might have been one of the reasons why the East Syrians adopted the liturgy of the apostles Addai and Mari as their ordinary anaphora. This anaphora was most probably composed in Syriac sometime between the third and fifth centuries. The absence of the words of Institution has puzzled scholars, and various theories have been put forward to explain this 'anomaly'.

Some scholars (Ratcliff 1928–1929; Dix 1945: 184) held that the anaphora never contained the institution narrative, as there existed similar Eucharistic prayers in the early centuries. Botte (1954), followed by Bouyer (1966: 146–52), argued that originally the anaphora must have had an institution, which was lost because of textual corruption or modification. In 1960s, Maccomber discovered the oldest manuscript of Addai and Mari from the church of Mar Esaʿya in Mosul which seems to date from the eleventh or twelfth century (Maccomber 1966). The Esaʿya text does not contain the institution and represents an earlier structure: Thanksgiving – Sanctus – Prayer of Intercession – Epiclesis – Doxology. Scholars have pointed out that its characteristics, both stylistic (redundancy in vocabulary, parallelism in phrasing) and theological are reminiscent of the Jewish prayer for the table. However, the assumption that Addai and Mari is purely Semitic in character and uninfluenced by Greek tradition is open to doubt.

Several East Syrian liturgical practices are traditionally attributed to the reforms of patriarch Išoʿyahb III, and/or with the usage of the 'Upper Monastery' (of Mar Gabriel and Mar Abraham, Mosul). Many new texts were incorporated in the twelfth and thirteenth centuries, in particular prose texts by Eliya III Abu Halim (d. 1190), verse texts by George Warda, and hymns (*ʿonyatha*) by Khamis bar Qurdahe (both thirteenth century).

Early Syriac baptism is characterised by the absence of a post-baptismal rite such as imposition of hands or anointing. Though a post-baptismal anointing was introduced into Syro-Antiochene baptism towards the end of the fourth century, it appeared only much later among the East Syrians. Now, East Syriac baptismal liturgy has a post-baptismal imposition of the hands followed by an anointing (absent in some manuscripts and even printed texts). The preparatory parts, such as exorcism and renunciation of Satan, are absent in East Syriac baptism. Baptismal fonts are called Jordan, a title regularly used in early Syriac tradition, which saw Christ's baptism as the foundation and model for Christian baptism. The most striking rite is the consecration of the oil, followed by that of the baptismal water.

East Syrians use two types of oil: oil previously consecrated by the bishop, called 'oil in the horn of anointing' (*qarna da-mshihuta*), and ordinary oil poured into a bowl or flagon (*laqna*), over which the priest recites a prayer, which includes an epiclesis. In consecrating it, the priest 'signs' the oil in the bowl *(laqna)* with the sign of the cross, that is a few drops of the oil in the 'horn (*qarna*) of anointing' are added. The epiclesis over the oil reads,

> may grace come from the gift of the Holy Spirit. . . . and be mingled with this oil, and give to those who are anointed with it a pledge of the resurrection . . . and may it reside and settle on this oil, and bless it and sanctify it and seal it in the name of the Father, and the Son and the Holy Spirit.

As in the West Syriac tradition, water is also blessed with an epiclesis and the pouring of the oil in the horn (*qarna*), in the form of a cross. The epiclesis asks, 'and may the same Spirit also come upon this water, so that it receives power for the assistance and salvation of those who are baptized in it'.

The oil in the *qarna* is used for the pre-baptismal anointing (or signing) of the forehead, as well as the post-baptismal signing. The new consecrated oil (in the bowl – *laqna*) is used for the pre-baptismal anointing of the whole body. Baptism is by immersion. Another striking rite is the 'loosing of the baptismal water from its consecration'. Following the concluding prayer, the priest pours a little ordinary water into the baptismal font, saying 'These waters have been consecrated with Amen and with the same Amen let them be loosed from their consecration, let them return unto their former nature'.

East Syrians celebrate three major hours: Matins (*Ṣapra*), Vespers (*Ramša*), and Night prayers (*Lelya*), followed by Vigil (*Qala d-Sahra*). At one time they also celebrated minor hours, known as *Subbaʿa* (Compline), *Qutta* (Terce), and *ʿEddana* (Sext) (as well as None), which disappeared by the ninth century as we can assume from the anonymous commentary on daily offices attributed to George of Arbel. However, Terce and Sext continued to be celebrated in Great Lent, and the remnants of Compline can be found in some feasts and that of Terce has survived in the *marmyata* (or Psalmody) in the pre-anaphora, and None in the initial psalmody of Vespers.

The norms regarding the celebration of the major hours were established by the patriarch Išoʿyahb III, at the 'Upper Monastery' (of Mar Gabriel) on the right bank of the Tigris in Mosul in 650–51. The patriarch left the monks free to follow their own customs in the celebration of the night offices.

East Syrians are perhaps the only easterners who have retained the early Christian custom of reciting a large number of psalms, a custom seemingly inherited from Lower Egypt, where the core of the offices comprised a series of psalms with prayer and prostration. The 150 psalms are divided into 20 *hullale*, which more or less correspond to the Greek *Kathismata*, and each of the *hullala* (sing.) is divided into two or three *marmiyata*. Each *marmita* (sing.) consists of two, three, or four psalms and is preceded by a prayer, which is generally based on the theme of the first psalm of the *marmita*. Each psalm has a *qanona* (refrain) given in red after the first or the second psalm. The composition of the *qanone* is attributed to the catholicos Mar Aba (536–552). The East Syrian psalter has a twenty-first *hullala* with the title 'the Canticles of blessed Moses' containing three *marmyata* [I: Ex 15: 1–21; Is 42: 10–13; 45: 8; II: Deut 32: 1–21ab; III: Deut 32: 21c–43]. Unlike the West Syrians, the East Syrians do not use the NT Canticles, Magnificat, and Beatitudes. The division of the psalter into *marmyata* must be older and *hullale* were arranged later. *Hullala* means 'shout of joy', or hallelujah at the end of the division and *marmita* means 'prayer' or 'exclamation'. Originally, *marmita* referred to the prayer which preceded a group of psalms.

WEST SYRIAC LITURGY

In the first half of the fifth century, the Antiochene Church adopted the Saint James Liturgy, the official anaphora of Jerusalem. The Syrian Orthodox Church, nicknamed 'Jacobite' (after Jacob Baradaeus, the sixth-century organiser), or 'Monophysite' (a name used by the Chalcedonians since the sixth century, as it was opposed to the dyophysite Christology of Chalcedon), inherited the Antiochene liturgy in its fifth-century form. When the non-chalcedonians were expelled from Antioch and the Eastern Roman Empire by the emperor Justin I (518–527), they took refuge in the Syriac-speaking areas of Mesopotamia in the region of the Persian borders. The Greek text of the liturgy was translated into Syriac probably before the end of the sixth century. A group of manuscripts bear the title *New and Correct Recension by Jacob of Edessa*, implying that Jacob made a more accurate Syriac translation on the basis of the Greek text of his time (hereafter NCR). The *Textus receptus* of the St James liturgy derives from NCR. In the thirteenth century, Barhebraeus (d. 1286) abridged the *Anaphora of St James* ('the shorter version'), which is currently used by all West Syriac churches in India.

The Eucharistic liturgy has the following structure:

1 Preparation rites
2 Pre-anaphora (the introductory rites, liturgy of the Word, censing, and the creed)
3 Kiss of peace
4 Trinitarian blessing and dialogue
5 Sanctus
6 Institution
7 Anamnesis
8 Epiclesis
9 Commemorations
10 Fraction
11 Lord's Prayer
12 'Holy things to the Holy'
13 Communion
14 Dismissal
15 Post-communion

The structure of the anaphora (nos. 3–14) was fixed as early as the time of Jacob of Edessa. The preparation rites and the post-communion, as well as the prayers to be said by the people and the deacon, were added later. The present form belongs to the fifteenth century.

The most characteristic trait of the Syrian Orthodox liturgy is the large number of anaphoras. About eighty are known, and a dozen are still in use. Generally speaking, with a few exceptions, the anaphoras follow the structure of Saint James, though the wording varies considerably. In the early Antiochene Eucharistic prayers, as attested by the *Apostolic Constitutions* (VIII, 12, 5–27), the prayer that followed the initial dialogue was a long thanksgiving addressed to the Father. The early Syriac version(s) of St James apparently followed this pattern. Thus some ancient anaphoras, which were modelled on St James, contain long thanksgiving prayers, usually with the title 'prayer of offering'. The *Anaphora of Timothy of Alexandria* offers an example of this (Anaphorae Syriacae 1939, I–1: 3–47). In NCR, the original thanksgiving prayer was abridged as follows:

> (*inaudibly*) Truly it is meet and right and fitting and due that we should glorify you, we should bless you, we should praise you, we should give thanks to you, the Maker of all creation visible and invisible.
>
> (AS II-2: 142)

The Sanctus enumerates the different angelic choirs, a characteristic of Antiochene anaphoras. Post-Sanctus briefly outlines the economy of salvation, which is continued in the institution narrative:

> In truth You are Holy, O King of the worlds and giver of all holiness. Holy is Your Son, our Lord Jesus Christ, and Holy is Your Holy Spirit who searches out your deep things, O God and Father. You are almighty, terrible, good, partaker of sufferings and especially towards Your creation, who made man from earth, having bestowed upon him the delights of paradise. But when he had transgressed your commandment and fallen, You did not disregard him, You did not leave him, O Good One, but you chastised him as a father fair of mercies, You called him through the Law, You educated him through the prophets, and finally You sent Your Only Begotten Son Himself to the world, that You might renew Your image (which was impaired in mankind): who, when He had come down and had become incarnate of Your Holy Spirit and of the holy and blessed Mother of God, the eternal-virgin Mary, conversed with man, accomplishing (*dabar*) everything for the salvation of our race.

Incarnation is seen as the renewal and restoration of the fallen human nature. Sometimes, prayers carefully articulate the Syrian Orthodox Christology, with its key terminology. The best example is the Post-Sanctus of the *Anaphora of Timothy of Alexandria*:

> When He was about to dwell among us, [He] came in the end of time and took for Himself our humanity; the Word became flesh; He neither took change nor alteration, but by the Holy Spirit He was conceived by Mary, the ever virgin and holy mother of God. [He took] a body having rational and intelligent soul, in the true and hypostatic unity; which was not an imaginary apparition. Without separation or division, He truly took a human body and soul and all that a man has, and in all things He resembled us except sin. He did not merely dwell among men, but while being perfect God the Word, He perfectly took flesh and became man. His divinity did not become humanity; but he remained in His divinity and took completely the human nature. He was not two, but one King, one Christ, one Lord, one God the Word incarnated who is revealed to us. He dwelt among

> men, affirmed the earth and blessed it; He restrained the waves of the sea. He was known by His deeds, revealed in power, conquered the human passions and put an end to the transgression of law, converted the erring, and destroyed the power of death from us, which conquered man in the beginning, and showed to be invincible in the end. Through the [human] body He caught hold of [the death] and that which was caught was destroyed. Through His death, He restored the glory of man who was destitute of glory.
>
> (AS I-1, 16–18)

This prayer is reminiscent of the Christology of Severus of Antioch and Philoxenus of Mabbug, whose key Christological concepts include the true and hypostatic union which was not an illusion, the oneness of God the Word incarnate, and the exclusion of any change in His divine nature after the incarnation.

In Syrian anaphoras, including the Syriac *Anaphora of St James*, the anamnesis is addressed to the Son (ending with a thanksgiving *ad Patrum*), whereas in the Greek version, it is addressed to the Father. Originally, the anamnesis must have been addressed to the Father as a prelude to the Epiclesis and the West Syrians might have modified it, most probably following an early Syro-Mesopotamian pattern. Thus the anaphora in *Testamentum Domini*, East Syrian Addai and Mari (only partly), and the Maronite Peter Sharar have retained this feature. As late as the ninth century, West Syrian anaphoras contained prayers addressed to Christ and in his commentary on the Eucharist; Moses Bar Kepha (d. 903) required such prayers to be corrected.

The Epiclesis of St James evokes the presence and work of the Holy Spirit in the economy of salvation and asks the Father 'to send down the Holy Spirit upon us and upon the offerings':

> (*Inaudibly*) Have mercy upon us, O God Almighty Father, and send upon us and upon these offerings that have been placed Your Holy Spirit, the Lord and life-giver, who is equal to You in throne, God the Father and to the Son, and equal in kingdom, consubstantial and co-eternal, who spoke in the law and the prophets, and in Your covenant, who descended in the likeness of a dove upon our Lord Jesus Christ in the river Jordan, who descended upon Your holy apostles in the likeness of fiery tongues.

The Epiclesis is followed by the great intercessions also known as 'diptychs', 'commemorations', or 'canons'. The intercessions consist of eighteen prayers, arranged in six canons, each of three prayers: one by the deacon, during which the celebrant says a prayer on the same theme inaudibly, and it is followed by an *ekphonesis* by the celebrant. Among the six canons, the first three commemorate the living (Orthodox prelates, believers, and rulers), and the last three the departed (apostles and saints, doctors, and the faithful). In the Greek St James and the Syriac *Anaphora of the Apostles*, intercessions are still a single prayer. The six-fold division was introduced probably in the eighth or ninth century.

In most of the ancient Eucharistic prayers, the fraction was a simple utilitarian rite which preceded communion. Originally, St James also seems to have followed this pattern. But by the twelfth century it became a complex rite with a long inaudible prayer, which was inspired by Dionysius Bar Salibi's commentary on the Eucharist (thus the prayer is attributed to him). The present rite consists of fraction, consignation, and commixture. Rubrics direct the celebrant to arrange the broken pieces in definite patterns (e.g. Lamb, Son of man, cross, or angel), a custom that appeared only after the thirteenth century.

The *Anaphora of St James* served as the main – if not the sole – model for the fixation of the structure and themes of the West Syrian anaphoras. Some of the earliest anaphoras might have influenced St James. The Old Syriac version of St James certainly served as the model for the structure of the sacramental celebrations, such as the consecration of baptismal water, the consecration of the Holy Chrism (or Myron, perfumed oil, as it is known in the East), ordination, the blessing of water on Epiphany, and the consecration of the churches. Thus they have retained a structure older than that of the *textus receptus* of St James.

It is rather difficult to give a list of the anaphoras in their chronological order. They are attributed to the apostles (St Peter, St John, St Thomas), evangelists (St Mark, St Luke), apostolic fathers (Ignatius of Antioch), pre-Nicene fathers (Sixtus of Rome), post-Nicene Greek fathers (Athanasius of Alexandria, St Basil, Gregory of Nazianzus, Cyril of Jerusalem, Cyril of Alexandria, Dionysius the Areopagite), and leading non-Chalcedonian fathers (Dioscorus of Alexandria, Severus of Antioch, Timothy of Alexandria, Philoxenus of Mabbug, Jacob of Edessa etc.).

The attribution of an anaphora to an apostle or a church father is rather arbitrary and probably implies that the liturgical text in question is a witness to a tradition that goes back to the early centuries. It is far from certain that the anaphoras that bear the names of the leading Syriac fathers are their genuine compositions. However, it is not unlikely that some of the anaphoras attributed to authors of the thirteenth century or later are correctly attributed. In some cases, two or more anaphoras are attributed to the same father, e.g. Jacob of Sarug (three), Dionysius Bar Salibi (three), and Dioscorus (two). The anaphoras attributed to leading Syriac figures were later known under the names of the apostles or some early church fathers. Thus in some manuscripts the *Anaphora of Peter of Kallinicus* (d. 591) is attributed to the Apostle St Peter, and that of Thomas of Harkel to the Apostle Thomas. Sometimes an anaphora that bears the name of a less well-known figure is later attributed to a leading church father, probably to achieve wider acceptance (e.g. the *Anaphora of John of Haran* is attributed to St John Chrysostom in later manuscripts).

The *Anaphora of the Twelve Apostles* (AS I-2: 203–227) is one of the oldest West Syrian anaphoras and was originally composed in Greek. It shares several prayers in common with the Byzantine *Anaphora of St John Chrysostom*. Both must have derived from a fourth-century Antiochene archetype.

The anaphora known as *Mkanašto* or *Compilation* (from the holy fathers) is composed of prayers taken from various anaphoras and exists in longer and shorter versions. The longer one was allegedly compiled by the patriarch John Bar Maʿdani (d. 1263).

Although the anaphoras follow the structure of St James, some of them have retained ancient features. The institution narrative of the *Anaphora of Thomas of Harkel* (also known as the anaphora of the Apostle Thomas) is an example:

> Rightly, when He has truly united Himself to the form of a servant, in order to accomplish the coming things of our salvation, He took bread and wine and He

> blessed it, sanctified it and broke it, and gave to His apostles saying: Take, partake [of them] and do thus; and as you receive them, believe and be assured that you are eating my body and drinking my blood for the commemoration of my death until I come.
>
> (AS II-3: 339)

Here, three liturgical units (the blessing of the bread, that of the chalice, and the introduction to the anamnesis) are conflated. The *Anaphora of the Patriarch John Yeshu Bar Shushan* (d. 1073) follows the same model. The *Anaphora of John the Elder* also has a similar structure, but the anamnesis has been separated.

These three anaphoras represent an ancient model, for which the nearest parallels can be found in the institution narrative of the *Testamentum Domini* and the Egyptian anaphora found in the *Deir Balyzeh Papyrus*. They probably represent the West Syrian anaphoras which resisted the pervasive influence of St James.

The oldest anaphoras seem to have been more influenced by St James than those composed in the second millennium. Generally speaking, ancient anaphoras are characterised by long and theologically rich prayers, and more recent compositions can be identified by their brevity and increasingly artificial ornamental language. The latter are often shorter and mediocre in language and content of the prayers.

A large number of anaphoras, as well as other liturgies, witness to the vitality of liturgical life and liturgical activity among the West Syrians as late as the fifteenth century. The Syrian Orthodox Church never made efforts to implement liturgical uniformity. Diverse liturgical practices were regarded as a sign of 'spiritual vigour', as Dionysius Bar Salibi (d. 1172) writes:

> The fact that people of every country pray differently, and have something which singles them out from the rest, goes to their credit, first because it indicates the wealth of their devotions and spiritual vigour, and secondly because it is a sign of the incomprehensibility of God, who wishes to be glorified in different ways in different countries and towns.
>
> (Varghese 2004: 3)

West Syrians have about a dozen baptismal liturgies, and most of them are in disuse. The ordo currently used in the Syrian Orthodox Church of Antioch is attributed to Severus of Antioch. According to manuscripts, Severus composed the text in Greek, which was translated into Syriac by Jacob of Edessa. This ordo of Severus was abridged by Barhebraeus (d. 1286) and is used in India. The ordo of Severus consists of two parts ('services'), and the first part has retained most of the elements of the catechumenate: inscription of names, insufflations, signing of the forehead without oil, exorcism, apotaxis, and syntaxis. The second part includes the signing of the forehead with oil, consecration of the water, pouring of Myron over the water, anointing of the whole body with olive oil, immersion, Chrismation, crowning, and communion. The consecration of the water follows the structure of the anaphora. The font is covered with a veil, which is removed at the beginning of the consecration. The priest breathes upon the water, signs it, and says the epiclesis with a waving of hands over the water, followed by its signing.

The two-fold division of the Severus ordo and the pre-baptismal anointing of the whole body are suppressed in the ordo of Barhebraeus.

Almost all the liturgical celebrations, including the daily offices and the lectionary, exist in several versions, most of them in manuscripts. The liturgical texts represent two major traditions, having their origin in two centres: Ṭur ʿAbdin in south-eastern Turkey and Mosul/Tikrit in Iraq. Mardin in Ṭur ʿAbdin was the seat of the patriarch of Antioch until 1924, while Mosul was that of the maphrian, the Syrian Orthodox primate in Persian territory. The two traditions are known popularly as 'Western and Eastern'. The Western rite represents the liturgical traditions of Antioch, Edessa, the Monastery of Qenneshre, and Melitene. The Eastern tradition follows the rites of Tikrit and Mosul, and it shares several features in common with the East Syriac liturgy.

The Syrian Orthodox liturgy, in its present form, is the result of the synthesis between Greek and Syriac (Edessa, Mosul, and Tikrit) traditions. In fact, the west Syriac liturgy was opened to Greek influence throughout its development. The Greek antiphons of Severus of Antioch were translated into Syriac in the early sixth century by Paul of Edessa and were later revised by Jacob of Edessa. The translation of Greek hymns and the adaptation of the Greek elements entered into a new phase in the tenth century, when northern Syria was conquered by the Byzantines (969–1084). The Greek Orthodox patriarchate of Antioch ('Melkite') was using Syriac, and their liturgical rite was replaced by that of Constantinople. Several Greek hymns were translated into Syriac for the use of the Melkites, and the Syrian Orthodox adopted some of them under the title 'Greek canons'. During this period, the Syrian Orthodox seem to have adopted the Byzantine *Octoechos*, the musical system in eight modes, attributing it to Severus of Antioch. Rich merchants from Tikrit immigrated to the newly occupied territories and financed the construction of new monasteries, where sometimes monks from the 'East' became abbots. This seems to have led to a synthesis of the 'Western' and 'Eastern' traditions. This synthesis is evident in some of the festal offices, where hymns from both traditions are given.

The breviary exists in at least in two versions: 'The Common Prayer' (*Šḥimo*) for the weekly cycle and 'The Festal Breviary' (*Penkito* or *Ḥudro*) for the annual cycle. Daily offices are divided into seven canonical hours (cf. Ps.119: 164), beginning with *Ramšo* (Vespers) and followed by *Sutoro* (Compline), *Lilyo* (Night), *Ṣapro* (Morning), and Third, Sixth, and Ninth hours. Each day and hour has fixed or dominant themes. For example, the ninth hour and the office of Saturday have for their theme the 'departed'. The theme of Sunday is always 'the Resurrection', and that of Wednesday is the 'Mother of God', while that for Friday is 'the Cross and the martyrs'. The balanced arrangement of the themes, the rich hymnody (most of them are the compositions of the poet-theologians like Saint Ephrem and Jacob of Sarug), and prayers of biblical inspiration illustrate the Syrian liturgical genius. The most characteristic Syrian orthodox prayer is *Sedro* (lit. a row, order, or series). A *Sedro* is a long prayer in the form of a series of expositions or meditations, usually preceded by a *Promiun* (introduction). Often, a *Sedro* summarises Syrian Orthodox theology.

A large number of commentaries (some of them in unpublished manuscripts) exist on the Eucharist, baptism and the consecration of the Myron. Most important among them are those by Jacob of Edessa (d. 708), George, bishop of the Arabs (d. 724),

John of Dara (ninth century), Moses Bar Kepha (d. 903), Dionysius Bar Salibi (d. 1171), and Barhebraeus (d. 1286).

The liturgical year begins with the 'Sunday of the Consecration of the Church' (first Sunday in November), followed by the 'Sunday of the Renewal of the Church', and the Sundays of Advent. Generally speaking, the liturgical year is divided into a cycle of seven periods, each consisting of approximately seven weeks, as follows:

1 From the Consecration of the Church to the Nativity: the Church and the events and persons associated with the birth of Jesus are the themes.
2 From Nativity to the Great Lent: Epiphany (Jan. 6) and the Presentation of Jesus in the Temple (Feb. 2) are the most important events commemorated. The *Nineveh fast* also falls in this period. The two Sundays that precede the Great Lent are dedicated for the memory of the departed priests and the faithful. Lent is the preparation for Easter, the celebration of the Resurrection of our Lord, and the living and the departed together prepare themselves for the great feast of our hope.
3 Great Lent: Great Lent is a period of repentance and reconciliation, and thus it begins and ends with the service of Reconciliation (*Shubkono*). The Gospel readings of the Sundays of Lent are on the healing miracles of Christ, which suggests that healing – that is the restoration of humanity to its original state – was the goal of the incarnation.
4 From Easter to Pentecost: the week that follows Easter is called the 'White (*hevoro*) days', as those who were baptised on Easter night used to wear white garments for a week. During the fifty days between Easter and Pentecost, the appearances of the risen Christ are commemorated.
5 From Pentecost to the Feast of the Apostles Peter and Paul (June 29): the theme of this period is the coming of the Holy Spirit and the growth of the Church.
6 From the Feast of the Apostles to the Feast of the Cross (Sept. 14): the feast of the Transfiguration (Aug. 6) and the feast of the Ascension of the Mother of God (Aug. 15) fall in this period.
7 From Feast of the Cross to the Sunday of the Consecration of the Church: the Second coming of Christ and its signs, and life in the coming world, are the themes.

The theme of the day or the season is presented in the Bible readings, *Promiun-Sedro*, and the hymns.

In church music, the Syrian Orthodox Church follows the *Octoechos*, a modal system in eight modes or tunes, analogous to the *Octoechos* of the Byzantine Church and the eight-mode Gregorian system. The Syrian Orthodox modal system has been attributed to Severus of Antioch. The chants are organised in an eight-weekly modal cycle in the following order: 1–5; 2–6; 3–7; 4–8; 5–1; 6–2; 7–3; and 8–4.

Canonical fasts are an important part of the Syrian Orthodox liturgical tradition. In addition to the weekly fasts of Wednesday and Friday, the Syrians have the following canonical fasts: (1) Advent fast: Dec. 1–25 (formerly Nov. 15–Dec. 25); (2) Nineveh fast: three days (three weeks before the Great Lent); (3) Great Lent for fifty days; (4) Apostles' fast (June 16–29); and (5) Ascension fast (Aug. 1–15).

The study of the history and theology of the Syriac liturgy is still in its initial stages. Apart from Baptism and Eucharist, we know very little about the historical developments of this ancient tradition. We are fortunate to have a large number of source materials, including liturgical commentaries, liturgical homilies, and liturgical texts. Some of these have been published over the last fifty years and translated into the major European languages. But the majority remains in manuscript form only. The manuscripts that are brought to Europe are catalogued and are available to scholars, but there are other important collections of Syriac manuscripts in West Asia, either in the possession of individuals, or else in church centres. They face serious threats of destruction or dispersion. It is vital that these be preserved, whether through digitisation or another method, in order to advance the study of Syriac liturgy.

BIBLIOGRAPHY

Anaphorae Syriacae. 1939-. 3 vols. Rome: Pontificium Institutum Studiorum Orientalium [Syriac text of 22 anaphoras with Latin translation].

Badger, G. P. 1852. *The Nestorians and Their Rituals.* 2 Vols. London: J. Masters.

Baumstark, Anton. 1910. *Festbrevier und Kirchenjahr der syrischen Jakobiten. Eine liturgiegeschichtliche Vorarbeit.* Studien zur Geschichte und Kultur des Altertums III, 3–5. Paderborn: Ferdinand Schöningh. Reprinted, New York, 1967.

Botte, B. 1954. L'épiclèse dans les liturgies syriennes orientales. *Sacris Erudiri* 6, 48–72.

Bouyer, Louis. 1966. *Eucharistie. Théologie et spiritualité de la prière eucharistique.* Paris: Desclée. Reprint, 1990.

Brock, S. P. 1972. Studies in the Early History of the Syrian Orthodox Baptismal Liturgy. *JThS* 23, 16–74.

———. 1988. Two Recent Editions of Syrian Orthodox Anaphoras. *Ephemerides Liturgicae* 102, 36–445.

———.2003. Gabriel of Qatar's Commentary on the Liturgy. *Hugoye* 6, 2, 197–248. Reprinted in *Fire From Heaven.* Ashgate: Variorum, 2006.

———.2004. Some Early Witnesses of the East Syriac Liturgical Tradition. *Journal of Assyrian Academic Studies* 18, 9–45.

———. 2008. *The Holy Spirit in the Syrian Baptismal Tradition.* Piscataway, NJ: Gorgias Press.

———. 2012. The Earliest Texts of the Syrian Orthodox Marriage Rites. *OCP* 78, 335–92.

Chabot, J. B. 1902. *Synodicon orientale ou recueil de synodes nestoriens.* Paris: Imprimerie nationale.

Cody, Alfred. 1982. The Early History of the Octoechos in Syria. *In:* N. Garsoian, T. Mathews, R. W. Thomson, ed., *East of Byzantium.* Washington, DC: Dumbarton Oaks Center for Byzantine Studies, 89–114.

Connolly, R. H. 1909. *The Liturgical Homilies of Narsai.* Cambridge: Cambridge University Press.

Connolly, R. H. and H. W. Codrington. 1913. *Two Commentaries on the Jacobite Liturgy By George Bishop of the Arab Tribes and Moses Bar Kepha, Together With the Syriac Anaphora of Saint James and a Document Entitled the Book of Life.* Oxford: Text and Translation Society. Reprint: Gregg: Farnborough, 1969.

De Smet, B. 1963. Le rituel du sacre des évêques et des patriarches dans l'Eglise syrienne d'Antioche. Traduction. *OS* 8, 165–212.

Dix, Gregory. 1945. *The Shape of the Liturgy.* London: Dacre/Black.

Gelston, A. 1991. *The Eucharistic Prayer of Addai and Mari.* Oxford: Clarendon Press.

Jammo, S.H. 1979. *La Structure de la messe chaldéenne*. OCA 207. Rome: Pontificium Institutum Orientalium Studiorum.

Jenner, K.D. 1997. The Development of the Syriac Lectionary Systems: A Discussion of the Opinion of P. Kannookadan. *The Harp* 10, 9–24.

Kadicheeni, Paul B. 1980. *The Mystery of Baptism: The Text and Translation of the Chapter 'On Holy Baptism' From the Causes of the Seven Mysteries of Timothy II, Nestorian Patriarch (1318–1332)*. Bangalore: Dharmaram Publications. [Reprint: Moran 'Etho 33. Kottayam: SEERI, 2015].

Kannookadan, P. 1991. *The East Syrian Lectionary: An Historico-Liturgical Study*. Rome: Mar Thoma Yogam Publications.

Maccomber, W. 1966. The Oldest known Text of the Anaphora of the Apostles Addai and Mari. *OCP* 32, 335–71.

———. 1973. A Theory on the Origins of the Syrian, Maronite and Chaldean Rites. *OCP* 39, 235–42.

———. 1977. A History of the Chaldean Mass. *Worship* 51, 107–20.

Maclean, A. J. 1894. *East Syrian Daily Offices*. London: Rivington, Percival, & Co.

Mannooramparampil, T., trans.1992. *John Bar Zoʿbi. Explanation of the Divine Mysteries*. OIRSI 157. Kottayam: Oriental Institute of Religious Studies.

Matéos, J. 1959. *Lelya-Sapra: Essai d'Interprétation des matines chaldéennes*. OCA 156. Roma: Pont. institutum orientalium studiorum.

Matheus, R. 2000a. *The Order of the Third Sanctification*. OIRSI 240. Kottayam: Oriental Institute of Religious Studies. [Eng tr. of the Anaphora of Mar Nestorius, with a study].

———. 2000b. *A Commentary on the Mass* [attributed to] *the Nestorian, George, Bishop of Mosul and Arbel* (tr. R.H.Connolly). OIRSI 243. Kottayam: Oriental Institute of Religious Studies.

Raes, A. 1960. Les ordinations dans la pontifical chaldéen. *OS* 5, 63–80.

Ratcliff, E. C. 1928–1929. The Original Form of the Anaphora of Addai and Mari: A Suggestion. *JThS* 30, 23–32.

Rouwhorst, G. 1996. Les lectionnaires syriaques. *In:* C. B. Amphoux and J. P. Bouhot, ed., *La lectures liturgiques des Épîtres catholiques dans l'Église ancienne*. Lausanne: Éditions du Zabre, 105–40.

———. 1997. Jewish Liturgical Traditions in Early Syriac Christianity. *VChr* 51, 72–93.

Spinks, B. D. 1977. The Original Form of the Anaphora of the Apostles: A Suggestion in the Light of Maronite Sharar. *Ephemerides Liturgicae* 91, 146–61.

———. 1999. *Mar Nestorius and Mar Theodore the Interpreter: The Forgotten Eucharistic Prayers of East Syria*. Grove Liturgical Studies 45. Cambridge: Grove Books.

———. 2013. *Do This in Remembrance of Me. The Eucharist From the Early Church to the Present Day*. London: SCM. [Syriac Liturgical Traditions, p. 141–70].

Taft, Robert. 1985. *The Liturgy of the Hours in East and West*. Collegeville: The Liturgical Press. [East Syriac Liturgy: pp. 225–37; West Syriac and Maronite traditions, 238–47].

Tarby, A. 1972. *La prière eucharistique de l'Église de Jérusalem*. Théologie Historique 17. Paris: Beauchesne.

Vadakkel, Jacob. 1989. *The East Syrian Anaphora of Mar Theodore of Mopsuestia. Critical Edition, English Translation and Study*. OIRSI 129. Kottayam: Oriental Institute of Religious Studies.

Varghese, B. 1989. *Les onctions baptismales dans la tradition syrienne*. CSCO 512, Subsidia 82. Louvain: Peeters.

———. 1997. Holy Week Celebrations in the West Syrian Church. *In:* Antonii Georgii Kollamparampil, ed. *Hebdomadae Sanctae Celebratio*. Rome: Edizioni Liturgiche, 165–86.

———. 1998a. Early History of the Preparation Rites in the Syrian Orthodox Anaphora. *In: Symposium Syriacum VII*. OCA 256. Roma: Pontificio istituto orientale, 127–38.

———. 1998b. *Dionysius Bar Salibi: Commentary on the Eucharist*. Moran 'Etho 10. Kottayam: SEERI. [Reprint: Piscataway, NJ: Gorgias Press, 2011].
———. 1999. *John of Dara: Commentary on the Eucharist*. Moran 'Etho 12. Kottayam: SEERI. [Reprint: Piscataway, NJ: Gorgias Press, 2011].
———. 2001. *The Syriac Version of the Liturgy of St James: A brief History for Students*. Alcuin/GROW Joint Liturgical Studies 49. Cambridge: Grove Books.
———. 2004. *West Syrian Liturgical Theology*. Ashgate: Aldershot.
———. 2006a. La Structure des liturgies sacramentelles. *In:* F.Cassingena-Trévedy et I.Jurasz, ed., *Les liturgies syriaques*. Études syriaques 3. Paris: Geuthner, 145–72.
———. 2006b. *Dionysius Bar Salibi: Commentaries on Myron and Baptism*. Moran 'Etho 29., Kottayam: SEERI.
———. 2007. East Syrian Liturgy During the Sassanian Period. *In:* Arafa Mustafa et al., ed., *Inkulturation des Christentums im Sasanidenreich*. Wiesbaden: Reichert, 269–80.
———. 2008a. Prayers Addressed to Christ in the West Syriac Tradition. *In:* Bryan D. Spinks, ed., *The Place of Christ in Liturgical Prayer. Trinity, Christology and Liturgical Theology*. Collegeville: Liturgical Press, 88–111.
———. 2008b. The Anaphora of St James and Jacob of Edessa. *In:* Bas ter Haar Romeny, ed., *Jacob of Edessa and the Syriac Culture of His Day*. Leiden: Brill, 239–64.
———. 2009a. West Syrian Anaphoras Other than St James and Their Theological Importance. *In:* John Berchmans and James Puthuparampil, ed., *The Liturgy of St James: Its Impact on Theologizing in India*. Pune: BVP Publications, 32–56.
———. 2009b. Moses Bar Kepha: Commentary on Baptism. *The Harp* 24, 55–82.
———. 2011. West Syriac Liturgy: One Hundred Years of Research. *The Harp* 27, 53–72.
———. 2012a. Saint Ephrem and the Early Syriac Liturgical Traditions. *St Vladimir's Theological Quarterly* 56, 17–49.
———. 2012b. John, Patriarch of Antioch. Homily on the Consecration of Myron. *The Harp* 26, 157–66.
———. 2014. *Moses Bar Kepha: Commentary on Myron*. Piscataway, NJ: Gorgias Press.
———. 2015. The Byzantine Occupation of Northern Syria (969–1085) and Its Impact on the Syrian Orthodox Liturgy. *PdO* 40, 447–67.
———. 2016. Bar Hebraeus: Mnarat Qudshe: Sixth Base on the Earthly Priesthood. *The Harp* 30, 147–229 [Syriac text and English translation].
———. 2017. *West Syrian Anaphoras*. Awsar Slawot'o 4. SEERI, Kottayam. [Syriac text and English translation of 33 anaphoras].
Winkler, G. 1978. The Original Meaning of the Pre-baptismal Anointing and Its Implications. *Worship* 52, 24–45.
Woolfenden, G. W. 2004. *Daily Liturgical Prayer. Origins and Theology*. Aldershot: Ashgate. [The East Syriac tradition, 121–47; The West Syriac and Maronite traditions, 149–70].
Yousif, P. 1990. *A Classified Bibliography on the East Syrian Liturgy*. Rome: Mar Thoma Yogam.

CHAPTER TWENTY-FOUR

HISTORIOGRAPHY IN THE SYRIAC-SPEAKING WORLD, 300–1000[1]

Philip Wood

The way in which histories were composed provide important indicators of how Syriac-speakers saw themselves and how they related to their neighbours and rulers. The selection of red-letter days in the past could be used to understand the present, whether the behaviour of men and states or the relationship between God and man.

I am reluctant to speak straightforwardly of Syriac historiography, because it seems to unduly privilege the language in which history was written. Certain historians, such as Michael the Syrian (d. 1199), did choose to emphasise the fact that they used Syriac and wrote histories that focused on miaphysite 'Suryayē'. But this use of history, and of the unity of language, ethnicity, and religion that it implies, were the perspectives of individuals. They were not shared by everyone and should not be considered 'natural', especially in the early parts of the period under discussion.

Instead, I have chosen to focus here on the ways in which the centres of Syriac scholarship such as Edessa were considered by historians. Therefore, I begin with the representation of Syriac culture in Greek and conclude with the reception of Syriac histories in Arabic. I argue that it is only in Arabic that we see the upgrading of the Syriac account of the formative past of Edessa to the rank of true history. Sources in Arabic also give us an insight into how much Syriac writing has been lost, especially from the Sasanian world.

SYRIAC CULTURE AND GREEK ECCLESIASTICAL HISTORY

The tradition of Greek ecclesiastical history is formed of a series of continuations of the work of Eusebius of Caesarea, who himself used and developed the Acts of the Apostles and the Gospels. The works of Socrates, Sozomen, and Theodoret in the fifth, and of Theodore Lector and Evagrius in the sixth, all fall into this tradition, which links the empire of Constantine and his successors to the deeds of the Gospel. From the final books of Eusebius's *Ecclesiastical History*, the genre came to focus on the deeds of emperors and bishops, and their efforts to preserve and extend orthodox religion and to maintain divine approval for the Roman Empire as a Christian state.

Sebastian Brock has observed that the significance of Eusebius as a source for church history can often lead modern historians to ignore the importance of Christianity outside the Roman world and to underplay the role of Syriac as a third cultural tradition of Christianity, a 'third lung for the church' (Brock 2005, 1992). But we should also remember that the tradition of ecclesiastical history did play a role in championing the early 'achievements' of Syriac-speaking Christians within the Roman world. Chief among these was the so-called *Abgar Legend*, which is first extant in Eusebius (*Church History* I, 13) and which the historian claimed to find in the city's archives. Here Abgar, the king of Edessa, corresponds with Jesus in Jerusalem, shortly before his arrest. Abgar tells Jesus that he has recognised him as the son of God after hearing of his miracles, and invites him to live in Edessa. Jesus replies that he cannot go, but he sends his disciple Addai to instruct the king in Christianity and dispatches a letter that will guarantee Edessa's invulnerability.

It is striking that Eusebius would give such prominence to the figure of Abgar. The king may function here as a kind of precursor to Constantine: a secular ruler who recognises the coming of Christ (Mirkovic 2004). But inclusion of the story also gives Edessa a role in the history of Christianity in the era of the Gospels, and already by the fourth century Edessa was being included on tours of the Holy Land (*Itinerarium Egeriae* 47). In other words, by recognising the supposed claim of an Edessene document, Eusebius had extended the boundaries of the world of the Gospels.

Eusebius's successors also devoted notable scenes to the cultural and political achievements of the Syriac world:

- hymnography and the works of Ephrem (Sozomen 3.16, 6.34; Theodoret 4.26)
- the holy man Julian Saba (Soz 3.14, 6.34; Thdt 4.24)
- Jacob of Nisibis and the defeat of the Persian invasion (Thdt. 2.26)
- Edessa's defiance against the pagan emperor Julian (Soz. 6.18)
- The martyrdoms of Christians in the Persian world under Yazdegard I (Soz 2.9–15; Thdt 5.38)

Most of these examples are set in Edessa and Nisibis. These narratives owe much to the position of these cities on the Persian border and their consequent role as indicators of Christian Roman steadfastness in the face of Persia.

These references in the ecclesiastical historians both confirmed and reflected the importance of Edessa as a missionary centre and, consequently, of the Syriac language as a high dialect for speakers of other Aramaic dialects (Brock 1994; Taylor 2002). This led to a growing significance of Syriac in the epigraphy and manuscript production of the lands west of the Euphrates, where Greek and Latin had long held a monopoly (Millar 2009: 49–54; Mango 1982). It is significant that when Theodoret of Cyrrhus, himself probably a Syriac-speaker, sought to praise the holy men of northern Syria in the fifth century, he traced their spiritual lineage back to two Mesopotamian ascetics of the fourth century, Jacob of Nisibis and Julian Saba (*Historia Religiosa* 1 and 2), who had both been praised by their near-contemporary Ephrem. The region around Edessa and Nisibis loomed large in the public imagination of ascetic piety: the cities provided an obvious starting point even for a hagiographic collection set in provinces further south (Wood 2010: 45–8).

THE SYRIAC PSEUDO-HISTORIES

However, the public image of the heroes of Edessa or Nisibis was still very much conditioned by historians and hagiographers writing outside this geographical and cultural milieu. Even where Syriac saints' lives described the famous figures mentioned above, Greek texts, and Syriac translations of the Greek, often became more prominent than the original Syriac versions.[2]

The principal exceptions to this pattern are Pseudo-histories, composed as extensions of significant scenes in Christian history. A key example is the *Doctrina Addai*, a fifth-century Syriac embellishment of the *Abgar Legend* that describes the role of Addai in converting Abgar and his nobles and the account he gives of an idealised ascetic Christianity. This text is unusual in receiving imitations in Greek and Armenian, and provides an example of the success of one Edessene in magnifying the fame accorded to his city by Eusebius (Debié 2010; Wood 2010: ch. 4; Brock 2004; Illert 2008).

A second exception is the sixth-century *Julian Romance*, which, like the *Doctrina*, emphasised the invulnerability of the city of Edessa and its role as a stronghold of orthodox Christianity. The *Romance* represents a highly embellished account of Edessa's resistance to Julian (Wood 2010: ch. 5; Drijvers 1999). We can consider these two texts, the *Doctrina* and the *Romance*, as apocrypha to the main historical canon of Eusebius and his continuators. They are Pseudo-historical embellishments of minor scenes in the canon that aim to exaggerate Edessa's role in foundational moments of Christian history in the Gospels and in the fourth century.

Finally, a third example of Pseudo-history that deserves mention here is the *Cave of Treasures*. This remarkable text was probably composed in the early sixth century in Julianist (miaphysite)[3] circles in northern Iraq (Minov 2013: 84–6). It is a Christian, Syriac re-writing of the Old Testament, which emphasises the existence of an ascetic ur-Christianity in the time of Adam that was passed on to various patriarchs, who resisted the varied temptations of the children of Cain. Several references in the text imply that its author straddled the thought-worlds of the East and West Syrians. The geography of the text emphasises Iranian Azerbaijan, which the author identifies with the Biblical land of Nod (Wood 2010: 118), and refers positively to some customs of Iranian Zoroastrianism (Minov 2013: ch. 4). But it also circulated under the name of Ephrem and refers to Abgar of Edessa (Minov 2013: 315–21, 363–8). Furthermore, it emphasises the divine favour given to the Aramaic language, which it identifies with Syriac. Syriac was associated with Edessa and was spoken there, whereas elsewhere it functioned as a high dialect for speakers of numerous different Aramaic dialects (Taylor 2002). This mixture of subjects suggests that the author is conscious of the need to emphasise the existence of a single language and ascetic religion that crossed political boundaries between Rome and Persia. The *Cave* circulated widely, in several different versions and languages (Minov 2013: 21–30).

WEST SYRIAN HISTORICAL WRITING IN THE SIXTH CENTURY

Two major extant works in Syriac continue the Eusebian tradition of ecclesiastical history, the works of Pseudo-Zachariah of Mytilene (written in 569) and John of Ephesus (written ca. 585). Both authors were from Amida. These histories are often classified according to their authors' miaphysite confession or the Syriac language in which they wrote. But John's church history remained wedded to the idea of a Christian Roman empire, with the deeds of emperors at its centre. He certainly attacks individual emperors, such as Justin II, as irrational heretics, but so too did Socrates and Sozomen in their criticism of the 'Arian' Valens. Likewise, John's criticism of individual Chalcedonian bishops does not seem to extend to all Chalcedonians. At points he imagines Chalcedonians and miaphysites as a single church, and his criticism of Chalcedonian extremists rests on their refusal to recognise miaphysite sacraments, rather than on their Christological beliefs.

John stretches the traditional borders of the genre: his willingness to give prominence to the Jafnid phylarch Mundhir in his attempts to reconcile different miaphysite factions in Book IV of his history is one striking example. But the Eusebian model of a universal church remained valid, and ecclesiastical history was not a genre that easily served communalist interests.[4] Later miaphysites did look back to John as the foundation of an independent 'communal' history, but their reading of him was selective and imposed the firm communal boundaries of their own days onto his text (van Ginkel 1998). John recorded the persecutions that gave miaphysites identity through shared suffering, but he did not consider the breach irrevocable (van Ginkel 1995: 182, 216; Menze 2008). John, ever hopeful for a reconciliation with the Chalcedonians, wrote on behalf of an 'orthodoxy in waiting' (Wood 2010: 175).

It is not necessary to place too much stress on John's history as part of a Syriac historiographical tradition. It might be more apt to see it as a work of ecclesiastical history in the Eusebian mould that was composed in Syriac. The same point could be made for Pseudo-Zachariah: he embeds a long miaphysite ecclesiastical history, originally composed in Greek, within his Syriac text, as Books III–VI, and follows Eusebius's precedent in including lengthy documentation (Greatrex et al. 2011: 19–28). John takes the whole of the eastern Mediterranean as his field, and his inclusion of the activities of missionaries beyond the frontier (in Nubia and in Arabia) has good precedents in Eusebius and the fifth-century historians. Pseudo-Zachariah of Mytilene does seek to 'improve' on Eusebius by referring to a hagiography of Pope Sylvester of Rome (Greatrex et al. 2011: 80), who allegedly baptised Constantine, but it is noteworthy that the Pseudo-histories of the *Doctrina* and the *Julian Romance* were omitted. Both the *Doctrina* and the *Romance* remained extraneous to the canon of sixth-century ecclesiastical history, even when composed in Syriac.

We can observe a very different pattern in the local histories of the same period, the *Chronicle of Edessa* (written ca. 550) and the *Chronicle of Pseudo-Joshua the stylite* (512). Both were composed in Edessa and drew on local archives. Neither have the miaphysite bias of the Syriac ecclesiastical histories of the same period, and the *Chronicle of Edessa* is noticeably pro-Chalcedonian and in favour of the emperor Justinian. The existence of both local chronicles is probably due to the high reputation of the archives held at Edessa. These were made famous by the reference in Eusebius to his use of the archives to discover the *Abgar Legend*. Whether or not Eusebius's claims were true, they were credible and stimulated the deposition of further documents, which would constitute raw material for the writing of local history (Segal 1970: 20–1).

The contents of the *Chronicle of Edessa* imply that the archival material included bishops' lists, records of local building and benefactions, and records of natural disasters. To this has been added references to church synods and a small number of significant events outside the city, such as the foundations of Tella and Amida by Constantius II (§19–20). Though the references in this short text are sparse, the lengthy account of the flood of the city in 202 draws on a detailed account that claims to have to have been composed under the Abgarid kings (§8). Witakowski has plausibly argued that the account of the flood derives from a more 'developed' text, an *Original Chronicle of Edessa*, which was drawn on by later chroniclers (Witakowski 1984/6).[5]

It is also important that the *Chronicle of Edessa* makes reference to several of the scenes of the history of the Syriac-speaking world made famous in the fifth century ecclesiastical historians. Julian Saba (§28), Jacob of Nisibis (§17), Ephrem (§30), Symeon the stylite (§69), the fifth-century persecutions in Persia (§54), Julian's Persian war (§26), and the 'heretic' Mani (§10) are all mentioned, even though the *Chronicle* does not regularly report heretics, holy men, martyrs, or warfare.

Pseudo-Joshua's *Chronicle* has a slightly different focus, and is more clearly presentist. It gives a vivid first-hand account of the Roman-Persian invasion of 502–6, including the fall of Amida and Edessa's resistance. But it too draws on archival material to give context to these events. They included recently published laws, the fluctuations of prices, death counts from famine, and the construction of public buildings (Trombley and Watt 2000: xxxii–xxxiv). Both Joshua and the Edessa *Chronicle* date their material according to the Seleucid era, and this may reflect the dating practices of local registers, which used this form alongside the imperial indiction (Trombley and Watt 2000: lii–liii). The Seleucid era would become a distinctive feature of West Syrian history writing and continued to be employed into the modern period (Debié 2015: 267–70).

Thus, in the sixth century, we should be reluctant to think of a single Syriac historical tradition. Historical writing can be divided into Pseudo-histories like the *Doctrina Addai*; Syriac writing in the Eusebian tradition of ecclesiastical history; and local chronicles. They all have different forms and concerns. However, we should also observe that all three were stimulated, in different ways, by the production of Greek ecclesiastical history. This is obviously true for the continuators like John of Ephesus, but we should remember that the Pseudo-histories are embellishments of key scenes in the Greek ecclesiastical histories. The *Chronicle of Edessa*, too, owes its interest in events outside the city to the authoritative selection of events by the Greek ecclesiastical historians.

WEST SYRIAN HISTORICAL WRITING IN THE SEVENTH TO EIGHTH CENTURIES

In addition to his *Ecclesiastical History*, Eusebius of Caesarea also composed the *Chronicon*. The second part of this work, the *Canons*, consisted of synchronic tables of regnal dates (the *fila regnorum*), annotated with notes on contemporary events (the *spatium historicum*) (Burgess 1999; Witakowski 2008; Debié 2015: 303–10). Though this form of historical writing fell out of use in Greek, it flourished in West Syrian writing in the seventh to ninth centuries. A number of 'minor chronicles' exist from this period, written in annalistic form and dated by the Seleucid era (Brock 1976; Palmer 2009). They were written by miaphysites, Maronites, and Melkites. They describe the controversies of the churches and local political history, and several give distinctive perspectives on the end of Roman rule in the Near East and the coming of the Arabs. The material is sparse, and its selection may have been intended to allow the reader to discern God's judgement on human behaviour (Palmer 1993: xxviii). I comment on these chronicles here with respect to their imagination of the Roman past and the rule of the Arabs in their own days.

The *Chronicle to 819* is especially interesting for its view of the past. This conceives of the third and fourth centuries almost exclusively through Edessene red-letter days: king Abgar; the founders of heresies that Ephrem opposed; the buildings of the Abgarids; Edessene bishops; Symeon the stylite. The chronicler has also added two further events of local significance: the miaphysite saint Barsauma of Samosata and the Persian invasion of Mesopotamia under Kavad I (which had been treated by Joshua the stylite). For this chronicler, writing in the miaphysite monastery of Qartmin, Edessene history has almost totally eclipsed knowledge of the wider church or of the Roman Empire. Though he is well informed about the regional politics of his day, the chronicler cannot see the past except through an Edessene lens. As we have seen, this lens was a construct of the identification of significant events made by the Greek ecclesiastical historians and the highlighting of the same events in local chronicles.

A second annalistic *Chronicle* that is worth discussing in detail is the *Zuqnin Chronicle*, composed in a monastery in northern Mesopotamia in ca.775. This text is striking for retaining the annalistic structure used by the 'minor chronicles' but pushing it to the breaking point by including large sections of Roman ecclesiastical history and contemporary reflections. Witakowski terms it a 'developed chronicle' (Witakowski 1987: 76–82). Parts I–III of the *Chronicle* are chiefly taken from Eusebius, Socrates, and John of Ephesus, while Part IV is made up of contemporary reflections on the rule of the Arabs and their wars (Witakowski 1987: 124–35; Brock 1980: 11–12). Interestingly, his coverage of the seventh century is very scanty, and he laments his lack of sources. Conrad (1991) and Wood (2011) have argued that the text was composed in several different layers, possibly involving a number of different authors, each with different criteria for inclusion that reflect changing political interests (also see Harrak 1998).

What is striking here is that universal Christian history in the Eusebian mode functions as the backdrop to very local events in the eighth century. On one hand, it illustrates the dramatic contraction of the worldview of one group of rural Christians. They no longer seem particularly connected to the rest of the Christian world, and they lose their residual loyalties to the Byzantine emperor after the wars of

Constantine V (Wood 2011). From the ʿAbbasid revolution onwards, the *Chronicle*'s chief concerns are the exactions of Mosuli tax collectors (Robinson forthcoming). Yet, at the same time, the fact that the *Chronicle* can appeal to this long set of predecessors may evoke a sense of past struggles and past glories helped by the persistence of a Christian solidarity under Arab rule.

The minor chronicles also provide an important insight into the early writing of history amongst the Arabs. Antoine Borrut has observed how the Arab king-lists preserved in these chronicles suppress the caliphates of ʿAli and Ibn al-Zubayr (Borrut 2014: 49–50). By a similar token, the *Zuqnin Chronicle* does not see the ʿAbbasid revolution of 750 in religious terms, but as an invasion of the Persians, which reflects how the event was seen locally by Muslims and Christians (Borrut 2014: 53; Borrut 2011: 151–2). Indeed, incidental references in the *Zuqnin Chronicle* give a good indication of the passage of the Arabisation of the countryside, in terms of intermarriage, linguistic change, religious conversion, or the creation of a cross-confessional regional identity (Wood 2011).

THEOPHILUS OF EDESSA AND DIONYSIUS OF TEL-MAHRE

The ʿAbbasid period saw the development of two more elaborate histories, by the Maronite scholar and astrologer Theophilus of Edessa (d. 785) and the Jacobite patriarch Dionysius of Tel-Mahre (d. 845). These were composed in a period when history writing in Greek had become rare (Whitby 2003: 492), and they serve as an illustration of the cultural significance of the Syriac-speaking world at this time. This salience of Syriac is related to the fact that Edessa and its environs survived the Arab Conquests relatively unscathed, and the role that Syriac-speakers acquired as translators of the products of Hellenic culture into Arabic (Conrad 1999; Tannous 2010).

However, neither of these major histories survives extant, and both must be reconstructed from later sources. Dionysius is attested through the *Chronicle of Michael the Syrian*; the *Chronicle of 1234*, and the *Ecclesiastical History* of Bar Hebraeus, while Theophilus is attested in the Arabic history of Agapius of Manbij, in the Greek *Chronicle* of Theophanes, and in Dionysius. It is best to underscore, therefore, the fact that comments on either historian depend on reconstructions, and there always remains the possibility that parallels between the texts that employ Theophilus or Dionysius are due, in fact, to other shared sources.[6]

Theophilus was a prodigious translator of Hellenic science at the court of al-Mahdi, and his chronicle may have provided a narrative that ran from the early seventh century to the consolidation of the rule of al-Mansur in 755 (Hoyland 2011: 20–1). As Robert Hoyland (2011: 34) observes, we should not simply think of him as a 'Christian under Muslim rule', but as an educated cosmopolitan. According to Dionysius, Theophilus composed a narrative without strict adherence to chronology, and it seems to have been densest towards the end of its range, during the end of the Umayyad period (Hoyland 2011: 23).

Much of the material that Hoyland attributes to Theophilus was 'secular', rather than ecclesiastical. It may be that, like his classical predecessors, he preferred not to continue his history into the reign of al-Mahdi because of the danger of commenting on the reign of his patron. The earlier part of the material that might be attributed to

Theophilus shows a markedly pro-Byzantine tone, unlike the material set in the 740s that has a sympathy for the Muslim government. This distinction may be explained by his use of Byzantine sources, which should be distinguished from Theophilus's own eyewitness account.

Dionysius's history was composed in sixteen books covering both secular and ecclesiastical material over the period 582–842 (Palmer 1993: 87–9). He made extensive use of Theophilus, but he also probably used minor Syriac chronicles, of the type surveyed above, and the histories of two magnate families from Edessa, the Rusafoye and the Gumoye (to which he was related) (Palmer 1993: 98–100). The overarching focus throughout his history are the deeds of the Jacobite patriarchs, their relations with the powers that be, and with prominent monasteries such as Qenneshre, Gubba Barraya, and Mar Mattai. This tendency becomes stronger as Dionysius becomes less dependent on the interests of his sources.

Though the chronicle must be constructed from later sources, we can still make some important observations about the differences between Dionysius's history and the minor chronicles of the previous centuries. Firstly, Dionysius conceives of himself as the heir to a chain of ecclesiastical historians: Eusebius, Socrates, John of Ephesus, and the obscure Cyrus of Batna, whose chronicle ended in 582 (Palmer 1993: 90–2). In this sense, we can draw a parallel to the *Zuqnin Chronicle*, where a prestigious historical tradition was continued in a remote corner of eighth-century Mesopotamia. But there is little sense from the final part of the *Zuqnin Chronicle* that the author(s) sought to emphasise their confessional difference from other Christians, and there is substantial sympathy with the military efforts of the Byzantines. The *Zuqnin Chronicle* received a miaphysite vision of the church history of the sixth century through John of Ephesus, but this is almost an incidental result of the fact that these texts were written in Syriac and that no alternative narratives were available to this isolated author. In Dionysius's case, by contrast, we know from his comments that he was able to use Theophilus, but also that he felt it necessary to edit out an alleged sectarian bias.

Dionysius wrote his history at the request of John, metropolitan of Dara, and he praises him for his training in the dogmas of orthodoxy 'from the softness of your fingernails until the silvering of your hair' (Palmer 1993: 90). The most distinctive feature of this focus on (miaphysite) orthodoxy is Dionysius's treatment of the Arab Conquests. Whereas the conquests themselves are barely treated in the *Zuqnin Chronicle*, Dionysius presents them as an act of liberation from Chalcedonian oppression: 'it was no light benefit for us to be freed from the tyranny of the Romans'. This should not be taken as a factual report of the feelings of seventh-century miaphysites, but a strategic re-imagination of the past by a patriarch embedded in struggles with contemporary Chalcedonians (Van Ginkel 2006). Dionysius also comments on his omission of any reference to the patriarchs of Rome or Constantinople (in a breach of tradition with predecessors like John of Ephesus) as a reflection both of political boundaries and of the deepening of Byzantine heresy after the acceptance of Monotheletism (Palmer 1993: 94). Dionysius's *Chronicle* can be read, therefore, as a symptom of the deepening confessional divide between Jacobites and Chalcedonians in the ʿAbbasid caliphate (cf. Morony 2005). Interestingly, he gives the separation a linguistic dimension that is not present in his predecessors: the Chalcedonians are said to have abandoned 'their language and literature' (Palmer 1993: 94). This likely refers to the greater use of Arabic among the Chalcedonians, an area in which they anticipated trends seen in other Christian groups, in contrast to the Jacobites' longer preference for Syriac, which remained marked into the period of the Crusades (Vollandt 2015: 27–33; Van Ginkel 2008).

EAST SYRIAN HISTORICAL WRITING IN THE FIFTH AND SIXTH CENTURIES

Historical writing in the Church of the East is even less unified than it was in the Roman world. In part, this was because the church was a much younger institution here: it was often subject to persecutions, of varying intensity, and catholicoi in Ctesiphon were only sporadically able to impose their authority. Furthermore, we should also remember that Syriac was not a native language in Sasanian Assyria or Babylonia, as it was in Edessa and Nisibis. For much of the east, we should imagine that speakers of numerous different Aramaic dialects were using Syriac as a Christian 'high language'.

In Late Antique Iraq, we are often the victims of fragmentary sources and must rely on reconstruction from later texts, often extant in Arabic, to trace the history writing of the pre-Islamic period. An important witness here is the tenth/eleventh century *Chronicle of Seert*, a Christian Arabic text that compiles substantial amounts of Syriac material and which covers the third to seventh centuries. In the fourth century, 'history' was primarily conceived through the hagiography of notable martyrs and holy men. This hagiographic tradition was adapted to produce a set of linked lives of the catholicoi of Ctesiphon in the second decade of the fifth century, in the aftermath of the sponsorship of the catholicos Ishaq by the shah Yazdegard I, which coincided with two embassies from the Romans. However, relations between the shah and the Christians of the empire broke down, and there was a corresponding lacuna in history writing until the end of the century (Wood 2013; Wood 2012: 116–9). Both the hagiographic and historical traditions of the fifth-century east may have been inspired by Eusebian models, in particular the hope for a Christian monarch in Yazdegard I, but this relationship is very hard to prove (Wiessner 1967: 35–6).

In addition to this patriarchal history, there was also a second stream of historical thought that had much more obvious links to the Roman world. The Persians had seized the city of Nisibis in 363, and this was a gate for Roman theological ideas until the seventh century. The influence of western ideas in the Persian world became especially strong after the expulsion of the Dyophysite school of Edessa to Nisibis in 484, and these scholars went on to play a major role in ensuring that the Church of the East as a whole leant towards that theological tradition (Gero 1981). One extant text produced in Nisibis was the *Cause of the Foundation of Schools*, which traces the transmission of divine *paideia* from the Creation to the author's own time. It is an intellectual history of the disciples of Theodore of Mopsuestia, the touchstone of orthodoxy for the Church of the East, but it also makes Ephrem an important link in the chain (Becker 2006; Wood 2012: 129–30).

However, there are only occasional reflections of this scholastic history in the histories composed around the court of the catholicos. It is only towards the end of the sixth century that we see an interest in western theology in the synods of the Church of the East, and that this corresponds with the transmission of Roman ecclesiastical history to writers in Ctesiphon.[7] Such histories helped the Church of the East to demonstrate its orthodoxy in terms understood and respected in the Roman world.

One important feature of this new awareness of 'western' ecclesiastical history is the attempt to 'work up' or invent semi-mythical founder figures from the early history of the Church of the East and link them to well-known orthodox figures in the Roman world. The earliest example of this is the correspondence attributed to the fourth century catholicos Papas, likely invented in the sixth century, which links him to Jacob of Nisibis and to Ephrem (Braun 1894). Here it is worth stressing the significance of Edessa and Nisibis as a 'mesh' through which the history of Mediterranean Christianity was received in the Sasanian world.

The texture of the later historical compilations made in Arabic suggest that these western histories were summarised or translated by many different authors, some of whom attempted to juxtapose this material with the 'indigenous' history of the patriarchate. The thirteenth-century bibliophile ʿAbdishoʿ of Nisibis wrote a substantial metrical poem listing, among other things, some fifteen historians. The earliest of these wrote in the late sixth century and may have been the men who summarised the western accounts (Wood 2013: ch. 5; Wood 2012: 123–9).[8]

EAST SYRIAN HISTORICAL WRITING IN THE SEVENTH TO NINTH CENTURIES

One East Syrian history from the mid-seventh century that has survived is the *Khuzistan Chronicle*. Though only thirty pages long in Guidi's edition, it gives a remarkable breadth of coverage of political and religious history during the wars of Hormizd IV, Khosrow II, and Heraclius and the Arab Conquest that followed. The author informs the reader that he will provide a mixture of *eqlesiasṭiqē and qosmoṭiqē*.[9] In context, this means both the history of churchmen and the deeds of the Sasanian shahs, and he appears to have understood his history as a continuation of two different historical traditions: the church histories that we have referred to above and the Sasanian royal histories. We should also note the presence of a number of extracts from the Sasanian histories in the *Chronicle of Seert*, which appear to have entered the Christian historical tradition before the reign of Hormizd IV (Wood 2013: 183–4, 187). The text is especially interesting for the prominence it gives to Yazdin bar Shamta, the Christian governor of much of northern Iraq under Khosrow II, whose son played a role in the shah's murder (§28).

The material in the *Chronicle of Seert* for the period 590–660 is especially dense. In part this is because of the tumultuous events of the period. But it is also a reflection of the presence of several different historical models. In this period, Christians showed increasing political prominence in Iraq, and this stimulated interest in secular models of history writing. To further complicate matters, the patriarchate, which had been the major patron of Christian historians in the east, was suppressed in 610, and this led Christian historians to hope for leadership from a number of different secular, ecclesiastical, and monastic sources and compose their histories accordingly. None of these histories is extant in Syriac, but the Arabic gives a good sense of the complexity of the way in which this period was handled (Wood 2013: ch. 7).

The *Chronicle of Seert* also incorporates a long series of monastic biographies that describe the foundations of monasteries. These are located across the former

Sasanian world, but are particularly clustered in northern Iraq. Similar biographies were collected in the ninth-century hagiographic collections of Thomas of Marga and Išoʿdenaḥ of Basra. Išoʿdenaḥ's hagiographies focus on monastic foundations, and the vast bulk of them are set in the late sixth to early eighth centuries, with a few later and earlier outliers, and this may well correspond to a genuine peak in monastic foundations in the late Sasanian and early Islamic period that was then systematically commemorated in the ninth century (Wood 2013: 150–3; Fiey 1972; Jullien 2008).[10]

THE ARABIC COMPILATIONS OF THE TENTH AND ELEVENTH CENTURIES

Many of the groups that had once spoken Syriac increasingly employed Arabic under Muslim rule. This trend is seen first among the Melkites, followed by the Church of the East and finally by the Jacobites. It is likely associated with the proximity of different Christian confessions to caliphal centres of government in Damascus and then in Baghdad. The same period also witnessed considerable migration of Christians within the caliphate, which broke down the earlier cantonment of 'Nestorians' in the east and Melkites and Jacobites in the west.

A number of lengthy Arabic histories were composed in this period by 'Nestorians' and Melkites, and these make great use of materials that were originally composed in Greek and Syriac. Here I will discuss two Nestorian texts, the *Chronicle of Seert* and the *Haddad Chronicle*, and two Melkite texts, the histories of Eutychius of Alexandria and Agapius of Manbij.

One feature that all of these texts share is the 'upgrading' of the Pseudo-histories discussed above as part of history proper. The *Chronicle of Seert* (PO 5, XXXIII–XXXIV) gives much more space to material derived from the Syriac *Julian Romance* than to the account derived from Socrates, and the compiler seems unable or unwilling to discriminate between the two. Eutychius and Agapius both make full use of the *Cave of Treasures* to fill out their discussion of the pre-Christian Near East. And Agapius (PO 5: 474–5) and the *Haddad Chronicle* (LVIII–LIX) give accounts of Addai and Abgar, drawn from the *Doctrina Addai*.

Two points need to be stressed here. The first is that, despite the origin of the *Julian Romance* and the *Cave of Treasures* in miaphysite circles, this was no impediment to their wide circulation. And the second is that texts that had once been 'apocryphal' were now treated as part of the canon. This may be in part because the Greek ecclesiastical histories were now harder to access and did not exist as single texts in Arabic translation that could be appealed to as a canonical vision of the past. Furthermore, the history of the period before Chalcedon did not bear the weight of justifying confessional divisions, which meant that it could be adapted more easily.

Another feature of these histories that should be stressed is their testimony to intercultural/interconfessional transmission. We have already seen important instances of this in Theophilus of Edessa, but our examples become more marked in texts of the tenth and eleventh centuries. The history of Elias of Nisibis (121–2/59 [AG 868–881]), for example, openly cites the Jacobite historian John of Ephesus, and the *Chronicle of Seert* incorporates a number of narratives of Melkite and Jacobite origin (Wood 2012: 139, 142).

We also find substantial use of Muslim historians in texts of this vintage. Agapius deploys a detailed Muslim text in his narrative on the ʿAbbasid revolution, and Elias of Nisibis's text is dominated by material of Muslim origin after the eighth century. The *Chronicle of Seert* (PO 13, CII–CIII) displays a slightly different phenomenon, which is the re-telling of the life of Muhammad to suit Christian political goals, in this case the presentation of the Christians of Najran as early allies of the Muslims against the Jews and pagans. Finally, we should note that this kind of exchange was not only one-way. Material of Syriac origin, such as the *Julian Romance* and the martyrdoms at Najran, is much more significant in al-Tabari's history (I. 840–43) than Greek material, which he seems not to have had access to.

CONCLUSIONS

I have argued that the Eusebian tradition of ecclesiastical history was a major stimulus to the recording of the past in Syriac. But this did not produce a single 'Syriac historical tradition' in the sixth century. After the Muslim conquests, historical writing in Syriac became increasingly dependent on sources available in Syriac, but even annalistic histories like the *Chronicle of Zuqnin* are still heirs to a Eusebian universal tradition, even if their contemporary information is highly parochial. In the ninth century we do see a marked confessionalisation of West Syrian history writing, which is partly a consequence of the ʿAbbasid sponsorship of the clergy as the leaders of distinct confessional groups.

East Syrian writing was also much inspired by the models and information provided by Eusebius and his successors. But East Syrian awareness of these 'Roman' models was limited to certain moments of cross-border contact.

Historical writing by Christians in Arabic in the ninth and tenth centuries also shows the hallmarks of earlier historical writing in Syriac: what was known of historical writing in Greek was often accessed through Syriac intermediaries, and Syriac Pseudo-historical material was increasingly incorporated into history proper.

NOTES

1 My thanks to Dan King, Scott Johnson, and Hartmut Leppin for their comments.

2 This included Ephrem (Amar 2011), Jacob of Nisibis (Peeters 1920), and Symeon the stylite (Harvey 1993).

3 The term 'Julianist' refers to the followers of Julian of Halicarnassus, who led a Miaphysite splinter group in the early sixth century. See Moss (2016).

4 Here I part company with Debié (2009: 113). In particular, I do not follow her in dating the dissolution of the genre of ecclesiastical history to the sixth-century persecution of Miaphysites (which was, in any case, intermittent). Muslim patronage of different Christian groups had a much stronger effect in the crystallisation of inter-communal boundaries.

5 But note Debié (2015: 77), who observes that it is unlikely that the chronicles of Edessa were ever 'closed texts'.

6 Different reconstructions of Dionysius are suggested in Abramowski (1940) (esp. the schema at 126–9) and Palmer (1993) (up to the 730s). Hoyland (2011) assembles the materials that might have been found in Theophilus. Note, however, that Papaconstantinou (2013), Conterno (2014), and Debié (2015: 27–31, 139–42) suggest that much of what has

been ascribed to Theophilus actually derives from a number of shared histories that were transmitted 'interculturally', including material composed by Muslim Arabs.

7 Goeller (1901) provides an example of the raw material that might have been extracted from the Western texts. Eusebius's *Chronicon* seems to have provided a skeleton for several of the ecclesiastical histories preserved in the *Chronicle of Seert*. This was probably received through a sixth-century (?) translation (Wood 2012: 131–3; Witakowski 1987: 78; Keseling 1927–8). Debié (2015: 223) challenges the attribution to Sergius of Beth Garmai.

8 The best attested of these lost historians is Daniel bar Maryam: Degen (1968).

9 On authorship, Nautin (1982).

10 Nautin (1974) argues that the *Chronicle* is written by Išoʿdenaḥ, which I do not find convincing.

BIBLIOGRAPHY

Primary Sources

Agapius, *History*. Ed. and tr. A. Vasiliev, PO 5, 7, 8, 11.

Bar Hebraeus, *Ecclesiastical History*. Ed. and tr. J. Abeloos and T. Lamy, *Gregorii Barhebraei Chronicon Ecclesiasticum*. 3 vols. Paris/Louvain, 1872–7.

Cave of Treasures. Ed. and tr. A. Su-Min-Ri, *La caverne des trésors: les deux recensions syriaques*. Louvain, 1987.

Chronicle of 819. Ed. A. Barsaum in J.-B. Chabot, *Anonymi auctoris chronicum ad 1234 pertinens I. Praemissum est Chronicon Anonymum ad A.D. 819 pertinens*. CSCO 81. Paris, 1920, 3–22. Tr. J.-B. Chabot, *Anonymi auctoris chronicum ad 1234 pertinens I. Praemissum est Chronicon Anonymum ad A.D. 819 pertinens*. CSCO 109. Louvain, 1937, 1–16.

Chronicle of Edessa. Ed. and tr. I. Guidi, *Chronica Minora* I. CSCO 1. Scriptores Syri 1. Paris, 1903, 1–13. Tr. I. Guidi, *Chronica Minora* I. CSCO 2. Scriptores Syri 2. Paris, 1903, 1–11.

Chronicle of Seert. Ed. A Scher and tr. F. Nau, F. Graffinn, R. Griveau et al., PO 4, 5, 7, 13.

Chronicle of Zuqnin. Tr. A. Harrak, *The Chronicle of Zuqnin, Parts III and IV A.D. 488–775, Translated From Syriac With Notes and Introduction*. Toronto, 1999.

Doctrina Addai. Ed. and tr. G. Phillips, *The Doctrine of Addai*. London, 1876. Tr. A. Desreumaux, *Histoire du roi Abgar et de Jesus*. Paris, 1993.

Elias of Nisibis, *Chronography*. Ed. and tr. E. Brooks and J.-B. Chabot, *Eliae metropolitae Nisibeni Opus chronologicum*. CSCO 62–3. Paris, 1909–10.

Eusebius of Caesarea, *Ecclesiastical History*. Ed. and tr. G. Bardy, Histoire ecclésiastique. SC 31, 41, 55, 73. Paris, 1952–60.

Eutychius, *History*. Ed. and tr. M. Breydy, *Das Annalenwerk des Eutychios von Alexandrien; ausgewählte Geschichten und Legenden kompiliert von Said ibn Batriq um 935 AD*. CSCO 471–2. Louvain, 1985.

Haddad Chronicle. Ed. B. Haddad, *Mukhtaṣar al-akhbār al-bīʿiya*. Baghdad, 2000.

Ishodnah of Basra, *Book of Chasitity*. Ed. and tr. J.-B. Chabot, *Mélanges d'archéologie et de l'histoire* 16 (1896), 225–90.

Itinerarium Egeriae. Ed. and tr. J. Wilkinson, *Egeria's Travels to the Holy Land*. 3rd edn., Warminster, 1999.

John of Ephesus, *Ecclesiastical History part II*, preserved in *The Chronicle of Zuqnin*. Ed. J.-B. Chabot, *Incerti auctoris Chronicon Pseudo-Dionysianum vulgo dictum II*. Paris, 1933. Tr. A. Harrack, *The Chronicle of Zuqnin*. Toronto, 1990; and W. Witakowski, *Pseudo-Dionysius of Tel-Mahre, Chronicle, Part III*. TTH 22. Liverpool, 1996.

John of Ephesus, *Ecclesiastical History part III*. Ed. and tr. E. W. Brooks, *Johnannis Ephesini Historia Ecclesiastica pars tertia*. CSCO 105/106. Louvain, 1935–6.

Joshua the Stylite, *Chronicle*. Ed. and tr. W. Wright, *The Chronicle of Joshua the Stylite, composed in Syriac A.D. 507*. London, 1882. Tr. F. Trombley and J. Watt, *The chronicle of Pseudo-Joshua the Stylite*. TTH 15. Liverpool, 2000.
Julian Romance. Ed. J. Hoffmann, *Iulianos der Abtreunigge: syrische Erzaehlung*. Leiden, 1880. Tr. H. Gollancz, *Julian the Apostate*. London, 1928.
Khuzistan Chronicle. Ed. and tr. I. Guidi, *Chronicum Anonymum*, in I. Guidi, *Chronica Minora* I. CSCO 1–2. Paris, 1903.
Michael the Syrian, *Chronicle*. Ed. and tr. J.-B. Chabot, *Chronique de Michel le Syrien, patriarche jacobite d'Antioche (1166–1199)*. Paris, 1899–1910.
Socrates, *Ecclesiastical History*. Ed. G. Hansen, *Sokrates. Kirchengeschichte*. GCS n.f. 1. Berlin, 1995.
Sozomen, *Ecclesiastical History*. Ed. J. Bidez and G. Hanson, *Sozomenus. Kirchengeschichte*. GCS n.f. 4. 2nd edn., Berlin, 1995.
Synodicon Orientale. Ed. and tr. J.-B. Chabot, *Synodicon orientale ou recueil de synodes nestoriens*. Paris, 1902.
Syriac *Life of Symeon the Stylite* (Vatican text). Tr. R. Doran, *Lives of Symeon the Stylite*. Kalamazoo, 1989, 101–201.
Theodoret, *Ecclesiastical History*. Ed. L. Parmentier and G. Hanson, *Theodoretus: Kirchengeschichte*. GCS n.f. 5. 3rd edn. Berlin, 1997.
Theodoret of Cyrrhus, *Religious History*. Ed. and tr. P. Canivet and A. Leroy- Molinghen, *L'histoire des moines de Syrie: Histoire Philothée*. Paris, 1979.
Thomas of Marga, *Book of Governors*. Ed. and tr. E. Wallis-Budge. London, 1883.
Zachariah of Mytilene, *Ecclesiastical History*. Ed. E. W. Brooks, *Historia ecclesiastica Zachariae Rhetori vulgo adscripta*. CSCO 83/84. Paris/Louvain, 1919–24. Tr. G. Greatrex, C. Horn, and R. Phenix, *The Chronicle of Pseudo-Zachariah: Church and War in Late Antiquity*. TTH 55. Liverpool, 2011.

Secondary Literature

Abramowski, R. 1940. *Dionysius von Tellmahre, jakobitischer Patriarch von 818–845. Zur Geschichte der Kirche unter dem Islam*. Abhandlungen für die Kunde des Morgenlandes 25.2. Leipzig: F. A. Brockhaus.
Amar, J. 2011. *The Syriac Vita Tradition of Ephrem the Syrian*. Leuven: Peeters.
Becker, A. 2006. *Fear of God and the Beginning of Wisdom: The School of Nisibis and Christian Scholastic Culture in Late Antique Mesopotamia*. Philadelphia: University Pennsylvania Press.
Borrut A. 2011. *Entre memoire et pouvoir: L'espace syrien sous les derniers Omeyyades et les premiers Abbassides. v. 72–193/692–809*. Leiden: Brill.
———. 2014. Vanishing Syria: Periodization and Power in Early Islam. *Der Islam* 91, 37–68.
Braun, O. 1894. Der Briefwechsel des Katholikos Papa. *Zeitschrift für katholische Theologie* 18, 162–82; 546–65.
Brock, S. P. 1976. Syriac Sources for Seventh-century History. *Byzantine and Modern Greek Studies* 2, 17–36.
———. 1979/80. Syriac Historical Writing: A Survey of the Main Sources. *Journal of the Iraqi Academy, Syriac Corporation* 5, 297–326.
———. 1992. Eusebius and Syriac Christianity. *In:* H. Attridge and G. Hata, ed., *Eusebius, Christianity, and Judaism*. Leiden: Brill, 212–34.
———. 1994. Greek and Syriac in Late Antique Syria. In Alan K. Bowman and Greg Woolf, ed., *Literacy and Power in the Ancient World*. Cambridge: Cambridge University Press, 149–160.
———. 2004. The transformation of the Edessa portrait of Christ. *Journal of Assyrian Academic Studies* 18, 46–56.

———. 2005. The Syriac Orient: A Third 'Lung' for the Church? *OCP* 71, 6–20.

Burgess, R. 1999. *Studies in Eusebian and Post-Eusebian Chronography.* Stuttgart: Franz Steiner.

Conrad, L. 1991. Syriac Perspectives on the Bilad al-Sham During the Abbasid Period. *In:* M. Bakhit and R. Schick, ed., *Bilad al-Sham During the Abbasid Period.* 2 vols. Amman: Lajnat Tārīkh Bilād al-Shām, II:1–44.

———. 1999. Varietas Syriaca: Secular and Scientific Culture in the Christian Bcommunities of Syria After the Arab Conquests. *In:* G. Reinink and A. Klugkist, ed., *After Bardaisan: Studies on Continuity and Change in Syriac Christianity in Honour of Professor Han J.-W. Drijvers.* Leuven: Peeters, 85–105.

Conterno, M. 2014. *La descrizione dei tempi all'alba dell'espanzione islamica. Un'indagine sulla storiografia greca, siriaca e araba fra Vii e VIII secolo.* Berlin/Boston: De Gruyter.

Croke, B. 1992. City chronicles of late antiquity. *In:* id., *Christian Chronicles and Byzantine History, 5th–6th Centuries.* Aldershot: Variorum, ch. IV.

Debié, M. 1999/2000. Record Keeping and Chronicle Writing in Antioch and Edessa. *Aram* 11/12, 409–17.

———. 2009. Syriac Historiography and Identity Formation. *Church History and Religious Culture* 89, 93–114.

———. 2010. Les apocryphes et l'histoire en syriaque. *In:* Françoise Briquel-Chatonnet and Muriél Debié, ed., *Sur les pays des Araméens chrétiens: Mélanges en honneur d'Alain Desreumaux.* Cahiers d'études syriaques 1. Paris: Geuthner, 63–76.

———. 2015. *L'écriture de l'histoire en syriaque. Transmissions interculturelles et constructions identitaires entre hellénisme et islam.* Late Antique History and Religion 12. Leuven: Peeters.

———. 2016. Christians in the Service of the Caliph: Through the Looking-glass of Communal Identities. *In:* A. Borrut and F. Donner, ed., *Christians and Others in the Umayyad State.* Late Antique and Medieval Islamic Near East 1. Chicago: Oriental Institute, 53–72.

Degen, E. 1968. Daniel bar Maryam: ein nestorianischer Kirchenhistoriker. *OC* 52, 45–80.

Drijvers, J.-W. 1999. The Syriac *Julian Romance.* Aspects of Jewish-Christian Controversy in Late Antiquity. *In:* G. Van Gelder and G. Reinink, ed., *All Those Nations: Cultural Encounters With and Within the Near East.* Gröningen: Styx, 31–42.

Fiey, J. 1972. Išoʿdnaḥ: métropolitain de Basra et son oeuvre. *OS* 11, 431–50.

Gero, S. 1981. *Barsauma of Nisibis and Persian Christianity in the 5th Century.* CSCO 426, Subs. 63. Louvain: Peeters.

Goeller, E. 1901. Ein nestorianisches Bruchstück zur Kirchengeschichte des 4 und 5 Jahrhunderts. *OC* 1 (1901): 80–97.

Greatrex, G., Phenix, R. and Horn, C. 2011. *The Chronicle of Pseudo-Zachariah Rhetor.* Translated Texts for Historians 55. Liverpool: Liverpool University Press.

Harrak, A. 1998. Arabisms in Part IV of the Syriac Chronicle of Zuqnin. *In:* R. Lavenant, ed., *Symposium Syriacum VII.* OCA 256 Rome: Pontificio Istituto Orientale, 469–98.

Harvey, S. A. 1993. The Memory and Meaning of a Saint: Two Homilies on Simeon Stylites. *Aram* 5, 222–35.

Hoyland, R. 1997. *Seeing Islam as Others Saw It: A Survey and Evaluation of Christian, Jewish and Zoroastrian Writings on Early Islam.* Princeton: Darwin Press.

———. 2011. *Theophilus of Edessa's Chronicle ca.590s–750s and the Circulation of Historical Knowledge in Late Antiquity and Early Islam.* Translated Texts for Historians 57. Liverpool: Liverpool University Press.

Illert, M. 2008. *Doctrina Addai; De imagine Edessena/Die Abgarlegende; Das Christusbild von Edessa.* Fontes Christiani 45. Turnhout: Brepols.

Jullien, C. 2008. *Le monachisme en Perse: la réforme d'Abraham le Grand, père des moines de l'Orient.* CSCO 622, Subs. 121. Leuven: Peeters.

Keseling, H. 1927–8. Die Chronik des Eusebius in der syrischen Überlieferung. *OC* 1927, 31–47, 225–39; 1928, 33–53.
Mango, M. M. 1982. Patrons and Scribes Indicated in Syriac Manuscripts, 411 to 800 AD. *In: XVI Internationaler Byzantinistenkongress* II/4. Jahrbuch der sterreichischen Byzantinistik 32,4. Vienna: Verlag der Österreichischen Akademie der Wissenschaften, 3–12.
Menze, V.-L. 2008. *Justinian and the Making of the Syrian Orthodox Church*. Oxford: Oxford University Press.
Millar, F. 2009. The Syriac Acts of Ephesus II. *In:* R. Price and Mary Whitby, ed., *Chalcedon in Context: Church Councils 400–700*. Translated Texts for Historians, Contexts 1. Liverpool: Liverpool University Press, 44–56.
Minov, S. 2013. *Syriac Christian Identity in Late Sasanian Mesopotamia: The Cave of Treasures in Context*. PhD Thesis. Hebrew University of Jerusalem.
Mirkovic, A. 2004. *A Prelude to Constantine: The Abgar Tradition in Early Christianity*. Studies in the Religion and History of Early Christianity 15. Frankfurt am Main: Peter Lang.
Morony, M. 2005. History and Identity in the Syrian Churches. *In:* J. J. van Ginkel, H. L. Murre-van den Berg, and T. M. van Lint, ed., *Redefining Christian Identity Cultural Interaction in the Middle East Since the Rise of Islam*. OLA 134. Leuven: Peeters, 1–33.
Moss, Y. 2016. *Incorruptible Bodies: Christology, Society and Authority in Late Antiquity*. Berkeley: University of California Press.
Nautin, P. 1974. L'auteur de la "Chronique de Seert": Isho'denaḥ de Basra. *RHR* 186, 113–26.
———. 1982. L'auteur de la "Chronique anonyme de Guidi": Élie de Merw. *RHR* 199, 303–14.
Palmer, A. 2009. Les chroniques brèves syriaques. *In:* M. Debié, ed., *L'historiographie syriaque*. Études syriaques 6. Paris: Geuthner, 57–87.
Palmer, A. with S. P. Brock and R.G. Hoyland. 1993. *The Seventh Century in the West Syrian Chronicles*. Translated Texts for Historians 15. Liverpool: Liverpool University Press.
Papaconstantinou, A. 2013. Review of R.G. Hoyland, *Theophilus of Edessa. LM* 126, 459–65.
Peeters, P. 1920. Jacob de Nisibe. *Analecta Bollandiana* 38, 287–373.
Robinson, C. Forthcoming. Al-ʿAttāf. b. Sufyān and Abbasid imperialism. *In: Festschrift for Ahmad Mahdavi Damghani*. Berlin.
Segal, J. B. 1970. *Edessa: the Blessed City*. Oxford: Clarendon Press.
Tannous, J. 2010. *Syria between Byzantium and Islam: Making Incommensurables Speak*. PhD Dissertation. Princeton University.
Taylor, D. 2002. Bilingualism and Diglossia in Late Antique Syria and Mesopotamia. *In:* J. Adams, M. Janse, and S. Swain, ed., *Bilingualism in Ancient Society: Language Contact and the Written Word*. Oxford: Oxford University Press, 298–331.
Trombley, F. and J. Watt. 2000. *The Chronicle of Pseudo-Joshua the Stylite*. Translated Texts for Historians 32. Liverpool: Liverpool University Press.
van Ginkel, J. J. 1995. *John of Ephesus: A Monophysite Historian in Sixth Century Byzantium*. PhD Dissertation. Gröningen.
———. 1998. Making History: Michael the Syrian and His Sixth Century Sources. *In:* R. Lavenant, ed., *Symposium Syriacum VII*. OCA 256. Roma: Pontificio Istituto Orientale, 351–8.
———. 2006. Michael the Syrian and His Sources: Reflections on the Methodology of Michael the Great as a Historiographer and Its Implications for Modern Historians. *JCSSS* 6, 53–60.
———. 2008. Aramaic Brothers or Heretics? The Image of East Syrians in the Historiography of Michael the Great. *The Harp* 23, 359–68.
Vollandt, R. 2015. *Arabic Versions of the Pentateuch: A Comparative Study of Jewish, Christian and Muslim Sources*. Leiden: Brill.
Whitby, L. M. 2003. The Church Historians and Chalcedon. *In:* G. Marasco, ed., *Greek and Roman Historiography in Late Antiquity: Fourth to Sixth Century AD*. Leiden: Brill, 447–93.

Wiessner, G. 1967. *Untersuchungen zur syrischen Literaturgeschichte I: Zur Martyrenüberlieferung aus der Christenverfolgung Shapurs II*. Abhandlungen der Akademie der Wissenschaften in Göttingen, Philologisch-historische Klasse III.67. Göttingen: Vandenhoeck & Ruprecht.

Witakowski, W. 1984/6. Chronicles of Edessa. *Orientalia Suecana* 33/35, 487–98.

———. 1987. *The Syriac Chronicle of Pseudo-Dionysius of Tel-Mahre: A Study in the History of Historiography*. Uppsala: Almqvist & Wiksell.

———. 2008. The Chronicle of Jacob of Edessa. *In*: B. Ter Haar Romeny, ed., *Jacob of Edessa and the Syriac Culture of His Day*. Leiden: Brill, 25–48.

———. 2011. Syriac Historiography. *In*: S. P. Brock, A. M. Butts, G. A. Kiraz, and L. van Rompay, ed., *Gorgias Encyclopedic Dictionary of the Syriac Heritage*. Piscataway: Gorgias Press, no.263.

Wood, P. 2010. *We Have No King But Christ. Christian Political Thought in Greater Syria on the Eve of the Arab Conquests*. Oxford: Oxford University Press.

———. 2011. The Chroniclers of Zuqnin and Their Times, c.720–775. *PdO* 36, 549–68.

———. 2012. The Sources of the Chronicle of Seert: Phases in the Writing of History and Hagiography in Late Antique Iraq. *OC* 96, 106–48.

———. 2013. *The Chronicle of Seert: Christian Historical Imagination in Late Antique Iraq*. Oxford: Oxford University Press.

CHAPTER TWENTY-FIVE

SYRIAC PHILOSOPHY

John W. Watt

By the time of the earliest-known Syriac author, Bardaiṣan of Edessa (154–222), the Syriac language area had long been subject to Greek influence. It is therefore natural to suppose that educated members of the upper classes there might have been interested in and familiar with Greek philosophy. Since Bardaiṣan's own works are all lost, we are largely dependent for his views upon the *Book of the Laws of the Countries*, a dialogue on fate and free will probably composed by his pupil Philip, in which Bardaiṣan is the protagonist. While it has been argued that he should be considered as primarily a theologian rather than a philosopher (Possekel 2006), it has also been thought that he was familiar with Stoicism and Epicureanism, and his analysis of fate and free will has been linked to the treatise *On Fate* (*Peri heimarmenēs*) of Alexander of Aphrodisias (Dihle 1979), although the importance ascribed to astrology in his worldview has also been held against this connection (Teixidor 1992: 92). While Bardaiṣan's ideas remained influential in the years after his death, we have no evidence for any other significant philosophical thinker in the Syriac world until Sergius of Resh῾aina (d. 536). It is often thought that, at least in the circles around or influenced by Ephrem (d. 373), there was considerable antagonism to the wisdom and philosophy of the Greeks in those years, but the later emergence of a lively interest in philosophy might lead one to ask if such interest was indeed totally absent, whether in Christian, pagan, or syncretistic (especially Bardesanite) circles. The earliest manuscript with Syriac philosophical texts, British Library Add. 14658 of the seventh century, contains in addition to Aristotelian and Bardesanite works a group of texts which, while probably assembled for the sake of training in rhetoric, nevertheless hints at an early Syriac interest in popular ethics (King 2011).[1]

LATE ANTIQUITY (CA. 500–750)

With the possible exception of Bardaiṣan, however, according to our available evidence the elite or higher school philosophy of the Greeks only reached the Syriac world in the late fifth or early sixth century. By that time, philosophy in the Greek world was concentrated in the schools at Alexandria and Athens (the closure of the latter being ordered by Justinian in 529) and dominated by Neoplatonism with a curriculum that, after some preliminaries of a more popular ethical nature, comprised a set of treatises of Aristotle followed by those of Plato. Those of Aristotle were to be read in a set order, commonly beginning with the logical and proceeding through those on practical philosophy, physics, and mathematics to the *Metaphysics*.[2] Subsequently, those of Plato were also to be studied in a prescribed sequence, culminating in the supposedly physical and theological treatises of *Timaeus* and *Parmenides*. The end (*telos*) to which the entire curriculum was dedicated was knowledge of the Neoplatonic One or, using a well-worn phrase from Plato himself, 'assimilation to God inasmuch as is possible'.

From the sixth century to the tenth and (more sporadically) to the thirteenth, those who wrote on philosophy in Syriac to a greater or lesser extent did so within this framework. Comparing the corpus of extant Syriac philosophical writings with the Late Antique Greek curriculum, the most obvious difference is the absence of Plato's works from the Syriac. In saying that Syriac philosophy to some extent followed the Late Antique Neoplatonic model, the first qualification to be noted, therefore, is that it appropriated only part of the curriculum. The focus on the Aristotelian treatises, to the exclusion of the Platonic, characterises Syriac philosophy all the way from the earliest prominent figure, Sergius of Resh'aina (d. 536), to the latest, Barhebraeus (d. 1286).

Sergius is the earliest of the three Syriac writers on Aristotelian philosophy known to us from the pre-Islamic period, the others being Proba and Paul the Persian. Sergius, who studied both philosophy and medicine in Alexandria, translated many treatises of Galen and the writings of Pseudo-Dionysius the Areopagite, wrote a commentary on the *Categories*, a shorter introduction to Aristotle's logic with particular reference to the *Categories*, an adaptation in Syriac of a cosmological treatise of Alexander of Aphrodisias (lost in the original Greek version but preserved in Arabic), a translation of the Pseudo-Aristotelian *De Mundo*, and a number of brief pieces mainly on logical questions (Hugonnard-Roche 2004: 123–42, and 2016; Watt in Hugonnard-Roche and Watt 2017: § 194). From Proba we have commentaries on Porphyry's *Eisagoge*, the *De interpretatione*, and the *Prior Analytics* I.1–7,[3] and from Paul an *Introduction to Logic* and an *Elucidation of the De interpretatione* (probably written in Persian but translated into Syriac and used within the Syriac environment). Also from this period we have anonymous translations of the *Eisagoge*, *Categories*, *De interpretatione*, and *Prior Analytics* I.1–7 (one or both of the last two possibly by Proba), and an anonymous commentary on the *Eisagoge*. Subsequently, in the early Islamic period, while there were a few East Syrian scholars of note (Theodore bar Koni, Silvanus of Qardu, Ḥenanisho' I, Isho'bokht), the most notable philosophical writers were four Syriac Orthodox scholars all associated at some time in their life with the monastery of Qenneshre on the Euphrates, to which it had migrated around 530 from its original home near Antioch: Severus Sebokht (d. 666/7), Athanasius of Balad (d. 686), Jacob of Edessa (d. 708), and George, bishop of the Arabs (d. 724). From these four, further translations and commentaries of the three logical works of Aristotle just mentioned are extant, as also a translation and commentary of the entire *Prior Analytics* by George, while by Jacob of Edessa there is (in his *Encheiridion*) a brief discussion of some passages of the *Metaphysics* (Brock 1993; Daiber 2012).

Surveying this list of extant works, it is clear that prior to the period of the 'Abbasid caliphate, when Arab interest in Greek philosophy is known to have arisen, we do not have direct evidence in Syriac for study of the complete Aristotelian curriculum as it was taught in the school of Ammonius at Alexandria. What was taught and studied in this period, and the related issue of the motivation for such study, is therefore a question to which different answers have been given.[4] It has to be remembered, however, that extant Syriac manuscripts represent only a fraction of what once existed in the language, especially from this early period, and that if other credible sources testify to the existence of works of which we have no knowledge through the direct manuscript tradition, that evidence should not be discounted. From one such source, the marginal notes in the Arabic manuscript of the *Organon* now in Paris (*Parisinus ar.* 2346), we know that George was not alone in producing a Syriac translation of the complete *Prior Analytics*, but that this was also done by Athanasius of Balad, who, furthermore, also made translations of the *Topics* and *Sophistical Refutations* (Hugonnard-Roche 1989: 516–17, 524, 526–8). Athanasius's translation of the *Topics* is also mentioned in a letter of the East Syrian patriarch Timothy I, and in addition he refers (*ep.* 48) to a translation by Athanasius of the *Posterior Analytics* (Heimgartner 2012: 89–92/74–7; Brock 1999: 238–46). It is clear, therefore, that the entire six-volume *Organon* (*Categories* to *Sophistical Refutations*) existed in Syriac in the pre-ʿAbbasid period, and it is hard to believe that translations would have been made of works for which there was little or no likelihood of finding any readers.

The other important point in this context concerns language. It is natural to suppose that translations of Aristotle or Porphyry were made for those who could not read Greek or only read it with difficulty, but the translators were not the only people who could understand it. There undoubtedly was a significant number of bilinguals in the Syriac language area, and if those who knew Greek are to be considered an 'elite', they may still have been a significant portion of those interested in philosophy, since philosophy was surely a fairly 'elite' activity. Sergius's commentary on the *Categories* was probably written before the earliest translation of the work, but even if not so, he undoubtedly did not assume (or probably know of) the existence of this translation (Hugonnard-Roche 2004: 23–33; King 2010a: 23, 39–79). If he wanted his readers to read Aristotle himself, he must have assumed they could do so in Greek, and probably many did. Around three hundred years later we find patriarch Timothy, who considered Syriac his native tongue but indicated that he had studied Greek and Arabic (*ep.* 19), comparing a passage of the *Posterior Analytics* in the Greek and Athanasius's translation (*ep.* 48). When therefore Timothy expressed his hope (*ep.* 19) to find commentaries on logic in the monastery of Mar Zaina by Olympiodorus, Stephanus, Sergius, or Alexander (Braun 1914/1915:127–9/85–6), while we must assume that in the case of Sergius he was thinking of Syriac, in those of the others we do not know whether he had in mind Syriac or Greek (or even both). Similarly, when Jacob of Edessa, who had a fine knowledge of Greek (and made a translation of the *Categories*), made reference to a number of passages of the *Metaphysics* (Furlani 1921), we do not know whether he was doing so from a translation which is no longer extant, or translating himself from a Greek text. We have thus to reckon with the possibility not only that more translations (and commentaries) were made in Syriac than those that have survived or are known to us, but also that some texts of (and commentaries on) Aristotle were studied in Greek by Syriac scholars without, during this period, being translated.

In order, therefore, to get a better idea of what Syriac scholars considered to be the content, as well as the aim, of philosophical study, we have to look beyond a mere list of their extant translations and works and find instances of the answers they themselves gave to these questions. In the case of the Qenneshre scholars, we are fortunate in having some very clear statements. Severus Sebokht wrote a short treatise on syllogisms which dealt only with those treated by Aristotle in *Prior Analytics* I.1–7. His work has therefore often been bracketed with that of Proba, with the implication that the study of logic in these circles never advanced beyond this point in the curriculum, the 'truncated *Organon*'. At the close of this treatise, however, Severus writes (Watt 2015a: 155–6):

> The student should first know that this book of the (*Prior*) *Analytics* is not for itself. On the contrary, as the book of *Categories*, which teaches (us) about simple namings, (leads us up) to the *De interpretatione*, which (teaches us) about the first combination of simple namings, (which in turn) leads us up to this book of the *Analytics*, so also this book of the *Analytics*, which teaches us about the construction together with the reduction again of categorical syllogisms, leads us up to the use of the logical treatise of the book of the *Apodeictics* [i.e. *Posterior Analytics*], which is the aim and fulfilment of the whole logical art, which (in turn) is the instrument (*organon*) of the whole of philosophy, which (in turn), according to a fine Platonic word or definition, is assimilation to God according to what is possible for man.

Severus's conception of philosophy is thus entirely consistent with that of the Alexandrian Neoplatonists (King 2015a; Hugonnard-Roche 2015: 55–7). Logical study attains its goal with the *Posterior Analytics*, not before, logic is an instrument (not a part) of philosophy, and the aim of philosophy is a Platonic 'assimilation to God'. The end (*telos*) of philosophy and the means to that end are standard items among the ten points in the prolegomena to Aristotelian philosophy of the Alexandrian commentators, and at the start of George's commentary on the *Categories* we have a corresponding Syriac prolegomenon, in the course of which he writes (Watt 2015a: 146):

> Point Four. What is the end of the Aristotelian philosophy? We say (it is) that we may know the one principal, cause, and creator of all. For the Philosopher demonstrates in the treatise called *Metaphysics* that the principal and cause is one, bodiless, from which everything has come into being.
>
> Point Five. What are the things which lead us to the end? We say that (it is) the doctrine of the things which are in time and change. For from these, by the intermediation of mathematics, we may ascend to those which are in a state always in like manner, and thus after bodiless substances (ascend) to the first cause of all.

George's prolegomenon is based on that of Philoponus, but this only emphasises the similarity of approach to philosophy between the Alexandrian (Christian) philosopher and that of the Qenneshre Aristotelians. The curriculum proceeds from logic through physics ('the doctrine of the things which are in time and change') and mathematics to metaphysics. Even in the Late Antique Greek sphere, however, the study of physics and mathematics in the context of Aristotelian philosophy was not limited to, or exclusively focused upon, Aristotle's own writings. While few if any writings of his could be found on mathematics, works of other authors on the quadrivium of arithmetic, geometry, astronomy, and music could take their place (Hadot 1990: 91). A certain relativising of the role of Aristotle's own physical treatises within the whole philosophical curriculum was therefore a consequence of the importance accorded the astronomical and cosmological works of Ptolemy and others (Scholten 1996: 386–406, 1997: 11–17, 62–3).[5] Sergius removed all references to the divinity of the heavenly bodies in his adaptation of a cosmological work of Alexander of Aphrodisias, while not going so far as to attack the idea of the eternity of the universe (King 2010b). Philoponus's rejection of this idea in his *Contra Aristotelem de aeternitate mundi*, however, and his introduction of philosophy into the hexaemeral tradition through his *De opificio mundi*, may have encouraged later Greek-reading Syriac Christians to take note of other approaches to natural philosophy beside that of Aristotle. The influence of his *De opificio mundi* can be detected in Jacob of Edessa's *Hexaemeron* (Wilks 2008),[6] and brief citations from both the *Contra Aristotelem* and the *De opificio mundi* have been preserved in Syriac,[7] though it is impossible to tell how much of them was translated.[8] There is good evidence for the study of mathematics and astronomy at Qenneshre, particularly in the writings of Severus Sebokht (Villey 2014a, 2015; Hugonnard-Roche 2014).

Sergius's commentary on the *Categories* does not have a prolegomenon to Aristotle in the same form as George and the Alexandrians, but in the first two (of the seven) chapters he discusses several of the same preliminary issues in a more discursive way, and in the course of this sets out his plans:

> The book written by (Aristotle) about simple namings is called *Categories*, that which he wrote about their first combination *De interpretatione*, that about the linkage of discourse is named *Analytics*, and that about the art of demonstrations itself is named *Apodeictics*. Together with this there is that called *Topics*, and that about the refutation of sophists which he named *Sophistical Refutations*. With these, therefore, this philosopher completed the whole art of logic, which is, as we have said, an instrument of philosophy and not a part of it. Some people say that the *Art of Rhetoric* which was composed by him is also part of the same (art) of logic. However, let us turn now to the subject itself and start to speak as (well as) we can about the aim of each one of these treatises, beginning the sequence with that on *Categories*, which is about simple namings, and similarly treating each of them one by one in the same way. Then we will go on to his other treatises, those on the parts of praxis [ethics], and on all natures [physics], teachings [mathematics], and the other ones which are called 'divine' [metaphysics].
>
> (Watt 2014a: 35)

We have no evidence of any commentary by Sergius other than that on the *Categories*. He may have died prematurely and unexpectedly,[9] or others which he wrote may not have survived. But it is nevertheless clear that his conception of Aristotelian philosophy was similar to that of the Neoplatonist teachers at Alexandria, of whom he was no doubt a pupil.

These teachers were pagans, but Sergius (together with his contemporary Philoponus) and the Qenneshre Aristotelians were Christians. Sergius's masters in Alexandria were undoubtedly religious, but it was a pagan religiosity that they saw justified by the culmination of their philosophical teaching, most notably embodied in the *Platonic Theology* of Proclus, Ammonius's teacher at Athens. An insight as to how Sergius resolved this conflict may be found in a brief treatise he prefaced to his translation of Pseudo-Dionysius.[10] In this treatise he identified seven different stages of *theoria* ('knowledge', 'contemplation'), six of which are woven, together with some overlap, from the Aristotelian curriculum and the teaching of Evagrius of Pontus. The Aristotelian components cover logic, physics, mathematics, and metaphysics, and the Evagrian the various stages in his theory of knowledge leading to the 'Kingdom of God'. The seventh and final stage, however, is from neither, but is of Neoplatonic inspiration: 'that which, like its finest flower, by means of all those (already) mentioned, touches, as far as is permitted, on the exalted radiance of the hidden divinity' and consists of a 'superabundance of non-knowledge and above knowledge' (Sherwood 1961: 122–4; Fiori 2008: 40–1).[11] In its present context, this clearly alludes to the teaching of Pseudo-Dionysius, who, as is well known, created a Christian Neoplatonic theology under the influence of Proclus's writings. It seems likely that Sergius would have encountered the latter in the school of Ammonius, and may have realised that the supposed convert of St Paul was in fact a literary disciple of Proclus. We cannot tell whether Sergius's own Neoplatonism was originally inspired by Pseudo-Dionysius, or first derived from Proclus and subsequently 'baptised' as a result of perceiving the similarities between the two. While the Qenneshre scholars might have adopted Aristotelianism, perhaps even before the migration from the Antioch region, quite independently of Sergius, it is nevertheless possible that his work was of significance for them, particularly in view of the attention also given to Pseudo-Dionysius (Watt 2011). The culmination of the Aristotelian curriculum according to Sergius's scheme has led to the suggestion that he envisaged Pseudo-Dionysius as a *Plato christianus* (Bettiolo 2005: 97–8).

THE EARLY ʿABBASID PERIOD (CA. 750–1000)

In the early ʿAbbasid period, during which Baghdad established itself as the intellectual centre of the Middle East, Arabic became an important language of philosophical discourse and was adopted for this purpose by Christians as well as Muslims. For many years, however, Syriac maintained its place alongside it among significant numbers of Christians. Unfortunately, for reasons to be discussed shortly, very little of what was accomplished in this sphere in Syriac has come down to us, and we are therefore largely dependent on Arabic references for our knowledge of it. Mention has already been made of the Paris manuscript of the Arabic *Organon*, and this is a source of great importance also for this period. From it we learn, for example, that already in the early ʿAbbasid years – or possibly in the immediately preceding ones – Syriac translations were made of the *Prior Analytics* and *Sophistical Refutations* by Theophilus of Edessa, who died in 785 (Hugonnard-Roche 1989: 517, 527), the latter also mentioned by the catalogue of Arabic bibliography, the *Fihrist* (Flügel 1871: 249; Dodge 1970: 601). The most important and prolific translators of philosophy in the period, however, were Ḥunain and his son Isḥāq.

Ḥunain and Isḥāq translated into both Syriac and Arabic. It is often supposed that their Syriac translations served merely as intermediaries facilitating an Arabic version, since an established Greek-to-Syriac, but no Greek-to-Arabic, translation tradition existed at the time, but this is not supported by the sources. The most important of these is the missive of Ḥunain to ʿAlī ibn Yaḥyā, extant only in Arabic, on the Syriac and Arabic translations of Galen (Bergsträsser 1925). In this he lists the translations known to him with their authors and patrons, where known. Patrons are mentioned for most of the Syriac translations made by him or his son, and these are mostly well-known and prestigious Syriac physicians, while none of the major patrons of the Arabic is known to have been a physician. Particularly striking is the fact that one of the Syriac physicians, Yuḥannā ibn Māsawayh, commissioned four Syriac translations of texts for which an Arabic version *already* existed. These Syriac translations were not therefore made to serve as the basis for an Arabic version, but to be used by practising Syriac physicians. Some other members of Ḥunain's circle, namely Ḥubaish and ʿIsā b. Yaḥyā, made their Arabic versions from the Syriac of Ḥunain, presumably because they either did not know Greek or found it more difficult. But the Syriac versions were not originally made for that reason, but to be read in Syriac by those who best understood, and made practical use of, their content (Strohmaier 1994: 1999–2011; Watt 2014c).

While unfortunately we do not have for the philosophical translations the information on the patrons that we possess for the medical, there is no reason to assume that the procedure was any different, namely that the Syriac translations were made for Syriac readers, and the Arabic for Arabic. The Syriac philosophical translations are known from the *Fihrist* and the 'Paris *Organon*', and from these we learn that Ḥunain translated in whole or in part *Categories*, *De interpretatione*, *Prior* and *Posterior Analytics*, *Physics* Book II, *De generatione et corruptione*, *De anima*, and *Metaphysics Lambda*, while Isḥāq completed his father's partial translations of *Prior* and *Posterior Analytics* and made a Syriac version of the *Topics*. The same sources also mention translations of the Greek Aristotelian commentators, but without providing the same amount of detail on the translators or even the language (Syriac or Arabic). There is, nevertheless, sufficient information there to conclude that several Greek commentaries were translated into Syriac, particularly some by Alexander, Themistius, Ammonius, Philoponus, Simplicius, and Olympiodorus (Watt 2014c).

From Ḥunain we know the names of some of the readers of his Syriac Galen translations, and from elsewhere (particularly Ibn Abī Uṣaibiʿa) we know that they were distinguished physicians. Although we do not have comparable information on the readers of his Syriac Aristotle, we can be confident that they did exist. Earlier in the period we know that Timothy was interested in Aristotle (cf. above),[12] and later we learn from the *Fihrist* that al-Marwazī, one of the teachers of Abū Bishr Mattā (d. 940), wrote exclusively in Syriac (Flügel 1871: 263; Dodge 1970: 629).[13] In ninth-century Baghdad, therefore, there was both a flourishing Syriac medical and philosophical culture, focused on Galen and Aristotle.

It is clear that more translations are attested for this period than for the preceding. It is possible that this could be down merely to our limited evidence; it has already been noted that more translations might have been made in the pre-ʿAbbasid years than those of which we are aware, while it is pertinent to observe that whereas at least some translations are extant from the earlier period, there are *none at all* from the ʿAbbasid.[14] Nevertheless, on the assumption that translation activity did indeed increase markedly during the latter, two reasons for it can readily be given. One is the declining familiarity with Greek, the other the more advantageous social and economic conditions. The wealth of the Syrians in ʿAbbasid Baghdad, not to mention the vibrant atmosphere of the new metropolis, enabled them to support this activity to a far greater degree than had previously been the case, and the decline of Graeco-Syriac bilingualism also made translations more necessary for those who wished to study either Galenic medicine or Aristotelian philosophy (Strohmaier 1991: 167–8). The rise of Arabic and the decline of the Christian population explain why the vigorous Syriac culture of this period, both medical and philosophical, has left no trace in the extant Syriac manuscript tradition. Very few Syriac manuscripts older than the thirteenth century have survived which are not among those taken from their homeland to Deir al-Suryān in Egypt (Brock 2004; Coakley 2011), and the philosophical and medical manuscripts of the early ʿAbbasid period were not among these. From the thirteenth century onwards, scribes willing to copy Syriac philosophical or medical works were generally more interested in those of Barhebraeus and others of the 'Syriac renaissance' or later, than those of Aristotle, Galen, or their Late Antique or ʿAbbasid period commentators (Watt 2014b: 429–33).

While Christians were important at all stages of the celebrated enterprise of the translation of Greek philosophy into Arabic (Stroumsa 2013), the decisive shift from Syriac to Arabic in philosophical writing by Christians appears to have occurred with Abū Bishr Mattā. He and his successors in the school of 'the Baghdad Aristotelians', principally Yaḥyā ibn ʿAdī (d. 974) and Ibn Zurʿa (d. 1008), translated into Arabic from Syriac those works in the Alexandrian curriculum of Aristotle for which no Arabic versions yet existed, as well as many of the Greek commentaries. They also themselves wrote Arabic commentaries on Aristotelian treatises (Endress and Ferrari 2012).[15] Their literary legacy therefore belongs to Arabic rather than Syriac literature, but they can also be said to belong in some way to 'the Syriac world'. Their immediate predecessors included al-Marwazī, who, as already noted, wrote only in Syriac.[16] Being ignorant of Greek, it was exclusively on Syriac that they depended for all their knowledge of Aristotle beyond what already existed in Arabic, and the curriculum to which they adhered was the Alexandrian Aristotelianism of the Syriac tradition (Watt 2011: 251–7).[17] It was this school that created the 'Paris *Organon*', from the marginalia of which, as already noted, comes much of our knowledge about the Syriac translations of Aristotle (Hugonnard-Roche 1991).

THE SYRIAC RENAISSANCE (THIRTEENTH CENTURY)

The time between the Baghdad Aristotelians and the 'Syriac renaissance' of the thirteenth century seems on the face of it to have been a comparatively barren one for philosophy in Syriac. The fact that a commentary covering the *Eisagoge* to the complete *Prior Analytics* was written in the period by Dionysius bar Ṣalībī (d. 1171) (Brock 2011), and also that in the thirteenth century manuscripts of Syriac translations of Aristotle stemming from the Baghdad period were still available to Syriac writers, both suggest, however, that interest in philosophy did not totally die out in Syriac Christianity, even if Arabic remained the preferred medium of philosophical writing. Around the turn of the twelfth/thirteenth century, a metrical work in Syriac by John bar Zoʿbī on the prolegomena to philosophy, seemingly following that of the Late Antique commentator David (Elias), is found in a number of manuscripts together with an anonymous metrical tract on the parts of philosophy. This tract, to which the writer of this period may have contributed merely the metrical form, is probably based on a much earlier Syriac translation of a lost Greek compilation drawn from a number of sources, including Porphyry and Ammonius (Daiber 1985).[18] John bar Zoʿbī was one of the teachers of Jacob bar Shakko (d. 1241), the second book of whose *Book of Dialogues* is the first major work on philosophy in the period of the Syriac renaissance. This (second) book is divided into two parts, the first on logic, the second on philosophy covering prolegomena, ethics, physics, mathematics, and metaphysics. Jacob also studied under the Muslim philosopher Kāmāl al-Dīn Mūsā b. Yūnus, and much in the philosophy section exhibits the influence of Arab learning and science (Ruska 1897). The section on logic, however, closely follows the old Alexandrian-Syriac tradition (Baumstark 1900: 181–210; Furlani 1927).

The most significant attempt to revive a secular literary tradition in Syriac in this period was that of Barhebraeus (d. 1286), whose vast output includes a number of works on philosophy (Takahashi 2005: 67–70). The most important of these is his *Cream of Wisdom*, a massive compendium of Aristotelian philosophy, divided into Logic, Theoretical Philosophy, and Practical Philosophy, with Theoretical Philosophy itself being divided into Natural Sciences and Metaphysics.[19] In this work, Barhebraeus's linkage to earlier Syriac tradition (he probably did not know Greek) consists mainly in his employment of the Syriac translations of Aristotle or other Greek authors, such as Nicolaus of Damascus. Beyond that, however, he depends on Arabic philosophers, especially Ibn Sīnā, whose *Shifāʾ* ('Cure') is the model both for the structure and much of the content of the *Cream*. In his *Chronicon syriacum*, Barhebraeus wrote that while Arab philosophers built on no other foundation than the Greeks, they nevertheless surpassed them, with the result that while they received that wisdom through Syriac translators, Syrians now find it necessary to seek wisdom from them (Bedjan 1890: 98; Budge 1932: 92). Similarly, in his Arabic *Historia dynastiarum*, he followed al-Qifṭī in asserting that while all translators of Aristotle from Greek into another language distorted his work in some way, al-Fārābī and Ibn Sīnā came closest to properly understanding it (Lippert 1903: 51; Watt 2010: 126–7). As in eastern Islam, Ibn Sīnā was more widely read than Aristotle himself, so in subsequent years Barhebraeus was more widely read than Aristotle. However, his attempt to revive a tradition of Syriac writing in philosophy, albeit one stamped by Arabic philosophers, had little or no success. While his own works were very popular among Syrians, resulting in many manuscripts now extant in numerous libraries, from these same libraries we know, to date, of no significant later Syriac philosophers. The works of Barhebraeus therefore represent, for the present at any rate, the final stage of Syriac philosophy.

POPULAR, ETHICAL, AND POLITICAL PHILOSOPHY

In addition to the theoretical philosophy stemming from the Neoplatonic Aristotelianism of the Alexandrian school, there existed a popular philosophy in the Syriac world directed towards matters of conduct and ethics, the possible early beginnings of which around the time of Bardaiṣan were noted above. This tradition, no doubt extending to a wider readership of broader educational range and interest than that of the theoretical philosophers, was of different origin from that of the theoretical, though still based on Greek authors and writings. Apart from the Pseudo-Aristotelian *On Virtues and Vices*, the main discursive texts translated were (whether genuine or pseudonymous) of Isocrates, Plutarch, Lucian, and Themistius, as well as some pseudonymous dialogues of Plato. There were also numerous collections of sayings, some attributed (pseudonymously) to more exalted philosophical authorities (such as Plato) than others (such as Sextus, in Syriac appearing as Pope Xystus). The translations, judged by the translation technique, probably belong mostly to the fifth century. They may be preserved in manuscripts which also contain works of a less popular nature, but directed nevertheless to a general readership,[20] or (sometimes additionally) in manuscripts evidently designed for monastic use (Brock 2003). There may have been comparable Syriac translations from the hand of Ḥunain and others during the ʿAbbasid era, but as we have no sources for that time comparable to those for the Syriac Galenic and Aristotelian translations, that remains rather speculative.[21]

Creative Syriac engagement with the longer among these works did not consist in the composition of commentaries, but in subtle modifications in their translation which not only made them more comprehensible to readers in the Syriac context, but also more consistent with Christian belief. This happened particularly with the texts of Plutarch, Lucian, and Themistius (Rigolio 2013). That at least two orations of Themistius[22] were translated into Syriac might seem surprising, since unlike the others in this group, Themistius was a post-Constantinian pagan best known in Greek as a theoretical (Aristotelian) and political (Platonic) philosopher, statesman, and public orator. Particularly in his public orations, he presented on the basis of a pagan monotheism a monarchic political philosophy centred around the idea of a philanthropic philosopher-king, which, *mutatis mutandis*, was shared by contemporary fourth-century Christian theologians, notably Gregory of Nazianzus, who were widely read in Syriac or Greek in the Syriac language area (Watt 2004). A Syriac version of unknown date of a treatise by Themistius on public administration is no longer extant, but was translated into Arabic by Ibn Zurʿa.[23] If it is considered likely that, given Themistius's reputation in Greek, more than the extant two Syriac orations were read (either in lost Syriac versions or in Greek) in the Syriac sphere in the pre-ʿAbbasid period, one may suppose that Syrians of that time had at their disposal a political philosophy from a pagan author consistent with what they could read in their Christian masters (Watt 2013). Alternatively, on the assumption that the treatise on public administration only attracted the interest of Syrians in ʿAbbasid times, and in the earlier period attention was directed only towards the two extant orations on personal ethics (maybe with others since lost), Themistius would initially have been conceived in the Syriac world as a teacher of individual virtue, and only subsequently thought of as the philosopher who complemented the concept of assimilation to God with the Middle and Neo-Platonic philosophy of felicitous community life on earth under a wise sovereign (Conterno 2014: 7–43).

NOTES

1 The texts in question are Pseudo-Isocrates *Ad Demonicum*, an *Apology* attributed to Melito of Sardis, the *Epistle* of Mara bar Serapion, the *Council* of Theano, and sayings

attributed to Pythagoras, Plato, and Menander. It has been suggested that some of these at least date back to the third century.

2 The logical treatises (the *Organon*) were *Categories*, *De interpretatione*, *Prior Analytics*, *Posterior Analytics*, *Topics*, *Sophistical Refutations*, and according to some but not all commentators, the *Rhetoric* and *Poetics*. They were generally prefaced by Porphyry's *Eisagoge*. The physical were *Physics*, *De caelo*, *De generatione et corruptione*, *Meteorology*, and possibly the *De anima*. There were alternative views as to which group (logic, physics, or ethics) should be studied first. Cf. Hadot (1990: 80–96).

3 The logical treatises as far as *Prior Analytics* I.1–7 constituted a 'truncated *Organon*', the study of which seems to have been attractive to many. See Hugonnard Roche (2004: 79–97).

4 One answer quite often given to the question of the motivation is that logic was useful to Syriac theologians in Christological debate, and this is often combined with the belief that the 'truncated *Organon*' was all of philosophy that was much studied by them in the pre-ʿAbbasid period (Gutas 2010: 14–15). There is, however, little or no evidence that Syriac theologians made much use of logic in Christological debate (King 2013), and however many were content with the 'truncated *Organon*', the interest of the major Syriac Aristotelians certainly went far beyond it (Watt 2009; Hugonnard-Roche 2013: 242–44).

5 This dual legacy of Aristotelian and mathematical (especially Ptolemaic) cosmology persisted in subsequent years in the Middle East and found notable expression in the work of al-Fārābī. Cf. Janos (2012: 16–26, 35–57, 119–28).

6 Later, in the ʿAbbasid period, Abū Bishr Mattā may have been strongly influenced by Philoponus's *Commentary on Aristotle's Physics* (Janos 2015: 164–9), and since Mattā was in touch with Syriac tradition, this might indicate that both the *Commentary on the Physics* and the *De opifio mundi* were read in Graeco-Syriac circles. See also Walker 2004.

7 It is perhaps significant that these citations are found together in the unique manuscript, British Library Add. 17214, foll. 72v–73r (*Contra Aristotelem*) and 73r (*De opificio mundi*). On the former, cf. Wildberg (1987: 148 [fr. 134] and 2010: 239–42). The latter is from *De opif. mundi* I.16 (Scholten 1997: 146, 20–23).

8 Another Syriac translation of a philosophical work of Philoponus (not extant in Greek) may, however, be noted here, that of his *Treatise concerning the Whole and the Parts*. Cf. King (2015b). On the interaction of scientific and religious ideas in the Syriac hexaemeral literature, cf. Debié 2014: 30–33.

9 This conclusion might be drawn from Pseudo-Zachariah 9.19 (Brooks 1921/1924: 136/94): 'Sergius died there [at Constantinople] *ʿgal*'.

10 The treatise appears to have been originally an independent piece and only subsequently attached to Pseudo-Dionysius. Since it is only transmitted in this form, its original title is unknown. The Italian translation of Fiori (2008) is more reliable than the French translation attached to the edition by Sherwood (1960–61).

11 On the interweaving of the diverse strands in Sergius's scheme, cf. Watt (2011: 241–4 and 2014a: 42–4) and slightly differently Fiori (2014: 77–86). Fiori considers that Sergius saw his curriculum 'incarnated' in Origen.

12 The idea that Timothy was interested in manuscripts of Aristotle for the purpose of supplying Arabic translations to Muslim caliphs and officials (Tarán and Gutas 2012: 87) is not credible. See Watt (2015b: 19–23), and more generally on Timothy's interest in philosophy, Berti (2009: 316–31).

13 Alongside the fact that al-Marwazī wrote 'about logic and other things' exclusively in Syriac, the *Fihrist* mentions that he was also a well-known physician in Baghdad.

14 Neither (with only an occasional possible exception) have Sergius's Galen translations known to Ḥunain survived to the present (about twenty-seven in number). See Kessel 2016.

15 The later members of the group were Ibn Suwār (d. 1017), Ibn al-Samḥ (d. 1027), and Ibn al-Ṭaiyib (d. 1043).

16 Al-Marwazī was one of the four to whom al-Fārābī in the later part of his 'Appearance of Philosophy in Islam' attributed the coming of philosophy to Baghdad (Endress-Ferrari 2012: 296–7). Although the bulk of al-Fārābī's narrative is of no historical worth, that does not apply to his naming of these four as immediate predecessors and teachers of Mattā and himself.

17 It was not solely due to 'the efforts of al-Kindī and his circle' that the Baghdad Aristotelians benefited from 'the permanent place' philosophy had won in the intellectual environment of Baghdad (Gutas 2010: 24). The readers of Ḥunain's and Isḥāq's translations were contemporary with al-Kindī, and earlier than that there was clearly a place for philosophy in the intellectual environment of Timothy and his circle. The Baghdad Aristotelians, who employed the Syriac and Arabic versions from Ḥunain's circle, were far closer in their focused Alexandrian Aristotelianism to Ḥunain's readers and al-Marwazī than to the more eclectic philosophy of al-Kindī, even though the latter did give some attention to Aristotle and the Baghdad Aristotelians may have adopted some cosmological ideas from al-Kindī. Al-Fārābī drew on both traditions, that of the Baghdad Aristotelians, and that of the *Neoplatonica arabica* and al-Kindī (Janos 2012: 14–22, 267–76).

18 In Daiber's opinion, neither the metrical character of the anonymous text nor its content constitutes a stringent proof that its author was John bar Zoʿbī.

19 Individual treatises of the work are gradually being published in the series Aristoteles Semitico-Latinus.

20 Notably British Library Add. 14658 and 17209. The former also contains, *inter alia*, the old anonymous translation of Aristotle's *Categories* and Sergius's commentary on the *Categories*.

21 On the Arabic translations of popular philosophy during the ʿAbbasid period, cf. Gutas 2012.

22 Or. 22 in the Greek tradition, and one *De virtute* not extant in Greek. Cf. Conterno (2014: 45–94).

23 There was an earlier Arabic translation by al-Dimashqī, but whether his exemplar was Greek or Syriac is not known. Themistius's authorship of the treatise has been disputed, but in Syriac and Arabic he was taken to be the author. Cf. Swain (2013: 22–91, 132–59) and Conterno (2014: 97–118).

BIBLIOGRAPHY

Baumstark, A. 1900. *Aristoteles bei den Syrern vom 5. bis 8. Jahrhundert*. Leipzig: B. G. Teubner.

Bedjan, P. 1890. *Gregorii Barhebraei Chronicon syriacum*. Paris: Maisonneuve.

Bergsträsser, G. 1925. *Ḥunain ibn Isḥāq über die syrischen und arabischen Galen-Übersetzungen*. Abhandlungen für die Kunde des Morgenlandes 17, 2. Leipzig: in Kommission bei F.A. Brockhaus.

Berti, V. 2009. *Vita e studi di Timoteo I, patriarca cristiano di Baghdad*. Paris: Association pour l'avancement des études iraniennes.

Bettiolo, P. 2005. Scuole e ambiente intellettuali nelle chiese di Siria. *In:* C. D'Ancona, ed., *Storia della filosofia nell' Islam medievale*. Turin: Einaudi, 48–100.

Braun, O. 1914/1915. *Timothei patriarchae I Epistulae*. CSCO 74/75. Paris: e Typographeo Reipublicae.

Brock, S. P. 1993. The Syriac Commentary Tradition. *In:* C. Burnett, ed., *Glosses and Commentaries on Aristotelian Logical Texts: The Syriac, Arabic and Medieval Latin Traditions*. Warburg Institute Surveys and Texts 23. London: Warburg Institute, 3–18.

———. 1999. Two Letters of the Patriarch Timothy From the Late Eighth Century on Translations From Greek. *Arabic Sciences and Philosophy* 9: 233–46.

———. 2003. Syriac Translations of Greek Popular Philosophy. *In:* P. Bruns, ed., *Von Athen nach Bagdad: zur Rezeption griechischer Philosophie von der Spätantike bis zum Islam*. Bonn: Borengässer, 9–28.

———. 2004. Without Mushē of Nisibis, Where Would We Be? *In:* R. Ebied and H. Teule ed., *VIII Symposium Syriacum = Journal of Eastern Christian Studies* 56: 15–24.

———. 2011. Dionysios bar Ṣalibi. *In:* S. P. Brock et al., ed., *Gorgias Encyclopedic Dictionary of the Syriac Heritage*. Piscataway, NJ: Gorgias Press, 126–7.

Brooks, E. W. 1921/1924. *Historia Ecclesiastica Zachariae Rhetori Vulgo Adscripta, II*. CSCO 84/88. Paris: e Typographeo Reipublicae.

Budge, E. A. Wallis. 1932. *The Chronography of Gregory Abû'l Faraj, the Son of Aaron, the Hebrew Physician, Commonly Known as Bar Hebraeus*. London: Oxford University Press.

Coakley, J. F. 2011. Manuscripts. *In:* S. P. Brock et al., ed., *Gorgias Encyclopedic Dictionary of the Syriac Heritage*. Piscataway, NJ: Gorgias Press, 262–4.

Conterno, M. 2014. *Temistio orientale*. Letteratura della Siria Cristiana 4. Brescia: Paideia.

Daiber, H. 1985. Ein vergessener syrischer Text. Bar Zo'bi über die Teile der Philosophie. *Oriens Christianus* 69: 73–80.

———. 2012. Die syrische Tradition in frühislamischer Zeit. *In:* U. Rudolph, ed., *Philososphie in der islamischen Welt, Band 1. 8.–10. Jahrhundert*. Grundriss der Geschichte der Philosophie begr. von Friedrich Ueberweg, völlig neu bearbeitete Ausgabe. Basel: Schwabe Verlag, 40–54.

Debié, M. 2014. Sciences et savants syriaques: une histoire multiculturelle. *In:* E. Villey, ed., *Les sciences en syriaque*. Études syriaques 11. Paris: Paul Geuthner, 9–66.

Dihle, A. 1979. Zur Schicksalslehre des Bardesanes. *In*: A. M. Ritter, ed., *Kerygma und Logos: Beiträge zu den geistesgeschichtlichen Beziehungen zwischen Antike und Christentum. Festschrift für Carl Andresen zum 70. Geburtstag*. Göttingen: Vandenhoeck & Ruprecht, 123–35.

Dodge, B. 1970. *The Fihrist of al-Nadīm*. New York: Columbia University Press.

Endress, G. and Ferrari, C. 2012. Die Bagdader Aristoteliker. *In:* U. Rudolph, ed., *Philososphie in der islamischen Welt, Band 1. 8.–10. Jahrhundert*. Grundriss der Geschichte der Philosophie begr. von Friedrich Ueberweg, völlig neu bearbeitete Ausgabe. Basel: Schwabe Verlag, 290–362.

Fiori, E. 2008. *Sergio di Resh'ayna. Trattato sulla vita spirituale*. Bose: Edizioni Qiqajon.

———. 2014. Un intellectuel Alexandrine en Mésopotamie. *In:* E. Coda and C. Martini Bonadeo, ed., *De l'Antiquité Tardive au Moyen Age. Études de logique aristotélicienne et de philosophie grecque, syriaque, arabe et latine offertes à Henri Hugonnard-Roche*. Études Musulmanes 44. Paris: Vrin, 59–90.

Flügel, G. 1871. *Kitāb al-Fihrist*. Leipzig: Vogel.

Furlani, G. 1921. Di alcuni passi della *Metafisica* di Aristotele presso Giacomo d'Edessa. *Rendiconti della Reale Accademia Nazionale dei Lincei. Classe di scienze morali, storiche e filologiche* 5: 268–73.

———. 1927. La Logica nei Dialoghi di Severus bar Shakko. *Atti del Reale Istituto Veneto di Scienze, Lettere ed Arti* 86,2: 289–348.

Gutas, D. 2010. Origins in Baghdad. *In:* R. Pasnau, ed., *The Cambridge History of Medieval Philosophy*. Cambridge: Cambridge University Press, 11–25.

Gutas, D. et al. 2012. Die Verbreitung philosophischen Denkens. *In:* U. Rudolph, ed., *Philososphie in der islamischen Welt, Band 1. 8.–10. Jahrhundert*. Grundriss der Geschichte der Philosophie begr. von Friedrich Ueberweg, völlig neu bearbeitete Ausgabe. Basel: Schwabe Verlag, 458–554.

Hadot, I. 1990. *Simplicius, commentaire sur les catégories, I*. Philosophia Antiqua 50. Leiden: Brill.

Heimgartner, M. 2012. *Die Briefe 42–58 des Ostsyrischen Patriarchen Timotheos I*. CSCO 644/645. Leuven: Peeters.

Hugonnard-Roche, H. 1991. Contributions syriaques aux études arabes de logique à l'époque Abbasside. *Aram* 3: 193–210.

———. 2004. *La logique d'Aristote du grec au syriaque*. Textes et traditions 9. Paris: Vrin.

———. 2013. Book Announcements & Reviews: Syriac Studies. *Studia graeco-arabica* 3: 233–44.

———. 2014. Mathématiques en syriaque. *In:* E. Villey, ed., *Les sciences en syriaque*. Études syriaques 11. Paris: Paul Geuthner, 67–106.

———. 2015. Questions de logique au VIIe siècle. Les épitres syriaques de Sévère Sebokht et leurs sources grecques. *Studia graeco-arabica* 5: 53–104.

———. 2016. Sergius de Rešʿainā. *In*: R. Goulet, ed., *Dictionnaire des philosophes antiques, VI*. Paris: CNRS Éditions, 214–27.

Hugonnard-Roche, H. and Elamrani-Jamal, A. 1989. L'*Organon*. Tradition syriaque et arabe. *In:* R. Goulet, ed., *Dictionnaire des philosophes antiques, I*. Paris: CNRS Éditions, 502–28.

Hugonnard-Roche, H. and J. W. Watt. 2018. Philosophie im syrischen Sprachbereich. *In:* C. Riedweg, C. Horn, and D. Wyrwa, ed., *Die Philosophie der Kaiserzeit und der Spätantike*. Teilband 3. Basel: Schwabe, chapter 16.

Janos, D. 2012. *Method, Structure, and Development in al-Fārābī's Cosmology*. Islamic Philosophy, Theology and Science 85. Leiden: Brill.

———. 2015. "Active Nature" and Other Striking Features of Abū Bishr Mattā ibn Yūnus's Cosmology as Reconstructed from his Commentary on Aristotle's *Physics*. *In*: D. Janos, ed., *Ideas in Motion in Baghdad and Beyond*. Islamic History and Civilization 124. Leiden: Brill, 135–77.

Kessel, G. 2016. Inventory of Galen's Extant Works in Syriac. *In*: J. C. Lamoreaux, ed., *Ḥunayn ibn Isḥāq on his Galen Translations*. Provo: Brigham Young University Press, 168–92.

King, D. 2010a. *The Earliest Syriac Translation of Aristotle's Categories*. Aristoteles Semitico-Latinus 21. Leiden: Brill.

———. 2010b. Alexander of Aphrodisias' *On the Principles of the Universe* in a Syriac Adaptation. *Le Muséon* 123: 159–91.

———. 2011. Origenism in Sixth Century Syria. The Case of a Syriac Manuscript of Pagan Philosophy. *In:* A. Fürst, ed., *Origenes und sein Erbe in Orient und Okzident*. Adamantiana 1. Münster: Aschendorff, 179–212.

———. 2013. Why Were the Syrians Interested in Greek Philosophy? *In:* P. Wood, ed., *History and Identity in the Late Antique Near East*. Oxford: Oxford University Press, 61–82.

———. 2015a. Logic in the Service of Ancient Eastern Christianity: An Exploration of Motives. *Archiv für Geschichte der Philosophie* 97: 1–33.

———. 2015b. Philoponus: A Treatise Concerning the Whole and the Parts. *In:* R. Sorabji et al., ed., *Philoponus: On Aristotle Categories 1–5 With a Treatise on the Whole and the Parts*. Ancient Commentators on Aristotle. London: Bloomsbury, 167–221.

Lippert, J. 1903. *Ibn al-Qifṭī's Taʾrīḫ al-ḥukamāʾ*. Leipzig: Dieterich'sche Verlagsbuchhandlung.

Possekel, U. 2006. Bardaisan of Edessa, Philosopher or Theologian? *Zeitschrift für antikes Christentum* 10: 442–61.

Rigolio, A. 2013. From "Sacrifice to the Gods" to the "Fear of God". Omissions, Additions and Changes in the Syriac Translations of Plutarch, Lucian and Themistius. *In:* M. Vinzent, ed., *Studia Patristica 64*. Leuven: Peeters, 133–43.

Ruska, J. 1897. Studien zu Severus bar Shakku's "Buch der Dialoge". *Zeitschrift für Assyriologie und verwandte Gebiete* 12: 8–41, 145–61.

Scholten, C. 1996. *Antike Naturphilosophie und christliche Kosmologie in der Schrift "De Opificio Mundi" des Johannes Philoponos*. Patristische Texte und Studien 45. Berlin: Walter de Gruyter.

———. 1997. *Johannes Philoponos. De opificio mundi/Über die Erschaffung der Welt, I*. Fontes Christiani 23/1. Freiburg: Herder.
Sherwood, P. 1960–61. Mimro de Serge de Rešayna sur la vie spirituelle. *L'Orient syrien* 4: 433–57; 6: 95–115, 122–56.
Strohmaier, G. 1991. Ḥunain ibn Isḥāq. An Arab Scholar Translating Into Syriac. *Aram* 3: 163–70.
———. 1994. Der syrische und der arabische Galen. *In:* H. Temporini et al., ed. *Aufstieg und Niedergang der römischen Welt* II. 37.2. Berlin: De Gruyter, 1987–2017.
Stroumsa, S. 2013. Philosophy as Wisdom. On the Christians' Role in the Translation of Philosophical Material Into Arabic. *In*: H. Ben-Shammai et al., ed., *Exchange and Transmission Across Cultural Boundaries. Philosophy, Mysticism and Science in the Mediterranean World*. Jerusalem: Israel Academy of Sciences and Humanities, 276–93.
Swain, S. C. R. 2013. *Themistius, Julian and Greek Political Theory Under Rome*. Cambridge: Cambridge University Press.
Takahashi, H. 2005. *Barhebraeus: A Bio-Bibliography*. Piscataway, NJ: Gorgias Press.
Tarán, L. and D. Gutas. 2012. *Aristotle Poetics*. Mnemosyne Supplements 338. Leiden: Brill.
Teixidor, J. 1992. *Bardesane d'Edesse: la première philosophie syriaque*. Paris: Éditions du Cerf.
Villey, E. 2014a. Qennešre et l'astronomie aux vi^e^ et viie siècles. *In:* E. Villey, ed., *Les sciences en syriaque*. Études syriaques 11. Paris: Paul Geuthner, 149–90.
———. 2014b. *Les sciences en syriaque*. Études syriaques 11. Paris: Paul Geuthner.
———. 2015. Ammonius d'Alexandrie et le Traité sur l'astrolabe de Sévère Sebokht. *Studia graeco-arabica* 5: 105–28.
Walker, J. 2004. Against the Eternity of the Stars: Disputation and Christian Philosophy in Late Sassanian Mesopotamia. *La Persia e Bisanzio. Atti dei convegni Lincei* 201: 509–37.
Watt, J. W. 2004. Syriac and Syrians as Mediators of Greek Political Thought to Islam. *Mélanges de l'Université Saint-Joseph* 57: 121–49.
———. 2009. *Al-Farabi and the History of the Syriac Organon*. Analecta Gorgiana 129. Piscataway, NJ: Gorgias Press.
———. 2010. Graeco-Syriac Tradition and Arabic Philosophy in Bar Hebraeus. *In:* H. Teule et al., ed., *The Syriac Renaissance*. Eastern Christian Studies 9. Leuven: Peeters, 123–33.
———. 2011. From Sergius to Mattā. Aristotle and Pseudo-Dionysius in Syriac Tradition. *In:* J. W. Watt and J. Lössl, ed., *Interpreting the Bible and Aristotle in Late Antiquity*. Farnham: Ashgate, 239–57.
———. 2013. Themistius and Julian: Their Association in Syriac and Arabic Tradition. *In:* A. J. Quiroga Puertas, ed., *The Purpose of Rhetoric in Late Antiquity*. Studien und Texte zu Antike und Christentum 72. Tübingen: Mohr Siebeck, 161–76.
———. 2014a. Sergius of Reshaina on the Prolegomena to Aristotle's Logic: The Commentary on the *Categories*, Chapter Two. *In:* E. Coda and C. Martini Bonadeo, ed., *De l'Antiquité Tardive au Moyen Age. Études de logique aristotélicienne et de philosophie grecque, syriaque, arabe et latine offertes à Henri Hugonnard-Roche*. Études Musulmanes 44. Paris: Vrin, 31–57.
———. 2014b. The Syriac Translations of Ḥunayn ibn Isḥāq and their Precursors. *In:* M. Tamcke and S. Grebenstein, ed., *Geschichte, Theologie und Kultur des syrischen Christentums. Beiträge zum 7. Deutschen Syrologie-Symposium in Göttingen, Dezember 2011*. Göttinger Orientforschungen: Syriaca 46. Wiesbaden: Harrassowitz, 423–45.
———. 2014c. Why Did Ḥunayn, the Master Translator Into Arabic, Make Translations Into Syriac? On the Purpose of the Syriac Translations of Ḥunayn and His Circle. *In:* J. Scheiner and D. Janos, ed., *The Place to Go. Contexts of Learning in Baghdad, 750–1000 C.E.* Studies in Late Antiquity and Early Islam 26. Princeton: Darwin Press, 363–88.
———. 2015a. The Prolegomena to Aristotelian Philosophy of George, Bishop of the Arabs. *In:* S. Griffith and S. Grebenstein, ed., *Christsein in der islamischen Welt. Festschrift für Martin Tamcke zum 60. Geburtstag*. Wiesbaden: Harrassowitz, 141–63.

———. 2015b. The Syriac Aristotelian Tradition and the Syro-Arabic Baghdad Philosophers. *In:* D. Janos, ed., *Ideas in Motion in Baghdad and Beyond: Philosophical and Theological Exchanges Between Christians and Muslims in the Third/Ninth and Fourth/Tenth Centuries*. Islamic History and Civilization 124. Leiden: Brill, 7–43.

Wildberg, C. 1987. *Philoponus. Against Aristotle, on the Eternity of the World*. Ancient Commentators on Aristotle. London: Duckworth.

———. 2010. Prolegomena to the Study of Philoponus' *Contra Aristotelem*. *In:* R. Sorabji, ed., *Philoponus and the Rejection of Aristotelian Science*. 2nd ed. Bulletin of the Institute of Classical Studies Supplement 103. London: Institute of Classical Studies, 239–50.

Wilks, M. 2008. Jacob of Edessa's Use of Greek Philosophy in His Hexaemeron. *In:* B. ter Haar Romeny, ed., *Jacob of Edessa and the Syriac Culture of His Day*. Leiden: Brill, 223–38.

CHAPTER TWENTY-SIX

SYRIAC MEDICINE

Grigory Kessel

INTRODUCTION[1]

The field of Syriac medicine is perhaps one of the least investigated and explored domains within Syriac intellectual culture. Yet owing to its decisive role during the late antique period for the transfer of Greek medical knowledge to the Islamic world, it should occupy a very special position, and the results of its study are appealing to both Classicists and historians of Greek and Islamic medicine. The study of Syriac medicine deals predominantly with medical literature, but also with theory and practice as they evolved over centuries within changing social and historical contexts (the surveys available differ in perspective and scope: Gignoux 2001a; Habbi 2001; Muraviev 2014; Pormann and Savage-Smith 2007: 17–21; Strohmaier 1994; on the Syriac scholarly milieu more broadly: Debié 2014).

Descriptions of Syriac medicine normally focus upon the relevant literary and social activity of Syriac Christians in the period between the sixth and the ninth centuries. However, this timeframe should not be taken to imply that before and after that period medical scholarship was non-existent, but rather that it was during those four centuries that the actual literary production in Syriac was carried out. What unites scholars of different ethnic backgrounds (Aramean, Iranian, Arab, and others) is the common literary medium, the Syriac language. Just as anywhere else in Roman Empire, the Aramaic-speaking Christians, some of whom were bilingual although living largely in the Hellenised territories, must have had medical practitioners among them. Thus it was not from a vacuum that the study of medicine, as well as an appreciation of Greek medical lore, entered the milieu of the Syriac Christians. The period that postdates the ninth century is better known to us, but by that time the literary output had become predominantly Arabic, and both scholars and physicians, albeit retaining (however, not always) their Christian faith, worked already within a different paradigm, that of Islamic medicine, when the scholars of various religious denominations could peacefully participate in a common discourse. The names of Sābūr ibn Sahl (d. 869), Abū al-Faraj ʿAbd Allāh Ibn al-Ṭayyib (d. 1048), Ibn Buṭlān (d. 1066), Ibn Jazlah (d. 1100), Ibn al-Tilmīdh (d. 1165), Ibn Muṭrān (d. 1190), Ibn al-Quff (d. 1286), and the ibn Bokhtīshūʿ family, may be related as the names of those who exerted the most significant impact. Some of the works of these authors occupied a prominent position in Islamic medicine and enjoyed widespread popularity (the details about their works can be found in Ullmann 1970).

A key factor that determined the development, significance, and impact of Syriac medicine was the permanent absence of a state system. The Syriac Christians always formed a minority while living in different, often confrontational, states of the Near and Middle East. Such political divisions did not restrain the flow and circulation of texts and knowledge, and thus it should come as no surprise that a text composed or translated somewhere in what is today Syria might, via ecclesiastical networks, reach such distant regions as Iran, the Persian Gulf, and India (Takahashi 2014). That eastwards vector may help to explain the penetration and dissemination of Greek medicine in the Middle East and beyond, but one should not forget that the Syriac Christians were undoubtedly also the vehicle that transmitted local medical traditions. Whereas the former process has been more thoroughly explored, the latter one has generally been neglected in scholarship due to the lack of sources. However, finding new texts and investigating existing ones more thoroughly will bring us to a better understanding of the integration and fusion of different medical traditions implemented by the Syriac Christians and the actual role they played in the formation of Islamic medicine, well known for its heterogeneous character (Pormann and Savage-Smith 2007: 35–6). For instance, one of the earliest Islamic medical encyclopaedias, the *Paradise of Wisdom* of ʿAlī ibn Sahl Rabban al-Ṭabarı, an East Syriac physician from Merw who late in his life converted to Islam (d. soon after 855), introduces in addition to the Greek sources also the principles of Indian medicine (Meyerhof 1931; Siggel 1950); slightly later al-Rāzī made a good use of the Syriac, Persian, and Indian sources in his *Comprehensive Book* (Kahl 2015).

A STANDARD HISTORICAL NARRATIVE

Any presentation of the history of Syriac medicine cannot fail to mention the two main periods that are closely associated respectively with the key figures of Sergius of Rēshʿaynā (d. 536) and Ḥunayn ibn Isḥāq (d. 873 or 877) (see, for example, Strohmaier 1998: 145–7). The rationale for such a framework lies in the distinctive features that marked those periods. Thus, Sergius was instrumental in bringing Greek medicine into the milieu of Aramaic-speaking Christians. The transfer was successfully implemented thanks to the introduction of the study of medicine into the school curriculum after the model of the Alexandrian tradition. The Hellenised eastern provinces of the Roman Empire had for centuries sustained the social institutions of medical practice, hence the science of medicine was not a foreign import in late antiquity and had long been pursued especially among the Greek-speaking population. Besides, early Syriac literature is notable for its particular attention to medical imagery, for example in the works of Ephrem of Nisibis. Be that as it may, Sergius's achievement consists not only in the translation of the standard Greek texts into Syriac, but also (and perhaps even more importantly) in the creation of the medical lexicon that made possible further medical scholarship in Syriac (Bhayro 2005). The extraordinary translation activity of Ḥunayn, his disciples and successors, came into being not due to the internal development of medicine within the Syriac milieu but rather because of the increasing interest in medicine within the Caliphs' courts (Gutas 1998). Despite the different historical context of his era, the tasks he implemented were basically the same as those faced by Sergius, namely the creation of the Arabic lexicon and the translation of Greek works into Arabic (on noticeable patterns in the two translation movements, see Freudenthal and Glasner 2014). Although the achievements of Ḥunayn have often been acclaimed, a closer study of contemporary accounts offers us the opportunity to hear other voices, not always so positive, concerning his reputation as a physician and a scholar (Olsson 2016).

THE STATE OF RESEARCH

Syriac medical literature once constituted a vast corpus of texts from which, regrettably enough, only mere fragments have come down to us. The first Syriac medical texts that reached Europe in the middle of the nineteenth century came from the famous library of the monastery of Deir al-Surian in Egypt. Other medical manuscripts were acquired in a similar way by collectors and scholars in the Near East at the end of that century and the first quarter of the twentieth. Relying on available manuscripts, scholars readily occupied themselves with their study (e.g. Schleifer undertook the mammoth task of identifying all the Galenic quotations in the *Syriac Book of Medicines*) and publication (Sachau 1870; Merx 1885; Pognon 1903; Budge 1913). This scholarly enthusiasm gradually began to wane, and some texts remained neglected. Beginning in the 1970s, the study of Syriac medicine took its second breath with such scholars as Rainer Degen and Philippe Gignoux. Whereas the former was planning to launch a publication series of all Syriac medical works (Degen 1972) which unfortunately never came to fruition, the latter was keenly interested in exploring connections between Syriac medicine and the Iranian tradition, as well as in pharmacology (Gignoux 2001b).

The beginning of the new millennium was marked by the appearance of a new generation of scholars. The studies of Siam Bhayro and Peter E. Pormann paid special attention to such previously under-researched aspects as medical nomenclature (Bhayro 2005) and translation techniques (Pormann 2012); Grigory Kessel made a preliminary study of the medical sources that had not been available to earlier researchers (Kessel 2012a; Kessel 2017a). The broader significance of Syriac medicine contributed positively to gaining the support of financial bodies. At the time of writing, three large-scale projects deal directly with Syriac medicine. One of these, 'The Syriac Galen Palimpsest: Galen's On Simple Drugs and the Recovery of Lost Texts through Sophisticated Imaging Techniques' (funded by the UK Arts and Humanities Research Council, and led by P.E. Pormann) aims at an in-depth study of the Syriac Galen Palimpsest (see below), applying cutting-edge multi-spectral imaging technologies to reveal the erased text. Another, 'From Babylon to Baghdad: Toward a History of the Herbal in the Near East' (funded by the European Research Council, and led by Robert Hawley), intends to produce an edition of the Syriac and Arabic version of Ḥunayn's medical compilation *On the Medicinal Properties of Foodstuffs*. The third, entitled 'Transmission of Classical Scientific and Philosophical Literature from Greek into Syriac and Arabic' (funded by the European Research Council and led by G. Kessel) sets out to create a trilingual, Greek-Syriac-Arabic, digital corpus of scientific literature to foster a close study of the historical development of scientific vocabulary and translation techniques.

SCHOOL SETTING

The origins of Syriac medicine must be traced in the context of the medical tradition as practised and studied in late ancient Alexandria (Iskandar 1976). It is now widely accepted that Sergius of Rēsh῾aynā's contribution to the field of philosophy cannot be detached from the commentary tradition of the Neoplatonic school in Alexandria (see ch. 25). The same pattern can be safely applied to his contribution to medicine. Moreover, Sergius himself exemplifies the Alexandrian type of scholar who combines Aristotelian philosophy and Galenic medicine. Both in his selection of texts to be translated and their interpretation he is heavily dependent on Alexandrian models (Hugonnard-Roche 1997).

Although our present knowledge of the curriculum, as well as of the educational procedures of the Syriac schools in general and of the School of Nisibis in particular, is far from presenting a complete picture (Becker 2006), what seems indisputable is that from the sixth century, the study of medicine became one of the disciplines taught at Nisibis as well as at other East Syriac centres of learning (see, for example, the canons of the School of Nisibis). One can observe that beginning from the sixth century, some sorts of hospices or infirmaries (referred to as *xenodocheia*) began to be attached to the schools. Some of these institutions were established by direct intervention of the ruling Sasanian shah. For example, the *Chronicle* of Pseudo-Zachariah of Mytilene reports how shah Khosrow I (531–579) established one *xenodocheion* (Zachariah 12.7; Greatrex et al. 2011: 455), apparently at the instigation of the Christian physicians present at his court (centuries later, the Christian physicians would come to advocate for their co-religionists before the ῾Abbasid Caliphs).

The school of Nisibis and its curriculum established an educational model that with some modifications persisted at least until the ninth century and shaped the intellectual climate. Thus many of the philosophical and psychological issues raised in the letters of catholicos Timothy I (such as providence, free will, nature of the soul, etc.) cannot be understood apart from the school tradition (Berti 2009, 2013, 2015). Moreover, Timothy I himself records that he paid for the foundation of a hospital (referred to as *xenodocheion* and *bīmāristān*) in Baghdad.

Medical practice was not foreign to East Syriac monasteries. Despite scant evidence, available accounts indicate that various medical treatments were familiar and performed by the monks. Thus, we know that in the monastery of Rabban Shabūr (located in Khuzistan) the use of cupping was quite common. One important source in this regard, Ibn Buṭlān's *Medical Manual for the Use of Monks and Country People*, has received absolutely no attention so far (the text is available in Jadon 1968).

TRANSLATIONS FROM GREEK

In considering translations from Greek, one needs to bear in mind that Syriac medicine, as we know it, derives from the late antique medical tradition, particularly as it existed in Alexandria. This should explain two important traits of Syriac medicine, especially in its earliest period. First, the works that happened to be translated into Syriac were those in circulation during the late antique period and, to be more precise, that were employed and produced in Alexandria (cf. the so-called 'the first rule of thumb in Graeco-Arabic studies' as presented in Gutas 1994).

Second, the study of medicine in the Syriac milieu was predominantly associated with the activity of schools and therefore it had to a large extent a 'scholastic' character.

It is hardly possible to enumerate the Greek works that were translated into Syriac, since most of the evidence comes from secondary sources that one can only rarely verify. However, based on more trustworthy sources (such as Ḥunayn's personal account of his translations of Galen's works [Bergsträsser 1925, but now available in a new edition and English translation, Lamoreaux 2016]), one can postulate that by the ninth century virtually the entire corpus of Galen's medical works extant in that period was available in Syriac (Degen 1981; Strohmaier 1994; Kessel 2016b). Thus, if Sergius must have translated two dozens of Galen's works (and nearly the whole of the Alexandrian canon of the sixteen books of Galen), Ḥunayn is credited with nearly a hundred. Besides Galen, the medical encyclopaedias of Oribasius, Aetius of Amida, Alexander of Tralles, and Paul of Aegina were also translated into Syriac, although mostly during the second period, that of the eighth to ninth centuries. Such encyclopaedias, themselves based on multiple sources, were in later times the only source of information, and many citations from lesser-known authors in fact derive from them. Given the close connection with the late antique Alexandrian medical tradition, one should assume that many of the medical works of the Alexandrian scholars and physicians were rendered into Syriac. Indeed, the scant available evidence attests to the availability of such material in Syriac beginning from the time of Sergius (who might have personally translated some of them) up until Ḥunayn (the later Syriac authors would have relied on Arabic versions rather than on Syriac). Christian anthropological treatises that contain much medical information, such as *On the Nature of Man* by Nemesius of Emesa (ca. 400) and *On the Making of Man* by Gregory of Nyssa (d. 394), were also rendered into Syriac (Zonta 1991 provides the identified excerpts of the former; the latter is preserved in full).

The very first Syriac medical texts to be edited were the extant fragments from the two treatises of Galen, *On the Properties of Foodstuffs* and the *Art of Medicine*. The age of the codex British Library Add. 17156, its translation techniques and the rendering of scientific vocabulary, suggest that both texts were translated by Sergius of Rēsh'aynā. Although the manuscript at present features just small parts of both of Galen's texts, it is likely that in its original form the codex contained both of them in their complete form. According to a recent study, the Syriac version of Galen's *On the Properties of Foodstuffs* is an accurate translation that displays its translator's creative approach towards the Greek text (Wilkins and Bhayro 2013).

One of the most well-known Syriac medical translations is a version of Hippocrates's *Aphorisms* (Figure 26.1), one of the most essential works in the history of medicine (edition and French translation: Pognon 1903). It has so far received considerably more attention than any other comparable work. The editor of the text, Henri Pognon (who acquired the unique manuscript in Aleppo in 1899) criticised the Syriac translation for being too literal and utterly unsatisfactory from the point of view of standard Syriac grammar, and he therefore assumed that it must have been produced in the earliest, pre-Islamic period of Syriac medicine, and maybe even by Sergius. The opposite opinion was expressed by Rainer Degen, who cautiously argued, based predominantly on indirect evidence, in favour of Ḥunayn's authorship (Degen 1978). It was Degen's opinion that became widely accepted and received additional support (Brock 1993; Overwien 2015). However, fresh in-depth studies have cast grave

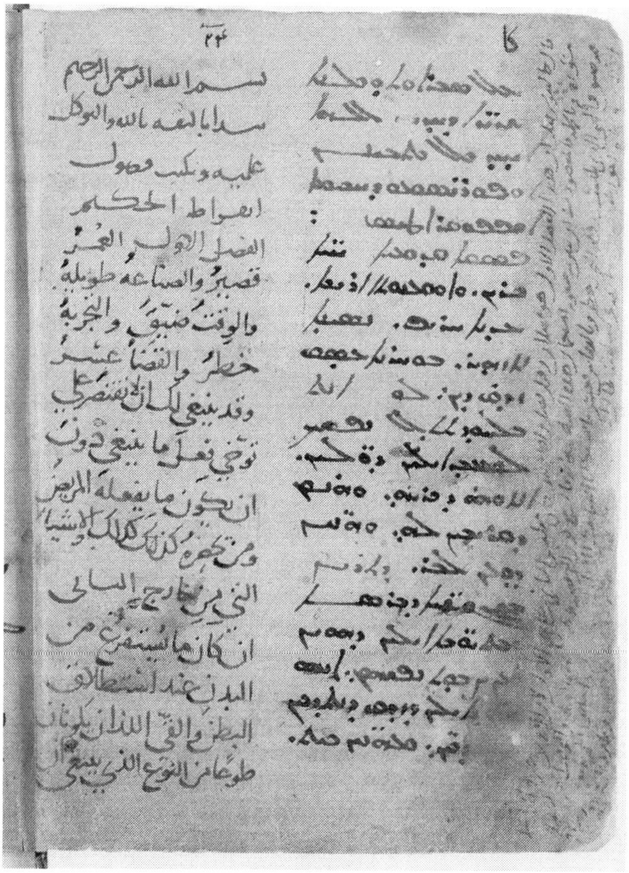

Figure 26.1 The beginning of the Syriac and Arabic versions of Hippocrates's Aphorisms (BNF arabe 6734, fol. 29v., dated 1205)

Source: © Bibliothèque nationale de France

doubt upon this widely accepted conviction and made it possible to dissociate the Syriac version from Ḥunayn, whilst attributing it to an earlier period of Syriac medical scholarship in the eighth century (Mimura 2017a, 2017b; Barry 2018).

Last but not least to be mentioned is the development of translation techniques. A widespread opinion about a customary dichotomy of free versus literal approaches cannot be any longer considered as self-evident. A. McCollum recently advanced a plea for its revision (McCollum 2015).

ORIGINAL WORKS

It is difficult to offer even an estimate of how much of the medical literature composed in Syriac is lost to us. There must have been a plentiful supply of texts, many of which were not merely treatises dealing with particular diseases and other medical issues but comprehensive encyclopaedias and handbooks (among them also revisions and adaptations of earlier works). Just a few treatises have survived in their complete form, whereas we know many more only in fragments. Besides these complete and fragmentary witnesses, another type of evidence for the study of Syriac medicine may be found in the texts belonging to the Islamic medical tradition. Many works originally composed in Syriac were eventually translated into Arabic, and thereby penetrated into Arabic medical treatises (Ullmann 1970: 100–3). Occasionally Syriac texts appear also in Hebrew versions (e.g. Bos and Langermann 2009), but we know next to nothing about that trajectory of the history of Syriac medicine.

A remarkable survivor among the original works is the *Questions on Medicine for Students*, one of the most influential medical treatises of the entire Middle Ages. It was begun by Ḥunayn ibn Isḥāq and completed by his nephew Ḥubaysh, who indubitably stuck to the teaching of his master (even though the larger part of the treatise was written by Ḥubaysh, traditionally it is Ḥunayn who is credited as its author). This work serves as an introduction to medicine and occupied a prominent position thanks to its question-and-answer format, not only in the Islamic world (in its Arabic version), but also in the Latin West (in at least two Latin translations that were made by Constantine the African and Mark of Toledo). The work aims to offer a digest of fundamental aspects of medicine and deals *inter alia* with such subjects as aetiology and symptoms of diseases, therapy, and diet. A number of Syriac manuscripts are extant, the oldest being Vat. sir. 192 (Figure 26.2), which contains the Syriac and Arabic texts in parallel columns and which dates to the beginning of the second millennium of the Common Era. The Syriac text was recently edited (Wilson and Dinkha 2010), although the edition must be used with caution (Kessel 2012c). The availability of the Syriac original easily lends itself to a detailed study of the treatise, particularly its sources and transmission history. It has been revealed that the work heavily depends on the literary output of the late antique Alexandrian medical school (Jacquart and Palmieri 1996). That conclusion needs to be verified based on a thorough source-critical analysis of the treatise. The very nature of a compilation that is based on other sources effectively blurs the line between translation and original work. The same is true for many other texts that cannot be qualified as translations in the strict sense. The loss of most of the primary sources employed (in this case, the Alexandrian medical treatises) makes it all the more difficult to evaluate properly the evidence of some Syriac sources. This point is of utmost significance for students of Greek medicine who are looking for witnesses to particular Greek texts (see, for instance, the valuable observations in Bhayro 2013).

As far as we know, Ḥunayn was eager to produce compilations. In addition to the introductory *Questions on Medicine* and a pharmacological compilation (see below), one further work, very modest in size compared to the other, may go back to Ḥunayn, entitled *Medical Questions Taken from the Works of Galen* (the text remains unedited).

Until now, it has been widely accepted that the largest medical text that has come down to us is the so-called *Syriac Book of Medicines*, discovered and later edited by E.A.W. Budge (Budge 1913). The title given by Budge suggests that what we are dealing with is a single homogeneous treatise. Many scholars have accepted that assumption, perhaps too naively. However, despite the somewhat misleading title, the ancient manuscript (dated by Budge to the twelfth century) found in a private collection in Alkosh, as well as a number of its extant apographs, contain three texts that are not genetically related. The first text deals extensively with therapy according to Galenic

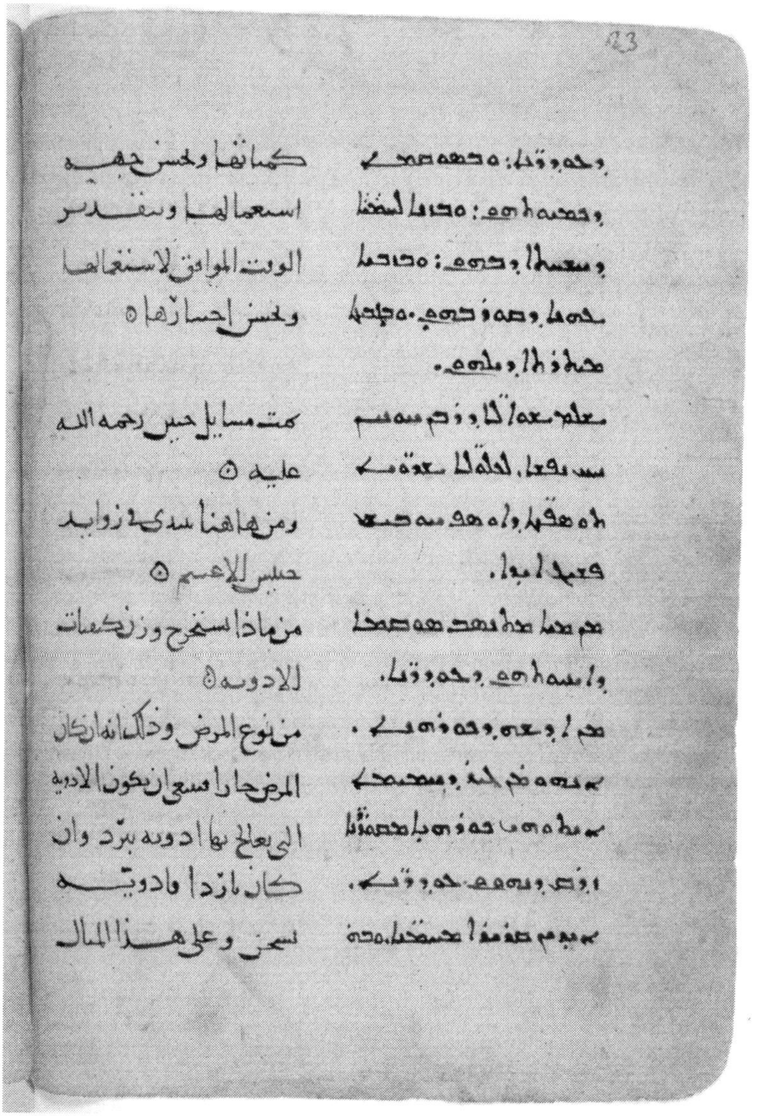

Figure 26.2 Ḥunayn, *Questions on Medicine for Students* (Vat. sir. 192, f.129v). A passage in the middle of the page explains that after Ḥunayn's death the work was continued by Ḥubaysh

Source: © Biblioteca Apostolica Vaticana

medicine and following, in the presentation of diseases, the principle 'from tip to toe'. The second text describes the relationship of the planets and the signs of the zodiac with human health. The third work provides a multitude of recipes, some of which are based on natural properties of certain substances, whereas others rely on their magical power (see also below, under 'Folk-medicine'). There is a widespread opinion among scholars that the texts published by Budge belong to one and the same work. However, since the second (astrological) and third (folk-medicine) texts are attested elsewhere in various forms and combinations, the presumed integrity of Budge's texts requires urgent revision and reconsideration.

As far as the 'Galenic' part is concerned, it has been established that it is essentially a compilation of two of Galen's works, *On the Affected Parts* and *On the Composition of Drugs According to Places in the Body*. However, as Bhayro argues, the compilation was accomplished not through the mechanical combination of different sources but creatively, by means of abridgement, reorganisation of the Hellenistic medical lore, and incorporation of indigenous Mesopotamian medicine (Bhayro 2013, 2015; a fragment edited in Fiori 2017 shows interesting parallels to the *Syriac Book of Medicines*).

Two further substanitial medical texts deserve a mention, although, unlike the texts introduced earlier, they have neither been edited nor studied thoroughly. By a quirk of fate, both manuscripts are damaged and are missing any decisive information about their authors and titles. They are preserved in the patriarchal library of the Syriac Orthodox Church near Damascus.

The older manuscript (Syrian Orthodox Patriarchate 12/25) contains a commentary on book six of the Hippocratic *Epidemics* and hence was called the *Syriac Epidemics* (Kessel 2012a, 2012b). Both in form and content, the *Syriac Epidemics* definitely belongs to the late Alexandrian medical tradition that flourished from the fifth to seventh centuries. Available evidence suggests that during that period, Alexandria boasted a number of scholars whose commentaries shaped the framework of mediaeval medicine in East and West. Although many dozens of texts were produced within that movement, only a handful survived.

Preliminary research demonstrates that the *Syriac Epidemics* is remarkably similar to a source used in the commentary on the sixth book of the Epidemics by John of Alexandria, who is known to us through a number of preserved texts. Since we know that John drew principally on the works of the Alexandrian iatrosophist Gesius, it seems likely that Gesius is also the author of the Greek text that was translated into Syriac. However, there is also reason to think that the *Syriac Epidemics* may be an original text, produced by a Syriac-speaking scholar relying on the commentary of Gesius.

Being produced sometime in eighth-century Persian Khuzistan (the city of Susa is mentioned in the colophon), the manuscript of the *Syriac Epidemics* is a unique document revealing intensive activity in the study of medicine in a region whose actual medical history is shrouded in mystery. Curiously, three Greek words jotted on the final leaf of the manuscript at about the same time as the main text persuasively testify to the spread and persistence of the knowledge of the Greek language in the region up until the eighth century, and thereby call into question the conventional point of view according to which the knowledge of Greek should have died out by that time.

The other Damascus manuscript (Syrian Orthodox Patriarchate 6/1) was copied in 1224 CE in Mosul and contains a medical encyclopaedia that will certainly occupy a prominent position among extant Syriac medical sources. The opening of the manuscript is missing but a preliminary study of the text suggests that it is a medical handbook (*Kunnāshā*) of Īšōʿ bar ʿAlī, a ninth-century physician and student of Ḥunayn ibn Isḥāq (Kessel 2017a). The seven books of the handbook appear to follow the model of Paul of Aegina's *Pragmateia* in both composition and content. The *Kunnāshā* covers all the standard subjects of the medical manuals: regimen and materia medica, symptoms and treatment of diseases (presented mutatis mutandis following the principle 'from tip to toe'), fevers, and poisons. The actual significance of the handbook in the history of Syriac and Arabic medicine is yet to be assessed, but there can be no doubt that it is a pivotal source that documents the development of Syriac medicine over a period of four centuries, at the time when it was establishing a foundation for the nascent science of medicine in Arabic.

Besides the extant witnesses to the Syriac texts, some texts have come down to us in their Arabic versions, and the great majority of those are attested solely as quotations. The œuvre of an East Syriac scholar Yūḥannā ibn Sarābiyūn (9th c.) may serve as a good example of the former. Ibn Sarābiyūn composed a medical compendium (*Kunnāshā*) in seven books which is lost in its Syriac original but does survive in Arabic, Latin, and Hebrew translations. Modelling his encyclopaedia after that of Paul of Aegina, Ibn Sarābiyūn deals with diseases 'from tip to toe', poisons, fevers, and recipes (Pormann 2004a, 2004b).

The *Comprehensive Book* of Abū Bakr Muḥammad ibn Zakarīyā' al-Rāzī (ca. 865–925 or 935) shows that Islamic scholars were well aware of, had access to, and made use of Syriac medical sources (Kahl 2015). In total, al-Rāzī provides citations from seven sources and the vast majority of those derive from the compendium of Yūḥannā ibn Sarābiyūn (194 quotations), a certain Shemʿōn (74 quotations, whose author should not be confused with the seventh-century monastic author Shemʿōn d-Ṭaybūtēh), an unidentified source referred to as 'Hūzāyē' which must have been a medical compendium produced in Khuzistan (228 quotations), a compendium of Ǧūrǧīs ibn Ǧibrīl ibn Bokhtīshūʿ (68 quotations), and to a lesser extent from an unknown medical compendium of Shlēmōn (19 quotations), Job of Edessa's *Book on Urine* (three), and the *Book on Dropsy* by Sergius of Rēshʿaynā (just one quotation). With the exception of the compendium of Yūḥannā ibn Sarābiyūn, none of the works is known to have survived either in Syriac or in Arabic translation. Hence, unquestionably the text of the *Comprehensive Book* must be used (with due caution to his handling of the sources) as an essential witness in the study of Syriac medical literature.

As mentioned earlier, from the ninth century onwards Syriac medical scholars and physicians preferred using Arabic to Syriac. This transformation may be what stands behind the dramatic loss of Syriac medical manuscripts (Watt 2014 argues that it was indeed the principal reason and did not occur because the Syriac versions served only as a utilitarian means for the production of Arabic translations). However, even with the switch to Arabic, there were both authors and readers who were interested in nurturing medical literary production in Syriac. A fine example of this contradictory period is offered by Barhebraeus (d. 1286), a maphrian of the Syrian Orthodox Church, who was not only a polymath and one of the best representatives of the so-called Syriac renaissance, but also a professional physician, who pursued his medical practice, for example, at the famous Nūrī hospital in Damascus and at the Mongol court as one of Hulagu's physicians (Micheau 2008). On the one hand, there is only a slight chance that any of some eight known works of Barhebraeus that deal with medicine was written in Syriac; in general, they pertain to Islamic medicine with little appreciation for original Syriac works (see, for instance, a provisional assessment of the recently discovered commentary on Hippocrates's *Prognostics* in Joosse 2013). These include a partial (reportedly, Barhebraeus died in the course of that work) Syriac translation of the *Canon* of Abū 'Alī Ibn Sīnā; an abridgment of Dioscorides's *On Medical Substances*; a commentary on Hippocrates's *Aphorisms* and *Prognostics*; an abridgment of a pharmaceutical work of al-Ghāfiqī (12th c.); and an epitome of Ḥunayn's *Questions on Medicine* (Takahashi and Yaguchi 2017 clearly show the way in which Barhebraeus produced the abridgments). On the other hand, while working in Syriac on his theological summa, *Candelabrum of the Sanctuary*, Barhebraeus deemed worthy of inclusion special sections dealing with the medicinal properties of plants and stones, as well as the anatomy of the human body. It has been suggested that the ultimate sources that Barhebraeus drew upon might well have been Dioscorides's *On Medical Substances* and Galen's *On the Powers of Simple Drugs* and *On the Utility of the Parts*, although the immediate sources cannot be pinpointed straightforwardly and may vary from the original sources to later compilations (a Pseudo-Aristotelian treatise *On Plants* that was possibly written by Nicolaus of Damascus [first century BCE]) and Islamic encyclopaedic works (for example, the *Eastern Discussions* of Fahkr al-Dīn al-Rāzī [1149–1209]). This case vividly represents the complexity of texts from this period.

FOLK-MEDICINE

Besides scholarly treatises, there is also a tradition of so-called folk-medicine that goes back in some of its parts to incantations from Late Antiquity and even from the Assyrian period (al-Jeloo 2012). The texts contain not only recipes, but also divinations, forecasts, charms, and amulets that were employed to guard against illnesses, demons, the evil eye, and other afflictions (Hunter 2009). They can usually be found either in pocket-sized book form or as a scroll and often bear the title *spar sammānē* (*Book of Medicines*). The contents of each book and scroll is individual, and it is unlikely that they ever had a fixed composition. It seems that, due to their connection with magic, such texts were not approved by the ecclesiastical authorities and most likely were condemned to destruction. However, wherever canonical discipline was less strict, the books of charms seem to have been copied and used rather freely even by priests and monks (in the East Syriac community in Turfan around the ninth–tenth centuries (Maróth 1984), and the East Syriac community in Hakkari region, from eighteenth to early twentieth centuries). Occasionally we find charms among the pharmacological recipes (the most notable example being the Syriac *Book of Medicines* that features an extensive section of more than 200 recipes and amulets). The texts under consideration reflect a blend of different cultures and traditions that were once active in the Mesopotamian region. The tradition of Greek medicine is echoed as well.

MEDICAL THEORY

The system of humoral pathology going back to Hippocrates and Galen but refined and systematised during Late Antiquity formed the backbone of Syriac medicine. In this theory, the body is thought to be made up of four humours: blood, phlegm, yellow bile, and black bile. Each humour was associated with two of the primary qualities (hot, cold, dry, and moist), one of the four seasons, and a mixture (sanguine, phlegmatic, choleric, and melancholic). An excess of the humours was considered harmful and therefore needed to be counterbalanced through diet, or removed through such measures as bloodletting or purging (Pormann and Sagave-Smith 2007).

While highlighting the centrality of the humoural pathology, one should not neglect that as far as the available sources allow us to tell, the Syriac physicians were open and perceptive also to other influences. Particularly, a study of the impact of Persian and Indian medical and pharmacological traditions remains a desideratum (for some observations, see Hawley 2016).

HOSPITALS

Syriac medicine is perhaps most remembered for the fact that twelve members of the Bokhtīshūʿ family served the caliphs as private physicians (from 765 when Ǧūrǧīs ibn Bokhtīshūʿ was summoned to Baghdad to treat Caliph al-Manṣūr, until 1058, when the last representative of the dynasty, ʿUbaydallāh ibn Ǧibrīl ibn Bokhtīshūʿ, died; see fig 26.4). Hailing originally from Gondēshāpūr, the family rose to great prominence in Baghdad and was involved in hospital medicine during ʿAbbāsid times. Older scholarship, relying on the late account of a historian al-Qifṭī (d. 1248), had a conviction that the foundation of the first hospital (the standard Arabic term *bīmāristān* is of Persian origin and appears also in Syriac sources, e.g. in a letter of Timothy I) in Baghdad during the reign of Caliph Hārūn al-Rashīd (786–809) was directly related to the presence of a medical school and a hospital in Gondēshāpūr, founded by Shāpūr I, which was the true oasis of the Greek medical tradition. Although this narrative is now often considered mythical, construed in order to support the Bokhtīshūʿ's primacy, it may still contain some trustworthy elements (Dols 1987; Abele 2008). For example, there must have been a *xenodocheion* (attached to the school, as in Nisibis) that may have accumulated particular authority in medicine before it was transformed into a more substantial institution for the provision of medical care. In general, at least from the seventh century, the Khuzistan region was indisputably an important area for the study of medicine, right up until the early Islamic period with many centres of scholarly and clinical activity. A unique piece of material evidence that comes from the region is the manuscript of the *Syriac Epidemics* (see above) that apparently was produced around the turn of the eighth century for a commissioner residing in Susa.

It ought to be mentioned here that special attention to the study of medicine as it emerged and developed in Khuzistan may have been determined by the strong presence of a Greek-speaking population that had been deported to the area as captives (Jullien 2006). That connection, however, requires further examination.

We hear about Syriac physicians of various denominations (Melkite, Syrian Orthodox, and East Syriac) also from other evidence. Especially well documented is the period of the Crusades (Eddé 1995; Pahlitzsch 2004; Nasrallah 1974). The Latin and Arabic chronicles left many accounts that can be used to reconstruct a network of physicians that traversed state borders during the wars. Moreover, Syriac physicians served as court physicians also for Chinese (Tang dynasty) and Mongol rulers (Shu 2007; Dmitriev 2005).

PHARMACOLOGY

Dioscorides's treatise *On Medical Substances* as well as Galen's *On the Powers of Simple Drugs*, the two chief Greek works on pharmacology, were both available in Syriac, although only the latter has reached us (for a survey see Bhayro and Hawley 2014). Some vestiges of the former in the translation of Ḥunayn are present in the *Lexicon* of

Bar Bahlūl (10th cent.), whereas for the latter we have at our disposal two manuscript witnesses (a study on Aramaic nomenclature of medicinal plants, Löw 1861, is still worth consulting). The one, British Library Add. 14661, contains Sergius of Rēshʿaynā's Syriac translation of books 6–8 of *On the Powers of Simple Drugs*, which provide a catalogue of drugs and their healing properties, and deal with herbs and plants in particular (Figure 26.3). Although the text has not been edited (save for a fragment published in Merx 1885), an ongoing study of the other witness, the so-called Syriac Galen Palimpsest, will hopefully provide us with a long-awaited edition. For the present it is possible to argue that in its original form the Syriac Galen Palimpsest (the original medical manuscript can be dated to the ninth century) may have contained the whole of Galen's treatise, although only about a half of it was re-used in the eleventh century on the Black Mountain near Antioch to produce the liturgical text which constitutes the upper text of the palimpsest (Bhayro, Hawley, Kessel and Pormann 2013; Hawley 2014; Kessel

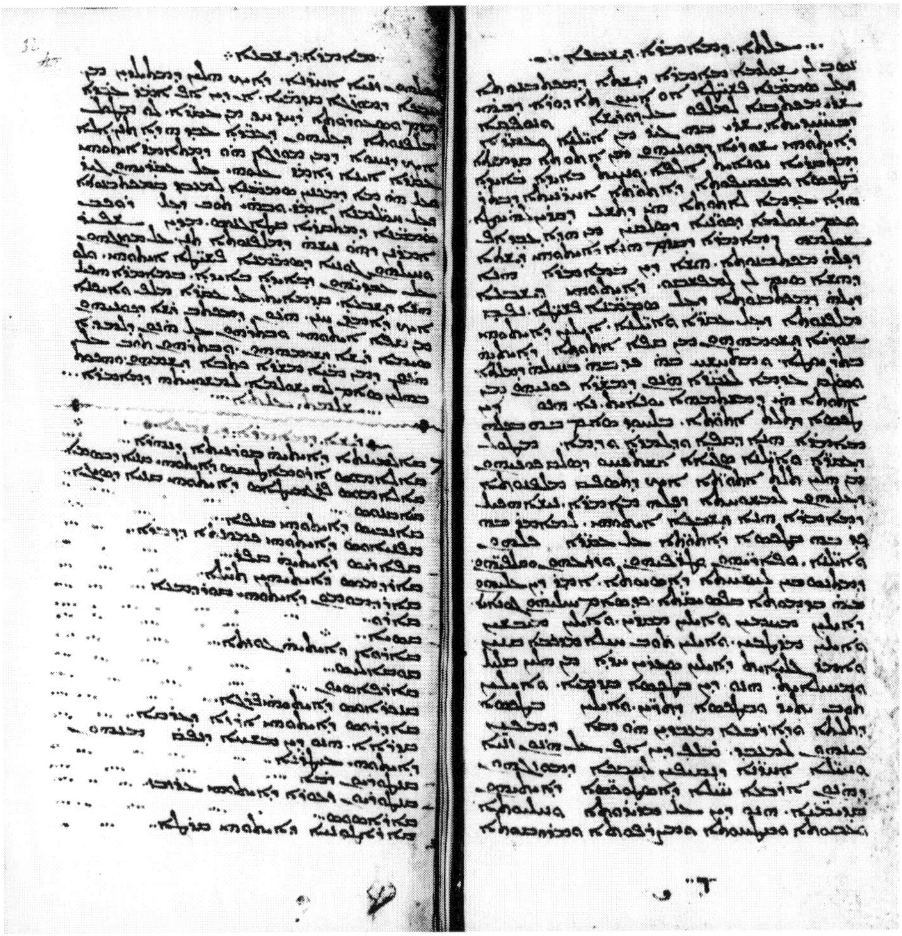

Figure 26.3 Galen, *On Simple Drugs* (BL Add. 14661, f.32v–33r). Final part of book six and the beginning of the list of the drugs treated in book seven

2016a). Those two treatises could have served as resources for the pharmaceutical word lists that are attested both independently and within other works (one such word list was found in the Cairo Geniza: Bhayro 2012, 2014, 2017a; Müller-Kessler 2017).

Many other texts dealing with pharmacology were once available in Syriac and of those only a handful have survived (a ninth-century fragment containing pharmacological recipes was recently edited, Fiori 2017). For example, Ḥunayn's compilation *On the Medicinal Properties of Foodstuffs* proves to be a source of immense significance as its author draws heavily on the works of Dioscorides, Galen, Hippocrates, Rufus of Ephesus, and others (Hawley 2008, 2010). There are also anonymous pharmacopoeia (one of those edited by Budge as a part of the Syriac *Book of Medicines*, on which see above) containing multiple recipes that, as shown by Gignoux, offer unique material into the study of pharmacological nomenclature in Syriac (Gignoux 1998, 1998/99). The lexicon of pharmacological terms compiled by Gignoux 2011 contains some seven hundred entries that reveal connections not only to Greek pharmacological lore but also to the Persian, Arabic, and Sanskrit medical traditions.

IMPACT

It would be too far-fetched to try to assess the full impact of Syriac medicine while most of the sources remain unedited and under-studied. Nevertheless, a few broad strokes may be painted. Its major contribution consists in the transmission of Greek medicine to the East (Dols 1989; for more on the background of the transmission, see Bhayro 2017b). On the one hand, Greek scientific texts were made available in a Semitic idiom through the creation of special scientific vocabulary and translation techniques (Daiber 1986). On the other hand, the open attitudes of Syriac scholars and physicians allowed them to integrate creatively Greek and other (Mesopotamian, Persian, Indian) traditions, to institutionalise the study of medicine (schools), and to organise the distribution of medical care (hospitals, infirmaries).

A broad appreciation towards medicine can easily be traced throughout the entire history of Syriac Christianity, leaving a substantial impact on many aspects of its intellectual culture as well as day-to-day life. One may come across medical allusions, references to medical theories, and a minute knowledge of anatomy and physiology in such unexpected genres as hagiography (e.g. the life of Mar Qardagh, Bruns 2008), poetry (e.g. a poem *Man as Microcosm* by Giwargis Warda, Gignoux 1999), biblical exegesis (Reinink 2003), and monastic theology (Kessel 2011, 2015). Voices occasionally raised against medicine indirectly demonstrate the widespread presence of medical theory and practice within the society and culture (see, for example, what the eighth-century monastic author Joseph Ḥazzāyā has to say on that subject, Kessel 2015: 147).

Fulfilling their missionary goals, Syriac Christians did not fail to transmit Greek medical lore even to such distant lands as China. For instance, there is a New Persian fragment of pharmacological content copied in Syriac script that was found among the Turfan manuscripts (Sims-Williams 2011) as well as Syriac glosses in the description of medicinal plants preserved in the ninth-century *Yǒuyáng Zázǔ* (a Chinese miscellany of legends, accounts, tales, and notes on plants, Santos 2010) and a fragment in Uighur (Zieme 2007; Takahashi 2014). A particularly notable impact was left in Cilician Armenia where the translations of Syriac medical works were carried out (Vardanyan 1982; Vardanian 1999). It remains, however, questionable to what extent

Syriac Christians contributed to the transmission of Greek medicine to other traditions. Thus, although it has been suggested that the transmission of Greek medicine to Persian Iran (as documented in *Dēnkard* and *Bundahishn*) was mediated by Syriac Christians (Delaini 2013), other channels cannot be excluded (see e.g. the case of the presence of Galenic medicine in Tibet, Yoeli-Tlalim 2012).

It is not unusual to find in Islamic medical sources, particularly those dealing with pharmacological nomenclature, references to their Syriac equivalents for the sake of facilitating the identification of particular drugs (Khan 2008; Käs 2010). Likewise, the recipes regularly mention substances employing words of Syriac origin (the proportion, however, of such works is always minute and insignificant).

Finally, the proliferation of medicine among Syriac Christians laid a foundation for the subsequent thriving of medical science in the Islamic milieu. Many medical works were composed by Christians in Arabic and some of those were well known, were widely copied, and reached Europe in Latin translation. A Latin translation of Yūḥannā ibn Sarābiyūn's compendium was earlier mentioned in passing. It is, however, the Latin version of Ḥunayn's *Questions* that dominated the manuals that served as introductions to medicine. Under the title *Isagoge Ioannitii ad Tegni Galieni*, the text was included in the *Articella* (a collection of texts that was used as a basis for medical training) which from around 1250 played a pivotal role within the curriculum of the emerging universities and was widely read and commented upon up until the sixteenth century. Of no less importance was the *Maintenance of Health* of the eleventh-century East Syriac physician and theologian Ibn Buṭlān, a synopsis of hygiene that enjoyed great popularity in Europe where it was known first in Latin translation (*Tacuinus sanitatis*) and later on become available in multiple vernacular versions; the text was also available in an abridged version and was enriched with picturesque illuminations of daily life. The work has a comprehensive character and tries to take into consideration all causes of sickness and health (the so-called six non-natural causes) with their variations, while the bulk of the book deals with foodstuffs.

DESIDERATA

It goes without saying that all the Syriac texts dealing with medicine deserve to be studied and edited. However, any comprehensive plan appears to be premature, as we do not know exactly which texts are extant. Therefore, one of the most urgent tasks is the preparation of a comprehensive inventory of all extant medical works and their manuscript copies. The pioneer contribution of Rainer Degen, who once set out to list all the texts and manuscript witnesses (Degen 1972), is outdated and needs to be revised. There has never been a better moment for compiling such an inventory because, thanks to digitalisation campaigns (for example, the multiple imaging projects run by the Hill Museum & Manuscript Library in different parts of the Middle East), thousands of previously unstudied manuscripts have become available in recent years that had previously been closed off to researchers. The sheer number of manuscripts can, however, be illusory. Among thousands of new manuscripts, texts with secular content are always exceptionally rare (e.g. Kessel 2017b).

The presence of medical texts hidden beneath palimpsests was known to scholars already in the nineteenth century (for example, in the British Library, Add. 14486, 14490 and 17127), but it is only very recently that the development of multi-spectral imaging technologies has begun to be applied to such cultural artefacts. The ongoing 'Syriac Galen Palimpsest Project' will hopefully provide a powerful impetus for the study of other medical palimpsests, the number of which known to us is growing thanks to digitisation projects (a previously unknown pharmacological fragment was recently identified by the author in one palimpsest preserved at the monastery of St Catherine, Sinai).

Another important direction for research is a study of quotations from the Syriac medical sources as found in Arabic medical treatises. Such quotations constitute unique evidence for otherwise lost works. Thus, for example, the Syriac quotations in the *Comprehensive Book* of al-Rāzī have been recently gathered, compiled and translated by Oliver Kahl (2015). Although the authorities al-Rāzī relied upon have long been known, this is the first time that the Syriac as well as the Persian and Sanskrit sources have become conveniently available. Other Arabic medical sources obviously deserve to be explored in a similar way. Additionally, prosopographical evidence about translators preserved in Arabic historiographical works, among which *The Best Accounts of the Classes of Physicians* of Ibn Abī Uṣaibiʿa (d. 1270) is the most prominent, likewise needs to be explored thoroughly and critically (for a survey of the principal translators see Overwien 2014).

Arabic translations often assert that they are based not directly on Greek originals but rather on Syriac intermediaries. Due to a lack of comparative material, scholars usually prefer to remain cautious and to doubt such statements. With more Syriac medical material to hand, it ought to become feasible to clarify the role played by the Syriac translations in the production of the Arabic ones. No small amount of confusion surrounds the so-called *Alexandrian summaries* of Galen's works preserved in Arabic. The question about their origin is not yet settled. And the two main possibilities (either that it was first produced in Greek and then translated into Arabic, or that it was prepared originally in Arabic) have now become entangled with the identified presence of some Syriac elements and parallels (see, for instance, Bos and Langermann 2015).

Next, one cannot achieve any appropriate degree of comprehension of a scientific work unless there is a clear understanding of the specialised vocabulary. Although some lexicographic research on Syriac pharmacological vocabulary has been done (Bhayro 2005; Gignoux 2011), the domains of anatomy, nosology, and therapy lie untapped (see Ford 2002 as a sample of the difficulties that such a study can present).

The proliferation of the medical sciences in the Syriac milieu, as well as the deep appreciation in which they are held by non-specialists, may be traced in texts that do not themselves deal specifically with medical issues (see the studies of alchemical texts in Martelli 2010 and Martelli 2017). In this respect Syriac lexicographic treatises deserve the most urgent attention (see, for instance, a ground-breaking study of the *Lexicon* of Bar Bahlūl in Pormann 2004a and now also Barry 2018).

Based on the research carried out thus far, it is becoming increasingly clear that Syriac medicine cannot be considered in isolation. Rather it is necessary to contextualise it while exploring its relationship to a number of adjacent medical traditions, such as the Alexandrian, Persian, and Islamic. It is through detailed comparative philological, historical, and sociological study that we shall be able to appreciate the actual contribution of generations of Syriac medical scholars and physicians. All in all, the history of Syriac medicine is yet to be written, and we may only guess what a proper study will bring about. What holds true is that the history of Syriac medicine belongs firmly within the more general history of science and medicine, even though a chapter about it can at present only be roughly mapped out.

Figure 26.4 *Book on the Characteristics of Animals* (BL Or. 2784, f.2v). The contents of the breviary derive from the works of pseudo-Aristotle and ʿUbaydallāh ibn Ǧibrīl ibn ʿUbaydallāh ibn Bokhtīshūʿ (d. 1058) who is tentatively to be identified as the individual depicted

Source: © The British Library Board

NOTE

1 The research leading to this article has received funding from the European Research Council under the European Union's Seventh Framework Programme (FP/2007–2013)/ERC Grant Agreement n. 679083 as part of the research project 'Transmission of Classical Scientific and Philosophical Literature from Greek into Syriac and Arabic' (HUNAYNNET), carried out at the Austrian Academy of Sciences.

BIBLIOGRAPHY

Abele, S. 2008. *Der politisch-gesellschaftliche Einfluss der nestorianischen Ärzte am Hofe der Abbasidenkalifen von al-Mansur bis al-Mutawakkil*. Hamburg: Kovač.

al-Jeloo, N. 2012. Kaldāyūthā: The Spar-Sammānė and Late Antique Syriac Astrology. *ARAM* 24, 457–92.

Barry, S. Ch. 2018. *Syriac Medicine and Ḥunayn ibn Isḥāq's Arabic Translation of the Hippocratic 'Aphorisms'*. Journal of Semitic Studies Supplement 39. Oxford: Oxford University Press.

Becker, A. H. 2006. *Fear of God and the Beginning of Wisdom: The School of Nisibis and the Development of Scholastic Culture in Late Antique Mesopotamia*. Philadelphia: University of Pennsylvania Press.

Bergsträsser, G. 1925. *Hunain ibn Ishāq über die syrischen und arabischen Galen-Übersetzungen*. Abhandlungen für die Kunde des Morgenlandes 17.2. Leipzig: Deutsche morgenländische Gesellschaft.

Berti, V. 2009. *Vita e studi di Timoteo I, Patriarca cristiano di Baghdad. Ricerche sull'epistolario e sulle fonti contigue*. Cahiers de Studia Iranica 41. Paris: Association pour l'avancement des études iraniennes.

———. 2013. Providenza, libertà e legame anima-corpo nella lettera 2 di Timoteo I a Rabban Bokhtīšō', archiatra di Hārūn al-Rašīd. *In:* C. Noce et al., ed., *Le vie del sapere in ambito siro-mesopotamico dal III al IX secolo. Atti del convegno internazionale tenuto a Roma nei giorni 12–13 maggio 2011*. OCA 293. Roma: Pontificio Istituto Orientale, 149–75.

———. 2015. *L'au-delà de l'âme et l'en-deça du corps. Morceaux d'anthropologie chrétienne de la mort dans l'Église syro-orientale*. Paradosis 57. Fribourg, Suisse: Academic Press.

Bhayro, S. 2005. Syriac Medical Terminology: Sergius and Galen's Pharmacopia. *Aramaic Studies* 3:2, 147–65.

———. 2012. A Judaeo-Syriac Medical fragment from the Cairo Genizah. *Aramaic Studies* 10:2, 153–72.

———. 2013. The Reception of Galen's Art of Medicine in the Syriac Book of Medicines. *In:* B. Zipser, ed., *Medical Books in the Byzantine World*. Eikasmós, Studi Online 2. Bologna: Pàtron Editore, 123–44.

———. 2014. Remarks on the Genizah Judaeo-Syriac Fragment. *Aramaic Studies* 12:2, 143–53.

———. 2015. Theory and Practice in the Syriac Book of Medicines: The Empirical Basis for the Persistence of Near Eastern Medical Lore. *In*: J. Cale, ed., *In the Wake of the Compendia: Infrastructural Contexts and the Licensing of Empiricism in Ancient and Medieval Mesopotamia*. Berlin: De Gruyter, 147–58.

———. 2017a. The Judaeo-Syriac Medical Fragment from the Cairo Genizah: A New Edition and Analysis. *In:* L. Lehmhaus and M. Martelli, eds., *Collecting Recipes: Byzantine and Jewish Pharmacology in Dialogue*. Science, Technology, and Medicine in Ancient Cultures 4. Berlin: De Gruyter, 273–300.

———. 2017b. On the Problem of Syriac "Influence" in the Transmission of Greek Science to the Arabs: The Cases of Astronomy, Philosophy, and Medicine. *Intellectual History of the Islamicate World* 5:3, 211–27.

Bhayro, S. and R. Hawley. 2014. La littérature botanique et pharmaceutique en langue syriaque. *In*: E. Villey, ed., *Les sciences en syriaque*. Études syriaques 11. Paris: Paul Geuthner, 285–318.

Bhayro, S., R. Hawley, G. Kessel, and P. E. Pormann. 2013. The Syriac Galen Palimpsest: Progress, Prospects and Problems. *JSS* 58:1, 131–48.

Bos, G. and T. Langermann. 2009. The Introduction of Sergius of Rēsh'ainā to Galen's Commentary on Hippocrates' On Nutriment. *JSS* 54:1, 179–204.

Bos, G. and T. Langermann. 2015. *The Alexandrian Summaries of Galen's on Critical Days*. Leiden: Brill.

Brock, S. P. 1993. The Syriac Background to Ḥunayn's Translation Techniques. *ARAM* 3, 139–62. Reprinted, *From Ephrem to Romanos*. Aldershot: Ashgate, ch. XIV.

Bruns, P. 2008. Von Bischöfen, Ärzten und Asketen – Schnittpunkte von Christentum und Medizin im spätantiken Sasanidenreich. *In*: G. Kiraz, ed., *Malphono w-Rabo d-Malphone: Studies in Honor of Sebastian P. Brock*. Gorgias Eastern Christian Studies 3. Piscataway, NJ: Gorgias Press, 29–42.

Budge, E. A. W. 1913. *Syrian Anatomy, Pathology and Therapeutics, or "The Book of Medicines"*. 2 vols. London: Oxford University Press.

Daiber, H. 1986. Semitische Sprachen als Kulturvermittler zwischen Antike und Mittelalter. Stand und Aufgaben der Forschung. *ZDMG* 136, 292–313.

Debié, M. 2014. Sciences et savants syriaques: une histoire multiculturelle. *In*: É. Villey, ed., *Les sciences en syriaque*. Études syriaques 11. Paris: Paul Geuthner, 9–66.

Degen, R. 1972. Ein Corpus Medicorum Syriacorum. *Medizinhistorisches Journal* 7:1–2, 114–22.

———. 1978. Zur syrischen Übersetzung der Aphorismen des Hippokrates. *Oriens Christianus* 62, 36–52.

———. 1981. Galen im Syrischen. Eine Übersicht über die syrische Überlieferung der Werke Galens. *In*: V. Nutton, ed., *Galen: Problems and Prospects*. London: Wellcome Institute for the History of Medecine, 131–66.

Delaini, P. 2013. *Medicina del corpo, medicina dell'anima. La circolazione delle conoscenze medico-filosofiche nell'Iran sasanide*. Indo-Iranica et orientalia 9. Milano: Mimesis.

Dmitriev, S. V. 2005. Samyj vlijatel'nyj xristianin Mongol'skoj imperii: Problemy rekonstrukcii biografii inozemca na mongol'skoj službe. *In*: N. P. Svistunov, ed., *Obščestvo i gosudarstvo v Kitae: XXXV naučnaja konferencija*. Moscow: Vostočnaja literatura, 66–104.

Dols, M. W. 1987. The Origins of the Islamic Hospital: Myth and Reality. *Bulletin for the History of Medicine* 61, 367–90.

———. 1989. Syriac Into Arabic: The Transmission of Greek Medicine. *ARAM* 1:1, 45–52.

Eddé, A.-M. 1995. Les médecins dans la société syrienne du VIIe/XIIIe siècle. *Annales Islamologiques* 29, 91–109.

Fiori, E. 2017. A Hitherto Unknown Medical Fragment in Syriac: Evidence of Recipes and Prescriptions from the Qubbet el-Ḫazne of the Umayyad Mosque in Damascus. *Aramaic Studies* 15:2, 200–29.

Ford, J. N. 2002. Two Syriac Terms Relating to Ophthalmology and Their Cognates. *JSS* 47:1, 23–38.

Freudenthal, G. and R. Glasner. 2014. Patterns of Medieval Translation Movements. *In*: E. Coda and C. M. Bonadeo, ed., *De l'antiquité tardive au Moyen Âge. Études de logique aristotélicienne et de philosophie grecque, syriaque, arabe et latine offertes à Henri Hugonnard-Roche*. Paris: Vrin, 245–52.

Gignoux, Ph. 1998. Le traité syriaque anonyme sur les medications. *In:* R. Lavenant, ed., *Symposium Syriacum VII: Uppsala University, Department of Asian and African Languages, 11–14 August 1996*. OCA 256. Roma: Pontificio Istituto Orientale, 725–33.

———. 1998/99. On the Syriac Pharmocopoeia. *The Harp* 11–12, 193–201.

———. 1999. Un poeme inedit sur l'homme-microcosme de Guiwarguis Wardā (13ème siècle). *In:* Ph. Gignoux, ed., *Ressembler au monde. Nouveaux documents sur la théorie du macro-microcosme dans l'antiquité orientale*. Turnhout: Brepols, 95–189.

———. 2001a. L'apport scientifique des chrétiens syriaques à l'Iran sassanide. *Journal asiatique* 289:2, 217–36.

———. 2001b. Medicina e farmacologia. *In:* S. Petruccioli, ed., *Storia della scienza, IV: Medioevo Rinascimento*. Rome: Istituto della Enciclopedia Italiana, 42–55.

———. 2011. *Lexique des termes de la pharmacopée syriaque*. Cahiers de Studia Iranica 47. Paris: Association pour l'avancement des études iraniennes.

Greatrex, G., C. Horn, and R. Phenix. 2011. *The Chronicle of Pseudo-Zachariah: Church and War in Late Antiquity*. TTH 55. Liverpool: Liverpool University Press.

Gutas, D. 1994. Pre-Plotinian Philosophy in Arabic (Other than Platonism and Aristotelianism): A Review of the Sources. *In*: W. Haase, ed., *ANRW*, Pt II,36.7. Berlin: de Gruyter, 4939–73.

———. 1998. *Greek Thought, Arabic Culture. The Graeco-Arabic Translation Movement in Baghdad and Early ʿAbbāsid Society (2nd–4th / 8th–10th centuries)*. London and New York: Routledge.

Habbi, J. 2001. Textes médicaux grecs en syriaque. *In*: G. Fiaccadori, ed., *Autori classici in lingue del Vicino e Medio Oriente. Atti del VI, VII, e VIII Seminario sul tema "Recupero di testi classici attraverso recezioni in lingue del Vicino e Medio Oriente"*. Roma: Istituto Poligrafico e Zecca dello Stato, 9–23.

Hawley, R. 2008. Preliminary Notes on a Syriac Treatise About the Medicinal Properties of Foodstuffs. *Semitica et Classica* 1, 81–104.

———. 2010. Three Fragments of Antyllus in Syriac Translation. *In:* F. Briquel-Chatonnet and M. Debié, ed., *Sur les pas des Araméens chrétiens. Mélanges offerts à Alain Desreumaux.* Cahiers d'études syriaques 1. Paris: Paul Geuthner, 241–56.

———. 2014. More Identifications of the Syriac Galen Palimpsest. *Semitica et Classica* 7, 237–72.

———. 2016. Words for Plants of Indian Origin in the Syriac Pharmacopoeia. *The Harp* 30, 45–58.

Hugonnard-Roche, H. 1997. Note sur Sergius de Rešʿaina, traducteur du grec en syriaque et commentateur d'Aristote. *In*: G. Endress and R. Kruk, ed., *The Ancient Tradition in Christian and Islamic Hellenism. Studies on the Transmission of Greek Philosophy and Sciences Dedicated to H. J. Drossaart Lulofs on His Ninetieth Birthday*. Leiden: Brill, 121–43.

Hunter, E. C. D. 2009. Magic and Medicine Amongst the Christians of Kurdistan. *In*: E. C. D. Hunter, ed., *The Christian Heritage of Iraq: Collected Papers From the Christianity of Iraq I-V Seminar Days*. Gorgias Eastern Christian Studies 13. Piscataway, NJ: Gorgias Press, 187–202.

Iskandar, A.Z. 1976. An Attempted Reconstruction of the Late Alexandrian Medical Curriculum. *Medical History* 20, 235–58.

Jacquart, D., and N. Palmieri. 1996. La tradition alexandrine des Masāʾil fī ṭ-ṭibb de Ḥunain ibn Isḥāq. *In*: A. Garzya, ed., *Storia e ecdotica dei testi medici greci. Atti del II Convegno Internazionale*. Napoli: M. D'Auria Editore, 217–36.

Jadon, S. Y. 1968. *The Arab Physician Ibn Buṭlān (d. 1066) Medical Manual for the Use of Monks and Country People*. PhD thesis. University of California. Los Angeles.

Joosse, N. P. 2013. A Newly-Discovered Commentary on the Hippocratic Prognostic By Barhebraeus: Its Contents and Its Place Within the Arabic *Taqdimat al-maʿrifa* Tradition. *Oriens* 41:3–4, 499–523.

Jullien, Ch. 2006. La minorité chrétienne "grecque" en terre d'Iran à l'époque sassanide. *In:* R. Gyselen, ed., *Chrétiens en terre d'Iran: Implantation et acculturation*. Cahiers de Studia Iranica 33, Chrétiens en terre d'Iran 1. Paris: Association pour l'avancement des études iraniennes, 105–42.

Kahl, O. 2015. *The Sanskrit, Syriac and Persian Sources in the Comprehensive Book of Rhazes*. Islamic Philosophy, Theology, and Science 93. Leiden: Brill.

Käs, F. 2010. *Die Mineralien in der arabischen Pharmakognosie. Eine Konkordanz zur mineralischen Materia medica der klassischen arabischen Heilmittelkunde nebst überlieferungsgeschichtlichen Studien*. 2 vols. Veröffentlichungen der Orientalischen Kommission, Akademie der Wissenschaften und der Literatur, Mainz 54. Wiesbaden: Harrassowitz.

Kessel, G. 2011. La position de Simon de Taibuteh dans l'éventail de la tradition mystique syriaque. *In:* A. Desreumaux, ed., *Les mystiques syriaques*. Études syriaques 8. Paris: Geuthner, 121–50.

———. 2012a. The Syriac Epidemics and the Problem of Its Identification. *In:* E. P. Pormann, ed., *Epidemics in Context: Greek Commentaries on Hippocrates in the Arabic Tradition*. Scientia Graeco-Arabica 8. Berlin: Walter de Gruyter, 93–117.

———. 2012b. Triseudemon Maximus Noster Sophista. The Evidence of One Syriac Text for the Identification of a Source Used in John of Alexandria's In Epid. VI. *In*: S. Fortuna et al., ed., *Sulla tradizione indiretta dei testi medici greci: i commenti. Atti del IV Seminario internazionale di Siena*. Pisa/Roma: Fabrizio Serra, 123–37.

———. 2012c. Review of Wilson, E. J., and Dinkha, S., Hunain Ibn Ishaq's "Questions on Medicine for Students": Transcription and Translation of the Oldest Extant Syriac Version (Vat. Syr. 192). *Hugoye: Journal of Syriac Studies* 15:2, 367–92.

———. 2015. "Life Is Short, the Art Is Long": An Interpretation of the First Hippocratic Aphorism By an East Syriac Monk in the 7th Century Iraq (Isaac of Nineveh, Kephalaia gnostica 3,62). *Zeitschrift für Antikes Christentum/Journal of Ancient Christianity* 19:1, 137–48.

———. 2016a. Membra disjecta sinaitica I: a reconstitution of the Syriac Galen Palimpsest. *In:* A. Binggeli et al., ed., *Manuscripta Graeca et Orientalia. Mélanges monastiques et patristiques en l'honneur de Paul Géhin*. OLA 243. Leuven: Peeters, 469–96.

———. 2016b. Inventory of Galen's Extant Works in Syriac. *In:* J. C. Lamoreaux, ed., *Ḥunayn Ibn Isḥāq on His Galen Translations*. Eastern Christian Texts 3. Provo: Brigham Young University Press, 168–92.

———. 2017a. A Syriac Medical Kunnāšā of Īšōʿ bar ʿAlī (9th c.): First Soundings. *Intellectual History of the Islamicate World* 5, 228–51.
———. 2017b. Field Notes on Syriac Manuscripts I: Two Medical Manuscripts Digitised By the Hill Museum & Manuscript Library. *Hugoye: Journal of Syriac Studies* 20:2, 419–34.
Khan, G. 2008. The Syriac Words in the Kitāb al-Mustaʿīnī in the Arcadian Library. *In:* Ch. Burnett, ed., *Ibn Baklarish's Book of Simples: Medical Remedies Between Three Faiths in Twelfth-Century Spain*. Studies in the Arcadian Library 3. Oxford: Arcadian Library/ Oxford University Press, 95–104.
Lamoreaux, J. C. 2016. *Ḥunayn Ibn Isḥāq on His Galen Translations*. Eastern Christian Texts, vol. 3. Provo: Brigham Young University Press.
Löw, I. 1861. *Aramæische Pflanzenamen*. Leipzig: W. Engelmann.
Maróth, M. 1984. Ein Fragment eines syrischen pharmazeutischen Rezeptbuches aus Turfan. *Altorientalische Forschungen* 11:1, 115–25.
Martelli, M. 2010. Medicina ed alchimia. 'Estratti galenici' nel corpus degli scritti alchemici siriaci di Zosimo. *Galenos* 4, 207–28.
———. 2017. Hippocrates in Two Syriac Alchemical Collections. *Aramaic Studies* 15:2, 230–51.
McCollum, A. C. 2015. Greek Literature in the Christian East: Translations Into Syriac, Georgian, and Armenian. *Intellectual History of the Islamicate World* 3, 15–65.
Merx, A. 1885. Proben der syrischen Übersetzung von Galenus' Schrift über die einfachen Heilmittel. *ZDMG* 39, 237–305.
Meyerhof, M. 1931. ʿAlī ibn Rabban aṭ-Ṭabarī, ein persischer Arzt des 9. Jahrhunderts n. Chr. *ZDMG* 85, 38–68.
Micheau, F. 2008. Les traités médicaux de Barhebraeus. *PdO* 33, 159–75.
Mimura, T. 2017a. Comparing Interpretative Glosses in the Syriac and Arabic Translations of the Hippocratic 'Aphorisms'. *Aramaic Studies* 15:2, 183–99.
———. 2017b. A Reconsideration of the Authorship of the Syriac Hippocratic Aphorisms: The Creation of the Syro-Arabic Bilingual Manuscript of the Aphorisms in the Tradition of Ḥunayn ibn Isḥāq's Arabic Translation. *Oriens* 45:1–2, 80–104.
Müller-Kessler, C. 2017. A Trilingual Pharmaceutical Lexical List: Greek – Aramaic – Middle Persian. *Le Muséon* 130:1–2, 31–69.
Muraviev, A. 2014, La médecine thérapeutique en syriaque aux IVe-VIIe siècles. *In:* É. Villey, ed., *Les sciences en syriaque*. Études syriaques 11. Paris: Paul Geuthner, 253–84.
Nasrallah, J. 1974. Médecins melchites de l'époque ayyubide. *PdO* 5, 189–200.
Olsson, J. T. 2016. The Reputation of Ḥunayn b. Isḥāq in Contemporaneous and Later Sources. *Journal of Abbasid Studies* 3:1, 29–55.
Overwien, O. 2014. Syriac and Arabic Translators of Hippocratic Texts. *In:* J. Jouanna and M. Zink, ed., *Hippocrate et les hippocratismes: médecine, religion, société, XIVe colloque international hippocratique*. Paris: Académie des Inscriptions et Belles-Lettres, 403–17.
———. 2015. The Paradigmatic Translator and His Method: Ḥunayn ibn Isḥāq's Translation of the Hippocratic 'Aphorisms' From Greek via Syriac Into Arabic. *Intellectual History of the Islamicate World* 3:1–2, 158–87.
Pahlitzsch, J. 2004. Ärzte ohne Grenzen: Melkitische, jüdische und samaritanische Ärzte in Ägypten und Syrien zur Zeit der Kreuzzüge. *In:* F. Steger and K. P. Jankrift, ed., *Gesundheit – Krankheit. Kulturtransfer medizinischen Wissens von der Spätantike bis in die Frühe Neuzeit*. Beihefte zum Archiv für Kulturgeschichte 55. Köln, Weimar and Wien: Böhlau, 101–19.
Pognon, H. 1903. *Une version syriaque des aphorismes d'Hippocrate*. Leipzig: J.C. Hinrichs.
Pormann, P. E. 2004a. *The Oriental Tradition of Paul of Aegina's Pragmateia*. Studies in Ancient Medicine 29. Leiden: Brill.
Pormann, P. E. 2004b. Yūḥannā Ibn Sarābiyūn: Further Studies Into the Transmission of His Works. *Arabic Sciences and Philosophy* 14, 233–62.
———. 2012. The Development of Translation Techniques From Greek Into Syriac and Arabic: The Case of Galen's on the Faculties and Powers of Simple Drugs, Book Six. *In:* R.

Hansberger et al., ed., *Medieval Arabic Thought: Essays in Honour of Fritz Zimmermann.* Warburg Institute Studies and Texts 4. London: Warburg Institute, 143–62.
Pormann, P. E. and E. Savage-Smith. 2007. *Medieval Islamic Medicine.* Edinburgh: Edinburgh University Press.
Reinink, G. J. 2003. Theology and Medicine in Jundishapur: Cultural Changes in the Nestorian School Tradition. *In:* A. A. MacDonald et al., ed., *Learned Antiquity: Scholarship and Society in the Near-East, the Greco-Roman World, and the Early Medieval West.* Groningen Studies in Cultural Change 5. Leuven: Peeters, 163–74.
Sachau, E. 1870. *Inedita syriaca: Eine Sammlung syrischer Übersetzungen von Schriften griechischer Profanliteratur.* Wien: Staatsdruckerei.
Santos, D. M. 2010. A Note on the Syriac and Persian Sources of the Pharmacological Section of the Yǒuyáng zázǔ. *Collectanea Christiana Orientalia* 7, 217–29.
Schleifer, J. 1926, 1927, 1928. Zum syrischen Medizinbuch. *Zeitschrift für Semitistik und verwandte Gebiete* 4, 70–122, 161–95; 5, 195–237; 6, 154–77, 275–99.
———. 1940, 1941–43, 1946. Zum syrischen Medizinbuch, II: Der therapeutische Teil. *RSO* 18, 341–72; 20, 1–32, 162–210, 383–98; 21, 157–82.
Shu, Sh. 2007. Nestoriane v Kitae – vrachi Chong Yi i Qin Ming-he. *Pismennye pamjatniki Vostoka* 1 [6], 148–50.
Siggel, A. 1950. *Die indischen Bücher aus dem Paradies der Weisheit über die Medizin des ʿAlī ibn Sahl Rabban aṭ-Ṭabarī.* Abhandlungen der Geistes- und Sozial Wissenschaftlichen Klasse, Jahrgang 1950, Nr. 14. Wiesbaden: Verlag der Akademie der Wissenschaften und der Literatur in Mainz.
Sims-Williams, N. 2011. Early New Persian in Syriac Script: Two Texts From Turfan. *Bulletin of the School of Oriental and African Studies* 74:3, 353–74.
Strohmaier, G. 1994. Der syrische und der arabische Galen. *ANRW* II.37.2, 1987–2017.
———. 1998. Medicine in the Byzantine and Arab World. *In:* M. D. Grmek, ed., *Western Medical Thought from Antiquity to the Middle Ages.* Cambridge, MA: Harvard University Press, 139–69.
Takahashi, H. 2014. Syriac as a Vehicle for Transmission of Knowledge Across Borders of Empires. *Horizons* 5:1, 29–52.
Takahashi, H. and N. Yaguchi. 2017. On the Medical Works of Barhebraeus. With a Description of the Abridgement of Ḥunain's 'Medical Questions'. *Aramaic Studies* 15:2, 252–76.
Ullmann, M. 1970. *Die Medizin im Islam.* Handbuch der Orientalistik, Abteilung I: Nahe und der Mittlere Osten, 6.1. Leiden: E.J. Brill.
Vardanyan, S. A. 1982. Ancient Armenian Translations of the Works of Syrian Physicians. *Revue des études arméniennes* NS 16, 213–19.
Vardanian, S. A. 1999. Medieval Armenian Medicine and Its Relations to Greek and Arabic Medicine. *In:* J. A. C. Greppin et al., ed., *The Diffusion of Greco-Roman Medicine Into the Middle East and the Caucasus.* Delmar and New York: Caravan Books, 199–210.
Watt, J. W. 2014. The Syriac Translations of Ḥunayn ibn Isḥāq and Their Precursors. *In:* M. Tamcke and S. Grebenstein, ed., *Geschichte, Theologie und Kultur des syrischen Christentums: Beiträge zum 7. Deutschen Syrologie-Symposium in Göttingen, Dezember 2011.* Göttinger Orientforschungen, I. Reihe: Syriaca 46. Wiesbaden: Harrassowitz, 423–45.
Wilkins, J. and S. Bhayro. 2013. The Greek and Syriac Traditions of Galen, De alimentorum facultatibus. *Galenos* 7, 95–114.
Wilson, E. J. and S. Dinkha. 2010. *Hunain Ibn Ishaq's "Questions on Medicine for Students": Transcription and Translation of the Oldest Extant Syriac Version (Vat. Syr. 192).* Studi e Testi 459. Roma: Biblioteca Apostolica Vaticana.
Yoeli-Tlalim, R. 2012. Revisiting 'Galen in Tibet'. *Medical History* 56, 355–65.
Zieme, P. 2007. Notes on Uighur Medicine, Especially on the Uighur Siddhasāra Tradition. *Asian Medicine* 3, 308–22.
Zonta, M. 1991. Nemesiana Syriaca: New Fragments From the Missing Syriac Version of the De Natura Hominis. *JSS* 36, 223–58.

CHAPTER TWENTY-SEVEN

THE MATERIAL CULTURE OF THE SYRIAN PEOPLES IN LATE ANTIQUITY AND THE EVIDENCE FOR SYRIAN WALL PAINTINGS

Emma Loosley

THE STATE OF RESEARCH IN THE FIELD

Over the later part of the twentieth and the beginning of the twenty-first centuries, there has been a major re-evaluation of the art and architecture of the Syriac-speaking world as archaeologists have uncovered new monuments that have caused a radical re-interpretation of the traditional assumption that the two Syriac church traditions, those of the Church of the East and the Syrian Orthodox Church, were largely aniconic. This is not only because more material has become available to us, but also because there has been a more nuanced understanding and interpretation of the relationship between the different church denominations in the Middle East. As Horn and Hunter wrote recently:

> distinct architectural traditions of the Diophysite Church of the East and the Monophysite Syrian Orthodox Church have emerged, complementing the theological and paleographic hallmarks that differentiated these branches of Syriac Christianity. . . . the discovery of decorated stucco-work and plastic arts has shed light on the decoration of churches, placing them within the larger context of Sasanian decorative arts and also challenging the so-called aniconic nature of the Church of the East.
>
> (Horn and Hunter 2012: 1111)

Perhaps in reaction to these changing perceptions, there has been a growth in the study of the material culture of the Late Antique Syrian peoples over the last few decades. Yet there remains a great deal of work to be done in this field. There is still no comprehensive overview of the subject and anyone seeking to study the issues further must either make use of medium-specific studies (Balty 1977; Donceel-Voûte 1988; Piccirillo 1993), books that include the material culture relating to a thematic issue (e.g. Trzionka 2007, which uses textual sources along with the evidence provided by material culture, represented largely in this case by amulets, medals, and other items of personal adornment, to reconstruct beliefs relating to the world of the supernatural in Late Antique Syria), or else rely on a variety of articles to build up a picture of the wider context. The one exception to this situation relates to the architectural record, in particular studies on the evolution of Syrian ecclesiastical architecture which has been, and continues to be, relatively well served both by survey volumes relating to particular countries (Krautheimer and Ćurčić 1992; Peña 1997) or regions (Tchalenko 1953) and by a number of site-specific monographs and articles. However even in this last category, notably in the work of Krautheimer and Ćurčić (1992), Syria is often pushed to the margins and seen as a provincial relation when compared to the artistic innovations being introduced in Rome and Constantinople.

ESTABLISHING THE RATIONALE FOR THE ESTABLISHMENT OF 'SYRIAN ART HISTORY' AND THE PARAMETERS OF RESEARCH

Therefore, it is the intention of this chapter to make the case for more study into Syrian art and architecture as a distinct category of material culture that deserves to be understood and studied on its own terms rather than being relegated, as it so often is, to a fringe subject on the outer edges of Byzantine material culture. If we are to argue for the originality and distinctiveness of a Syrian form of artistic expression, then it is necessary to look for the earliest evidence of this type of art. Perhaps surprisingly for a visual culture that is so strongly tied to a Christian identity, the roots of Syrian art in the sense of an artistic tradition linked to a cultural movement based around Syriac language and ethnicity began in the first three centuries of the Christian era but were explicitly pagan in origin.

The first artefacts that can be placed in this category are a series of funerary mosaics that first came to wider attention in the mid-twentieth century and were published by Segal in his seminal study on the city of Edessa (Segal 1970). By the time that Segal published his book, a number of these mosaics had already been destroyed or stolen and were only known through surviving line drawings, making it difficult to quantify how many of these mosaics had been discovered in all. This situation remained the same throughout the latter part of the century and gained wider attention when the Dallas Museum of Art purchased a mosaic of Orpheus at a Christie's auction in 1999 (Figure 3.4).[1] A study by John Healey (2006) of the inscription on the mosaic was instrumental in tying it to Edessa and strengthening the legal argument for its return to Turkey. This case therefore highlights the necessity of developing the study of Syrian art; in this instance, a relative dearth of art historical articles on Edessene mosaics meant that the arguments for the Edessene provenance of the artefact rested on palaeographic analysis rather than on an art historical evaluation.[2]

The current state of research into this genre has thus far produced articles concentrating on a single mosaic or provided a brief overview of a topic such as funerary imagery, but we still await a comprehensive monograph on the subject that attempts to place this imagery firmly within the wider regional context and identify how Eastern influences such as the art of Palmyra and the Sasanian Empire have been blended with the Graeco-Roman imagery known to us from Antioch. Perhaps most significantly for the study of Edessene art, we need to research how these mosaics relate to contemporary evidence from Zeugma, which was only approximately 100 km away from Edessa and yet worked in a style that placed the city firmly within a Hellenised rather than a Semitic context.

The relationship between the early Syriac-speaking world and its Greek-speaking neighbours is further complicated by the fact that in 2000, Balty and Briquel Chatonnet published six panels with Greek mythological scenes that were clearly executed in the Edessene idiom and possessed estrangela inscriptions that further tied the panels to Edessa as their place of origin. Four of these panels now reside in the Bible Lands Museum in Jerusalem and two are in private collections. Five of the panels, including all four in Jerusalem, depict episodes and characters relating to the Trojan epic. The sixth panel has a more complex Promethean theme, which is the subject of an article by Bowersock (2001). All six panels have been dated on stylistic and epigraphic grounds by Balty and Briquel Chatonnet to the third century. They remain an intriguing addition to the canon of Syrian art as they show that there was a clear knowledge of Greek literature and mythology in Edessa but that by the first centuries CE, there was already a movement towards a distinct 'Syrian' or 'Syriac' visual culture that was beginning to spread in regions where Syriac was the vernacular language.

Therefore, although Syrian art in the sense of a visual culture tied to the Syriac-speaking peoples is normally interpreted as a wholly Christian phenomenon, it is important to note that a distinctively Syrian idiom evolved in parallel with the written language, and that these mosaics can be viewed on many levels as the visual accompaniment to the inscriptions catalogued by Drijvers and Healey (1999). Having developed in the first three centuries CE in Edessa and its environs, this Syrian form of art spread to the south and east to Syria and Mesopotamia, where it blended elements of the Hellenistic visual repertoire with the Persian and Semitic currents found in the Sasanian Empire and regional centres of influence such as Palmyra. This rapidly evolving form of art utilised a formal and stylised representation of figures that was generally more static and less fluid than the Hellenised images found at sites like Antioch and Zeugma. The front-facing poses and rigid placement of many of the figures perhaps more closely resembles the funerary portraits of Palmyra than any other regional culture, which seems unsurprising given that the two city-states flourished in the first three centuries CE and both spoke Aramaic dialects, giving them a shared Aramaic and Syro-Mesopotamian origin and wider cultural milieu.

These cultural interactions took place not only in different fields of art but also in the evolution of regional architecture. Just as the first- to third-century mosaics originating in Edessa showed figures in clothes, headdresses, and jewellery that are closely comparable with the attire and personal adornments carved on the funerary busts of Palmyra (Figure 27.1), so on the southern edges of Edessa the fifth-century monastery of Dayr Yakub was built around a Palmyrene-style tomb tower. The tower's pagan funerary inscription was left *in situ* as a substantial monastic cloister was built around it with locally quarried limestone in an architectural style akin to that of the monasteries on the Syrian limestone massif to the south. However, it must not be forgotten that Syrian art and architecture evolved in the marginal space left between two great world empires and therefore developed in a symbiotic relationship with the visual languages of the Hellenistic and Persian worlds, adopting and discarding their motifs as expedient in their pursuit of a Syrian visual identity.

Figure 27.1 Edessene funerary mosaic, Şanliurfa Museum, Turkey

Source: Author

THE FIFTH AND SIXTH CENTURIES: SYRIAN CULTURE AT THE CROSSROADS

As outlined above, the geographical location of the Syrian world meant that influences affected its material culture in a variety of ways. However, it was in the sixth century, as the consequences of the Council of Chalcedon began to crystallise, that adopting a distinctively Syrian artistic idiom amounted to a statement of religious identity (and by extension a declaration of political intent) for the first time. In the earlier centuries of the Common Era, Syrian art denoted a certain ethnicity and, perhaps, an allegiance to a local ruler or ancestral gods. The theological controversies of the fifth century meant that by the sixth century, the political and religious landscape had changed dramatically, and architectural and artistic choices could be taken to indicate a particular theological worldview in some quarters; specifically for Syrians it identified a patron as a partisan of the Chalcedonian or anti-Chalcedonian camps. This can perhaps be most clearly articulated in visual terms by two radically different artistic styles linked to sixth-century Edessa.

The famous Rabbula Gospels now residing in the Bibiliotheca Laurenziana in Florence (Figure 27.2) have been the source of some dispute, as a colophon dated 586 links them to the monastery of Beth Mar Yohannon of Beth Zagba. This monastery has never been comprehensively identified and could have been anywhere in Syria or Mesopotamia, although at least one scholar links it to Edessene scribes (Mundell Mango 1983). The famous image of Christ crucified between the two thieves wearing a long *colobium* and flanked in the sky above by solar and lunar imagery demonstrates a different iconographic tradition to the imperial and courtly styles that were increasingly dominating the Christian imagery of Rome and Constantinople. The careful framing of the scene with two high mountains towering above the crosses of the thieves flanking Christ creates a valley that is broken in the pictorial field by the

Figure 27.2 Crucifixion from the Rabbula gospels. From Cod Pluteus I, 56, fol.13r

Source: Courtesy of the Biblioteca Medicea Laurenziana, Firenze

taller cross of Christ himself. In the gaps between His head and the mountains, we have the sun to His right and a crescent moon to His left. Whilst the conflation of solar imagery with imperial propaganda and its adoption into Christian iconography is well known and has been widely discussed, particularly in relation to the imagery of Constantine (e.g. Bardill 2012: 335), most of the discussion has related to the Romanised Sol and Luna cults, whereas here the imagery presented in the Rabbula Gospels is closer to that of the Palmyrene triads of Bel with Aglibol (moon) and Iarhibol (sun) or Baalshamin with Aglibol (moon) and Malakbel (sun) (Dirven 1999: 164), or that of the cult of the moon-god Sin in Ḥarran. The conflation of a fiery halo with a crescent moon at Palmyra seems to be a much closer influence on the Rabbula image than the representations of Helios driving his chariot known from synagogue pavements in the Holy Land.

Unfortunately, the comparative scarcity of any extant imagery securely dated to the fifth and sixth centuries makes it difficult to come to any firm conclusions about Syrian art and religious iconography during this period. As with the earlier centuries discussed above, the largest body of visual material still extant comprises mosaic pavements, as this was the most durable art form and therefore remains the medium most likely to survive. Across the region, a large number of floor mosaics have survived and a high proportion of these come from churches. However, this does not tell us a great deal about Christian imagery, as there was a tradition of paving ecclesiastical floors with secular or pagan scenes, as it was not acceptable for the faithful to tread on sacred figures. Although many of these mosaics followed the classical tradition and were heavily influenced by the artistic traditions of the later Roman Empire, in Syria we see elements of vernacular culture emerging in the more stylised representation of figures and animals. In some cases, inscriptions utilise Syriac rather than Greek, as in the mosaic from Umm Ḥartin now in the Museum of Ma'arrat Nu'man (Shehade 1997) and the martyrium of St John discovered at Nabgha in the vicinity of Jarablus (Sabbagh et al. 2008). Intriguingly, despite its early prominence in Syriac culture, Edessa was thought not to have any mosaics from this period until the discovery of a presumed sixth-century villa in the Haleplibahçe area of the city in 2006 (Karabulut et al. 2011). The 'Villa of the Amazons', as the site has been named by archaeologists, reprises Homeric themes as with the third-century panels mentioned above. However, as the name suggests, the most complete and striking chamber is that depicting four Amazonian queens hunting wild animals (Figure 27.3). In other rooms, motifs include wild animals, water fowl, a young black man leading a zebra, and a personification of *Ktisis* (Foundation or Creation). Although different levels of skill are clearly displayed in the work, with the Amazonian mosaic demonstrating the highest level of both design and execution, what is unusual is that stylistically the nearest comparison with these mosaics are the floors still extant at the Great Palace

Figure 27.3 Amazonian Queen, Villa of the Amazons, Şanliurfa, Turkey

Source: Author

in Constantinople. The style closely echoes the art of the Imperial Court (Jobst et al. 1997) and therefore, despite its location, we cannot place the Haleplibahçe mosaics within the contexts of 'Syrian' art, despite the location in which they were discovered as, in this case, it seems clear that artisans were transported from elsewhere to Mesopotamia to undertake this commission probably at the behest of a senior Byzantine administrator or military figure.

This means that we must view the borders of Syrian art as being fluid and ever changing, as well as being permeable, so that it is possible to find other forms of visual culture such as Byzantine or Persian art co-existing alongside more native and vernacular visual expression.

The last category of Syrian art to be considered in this period raises the same questions about cultural interactions and the definition of a 'Syrian' form of iconography and stylistic development. This is the corpus of metal objects that have survived and that are now in major museums or private collections. Because of their intrinsically valuable nature as well as their portability, it is even more difficult to answer questions relating to the production and market for these items than it is with other easily moveable items such as manuscripts. Obviously this is not the place to rehearse all the arguments relating to Syrian silver and bronze objects, and so we shall content ourselves with a single example that highlights some of the difficulties in defining what is meant by 'Syrian art' in this period.

Throughout the twentieth century, there has been a sporadic debate into the provenance of a group of bronze thuribles that the academic literature refers to as 'Syrian' censers. These objects first came to Western notice when a small number of them were brought back to Europe by travellers in the Near East and Asia Minor. In actual fact, only one of these thuribles has ever been conclusively provenanced as coming from a Syrian location, and others bought by travellers in eastern Asia Minor often have only vague information as to where exactly they were acquired. The censer known to have been acquired in Syria is now in the British Museum in London, having been sold to them by Sir Richard Francis Burton in the nineteenth century. Whilst the find spot of an archaeological artefact can never be taken as indicating the place of manufacture of that object, there still can be an argument made that – given the discovery of a number of hoards of Syrian liturgical objects ranging in date from the sixth- to seventh-century Kaper Koraon treasure (the name given to a haul of four different collections of silver objects) in the early twentieth century to the 1982 discovery of Crusader-era silver liturgical objects at Reșafa – if they were Syrian in origin, one would expect to find more traces of them in the contemporary Syrian archaeological record. In fact, recent research suggests[3] that the thuribles have been found in the largest numbers in the Caucasus (both Georgia and Armenia) with other clusters in Eastern Asia Minor and the Holy Land. This would suggest either a more northerly origin for the objects or else that they were items manufactured for export by pilgrims to the Holy Land.

Whatever the case, the portable nature and intrinsic value of metal objects meant that they had a value as items of exchange throughout their existence and this means that the question of defining a 'Syrian' form of metalwork in this period has yet to be explored in any meaningful manner. However, if, as argued above, there is a case for a distinct Syrian school of art in other media and bearing in mind the much-prized nature of Damascene metalwork throughout history, this is a question that deserves further exploration.

BEYOND THE ORIGINS OF SYRIAN ART: THE SYRIAN TRADITION OF WALL PAINTING

In 2009, Mat Immerzeel published *Identity Puzzles: Mediaeval Christian Art in Syria and Lebanon* and attempted to shed light on the complex issue of how, or if it is even possible, to attribute a doctrinal identity to the mediaeval frescoes and icons of Syria and Lebanon. This was followed a year later by Bas Snelders's work on the Syrian Orthodox art of mediaeval Mosul (Snelders 2010). Both books were related to a wider research project looking at issues of Syrian Orthodox identity. They clearly highlighted the difficulties of scholars working in the field; in Lebanon, it is extremely difficult to identify the confessional identity of the artists or their patrons in a wide variety of cases. In Syria, it is easier to find a record of which denomination occupied a site in the Middle Ages, but information concerning the artisans who undertook the commissions is lacking. In the Mosul region, there is a reasonable amount of manuscript and sculptural evidence, but very little remains in the way of fresco paintings.

In a chapter of this length, there is not room to fully address the issues relating to questions about the confessional identity of the artisans. Therefore, what follows will be a discussion of the only two complete cycles of wall paintings still extant in the Syrian world. They will be briefly contextualised before their content is considered and further avenues for research are highlighted. One of the cycles is well known and has been published in the past, whereas the other remains largely unpublished and, aside from local people, is familiar only to a small group of specialists. Therefore, we will proceed chronologically and from the known to the unknown in this brief overview of Syrian visual art.

The monastery of Mar Musa al-Habashi, Nebek

In 1992, Erica Dodd published the first article on the mediaeval frescoes of the monastery of Mar Musa al-Habashi (St Moses the Abyssinian or Ethiopian) east of Nebek in the Qalamoun region of Syria (Dodd 1992, 2001).[4] The site had been abandoned in the early nineteenth century and, although widely known amongst the local community and academics in Syria and Lebanon, had not been extensively studied. In part, this neglect can be attributed to the Eurocentric disdain for Byzantine culture most famously typified by the work of Gibbon's *Decline and Fall*. This tradition of viewing Byzantine or oriental Christian art as inferior is illustrated by the reaction of Sir Richard Francis Burton, who on visiting Deir[5] Mar Musa in 1870 referred to the frescoes as 'the vilest of daubs' (Burton and Drake 1872: 274). When Byzantine art became a more popular area of study again in the twentieth century, Deir Mar Musa was still largely ignored, as the cycle was viewed as a vernacular art form that derived from a Byzantine source, rather than being studied as an expression of Syrian visual culture. Even today, the frescoes are most often viewed as a regional variant of Byzantine art and compared to the frescoes of Cappadocia (for example), rather than being viewed as a purely Syrian phenomenon (e.g. Westphalen 2007: 106). Whilst it is absolutely correct to evaluate the cycle within its wider contextual framework as a series of paintings that were created in a Muslim-majority society where the Christian population had strong cultural affinities with the cultural traditions of the Byzantine Empire, this is also to relegate Deir Mar Musa to the level of a provincial curiosity rather than seeing the frescoes as the sole surviving representative of mediaeval Syrian wall painting. Although we have fragments of other cycles with which to contextualise the images within the wider region, notably the surviving paintings in nearby Qara, fragments from Homs and Ma'arrat Saydnaya and the Crusader imagery still extant from the castles of Krak des Chevaliers and Marqab, it should be underlined that these examples are linked to the Rum Orthodox and Catholic traditions. Issues of how artisans may or may not have worked across confessional boundaries are complex and difficult to unravel and must therefore be left aside for the purposes of this chapter.

When viewed in this way, questions relating to the naivety and simplicity of some of the images can instead be seen as elements of a different visual language that reflected the non-Chalcedonian doctrinal beliefs of the monks who inhabited the monastery. As there is little space to devote to the scheme, the following discussion will concentrate mainly on the west wall of the chapel. This also means that the analysis below will only consider the topmost layer of the three superimposed schemes in the chapel. This uppermost level can be clearly dated by a painted inscription to 1208–1209 and therefore we can be specific in stating that we are dealing with an early thirteenth-century decorative scheme (Den Heijer et al. 2007: 167).

The west wall is the most complete section of the cycle still extant and is also a clear statement of oriental Orthodox belief. In brief, the scheme has saints on the pillars that support the north and south arcades of the nave, with the four evangelists in the four spandrels above the pillars and martyr saints riding to the east on the walls above. In the east is a small semi-domed apse with the Virgin and Christ Emmanuel in the centre, flanked by the fathers of the church on the curve of the apse, but the scene in the semi-dome has been lost. Above, Christ dominates the east wall, flanked by the apostles, and above them, on either side of a small window, are the remnants of an Annunciation scene, which was largely looted in the 1980s. There are isolated scenes in the north and south aisles, but lack of space means that there is no room to discuss them here, except to note the baptism of Christ at the east end of the northern aisle flanked by an image of Symeon Stylites and an angel.

Returning to the west wall, the viewer is confronted with a scene of the Last Judgment that dominates the small chapel (Figure 27.4). On the left as the viewer faces the image are the elect and on the right are the damned. Between these two categories are angels holding the scales of justice, and there are angels and demons on their respective sides of the scene waiting to receive the souls allocated to them. Above the scales in the centre of the scene are Adam and Eve, who have the *Hetoimasia* and the instruments of the Passion above them. At the very top of the wall, angels flank a window and beneath them the apostles are divided on either side of the *Hetoimasia*. The background of the wall is predominantly blue, but beneath the feet of the right-hand apostles, it turns a russet red to visually evoke hell and damnation. On the left (blue) side we have the three patriarchs (Abraham, Isaac, Jacob) and the Virgin each cradling a trayful of heads representing the souls of the saved.[6] Beneath the patriarchs, groups of figures are clustered together, and these figures are clearly labelled as saints and other biblical figures such as King David. On the lowest level, the confessional identity of the church becomes abundantly clear. Beside an angel receiving the scales of the just, St Peter stands before a pink brick wall holding the keys of heaven. Behind the wall stand haloed figures carrying small crosses and each figure, both male and

Figure 27.4 The Last Judgement, west wall, Deir Mar Musa al-Habashi, Nebek, Syria

Source: Author

female, wears the distinctive hood bearing thirteen crosses still worn today by Syrian Orthodox (and Coptic) monks and nuns. Therefore, the image sends a clear message that only the non-Chalcedonians are assured of entering Paradise.

On the other side, in stark contrast, sinners are arranged in a perceived order of transgression. The lowest level, against a background of pink rock which is the floor for the elect, shows naked sinners tormented by snake-like forms that demonstrate punishment for the sins of the flesh. Above, swaddled figures with only their heads uncovered are pictured beside symbols highlighting their faults – a sword for violence, money for usury or theft, and so on. In the red zone, we have what are clearly meant to be foreign priests with exotic headgear who could represent Jews or Zoroastrians and other beliefs. Above them, Muslim imams are clearly identified by their robes and turbans. Finally, the highest rung of hell is reserved for Christian clergy who are obviously intended to represent the Chalcedonian churches and their erroneous doctrine. In short, it is immediately obvious to a viewer acquainted with the dress of Syrian clergy that this wall is a statement of the orthodoxy of Syrian Orthodox non-Chalcedonian Christology, and the image makes a strong assertion that the consequences of theological error lead to damnation. If such a worldview is still so readily recognisable to a contemporary audience, we can be sure that the impact of the message was still more forceful at the time that the paintings were executed and these doctrinal beliefs and conflicts played a more significant part in the lives of mediaeval Christians. Bearing this in mind, it seems incorrect to place this scheme under the wider umbrella of 'Byzantine Art'; instead, it would appear more appropriate to use Deir Mar Musa as a starting point for developing our understanding of mediaeval Syrian visual culture as a distinct indigenous form of artistic expression.

In turn this leads on to our next example, which lies around 35 km north-west of Deir Mar Musa as the crow flies, although a mountain range divides the two sites, and was executed some five hundred years later, in the eighteenth century.

The Church of St Sergius and St Bacchus, Sadad

The wall paintings in the Church of St Sergius and St Bacchus in the small town of Sadad are the sole surviving examples of eighteenth-century wall painting in Syria. Unlike at Deir Mar Musa, in the case of the Sadad images there are no contemporary wall paintings of any kind in Syria, or indeed in the wider region. In light of this fact, the scarcity of published academic research on the paintings is even more surprising and highlights the need for more research in this field.[7] Unlike at Mar Musa, we cannot call the paintings in Sadad a cycle as they represent a series of tableaux that do not present an overarching theological narrative. Rather we are dealing with a succession of images that depict isolated biblical episodes in tandem with scenes from the lives of notable saints, with a particular emphasis on regional cults. In addition, there are portraits of the patron and other contemporary figures in the sanctuary of the church, a subject to which we shall shortly return.

The dedication of the Church to Sts. Sergius and Bacchus shows that there is a desire to venerate local figures. Sadad is approximately 220 km across the desert from Reṣafa, which is where Sergius and Bacchus are traditionally believed to have been martyred by fellow Roman army officers because they had adopted the Christian faith. As well as the titular saints, the scheme also includes images of Mar Elian esh-Sharqi (St Julian of the East) whose sarcophagus formed the heart of the monastery named after him in nearby Qaryatayn[8] and of Mar Musa al-Habashi with the painting of Mar Musa providing the earliest visual representation of the saint in Syria. Other figures, such as St Elias and St Kyriakos, are popular figures but are less closely tied to the central desert region of Syria than the figures mentioned above.

What is perhaps most intriguing about these paintings is the procession of figures in Syrian Orthodox clerical garb that flank the scene of the Presentation of Christ in the Temple across the flat east wall of the church. It is from these images that we can ascertain that the paintings were executed during, or shortly after, the episcopacy of Bishop Dioskoros Sarukhan; possibly paid for by Sarukhan himself as he figures prominently in the scene (Loosley 2009). He was appointed to the diocese of Nebek and Deir Mar Musa in 1733, with Sadad subsequently appended to his diocese. In 1748, Dayr Mar Elian and Homs were added to his territories when the local bishop was raised to the Metropolitanate of Jerusalem (Kaufhold 1995). Therefore this scheme perhaps reflects the amalgamation of the two dioceses as, in this context, the choice of saint on the walls suggests that the paintings were intended to evoke the major cults of the region, which now all lay under the direct jurisdiction of Sarukhan. He is recorded as dying on 11 February 1769 in Sadad at the age of 110 (Kaufhold 1995: 80–1). This suggests that the church was decorated at some point after 1748, when all the monasteries in the region came under his control, and before his death in 1769, assuming that he was still living when the paintings were executed.

Just as the style of dress makes the affiliation of the clergy clear, it also tells us a great deal about the stylistic influences that shaped the artistic tradition. The clerical garb is typically Syrian, and the monastic saints wear robes akin to those worn by Sarukhan and his brethren, but the dress of the prophet Jonah and the military saints shows a strong Persian influence. Jonah in particular is distinguished by his cap enfolded in a large swathed turban and his short-sleeved tunic over a longer armed shirt (Figure 27.5), and Mar Musa al-Habashi is dressed in the same style with a long tunic over an under-shirt and leggings despite wearing a crown to denote his royal African lineage. This shows us that the painter was familiar with Persian fashions, as these would not have been typical attire for eighteenth-century desert Syrians. Therefore, we are once again faced with questions as to how far we are dealing solely with a Syrian artistic idiom and how far the artist adapted images he had seen in printed books circulating in Syria to evolve a syncretistic art form that mixed Syrian vernacular imagery with new styles coming from both East and West, with the advent of European printed books entering the Levant. Yet again, a lack of comparative data limits our conclusions, but the area remains ripe for future research.

CONCLUSION: PLACING SYRIAN ART CENTRE STAGE

As this chapter has made clear, for a long time Syrian art has been viewed as a sideshow. It has been consigned to the margins and regarded as a provincial, vernacular offshoot of Byzantine art by many art historians, whilst others have seen it as the product of artistic syncretism on the borders of the Byzantine and Persian empires. Whilst the cultural borrowings from both traditions are very clear, it is the contention of this author that we must now consider Syrian artistic production as being more than a simple synthesis of two foreign visual languages but actually a new phenomenon that gives expression to a Syriac-speaking Christianity that was firmly rooted in its native Syrian and Mesopotamian material culture. This distinctively Syrian idiom has been widely overlooked because relatively little evidence for it is still extant compared to neighbouring cultures and because it was, ultimately, the art of the 'losing side' in the fallout from the Council of Chalcedon. There were fewer non-Chalcedonian Syrians in the west of the country, and the Syrian heartlands of what is now south-east Turkey have suffered numerous displacements of population. This

Figure 27.5 Jonah and the Whale, Church of St Sergius, Sadad, Syria

Source: Author

even continues to the present day as native Christians find themselves caught between the Turkish government and resurgent Kurdish nationalists, and that is without considering the tragedies that have befallen Syria. The art history of the Syriac-speaking peoples has yet to be written, but it is hoped that this chapter has offered a starting point and raised wider questions about how this field can, and should, be explored further.

NOTES

1 See http://lootingmatters.blogspot.co.uk/2012/12/dallas-and-orpheus-mosaic.html (accessed 21.03.16) for a discussion of the theft and subsequent restitution to Turkey of the mosaic.

2 There are naturally a handful of academic articles on this subject. See for example Desreumaux (2000); Bowersock (2001); Colledge (1994); and Salman (2008). Edessene mosaics have also been mentioned in more general survey or thematic books on mosaics (Dunbabin 1999; Bowersock 2006).

3 See the forthcoming monograph by the present author on the relationship between Syria and Georgia in Late Antiquity. More information may be found at http://architectureandasceticism.exeter.ac.uk. This site is funded by the European Research Council under the European Union's Seventh Framework Programme (FP7/2007–2013) / ERC grant agreement n° 312602.

4 In the opinion of the current writer, Dodd (2001) does not significantly add to Dodd's original findings and the 1992 article remains the most useful discussion of the paintings.

5 'Monastery' in Arabic is usually transliterated as 'Dayr' in English. However, the strong French influence on the community of Mar Musa who inhabit the monastery today mean that all literature on the site refers to 'Deir Mar Musa' after the French manner of transliteration.

6 A similar composition of the Three Patriarchs, but in this case without the Virgin and the souls represented as small figures rather than merely heads, was discovered at Deir al-Surian in Wadi Natrun, Egypt. The monastery was inhabited by both Coptic and Syrian Orthodox monks between the ninth and sixteenth centuries and so shares strong doctrinal and cultural links with Deir Mar Musa, even if stylistically the paintings obviously bear clear Coptic influences. The paintings have been part of an ongoing restoration project by the Universtiy of Leiden since 1995 under the direction of Karel Innemee. See www.universiteitleiden.nl/en/research/research-projects/archaeology/the-mural-paintings-of-deir-al-surian (accessed 16.06.16) for further details.

7 Although at the time of the outbreak of the Syrian civil war a team of conservators from the Directorate General of Antiquities and Museums (DGAM) under the direction of Ms. Nada Sarkis was engaged in cleaning and consolidating the paintings, they remain almost entirely unpublished. They were discussed in a brief article by Enno Littmann (1928–29) and in a presentation at the 2009 Middle Eastern Studies of America (MESA) Annual Conference on 21–24 November in Boston, in a conference paper (Loosley 2009).

8 This monastery was destroyed by the so-called Islamic State in August 2015.

BIBLIOGRAPHY

Balty, Janine. 1977. *Mosaïques antiques de Syrie*. Bruxelles: Centre belge de recherches archéologiques à Apamée de Syrie.

Balty, Janine, and F. Briquel Chatonnet. 2000. Nouvelles Mosaïques Inscràites D'Osrhoène. *Monuments et Mémoires, Fondation Eugène Piot* 79, 31–72.

Bardill, Jonathan. 2012. *Constantine, Divine Emperor of the Christian Golden Age*. Cambridge: Cambridge University Press.

Bowersock, Glen W. 2001. Notes on the New Edessene Mosaic of Prometheus. *Hyperboreus* 7, 411–6.

———. 2006. *Mosaics as History: The Near East From Late Antiquity to Islam*. Cambridge, MA and London: The Belknap Press of Harvard University Press.

Burton, Richard Francis, and Charles F. Tyrwhitt Drake. 1872. *Unexplored Syria*. London: Tinsley Brothers.

Colledge, Malcolm A. R. 1994. Some Remarks on the Edessa Funerary Mosaics. *In:* Jean-Pierre Darmon and Alain Rebourg, ed., *La Mosaïque gréco-romaine IV. Actes du IVe Colloque*

International pour l'Étude de la Mosaïque Antique (Trèves, 8–14 août 1984). Paris: Supplément au Bulletin de l'A.I.E.M.A., 189–97.

Den Heijer, Johannes, Bas ter Haar Romeny, Mat Immerzeel, and Stephan Westphalen. 2007. Deir Mar Musa: The Inscriptions. *Eastern Christian Art in its Late Antique and Islamic Contexts* 4, 133–85.

Desreumaux, Alain. 2000. Une Paire de Portraits sur Mosaïque avec leurs Inscriptions Édesséniennes. *Syria* 77, 212–15.

Dirven, Lucinda. 1999. *The Palmyrenes of Dura-Europos: A Study of Religious Interaction in Roman Syria*. Leiden: Brill.

Dodd, Erica Cruikshank. 1992. The Monastery of Mar Musa al-Habashi, near Nebek, Syria. *Arte mediaevale*, 2nd Ser. VI, 61–144.

———. 2001. *The Frescoes of Mar Musa al-Habashi: A Study in Medieval Painting in Syria*. Studies and Texts 139. Toronto: Pontifical Institute of Mediaeval Studies.

Donceel-Voûte, Pauline. 1988. *Les pavements des églises byzantines de Syrie et du Liban*. Louvain-la-Neuve: Publications d'Archéologie et d'Histoire de l'Art de l'Université Catholique de Louvain 69.

Drijvers, Han J.W. and John F. Healey. 1999. *The Old Syriac Inscriptions of Edessa and Osrhoene*. Leiden and Boston: Brill.

Dunbabin, Katherine M.D. 1999. *Mosaics of the Greek and Roman World*. Cambridge: Cambridge University Press.

Healey, John F. 2006. A new Syriac mosaic inscription. *JSS* 51, 313–27.

Horn, Cornelia, and Erica C D. Hunter. 2012. Christianity in the Late Antique Near East. *In:* Dan T. Potts, ed., *A Companion to the Archaeology of the Ancient Near East*. Oxford: Wiley Blackwell, 1095–112.

Immerzeel, Mat. 2009. *Identity Puzzles: Mediaeval Christian Art in Syria and Lebanon*. Leuven: Peeters.

Jobst, Werner, Behçet Erdal, and Christian Gurtner. 1997. *Istanbul: The Great Palace Mosaic*. Istanbul: Arkeoloji ve sanat yayinlari.

Karabulut, Hasan, Mehmet Önal, and Nedim Dervişoğlu. 2011. *Haleplibahçe Mozaikleri. Şanliurfa/Edessa*. Istanbul: Arkeoloji ve sanat yayinlari.

Kaufhold, Hubert. 1995. Notizen über das Moseskloster bei Nabk und das Julianskloster bei Qaryatain in Syrien. *OC* 79, 48–119.

Krautheimer, Richard, and Slobodan Ćurčić. 1992. *Early Christian and Byzantine Architecture*. New Haven: Yale University Press.

Littmann, Enno. 1928–29. Die Gemälde der Sergios-Kirche in Sadad. *OC* 25–26, 288–91.

Loosley, Emma. 2009. *Sarukhan and His Legacy: Sadad as a Western Outpost of Mesopotamian Fresco Painting*. Presentation. Available at www.academia.edu/14918876/Sarukhan_and_his_Legacy_Sadad_as_a_western_outpost_of_Mesopotamian_Fresco_Painting

Mundell Mango, Marlia. 1983. Where Was Beth Zagba? *Harvard Ukrainian Studies* 7, 405–30.

Peña, Ignacio. 1997. *The Christian Art of Byzantine Syria*. Reading: Ithaca Press.

Piccirillo, Michele. 1993. *The Mosaics of Jordan*. Amman: American Center of Oriental Research.

Sabbagh, Rana, Fayez Ayash, Janine Balty, Françoise Briquel Chatonnet, and Alain Desreumaux. 2008. *Le Martyrion Saint-Jean dans la moyenne vallée de l'Euphrate: Fouilles de la Direction Générale des Antiquités à Nabgha au nord-est de Jarablus*. Damascus: Ministère de la culture. Direction Générale des Antiquités et des Musées.

Salman, Barış. 2008. Family, Death and Afterlife According to Mosaics of the Abgar Royal Period in the Region of Osroene. *Journal of Mosaic Studies* 1–2, 103–15.

Segal, J. B. 1970. *Edessa 'The Blessed City'*. Oxford: The Clarendon Press.

Shehade, Kamel. 1997. *The Mosaics of Al-Ma'arra Museum*. Kaslik: Institut d'Art Sacré.

Snelders, Bas. 2010. *Identity and Christian-Muslim Interaction: Mediaeval Art of the Syrian Orthodox From the Mosul Area*. Leuven: Peeters.
Tchalenko, Georges. 1953. *Villages antiques de la Syrie du Nord. Le Massif du Bélus à l'époque romaine*. Bibliothèque archéologique et historique 50. Paris: Paul Geuthner.
Trzionka, Silke. 2007. *Magic and the Supernatural in Fourth-Century Syria*. London and New York: Routledge.
Westphalen, Stephan. 2007. Deir Mar Musa: Die Malschichten 1–3. *Eastern Christian Art in Its Late Antique and Islamic Contexts* 4, 99–126.

CHAPTER TWENTY-EIGHT

CHURCHES IN SYRIAC SPACE
Architectural and liturgical context and development

Widad Khoury

This essay is an attempt at a comprehensive approach to the great series of churches that emerged and developed in the Middle East in an environment that was especially marked out by the Syriac culture of the Syrian Christians, in addition to its rich Graeco-Roman architectural heritage.[1] This reflection took its first steps in 2012 thanks to the initiative of the *Société d'études Syriaques*, which organised a conference dedicated to this subject organised by Françoise Briquel-Chatonnet. It was in this context that specialists of ecclesiastical architecture in the various regions of the Middle East met to discuss the results of their work.

Naturally, Syria occupies a prominent place in the centre of this world in its role as the place of origin of Christianity's diffusion as well as the birthplace of the important Syriac culture. This significance is due also to its geographical position and the large number of churches it houses, their wealth, and the quality of their preservation. The presentation of the research that was carried out across this enormous Syrian heritage, its regional context, its liturgical forms and structures, and its developments, were published in the proceedings of the symposium by Widad Khoury and Bertrand Riba (Khoury and Riba 2013b), together with the results of the research carried out in the other eastern regions of Syriac culture. It was in this same context that Jean-Pierre Sodini presented the conclusion of all these contributions (Sodini 2013: 541–7), forming thereby the second stage of general reflection and also opening up paths for the development of the present study.

INTRODUCTION: THE CONCEPT OF A SYRIAC CHURCH AND ISSUES RELATING TO ITS PATTERN

This study opens with defining the scope of the field, a fundamental question raised by, amongst others, Françoise Briquel-Chatonnet and repeated by Jean-Pierre Sodini: Is the concept of a 'Syriac church' meaningful? Then adding,

> the question that arises for us today is this: Is there a model common to speakers of Syriac, diffused in its basic pattern over the whole geographical region of this community, that is distinct from other churches in the same territory, e.g. Greek

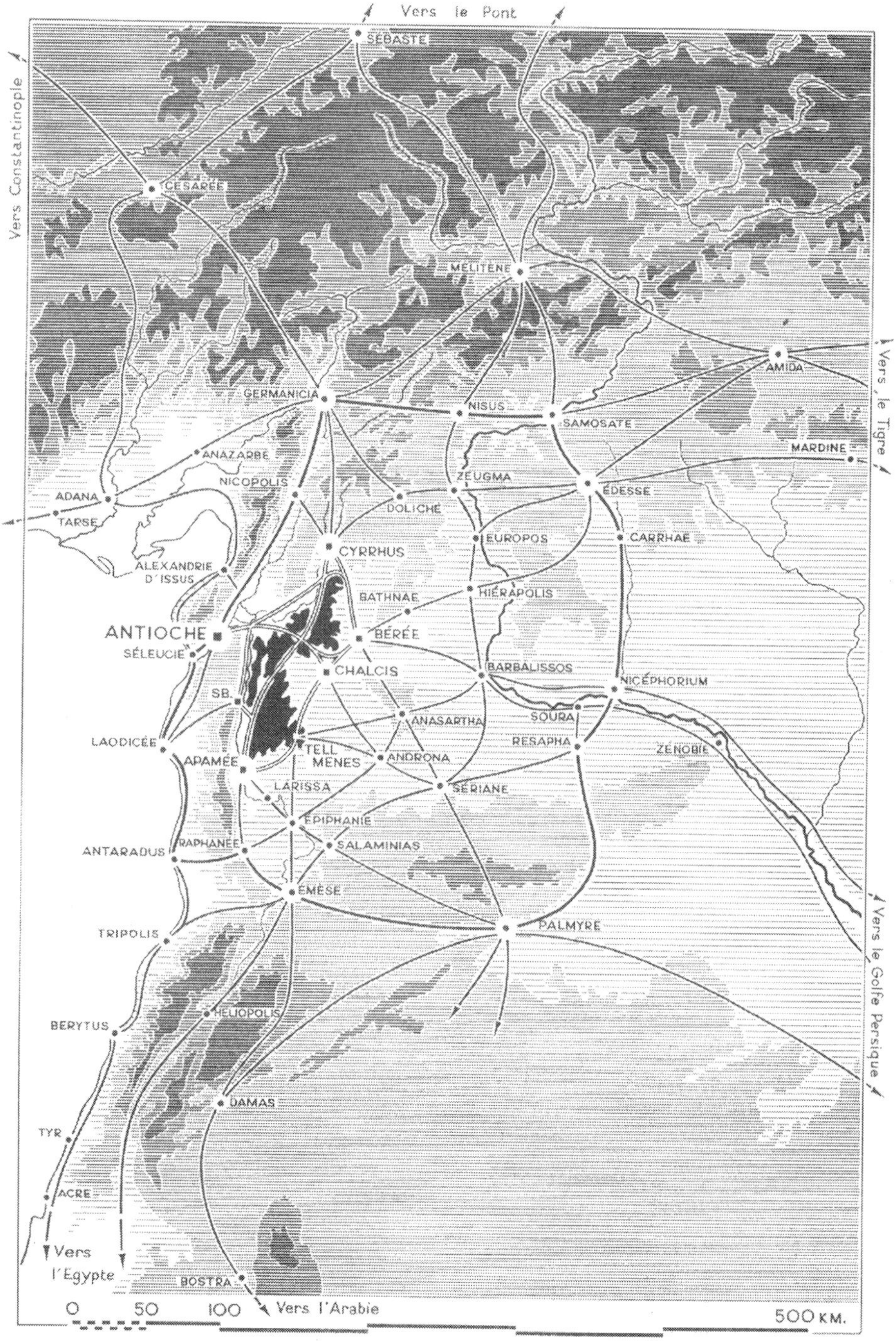

Figure 28.1 Main routes of Byzantine Syria, and location of the Limestone Massif

> or Coptic? Within this (Syriac) series, is the inevitable diversity that is present mostly a geographical diversity or does it relate to the denominations/church groupings? In the same region, do the churches belonging to different communities all follow the same pattern?
>
> (Briquel-Chatonnet 2013: 1–6)

These questions have been the subject of several specific or partial reflections that have been taken up and developed in the present study, and I hope to rephrase and/or supplement the answers to those questions in the light of regional monographs covering the whole expanse of the territory of Syriac churches, namely answers that correspond to the realities in the field, to the reflections of Jean-Pierre Sodini, and to our previous research (Khoury and Riba 2013b). The aim is to end up with a general presentation covering the 'Syriac axis' that runs from the Limestone Massif to India and China, showing what was not included in that axis, despite a similarity of audience or language, namely the Arab-Muslim axis (Sodini 2013). The geographical coverage is therefore a wide sweep from west to east through the regions that testify to a Syriac presence, from Syria itself, to the Indus and China by way of south-east present-day Turkey, Iraq, Iran, Central Asia, Southern Jordan, Arabia, the African Indian Ocean coast, and on to India and China. Were all these people truly or uniquely speaking Syriac? And if so, which ones among them and in what periods?

THE STATE OF RESEARCH: ISSUES OF LANGUAGE AND COMMUNITY

Research on Syriac churches took shape initially based on the great publications of M. De Voguë (Vogüe 1865–77) which revealed to the world the incredible architecture of the Near East, while also presenting it with a social and cultural mosaic unique in its richness. The publications of the American archaeological missions to Syria (AAES, American Archaeological Expedition to Syria, 1903–1930, and PAES, Publications of the Princeton University Archaeological Expeditions to Syria, 1904–1905) were followed by a series of important studies of churches and Christian monuments accomplished by French researchers and missions (J. Lassus, G. Tchalenko, J.-P. Sodini, G. Tate). The work of the Franciscan fathers spanned decades (Peña et al. 1975, 1980, 1983, 1987, 1990, 1999, 2003), itself instigating further research by Syrians (W. Khoury, M. Abdelkarim) and a return of a much broader level of interest (see e.g. works by J.-L. Biscop, J.-P. Foudrin, J. Gaborit, M.-Ch. Comte, D. Pieri, A. Michel, N. Baudry, B. Riba). The Syro-French Mission for Syriac Inscriptions in Syria created and directed by Francoise Briquel-Chatonnet and Widad Khoury initiated multi-disciplinary new research aiming at an optimal approach to the inscriptions through a full understanding of their urban and architectural context (Briquel-Chatonnet et al. 2004–05). Outside the Near East, alongside the ancient and pioneering authors of the nineteenth and early twentieth centuries, a series of regional studies successively covered Jordan, Arabia, Tur ʿAbdin, Iraq, Arabia, and Iran (F. Alpi, P.-L. Gatier, O. Callot, F. Villeneuve, B. Geyer, J.-M. Fiey, M. Mouton, M. Tardieu, Ch. Robin). The churches of India and China were also studied, but their antiquity and their community affiliations could not be established with certainty because of either their state of deterioration or else a complete lack of specific archaeological data. In general, these studies focused on historical, epigraphic, and archaeological data and dealt separately with the urban and economic aspects of the surrounding area. They particularly focused on the forms and decorations of regional religious monuments and on the major artistic trends that influenced their construction.

Sodini traces a new path through several synthetic articles on churches, baptisteries, liturgy, and the spatial organisation of churches (Sodini 2006, and in many other works). It is thanks to his support and encouragement that Syrian churches are tackled from a global point of view in the synthesising essay on the Syrian Churches (Khoury and Riba 2013a) and the first research essay on the possible community affiliation of churches (Khoury and Riba 2013b).

Indeed, the case of the Proto-Byzantine churches that are located specifically in Syria is the most favourable one in which to find the answer to the thorny problem posed by the simultaneous presence of different language communities and different religious affiliations within towns and villages having several churches. On the one hand, the presence of Greek culture – introduced from the fourth century onwards and established in the Semitic regions of the Near East, where the Greek language penetrated to varying degrees a population otherwise defined by the use of different Aramaic dialects, of which Syriac, being derived from the specifically Aramaic city of Edessa and the province of Osrhoene – became the standard cultural and liturgical language for many communities in northern Syria. On the other hand, the Christological struggles (Sodini 2013: 546–7; in this volume, see chapters 6 and 22) constituted a decisive factor in the division between the Greek Orthodox Church (Chalcedonian) and the Syriac Orthodox Church (miaphysite). Moreover, it seems legitimate to consider whether the models that emerged were directly related to the ways in which communities were organised around places of Christian worship and to observe whether the epigraphy, architecture, and spatial organisation of churches in any way reflects distinct theological or linguistic groupings. To these two reasons may be added the great number and the good state of preservation of the monuments and churches on Syrian land, which have made it possible both to carry out detailed studies and then to make the necessary comparisons.

In this framework, the present study starts out from Maʾramaya (Fernandez and Khoury 2008), one of the villages of the Limestone Massif, which was occupied from the fourth to the ninth centuries with a single church (Figures 28.2–3).

This single-nave building, probably built in the fourth century, contains Greek, Syriac, and Arabic inscriptions indicating that the faithful, who certainly derived from different communities at the very least from the sixth century as was the case throughout the region, nevertheless had no need to build a second church and followed all their liturgical services in one and the same church (Figure 28.4).

In this connection, there are several written sources that can briefly illuminate through some significant examples the linguistic problems that could arise in Syria. These sources show an important contrast between cities, where Greek is the language of use, and the countryside where Aramaic remains the popular language despite the presence of plenty of epigraphic evidence in Greek. This phenomenon is observable until, at the end of the fourth century, John Chrysostom exhorted the city-dwellers not to ridicule the rural people who knew no Greek who came to Antioch at Easter.

In the same way, even though the writings of Theodoret of Cyrrhus were all written in Greek, we know that the bishop addresses the dependent villagers of his diocese

Figure 28.2a Church of Ma'ramaya, southern façade and baptistery at the eastern extremity of the portico

Figure 28.2b Lintel with three cross motifs

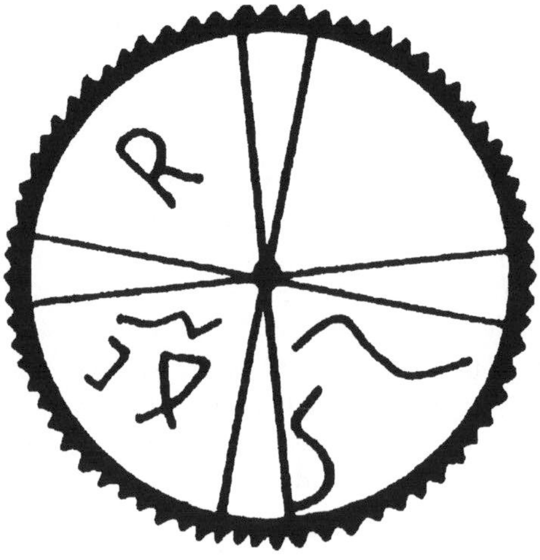

Figure 28.2c Detail of the Greek cross of the central motif showing Greek characters

Figure 28.3a Church of Ma'ramaya, eastern façade

Figure 28.3b Syriac inscription from the sixth century carved on a block of the facade

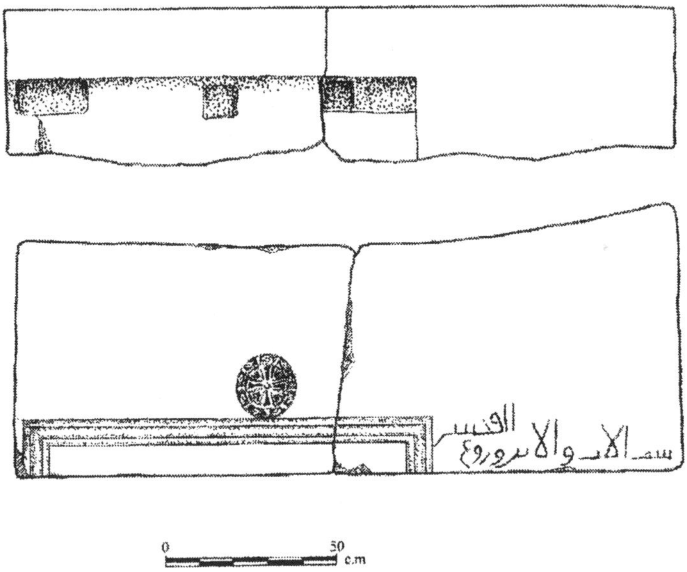

Figure 28.4a Church of Ma'ramaya, Arabic Christian inscription carved on the lintel of the baptistery

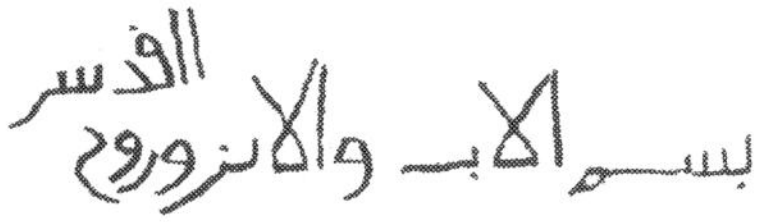

Figure 28.4b Arabic Christian inscription 'In the Name of the Father and the Son and the Holy Spirit'

Figure 28.4c Chrism motif carved in the centre of the baptistery lintel

in Aramaic. Saint Jerome, for his part, was forced to 'learn Syriac to communicate with his neighbours' in the region of Chalcis (Festugière 1959: 416). In cities whose ancient Semitic names are often preserved alongside the Greek name imposed by the founder, the cultural currents are more varied. Although Greek culture and language remained firmly established in those cities, many Edessene personalities, such as Eusebius, Bishop of Emesa (Ḥomṣ), knew Greek and actively participated, from the fourth century, in the political and religious life of the city (Canivet and Canivet 1987: 137). In urban centres oriented towards the East, Aramaic was more common. This is the case in Palmyra where the official texts are engraved in both languages, but especially so in Edessa where the organisation of the city was carried out on the classic model but whose life was carried on primarily through the use of the local Aramaic dialect. It was this dialect that gave rise to an abundant Syriac literature whose influence spread through Mesopotamia and northern Syria among Aramaic-speaking Christians.

Reflection on the problem posed by different communities in towns and villages possessing several churches was a result of the previous study of single-church sites turning to those sites having two churches, and later those with several. When looked at together and in context, the churches found at two-church sites seem more complementary than separated. Churches whose doors opened onto a common courtyard leading to a martyrion or baptistery in its annexes could hardly house warring groups (Khoury 1996). By occupying respectively the centre and the outskirts of a village, they complemented one another, as well as their liturgical devices, one as a parish church, the other as a sanctuary (Khoury 1996; Khoury and Riba 2013b). A greater number of churches corresponds to the enlargement of the village or the development there of a pilgrimage site.

In this respect it is to be emphasised that despite the quarrels between Arians and Niceans, and later between strict Niceans and Meletians, that led to the expulsion of the one group by the other from the different churches of Antioch, and despite the confrontations attested between Chalcedonians and miaphysites in time of Severus of Antioch (Alpi 2010), the relationships between those communities were nuanced and varied. In fact, the field data show the coexistence of Greek and Syriac inscriptions in the same churches and thus testify to the presence of different linguistic communities. This points to a certain degree of mixture between the communities.

The architecture of ecclesiastical monuments reflects essentially the same picture, where liturgical differences blur together, the gradual decline of specifically Syriac liturgical traits giving way to others more in keeping with the Christian Mediterranean centres.

The presence of several churches in the villages is to be explained by the development of the villages themselves, especially their concern to attract pilgrims en route to Jerusalem or even to Qalʿat Semʿan. As for the presence of several baptisteries, that corresponds to the concern to manage expanding communities in which both adults and young children were baptised, as at Qalʿat Semʿan or Halabiyye. Some two- or three-church complexes belong to a single ensemble where the churches coordinated their services, with probably even common processions and the establishment of ad hoc liturgies, as was recently proposed for Reṣafa. In the villages, the maintenance of a single bêma church strongly suggests the unity of the community, perhaps with variations of choice from one village to another, yet above all tolerant in spite of the dogmatic nuances sometimes suggested by some lintel inscriptions (Sodini 2013: 545).

It is true that the miaphysite monks did sometimes push their propaganda, especially during the reign of Anastasius, when, during the episcopates of Severus of Antioch and Peter of Apamea, they were especially violent towards Chalcedonian monks of Apamene, who were trying to give assistance to the monks of Telanissos. A double hierarchy was then established and the dogmatic positions became irreconcilable. A Chalcedonian monastery was built towards the middle of the sixth century for a new Symeon the Stylite, imitating in his own way his namesake's life, with the blessing of the patriarch of Antioch. By that time, the sanctuary at Qalʿat Semʿan had fallen into the hands of the miaphysites, wasted away, and was only frequented by the peasants of the neighbourhood. According to Evagrius Scholasticus, the secretary of the Patriarch Gregory (570–592) reports the story of the two stylites ignoring the reasons for this substitution. But the architecture of churches and convents in no way reflects these deep ruptures, either in this case or in others (Sodini 2013: 545).

FROM HOUSE CHURCH TO BASILICA

The written sources for the first centuries of Christianity, from the epistles of Saint Paul to Eusebius, were initially the only means of reconstructing the framework in which the first Christians lived. The testimony of these sources indicates that Christians gathered in the homes of private individuals before taking possession of one of them for permanent use. In the absence of Christ having given any specific liturgical instructions, the cult required only a room of some form and a room to share a meal in memory of the Last Supper. Only baptism required a special arrangement (Lassus 1947: 1–19; Grabar 1966a: 65–71). The texts have, however, made it possible to appreciate that in general a primitive church consisted of a house with several spaces where the Christian life developed, which housed whatever was necessary for the liturgy and which had a staff. This is confirmed by the extant report of a search of the church of Cirta (Lassus 1947: 3), which contains an entire and detailed account of the action of the chief magistrate, who visited all the rooms and who even drew up an inventory of their contents, which gives us a good sketch of the architecture of the place and of the people who took care of it.

The unique discovery in 1931/2 in Dura Europos of the Domus Ecclesiae dating from the first half of the third century (Rostovtzeff 1938) came to back up this general description and to give substance to one of its possible forms. The Christian house-churches merged with the private houses and differed among themselves as much as the architecture of the latter in the different parts of the Roman world (Figures 28.5–8).

The Domus Ecclesiae consisted of a set of rooms grouped around a square central courtyard, with the southern rooms being built on two floors. The upper rooms were used as a dwelling-place for the staff in charge of the premises while the ground floor was devoted to worship. The room in the south-west corner, which was the best preserved, was a baptistery recognisable by the baptismal font which occupies the western wall and is covered with a canopy in the form of a barrel vault resting on two columns. The room also preserves part of the wall paintings on the east side, under the canopied arch: the good pastor and, below, Adam and Eve after the fall.

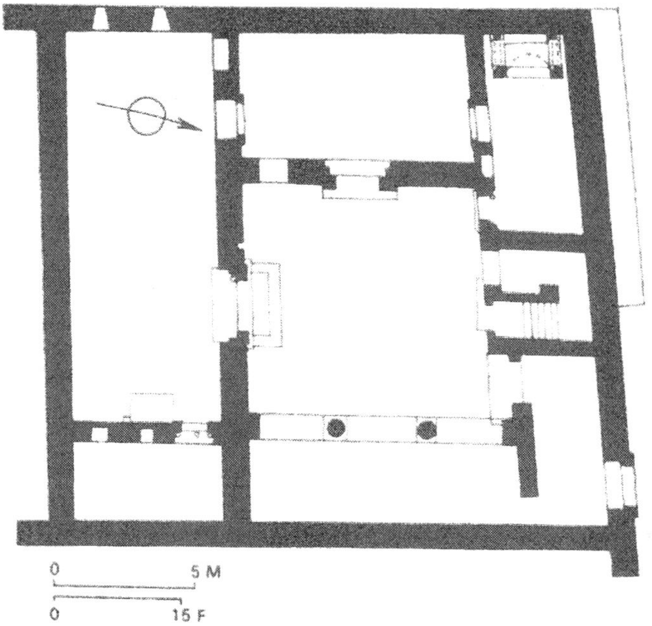

Figure 28.5a Plan of the Domus Ecclesiae

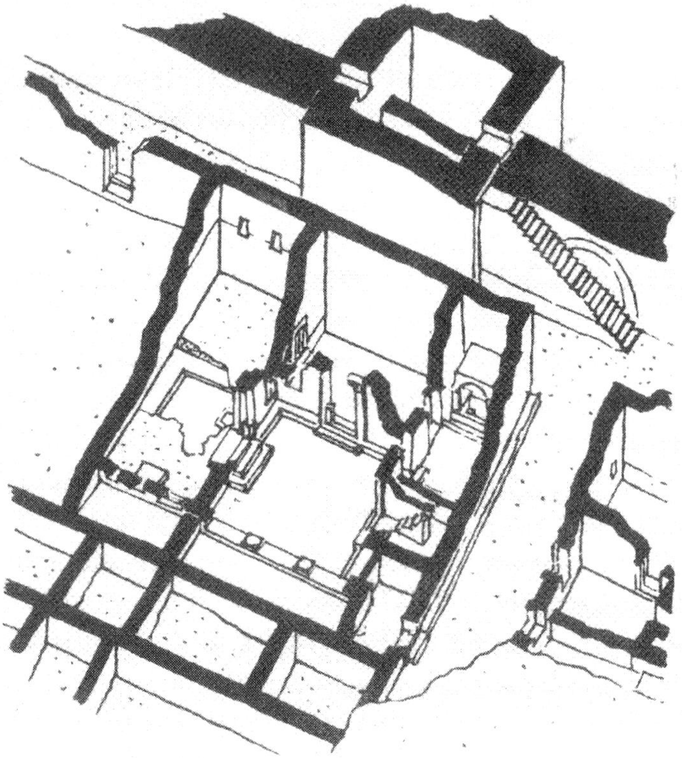

Figure 28.5b Isometric view of the Domus Ecclesiae

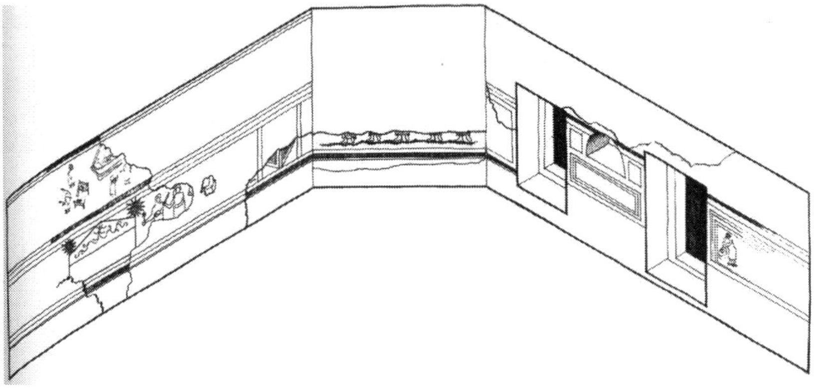

Figure 28.6 Distribution of painted scenes inside the Domus Ecclesiae

Source: Courtesy of J. P. Sodini

Figure 28.7a Baptismal font against the western wall of the Domus Ecclesiae

Figure 28.7b The good Pastor and, below, Adam and Eve after the fall

Figure 28.8a The healing of the paralytic

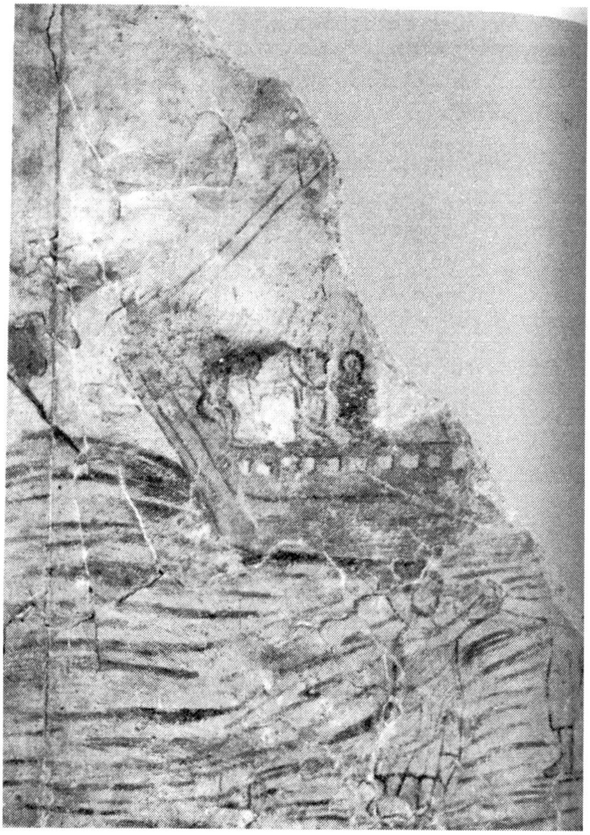

Figure 28.8b Christ walking on the water

Figure 28.8c The holy women at the tomb holding torches

Figure 28.8d Samaritan woman near the well

On the north wall are painted several scenes: above, the healing of the paralytic and Christ walking on the water; below, the holy women at the tomb holding torches. Five women are shown on the east wall, and in a niche on the south the fight between David and Goliath; the Samaritan woman drawing water from a well is shown on the west wall near the canopy.

The south side is entirely occupied by a large elongated room suggesting that this is where the liturgy was held. It is accessible by two doors, one opening onto the courtyard and the other into the room to the west. This may have served for the common meal but perhaps for other purposes such as housing goods. In any case the early Christians sought a place for the carrying on of the Christian life together or for holding the liturgy.

Constantine, proclaimed emperor by his generals, defeated his rivals in 312. He proclaimed the Edict of Milan in 313 and took his place at the head of the empire in 323. Although he was not baptised until shortly before his death, Christianity became a freely and publicly practiced religion. The church recovered its confiscated property and acquired the right to own property and to construct buildings for meetings. The broadening of Christianity was given momentum by the granting of privileges and immunities to the Church and by the convening of the first ecumenical council at Nicaea (325), where Arius was condemned and where fundamental laws were enacted in favour of the Church.

In 326, Constantine chose the ancient city of Byzantium as the capital of the empire, to become Constantinople, one of the most important cities in the world. The emperor opened a new page in the history of Roman architecture by contributing to the construction and diffusion of places of Christian worship, the churches. And it was with the support of his mother Helen that he built those important churches that marked a new stage in Roman architecture in both West and East.

Only some of these churches are known, and often only in written testimony (Testini 1980), but all in all, researchers agree on the key locations and their 'basilical' forms. We think in particular of the five churches built in Rome and the Church of the Apostles in Constantinople, where the emperor himself was to be buried (Figure 28.9). The Holy Land was at the centre of Constantine's and his mother Helen's devotion. The Church of the Anastasis (Resurrection) in Jerusalem, built on the site where the cross of Christ was unearthed during work conducted by the emperor's mother, was the standout monument, built around the tomb of Christ (Biddle 1999). The Basilica of Eleona was erected on the Mount of Olives, the Church of the Nativity in Bethlehem, and the Church of the Annunciation in Nazareth. Tyre was given by the emperor a cathedral where Eusebius gave the dedicatory speech in 324. Polygonal forms are attested: at Antioch, the emperor built the largest of all these churches, known as the *Domus Aurea*, so-named because of its golden dome. There were also many other churches in different regions of the empire, and which gave impetus to ecclesiastical architecture and its development.

Imperial initiatives followed one after the other, although the reign of Theodosius was more associated with the destruction of pagan cult sites. Emperor Leo established the shrine of Qal'at Sem'an around the base of the last column of Saint Symeon the Stylite; and many churches were built during the reign of Anastasius, including the church of Kafret 'Aqab. Qasr ibn Wardan, together with the churches and city of Reṣafa/Sergiopolis, were renewed by Justinian, to whom is attributed the largest

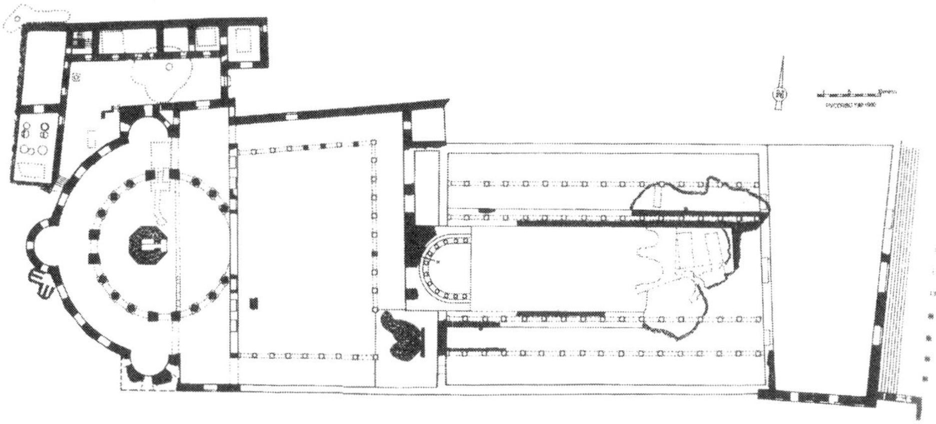

Figure 28.9a Plan of the Church of the Holy Sepulchre, Jerusalem

Source: Courtesy of Virgilio Corbo

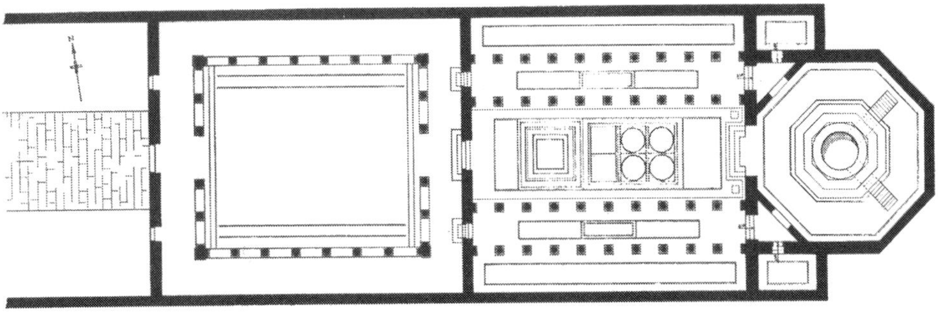

Figure 28.9b Plan of the Church of the Nativity, Bethlehem

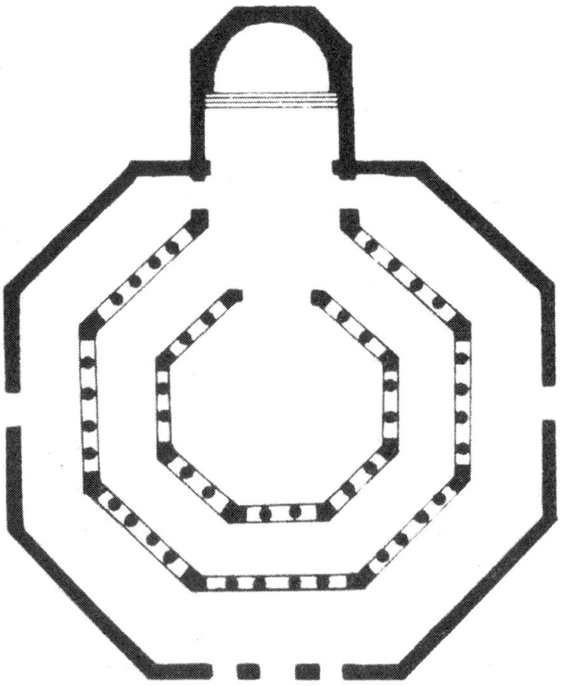

Figure 28.9c Hypothetical reconstruction of the octagon of the 'Domus Aurea' in Antioch

Source: Courtesy of J. P. Sodini

number of churches. Justin II followed his example, and it was during his reign that the pilgrimage churches were built at the end of the sixth century. The final churches of the Proto-Byzantine period, before the Arab Conquest of the Near East, were built under Heraclius.

Imperial interventions by their complex and multifaceted nature at first sight seem to fill an immense space in which we must look to other individual studies in order to find alternative patterns of church building. In the first place, urban expansion necessitated the addition of numerous buildings, the shapes and dimensions of which vary from place to place. The economic prosperity of the region also motivated this activity and sometimes led to embellishments, enlargements, and restorations carried out by the church itself or from different donations. The initiative of the faithful themselves was especially attached to the cult of the martyrs and thus in the churches played a significant role not only in building works but above all in influencing the wide variety of decorative schemes and religious layouts.

CHURCHES

The Syriac western nucleus

The first churches of the Syriac world are those which appeared and developed in Syria between the fourth and seventh centuries in a multilingual, multi-confessional environment in which, throughout this period, they merged with one another and confronted one another in a variety of different religions and schisms. It is an archaeological heritage extremely rich in the number of its monuments, in its architecture, and in its well-preserved decorations. An attempt will be made to highlight the main features and to give a general overview of ecclesiastical, spatial, and liturgical architecture. Finally, we shall identify the common and the specific features and discuss the influences to which the Syrian basilicas attest, before finally giving some consideration to their place in the early Christian era.

Location

Three geographical areas are to be defined within the framework of this presentation: the first is the more limited region of late antique Byzantine Syria itself; the second consists of Iraq, the Persian Gulf and western Iran, while the third extends from eastern Iran to include India and China, these latter two regions together corresponding to the wider extension of Syriac influence. Within Syria itself, the remains of the numerous basilicas are unevenly divided into several more- or less-dense groupings, and consist of three main archaeological areas. The first is 'northern Syria', comprising a vast territory of contrasting natural conditions, including the Syrian coast, the Limestone Massif, the eastern basalt plateaux, and the eastern steppe to the banks of the Euphrates and beyond to the region of Edessa (Figure 28.1; 28.10).

The ancient provinces of Syria I, Syria II, Euphratesia, and Osrhoene belong to this sector. The area to the east and south of Aleppo, however, will be considered as an integral part of a separate area known as 'central Syria', which represents an important archaeological area between the Limestone Massif and the basaltic massifs of southern Syria. In the context of this presentation, it includes the territory on the north–south axis between Aleppo and Ḥama, passing through Chalcis, and on the

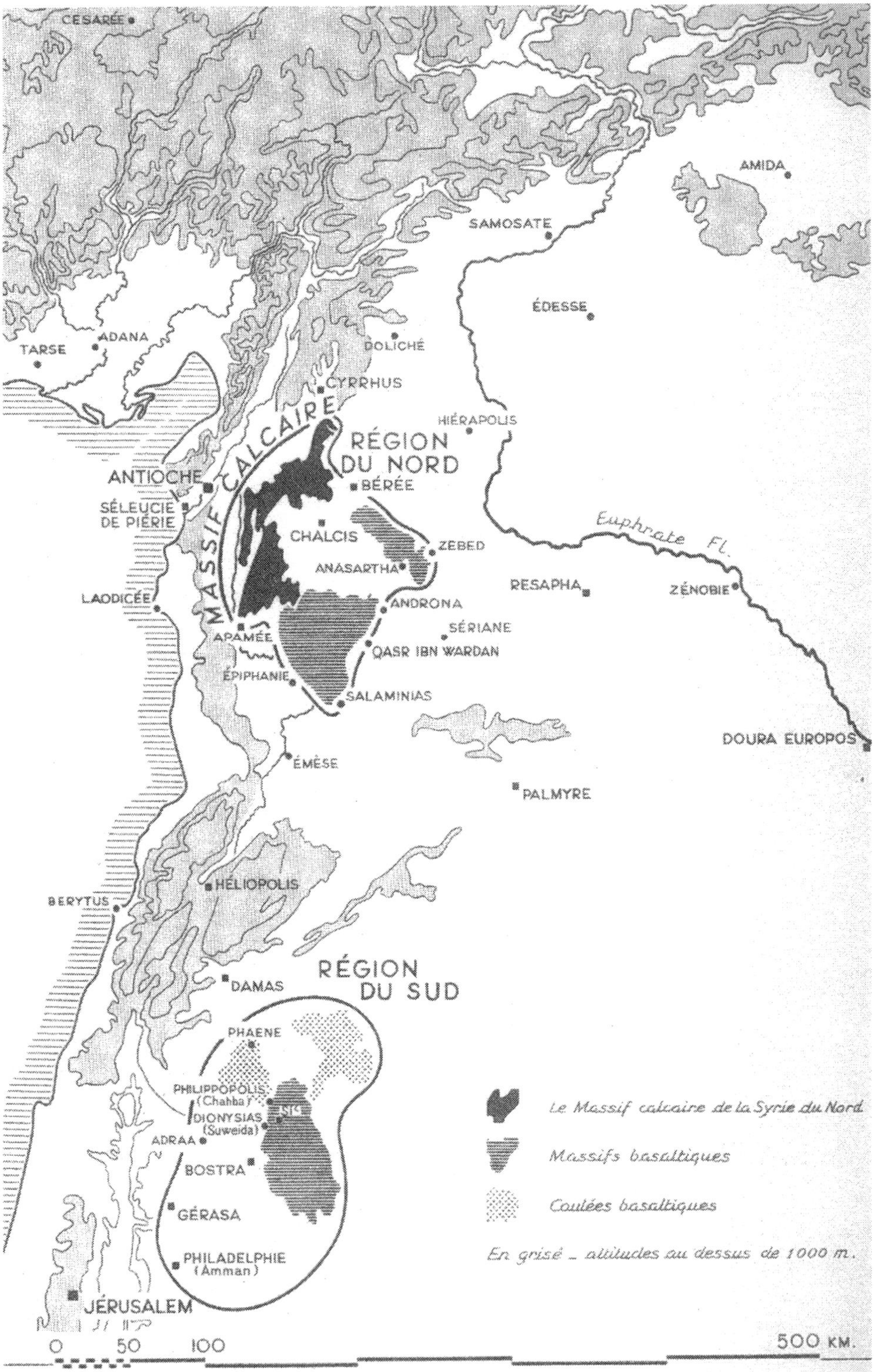

Figure 28.10a Archaeological regions of Syria

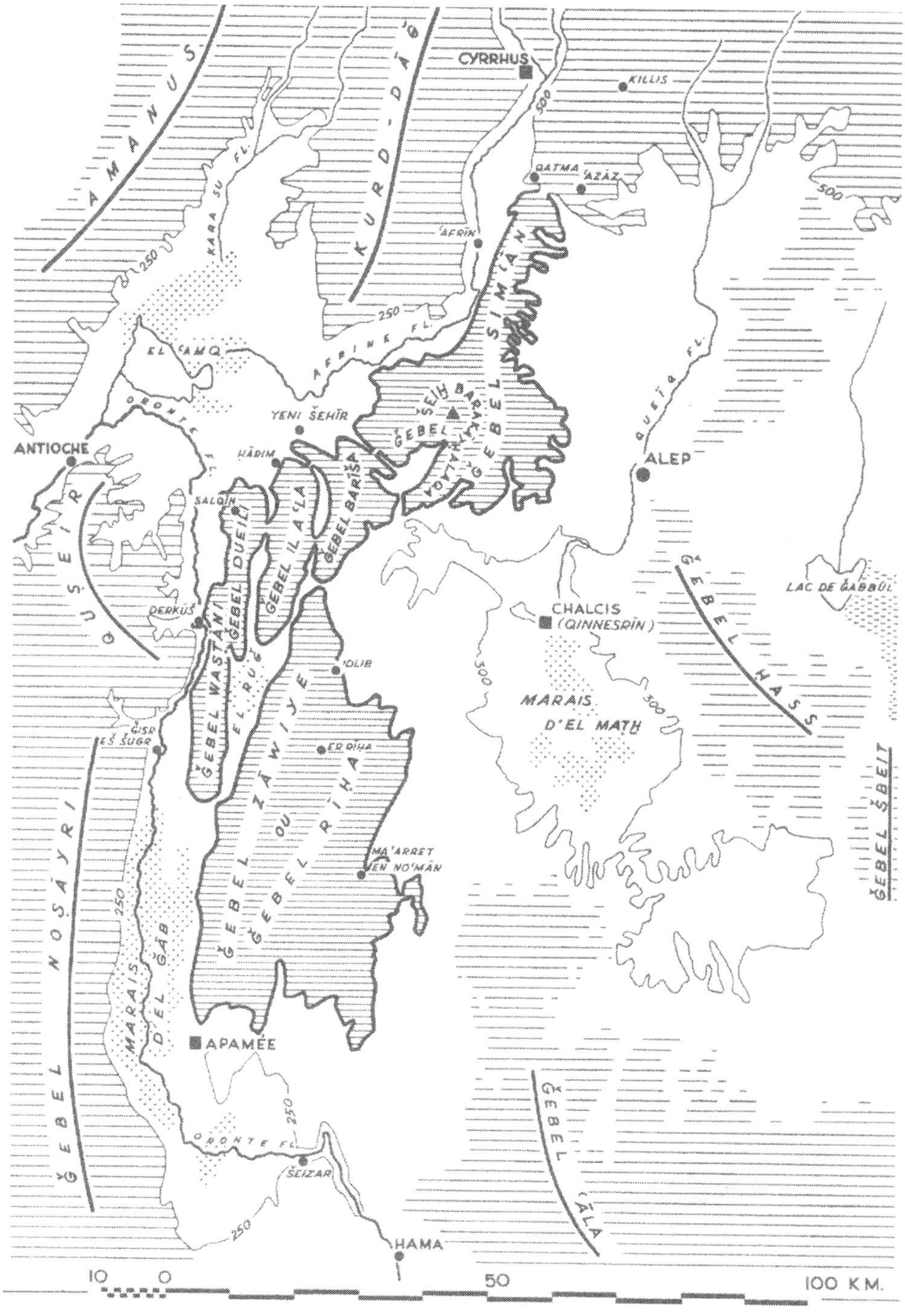

Figure 28.10b Toponymy of the Limestone Massif

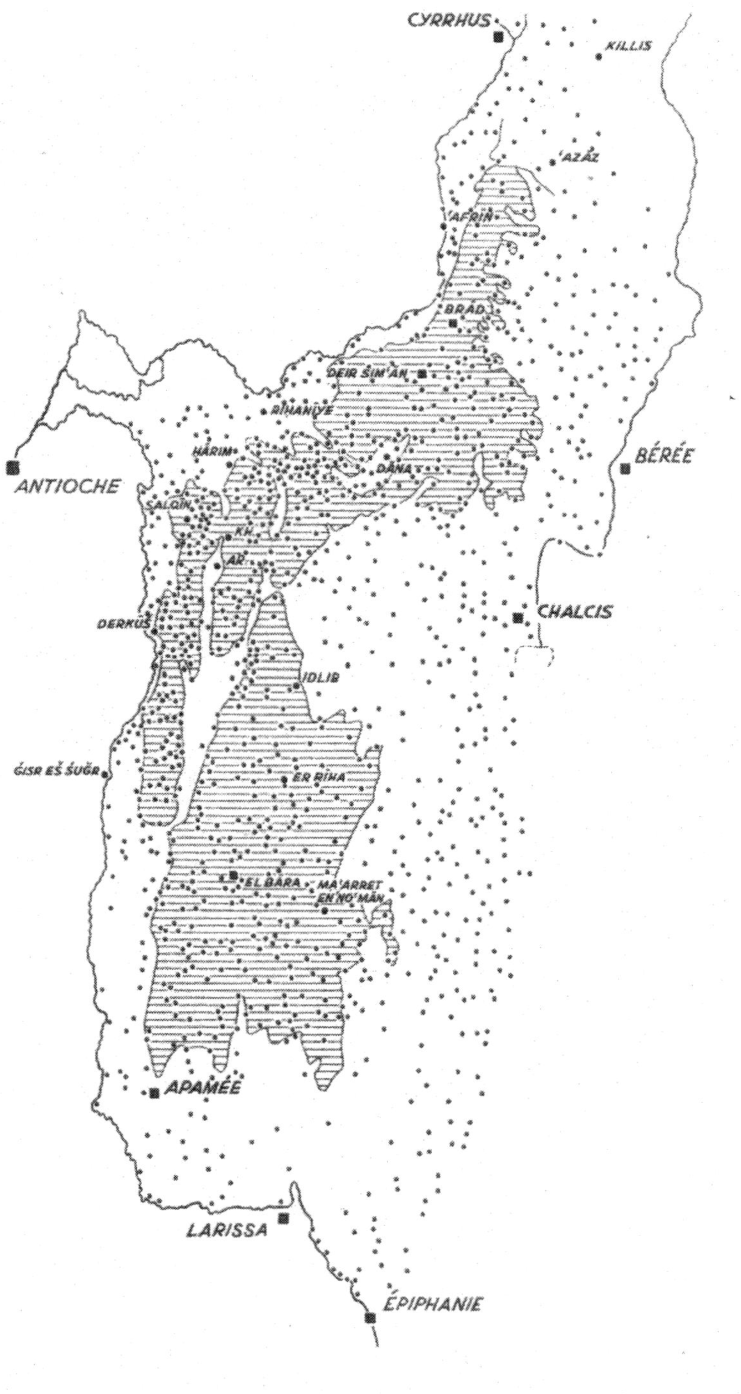

Figure 28.10c Distribution of inhabited locations in the Limestone Massif in Late Antiquity

east–west axis from Ḥama to the Euphrates through Palmyra. It thus includes parts of the former provinces of Syria I, Syria II, Euphratesia, and Phoenicia II. Third, there is 'southern Syria', which comprises the entire basaltic territory that stretches south and south-east of Damascus, between the Jawlān in the west and the desert to the east and south. The churches belonging to this zone of the province of Arabia are located within the administrative boundaries, a few dozen kilometres south of Damascus.

The churches of the Limestone Massif

From the fourth century onwards, the planting of churches in the villages was naturally carried on at the peripheries of the old centres of the imperial era (Khoury and Riba 2013b). Others occupy a central position in the village, on the site of an ancient temple (Brād), while the old sanctuaries of the high places, built on the highest peaks of the region, were redesigned into monastic complexes (Callot 1997). Some pagan sanctuaries, such as the Hūarte mithraeum, were also replaced by places of Christian worship (Gawlikowski 2013). The ecclesiastical complexes, sometimes delimited by an enclosure wall like the ancient temples, consist of a church preceded by a portico and a courtyard, most often situated to the south, around which gravitate various buildings, such as the dwellings of the clergy, a martyrion, and a baptistery. Other ensembles are characterised by the presence of two churches, as at Banassara and Fassūq where the basilicas, arranged on either side of a courtyard, played a complementary role. They are also found elsewhere in Syria with a different organisation (Figures 28.11–13).

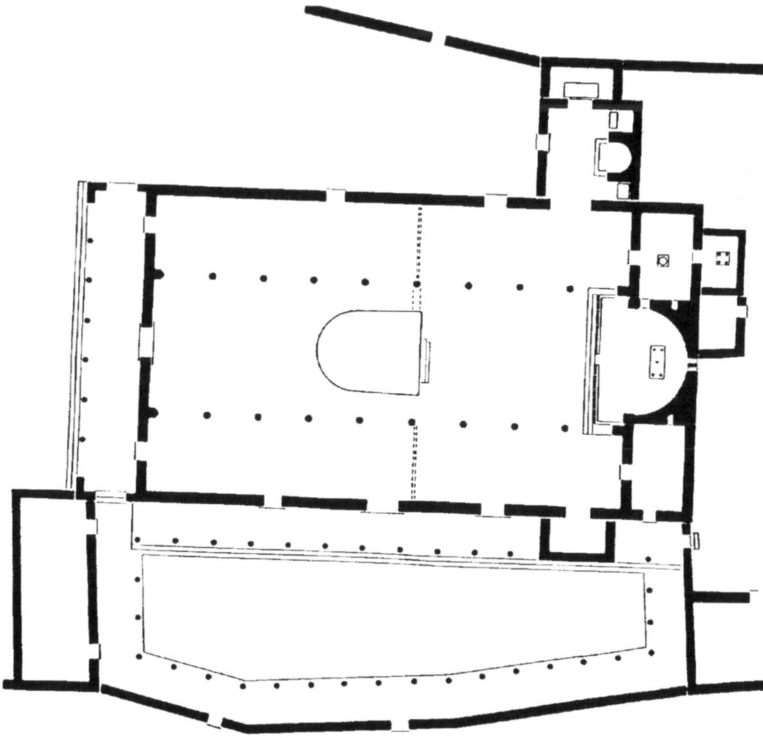

Figure 28.11 The church of Julianos established in a Roman temple

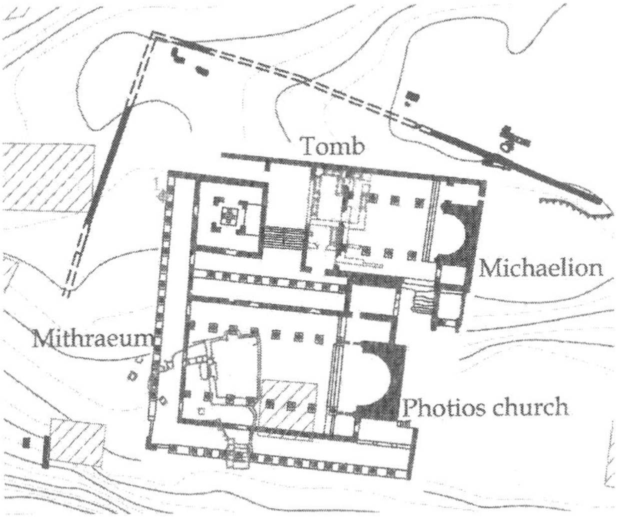

Figure 28.12a Hūarte church

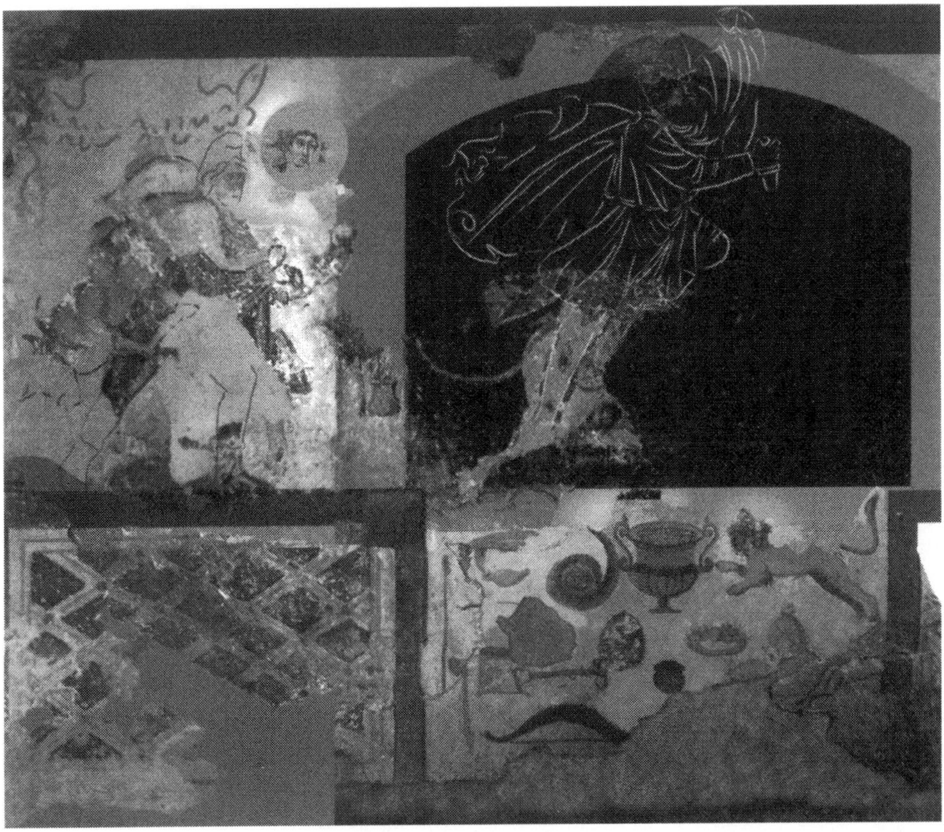

Figure 28.12b Detail of the Mithraeum fresco beneath the church of Phocas

Source: © Syro-Polish mission in Hūarte

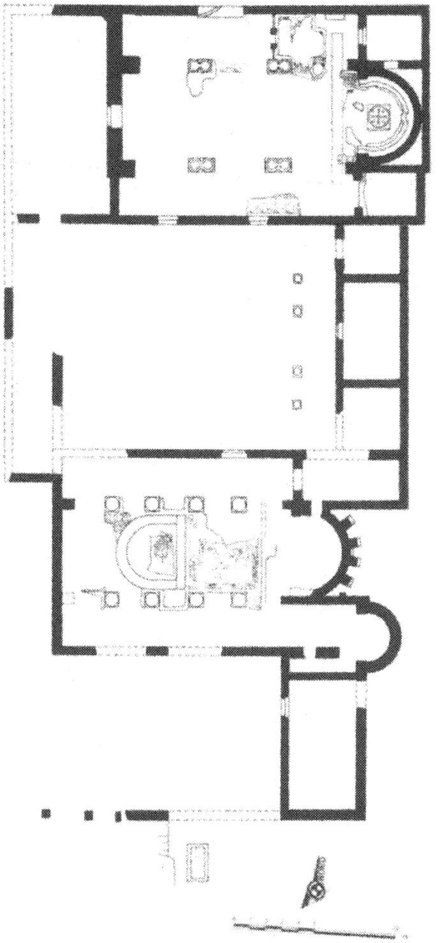

Figure 28.13a Ecclesial complex of Banassara

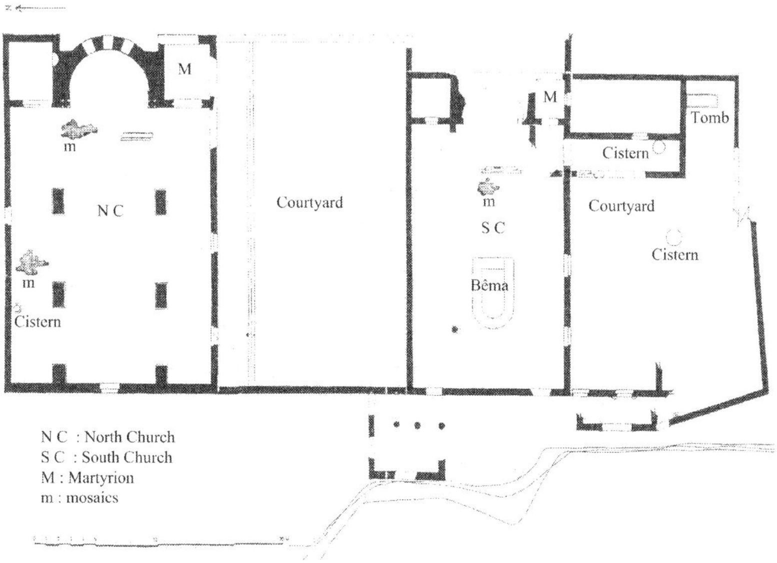

Figure 28.13b Ecclesial complex of Fassūq

The basilica plan, which is the dominant model in the region despite some exceptions, is reflected in churches with single aisles or three naves. Churches with a single nave (Figure 28.20), known from the fourth century especially in the north, such as at Qirkbīze, Nūrīye, Ishrūq, Maʾaramāyā, and Bānaqfūr (Strube 1986: 109–23), continue until the end of the sixth. These buildings sometimes have a rectangular chevet without lateral chambers, or else a tripartite chevet, the outlines of which sometimes protrude from the lateral facades. The division of the sanctuary sometimes took place towards the end of the fifth century (Tchalenko 1990: 153). Other single-nave chapels (Ḫarāb Sulṭān, Bāʿūde, Bardḫān) are provided with a semi-circular apse enclosed within a straight chevet (Peña et al. 1999: 107). The prominent apse is attested fairly early in Nūrīye (Peña et al. 1987: 177–8), and then becomes more common from the end of the fifth century. It may be associated with basilicas as in Ṭurīn East (Khoury and Castellana 1990: 18; Peña et al. 1999: 157) and at Kefert ʿAqab South (Riba 2018). The rectangular cella is also known in the sixth century as in Burǧke and Sitt er-rūm (Figures 28.14–15).

The old three-nave basilicas have elongated plan, narrow spans and aisles, a shallow semi-circular apse, and the tripartite chevet canonical in northern Syria. In Syria I, the point of access to the church was initially on the south side in accordance with a plan derived from domestic architecture, and then increasingly on the west and north sides as at Sinhar, while the churches of Syria II adopted the basilical plan right away. At the

Figure 28.14a Fourth-century single-nave church, Bānaqfūr

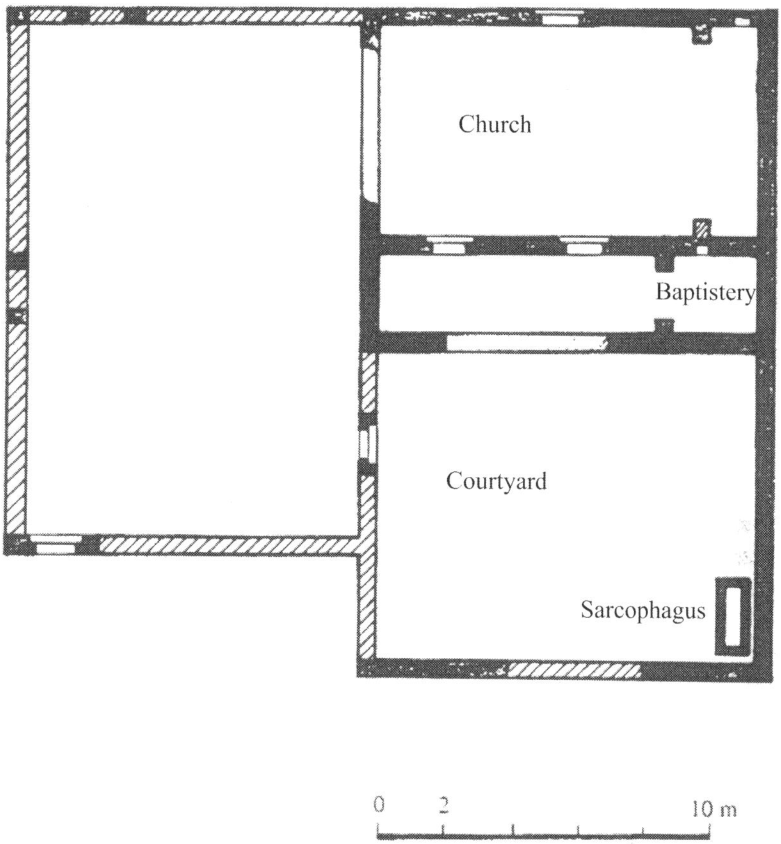

Figure 28.14b Ma'aramāyā

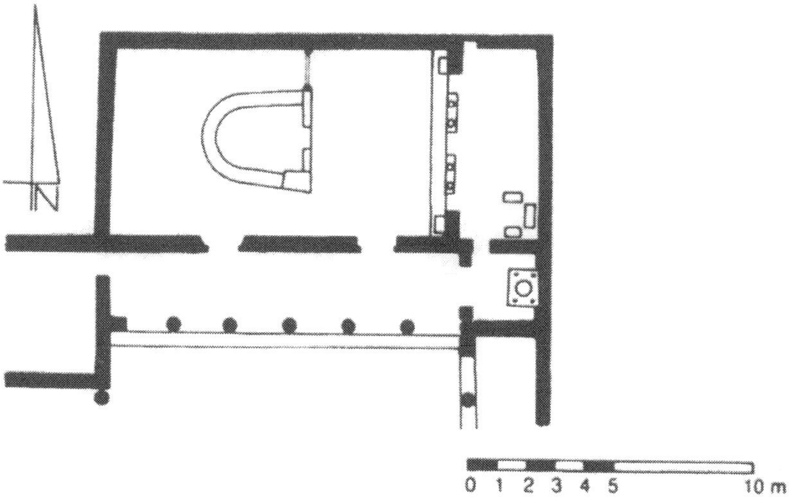

Figure 28.14c Qirkbīze

Figure 28.15a Single-nave chapel, Sūrqānya (sixth century), southern façade

Source: © Syrian-French Mission for Syriac Inscriptions

Figure 28.15b Single-nave chapel, Deiruné

Source: © Syrian-French Mission for Syriac Inscriptions

turn of the fifth century, important innovations may be observed as in the basilica of Julianos at Brād: the presence of points of access on three sides of the building including an axial monumental gate, the appearance of the triple bay, and windows provided with a semi-circular notched lintel become general at the same time as the cornice running around the top of the exterior walls (Figure 28.14). In Ǧebel Barisa, five churches of Markianos Kyris of Bābisqā (390–407), Bāʿūde (392/3), Ksēǧbe (414), Dārqītā (418), and Qarṣ el-Banāt (420) all show the same structural and decorative evolution that marks out the space of these churches and their ornamentation (Figures 28.16–17).

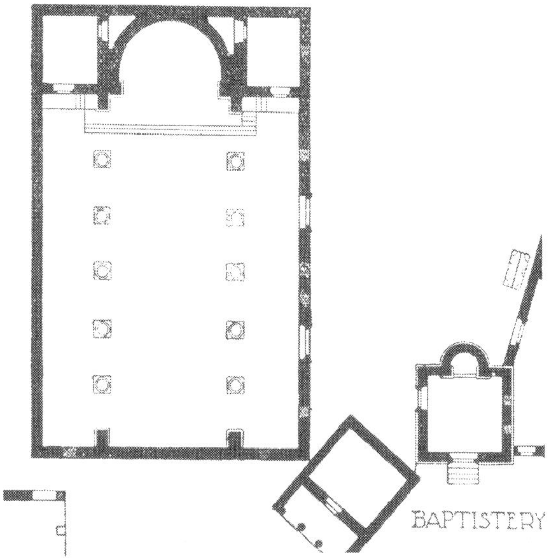

Figure 28.16a Darqita, St Paul and Moses Church of Markianos

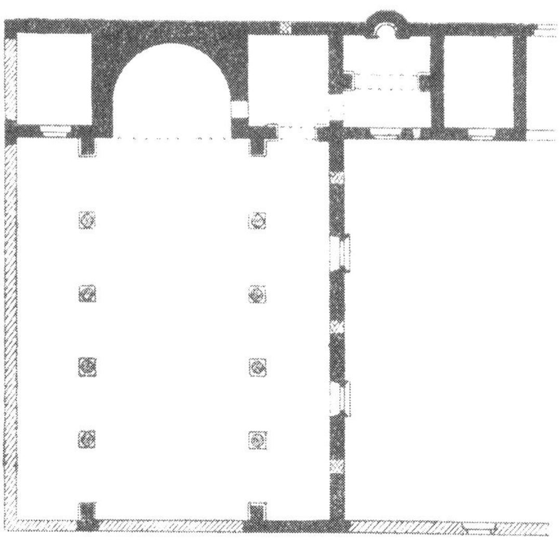

Figure 28.16b Ksēǧbe, Church of Markianos

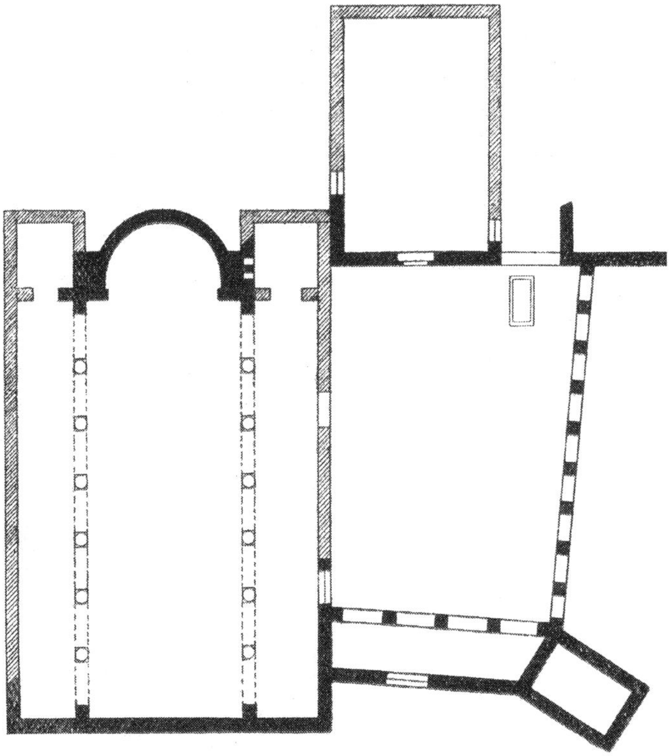

Figure 28.16c Babisqa, Church of Markianos

Figure 28.17a, b, c Decorated capitals from Markianos's church of Ksēğbe

Figure 28.17a, b, c (continued)

The considerable expansion in the cult of relics, combined with the economic and demographic growth extending across the whole of northern Syria, gave rise to an intense period of construction from the 480s. This phenomenon sometimes led to an expansion of the primitive village churches, but more particularly by the addition of one or more pilgrimage basilicas designed to accommodate numerous worshippers. Some buildings retain their local character, as does the western church at Baqirḥa (Figure 28.18). Others belong to the lineage of the great churches built after the prestigious Qalʿat Semʿān shrine built between 476 and 490 (Figure 28.19). This vast group dedicated to Saint Symeon the Elder, itself the result of imperial initiative, introduced architectural and ornamental innovations which then spread rapidly across Syria (Sodini 2010: 318).

It is essentially the colonnaded chevet that is taken up, with different variants, in several churches of the region. At the same time, the influx of pilgrims led to a reconsideration of the interior space of the nave. Pillars replace arches to give more volume and unity to the interior volume of the church. These supporting elements made it possible to go beyond the limits of the arch-on-columns which were preponderant in the Limestone Massif. Among the thirteen basilicas known in the region, mostly located in the Ǧebels Il-Aʿla (Tchalenko 1953–58) and Waṣṭāni (Khoury and Castellana 1990), it is those at Banassara North (Khoury 2005a) and Kefert ʿAqab South (Riba 2018) that have the distinctive characteristic of combining the shape of the pillar with that of the column. Some pillars, provided with lateral buttresses

Figure 28.18a Western façade and narthex of the western church at Baqirḥa

Figure 28.18b Eastern façade of the western church at Baqirḥa

Figure 28.18c Lintel with Syriac and Greek inscriptions on the western door of the western church at Baqirḥa

Source: © Syrian-French Mission for Syriac Inscriptions

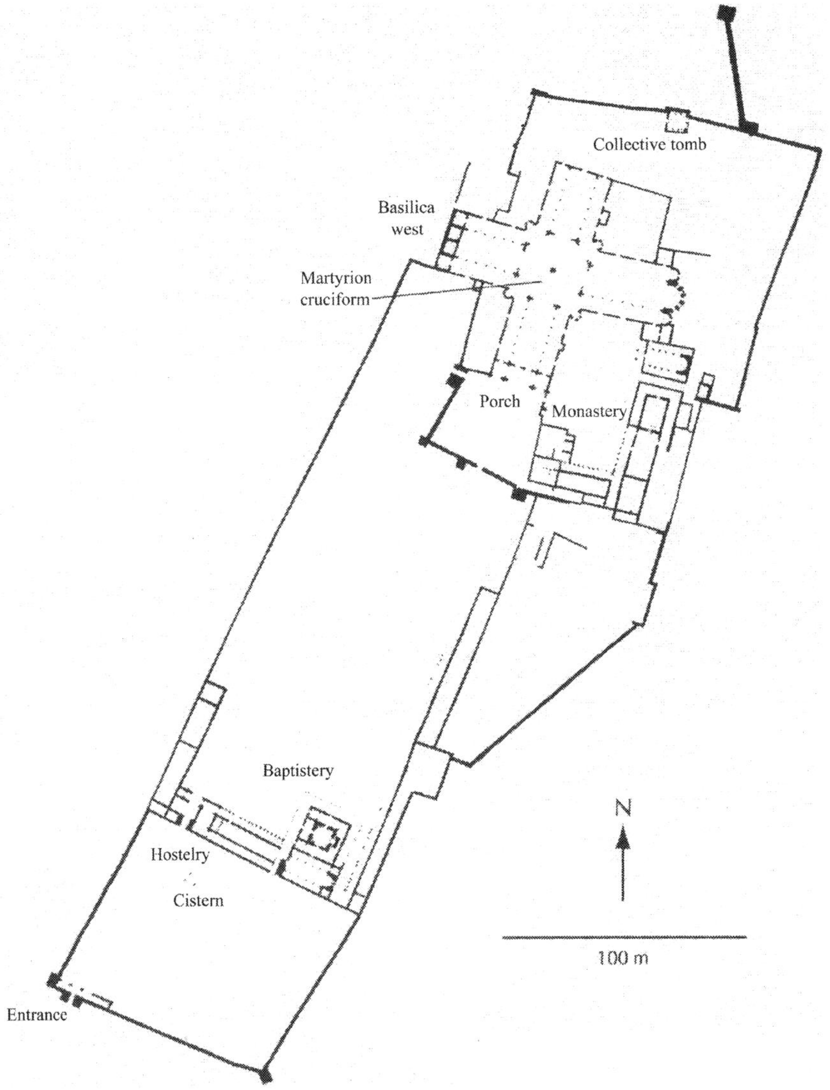

Figure 28.19 General plan of the monastery complex of Qal'at Sem'ān

Source: Courtesy of Jean-Luc Biscop

(Figure 28.20), are cruciform as at Ruweiḥa; others, with only one, are T-shaped as in Ṭurīn (Khoury and Castellana 1990).

The most common type of chevet is an apse enclosed inside a straight wall across the whole width of the building. In some cases, the apsidal form of the sanctuary is lost in favour of a rectilinear partitioning of the tripartite sanctuary. The chevet with semi-circular apse, partially enclosed between lateral chambers, was known in the fourth century at Fafertīn (Tchalenko and Baccache 1979: 44, fig. 84) and appears elsewhere in the fifth and sixth centuries, e.g. in the churches of Bāsūfān, Deir Turmānīn, Bānqūsa (Figure 28.21), 'Aršīn and others.

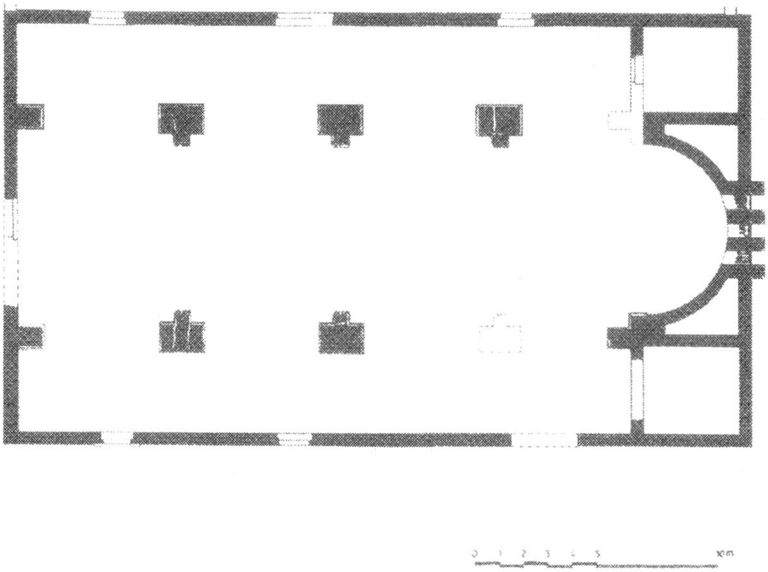

Figure 28.20 Ṭurīn, western church II with T-shaped pillars

Figure 28.21 Partially enclosed apse of the southern church of Bānqūsa

Some three-nave churches have a principal projecting apse as at Qalblōze (Figure 28.22), Kīmar East, and E3 at El-Bāra. Finally, there is the chevet with three prominent apses of the east basilica at Qalʿat Simʿan (Figure 28.23) (Biscop and Sodini 1984: 269–75), whose model is reproduced in Kefert ʿAqab and north of Laodicea, in the church of Bahr al Midan, formerly El-Dyar (Riba 2012).

Figure 28.22a, b Projecting apse, Qalblōze

Figure 28.22c Interior of projecting apse, Qalblōze

Figure 28.23 Three prominent apses of the eastern basilica, Qalʿat Semʿān

The churches of central Syria

The well-preserved churches of the Reṣafa pilgrimage complex are the best known in the region but do not represent a characteristic evolution. In general, the churches are preceded by a portico and are located in the centre of a complex provided with various annexes. The dimensions and the degree of attention given to these ensembles vary according to the locality. There is a variant on this organisation in Al-Ruhaiyah (Figure 28.24), where three basilicas are gathered around a courtyard (Butler 1920: 23–4), and again in Andarin, where the basilica is located in the centre of the kastron. Some of them are provided with towers, as in Zebed, Al-Habbat, and Tell Draham (Mouterde and Poidebard 1945, 2: 94).

The plans of these churches are of the type of the three-nave Syrian basilica, covered with a frame roof and equipped with a tripartite sanctuary. Pillars as well as the columns are attested from as early as the fourth century as at Iʿǧāz (Lassus 1947: 177, 236), and continued to be used during the following centuries. In Ḥawarīn, all the identified churches are pillared (Khoury 2005b: 299–316). Some are flanked by lateral buttresses designed to carry the frame of the main nave as in Reṣafa in the Basilica of the Holy Cross and in Ḥalabiyye. The points of access on both the south side and the west, together with the porticos being more numerous in front of the west facades, nevertheless suggest a certain preference for this western side of the churches. We can note the presence of a tribelon (triple-arched opening) in certain buildings: Dibsi

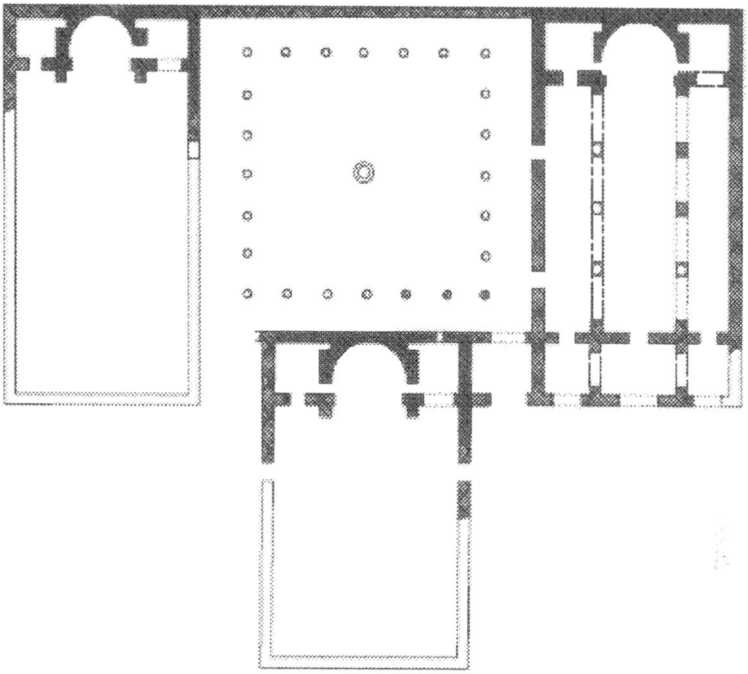

Figure 28.24 Ecclesial ensemble with three basilicas, al-Ruhaiyah

Farağ (Harper and Taylor 1975, fig. F; Donceel-Voûte 1988: 78, fig. 46), the Holy Cross in Reṣafa, and the cathedral of Kerratīn (Butler 1920: Plate 10), recalling the E4 church of El-Bāra (Sodini 1989a: 360, fig. 90) and that of Ras el-Bassit (Beaudry 2005: 119–36).

Aside from the rectilinear chevet, there are some variants, such as churches with semi-circular apses enclosed between annexes as at Andarīn and Reṣāfa. In Qaṣr Abu Samra and Dibsi Farağ (Lassus 1947, 1: 154, fig. 156), the apse is set back from the projecting appendages as at Palmyra (Gabriel 1926: 88–90, pl. 16; Lassus 1947: 168) and at Ḥalabiyye (Lauffray 1991: fig. 21). The Kanasir church has three prominent apses enclosed in a polygonal massif (Burton and Drake 1872: II, 181) The less numerous single-nave churches are attested in Deir Nawa, Andarīn, and elsewhere. They show the same variations in access points and chevets as attested in the northern region (Figures 28.25–26).

Churches of southern Syria

The groups of churches in this region follow the plans and technical processes used in the general architecture of the region, where the presence of basalt and the absence of wood led to the construction of 'Pseudo-basilicas' with transverse arches perpendicular to the axis of the nave to support a stone slab covering. The single-nave and

Figure 28.25a Tripartite eastern church, Ḥalabiyye, Central Syria

Source: © Syrian-French Mission in Zenobia

Figure 28.25b Tripartite central church, Palmyra, Central Syria

Figure 28.26a Lateral buttresses carrying the nave of the Holy Cross Basilica, Reṣafa, Central Syria

Figure 28.26b Rectilinear chevet in al-Rouhbane church, Ḥawarīn, Central Syria

three-nave churches, often with a western portico, are distinguished only by the presence of an apse. They are integrated into an ensemble surrounded by a courtyard designed on the model of a house (Lassus 1947: 25–8). The church of Julianos of Umm al-Jimāl of 345 (Butler 1920: 173–6) is one of the earliest examples of this local architecture.

In Taḥfa there are three-nave churches constructed according to this method, which were later replaced in the fifth century by longitudinal arches (Lassus 1947: 47–53; Restle 1989: 374), which were required by the adoption of the basilica plan and the framework roof. These basilicas are known in Boṣrà and Umm al-Jimāl, in the 'cathedral' dated 557. The two types of arches are found in the church of Šahbā and the use of columns is observed in Shaqrā and Boṣrà.

The tripartite chevet developed slowly over the course of the sixth century when the annexes were contemporaneous with the construction of the building. The chevets of the basilicas of southern Syria are diverse, as may be seen in the fifteen churches of Umm al-Jimāl (Lassus 1947: 61) (Figure 28.27). The single-nave chapels multiplied from the second half of the sixth century. These buildings of small dimensions often constitute the centre-point of a monastic complex, such as the northern church of Ḥīt (Figure 28.28), which is characterised by a rectangular sanctuary (Khoury and Riba 2013).

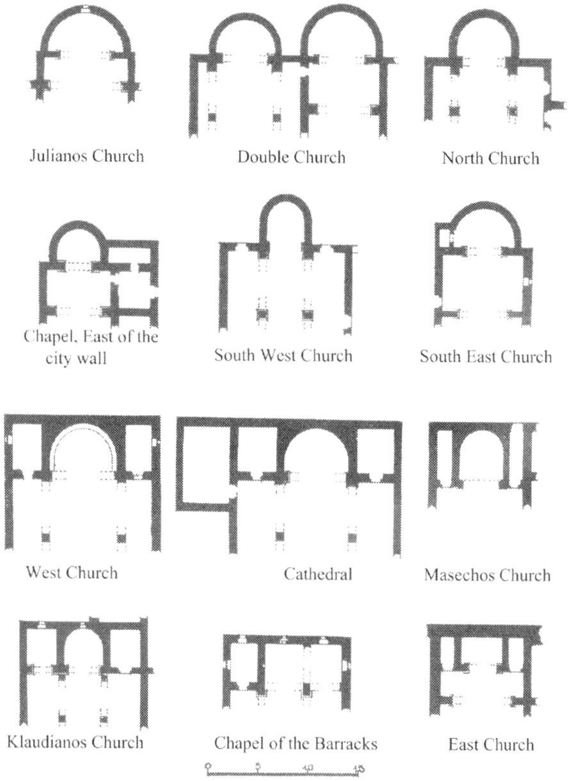

Figure 28.27 Different forms of chevet in southern Syria

Figure 28.28 Aerial view of the northern church, Ḥīt, Southern Syria

Prestige architecture

Parallel to the basilicas, an architecture of prestige, with a centred or cruciform plan, also developed. Both types can be found in the martyrion of Qalʿat Semʿān: the central octagon surrounding the stylite's column marks the starting point for four three-nave basilicas. The baptistery, similar to the central nucleus of the martyrion, is enclosed inside a square building (Figure 28.30). This plan is imitated, albeit with variations, in the monastery dedicated to Saint Symeon the Younger, completed in 551 (Mécérian 1964). The free-cross plan is well represented by the fourth-century church of Antioch Qausiye (Figure 28.29). Buildings with an enclosed cross, however, offered a plan well adapted to the tripartite arrangement of the chevet, as at Andarīn (Butler 1920: 56, fig. 50), Reṣāfa, and Qaṣr Ibn Wardan. The Gold Church in Antioch (Lassus 1947: 109; Goilav 2010) and the martyrion of Ḥomṣ (Saliby and Griesheimer 1999: 383–400) were both built on an octagonal plan.

We may note also the polygonal buildings associated with the churches in Deir Sētā (Figure 28.31) (Butler 1929: 155; Lassus 1947: 226; Khoury 1987: 97–110), Deir Sunbul, and also Mirʿayāh and Mūgleyyā. The church of Faʾlūl (Butler 1920: 96, fig. 113), with its central plan, has a rotunda like that at Apamea (Balty 1977: 145). Finally, tetraconch churches become very popular (Kleinbauer 1973: 89–114) from the end of the fifth century at Seleuceia

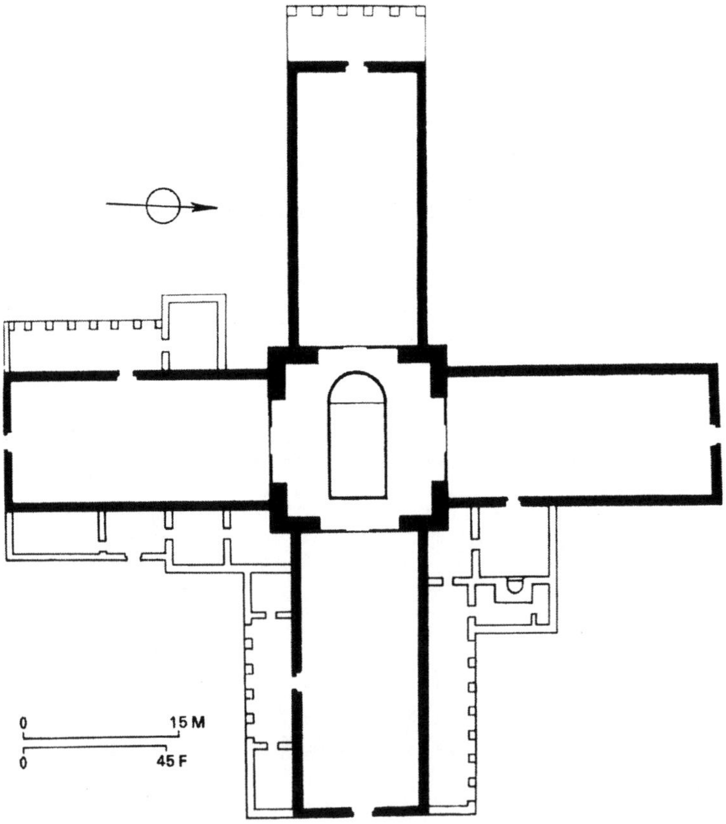

Figure 28.29 The cross-shaped church of Saint Babylas, Antioch-Qausiye

Figure 28.30a The cross-shaped church of the Martyrium, Qalʿat Semʿān

Source: Yves Guichard

Figure 28.30b Eastern basilica of the Martyrium, Qalʿat Semʿān

Figure 28.31a South-western façade of the Martyrium, Deir Seta

Figure 28.31b South-eastern façade of the Martyrium, Deir Seta

Pieri (Campbell 1941 III: 35), Apamea (Balty 1976: 31–46), in the martyrion of Reṣāfa (Brands 2002: 123, fig. 15), and in Ḥawarīn (Khoury 2005b: 312–13) (Figure 28.32).

The central-planned buildings developed in Boṣrà in the sixth century. The remarkable cathedral (Blanc et al. 2007; Blanc and Piraud-Fournet 2010) has a square plan containing a central circular space 30 m in diameter edged by a colonnade, an ambulatory, and a polygonal chevet. The church of Saints Sergius, Bacchus, and Leontes in Boṣrà also features a centred plan with a quatrefoil inner colonnade. The church of Ezra' has exedrae formed at the corners, a nucleus with eight octagonal angular pillars, and an octagonal apse (Figure 28.33).

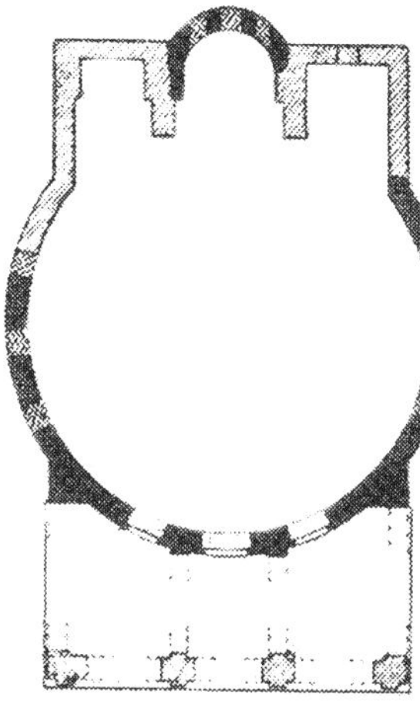

Figure 28.32a Archangels's Church, Fa'lūl

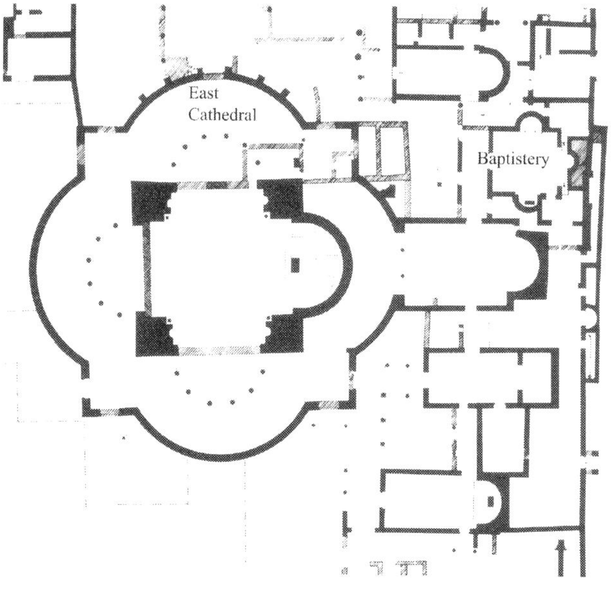

Figure 28.32b Apamea Cathedral

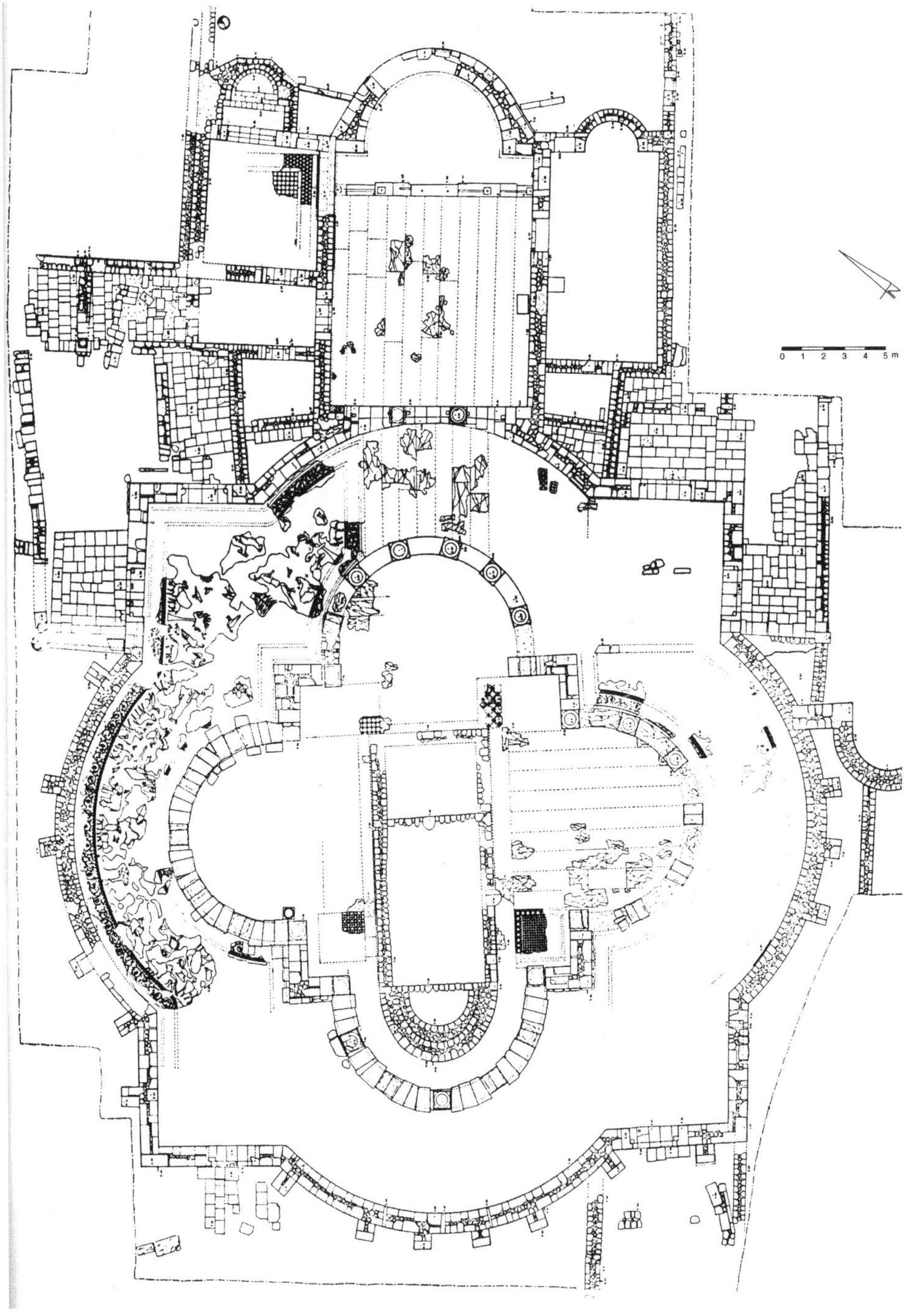

Figure 28.32c Martyrium of Seleuceia Pieri

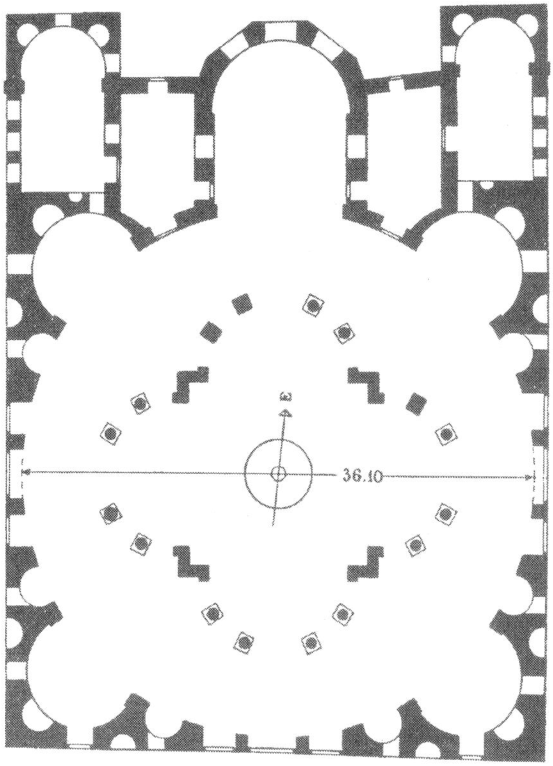

Figure 28.33a Bosra Cathedral

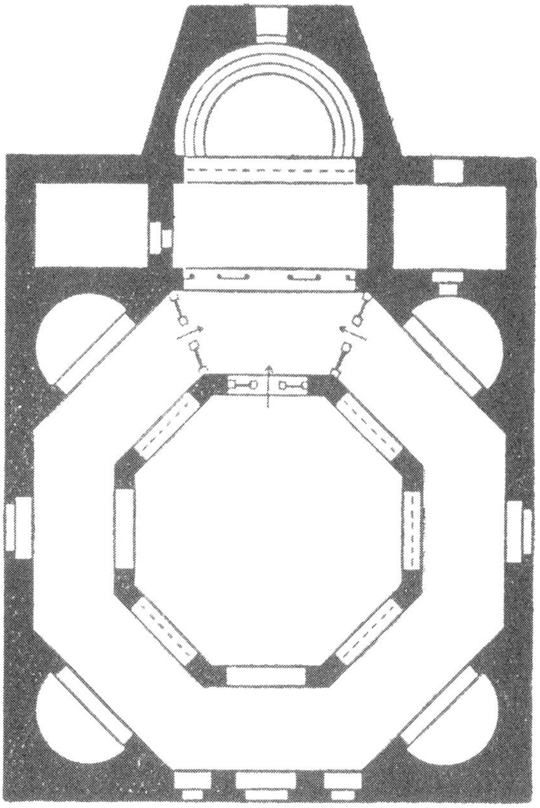

Figure 28.33b Church of St George, Ezra'

THE SPATIAL AND LITURGICAL ARRANGEMENT OF CHURCHES

During the first quarter of the fifth century, certain liturgical distinctions emerged in the different regions of Syria (Balty 1980: 465–81). Generally, in the Antiochene, the martyrion opens through an arch on the lower south side, while on the north the diaconicon communicates by means of gates with the collaterals and with the apse. In the Apamene and 'central Syria', this liturgical disposition is reversed as at Serğilla and Kefert ʿAqab. At Ras al-Bassit, the two annexes each open onto the apse by a door and onto the sides through an arch (Beaudry 2005: 119–36). In the sanctuary, the synthronon, welcoming members of the clergy, is common in the Apamene, but is also attested in some churches in north Syria, including St Symeon, Deir Semʿān (Azpeitia 2005: 44–5), Banassara North (Khoury 2005a: 259, pl. 8), and Maʾchouqa and Ras el-Bassit. It is known in Euphratesia, at Dibsi Faraj and in three basilicas in Reṣāfa (Ulbert 1986: 25–32, 136–7), also at Palmyra, in Lebanese Phoenicia (Gawlikowski 1993, 2008), and at Boṣrà in southern Syria. The most widespread type of barrier dividing the choir from the nave of the church is made of stone panels held by low pillars arranged on either side of a central entrance. The whole was surmounted by a curtain supported by a rod. In Kefert ʿAqab, the chancel was closed by a metal grid on either side of a short solea closed off by a wooden barrier. Except in the Apamene, churches do not have any galleries or U-shaped sides, except for those arranged above the porches and those of the terrace on the south side of the church of Qalblōze (Tchalenko 1990).

The bêma (Figure 28.34), better known in the Antiochene, is attested in several churches of the Apamene: in Saint-Maurice in Apamea (Balty 2013), Hir eš Šeiḫ in Umm Ḥerteyn (Donceel-Voûte 1988: 193, fig. 165), Qumhane and Tayyibet

Figure 28.34a Bêma facing the apse at Kafr Daret Azzeh church

Figure 28.34b The bêma of Kirkbisé church

Figure 28.34c Throne of the bêma at Kirkbisé

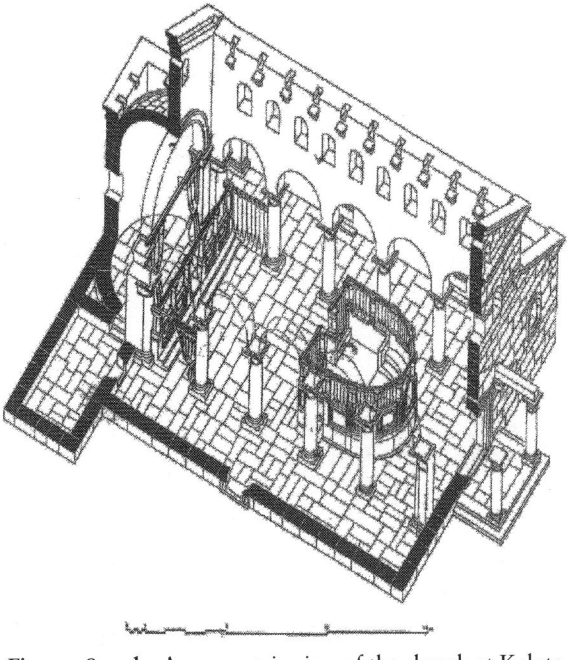

Figure 28.34d Axonometric view of the church at Kalota

Figure 28.34e Reconstruction of the bêma of the Holy Cross Church, Reṣafa

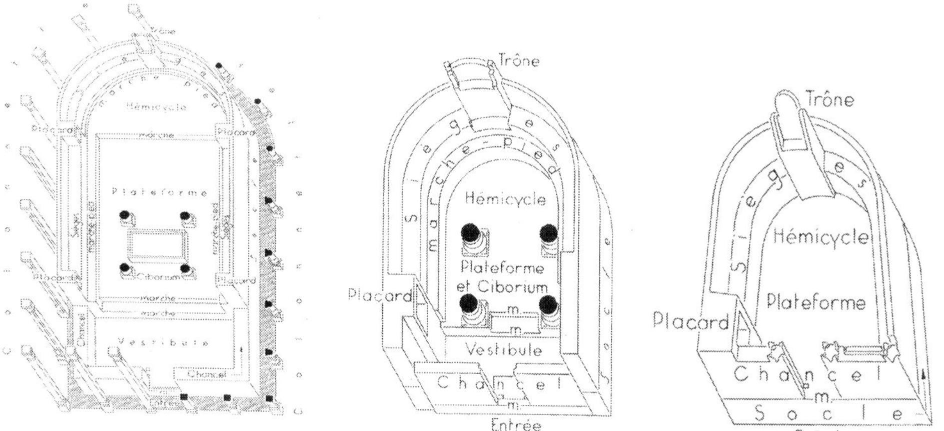

Figure 28.34f Schematic presentation of three variants of the bêma

el-Imam (Zaqzuq and Piccirillo 1999: 453–4, fig. 3), at Dibsi Faraj and Reṣāfa, Al-Firjah, Rayan, and Zebed. They vary in their dimensions and arrangements, but they seem to have been used like an ambon for the reading of the sacred text, for housing seats for members of the clergy, and/or for an altar. The bêma is always added to the centre of churches of martyr cults, richly decorated with polished columns and surmounted by a cross at its semi-circular end, thereby evoking the Holy Sepulchre.

Finally, the ambon is common in the Apamene (Ḥuarte, Deir Soleib, and Mūgleyyā), in Euphratesia (Reṣāfa, Dibsi Faraj, and Halabiyye), in Lebanese Phoenicia, at Palmyra, and in the Antiochene (Deir Semʿān, Baʿūde, Bafetīn, and Banassara). On the other hand, in Osrhoene and Mesopotamia, it is part of the essential equipment of the Syro-oriental liturgy, as in the church of the tell at Hassake, which presents a circular ambon carried by mini columns (Khoury and Riba 2013b). This installation is similar to others, especially that of the church of Tell aš-Šayḫ Ḥasan (Roumi 1975: 227–30) located in the Ṭur ʿAbdin. The church of Hassake also shows the masonry corridor (*shqaqonā*), which connects the ambon to the sanctuary, a typical arrangement in the East Syriac area (Figure 28.35). This narrow passage, which was to be flanked by decorated plates, is attested also in Palmyra and Bazyan.

Figure 28.35a Tell Hassake church with shqaqonā and ambon

Figure 28.35b Detail of the circular ambon

Figure 28.35c, d, e, f Decorated capitals of Tell Hassake church

Figure 28.35c, d, e, f (continued)

Figure 28.35c, d, e, f (continued)

Moreover, the spatial organisation and the existence of certain arrangements make it possible to draw parallels between the churches of these regions and those of northern Syria. The form of the Nestorian church as described by Connolly (1913) on the basis of an anonymous 10th/11th-century account of the Nestorian liturgy includes many readily anticipated features (Lassus 1950: 236–52), even though this *expositio* does not mention the chapel of the martyrs (Figure 28.36). There is also no masonry corridor, but several indications pointed out by Sodini underline the importance accorded to the space between the bêma and the sanctuary in the liturgy of the churches of northern Syria (Sodini 2006: 257–9).

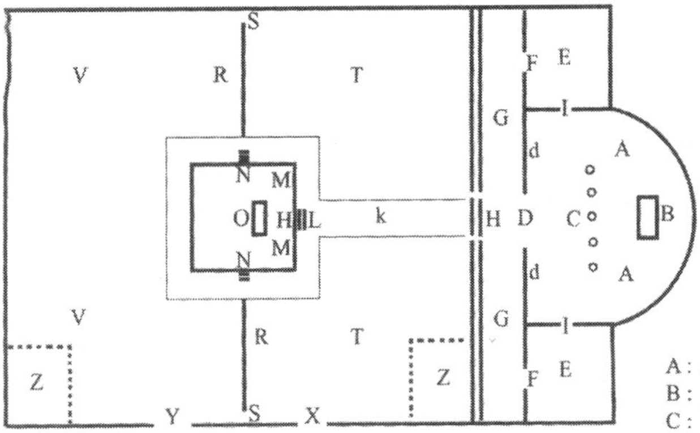

Delineatio Ecclesiae
Adapted from Connolly, after *Expositio Officiorum Ecclesiae*

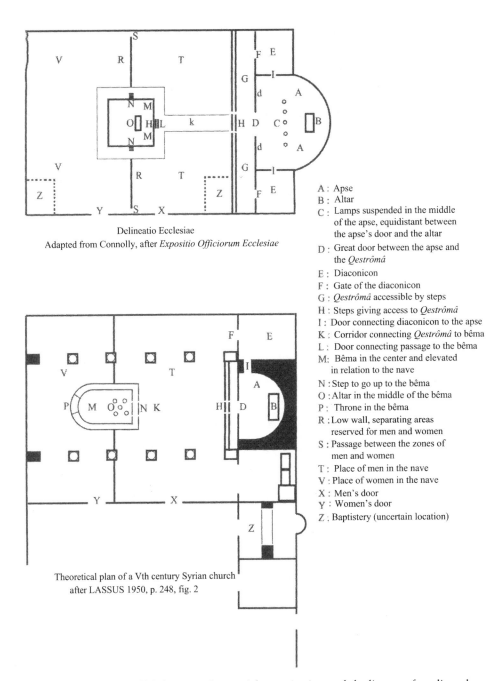

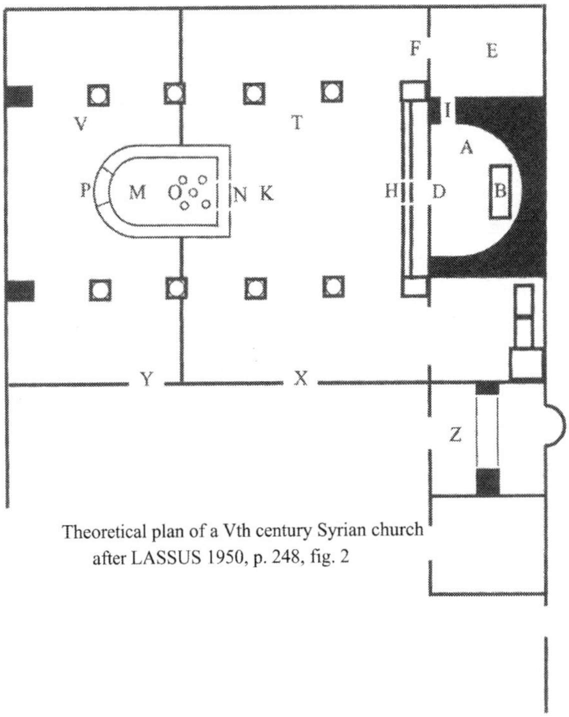

Theoretical plan of a Vth century Syrian church
after LASSUS 1950, p. 248, fig. 2

A : Apse
B : Altar
C : Lamps suspended in the middle of the apse, equidistant between the apse's door and the altar
D : Great door between the apse and the *Qestrômâ*
E : Diaconicon
F : Gate of the diaconicon
G : *Qestrômâ* accessible by steps
H : Steps giving access to *Qestrômâ*
I : Door connecting diaconicon to the apse
K : Corridor connecting *Qestrômâ* to bêma
L : Door connecting passage to the bêma
M: Bêma in the center and elevated in relation to the nave
N : Step to go up to the bêma
O : Altar in the middle of the bêma
P : Throne in the bêma
R : Low wall, separating areas reserved for men and women
S : Passage between the zones of men and women
T : Place of men in the nave
V : Place of women in the nave
X : Men's door
Y : Women's door
Z : Baptistery (uncertain location)

Figure 28.36 Parallels between the spatial organisation and the liturgy of mediaeval Mesopotamian churches and the ancient churches of northern Syria

CONVERGENCE AND DIFFUSION: PATTERNS OUTSIDE OF SYRIA

North-east Proto-Byzantine Syria: the Edessa region

In the north-east of Proto-Byzantine Syria in Nisibis (Nusaybin), the church of Mar Yaʿqub is a unique monument that, according to its epigraphic dating, belongs to the early history of Christian monuments (Figure 28.37). Justine Gaborit was able to complete the study of the complex and to publish the final developed plan of a tripartite basilica based around a central nucleus (Gaborit and Thébault 2013).

Figure 28.37a Church of Mar Yaqub, western façade

Figure 28.37b Mar Yaqub, details of a lintel

Source: © J. Gaborit & G. Thébault

Dedicated to Jacob I, bishop of Nisibis 308–338, founder of a famous theological school, it was built in 359 under Bishop Vologeses and the priest Akepsimas. This date is to be retained despite the presence of arches and decorative elements reminiscent of sixth-century churches: for the use of horseshoe arches is attested at St Simeon, rinceaux of acanthus scrolls may be found on the lintels of the churches of Deir Seta (Khoury 1987), and the door frames with their friezes resemble those at Reṣafa. The naturalistic representation is attested in the churches of Baricha, Bankoussa, and Sheikh Sleiman. The patterns of double rows of helical leaves are comparable with the decoration of St Sophia. But this neat decoration combining inventiveness with technical mastery may have originated in the Roman cities of Hatra and Palmyra, whose architecture was influenced by Sasanian art. By this route we can more easily understand the fourth-century dating of Mar Ya'qub, a key monument of Eastern Christian art.

Around Mar Ya'qub, as elsewhere in the Edessene region, churches, and even monasteries did not have a real communal identity. Until the sixth century, it was only the patriarch of Antioch who, due to his imperial patronage, was officially able to manage the Christian communities. With the Arab Conquest of the seventh century, the borders between Eastern and Western Syriac disappear and Byzantine influence becomes more restricted. This situation was favourable for the separation of groups and encouraged the emergence in the eighth century of architectural innovations linked to the development of local workshops supporting local identities. Many church naves, especially those in the monasteries, became transverse as happened at Mar Ya'qub in Ṣalaḥ (Figure 28.38).

The external oratory, which was to become the house of prayer, was introduced, as were lateral pillars, large apse archivolts, and monumentally sized sculptured crosses.

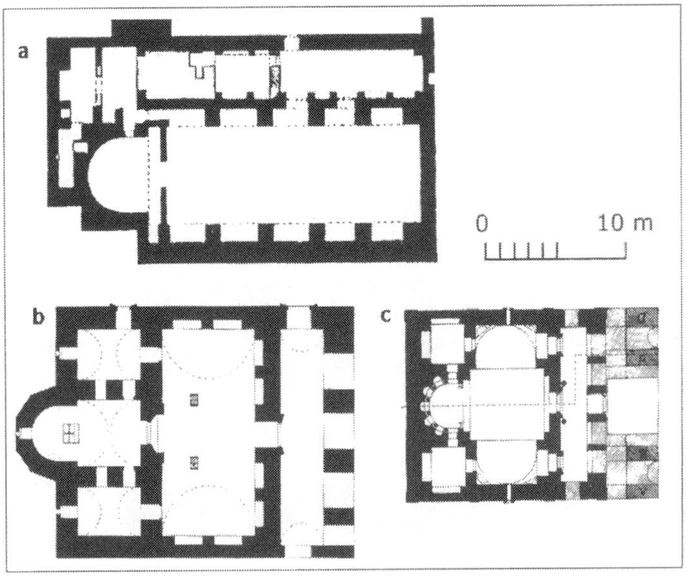

Figure 28.38 a: Mor 'Azozoyel, Keferzi; b: Mor Ya'qub, Ṣalaḥ; c: Mor Aloho, Hab

At the time of the Syriac renaissance (twelfth–thirteenth centuries), the development of churches in the Ṭur ʿAbdin follows that of local Eastern architecture, now under the influence of Muslim culture (Keser-Kayaalp 2013).

To the east of the Euphrates, in the north of Mesopotamia, the church of Bazian (Déroche and Ali Amin 2013), built against the wall on the inside of a fortified enclosure, makes it possible to observe an association of influences distinctive of the two banks of the Euphrates. On the one hand, the orientation of its plan continues the tradition of the Syrian basilicas: it has three naves separated by two rows of columns and a bêma and is preceded by a portico to the south and a narthex to the west (Figure 28.39).

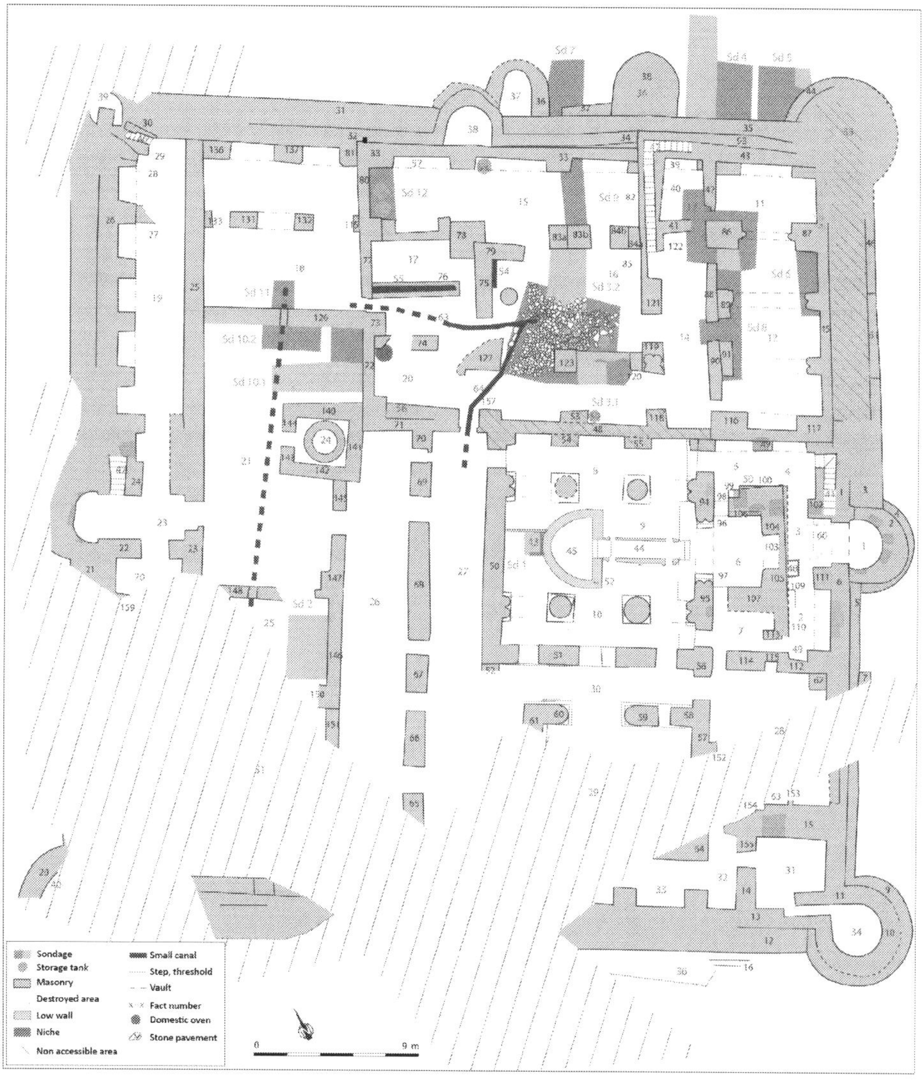

Figure 28.39a Plan of the church of Bazian

Source: © French mission Bazyan

Figure 28.39b General view of Bazian church

Source: © French mission Bazyan

Figure 28.39c Shqaqona Tell Hassakeh church

Figure 28.39d Shqaqona of central church at Palmyra

Source: © French mission Bazyan

On the other hand, the construction techniques, certain architectural details, and the decorative scheme are all owed to local traditions: columns and walls are constructed of rubble-bound mortar, as at the church of the Tell at Hassakeh (Khoury and Riba 2013b). The sanctuary, accessible by an axial entrance, opens through two side doors onto a peripheral corridor.

The decoration is marked by the use of moulded stucco, scriptures, and small circular motifs known in Mesopotamia since the second millennium BCE and in vogue during the Sasanian era.

The inscriptions are mostly liturgical, while the presence of incised and painted plaques bearing stylised crosses is better attested to the north where the necessary stone is available. There are two schemes that continued to be in use from the sixth to the nineteenth centuries: the eastern church with its Chaldean branch, and the Orthodox or Catholic Syriac church, whose nave and sanctuaries are tripartite and separated by a wall open to an axial gate (Figure 28.40). The bêma, when it exists, is connected to the sanctuary by a narrow passage, as in the churches of el-Ḥira XI, al-Kenisa, and elsewhere. Martyrions may be present, as at Mar Behnam (Harrak 2013) (Figure 28.41) or the church of the monastery of Rabban Hormizd, whose foundation dates from the fourteenth century. This last, partly formed from a cave, has a single nave, the dome of the sanctuary is decorated by muqarnas, and the tomb of the saint is integrated into the monastic complex (Brelaud 2013).

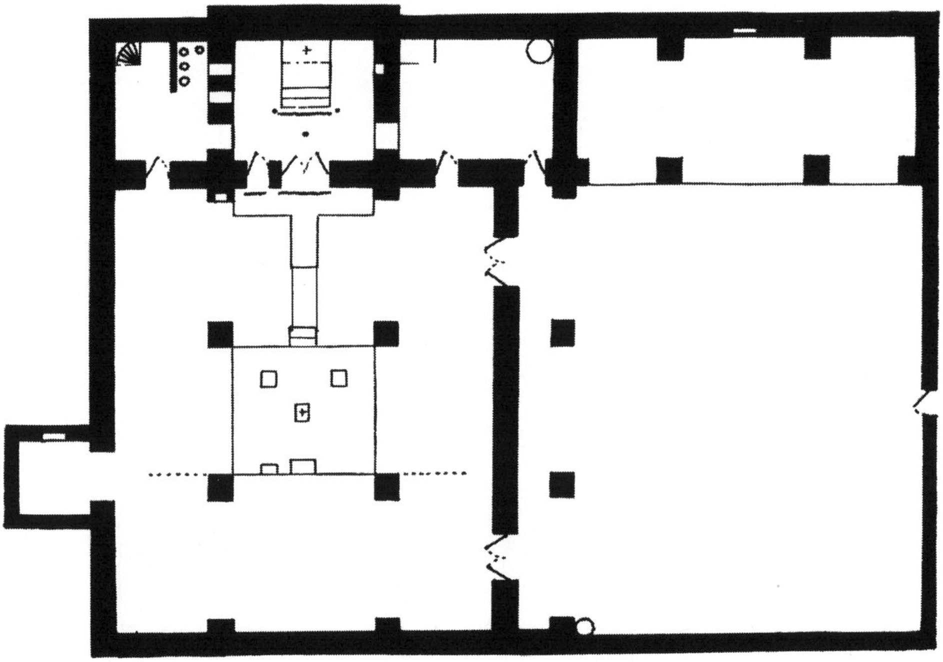

Figure 28.40a The Chaldaean scheme of the Syriac Church

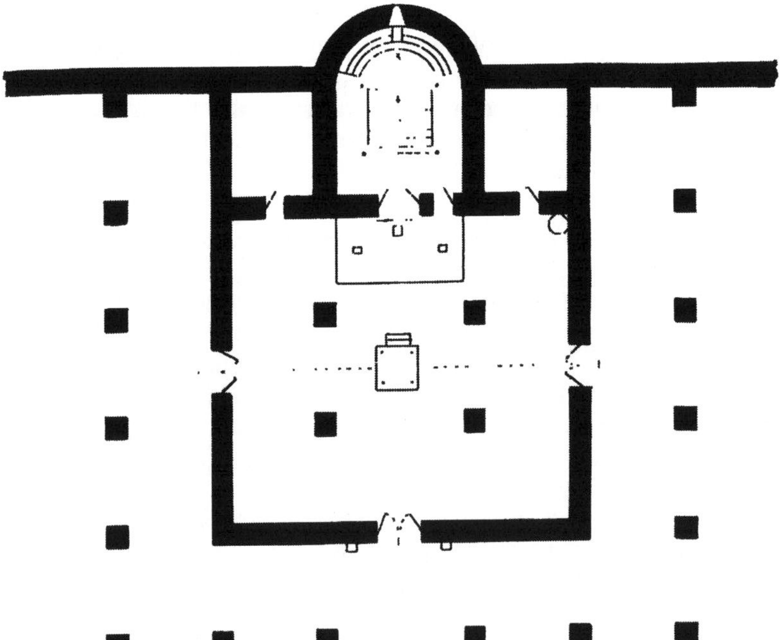

Figure 28.40b The Orthodox and Catholic scheme of the Syriac Church

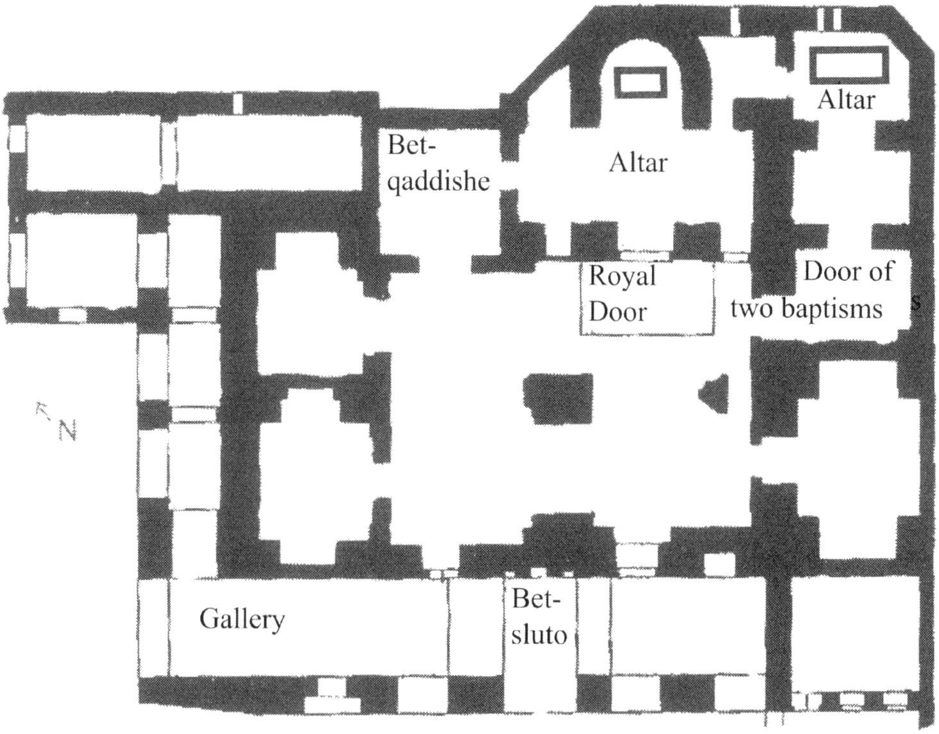

Figure 28.41a Monastery of Mar Behnam near Mosul

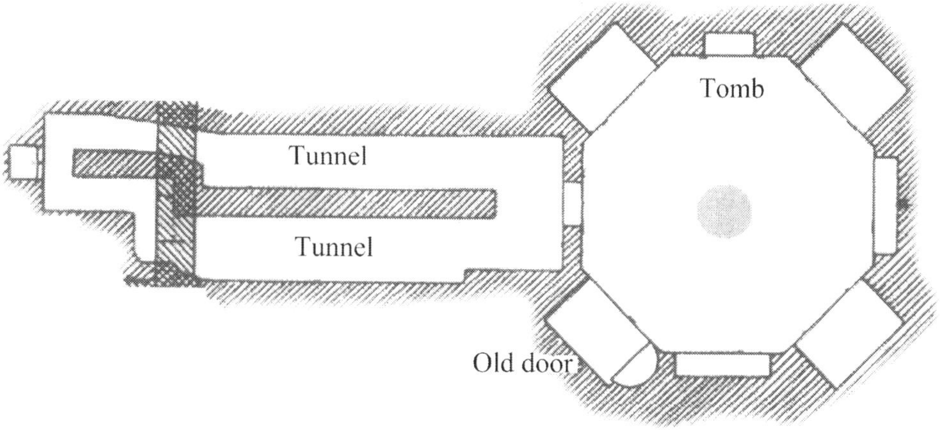

Figure 28.41b Martyrion of Mar Behnam near Mosul

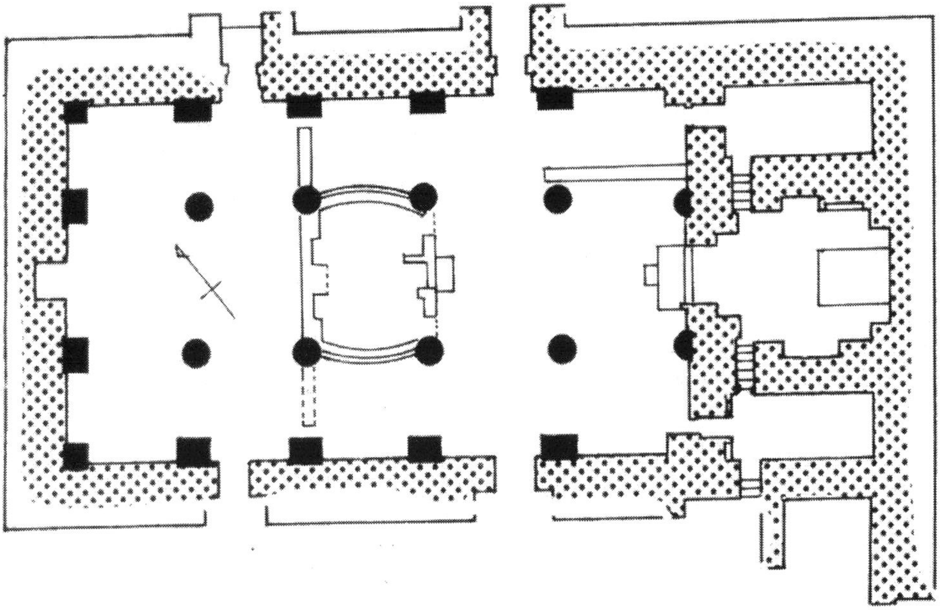

Figure 28.41c Church of El-Ḥira XI

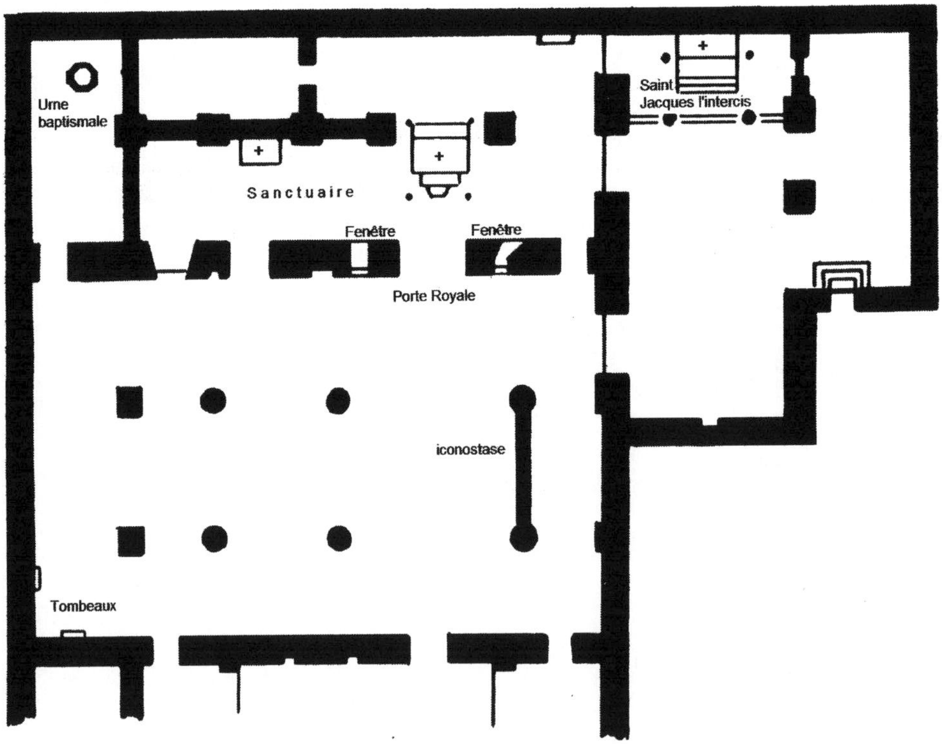

Figure 28.41d Church of El-Tahira, Mosul

Churches of the province of Arabia

In the province of Arabia, the major urban centres are quite distinct from the village communities since most of their churches have an architecture more akin to that of the monumental buildings of the Hellenised and Romanised Mediterranean regions (Michel 2013). In the village context, architecture is marked by the use of local building materials and techniques. The liturgical arrangements present a broad homogeneity, and even without any detailed knowledge of the liturgy practiced in a particular church, it is clear that there is a close relationship with the buildings of the provinces of Palestine under the patriarchate of Jerusalem. And although they belong to the jurisdiction of the patriarchate of Antioch, these churches belong to a liturgical tradition different from that of the Syriac context.

In Transjordan at Kilwa (Bell 2000: 76), near a settlement, five small cells are built with different fittings around a church. The latter consists of a single oriented nave, with semi-circular apse, flanked by two niches. It is accessible by two gates to the south and west and has two crosses engraved on its blocks, similar to those engraved on the walls of other cells (Farès 2013). It is a monastic complex with a cistern, a common room, and a tomb, which was supposed to be connected with the rocky hermitage hewed out of the nearby rock flank (Horsfield et al. 1933: 383; Horsfield 1943: 74) (Figure 28.42).

Arab populations of different types, speaking Arabic and belonging to sedentary or pastoral circles, used to meet and communicate in monasteries and churches for many different purposes. Rock hermitages in the steppes, village churches, rural

Figure 28.42a Church of Kilwa

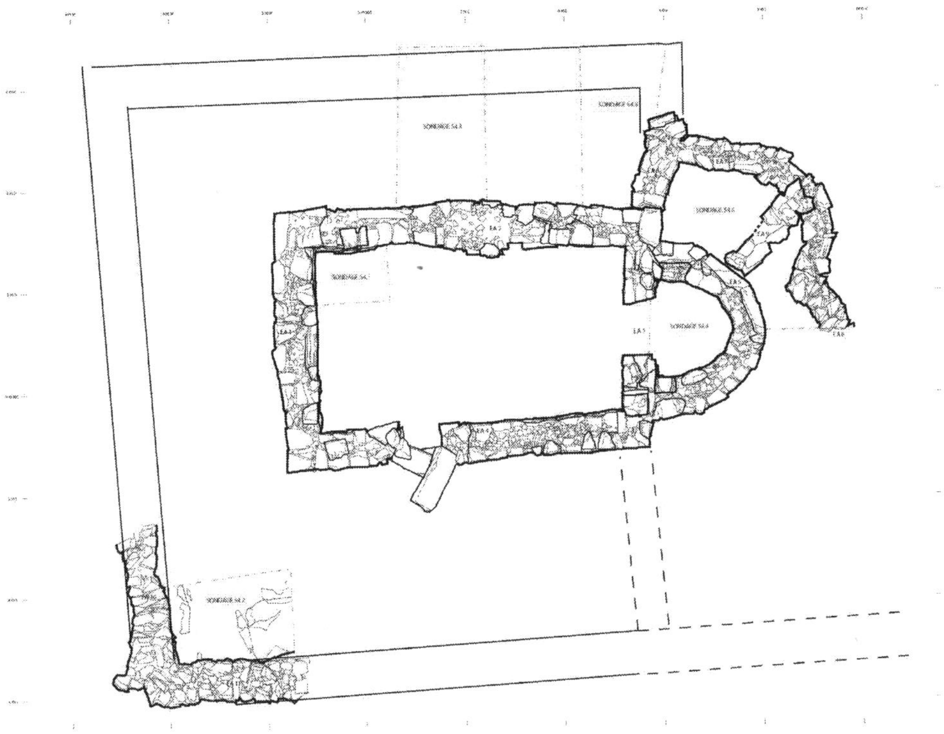

Figure 28.42b Church of Kilwa plan

monasteries, and great pilgrimage sites are places where mutual relations between these two worlds were woven together and where cultural and practical ideas were transmitted (Fowden 2013). The pastoral environment is known from various sources, including the lives of saints, ecclesiastical stories, and graffiti. These hostile spaces, almost devoid of agriculture, constituted the life setting of the hermits and the breeders attracted by spirituality, and by the impressing aspect of the hermitages hewed from the rock.

Always built near a water source and a road, these hermitages were composed of prayer and meeting spaces, guest accommodation, and monks' cells. The best known are those in Palestine such as the 'Chariton' (Hirschfeld 1992: 23–4, 229–33), founded by the monk himself beside the source of Ein en-Natouf and which is the most important example of a laura in the Judean desert. We also think of Theoctistus in Ein er-Rashash and others. These hermitages were established among the rocks, close to a water supply and to roads linking the nomadic environment with that of the sedentary Christians. They recall the Christian locations at Qusayr near Karbalā' and Kilwa, whose vocation is confirmed by an Arabic inscription: 'In the name of God, this is the protected territory of the community of Thecla, originating in Iqlîm'. The best-documented hermitage is that of Centum Putea (Dussaud 1927) at Bir Jazal. It offers a model pattern of organisation (Abou Sekeh 2017): located near a water supply next to the Palmyra-Hama road, it is entirely carved into the rock and includes a common block in the centre, the individual cells of

Figure 28.43 View of the hermitage of Centum Putea near Bir Jazal

Source: Abou Sekeh

the monks carved out separately, as well as the guest house which was added later (Figure 28.43).

Churches and monasteries, which played an important role in the Christianisation of the Arabs, continued to be places of encounter until the ninth century. Those of al-Ḥīra and the plain of Ghūṭa-Basra, located on the fringes of the sedentary settlements, are examples of meeting places of populations of different origin, gathering together for a variety of communal activities. They consist of ensembles composed of houses, churches, and monasteries interspersed with spaces and gardens opening on the pasturages and surrounded by huts, tents, and other ephemeral structures. The rural monasteries were developing, and the great churches were becoming sites of pilgrimage, such as at the martyrion of Symeon the Stylite and the sanctuary of St Sergius in Reṣāfa, which attracted an enormous number of Arabs. These places contributed to the creation of close relations and exchanges between all types of populations, nomadic or sedentary, who were thereby put in contact with the Christian hierarchy. Notable in this connection was Aḥudemmeh Metropolitan for Eastern Mesopotamia, and John the bishop of Euroia/Hawarine (Khoury 2005b), who is presented as the bishop of the Arabs (Feissel 1985). In addition to the large centres, the simple churches built in the areas where the nomads would return seasonally made possible a unity of faith among such a variety of populations. These churches represented a fusion of elements of varying inspiration.

In Kuwait and in the Persian Gulf (Salles and Callot 2013), there are but a few traces of churches, at Akkaz and al-Qoussour (Figure 28.44). The first of these sites offers the plan of a modest rectangular building with three bays with a choir flanked by two lateral chapels. Among its rarer characteristics are the fragments of a stucco cross dating to between the fifth and the seventh centuries. At al-Qoussour are the remains of two churches that have been superimposed on a podium preceded by five steps. The old church, of which only the gate has been identified, had to be destroyed at an early date and was replaced by a larger one. We may therefore infer the existence of an ecclesiastical complex, an important and

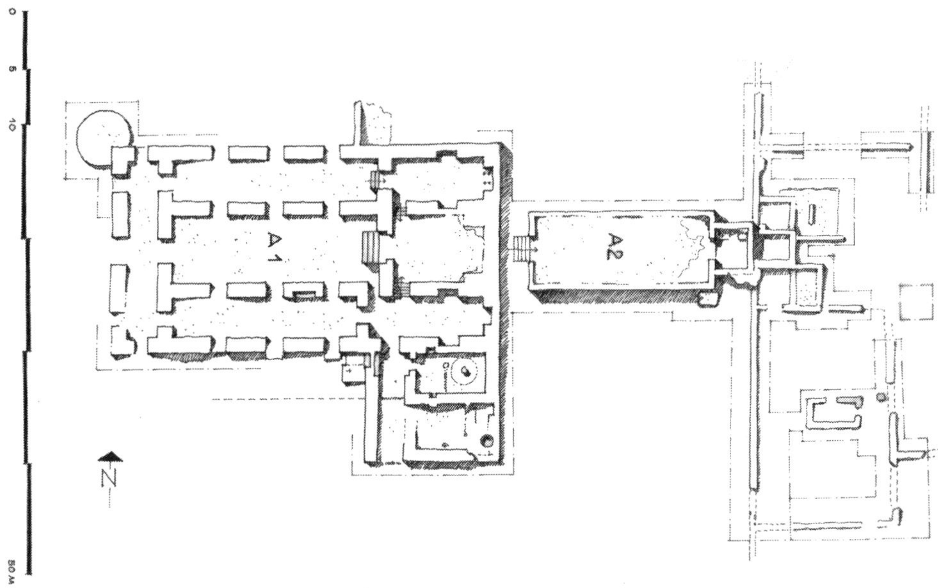

Figure 28.44 The church of al-Qoussour

well-designed establishment. A third little-studied church is that at Jubayl (Saudi Arabia). Its plan consists of a room with three naves and two chapels attached to the sanctuary. Some of its decorative motifs date back to the end of the sixth or the beginning of the seventh century. Among them are two crosses with dove-tailed branches terminated by two pearls surmounting a triangular base, which recall the hill of Calvary.

Overview of Syrian churches in Iran, India, Central Asia, and China

The Hakkari churches in the north-western corner of present-day Iran are very recent or at least not especially old and may go back through many stages of maintenance and repair to much older buildings and to a liturgy that has retained primitive characteristics (Hellot-Bellier 2013). The clay churches characteristic of Ormia-Salmas are known today only by the description of the church of Khorsrowa made in 1845 by Bishop Isoyaw Melchisedeq of Salmas. The small stone churches of Mar Touma of Beloulan and Mart Maryam are single-nave constructions, simply decorated with discreet wooden doors and a low, flat-winged roof (Figure 28.45).

Other churches such as Mar Sergius-Bacchus and Mar Petros-Mar Polos have two naves and no bêma, but are equipped with a qestroma with sarcophagi in the first, and two ambons in the second.

All in all, these churches, which do not necessarily have a courtyard, are simple, rustic, and carry very little decoration. Their naves are narrow, vaulted, without windows, and open to the south through a single door. The baptistery is at the south-east corner, a diaconicon is rare, and in the sanctuary, closed off by a curtain, the altar is

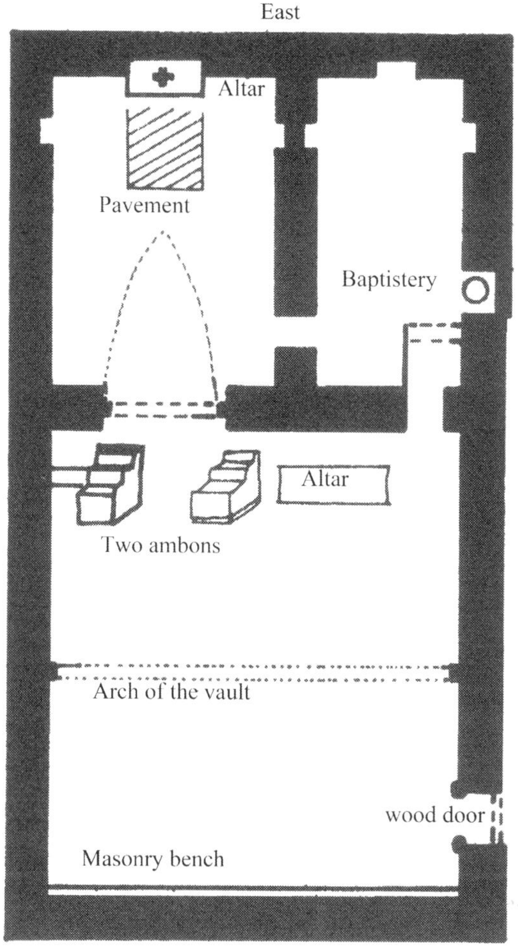

Figure 28.45a Church of Mar Touma of Beloulan

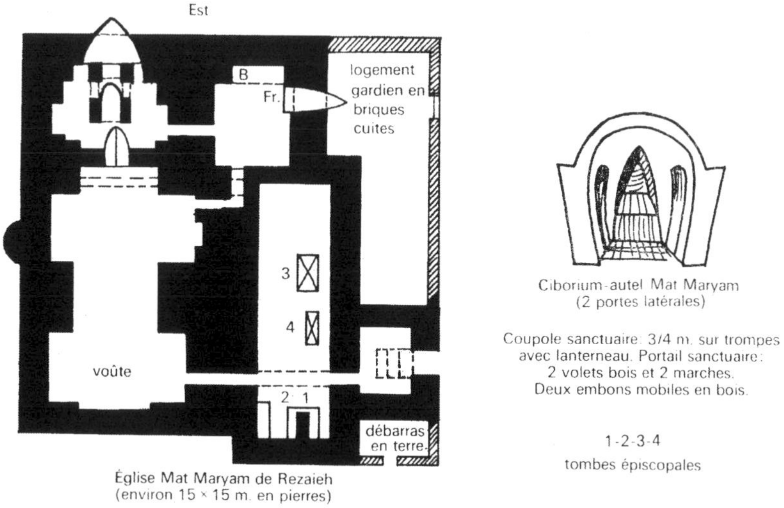

Figure 28.45b Church of Mart Maryam

attached to the wall. The walls of the Chaldean churches carry stations of the cross and images. The churches with tripartite sanctuaries had a central altar flanked by the baptistery and the sacristy or diaconicon. The division between men and women seems to correspond to the Syriac order, according to which men and women entered the church by two different lateral doors, the men standing near the sanctuary to the east and the women to the west.

Kerala

In Kerala, the origins of those churches known as the 'churches of the Christians of St Thomas' remain obscure, but their three-part arrangement probably originates from an ancient Syriac model (Thekeparampil et al. 2013). To the east is the tower-sanctuary (*Quds Qudsin*) with its thick walls, raised on a chamfer, covered with a semi-cylinder vault, and open to the west through an arch raised on engaged pillars. The central part, the *haykla*, with a single nave which rests against the arch of the sanctuary, is the locus of the liturgy which houses the bêma, the baptismal foundations, and the pulpit. To the west, a gallery called the *mondalam* constitutes the meeting space itself together with the passage giving access to the main door. It is always preceded by a monumental cross located a few metres off the axis of the whole complex. The Syriac churches of Kerala testify to a history during the course of which developed a synthesis consisting of a Syro-oriental structure, built in a Hindu context, and further enriched through contact with Syrian, Mesopotamian, Indian, and Portuguese styles. The result has produced original Syriac buildings under which it is impossible to detect the original edifices (Figure 28.46).

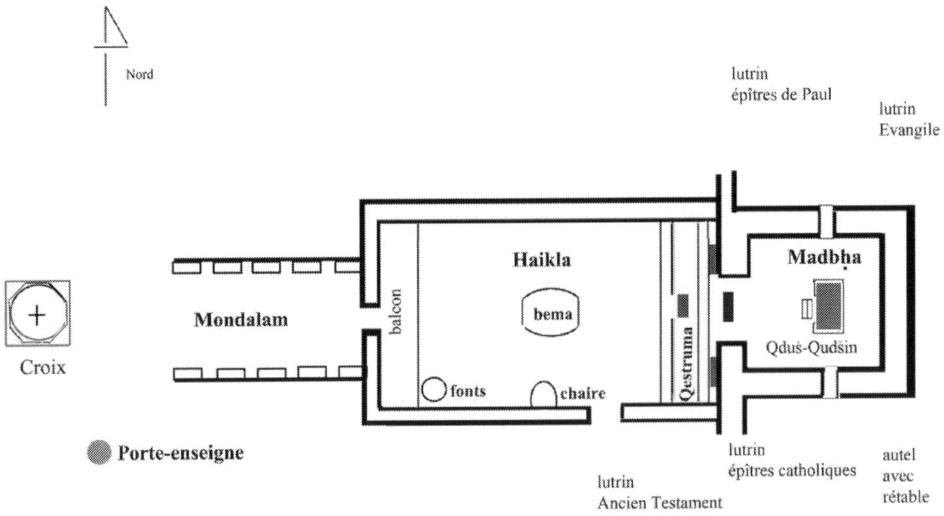

Figure 28.46a Schematic plan of the Syriac Church in Kerala

Figure 28.46b Church of Kudamaloor

China and Central Asia

In China (Borbone 2013), a stable Christian presence seems to have been attested in the time of catholicos Timothy I (780–823). The sources also mention Mongol tent-churches, and Marco Polo mentions a church of Saint John the Baptist. These churches were built with materials similar to those of the churches of the East Syriac Church and of Mesopotamia. These resemblances are also apparent in their rectangular oriented plans, with a distinct sanctuary, a baptistery to the south, and an oven. Numerous niches contained bone remains corresponding to the martyrion. The naves bear no trace of a bêma, but with the current state of research it cannot be known for certain whether this is merely because they were always constructed of wood, or whether in fact they did not exist in the region at all. The churches of Ugrut in Uzbekistan and of Ak Beshim in Kyrgyzstan (Figure 28.47) show affinities with those of Kurdistan, and may be partitioned or juxtaposed, double or triple, and each has an altar.

CONCLUSION

The major architectural features of Syriac churches have now emerged from this review of the churches throughout the various parts of the substantial territory in which Syriac churches have spread. Syria, the nucleus of birth and expansion of the

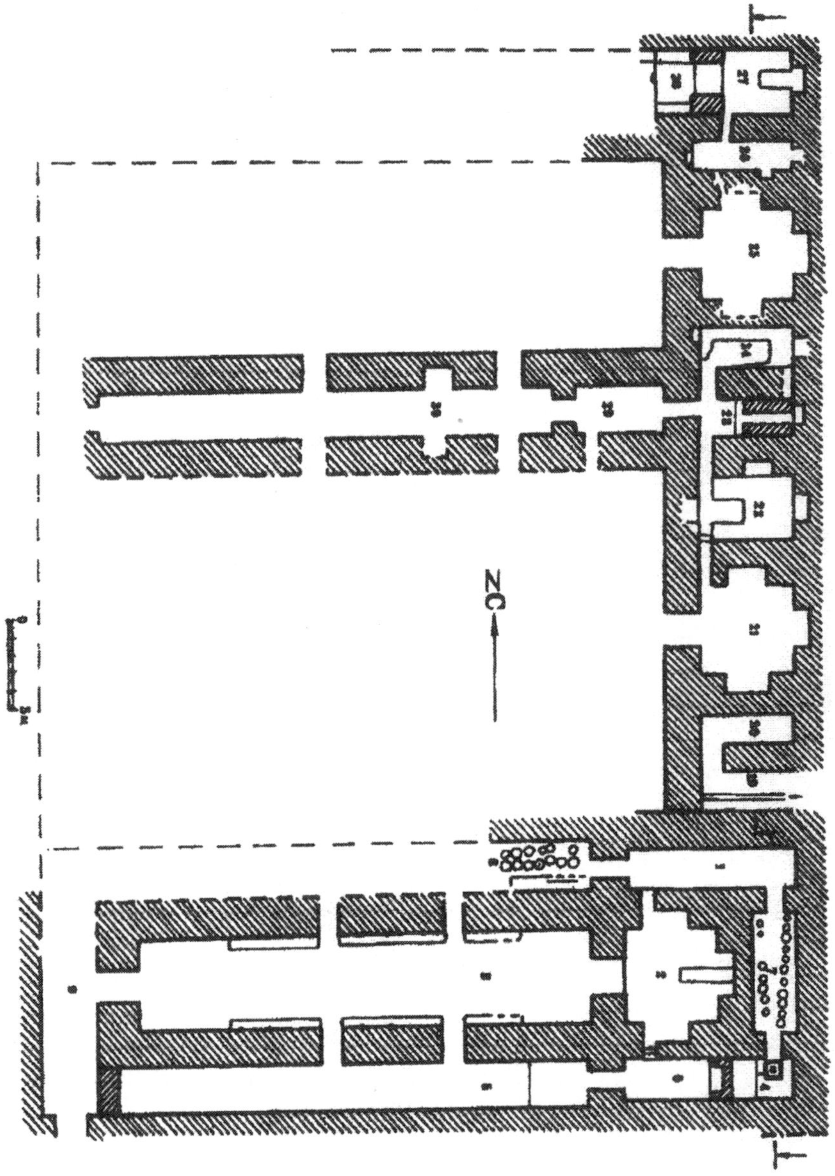

Figure 28.47 Ensemble of Ak Beshim (8th to 11th centuries)

Syriac world, one of the richest provinces of the Eastern Roman Empire, is a vast territory in which the rapid spread of Christianity gave rise to the construction of edifices of worship from the third and fourth centuries.

This region, where Greek and Aramaic culture coexisted, held a privileged place between Constantinople, the political capital of the empire, and Jerusalem, a religious centre where the Martyrion, Golgotha, and the Church of the Anastasis formed the heart of the network of holy places. This situation, combined with the extraordinary expansion of the cult of relics, is reflected in the Syrian territory by the emergence of innumerable places of worship both in the larger urban centres as well as in the smallest villages.

Until the sixth century, and even beyond, the faithful of different linguistic or communal identities shared their churches despite the influence of the patriarchal capital of the Eastern Diocese in northern Syria, churches that were characterised by an Aramaic Syriac identity shaped and perpetuated through Edessa.

The constants observed in the Syrian churches are partly explained by the desire to bring Christians together at a time marked by the increasing popularity of the pilgrimage, which contributed to the cohesion of society and encouraged the growth of specific localities under the tutelage of the patriarchate of Antioch.

This phenomenon, encouraged by the imperial power, was further favoured by a Christian évergétisme, which in turn brought about a multiplication of churches whose number even within each locality continues to astonish. In urban as well as in rural areas, full measures are taken in order to attract the faithful and to establish the reputation of the religious complexes, which represent many stages in the pilgrimage to the holy places along the main and even along the secondary roads.

Beyond the overall uniformity that characterises the Syrian basilical model within the unified provinces under the patronage of the patriarchate of Antioch (in which the early Syriac churches lie), the rule of Constantinople and the radiance of Jerusalem also served to locate Syrian ecclesiastical architecture at the very centre of a network of pilgrimage routes which developed between these two fundamental poles of the Byzantine Empire and which remained significant until the seventh century. In this context, the architectural characteristics and decoration patterns of the Syriac churches emerged and developed through the medium of the Syrian Antiochene basilicas. As we have seen, such characteristics include the following:

- Two entrances were opened into the southern facade: an eastern one for men and a western one for women, permitting each group to access the corresponding part of the nave.
- The sanctuary (*haykla*) elevated by two steps is oriented and ends with a semicircular apse (*qanke*) flanked by two annexes. Communication doors allowed the clergy to access these spaces directly. On the other hand, it opened by a central door onto a transverse passage separating it from the room.
- The bêma in the centre of the nave is connected to the *qestroma* by a passageway, a device dedicated to the oral liturgy, the forms of which vary according to the region.
- The baptistery (*ma'muditha*) is attested but its location is uncertain.
- The martyrion (*beth sahde*), a place dedicated to saints and martyrs, takes various forms and occupies different locations.

These patterns and characteristics, together with a degree of local variation, are clearly present in those parts of the Syriac world that extended to the east of Syria proper. Here the churches form three interconnected groups belonging to different periods: east of the Euphrates, Arabia, and the Asian area.

In the Edessene region and to the east of the Euphrates, with the exception of Mar Ya'qub of Nisibis, the unique well-preserved monument was built in 359. In Tur

ʿAbdin, most churches display the same patterns, in particular the transverse nave and in some cases special martyr chapels. Following the Arabic conquest, decoration patterns emerge that are typical of local workshops. Two narrow naves, ambon, *qestroma*, and sarcophagi appear in the churches of Hakkari. Tripartite sanctuaries and baptisteries are also attested.

In the same way, the church of Bazian (northern Iraq) shows both the continuity of the traditions of the Syrian basilica and the distinctive features of local architecture and techniques related to the nature of the local materials. Such typical features appear more clearly in Mosul and el-Ḥira, where there are three models dating back to the first millennium: the Chaldean plan, the orthodox type with transverse hall, and the polygonal martyr chapels.

Apart from three Syriac monasteries located in Jericho, Gaza, and el-Mshash in Palestine, it was the Greek religious tradition that principally influenced the churches of the province of Arabia, which was particularly attached to the patriarchate of Jerusalem. They were also under the jurisdiction of the patriarchate of Antioch and shared architectural traits with the Syrian churches, with the exception of the centred plan.

In the Persian Gulf and Arabia (present Saudi Arabia), three churches were studied. They date back to the sixth and seventh centuries and show similarities with Iraqi churches and motifs. The church of Kilwa, located in a roadside stop where Arabs used to meet, does not offer liturgical features indicating any special identity.

In Central Asia and China, sanctuaries are located in the eastern part of the churches. Their layouts recall the Mesopotamian plans. There is always a baptistery but niches replace the Martyrion and naves may be double or triple.

In Kerala, a three-part arrangement is widespread: (1) the altar (*madbeha*); (2) the sanctuary (*haykla*), with a single nave housing the bêma, the baptismal font and the pulpit; and (3) a meeting space (*mondalam*) near the entrance. Consecutive styles together with Mesopotamian, Indian, and Portuguese influences have conspired to hide the original layout, but these Keralese churches still preserve even today a genuine Syriac tradition.

NOTE

1 This essay was achieved thanks to the kind support and understanding of Vincent Déroche, director of the Byzantine World CNRS, Paris. My sincere thanks go also to the encouragement of Brigitte Pitarakis and the help of Marie-Christine Comte. I would like to express my thanks to the editor of this volume for his generous support and assistance in the publication of this article. All drawings and photographs, where the source or copyrights are not mentionned, belong to the author, to the Syrian mission of Banassara and Jebel Wastani, and to the Syrian-French Mission of Prospecting Syriac Inscriptions of Syria. I would also like to express my thanks to the editor Daniel King for his generous support and assistance in the publication of this article.

BIBLIOGRAPHY

Abou Sekeh, Fadia. 2017. Die Eremiten der Hohlenkloster das Beispiel der Felsenkloster in Phoenice Libanensis, Syrien. *Hortus Artium Medievalum* 23 (Living and Dying in the Cloister. Monastic Life From the 5th to the 11th Century), 96–106.

Alpi, Frédéric. 2010. *La Route royale – Sévère d'Antioche et les Églises d'Orient (512–518)*. Bibliothèque archéologique et historique 188. Beyrouth: Presses de l'Ifpo.

Azpeitia, Johanne. 2005. Deir Sim'ān, monastère nord-est: présentation de l'église. *In:* Baratte et al. 2005, 34–54.
Balty, Janine. 1976. L'évêque Paul et le programme architectural et décoratif de la cathédrale d'Apamée. *In:* P. Ducrey, ed., *Mélanges d'histoire ancienne et d'archéologie offerts à Paul Collart.* Bibliothèque Historique Vaudoise: Lausanne, 31–46.
———. 1980. Sur la date de la Syria Seconda. *Syria* 57, 465–81.
———. 2013. Maurice, un saint d'Apamée: témoignages littéraires et monuments. *In:* Charpentier and Puech 2013, 223–33.
Balty, Janine, and Jean-Charles Balty. 2004. Nouveaux exemples de 'Bêma' syrien. *In:* Ma. Blázquez Martínez and A. González Blanco, ed., *Sacralidad y Arqueologia, homenaje al Prof. Thilo Ulbert al cumplir 65 años.* Antigüedad y cristianismo, 21. Murcia: Universidad de Murcia, Servicio de Publicaciones, 447–57.
Balty, Janine, and J. Napoleone-Lemaire. 1974. *L'église à atrium de la grande colonnade.* Fouilles d'Apamée de Syrie I, 1. Bruxelles: Centre belge de recherches archéologiques à Apamée de Syrie.
Baratte, F., V. Déroche, C. Jolivet-Levy, and B. Pitarakis, ed. 2005. *Mélanges Jean-Pierre Sodini.* Travaux et Mémoires 15. Paris: Association des amis du centre d'histoire et civilisation de Byzance.
Beaudry, Nicolas. 2005. Formes architecturales et géographie historique: l'église de Bassit et le corpus nord-syrien. *In:* Baratte et al. 2005, 119–36.
Bell, Gertrude. 2000. *The Arabian Diaries, 1913–1914.* Re-edited by Rosemary O'Brien. Syracuse University Press.
Biddle, Martin. 1999. *The Tomb of Christ.* Stroud: Sutton Publishing, 1999.
Biscop, Jean-Luc. 1987. Églises syriennes apparentées à Qal'at Sem'ān: les exemples de Turin et de Fassouq dans le gebel Wastani. *Syria* 64, 107–29.
———. 2005. Le chantier du martyrium de Saint-Syméon, du dessin à la mise en œuvre. *In:* Baratte et al. 2005, 11–36.
———. 2011. Qal'at Sem'an et Deir Sem'an: naissance et développement d'un lieu de pèlerinage durant l'antiquité tardive. *In:* J.-M. Spieser, ed., *Architecture paléochrétienne.* Gollion: Infolio, 11–59.
Biscop, Jean-Luc, and Jean-Pierre Sodini. 1984. Qal'āt Sem'an et les chevets à colonnes de Syrie du Nord. *Syria* 61, 267–330.
Blanc, Pierre-Marie, Jean-Marie Dentzer, and Jean-Pierre Sodini. 2007. La grande église à plan centrée (ou "cathédrale de l'Est"). *In:* Dentzer-Feydy et al. 2007, 137–46.
Blanc, Pierre-Marie, and Pauline Piraud-Fournet. 2010. La grande église du quartier est de Bosra. *In:* M. al-Maqdissi, F. Braemer, J.-M. Dentzer, ed., *Hauran V. La Syrie du Sud du Néolithique à l'Antiquité tardive.* Bibliothèque archéologique et historique 191. Beyrouth: Institut français du Proche-Orient, 275–88.
Borbone, Pier Giorgio. 2013. Les églises d'Asie centrale et de Chine: état de la question à partir des textes et des découvertes archéologiques: essai de synthèse. *In:* Briquel-Chatonnet 2013, 441–65.
Brands, G. 2002. *Resafa VI. Die Bauornamentik von Resafa-Sergiupolis. Studien zur spätantiken Architektur und Bauausstattung in Syrien und Nordmesopotamien.* Deutsches archäologisches Institut, Resafa VI. Mainz: Verlag Philipp von Zabern.
Brelaud, Simon. 2013. Un programme de restauration exceptionnelle au nord de l'Irak: les églises du monastère de Rabban Hormizd. *In:* Briquel-Chatonnet 2013, 381–90.
Briquel-Chatonnet, F. ed. 2013. *Les églises en monde syriaque.* Études syriaques 10. Paris: Geuthner.
Briquel-Chatonnet, F., A. Desreumaux, and W. Khoury. 2004–05. Inscriptions syriaques de Syrie: Premiers résultats. *Annales Archéologiques Arabes Syriennes* XLVII–XLVIII [2008], 187–95.

Burton, R. F., and C. F. Tyrwhitt Drake. 1872. *Unexplored Syria. Visits to the Libanus, the Tulúl el Safā, the Anti-Libanus, the Northern Libanus, and the Aláh*. London: Tinsley Bros.
Butler, Howard Crosby. 1920. *Syria, Publications of the Princeton University Archaeological Expeditions to Syria in 1904–1905 and 1909. 2. Architecture, Section B, Northern Syria.* Leiden = *PAES* II B.
———. 1929. *Early Churches in Syria: Fourth to Seventh Centuries*. Princeton Monographs in Art and Archaeology. Princeton.
Callot, Olivier. 1997. La christianisation des sanctuaires romains de la Syrie du Nord. *Topoi* 7, 735–50.
Campbell, S. 1947. *In:* R. Stillwell et al., ed., *Antioch-on-the-Orontes, III*. Princeton: Princeton University Press.
Canivet, Marie-Thérèse, and Pierre Canivet. 1980. A Huarte en Syrie, une église primitive du IVe siècle. *Archeologia* 138, 54–7.
———. 1987. Ḥuārte: Sanctuaire chrétien d'Apamène (IVe – VIe siècle). Paris: Geuthner.
Charpentier, G., and V. Puech, ed. 2013. *Villes et campagnes aux rives de la Méditerranée ancienne. Hommages à Georges Tate*. Topoi Supplement 12. Lyon: Maison de l'Orient Méditerranéen.
Comte, M.-C. 2012. *Les reliquaires du Proche-Orient et de Chypre à la période protobyzantine (IVe-VIIIe siècles). Formes, emplacements, fonctions et cultes*. Bibliothèque de l'Antiquité tardive 20. Turnhout: Brepols.
Connolly, R. H. 1911, 1913. *Anonymi Auctoris Expositio Officiorum Ecclesiae*. CSCO 64, 71, 72, 76, Scriptores Syri series secunda 91, 92. Paris: E Typographeo Reipublicae.
Dentzer-Feydy, J., M. Vallerin, Th. Fournet. 2007. *Bosra. Aux portes de l'Arabie*. Guides archéologiques de l'Institut français du Proche-Orient 5. Damas: Institut français du Proche-Orient.
Déroche, Vincent, and Narmin Ali Amin. 2013. La fouille de Bazyan (Kurdistan irakien): un monastère nestorien? *In:* Briquel-Chatonnet 2013, 363–80.
Desreumaux, Alain. 2013. Les églises, leur architecture et leurs aménagements dans les inscriptions syriaques. *In:* Briquel-Chatonnet 2013, 491–520.
Donceel-Voûte, Pauline. 1988. *Les pavements des églises byzantines de Syrie et du Liban: décor, archéologie et liturgie*. Publication d'histoire de l'art et d'archéologie de l'Université catholique de Louvain 69. Collège Erasme: département d'Archéologie et d'Histoire de l'Art, Louvain-la-Neuve.
Dussaud, René. 1927. *Topographie historique de la Syrie antique et médiévale*. Bibliothèque archéologique et historique 4. Paris: Geuthner.
Duval, Noël. 2003. Architecture et liturgie dans la Jordanie byzantine. *In:* id., *Journée d'études sur les églises de Jordanie et leurs mosaïques*. Bibliothèque archéologique et historique 168). IFPO, Beyrouth: Institut français du Proche-Orient, 35–114.
Farès, Saba. 2013. Communauté monastique chrétienne en Transjordanie méridionale: l'église de Kilwa. *In:* Briquel-Chatonnet 2013, 225–36.
Farioli Campanati, R., and N. Masturzo. 2007. L'église des Saints Serge, Bacchus et Léonce et le palais "épiscopal" Saint-Serge. *In:* Dentzer-Feydy et al., 2007, 155–60.
Feissel, Denis. 1985. Magnus, Mégas et les curateurs des "maisons divines" de Justin II à Maurice. *Travaux et Mémoires* 9, 465–76.
———. 1995. Bulletin épigraphique. Syrie, Phénicie, Palestine, Arabie. *Revue des Études grecques* 108, 544–9.
Fernandez, Romualdo, and Widad Khoury. 2008. A propos d'une église de l'époque arabe dans le Massif calcaire: Ma'ramaya dans le Jebel Baricha. *In:* C. Roche, ed., *D'Ougarit à Jérusalem. Recueil d'études épigraphiques et archéologiques offert à Pierre Bordreuil*. Orient et Méditerranée 2. Paris: de Boccard, 333–7.
Festugière, A. J. 1959. *Antioche paienne et chrétienne: Libanius, Chrysostome et les moines de Syrie*. Paris: de Boccard.

Fiey, Jean-Maurice. 1965–68. *Assyrie Chrétienne: contribution à l'étude de l'histoire et de la géographie ecclésiastiques et monastiques du nord de l'Iraq*. Vols. I–III. Beyrouth: Imprim. Catholique.

———. 1979. *Communautés syriaques en Iraq et en Iran des origines à 1552*. London: Variorum.

Fourdrin, Jean-Pascal. 1985. Les églises à nefs transversales d'Apamène et du Tur 'Abdin. *Syria* 62, 319–35.

Fowden, Elizabeth Key. 2013. Des églises pour les Arabes, pour les nomades? *In:* Briquel-Chatonnet 2013, 391–420.

Gaborit, Justine, and Gérard Thébault, with Abdurrahman Oruç. L'église Mar-Ya'qub de Nisibe. *In:* Briquel-Chatonnet 2013, 289–330.

Gabriel, Albert. 1926. Recherches archéologiques à Palmyra. *Syria* 7, 71–92.

Gatier, P.-L. (in collaboration with Denis Feissel). 2013. Bulletin épigraphique. Syrie, Phénicie, Palestine, Arabie. *Revue des Études grecques* 126, 581–92.

Gawlikowski, Michel. 1993. Rapports des missions actives à Palmyre 1990–1991. *Syria* 70, 561–3.

———. 2008. The Cathedral of Palmyra. *In:* XV *Congreso International de Arqueología Cristiana*, Sesión I: Obispo y topografia urbana, Toledo, 517–26.

———. 2013. Houarté, un village d'Apamène. *In:* Charpentier and Puech, 261–70.

Goilav, Ana-Maria. 2010. Proposal for the Reconstruction of the Golden Octagon. *In:* C. Saliou, et al., ed., *Les sources de l'histoire du paysage urbain d'Antioche sur l'Oronte*. Université Paris 8: Paris, 159–79.

Grabar, André. 1966a. *Le premier Art Chrétien*. Univers des Formes. Paris: Gallimard.

———. 1966b. *l'Âge d'or de Justinien, de la mort de Théodose à l'islam*. Univers des Formes. Paris: Gallimard.

Hadjichristophi, P. 1998. L'île aux cent basiliques. *Le Monde de la Bible* 112, 38–43.

Harper, R. P. 1980. Ahtis, Neocaesareia-Qasrin-Dibsi Faraj. *In:* J.-Cl. Margueron, ed., *Moyen Euphrate: zone de contacts et d'échanges*. Leiden: Brill, 327–48.

Harper, R. P., and J. Wilkinson Taylor. 1975. Excavations at Dibsi Faraj- Northern Syria, 1974–1975. A Preliminary Note on the Site and Its Monuments With Appendix. *DOP* 29, 319–38.

Harrak, Amir. 2013. Son architecte est saint Paul: l'architecture traditionnelle des églises de la Mésopotamie. *In:* Briquel-Chatonnet 2013, 331–62.

Hellot-Bellier, Florence. 2013. Églises de l'Azerbaidjan iranien et du Hakkari. *In:* Briquel-Chatonnet 2013, 421–41.

Hirschfeld, Yizhar. 1992. *Judean Desert Monasteries in the Byzantine Period*. New Haven: Yale University Press.

Horsfield, G., A. Horsfield, and N. Glueck. 1933. Prehistoric Rock-Drawings in Transjordan. *American Journal of Archaeology* 37/3, 381–6.

Horsfield, A. 1943. Journey to Kilwa, Transjordan. *The Geographical Journal* 102(2), 71–77.

Keser-Kayaalp, Elif. 2013. Églises et monastères du Tur 'AbdIn: les débuts d'une architecture "syriaque". *In:* Briquel-Chatonnet 2013, 331–62.

Khoury, Widad. 1987. *Deir Seta: prospection et analyse d'une ville morte inédite en Syrie*. 2 vol. Damas: Dar Tlass.

———. 1996. Les basiliques doubles de Fassouq et de Banassara (Jebel Wastani). *Antiquité tardive* 4, 160–3.

———. 2005a. Banassara, un site de pèlerinage dans le Massif calcaire, Rapport sur les travaux menés en 2002–2004. *Syria* 82, 225–66.

———. 2005b. Hawarine. Premiers résultats, campagnes 2003–2004. *In:* F. Baratte et al., ed., *Mélanges Jean-Pierre Sodini*. Travaux et Mémoires 15. Paris: Association des amis du Centre d'histoire et civilisation de Byzance, 299–316.

Khoury, Widad, and Pasquale Castellana. 1990. Fruhchristliche Städe in Nordlichen Jebel Wastani. *Antike Welt* 21/1, 14–25.

Khoury, Widad, and Bertrand Riba. 2013a. Les églises de Syrie (IVe-VIIe siècle): essai de synthèse. *In:* Briquel-Chatonnet 2013, 41–106.

———. 2013b. Peut-on discerner des modèles reliés à des communautés ecclésiales ou linguistiques en Syrie du Nord ? (IVe-IXe siècle). *In:* Briquel-Chatonnet 2013, 107–30.

Kleinbauer, W. E. 1973. The Origin and Functions of the Aisled Tetraconch Churches in Syria and Northern Mesopotamia. *DOP* 27, 89–114.

Lassus, J. 1947. *Sanctuaires chrétiens de Syrie. Essai sur la genèse, la forme et l'usage liturgique des édifices du culte chrétien, en Syrie, du IIIe siècle à la conquête musulmane*. Bibliothèque archéologique et historique 42. Paris: Geuthner.

———. 1950. Liturgies nestoriennes médiévales et églises syriennes antiques. *RHR* 137.2, 236–52.

Lauffray, Jean. 1991. *Halabiya-Zenobia, place forte du limes oriental et la Haute-Mésopotamie au VIe siècle*, II. Paris: Geuthner.

Margalit, S. 1990. The Bi-apsidal churches in Palestine, Jordan, Syria, Lebanon, and Cyprus. *Liber Annus* 40, 321–34.

Mécérian, Jean. 1964. *Expédition archéologique dans l'Antiochène occidentale*. Mélanges de l'Université Saint-Joseph: Beyrouth.

Michel, Anne. 2001. *Les églises d'époque byzantine et umayyade de Jordanie (provinces d'Arabie et de Palestine), Ve-VIIIe siècles: typologie architecturale et aménagements liturgiques*. Bibliothèque de l'Antiquité tardive 2. Brepols: Turnhout.

———. 2013. Les églises de la provincia Arabia, particularités de structures et de répartition. *In:* Briquel-Chatonnet 2013, 197–224.

Mouterde, R., and A. Poidebard. 1945. *Le Limes de Chalcis. Organisation de la steppe en Haute Syrie romaine*. Bibliothèque archéologique et historique 38. 2 vols. Paris: Geuthner.

Naccache, Alice. 1999. Les influences orientales dans les décorations architecturales de la Syrie du Nord. *Annales archéologiques arabes syriennes* 43, 193–4.

Naccache, Alice, and George Tate. 1995. Le village de Deir Sunbul. *MUSJ* 52, 371–489.

Peña, Ignacio. 2000. *Lieux de pèlerinages en Syrie*. Studium Biblicum Franciscanum, Collectio Minor 38. Milan: Franciscan Printing Press.

Peña, Ignacio, Pasquale Castellana, and Romualdo Fernandez. 1975. *Les stylites syriens*. Studium Biblicum Franciscanum, Collectio Minor 16. Milan: Franciscan Printing Press.

———. 1980. *Les reclus syriens. Recherches sur les anciennes formes de vie solitaire en Syrie*. Studium Biblicum Franciscanum, Collectio Minor 23. Milan: Franciscan Printing Press.

———. 1983. *Les cénobites syriens*. Studium Biblicum Franciscanum, Collectio Minor 28. Jerusalem: Franciscan Printing Press.

———. 1987. *Inventaire du Jebel Baricha. Recherches archéologiques dans la région des villes mortes de la Syrie du Nord*. Studium Biblicum Franciscanum, Collectio Minor 33. Jerusalem: Franciscan Printing Press.

———. 1990. *Inventaire du Jebel El-ʿAla. Recherches archéologiques dans la région des villes mortes de la Syrie du Nord*. Studium Biblicum Franciscanum, Collectio Minor 31. Jerusalem: Franciscan Printing Press.

———. 1999. *Inventaire du Jébel Wastani. Recherches archéologiques dans la région des villes mortes de la Syrie du Nord*. Studium Biblicum Franciscanum, Collectio Minor 36. Jerusalem: Franciscan Printing Press.

———. 2003. *Inventaire du Jébel Doueili. Recherches archéologiques dans la région des villes mortes de la Syrie du Nord*. Studium Biblicum Franciscanum, Collectio Minor 43. Jerusalem: Franciscan Printing Press.

Restle, Marcell. 1989. Les monuments chrétiens de la Syrie du Sud. *In:* J.-M. Dentzer and W. Orthmann, ed., *Archéologie et histoire de la Syrie. 2, La Syrie de l'époque achéménide à l'avènement de l'Islam*. Schriften zur vorderasiatischen Archäologie 1. Saarbrücken: Saarbrüker Druckerei und Verlag, 373–84.

Riba, Bertrand. 2012. L'église de l'Est et les inscriptions du village de Kefert ʿAqab. *Syria* 89, 213–27.

———. 2014. Le village de Kefert ʿAqab: un site inédit du gebel Wastâni dans le Massif calcaire de la Syrie du Nord. *Semitica et Classica* 7, 147–67.

———. 2016. Quelques remarques sur les activités liées à l'architecture et au décor sculpté en Antiochène. *Syria* 93, 353–68.
———. 2018. *Étude monographique du village de Kafr ʿAqāb, un site du ğebel Waṣṭāni (Massif Calcaire de Syrie du Nord)*. Bibliothèque de l'Antiquité tardive. turnhout: Brepols.
Rostovtzeff, M. I. 1938. *Dura-Europos and its Art*. Oxford: Clarendon Press.
Roumi, M. 1975. L'église du tell d'as-Sayh Hasan: notes préliminaires. *Bulletin d'études orientales* 28, 227–30.
Saliby, N., and M. Griesheimer. 1999. Un martyrium octogonal découvert à Homs (Syrie) en 1988 et sa mosaïque. *Antiquité tardive* 7, 383–400.
Salles, Jean-François, and Olivier Callot. 2013. Les églises antiques de Koweit et du golfe Persique. *In:* Briquel-Chatonnet 2013, 237–68.
Sodini, Jean-Pierre. 1975. Note sur deux variantes régionales dans les basiliques de Grèce et des Balkans. *Bulletin de correspondance hellénique* 99, 581–8.
———. 1988. Géographie historique et liturgie: l'opposition entre Antiochène et Apamène. *In:* H. Ahrweiler, ed., *Géographie historique du monde méditerranéen*. Byzantina Sorboniensa 7. Paris: Publications de la Sorbonne, 203–20.
———. 1989a. Les églises de Syrie du Nord. *In:* J.-M. Dentzer and W. Orthmann, ed., *Archéologie et histoire de la Syrie. 2, La Syrie de l'époque achéménide à l'avènement de l'Islam*. Schriften zur vorderasiatischen Archäologie 1. Saarbrücken: Saarbrüker Druckerei und Verlag, 347–72.
———. 1989b. Compte rendu de *Églises syriennes à bêma* de G. Tchalenko. *Antiquité tardive* 1, 242–53.
———. 2006. Archéologie des églises et organisation spatiale de la liturgie. *In:* F. Cassingena-Tréverdy and I. Jurasz, ed., *Les liturgies syriaques*. Études syriaques 3. Paris: Geuthner, 229–66.
———. 2007. Saint Syméon, lieu de pèlerinage. *Les cahiers de Saint-Michel de Cuxa* 38, 107–20.
———. 2010. Saint-Syméon: l'influence de saint-Syméon dans le culte et l'économie de l'Antiochène. *In:* J. La Genière, A. Vauchez, and J. Leclant, ed., *Les sanctuaires et leur rayonnement dans le monde méditerranéen de l'antiquité à l'époque moderne*. Cahiers de la Villa Kérylos 21. Paris: Académie des Inscriptions et Belles-Lettres, 285–322.
———. 2013. Conclusions. *In:* Briquel-Chatonnet 2013, 541–68.
Strube, Christine. 1986. Hauskirche und Einschiffige Kirche in Syrien: Beobachtungen zu den Kirchen von Marmaya, Isruq, Nuriye und Banaqfur. *In:* Otto Feld and Urs Peschlow, ed., *Studien zur spätantiken und byzantinischen Kunst: Friedrich Wilhelm Deichmann gewidmet. I*. Römisch-Germanisches Zentralmuseum Mainz. Forschungsinstitut für Vor- und Frühgeschichte. Monographien 10. Bonn: Habelt, 109–23.
Tchalenko, George. 1953–58. *Villages antiques de la Syrie du Nord: le massif du Bélus à l'époque romaine*. Bibliothèque archéologique et historique 50. 3 vols. Paris: Geuthner.
———. 1990. *Églises de village de la Syrie du nord. III, Texte. Églises syriennes à Bêma*. Bibliothèque archéologique et historique 105. Paris: Geuthner.
Tchalenko, George, and Eugène Baccache. 1979. *Églises de village de la Syrie du Nord. I, Planches*. Bibliothèque archéologique et historique 105. Paris: Geuthner.
Testini, P. 1980. *Archeologia Cristiana*. 2nd ed. Rome: Edipuglia.
Thekeparampil, Jacob, Thomas Koonammakkal, and Alain Desreumaux. 2013. Les églises des chrétiens de saint Thomas au Kérala. *In:* Briquel-Chatonnet 2013, 467–90.
Ulbert, Thilo. 1986. *Resafa. II, Die Basilika des Heiligen Kreuzes in Resafa Sergiupolis*. Mainz am Rhein: Von Zabern.
Vogüe, Melchior de. 1865–77. *Syrie Centrale: architecture civile et religieuse du Ier au VIIe siècle*. 2 vols. Paris: Baudry.
Youssif, Pierre. 2006. Le déroulement de la messe chaldéenne. *In:* F. Cassingena-Tréverdy and I. Jurasz, ed., *Les liturgies syriaques*. Études syriaques 3. Paris: Geuthner, 59–99.
Zaqzuq, A., and M. Piccirillo. 1999. The Mosaic Floor of the Church of the Holy Martyrs at Tayibat al-Imam – Hamah, in Central Syria. *Liber Annus* 49, 443–64.

CHAPTER TWENTY-NINE

WOMEN AND CHILDREN IN SYRIAC CHRISTIANITY

Sounding Voices

Susan Ashbrook Harvey

Historians often lament the silence of women and children in our ancient Syriac sources. To our knowledge, there is no surviving Syriac text authored by a woman (of which we can be certain) until modern times, and of course, nothing by children. Moreover, the vast majority of our extant Syriac literature was produced and transmitted by male monastic communities and ecclesiastical authorities. Thus the larger Syriac corpus – rich, diverse, and brilliant as it is – is often quite simply not interested in matters of women or children.

To grasp the crucial contribution of women and children to Syriac Christianity, I suggest that we start from that social location where their voices were heard often, repeatedly, loudly and clearly, in public, and as publicly significant: Christian liturgy. That is, I propose liturgy as a historical location of social consequence. Consider, for example, this short verse from a mid-fourth-century hymn written by the great Syriac poet Ephrem the Syrian, as part of the Easter celebration:

> This joyful festival is entirely made up of tongues and voices:
> innocent young women and men sounding like trumpets and horns,
> while infant girls and boys resemble harps and lyres;
> their voices intertwine as they reach up together towards heaven,
> giving glory to the Lord of glory.
> Blessed is He for whom the silent have thundered out!
> (*On the Resurrection* 2.2; Brock and Kiraz 2006: 170–1)

Indeed, women and children were not silent in ancient Syriac communities, rural or urban, whether in domestic, civic, or monastic contexts! The place where historians can best access their voices, I suggest, is in the devotional activity that liturgy encompassed. For the present essay, I focus on the foundational era of Late Antiquity (fourth through seventh centuries CE). I turn first and most extensively to the voices of women. They will lead us, in turn, to those of children.

SERVING WOMEN/SINGING WOMEN

Late Antique Syriac Christianity attests two public roles for women that appear distinctive to its communities, in comparison with what we know of Greek or Latin-speaking regions. One was the ecclesiastical office of Daughter of the Covenant, a publicly visible office from the early fourth through perhaps the tenth centuries, different in its requirements from the female diaconate or the monastic vocation of nuns. The second were the non-monastic women's liturgical choirs that were a prominent part of civic life from the mid-fourth century onwards, and which continue still in Syriac Orthodox churches of the present day (Bakker Kellogg 2013). Though closely identified in Late Antiquity, the two are historiographically visible in different ways. Between the fourth and seventh centuries, both become strongly evident in our sources, serving to articulate distinctive Syriac modes of piety.

The Covenanters – or, Sons and Daughters of the Covenant (*Bnay* and *Bnat Qyama*) – were members of a formal ministry that appears in Syriac sources by the early fourth century, in both Roman and Persian territories (see chapter 5 in this volume; Nedungatt 1973; Griffith 1993; Tabé 1998; Macina 1999; Koltun-Fromm 2001; Harvey 2005). These were men and women under vows of celibacy and simplicity who worked in the service of their local church community. They lived in houses with other Covenanters, or with parents, but separately from the general population. In martyr accounts both Roman and Persian, Daughters of the Covenant are mentioned among those persons targeted for persecution and martyrdom, along with Sons of the Covenant, deacons, and clergy. The early historical sources that mention their presence do not identify their precise terms or duties. Yet Daughters of the Covenant were clearly evident in their societies as a group, and of some import to governing officials when seeking public identification of Christians. This type of civic visibility for Daughters of the Covenant was repeatedly re-inscribed over subsequent centuries when historical narratives or chronicles mentioned civic religious processions in times of danger, suffering, or sorrow. Such processions carried strong liturgical inflection: led in order by bishops, clergy, Covenanters, and then lay people in their respective ranks, as prayers, songs, and laments were sung by all (e.g. Ps.-Joshua the Stylite, *Chronicle*, 36, 43; Trombley and Watt 2006: 35–6, 45).

In the fifth century, canonical rules for the Covenanters began to appear, again in both Roman and Persian territory (e.g. Vööbus 1960: 34–50; idem 1982: 85 text/72 trans.). These provided guidelines as to appropriate dress, living arrangements, acceptable types of employment, and proper decorum for conduct in public. In general, the sources present Covenanters as performing a ministry of good works, in assistance to clergy and bishops. For example, Daughters of the Covenant in fifth-century Edessa served in a women's hospital established under the bishop Rabbula (Doran 2006: 100). The duties of the Daughters of the Covenant were complementary to, but not the same as, those of women deacons whose assigned work often included sacramental aspects (Brock 1998). Nor did the rise of women's monasticism eclipse the roles or work of the Daughters of the Covenant, whose ministry remained in the civic context of the local worshipping community (Jullien 2010).

Daughters of the Covenant may have been similar to consecrated virgins in Greek or Latin churches of the same time, called by different titles (*canonicae* or *subintroductae*; see especially Macina 1999). But in one key respect Daughters of the Covenant differed, and it was this difference that no doubt allowed this office to flourish for some centuries to come while their Greek and Latin counterparts disappeared. This was the ministry of liturgical song, identified in various ecclesiastical canons as their primary religious duty (Rabbula canons 20, 27, Vööbus 1960: 41, 43; Maruta canon 41, Vööbus 1982: 85 text/72 trans.).

The singing of women's choirs resounded through Late Antique Syriac liturgy (Harvey 2012). Occasionally mentioned in fourth-century sources, from the early fifth century onwards Syriac women's choirs were canonically prescribed in both Roman and Persian territory. Greek or Latin liturgies included choirs of nuns for special services, such as Easter, or important funerals. But in Syriac churches, women's choirs – consecrated but not monastic – were an integral part of daily and weekly civic worship in addition to special occasions.

Women's liturgical choirs are mentioned or discussed in a variety of Late Antique Syriac sources: hymns, homilies, ecclesiastical canons, and hagiography. Interestingly, they become historically visible during Late Antiquity, a time when the broader church institution was increasingly regulating and marginalising women's roles, phasing out the offices of widow and woman deacon, and institutionalising women's monasticism with greater constraints as the early ecumenical councils of the church established normative structures.

More surprising perhaps is the nature of their ministry. For Syriac commentators and ecclesiastical canons alike clearly state that the women's choirs sang the *madraše*, the doctrinal hymns through which congregations received instruction in right belief and proper biblical understanding. Greek canonical manuals of the time expressly forbid women to teach on doctrinal matters related to Christ and his saving passion (e.g. *Didascalia*, chapter 15). Yet these are precisely the theme of Syriac *madraše*; the great variety of hymns on the Virgin Mary provide eloquent examples (Brock 2010). As Jacob of Sarug notes, the very sound was arresting: 'A new sight of women uttering the proclamation (*karuzuta* = *kerygma*)/and behold, they are called teachers among the congregations' (*On Ephrem*, v. 42 = Amar 1995: 34–5). The designation *malpanyatha*, '(female) teachers', a term ordinarily employed in the masculine (*malpane*) for distinguished teachers and scholars of doctrine, was also used for the choirs in the anonymous *Life of Ephrem* (*Vita Ephremi*, 31 = Amar 2011: 71 text/77 trans.).

The Syriac women's choirs are wholly anonymous in our sources. They are discussed without reference to singers or places. While Late Antique sources at times referred to exceptional individual liturgical singers, Syriac women's choirs were treated collectively and without differentiation. Nonetheless, their singing was identified as authoritative in the eyes of the church: it was acknowledged to be theologically and religiously significant. The contrast here is to the charismatic authority of the individual holy woman, whose capacity for spiritual instruction was highly respected in Late Antique society in general (and to which we will turn below). The teaching performed by Syriac women's choirs differed substantially from this model, both in nature and in kind. Their teaching communicated the corporately defined doctrines of the Church, not the special insight or charismatic wisdom of a holy individual.

But what precisely was their authority? According to Syriac tradition, St Ephrem himself founded the choirs during the fourth century, specifically to sing his *madraše* and provide right teaching to the congregations. Although Ephrem addressed women's choirs in his hymns, he made no such claim for his part. In the sixth century, however, Jacob of Sarug and the anonymous *Life of Ephrem* both contend that women's choirs were established by Ephrem as a response to the danger of popular and seductive heretical hymns. Seeking to combat falsehood with truth, Ephrem chose women's voices as his instrument (Jacob of Sarug, *On Ephrem*, vv. 96–116 = Amar 1995: 48–53; *Vita Ephremi*, 31 = Amar 2011: 70–4 text/76–80 trans.). Such a genealogy lent irrefutable weight to the singing of women's choirs, tying their validity and their justification to the greatest of Syriac saints. At the same time, the need to designate this legacy may also indicate that these choirs were controversial (McVey 2007). Jacob suggests as much. Calling Ephrem 'a godly philosopher in his actions', Jacob offered high praise to the saint for his visionary work:

> Our sisters also were strengthened by you [Ephrem] to give praise;
> For women were not allowed to speak in church [cf. 1 Cor. 14:34].
> Your instruction opened the closed mouths of the daughters of Eve;
> And behold, the gatherings of the glorious (church) resound with their melodies.
> (*On Ephrem*, vv. 26, 40–1 = Amar 1995: 31, 35)

Syriac church canons in a variety of collections prescribed that women's choirs should sing the *madraše* and the Psalms. Other sources – such as Jacob just quoted – drew attention to the sound of their singing. The anonymous *vita* of Ephrem stressed both the instructional aspect of Ephrem's work with the Daughters of the Covenant, as well as the beauty of their voices:

> [The Daughters of the Covenant] would surround [Ephrem] like a flock of pure partridges and he resembled an eagle perched among doves being instructed by him, a sweet master with a pure melody. It was likewise fitting for the church which rang with the melodies of chaste women.
> (Amar 2011: 78)

The sonic impact of these voices was wondrous:

> My friends, who would not be astounded and filled with fervent faith to see the athlete of Christ [Ephrem] amid the ranks of the Daughters of the Covenant as they chanted songs, hymns, and melodies? Their songs resemble the songs and ethereal melodies of spiritual beings who chant to the spirits of humans with the sweetness of their songs.
> (Amar 2011: 80)

Jacob of Sarug draws attention to the sound of the women's choirs in a number of his homilies. In his homily *On the Partaking of the Holy Mysteries*, he instructs the congregation to 'pay heed to the hymns (sung) by virgins with glorious voices', which he terms a God-given gift to the churches (*On Partaking*, ll. 131–2 = Harrak 2009: 18). In his festal homilies, he exalts their singing in honour of the feasts. Most notably, he celebrates the choirs at length in his homily commemorating Ephrem (Amar 1995). Here, he praises the women's choirs in lavish terms, citing their 'joyful sound' (v. 59), their 'resounding melodies' (v. 41), the power of their 'soft tones' (v. 152), and their 'instructive' songs (v. 114). He presents Ephrem's establishment of the choirs as an act of theological brilliance, for by joining their voices to liturgy the choirs signified the fulfilment of the promise of salvation for all: 'Your teaching [O Ephrem] signifies an entirely new world;/for yonder in the kingdom, men and women are equal' (v. 43 = Amar 1995: 35). Citing the equal participation of men and women in the sacraments of baptism and Eucharist, he calls on women to sing out with men in church, overturning the old dispensation that had punished women with silence because of Eve. Now, because of the Virgin Mary, women should take their rightful place, joyfully adding their voices to those of men.

> Until now, your gender was brought low because of Eve;
> but from now on, it is restored by Mary to sing Alleluia!
> . . .
> Uncover your faces to sing praise without shame
> to [Christ] the One who granted you freedom of speech by his birth.
> (vv. 111, 113 = Amar 1995: 53)

Late Antique Syriac liturgies highlighted women's voices in other ways. Syriac hymns and homilies were filled with stories of the Bible, many featuring biblical women (Harvey 2010). Delighting to explore and elaborate the biblical accounts, liturgical poets such as Ephrem, Jacob of Sarug, Narsai of Nisibis, and others presented biblical figures in vivid terms, with striking characterisations and, often, with dialogues and monologues of lively imagined speech – a favoured technique of Late Antique Syriac poets. Since the Bible itself often did not highlight women's speech in this way, Syriac hymns and homilies thus brought these women of the biblical past into striking relief as favoured exemplars of the life of faith. The list of such women is extensive: from the Old Testament, Eve, Sarah the wife of Abraham, Tamar the daughter-in-law of Judah, Rahab the prostitute, Ruth the Moabite, Potiphar's Wife, Jephthah's Daughter, the Widow of Sarepta, the Shunammite Woman, Susannah, and the Maccabean Mother; and from the New: the Virgin Mary, Elizabeth the mother of John the Baptist, Anna the Prophetess, Mary and Martha the sisters of Lazarus, Mary of Bethany, Mary Magdalene, the Sinful Woman of Luke 7, the Canaanite Woman, the Haemorrhaging Woman, the Samaritan Woman, and others. All were celebrated in liturgy in song and chant offered by clergy and choirs, joined with responses by the congregation.

The different forms of Syriac liturgical poetry – hymns, homilies, and prayers – are noteworthy for their lyrical beauty. They also stand out for their vivid use of drama, pathos, humour, and delight. In such texts, for example, the fiercely determined Widow of Sarepta bullied the prophet Elijah into action when even God has failed to move the obstinate prophet (Brock 1989). A canny and perceptive Virgin Mary argued with the Archangel Gabriel about how pregnancy happens, and earnestly again with her husband Joseph as to her purity; she sang poignant lullabies to her new-born son Jesus (Brock 2010). Eve wept bitter lament over her sons Cain and Abel, or sang her joy at Christ's saving mercy (Harvey 2015). Syriac hymns and homilies presented biblical women in a rich tapestry of variations on a simple theme: the true life of faith required righteous behaviour, boldly performed, 'with a loud voice' – a phrase used repeatedly for these different Biblical women, and also, significantly, for the women's choirs who sang their stories in hymns and whose singing framed the homilies intoned by male clergy (Harvey et al. 2016).

In Syriac hymns and homilies, women of the Bible were repeatedly characterised as 'wise', 'perceptive', 'discerning'. They are presented as learned and knowledgeable about Scripture and about God's teaching. They are praised for speaking out, for refusing to be silent, for shouting, for proclaiming God's truth, for refusing to be hindered by men or social convention. They are presented as active agents, independent in thought and deed, fearless in their faith (e.g. Ephrem, *Hymns on Virginity*, 22, 23, 25, 26 = McVey 1989: 354–81; Harvey et al. 2016). Real voices female and male performed the imagined and remembered voices of biblical women, in the context of the gathered congregations of the church. Singing women's voices instructed Syriac Christians in models of faith.

Liturgy was also a location for celebrating women saints. Syriac Christianity produced an impressive cadre of prominent women saints and martyrs, both historical and legendary. Figures such as Pelagia of Antioch, Mary of Qidun, Febronia of Nisibis, and Marina/Marinus of Qannoubis were commemorated in notable hagiographies, hymns, and prayers sung and heard in liturgical gatherings. Their stories were transmitted widely in ancient and mediaeval Christianity more broadly, circulating in Syriac, Greek, Latin, Coptic, Arabic, and other languages (Fiey 1966; Petitmengin 1981; Brock and Harvey 1998; Saint-Laurent 2012; Hélou 2013). At times, hymns were composed in the imagined voices of women saints as they were for biblical women (Brock 2012). One presents a piercing lament in the voice of the penitent harlot Mary of Qidun (Brock and Harvey 1998: 37–9). Another in the form of a dialogue presents St Marina (disguised as the monk Marinus) in viscerally dramatic dialogue with Satan, in which she will be victorious (Brock 2008). This hymn belonged to a rich liturgical celebration of Marina, preserved particularly in Maronite tradition (Hélou 2013).

In part, the imagined speeches of biblical women or women saints, liturgically performed and celebrated, were the rhetorical vehicle that enabled Syriac poets to present women as generic models of faith, exemplifying virtues applicable to men as well as women. In the biblical or hagiographical stories, these speeches took place in narratively identified public, civic locations and contexts, just as their words were performed in the public context of liturgy. These sainted women then became not so much 'women' as 'faithful Christians'. Their words, like the model of faith they presented, belonged to all. As such, they represented an inclusive understanding of the Christian community, not always evident through moral instruction that favoured men explicitly.

Syriac liturgical presentation of biblical women and female saints – with their loud, bold voices – was ritually framed by the singing of women's choirs, whose own voices echoed also through homilies and prayers. Again, real and imagined voices interacted. Consider this passage from Jacob of Sarug's fourth homily on Elisha:

> The sound of Your praise [O Lord] thunders awesomely among the congregations,
> And through it the impudent song of idolatry was silenced.
> . . .
> By the sweet voices of the young women who sing Your praise
> You have captured the World so that all of it would be moved to Your praise.
> (ll. 21–30 = Kaufman 2010: 176)

WOMEN AND CHILDREN: MODES OF TEACHING

Let us add children to this picture. Historiographically speaking, where the women are found, there, too, are the children. In the religious lives of Late Antique Syriac communities, this was true liturgically and also in devotional piety. Children were tonsured as Sons and Daughters of the Covenant, and sang with gusto accordingly, as both Ephrem and Jacob of Sarug delighted to point out (e.g. Ephrem, *On the Resurrection* 2 = Brock and Kiraz 2006: 170–9; Jacob, *Against the Jews* 7: 529–41 = Albert 1976: 216–7). Their ministry as Covenanters and their singing were understood to be formative for their later roles in the community.

For example, in the early sixth century, a solitary ascetic named Simeon roamed the border mountains between the Roman and Persian empires. There, to his horror, Simeon stumbled on a semi-nomadic community with only the faintest notion of Christianity. At once, he set about establishing a canonically ordered religious life for the people. Among his first acts was the tonsuring of boys and girls as Covenanters. This he did by bribing the little ones with promises of presents, then locking the doors and tonsuring them! When the parents discovered this, to their profound dismay, they objected that they needed the children to help with their herds. But Simeon would not budge: divine punishment smote the families that refused to let their children participate. Simeon then set to work, with eighteen boys and twelve girls as a start.

> But for those who had been tonsured he made tablets for writing, and wrote for them, and thus he would frequently sit with patience as in a school and would teach them, boys and girls together. And down to the time when they reached an age at which they might receive harm from one another, within four or five years, they learned the psalms, and the Scriptures; and thus thenceforward loud choirs were to be heard at the service.
>
> (*Lives of the Eastern Saints* 16 = Brooks 1923: 238)

Twenty-six years later, the blessed Simeon went peacefully to his death, content that 'these disciples of his also had become grown women and men, and they were now becoming readers and Daughters of the Covenant, and they were themselves teaching others also' (*Lives* 16 = Brooks 1923: 248). The boys had grown into men entering church offices, while the girls continued in the ministry of the Covenanters, teaching, serving, and singing.

In addition to their (loud) voices offered in liturgy, children were present with their mothers especially in the daily devotional activities of villages and towns. Mothers could be powerful influences on their children's religious formation, as in the cases of Rabbula of Edessa or John of Tella, for both of whom fiercely determined mothers oversaw their religious education, leading eventually to their future careers as bishops. (*Life of Rabbula*, Doran 2006: 66–8; *Life of John of Tella*, Brooks 1907: 39–45 text/27–31 trans.). Historical sources as well as hagiography often note that mothers took their children regularly to visit local holy men or women for spiritual instruction and counsel. A frequent trope in hagiography, it also occurs in texts of personal memory. Theodoret of Cyrrhus fondly recalled that his mother often took him to visit the holy men of his region. A favourite memory was of Peter the Galatian, who lived in an abandoned tomb: 'He often sat me on his knees and fed me with grapes and bread; my mother, who had had experience of his spiritual grace, ordered me to reap his blessing once each week' (*History of the Monks* 9.4 = Price 1985: 83).

Holy women, too, were sought out in this way. The early-seventh-century Syriac mystic Sahdona described his childhood in a village of northern Iraq, where his mother often took him to visit an elderly local woman solitary named Shirin. In her eighties when he was a child, Shirin had long served the local people as a source of spiritual teaching and counsel. She is not identified as a nun nor as a Covenanter. Her practice consisted of living alone, following a simple ascetic regime, singing the daily prayer services, and studying the Bible, hagiography, and theological writings. Sahdona tells us that her fame as a holy woman was such that abbots and monks as well as local laity flocked to her hut regularly, 'for lessons in sanctity with her, wanting to receive her blessing'. Moreover, he wrote,

> Women in particular frequented her company, seeing that she was someone to whom they found access easy . . . They greatly profited from her, both from talking with her and just from seeing her . . . And ever since I was a child [my mother] would exhort me to choose to live a life to conform with Shirin's.
>
> (*Shirin*, 77–8; Brock and Harvey 1998: 180–1)

In this way, local holy women no less than biblical women served as moral exemplars and as wise counsellors for their communities, including contribution to the religious formation of children. Although there are no surviving Syriac texts authored by women, yet there are a number of such testimonies that make clear that women served as important teachers, mentors, and leaders in Syriac villages, towns, and cities in just such manner.

In Syriac hagiography, it was not uncommon for young children – girls and boys, both – to take themselves to monasteries, or to seek service with a local holy man or woman. John of Ephesus recounted the life of a recluse Mary, who apprenticed herself to a local hermit at the age of ten, leading to a long and fruitful ascetic career of her own (*Lives of the Eastern Saints* 28 = Brooks 1924: 559–62); and the nun Susan, who ran away to a convent at the age of eight, eventually becoming its leader during a time of persecution (*Lives* 27 = Brooks 1924: 541–58; Brock and Harvey 1998: 133–41). And of course, John himself was dedicated to a monastery at the age of four by his parents, in thanksgiving for the saving of his life as a baby by the monastery's stylite, Maro (*Lives* 4 = Brooks 1923: 60–4). These were often wholly informal arrangements, as so much of Syriac monastic life could be. They were not always the result of rebellion or rupture in a family, although Syriac hagiography also engaged that trope (Vuolanto 2009; Hatlie 2006).

Just as women martyrs or saints were celebrated liturgically as models of faith for the entire congregation, so, too, were the stories of children who suffered martyrdom, or who grew into holy careers, or whose lives were transformed by healing miracles (Horn 2006, 2009; also Horn and Martens 2009). Publicly told and transmitted, the stories of holy children were part of their religious formation as well as contributing to the edification of the larger community.

At times, families or households became monasteries, so to speak, with family members adopting an ascetic life together much like Shirin's. A basic ascetic regimen, combined with singing the daily services, characterised these households. Sometimes the families stayed together. Sometimes they separated on gender lines, fathers and sons in one house, mothers and daughters in another (*Lives of the Eastern Saints*, 21, 31 = Brooks 1923: 283–98, 1924: 576–85; Harvey 1996). In the case of the widow Euphemia and her daughter Maria in the sixth-century city of Amida, their work included extensive ministry to the city's poor, sick, and needy. Their active ministry combined with substantial liturgical service brought these two women over the course of thirty years to a position of great public prominence. The city's officials complained, 'the citizens revere and honor them more than the bishops!' (*Lives*, 12 = Brock and Harvey 1998: 124–33, at 131).

It is worth noting that such devotional work with children, both female and male, invariably included basic education so that they could read and study Scripture, hagiography, and theological and ascetical texts. Literacy for girls as well as boys was stressed in our Syriac hagiographical and monastic sources. The sixth-century epic romance of St Febronia, for example, presents a highly stylised portrait of the convent as a place of valued education and intellectual vitality. Not only did the nuns study together and read to one another, but they did so also with women visiting from the local community. Roughly contemporary with this hagiography is a sixth-century Syriac manuscript, British Library Add. 14,652, containing a compilation known as the 'Book of Women' (*kthaba d-neshe*). This compilation, which circulated over some centuries in Syriac, consisted of the lives of five biblical women: Ruth, Esther, Susanna, Judith, and Thecla (the companion of Paul). Although badly damaged, the colophon for Add. 14,652 indicates that the manuscript belonged to an abbess named Maryam (Wright 1872: 652a; Burris and Van Rompay 2002). This colophon offers the barest glimpse of women's monastic literacy, but in the context of the larger picture presented here, one we should take seriously.

In the interests of a balanced picture, of course, one should note that the sounds of women and children were not always appreciated. In the anonymous *Life of Ephrem*, children's choirs established by the heretic Bardaiṣan were the real source of dangerous teaching that spurred Ephrem to holy war through song (*Vita Ephremi*, 31 = Amar 2011). Jacob of Sarug complained that seductive songs from public theatres were especially attractive to children, who hummed them after the shows were finished (*On Spectacles Hom* 3 = Moss 1935: 105). Jacob also derided the sounds of pagan women's choirs (*Hom. 4 on Elisha*, ll. 27–8 = Kaufman 2010: 176–7), as well as the wailing sound of women mourners (*On the Partaking*, l. 157 = Harrak 2009: 21–2; *On the Departed*, Connolly 1910). Again, in late sixth century, in Persian territory, the hermit Elisha was disturbed by the sound of women's weaving rods (Thomas of Marga, *Book of Governors* 1.9 = Wallis Budge 2003 [1893]: 29 text/53 trans.). Around the same time, a group of seventy monks in the Iraqi hinterland left their monastery when it was announced that a school would be established nearby. They complained that the sounds of lessons in reading and psalmody would ruin their contemplative practices (*Book of Governors* 2.8 = Wallis Budge 2003 [1893]: 74–5 text/148–9 trans.). The voices of women and children might harm, just as they also might guide, teach, inspire, or save. What is certain is that they were meaningful, for ill or for good. Their voices mattered.

CONCLUSION: SOUNDING PRESENCE

One year during the fifth century, as Simeon the Stylite stood on his column outside the town of Tell-Neshe, severe famine struck the region. In desperation, people flocked to the stylite to seek his intercession on their behalf. Their petition took the form of liturgical participation.

> An innumerable crowd collected; the mountains were covered and the land filled with men and women. The [stylite's] enclosure was filled inside and out from one end to the other. They brought small boys who were learning the alphabet and placed them before him as their teachers sang antiphonally in Greek, 'Kyrie eleison'. When the saint saw all this – the priests, with their heads covered in dust standing in sorrow and distress, men and women within and without raising their voices on high, those children like innocent lambs, the sun as hot as summer – he was deeply distressed and his heart opened.
>
> (*Syriac Life of Symeon*, 75 = Doran 1992: 156)

In this scene of crisis and solace, the population of the region gathered together as a liturgical community in the presence of their local saint. Young and old, male and female, lay and ordained, they raised their voices in song. Everyone participated; every voice contributed. Such moments rendered women and children visible in ancient Syriac literature.

Devotional life in Late Antique Syriac Christianity fits loosely at best into an officially designated structure of liturgical practice, conducted with and under ecclesiastical supervision. That devotional life included lay people, clerics, and various other religious such as Covenanters, monastics, and deacons male and female. There were official roles (ecclesiastical offices), official spaces (church buildings, shrines, monastic buildings), and official activities (liturgical practices of various sorts, daily, weekly, festal, and other). Women and children are visible in the surviving Syriac sources in all of these contexts.

But women and children are not only visible in the literary sources. Their voices sounded loudly and clearly in all of these social locations and contexts. Their religious singing was a constant accompaniment in the ordinary lives of Late Antique villages, towns, and ascetic communities, whether lay or monastic. So, too, it would appear, were women's voices as religious teachers, instructors, and counsellors, whether historical persons (like Shirin) or as imaginatively remembered (biblical women or women saints).

When we take as our frame the public ministry of women, as Daughters of the Covenant and as choirs, the larger picture of women and children in the Late Antique Syriac world gains a far richer texture. If one examines the sources closely, Syriac hagiographical and historiographical texts are just as likely to identify women by official titles (Daughter of the Covenant, widow, woman deacon) as they are *without* such titles. Women like Shirin or Euphemia and Maria, or the family ascetics of whom John of Ephesus wrote, were not identified as formally consecrated or tonsured or holding such offices. Yet their public presence and activity is never presented as surprising, scandalous, or uncommon in Syriac sources. Rather, I suggest, women and children in local communities – villages, towns, cities, countryside – lived in a social and cultural context framed by what became in Late Antiquity the familiar sound of women and children in public religious work. Because there were official versions of these activities (Daughters of the Covenant, liturgical choirs), there could also be informality and social flexibility. When women and children behaved in these recognisable terms, they performed lifestyles familiar and acceptable in their local communities. What were the necessary components of such performance? A simple ascetic regimen of chastity and voluntary poverty, a disciplined prayer life expressed through daily liturgical practice, ministry to the needy, and ministry of spiritual counsel. And in constant accompaniment to all of these efforts, an ever-present sound of song.

As historians, we may lament the loss of words or evidence. The least we can do, then, is to honour the memory of Syriac women's voices, and their children's with them, so beloved in Late Antiquity, and still.

BIBLIOGRAPHY

Albert, M. 1976. *Jacques de Saroug, Homélies contre les Juifs*. PO 38.1, No. 174. Turnhout: Brepols.

Amar, J. P. 1995. *A Metrical Homily on Holy Mar Ephrem By Mar Jacob of Sarug*. PO 47.1, No. 209. Turnhout: Brepols.

———. 2011. *The Syriac Vita Tradition of Ephrem the Syrian*. CSCO 629–30/ Scr. Syr. 242–43. Louvain: Peeters.

Bakker Kellogg, S. 2013. *Fragments of a Liturgical World: Syriac Orthodox Christianity and the Dutch Multiculturalism Debates*. Ph.D. diss. University of California, Santa Cruz.

Brock, S. P. 1989. A Syriac Verse Homily on Elijah and the Widow of Sarepta. *LM* 102.1–2, 93–113.

———. 1996. Deaconesses in the Syriac Tradidion. *In:* P. Vazheeparampil, ed., *Woman in Prism and Focus: Her Profile in Major World Religions and in Christian Traditions*. Rome: Mar Thomas Yogam, 205–18.

———. 2008. St. Marina and Satan: A Syriac Dialogue Poem. *Christiana Orientalia* 5, 35–57.

———. 2010. *Bride of Light: Hymns on Mary From the Syriac Churches*. Piscataway, NJ: Gorgias.

———. 2012. L'hagiographie versifiée. *In:* A. Binggeli, ed., *L'hagiographie syriaque*. Études syriaques 9. Paris: Geuthner, 113–26.

Brock, S. P. and S. A. Harvey. 1998. *Holy Women of the Syrian Orient*. Berkeley: University of California Press.

Brock, S. P. and G. A. Kiraz. 2006. *Ephrem the Syrian: Select Poems*. Piscataway, NJ: Gorgias.

Brooks, E. W. 1907. *Vitae Virorum apud monophysitas celeberrimorum*. CSCO 7–8/ Scr. Syr. 7–8. Louvain: Durbecq, Secrétariat du CorpusSCO.

———. 1923–25. *John of Ephesus, Lives of the Eastern Saints*. PO 17–19. Paris: Firmin Didot.

Burris, C. and L. van Rompay. 2002. Thecla in Syriac Christianity: Preliminary Observations. *Hugoye: Journal of Syriac Studies* 5.2, 225–36.

Connolly, H. 1910. A Homily of Mar Jacob of Serugh on the Memorial of the Departed and on the Eucharistic Loaf. *Downside Review* 29 (n.s. 10), 260–70.

Doran, R. 1992. *The Lives of Simeon the Stylite*. Kalamazoo: Cistercian Publications.

———. 2006. *Stewards of the Poor: the Man of God, Rabbula, and Hiba in Fifth-Century Edessa*. Kalamazoo: Cistercian Publications.

Fiey, J.-M. 1966. Une hymne nestorienne sure les saintes femmes. *Analecta Bollandiana* 84, 77–110.

Griffith, S. H. 1993. Monks, "Singles", and the "Sons of the Covenant": Reflections on Syriac Ascetic Terminology. *In:* E. Carr et al., ed., *Eulogema: Sudies in Honor of Robert Taft*. Studia Anselmiana 110 / Analecta Liturgica 17. Rome: Centre Studi S. Anselmo, 141–60.

Harrak, A. 2009. *Jacob of Sarug's Homily on the Partaking of the Holy Mysteries*. The Metrical Homilies of Mar Jacob of Sarug 17. Piscataway, NJ: Gorgias.

Harvey, S. A. 1996. Sacred Bonding: Mothers and Daughters in Early Syriac Hagiography. *Journal of Early Christianity* 4.1, 27–56.

———. 2005. Revisiting the Daughters of the Covenant: Women's Choirs and Sacred Song in Ancient Syriac Christianity. *Hugoye: Journal of Syrirac Studies* 8.2, 125–49.

———. 2010. *Song and Memory: Biblical Women in Syriac Tradition*. Milwaukee: Marquette University Press.

———. 2012. Performance as Exegesis: Women's Liturgical Choirs in Syriac Tradition. *In:* B. J. Groen, S. Alexopoulos, and S. Hawkes-Teeple, ed., *Inquiries into Eastern Christian Worship: Acts of the Second International Congress of the Society of Oriental Liturgy*. Leuven: Peeters, 47–64.

———. 2015. Encountering Eve in Syriac Tradition. *In:* M. Doerfler, E. Fiano, and K. Smith, ed., *Syriac Encounters: Papers From the Sixth North American Syriac Symposium*. Leuven: Peeters, 11–49.

———. 2016. Bearing Witness: New Testament Women in Early Byzantine Hymnography. *In:* D. Krueger and R. Nelson, ed., *The New Testament in Byzantium*. Washington, DC: Dumbarton Oaks Publications, 205–19.

Harvey, S. A., S. P. Brock, R. Durmaz, R. S. Falcasantos, M. Payne, and D. Picus. 2016. *Jacob of Sarug's Homilies on the Women Whom Jesus Met*. Texts from Christian Late Antiquity 44. Piscataway, NJ: Gorgias Press.

Hatlie, P. 2006. The Religious Lives of Children and Adolescents. *In:* D. Krueger, ed., *Byzantine Christianity*. Minneapolis: Fortress, 182–200.

Hélou, C. 2013. *Sainte Marina: Moniale déguisée en habit de moine dans la tradition maronite*. Patrimoine Syriaque 6. Kaslik, Liban: Parole de l'Orient.

Horn, C. B. 2006. Children and Violence in Syriac Sources: The *Martyrdom of Mar Talya' of Cyrrhus* in the Light of Literary and Theological Implications. *PdO* 31, 309–26.

———. 2009. Raising Martyrs and Ascetics: A Diachronic Comparison of Educational Role-Models for Early Christian Children. *In:* C. B. Horn and R. R. Phenix, ed., *Children in Late Ancient Christianity*. Studien und Texte zu Antike und Christentum 58. Tübingen: Mohr Siebeck, 293–316.

Horn, C. B. and J. W. Martens. 2009. *'Let the Little Children Come to Me': Childhood and Children in Early Christianity*. Washington, DC: The Catholic University of America Press.

Jullien, F. 2010. Le monachisme feminine en milieu syriaque. *In:* F. Jullien, ed., *Le monachisme syriaque*. Études syriaques 7. Paris: Geuthner, 65–87.

Kaufman, S. A. 2010. *Jacob of Sarug's Homilies on Elisha*. The Metrical Homilies of Mar Jacob of Sarug 23–28. Piscataway, NJ: Gorgias.

Koltun-Fromm, N. 2001. Yokes of the Holy Ones: Embodiment of a Christian Vocation. *Harvard Theological Review* 94, 205–18.

Macina, M.R. 1999. Les *bnay* et *bnat qyama* de l'Église syriaque: Une piste philologique sérieuse. *In:* Centre d'Études et de Recherches Orientales (CERO), *Le Monaschisme Syriaque du VIIe siècle à nos jours*. Patrimoine Syriaque Actes du colloque VI. Antélias, Liban: Éditions de CERO, 13–50.

McVey, K. 1989. *Ephrem the Syrian: Hymns*. New York: Paulist.

———. 2007. Ephrem the Kitharode and Proponent of Women: Jacob of Sarug's Portrait of a Fourth-Century Churchman for the Sixth Century Viewer and Its Significance for the Twenty-first Century Ecumenist. *In:* S.T. Kimbrough, ed., *Orthodox and Wesleyan Ecclesiology*. Crestwood: St. Vladimir's Seminary Press, 229–53.

Moss, C. 1935. Jacob of Serugh's Homilies on the Spectacles of the Theatre. *LM* 48, 87–112.

Nedungatt, G. 1973. The Covenanters of the Early Syriac-Speaking Church. *OCP* 39, 191–215, 419–44.

Petitmengin, P. 1981. *Pélagie la Pénitente: métamorphoses d'une legend.* Paris: Études augustiniennes. 2 Vols.

Price, R. M. 1985. *Theodoret of Cyrrhus, History of the Monks of Syria.* Kalamazoo: Cistercian Publications.

Saint-Laurent, J.-N. 2012. Images de femmes dans l'hagiographie syriaques. *In:* A. Binggeli, ed., *L'hagiographie syriaque.* Études syriaques 9. Paris: Geuthner, 201–24.

Tabé, E. 1998. Les Bnay wa Bnoth Qyomo. *In:* Centre d'Études et de Recherches Pastorales (CERP), *Le Monachisme Syriaque aux premiers siècles de l'Église, IIe-Début VIIe siècle.* Patrimoine Syriaque, Actes du colloque V, Antélias, Liban: Éditions du CERP, 55–60.

Trombley, F. R. and J. W. Watt. 2006. *The Chronicle of Pseudo-Joshua the Stylite.* Liverpool: Liverpool University Press.

Vööbus, A. 1960. *Syriac and Arabic Documents Regarding Legislation Relative to Syrian Asceticism.* Stockholm: ETSE.

———. 1982. *The Canons Ascribed to Maruta of Maipherqat and Related Sources.* CSCO 439–40/ Scr. Syr. 191–2. Leuven: Peeters.

Vuolanto, V. 2009. Choosing Asceticism: Children and Parents, Vows and Conflicts. *In:* C. B. Horn and R. R. Phenix, ed., *Children in Late Ancient Christianity.* Studien und Texte zu Antike und Christentum 58. Tübingen: Mohr Siebeck, 255–92.

Wallis Budge, E. A. 2003 [1893]. *The Book of Governors: The Historia Monastica of Thomas Bishop of Marga AD 840.* Piscataway, NJ: Gorgias. 2 Vols.

Witakowski, W. 1996. *Pseudo-Dionysius of Tel-Mahre, Chronicle, Part III.* Liverpool: Liverpool University Press.

Wright, W. 1872. *Catalogue of Syriac Manuscripts in the British Museum*, Vol. 2. London: British Museum.

CHAPTER THIRTY

SYRIAC AGRICULTURE 350–1250

Michael J. Decker

'Syrians', or Syriac-speakers (*suryaye*), played a significant role in the agrarian history of the Middle East. There are difficulties in limiting 'Syriac' agriculture to the regions were Syriac was spoken at the end of Late Antiquity, e.g. in the lands of northern Mesopotamia around Edessa and along the Levantine coast, especially in the Lebanon mountains. In Palestine, Syriac inscriptions attest to Syrian monks in monasteries in the western Galilee and north through the region of Damascus, the Golan, and the Hauran, where dialects of Aramaic were spoken into the fourteenth century, according to Bar Hebraeus (Contini 1987; Hoyland 2009; Ashkenazi and Aviam 2012: 282; Griffith 1997). This is due to the rather wide-ranging nature of Syriac-speakers, who were active missionaries, monks, travellers, and merchants whose activities spread east and southward for great distances. These eastern diasporas took Syrians into the traditional Aramaic strongholds of southern Mesopotamia. In Mesopotamian communities of large numbers of Aramaic-speakers, including the 'Nabataeans', who were Aramaic-speakers but not necessarily Syriac-speakers, we have nonetheless considerable overlap in cultural and linguistic heritage. It is thus not unreasonable to include within the Syriac milieu other Aramaic-speaking minorities, such as the 'Nabataeans' of Mesopotamia (not to be confused with the Nabataeans of Arabia), Sabaens, and Mandaeans. This is underscored by the lack of clarity in the Arabic authors who describe the agrarian people of Mesopotamia as 'Nabataeans' and by the preservation of their agricultural and religious traditions in Syriac in the *Nabataean Agriculture* (Graf and Fahd 2012).

Communities of Syriac- and other Aramaic-speaking farmers and scholars were fully integrated into the economic systems of the empires to which they were subject throughout Late Antiquity and through the central mediaeval period. Moreover, Syriac scholars were aware of Hellenic technical treatises on farming and translated these. The circulation of such texts probably also implies that Syriac landowners were interested in current land management practices that had reached a high level of development over much of the Levant and Mesopotamia, especially following the conquests of Alexander when Mesopotamian, Egyptian, and Mediterranean methods circulated freely in and beyond the large territorial empires of the Didachoi. The probable involvement (though not without controversy among scholars) of

East Syrian monks in the transferal of silk worms to Byzantium in the sixth century underscores an interest in plants and their products in keeping with the theoretical interests just noted.

Similar to Jewish populations, Syriac-speaking settlements stretched from Palestine, where rain-fed agriculture was the norm, to lowland Mesopotamia, where farming was traditionally supported by perennial irrigation, predominantly from canals excavated by the state and maintained under state coercion by communities along their banks. Thanks to the Babylonian Talmud, redacted ca. AD 500, we are well-informed about farming in Lower Mesopotamia during Late Antiquity. There, significant urban populations at places like Peroz-Sapor, Ctesiphon, Sura, al-Hira, and others created markets for substantial quantities of agrarian produce and allowed merchant networks and specialist trades to thrive. The expansion of Christianity and the mendicant nature of the Syrian clergy no doubt stimulated intellectual and physical contacts and helped to erode the physical barriers erected by the Romans and Sasanians. Syrian traders were among these communities, as attested by the expansion of Syriac Christianity along the early Silk Roads and to the Kerala coast of India. In their eastern travels, it is likely that Syriac travellers brought back botanical knowledge and actual specimens of new crops or new crop varieties from Central Asia and India.

The environment inhabited by Syriac-speakers ranged from semi-arid upland terrain dominated by continental climates, as around Amida (Diyarbekir) and the Ṭur ʿAbdin, to lowland subtropical semi-arid and arid zones in Iraq. Along the coastlands, the Mediterranean climate was characterised by long, dry summers with cool, rainy winters, while in the mountainous regions heavy snowfalls were common. Significant environmental changes occurred in Late Antiquity. Longer-term climate oscillations affected the agrarian communities of Syriac lands. The advent of the 'Late Antique Little Ice Age' or 'Vandal Minimum' coincided with a period of global cooling that lasted ca. AD 500–800. Late Antiquity also witnessed a shift in millennial-scale precipitation trends thought to be functions of the North Atlantic air currents and ocean temperatures. The expression of these periodic oscillations produced cooler, drier weather in Syria-Palestine after AD 500 and a shift to heavier winter storm precipitation in Anatolia and northern Mesopotamia. The latter regions became cooler and wetter ca. AD 500–750, then drier from ca. 750–950, and finally wetter again in the centuries from ca. 950 through 1450 (Haldon et al. 2014). In southern Syria, the long-term change in precipitation has been linked both to the arrival of Arab tribesmen in the wake of the Muslim conquests but also to a concurrent decline in overall agricultural activity beginning in the seventh century and possibly recorded in the pollen record (Kedar 1985). Volcanic activity is likely responsible for severe climatic instability around AD 536, when the so-called Dust Veil Event occurred. Probably caused by massive eruptions at Ilopango (El Salvador), proto-Krakatoa (Indonesia), or both, the Dust Veil Event was caused by atmospheric haze that blocked solar radiation (Baillie and Mcaneney 2015; Baillie 1994; Toohey et al. 2016). Tree-ring data from around the globe indicate poor growing conditions, and literary sources support this: in the Latin west, Cassiodorus witnessed a summer of drought and frosts with widespread crop failures. In some areas the effects of the AD 536 Dust Veil Event may have been felt as late as 550 (Gräslund and Price 2012). These trends coincided with the advent of the so-called Mediaeval Warm

Period beginning ca. AD 800 and extending into the fifteenth century, which was caused by increased solar activity and a lower level of volcanic activity than in prior centuries. By the ninth century, the climate of Anatolia and northern Mesopotamia had once again changed, becoming moister and apparently more hospitable both to agriculture and herding, a climate situation that prevailed until around the middle of the fifteenth century (Haldon et al. 2014). Thus, across the Late Antique and mediaeval periods, drought and other severe weather events were common events that could threaten the harvests and health of entire regional populations; some periods seem to exhibit more instability in this regard than others, but the explanation for this could be as simple as source bias.

Beyond the climate and landscape, there were other environmental issues to contend with, such as plant diseases which could blight an entire harvest, or the dreaded locust, whose arrival occurred erratically and whose swarms could number in the billions. A swarm in AD 500 sparked a famine in a belt from the Persian side of the frontier east of Amida, through Reshaina (Constantia; modern Viranşehir) to Edessa (Trombley and Watt 2000: 37). Another locust swarm passed through the region in the spring of 785 and wrought widespread destruction. Other arrivals are reported in 804 and 808/9 (Morony 2000: 155; Chabot 1901: III, 19). Locust hatches that caused regional damage are recorded in Michael the Syrian's chronicle in 1080–1, 1120–1, 1136, and 1195–6 (Morony 2000: 156; Chabot 1901: III, 177, 208–9, 238–9, 243, 413).

Disease was also a critical part of the agrarian environment that affected rural communities. The well-known pandemic of AD 542, the Justinianic Plague, remains of unknown demographic significance. Several accounts, however, including that of John of Ephesus, indicate that there was widespread mortality in both the cities and rural areas. Increasing the likelihood of its serious harm to society is the cyclical nature of the bubonic plague outbreaks which occurred at fairly regular intervals until vanishing from the Levant and Mesopotamia around 750. The *Zuqnin Chronicle* records plague in 542–3, 546–7, at Amida (Diyarbekir) in 557–8, 704–5, and 743–4 (Harrak 1999: 96, 119, 148, 166). The plague is last noted in the Middle East around 750; it apparently made little demographic impact until the Black Death of the mid-fourteenth century (Stathakopoulos 2004).

Most of Mesopotamia lay outside the 200 mm isohyet where dry farming was not impossible, but was limited and depended on special conditions. This 'zone of uncertainty' was better farmed using hydraulic agriculture, which required high levels of investment but could be counted on for more reliable returns. One should not mistake the engineering interventions of the Late Antique and mediaeval periods as having tamed the Tigris and Euphrates. The rivers remained large and unruly; the Tigris in particular was prone to unpredictable and violent flooding. These tragic rises in the river swept away dams, weirs, bridges, roads, and settlements and destroyed fields and crops. In addition to the threat of flooding, which could destroy canals, normal flows of water carried sediments that threatened to choke the canal network. The system therefore required constant cleaning and maintenance to ensure the integrity of weirs and ditches. In addition, salinisation of soil was a constant threat on irrigated land; the build-up of salts in the soil remained a persistent problem in irrigated farming regimes and plagued farmers throughout the ancient and mediaeval eras (El Faiz 1990).

Nonetheless, by Late Antiquity the canals of the region were quite well developed, thanks to investment which gathered pace in the late Sasanian era. The potential of the northern Euphrates and Tigris was limited both by their forming part of imperial political boundaries and by their geology, notably the bluffs of the Upper Euphrates and lack of a wide, easily irrigable plain there. The Muslim conquest removed the political impediments to development, and it is therefore unsurprising that considerable Umayyad investment occurred precisely in this region, especially in the watersheds of the Balikh, around Raqqa, and along the Khabur River where there is evidence of settlement expansion and agricultural intensification in the seventh–tenth centuries (Decker 2011). The early Muslims had a reputation for developing irrigation networks; the people of Balis (Barbalissos) were said to have approached ʿAbd al-Malik and demanded that he provide an irrigation canal, whereupon the caliph had the Nahr Maslama built or restored (Ibn Shaddad 1984: 6). Hisham had canals dug from the Euphrates. Major canals branched off the Tigris, notably the Nahrawan canal, originating on the lower Diyala River in the vicinity of Tikrit and flowing across the plain to join the Tigris River at Madharaya; the Persian *shah* Khosrow I (531–79) had enlarged this system greatly by having dug a canal from the east bank of the Tigris to join the Diyala (Morony 2012). The Sasanian era canal systems in central and southern Mesopotamia are estimated to have supplied irrigation to some 8,000 km^2 (Adams 1965: 77). The Diyala continued to be developed in the ʿAbbasid era, but conditions in Iraq began to deteriorate with the time of troubles in the tenth century. The Seljuk rulers of Iraq tried, but ultimately failed, to restore considerable portions of the Nahrawan which was largely derelict by the thirteenth century (Le Strange 1905: 37). Syriac- and Aramaic-speakers played a significant role in these irrigation schemes. The Nabataeans of Mesopotamia, eastern Aramaic-speakers, including the community of at-Tib are mentioned by Yaqut (d. 1229) as still speaking Aramaic and tracing their descent from Seth, perhaps a reference to Mandaean or Sabian practitioners. In this portion of eastern Iraq, farming was possible among the predominantly Mandaean population through irrigation from the Nahr at-Tib. Another Nabataean named Hassan helped al-Hajjaj ibn Yusuf (d. 714) drain the southern marshlands of Iraq (Le Strange 1873: 64, 42). In Khuzistan, major Sasanian irrigation projects served to support farming around the cities of Gundeshapur, Karkeh, Susa, and Sustar. From Shapur I (r. 242–72), who deported thousands of captives from Antioch, including the Christian Bishop Demetrianos in the middle of the third century, the development of the Khuzistan Plain gathered pace, and the urban centres noted above may have supported as many as 100,000 people (Christensen 1993).

In Roman Syria, Syriac-speakers were common in rural areas as far south as Emesa (Homs) and along some reaches of the desert fringe around Epiphaneia (Hama), where at least three Syriac inscriptions recorded indicate a Late Antique presence near Androna (al-Andarin) (Butler and Littmann 1905). Androna and its vicinity witnessed considerable agricultural investment and intensification during the fifth through seventh centuries, including a network of underground drainage galleries (*qanats*) and associated reservoirs and distribution channels, as well as the use of *saqiyas* (gear-driven water-lifting machines). Archaeological evidence for the use of *saqiyas* are found from Palestine through northern Syria (Decker 2009b: 198–202). At Dara, the Romans built a sizeable hydraulic infrastructure, including a large dam, though perhaps not the arch dam that the sixth-century historian Procopius seems to describe (Garbrecht and Vogel 1991). Dams, weirs, cisterns, and other hydraulic technologies, such as watermills, were a normal part of the countryside around Amida and elsewhere in Syria (Wilson 2003: 115–41).

The major crops of Syriac farmers were the same as other Byzantine and Sasanian subjects. In areas blessed with a Mediterranean climate, such as the Levantine coast of central and north Syria, a regime dominated by the well-known Mediterranean triad of grain, wine, and olive oil prevailed. This is also true of certain parts of southwestern Iran, where olives are able to grow. In mountainous and temperate regions, animal fats generally replaced olive oil. Grain, the main food staple, provided the majority of calories for most individuals. Numerous varieties of wheat and barley were grown. Wheat was preferred for its palatability and the quality of bread it rendered. Barley bread was considered inferior to wheat, being generally coarser and less easily digested. Barley was the main food for the poor throughout the pre-industrial Middle East but remained a vital plant for human consumption as well as a major component of the diet of stall-fed animals. Archaeological evidence from the Late Antique and mediaeval Fertile Crescent underscores the importance of wheat and barley in the diet. Excavation in the Euphrates valley indicates that barley dominated there from the Sasanian-ʿAbbasid periods (Decker 2011). Barley was generally a hardier grain, able to adapt better than wheat to the saline soils that frequently plagued irrigated agriculture, and is also typically more disease resistant than wheat. Another important grain crop was millet, a shorter-season grain that tolerated the hot summer growing season in Mesopotamia. During the famine of 501–2, ps.-Joshua records that the Edessenes planted millet as an emergency summer crop after their winter-sown wheat crop (and barley likely as well) had failed (Trombley and Watt 2000: 38).

The eleventh-century *Kitab al-Hawi*, an anonymous mathematical treatise, lists the following four categories of crops growing in Iraq, organised by value for purposes of assessment and taxation. Among these common crops were sesame, wheat, barley, cumin, mustard, coriander, caraway, poppy, lucerne (alfalfa), chickpeas, haricot beans, lentils, linseed, cress, fenugreek, safflower, raisins, sumac, almonds, hazelnuts, hemp, rice, millet, and oats (El-Samarraie 1972: 81). Missing from this list is olive, the major oil crop of the Mediterranean. Sesame and safflower would have provided cooking oil in places where olive did not grow, but olive oil was probably imported into Iraq in some quantity, as it was to Egypt (Goitein 1967: 120). Sesame oil was the primary cooking oil in Iraq (Newman 1932: 101). Major tree crops included dates, pistachio, fig, pomegranate, almond, and hazelnuts, among others (El-Samarraie 1972: 81).

Palæobotanical evidence from central and eastern Turkey and Iran offers insights into specific regional agricultural trends of the past. Well-dated pollen recovered from Lake Nar in Cappadocia suggest that the period from AD 670 to 950, which corresponds to a general decline in Byzantine political and economic power, witnessed a considerable decrease in pollen associated with human activity on the landscape. Tree pollens from species such as pine, normally indicative of low frequency human exploitation, increased markedly at this time. This contrasts with the centuries prior (AD 300–670), in which species like sweet chestnut, walnut, vine, rye, and wheat are detectable in the record; these appear to indicate much more widespread settlement and agrarian activity in central Asia Minor (England et al. 2008: 1238). Around

Lake Urmia, in north-west Iran, study of pollen cores indicate that the cultivation of fruit trees peaked during the Sasanian period and declined from the Early Islamic era onwards, supporting the view of demographic or political instability that undermined the efforts of those who would invest in such long-term projects as the planting and nurturing of fruit trees (Djamali et al. 2009). Isotope and pollen evidence from south-west Iran, on the other hand, suggests human intervention in the landscape as steadily increasing from the Sasanian era through the early Islamic period and later (Jones et al. 2015).

Wine was produced in considerable quantities in the Levant and Mesopotamia. Mar Mari, the apostle to Seleucia, found that the inhabitants were wont to spend their time in a perpetual state of drunkenness (Harrak 2005: 43). Mesopotamian wine was shipped down the rivers and consumed domestically, though quantities were also exported throughout the Parthian, Sasanian, and early Islamic eras. One probable marker of this trade is the long (about 800 cm in height), cylindrical, handless, and neckless amphorae, the so-called Torpedo jar, remains of which are found throughout the Gulf, along coastal north-west India and as far south as Sri Lanka (Tomber 2007, 2008: 39–42, 112–13, 126–8). While there was certainly a longstanding appetite for alcoholic beverages in general in India and the Gulf, perhaps some of the traffic in wine was due to the demands of eastern Christian communities, who required the beverage for the Eucharist. The fate of wine production following the establishment of the ʿAbbasids is unclear. However, several caliphs were certainly wine drinkers, and the presence of sizeable Jewish and Christian communities who used wine in ritual and who had no prohibitions against the consumption of alcohol favours the continuation of widespread wine growing.

During Late Antiquity and into the early Islamic period, the Fertile Crescent witnessed the arrival or expansion of crops that were relative newcomers to the region. Rice arrived from India during the Hellenistic period and diffused slowly northwards and westwards throughout the Sasanian and Roman empires. Rice was a minor crop in the diet as a whole but regionally important. Farmers cultivated rice from the Sawad (southern Iraq), along the rivers and as far north as the Caucasus (Decker 2009a). Rice farming prior to the Arab Conquests is also known in Palestine, the Syrian Golan, and in the region of Antioch, and was prominent in the territory of Kaskar (Kashkar) opposite the future site of Wasit (Le Strange 1905: 43). Muslim historians and geographers indicate a similar crop regime from the seventh through the tenth centuries. Tabari (d. 923) for instance, notes that the assessment under the caliph Muʿawiyah (661–80) was so thorough that it counted 'even the husks of rice' (Hawting 1989: 36–7).

Another recently cultivated crop that spread widely under Islam was cotton, which by the tenth century was grown in the Levant as far north and west as the Cilician Plain, according to recent archaeobotanical finds at Kinet Höyük (Ramsay and Eger 2015). Landowners devoted ever greater acreage to cotton from the Sasanian period onwards, with the crop becoming a major staple in Khuzistan and on the Iranian plateau, in many instances stimulated by Muslim landowners looking for a profitable crop suited to the hot and dry conditions that prevailed there. Given sufficient irrigation, the semi-arid landscapes of the Fertile Crescent and Iranian plateau were well suited to cotton; a combination of cultural and ecological factors favoured its advancement and spread throughout the Islamic world. Khuzistan, which continued to host a sizeable Syrian community, was a major cotton growing area, and the cities there were famous for their textile and dye works as well (Bulliet 2011). In the fourteenth century, cotton flourished in the Syriac heartland of Ṭur ʿAbdin (Le Strange 1873: 96).

Animal husbandry was ubiquitous in the ancient and mediaeval worlds. Animals provided the necessary calories, via meat or milk or via eggs that sustained some communities in difficult environmental landscapes. Syriac sources frequently refer to Arab pastoralists (ṭayyaye) who moved throughout the semi-arid landscapes of the Jazira, around Edessa and through highland pastures. Conflict was not uncommon between sedentary peoples and pastoralists, as in 772–3 when tribesmen of the Banu Taghlib and Maʿd moved into the foothills of the Jazira; their cattle devoured the pasture there, leaving none for the cattle belonging to the sedentary farmers (Morony 2000: 154). More often relationships were characterised by peaceful, if not harmonious, coexistence. Animal products were important in settled groups as well, where they supplemented the meagre diets enjoyed by the majority of the population. Semi-nomads, or more rarely true nomads who were always on the move, were common throughout the Fertile Crescent, especially in the semi-arid steppelands of the Syrian Desert and on the Iranian plateau, as well as throughout the borderlands of the Gulf and over much of the Arabian Peninsula. Sheep, goat, and camels provided not only meat and milk protein, calories, and other critical food items, but also raw materials (sinew, horn, hides) for clothing, shelter, and tools. Horses were expensive to maintain and therefore used mostly by upper classes who could afford them. Peasants and poorer townsfolk relied on asses for local transport, and donkey caravans appear frequently in rabbinic literature and by Late Antiquity had been the normal means of long-distance transport for more than a millennium (Veenhof 2009; Förster 2007; Decker 2009b: 249–52). In areas where tilled land was widespread, such as the Syrian Hauran and the Jazira (Upper Mesopotamia), cattle (*bos taurus*) provided the main form of traction, for pulling ploughs, sledges, cartage, and other laborious tasks, such as driving *saqiyas* or other water-lifting devices. The plough ox was probably the most important asset that a farmer could possess, allowing one to cultivate a much greater area than hoeing or other forms of manual tillage. Animal disease, such as bubonic plague or rinderpest, became the scourge of cattle-rearing peoples in the Levant and the Mediterranean following its introduction from the Asian steppe, probably from the fourth century AD onwards (Spinage 2003: 88–9). Archaeozoological study provides important insights into the ancient and mediaeval diets of Syriac lands. At Zeugma, for example, finds of animal bones indicate that pork declined in the diet during Late Antiquity, giving way to cattle and, in the Early Islamic period, to sheep and goat. Cattle remained prominent in the record, indicating their continued use as animals for ploughing and other heavy labour (Rousseau et al. 2008).

Around Antioch (Antakya) and Aleppo (Haleb) and in the plains north and east of Homs and Hama, home to a sizeable Syriac population, there is ample evidence of intensive mixed-farming practices (Decker 2009b). The integration of animal husbandry within a Mediterranean mixed-farming regime of vines, cereals, and olives became especially prominent from the fourth century AD at the latest. In some regions, intensive agriculture continued uninterrupted beyond the seventh-century Muslim Conquests, since the principal drivers of this kind of farming were both the large urban centres in the region, especially Antioch and Apamea, as well as overseas demand driven by the export of surplus consumed by state levies of the *annona* as well as overseas private trade. We get a glimpse of Syrian merchants operating in northern Mesopotamia in the histories of Zachariah of Mitylene; among these merchants were those who carried grain and other local products up to the army at Amida during the war of Anastasius (Greatrex et al. 2011: §5.7). There we find that the vineyards of the region of the upper Euphrates supplied wine to merchants from Cappadocia, whose region did not produce sufficient quantities or qualities of wine. It is unclear where this wine was bound, but there is material evidence for both the production of surplus wine and oil in predominantly Syriac-speaking regions around Melitene, Amida, and the Ṭur ʿAbdin, as well as northern Syria, throughout the fifth–seventh centuries. The fortune of local elites was undoubtedly built, at least in part, upon ownership of landed estates. Among the best known of these prominent large-estate owners was Magnos the Syrian (d. ca. 582) who came from Huwwarin in central Syria. Magnos was probably, though not certainly, a Syriac-speaker. He rose to great prominence under Justin II and Tiberius, holding in 566 the office of *comes sacrarum largitionum*. Magnos managed lands around Huwwarin, but also at one time or another imperial lands in Pamphylia and the large former imperial estate of the Persian defector Hormisdas, brother of the Persian shah Shapur II (309–79). When Magnos arrested the Ghassanid phylarch Mundhir in 584, the Ghassanids plundered his fortified compound, presumably at Bab el-Hawa where they seized quantities of gold, silver, and servants but also stores of grain, wine, and oil as well as large numbers of animals (Payne Smith 1860: 387). While we cannot be sure about Magnos's linguistic and ethnic identity (inscriptions mentioning him are in Greek but this is hardly conclusive), others are more certain. We can more confidently place within the Syriac milieu the family of Iwannis Rusafoyo and his son Sergios. Iwannis was so wealthy from the produce of his estates that he was able to lavishly entertain the deposed Sasanian shah Khosrow II (590–628), in the process laying out a fortune in precious vessels. Allegedly insulted by Iwannis's wife, Khosrow later exacted revenge by imprisoning her and carrying off her household into captivity. Only later was her son Sergios released and restored to his now despoiled properties. Among the capital left to Sergios we find listed villages, orchards, mills, and shops (Kennedy 2010).

Ownership of entire villages was common throughout the Levant and Mesopotamia, no doubt with the assurance of an inherited labour force as well. If the written sources are accurate in their portrayal of the incessant warfare of the late sixth and early seventh centuries, violence must have damaged farming communities in northern Syria and Mesopotamia. Armies on the march foraged and devastated crops, besieged cities, and sometimes sacked them, thus temporarily destroying lucrative market centres. Perhaps most disruptive of all was the taking of captives. Some Roman and Sasanian raids read like giant captive-taking operations, such as the 573 campaign of Khosrow II who is said to have seized tens of thousands of people (from 92,000 to 292,000 depending on the source) from the city of Apamea (Perry et al. 2011). The Roman invasion of Arzanene on the left bank of the Upper Tigris in 578 resulted in the capture of (allegedly) some 100,000 prisoners, a portion of whom were sent to Cyprus (Whitby and Whitby 1986: 97). Such massive transfers of people through captivity or through the flight of refugees into other parts of the empires disrupted agriculture and diminished the availability of labour in certain places while expanding the capacity of others. Populations were also moved to settle the lands around Nisibis following the end of the Roman-Persian war in 363. Shapur II (309–79) transplanted thousands more prisoners, including many Christians, from Amida, Bezabde (Cizre), and Sinjar to Khuzistan and the vicinity of the Karkeh River (Christensen 1993: 110). According to the late-ninth- or early-tenth-century *Chronicle of Seert*, Shapur provided houses and farmland for these prisoners (Howard-Johnston 2010: 325; Wood 2013: 221–3). One of the largest hauls of prisoners seems to have been taken during the Roman-Persian War between Anastasius and Kavad I (488–531). The latter, according to ps.-Joshua, numbered more than 80,000, and these were removed to Khuzistan. In 501–2, Lakhmid raiders seized 18,500 around Ḥarran and Edessa. Under Khosrow I, the seizure and transplantation of Roman prisoners reached great proportions; John of Ephesus claims that up to 275,000 prisoners from Dara, Apamea, and elsewhere in Syria and Mesopotamia were settled in Persia, though we are not told where. Even while these figures must be exaggerated, they nonetheless indicate considerable potential disruptions in the farming communities, among the free peasantry and estate dependents throughout Late Antiquity, a situation which improved somewhat in the Umayyad and ʿAbbasid periods, when relatively strong central state control secured many of the Syriac lands from serious foreign depredations.

The sundering of these areas from Roman control over the course of the seventh century had serious repercussions for the economy. The large-scale exports of wine and olive oil that had formerly been shipped from the coastal plains and hills to Constantinople and as far afield as Crimea, Ethiopia, and Britain plunged following the Muslim conquests. While abundant material evidence suggests that the southern Levant and Egypt continued to thrive following the conquests, the picture for the northern Levant is far less complete or compelling. With the evaporation of Roman state structures, the disruption and flight of some elites, and the sundering of networks that began with the Sasanian conquest and could hardly have been restored by the time of the Muslim conquests, it is hard to imagine that the economy of northern Oriens and the Syriac Christian population fared particularly well from the early decades of the seventh century. Indeed, a picture of agrarian crisis is evident in the anxiety expressed in the well-known *Apocalypse of Pseudo-Methodius*, probably written by a Jacobite priest around the early 690s, when ʿAbd al-Malik restored Umayyad authority in the north of Mesopotamia. ʿAbd al-Malik initiated a census of Syriac Christians in Mesopotamia. According to Baladhuri (d. 829), the caliph decreed that:

> Everyone go to his region, village, and father's house and register his name, his lineage, his crops and olive trees, his possessions, his children, and everything he owned. From this time tax began to be levied *per capita*; from this time all manner of evils were visited upon the Christian people. For until this time kings had taken tribute on land rather than on the person . . . And this was the first census that the Arabs carried out.
>
> (Hoyland 2008: 15)

This intrusive assessment, reminiscent of the fiscal reforms of Diocletian of the late third and early fourth centuries, created a crisis in the Syriac Christian community.

Many apparently apostatised in order to escape paying the *kharaj* or *jizya*, as is well-attested in other communities in Mesopotamia (Reinink 2006). In all likelihood, heavy-handed measures of this kind encouraged the abandonment of the countryside and the movement of converts as *mawali* into the orbit, often in cities such as Kufa or Basra, of urban Arab elites. Al-Hajjaj disallowed conversions of many fellahin in Mesopotamia due to the threat of diminished taxation and perhaps labour on the lands of Iraq as well (Dietrich 2012). While the Umayyads and early ʿAbbasids invested heavily in Mesopotamia, the latter favouring it as their centre of power in part because of its productive landscape, the fragmentation of the later ʿAbbasids led to a decline in agriculture from the late tenth century onwards. Regionalisation and the attendant fracture of political and administrative powers of coercion and internecine strife contributed to the decay of hydraulic agriculture in the ʿAbbasid breadbasket. In the eleventh and twelfth centuries, the Ayyubids and Seljuks could not mend nor maintain the vast infrastructure they had inherited. While scholars debate whether the evidence from mediaeval Mesopotamia indicates a fiscal or an agricultural crisis, the preponderance of evidence favours the latter (Campopiano 2012).

Nonetheless, Syriac communities remained integrated into the expansive economy of the early caliphate and the wealthy continued to conduct specialised production. In the vita of St Simeon ('of the Olives') (d. 734), abbot of the Monastery of Qarṭamin (Mor Gabriel) in the Ṭur ʿAbdin, and later bishop of Ḥarran, we find the saint planting 12,000 olive trees, oil from which was sold throughout the region and the cash from which supported his flourishing religious house. From the fourth to the thirteenth centuries, monastic houses were integrated into the agricultural economy, owning land, investing in agricultural capital, and buying, selling, or bartering livestock and other agricultural products. The monastery of Deir Dehes in the Antiochene Limestone Massif was founded perhaps in the fourth century. Deir Dehes housed double olive oil presses comprised of two rotary millstones used to crush the olives into a paste, which was then loaded into the two lever-and-screw-type presses in order to extract the oil. These installations represent considerable investment on the part of the religious house and could process far in excess of subsistence need; the surplus oil must have been bartered or sold, as was common throughout the Limestone Massif in the fourth to seventh centuries. The Deir Dehes presses functioned at least until the sixth century, and there is evidence of occupation at the monastery as late as the ninth century (Biscop 1997: 21–5, 49).

Byzantine incursions increased in the middle ʿAbbasid centuries, however, and in the tenth century especially, eastern Christians were deported to Byzantine lands in Anatolia where they were settled, presumably to re-Christianise the landscape as well as to increase its agricultural productivity (Dagron 1976). With the arrival of the Mongols, much of the rural landscape of Syria was affected by warfare and emigration. Ibn Shaddad notes that settlements in the Jund Qinnasrin were abandoned, among the city of Balis (Barbalissos/Meskene), the Syrian monastery in Resafa, and others (Ibn Shaddad 1984: 13, 19–22). On the whole, however, the Mongol period was a good time for the Syriac communities of the Middle East and beyond; Syriac communities were spared the sack of Baghdad in 1258 and the Mongols employed a number of Syriac Christians in the imperial bureaucracy. But following the Mamluk conquest of Crusader Palestine and Mongol Syria, Christians suffered from Muslim reprisals (Micheau 2008: 387–8). Syrian Christian prosperity and influence in the countryside waned.

Syriac communities nonetheless remained on the land and were important in the transmission of botanical and agricultural knowledge. Especially under the Umayyads and ʿAbbasids, Syrians transplanted into Sasanian Persia became critical foci for the spread of Syriac language and knowledge. The school at Jundishapur (Gondesapur) was critical in the translation of Greek texts into Pahlavi and later into Arabic, especially in the natural sciences. Numerous Greek technical treatises were translated from Greek into Arabic, among them important botanical and technical texts, such as the *Synagogê geôrgikon epitêdeumaton*, a Late Antique encyclopaedia of Graeco-Roman farming practices (Decker 2007; Lagarde 1967). Syriac was also the language of the well-known but controversial tome, the *Nabataean Agriculture* (*al-Filaḥa an-Nabaṭiyya*) (Fahd 1993–8). This massive work, attributed to the ʿAbbasid-era author Ibn Waḥšiya (d. 930/31) and once dismissed as a forgery by the prominent orientalist Theodore Nöldeke, has since been edited and studied by Toufic Fahd (Fahd 1952, 1969). Fahd and, more recently, Hämeen-Anttila (2006: 87), judge the work an authentic compilation of earlier material that was translated from a group of Syriac originals. The *Nabataean Agriculture* formed the basis of the bulk of agronomic knowledge that circulated throughout the mediaeval Islamic world. The text offers insights into folklore, religious beliefs, and the daily life of the inhabitants of Mesopotamia in a broad timeframe ranging from Graeco-Roman antiquity through the tenth-century redaction and translation by Ibn Waḥšiya. In terms of agricultural history, the *Nabataean Agriculture* is a trove of information, providing details on the management of water and estates as well as the cultivation and uses of scores of plants. Some twenty-three aromatic plants are discussed, including cedar, bitter orange, banana, lemon, hawthorn, and plane. Nearly sixty kinds of fruiting and non-fruiting trees are discussed, along with their properties. There are also voluminous sections on grains, legumes, and oil seeds, as well as the botanical characteristics of plants. While it is uncertain how many of certain types of plants were cultivated in Mesopotamia (such as storax, *Liquidambar orientalis*, which even in antiquity is thought to have been limited to a small corner of south-western Asia Minor), the information is rich and indispensable for those who wish to understand agronomy and practice in the Late Antique and mediaeval Fertile Crescent.

Agriculture in the lands forming the arc from the coast of Lebanon through the Jazira to the Plain of Nineveh certainly ebbed and flowed in response to local environmental and political pressures, but on the whole there was considerable continuity. Despite the character of the inland 'zone of uncertainty', the region remained politically and economically important, lying in and along the frontiers of Mongol-Mamluk power and later along the fault line of the Ottoman and Safavid empires. Through the vagaries of political strife, environmental flux, and demographic instability (often human-made), the farmers of the Fertile Crescent adapted and persisted. But theirs was not a timeless story akin to fable, but rather a series of successes and failures, of expansion and retraction, a mingling of ancient technique and structures with, in certain times and spaces, new methods developed locally or imported from half a world away. Syrian farmers and elites remained prominent in the agrarian life of the ancient and mediaeval periods over much of the Near East. Most formed the rural villagers and cultivators, the 'Nabataeans' who practiced traditional methods of farming and herding and passed on their local knowledge within their families over centuries. At least some Syrian elites, though, viewed the land differently and thought more economically about the land and its products. Still others (and these need not be different) were scholars interested in gathering, preserving, and presumably applying the wisdom accumulated over centuries of farming in the Levant and Mesopotamia. It is through these texts, and through the scant surviving archaeological remains of farming installations and tools, that we glimpse the Syriac farmers of the past and understand their important role in world history.

BIBLIOGRAPHY

Adams, R. M. 1965. *Land Behind Baghdad: A History of Settlement on the Diyala Plains.* Chicago: University of Chicago Press.

Ashkenazi, J. and M. Aviam. 2012. Monasteries, Monks, and Villages in Western Galilee in Late Antiquity. *Journal of Late Antiquity* 5, 269–97.

Baillie, M. G. L. 1994. Dendrochronoloy Raises Questions About the Nature of the AD 536 Dust-veil Event. *The Holocene* 4, 212–17.

Baillie, M. G. L. and J. Mcaneney. 2015. Tree Ring Effects and Ice Core Acidities Clarify the Volcanic Record of the First Millennium. *Climate of the Past* 11, 105–14.

Biscop, J.-L. 1997. *Deir Déhès, monastère d'Antiochène: étude architecturale.* Beirut: Institut français d'archéologie du Proche-Orient.

Bulliet, R. W. 2011. *Cotton, Climate, and Camels in Early Islamic Iran: A Moment in World History.* Chichester: Columbia University Press.

Butler, H. C. and E. Littmann. 1905. Preliminary Report of the Princeton University Expedition to Syria. *American Journal of Archaeology* 9, 389–410.

Campopiano, M. 2012. State, Land Tax and Agriculture in Iraq From the Arab Conquest to the Crisis of the Abbasid Caliphate (Seventh-tenth Centuries). *Studia Islamica* 107, 1–37.

Chabot, J.-B. 1901. *Chronique de Michel le Syrien, Patriarche Jacobite d'Antioche, Tome II.* Paris: Ernst Leroux.

Christensen, P. 1993. *The Decline of Iranshahr: Irrigation and Environments in the History of the Middle East, 500 BC to AD 1500.* Copenhagen: Museum Tusculanum.

Contini, R. 1987. Il Hawran preislamico: Ipotesi di storia linguistica. *Felix Ravenna* 4, 25–79.

Dagron, G. 1976. Minorités ethniques et religieuses dans l'Orient byzantin à la fin du Xe et au XIe siècle: l'immigration syrienne. *Travaux et Mémoires* 6, 177–216.

Decker, M. 2007. The Authorship and Context of Early Byzantine Farming Manuals. *Byzantion* 77, 106–15.

———. 2009a. Plants and Progress: Rethinking the Islamic Agricultural Revolution. *Journal of World History* 20, 187–206.

———. 2009b. *Tilling the Hateful Earth: Agricultural Production and Trade in the Late Antique East.* Oxford: Oxford University Press.

———. 2011. Settlement and Agriculture in the Levant, 6th–8th Centuries. *In:* A. Borrut, ed., *Le Proche-Orient de Justinien aux abbassides: peuplement et dynamiques spatiales: actes du colloque "Continuités de l'occupation entre les périodes byzantine et abbasside au Proche-Orient, VIIe-IXe siècles," Paris, 18–20 octobre 2007.* Turnhout: Brepols, 1–7.

Dietrich, A. 2012. Al-Hadjdjadj b. Yusuf. *In:* P. Bearman et al., ed., *Encyclopaedia of Islam, Second Edition.* Leiden: Brill, 3:39–43.

Djamali, M., J.-L. De Beaulieu, V. Andrieu-Ponel, M. Berberian, N. F. Miller, E. Gandouin, H. Lahijani, M. Shah-Hosseini, P. Ponel, and M. Salimian. 2009. A Late Holocene Pollen Record From Lake Almalou in NW Iran: Evidence for Changing Land-use in Relation to Some Historical Events During the Last 3700 Years. *Journal of Archaeological Science* 36, 1364–75.

El Faiz, M. 1990. Salinité et Histoire de l'Irak pré-islamique. *Journal of the Economic and Social History of the Orient/Journal de l'histoire economique et sociale de l'Orient* 33, 105–16.
El-Samarraie, H. Q. 1972. *Agriculture in Iraq During the 3rd Century AH*. Beirut: Librairie du Liban.
England, A., W. J. Eastwood, C. N. Roberts, R. Turner, and J. F. Haldon. 2008. Historical Landscape Change in Cappadocia (Central Turkey): A Palaeoecological Investigation of Annually Laminated Sediments From Nar Lake. *The Holocene*, 18 1229–45.
Fahd, T. 1952. Materiaux pour l'histoire de l'agriculture en Irak: al-Filāḥa n-nabaṭiyya. *Handbuch der Orientalistik*, I.VI.1, 276–377.
———. 1969. Retour à Ibn Waḥšiyya. *Arabica* 16, 83–8.
———. 1993–98. *Ibn Waḥšiya: al-Filaḥah al-Nabaṭīyah*. Damascus, al-Ma'had al-'Ilmi al-Faransi lil-Dirasat al-'Arabiyah.
Förster, F. 2007. The Abu Ballas Trail: A Pharaonic Donkey-caravan Route in the Libyan Desert (SW-Egypt). *In:* O. Bubenzer et al., ed., *Atlas of Cultural and Environmental Change in Arid Africa*. Africa Praehistorica 21. Cologne: Heinrich-Barth-Institut, 130–3.
Garbrecht, G. and A. Vogel. 1991. Die Staumauern von Dara. *In:* K. Witwer, ed., *Historische Talsperren*. Stuttgart: Wittwer, 2:263–76.
Goitein, S. D. 1967. *A Mediterranean Society: The Jewish Communities of the Arab World as Portrayed in the Documents of the Cairo Geniza. Vol 1: Economic Foundations*. Berkeley: University of California Press.
Graf, D. F. and T. Fahd. 2012. Nabaṭ. *In:* P. Bearman et al., ed., *Encyclopaedia of Islam, Second Edition*. Leiden: Brill, 7:834–8.
Gräslund, B. and N. Price. 2012. Twilight of the Gods?: The 'Dust Veil Event' of AD 536 in Critical Perspective. *Antiquity* 86, 428–43.
Greatrex, G., R. R. Phenix, and C. B. Horn. 2011. *The Chronicle of Pseudo-Zachariah Rhetor: Church and War in Late Antiquity*. Liverpool: Liverpool University Press.
Griffith, S. H. 1997. From Aramaic to Arabic: The Languages of the Monasteries of Palestine in the Byzantine and Early Islamic Periods. *DOP* 51, 11–31.
Haldon, J., N. Roberts, A. Izdebski, D. Fleitmann, M. Mccormick, M. Cassis, O. Doonan, W. Eastwood, H. Elton, and S. Ladstätter. 2014. The Climate and Environment of Byzantine Anatolia: Integrating Science, History, and Archaeology. *Journal of Interdisciplinary History* 45, 113–61.
Hämeen-Anttila, J. 2006. *The Last Pagans of Iraq: Ibn Waḥshiyya and His Nabatean Agriculture*. Leiden, Brill.
Harrak, A. 1999. *The Chronicle of Zuqnīn, Parts III and IV: AD 488–775: Translated From Syriac With Notes and Introduction*. Toronto: PIMS.
———. 2005. *The Acts of Mār Mārī the apostle*. Atlanta: Society of Biblical Literature.
Hawting, G. R. 1989. *The History of al-Tabari Vol. 20: The Collapse of Sufyanid Authority and the Coming of the Marwanids: The Caliphates of Mu'awiyah II and Marwan I and the Beginning of the Caliphate of 'Abd al-Malik AD 683–685/AH 64–66*. Albany: SUNY Press.
Howard-Johnston, J. D. 2010. *Witnesses to a World Crisis: Historians and Histories of the Middle East in the Seventh Century*. Oxford: Oxford University Press.
Hoyland, R. 2008. Jacob and Early Islamic Edessa. *In:* R. B. ter Haar Romeny, ed., *Jacob of Edessa and the Syriac Culture of His Day*. Leiden: Brill, 11–24.
———. 2009. Late Roman Provincia Arabia, Monophysite Monks and Arab Tribes: A Problem of Centre and Periphery. *Semitica et Classica* 2, 117–39.
Ibn Shaddad, M. I. A. 1984. *Description de la Syrie du nord*. Damascus: Institut français de Damas.
Jones, M. D., M. Djamali, J. Holmes, L. Weeks, M. J. Leng, A. Lashkari, K. Alamdari, D. Noorollahi, L. Thomas, and S. E. Metcalfe. 2015. Human Impact on the Hydroenvironment of Lake Parishan, SW Iran, Through the Late Holocene. *The Holocene* 25(10), 1651–61.

Kedar, B. Z. 1985. The Arab Conquests and Agriculture: A Seventh-century Apocalypse, Satellite Imagery, and Palynology. *Asian and African Studies* 19, 1–15.

Kennedy, H. 2010. Syrian Elites From Byzantium to Islam: Survival or Extinction? *In:* J. F. Haldon, ed., *Money, Power and Politics in Early Islamic Syria a Review of Current Debates*. Burlington, VT: Ashgate, 181–98.

Lagarde, P. D. 1967. *Geoponicon in Sermonem Syriacum Versorum Quae Supersunt*. Osnabrück: O. Zeller.

Le Strange, G. 1873. *Lands of the Eastern Caliphate*. New York: Barnes and Noble.

———. 1905. *The Lands of the Eastern Caliphate: Mesopotamia, Persia, and Central Asia, From the Moslem Conquest to the Time of Timur*. Cambridge: Cambridge University Press.

Micheau, F. 2008. Eastern Christianities (Eleventh to Fourteenth Century): Copts, Melkites, Nestorians and Jacobites. *In:* M. Angold, ed., *The Cambridge History of Christianity*. Cambridge: Cambridge University Press, 371–403.

Morony, M. 2000. Michael the Syrian as a Source for Economic History. *Hugoye* 3, 141–72.

———. 2012. Al-Nahrawan. *In:* P. Bearman et al., ed., *Encyclopaedia of Islam, Second Edition*. Leiden: Brill, 7:912–3.

Newman, J. 1932. *The Agricultural Life of the Jews in Babylonia Between the Years 200 C.E. and 500 C.E.* London: Oxford University Press.

Payne Smith, R. 1860. *The Third Part of the Ecclesiastical History of John, Bishop of Ephesus*. Oxford: Oxford University Press.

Perry, J. R., A. Shaphur Shahbazi, and E. Kettenhofen. 2011. Deportations. *Encyclopedia Iranica* Vol. VII, Fasc. 3, 297–312. Online: www.iranicaonline.org/articles/deportations.

Ramsay, J. and A. Eger. 2015. Analysis of Archaeobotanical Material From the Tüpraş Field Project of the Kinet Höyük Excavations, Turkey. *Journal of Islamic Archaeology* 2, 35–50.

Reinink, G. J. 2006. Following the Doctrine of the Demons: Early Christian Fear of Conversion to Islam. *In:* J. N. Bremmer, Wout J. van Bekkum, and Arie L.Molendijk, ed., *Cultures of Conversions*. Leuven: Peeters, 127–38.

Rousseau, G., C. Guintard, and C. Abadie-Reynal. 2008. La gestion des animaux à Zeugma (Turquie): étude des restes fauniques du chantier 9 (époques hellénistique, romaine, byzantine et islamique). *Revue Médecine Vétérinaire* 159, 251–75.

Spinage, C. A. 2003. *Cattle Plague: A History*. New York: Kluwer Academic/Plenum Publishers.

Stathakopoulos, D. C. 2004. *Famine and Pestilence in the Late Roman and Early Byzantine Empire: A Systematic Survey of Subsistence Crises and Epidemics*. Aldershot: Ashgate.

Tomber, R. 2007. Rome and Mesopotamia – Importers Into India in the First Millennium AD. *Antiquity* 81, 972–88.

———. 2008. *Indo-Roman Trade: From Pots to Pepper*. London: Duckworth.

Toohey, M., K. Krüger, M. Sigl, F. Stordal, and H. Svensen. 2016. Climatic and Societal Impacts of a Volcanic Double Event at the Dawn of the Middle Ages. *Climatic Change* 136(3), 1–12.

Trombley, F. R. and J. W. Watt. 2000. *The Chronicle of Pseudo-Joshua the Stylite*. Liverpool: Liverpool University Press.

Veenhof, K. R. 2009. Ancient Assur: The City, Its Traders, and Its Commercial Network. *Journal of the Economic and Social History of the Orient* 53, 39–82.

Whitby, M. and M. Whitby. 1986. *The History of Theophylact Simocatta: An English Translation With Introduction*. Oxford: Oxford University Press.

Wilson, A. I. 2003. Classical Water Technology in the Early Islamic World. *In:* C. Bruun and A. Saastamoinen, ed., *Technology, Ideology, Water: From Frontinus to the Renaissance and Beyond*. Rome: Institutum Romanum Finlandiae, 115–41.

Wood, P. 2013. *The Chronicle of Seert: Christian Historical Imagination in Late Antique Iraq*. Oxford: Oxford University Press.

PART V

SYRIAC CHRISTIANITY BEYOND THE ANCIENT WORLD

CHAPTER THIRTY-ONE

SYRIAC CHRISTIANITY IN CENTRAL ASIA

Mark Dickens

This chapter discusses the textual and archaeological evidence for Syriac Christianity in Central Asia from the pre-Islamic period to the Timurid era (late second–fifteenth centuries; for more on this general topic, see Malek and Hofrichter 2006; Winkler and Tang 2009; Tang and Winkler 2013). Scholarly consensus on what constitutes Central Asia is not uniform. It is understood here to be the area bounded by the Hindu Kush, Pamir, Karakorum, and Kunlun mountain ranges to the south, the Gansu Corridor to the east, and the Caspian Sea to the west. Central Asia does not have a clearly defined northern boundary, but gradually merges with the steppe, taiga, and tundra of Russia. Thus, it comprises the modern-day territories of northern Afghanistan, Turkmenistan, Uzbekistan, Tajikistan, Kazakhstan, Kyrgyzstan, Xinjiang, and Inner Mongolia (the latter two in China), with many scholars also including Mongolia and the Russian steppe north of Kazakhstan.

Historically speaking, Central Asia has formed a vast cultural area between Iran, India, China, and Russia, inhabited mainly by speakers of Indo-European, Turkic, or Mongolic languages. The region includes some of the tallest mountains, harshest deserts, and lowest depressions on earth. Over the centuries, rivers like the classical Oxus (Amu Darya) and Jaxartes (Syr Darya) have fed various lakes and inland seas and provided extensive irrigation for the few places where agriculture is possible. In the deserts and on the steppes dominating Central Asia, however, the economy has typically been based on pastoral nomadism and transcontinental commerce along the trade network now called the Silk Road.

THE EARLY EXPANSION OF SYRIAC CHRISTIANITY INTO KHORASAN AND BACTRIA

As noted elsewhere in this volume, the Church of the East was established in Persia during the Parthian Empire (247 BCE–224 CE) and played a significant role in Persian society under the subsequent Sasanian Empire (224–651 CE). It was thus from Persia that Syriac Christianity spread eastward into Central Asia and then China. However, despite its predominance, the Church of the East was not the only church involved in Central Asia. At various times, the Melkites (Dauvillier 1953;

Parry 2012), Syrian Orthodox (Dauvillier 1956), and Armenians (Dauvillier 1974) were also present. Additionally, alongside Syriac as its primary liturgical language, the Church of the East also employed local languages (e.g. Middle Persian, Sogdian, New Persian, and Old Uyghur) in Central Asia, as extant Christian texts and inscriptions attest. Central Asian Christians were rarely native Syriac speakers or writers, but the language and script nonetheless played a crucial role in their religious life.

The *Book of the Laws of Countries* (written in the late second century by a pupil of the philosopher Bardaiṣan) gives us the earliest reference to Christians in Central Asia, namely the inhabitants of 'Beth Qashan' (Drijvers 1965: 60/61),[1] indicating the Kushan Empire (ca. 30–ca. 225). Kushan territory included northern India, Bactria (northern Afghanistan), and parts of Sogdiana (Uzbekistan and Tajikistan), but Eusebius's Greek *Praeparatio evangelica* (early fourth cent.) specifically translates the Syriac ethnonym in Bardaiṣan as 'Bactrians' (Gifford 1903: 302). Eḷishe Vardapet (d. 475) also mentions Christians 'reaching even the land of the Kushans' during the reign of either Shāpur II (r. 310–379) or Shāpur III (r. 383–388), long after the end of Kushan rule (Thomson 1982: 111).

The Syriac *Doctrine of the Apostles* (ca. 250) states that many countries in the East 'received the hand of the priesthood of the apostles' from Aggai, even as far as 'the land of Gog and Magog' (Cureton and Wright 1864: 34–5/34), a claim repeated in the Christian Arabic *Kitāb al-Majdal*, 'Book of the Tower' (Gismondi 1899: 3/2). This latter work is frequently referred to under the name(s) of ʿAmr ibn Mattā, Mārī ibn Sulaymān, and/or Ṣalībā ibn Yuḥannā, and was probably originally written in the eleventh century and then subsequently continued in the fourteenth (Holmberg 1993; Landron 1994: 99–108). No location is given, but Gog and Magog are typically associated in Syriac literature with nomads living on the northern steppe.

More historically grounded references are found in the *Synodicon Orientale* (late eighth cent.), which contains the synodical records of the Church of the East. These inform us of bishops of Merv and Herat (from Iranian Khorasan, now in Turkmenistan and Afghanistan, respectively) at the Synod of Dadišoʿ (424) and a metropolitan of Merv at the Synod of Yusuf (554) (Chabot 1902: 43/285, 109/366). Both the *Fiqh an-Naṣrānīya* of Ibn aṭ-Ṭayyib (d. 1043) and the *Nomocanon* of ʿAbdishoʿ bar Berikha (1290) mention a metropolitan or bishop of Merv during the time of catholicos Isaac I (r. 399–410) (Hoenerbach and Spies 1957a: 121; Hoenerbach and Spies 1957b: 123; Mai 1838: 304/141). This is unrecorded in the *Synodicon Orientale*'s record of the Synods of Isaac (410) or Yahbāllahā I (420); however, since half of the bishops at these two synods did not indicate their see cities, it is possible that Merv was represented at one or both of them (Chabot 1902: 35–6/274–5, 42/283–4).

Due to its strategic location on the eastern flank of the Persian Empire, Merv was an extremely important city for the Persians (and subsequently for the Muslims). It was also a key staging post for missions sent out by the Church of the East into Central Asia. According to a legend extant in Syriac, Sogdian, and Christian Arabic texts, Christianity was established in Merv by Barshabbā (Chabot 1896: §36; Scher 1910: 141–6; Gismondi 1899: 26–7/23; Sims-Williams 1988 [1989]; Brock 1995), probably reflecting the bishop of the same name from Merv present at the Synod of 424.

Later metropolitans of Merv occasionally caused trouble for the catholicos-patriarch, including David of Merv, who consecrated one of two rival patriarchs during a time of schism in the Church of the East in 524 (Scher 1911: 57; Gismondi 1896–1897:

38/22–3) and Joseph of Merv, who challenged the leadership of patriarch Timothy I (r. 780–823) before eventually converting to Islam (Budge 1893a: 198; 1893b: 385; Gismondi 1899: 72/63; Wilmshurst 2016: 361–3/360–2). Merv and Herat continued for centuries to play vital roles in the growth and expansion of the Church of the East, as documented by Fiey (1973: 75–87, 89–92). Surprisingly, only a few Christian artefacts have been found in and around Merv (Lala Comneno 1997: 31). A large building excavated there called Kharoba Koshuk (11th–12th cent.?) has been interpreted as a Christian church, but this is disputed by some (Lala Comneno 1997: 28–30; Herrmann 1999: 103–5, 180–1, 223–4; Borbone 2013: 452–3).

We lack information on Christianity in Bactria between the end of the Kushan Empire (ca. 225) and the sixth century, when several sources give evidence of Christian activity beyond the eastern borders of the Sasanian Empire, specifically in the territory of the Hephthalites (or 'White Huns'), who ruled north and south of the Amu Darya (ca. 467–561). Cosmas Indicopleustes's *Christian Topography* (547–549) describes Christian communities and clergy amongst the 'Bactrians and Huns' (McCrindle 1897: 119–20). The *Biography of Mar Aba* (after 552) describes how the Hephthalite ruler sent a Hephthalite Christian priest to Khosrow I Anushirvān ca. 550, requesting that patriarch Mar Aba I (r. 540–552) ordain him as a bishop for 'the whole kingdom of the Hephthalites' (Bedjan 1895: 266–9; Braun 1915a: 217–18; Mingana 1925: 304–5; Peeters 1946: 108; Pigulevskaya 1963: 335). The Christian Arabic *Chronicle of Seert* (between 864 and 1020) recounts the same story, referring to the Hephthalites merely as 'the barbarians' (Scher 1911: 78). This evangelistic activity amongst the Hephthalites should not be confused (as in Mingana 1925: 302–4) with a separate Armenian mission to the Caucasian Huns described in the *Chronicle of Pseudo-Zachariah Rhetor* (Greatrex et al. 2011: 452–4).

The Hephthalite bishop's see was doubtless in Badisi (Badghis, an important Hephthalite centre in NW Afghanistan), mentioned at the Synod of Ishoʿyahb I (585), which also furnishes the first reference to a metropolitan of Herat. By this time, however, the see of Badghis was no longer under Hephthalite control; they had been crushed by the resurgent Sasanian Empire and the nascent First Türk Empire (552–659) between 556 and 561, their territory partitioned between those two imperial powers. Indeed, these are the last records of any bishops or metropolitans from Central Asia participating in synods of the Church of the East (Chabot 1902: 165/423). However, the *Kitāb al-Majdal* does mention metropolitans being consecrated for Herat under the patriarch Joshua bar Nun (r. 823–828) and for both Herat and Merv under Mari II bar Tobi (r. 987–999) (Gismondi 1896–1897: 66/38, 94–5/55), not to mention references to metropolitans for both cities in later sources discussed below.

SYRIAC CHRISTIANITY SPREADS TO SOGDIAN AND TURKIC TERRITORY

Dating the spread of Christianity from Khorasan and Bactria northward to Samarqand (Uzbekistan) is more complicated, due to disagreement amongst sources regarding its addition to the episcopal hierarchy. The relevant sources only mention a metropolitan of Samarqand, never a bishop. Perhaps, due to its importance, it received a metropolitan from the start, as was the case with the Turks under Timothy I, discussed below. There is no mention of Samarqand's metropolitan ever attending any synods of the Church of the East, probably due to the city's distance from Seleucia-Ctesiphon. However, the metropolitan of Samarqand was present at the election of patriarch Yahbāllahā III (r. 1281–1317; see below) (Bedjan 1895: 37; Montgomery 1927: 46; Budge 1928: 156). Due to their remoteness from the ecclesiastical centre, 'exterior' metropolitans (including Merv, Herat, and Samarqand) were permitted to consecrate bishops without personally conferring with the patriarch or even having other metropolitans present at the consecration, as we learn from Ibn aṭ-Ṭayyib (Hoenerbach and Spies 1957a: 124; Hoenerbach and Spies 1957b: 126) and the Syriac *Liber Patrum* (late 13th–early 14th cent.) (Vosté 1940b: 24–5).

Regarding Samarqand's elevation to the metropolitanate, ʿAbdishoʿ bar Berikha's *Nomocanon* reports unnamed authorities claiming that a metropolitan was appointed for the city during the patriarchate of either Ahai (r. 410–414) or Shila (r. 503–523) (Mai 1838: 304/141). However, these dates are far too early, since they predate the appointment of a metropolitan for Merv. Slightly more helpful is Ibn aṭ-Ṭayyib's statement that metropolitans were appointed for Ḥolwān (western Iran), Herat, Samarqand, India, and China during the patriarchate of Ishoʿyahb (Hoenerbach and Spies 1957a: 121; Hoenerbach and Spies 1957b: 123; Sachau 1919: 23–5). However, based on other sources, the author has clearly conflated at least two (and maybe all three) patriarchs named Ishoʿyahb.

The *Synodicon Orientale* confirms that Ishoʿyahb I (r. 582–596) established Herat's metropolitan, while ʿAbdishoʿ's *Nomocanon* credits Ishoʿyahb II (r. 628–646) with giving Ḥolwān a metropolitan (Mai 1838: 304/141). Lacking information about India's elevation to the episcopate, we must consider instead China's status. The Chinese-Syriac Xi'an 'Nestorian' Stele (781; see below) describes how Aluoben received a title equivalent to Syriac *Mar* (generally used only by bishops, metropolitans, and patriarchs) during the reign of Gaozong (r. 650–683), concurrent with the patriarchate of Ishoʿyahb III (r. 650–658); thus, an earlier date for a Chinese metropolitan is unlikely (Pelliot and Dauvillier 1984: 26–7, 45). Unfortunately, this sheds no light on the Samarqand metropolitanate.

Further confusing the situation, the *Nomocanon* of ʿAbdishoʿ bar Berikha claims that metropolitans were established for Herat, Samarqand, and China during the patriarchate of Ṣalībā-Zakhā (r. 714–728) (Mai 1838: 304/141). If so, perhaps they had to be re-established after a vacancy in the patriarchate (700–714), as Young (1974: 47) suggests. Whichever Ishoʿyahb established the metropolitan of Samarqand, it was during a turbulent time in Central Asian history, with the Eastern and Western Turkic Qaghanates, the Chinese and Sasanian empires, and the Arab Caliphate all competing for power in the region. Since Samarqand and the other Sogdian city-states were under constant pressure from the invading Arabs, a political dimension to the appointment of a metropolitan for Samarqand is likely, as was probably the case with the Hephthalites and the Turks (Dickens 2010: 130–1).

Other sources describe Christian activity which may have been connected with the appointment of Samarqand's metropolitan during this period. Thus, Theophylact Simocatta (late 620s) mentions Turks captured by the Persians in 591 (during the patriarchate of Ishoʿyahb I) who, on the advice of Christians, had had crosses tattooed on their foreheads while still young (presumably several decades earlier) in order to ward off the plague (Whitby and Whitby 1986: 146–7). However, it is unclear whether these Christians were Persians, Sogdians, Hephthalites, or others, and tattooed crosses are not synonymous with conversion. Where these Turks had grown up is also not clear, but it could easily have been Sogdiana, after the aforementioned defeat of the Hephthalites, when Turks increasingly moved into the area.

Equally significantly, the mission of Aluoben, dispatched by patriarch Ishoʿyahb II to China and recorded on the Xi'an Stele, must have passed through Central Asia before it arrived in Chang'an (Xi'an) in 635. In addition to those who came from Persia with Aluoben, the envoys may have included Central Asians, particularly if the mission accompanied an embassy from Samarqand that arrived in China that year (Pelliot and Forte 1996: 359–61). However, the non-Syriac names on the Xi'an Stele are all Middle Persian, not Sogdian (Hunter 2009); in contrast, the Luoyang pillar (814/15) describes a Christian community which is obviously Sogdian in origin (Tang 2009a).

The Syriac *Khuzistan Chronicle* (ca. 660–680) reports the conversion and baptism of a minor Turkic ruler and his army ca. 644 (they may have been Hephthalites, now absorbed into the First Türk Empire and often called Turks in the sources). This feat was accomplished during the patriarchate of Ishoʿyahb II by Eliya, Metropolitan of Merv, in the context of a display of weather magic by Turkic priests accompanying the warriors. It took place near either the Amu Darya or the Murghab River (near Merv), as a result of which Eliya 'made disciples of many people from the Turks and from other peoples' (Guidi 1903a: 34–5; 1903b: 28–9; Mingana 1925: 305–6; Hunter 1989/1991: 157–60). The event took place between the Chinese defeat of the Eastern Türk Qaghanate (630) and the Western Türk Qaghanate (659), a time of intense instability in both Iran and Central Asia, due to the Arab invasion and collapse of the Sasanian Empire. However, it was clearly also a time of expansion for the Church of the East. Thus, political turmoil and missionary zeal provided the context for this conversion event. As the Muslim historian al-Ṭabarī (ca. 920) notes, Eliya was also responsible for giving a proper burial to the last Sasanian shah, Yazdegerd III (r. 632–651) (Humphreys 1990: 89) and, according to the *Chronicle of Seert*, for composing a now-lost *Ecclesiastical History* (Assemani 1721–28: III, 1, 148; Scher 1919: 193).

Finally, Ishoʿyahb III refers in his Letter XXI (651) to 'more than twenty bishops and two metropolitans in the East' (Duval 1904: 280; 1905: 202; Fiey 1970: 40–1), unfortunately without specifying which metropolitans are meant. Did he consider Merv and Herat (already in existence since the sixth century) to be 'in the East'? If not, was he referring to two of the three metropolitans further east appointed by 'Ishoʿyahb' according to Ibn aṭ-Ṭayyib, possibly China and Samarqand, as Young (1974: 47, 91–2) suggests? This time just prior to the Arab invasion also witnessed the arrival of the Syrian Orthodox hierarchy in Central Asia, with the appointment of a bishop of Herat under the first maphrian Marutha of Tagrit (r. 628–649) (Wilmshurst 2016: 347/346; Scher 1919: 225). Thus, by the advent of Islam, Syriac Christianity was well established not only south of the Amu Darya, in Khorasan and Bactria, but also north of the river, amongst Iranian and Turkic speakers in Sogdiana and adjacent areas.

CENTRAL ASIAN SYRIAC CHRISTIANITY UNDER EARLY MUSLIM RULE

The Arab Conquest of the Persian Empire lasted barely two decades until the death of Yazdegerd III (651), but it took much longer to bring Central Asia north of the Amu Darya under control; final victory came only after the Battle of Talas (751). Even after political control was established, the process of Islamisation continued well into the ninth century. The military conquest of Central Asia took place largely under the Umayyad Caliphate (661–750), during which the Arabs faced competition in Central Asia from the Chinese Tang dynasty (618–907), the Second Türk Empire (682–742), and even the Tibetan Empire (618–842). Several references to Christianity in Central Asia which can be dated to the Umayyad period suggest elements of conflict between the invading Muslims and Christians living there.

Narshakhī's *History of Bukhara* (943/44) mentions a Christian church converted into a mosque (a common occurrence in areas conquered by Muslims) after Arab forces under Qutayba ibn Muslim captured Bukhara in 709 (Frye 1954: 53). Also of interest is Al-Ṭabarī's reference to the Sogdian ruler Dewāshtich (Dīwāshinī) being crucified in 722 'on a (Christian) burial place' between Bukhara and Samarqand (Powers 1989: 178). More problematic is the *Tezkere* of Imam Muḥammad Ghazalī (d. 739), which describes a prince of Kashgar named Sherkianos fighting against the Muslims in the eighth century (Grenard 1898: 15–25; Blochet 1925–1926: 24–36). Grenard's translation of 'Cher Kianos' is not accompanied by the original Turkic text; Blochet suggests it represents Sergianos, but the text does not identify him as a Christian.

More concrete and lacking indications of religious conflict are various archaeological finds from this time period. An ostracon found in Panjikent (Tajikistan, late seventh/early eighth centuries) with portions of Psa. 1–2 written on it in Syriac has errors indicating the scribe spoke Sogdian (Paykova 1979). A processional cross inscribed in Pahlavi script mentions the Church of Herat and a date (507 or 517), possibly referring to the Bactrian era calendar beginning in 232 CE (thus, 739 or 749 CE) (Gignoux 2001). Also dating from the seventh/eighth centuries are Christian burial sites (including ossuaries with crosses) found at Mizdaxkan (Khwarezm), Afrasiyab (the ancient site of Samarqand), Aq-Beshim (Kyrgyzstan), and Panjikent (Grenet 1984: 146–7, 160, 185–6, 265, 329).

A large number of coins with crosses on them (7th–8th cent.) from Samarqand, Bukhara, Tashkent, and other locations in Sogdiana suggest that these cities had Christian rulers before and during the Arab invasion (Semenov 1996: 60–1; Naymark 2001: 178–295; Ashurov 2015: 174–8). Finally, several silver plates of Central Asian (perhaps Sogdian) provenance with biblical scenes dating from the seventh–tenth centuries have been found in the Ural region (Klimkeit 1993: 480–2; Semenov 1996: 66–7; Klein 2000: 107–8, 368–9; Baulo 2000, 2004). By contrast, a jar inscribed in Syriac found in the Surkhandarya Region of Uzbekistan (undated) is likely a magic bowl mentioning Ishtar and Lilith, reminding us that Central Asian Christianity was influenced by earlier religious ideas (Gignoux 1996).

The Umayyads were overthrown in 750 by the ʿAbbasids (750–1258), who then defeated the Chinese at the Battle of Talas (751), thus securing control of Central Asia west of the Tian Shan Mountains and south of the nomadic steppe until the late ninth century, after which various Persian and Turkic dynasties arose (discussed below). There are several key references to Christianity in Central Asia during the period of ʿAbbasid hegemony. The aforementioned Xi'an Stele (781) was erected by 'Mar Yazdbozid, priest and chor-bishop of Khumdān (Xi'an)', whose father had been a priest from 'Balkh, a city of Tokharistan', another name for Bactria (Pelliot and Dauvillier 1984: 35–8, 47, 55–7, 64–5, 72–4; Lieu 2009: 235–6; Deeg 2013).

Coincidentally, this stele was erected at the beginning of the patriarchate of Timothy I (r. 780–823), who promoted the missionary expansion of the Church of the East. In his Letter XLI (782/83), he mentions the conversion of an unidentified 'king of the Turks with his whole territory', who had subsequently asked the patriarch to 'appoint a Metropolitan for the territory of his kingdom' (Bidawid 1956: 46/124; Labourt 1904: 43; Mingana 1925: 306; Gismondi 1899: 73/64). In Timothy's Letter XLVII (792/93), he mentions having consecrated 'a metropolitan for the Turks' and intending to do the same for the Tibetans (it is unknown whether this happened) (Braun 1901: 308–11; Labourt 1904: 43; Mingana 1925: 306; Dauvillier 1948: 291–6; Uray 1983).

These Turks were probably the Qarluqs, living on the steppe north of Tashkent. Several Muslim historians describe how their capital Talas (Taraz, Kazakhstan) was captured in 893 by the Sāmānids (based in Bukhara), after which the church there was converted into a cathedral mosque; various Christian artefacts discovered in Talas/Taraz support the idea of a Christian presence there (Frye 1954: 86–7; Dickens 2010: 127–9). Al-Muqaddasī (985) observes that the mosque in Mīrkī (160 km east of Talas/Taraz) 'was formerly a church' (Collins 1994: 246; le Strange 1905: 487), suggesting that converting churches into mosques was a common occurrence after the Sāmānid defeat of the Qarluqs.

References in Thomas of Marga's *Book of Governors* (840) to Timothy dispatching missionaries to 'countries of the barbarians who were remote from all understanding and a decent manner of life' (Budge 1893a: 252, 1893b: 467–8) have been understood by some as a reference to Central Asia (Mingana 1925: 306–8), but this is unclear in the text. Descriptions of 'other barbarians who live beyond them . . . ends of the East . . . countries beyond Gīlān and Dailōm' (on the southern shore of the Caspian Sea) are too vague to associate with any particular region. More certain are several important references to Christianity in Merv and Khwarezm at this time. Isho'denaḥ of Baṣrā's *Book of Chastity* (849/50) mentions several monasteries near Herat or Merv and a Palestinian monastery founded by a native of Merv during the eighth/ninth centuries (Chabot 1896: §14, 36, 37, 87; Gismondi 1896–1897: 61/35). Isho'dad of Merv (fl. ca. 850), bishop of Ḥdatta in northern Iraq, was a seminal biblical exegete in the Church of the East (Gismondi 1896–1897: 72/42). A list of metropolitans in the Church of the East prepared by Eliya Jawharī, metropolitan of Damascus (after 903), includes Herat, Merv, and Samarqand (Assemani 1721–28: II, 458–60), but not the metropolitan of the Turks established by Timothy I, probably because Eliya wrote after the aforementioned Muslim capture of the Qarluq Turk capital, when the metropolitanate was probably abolished by the victorious Sāmānids.

During the period when 'Abbasid authority in Central Asia was declining, 'Abdisho' bar Berikha's *Nomocanon* describes how patriarch Theodosius (r. 853–858) mentioned Merv, Herat, and Samarqand in the context of reforming the 'exterior metropolitans', thenceforth requiring them only to send a written report to the patriarch once every six years (rather than making regular personal visits), due to their great distance from the ecclesiastical centre (Mai 1838: 308/146). This devolution of ecclesiastical authority mirrored the political independence increasingly evident in parts of the 'Abbasid Caliphate further from the centre, particularly Central Asia. A quite different persepective on Central Asian Christianity is found in the *Book of Religion and Empire* (ca. 855), by Ibn Rabban Al-Ṭabarī (a Muslim writer whose

Christian father came from Merv): 'Outside these countries [those of the Greeks, Franks, "tent-dwelling Turanians" and Armenians] what Christians are to be found in the country of the Turks except a small and despicable quantity of Nestorians scattered among the nations?' (Mingana 1922: 156–7). From the same period comes a Sogdian inscription dated to 841/42 from Ladakh (N. Pakistan) accompanied by a cross; the former was probably inscribed by a Buddhist, the latter by a Christian travelling between Central Asia and India or Tibet, likely on a trade or diplomatic mission (Sims-Williams 1993). Crosses inscribed on boulders have also been found to the NW in Gilgit (N. Pakistan), possibly left by Christian traders travelling on the same route (Klimkeit 1979: 103).

The early ʿAbbasid period gives us more information on the different churches present in Central Asia, beginning with the Syrian Orthodox. Timothy I was obviously concerned about affairs in Herat, urging in his Letter XXV (799/804) that a young logician be made metropolitan of the city, in order to do battle with the Syrian Orthodox 'Severians' there (Braun 1915b: 141–2; Braun 1915c: 96). A different Central Asian connection may be indicated by the name of the Syrian Orthodox maphrian Yoḥannan of Beth Kionaya (r. 759–785) (Wilmshurst 2016: 357/356). Does it reflect an ethnic connection with the Chionites (from Pahl. *Xyōn/Hyōn*), 'a tribe of probable Iranian origin that was prominent in Bactria and Transoxania [territory north of the Oxus] in late antiquity' (Felix 1991: 485)?

This era brought another Church to Central Asia, as a result of the capture of some Melkite (Syriac-speaking Greek Orthodox) Christians transported to Shāsh (Tashkent) by Caliph al-Manṣur in 762 (Parry 2012: 96–8). The polymath al-Birunī (ca. 1000) – who spent much of his life in Central Asia, whether his native Khwarezm, Bukhara, or the Ghaznavid court – specifically mentions the festivals of both 'Nestorian' and 'Melkite' Christians in Khwarezm and informs us of a Melkite metropolitan in Merv during his time (Sachau 1879: 282–313; Griveau 1915: 291–312). Al-Birunī was unable to explain the calendar of the 'Jacobites', having never met anyone who 'knew their dogmas' (Sachau 1879: 312).

The Khwarezmian court in Konye-Urgench (Turkmenistan) in al-Birunī's time was home to two famous Central Asian scholars, the Muslim Ibn Sīnā (Avicenna) (d. 1037) and the Christian Abū Sahl al-Masīḥī (d. after 1002), the author of several works, most notably 'The Book of the Hundred on Medicine', and allegedly Ibn Sīnā's teacher (Bedjan 1890: 195; Budge 1932: 176; Karmi 1978). Christian artefacts from Khwarezm include the aforementioned Christian ossuaries from Mizdaxkan and several slabs (gravestones?) with crosses preserved in Konye-Urgench (Lala Comneno 1997: 33). In the context of discussing a passage from William of Rubruck (ca. 1255), Pelliot (1973: 117–8) argues convincingly that references to 'people called Koltink' [Soldains], possessing their own language and using Greek letters and the Greek rite . . . [who] obey the patriarch of Antioch' but live in 'the kingdom of Khwarazmia', mentioned in *The Flower of Histories of the East* by Hetʿum (1307), must refer to the remnants of the aforementioned Melkites, with 'Soldains' a variant of 'Sogdians' (Bedrosian 2004: §4).

Thus, as ʿAbbasid power eroded in Central Asia, three branches of Syriac Christianity could be found throughout the region, including Khorasan, Bactria, Khwarezm, Sogdiana, and Qarluq territory north of Sogdiana. Whether Christianity had penetrated into the Tarim Basin (Xinjiang province, China) by this time is uncertain.

The probable adoption of Christianity as the official religion of the Qarluqs was a significant (but short-lived) development, paralleling the adoption of Judaism by the Turkic Khazars, Manichaeism by the Turkic Uyghurs, and Buddhism by the Tibetans at roughly the same time.

CENTRAL ASIAN SYRIAC CHRISTIANITY UNDER NON-ARAB POLITIES

As noted already, Arab authority in Central Asia was eventually replaced by Persian and Turkic states, essentially independent but owing token loyalty to the caliph in Baghdad: the Persian Sāmānid Dynasty in Mawara'n-nahr (the Arabic term for Transoxania) (875–999), the Turkic Qarakhanid Dynasty in Eastern (and later Western) Turkistan (ca. 943–1212), and the Turkic Ghaznavid Dynasty in Afghanistan and northern India (962–1163). Beyond the *Dar al-Islam*, the Uyghur Kingdom of Qocho in Turfan (ca. 860–1284) emerged from the overthrown Uyghur Empire in Mongolia (744–840). In both Uyghur states, Manichaeism was the main religion, eventually displaced in Turfan by Buddhism. Various sources confirm the continuing vitality of Christianity in Mawara'n-nahr during this period. Ibn al-Faqīh (ca. 902) includes the doors on the church of Samarqand in a list of the most impressive sites on earth (Massé 1973: 297). Ibn Ḥawqal (988) mentions three Christian sites in Central Asia: (1) a church just north of Herat, also mentioned by Ḥamd Allāh Mustawfī (after 1335) (le Strange 1919: 150); (2) a monastery in Sogdiana, recently excavated near Urgut, 40 km SE of Samarqand; and (3) a village near the city of Shāsh (Tashkent) (Kramers and Wiet 1964: 424, 478, 485; Ouseley 1800: 218, 257, 265).

Based on archaeological finds, including a bronze censor with biblical scenes found long before the Urgut monastery was excavated (Zalesskaja 1971; Lala Comneno 1997: 35), the monastery was probably established in the seventh century and inhabited up to the thirteenth (Savchenko and Dickens 2009; Savchenko 2010). Dozens of Syriac inscriptions (Figures 31.1–4) left on nearby cliffs (including Syriac, Arabic, Persian, and Turkic names) suggest that many Christians visited the vicinity and held vigil there (Dickens 2017 provides the text of all legible inscriptions). Summarising conditions in the region of al-Mashriq – defined as 'the territories of the Sāmānids' – al-Muqaddasī comments that 'many Jews are here, few Christians, some Magians' (Collins 1994: 7, 284), but the general reference does not precisely locate these Christians. In contrast, al-Nadīm's *Fihrist* (ca. 988/89) mentions Sogdiana as 'an abode of the Turks' whose people are 'dualists [Zoroastrians] and Christians' (Dodge 1970: 33), likely describing an earlier situation, since the region had been largely Islamised by his time.

Several archaeological sites in former Sogdian territory (all now in Uzbekistan) containing cross-shaped elements (many of them underground edifices) have also been proposed as Christian sites. This is unclear in some cases (especially where identifiable Christian artefacts were not found), but seems possible in others. These suggested sites have been grouped into those supposedly serving as churches, monasteries, or other places of communal worship and those located in private homes, used for family worship. The communal structures (7th–9th cent.) include Korxona, SE of Tashkent; Qosh-tepa, near Qarshi, SW of Samarqand; Kojar-tepa, also near Qarshi; and Samarqand, where baked bricks laid in the form of a cross were found in an underground

Figure 31.1 Inscriptions from Urgut, showing two occurrences of the name Sargis

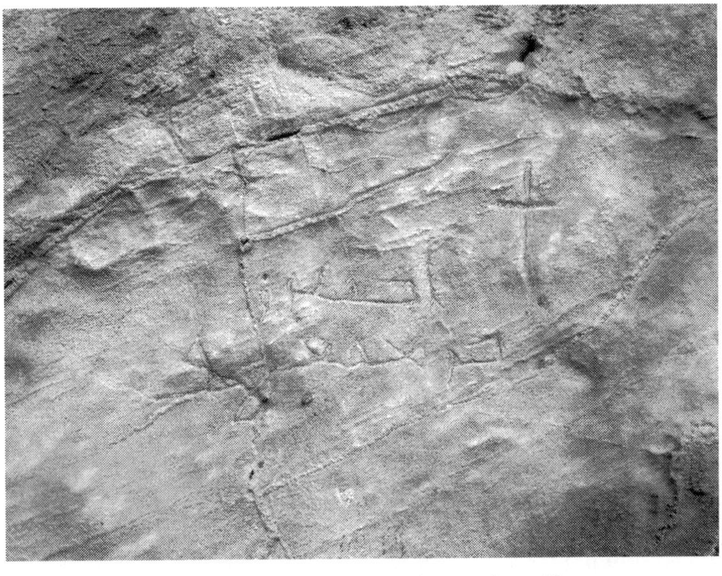

Figure 31.2 Inscription and cross from Urgut

Figure 31.3 Inscriptions with crosses from Urgut

Figure 31.4 Persian inscription in Syriac script from Urgut

structure near the Registan square. The private structures (6th–10th cent.) include Kultepa, also near Qarshi; Afrasiyab (Samarqand), where a portable oven stamped with the image of a cross and medical paraphernalia were discovered in an underground structure; and O'zgan III-Shahristan, Ferghana Valley (Raimqulov 1999, 2000).

More certain is the Christian provenance of various crosses of gold, silver, bronze, copper, nephrite, and bone, dating from the seventh to the fourteenth centuries, found throughout territories where Sogdians were prevalent before and after the Arab Conquest (Sogdiana, Ferghana, and Semirechye). Many of them are pectoral crosses, often discovered in burial sites. These include crosses from (1) Tajikistan (Dashti-Urdakon, near Panjikent); (2) Uzbekistan (Afrasiyab, Samarqand; Durmen, near Samarqand; Qashqadarya; Kanka, near Tashkent; Quva, Ferghana Valley); (3) Kyrgyzstan (Krasnaya Rechka, Burana, Aq-Beshim, Toru Aygyr); and (4) Kazakhstan (Kostobe, near Taraz; Talgar). Many of these crosses were locally made, as evidenced by the discovery of casting moulds in Merv and Rabinjan, between Bukhara and Samarqand (Rott 2006; Savchenko and Dickens 2009: 131–2, 297, 299; Savchenko 2010: 77).

There is abundant evidence of the presence of Christians around the Tarim Basin at this time, much of it related to the Uyghur Kingdom in Turfan. Gardīzī (ca. 1050) describes Christians, 'Dualists' (probably Manichaeans), and Buddhists in the realm of the Toquz Oghuz (as the Uyghurs were often called) and notes two Christian churches in Khotan, on the southern perimeter of the Tarim Basin (Martinez 1982: 134, 141). The prevalence of Christians in the Uyghur Kingdom is also affirmed by the anonymous author of the *Ḥudūd al-ʿĀlam* (982), who mentions five Sogdian 'villages of Bek-Tegin' in the Toquz Oghuz realm in which lived Christians, Zoroastrians, and others (Minorsky 1970: 95, 274). A much later writer, John of Plano Carpini, in his *History of the Mongols* (after 1247), inflates the role of Christianity amongst the Uyghurs when he writes 'These people, who are Christians of the Nestorian sect, he [Chinggis Khan] defeated in battle, and the Mongols took their alphabet' (Dawson 1955: 20–1). Similarly, the *Tartar Relation* (1247), a transcript of Carpini's initial report of his mission, mentions 'the country called Uighur, whose inhabitants were Christians of the Nestorian sect' (Skelton et al. 1965: 58).

Also dating from this period is the crucially important corpus of approximately 1,100 Christian textual fragments in Syriac, Sogdian, New Persian, and Uyghur Turkic found at Turfan in the early twentieth century, usually dated to between the ninth and the thirteenth/fourteenth centuries (Sims-Williams 2012; Hunter and Dickens 2014; Zieme 2015), plus a smaller number of Christian texts from Dunhuang (Sims-Williams and Hamilton 1990: 51–76; Klein and Tubach 1994; Duan 2001; Yakup 2002) and Qara Qoto/Kharakhoto (Pigoulewsky 1935–1936; Zieme 2006; Zieme 2013), both east of Turfan (Figures 31.5–14). The European expeditions which collected these manuscripts also found a few Christian artefacts, including the remains of a church building in Qocho, Turfan, with several wall paintings (Figure 31.15) (Bussagli 1978: 111–4; Parry 1996: 161–2; Lala Comneno 1997: 45–7; Borbone 2013: 458–60) dated to the seventh/eighth centuries (Yaldiz et al. 2000: 224), and a silk painting from Dunhuang (Figure 31.16) of a figure commonly interpreted as a Christian saint rendered in the style of a Buddhist bodhisattva (Whitfield 1982: 322; Parry 1996: 150–1, 159–60). However, it is possible that the latter may in fact be a Manichaean image of Jesus (an important figure in Manichaeism), given similarities (namely, a cross on the chest) with a Manichaean painting of Jesus from Fujian, China, recently re-identified at Seiunji Temple (Kofu, Japan), especially since the Dunhuang silk painting was found in the same cave as the Chinese Manichaean Hymnscroll, which includes three Manichaean hymns to Jesus (Gulacsi 2009, especially 96, n. 12,

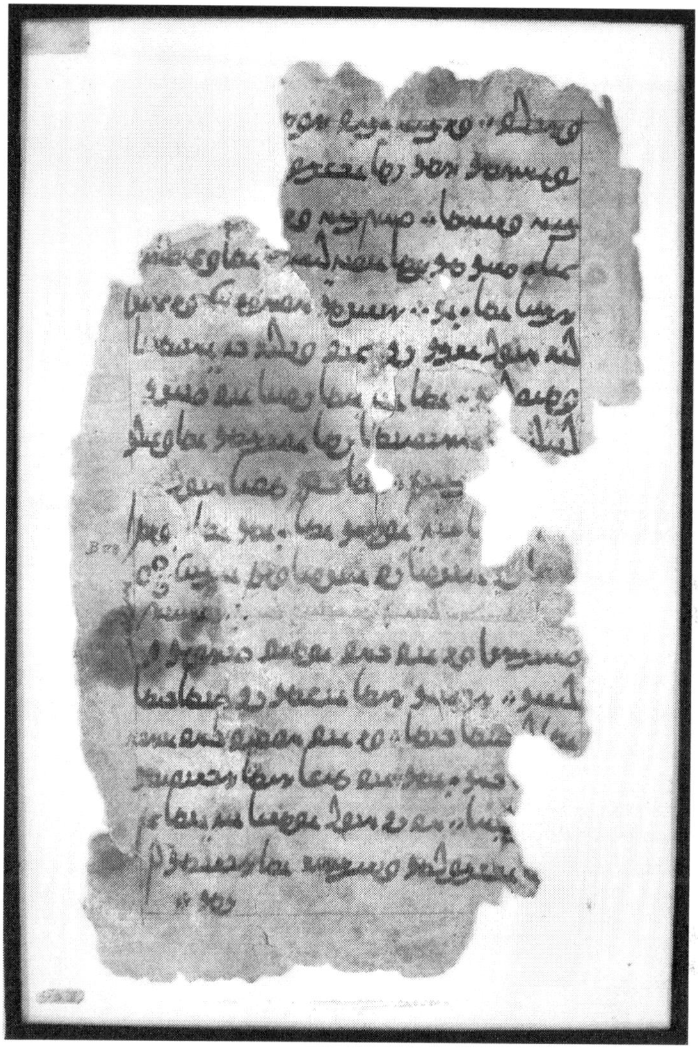

Figure 31.5 Sogdian translation of Nicene Creed from Turfan, with Syriac rubric (MIK III 59)[2]

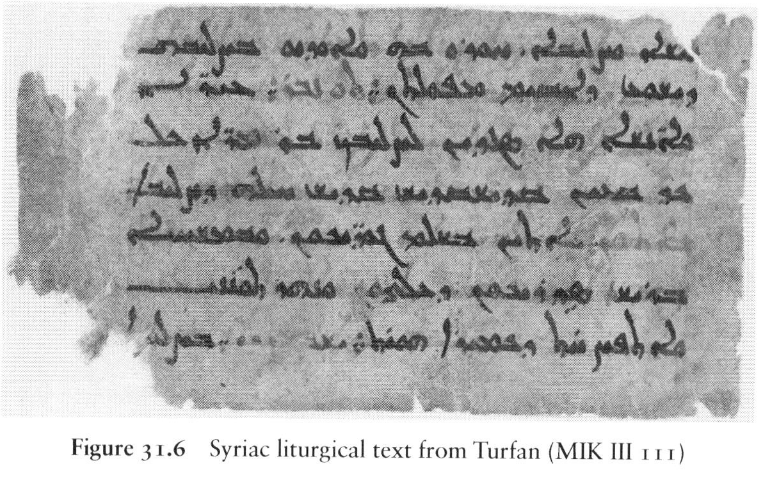

Figure 31.6 Syriac liturgical text from Turfan (MIK III 111)

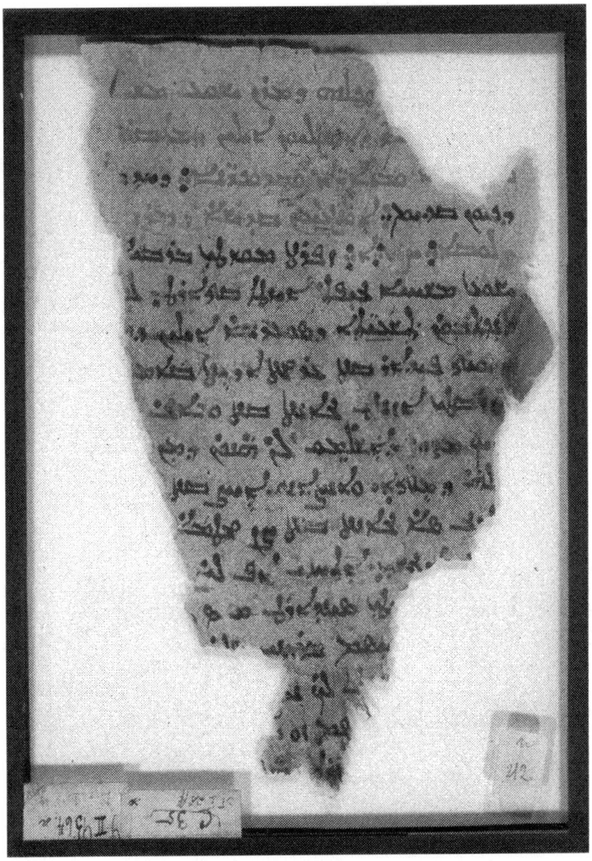

Figure 31.7 Bilingual Syriac-Sogdian lectionary from Turfan (n212)

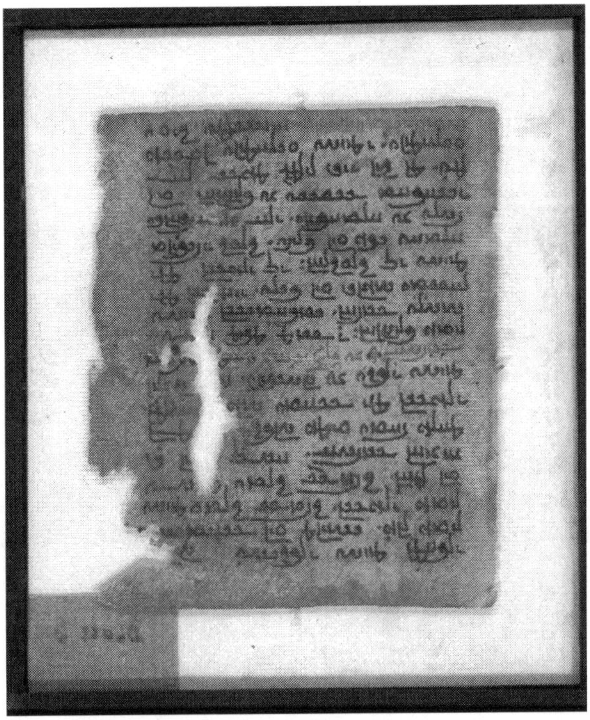

Figure 31.8 Middle Persian psalter from Turfan (ps06)

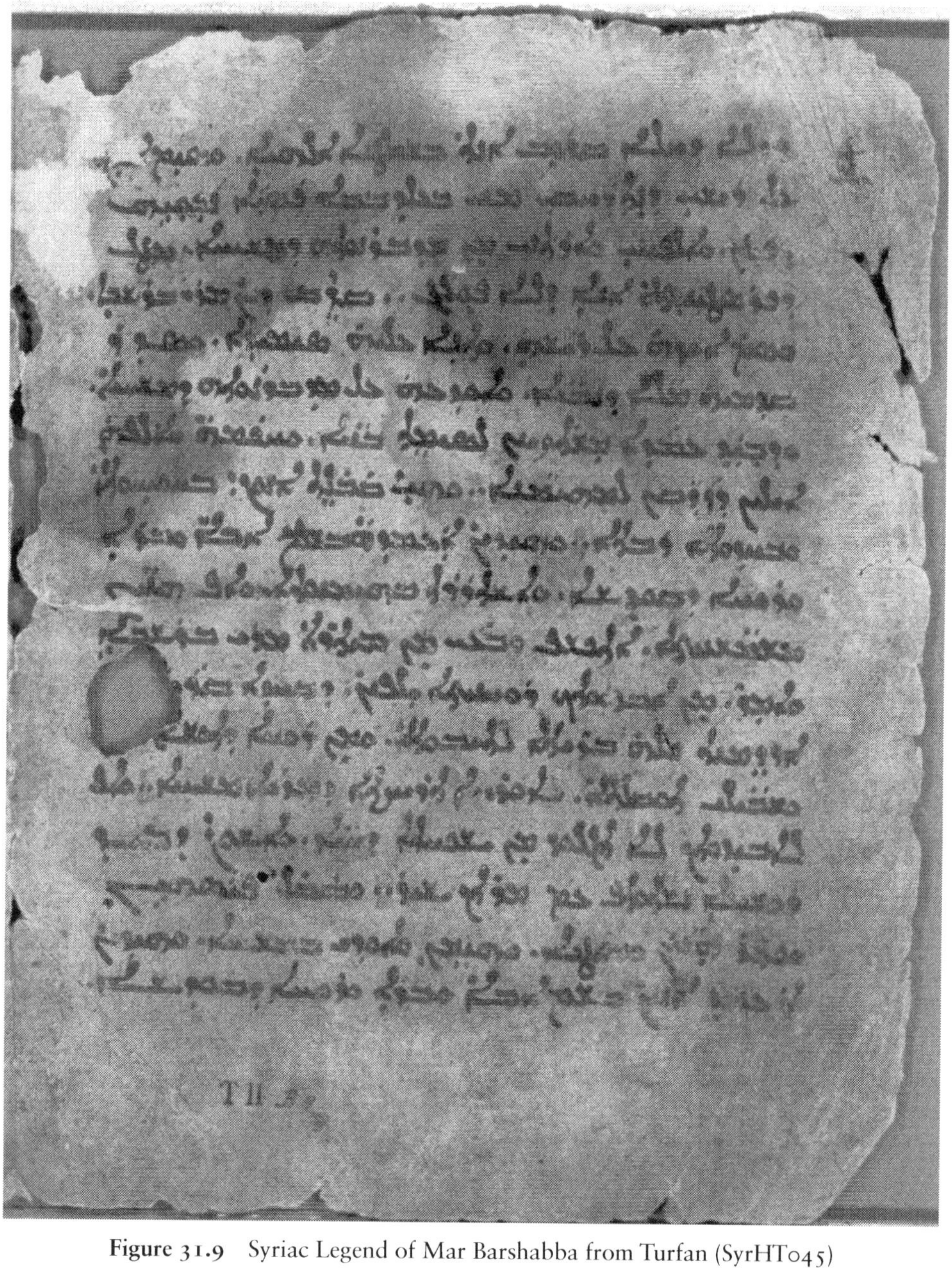

Figure 31.9 Syriac Legend of Mar Barshabba from Turfan (SyrHT045)

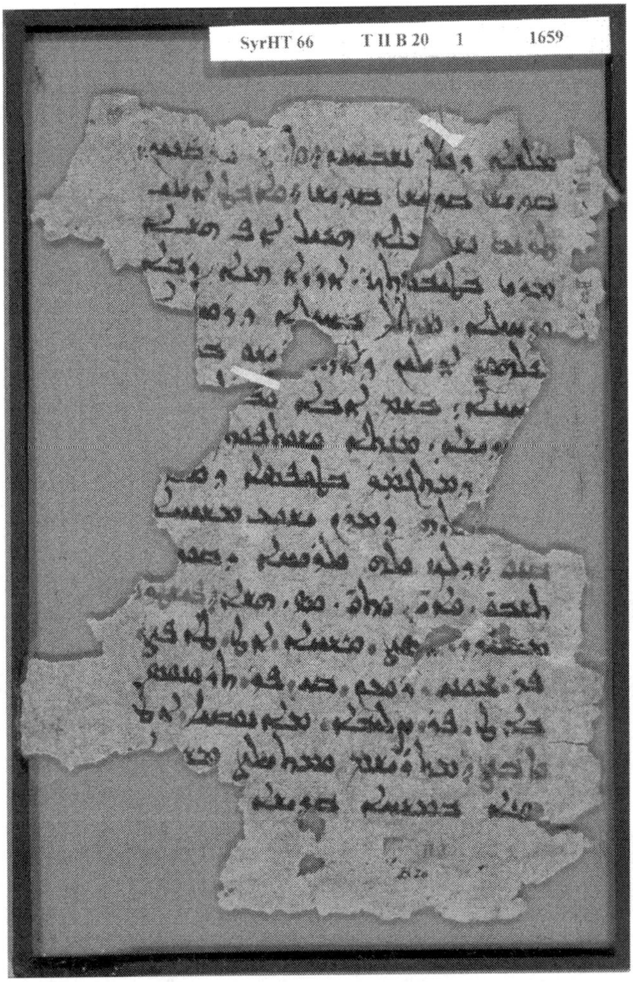

Figure 31.10 Syriac baptismal service, with instructions to the priest in Sogdian from Turfan (SyrHT066)

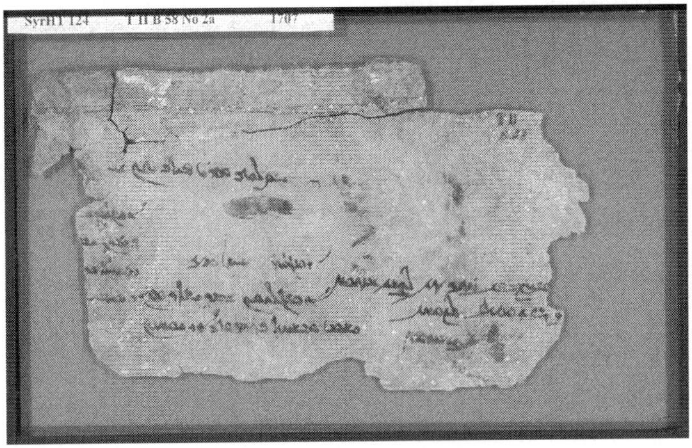

Figure 31.11 Graffiti in Syriac and Uyghur on blank side of folio from Syriac Hudra from Turfan (SyrHT124)

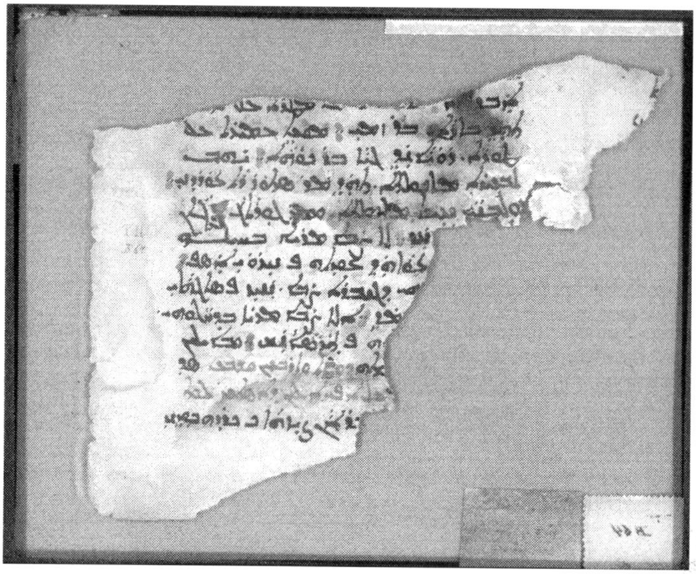

Figure 31.12 Bilingual Syriac-Persian psalter from Turfan (SyrHT153)

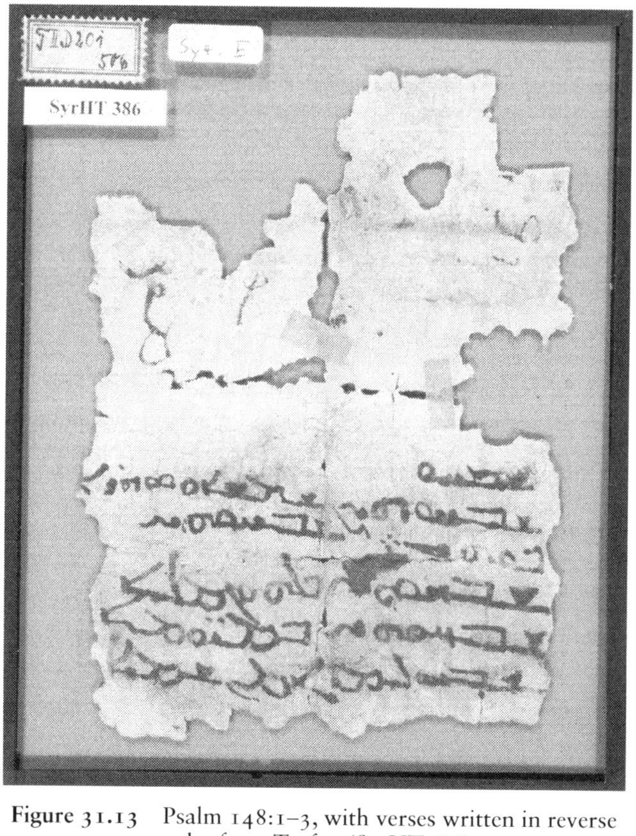

Figure 31.13 Psalm 148:1–3, with verses written in reverse order from Turfan (SyrHT386)

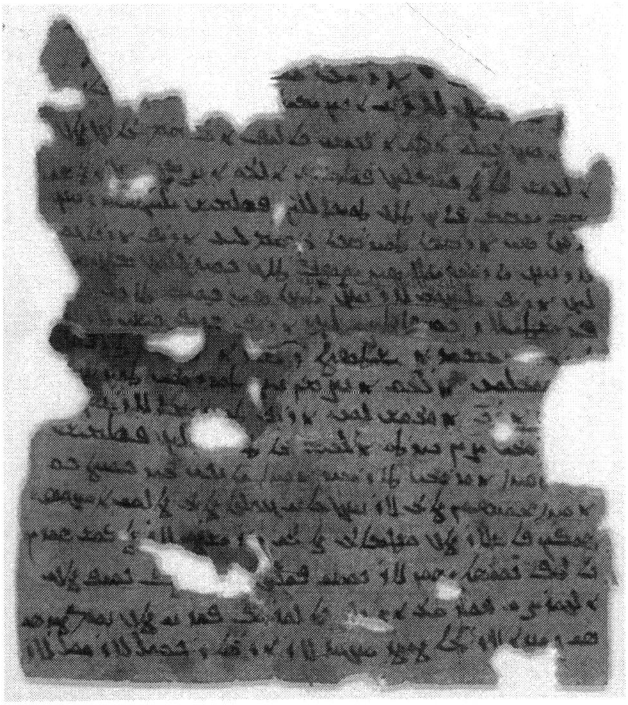

Figure 31.14 Christian wedding blessing, Uyghur in Syriac script, from Turfan (u7264)

Figure 31.15 Wall painting from a ruined church building in Qocho, Turfan, probably showing a Christian priest and three female worshippers (now located in the Museum für Asiatische Kunst, Berlin)

Figure 31.16 Silk painting from Dunhuang of a possible Christian figure wearing a pectoral cross and a crown/headdress with a cross

Source: © The British Library Board

98, n. 17, 106; Yoshida and Furukawa 2015: 141–7, 183–95). The origins of Christianity in Turfan, Dunhuang, and Qara Qoto are unclear. Possibly the Chinese imperial edict of 845 forcing Buddhist, Zoroastrian, and Christian monasteries in China to close and monastics to return to secular life was a catalyst for some Christians, especially those accustomed to monastic life, to move to the multicultural and religiously diverse Uyghur state in Turfan.

In addition to the Uyghurs, there are several references to Christian Turks during this period. An unknown biblical interpreter who composed the Syriac *Gannat Bussāmē* ('Garden of Delights', ca. 900), a commentary on the lectionary readings of the Church of the East, is called 'the Interpreter of the Turks' in ʿAbdishoʿ bar Berikha's *Catalogue of Syriac Writers* (ca. 1318) (Assemani 1721–28: III, 1, 188; Badger 1852: 374; Scher 1906: 28–9). It is unclear whether he taught Christianity to the Turks or was a Turk himself. The author of the *Gannat Bussāmē* cites several biblical expositors with connections to Merv, including Theodore of Merv (ca. 540), Eliya of Merv (ca. 660), and Ishoʿdad of Merv (ca. 850), reminding us of the important role which that city played in the spiritual life of the Church of the East (Chabot 1906: 491–5; Assemani 1721–28: III, 1, 147–8; Badger 1852: 371; Reinink 1988: xxix–xxx, xxxvii–xxxix, xlii–xliii). Finally, could there be a connection with the Sogdians in the name of Timothy, known as Sogdi, metropolitan of the Syrian Orthodox monastery of Mar Mattai from shortly after 1074/75 until sometime after 1111/12 (Wilmshurst 2016: 409/408)?

A major event in the history of Turkic Christianity is recorded in the *Kitāb al-Majdal* and Bar Hebraeus's Syriac *Chronicon Ecclesiasticum* (1286), namely a report from metropolitan ʿAbdishoʿ of Merv about the conversion of 200,000 Turks to Christianity in 1007/08 (Assemani 1721–28: III, 2, 484–5; Gismondi 1899: 112–3/99–100; Wilmshurst 2016: 399/398; Mingana 1925: 308–9). Bar Hebraeus calls them Keraits, but this likely reflects a later situation in the Mongol Empire when the Keraits were well-known as Christians (Hunter 1989/1991); it has been argued that the Turks in question were probably the Öngüt, mentioned below (Atwood 2014). Writing in his *Kitāb al-Majālis*, 'Book of Sessions', approximately when this conversion event occurred, Eliya, Metropolitan of Nisibis (r. 1008–1023) mentions the Turks, Romans, Franks, Bulgars, Copts, Nubians, Armenians, Syrians, Persians, and Chinese amongst the nations that had 'entered the religion of Christianity . . . because of the divine miracle that led them to it' (Assemani 1721–28: III, 1, 270–1; Cheikho 1922: 267; Landron 1994: 159). It is unclear which 'Turks' Eliya meant, but perhaps it was those referred to by the *Kitāb al-Majdal* and Bar Hebraeus. Baumer (2006: 212) suggests that the ruins of a cruciform complex (11th–12th cent.) at Sum Huh Burd in Dundgov aimag (Middle Gobi province), Mongolia, might be 'a Christian-Nestorian shrine . . . here in the area of the Christian Kerait'.

In summary, Syriac Christianity continued to thrive under the Iranian and Turkic-speaking dynasties that succeeded the ʿAbbasids in Central Asia, not only in Khorasan and Sogdiana, but significantly also in the Tarim Basin to the east and amongst various Turkic groups living to the north, including either the Keraits or the Öngüt. As in previous periods, Merv and Samarqand continued to play important roles in the geographic expansion and spiritual vitality of the Church of the East.

SYRIAC CHRISTIANITY SPREADS FURTHER NORTH AND EAST UNDER THE SELJÜKS

When the Seljük Turks defeated their rivals the Ghaznavids (1040) and then captured Baghdad (1055) to become the official protectors of Islam, they ushered in a new era when Muslim Turks ruled the Middle East. In Central Asia, political power was shared between the Great Seljük Empire (1037–1194) and the rival Qarakhanid dynasty, later to be joined by the Khwarezmshah Empire (1077–1220) and the Qara-khitai Khanate (1124–1218). Despite these groups competing for territory in Central Asia and thoughout the Middle East, prelates of the Church of the East in Central Asia still had a role to play in keeping the political centre informed of happenings on the periphery of the Caliphate, as when Bar Hebraeus's *Chronicon Syriacum* (1286) mentions a letter about invading hordes from the east written by 'the Nestorian Metropolitan of Samarqand' in 1046/47 which was read out to the Caliph in Baghdad (Bedjan 1890: 228–9; Budge 1932: 204–5).

There are several enigmatic references to Christianity amongst the Turkic Qipchaqs (or Cumans), living on the northern steppe during this period and the succeeding Mongol era. However, we must first dispel the idea in some literature that the Seljüks were originally Christian, by virtue of the dynasty's founder, Seljük, having two sons named Mika'il (Michael) and Musa (Moses) and a grandson named Dawud (David) (Bedjan 1890: 218; Budge 1932: 196; Barthold 1901, 42–3). It is far more likely that they took these names when Seljük served the Jewish Khazar ruler. The Oghuz Turks, from whom the Seljüks separated, are called Christians by the Persian writer Qazwīnī (d. 1283/84), but their faith 'seems to reflect the incorporation of oral traditions about Christianity into Turkic shamanistic practices' (Dickens 2010: 125–6).

Concerning the Qipchaqs, Marvazī (1120) describes the Qūn (one of the tribes in the Qipchaq confederation) as 'Nestorian Christians' (Minorsky 1942: 29–30, 95–100; Pritsak 1982: 328–31), and Michael the Syrian (1195) briefly discusses Christianity amongst the Cuman, noting that 'their customs are confused', perhaps a reference to their 'Nestorian' background (Chabot 1899–1910, Vol. III: 155; Vol. IV: 570–1). The Christianisation of the Qipchaqs was likely the result of missionary efforts by the Church of the East based in Merv, Samarqand, or somewhere else in Central Asia, but we lack information on any ecclesiastical hierarchy established amongst them. Later on, there was a Catholic mission to the Qipchaqs living north of the Black Sea, as indicated by the famous *Codex Cumanicus*, divided into two sections: the 'Interpreter's Book' (1293–1295) and the 'Missionaries' Book' (ca. 1330–1340) (Bang 1914; Ligeti 1981; Golden 1992).

Passing through the area in 1332/3, the traveller Ibn Baṭṭuṭa hired waggons from Christian Qipchaqs north of the Black Sea and mentioned Qipchaqs amongst the Christian residents of Sarai, the capital of the Qipchaq Khanate (Golden Horde) (Gibb 1929: 142, 166). A similar story occurs in the largely invented *Book of Knowledge of all Kingdoms* (14th cent.), where the anonymous author recounts how he 'entered the Sea of Sara in a boat of Christian Komans' and mentions 'the kingdom of Sant Estopoli [Sevastopol], which belongs to Koman Christians' (Marino 1999: 87, 97). Presumably these Christians were part of the same community that the

Catholic missionaries were working with; it seems that their 'Nestorian' roots had prepared them for proselytisation by other branches of Christianity, a phenomenon also seen in Mongol China. For more on Christianity amongst the Qipchaqs, see Golden (1998: 217–22).

There are also references from the mid-twelfth century to Christianity on the rim of the Tarim Basin. The semi-legendary *Tezkere* of Maḥmud Karam Kabulī (fl. ca. 1155) portrays Muslim conflict with a Christian governor of Aqsu and a Christian king of Khotan in the twelfth century (Grenard 1898: 44–6). As noted above, separating historical elements from these hagiographical legends is challenging. More tangible evidence for Christianity in Khotan, possibly from the Mongol era, comes from a bronze cross inscribed in Chinese. It has been read as 'Supreme altar of the Cross', a reading questioned by some (Devéria 1896: 435–7; Pelliot 1914: 644; Dauvillier 1953: 71). The shorter version of the *Kitāb al-Majdal* (early 14th cent.) mentions a metropolitan of Kashgar during the patriarchate of Bar Ṣawmā (r. 1134–1136) and two consecutive metropolitans consecrated for the same city under patriarch Eliya III (r. 1176–1190) (Gismondi 1896–1897: 105/61, 111/64). Unfortunately, no other bishops or metropolitans are mentioned in Kashgar outside the twelfth century (Fiey 1993: 101–2), apart from the city's placement in the list of metropolitans from the *Kitāb al-Majdal*, discussed below.

Very similar to the aforementioned *Tezkere* are legends arising after the death of Khoja Ahmad Yassavī (founder of an important Sufi *tariqah*, d. 1166), which record conflict between Muslims and Christians (including rulers and whole towns) during the Muslim conquest of Central Asia. According to these accounts, important urban centres with Christian populations and/or rulers once included Ferghana, Uzgand (Uzgen), Osh and Shāsh (Tashkent) in or near the Ferghana Valley, and Kashgar and Aqsu in the Tarim Basin. However, the stories are very difficult to date and the legendary aspects of these hagiographies need to be considered when attempting to recover any historical facts (DeWeese 1990). In contrast, al-Shahrastānī's *Book of Religions and Sects* (1127/28) mentions only Zoroastrians and Mazdakites in Sogdiana (Gimaret and Monnot 1986: 665–6, 673).

Finally, there are enigmatic references in the twelfth century to one or possibly two Syrian Orthodox bishops named Bar Turkaya, 'Son of the/a Turk'. Michael the Syrian and Bar Hebraeus's *Chronicon Ecclesiasticum* both mention the patriarch Yoḥannan X bar Mawdyono (r. 1129–1137) appointing a 'Bar Turkaya' as bishop of Mabbug (Chabot 1899–1910, Vol. III: 238–9; Vol. IV: 615–6; Wilmshurst 2016: 169/168) and/or bishop of Tel Bashir (Chabot 1899–1910, Vol. III: 298–9; Vol. IV: 649–50; cf. Vol. III: 478, n. 4; Wilmshurst 2016: 181/180). It is unclear whether the name of the bishop(s) in question indicated Turkic ethnicity, but this is certainly a possibility, since the dioceses mentioned were in territory ruled by the Seljüks (if so, this might imply mixed parentage or conversion from Islam to Christianity). Thus, Syriac Christianity by this period had become established well beyond the initial ecclesiastical bases of Merv and Samarqand, as indicated by the references to metropolitan bishops in Kashgar and Christianity amongst the Qipchaq-Cumans on the northern steppe.

THE FINAL STAGE OF SYRIAC CHRISTIANITY UNDER THE MONGOLS AND TIMURIDS

Mongol power in Central Asia was consolidated by their defeat of the Qarakhitai (1218) and Khwarezmshah (1220) empires. After the death of Chinggis Khan (1227), the unified Mongol Empire he had forged evolved into four separate states: the Il-khanate in Persia (1256–1335), the Chaghatayid Khanate in Central Asia (1242–1347), the Qipchaq Khanate (Golden Horde) on the northern steppe (1256–1360), and the Yuan dynasty in Mongolia and China (1260–1368). Under Chinggis Khan and his immediate successors – Ögedei Khan (r. 1229–1241), Güyüg Khan (r. 1246–1248), Möngke Khan (r. 1251–1259), and Qubilai Khan (r. 1260–1294) – there was an intentional policy of religious tolerance, as Juvaynī (1259) indicates (Boyle 1958: 26); for a more nuanced evaluation of Mongol religious policy, see Jackson 2005. However, beginning in 1295 and continuing up to the mid-fourteenth century, the rulers of the Il-khanate, the Qipchaq Khanate, and the Chaghatayid Khanate gradually converted to Islam, along with the majority of their Turko-Mongolian troops. Christianity continued to exist in all three domains after the rulers' adoption of Islam, but it did so in a weakened position, eventually disappearing in Central Asia under the Timurid dynasty (1369/70–1506).

Before that disappearance, however, there are numerous references to Christianity during the Mongol era, thanks to the many extant primary sources in Arabic, Armenian, Chinese, mediaeval Latin or Italian, Persian, and Syriac. There is evidence of Christianity flourishing amongst several Turkic groups during this period. The ruling elites of the Christianised Kerait/Kereyid (Atwood 2004: 295–7) and Öngüt/Önggüd Turks (Atwood 2004: 424–5; Borbone 2005; Baumer 2006: 201–5; Borbone 2008a) developed marriage alliances with the Mongol nobility. Christian rulers of the Kerait before the Mongol Empire include Marghuz (Marcus) Buyruq Khan (r. 1125–1140), his son Quryaqus (Cyriacus) Buyruq Khan (r. 1140), and most importantly his grandson Toghrul Wang Khan (r. 1150–1203), initially Chinggis Khan's mentor and later his rival, whom Chinggis defeated; Toghrul was later associated by Marco Polo (after 1296) with the legend of Prester John (Boyle 1958: 35–8; Bedjan 1890: 409–10; Budge 1932: 352–3; Moule and Pelliot 1938: 63–8; Togan 1998: 65–103, 170–3). *The Secret History of the Mongols* (1228?) describes how Toghrul and his associates had 'made magic strips and uttered the prayer *Abui babui*' when 'pleading for a son who was yet to come [be born]'; could the prayer name (accompanied by obviously shamanistic practices) represent the Syriac title of the Lord's Prayer, *Abun dbashmayo* (de Rachewiltz 2004: 94)?

Despite hopeful reports from Western envoys and the general policy of religious tolerance in Mongol territory, few Mongol rulers genuinely adopted Christianity; Sartaq, ruler of the Golden Horde (r. 1256–1257) is a notable exception. Juvaynī, Kirakos Gandzakets'i (1266/67), Vardan Arewelts'i (1267), and Bar Hebraeus all affirm Sartaq's faith (Boyle 1958: 268; Bedrosian 1986: §55, §58; Bedrosian 2007, §90; Bedjan 1890: 465; Budge 1932: 398). Less convincingly, Bar Hebraeus calls Güyüg Khan 'a true Christian' (Bedjan 1890: 481; Budge 1932: 411), while Het'um claims that Möngke Khan and Qubilai Khan converted or promised to do so (Bedrosian 2004: §19, §23–24), but there is no evidence to support these claims. William of Rubruck is generally sceptical of any stories that rulers had converted or been baptised (Jackson 1990: 114–22, 172, 187–8).

Even more naïve is the claim by Guillaume de Nangis (ca. 1285–1300) that the Il-khan Ghazan Khan (r. 1295–1304), a devout Muslim, had converted shortly before ascending to the throne, especially since this is followed in 1303 by Ghazan's promise to convert in exchange for a Christian invasion of the Middle East (Guizot 1825: 236, 247). In contrast, after Chinggis Khan consolidated his power, numerous Christian Kerait princesses married into his family, notably a niece and granddaughter of Toghrul Wang Khan: Sorqaqtani Begi (d. 1252, mother of Möngke Khan, Qubilai Khan, and Hülegü Khan) and Doquz Khatun (d. 1265, wife of Hülegü, the conqueror of Baghdad) (Bedjan 1890: 465, 488, 491, 521; Budge 1932: 398, 417, 419, 444; Boyle 1958: 550–3; Bedrosian 2007, §90, §97; Atwood 2004: 511–2, 541–2; Tang 2006; Borbone 2009).

Writing about the Il-khanate, Armenian historians in particular make much of Hülegü (r. 1256–1265) and Doquz Khatun's favouritism towards Christians. Stephen Orbelian (1299) compares them to Constantine and Helen, an equation perhaps confirmed by an image in an illustrated Syriac gospel (Brosset 1864: 234–5; Fiey 1975), while Vardan Arewelts'i recounts a conversation with 'the benevolent and mild-mannered' Hülegü (who was a Buddhist) on spiritual matters (Bedrosian 2007, §96). The favour shown to Christians continued under Abaqa Khan (r. 1265–1282) and Arghun Khan (r. 1284–1291), as indicated by coins they issued with Arabic legends reading 'In the name of the Father, the Son and the Holy Spirit, One God' (Drouin 1896: 514, 521; Blochet 1906: 59). Pope Nicholas IV (r. 1288–1292) wrote letters to Christian wives of both khans (Ryan 1998: 417–8). The *History of Mar Yahbāllahā* (see below) notes that Arghun had his son baptised in 1281 (Bedjan 1895: 88; Montgomery 1927: 74; Budge 1928: 199). This was Kharbanda, the son of the Christian queen Urug Khatun. Baptised as Nicholas, he later converted to Islam and, ruling as Sultan Öljeitü (r. 1304–1316), strengthened the policy of Islamisation begun under his brother Ghazan Khan (r. 1295–1304) (Bedjan 1895: 147–9; Budge 1928: 255–7; Atwood 2004: 108, 199, 234–5, 598).

Bar Hebraeus even speaks favourably of Sultan Ahmed (r. 1282–1284), the first Muslim Il-khan, and notes that Ahmed's mother Qutui Khatun commanded the Christians in 1279 to renew their custom of blessing the waters at Epiphany (Bedjan 1890: 539–40, 548; Budge 1932: 460, 467). Although this does not clarify her religious persuasions, she was apparently responsible for Yahbāllahā III being released from prison later on (Bedjan 1895: 43; Montgomery 1927: 49; Budge 1928: 161). Nevertheless, the status of Christians was gradually eroded by internecine fighting between the descendants of Hülegü and the conversion of the ruling Il-khanid house to Islam, beginning under Ghazan Khan. Even Baidu Khan (r. 1295), the last khan to show favour to Christians, presented himself as both a Christian and a Muslim, as Bar Hebraeus's continuator notes (Bedjan 1890: 593–4; Budge 1932: 505).

A significant Christian ruler in the Mongol heartland was 'King George' (Syr. Giwargis, Turk. Körgüz, Chin. Kuolijisi) of the Öngüt (r. 1294–1298), converted to Catholicism by John of Montecorvino (writing in 1305–1306). Various European writers identify him as a descendent of Prester John or even equate him with that mythical Christian ruler (Moule and Pelliot 1938: 181–3; Dawson 1955: 225–6; Boyle 1971: 326–8; Paolillo 2009; Marsone 2013; Tang 2013). A Syriac gospel book, likely intended for George's sister Sara and written in gold ink on blue paper, is preserved in the Vatican Library (Borbone 2006a; Baumer 2006: 203). Chinese and Syriac inscriptions almost certainly left by George in 1298 have been discovered at Ulaan Tolgoi in Mongolia (Osawa and Takahashi 2015).

There were several prominent Christians who served under the Grand Khans or the Il-khans. The Uyghur Chinqai (d. 1252), Naiman Qadaq (d. 1251), and Kerait Bulghai (d. 1264) were chief scribes, judges, and court administrators, while the Naiman Kitbuqa/Ked-Buqa (d. 1260) was a military commander under Hülegü (Boyle 1958: 259, 572, 605; Boyle 1971: 184, 188; Jackson 1990: 173, 192; Bedrosian 2007, §92; Atwood 2004: 103, 295, 666; Buell 1994). The case is less clear with Eljigidei (d. 1251), chief military commander in the Middle East under Güyüg Khan, who dispatched a letter to Louis IX of France in 1248 proposing an alliance between the Mongols and the Christians against the Muslims, as recorded by Vincent of Beauvais (1253), Matthew Paris (1273), Guillaume de Nangis, and others (Howorth 1876: 77–8; Giles 1854: 419–20; Lespinasse 1877: 86–9).

The letter, delivered by David and Mark, two Christians from Mosul, describes the Mongol intention as 'the benefit of Christianity' and urges equal treatment of all Christian sects. The envoys told Louis that Eljigidei was a Christian, along with Güyüg Khan, his mother, his sons, and other nobles (Lespinasse 1877: 97) but, as Pelliot (1931: 150–75) notes, assessing the authenticity of the letter is difficult, and some of the Christian envoys' supplementary information is erroneous or fabricated. Indeed, Möngke Khan later denounced David as a liar (Jackson 1990: 249). A letter written earlier in 1248 in the typical Mongol fashion (with threats and demands) to Pope Innocent IV (r. 1243–1254) from Eljigidei's predecessor Baiju (d. 1260), was delivered by Aybeg (Turk. 'moon-prince', Rásonyi and Baski 2007: 12–14) and Sargis, whose Turkic and Syriac names perhaps indicate a Christian community in Baiju's camp similar to that discussed below connected with the Semirechye gravestones (D'Ohsson 1834: 229–30; Pelliot 1931: 128–9).

Also playing a key role in both Mongolia and Iran was Simeon Rabban-ata, 'a pious, God-loving man of Syrian nationality' [describing his Syriac connections, not ethnicity] who defended the interests of Christians in eastern Iran and Armenia from ca. 1235 on, as Kirakos Gandzakets'i (writing in 1241) relates (Bedrosian 1986: §33; Pelliot 1931: 48–50). Based in Tabriz, he functioned as an intermediary between the Church of the East and the papacy of Innocent IV (Pelliot 1931: 29–42). A complementary account is found in Vincent of Beauvais, who describes Rabban-ata as a former confidante of 'King David' (here, Toghrul Wang Khan) and his 'daughter' (perhaps Sorqaqtani Begi?) who later functioned as a counsellor, confessor, and diviner in the Mongol court before he was sent to Tabriz (Pelliot 1931: 42–7). His title combines Syr. *Rabban*, 'master' and Turk. *ata*, 'father'; if not of Turkic (Kerait?) origin himself, he was obviously used to functioning in a Mongol-Turkic environment. A Chinese funerary inscription describes how he was 'in charge of the affairs of his religion' under Güyüg Khan (Pelliot 1931: 52–3).

Bar Hebraeus mentions several Central Asian Christians who served the Il-khanate in Iran. Samdagu, 'a splendid Mongol Christian youth', led the siege and recapture of Mosul in 1260/61 (Bedjan 1890: 519; Budge 1932: 443), about the same time that 'a

Christian Hun' named Tay Qutlugh (Turkic for 'blessed colt'), presumably a member of the Mongol army, was summoned to arrest and kill the murderers of Dionysius ʿAngur (r. 1252–1261), rival of the Syrian Orthodox patriarch Yoḥannan XII bar Maʿdani (r. 1252–1263) (Wilmshurst 2016: 267/266). Later, Eshimut, a Christian Uyghur ascetic, served the Il-khan Abaqa ca. 1275/76–1284 (Bedjan 1890: 535, 539, 542, 554; Budge 1932: 456, 459–60, 462, 472; Rásonyi and Baski 2007: 270). A Christian connection can also be seen in the story recounted by Juvaynī of the Uyghur Körgüz, governor of Iran and then Khorasan (1235/36–1242/43), who apparently converted from Christianity (given his name) to Buddhism and then Islam (Boyle 1958: 489–507, 534–9; Atwood 2004: 320–1).

There are numerous references to Christians of other ecclesiastical backgrounds in Central Asia during this period, including Syrian Orthodox, Melkites, Armenians, and Latin Christians (the latter ultimately part of a concerted papal effort to convert the Mongols, as well as the 'heretical Nestorians'). William of Rubruck and Marco Polo are particularly good sources of information on the different branches of Christianity in the region under the Mongols, as well as the locations of Turkic Christians in the region. Rubruck describes 'Nestorians' near Qayaliq (about 450 km north of Lake Issyq-Köl) and elsewhere in the territory of the Uyghurs (Jackson 1990: 148–52, 157, 165; Pelliot 1973: 113–23). Polo mentions Christians in Kashgar, Samarqand, Yarkand, Tangut, Qara-khoja in 'Uyghuristan' (Turfan), 'Ghinghintalas' (Barkul = Bars-köl), and 'Tenduc' (Öngüt territory); he describes a miraculous church in Samarqand with a pillar suspended in mid-air, but whether he visited the city himself is questionable (Moule and Pelliot 1938: 143–6, 150–1, 156, 158, 178–9, 181–3; Borbone 2013: 447–9).

The Chinese *Journey to the West of Qiu Changchun* (1228), which records the journey of the Taoist scholar Changchun to see Chinggis Khan in the Hindu Kush in 1221–1223, describes how, when camped to the east of Luntai (Bügür or Bayingol), between Turfan and Aqsu on the northern edge of the Tarim Basin, 'the head of the Tarsā [Chin. *Diexie-tarsā* was a common Persian term for Christians in Central Asia] came to meet us', reminding us that there were still Christian communities in the oasis cities ringing the Tarim Basin in the thirteenth century (Waley 1931: 82; Standaert 2001: 45). Another reference to the *tarsā* during the Mongol era occurs in Hetʿum, who describes the inhabitants of 'the kingdom of Tars' as

> Eo'gur [Uyghurs]. They have always been idolators [sic] and at present still are, excepting the kin of those kings who came, guided by a vision of the Star to Bethlehem in Judea to worship the birth of the Lord. Even now one may find many grandees and nobles among the Tartars who are descended from that line, and who firmly hold the faith of Christ.
>
> (Bedrosian 2004: §2)

Slightly later, Mustawfī includes Tarsiyān and Uighūr' in his list of kingdoms lying outside Iran, again equating Christians and Uyghurs (le Strange 1919: 249).

One of the most important texts from this period is the *History of Mar Yahbāllahā* (after 1317) (Pelliot 1973: 239–88; Borbone 2000), which narrates the travels of the Turkic monks Marqos and Rabban Ṣawmā from Khanbaliq (Beijing), via Marqos's hometown of Koshang – either Olon Sume (Borbone 2015: 138) or 'the southern political center of the Önggüts' (Paolillo 2006: 373) in Öngüt territory (Bedjan 1895: 14; Montgomery 1927: 33; Budge 1928: 135; Pelliot 1973: 251–5, 259–61), to Baghdad (ca. 1277–1279). Shortly after, Marqos was appointed Metropolitan of 'the flock of Khitai and Öng' (referring to Northern China and Öngüt territory) by Denḥā I (r. 1265–1281) (Bedjan 1895: 28–9; Montgomery 1927: 41; Budge 1928: 148; Dauvillier 1948: 302–4). When Denḥā died, the Öngüt monk was elected Yahbāllahā III, the first and only Turkic patriarch of the Church of the East (r. 1281–1317) (Bedjan 1895: 32–8; Montgomery 1927: 43–6; Budge 1928: 151–6; Wilmshurst 2016: 463/462).

Yahbāllahā's ethnicity was so significant that his identity as a Turk is specifically noted in lists of patriarchs assembled by continuators of the *Book of the Bee* (ca. 1222) and Eliya Jawharī, as well as a *memrā* in honour of Yahbāllahā (1295) (Budge 1886: 135/119; Assemani 1721–28: II, 391–2; Vosté 1929). Rabban Ṣawmā (who may have been Uyghur or Öngüt; see Pelliot 1973: 247–8) was appointed visitor-general by Denḥā I and subsequently sent on a diplomatic mission to Europe (1287–1288) by Yahbāllahā III and Arghun Khan; while in Rome, in response to questioning by the cardinals, he declared, 'Many of our fathers have gone to the lands of the Mongols, Turks and Chinese and have taught them, and today there are many Mongol Christians' (Bedjan 1895: 57; Montgomery 1927: 56; Budge 1928: 174).

The various 'professions of Catholic faith' made by the embattled Yahbāllahā III in letters to the popes Boniface VIII (1302) and Benedict XI (1304) (Chabot 1895: 249–56; Tisserant 1931: 222–3) should be understood in the context of the Church of the East facing increasing hostility and persecution in the Mongol Il-khanid realm. By contrast, the Syro-Turkic patriarchal seal affixed to these letters gives fascinating insight into the cultural climate in which his church functioned under the Mongols (Hamilton 1972). The prevalence of Christianity amongst Turkic peoples at this time is well-expressed in the optimistic introduction to the *History of Mar Yahbāllahā*: 'Today the Turks have bound their necks under the yoke of divine lordship, and they believe and whole-heartedly affirm the word of our Lord' (Bedjan 1895: 2; Budge 1928: 123).

Also of importance for understanding Christianity under the Mongols are texts listing the metropolitans of the Church of the East; however, differences between these lists show how difficult it is to reconstruct the ecclesiastical hierarchy in Central Asia during this period. Thus, the only Central Asian metropolitans recorded in ʿAbdishoʿ bar Berikha's *Order of Ecclesiastical Judgements* (1315/16) are Merv, twinned with Nishapur, the Turks, and Herat, but not Samarqand (Chabot 1902: 618–20; Vosté 1940a, 56–7)! By contrast, the continuator of the *Kitāb al-Majdal* (14th cent.) gives a much more extensive list of metropolitans, including Merv, Herat, Samarqand, Turkistan, Khanbaliq and Al-Faliq, Tangut, Kashgar, and Navekath, but there is no indication of the total number of bishops overseen by these ecclesiastical provinces, beyond the general statement that 'each one of these metropolitans has bishops under him, some twelve, some six', probably more reflective of the situation in Mesopotamia/Iraq than in Central Asia (Gismondi 1896–1897: 126/73; cf. Siouffi 1881: 95).

It is unclear whether the metropolitanate of Turkistan was a restoration of Timothy's earlier metropolitanate of the Turks. If so, it may have included some of the Turkic groups amongst whom Christians flourished under Mongol rule: the aforementioned

Kerait, Öngüt, and Uyghurs, plus the Mongolic-speaking Merkit/Merkid and Turkic-speaking Naiman (Atwood 2004: 347, 397–8). From the latter came Küchlüg, the usurper of the Qarakhitai Empire (r. 1211–1218), who had grown up a Christian (Boyle 1958: 64, 65; Jackson 1990: 23, 122–3; Tang 2009b). Navekath was in the Chu River Valley (Kyrgyzstan), only 400 km north of its twin see city of Kashgar, but the harsh mountainous terrain between the two would have made travel and communication from one to the other very difficult (Dauvillier 1948: 288–91; Klein 2000: 136–9).

The see of Khanbaliq and Al-Faliq has been reinterpreted as Besh-baliq and Almaliq, two important cities along the northern Silk Road in the Chaghatayid Khanate (Sachau 1919: 22; Dauvillier 1948: 305–7). Given the significant number of Christian gravestones found near Almaliq (see below), there was presumably a sizeable Syriac-speaking Christian community there. A Catholic bishopric was established in Almaliq probably in the 1320s; however, seven residents of the Catholic friary at Almaliq, including the bishop, were martyred in 1339, as John of Marignolli (passing through the area in 1354–1355) and Bartholomew of Pisa (d. 1361) both recount (Yule and Cordier 1914: 31–3, 212; Standaert 2001: 75–6). Bartholomew narrates how the 'emperor', meaning the Chaghatayid khan Changshi (r. 1334–1338), was very favourable towards the Franciscan friars, possibly a result of having had a Christian wife, Alma Khatun (Klein 2000: 258–60; Baumer 2006: 210).

Tangut refers to both the Tangut people and their territory (situated in the Chinese provinces of Gansu, Ningxia, Shanxi, and Shaanxi and formerly the Xi Xia or Tangut Empire, 1038–1227). The *History of Mar Yahbāllahā* and the *Kitāb al-Majdal* praise the Tangut Christians for their ardent belief and note the presence of the metropolitan of Tangut at the patriarchal election of Yahbāllahā III; sadly, plotting by the metropolitan subsequently landed the patriarch in prison under Ahmed Khan (Bedjan 1895: 17–18, 33, 40–2; Montgomery 1927: 34–5, 43, 47–8; Budge 1928: 137–8, 152, 159–61; Gismondi 1896–1897: 124/71–2; Siouffi 1881: 92; Dauvillier 1948: 310–11).

Smbat Sparapet's letter from Samarqand (1248–1250) affirms the strength of Christianity in Tangut, noting it as 'the land from which came the Three Kings to Bethlem [sic] to worship the Lord Jesus' (Yule and Cordier 1915: 162; Lespinasse 1877: 92). It may be to the Tangut people that Plano Carpini refers when he describes the 'Kitayans' as having 'an Old and New Testament . . . lives of the Fathers and hermits and buildings made like churches . . . They worship one God, they honour Our Lord Jesus Christ, and they believe in eternal life, but they are not baptised' (Dawson 1955: 21–2), a passage repeated in the *Tartar Relation* (Skelton et al. 1965: 62). However, Pelliot (1973: 36–7) suspects that the original source is describing the typical mixture of Confucianism and Buddhism found in China at the time. Tangut Christianity can probably also be connected with the aforementioned texts from Qara Qoto, an important Tangut city.

A significant source of information on Christian communities in Central Asia during the Mongol era is a large corpus of Christian gravestones (about 600), mostly found in the 'Seven Rivers' region (*Semirechye* in Russian, *Yeti Su* in Turkic), in two sites near Bishkek (Kyrgyzstan): Karajigach and Burana (Figure 31.17) (Chwolson 1890; Chwolson 1897; Dickens 2009: 14–17). The majority of the gravestones are inscribed in Syriac or the Middle Turkic dialect spoken in the area, written in the Syriac script. Smaller collections of Christian gravestones come from three other

Figure 31.17 Gravestone from Kyrgyzstan

locations now in China: Almaliq, Xinjiang (Kokovtsov 1904–1905 [1906]); the traditional territory of the Öngüt in Inner Mongolia (Halbertsma 2015); and Quanzhou (Zayton) in Fujian province (Lieu et al. 2012). The preponderance of Turkic inscriptions in Syriac or Uyghur script from Quanzhou suggests that the Christian community there was mostly Central Asian in origin.

In addition to gravestones, the Öngüt Christians may have left behind two churches in Olon Sume – one 'Nestorian' and one Catholic (Egami 1952; Borbone 2013: 460–1) – and numerous small bronze objects, many shaped as crosses or doves, from the Ordos region of Inner Mongolia (Hambis 1947–50). Further evidence of Christian activity in Inner Mongolia during this time comes from Turkic 'graffiti' in Syriac script left in the 'White Pagoda' near Hohhot, Inner Mongolia, possibly dating to 1221 (Borbone 2008b), and a funerary tile from Chifeng, dating to 1253, containing a Turkic text in Uyghur characters and a short Syriac text (Borbone 2006b).

Near the Semirechye gravestone sites, two church buildings have been excavated in Aq-Beshim, both probably from the eighth century (Clauson 1961: 2–3; Hambis 1961; Klein 2004; Borbone 2013: 455–8). In one was found a cross with a Sogdian inscription (10th–11th cent.) (Klein and Reck 2004). Artefacts discovered in nearby Krasnaya Rechka include the rim of a stone jar (late 8th–early 10th cent.) with an inscription in Sogdian script dedicated to *yrwytkyn mlp'ny*, 'Yaruq-tegin the teacher' (Livshits 2006; Lurje 2010: № 1517) and a brick (11th or 12th cent.) inscribed with the words *Giwargis Temurchi*, 'George the Blacksmith' in Syriac script (Borisov 1963). This data suggests that the Christian community which left the gravestones had probably been present there for at least six centuries, living under the rule of the Second Türk Empire, the Türgesh and Qarluq Qaghanates, the Qarakhanid Qaghanate, the Qara-Khitai Khanate, and the Mongol Empire.

The Semirechye stones date between 1200/01 (Chwolson 1897: № 2) and 1344/45 (Chwolson 1890: № 56), roughly corresponding to the time of Mongol rule. Dates on the stones are given using the Seleucid calendar and/or the Sino-Turkic twelve-year animal-cycle (Bazin 1991: 413–29). Most names are Syriac or Turkic, a few are Arabic or Persian; nearly all the deceased must have been Turkic speakers. One popular Turkic male name from the corpus is a word found in Maḥmud al-Kāshgharī's *Dīwān Lughāt at-Turk* (1072): *bachāq* 'Christian fast (*ṣawm an-naṣārā*)' (Dankoff and Kelly 1982: 313; Clauson 1972: 293; Rásonyi and Baski 2007: 93). It is likely that these Christians were descendants of earlier Turks, perhaps the Qarluqs, given their location in the traditional territory of the latter.

Approximately two-thirds of the 300 males represented held positions in the church, whether as priests, church visitors, scholars, archdeacons, chor-bishops, biblical interpreters, teachers, ecclesiastical administrators (e.g. 'head of the church'), exorcists, sacristans, or musicians. However, the only bishop commemorated on a gravestone is an Armenian (Marr 1894). There are also several non-ecclesiastical administrative or military titles, including *tuman begi*, 'chief of 10,000'; *rav ḥaylā*, 'commander or military governor', *amir* and *ispasalar* 'commander-in-chief' (Chwolson 1890: 124–9; Chwolson 1897: 53–4). Thus, this Turkic Christian community was involved not only in church life, but also in the broader society, notably the military.

The gravestones may give us insight into how other Central Asian Christian communities probably declined during the fourteenth century, due primarily to the arrival of the plague between 1337 and 1339 (nearly twenty percent of the Semirechye stones are from this period) and secondarily to conversion to Islam (Chwolson 1890: № 44). Other sources from this period also give indications of the impending demise of Central Asian Christianity. Juzjānī (1260) describes the destruction of a Christian church in Samarqand by local Muslims in 1259 after a young Christian converted to Islam and subsequently died at the hands of a Mongol ruler partial to Christianity (Raverty 1881: 1288–90). Baumer (2006, 169) suggests plausibly that this is the source of the story noted above that Polo relates of the Samarqand church.

For the time being, Central Asian Christians in China fared better. Mar Sargis, whose family was from Samarqand, had a distinguished career in service to the Mongols from 1268 to at least 1295, during which he was able to build seven Christian monasteries (Pelliot 1963: 774–6; Ligeti 1972). The Chinese *Annals (Gazetteer) of Zhenjiang of the Zhishun Period* (1332), which records information about him, describes Samarqand as 'a land where the *Yelikewen* [Chinese for *ärkägün*, "Christians" (Baumer 2006: 219)] practice their religion' and mentions the same story that Polo does about a church with a suspended pillar; the surname 'An' of one of Sargis's assistant administrators, An Chenheng, signifies the origins of the latter in Bukhara (Moule 1930: 145–50, 156–7). However, as Rashiddudin (1310) recounts, conflict between Christians and Muslims at the court of Qubilai Khan increased during this time (Boyle 1971: 293–5), and when the Ming dynasty replaced the Yuan dynasty (1368), Central Asian Christianity in China had apparently ceased to exist.

By the fifteenth century, only a few sources mention Christians in Central Asia and then only in Samarqand and possibly Turfan. A report by Ruy González de Clavijo, the Castilian ambassador to Timur (1403–1405), mentions Christians captured by Timur who were resident in Samarqand, without specifying their ethnicity or ecclesiastical allegiance (Markham 1859: 171). However, by the time of Timur's grandson, Ulugh Beg, who ruled in Mawara'n-nahr (r. 1411–1449), relations between local Christians and Muslims had deteriorated significantly, according to an anecdote in the *History of Tamerlane and His Successors* by T'ovma Metsobets'i (early fifteenth century), which narrates how Ulugh Beg 'ordered all Christians to apostatize or be killed' after 'an impure Syrian Nestorian [priest]' committed an immoral act. As a result of this, some Christians 'chose death, while many lost the faith' (Bedrosian 1987: §19).

Two further sources discuss what appear to be syncretistic remnants of Christianity in the Turkic world. The first is the *Travels of Johann Schiltberger* (after 1427), where the author, a German captive of various Turkic rulers, describes accompanying Edigü (founder of the Noghay Horde) and his protégé Chakri Khan of the Golden Horde on an expedition of conquest to 'Ibissibur' (Sibir, east of the Urals and north of the Kazakh steppe, later the short-lived Siberian Khanate). Schiltberger notes,

> the people in this country believe in Jesus Christ like the three kings who came and brought offerings to Christ at Bethlaem [sic] . . . and they have a picture, which is a representation of our Lord in a manger, as the three holy kings saw him . . . They have this also in their temples, and say their prayers before it.
>
> (Telfer 1879: 35–6)

The second source is the *Tarikh-i Khata'i* (1494/95), a Turkish translation of a Persian report of an embassy to China from the Timurid ruler Shah Rukh in Herat which passed through Turfan in the summer of 1420, observing that 'many of the inhabitants . . . were infidels and they worshipped the cross'. Similarly in Qamul (400 km east of Turfan), in 'a large idol-temple . . . the image of a marvellous cross was set up . . . in front of that cross a copper image . . . was set up' (Bellér-Hann 1995: 159). These presumably represent the gradual absorption of the remnants of Christianity by Buddhism, by this time the dominant religion along the northern rim of the Tarim Basin.

How and when Syriac Christianity finally vanished in Central Asia – after a presence of more than 1,200 years – is unknown, but in addition to the textual and archaeological evidence presented here, echoes of it remained in personal names and stories after Central Asian Christians vanished from the sources. Thus, we hear of an official named Mar-Hasia (Syr. 'Right Reverend', 1388–1403) and a khan named Mar-Körgis (r. 1455?–1466?) in the Northern Yuan dynasty, established by the remnant of the Chinese Yuan dynasty after their downfall (Atwood 2004: 408). Somewhat later, the Portuguese Jesuit Benedict (Bento de) Goës, who spent a year (1603–1604) in Yarkand before travelling on to China, relates that priests in the Kingdom of Kashgar were called 'Cashishes' (from Syr. *qashīshē*, 'priests') and the ruler of 'Cialis' (probably Qarashahr or Korla, 350 or 390 km SW of Turfan, respectively) admitted that 'his own ancestors [from Kashgar] had been professors of their [Christian] faith' (Yule and Cordier 1916: 223, 233; Wessels 1924: 34–5). Syriac Christianity in Central Asia was gone, but not entirely forgotten.

NOTES

1 Page references separated by a slash indicate the Syriac or Arabic text followed by the translation.

2 All images of the Turfan manuscripts are reproduced courtesy of the Berlin-Brandenburgische Akademie der Wissenschaften.

BIBLIOGRAPHY

Ashurov, B. 2015. Inculturation matérielle de l'Église d'Orient en Asie centrale: témoignages archéologiques. *In*: P. G. Borbone and P. Marsone, ed., *Le christianisme syriaque en Asie centrale et en Chine*. Études syriaques 12. Paris: Geuthner, 161–83.

Assemani, J. S. 1721–28. *Bibliotheca Orientalis Clementino-Vaticana, Tom. II, III,1–2*. Rome: Typis Sacrae Congregationis de Propaganda Fide.

Atwood, C. P. 2004. *Encyclopedia of Mongolia and the Mongol Empire*. New York: Facts on File Publications.

———. 2014. Historiography and Transformation of Ethnic Identity in the Mongol Empire: The Öng'üt Case. *Asian Ethnicity* 15, no. 4, 514–34.

Badger, G. P. 1852. *The Nestorians and Their Rituals, Vol. II*. London: Joseph Masters.

Bang, W. 1914. Der Komanische Marienpsalter. *Abhandlungen der Königlichen Gesellschaft der Wissenschaften zu Göttingen. Philologisch-Historische Klasse* 13 (N.F.), no. 1, 241–76.

Barthold, W. 1901. *Zur Geschichte des Christentums in Mittel-Asien bis zur mongolischen Eroberung*. Turnhout and Leipzig: J. C. B. Mohr.

Baulo, A. V. 2000. Silver Plate From the Malaya Ob. *Archaeology, Ethnology & Anthropology of Eurasia* 4, no. 4, 143–53.

———. 2004. Connection Between Time and Cultures (Silver Plate from Verkhnee Nildino). *Archaeology, Ethnology & Anthropology of Eurasia* 3, no. 19, 127–36.

Baumer, C. 2006. *The Church of the East: An Illustrated History of Assyrian Christianity*. London and New York: I.B. Tauris.

Bazin, L. 1991. *Les systèmes chronologiques dans le monde turc ancient*. Bibliotheca orientalis Hungarica 34. Budapest: Akadémiai Kiadó.

Bedjan, P. 1890. *Gregorii Barhebraei Chronicon Syriacum*. Paris: Maisonneuve.

———. 1895. *Histoire de Mar-Jabalaha, de trois autres patriarches, d'un prêtre et de deux laïques, nestoriens* (2nd ed.). Leipzig: Otto Harrassowitz.

Bedrosian, R. (trans.). 1986. *Kirakos Gandzakets'i's History of the Armenians*. New York: Sources of the Armenian Tradition [Available at www.rbedrosian.com/Downloads/Kirakos_Gandzaketsi.pdf].

———. 1987. *The History of Tamerlane and His Successors by Vardapet T'ovma Metsobets'i*. New York: Sources of the Armenian Tradition [Available at rbedrosian.com/tm2.htm].

———. 2004. *Het'um the Historian's History of the Tartars*. Long Branch: Sources of the Armenian Tradition [Available at rbedrosian.com/Downloads/Hetum.pdf].

———. 2007. *Vardan Arewelts'i's Compilation of History*. Long Branch: Sources of the Armenian Tradition [Available at rbedrosian.com/vaint.htm].

Bellér-Hann, I. 1995. *A History of Cathay: A Translation and Linguistic Analysis of a Fifteenth-Century Turkic Manuscript*. Indiana University Uralic and Altaic Series 162. Bloomington: Indiana University.

Bidawid, R. 1956. *Les lettres du patriarche nestorien Timothée I: étude critique avec en appendice la lettre de Timothée I aux moines du couvent de Mār Mārōn*. Studi e Testi 187. Città del Vaticano: Biblioteca Apostolica Vaticana.

Blochet, E. 1906. Les monnaies mongoles de la collection Decourdemanche. *ROC* 11, 50–9, 113–29.

———. 1925–26. La conquête des états nestoriens de l'asie centrale par les shiïtes. *ROC* 25, 3–131.

Borbone, P. G. 2000. *Storia di Mar Yahballaha e di Rabban Sauma: Un orientale in Occidente ai tempi di Marco Polo*. Torino: Silvio Zamorani editore.

———. 2005. Some Aspects of Turco-Mongol Christianity in the Light of Literary and Epigraphic Syriac Sources. *Journal of Assyrian Academic Studies* 19, no. 2, 5–20.

———. 2006a. Princess Sara's Gospel Book: A Syriac Manuscript Written in Inner Mongolia? *In*: R. Malek and P. Hofrichter, ed., *Jingjiao: The Church of the East in China and Central Asia*. Sankt Augustin: Institut Monumenta Serica, 347–8.

———. 2006b. Peshitta Psalm 34:6 From Syria to China. *In*: W. Th. van Peursen and R. B. ter Haar Romeny, ed., *Text, Translation, and Tradition: Studies on the Peshitta and Its Use in the Syriac Tradition*. Monographs of the Peshitta Institute Leiden 14. Leiden: Brill, 1–10.

———. 2008a. Syroturcica 1. The Önggüds and the Syriac Language. *In*: G. A. Kiraz, ed., *Malphono w-Rabo d-Malphone: Studies in Honor of Sebastian P. Brock*. Piscataway, NJ: Gorgias Press, 1–17.

———. 2008b. Syroturcica 2: The Priest Särgis in the White Pagoda. *Monumenta Serica* 56, 487–503.

———. 2009. "Saint Hülegü and Doquz Khatun": Syriac Perspectives on Mongol Rule (13–14th Century Iran/Iraq). *Mongolica: an International Annual of Mongol Studies* 22/43, 102–12.

———. 2013. Les églises d'Asie centrale et de Chine: état de la question à partir des textes et des découvertes archéologiques. *In*: F. Briquel Chatonnet, ed., *Les églises en monde syriaque*. Études syriaques 10. Paris: Geuthner, 441–65.

———. 2015. Les "provinces de l'extérieur" vues par l'Église-mère. *In*: P. G. Borbone and P. Marsone, ed., *Le christianisme syriaque en Asie Centrale et en Chine*. Études syriaques 12. Paris: Geuthner, 121–59.

Borisov, A. Ya. 1963. Epigraficheskie Zametki. *Epigrafika Vostoka* 15, 51–7.

Boyle, J. A. (trans.). 1958. *The History of the World-Conqueror* (2 vols). Manchester: Manchester University Press.

———. 1971. *The Successors of Genghis Khan*. New York and London: Columbia University Press.

Braun, O. 1901. Ein Brief des Katholikos Timotheos I über biblische Studien des 9 Jahrhunderts. *Oriens Christianus* 1, 299–313.

———. 1915a. *Ausgewählte Akten persischer Märtyrer*. Bibliothek der Kirchenväter 22. Kempten and München: J. Kösel.

———. 1915b. *Timothei Patriarchae I Epistulae I*. CSCO 74/Syr. 30. Paris: J. Gabalda.

———. 1915c. *Timothei Patriarchae I Epistulae I*. CSCO 75/Syr. 31. Paris: J. Gabalda.

Brock, S. P. 1995. Bar Shabba/Mar Shabbay, First Bishop of Merv. *In*: M. Tamcke et al., ed., *Syrisches Christentum weltweit: Festschrift Wolfgang Hage*. Studien zur Orientalischen Kirchengeschichte 1. Münster: LIT Verlag, 190–201.

Brosset, M. 1864. *Histoire de la Siounie par Stéphannos Orbélian, Vol. I*. Saint-Petersburg: Eggers et Cie.
Budge, E. A. W. 1886. *The Book of the Bee*. Oxford: Clarendon Press.
———. 1893a. *The Book of Governors: The Historia Monastica of Thomas Bishop of Margâ. Vol. I: The Syriac Text*. London: Kegan Paul, Trench, Trübner & Co.
———. 1893b. *The Book of Governors: The Historia Monastica of Thomas Bishop of Margâ. Vol. II: English Translation*. London: Kegan Paul, Trench, Trübner & Co.
———. 1928. *The Monks of Kûblâi Khân, Emperor of China*. London: Religious Tract Society.
———. 1932. *The Chronography of Gregory Abû'l Faraj, the Son of Aaron, the Hebrew Physician, Commonly Known as Bar Hebraeus, Being the First Part of His Political History of the World, Vol. I*. Oxford: Oxford University Press.
Buell, P. D. 1994. Chinqai (1169–1252): Architect of Mongolian Empire. *In*: E. H. Kaplan and D. W. Whisenhunt, ed., *Opuscula Altaica, Essays Presented in Honor of Henry Schwarz*. Bellingham: Western Washington University, 168–86.
Bussagli, M. 1978. *Central Asian Painting*. London: Macmillan.
Chabot, J.-B. 1895. *Histoire de Mar Jabalaha III, Patriarche des Nestoriens (1281–1317) et du moine Rabban Çauma*. Paris: Ernest Leroux.
———. 1896. Le livre de chasteté composeé par Jésusdenah, évêque de Baçrah. *Mélanges d'Archéologie et d'Histoire* 16, 225–83, 221–71 [Syriac text].
———. 1899–1910. *Chronique de Michel le Syrien, Patriarche Jacobite d'Antioche 1166–1199*. 4 vols. Paris: Ernest Leroux.
———. 1902. *Synodicon Orientale ou Recueil de Synodes Nestoriens*. Notices et extraits des manuscrits de la Bibliothèque Nationale et autres bibliothèques 27. Paris: Imprimerie Nationale.
———. 1906. Note sur l'ouvrage syriaque intitulé Le Jardin des Délices. *In*: C. Bezold, ed., *Orientalische Studien: Theodor Nöldeke zum siebzigsten Geburtstag, Band I*. Gieszen: Alfred Töpelmann, 487–96.
Cheikho, L., ed., 1922. Majālis Īliyya muṭrān Naṣībīn. *Al-Machriq* 20, no. 3, 267–72.
Chwolson, D. 1890. Syrisch-Nestorianische Grabinschriften aus Semirjetschie. *Mémoires de l'Académie impériale des sciences de St.-Pétersbourg*, Ser. VII, Tom. XXXVII.
———. 1897. *Syrisch-Nestorianische Grabinschriften aus Semirjetschie. Neue Folge*. St. Petersburg: Imprimerie de l'Académie Impériale des Sciences.
Clauson, G. 1961. Ak Beshim – Suyab. *Journal of the Royal Asiatic Society*, 1–13.
———. 1972. *An Etymological Dictionary of Pre-Thirteenth Century Turkish*. Oxford: Clarendon Press.
Collins, B. A. 1994. *Al-Muqaddasi. The Best Divisions for Knowledge of the Regions*. Reading: Garnet Publishing.
Cureton, W. and W. Wright. 1864. *Ancient Syriac Documents Relative to the Earliest Establishment of Christianity in Edessa and Neighbouring Countries*. London: Williams and Norgate.
Dankoff, R. and J. Kelly. 1982. *Maḥmūd al-Kāšγarī. Compendium of the Turkic Dialects (Dīwān Luγāt at-Turk), Part I*. Sources of Oriental Languages and Literatures 7, Turkish Sources VII. Cambridge, MA: Harvard University Press.
Dauvillier, J. 1948. Les Provinces Chaldéennes 'de l'Extérieur' au Moyen Age. *In: Mélanges offerts au R. P. Ferdinand Cavallera*. Toulouse: Bibliothèque de l'Institut Catholique, 260–316.
———. 1953. Byzantins d'asie centrale et d'extrême-orient au moyen age. *Revue des Études Byzantines* 11, 62–87.
———. 1956. L'expansion de l'Eglise Syrienne en Asie Centrale et en Extreme-Orient. *L'Orient Syrien* 1, 76–87.

———. 1974. Les Arméniens en Chine et en Asie Centrale au Moyen Age. *In: Mélanges de Sinologie offerts à Monsieur Paul Demiéville, Vol. II.* Bibliothèque de l'Institut des Hautes Études Chinoises XX. Paris: Presses Universitaires de France, 1–17.
Dawson, C. 1955. *The Mongol Mission.* London: Sheed and Ward.
Deeg, M. 2013. A Belligerent Priest – Yisi and His Political Context. *In*: L. Tang and D. W. Winkler, ed., *From the Oxus River to the Chinese Shores: Studies on East Syriac Christianity in Central Asia and China.* Orientalia – Patristica – Oecumenica 5. Wien: LIT Verlag, 107–21.
de Rachewiltz, I. 2004. *The Secret History of the Mongols.* Brill's Inner Asian Library 7/1. Leiden and Boston: Brill.
Devéria, M. G. 1896. Notes d'épigraphie mongole-chinoise. *Journal Asiatique* Ser. IX, Tom. VIII, 94–128, 395–443.
DeWeese, D. 1990. Yasavian Legends on the Islamization of Turkistan. *In*: D. Sinor, ed., *Aspects of Altaic Civilization III: Proceedings of the Thirtieth Meeting of the Permanent International Altaistic Conference.* Indiana University Publications, Uralic and Altaic Series 145. Bloomington: Indiana University, 1–19.
Dickens, M. 2009. Syriac Gravestones in the Tashkent History Museum. *In*: D. W. Winkler and L. Tang, ed., *Hidden Treasures and Intercultural Encounters: Studies on East Syriac Christianity in China and Central Asia.* Orientalia – Patristica – Oecumenica 1. Wien: LIT Verlag, 13–49.
———. 2010. Patriarch Timothy I and the Metropolitan of the Turks. *Journal of the Royal Asiatic Society* 20, 117–39.
———. 2017. Syriac Inscriptions near Urgut, Uzbekistan. *Studia Iranica* 46, 205–60.
Dodge, B. 1970. *The Fihrist of al-Nadīm: A Tenth-Century Survey of Muslim Culture.* 2 vols. Records of Civilization: Sources and Studies 83. New York: Columbia University Press.
D'Ohsson, C. 1834. *Histoire des Mongols, depuis Tchingiz-Khan jusqu'a Timour Bery ou Tamerlan*, Vol. II. Le Haye and Amsterdam: Les Freres van Cleef.
Drijvers, H. J. W. 1965. *The Book of the Laws of Countries: Dialogue on Fate of Bardaiṣan of Edessa.* Semitic Texts with Translations 3. Assen: Van Gorcum & Co.
Drouin, E. 1896. Les monnaies mongoles. *Journal Asiatique* Ser. IX, Tom. VII, 486–544.
Duan, Q. 2001. Bericht über ein neuentdecktes syrisches Dokument aus Dunhuang/China. *OC* 85, 84–93.
Duval, R. 1904. *Išō'yahb III Patriarcha Liber Epistularum.* CSCO 11/Syr. 11. Paris: Typographeo Reipublicae.
———. 1905. *Išō'yahb III Patriarcha Liber Epistularum.* CSCO 12/Syr. 12. Paris: Typographeo Reipublicae.
Egami, N. 1952. Olon-sume et la découverte de l'église catholique romaine de Jean de Montecorvino. *Journal Asiatique* 240, 155–67.
Felix, W. 1991. Chionites. *Encyclopaedia Iranica* 5, 485–7.
Fiey, J.-M. 1970. Išō'yaw le Grand. *OCP* 36, 5–46.
———. 1973. Chrétientés syriaques du Horāsān et du Ségestān. *Le Muséon* 86, 75–104.
———. 1975. Iconographie syriaque: Hulagu, Doquz Khatun . . . et six ambons? *LM* 88, 59–68.
———. 1993. *Pour un Oriens Christianus Novus.* Beiruter Texte und Studien 49. Beirut and Stuttgart: Franz Steiner.
Frye, R. N. 1954. *The History of Bukhara.* Cambridge, MA: Mediaeval Academy of America.
Gibb, H. A. R. 1929. *Ibn Battuta: Travels in Asia and Africa, 1325–1354.* London: George Routledge & Sons.
Gifford, E. H. 1903. *Eusebii Pamphili Evangelicae Praeparationis Libri XV.* Oxford: Oxford University Press.
Gignoux, P. 1996. Une nouvelle jarre inscrite en syriaque d'asie centrale. *In: La Persia e l'Asia Centrale da Alessandro al X Secolo.* Atti dei Convegni Lincei 127. Rome: Accademia Nazionale dei Lincei, 39–48.

———. 2001. Une croix de procession de Hérat inscrite en pehlevi. *LM* 114, 291–304.
Giles, J. A. 1854. *Matthew Paris's English History From the Year 1235 to 1273, Vol. III.* London: Henry G. Bohn.
Gimaret, D. and G. Monnot. 1986. *Shahrastani: Livre des religions et des sectes, Vol. I.* Paris: Peeters/UNESCO.
Gismondi, E. 1896–1897. *Maris Amri et Slibae. De Patriarchis Nestorianorum. Commentaria, Pars Altera (Amri et Slibae).* Rome: C. de Luigi.
———. 1899. *Maris Amri et Slibae. De Patriarchis Nestorianorum. Commentaria, Pars Prior (Maris).* Rome: C. de Luigi.
Golden, P. B. 1992. Codex Cumanicus. *In*: H. B. Paksoy, ed., *Central Asian Monuments.* Istanbul: Isis Press, 33–63.
———. 1998. Religion Among the Qıpčaqs of Medieval Eurasia. *Central Asiatic Journal* 42, 180–237.
Greatrex, G., R. R. Phenix and C. B. Horn. 2011. *The Chronicle of Pseudo-Zachariah Rhetor: Church and War in Late Antiquity.* TTH 55. Liverpool: Liverpool University Press.
Grenard, F. 1898. *J.-L. Dutreuil de Rhins. Mission scientifique dans la haute Asie, 1890–1895. Partie 3, Histoire, Linguistique, Archéologie, Géographie.* Paris: Ernest Leroux.
Grenet, F. 1984. *Les pratiques funéraires dans l'Asie centrale sédentaire de la conquête grecque à l'islamisation.* Publications de l'U.R.A. 29, Memoire No. 1. Paris: Editions du Centre national de la recherche scientifique.
Griveau, R. 1915. *Les Fêtes des Melchites, par al-Birouni.* PO X, Fasc. 4. Paris: Firmin-Didot.
Guidi, I. 1903a. *Chronica Minora: Chronicon anonymum de ultimis regibus Persarum.* CSCO 1/Syr. 1. Paris: Typographeo Reipublicae.
———. 1903b. *Chronica Minora: Chronicon anonymum de ultimis regibus Persarum.* CSCO 2/Syr. 2. Paris: Typographeo Reipublicae.
Guizot, F. 1825. *Chronique de Guillaume de Nangis.* Paris: J.-L.-J. Brière.
Gulacsi, Z. 2009. A Manichaean "Portrait of the Buddha Jesus": Identifying a Twelfth- or Thirteenth-century Chinese Painting From the Collection of Seiun-ji Zen Temple. *Artibus Asiae* 69, no. 1, 91–145.
Halbertsma, T. 2015. *Early Christian Remains of Inner Mongolia: Discovery, Reconstruction and Appropriation.* 2nd ed. Leiden: Brill.
Hambis, L. 1947–50. Notes sur quelques sceaux-amulettes nestoriens en bronze. *Bulletin de l'École Française d'Extrême Orient* 44, 483–518.
———. 1961. Communication: Ak-Bešim et ses sanctuaires. *Comptes-rendus des séances de l'Académie des Inscriptions et Belles-Lettres*, 124–38.
Hamilton, J. 1972. Le texte turc en caractères syriaques du grand sceau cruciforme de Mār Yahballāhā III. *Journal Asiatique* 260, 155–70.
Herrmann, G. 1999. *Monuments of Merv: Traditional Buildings of the Karakum.* London: Society of Antiquaries of London.
Hoenerbach, W. and O. Spies. 1957a. *Ibn aṭ-Ṭaiyib, Fiqh an-Naṣrānīya: "Das Recht der Christenheit" II.* CSCO 167/Ar. 18. Louvain: Imprimerie Orientaliste L. Durbecq.
———. 1957b. *Ibn aṭ-Ṭaiyib, Fiqh an-Naṣrānīya: "Das Recht der Christenheit" II.* CSCO 168/Ar. 19. Louvain: Imprimerie Orientaliste L. Durbecq.
Holmberg, B. 1993. A reconsideration of the Kitāb al-Mağdal. *PdO* XVIII, 255–73.
Howorth, H. H. 1876. *History of the Mongols, From the 9th to the 19th Century, Part III: The Mongols of Persia.* London and New York: Longmans, Green & Co.
Humphreys, R. S. 1990. *The history of al-Ṭabarī: Ta'rīkh al-rusul wa'l-mulūk XV: The Crisis of the Early Caliphate.* Albany: State University of New York Press.
Hunter, E. C. D. 1989/1991. The Conversion of the Kerait to Christianity in A.D. 1007. *Zentralasiatische Studien* 22, 142–63.

———. 2009. The Persian Contribution to Christianity in China: Reflections in the Xi'an Fu Syriac Inscriptions. *In*: D. W. Winkler and L. Tang, ed., *Hidden Treasures and Intercultural Encounters: Studies on East Syriac Christianity in China and Central Asia*. Orientalia – Patristica – Oecumenica 1. Wien: LIT Verlag, 71–85.

Hunter, E. C. D. and M. Dickens 2014. *Syrische Handschriften. Teil 2. Syriac Manuscripts From the Berlin Turfan Collection*. Verzeichnis der Orientalischen Handschriften in Deutschland 5, 2. Stuttgart: Franz Steiner.

Jackson, P. 1990. *The Mission of Friar William of Rubruck: His Journey to the Court of the Great Khan Möngke 1253–1255*. London: Hakluyt Society.

———. 2005. The Mongols and the Faith of the Conquered. *In*: R. Amitai and M. Biran, ed., *Mongols, Turks and Others: Eurasian Nomads and the Sedentary World*. Leiden: Brill, 245–90.

Karmi, G. 1978. A Mediaeval Compendium of Arabic Medicine: Abū Sahl al-Masīḥī's "Book of the Hundred." *Journal for the History of Arabic Science* 2, 270–90.

Klein, W. 2000. *Das nestorianische Christentum an den Handelswegen durch Kyrgyzstan bis zum 14. Jh*. Silk Road Studies III. Turnhout: Brepols.

———. 2004. A Newly Excavated Church of Syriac Christianity Along the Silk Road in Kyrghyzstan. *Journal of Eastern Christian Studies* 56 (Symposium Syriacum VII), 25–47.

Klein, W. and C. Reck. 2004. Ein Kreuz mit sogdischer Inschrift aus Ak-Bešim/Kyrgyzstan. *ZDMG* 154, 147–56.

Klein, W. and J. Tubach. 1994. Ein syrisch-christliches Fragment aus Dunhuang/China. *ZDMG* 144, 1–13, 446.

Klimkeit, H.-J. 1979. Das Kreuzessymbol in der zentralasiatischen Religionsbegegnung. *Zeitschrift für Religions- und Geistesgeschichte* 31, 99–115.

———. 1993. Christian Art on the Silk Road. *In*: T. W. Gaehtgens, ed., *Künstlerischer Austausch. Artistic Exchange: Akten des XXVIII. Internationalen Kongresses für Kunstgeschichte, Berlin, 15.–20. Juli 1992*. Berlin: Akademie Verlag, 477–88.

Kokovtsov, P. K. 1904–1905 [1906]. Xristiansko-sirijskija nadgrobnyja nadpisi iz Almalyka. *Zapiski Vostochnogo Otdelenija Imperatorskogo Russkogo Arkheologicheskogo Obshchestva* 16, 190–200.

Kramers, J. H. and G. Wiet. 1964. *Ibn Hauqal: Configuration de la Terre (Kitab Surat al-Ard)*. 2 vols. Paris: G.-P. Maisonneuve.

Labourt, J. 1904. *De Timotheo I Nestorianorum Patriarcha (728–823) et Christianorum Orientalium condicione sub Chaliphis Abbasidis*. Paris: Victor Lecoffre.

Lala Comneno, M. A. 1997. Nestorianism in Central Asia During the First Millennium: Archaeological Evidence. *Journal of Assyrian Academic Studies* 11, no. 1, 20–69.

Landron, B. 1994. *Chrétiens et Musulmans en Irak: Attitudes Nestoriennes vis-à-vis de l'Islam*. Paris: Cariscript.

Lespinasse, R. de. 1877. *Vie et vertus de saint Louis, d'après Guillaume de Nangis et le confesseur de la reine Marguerite*. Paris: Société Bibliographique.

Le Strange, G. 1905. *The Lands of the Eastern Caliphate: Mesopotamia, Persia, and Central Asia, From the Moslem Conquest to the Time of Timur*. Cambridge: Cambridge University Press.

———. 1919. *The Geographical Part of the Nuzhat-al-Qulūb composed by Ḥamd-Allāh Mustawfī of Qazwīn in 740 (1340)*. Leyden and London: E. J. Brill and Luzac & Co.

Lieu, S. N. C. 2009. Epigraphica nestoriana serica. *In*: W. Sundermann, A. Hintze and F. De Blois, ed., *Exegisti Monumenta: Festschrift in Honour of Nicholas Sims-Williams*. Wiesbaden: Harrassowitz, 227–46.

Lieu, S. N. C., L. Eccles, M. Franzmann, I. Gardner and K. Parry 2012. *Medieval Christian and Manichaean Remains From Quanzhou (Zayton)*. Corpus Fontium Manichaeorum: Series Archaeologica et Iconographica II. Turnhout: Brepols.

Ligeti, L. 1972. Les sept monastères nestoriens de Mar Sargis. *Acta Orientalia Academiae Scientiarum Hungaricae* 26: 169–78.

———. 1981. Prolegomena to the Codex Cumanicus. *Acta Orientalia Academiae Scientiarum Hungaricae* 35: 1–54.

Livshits, V. A. 2006. Sogdijtsy daryat xum nestorianskomu uchitelyu Yarukteginu. *In*: B. Lourié and A. Mouraviev, ed., *Universum Hagiographicum. Mémorial R. P. Michel van Esbroeck, s. j. (1934–2003)*. Scrinium 2. Saint-Petersburg: Byzantinorossica, 365–70.

Lurje, P. 2010. *Personal names in Sogdian texts*. Iranisches Personennamenbuch, Band II, Faszikel 8. Wien: Österreichischen Akademie der Wissenschaften.

Mai, A. 1838. *Scriptorum veterum nova collectio e vaticanis codicibus edita ab A.M., Vol. X*. Rome: Typis Collegi Urbani.

Malek, R. and P. Hofrichter, ed., 2006. *Jingjiao: The Church of the East in China and Central Asia*. Sankt Augustin: Institut Monumenta Serica.

Marino, N. F. 1999. *El libro del conoscimiento de todos los reinos (The Book of Knowledge of All Kingdoms)*. Medieval and Renaissance Texts and Studies 198. Tempe: Arizona Center for Medieval and Renaissance Studies.

Markham, C. R. 1859. *Narrative of the Embassy of R. Gonzalez de Clavijo to the Court of Timour, at Samarcand, A.D. 1403–6*. London: Hakluyt Society.

Marr, N. 1894. Nadgrobnyj kamen' iz Semirechija, s armjansko-sirijskoj nadpisju 1323 g. *Zapiski Vostochnogo Otdelenija Imperatorskogo Russkogo Arkheologicheskogo Obshchestva* 8, 344–9.

Marsone, P. 2013. Two Portraits for One Man: George, King of the Önggüt. *In*: L. Tang and D. W. Winkler, ed., *From the Oxus River to the Chinese Shores: Studies on East Syriac Christianity in Central Asia and China*. Orientalia – Patristica – Oecumenica 5. Wien: LIT Verlag, 225–36.

Martinez, A. P. 1982. Gardīzī's Two Chapters on the Turks. *Archivum Eurasiae Medii Aevi* 2, 109–217.

Massé, H. 1973. *Ibn al-Faqīh al-Hamadānī: Abrégé du livre des pays*. Damascus: Institut Français de Damas.

McCrindle, J. W. 1897. *The Christian Topography of Cosmas, an Egyptian Monk*. London: Hakluyt Society.

Mingana, A. 1922. *The Book of Religion and Empire*. Manchester: University of Manchester Press.

———. 1925. The Early Spread of Christianity in Central Asia and the Far East: A New Document. *BJRL* 9, 297–371.

Minorsky, V. 1942. *Sharaf al-Zamān Ṭāhir Marvazī on China, the Turks and India*. James G. Forlong Fund XXII. London: Royal Asiatic Society.

———. 1970. *Ḥudūd al-'Ālam: 'The Regions of the World'* (2nd ed.). E. J. W. Gibb Memorial Series, N.S. 11. London: Luzac & Co.

Montgomery, J. A. 1927. *The History of Yaballaha III, Nestorian Patriarch, and of His Vicar Bar Sauma*. New York: Columbia University Press.

Moule, A. C., 1930. *Christians in China Before the Year 1550*. London: Society for Promoting Christian Knowledge.

Moule, A. C. and P. Pelliot. 1938. *Marco Polo: The Description of the World, Vol. I*. London: George Routledge & Sons.

Naymark, A. 2001. *Sogdiana, Its Christians and Byzantium: A Study of Artistic and Cultural Connections in Late Antiquity and Early Middle Ages*. Dissertation. Bloomington: Indiana University.

Osawa, T. and H. Takahashi. 2015. Le prince Georges des Önggüt dans les montagnes de l'Altaï de Mongolie: les inscriptions d'Ulaan Tolgoi de Doloon Nuur. *In*: P. G. Borbone and

P. Marsone, ed., *Le christianisme syriaque en Asie centrale et en Chine*. Études syriaques 12. Paris: Geuthner, 257–90.

Ouseley, W. 1800. *The Oriental Geography of Ebn Haukal, an Arabian Traveller of the Tenth Century*. London: Oriental Press.

Paolillo, M. 2006. A Nestorian Tale of Many Cities. *In:* R.Malek and P. Hofrichter, ed., *Jingjiao: The Church of the East in China and Central Asia*. Sankt Augustin: Institut Monumenta Serica, 357–73.

———. 2009. In Search of King George. *In*: D. W. Winkler and L. Tang, ed., *Hidden Treasures and Intercultural Encounters: Studies on East Syriac Christianity in China and Central Asia*. Orientalia – Patristica – Oecumenica 1. Wien: LIT Verlag, 241–55.

Parry, K. 1996. Images in the Church of the East: The Evidence From Central Asia and China. *BJRL* 78, no. 3, 143–62.

———. 2012. Byzantine-Rite Christians (Melkites) in Central Asia in Late Antiquity and the Middle Ages. *Modern Greek Studies, Australia and New Zealand* 16, 91–108.

Paykova, A. V. 1979. The Syrian Ostracon From Panjikant. *LM* 92, 159–69.

Peeters, P. 1946. Observations sur la vie syriaque de Mar Aba, Catholicos de l'église perse (540–552). *Miscellanea Giovanni Mercati, Vol. V*. Studi e Testi 125, 69–112.

Pelliot, P. 1914. Chrétiens d'asie centrale et d'extrême-orient. *T'oung Pao* 15, 623–44.

———. 1931. *Les Mongols et la papauté*. Extrait de la Revue de l'Orient Chrétien. Paris: Librairie Auguste Picard.

———. 1963. *Notes on Marco Polo, Vol. II*. Oeuvres Posthumes de Paul Pelliot. Paris: Imprimerie Nationale.

———. 1973. *Recherches sur les chrétiens d'Asie centrale et d'Extrême-Orient [Vol. 1]*. Oeuvres Posthumes de Paul Pelliot. Paris: Imprimerie Nationale.

Pelliot, P. and J. Dauvillier 1984. *Recherches sur les chrétiens d'Asie centrale et d'Extrême-Orient [Vol.] 2, 1: La Stèle de Si-ngan-fou*. Oeuvres Posthumes de Paul Pelliot. Paris: Éditions de la Fondation Singer-Polignac.

Pelliot, P. and A. Forte 1996. *L'inscription nestorienne de Si-ngan-fou*. Kyoto and Paris: Scuola di Studi sull'Asia Orientale and Collège de France.

Pigoulewsky, N. 1935–1936. Fragments syriaques et syro-turcs de Hara-hoto et de Tourfan. *ROC* 30, 3–46.

Pigulevskaya, N. 1963. Mar Aba I: une page de l'histoire de la civilisation au VIe siècle de l'ère nouvelle. *In: Mélanges d'orientalisme offerts à Henri Massé à l'occasion de son 75ème anniversaire*. Tehran: Tehran University, 327–36.

Powers, D. S. 1989. *The history of al-Ṭabarī: Ta'rīkh al-rusul wa'l-mulūk, Vol. XXIV: The Empire in Transition*. Albany: State University of New York Press.

Pritsak, O. 1982. The Polovcians and Rus. *Archivum Eurasiae Medii Aevi* 2, 321–80.

Raimqulov, A. A. 1999. Korxona – o'rta osiyodagi qadimiy nasroniylar cerkov – monastir. *Istoriia material'noi kul'tury Uzbekistana* 30, 213–22.

———. 2000. Novyje Arxeologicheskije Materialy k Istorii Xristianstva Srednej Azii. *In*: Yu. E. Berezkin, ed., *The Interactions of Cultures and Civilisations: In Honor of V. M. Masson*. St. Petersburg: Russian Academy of Sciences, 232–8.

Rásonyi, L. and I. Baski 2007. *Onomasticon Turcicum: Turkic Personal Names*. 2 vols. Indiana University Uralic and Altaic Series 172/I & II. Bloomington: Indiana University.

Raverty, H. G. 1881. *Tabaḳāt-i-nāṣirī: A General History of the Muḥammadan Dynasties of Asia, Including Hindūstān, From A.H. 194 (810 A.D.), to A.H. 658 (1260 A.D.), Vol. I*. London: Gilbert & Rivington.

Reinink, G. J. 1988. *Gannat Bussame I. Die Adventssonntage*. CSCO 502/Syr. 212. Louvain: E. Peeters.

Rott, P. G. 2006. Christian Crosses From Central Asia. *In*: R. Malek and P. Hofrichter, ed., *Jingjiao: The Church of the East in China and Central Asia*. Sankt Augustin: Institut Monumenta Serica, 395–401.

Ryan, J. D. 1998. Christian Wives of Mongol Khans: Tartar Queens and Missionary Expectations in Asia. *Journal of the Royal Asiatic Society* 8, 411–21.

Sachau, E. 1879. *The Chronology of Ancient Nations*. London: Oriental Translation Fund of Great Britain & Ireland.

———. 1919. Zur Ausbreitung des Christentums in Asien. *In: Abhandlungen der Preussischen Akademie der Wissenschaften, Phil.-hist. Klasse*. Jahrgang 1919, Nr. 1. Berlin: Verlag der Akademie der Wissenschaften.

Savchenko, A. 2010. Östliche Urkirche in Usbekistan. *Antike Welt* 2, 74–82.

Savchenko, A. and M. Dickens 2009. Prester John's Realm: New Light on Christianity Between Merv and Turfan. *In*: E. C. D. Hunter, ed., *The Christian Heritage of Iraq*. Gorgias Eastern Christian Studies 13. Piscataway, NJ: Gorgias Press, 121–35.

Scher, A. 1906. Étude Supplémentaire sur les Écrivains Syriens Orientaux. *ROC* 11, 1–32.

———. 1910. *Histoire Nestorienne (Chronique de Séert), Première Partie (II)*. PO V, Fasc. 2. Paris: Firmin-Didot.

———. 1911. *Histoire Nestorienne (Chronique de Séert), Seconde Partie (I)*. PO VII, Fasc. 2. Paris: Firmin-Didot.

———. 1919. *Histoire Nestorienne (Chronique de Séert), Deuxième Partie (II)*. PO XIII, Fasc. 4. Paris: Firmin-Didot.

Semenov, G. L. 1996. *Studien zur sogdischen Kultur an der Seidenstraße*. Studies in Oriental Religions 36. Wiesbaden: Harrassowitz Verlag.

Sims-Williams, N. 1988 [1989]. Baršabbā. *Encyclopaedia Iranica* 3, 823.

———. 1993. The Sogdian Inscriptions of Ladakh. *In*: K. Jettmar, ed., *Antiquities of Northern Pakistan: Reports and Studies. Rock Carvings and Inscriptions Along the Karakorum Highway* 2. Mainz: Verlag Philipp von Zabern, 151–63.

———. 2012. *Mitteliranische Handschriften: Teil 4. Iranian Manuscripts in Syriac Script in the Berlin Turfan Collection*. Verzeichnis der Orientalischen Handschriften in Deutschland 18, 4. Stuttgart: Franz Steiner.

Sims-Williams, N. and J. Hamilton. 1990. *Documents turco-sogdiens du IX*^{e}*-X*^{e} *siècle de Touen-houang*. Corpus Inscriptorum Iranicarum, Part II, Vol. III. London: School of Oriental and African Studies.

Siouffi, M. 1881. Notice sur un patriarche nestorien. *Journal Asiatique*, Ser. VII, Tom. XVII, 89–96.

Skelton, R. A., T. E. Marston and G. D. Painter. 1965. *The Vinland Map and the Tartar Relation*. New Haven and London: Yale University Press.

Standaert, N. 2001. *Handbook of Christianity in China, Volume One: 635–1800*. Handbuch der Orientalistik IV, 15/1. Leiden: Brill.

Tang, L. 2006. Sorkaktani Beki: A Prominent Nestorian Woman at the Mongol Court. *In*: R. Malek and P. Hofrichter, ed., *Jingjiao: The Church of the East in China and Central Asia*. Sankt Augustin: Institut Monumenta Serica, 349–55.

———. 2009a. A Preliminary Study on the *Jingjiao* Inscription of Luoyang: Text Analysis, Commentary and English Translation. *In*: D. W. Winkler and L. Tang, ed., *Hidden Treasures and Intercultural Encounters: Studies on East Syriac Christianity in China and Central Asia*. Orientalia – Patristica – Oecumenica 1. Wien: LIT Verlag, 109–32.

———. 2009b. Medieval Sources on the Naiman Christians and on Their Prince Küchlüg Khan. *In*: D. W. Winkler and L. Tang, ed., *Hidden Treasures and Intercultural Encounters: Studies on East Syriac Christianity in China and Central Asia*. Orientalia – Patristica – Oecumenica 1. Wien: LIT Verlag, 257–66.

———. 2013. Rediscovering the Ongut King George: Remarks on a Newly Excavated Archaeological Site. *In*: L. Tang and D. W. Winkler, ed., *From the Oxus River to the Chinese Shores: Studies on East Syriac Christianity in Central Asia and China*. Orientalia – Patristica – Oecumenica 5. Wien: LIT Verlag, 255–66.

Tang, L. and D. W. Winkler. 2013. *From the Oxus River to the Chinese Shores: Studies on East Syriac Christianity in Central Asia and China*. Orientalia – Patristica – Oecumenica 5. Wien: LIT Verlag.

Telfer, J. B. 1879. *The Bondage and Travels of Johann Schiltberger, a Native of Bavaria, in Europe, Asia, and Africa, 1396–1427*. London: Hakluyt Society.

Thomson, R. W. 1982. *Eḷishē: History of Vardan and the Armenian War*. Cambridge, MA: Harvard University Press.

Tisserant, E. 1931. L'Eglise Nestorienne. *Dictionnaire de Théologie Catholique* 11, 157–225.

Togan, I. 1998. *Flexibility and Limitation in Steppe Formations: The Kerait Khanate and Chinggis Khan*. The Ottoman Empire and its Heritage 15. Leiden: Brill.

Uray, G. 1983. Tibet's Connections With Nestorianism and Manicheism in the 8th–10th Centuries. *In*: E. Steinkellner and H. Täuscher, ed., *Contributions on Tibetan Language, History, and Culture*. Wiener Studien zur Tibetologie und Buddhismuskunde 11. Wien: Universität Wien, 399–429.

Vosté, J.-M. 1929. Memra en l'honneur de Iahballaha III. *LM* 42, 168–76.

———. 1940a. *Ordo Iudiciorum Ecclesiasticorum, collectus, dispositus, ordinatus et compositus a Mar ʿAbdišoʿ Metropolita Nisibis et Armeniae*. Codificazione Canonica Orientale, Fonti, Serie II – Fascicolo XV. Caldei – Diritto Antico II. Città del Vaticano: Typis Polyglottis Vaticanis.

———. 1940b. *Liber Patrum*. Codificazione Canonica Orientale, Fonti, Serie II – Fascicolo XVI, Caldei – Diritto Antico III. Città del Vaticano: Typis Polyglottis Vaticanis.

Waley, A. 1931. *The Travels of an Alchemist: The Journey of the Taoist Ch'ang-Ch'un From China to the Hindukush at the Summons of Chingiz Khan*. London: George Routledge & Sons.

Wessels, C. 1924. *Early Jesuit Travellers in Central Asia, 1603–1721*. The Hague: Martinus Nijhoff.

Whitby, M. and M. Whitby. 1986. *The History of Theophylact Simocatta*. Oxford: Clarendon.

Whitfield, R. 1982. *The Art of Central Asia: The Stein Collection in the British Museum, Vol. 1: Paintings From Dunhuang, I*. Tokyo: Kodansha.

Wilmshurst, D. 2016. *Bar Hebraeus The Ecclesiastical Chronicle: An English Translation*. Gorgias Eastern Christian Studies 40. Piscataway, NJ: Gorgias Press.

Winkler, D. W. and L. Tang. 2009. *Hidden Treasures and Intercultural Encounters: Studies on East Syriac Christianity in China and Central Asia*. Orientalia – Patristica – Oecumenica 1. Wien: LIT Verlag.

Yakup, A. 2002. On the Interlinear Uyghur Poetry in the Newly Unearthed Nestorian Text. *In:* S.-C. Raschmann and M. Ölmez, ed., *Splitter aus der Gegend von Turfan: Festschrift für Peter Zieme anlässlich seines 60. Geburstags*. Istanbul and Berlin: Safak Matbaacilik, 409–17.

Yaldiz, M., R. D. Gadebusch and R. Hickmann. 2000. *Magische Götterwelten: Werke aus dem Museum für Indische Kunst Berlin*. Berlin: Staatliche Museen zu Berlin – Preußischer Kulturbesitz, Museum für Indische Kunst.

Yoshida, Y. and S. Furukawa (ed.). 2015. 中国江南マニ教絵画研究 [Studies of the Chinese Manichaean paintings of South Chinese origin preserved in Japan]. Kyoto: Rinsen.

Young, W. G. 1974. *Patriarch, Shah and Caliph*. Rawalpindi: Christian Study Centre.

Yule, H. and H. Cordier. 1914. *Cathay and the Way Thither, Vol. III: Missionary Friars – Rashiduddin – Pegolotti – Marignolli*. London: The Hakluyt Society.

———. 1915. *Cathay and the Way Thither, Vol. I: Preliminary Essay*. London: The Hakluyt Society.

———. 1916. *Cathay and the Way Thither, Vol. IV: Ibn Batuta – Benedict Goës – Index*. London: The Hakluyt Society.

Zalesskaja, V. N. 1971. K Voprosu o Datirovke Nekotoryx Grupp Sirijskix Kul'tovyx Predmetov. *Palestinskij Sbornik* 23, no. 86, 84–91.

Zieme, P. 2006. A Cup of Cold Water: Folios of a Nestorian-Turkic Manuscript From Kharakhoto. *In*: R. Malek and P. Hofrichter, ed., *Jingjiao: The Church of the East in China and Central Asia*. Sankt Augustin: Institut Monumenta Serica, 341–5.

———. 2013. Turkic Christianity in the Black City (Xaraxoto). *In*: L. Tang and D. W. Winkler, ed., *From the Oxus River to the Chinese Shores: Studies on East Syriac Christianity in Central Asia and China*. Orientalia – Patristica – Oecumenica 5. Wien: LIT Verlag, 99–104.

———. 2015. *Altuigurische Texte der Kirche des Ostens aus Zentralasien*. Gorgias Eastern Christian Studies 41. Piscataway, NJ: Gorgias Press.

CHAPTER THIRTY-TWO

SYRIAC CHRISTIANITY IN CHINA

Hidemi Takahashi

INTRODUCTION

There have been two main periods in which Christians using Syriac as their liturgical language were present in significant numbers in the traditionally Han Chinese areas of China, under the rule of the Tang Dynasty (618–907) and under the rule of the Mongols, who began their conquest of the core areas of China in the first half of the thirteenth century and later founded the Yuan Dynasty (1271–1368). The official Chinese records from the early Tang period refer to Christianity in China as the religion of Persia (*Bosi* 波斯) and, after 745, as that of the Roman (or Byzantine) Empire (*Da Qin* 大秦), while the Christians themselves called their religion *Jingjiao* 景教, a term which is usually understood to mean the 'religion of light', although a recent suggestion by Lieu (2013: 133–7, 2014: 374–6) associates the name with the usual Middle Persian term for 'Christian', *tarsāg* (lit. '(God) fearer'), giving it the meaning 'religion of fear/awe'. Under the Yuan, the Christians in China were normally referred to in Chinese as the *Yelikewen* 也里可温, a term whose origin remains a mystery (Tang 2011: 53–7). The majority of the Christians present in China during the Tang period were evidently of Iranian origin and speakers of such languages as Persian and Sogdian, while the Christians under Mongol rule were for the most part speakers of Turkic languages. There was probably never any widespread knowledge of the Syriac language among the Christians in China, but during both periods the community of Syriac-rite Christians, who were mostly, if not exclusively, members of the Church of the East, maintained its ties with the mother Church in the West, and thus constituted an important, if somewhat unusual, branch of that church and of the world of Syriac Christianity.

The academic study of Syriac Christianity in China has a long history going back at least to the discovery of the famous Xi'an Stele in 1625 (cf. Ferreira 2014: 7–44), but it is also a field that has seen rapid advances in the past few decades.[1] In what follows, an attempt will be made to provide an outline of what we know about the history of Syriac Christianity in China, highlighting in the process some of the more important new findings.

SYRIAC CHRISTIANITY IN CHINA IN THE TANG PERIOD

Principal sources

Sources composed by the Syriac Christians in the Middle East give us varying accounts of the earliest Christian missions to China. The tradition of making St Thomas the apostle of China (cf. Nicolini-Zani 2006: 84–6), which appears in such East Syrian sources as Ibn al-Ṭayyib's *Fiqh al-naṣrānīya* (ed. Hoenerbach and Spies 1956–57: II.138), ʿAbdīshōʿ bar Brīkā's *Nomocanon* (Mai 1838: 317a), and the Chaldean breviary, may have originated as early as the late Sasanian period (Tubach 1995/96). Although it is possible that individual Christians travelling along the Silk Road reached China before the seventh century, there is little historical evidence to support the tradition reported by ʿAbdīshōʿ (*Nomocanon*, 304a) which credits the Church of the East catholicoi Aḥā I (410–414) and Shīlā (503–523) with the erection of a metropolitan see for China. ʿAbdīshōʿ himself gives the credit to Ṣlībā Zkā (714–728), while Īshōʿyahb (probably Īshōʿyahb III, 649–659) is given the honour by Ibn al-Ṭayyib (*Fiqh al-naṣrānīya*, II.121). The existence of a metropolitan see for China in the time of Timothy I (780–823) is assured by his letter mentioning the death of a 'metropolitan of Bēt Ṣīnāyē' (Letter 13, Braun 1914: text 109, trans. 72) and by the report by Thomas of Marga, told on the authority of Timothy, of David, a monk of the monastery of Bēt ʿAbē, being elected metropolitan for Bēt Ṣīnāyē (*Book of Governors*, Budge 1893: text 238, trans. 448).

For a more detailed account of the history of Syriac Christianity in China during the Tang period, we are naturally reliant on Chinese literary sources and other monuments discovered in China. The Chinese sources based on the official records of the period occasionally refer to the Christians. More substantial information, however, is to be gained from the materials left by the Christians themselves, the most important of such items being the Xi'an Stele, often referred to in the past as the 'Nestorian Stele' and more properly called *Da Qin Jingjiao liuxing Zhongguo bei* 大秦景教流行中國碑 ('Monument on the propagation of the Religion of the Light of Da Qin in China'). The main Chinese text of the monument, which was originally erected in 781 and has been the subject of much study since its rediscovery on the western outskirts of the former Tang capital Chang'an (modern Xi'an) in 1625, contains an exposition of the teachings of *Jingjiao* and an account of its history in China since the arrival of Aluoben, followed at the end by an eulogy of Yisi 伊斯/Yazdbōzīd, the sponsor of the Stele, and a summary in verse of the preceding historical account. The Chinese text is accompanied by a brief Syriac text recording the circumstances of the erection of the monument, as well as a list of the clerics present in China at the time, in Syriac and in Chinese (Figures 32.1–2).

Beyond those on the Xi'an Stele and the Luoyang Pillar mentioned below, the only other extant literary texts composed by the Christians in Tang China are to be found in the documents which were, or are purported to have been, discovered in Dunhuang in the early part of the twentieth century (cf. Deeg 2015: 204–12):

1 *Xuting Mishisuo jing* 序聽迷詩所經 ('Book of Jesus-Messiah' or 'Book of listening to the Messiah')

Figure 32.1 Xi'an Stele

Source: © University of Birmingham 2008

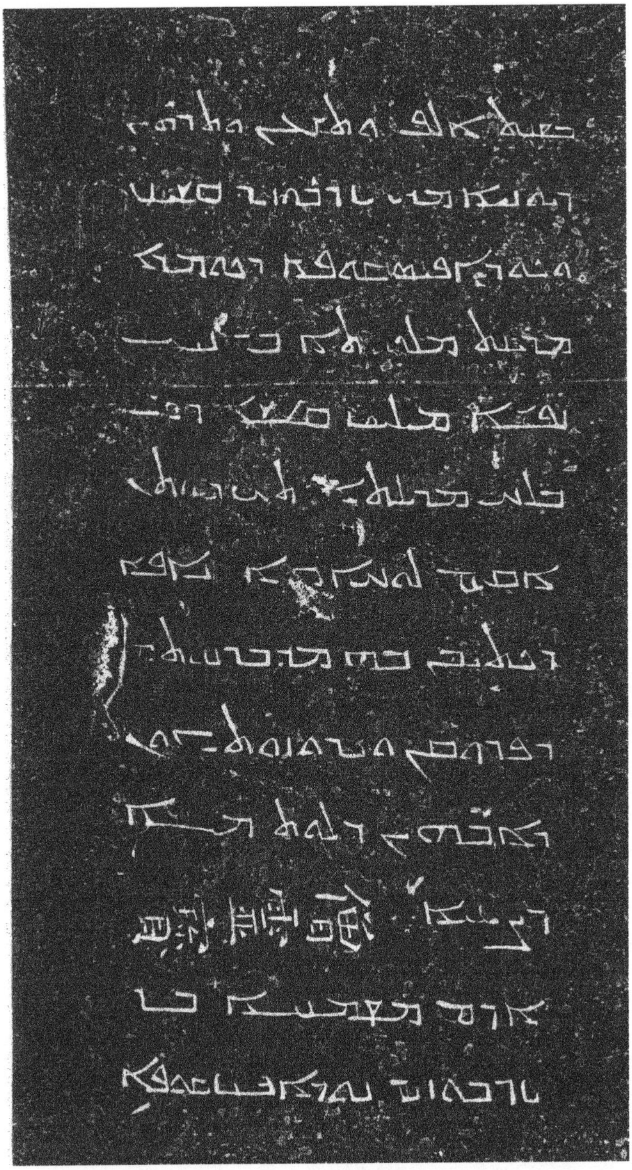

Figure 32.2 Xi'an Stele donor statement

2 *Yishenlun* 一神論 ('Discourse on the One God', consisting of three treatises)
3 *Da Qin Jingjiao Sanwei mengdu zan* 大秦景教三威蒙度讚 ('Hymn in adoration of the Holy Trinity')
4 *Zunjing* 尊經 ('Book of Honour' or [list of] 'Venerable books')
5 *Zhixuan anle jing* 志玄安樂經 ('Book on attaining profound peace and joy')
6a Beginning of *Da Qin Jingjiao Xuanyuan zhiben jing* 大秦景教宣元至本經 ('Book of proclamation of the highest origin of origins')

6b End of *Da Qin Jingjiao Xuanyuan zhiben jing*
7 *Da Qin Jingjiao Dasheng tongzhen guifa zan* 大秦景教大聖通真歸法讚 ('Hymn of praise for the Transfiguration of Our Lord')

Of these documents, nos. 3 and 4 are found together in a single manuscript now in Paris (Bibliothèque national, Pelliot chinois 3847). Of the remaining manuscripts, nos. 1, 2, 5, and 6a are now in the Kyōu Shooku library in Osaka.[2] The remaining two documents (6b and 7), missing today, are now considered to be forgeries. While some doubt has been cast also on the authenticity of the items now in Osaka (especially nos. 1 and 2), it is generally agreed that these manuscripts, even if they are later copies, contain texts which were originally composed in the Tang period.

Important information on Christianity in China is sometimes also provided by inscriptions. To the funerary inscriptions which have been known for some time, a number of new additions have been made since the turn of the twenty-first century in the area around Luoyang, the former eastern capital of the Tang. The first and foremost of these is the octagonal pillar (Figures 32.3–6), resembling in its form the Buddhist *dhāraṇī* pillars, whose discovery was announced in 2006, and which, though now missing its lower parts, bears a text of *Xuanyuan zhiben jing* complementing the incomplete text of the same piece found in the Dunhuang manuscript (no. 6a above), as well a historical note recording the circumstances of its erection apparently in 814/5 and its removal to another location in 829 (Ge 2009; Tang 2009; Nicolini-Zani 2009). This has since been followed by the discovery, in 2009, of a Christian burial niche at the north-western end of the famous Longmen Grottoes (Jiao 2013; Zhang and Zheng 2014; Wenzel-Teuber 2014), as well as by that of the epitaphs, unearthed in 2010, of an apparently Christian court official by the name of Hua Xian 花獻 (d. 827) and his wife An shi 安氏 (Mao 2014; Wu 2014–15; id. 2015a: 217–36; id. 2015b: 247–66; Fukushima 2016; cf. Tang 2016, expressing doubts on the authenticity of the epitaphs).

History of the Church in China during the Tang period

The history of Christianity in Tang-period China as recounted in the Xi'an Stele begins with the arrival of Aluoben 阿羅本 in Chang'an in 635. From the Xi'an Stele, as well as the transcript of the official record in *Tang huiyao* (*juan* 49, p. 864), we learn that in 638 Aluoben was granted permission by emperor Taizong (626–649) to establish a monastery in Chang'an after an examination of his teachings. For the imperial authorities to examine the doctrines of the new religion, materials must have been made available in Chinese, and it is often assumed that two of the Jingjiao documents from Dunhuang, *Xuting Mishisuo jing* and *Yishenlun* (nos. 1 and 2 in the list above), which share an unpolished Chinese style and are more 'biblical' in content than the other Jingjiao documents, were among the materials presented to the imperial court on that occasion. *Yishenlun*, in fact, refers to the passage of 'not quite 641 years' since the Incarnation (col. 366; trans. Saeki 1937: 226; Tang 2002: 179; Nicolini-Zani 2006: 260). Syriac authors give different dates for the birth of Christ (Bernhard 1969: 119–25), but if the author of *Yishenlun* placed it in December 307 A.Gr. (6 BC), like Īshōʿdād of Merv (fl. ca. 850; ed. Gibson 1911: II.25), this would allow

Figure 32.3 Luoyang Pillar

Source: Megumi Fukushima

us to date the composition of the work to 947 A.Gr. (AD 635/6), just when Aluoben and his collaborators would have been preparing such a work.

The original language and form of the name 'Aluoben' remains unclear; suggestions include the Syriac honorific title *rabban* and Persian Ardābān (Nicolini-Zani 2006: 103; Takahashi 2008: 639). *Tang huiyao* describes him as a monk from Persia (*Bosi*), and it is quite possible that he was sent to China from the Sasanian court. It appears that Christianity in the form brought to China by Aluoben was conceived of by the authorities there for a long time as a 'Persian' religion, since it was only by an edict issued in 745 that the Christian monasteries in Chang'an and Luoyang,

Figure 32.4 Luoyang Pillar detail

Source: Megumi Fukushima

Figure 32.5 Luoyang Pillar detail

Source: Megumi Fukushima

Figure 32.6 Rubbing of the inscription from the Luoyang Pillar (first four sides)

formerly called 'Persian monasteries', were renamed 'Da Qin monasteries' (Forte 1996a: 353–5).

As was the case with the St Thomas Christians in India, the Syriac Christians in China were placed under the jurisdiction of bishops sent to them from the centre of the Church in Mesopotamia. In the list of clerics on the Xi'an Stele, the same person is called Mār Yōḥannān the bishop (*episqōpā*) in Syriac and *dade* Yaolun 大德曜輪 in Chinese, whence it is assumed that the term *dade*, originally a Buddhist title, is used there as equivalent to 'bishop' (or 'metropolitan'). Besides Yaolun, the historical section of the text of the Stele names three persons as *dade*: Aluoben, Jilie 及烈 ('Gabriel'), and Jihe 佶和 (probably an abbreviated transcription of 'Gīwargīs/George'), the last of whom arrived in China in 744.

The text of the Stele indicates that Jilie, together with the 'head-of-monks' (僧首, abbot?) Luohan 羅含, was responsible for the revival of the Church in China in the first half of the eighth century after it had come under attack from the Buddhists and 'lowly scholars' (probably Daoists; Deeg 2015: 202f.) at the end of the seventh century and at the beginning of the eighth. Jilie of the Xi'an Stele is no doubt to be identified with the 'Persian monk Jilie' who appears in the Chinese sources in connection with an event that took place in 714,[3] as well as the '*dade* monk Jilie' who arrived in Chang'an in 732 in the company of Pannami 潘那密, an envoy of the 'King of Persia'.[4] The record for 714 tells us how the palace censor Liu Ze 柳澤 (d. 734) admonished the emperor against accepting the 'articles full of strange devices and wonderful designs' (奇器異巧) which Zhou Qingli 周慶立, the commissioner for maritime trade in Lingnan 嶺南, had prepared together with Jilie in Guangzhou (Canton). We are unfortunately left in the dark about the exact nature of these strange and wonderful devices, but the record is highly interesting in suggesting the use of the southern sea route as an alternative to the land route by Christians travelling to China in this period (cf. Luo 1966: 71–86). The record for 732 underscores again the association of the Christians in China with Persia, or rather with the Persian elite in exile in Central Asia. It will be remembered in this connection that Pērōz, the son of the last Sasanian king Yazdegerd III (632–651), who sought refuge in China and who in 677 made a request for a second Christian monastery to be built in Chang'an (Forte 1996a: 355; Riboud 2015: 55), had been granted the title of 'King of Persia' by emperor Gaozong in 662 and was succeeded in that title by his son Narses, who, after his unsuccessful attempt to regain the land ruled by his forefathers, spent over twenty years in Tokharistan (Bactria) before returning to China in 708 (Forte 1996b: 403–5), and that frequent embassies from 'Persia' to China are mentioned even after 732, especially in the years leading up to 751.[5]

The situation on the western peripheries of the Tang Empire underwent a major change between Narses's time and the erection of the Xi'an Stele in 781, especially with the decisive victory of the Arabs at the Battle of Talas River in 751, but the connection of the Christian community in China with Tokharistan is still evidenced in the Stele by the fact that its sponsor Yisi/Yazdbōzīd, a former military commander turned cleric, was a native of Balkh in Tokharistan. Another interesting fact about the group of people responsible for the Stele is that Jingjing/Adam, the author of the text of the Stele, is reported to have collaborated with the Buddhist monk Prajñā, a recent arrival from Kāpiśī (the region around Kabul), in translating the Buddhist *Six Pāramitās Sutra* into Chinese in around 782 (Takakusu 1896). On the basis of a detailed examination of the people associated with the project, Nakata (2011) suggests that this seemingly unusual collaboration between Buddhist and Christian clerics was promoted by the ascendant political faction in the capital led by the eunuchs in command of the Imperial Guard (禁軍), who sought to enlist the support of the Central Asian émigrés forced from their land by the advances made by the ʿAbbasids.

The latter group, including Sogdians and Bactrians, as well as those from south of the Hindu Kush, would have counted among them both Buddhists and Christians, so that it would have been expedient to promote an alliance between the two religious groups. If the people behind the erection of the Stele were members of an anti-ʿAbbasid coalition, this may also help explain why the text of the Stele, erected in 781, names Ḥnānīshōʿ II (773–779/8) as the head of the church, rather than Timothy I, who was made catholicos with the backing of the caliphate (Deeg 2016).

Besides the text of the Xi'an Stele, four of the Christian documents discovered in Dunhuang, *Sanwei mengdu zan*, *Zunjing*, *Zhixuan anle jing*, and *Xuanyuan zhiben jing* (nos. 3–6 in the list above) are generally thought to be the work of either Jingjing or a group of people working under his direction. It has long been noted that these texts are peppered with Buddhist terminology and generally have a much stronger Buddhist colouring than the two Jingjiao texts that are believed to date from the seventh century. Of the four texts, *Sanwei mengdu zan* is a paraphrase of the Greater Doxology (*Gloria in excelsis Deo*), but the others have no known counterparts in Syriac or any other Christian literature, and although their content is recognisably Christian, in their form they have been found to be modelled on the Buddhist texts of the period (Nicolini-Zani 2006: 166–71). In translating Christian concepts into Chinese, it was perhaps inevitable that one should avail oneself of the vocabulary created by another foreign religion that had arrived in China some centuries earlier (Nicolini-Zani 2006: 180), but if, as has been suggested, the project Jingjing was involved in was aimed at forging an alliance between the Buddhists and the Christians, that would give us an additional explanation for the Buddhist colouring of the texts associated with him.

The texts associated with Jingjing, and the Xi'an Stele in particular, provide us with a snapshot, as it were, of the Church in China in the latter half of the eighth century. We have little information about the situation of the Church in the years after 781. A hint of the activities of a Christian monk in China in the first half of the ninth century is provided by *Youyang zazu* 酉陽雜俎, an encyclopaedic work compiled by Duan Chengshi 段成式 (803–863), where we are given, on the basis apparently of information provided by a monk from the land of Fulin 拂林 ('Rome') called either Luan or Wan (鸞/彎), the properties of a number of plants that grow outside of China with their names in the languages of Bosi (Persia) and Fulin.[6] Nine, at least, out of the eleven 'Fulin' names given there can be identified as transcriptions of Syriac plant names. Whether he was a Melkite (from the Melkite community in Central Asia), as has been argued by Lin Ying (2006: 41–51; 2007), or a member of the Church of the East, as would appear more likely, the monk Luan/Wan who was able to inform Duan Chengshi of these plant names in Syriac and Persian is likely to have been a cleric of a Syriac-rite church.

The accounts of the history of Christianity in Tang China usually come to an end with the imperial edict of 845. Although emperor Wuzong's edict proscribing 'foreign religions' was aimed primarily at Buddhists, it was to have a more devastating effect on the smaller 'foreign' religions in China, including Christianity, as well as Manichaeism and Zoroastrianism. When combined with other factors, such as the increasing political instability of the late Tang period and the resultant difficulty of travel along the Silk Road, as well as the weakening of the mother Church in the West, it was to lead to the disappearance of Christianity from China in any organised form in the following centuries.

The Christian community in China during the Tang period

The Christian community in China during the Tang period probably consisted mainly of Iranian immigrants from Central Asia. The official Chinese records tend, as we have seen, to emphasise the Persian connection of the Church, and this link with Persia is also evidenced by the Persian names borne by the clerics mentioned on the Xi'an Stele, such as Yazdbōzīd, Māhdād-Gushnāsp, Mshīḥādād, Īzadspās, and Gīgōy. The Iranian element is also reflected in the words of Iranian origin that appear in the Chinese Jingjiao documents (Takahashi 2014b: 335, 338). While some of these words could be either Persian or Sogdian, as in the case of 達娑 (LMC tɦat-sa, 'Christian')[7] of the Xi'an Stele (cf. Middle Pers. tarsāg, Sogd. tarsāk), two, at least, are better interpreted as transcriptions from Sogdian (糸怒 LMC ʂəm-nuǝ̆, 'Satan', Sogd. šmnw; 耀森文 LMC jiaw-ʂəm-ʋjyn, 'Sunday', Christian Sogd. ywšmbd) (Yoshida 2017: 159–162; id. forthcoming). A further probable instance of transcription from Sogdian is 岑穩僧 of *Zunjing* (LMC tʂɦəm-ʔun səə̆ŋ; also 岑穩僧伽 in *Zhixuan anle jing*, col. 12f.) which has been interpreted to represent the Sogdian name for 'Simon Peter' (Šamγōn Sang, where *sang* = 'stone/rock', cf. Syr. Šemʿōn Kēpā). This Sogdian component of the community is something that has come into greater evidence through the recent discoveries in Luoyang, with all the persons named in the 'dhāraṇī' pillar bearing family names associated with cities in Sogdiana, and with the character 石 read above the burial niche in the Longmen Grottoes suggesting a connection with Shiguo 石國 (Čāč/Tashkent).

The mention of a 'teacher of reading' (*maqryānā*) on the Xi'an Stele indicates that there was provision for teaching of the reading of the scriptures, presumably in Syriac. We do not know in what language the liturgy was normally celebrated. Of the documents discovered in Dunhuang, *Sanwei mengdu zan*, a paraphrase, as mentioned above, of the Greater Doxology, is written in verse, and was undoubtedly intended to be sung in the liturgy, while some of the titles of the texts mentioned in *Zunjing*, such as *Wushana-jing* 烏沙郍經 ('Hosanna sutra') and *Shilihai-jing* 師利海經 ('Apostle sutra', i.e. the book of Pauline readings), are suggestive of liturgical usage, so that it is likely that part, at least, of the liturgy was being celebrated in Chinese.

As regards the geographical spread of the Christian communities (cf. Nicolini-Zani 2006: 112–23), when the Xi'an Stele tells us that emperor Gaozong (650–683) ordered Christian monasteries to be constructed in every prefecture of the land, of which there were approximately 360, that is clearly to be taken as an exaggeration. More credence can be given to the passage of the Stele telling us that emperor Suzong (756–762) ordered monasteries to be built in five commanderies (*jun* 郡) including Lingwu 靈武 (in present-day Ningxia), and it seems likely that there were Christian communities, besides those in Chang'an and Luoyang, in at least some of the cities along the Silk Road. The presence of Christians in Guangzhou on the southern coast of China in a relatively early period is suggested by the sojourn of Jilie there mentioned above, while the existence of a community there at a later date is indicated by al-Sīrāfī (see below). A possible presence of Christians elsewhere in China is suggested, for example, by the epitaph of An Yena 安野郍 in Guilin (Luo 1966: 87–96; Yoshida 1996: 75; cf. Du 2013: I.7), even if her identification as a Christian may require some further corroboration.

The titles borne by the clerics on the Xi'an Stele give us an idea of the ecclesiastical organisation of the community (cf. Nicolini-Zani 2006: 101–5; Riboud 2015: 53). Besides bishop Yōḥannān/*dade* Yaolun, we seem to have three chorepiscopoi (Yazdbōzīd/Yisi, Adam/Jingjing, and Mār Sargīs/Jingtong 景通, the last apparently named twice), and two archdeacons, one of them, Gabriel/Yeli 業利, bearing the additional title of the 'head of the church of Kumdan (Chang'an) and Sarag (Luoyang)' in Syriac and of 'temple-lord' (*sizhu* 寺主, 'abbot'?) in Chinese, and the other, Gīgōy/Xuanlan 玄覧, styled 'archdeacon of Kumdan and teacher of reading'. Two originally Buddhist Chinese titles transcribed into Syriac are given to two of the chorepiscopoi, Adam who was 'P'PŠY (*fashi* 法師, lit. 'law-master') of Ṣinistan', and Mār Sargīs who was 'ŠY'NGTSW'' (*shangzuo* 上座, lit. 'upper-seat', corresponding to Sanskrit *sthavīra*, 'elder'). The Stele names twenty-five other priests, four of whom have the additional title of 'solitary' (*īḥīdāyā*), while one is called the 'priest of the tomb' and another 'priest and elder' (*sābā*). We also have two deacons, one of them being Adam, the son of Yazdbōzīd, the other a 'deacon and solitary', as well as a sacristan (*qanqāyā*). In most cases the Syriac names are followed by Chinese names, prefixed almost invariably with the Chinese title 'monk' (*seng* 僧), with the exception of the bishop, *dade* Yaolun, and the priest Yaʿqōb/Yejumo 耶俱摩, who also differs from others in having a three-character Chinese name and who has the Chinese title of *laosu* 老宿, a term used in Buddhist Chinese, like *shangzuo*, as equivalent of *sthavīra*, 'elder'. The title *seng* is attached also to those who bear no ecclesiastical titles in Syriac. It may be that these people were bearers only of minor orders.

Precious information on the lay community surrounding the monastery (or monasteries) in Chang'an is provided by two funerary inscriptions originally discovered, respectively, in 1955 and 1980. The first is that of Mi Jifen 米繼芬 (714–805), a military officer, whose father had been sent to China from Miguo (米國, Māymurgh) in Sogdiana as a 'hostage', and whose elder son followed him into service in the imperial army, while his younger son Siyuan 思圓 (or Huiyuan 惠圓), the inscription tells us, 'lived in the Da Qin monastery' (Ge and Nicolini-Zani 2004). The other is the epitaph of Li Wenzhen 李文貞 (Li Su 李素, 744–817), whose grandfather, scion of a Sasanian aristocratic family, had come to China likewise as a hostage, and who himself worked as an astronomer in the imperial observatory. This Li Wenzhen is most likely to be the same person as the 'monk Wenzhen/Lūqā' mentioned, without any ecclesiastical title in Syriac, on the Xi'an Stele (Rong 2001; cf. Nicolini-Zani 2006: 77, 103, 110). The two inscriptions serve to confirm the Persian and Sogdian origin of the Christian community in China. The epitaph of Mi Jifen, together with the case of Yazdbōzīd, underscores the military connections of the community, while that of Li Wenzhen is of note in suggesting how these Christians, as in the case also of Luan/Wan of *Youyang zazu*, might have been appreciated for their scientific knowledge in China (cf. Nicolini-Zani 2006: 108f.).

The Christians in China after 845

We have little knowledge of the fate of the Christians in China after the events of 845. The mention by Abū Zayd al-Sīrāfī (*Silsilat al-tawārīkh*, Reinaud 1845: text 63, trans. 63) of Christians (*naṣārā*), alongside Muslims, Jews, and Zoroastrians, among the groups massacred in Guangzhou during the rebellion of Huang Chao in 878/9 suggests that a Christian community still existed in that city at that date. From the end of the tenth century, we have the account of a Najrānī monk who had been sent to China by the catholicos around 970 and had found that the Christian community there had vanished save for one man (Ibn al-Nadīm, *Fihrist*, ed. Flügel 1872: II.349, trans. Dodge 1970: 837).

One recent discovery throws important further light on the possible afterlife of Christian communities in China. Among the Chinese Manichaean documents discovered in Xiapu County 霞浦縣 in northern Fujian in 2008 (Kósa 2013/14; Ma 2015) is a piece entitled *Jisizhou* 吉思呪 (text in Lin 2014: 471f.; images in id. 2015: 130f.; see also Ma Xiaohe 2016; Wang and Lin 2018). 'Jisi' in the title is a shortened form of Yihuojisi 移活吉思, which in turn is a Chinese rendition of the name 'George/Gīwargīs', or rather probably of 'Yiwarkis', evidently a vernacular form of the name attested in Sogdian and Turkic documents from Dunhuang and Turfan (Sims-Williams and Hamilton 1990: 64f., 68; Reck 2006: 274; Zieme 2015: 38, 188). The prayer is based on the Acts of St George, and its contents show a close affinity in particular with the Syriac and Sogdian versions of the Acts. It is unclear when and how this Christian prayer became part of the Manichaean tradition, but if, as suggested by Ma (2014: 365, 375f.), the work called *Qisijing* 訖思經 which appears in a list of Manichaean books proscribed by the authorities in 1120 (*Song huiyao jigao*, ed. 1957: 6534) is related to our piece, it would indicate that the story of St George had become a part of the Manichaean tradition before that date, and this in turn suggests that some descendants of the Tang-period Christians had been absorbed by the middle of the Song period into the Manichaean community, bringing with them the story of one of their beloved saints.

SYRIAC CHRISTIANITY IN CHINA IN THE MONGOL PERIOD

Sources and relics

Sources available for the history of Syriac Christianity in China during the Yuan period are more diverse than those available for the Tang period. Much information on the more important Christian figures and on the status of the Christians under Yuan rule is to be gathered from the principal Chinese sources based on official records such as the *Yuanshi* 元史 and *Yuan Dianzhang* 元典章 (van Mechelen 2001: 43f.). A particularly interesting account of the Christians in and around Zhenjiang, an important commercial centre on the Yangtze River, is provided by *Zhishun Zhenjiangzhi* 至順鎮江志, the local gazetteer of the area compiled in the Zhishun era (1330–1333). Of the European sources, the accounts left by the Latin missionaries, such as William of Rubruck (1220–1293) and John of Montecorvino (1247–1328), along with the *Travels* of Marco Polo (1254–1324), provide important information on the Syriac-rite Christians they encountered in China (van Mechelen 2001: 46–51; Tang 2011: 9–14). Among the sources composed in the Middle East, the Persian histories of Juwaynī (*Tārīkh-i jahān-gushā*) and Rashīd al-Dīn (*Jāmiʿ al-tawārīkh*) are of relevance. The most important Syriac source is the *History of Mar Yahbalāhā*, the first part of which gives us an account of the journey of Rabban Ṣawmā and the monk Marqōs, the future catholicos Yahbalāhā III (1281–1317), from their home in China to the Middle East.

Unlike in the Tang period, we have no indication of Syriac-rite Christians composing specifically Christian texts in Chinese in the Yuan period, although a number of scholars who were either Christians or of Christian descent played a significant role in the Chinese literary scene of the day, including the Önggüt-born Zhao Shiyan 趙世延 (1257–1336) and Ma Zuchang 馬祖常 (1278–1338) (see Ch'ên 1966), as well as Jin Hala 金哈剌 (Jin Yuansu 金元素, d. after 1368), a collection of whose poems has only relatively recently been re-discovered (Xiao 1995; Duan 2010).

The language used in the vast majority of the relics left behind by the Syriac-rite Christians is Turkic, usually written in Syriac characters ('Syro-Turkic'). Such relics, funerary inscriptions for the most part, have been discovered in Inner Mongolia, near Beijing, and in two cities in the south-east of China, Yangzhou 揚州, on the Yangtze opposite Zhenjiang, and Quanzhou 泉州, the main maritime port city of China in this period.

A large number of Christian gravestones have been found in the northern part of the former Önggüt territory in Inner Mongolia, especially in and around Olan Süme, the northern capital of the Önggüt (Halbertsma 2005; Niu 2006; id. 2008: 67–102). The finds from Olan Süme include the bilingual epitaph of Abraham Tömüras (dated 1327), a former military governor (*daruyači*) of Jingzhaofu 京兆府 (Xi'an), in Chinese and Turkic, with the Turkic text written twice in Syriac and Uighur characters. Another relatively long epitaph from Olan Süme, dated 1290, has the opening Trinitarian formula in Syriac, but is otherwise in Syro-Turkic. Apart from these two, the remaining gravestones bear only short inscriptions, usually simply stating the name and title of the buried. Among the large number of graffiti left by the pilgrims in the 'White Pagoda' (Wangbu Huayangjing ta 萬部華嚴經塔) (Figure 32.7) on the site of Fengzhou 豐州, the southern capital of the Önggüt, on the eastern outskirts of Köke Qota (Hohhot), we find at least seven inscriptions in Syro-Turkic left by the priest Särgis (Borbone 2013; cf. Zieme 2015: 175f.), as well as a recently discovered inscription left by a group of five pilgrims, two of whom had the clearly Christian names of Pilipoẓ ('Philip') and Yušimut ('Sunday', cf. Zieme 2015: 188–91). The main part of this inscription, recording the visit of the five in Turkic in Uighur script, is followed by several words in Syriac, including *ʿabdāk* 'your servant' and what is probably the beginning of the name *Pīlīpōs* (Bai and Matsui 2016; Matsui 2016: 289).[8]

From Chifeng 赤峰, further east in Inner Mongolia, we have the epitaph of the military commander Yawnan (d. 1253) (Hamilton and Niu 1994; Wang 2000), whose family may have come from Almalïq (Ma Xiaolin 2016). The text of this epitaph is in Uighur script, but above the main text is a cross surrounded by the words of Psalm 34:6 in Syriac. The same verse of the Psalms is also quoted on one of the two stone blocks with crosses found at the 'Temple of the Cross' 十字寺 in Fangshan 房山 to the south-west of Beijing (Borbone 2006ab), as well as on a bronze mirror bearing a cross recently found in Inner Mongolia and now in the National Museum in Beijing (Niu 2017). As has been suggested by Borbone (2006b: 9f.), these words of the Psalms may have been copied, together with the cross, from an illustration in a Gospel manuscript.

From southern China, we have two gravestones from Yangzhou, one without any remaining inscription discovered in 1929 in the grounds of the mausoleum of the Muslim *sayyid* Puhadin 普哈丁/Bahāʾ al-Dīn (Saeki 1935: 964–8; id. 1937: 434f.; Guo 2014), and the bilingual Turkic-Chinese gravestone of Elizabeth (Yelishiba 也里世八,

Figure 32.7 Newly-Discovered Inscription in the White Pagoda near Hohhot

Source: Dai Matsui

d. 1317) discovered in 1981 (Geng et al. 1996; Franzmann 2013), as well as a large number of gravestones from Quanzhou (Wu 2005: 365–440; Lieu et al. 2012). Around twenty of the Syriac-rite Christian gravestones from Quanzhou have inscriptions. One of them, that of bishop Mār Shlēmōn (d. 1313), is bilingual in Syro-Turkic and Chinese (Lieu et al. 2012: 206–9; Franzmann 2015); nine others are in Syro-Turkic, while one is in Uighur script (Lieu et al. 2012: 131–3), and the rest are in Chinese, either in Chinese characters or in Phagspa.

It is to be assumed that there were Syriac manuscripts in circulation in China during the Yuan period, even luxury ones, as is suggested by Marco Polo's account of Qubilai Khan having the Christians bring him a book of the Gospels for a ceremony at Easter in Khanbaliq (Ramusio 1559: 20F; trans. Moule and Pelliot 1938: I.201; cf. Hage 1978: 140). One such luxury manuscript which, however, probably never reached China, is the Gospel manuscript copied in gold ink for the Önggüt Christian princess Sarā (Ärä'öl/Äroġul/Yeliwan 葉里彎/也里完, d. 1306) in 1298 (MS. Vatican, syr. 622, olim Diyarbakır 9 Scher; see Borbone 2003; id. 2015b: 227). Only a small number of Syriac and Syro-Turkic manuscripts that are likely to have been in use in and around the core area of China in the Mongol period have come down to us, all of them in a fragmentary state. These include the two liturgical fragments in Syriac from Dunhuang, discovered, respectively, some time before 1991 (Klein and Tubach 1994; cf. Kaufhold 1996) and in 1995 (Duan 2001), as well as the liturgical and para-liturgical fragments in Syriac and Syro-Turkic from Qara Qota (Kharakhoto) (Smelova 2015; Muto 2016). Another liturgical fragment, now lost, was discovered around 1925 in a room above the southern gate (*Wumen* 午門) of the Forbidden City in Beijing (Saeki 1935: 751–90; id. 1937: 315–33; Taylor 1941). What by all appearances is another fragment of the same manuscript has recently been located in the library of the Academia Sinica in Taipei (Muraviev 2012; Zieme 2015: 147f.; cf. Tang 2015: 81f., n. 61). The material preserved in the Taipei fragment includes a part of the marriage rite (rite of consent) in New Persian written in Syriac characters, as well as marginal glosses giving liturgical instructions in Uighur in Uighur script, suggesting that the owner of the manuscript was an Uighur-speaking cleric who might sometimes have had occasion to officiate in the marriage of Persian speakers.

Some aspects and personalities of Christianity in Mongol-period China

The re-emergence of Syriac-rite Christianity in China in the thirteenth century is largely due to the Mongol conquest of the land. The Mongol rulers themselves were not Christians, but they were closely allied, often through marriage, with a number of Turkic-speaking tribes, such as the Kereit and the Önggüt, who had been Christianised in an earlier period through the missionary activities mainly of the Church of the East. The Mongol rule over China resulted in the movement of a significant number of Christians from such Turkic tribes into China, where they were given privileges above those of the native Chinese population and were often employed as administrators, as well as engaging in trade and other activities. The period of Mongol rule also saw the presence in China of Christians other than members of the Church of the East, such as the Latin missionaries and Alan mercenaries.

As in the earlier period, the hierarchs at the head of the Church of the East community in China were evidently sent from the mother Church in the West. The *History of Mar Yahbalaha* provides us with the names of two metropolitans of China, Mār Gīwargīs (ca. 1248) and Mār Nestōrīs (ca. 1263), from whom Rabban Ṣawmā and Marqōs, respectively, received their tonsure.[9] We know of two further metropolitans who, however, never reached China after their ordination, Shemʿōn bar Qalīg, a native of Ṭūs in Khorasan, who rebelled against catholicos Denḥā I (1265–1281) in 1279 and later died in prison, and the future catholicos Yahbalāhā, ordained metropolitan of 'Katay and Ong' (i.e. of China and the Önggüt) shortly before his elevation to the catholicate in 1281.[10] The sources also mention a metropolitan see of Tangut for this period, but Īshōʿsabran, the only metropolitan known by name, was deprived of his office for his complicity in a plot against Yahbalāhā in 1282, so that the see may never have had a resident incumbent.[11]

The custom of the Mongol rulers receiving their consorts from their often Christian Turkic allies resulted in Christian ladies occupying the highest positions in the realm that they could as women. The most famous of such ladies was Sorqaqtani Beki (d. 1252), a Kereit princess who married Genghis Khan's youngest son Tolui and gave birth to the great khans Möngke (1251–1259) and Qubilai (1260–1294), as well as the Ilkhanid Hülegü (1256–1265).

Among the highest-ranking male Christians in the empire were the chiefs of the Önggüt tribe, who rallied to the side of Genghis Khan at an early stage and were rewarded for their loyalty by being given the privilege of receiving imperial princesses in marriage (Atwood 2014). The best known of these Önggüt chiefs is Gīwargīs/Kuolijisi 闊里吉思 (d. 1298), who was raised to the rank of Prince of Gaotang 高唐王 in 1294 by his brother-in-law cum father-in-law Temür Öljeitü (Chengzong, 1294–1307). The Chinese sources portray him as a patron of Confucianism, while the Franciscan John of Montecorvino claims to have converted him from 'Nestorianism' to Catholicism (Marsone 2013). The recently discovered inscriptions in Chinese and Syriac, left by the prince on a mountain pass at Ulaan Tolgoi in western Mongolia just before his capture and death at the hands of his enemies, suggest that the prince remained true to the end to the Christian faith of his forefathers (Osawa et al. 2015). At the same time, the sources tell us how the prince and his family also patronised other religions, including Buddhism and, increasingly, Daoism, indicating how the different religious groups vied for the support of such powerful figures (Osawa and Takahashi 2015).

Gīwargīs was also the brother of Princess Sarā for whom the manuscript now in the Vatican Library was copied in 1298. That princess was married to Altan-Buqa (created Prince of Qin 秦王 in 1287), the brother of the powerful Muslim prince Ananda (Prince of Anxi 安西王, d. 1307), who held large tracts of western China, including much of the former Tangut territory, as his fief (Dunnel 2014), and she is reported to have been killed in an earthquake in 1306 at Kaichenglu 開成路 (in Guyuan City in southern Ningxia), the summer residence of the Prince of Anxi (*Yuanshi*, *juan* 21, ed. 1976: 471). Although the Tangut Empire had been erased from the map by Genghis Khan's army in 1227, the Persian historian Rashīd al-Dīn constantly refers to Ananda as the ruler of the 'province' or 'kingdom' of Tangut (*wilāyat/mamlakat-i Tangqūt*),[12] so that the Christians in the Middle East may have conceived of Ananda's fief in the same way, and if so, the decision to erect the see of Tangut may have been connected with the presence of the Christian princess there.

A Syriac-rite Christian with a quite different background who played an important role both in the imperial bureaucracy and in the life of the Christian community in China is Aixue 愛薛 (d. 1308).[13] We do not know exactly where he originated, but he was granted the posthumous title of 'loyal and devoted prince of Fulin' 拂林忠獻王 and he is described as being from 'Fulin' in the *Yuanshi* (*juan* 134, ed. 1976: 3249) and in the text of the commemorative stele composed by Cheng Jufu 程鉅夫 (*Quan Yuanwen*, vol. 16: 324). Cheng describes him further as lacking no knowledge of the 'various languages of the West, calendrical astronomy and medicine'. Aixue entered

Figure 32.8 Syriac inscription with the words of Psalm 125 (124):2 at Ulaan Tolgoi

Source: Takashi Osawa

the service of the Mongols under Güyük Khan (1246–48), and worked in the agencies for calendrical astronomy and medicine under Qubilai. He was sent on a mission to the West around 1283, and appears in Rashīd al-Dīn's *Jāmiʿ al-tawārīkh* as ʿĪsā the translator (*kelemechi*). Upon his return from the West in 1287, Aixue was made the director of the Palace Library 秘書監, and two years later in 1289, the director of Chongfusi 崇福司, the government office which oversaw the affairs of the Christians (cf. Tang 2011: 128f.), and which may have been established at Aixue's instigation (Yin 2016: 317). He was succeeded in his office at Chongfusi by his eldest son Yeliya 也里牙 (Eliyā), while a younger son, Luha 魯哈 (Lūqā), succeeded him as the head of the medical bureau.

Another Christian whose career was aided by the medical connections of his family was Mār Sargīs (Ma Xuelijisi 馬薛里吉思), of whom we hear in the text of a stele (erected in 1281) reproduced in the entry on the Xingguo Monastery 興國寺 in Zhenjiang in the *Zhishun Zhenjiangzhi*.[14] Mār Sargīs stemmed from a family of physicians from Samarkand whose members had been recruited into the imperial service after a successful treatment of Genghis Khan's youngest son Tolui. Mār Sargīs, known to Marco Polo as Marsa(r)chis (Moule and Pelliot 1938: II.xliv, I.323), was appointed assistant governor of the Zhenjiang Circuit in 1277 and founded seven Christian monasteries in the area during his tenure of office there. Besides for the information it provides on Mār Sargīs' family and the monasteries he founded, the passage is also of interest in that it gives us, with its brief discourse on the Christian cross, a glimpse of the Christian doctrine taught at the time in China, and in that the bishop Maer Xili 麻兒失理 mentioned there can be identified with the bishop Mali Xilimen 馬里失里門 (Mār Shlēmōn, d. 1313) whose epitaph has been found in Quanzhou (Moriyasu 2011: 348–57). When the *Zhenjiangzhi* tells us that the bishop came from the 'land of the Buddha' (*foguo* 佛國), this is probably to be emended to read the 'land of Fulin' as was already suggested by Saeki (1937: 515), especially in the light of the association we have seen above of Aixue with 'Fulin', as well as the poem by the Önggüt-born Jin Yuansu addressed to Rabban Yuanming 元明列班 of the Xingming Monastery 興明寺 in Quanzhou, in which he talks of the teaching preserved in the monastery as coming from 'Fulin'.[15]

The *Zhishun Zhenjiangzhi* also gives some further interesting information about the Christian community in the area. From the population statistics in *juan* 3, we learn that there were 215 Christians (*Yelikewen*) in the area in around 1330, making up 1.6% of the non-native residents and 0.033% of the total population (ed. 1990: 93; Moule 1930: 161–3; Tang 2011: 115f.). While the passage of the *Zhenjiangzhi* on the Xingguo Monastery talks in favourable terms about Christianity, we have some indications of the incipient decline of Christianity in the area in the parts of the work that immediately follow, such as the passage on the Bore Convent 般若院, where we hear of the Buddhists taking, or regaining as they claimed, the possession of two of the monasteries founded by Mār Sargīs with the help of the imperial authorities in 1311 (*juan* 9, ed. 1990: 387f.; Moule 1930: 152–5).

Such factors as the minute number of its adherents within the total population and competition from other far more populous religious groups, along with the increasing political instability in Central Asia, explain why Christianity was unable to survive in China when it no longer had the protection it had received from the Mongol overlords. One remarkable relic which gives us some hints about the fate of the Christians who remained in China after the fall of the Yuan is a manuscript now in Manchester (John Rylands Library, Syriac 4; see Coakley 1993: 120–3 and figure 2). The manuscript was copied at the request of Jesuit missionaries around 1725 by 'Lieou yu si', a Muslim court official holding the office of 'tong koan tching', on the basis of an older Syriac manuscript dated AD 752/3, which according to Lieou had been brought to China by his ancestors at the time of the Mongol rule. The copyist can be identified with Liu Yuxi 劉裕錫, who became the supervisor of the Winter Office (dongguanzheng 冬官正) in the Directorate of Astronomy in March 1725 (Chang 2015: 195–8). Liu Yuxi and his younger brother Liu Yuduo 劉裕鐸, one of the two editors-in-chief of the medical work *Yizong jinjian* 醫宗金鑑, were members of the Muslim community at Niujie 牛街 in Beijing (*Gangzhi*, ed. 1991: 11). If what Liu Yuxi told the Jesuits about his ancestors bringing the original manuscript to China is true, it becomes likely that he and his brother were descendants of Syriac-rite Christians, and that some, at least, of those Christians who came to China in the Yuan period survived by being absorbed into the Muslim community there, retaining in some cases the tradition of transmitting through the family the knowledge and skills that they had brought with them, such as those of astronomy and medicine.

CONCLUSION

Considered as a missionary endeavour, the efforts made by the Church of the East in China might be seen as a failure. The Church does not seem to have gained any significant number of local converts either in the Tang or the Yuan period, and their membership was largely limited to immigrants of Iranian or Turkic origin and their sometimes Sinicised descendants. The dependence of the Church in China on the protection of groups seen to be 'foreign' by the local population, be it the exiled Persian aristocracy of the Tang period or the Mongol rulers of the Yuan period, hastened its decline when that protection could no longer be maintained. The way in which the Christian communities disappeared, through emigration and absorption into other religious communities, also tells us about the disadvantage of the centralised hierarchical system of the Church, which made it difficult for the distant local communities to survive when the political situation hindered communication with the centre of the Church and the centre itself was weakened.

At the same time, the meeting of Syriac Christianity with the local Chinese culture produced some remarkable results, the best representative of which is the Xi'an Stele, along with the other Christian texts composed in the Tang period and the Chinese-style Christian gravestones of Quanzhou and Yangzhou. These relics from the past tell us what can happen when a religious community like that of the Syriac Christians comes into contact with a population with a strongly embedded cultural tradition such as that of China. Furthermore, such relics left behind by the Syriac-rite Christians are still being discovered today, while the older finds are still capable of yielding new interpretations and providing us with new insights. It is such factors as these that have made and continue to make the history and culture of Syriac Christianity in China a fascinating field of study.

NOTES

1 A comprehensive list, compiled by Malek and Nicolini-Zani, of publications in the field up to just after the turn of the twenty-first century can be found in the proceedings of the first of a series of conferences on the subject held in Salzburg (Malek and Hofrichter 2006: 499–698), while much of the latest findings in the field can be found in the proceedings of those conferences (Malek and Hofrichter 2006; Winkler and Tang 2009; Tang and Winkler 2013; Tang and Winkler 2016). Also of importance in providing the latest information on various aspects of the subject are the papers in the volume devoted to it in the series Études syriaques (Borbone and Marsone 2015). Among the publications from the first half of the twentieth century, those by Moule (1930) and Saeki (1935, 1937) in particular are still of importance in that they bring together many of the important source texts. For the translation and study of the Xi'an Stele, the posthumous publications of Pelliot's work (1984, 1996) still remain the points of reference, although newer translations (Nicolini-Zani 2006: 191–214; Ferreira 2014; Eccles-Lieu 2016; Deeg 2018) and important new studies are also available. New European-language translations of the Chinese Christian documents from Dunhuang can be found in the monographs by Tang (2002) and Nicolini-Zani (2006), the latter of which includes a particularly useful account of Christianity in China during the Tang period based on the latest information available at the time of publication. As recent monographs on Syriac Christianity in China during the Yuan period, mention might be made of Tang (2011), Yin (2012) and, though covering a somewhat narrower field of Inner Mongolia, Halbertsma (2015).

2 Respectively, Tonkō Hikyū collection 459, 460, 13, 431; colour images in Kyōu Shooku (2009–13: 1.128, 132, 5.396f., 6.83–96); cf. Nicolini-Zani (2016).

3 *Tang huiyao*, *juan* 62, ed. 1955: 1078; *Cefu yuangui*, *juan* 546, ed. 2006: 6243 (trans. of part of passage in Saeki 1937: 94); cf. *Xin Tangshu*, *juan* 112, ed. 1975: 4176.

4 *Cefu yuangui*, *juan* 971, 975, ed. 2006: 11240, 11286 (trans. Saeki 1937: 459).

5 *Cefu yuangui*, *juan* 971, ed. 2006: 11243f.; cf. Nakata (2011: 180).

6 *Youyang zazu*, *juan* 18, ed. 1981: 178–80; cf. Santos (2010), Takahashi (2014a: 42f). To the identification of Syriac terms made by earlier scholars, one should add 阿梨訶咃 (LMC ʔa-li-xa-ta, 'long pepper'), < Syriac *arrīkātā* (lit. 'long' [fem. pl.], sc. *pelplē*); and 阿梨去伐 (LMC ʔa-li-kʰiə̌-fɦaːt, *Cassia fistula*), < Syriac ʾlyqbr (*alīqbar/ēlīqbar*).

7 LMC: Late Middle Chinese pronunciation according to the reconstruction of Pulleyblank (1991).

8 On a further newly identified Syro-Turkic inscription, left by a group of three pilgrims calling themselves Buyan Temür, Nathaniel (ntn'yl), and John (ywḥnn) in the Yulin Grottoes 榆林窟 (Cave 16) to the east of Dunhuang, see Matsui (2017: 100f. and Plate 5).

9 *History of Mar Yahbalaha*, ed. Bedjan (1895: 7, 11); trans. Borbone (2009: 52, 54); cf. Dauvillier (1948: 301); Fiey (1993: 104).

10 Barhebraeus, *Chronicon ecclesiasticum*, ed. Abbeloos and Lamy (1872–77: II.449, 451); trans. Wilmshurst (2016: 460, 462); *History of Mar Yahbalaha*, ed. Bedjan (1895: 29); trans. Borbone (2009: 62); cf. Borbone (2015a: 133f).

11 *History of Mar Yahbalaha*, ed. Bedjan (1895: 33, 40–6); trans. Borbone (2009: 63, 66–8); cf. Dickens (2015: 26f.); Borbone (2015b: 132, 134f). *The Book of the Tower* (Gismondi 1896–99: II, text 123) evidently errs in having Yahbalāhā ordained for the see of Tangut; the persistent notion of a double see of Tangut-China, whose origins can be traced back to J. S. Assemani (1719–28: III/2, 523, 784; cf. Fiey 1993: 44, 137), is not otherwise supported by the primary sources.

12 *Jāmiʿ al-tawārīkh*, ed. Raushan and Mūsawī (1994/5: 866, 910, 913, 949f., 952f.); trans. Thackston (1998–99: 422, 446f., 464–7).

13 On Aixue, see Pelliot (1914: 638–41); Moule (1930: 228–33); and further literature cited at Takahashi (2014a: 44, n. 35); also Kim (2006); Yin (2014b).

14 *Zhishun Zhenjiangzhi*, *juan* 9, ed. 1990: 367–8; cf. Moule and Giles (1915); Moule (1930: 146–65); Saeki (1937: 510–15); Yin (2009); Tang (2011: 133–8).

15 Xiao (1995: 5); Yin (2014a: 399f.); ead. (2016: 325); Liu (2016: 170): 寺門常鎖碧苔深,千載燈傳自苐林, 明月在天雲在水, 世人誰識老師心 ('The gate of the monastery is always locked, and the green moss has grown deep. The millennium-old lamp of teaching comes from Fulin. The bright moon is in the sky, and the clouds are [reflected] in water. Who out of the worldly people can fathom the heart of the old master?'). Xingming Monastery is also named in the epitaph of its abbot Wu Anduonisi (d. 1306) found in Quanzhou (Lieu et al. 2012: 141f.).

BIBLIOGRAPHY

Chinese primary sources

Cefu yuangui 冊府元龜. Nanjing: Fenghuang Chubanshe, 2006 (12 vols.).

Gangzhi 岡志: *Beijing Niujie zhishu: 'Gangzhi' (xiudingben)* 北京牛街志书—《冈志》（修订本）(annotated by Liu Dongsheng 刘东声 and Liu Shenglin 刘盛林). Beijing: Beijing Chubanshe, 1991.

Quan Yuanwen 全元文. Nanjing: Jiangsu Guji Chubanshe, 1997–2005 (60 vols.).

Song huiyao jigao 宋會要輯稿. Beijing: Zhonghua Shuju, 1957 (8 vols.).

Tang huiyao 唐會要. Beijing: Zhonghua Shuju, 1955 (3 vols.).

Xin Tangshu 新唐書. Beijing: Zhonghua Shuju, 1975 (20 vols.).

Youyang zazu 酉陽雜俎. Beijing: Zhonghua Shuju, 1981.
Yuanshi 元史. Beijing: Zhonghua Shuju, 1976 (15 vols.).
Zhishun Zhenjiangzhi 至順鎮江志. Nanjing: Jiangsu Guji Chubanshe, 1990.

Other primary and secondary literature

Abbeloos, J. B., and T. J. Lamy, ed. 1872–77. *Gregorii Barhebraei Chronicon ecclesiasticum.* 2 parts [3 vols.]. Louvain: Peeters.

Assemani, J. S. 1719–28. *Bibliotheca orientalis clementino-vaticana.* 3 vols. Rome: Sacra Congregatio de Proparanda Fide.

Atwood, C. 2014. Historiography and Transformation of Ethnic Identity in the Mongol Empire: the Öng'üt Case. *Asian Ethnicity* 15/4, 514–34.

Bai Yudong 白玉冬 and D. Matsui 松井太. 2016. Fufuhoto Hakutō no Uiguru-go daiki meibun フフホト白塔のウイグル語題記銘文. *Studies on the Inner Asian Languages* 内陸アジア言語の研究 31, 29–77.

Bedjan, P., ed. 1895. *Histoire de Mar-Jabalaha, patriarche, et de Raban Sauma.* 2nd ed. Paris/Leipzig: Harrassowitz.

Bernhard, L. 1969. *Die Chronologie der Syrer.* Vienna: Böhlau.

Borbone, P. G. 2003. I Vangeli per la principessa Sara. Un manoscritto siriaco crisografato, gli Öngüt cristiani e il Principe Giorgio. *Egitto e Vicino Oriente* 26, 63–82.

———. 2006a. I blocchi con croci e iscrizione siriaca da Fangshan. *OCP* 72, 167–87.

———. 2006b. Peshitta Ps. 34:6 from Syria to China. *In*: W. T. van Peursen and R. B. ter Haar Romeny, ed., *Text, Translation and Tradition: Studies on the Peshitta and Its Use in the Syriac Tradition Presented to Konrad D. Jenner on the Occasion of His Sixty-Fifth Birthday.* Leiden: Brill, 1–10.

———, ed. and trans. 2009. *Storia di Mar Yahballaha e di Rabban Sauma. Cronaca siriaca del XIV secolo.* Moncalieri: Lulu Press.

———. 2013. More on the Priest Särgis in the White Pagoda: The Syro-Turkic Inscriptions of the White Pagoda, Hohhot. *In*: Tang and Winkler 2013, 51–65.

———. 2015a. Les "provinces de l'extérieur" vues par l'Église-mère. *In*: Borbone and Marsone 2015, 121–59.

———. 2015b. An Önggüd Gravestone in the Musée Guimet, Paris, and Its Inscription. *In*: P. Fedi and M. Paolillo, ed., *Arte dal Mediterraneo al Mar della Cina. Genesi ed incontri di scuole e stili. Scritti in onore di Paola Mortari Vergara Caffarelli.* Palermo: Officina degli studi medievali, 221–31.

Borbone, P. G., and P. Marsone, ed. 2015. *Le christianisme syriaque en Asie centrale et Chine.* Paris: Geuthner.

Braun, O., ed. and trans. 1914. *Timothei patriarchae I epistulae.* 2 vols. CSCO 74, 75. Paris: Gabalda/Leipzig: Harrassowitz.

Budge, E. A. W., ed. and trans. 1893. *The Book of Governors: The Historia Monastica of Thomas Bishop of Margâ A.D. 840.* 2 vols. London: Kegan Paul, Trench, Trübner & Co.

Chang, Ping-Ying. 2015. *Chinese Hereditary Mathematician Families of the Astronomical Bureau, 1620–1850.* Ph.D. dissertation. City University of New York.

Ch'ên Yüan 陳垣. 1966. *Western and Central Asians in China under the Mongols* (trans. Ch'ien Hsing-hai 銭星海 and L. C. Goodrich). Los Angeles: University of California.

Coakley, J. F. 1993. A Catalogue of the Syriac Manuscripts in the John Rylands Library. *Bulletin of the John Rylands Library* 75, 105–207.

Dauvillier, J. 1948. Les provinces chaldéennes "de l'extérieur" au Moyen Age. *In*: *Mélanges offerts au R. P. Ferdinand Cavallera.* Toulouse: Institut catholique de Toulouse, 261–316 [Reprinted in id., *Histoire et institions des Eglises orientales au Moyen Age.* London: Variorum, 1983. I].

Deeg, M. 2015. La littérature chrétienne orientale sous les Tang: un bref aperçu. *In*: Borbone and Marsone 2015, 199–214.
———. 2016. An Anachronism in the Stele of Xi'an – Why Henanisho? *In:* Tang and Winkler 2016, 243–51.
———. 2018. *Die Strahlende Lehre: Die Stele von Xi'an*. Vienna: LIT.
Dickens, M. 2015. Le christianisme syriaque en Asie centrale. *In*: Borbone and Marsone 2015, 5–39.
Dodge, B., trans. 1970. *The Fihrist of al-Nadīm: A 10th Century AD Survey of Islamic Culture*. New York: Columbia University Press.
Du Haijun 杜海军. 2013. *Guilin shike zongji jixiao* 桂林石刻総集輯校. 3 vols. Beijing: Zhonghua Shuju.
Duan Hairong 段海蓉. 2010. Yuandai Fulin shiren Jin Hala jiyu Dongnan de shiyong 元代茀林诗人金哈剌寄寓东南的诗咏 [On Jinhala's Poems in the Yuan Dynasty]. *Journal of Xinjiang University (Philosophy, Humanities & Social Sciences)* 新疆大学学报（哲学・人文社会科学版）38/1, 117–21.
Duan Qing 段晴. 2001. Bericht über ein neuentdecktes syrisches Dokument aus Dunhuang/China. *OC* 85, 84–93.
Dunnel, R. W. 2014. The Anxi Principality: [un]Making a Muslim Mongol Prince in Northwest China during the Yuan Dynasty. *Central Asiatic Journal* 57, 185–200.
Eccles, L., and S. Lieu. 2016. *Stele on the Diffusion of the Luminous Religion of Da Qin (Rome) in the Middle Kingdom*. www.mq.edu.au/__data/assets/pdf_file/0007/55987/Xian-Nestorian-Monument-27-07-2016.pdf [Accessed October 2016].
Ferreira, J. 2014. *Early Chinese Christianity: The Tang Christian Monument and Other Documents*. Strathfield (N.S.W.): St. Paul's.
Fiey, J. M. 1993. *Pour un Oriens christianus novus: répertoire des diocèses syriaques orientaux et occidentaux*. Stuttgart: Steiner.
Flügel, G., ed. 1872. *Kitâb al-Fihrist*. 2 vols. Leipzig: Vogel.
Forte, A. 1996a. The Edict of 638 Allowing the Diffusion of Christianity in China. *In*: Pelliot 1996, 349–73.
———. 1996b. On the So-Called Abraham from Persia: A Case of Mistaken Identity. *In*: Pelliot 1996, 375–428.
Franzmann, M. 2013. Yangzhou and Quanzhou: Ongoing Research on Syro-Turkic Inscriptions. *In*: Tang and Winkler 2013, 83–92.
———. 2015. The Epitaph of Mar Solomon, Bishop of South China, Administrator of Manicheans and Nestorians. *Open Theology* 1, 293–300.
Fukushima, M. 福島恵. 2016. Tōdai ni okeru Keikyōto boshi: shinshutsu "Ka Ken boshi" wo chūshin ni 唐代における景教徒墓誌—新出「花献墓誌」を中心に [The Epitaph of Nestorian in Tang Dynasty: In the Center of Newly Found "Epitaph of Hua Xian (花献)"]. *The Tōdaishi-Kenkyū: The Journal of Tang Historical Studies* 唐代史研究 19, 42–76.
Ge Chengyong 葛承雍, ed., 2009. *Jingjiao yizhen: Luoyang xin chu Tangdai Jingjiao jingchuang yanjiu* 景教遺珍—洛陽新出唐代景教經幢研究 [*Precious Nestorian Relic: Studies on the Nestorian Stone Pillar of the Tang Dynasty Recently Discovered in Luoyang*]. Beijing: Wenwu Chubanshe.
Ge Chengyong and M. Nicolini-Zani. 2004. The Christian Faith of a Sogdian Family in Chang'an during the Tang Dynasty. *Annali dell'Università degli studi di Napoli "L'Orientale"* 64, 181–96.
Geng Shimin, H.-J. Klimkeit and J. P. Laut. 1996. Eine neue nestorianische Grabinschrift aus China. *Ural-altaischer Jahrbücher N.F.* 14, 164–75.
Gibson, M. D., ed. and trans. 1911. *The Commentaries of Isho'dad of Merv, Bishop of Ḥadatha* (c. 850 A.D.). 3 vols. Cambridge: Cambridge University Press.
Gismondi, H., ed. and trans. 1896–1899. *Maris Amri et Slibae De patriarchis Netorianorum commentaria*. 2 parts. Rome: C. de Luigi.

Guo Chengmei 郭成美. 2014. Yangzhou Puhadingyuan shoucang yi tong Jingjiao mugai canshi 扬州普哈丁园收藏一通景教墓盖残石. *In*: Zhongguo Huizu Xuehui 中国回族学会, ed., *The Hui Nationality Area Build a Well-Off Society in an All-Round Way* 回族地区全面建成小康社会 第二十一次全国回族学研讨会论文集. Yinchuan: Ningxia Renming Chubanshe, 83–88.

Hage, W. 1978. Einheimische Volkssprachen und syrische Kirchensprache in der nestorianischen Asienmission. *In*: G. Wießner, ed., *Erkenntnisse und Meinungen II*. Wiesbaden: Harrassowitz, 131–60.

Halbertsma, T. 2005. Some Field Notes and Images of Stone Material from Graves of the Church of the East in Inner Mongolia, China (With Additional Rubbings of Seven Stones by Wei Jian). *Monumenta serica* 53, 133–244.

———. 2015. *Early Christian Remains of Inner Mongolia*. 2nd ed. Leiden: Brill.

Hamilton, J., and Niu Ru-Ji. 1994. Deux inscriptions funéraires turques nestoriennes de la Chine orientale. *Journal asiatique* 282, 147–64.

Hoenerbach, W., and O. Spies, ed. 1956–57. *Ibn aṭ-Ṭayyib. Fiqh an-naṣrānīya: "Das Recht der Christenheit"*. CSCO 161, 167. Louvain: Durbecq.

Jiao Jianhui 焦建辉. 2013. Longmen shiku Hongshigou Tangdai Jingjiao yiji diaocha ji xiangguan wenti tantao 龙门石窟红石沟唐代景教遗迹调查及相关问题探讨 [The Nestorian Relic of Hongshigou Valley in Longmen Grottoes and the Related Issues]. *Study on the Cave Temples* 石窟寺研究 4, 17–22.

Kaufhold, H. 1996. Anmerkung zur Veröffentlichung eines syrischen Lektionarfragments. *ZDMG* 146, 49–60.

Kim Ho Dong. 2006. A Portrait of a Christian Official in China under Mongol Rule: Life and Career of 'Isa Kelemechi (1227–1308). *In*: G. Bamana, ed., *Christianity and Mongolia Past and Present: Proceedings of the Antoon Mostaert Symposium on Christianity and Mongolia*. Ulaanbaatar: Antoon Mostaert Mongolian Study Center, 41–52.

Klein, W., and J. Tubach. 1994. Ein syrisch-christliches Fragment aus Dunhuang/China. *ZDMG* 144, 1–13, 446 (plate).

Kósa, G. 2013/14 [2015]. The Fifth Buddha: An Overview of the Chinese Manichaean Material from Xiapu (Fujian). *Manichaean Studies Newsletter* 28, 9–30.

Kyōu Shooku 杏雨書屋. 2009–2013. *Tonkō Hikyū. Eihen-satsu* 敦煌秘笈 影片册. 9 vols. Osaka: Takeda Kagaku Shinkō Zaidan.

Lieu, S. N. C. 2013. The 'Romanitas' of the Xi'an Inscription. *In* Tang and Winkler 2013, 123–40.

———. 2014. Epigraphica Nestoriana Serica (II). *In*: Zhang Xiaogui 张小贵 et al., ed., *San yijiao yanjiu: Lin Wushu xiansheng guxi jinian lunwenji* 三夷教研究—林悟殊先生古稀纪念论文集. Lanzhou: Lanzhou Daxue Chubanshe, 360–80.

Lieu, S. N. C., L. Eccles, M. Franzmann, I. Gardner and K. Parry. 2012. *Medieval Christian and Manichaean Remains from Quanzhou (Zayton)*. Tournhout: Brepols.

Lin Wushu 林悟殊. 2014. *Monijiao huahua bushuo* 摩尼教華化補説. Lanzhou: Lanzhou Daxue Chubanshe.

———. 2015. Fujian Xiapu chaoben Yuandai Tianzhujiao zanshi bianxi – fu: Xiapu chaoben Jingjiao 'Jisizhou' kaolüe 福建霞浦抄本元代天主教赞诗辨释 – 附：霞浦抄本景教《吉思呪》考略. *The Western Regions Studies* 西域研究 4, 115–34.

Lin Ying 林英. 2006. *Tandai Fulin congshuo* 唐代拂菻丛说 [*Fulin the Ruler of Treasure Country: Byzantium in the Tang Society AD618–907*]. Beijing: Zhonghua Shuju.

———. 2007. Fulin Monks: Did Some Christians Other than Nestorians Enter China during the Tang Period? *Proche-Orient chrétien* 57, 24–42.

Liu Jiawei 刘嘉伟. 2016. Yuandai Fulin shiren Jin Hala chuyi 元代茀林诗人金哈剌刍议. *Wenxue yichan* 文学遗产 2016/3, 166–175.

Luo Xianglin [Lo Hsiang-lin] 羅香林. 1966. *Tang Yuan er dai zhi Jingjiao* 唐元二代之景教 [*Nestorianism in the T'ang and Yüan Dynasties*]. Hong Kong: Institute of Chinese Culture.

Ma Xiaohe 馬小鶴. 2014. *Xiapu wenshu yanjiu* 霞浦文書研究. Lanzhou: Lanzhou Daxue Chubanshe.

———. 2015. Remains of the Religion of Light in Xiapu (霞浦) County, Fujian Province. *In*: S. G. Richter et al., ed., *Mani in Dublin: Selected Papers from the Seventh International Conference of the International Association of Manichaean Studies in the Chester Beatty Library, Dublin, 8–12 September 2009*. Leiden: Brill, 228–58.

———. 2016. Sutewen "Sheng Qiaozhi shounanji" yu "Jisizhou" 粟特文《聖喬治受難記》與《吉思咒》[Chinese Essentials of Martyrdom of George]. *Newsletter for International China Studies* 國際漢學研究通訊 12, 45–75.

Ma Xiaolin 马晓林. 2016. Yuandai Jingjiao renmingxue chutan: yi qianju Jining de Alimali Jingjiao jiazu wei zhongxin 元代景教人名学初探 – 以迁居济宁的阿力麻里景教家族为中心 [A Preliminary Study on the Anthroponomy of Nestorians in the Yuan Dynasty: A Case Study on an Immigrant Family from Almaliq to Jining]. *Journal of Peking University (Philosophy and Social Sciences)* 北京大学学报 (哲学社会科学版) 53/1, 134–40.

Mai, A., ed., 1838. *Scriptorum veterum nova collectio*, tomus X. Rome: Collegium Urbanum.

Malek, R., and P. Hofrichter. ed., 2006. *Jingjiao: The Church of the East in China and Central Asia*. Sankt Augustin: Institut Monumenta Serica.

Mao Yangguang 毛阳光. 2014. Luoyang xin chutu Tangdai Jingjiaotu Hua Xian ji qi qi Anshi muzhi chutan 洛阳新出土唐代景教徒花献及其妻安氏墓志初探 [A Study of the Epigraph of Nestorian Hua Xian and His Wife Ann of Tang Dynasty from Luoyang]. *The Western Regions Studies* 西域研究 2, 85–91.

Marsone, P. 2013. Two Portraits for One Man: George, King of the Önggüt. *In*: Tang and Winkler 2013, 225–35.

Matsui, D. 松井太. 2016. Meng Yuan shidai Huihu Fojiatu he Jingjiaotu de wangluo 蒙元时代回鹘佛教徒和景教徒的网络 (trans. Bai Yudong 白玉冬). 蒙元时代回鹘佛教徒和景教徒的网络 *(trans. Bai Yudong* 白玉冬*)*. *In*: Xu Zhongwen 徐忠文 and Rong Xinjiang 荣新江, ed., *Make Boluo, Yangzhou, Sichou zhi lu* 马可·波罗 扬州 丝绸之路 [Marco Polo, Yangzhou, the Silk Road]. Beijing: Beijing Daxue Chubanshe. 283–93.

———. 2017. Tonkō Sekkutsu Uiguru-go Mongoru-go daiki meibun shūsei 敦煌石窟ウイグル語・モンゴル語題記銘文集成. *In*: D. Matsui and S. Arakawa, ed., *Tonkō Sekkutsu tagengo shiryō shūsei* 敦煌石窟多言語資料集成 [Multilingual Source Materials of the Dunhuang Grottoes]. Tokyo: Research Institute for Languages and Cultures of Asia and Africa, Tokyo University of Foreign Studies, 1–162.

Moriyasu, T. 2011. The Discovery of Manichaean Paintings in Japan and Their Historical Background. *In*: J. A. van den Berg et al., ed., *'In Search of Truth': Augustine, Manichaeism and Other Gnosticism: Studies for Johannes van Oort at Sixty*. Leiden: Brill, 339–60.

Moule, A. C. 1930. *Christians in China before the Year 1550*. London: Society for Promotion of Christian Knowledge.

Moule, A. C., and L. Giles. 1915. Christians at Chên-chiang fu. *T'oung pao* 16, 627–86.

Moule, A. C., and P. Pelliot, ed. and trans. 1938. *Marco Polo. The Description of the World*. 2 vols. London: Routledge.

Muraviev, A. 2012. The New Persian Marriage Contract in the Manuscript from Turfan. *In*: Academia Turfanica, ed., *The History Behind the Languages: Essays of Turfan Forum on Old Languages of the Silk Road* 语言背后的历史:西域古典语言学高峰论坛论文集. Shanghai: Shanghai Guji Chubanshe, 160–4.

Muto, S. 2016. The Exorcism in the Newly Found Khara-Khoto Syriac Document. *In* Tang and Winkler 2016, 147–51.

Nakata, M. 中田美絵. 2011. Hasseiki kōhan ni okeru Chūō Yūrashia no dōkō to Chōan bukkyōkai: Tokusō-ki "Daijō rishu roku haramitta kyō" hon'yaku sankasha no bunseki yori 八世紀後半における中央ユーラシアの動向と長安仏教界—徳宗期『大乗理趣六波羅

蜜多経』翻訳参加者の分析より [The Buddhist Circle in Chang'an and the Movements amongst Central Eurasia during the Latter Half of the Eighth Century: From the Study on Participants in Translation of *Dacheng Liqu Liu Boluomiduo Jing* 大乗理趣六波羅蜜多経 during the Era of the Emperor 德宗]. *Bulletin of the Institute of Oriental and Occidental Studies, Kansai University* 関西大学東西学術研究所紀要 44, 153–89.

Nicolini-Zani, M. 2006. *La via radiosa per l'oriente. I testi e la storia del primo incontro del cristianesimo con il mondo culturale e religioso cinese (secoli VII-IX)*. Magnano: Qiqajon.

———. 2009. The Tang Christian Pillar from Luoyang and Its *Jingjiao* Inscription: A Preliminary Study. *Monumenta serica* 57, 99–140.

Nicolini-Zani, M. (in collaboration with H. Takahashi). 2016. The Dunhuang *Jingjiao* Documents in Japan: A Report on Their Reappearance. *In*: Tang and Winkler 2016, 15–26.

Niu Ruji 牛汝极 2006. Nestorian Inscriptions from China (13th–14th Centuries). *In*: Malek and Hofrichter 2006, 209–42.

———. 2008. *Shizi lianhua: Zhongguo Yuandai Xuliyawen Jingjiao beiming wenxian yanjiu* 十字莲花 中国元代叙利亚文景教碑铭文献研究 [The Cross-Lotus: A Study on Nestorian Inscriptions and Documents from Yuan Dynasty in China]. Shanghai: Shanghai Guji Chubanshe.

———. 2017. Xin faxian de shizi lianhua Jingjiao tongjing tuxiang kao 新发现的十字莲花景教铜镜图像考 [A Study of the Cross Lotus Design on Newly-Found Nestorian Bronze Mirror]. *The Western Regions Studies* 西域研究 2, 57–63.

Osawa, T., G. Lkhundev, S. Saitou and H. Takahashi. 2015. "As the Mountains Surround Jerusalem": Two Syriac Inscriptions at Ulaan Tolgoi (Doloon Nuur) in Western Mongolia. *Hugoye* 18/1, 181–96.

Osawa, T., and H. Takahashi. 2015. Le prince Georges des Önggüt dans les montagnes de l'Altaï de Mongolie: les inscriptions d'Ulaan Tolgoi de Doloon Nuur. *In*: Borbone and Marsone 2015, 257–90.

Pelliot, P. 1911. Deux titres bouddhiques portés par des religieux nestoriens. *T'oung pao*, ser. II, 12, 664–70.

———. 1914. Chrétiens d'Asie centrale et d'Extrême-Orient. *T'oung pao*, ser. II, 15, 623–44.

———. 1984. *Recherches sur les chrétiens d'Asie centrale et d'Extrême-Orient. II, 1: La Stèle de Si-ngan-fou*. Paris: Fondation Singer-Polignac.

———. 1996. *L'inscription nestorienne de Si-ngan-fou* (edited with supplements by A. Forte). Kyoto: Scuola di Studi sull'Asia Orientale-Paris: Collège de France, Institut des Hautes Études Chinoises.

Pulleyblank, E. G. 1991. *Lexicon of Reconstructed Pronunciation in Early Middle Chinese, Late Middle Chinese, and Early Mandarin*. Vancouver: UBC Press.

Ramusio, G. B. 1559. *Navigationi et viaggi*. vol. 2. Venice: Giunti.

Raushan, M., and M. Mūsawī, ed. 1994/5 [1373 h.sh.]. *Jāmiʿ al-tawārīkh-i Rashīd al-Dīn Faḍl-Allāh Hamadānī*. 4 vols. Tehran: Nashr-i Alburz.

Reck, C. 2006. *Berliner Turfanfragmente manichäischen Inhalts in soghdischer Schrift*. Stuttgart: Steiner.

Reinaud, [J. T.], ed. and trans. 1845. *Relation des voyages faits par les Arabes et les Persans dans l'Inde et à la Chine dans le IXe siècle de l'ère chrétienne*. 2 vols. Paris: l'Imprimerie royale.

Riboud, P. 2001. Tang. *In*: N. Standaert, ed., *Handbook of Christianity in China. Volume One: 635–1800*. Leiden: Brill, 1–42.

———. 2015. Le christianisme syriaque à l'époque Tang. *In*: Borbone and Marsone 2015, 41–61.

Rong Xinjiang 栄新江. 2001. Yige rushi Tangchao de Bosi jingjiao jiazu 一个入仕唐朝的波斯景教家族. *In*: id., *Zhonggu Zhongguo yu wailai wenming* 中古中国与外来文明. Beijing: Sanlian Shudian, 238–57.

Saeki, Y. 佐伯好郎. 1935. *Keikyō no kenkyū* 景教の研究. Tokyo: Tōhō Bunka Gakuin.

———. 1937. *The Nestorian Documents and Relics in China*. Tokyo: The Toho Bunkwa Gakuin.

Santos, D. M. 2010. A Note on the Syriac and Persian Sources of the Pharmacological Section of the Yǒuyáng zázǔ. *Collectanea Christiana Orientalia* 7, 217–29.

Sims-Williams, N., and J. Hamilton. 1990. *Documents turco-sogdiens du IXe-Xe siècle de Touen-houng*. London: School of Oriental and African Studies.

Smelova, N. 2015. Manuscrits chrétiens de Qara Qoto: nouvelles perspectives de recherche. *In*: Borbone and Marsone 2015, 215–37.

Takahashi, H. 2008. Transcribed Proper Names in Chinese Syriac Christian Documents. *In*: G. A. Kiraz, ed., *Malphono w-Rabo d-Malphone: Studies in Honor of Sebastian P. Brock*. Piscataway, NJ: Gorgias Press, 631–62.

———. 2014a. Syriac as a Vehicle for Transmission of Knowledge across Borders of Empires. *Horizons* (Seoul) 5/1, 29–51.

———. 2014b. Transcription of Syriac in Chinese and Chinese in Syriac Script in the Tang Period. *In*: J. den Heijer, A. Schmidt and T. Pataridze, ed., *Scripts Beyond Borders: A Survey of Allographic Traditions in the Euro-Mediterranean World*. Louvain: Peeters, 329–49.

Takakusu, J. 1896. The Name of "Messiah" Found in a Buddhist Book; The Nestorian Missionary Adam, Presbyter, Papas of China, Translating a Buddhist Sûtra. *T'oung pao* 7, 589–91.

Tang, L. 2002. *A Study of the History of Nestorian Christianity in China and Its Literature in Chinese*. Frankfurt: Peter Lang.

———. 2009. A Preliminary Study on the *Jingjiao* Inscription of Luoyang: Text Analysis, Commentary and English Translation. *In*: Winkler and Tang 2009, 109–32.

———. 2011. *East Syriac Christianity in Mongol-Yuan China*. Wiesbaden: Harrassowitz.

———. 2015. Le christianisme syriaque dans la Chine des Mongols yuan: diffusion, statut des chrétiens et déclin (XIIIe-XIVe siècles). *In*: Borbone and Marsone 2015, 63–88.

———. 2016. Critical Remarks on a So-Called Newly Discovered *Jingjiao* Epitaph from Luoyang with a Preliminary English Translation. *In*: Tang and Winkler 2016, 27–40.

Tang, L., and D. W. Winkler, ed. 2013. *From the Oxus River to the Chinese Shores: Studies on East Syriac Christianity in China and Central Asia*. Vienna: LIT Verlag.

———, ed. 2016. *Winds of Jingjiao: Studies on Syriac Christianity in China and Central Asia*. Vienna: LIT Verlag.

Taylor, W. R. 1941. Syriac Mss. Found in Peking, *ca*. 1925. *JAOS* 61, 91–7.

Thackston, W. M., trans. 1998–99. *Rashiduddin Fazlullah's Jami'u't-tawarikh*, 3 vols. Cambridge, MA: Harvard University, Department of Near Eastern Languages and Civilizations.

Tubach, J. 1995/96. Der Apostel Thomas in China. Die Herkunft einer Tradition. *The Harp* 8–9, 397–430.

van Mechelen, J. 2001. Yuan. *In*: N. Standaert, ed., *Handbook of Christianity in China. Volume One: 635–1800*. Leiden: Brill, 43–111.

Wang Dafang 王大方. 2000. Nei Menggu Chifengshi Songshanqu chutu Wokuotai Han shiqi de gu Huihuwen Jingjiao cibei kao 内蒙古赤峰市松山区出土窝阔台汗时期的古回鹘文景教瓷碑考, *Journal of Inner Mongolia Normal University (Philosophy & Social Science)* 内蒙古师大学报 (哲学社会科学版) 29/5, 42–4.

Wang Yuanyuan 王媛媛 and Lin Wushu 林悟殊. 2018. Discovery of an Incantation of St. George in Ritual Manuscript of a Chinese Folk Society. *Monumenta Serica* 66, 115–130.

Wenzel-Teuber, K. 2014. "Nestorianische" Grabnische in den Longmen-Grotten vermutlich bisher frühester christlicher Grabfund in China. *China heute* 33/1 (181), 4–5.

Wilmshurst, D., trans. 2016. *Barhebraeus. The Ecclesiastical Chronicle: An English Translation*. Piscataway, NJ: Gorgias Press.

Winkler, D. W., and L. Tang, ed., 2009. *Hidden Treasures and Intercultural Encounters: Studies on East Syriac Christianity in China and Central Asia*. Vienna: LIT Verlag.

Wu Changxing 吳昶興. 2014–15. Luoyang Huashi fufu shendao muzhiming: Hanren Jingjiaotu de xin faxian 洛陽花氏夫婦神道墓誌銘：漢人景教徒的新發現. *Jidujiao yu Huaren wenhua shehui yanjiu zhongxin tongxun* 基督教與華人文化社會研究中心通訊 (Research Center for Chinese Christianity, Chung Yuan Christian University) 4 (2014), 1–3; 5 (2015), 1–3.

———, ed. 2015a. *Da Qin Jingjiao liuxing Zhongguo bei: Da Qin Jingjiao wenxian shiyi* 大秦景教流行中國碑：大秦景教文獻釋義 [*Da Qing Jingjiao Liuxing Zhongguo Bei (The Xian Stele): Text Analyses with Commentaries on Documents of Da Qin Jingjiao*]. Hong Kong/New Taipei: Olive Publishing.

———. 2015b. *Zhen chang zhi dao: Tangdai Jidujiao lishi yu wenxian yanjiu* 眞常之道：唐代基督教歷史與文獻研究 [*The True and Eternal Way: Bibliographic Research of Assyrian Church of the East in Tang Dynasty*]. New Taipei: Taiwan Jidujiao Wenyi Chubanshe.

Wu Wenliang 吴文良. 2005. *Quanzhou zongjiao shike (zengdingben)* 泉州宗教石刻（增订本）(revised by Wu Youxiong 吴幼雄). Beijing: Kexue Chubanshe.

Xiao Qiqing 蕭啟慶. 1995. Yuan Semu wenren Jin Hala ji qi "Nanyou yuxing shiji" 元色目文人金哈剌及其《南遊寓興詩集》. *Chinese Studies* 漢學研究 (Taipei) 13/2, 1–14.

Yin Xiaoping 殷小平. 2009. On the Christians in Jiangnan during the Yuan Dynasty According to *The Gazetteer of Zhenjiang of the Zhishun Period 1329–1332*. *In*: Winkler and Tang 2009, 305–19.

———. 2012. *Yuandai Yelikewen kaoshu* 元代也里可温考述. Lanzhou: Lanzhou Daxue Chubanshe.

———. 2014a. *Chongfu Si* and *Zhangjiao Si*: On the Christian Administration in Yuan China. *In*: *San yijiao yanjiu: Lin Wushu xiansheng guxi jinian lunwenji* 三夷教研究—林悟殊先生古稀纪念论文集. Lanzhou: Lanzhou Daxue Chubanshe, 381–404.

———. 2014b. Yuandai Chongfusi Ai Xue shishi bushuo 元代崇福使爱薛史事补说 [Supplements to the Historical Events of Director Ai Xue of Chongfu Office of Yuan Dynasty]. *Western Regions Studies* 西域研究 3, 95–103.

———. 2016. The Institution of *Chongfu Si* of the Yuan Dynasty. *In*: Tang and Winkler 2016, 311–29.

Yoshida, Y. 1996. Additional Notes on Sims-Williams' Article on the Sogdian Merchants in China and India. *In*: A. Cadonna and L. Lanciotti, ed., *Cina e Iran: da Alessandro Magno alla dinastia Tang*. Florence: Olschki, 69–77.

——— 吉田豊. 2017. Chūgoku, Torufan oyobi Sogudiana no Sogudojin Keikyōto: Ōtani Tankentai shōrai Saiiki bunka shiryō 2497 ga teiki suru mondai 中国，トルファンおよびソグディアナのソグド人景教徒ー大谷探検隊将来西域文化資料2497が提起する問題 [Christian Sogdians in China, Turfan, and Sogdiana: Problems Raised by a Christian Sogdian Text Ōtani 2497]. *In*: T. Irisawa and K. Kitsudo, ed., *Essays on the Manuscripts Written in Central Asian Languages in the Otani Collection: Buddhism, Manichaeism, and Christianity* 大谷探検隊収集西域胡語文献論叢ー仏教・マニ教・景教. Kyoto: Research Institute for Buddhist Culture/Research Center for World Buddhist Cultures, Ryukoku University, 155–175.

———. Forthcoming. Sogdian Christians in Sogdiana, Turfan, and China. *In* Proceedings of the conference "From Tajikistan to Turfan: Traces of Cultural Heritage of Sogdians", Dushanbe, September 2015.

Zhang Naizhu 张乃翥 and Zheng Yaofeng 郑瑶峰. 2014. Wenhua renleixue shiyu xia Yi Luo he yan'an de Tangdai Huren buluo: yi Longmen shiku xin faxian de Jingjiao yiku wei yuanqi (shang) 文化人类学视域下伊洛河沿岸的唐代胡人部落—以龙门石窟新发现的景教瘗窟为缘起(上) [The Community of Central Asians on the Banks of the Yi and Luo Rivers from the Perspective of Cultural Anthropology: The Case of the Newly Discovered Nestorian Burial Niche in Longmen Grottoes (I)]. *Study on the Cave Temples* 石窟寺研究 5, 154–74.

Zieme, P. 2015. *Altuigurische Texte der Kirche des Ostens aus Zentralasien*. Piscataway, NJ: Gorgias Press.

CHAPTER THIRTY-THREE

SYRIAC CHRISTIANITY IN INDIA

István Perczel

INTRODUCTION

The most numerous branch of Syriac Christianity in the world is that of the Syrian Christians of India.[1] Although monuments, historical records, and oral tradition indicate the erstwhile existence of branches of the same community on the Coromandel Coast[2] in Mailapur (today a suburb of Chennai) in Tamil Nadu as well as in Sri Lanka, when the Portuguese re-discovered India in the late fifteenth century, they found Christian populations only in the central and southern parts of the Malabar Coast (also called Malankara and, by the Portuguese, *a Serra*).[3]

At present, due to colonial interventions and the activity of Middle Eastern missionaries coming to India from diverse Syrian churches throughout history, the Indian Syrian Christians belong to at least eight different jurisdictions. Yet, as these Christians have been an integral part of the local Indian society that was based, since the Middle Ages, on strict caste hierarchy, more fundamental and more ancient than their ecclesiastic divisions of modern times is their unity as a caste of Indian society, divided only by their separation into two sub-castes: 'Those of the northern side' (*Vaṭakkumbhāgar*) and 'Those of the southern side' (*Tekkumbhāgar*). Nobody really knows the real origin of these names, which is clad in legends. Both these communities had a relatively high standing in the complicated caste structure of South Indian society, being close to the dominant *śūdra* caste, the Nāyars. In fact, the specificity of the caste system of the Malabar Coast was the lack of the *kśātriya* and *vaiśya* castes. The matrilineal *śūdra* Nāyars constituted the warrior and land-tenant class among the Hindus, from among whom the local kings emerged. The latter were given by the brahmins the rank of *kśātriya* at the moment of enthronement, but this did not touch their entire family. The role of the missing *vaiśyas* was filled by certain non-polluting Hindu craftsmen castes and by the non-Hindu merchant communities: Jews, Christians, and Muslims in the Middle Ages and early modernity (Susan Thomas 2002: 7–8), but also Jains, Buddhists, and Zoroastrians in the earlier mediaeval period. While the 'Northists' are more numerous and more integrated into the surrounding society, the 'Southists', who trace their origins back to a group of early Syrian Christian settlers, were until recently strictly endogamous, not intermarrying with anyone, including their Northist fellow Christians, and boast that they are thereby preserving pure Semitic blood.[4] While both sub-castes belonged to the same church organisation, their churches and clergy were strictly separated, which fact had greatly scandalised the Portuguese missionaries, who tried in vain to unite the two 'sides'.

According to the data released by the churches, this community numbers altogether around eight million members (Menachery-Balakrishnan-Perczel 2014: 582–91). They are being called Syrian Christians (*suṟiyāni nasrāṇikal*), Saint Thomas Christians (*Mār Tōma nasrāṇikal*), or Māppiḷḷa Christians (*nasrāṇi māppiḷḷamar*). Yet, originally they seem to have called themselves simply 'Christians' (*nasrāṇikal*), as there were no other Christians in India from whom they needed to distinguish themselves. Nevertheless, as the above denominations reveal important aspects of the history and the life of the community, it is convenient to begin with these.

THE NAMES OF THE GROUPS

Syrian Christians

The mother tongue of the indigenous, pre-colonial Indian Christians is Malayalam, a Dravidian language akin to Tamil, Kannada, and Telugu. Yet they identify themselves as Syrian Christians, because, before their forced submission by the Portuguese colonisers to the Roman Catholic Church, they had belonged to the Church of the East, that is, to the Persian Church. Even the Malayalam name for Syrian Christian (*Suṟiyāni*) is borrowed from the Persian *Soryāni*, meaning the Christian ethnicity of the Sasanian Empire.The forced Latinisation had made these Christians forget to a certain extent their Persian origins but had only reinforced their feeling of Syrian identity. They cherished Syriac as their liturgical language and, also, the language of their theology and elite culture, and revered as their teachers (*malpān*, plural: *malpānmar*, from the Syriac *malpāna*) and leaders those local priests who knew good Syriac. The cultivation of Syriac constituted their principal connecting link and opening towards the West Asian mother churches and thus served, besides its liturgical use, as the *lingua franca* for official correspondence with the representatives of those churches.

Furthermore, as the Syrian Christians constituted a relatively high caste of Indian society (bearing in mind that they ranked below the *śūdra* Nāyars), Syriac also played a role analogous to that of Sanskrit among the Brahmins: that of a sacred literary language, the good knowledge of which was one of the constituting factors of the community's priestly elite (Perczel 2009). After the arrival of the Portuguese colonisers following Vasco da Gama's discoveries in 1498, the European missionaries had to deal with this situation. Before long, they had to recognise that, if they wanted their missionary work to be successful, they had to carry it on in Syriac. Thus, Syriac became the main linguistic vehicle of Catholic missions too. Recent research by the SRITE project[5] has uncovered a large quantity of early modern literature written in Syriac, produced in India by Western missionaries, mainly by Jesuits. Moreover, while a Franciscan attempt to educate Roman Catholic priests in Latin-speaking seminaries inevitably failed (Thekkedath 1988: 34–6), from 1587 onwards the Jesuits trained their seminarians in Syriac at Vaipicotta Seminary in Chennamangalam, a decision that was accompanied by much success (Thekkedath 1988: 56–9, 86–90).

The Latinisation of the liturgy also had of necessity to take the form of translating the Latin prayers into Syriac and to write new Syriac liturgical texts reflecting the Tridentine doctrines. Syriac language and culture gained a special new emphasis because of the activity of two 'Western' missionaries of exceptional erudition. One of them was Mar Abraham (d. 1597), the last Persian metropolitan of the Indian Syrian Christians who, around 1556, came as a Nestorian bishop and, in 1568, returned from Rome as a Catholic Chaldean bishop. The other was the Catalan Jesuit Francisco Roz (1559–1624), professor of Syriac at the Vaipicotta Seminary and then, from 1599, bishop of Angamaly and finally, from 1608, archbishop of Kodungallur (Cranganore). It was due to the activity of these two great scholars in opposition that the fight for the souls of the Indian Christians took the form of a *Kulturkampf* conducted in Syriac (Perczel 2018b). Also, it is during these early colonial times that we witness the appearance and multiplication of dated and undated Syriac inscriptions, while all the earlier inscriptions are in Malayalam and Tamil (Briquel Chatonnet, Desreumaux and Thekaparampil 2008: 24; Perczel 2009: 292–4), as well as the multiplication of Syriac manuscripts imported to or written in India (Van der Ploeg 1983: *passim*; Perczel 2009: 292).

When, in 1653, the community revolted against the colonial and missionary endeavours of the Portuguese and the Jesuits (Thekkedath 1972), new West Asian missionaries were invited, who also communicated and taught in Syriac. This only enhanced the *Kulturkampf* started by Mar Abraham and Francisco Roz and the significance of the Syriac language in it. Syriac has remained a means of communication and creation for a small layer of learned elite until modern times. Thus, in the first half of the twentieth century, two great scholars, Mar Abimalek Timotheos Qelayta (1878–1945), the metropolitan of the Indian Syrian Chaldean (that is, Nestorian) Church (Mar Aprem 1975), and Placid Podipara CMI (1895–1985), the greatest Catholic theologian of the Syro-Malabar Catholic Church (Thomas Kalayil 2007: xxvii–lix), corresponded in eloquent Classical Syriac, although both of them were perfectly fluent in English, and Mar Timotheos also knew Malayalam, the mother tongue of Fr. Placid.[6] The latest great teacher of Syriac language and culture, who translated the Syrian Orthodox liturgy into Malayalam and wrote poetry in Syriac, Fr. Kurien Kaniamparampil, who also bore the title of the great Malankara Malpan (the Teacher of all Malankara), died in 2015, at the age of 104 (Pulickavil Achen 2003).

Saint Thomas Christians

According to the unanimous founding traditions of the community, the first Indian Christians were converted and baptised by the Apostle Thomas. This tradition is deeply rooted, even the date AD 52 being widely claimed as indicating the date of the Apostle's arrival in India. Its historical authenticity has been widely debated but should not concern us here.[7] What is important to note is that South India was linked into the network of Roman trade routes by sea and land and that, from the first century AD, there was very close communication between the eastern Mediterranean and the South Indian ports, the most important of which was Musiris.[8] This is independently testified in written sources, such as the *Periplus of the Erythraean Sea*, Strabo's *Geography*, and most importantly, by the 'Musiris Papyrus' kept in Vienna[9] as well as by the recent excavations of the site of Musiris at Pattanam, near North Paravur. It was these intense trade relations that had made possible the early Christian missionary activity in India.

Local Christian tradition connects the earliest such missionary efforts to the figure of the apostle Saint Thomas, which is celebrated by an abundant folklore. There are a number of ballads celebrating the deeds of the apostle, most of which are connected to performative events (Nedungatt 2008: 355–67). Such are the *Vīraṭiyān Pāṭṭu*, or Viradiyan Song, performed at festive Christian occasions by a Hindu caste called Viradiyan (from the Malayalam adjective *vīram*: 'strong', 'brave', but originally meaning 'chief of slaves' [Gundert 1872: 874]), but also called Pāṇar, 'Bards', 'Singers' (Gundert 1872: 599), who perform to the accompaniment of a string instrument called *villu*. The Pāṇar (plural of Pāṇan) are the bards who traditionally perform historical songs for high-caste Indians, among whom the Christians also belong. The Pāṇar are, in this sense, bearers of the historical consciousness of these communities.

Another ballad is the *Mārggam Kaḷi Pāṭṭu*, that is, the 'Song of the Drama of the Way', 'Way' meaning here the Christian religion. This historical song and dancing drama was originally performed uniquely by men at weddings and other feasts. It has different versions sung by the Northist and Southist sub-castes of Christians. In its currently known Southist form, attributed to Anjilimuṭṭil Iṭṭi Tōmman Kattanār (d. 1659), one of the leaders of the great revolt against the Portuguese in 1653, it contains fourteen stanzas. It retells the stories of the Acts of Thomas, placing them, however, in the court of the Cōḷa emperor in Mailapur and adding to it the local legend of the death of the apostle pierced with a lance by a Brahmin (Barboza 1990: 25–41).

The most famous and extensive ballad is the *Rambān Pāṭṭu*, the 'Song of the Teacher (Thomas)', which contains 448 lines (Hosten 1931). Yet, this ballad, in its present form, cannot be earlier than the second half of the seventeenth century (Perczel 2006: 416–17). These ballads recount the arrival of the apostle, his missionary activities, his miracles and death, which they place, without exception, in Mailapur. Yet they differ as to Thomas's port of landing. While the *Rambān Pāṭṭu* indicates Maliankara (traditionally understood as Kodungallur),[10] the *Mārggam Kaḷi Pāṭṭu* places the port of landing in Mailapur. While these are the most important folk songs concerning the life and death of the apostle, there are innumerable other stories told in diverse localities: Saint Thomas is ever-present in the imagination of the Saint Thomas Christians and is as much inalienable to their identity as is Saint Peter to the Catholic Church.

In the colophon of the earliest extant Syriac manuscript copied in India, Ms Vaticanus syriacus 22, dated 1301 and copied in Śenglē/Śenjlī in the Malabar Coast, the scribe, a young deacon called Zachariah, son of Joseph, son of Zachariah, commemorates the then metropolitan bishop of India, Mar Jacob, and calls him the holder of the apostolic see of Saint Thomas (Van der Ploeg 1983: 3–4, 187–9).[11] This shows that the idea that the Indian Christians had issued from Saint Thomas's apostolic mission was not only deeply rooted in the conscience of the Indian community but was also accepted by their mother Church in Persia.

The divided testimony of the poetic tradition as to the place of arrival corresponds to a similar variation observed in local church histories. While the most generally held tradition indicates Maliankara (Kodungallur) as Thomas's place of arrival, an important tradition places it in Mailapur. The latter tradition is recorded in a history, redacted in Malayalam and Syriac, whose manuscripts are now preserved in Leiden.[12] Also, the tomb of the apostle was venerated from time immemorial in Mailapur, as was observed by early travellers, such as Marco Polo in 1293.[13] These traditions coincide perfectly with the early Portuguese reports and indicate an important historical fact: the original core and centre of the community was not at the Malabar Coast as today, but at the eastern Coromandel Coast, and was later destroyed due to historical calamities, either an encroachment of the sea upon the city of Mailapur, a war, or a persecution (Mundadan 1984: 71–8). The rise of the Christianity of the western coast may be related to this disaster, whose dating thus becomes crucial for understanding the mediaeval history of the community.

There are also other stories about the early evangelisation of India. According to Eusebius and Jerome, Pantaenus, the second-century Alexandrian teacher, visited India, where he found that the Indian Christians had been evangelised by the apostle Bartholomew and were reading the gospel according to Matthew written in the Hebrew tongue (which must mean Aramaic).[14] The difficulty in interpreting this report lies in the fact that the name India in antiquity simply meant the place from where the spices came: thus, any region from the Arab peninsula to the real India could be denominated as 'India'. Yet, Jerome specifically speaks of Pantaenus's mission to the Brahmins, which should indicate South Asia (unless this is just a gloss on Eusebius's text). If Eusebius and Jerome are reliable here, this report would preserve the memory of an early – second-century – Alexandrian connection preceding

Figure 33.1 Pilgrimage to the Mount of Malayathur, for venerating the footsteps of Saint Thomas imprinted in a rock

Source: István Perczel

Figure 33.2 Pilgrimage to the Mount of Malayathur

Source: István Perczel

Figure 33.3 An early statue of Christ, probably from the second half of the sixteenth-first decades of the seventeenth century. Lacking European models, the local artist represented Christ upon the model of the Buddha. The pedestal decorated with lotus flower is the same as that of the Hindu gods, while the cloth of the little Jesus is that worn by the contemporary Christians/Christian priests. The binding of the belt in the form of the Egyptian hieroglyphic sign ankh on this and other statues indicates that this was the distinguishing mark of the Christian clothing on the Malabar coast and may be one of the distant relics of an early Egyptian connection

Source: Courtesy of the Rev. Dr. Ignatius Payyappilly

the one with the Persian Church (Dihle 1963). Given the intense trade connections between the South Indian and the Red Sea ports, this hypothesis stands to reason. Also, there are some signs in the local tradition of surviving elements of specifically Egyptian customs.

Māppiḷḷa Christians

The Māppiḷḷa Christians (*nasrāṇi māppiḷḷa*) share their epithet with two other groups of similarly Western origin and similar status in Indian society: the Jewish Māppiḷḷa (*jūta māppiḷḷa*) and the Muslim Māppiḷḷa (*cōnaka māppiḷḷa*) communities of the Malabar Coast. *Māppiḷḷa* means 'the son of the maternal uncle' and, hence, the ideal bridegroom for some exogamous Hindu castes.[15] The name indicates that these Abrahamic communities came into existence, at least partially, through the intermarriage of West Asian merchants with local Indian women. This was possible because the Hindu Nāyar caste, which provided the bulk of the soldiers in Malankara society and from among whom the local kings also emerged, was exogamous and matrilineal, meaning that they intermarried with other castes, while the inheritance was passed on from maternal uncle to nephew. Moreover, there was a loose concept of marriage among the Nāyars. Nāyar women also acted as concubines to the young Brahmins, as the custom among the Brahmins was to marry only the first-born son to a Brahmin girl, so that the entire landed property of the family becomes his inheritance. The other sons had Nāyar concubines, so that their children also became members of the Nāyar caste and inherited from their maternal uncle only (Susan Thomas 2002: 9–12).

The Nāyar women were the ideal partners for West Asian merchants, who came to India via the monsoon winds and had to stay there for six months at least, until they could return to the West. This led to relatively easy solutions for the Muslim merchants, whose law permitted temporary marriages (*mutʿa*) for facilitating trade (Gamliel 2018b: 204). As a result, a Muslim Māppiḷḷa community was formed, which, while observing the commandments of the Qurʾan and the Shariah, still follows the matrilineal customary laws of the Nāyars, a fact that stupefied the more traditional Muslim visitors and members of the community (Shaykh Zainuddin Makhdum 2009: 40). To follow a similar practice would have been much more difficult for the Jewish merchants; however, there are among the Cairo Genizah some documents testifying to intermarriage between Jewish merchants and the local Indian communities. These are those relative to the marriage of the merchant Abraham ben Yijū with a Nāyar woman, Aśu, whom he allegedly 'bought' as a 'slave' as soon as he arrived in Mangalore, and freed from servitude before renaming her 'Berākhā, daughter of Abraham'[16] (Goitein and Friedman 2007: 55–7, 632–4; Ghosh 1993; Gamliel 2018b). These unique documents show how intermarriage with local women had to be handled according to Jewish halakhic rules. In fact, Aśu could not have been a slave but a Nāyar girl as, in his letters, Abraham ben Yijū speaks about his 'brother-in-law Nāyar' who was also his business partner. Yet, it was through the ceremony of manumission that Aśu could be integrated into the Jewish community (Goitein and Friedman 2007: 638; 660; 774; Ghosh 1993: 226–8; Gamliel 2018b).[17] That this combination of Indian Nāyar customary law and Jewish halakhic rules was not without problems is indicated by the legal attacks upon the validity of ben Yijū's marriage and upon his children's right of inheritance, attacks that he was obliged to repel as soon as he returned to Yemen (Goitein and Friedman 2007: 73–6; Gamliel 2018b: 208–9).

The legendary traditions of the Christians record a similar case. According to these, the first Persian/Syrian merchant who settled on the Malabar Coast was Thomas of Kana, from whom both sub-castes of the Māppiḷḷa Christians, that is the Northists and the Southists, trace their origins. According to an ancient tradition of the Southists, recorded by the Portuguese travellers of the sixteenth–seventeenth centuries, Thomas of Kana had become very rich due to his business in Malankara. As he was constantly travelling, he kept two houses, one in Kodungallur and one in the North. In these two houses he kept two wives, a Syrian Christian in Kodungallur and a slave from the Nāyar caste, whom he baptised, in the North. In this way, the Southists would be the descendants of Thomas's legitimate wife, while the Northists would issue from his illegitimate relationship with the Nāyar woman (Gouvea 1606: fol. 4v; Malekandathil 2003: 18–20). Contrary to this, the Northists relate that they are the descendants of Thomas of Kana from his legitimate wife, who was a high-caste Hindu (a Nāyar), while the Southists issued from a concubine from the *Maināttu* washermen's caste (Mundadan 1984: 95–8). Apparently, these ethno-histories are aimed at celebrating one's own caste and vilifying the other, but they also preserve memories of the formation of the communities through the intermarriage with local matrilineal castes, such as the Nāyars and the *Maināttus*. In fact, most probably, intermarriage did not occur only with the higher castes.

As to the relationship with the Nāyar caste, the Portuguese chroniclers recorded that, in the sixteenth century, marriage between the Māppiḷḷa Christians and the Nāyars was considered normal and did not transgress the rules of pollution (Dionysio 1578: DI XI, 137; Monserrate 1579: foll. 149–51; T. K. Joseph 1928: 29–30; Mundadan 1984: 96; Bayly 2003: 252). The Christians also had a shared culture with the Nāyars. The communities practised the traditional South Indian martial art of *kaḷarippayaṯṯu*, served in the armies of the local kings, followed similar rituals, and enjoyed similar social privileges. These privileges were bestowed upon them by royal decrees, some of which are extant to the present day. Besides being involved in trade and warfare, at an unspecified date the Māppiḷḷa Christians also engaged in spice plantation, which resulted in their moving their settlements from the coastal area towards the low ranges of the Western Ghats (Malekandathil 2010: 9ff).

The term Māppiḷḷa thus reveals the manifold embeddedness of the Indian Syrian Christians. It indicates their origin from West Asian merchants who settled on the Malabar Coast, their shared culture and social status with the other two Abrahamic communities of the Coast, as well as their entangled relationship with the local Hindu communities, especially with the Nāyar caste, with whom they intermarried. Yet they differ from their Muslim Māppiḷḷa neighbours in that they were constituted of two layers: of local Indians converted by early missions and of the descendants of the West Asian merchants, who intermarried not only with the local Hindu matrilineal castes, but also with their Christian co-religionists whom they found in South India. Yet, the taboo of intermarriage between the Northists and the Southists, as well as the deep tensions between them, indicate that this relationship was far from unproblematic.

In the following, I will give a brief outline of the history of the community. At present, I will focus my attention on the early history, that which preceded the colonial

Figure 33.4 Participants in the feast of Mor Baselios Yaldo in Kothamangalam, 2 October 2007. Mor Baselios Yaldo was an Antiochian Syrian Orthodox missionary bishop, who came to India in 1685. Christians and Hindus together participate in the feast

Source: István Perczel

conquest of the Portuguese, as this period is shrouded in legends, which have given rise to much misunderstanding. Yet, recent advances in South Indian and Indian Ocean historiography as well as in the study of the extant ancient epigraphic material, and also the SRITE project for the survey of local Christian archives, now permit us to formulate a new synthesis about the early history of the Indian Syrian Christian community.

HISTORY

The early mediaeval period

The Persian mission

The possibility of an early Alexandrian mission and of early connections with Egypt and Alexandria corresponding to the period of intense Indo-Roman trade exchanges has been mentioned above, concerning the St Thomas traditions.[18] Yet, in the earliest period for which we have firm historical records from both sides of the East–West relation, we find a tight connection between the Persian Church and South India. This must have to do with the rivalry between the Roman and the Persian empires for dominating the India trade in which, apparently, the Persians increasingly acquired the upper hand (Malekandathil 2010: 1–13). When the Alexandrian merchant

Cosmas Indicopleustes sailed to India in the early sixth century, he found Christian communities along the Indian Coast, which were under a bishop consecrated in Persia (Cosmas, *Christian Topography*, 3.65 – Wolska-Conus 1968, 503–5). He also reports the presence of a church in Taprobane (Sri Lanka), where constant liturgical services were held by a priest and a deacon ordained in Persia, serving the visiting Persian merchants (Cosmas, *Christian Topography*, 11.14 – Wolska-Conus 1973, 343–5). The Greek word *Persis* most probably means here the province of Fars, so that the bishop could have been consecrated in Rew Ardashir. These sparse remarks may indicate more than the mere presence of visiting Persian merchants in mainland India, otherwise the consecration of a bishop for the community would not have been necessary.

What was the liturgical language used in the South Indian churches in those times? We do not have local sources to decide this question. The language of the liturgical service in the Persian Church was Syriac, so one would suppose that the liturgy was served in this language in the entire South Asian region. Yet, the Chronicle of Se'ert reports that, at the beginning of the sixth century, Ma'ana, metropolitan of Fars, translated liturgical texts from Syriac to Middle Persian and sent the books 'to the maritime lands (the Persian Gulf) and India' (Chronicle of Se'ert: IX, PO 7.2, 117). From this note, some scholars have drawn the conclusion that the liturgical language of Fars and India was, from the sixth century to the eleventh, Middle Persian (Gropp 1991; Malekandathil 2010: 9). Yet, a careful reading of the text does not confirm this interpretation. The Arabic of the Chronicle of Se'ert uses precise Syriac terms for what has been translated: *madrāšē* – that is, exegetical expositions or doctrinal hymns; *memrē* – that is, sermons, teaching poems; and *ōnyāṯā* 'sung in the church' – that is, the anthems of the changing feasts. These are all parts of the teaching elements in the liturgy and are additions to the main part, which consists of the anaphora and the daily liturgy. Had Ma'ana wanted to replace the Syriac liturgy with the Persian text, he should have started with the anaphora and the daily prayers. Thus, nothing indicates here that the translations were meant to replace the Syriac liturgy but, rather, they seem to have been intended to explain it and make it comprehensible for those whose mother tongue was Middle Persian. Therefore, we may suppose that the liturgical language of the Indian Church was, ever since it had joined the Church of the East, Syriac, and that the Persian translation was meant to serve the visiting Persian merchants, whom Cosmas mentions also in Taprobane/Sri Lanka. With this caveat for the liturgy, one must admit that the importance of Middle and Early New Persian for mediaeval Indian Christianity was paramount.

Thomas of Kana and the lost copper plates

How did the Indian Christian community join the Church of the East? According to local tradition, this event is connected with the arrival of the rich Persian merchant who, together with his two wives who became the origins of two communities, was mentioned above: Thomas of Kana, or, in Malayalam, Knāyi Tōmman. Current tradition also assigns a date to his arrival, 345 CE, and knows of about 72 families who arrived together with him. It is reported that Thomas arrived in *Mahādēvarpattanam*, the 'City of the Great God' (Śiva), which is placed either in Kodungallur or, by early seventeenth-century Portuguese sources, in the neighbourhood of North Paravur, precisely where the site of Musiris is being excavated. It is said that he built a church and a Christian settlement there. Further, with the help of a bishop and clergymen belonging to the Church of the East, who accompanied him, he reorganised the religious life of the Christians who, by that time, had fallen to such spiritual indigence that they were intermarrying with the Nāyars and their lifestyle did not differ from that of the latter. The early Portuguese reports tell similar stories albeit with much variation, even as to the dates concerned which vary from the first Christian centuries to the ninth (Mundadan 1984: 90–5).

At the source of all these stories lies a document, now lost, which was written on copper plates and whose only remnant is a Portuguese translation contained in a text entitled 'Narrative about Malankara–written in 1604' (*Relação sobre a Serra–feito em 1604*), now kept in the British Library (MS BL Add. 9853),[19] which scholars suppose to have been written by Francisco Roz S.J., the first European archbishop of the Syrian Christians (Mundadan 1984: 4).[20] These copper plates were in the custody of the Syrian metropolitan Mar Jacob (in Malabar between 1504 and 1549) who, because of his poverty, pawned them to an anonymous person from whom, upon Mar Jacob's request, the plates were redeemed by the treasurer of the Portuguese factory in Cochin, Pero de Sequeira. According to de Sequeira's testimony, the grant was written on two plates, written on both sides. De Sequeira showed them to the governor of Kochi, Martim Afonso de Sousa, who had them translated by a Jew who was able to read the *Vaṭṭeḻuttu* script.[21] Later the plates were lost, so that what we have now is the Portuguese translation made on the basis of the Malayalam reading of the Jewish interpreter (Goes 1619: 77–78; Monteiro d'Aguiar/Hosten 1930/1997: 183–5; Schurhammer 1963: 348). According to this translation, the king of Kodungallur donated *Mahādēvarpattanam* to Thomas, and gave seventy-two houses to the families that came together with him. Hence the tradition of a first Persian settlement on the Malabar Coast, which had arrived in the fourth century and included entire settler families. Because of the early date attributed to this settlement, it is believed that Thomas of Kana and the clerics who came with him were those who established the original connection with the Church of the East. This tradition is firmly believed by most of the Syrian Christians (Malekandathil 2010: 2).

Yet, although the copper plates are believed to have been lost, the tradition can and should be corrected as to the nature and the date of the migration. As it has been demonstrated by T. K. Joseph, the motif of seventy-two houses or families comes from a misreading of the phrase *eḻupattiraṇḍu viṭupēru*, 'seventy-two privileges', a necessary component of all these copper plate grants, by reading instead of *viṭu* with short i, *vīṭu*, 'house', with long ī (T. K. Joseph 1929: 199; Schurhammer 1963). Thus, it was not entire families, but single settlers who arrived with Thomas and received the seventy-two privileges of the *Añcuvaṇṇam* and *Manigramam* trade guilds, being those of the foreign merchants trading with the local ones, and consisting of Jewish, Christian, Zoroastrian and, in view of the probable date of the arrival, Muslim members (Subbarayalu 2012: 176–87). Apparently, those settlers intermarried with the local women.

Definitively, the fourth-century date should also be corrected. The Leiden manuscripts mentioned above connect the arrival of the colonist group of Thomas of Kana with the destruction of the main settlement of the Christians in Mailapur, the result of the persecutions of Māṇikkavācakar, a ninth-century Śaiva saint, one of the founders of Śaiva *bhakti* (devotion) whose fifty-one hymns entitled *Tiruvacāgam* ('The Sacred Word') constitute the eighth volume of the Tamil Śaiva canon of devotional hymns. Mānikkavācakar is also considered the author of the *Tiruccirrambalakkōvai*, a mystical love-poem in 400 stanzas. According to tradition, he lived in the ninth century and was the son of a minister of a Pāndya king (Nilakanta Sastri 1975: 335; Mundadan 1984: 74; Champakalakshmi 2011: 63). Although the *bhakti* hagiographic works do not mention any tension between the movement and the Christian community, they are replete with violent acts against the Jains and the Buddhists (Champakalakshmi 2011: 438–60). Traditionally, the Indian Christians were also called Buddhists by Hindu sources. Besides the Leiden histories, most Portuguese reports of the late sixteenth century tell similar stories and know of the arrival of Thomas in Kodungallur following the destruction of Christianity in Mailapur. Those which depend on the lost copper plates also date the arrival to the ninth century (Mundadan 1984: 91).[22]

Maruvān Sapir Īśō and the Kollam copper plates[23]

Placing Thomas of Kana's arrival in the ninth century would make his arrival relate to another settler group that arrived in Kollam sometime after 825, the founding date of the city and the beginning of the Malayalam era. Thus, if the arrival of Thomas's community is to be placed in the ninth century, this was not the moment when the link with the Persian Church was established. There are concordant data indicating that, at an earlier time, the principal point of contact of the Persian merchants and the Persian Church with India was in Mailapur, which was also the see of the bishop of India (Gouvea 1606: 5v–6r, Malekandathil 20, 03: 25–6). The ninth-century colonisation and the arrival of Persian bishops at the Malabar Coast was most probably the result of the destruction of the community at the eastern coast and the transfer of the community's centre of gravity to the West.

We are much better informed about the arrival of the settler community that arrived in Kollam, given that the royal grant of the privileges given to them is extant on five copper plates dated to 849 AD (see fig 33.5).[24]

The grant recorded on the plates was donated by Ayyaṉ Aṭikal Ṭiruvaṭikaḷ ('His Highness the Ruler of Ay'), the governor of Vēṇāṭu,[25] in the fifth year of the Cēra emperor Stāṇu Ravi, that is, in 849. As was the case with the lost Thomas of Kana plates, so the Kollam plates are also a grant for the foundation of a settlement, or emporium (*nagaram*) situated in the seaport, around a sanctuary called *Tarisāppaḷḷi*. The latter is most probably a composite word from the Malayalam *paḷḷi* 'settlement', 'non-Hindu sanctuary', and *tarsā*, the Early New Persian variant of the Middle Persian *tarsāk* (*tls'k'*), derived from *tars* (*tls*), 'fear', and meaning 'the one who fears', 'God-fearer', 'a Christian' (Mackenzie 1971: 82), so that *Tarisāppaḷḷi* would mean 'a Christian place of worship'.[26] Apparently, the denomination follows the community's self-identification, from which we understand that it was Persian speaking.

The community attached to the church receives servant families (apparently as slaves) 'to guarantee that the church is not lacking anything in the form of oil etc. by sowing what is to be sown and giving what is to be given' (Narayanan 1972: 92), the right of self-governance, and exemption from taxes and is granted large incomes and the right to levy tolls and taxes. 'To guarantee that the church is not lacking anything in the form of oil' seems to be a symbolic expression, meaning that extensive privileges are given to a community centred on a place of worship. Similar expressions are used in Cēra grants given to Hindu, Buddhist, and Jain communities. This is also evidence for the official acceptance of the worship conducted in the *Tarisā* sanctuary.

It is said in the grant that the church (or the church community) was founded by one Maruvān Sapir Īśō, whose name is a Persian-Syriac composite. Maruvān is a common Persian name, often used by Christians (Gignoux, Jullien and Jullien 2009: 98), Īśō is the East Syriac pronunciation of Jesus, a name much used among the Nestorian Christians, while *sapir* means 'learned', 'erudite' in Syriac. Thus, the name probably means Maruvān Jesus, the Learned one. This name has been often identified with the East Syrian name Sabrishoʿ, 'Hope in Jesus', but this is contradicted by the other variant, in which it is found in the inscription, *Ēśō da-Tapir āyi*. This seems to be a Syriac-Malayalam composite: *Ēśō* (Syriac: Jesus), *da* (Syriac: who), *Tapir* (Syriac, to be read as *Sapir*: learned), *āyi* (Malayalam: is): 'Jesus, who is [the] Learned'. The name Sabrishoʿ, usually used as a name for clerics, could not be written this way.[27]

It is understood that the privileges are witnessed by Muslim, Christian, Zoroastrian, and Jewish witnesses. The Muslims sign in Arabic written in Kufic script, the Christians and the Zoroastrians in Middle Persian written in Pahlavi characters, and the Jews in Early Judaeo-Persian written in Hebrew script (Cereti 2009). This shows that, by the mid-ninth century, the languages of the trans-Arabian Sea maritime trade were Arabic and Persian, the latter being shared by the three religious communities.

The God venerated in the church is referred to as *tevar*, 'deity', without any specification of who this deity is. In fact, the copper plates are not a religious but a purely legal document, which is given to receive a rich foreign merchant community, to settle them, and to give them the traditional privileges of the Malankara aristocracy. In the local Christian tradition, Sapir Īśō is remembered as a rich merchant who settled in Kollam and brought with him two bishops with Persian names, Mar Śābūhr and Mar Afrahāt (Marxabro and Marprohd in the Portuguese documents),[28] who were to be venerated as the great saints of the Malankara Church and to whom many churches were dedicated (Gouvea 1606: 5r; Malekandathil 2003: 21–2; Mundadan 1984: 103–7).

What was the occasion for the arrival of this new settler community? Antonio Gouvea says that they arrived 'a few years after the founding of the city of Coulão' (Kollam) (Gouvea 1606: 4v–5r; Malekandathil 2003: 20–1). From this narrative, we learn that the colony of Maruvān Sapir Īśō came after the founding of Kollam, whence the Malayalam era starts. Apparently, Kollam was founded in 825 as a new port city, where the king invited foreign merchants, Muslim Arabs, Christians, Zoroastrians, and Jews to settle. So, most probably, the founding and building of the *Tarisāppaḷḷi* is posterior to 825 and should be dated around the 840s (Narayanan 1972: 32). Thus, the Malayalam era begins with the founding of a new port city by the emperor Stāṇu Ravi but is not connected to Sapir Īśō himself. Because of this, the view that is generally held, namely that Kollam was founded by Sapir Īśō, who arrived in the year 823, should be revised. So also should be revised the widespread misreading of the name Maruvān Sapir Īśō as Mar Sabrishoʿ and his identification with one of the bishops, Mar Śābūhr, based on one of the Portuguese transcriptions of the latter's name as Mar Sapor (Malekandathil 2010: 38ff). The grant is clearly given to a lay merchant community, which is identified as Christian (*tarsā – tarisā*).

The foundation and growth of the port city of Kollam is to be linked to the intense conflict between the Cēra emperors, whose capital was Magodaiyapattanam, near Kodungallur, and the Pāndyas, centred on Madurai. In the early ninth century, the Pāndyas attacked the kingdom of Ay and occupied it, together with its capital and port city, Vizhinjam, 15 km south of present-day Tiruvananthapuram/Trivandrum, while the Cēras moved in and occupied the Vel country, to the north of Ay. It was the loss of Vizhinjam, an ancient port with remnants of Indo-Roman trade – perhaps identical with the ancient Balita/Valita described in the Periplus – to the Pāndyas, which prompted the foundation of Kollam as a rival port (Periplus 56; Narayanan 1972: 32–3). Apparently, under the ninth-century Pāndyas, a Hindu restoration took place in present-day Tamil Nadu, also introducing the new *bhakti* movement (a devotional form of Hinduism) which aimed to sweep away Buddhism, Jainism, and Christianity (Champakalakshmi 2011: 438–60). At the same time, their Western neighbours and rivals, the Cēras, were practicing religious tolerance, even religious pluralism. There are also copper plate charters concerning Cēra donations to a Buddhist monastery (*vihara*) (Narayanan 1972: 9–16, 65–9), to Jain temples (Narayanan 1972: 17–22, 70–8), and to Jewish merchants (Narayanan 1972: 23–30, 79–85). This attitude attracted foreign merchants, be they Jewish, Zoroastrian, Christian, or Muslim, to populate the new port city of Kollam. If indeed the Christians were expelled from the Pāndya Empire, it is comprehensible that the Cēras, who fought the Pāndyas, gave them shelter. Thus, the foundation of the *Tarisāppaḷḷi* must have been part of a complex process of the decline of the Christian merchant community at the Coromandel Coast and its parallel rise at the Malabar Coast.

As to the arrival of the two bishops, we cannot know anything for sure about them. While the most general tradition links this event to the foundation of the *Tarisāppaḷḷi*, it is also possible that the bishops arrived later. Francisco Roz recorded that the remnants of these saints (called *kadišaŋŋal*: Malayalam plural from the Syriac *qadišā*, 'saint') lay buried in the Kollam church, where there were also inscriptions, which were neither in Malayalam nor in Syriac but looked to him Abyssinian (Mundadan 1984: 105). We have no reason to doubt Roz's great erudition, but I would rather suggest that he had probably seen Pahlavi characters, which would better fit the Persian origin of the bishops.

The contribution of the indirect text tradition of the Kollam copper plates

The hitherto neglected indirect text tradition of the Kollam copper plates permits us to formulate a new hypothesis concerning the provenance not only of the Kollam copper plates but also of the Thomas of Kana copper plates and, eventually, to give a dating for the latter. This indirect tradition seems to have first been subjected to analysis by Jacob Kollaparambil in a mimeographed publication of limited distribution (Kollaparambil 1995: 17–44), but it has never been properly taken into consideration in the scholarly literature.

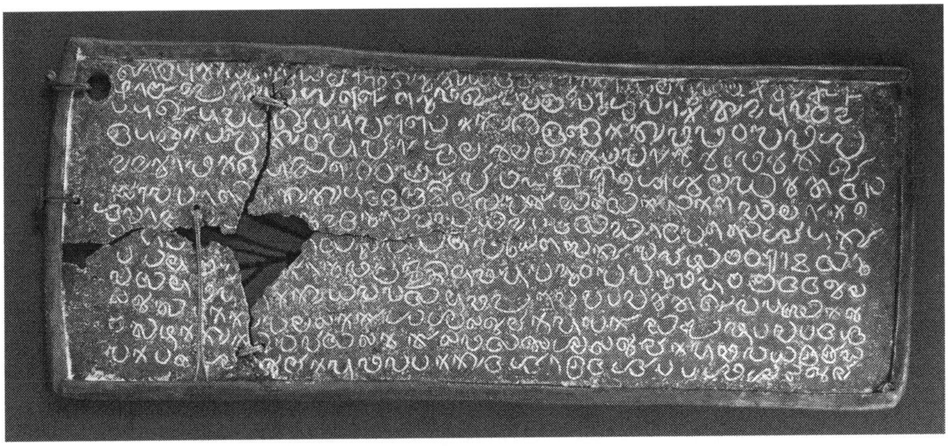

(a)

(b)

Figure 33.5a, b, c Plate 2/2, 5/1 and 5/2 of the Kollam copper plates. Plate 2/2 (a) is written in Old Malayalam, in *Veṭṭeḻuttu* script; Plate 5/1 (b) contains the Muslim signatures in Kufic Arabic and the Christian signatures in Middle Persian, in Pahlavi script; Plate 5/2 ((c), opposite) contains the Zoroastrian signatures in Middle Persian, in Pahlavi script and the Jewish signatures in Judaeo-Persian, in Hebrew script

Source: Kesavan Veluthat

(c)

Figure 33.5a, b, c (continued)

Two transcripts of the Kollam copper plates are extant. Francisco Roz had a transcript of the entire document made by a certain Itimani Kattanar into Garshuni Malayalam script in 1601.[29] Later, John Baptist Multedo of St. Teresa, bishop of Varapuzha (1714–1750), had another transcript made in Grandha or *Ārya eḻuttu* of the original *Veṭṭeḻuttu*, which was interpreted by a certain Mattai Kattanar from Angamaly in poor Portuguese for the French traveller and Indologist, A. H. Anquétil du Perron in 1758. Du Perron then translated the Portuguese interpretation of Mattai Kattanar into French and included it in his travelogue in the introduction to his translation of the Zend Avesta. The *Ārya eḻuttu* transcript itself was lost and has not to date been located.[30]

Both the Garshuni Malayalam transcript and the French text of Anquétil du Perron arrange the five plates precisely in the order which was recently established by Raghava Varier and Kesavan Veluthat on the basis of internal criteria, while earlier scholarship considered the two sets of copper plates as containing two separate grants. Moreover, while the text of the first three plates in the direct tradition is similar in the indirect text tradition to that on the extant plates, the fourth differs from the others palaeographically and contains much less text than the others. Its text is interrupted where the signatures of the local dignitaries, a necessary part of the mediaeval royal copper plate grants, begins. From the indirect text tradition, it can be established beyond any reasonable doubt that the currently extant fourth plate is only the first part of a copy of the lost fourth plate. In fact, it was a general habit that, when a document was damaged but was still partly legible, a copy of it was made to replace the original. However, since in this case the copyists did not posess the same skills as the scribes of the original document, two plates were used for copying the content of the fourth plate, the second of which was later lost. The Garshuni Malayalam transcript and the French text of Anquétil du Perron (of necessarily poor quality) permit the reconstruction of the missing part of the original fourth plate.

The currently extant fourth plate contains the concluding formula of the original royal grant, after which the signatures of the local dignitaries begin. However, the text is interrupted in the middle of the second name but continues in du Perron's French text, which contains the names of seventeen dignitaries, some of them also mentioned in the main text.[31] The signatures were not copied in the Garshuni Malayalam text. After that comes a paragraph, extant in both witnesses, about Thomas of Kana and the grants he received, with a date given according to astronomical constellations and other precious information. Yet this paragraph is odd. It appears to be like the beginning of a grant containing the usual formulae of the Cēra grants, but its text is interrupted. What follows next is the signatures in Arabic and Persian. These may, or may not, correspond to the members of the merchant guilds *Añcuvaṇṇam* and *Manigramam* mentioned in the text of the *Tarisāppaḷḷi* plates but their exact meaning becomes ambiguous because of the last paragraph.

Now my hypothesis is that this paragraph is nothing other than the first part of the lost Thomas of Kana copper plates, of which we possess only the imprecise Portuguese translation and that the two sets once belonged together as a single document witnessing the privileges received by the Christian community through the two grants given to the two settler groups. According to this hypothesis, none of the copper plate sets was the original document, but they were parts of a unified copy of the two grants. Sometime during the history of the community, the two parts of the grants were separated, so that the group centred on Kodungallur kept the Thomas of Kana grant, and the one centred on Kollam kept the *Tarisāppaḷḷi* grant. But the separation could not be made perfectly, as the copy of the Thomas of Kana grant began immediately after the signatures of the *Tarisāppaḷḷi* grant on the same plate. So the first paragraph of the Thomas of Kana grant became cut off from the main text.

Besides the above arguments, the following also seem to confirm this hypothesis: 1) there is no date of the Thomas of Kana grants in the Portuguese text, most probably because the date–as is the usual practice of the Cēra grants–is contained in the first paragraph; 2) according to the narrative of Damião de Goes (Goes 1619: 77/4; Monteiro d'Aguiar/Hosten 1930/1997: 184–5) the Thomas of Kana plates, two in number, were "written on both sides", while at the same time, "it was customary to leave blank the obverse of the first plate" (Monteiro d'Aguiar/

Hosten 1930/1997: 186): this is an indication that the Thomas of Kana plates were not an independent document–indeed, on the first plate of the Tarisāppaḷḷi grant the obverse side is left blank.

If such was the case, it is difficult to decide to which grant the Arabic and Persian signatures had belonged originally, as they could belong to either of the two, or to both, as the plate with the Arabic and Persian signatures must have been the last plate of the entire document. It is even possible that the signatories were witnessing the faithfulness of the copy containing the two documents. If the dating through astronomical constellations could be deciphered, we would know the precise date of the Thomas of Kana grants. Yet even so, it appears that Francisco Dionysio had the correct information: Thomas of Kana came after, and not before, Maruvān Sapir Īśō.[32]

The Persian crosses

It is to this period of a strong presence of Persian Christian merchants (sixth–ninth centuries) that one might link the Persian crosses found along maritime South India and Sri Lanka. These are granite crosses in bas-relief, with four equal branches, placed on a three-graded pediment, with the representation of the two wings placed on the crown of the Sasanian king, so that the cross occupies the original place of the crescent and the star on the crown.[33] The wings have been stylised so that they resemble floral motifs. On some of the bas-reliefs a dove is descending on the cross, representing the descent of the Holy Spirit at Christ's baptism, while on other crosses the dove becomes a mere 'bud' at the top of the cross. There are nine such crosses extant at the following locations. In Tamil Nadu: Mailapur; in Goa: Pilar; in Sri Lanka: Anuradhapura; in Kerala: Kottayam-Valiyapally – two crosses (fig 33.6); Alangad; Muttuchira (fig 33.7); Kothanallur; and Kadamattam (fig 33.8). The ones in Mailapur, Pilar, Kottayam, Alangad, and Muttuchira bear the same inscription in faithful copies, the Kadamattam cross is an epigraphically poor imitation, while the ones in Kothanallur and Anuradhapura are now without any inscription (Cereti, Olivieri and Vazhuthanapally 2002: 293–300). Several attempts at deciphering have been offered for the Mailapur cross, which was unearthed by the Portuguese in 1547 and to which miraculous powers were attributed. The latest one is by Carlo G. Cereti:

> Our Lord Christ, have pity on Sabrīšōʿ, (son) of Čahārbōxt, (son) of Sūray, who bore (brought?) this (cross).
>
> (Cereti, Olivieri and Vazhuthanapally 2002: 297)

The name Sabrīšōʿ for the commissioner of the cross was proposed already by Philip Gignoux (Gignoux 1995: 416). Yet, Gignoux's and Cereti's unanimous reading for this personal name is *splyš<'w>*, which I would interpret as Sapir Īśō' rather than Sabrīšōʿ, given that the Pahlavi script distinguishes between the letters *beth* and *pe* (see in the same inscription the name Čahārbōxt [*č'hrbōxt*]). As, unlike Sabrīšōʿ, Sapir Īśō is a unique name, the question arises whether the cross, or its putative lost model, was commissioned by the same person who is said to have founded the community that received the privileges of the Kollam copper plates.

Figure 33.6 One of the Persian crosses in Kottayam

Source: Fabian da Costa

If one accepts the hypothesis, which has been formulated several times (Cereti, Olivieri and Vazhuthanapally 2002: 294), according to which all the other Persian crosses are replicas of the one in Mailapur, this phenomenon would stand in need of an explanation. Hypothetically, I would connect this to the spread or expulsion of the Persian Christian communities from Mailapur, which, when spreading to the Malabar Coast, reproduced a religious symbol that had been at the core of the community's worship in Mailapur. Thus, it seems that the verifiable written history of the Christian community on the Malabar Coast begins in the ninth century.

Apparently, even after the expulsion, Mailapur had preserved its symbolic importance, as Marco Polo in 1293 still reported on the veneration of the tomb of the Apostle, kept by Christian guardians (Marco Polo 1908: 363–5).

Figure 33.7 The Muttuchira Persian cross

Source: Fabian da Costa

The period preceding the arrival of the Portuguese (849–1498)

Very little can be known about the mediaeval history of the community between the ninth century and the arrival of Vasco da Gama in Kozhikode in 1498.

One important, though little-studied, document is a grant written in Tamil and carved on a granite stele[34] (fig 33.9; Ramanatha Ayar 1927: 176–80). It was given by an unnamed king of Travancore to a Christian community in Kumari-muṭṭam, two kilometres to the north-west of Cape Comorin, the southernmost point of India, another ancient port mentioned in the Periplus under the name Komar (Periplus 58–59). The grant is dated to 1494, four years before the arrival of Vasco da Gama, and gives privileges to the Christian church community of Kumari-muṭṭam, very similar to those of the Kollam copper plates. It states that 'for the coconut oil (required) for the lamps in the church (*paḷḷi*) at Kumari-muṭṭam', the community is entitled to levy a series of taxes in the harbour, such as those on fishing nets, on boats loading and unloading in the harbour, on cargos sold in the harbour, on paddy fields, and on fish caught in the port. Also, it is stated that those living within the four boundaries – apparently within

Figure 33.8 The Persian cross of Kadamattam. The inscription around the cross is an imitation of Pahlavi characters, while the entire bas-relief is a schematic imitation of the Mailapur cross

Source: István Perczel

the emporium (*nagaram*) belonging to the church – should be exempt from all kinds of taxes, such as the taxes on the right-handed and left-handed castes,[35] the military cess, and other imposts.

A comparison of this document with the Kollam plates, written 645 years earlier, reveals a steady pattern: South Indian rulers were establishing Christian trading communities in the trading cities and ports, which they founded or ruled. To attract these communities, they were offering broad financial and legal privileges related to the religious services performed in the churches (the burning of oil), comparable to the royal privileges given to Brahmin or Jain temples or to Buddhist monasteries. The exemption from the taxes levied 'on the right-handed and left-handed castes' shows that the importance of these merchant communities for the local economy warranted their liberation from the local hierarchical order, so that they were granted almost complete autonomy, while the community's religious freedom was fully respected.

This practice did not change much after the advent of the European colonisers. In 1796, Rāma Varma IX, the king of Kochi, also called Śaktan Tampurān ('the Mighty Ruler'), founded the city of Thrissur, which he designed as a new trade centre. For so doing, he settled in Thrissur fifty-two Christian merchant families, of the Syrian Chaldean confession. In 1815 he built them a church and granted them freedom of religion and independence from the then ruling European hierarchy (Mar Aprem 1983: 30–5). This community became the kernel of the modern Nestorian Church of India.

We know even less about the liturgical and ecclesiastical life of the community in this period. As mentioned above, the first extant Syriac text that was written in Kerala dates from 1301 (MS Vat. syr. 22, Van der Ploeg 1983). This is a lectionary of the readings of the letters of St Paul for the whole year, according to the order followed in the church of Kokhe, the cathedral church of Seleucia-Ctesiphon, the see of the Nestorian catholicos-patriarchs of the East. It was copied in Kodungallur by a young deacon of fourteen years of age. All the other early Syriac manuscripts are from the sixteenth century and testify to the fact that the bishops coming from the Church of the East in the early modern period were bringing with them their own Syriac books, which were held in high esteem by the community.

The relationship of these communities with the Persian Church depended on the financial strength of the community concerned as well as on the linguistic skills of its elite. To have a normal church life, a bishop, or bishops, had to reside in India, to consecrate the holy orders who performed the liturgical practices, teach the clergy, and maintain contact with the mother church. The community had to pay for the mission to bring the bishop(s) from the headquarters of the Persian Church, and for gifts to the catholicos-patriarch; also, it had to cover the expenses of the bishops as long as they stayed in India. The recently discovered accounts of a mission sent to the Chaldean catholicos-patriarch Yoḥannān Hormizd in 1796 testify to the immense financial burden that all this laid on the community (Perczel 2013: 431–5). This resulted in the fact that contact with the mother church was intermittent. Portuguese sources relate that, until not long before the Portuguese arrived in India, there was a long period of interruption in these contacts, so much so that there were no priests left in the Indian Church, but only a deacon who was forced to celebrate the liturgy for the faithful (George of Christ 1578: DI XI, 130; Gouvea 1606: 5v–63; Malekandathil 2003: 25–6). It was from this state of affairs that, in 1490, a mission was sent to Gazarta d-Beth Zabday (modern Cisre in Eastern Turkey), to catholicos Šem'on IV Basidi, with the participation of Deacon Joseph and a certain George, from the influential Pakalomaṭṭam family (fig 33.12). As a result, Joseph and George were consecrated priests and two bishops, Mar Thomas and Mar John, came to India (Vallavanthara 1984). Mar Thomas soon returned to Gazarta to carry home the gifts of the Indian faithful and was dispatched again in 1503 with three more bishops, Mar Jacob, Mar Yahbalāhā, and Mar Denḥā (Assemani 1725: III/1, 590–2). In Malabar, these bishops received the honorary name *Mārābhanmār* (Syro-Malayalam: from the Syriac

Mar Abba, 'holy Father' plus the Malayalam plural suffix *-mar*; MS Mannanam Malayalam 3: fol. 9r; Perczel 2018a: 98–9) and were the object of great veneration. Together with Joseph and George – the latter of whom became the first archdeacon, an important position denoting the local leader of the Christians[36] – they were responsible for the re-introduction and the blossoming of Syriac learning in Kerala. It is from this time that Syriac manuscripts start to arrive in India and to be written there – at least, this is the impression one gets from a survey of the Indian manuscript archives. It was also from this time that a local elite cultivating the knowledge of

Figure 33.9 The Kumari-muṭṭam inscription, currently kept in the Padmanabhapuram Palace Museum in Tamil Nadu. Language and script: Tamil

Source: István Perczel

Figure 33.10 Traditional decorative motifs: monkeys holding a baptismal font, Kanjoor

Source: István Perczel

Figure 33.11 Traditional decorative motifs: worshipping angel from the pedestal of a cross, Koratthy

Source: István Perczel

Syriac began to develop. Finally, it is only from this time onwards that we know the names and histories of all the Syrian bishops and missionaries who arrived in India.

The Portuguese period

When the Portuguese arrived in India, they encountered a revitalised Church, an aristocratic and well-to-do Christian community, and a blossoming Syriac culture. This was the opportunity for mutual discoveries. It was the second Portuguese armada, under the leadership of Pedro Alvares Cabral, reaching Kodungallur in the year 1500, which first met the Indian Christians. Immediately, the Christians sent to Portugal their envoys, Joseph, who had participated in the 1490 mission to Persia, and his brother who died during the journey to Europe. Joseph, who met the Portuguese king, the pope, and the signoria in Venice, gave the first detailed account of Indian

Christianity to the Europeans before returning to India to inform his community about Europe (Vallavanthara 1984; Perczel 2015). From that time on, a good number of Indian Christians visited Europe sailing on Portuguese ships. The local documents that originate from this period testify to a great openness and curiosity towards the novelties coming from Europe (Perczel 2015).

When Vasco da Gama landed a second time in 1502, in Kochi, the Christians offered him a rod, which they claimed was the sceptre of their legendary former kings, whose dynasty, called Villarvattam, had earlier become extinct.[37] They therefore wanted to entrust themselves to the protection of the powerful foreign Christian king, whose envoys had arrived in India (Gouvea 1606: 5r; Malekandathil 2003: 23; Mundadan 1984: 163–4). Their offer was accepted and, from that time onward, the Portuguese acted as the powerful protectors of the Christians, representing their interests before the local kings.

In 1503, the Portuguese met four from among the *Mārābhanmār* and concelebrated with them in the Portuguese church of Cannanore. The bishops sent a report in Syriac about the Portuguese arrival to their catholicos-patriarch Mar Eliah V, this being the first Indian report about the Portuguese conquests and their wars against the Zamorin of Calicut and his Muslim allies.[38] They also reported on the first attempts – under Portuguese protection – at repopulating with Christians the city of Mailapur around the tomb of Saint Thomas (Assemani 1725: III/1, 589–99;

Figure 33.12 The tombs of the Pakalomaṭṭam archdeacons in Kuravilangad. Important priests were buried under semi-cylindrical tombstones, none of which bears any inscription. The earliest funerary inscriptions date from the late sixteenth century

Source: István Perczel

Schurhammer 1963: 333–8). The bishops exulted in the Portuguese victories and the destruction of the Muslims, who were the main competitors of the Christian merchants in the trans-Arabian Sea trade. In every way, the first half of the sixteenth century witnessed close collaboration between the local Christians and the Portuguese colonisers, who powerfully represented before the local kings the interests of their Christian interlocutors, resulting in the rise of the latter's social prestige and economic power (Schurhammer 1963: 338). The cultivation of pepper was in the hands of the Christians, and they were happy to sell their pepper to the Portuguese. Moreover, the Portuguese fought the Muslims and imposed restrictions on their merchants, which strengthened the position of the Syrian Christians in the Indian Ocean trade.[39] One contention remained, however: the Portuguese attempted to Latinise the liturgical life and culture of the Syrian Christians, in which task they found a ready ally in Mar Jacob, while the local Christians, led by Mar Denḥā, the only other remaining bishop out of the five, were resistant to these attempts and clung on to their East Syriac culture (Mundadan 1984: 287–347). Mar Denḥā – often referred to by the Portuguese sources complaining about him as 'the younger bishop' – animated the resistance against the European missionaries and continued to teach the East Syrian customs to the local Christians (Mundadan 1984: 304–9). He retired to the inner lands, keeping himself away from the reach of the Portuguese dominating the seashore; he was buried in the southern wall of the church of Kadamattam (figs 33.13–14) (MS Mannanam Malayalam 3: fol. 9r; Perczel 2018: 98–100).[40]

By the mid-sixteenth century, matters were changing in Europe, the Middle East, and India. The Counter-Reformatory Council of Trent (1545–63) inaugurated a strict dogmatic turn in the Catholic Church. In 1552, the Chaldean Church was formed from that part of the Church of the East which united with Rome under its first patriarch, John Sulaqa (1553–55). In India, the Portuguese fought successfully against the Zamorin and the Muslims, so that they felt safer in their positions and were ready to tighten their grip on all the local populations. As a result, the relatively tolerant attitude of the Portuguese, allowing for, even if not approving of, differences, gradually changed. After the split within the Church of the East, both the Chaldean and the Nestorian factions sent missionary bishops to India, to ensure the loyalty of the Indian faithful (Mar Aprem 1983: 24). From this, a complicated and entangled strife emerged, in which East Syrian prelates competed with each other and with the Europeans for ensuring the affiliation to their churches, while the Europeans intermittently fought against all of them, or contracted temporary alliances with some of them.

From the middle of the sixteenth century, the Jesuits began to arrive in Malabar and gradually took control of the bulk of the missionary work from the Franciscans (Mundadan 1984: 322–3; Thekkedath 1988: 56–9). This resulted in a change in the way the mission was conducted. The Jesuits possessed a good knowledge of the local language, Malayalam; while some of them, the most significant being Francisco Roz, who from 1587 was professor of Syriac at the Vaipicotta Jesuit seminary in Chennamangalam, were excellent Syriacists. He was capable of reading and judging the Syriac texts used by the community and was scandalised at their 'Nestorian' content (Roz 1586; Hausherr 1928). Centred on Vaipicotta (fig 33.16), the Jesuits started to create a new Tridentine Catholic literature in Syriac and Malayalam, which was destined to replace the local culture, deemed to be 'Nestorian'. Yet the Māppiḷḷa Christians,

Figure 33.13 St George Jacobite Church, Kadamattam, where Mar Denḥā resided in his last years

Source: Fabian da Costa

Figure 33.14 A granite plaque inscribed in Syriac and Malayalam, commemorating the finding of Mār Denḥā's bones in 1990, in the southern wall of the church. The Syriac inscription says: 'The holy relics of the venerable priest of Kadamattam, which were found here on the first day of the month of Adar (March) in the year 1990 of our Lord, are placed here.' Yet, the Malayalam only says: 'Here are the holy relics of a father found on the 1 March 1990.' The bones attributed to the Kadamattam priest, a famous magician, seem to be in fact those of Mār Denḥā

Source: Susan Visvanathan

whilst being open to the Jesuits and their accommodationist strategies, also clung to their cultural heritage, so that the texts and the cultural trends became combined and gave rise to a unique early modern culture, with Syriac as the lingua franca (Perczel 2009; Perczel 2018b).

The Jesuits had a complicated relationship with the East Syrian bishop who had emerged as the great leader of the St Thomas Christians during the second half of the sixteenth century: Mar Abraham, who came first to India before 1556 as a Nestorian bishop, and then, in 1563, joined the Chaldean patriarch Mar Abdisho IV (1555–1567), before going to Rome to visit the pope and receive a new consecration as a Chaldean bishop in 1565 (fig 33.17). Mar Abraham, who returned to India in 1568, transferred

Figure 33.15 Ruins of the Portuguese fort at Kodungallur/Cranganore

Source: István Perczel

his see from Cranganore on the seashore, where the Portuguese could have easily reached him, to inland Angamaly, thus following the example of Mar Denḥā. In 1576, Mar Abraham opened his community to the Jesuit mission. In 1583, Alessandro Valignano, the Jesuit visitor of the missions in the Indies, and Mar Abraham held a synod in Angamaly, which introduced a thorough Latinisation of the ecclesiastical customs of the Suriyāni.[41] Yet, the community continued to use their Syriac liturgical books. In 1597 Mar Abraham died, opening the door to a more thorough European takeover of the Malankara Church (Perczel 2018b: 217ff.).

All these attempts culminated in the Synod of Diamper (Udayamperur), held in 1599, when both the East Syrian and the Indian customs of the Māppiḷḷa Christians were condemned. The East Syriac Biblical canon and liturgical books had to be corrected based on Latin texts, a list of heretical books was established, and these books were condemned to be burnt (Thaliath 1958). Hence the widespread view, repeated in innumerable scholarly publications, that the age-old tradition of the Saint Thomas Christians was destroyed at the Synod. Yet, this view needs to be revised. Most of the books condemned were Middle Eastern compositions well known from elsewhere (Chabot 1909). They were taken to India by the East Syrian prelates who had arrived after 1490. Also, the destruction was only partial. On the one hand, the Syrian Christian community jealously preserved the condemned books and continued to use and copy them. On the other hand, the Portuguese apparently also preserved the condemned books, some of which have been found by recent research (Perczel 2006).

Figure 33.16 Ruins of the Jesuit seminary at Vaipicotta/Chennamangalam

Source: István Perczel

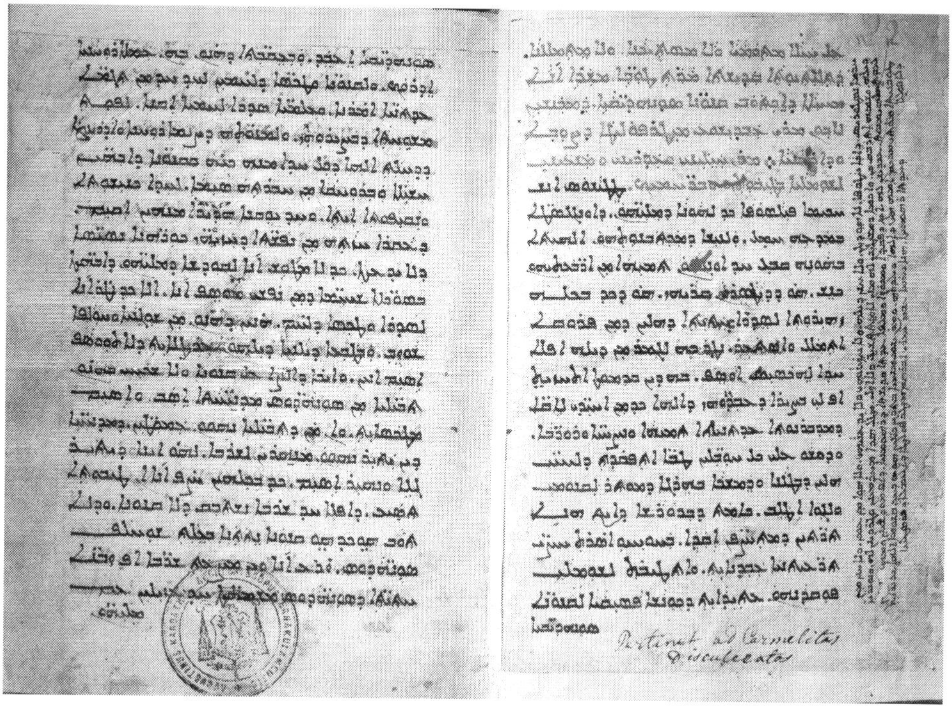

Figure 33.17 First pages of Mar Abraham's personal copy of the Nomocanon of Abdisho – Chaldean version copied for Mar Abraham in Gazarta, in 1563. On the right margin, Mar Abraham's 'Curse on Nestorius,' rejecting both the person of Nestorius and the allegation that the Church of the East had ever been Nestorian and, so, heretic. At bottom right, Latin inscription: Pertinet ad Carmelitas Discalcatos ("This book belongs to the Discalced Carmelites"). Apparently, the book was condemned to be burnt at the Synod of Diamper but was preserved by the Jesuits, from whom it went to the Carmelite library of Varapuzha/Verapoly. It was rescued from there by Mar Louis Pazheparambil, who became the first bishop of the Syro-Malabar Catholic Church in 1896. Mar Louis was expelled from the Carmelite order in 1875. The manuscript is now in the Archdiocesan Archives of the Ernakulam-Angamaly Archdiocese of the Syro-Malabar Church

Source: Courtesy of the Rev. Dr Ignatius Payyappily, Chief Archivist

Francisco Roz became the first European archbishop of the Saint Thomas Christians (1599–1624). A champion of accommodation and a supporter of Roberto de Nobili's mission in Madurai, he oversaw and participated in the creation of a huge quantity of new Catholic Syriac literature in India (fig 33.18). He was loved and respected for his knowledge by the Indian faithful, and his tenure marked a peaceful period of coexistence between the Europeans and the Māppiḷḷa Christians (Perczel 2018b: 216–23). Yet, under the Jesuit archbishops that followed him in the see of Cranganore, the situation deteriorated, finally leading to a revolt of the community against the Portuguese and the Jesuits, the celebrated Oath of the Slanting Cross (*kūnan kuriśu satyam*). The Christians rejected their obedience to the Portuguese and the Jesuits, the then archdeacon, Thomas Pakalomaṭṭam, was consecrated metropolitan of India with the name Mar Thoma, and the community pledged their obedience to the Chaldean patriarch (Thekkedath 1972; Thekkedath 1988: 91–100).

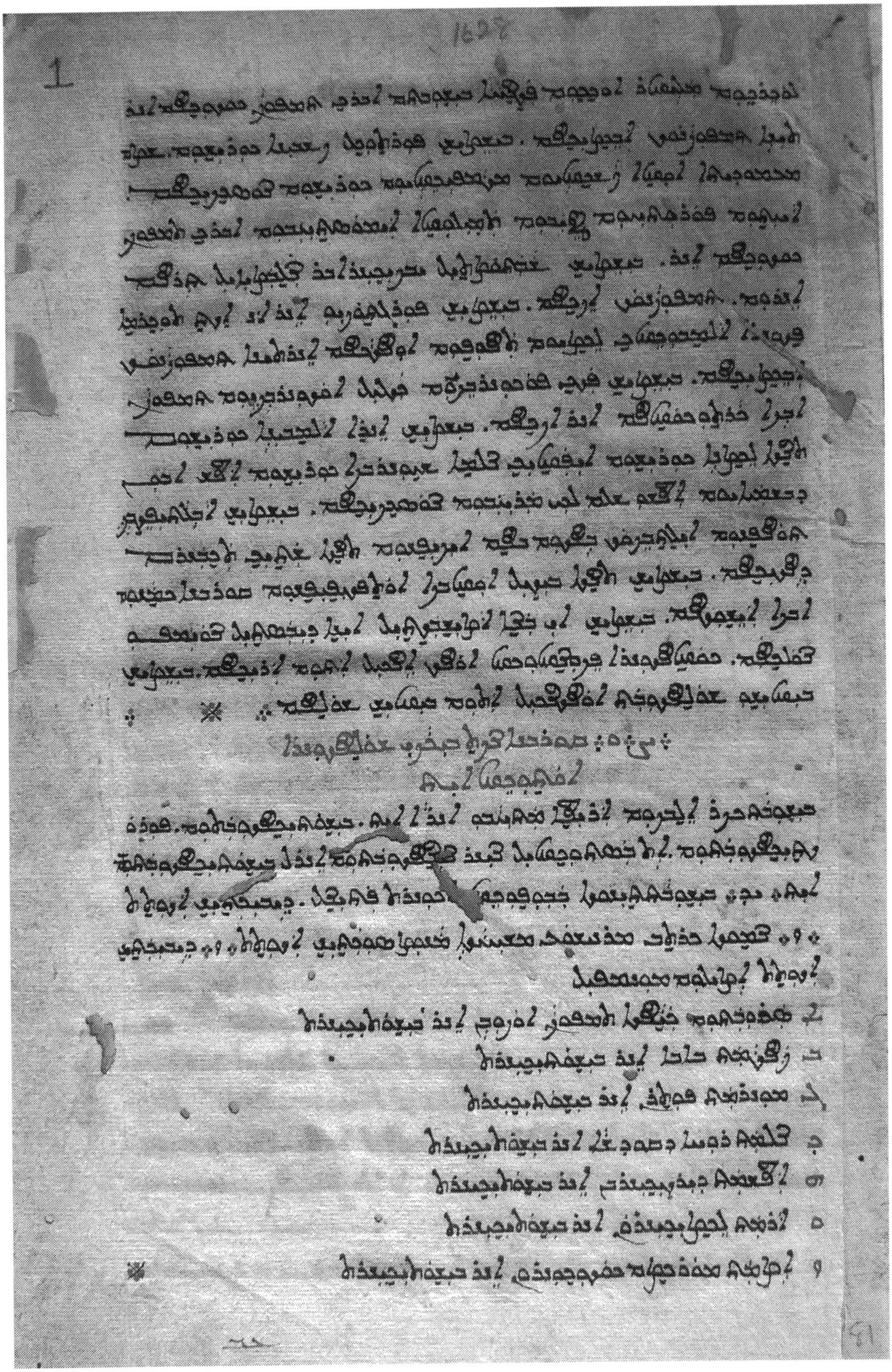

Figure 33.18 First page of the extant copy of the Church Statutes of Francisco Roz, written in Malayalam, in Garshuni Malayalam characters, in 1607. The text begins with the last part of the fifth canon and the beginning of the sixth, regulating the celebration of the mass by the parish priests. The manuscript is kept in the State Archives of Ernakulam and was digitised by the SRITE project

Source: Courtesy of the Rev. Dr. Ignatius Payyappilly

Figure 33.19 St Mary's Orthodox Church in Thiruvithamcode, Tamil Nadu. View from the South. Built in the first years of the seventeenth century, this is one of the first churches built according to the prescriptions of the Synod of Diamper. It does not have a church tower above the sanctuary, which is illuminated by small windows (the sanctuary of the earlier churches was entirely closed). Its decoration is similar to that of the Hindu temples

Source: István Perczel

Figure 33.20 Bas-relief in granite above the entry of the Thiruvithamcode church. It represents the adoration of the Holy Sacrament, a Roman Catholic devotional practice introduced by the Portuguese. Note the decorative elements characteristic of the late Vijayanagaram iconography of Indian art

Figure 33.21 Upper part of the open-air cross in Korathy, with Syriac inscriptions. On the upper cross-beam: "This is Jesus of Nazareth, the King of the Jews" (Jn 19:19); on the trunk in-between the cross-beams: "Yah" – the East Syriac name for God; on the lower cross-beam: "Behold, the Lamb of God, who takes away the sin of the world" (Jn 1:29). The usage on the crosses of these scriptural passages is a Latin influence, while the lack of the Corpus Christi and the divine name Yah belong to the East Syriac tradition. The earliest extant Syriac inscriptions date from the second half of the sixteenth century

Source: István Perczel

After the Portuguese

After this, a long period of strife and schism emerged. In 1663, the Dutch conquered Cochin and the Malabar Coast, ending the Portuguese hegemony which in turn meant the expulsion of the Jesuits. At that moment, an indigenous priest, Mar Parambil Cāndi Kuriētu (Alexandre de Campos) was consecrated as rival bishop for the Roman Catholics and, gradually, the community split into two (Thekkedath 1988: 100–9; Perczel 2016b: 50–1, 264–5). Mar Thoma finally obtained consecration from a Syrian Orthodox (Jacobite) bishop, Mor Gregorios abd'al-Jalīl, formerly abbot of Saint Mark's Monastery and patriarch of Jerusalem, who came to India in 1665 and resided in North Paravur until his death in 1681. The Syrian Orthodox liturgy and customs were introduced by a subsequent mission by Mor Baselios Yaldo (fig 33.4) and Mor Iyovannis Hidayat Allah, which arrived in 1685. Subsequent missions from the Syrian Orthodox Church led to the gradual formation of a semi-independent community under the spiritual leadership of the Antiochian Syrian Orthodox patriarch under the de facto jurisdiction of the Pakalomaṭṭam Mar Thoma metropolitans, who bequeathed their office from uncle to nephew until the extinction of the family in 1809. This branch of the community is called the New Faction (*puttan kūṟu*), while those who remained within the Catholic Church are called the Old Faction (*paḻaya kūṟu*) (Thekkedath 1988: 100–9).

As a result of subsequent schisms, not unrelated to the influence of the colonial powers, these two factions suffered from further divisions. Today, the Old Faction is divided into two local churches: the Syro-Malabar Catholic Church of Roman Catholic confession, and the Chaldean Syrian Church, or Assyrian Church of the East in India, of Nestorian confession. The New Faction is divided between six local churches, among which three are of miaphysite confession, one is Catholic, and two are Protestant. Of miaphysite confession are the Malankara Jacobite Syrian Orthodox Church under the jurisdiction of the Antiochian patriarch; the autocephalous Malankara Orthodox Syrian Church under the jurisdiction of their local catholicos, residing in Devalokam, Kottayam; and the autocephalous Malabar Independent Syrian Church under its metropolitan in Thozhiyur. Of Catholic confession is the Syro-Malankara Catholic Church, which separated from the miaphysites in 1932 and follows the liturgical practice of the Syrian Catholic Church of Antioch. Of Protestant confession are the Mar Thoma Syrian Church of Malabar, belonging to the Episcopalian tradition, under its metropolitan residing in Thiruvalla, and the Saint Thomas Evangelical Church, which recently separated from the Mar Thoma Church (Menacherry-Balakrishnan-Perczel 2014: 565–9, 582–91).

NOTES

1 I am not using in this case the neologism 'Syriac Christian', as the community itself does not use it but calls itself 'Syrian' (*Suriyāni* in Malayalam).

2 Coromandel is the Portuguese name for the south-eastern coast of India. The name seems to have been derived from the Tamil *Cōla mandalam/Cōra mandalam*, 'the country of the Cōla emperors'. The Arab name for the eastern coast was *Ma'bar* ('Passage'/'Crossing') (Mundadan 1984: 49).

3 *Malankara*, *Malayankara*, and *Malayālam* mean 'the Mountainous region', the region of the Western Ghats (Malayam), in Malayalam (Gundert 1872, 2013: 729). The Portuguese translated the name as '*a Serra*'. Derivatively, Malabar has the same meaning. In fact, the word *malavāram*, from which the toponym Malabar is derived, means 'hill-produce' (Gundert 1872, 2013: 730). The word *Malibar* was used to indicate the entire south-western coast by the Jewish, Christian, and Arab traders, from whom the Portuguese adopted it. *Malayālam* has been used to denote the language of the 'Mountainous region' only since the 19th century.

4 Among the *Tekkumbhāgar* in modern times there prevails the legend that they are of Jewish Christian origin, which has also been taken at face value by certain Western scholars [Frykenberg 2008: 112–13].

5 The SRITE project (from the Syriac word for manuscripts) is an ongoing international project to digitise, catalogue, and exploit for scholarship the manuscript archives of the Indian Syrian Christians. Hitherto some 1,200 Syriac and Syriac (Garshuni) Malayalam paper manuscripts and 60,000 Malayalam palm-leaves have been digitally preserved. While the institutions participating in the project were – besides the Indian custodians – Central European University Budapest, Tübingen University, and Hill Museum and Manuscript Library, Collegeville MN (HMML), the digital images are preserved, archived, and distributed by HMML. The manuscripts are being published at the vHMML reading room (https://www.vhmml.org/readingRoom/).

6 We have found and digitised the correspondence of Mar Timotheos and Placide Podipara, kept in the archives of Dharmaram College in Bangalore and of the Metropolitan's House in Thrissur.

7 The latest comprehensive study of great erudition, championing the historicity of the Indian apostolate of Saint Thomas, is Nedungatt 2008.

8 The placename Musiris is attested in ancient sources, such as the Musiris Papyrus or the Tabula Peutingeriana, the copy of a first-century Roman map. *Mucciri* is in fact a Dravidian word, meaning 'harelip' ('three lips') (Gundert 1872: 753). The name indicated the delta of the Periyar river, where Musiris was situated. The delta and the port of Musiris were destroyed by a tsunami in 1341 CE, which led to the rise of Kozhikode and Kochi as the new centres of international maritime trade.

9 This is Papyrus Vindobonensis Graecus 40822 from the first century CE, from Berenike or Myos Hormos at the Red Sea, containing the renewal of an original contract made in Musiris. The merchant took a loan for purchasing his products, which he warrants with the whole value of the cargo remaining after payment of taxes. The products are brought from Musiris by an Egyptian ship called Hermapollo. The papyrus is a witness to the intense trade relations between India and the Mediterranean, and also to the fact that Greek was the international language of trade along these routes (Casson 1990; De Romanis 2012).

10 *Maliankara* is a version of the name *Malayankara*. In fact, the word means the entire region of the Western Ghats (see above, note 2).

11 MS Vaticanus Syriacus 22 (online: https://digi.vatlib.it/view/MSS_Vat.sir.22), the colophon is found at foll. 93r–94v. On fol. 93v-94r, the scribe writes: "This holy book was copied in the royal (or capital: *arśakāyā*), renowned and famous city of Śenglē (or, perhaps, Śenjlī), which is in Malabar, in the land of India, in the holy church named after Mar Quriaqos, the glorious martyr . . . when Mar Jacob, Metropolitan Bishop was the overseer and governor of the holy see of Saint Thomas the Apostle, that is to say governor of us and of all the holy Church of the Christian India." Śenglē/Śenjlī corresponds to the sinjlī (سنجلي), śinklī (شنكلي) and sanjā (سنجا) of the Arab geographers and to the Shingly of the early modern Cochini Jewish traditions of origin (on the mediaeval and early modern Shingly traditions, see Gamliel 2018a, here 64). Van der Ploeg reads the name as Shengala and identifies the city with Kodungallur (Van der Ploeg 1983, 3). Yet the word is clearly vocalised as Śenglē/Śenjlī, while the identification, based on the early modern Paradeśi ("foreigner": European immigrant) Jewish traditions, lacks sufficient foundation (see Gamliel 2018a).

12 The original text of this church/community history was written in Malayalam and is contained in MS Leiden Or. 1214. It was sent to Leiden, together with a Syriac translation, contained in MS Leiden Or. 1213, by the Nestorian metropolitan Mar Gabriel (in India from 1704 to 1730). The Syriac text with an earlier Latin translation was published by Samuel Giamil (Brevis historia, Giamil 1902: 552–64). The Malayalam original remains unpublished.

13 Marco Polo (tr Masefield 1908), III.17, 363–5.

14 Eusebius, Ecclesiastic History V.10.3, and Jerome, Letter 70.4, and *De viris illustribus* 36.

15 Explanation given by Venugopala Panicker, communication to the author by Dr. Ophira Gamliel. According to this explanation, *māppiḷḷa* is a word composed of *māman*, 'maternal uncle', and *piḷḷa*, 'child'. Gundert gives the following meanings: 'a bridegroom', 'son-in-law', and 'honorific title given to the colonists from the West' (Gundert 1872: 739).

16 It is a prescription of the slave-manumission ceremony that the newly liberated slave should be called the son/daughter of the former master.

17 I owe this interpretation to Ophira Gamliel. Goitein and Friedman do not doubt that Aśu could be a real slave-girl.

18 On the question of how much these exchanges can be considered real trade, see Rajan Gurukkal 2016.

19 I warmly thank Dr Péter Tóth, Curator of Ancient and Medieval Manuscripts at the British Library, for providing me with a copy of the relevant pages from the manuscript.

20 Mundadan refers to this document under the title '*Relação da Serra*' and attributes it to Roz. Yet in the text the document bears the title '*Relação sobre a Serra–feito em 1604*' and is anonymous. In the contemporary table of contents of the manuscript, the same document bears the title 'Narrative about the Christianity of Malankara from 1604' (*Relação da Christandade da Serra de 1604*). The manuscript contains yearly reports on the south-eastern provinces of the Jesuits, most of them bearing the title 'Annual of the South' (*Annual do Sul*). Yet one of the items is explicitly identified as 'Narrative about the Christianity of San Thomè by the lord bishop Francisco Roz' (*Relação da Christandade de S. Thomè feyta pelo Sor Bispo Dom Francisco Roz*), which, according to its place in the manuscript, must be dated 1602.

21 *Veṭṭeḻuttu* ('engraved script') or *Vaṭṭeḻuttu* ('round script') is the name of one of the Dravidian scripts used in the Middle Ages for writing southern Dravidian languages, namely Tamil and Malayalam. In the Malayalam context, it was replaced by Grandha or *Ārya eḻuttu* ('Arya script'), the ancestor of Modern Malayalam, only in the seventeenth century. Earlier the Grandha alphabet had been used only for writing Sanskrit.

22 In fact, Francisco Dionysio, the Jesuit Rector of Cochin, dates the arrival of Thomas of Kana to precisely the date of the foundation of Kollam: 825 (Dionysio 1578: 137). However, Dionysio also says that Thomas came after Maruvan Sapir Īšō, which seems to be correct, as we shall see shortly.

23 In preparing this section, I benefited from the knowledge of the material prepared as a result of the two-year project funded by the British Arts and Humanities Research Council and directed by Elizabeth Lambourn: 'A Persian church in the land of pepper – routes, networks and communities in the early medieval Indian Ocean', which ran from 2011 to 2013 (Grant reference: AH/I025948/1). I thank Elizabeth Lambourn and the members of the team, especially Kesavan Veluthat and Philip Wood, for sharing the material of the project with me. The project results will be published in two volumes in 2019.

24 Latest English translation in Narayanan (1972: 91–4). There is a new arrangement of the plates, made by M. R. Raghava Varier and Kesavan Veluthat and a new transcription and translation, too (Rhagava Varier-Kesavan Veluthat 2013: 109–13, in Malayalam). Earlier, the five plates were considered as belonging to two different grants given at different times, but the two scholars have proven beyond doubt that all the plates belong together. A new English translation by the two authors is forthcoming in the two-volume publication of the Kollam plates project. Here I am citing Narayanan's translation.

25 *Vēṇāṭu* was one of the regions under the rule of the Cēra emperor. Later it became the kingdom of Travancore.

26 As far as I know, this etymology was first proposed by W. B. Henning (1958: 51). Recently, Philip Wood and Sunish George Alumkkal suggested it to the team working on the Kollam plates, which has accepted it.

27 This reading of the form *Ēśō da-Tapir āyi* as a mixed Syriac-Malayalam name form is a new proposal, first published here. Narayanan, for one, leaves the two forms unexplained (Narayanan 1972: 91–2).

28 So Gouvea (1606: 5r) and the Acts of the Synod of Diamper (Da Cunha Rivara 1862: 476–7).

29 The Garshuni Malayalam text was copied into MS BnF Syr 186, foll. 127–30, and discovered by Jacob Kollaparambil, who published its facsimile with modern Malayalam transcription (Kollaparambil 1995: 17–26). According to Kollaparambil, the folios containing the text did not originally belong to the Paris manuscript but are the missing folios 57–60 of MS ARSI Goa 58 in the Archives of the Society of Jesus in Rome, containing the text of the *Historia do Malavar* of Diogo Gonçalves S. J. written in 1615. I owe the information

about this publication to Fr Francis Thonippara CMI, who gave it to me in August 2016. Garshuni Malayalam is a local alphabet used by the Syrian Christians of South India to write Malayalam. This is a right-to-left script using the 22 East Syriac consonants and semi-consonants plus 8 Dravidian consonantal letters from one of the Old Malayalam alphabets, namely the *Tekken-Malāyaḻma*, the southern variant of *Veṭṭeḻuttu*, and also later on a avariable number of Grandha letters. The vowels are indicated by the Syriac vowel signs. I was reading the Garshuni text together with Prof. Susan Thomas whom I warmly thank for this collaboration.

30 The story is related in Anquétil du Perron 1771: clxxi–iv, and the French translation may be found at clxxv–viii.

31 This was already observed by Kollaparambil 1995: 44.

32 This interpratation is an elaboration upon that of Kollaparambil 1995: 17–19, proposing a new hypothesis. Kollaparambil's hypothesis was that the inclusion of a paragraph on Thomas of Kana in the fourth Kollam plate testifies to the anteriority of the Thomas of Kana mission relative to the *Tarisāppaḷḷi* grant. Yet these suggestions are of a tentative nature due to the need for further study by a team representing a number of disciplines and language skills.

33 I have learned this interpretation concerning similar crosses in Georgia from a lecture by Stephen Rapp at a summer university course held at CEU Budapest in July 2017. The wings are interpreted as parts of a lotus flower by J. Vazhuthanapally in Cereti, Olivieri and Vazhuthanapally (2002: 290). Similarly, in Perczel (2016a: 45), I still interpreted them as floral motives.

34 Now the stele is stored in the museum of Padmanābhapuram Palace, as witnessed by the author. The erection of four such steles at the four ends of the Christian settlement was ordered by the royal decree.

35 The right-handed and left-handed groups designated shifting social categories throughout the ages. According to Y. Subbarayalu, by the fifteenth century, 'the Right and Left groups comprised of all the direct producers, namely the cultivators, artisans, commercial castes and other servicing castes' (Subbaralayu 2012: 173).

36 Until recently, the received wisdom had been that the office of the archdeaconate originated in very early times, perhaps after the supposed fourth-century arrival of Thomas of Kana (Kollamparampil 1972: 79–80). However, I believe it is now proven that all the sources indicate that the first archdeacon was George Pakalomaṭṭam, consecrated in 1490 (Perczel 2015).

37 This seems to be an apocryphal tradition, perhaps invented to enhance the prestige of the local Christians. It is true that the putative tombstone of the last Villarvattam king, called Thomas, who allegedly died in the year 1500, is still extant in the wall of the Udayamperur church (Ramanatha Ayyar 1927: 68–71 – Ayyar's transcription and conclusions are to be modified); however, the inscription is clearly a fake from the seventeenth to eighteenth centuries. Upon my request, the inscription was recently studied by Prof. Raghava Varier and Prof. Kesavan Veluthat who have come to this conclusion (e-mail exchange 21–24.10.2017).

38 The next one is Shaykh Zainuddin Makhdum senior's *Tahrid ahlil iman 'ala jihadi 'abdati sulban* ('Exhortation to the followers of the Faith to the holy war against the followers of the Cross') written sometime before 1522 which shortly summarises the misdeeds of the Portuguese, in order to exhort the Muslims to jihad against them (Zaynuddin Makhdum sr. 2012). The first detailed chronicle of the fight of the Muslims in alliance with the Portuguese is the *Tuḥfat al-Mujāhidīn* written sometime after 1583 (Nainar 2009).

39 This was bitterly resented by the Muslims, as testified to by the *Tuḥfat al-Mujāhidīn* (Nainar 2009: 52).

40 Schurhammer thought that Mar Denḥā had died not long after his arrival in India (Schurhammer 1963: 338). Mundadan tentatively identified the 'younger bishop' with Mar

Denḥā (Mundadan 1984: 286) but rejected this hypothesis some pages later (ibid: 313). Yet surely the 'younger bishop' is Mar Denḥā. His remains were found in 1991 in the wall of the Kadamattam church but were erroneously identified with those of his pupil, Pozhiyeduttu Paulose, a famous white magician: the 'Kadamattam priest' of the folktales (Perczel 2018a: 100).

41 On this synod, see Thazhath (1987: 130–1). Its acts have been lost. Earlier I thought that a unique manuscript written in Garshuni Malayalam (Dharmaram College MS Syr 32 [= Gar Mal 2]), found and rescued by the great Church historian Mathias Mundadan CMI, contains the second half of the Synod's canons (Perczel 2014: 274–82; Perczel 2018b: 212, n. 80). Unfortunately, I was wrong. There has been a binding error and the second half of the Acts of the Synod of Diamper (sixth and seventh sessions) are bound first. This means, however, that we have the full text of the Garshuni Malayalam Acts of the Synod of Diamper. I was reminded of this error by Fr Joseph Roby Alenchery, whom I warmly thank for this correction.

BIBLIOGRAPHY

Primary Sources

Brevis notitia historica circa Ecclesiae Syro-Chaldaeo-Malabaricae statum. *In:* Samuel Giamil. 1902. *Genuinae relationes inter sedem apostolicam et Assyriorum orientalium seu Chaldaeorum ecclesiam* [ܟܬܒܐ ܕܡܫܘܬܦܘܬܐ ܕܥܕܬܐ ܕܟܠܕܝܐ ܥܡ ܟܘܪܣܝܐ ܫܠܝܚܝܐ ܕܪܗܘܡܝܐ]. Rome: Loescher, 552–64.

Chronicle of Se'ert: Scher, Addai, ed.&tr., 1908, 1910, 1911, 1919. *Histoire nestorienne inédite: Chronique de Séert.* PO 4.3, 5.2, 7.2, 13.4.

Cosmas Indicopleustes, *Christian Topography.* W. Wolska-Conus, ed., 1968, 1970, 1973. *Topographie chrétienne.* 3 vols. Sources chrétiennes 141, 159, 197. Paris: Éditions du Cerf.

Diamper Synod, Acts of: da Cunha Rivara, J. H., ed., 1862/1992. *Archivo Portuguez-Oriental, Fasciculo 40 que contem os Concilios de Goa e o Synodo de Diamper.* Nova-Goa: Imprensa Nacional. Reprint: New Delhi: Asian Educational Services, 1992, 283–556.

Dionysio. 1578. Relatio P. Francisci Dionysii S. I. De Christianis S. Thomae Cocini 4 Ianuarii 1578. *In:* Josephus Wicki, S. I. 1970. *Documenta Indica* XI (1577–1580). Roma: Institutum Historicum Societatis Iesu, 131–43. Online at: https://babel.hathitrust.org/cgi/pt?id=mdp.39015078388348;view=1up;seq=221.

Funerary Inscription of the Last Villarvattam King. *In*: A. S. Ramanatha Ayyar. 1927. *The Travancore Archaeological Series* VI/1, 68–71.

George of Christ. 1578. Rev. Georgius de Christo, Archidiaconus Christianorum S. Thomae, P. E. Mercuriano, praep. gen. S. I. Cocino 3 Ianuarii 1578, *In*: Josephus Wicki, S. I. 1970. *Documenta Indica* XI (1577–1580). Roma: Institutum Historicum Societatis Iesu, 129–31.

Goes, Damião de. 1619. *Chronica do Felicissimo Rey Dom Emmanuel da gloriosa memoria.* Lisbon: Antonio Alvares.

Gouvea, Antonio. 1606. *Jornada do Arcebispo de Goa Dom Frey Aleixo de Menezes Primaz da India Oriental, Religioso da Orden de S. Agostino.* Coimbra: Officina de Diogo Gomez. English translation: Malekandathil, Pius. 2003. *Jornada of Dom Alexis de Menezes: A Portuguese Account of the Sixteenth Century Malabar.* Kochi: LRC Publications.

Kollam Copper Plates: Malayalam text in M. R. Raghava Varier and Kesavan Veluthat. 2013. *Tarisāppaḷḷippaṭṭayam (Caritram).* Kottayam: Sahithya Pravarthaka C. S. Ltd., 109–13. English translation: M. G. S. Narayanan. 1972. *Cultural Symbiosis in Kerala.* Trivandrum: Kerala Historical Society, 91–4.

Kumari-Muṭṭam Tamil Inscription: A. S. Ramanatha Ayyar. 1927. *The Travancore Archaeological Series* VI/1, 176–80.

Letter of Mar Thomas, Mar Yahballāhā, Mar Jacob and Mar Denḥā to Patriarch Mar Eliah V: Josephus Simonius Assemani. 1725. *Bibliotheca Orientalis Clementino-Vaticana*, vol. III/1. Rome: Sacrae Congregationis de Propaganda Fide, 589–99.

Marco Polo the Venetian, The Travels of: Trans. John Masefield. 1908. Everyman's Library. London-New York: J. M. Dent and Sons-E. P. Dutton and Co.

Märggam Kaḷi Pāṭṭu (The Song of the Drama of the Way): Trans. T. K. Joseph. 1931. *In*: H. Hosten S.J., *The Song of Thomas Ramban or Mr. T. K. Joseph, vs Fr. Romeo Thomas, T. O. C. D. and Others*. Darjeeling. Reprinted in George Menachery. 1998. *Indian Church History Classics Volume One: The Nazranies*. Pallinada, Ollur, Thrissur: The South Asia Research Assistance Services, 522–5.

Monserrate, Antonio de, S.J. 1579. *Informacion de los Christianos de S. Thomé*. Manuscript preserved in Rome, *Archivum Romanum Societatis Jesu*, MS Goa 33.

Periplus Maris Erythraei: K. Müller. 1855/1965. *Geographi Graeci minores*, vol. 1. Paris: Firmin Didot, 515–62. Reprint: Hildesheim: Olms, 1965.

Relação sobre a Serra. British Library, Add 9853, ff. 86 (525)–99 (539).

Roz, Francisco, S.J., *De erroribus Nestorianorum qui in hac India orientali versantur*. Published under the title, "Inédit latin-syriaque de la fin de 1586 ou du début de 1587, retrouvé par le P. Castets S. I., missionaire à Trichinopoly", in I. Hausherr. 1928. *Orientalia Christiana* 11,1 (40), 1–35.

Rambān Pāttu (Song of the Teacher [Thomas]): Trans. T. K. Joseph. 1931. In: H. Hosten S.J., *The Song of Thomas Ramban or Mr. T. K. Joseph, vs Fr. Romeo Thomas, T. O. C. D. and Others*. Darjeeling. Reprinted in George Menachery. 1998. *Indian Church History Classics Volume one: The Nazranies*. Pallinada, Ollur, Thrissur: The South Asia Research Assistance Services, 520–2.

Zaynuddin Makhdum sr. 2012. *Tahrid ahlil iman 'ala jihadi' abdati sulban* (Exhortation to the followers of the Faith to the holy war against the followers of the Cross). Trans. K. M. Mohamed. Calicut: Other Books.

Zaynuddin Makhdum jr. 2009. *Tuḥfat al-Mujāhidīn*: A Historical Epic of the Sixteenth Century. Trans. S. Muhammad Husayn Nainar. Kuala Lumpur: Islamic Book Trust.

Secondary Literature

Anquétil du Perron, Abraham Hyacinth. 1771. *Zend-Avesta, Ouvrage de Zoroastre, Contenant les Idées Théologiques, Physiques & Morales de ce Législateur, les Cérémonies du Culte Religieux qu'il a établi, & plusieurs traits importans relatifs à l'ancienne Histoire des Perses*. Tome premier, première partie. Paris: N. M. Tilliard.

Bayly, Susan. 2003. *Saints, Goddesses and Kings: Muslims and Christians in South Indian Society, 1700–1900*. Cambridge: Cambridge University Press.

Barboza, Francis Peter. 1990. *Christianity in Indian Dance Forms*. Sri Garib Dass Oriental Series 114. Delhi: Sri Satguru Publications.

Briquel Chatonnet, Françoise, Alain Desreumaux, and Jacob Thekaparampil. 2008. *Recueil des Inscriptions Syriaques, Tome I: Kérala*. Paris: De Boccard.

Casson, L. 1990. New Light on Maritime Loans: P. Vindob. G 40822. *ZPE* 84, 195–206.

Cereti, Carlo G. 2009. The Pahlavi Signatures on the Quilon Copper Plates (Tabula Quilonensis). *In:* Werner Sundermann, Almut Hintze and François de Blois, ed., *Exegisti Monumenta: Festschrift in Honour of Nicholas Sims-Williams*. Wiesbaden: Harrasowitz, 31–50.

Cereti, Carlo G., Luca M. Olivieri, and Fr. Joseph Vazhuthanapally. 2002. The Problem of the Saint Thomas Crosses and Related Questions: Epigraphical Survey and Preliminary Research. *East and West* 52, 1/4 (December 2002), 285–310.

Chabot, Jean-Baptiste. 1909. L'autodafé des livres syriaques du Malabar. *In: Florilegium Melchior de Voguë*. Paris: Imprimerie Nationale, 613–23.

Champakalakshmi, R. 2011. *Religion, Tradition and Ideology: Pre-Colonial South India*. New Delhi: Oxford University Press.

de Romanis, Francesco. 2012. Playing Sudoku on the Verso of the 'Muziris Papyrus': Pepper, Malabathron and Tortoise Shell in the Cargo of the *Hermapollon*. *Journal of Ancient Indian History* 27, 77–101.

Dihle, Albrecht. 1963. Neues zur Thomas-Tradition. *Jahrbuch für Antike und Christentum* 6, 54–70.

Frykenberg, Robert Eric. 2008. *Christianity in India: From Beginnings to the Present*. Oxford History of the Christian Church. Oxford: Oxford University Press.

Gamliel, Ophira. 2018a. Back from Shingly: Revisiting the Premodern History of Jews in Kerala. *In*: *The Indian Economic and Social History Review* 55,1, 53–76.

———. 2018b. Aśu the Convert: A Slave Girl or a Nāyar Land Owner? *In*: Entangled Religions. *Interdisciplinary Journal for the Study of Religious Contact and Transfer* 6, 201–46.

Gignoux, Philippe. 1995. The Pahlavi Inscription on Mount Thomas Cross (South India). *In:* Ziony Zevitt, Seymour Gittin and Michael Sokoloff, ed., *Solving Riddles and Untying Knots: Biblical, Epigraphic, and Semitic Studies in Honor of Jonas C. Greenfield*. Winona Lake: Eisenbrauns, 411–22.

Gignoux, Philippe, Christelle Jullien, and Florence Jullien. 2009. *Iranisches Personennamenbuch, Band VII: Iranischen Namen in Semitischen Nebenüberlieferungen, Faszikel 5: Noms propres syriaques d'origine Iranienne*. Vienna: Verlag der Österreichischen Akademie der Wissenschaften.

Ghosh, Amitav. 1993. *In an Antique Land*. New York: A. A. Knopf.

Goitein, S. D. and Mordechai A. Friedman. 2007. *India Traders of the Middle Ages: Documents From the Cairo Geniza. "India Book" Part One*. Leiden: Brill.

Gropp, Gerd. 1991. Christian Maritime Trade of Sasanian Age in the Persian Gulf. *Internationale Archäologie* 6, 83–8.

Gundert, Hermann. 1872. *A Malayalam and English Dictionary*. Mangalore: C. Stoltz. Reprint 2013_4: ഡോ. ഹെർമ്മൻ ഗുണ്ടർട്ട്, മലയാളം ഇംഗ്ലീഷ്നി ഘണ്ടു. Kottayam: Sahitya Pravarthaka C.S. Ltd.

Gurukkal, Rajan. 2016. *Rethinking Classical Indo-Roman Trade: Political Economy of Eastern Mediterranean Exchange Relations*. New Delhi: Oxford University Press.

Henning, W. B. 1958. Mitteliranisch. *In: Handbuch der Orientalistik*. 1. IV. *1*. Leiden: Brill, 20–130.

Joseph, T. K. 1928. Malabar Miscellany, ch. V: A Râjasiṁha Inscription at Tâḻêkkâḍ in Cochin. *The Indian Antiquary* 57 (February 1928), 24–30.

———. 1929. Malabar Miscellany, ch. VII: The Malabar Christian Copper-Plates. *Indian Antiquary* 58 (January 1929), 13–16.

Kalayil, Thomas C. M. I., Antony Narithookil C. M. I., and James Kurianal. 2007. How Good and Great Fr. Placid Was! Biographical Sketches and Reminiscences. *In:* Thomas Kalayil and Josey Kollammalil C. M. I., ed., *Collected Works of Rev. Dr. Placid J. Podipara C.M.I* I–V. Mannanam, Kerala, India: Sanjos Publications, vol. I, xxvii–lix.

Kollamparampil, Jacob. 1972. *The Archdeacon of All-India*. The Syrian Churches series 5. Kottayam: Catholic Bishop's House.

———. 1995. Malayalam Paleography. *Mimeographed internal publication*. Rome.

Mackenzie, D. N. 1971. *A Concise Pahlavi Dictionary*. London: Oxford University Press.

Malekandathil, Pius. 2010. *Maritime India: Trade, Religion and Polity in the Indian Ocean*. New Delhi: Primus Books.

Menacherry, Joseph, Uday Balakrishnan, and István Perczel. 2014. Syrian Christian Churches in India. *In:* Lucian Leustean, ed., *Eastern Christianity and Politics in the Twenty-First Century*. London: Routledge, 563–97.

Monteiro D'Aguiar, Rev. 1930/1997. "The Magna Charta of the St. Thomas Christians", translated from Portuguese and annotated by Rev. H. Hosten, S.J. *Kerala Society Papers*, series 4, 169–93. Reprint: Thiruvananthapuram: The State Editor, Kerala Gazetteers, 1997.

Mar Aprem. 1975. *Mar Abimalek Timotheus: A Biography*. Trichur: Mar Narsai Press.
———. 1983. *The Chaldean Syrian Church of the East*. Delhi: I.S.P.C.K.
Mundadan, Mathias. 1984. *History of Christianity in India, Vol. 1: From the Beginning Up to the Middle of the Sixteenth Century (up to 1542)*. Bangalore: Church History Association of India.
Narayanan, M. G. S. 1972. *Cultural Symbiosis in Kerala*. Trivandrum: Kerala Historical Society.
Nedungatt, George S.J., 2008. *Quest for the Historical Thomas, Apostle of India: A Re-reading of the Evidence*. Bangalore: Theological Publications in India.
Nilakanta Sastri, K. A. 1975. *A History of South India: From Prehistoric Times to the Fall of Vijayanagar*, 4th edition. New Delhi: Oxford University Press.
Perczel, István. 2006. Language of Religion, Language of the People, Languages of the Documents: The Legendary History of the Saint Thomas Christians of Kerala. *In:* Ernst Bremer et al., ed., *Language of Religion – Language of the People: Judaism, Medieval Christianity and Islam*. Mittelalter Studien 11. Munich: Wilhelm Fink Verlag, 387–428.
———. 2009. Classical Syriac as a Modern *lingua franca* in South India Between 1600 and 2006. *ARAM* 21, 289–321.
———. 2013. Some New Documents on the Struggle of the Saint Thomas Christians to Maintain the Chaldaean Rite and Jurisdiction. *In:* Peter Bruns and Heinz Otto Luthe, ed., *Orientalia Christiana: Festschrift für Hubert Kaufhold zum 70. Geburtstag*. Wiesbaden: Harrassowitz, 415–36.
———. 2014. Garshuni Malayalam: A Witness to an Early Stage of Indian Christian Literature. *Hugoye: Journal of Syriac Studies* 17 (2), 263–323.
———. 2015. Cosmopolitismes de la Mer d'Arabie: Les chrétiens de saint Thomas face à l'expansion Portugaise. *In:* Corinne Lefèvre, Ines Županov and Jorge Flores, ed., *Cosmopolitismes en Asie du Sud: Sources, intinéraires, langues (XVIe-XVIIIe siècle)*. Collection Puruṣārtha 33. Paris: Éditions de l'École des hautes études en sciences sociales, 143–69.
———. 2016a. Monuments of Indian Christian Art: Problems of Genres, Dating and Context. *In:* Alan Chong et al., ed., *Christianity in Asia: Sacred Art and Visual Splendour*. Singapore: Asian Civilisations Museum, 38–49.
———. 2016b. Prayer Book of Mar Parampil Ćāndi Kuriātu. *In:* Alan Chong et al., ed., *Christianity in Asia: Sacred Art and Visual Splendour*. Singapore: Asian Civilisations Museum, 50–1.
———. 2018a. Some Early Documents About the Interactions of the Saint Thomas Christians and the European Missionaries. In: Mahmood Kooria and Michael Naylor Pearson, ed., *Malabar in the Indian Ocean: Cosmopolitanism in an Indian Ocean Region*. New Delhi: Oxford University Press, 76–120.
———. 2018b. Accommodationist Strategies on the Malabar Coast: Competition or Complementarity? *In:* Pierre-Antoine Fabre and Ines G. Županov, ed., *The Rites Controversy in the Early Modern World*. Leiden: Brill, 191–232.
Pulickavil, Achen. 2003. *Malankarayudae Manideepam (Light of Malankara): Kaniamparampil Achen*. Trans from Malayalam by Dr. K. M. Cherian. Kozhencherry: Syrian Orthodox Bible Society of India.
Rajan, Gurukkal. 2016. *Rethinking Classical Indo-Roman Trade: Political Economy of Eastern Mediterranean Exchange Relations*. New Delhi: Oxford University Press.
Schurhammer, Georg S. J. 1963. *Orientalia*. Rome-Lisbon: Institutum Historicum Societatis Iesu-Centro de Estudos Historicos Ultramarinos.
Subbarayalu, Y. 2012. *South India Under the Cholas*. New Delhi: Oxford University Press.
Susan Thomas. 2002. *Property Relations and Family Forms in Colonial Keralam*. Ph.D. thesis defended at Mahatma Gandhi University, Kottayam. Online at: http://shodhganga.inflibnet.ac.in/handle/10603/566?mode=full (last accessed on 18.02.2018).
Thaliath, Jonas. 1958/1999. *The Synod of Diamper*. OCA 152. Rome: Pontificium Institutum Orientalium Studiorum. Reprint: Bangalore: Dharmaram Vidya Kshetram, 1999.

Thazhath, Andrews. 1987. *The Juridical Sources of the Syro-Malabar Church (A Historico-Juridical Study)*. Vadavathoor, Kottayam: Paurastya Vidyāpīṭham, Pontifical Oriental Institute of Religious Studies.

Thekkedath, Joseph. 1972. *The Troubled Days of Francis Garcia S.J., Archbishop of Cranganore 1641–59*. Analecta Gregoriana 187. Roma: Università Gregoriana Editrice.

———. 1988. *History of Christianity in India, Vol. 2: From the Middle of the Sixteenth Century to the End of the Seventeenth Century (1542–1700)*. Bangalore: Church History Association of India.

Vallavanthara, Antony, C. M. I. 1984. *India in 1500 AD: The Narratives of Joseph the Indian*. Mannanam: Research Institute for Studies in History. Reprint: Piscataway, NJ: Gorgias Press, 2010.

Van der Ploeg, J. P. M. 1983. *The Christians of St. Thomas in South India and Their Syriac Manuscripts*. Rome/Bangalore: Center for Indian and Inter-Religious Studies/Dharmaram Publications.

CHAPTER THIRTY-FOUR

THE RENAISSANCE OF SYRIAC LITERATURE IN THE TWELFTH–THIRTEENTH CENTURIES

Dorothea Weltecke and Helen Younansardaroud

THE PERIOD AND THE TERM 'SYRIAC RENAISSANCE'

Western scholars of the early twentieth century did not hold this period of Syriac literature in high esteem (Wright 1894: 259; Chabot 1935: 114). It was this frequently arrogant attitude that motivated the Syriac Orthodox patriarch Ignatius Aphrem I Barsoum (1887–1957) to write his own presentation. Apart from documenting a wealth of knowledge about works that even today have not been edited, the patriarch's view is vital for the understanding of this period in general: works of the twelfth and thirteenth centuries are still part and parcel of the active life of the Syriac churches; they are known, valued, and used (Barsaum 1987).

The concept of a Syriac renaissance was introduced by Anton Baumstark (1922: 285). Modern research has rendered parts of Baumstark's presentation outdated, but his term 'Syriac renaissance' has endured. The German scholar also pointed out parallel developments in other Eastern Christian literatures such as Armenian, Georgian, and Coptic. In recent years, this idea has been confirmed (Teule 2010). Consequently, Mat Immerzeel (2004: 13–15) has suggested the adoption of the term 'Christian renaissance' to include also art history in the concept.

Generally speaking, the societies of the twelfth and thirteenth centuries experienced a period of great dynamism. Asia, Europe, and Northern Africa formed once again an interconnected space; science and all kinds of cultural endeavours prospered (Arnason 2004). While the efforts for union between Chalcedonian and non-Chalcedonian churches did not result in formal agreements, the scholars of the time were prepared for reconciliation and tolerance. Even though the Crusades and other wars brought hardships to the population, the churches of the Syriac tradition even expanded geographically, especially in the thirteenth century (1272–1368) (e.g. Winkler and Tang 2013). The Islamisation of the Mongols at the turn of the thirteenth to the fourteenth centuries is generally seen as marking the end of this period.

The term 'renaissance' as a designation for mediaeval cultures East or West was first used in the early twentieth century to highlight the achievements of those periods and to correct their negative image (Haskins 1927; Mez 1937). Accordingly, Baumstark's preference for the term may be understood in this sense. Yet in the context of current studies, the term Syriac renaissance has methodological disadvantages, since 'renaissance' is now understood as something rather more than a 'cultural revival'. The concept is envisaged as being a watershed in European cultural history, resulting in radical new attitudes towards the past and the future, in a hotbed of European modernity in science, politics, and philosophy. While Herman Teule suggested the literature of the period to be characteristic of a revival of ancient sources, religious and denominational openness, and an exhaustive use of Arabic science (Teule 2010: 95–112), not every scholar seems to agree with this description (Haar Romeny 2010). However, the idea, that the period has specific features that distinguish it from former and later ones is not disputed. In our view, the writers of the period are united by their common efforts to renew the Syriac tradition by every means possible, from the past or present, from native or foreign sources.

For this programme, the only extant versified catalogue of writers in Syriac, which was compiled by ʿAḇdīshōʿ bar Brīḵā (d. 1318), may serve as a symbol: ʿAḇdīshōʿs work displays a new regard towards past achievements. At the same time, he was also aware of Arabic lists of scholars (*ṭabaqāt*). While he strove to create something equal in value to *ṭabaqāt*, he invented something new. After all, his work became the chief source for all modern histories of Syriac literature, as was acknowledged by Baumstark (1922: 5).

AWARENESS OF SYRIAC

Syriac was considered the sacred language of Christ. All of the churches of the Syriac tradition can be seen to value the language very highly during this period (Rubin 1998). They revived and improved its liturgical use and provided the communities with biblical texts, prayer books, and liturgical material (e.g. Brock 1990). The main body of extant Syriac writing from this period comes either from the Syriac Orthodox Church or from the Church of the East.

The population of the churches in the Syriac tradition in western Asia still often spoke various forms of Syriac. For illiterate people, writers produced works in easy language to listen to or to sing. To be skilled in the written language, however, was a matter of access to schooling and classical literature and of comprehensive learning. Certain remarks in relation to the spoken languages in the Syriac grammar written by polymath and maphrian Grigorios Abū l-Farağ bar ʿEḇrōyō (1225/6–1286) (Barhebraeus) shed light on the variations, but the first documents of the spoken language date only from the sixteenth and seventeenth centuries (Mengozzi 2002). During the twelfth and the thirteenth centuries, the teaching of Syriac took place within the frame work of the church. Bar ʿEḇrōyō required the bishops to provide compulsory schooling for all boys to learn at least the basic elements of the language, of secular learning as well as the Christian teachings (*Nomocanon* VII, 9). Even if this remained an ideal, the communities then as now strove as best they could to transmit the tradition.

However, it is important not to confuse the state of Classical Syriac learning with the state of learning in general (Kawerau 1960). Neither should the fact that clerics did not always speak or write Arabic mislead Western scholars to impute the mediaeval European situation to Syriac Christians. Members of the churches of the Syriac tradition depended on an education outside the church schools and had to study

Arabic or Persian to proficiency (see below, Philosophy and natural science; Samir 2005; for an example, Kedar and Kohlberg 1995).

Hence, unlike the case of the translations from Arabic into Latin, the literature of the Syriac renaissance that was based on Arabic learning was not intended primarily to introduce the contents of higher learning into the Syriac communities. Rather, authors were reacting to the general appreciation of Arabic literature by demonstrating the possibilities of Syriac. One distinctive feature of the Syriac literature of this period is the existence of bilingual texts (e.g. Syriac/Arabic), which were produced especially where mutual understanding and communication between two cultures were of particular importance.

GRAMMAR AND LEXICOGRAPHY

Despite the predominance of Arabic and because of the great interest that Syrian writers directed towards their language, such writers studiously maintained the rules of correct reading and writing as well as standards and styles for their literary language, as transmitted by works of grammar and lexicography. One of the first of these in this period was Eliyā bar Shīnāyā of Nisibis (975–1046), an eleventh-century bishop of the Church of the East with a remarkable breadth of knowledge, who composed important works in both Syriac and Arabic. He was famous as a theologian, historian, grammarian, and lexicographer. His Syriac work on grammar (*Turrāṣ mamllā suryāyā*, ed. Gottheil 1887) and his Arabic-Syriac dictionary, *Kitāb al-Tarğumān fī ta'līm luġat as-Suryān*, show his deep interest in Syriac grammatical and linguistic science (Weninger 1994). Another grammarian originating from Nisibis is the East Syrian Īshō'yahḇ bar Malkōn (late 12th–early 13th cent.), whose work is based on Eliyā's grammar as reported by Gottheil in his 1887 edition. Bar Malkōn came from Dunaysir, today Kızıltepe, not far from Mardin, and was bishop of Mardin. When he became metropolitan bishop of Nisibis and Armenia, he changed his name from Yauseph into Īshō'yahḇ. He wrote on different topics in Arabic and Syriac, e.g. a metrical tract on questions of grammar in Syriac entitled *Mṣidtā ḏ-Nuqzē*, 'Net of points' (Wright 1894: 256–7; Merx 1889: ch. VIII), and *Manhrānūṯā ḇa-grammaṭīqī suryāytā*, 'Elucidation in Syriac grammar', a work in two columns of forty-seven chapters of different lengths (Scher 1905: 72–3; Graf 1947: 208–10; Teule 2007a). Yōḥannān bar Zō'bī (12th/13th cent.), an East Syrian monk of Bēṯ Qōqā in Adiabene (North Mesopotamia) near Erbil, worked on spirantisation, an important aspect of Syriac phonology. He was a highly esteemed teacher of language and philosophy (see below, Philosophy and natural science), far beyond the boundaries of his church, and is today best known as a grammarian. Bar Zō'bī mentions Eliyā of Nisibis in his grammar by name and seems to depend largely on Eliyā's grammar (ed. Gottheil, 8). His work on spirantisation was published by Georges Bohas 2005. According to Volkmer (2008: 352), in his approach to Syriac grammar, Bar Zō'bī 'tends to consider Syriac in its own right apart from the interpretive framework of Arabic grammar, a unique indigenous perspective'.

Ya'qōḇ bar Shakkō (died 1241) of the Syriac Orthodox Church, born in Barṭella (about 20 km east of Mosul) and a monk at the Mōr Mattay monastery who studied under Bar Zō'bī, also participated in the debate on Syriac. Bar Shakkō devoted sections of his 'Book of Dialogues' on grammar, poetry, and metre (Martin 1879:

68–70; Sprengling 1916). He also followed Eliyā of Nisibis closely. Maphrian Bar ʿEḇrōyō too was greatly concerned to cultivate the Syriac language as is evident from his *Kṯōḇō ḏ-ṣemḥē*, 'Book of Splendours' (ed. Moberg 1913), and other grammatical works (Takahashi 2005; Farina 2016).

PHILOSOPHY AND NATURAL SCIENCE

The state of secular learning during the period of the Syriac renaissance is often considered by Western scholars to have been poor, but the remains of Syriac writing do not permit us to speak with certainty about the state of studies at that time. The Syrians were still respected all over Asia for their knowledge. Some individuals were physicians at important courts such as that of the ʿAbbasids in Baghdad (Baumstark 1922: 306 etc.), and a Syrian physician initiated a medical bureau in the capital under Qubilai Khan (1260–94). Often their names were Arabic and mentioned as such in the Syriac chronicles, because scientists preferred to read and write in Arabic rather than Syriac so as to take part in the world of scientific discourse (Takahashi 2014b: 43–5; Weltecke 2008). Their books had little chance of survival. Because of the low estimation in which the remnants are held in Western scholarship, not even all that is extant in Syriac has been edited and studied by modern scholars (Takahashi 2012, 2010).

One of these unedited works is a large commentary by metropolitan Dionysius bar Ṣalīḇī (d. 1171) on Aristotle's *Organon*, considered the propaedeutic basis of all learning (Hugonnard-Roche 1989; along with other works by this author). It is the only extant philosophical work in Syriac from the twelfth century. The commentary is preserved in the same manuscript as the Syriac epitome of a work by Nikolaus of Damascus (d. 64) on physics and metaphysics (Wright and Cook 1901: 1009–17; Takahashi 2012). During this period, many more of the writings of Nikolaus must have been available in Syriac, because he was used in all of the extant philosophical works of the Syriac renaissance (Watt 2010). The codicological context supports the assumption that the Syrians had preserved their ancient Aristotelian translations together with the commentaries of Nikolaus and other authors. While Dionysius taught in this conservative manner, the thirteenth century masters also included a second tradition. They received new developments from Arabic philosophy and the contemporary discussion on the value of the works of Ibn Sīnā (980–1037) (Watt 2010: 130–3). As the Cambridge manuscript indicates, both avenues coexisted side by side even beyond the Syriac renaissance.

Astronomy was one of the mathematical arts and at the same time, in the form of predictive astrology, was considered by rulers to be a powerful tool, the reservations of clerics notwithstanding. While no Syriac writings on astronomy are extant from our period, historical records inform us that Syrians were active in this field even in the most exclusive circles and took part in the controversies on all sides (Weltecke 2003b). One of them, Theodore of Antioch (d. before 1244), became physician, philosopher, translator, and astrologer at the court of emperor Frederick II. Traces of his work are extant in Latin (Kedar and Kohlberg 1995; Burnett 1995). The Almagest, Ptolemy's treatise on the movement of celestial bodies, must have been translated into Syriac, and vestiges of it have been detected in the works of two of the thirteenth-century masters, *maphriān* Bar ʿEḇrōyō and bishop Yaʿqōḇ bar Shakkō (Takahashi 2014a).

The didactic function of the works of all of the thirteenth-century masters is especially marked in the unedited works of Bar ʿEḇrōyō's and Yaʿqōḇ teacher, the priest-monk Yōḥannān bar Zōʿbī. Yōḥannān wrote short metrical introductions to philosophy for his pupils (for the grammar, see above Grammar and lexicography; the introductions are extant in Berlin Syr. 69/Sachau 72, see Sachau 1899: 265ff.; Daiber 1985). Bar ʿEḇrōyō and Yaʿqōḇ – as well as Theodore of Antioch before them – had also studied natural philosophy in Mosul with Kamāl ad-Dīn ibn Yūnus (1156–1242) and Nāsīr ad-Dīn al-Ṭūsī (1201–1274), whose influence on their works is very marked, as also is that of Faḫr ad-Dīn ar-Rāzī (1149–1209) (Takahashi 2006).

Both Bar ʿEḇrōyō and Yaʿqōḇ covered the entire Aristotelian corpus and also were open to Neoplatonic strands present in contemporary Arabic debate. Among shorter works, each compiled a vast systematic introduction to all parts of philosophy, which are today considered exceptionally well informed and diligently balanced. Yaʿqōḇ Bar Shakkō wrote the *Kṯōḇō ḏ-dialogu*, 'Book of Dialogues', as questions and answers between pupil and teacher in two parts (Furlani 1926/7; see also recent works by Takahashi, Teule, Watt). The first covers the topics concerning the use of language, rhetoric, logic, and dialectics. The second covers mathematics, physics, that is, the entire natural world, philosophy of the practical world (economics, politics, ethics), and, in place of metaphysics, a rational theology. The large comprehensive work by Bar ʿEḇrōyō is the *Kṯōḇō ḏ-hewaṯ ḥekmeṯō*, 'Book of the Cream of Wisdom', which he wrote at the very end of his life between 1285 und 1286 (Takahashi 2005: 68, 245). In the first of the four parts he presented logic in the order of the traditional Organon (Hugonnard-Roche 2008), in the second the natural world, i.e. physics (Takahashi 2004; Schmitt 2017), in the third metaphysics, and in the last practical philosophy (Joosse 2004; Watt 2005). While using the works of al-Ṭūsī and Ibn Sīnā as models, even translating entire parts of these at times, Bar Shakkō and Bar ʿEḇrōyō drew on the traditional Syriac translations as a quarry for terminology. Bar ʿEḇrōyō developed a large number of appropriate neologisms to adapt the material to the Syriac language. Like the summaries of the Latin masters of the thirteenth century, these writings could be used as textbooks for higher education. Students had to be already versed either in Syriac or in (natural) philosophy in the Arabic dress and were encouraged to use Syriac in secular learning. Rather than being original works on science, these texts are highly creative in their masterly renovation of Syriac.

SECULAR LITERATURE

Little can be said about secular literature, because the given conditions of the age it had no chance of survival. However, historical records and laws mention in passing a lively culture of storytelling. Professionals like physicians would also relate stories about famous kings or anecdotal matters to entertain each other in learned circles; communities would enjoy diversion with all sorts of performances, music, songs, and stories at festivities such as banquets and weddings. These forms of secular entertainment were not always looked upon with approval by the clerical authorities. Especially in times of tribulation, adherence to piety was demanded by strict reform clerics such as Dionysius bar Ṣalīḇī, and secular means of entertainment were discouraged (Weltecke 2003a).

It is only Bar ʿEḇrōyō who actively responded to the popularity of secular stories and secular genres of literature. In accordance with his project to always provide his flock with alternatives in Syriac and with a Christian setting, he even strove to produce something equal to Arabic *adab* literature in Syriac with his 'Collection of delightful stories' (ed. Wallis Budge 1897 as *The Laughable Stories*). For this collection, which has received little scholarly attention, he took notes and excerpts from the *Kitāb Naṯr ad-durr* of Abū Saʿīd Manṣūr ibn al-Ḥusayn al-Ābī (d. ca. 421/1030), a compilation of short narratives from scripture and oral traditions. These stories Bar ʿEḇrōyō adapted for the Syriac Christian environment, but they remain at the same time within the framework of the norms of *adab* (Marzolph 1985). Bar ʿEḇrōyō is also known as a writer of secular poems on love, friendship, satire, and nature. For these, too, he used Arabic models or even translated material into Syriac (Takahashi 2005: 77).

THEOLOGY – POETRY AND PROSE

The bulk of extant literature, be it poetry or prose, is unsurprisingly theological in nature, covering all the different fields of theology from spiritual theology, exegesis, dogmatic teaching, apology, and polemics. This literature in Syriac arose from the need for a religious orientation in their own prestige language on the part of believers. Here, poetry continued to flourish in the Syriac communities. Many authors are not known to the West as yet, because their poems on holidays, saints, penitence, mourning etc. have only rarely been edited. It is noteworthy that patriarch Barsaum especially praises the quality of these poems, the lasting popularity of which may be seen in their use in the Syrian churches to this day (Barsaum 1987: 334–6). Interesting also is the way in which the Syriac authors incorporate theological theoretical knowledge into their poetical works of very high quality confirming the truth of Christianity.

In the field of liturgy and liturgical poetry, Eliyā of Nisibis's literary production is very rich indeed. He wrote various liturgical texts in Syriac which occur in the service books of the Church of the East. Among his many works that remain unedited, especially worthy of mention is his *Kitāb Kitāb al-Mağālis* (trans. Horst 1886), an apologetic treatise in Arabic based on biblical sources defending the truth of Christianity. He also composed the *Kitāb al-mağālis*, 'Book of sessions', which include religious discussions related to his linguistic interests with the famous Islamic scholar and statesman Abū al-Qāsim al-Mağribī. According to David Bertaina (2011: 197) the disputation has a vital aim, 'to recognize scientific achievement by Syriac scholars, (and) to strengthen the rational arguments for the Christian faith'.

Khāmīs bar Qardāḥē (13th cent.?), a priest in or near Arbela, was a very productive East Syriac poet and famous especially for his collection of *ʿonyāṯā* (anthems in which alternate verses were sung by the choir), which were continuously copied from the fourteenth to the nineteenth centuries. His *Turgāmē* (expository anthems preceding the Epistle and Gospel) have a liturgical purpose (ed. Khadbshaba 2002; Mengozzi 2014; Pritula 2014).

Already, in the field of poetry, besides hymns for various feasts of the liturgical year, he wrote poems on secular topics and many epigrams or *Tarʿē ḏ-mušḥāṯā* on different subjects (e.g. love, wisdom, flowers). The poems attributed to Khāmīs with the title *Soġyāṯā ḏ-ʿal ḥamrā*, or wine songs, inspired from the Arabic *Khamriyya* (Bencheikh 1978), are transmitted together with a poem of 120 lines by Bar ʿEḇrōyō belonging to the same genre (Taylor 2010: esp fn. 11). According to Taylor (2010: 51), in his wine songs Khāmīs was 'not merely parroting the Arabic (and perhaps Persian) examples of Khamriyya available to him, but he appears to have been thoroughly reworking their themes within the framework of his Christian faith and doctrine'.

Another famous hymn-writer (the genre of *ʿonīṯā*) of this period in the Church of the East is Gīwargīs Wardā (13th cent.?). His *ʿonyāṯā* with biblical and theological contents are used in holiday services up to the present day. Among these he wrote hymns on other subjects such as a description of different calamities such as the famines and plagues of the Mongol period through which he lived. Pritula 2015 identifies a radical change in the character of Wardā's poetry. Wardā's aim, as the creator of a new genre inspired possibly by Persian poetry, seems to have been to arrange traditional poetry into a new formalistic poetic form (Nicák 2016).

To the list of East Syrian authors in the *ʿonīṯā*-tradition one might add Gabriel Qamṣā (d. ca. 1300), metropolitan bishop of Mosul, though his work mostly remained unpublished (Baumstark 1922: 323; Wright 1894: 284–5; sample in Cardahi 1875: 107–13).

In this respect, it is important to mention also ʿAḇdīshōʿ bar Brīḵā's *Paradise of Eden* (ed. d-Bēt Qelayta 1916). This book is a collection of fifty *mēmrē* or *maqāma* with theological content (*maqāma* meaning exhortation and being a narrative genre of Arabic prose literature composed of episodes centring on a common hero, in which the word *maqāma* denotes the overarching story). It consists of two parts of twenty-five *mēmrē* each. The first part, which is composed of over 2,626 verses, is named after Enoch, as we learn from the author's introduction. The second part, which comprises over 2,000 verses, is dedicated to Eliyā. ʿAḇdīshōʿ lists the various ornamental figures employed in his work, including his various types of wordplay. He states that he used these means in order to praise God and to preach in a manner that would encourage his people to return to their faith.

With his masterly command of Syriac, ʿAḇdīshōʿ dealt with diverse religious and dogmatic topics, for example with the questions of trinity and unity in *mēmrē* 1, 26, 27, 31, and 32. Repeatedly he applied the form of *mēmrē* to biblical themes, for example in the story of the lost son in *mēmrē* 7 and 8. Many questions dealing with asceticism are treated in *mēmrā* 5, while philosophical issues are represented in *mēmrā* 18. The fifty *mēmrē* in the *Paradise of Eden* draw on a wide variety of sources. The most common, which ʿAḇdīshōʿ himself mentions, is the Bible, and rather often a part of a verse is actually a biblical quotation. ʿAḇdīshōʿ wanted to demonstrate by his work that Syriac is no less suitable for the art of poetry than Arabic. He mostly uses his favourite verse-types, consisting of lines of seven, six, and twelve syllables, and more rarely those consisting of four or ten. Up to the present, ʿAḇdīshōʿ's *maqāma* enjoy an undiminished popularity among educated people in all the Syrian communities and the work circulates in countless copies. Often the Syriac vocabulary is listed after each *mēmrā*, and ʿAḇdīshōʿ's explanations of neologisms of his own and loanwords in Syriac are added. Robert Payne Smith's *Thesaurus Syriacus* (1868–1901) contains numerous citations of ʿAḇdīshōʿ's *Paradise*.

An important aspect of ʿAḇdīshōʿ's language is the extent of his linguistic creativity. He composed a second book entitled *Kṯāḇā ḏ-Margānīṯā ʿal šrārā ḏa-ḵresṭyānūṯā*,

'Book of the Pearl on the Truth of Christianity' (see bibliography for editions and translations). This work was the result of prompting by his patriarch Yahḇallāhā III, who urged ʿAḇdīshōʿ to write another book on material he had already covered, only this time smaller in size. ʿAḇdīshōʿ divided his book into five parts: (a) Concerning God; (b) Creation; (c) the Christian dispensation; (d) the sacraments of the Church; and (e) the things that pre-figure the world to come.

Considering the nature of the subjects treated in the *Margānīṯā*, the work is remarkable for its conciseness, clarity, and simplicity. The topic of the sacraments of the Church, or Sacramental Theology, especially concerning the Syriac concept of *rāzā*, was a topic for discussions sponsored in 2003 by the Pro Oriente Foundation, based in Vienna, with the goal of promoting dialogue within the churches of the Syriac tradition. In a synod held in 2001, the Assyrian Church of the East reaffirmed the list of the seven *rāzē* that are found in ʿAḇdīshōʿ bar Brīḵā's *Margānīṯā* (Winkler 2003: 141ff.). These seven *rāzē* are the Priesthood, Baptism, the Oil of Unction, the Oblation, the Holy Leaven, Absolution and Repentance, and Matrimony and Virginity (Badger 1852: 404–12). ʿAḇdīshōʿ also worked as a copyist. In the year 1284, during his tenure as bishop of Shīġār and of Bēṯ ʿArābāyē, he also completed an Evangelistary.

Less complicated in language but also very popular were works of spiritual literature. The compilation of narrations, exempla, and exegetical stories by the metropolitan Shlēmōn bar Baṣrā (fl. 1222) was very popular and in use at least until the nineteenth century. His 'Book of the Bee' presented these stories while following the order of the history of salvation from creation to the end times (Baumstark 1922: 309). In his 'Book of the Dove' written at the end of his life, Bar ʿEḇrōyō compiled a work for the edification of monks, on their practical and spiritual way of life, embedding these rules in a relation of his own doubts and his development from dogmatical theory to mystical practice, once again drawing on his readings of Al-Ġazālī (1058–1111) (Takahashi 2005: 66, 212–22; Pinggéra 2000).

The numerous official negotiations between the Latin Church, the Greek Orthodox Church, and the non-Chalcedonian churches during the twelfth and thirteenth centuries, the inter-denominational disputes, as well the need for defence against Islam, all spurred the production of theological literature that explained and highlighted differences and boundaries. Members of the hierarchy formulated expositions of faith and prepared dogmatical and polemical treatises for the preparation of negotiations and as statements within the ongoing exchange (e.g. Rabo 2015). As we have already seen, many of the authors mentioned here took part in these debates and several theological works related to them in some way. One prominent and widely read polemicist of the Syriac Orthodox Church was Dionysius bar Ṣalīḇī (Rabo 2014), who wrote a systematic tract on polemics against other Christian denominations as well as against Islam. The latter contains a detailed description of the development of the Islamic schools and displays a thorough reading of the Qurʾān. Dionysius's treatise also contains the largest number of Syriac quotations of the Qurʾān (for a selection of his works, see bibliography). Moreover, Dionysius was active in the internal theological debates spurred by the re-conquest of the city of Edessa and the dispute on the providence of history. His goal was to affirm the teachings of the Syriac Orthodox Church and to warn a doubting flock against apostasy (Weltecke 2002).

Īshōʿyahḇ bar Malkōn's works on theological themes as well as his letters are largely written in Arabic. Among them, his treatise on the veneration of icons and the holy cross addressed to members of two different religions, Jews and Muslims (Teule 2007a), plays an important role in many East Syrian theological and apologetical writings. Bar ʿEḇrōyō, for one, had also always taken an active part in these disputations. In his old age, however, he wanted to overcome all these arguments about words and to foster tolerance as well as unity among all Christians, a task stressed in his 'Book of the Dove'.

Another outcome of the widely felt need to elucidate and confirm the teachings of the churches in Syriac are the monumental theological summaries of this period written by systematic theologians. Yaʿqōḇ bar Shakkō, for example, is also the author of a theological compilation dated 1231, which is called the 'Book of Treasures' (Teule 2007b). Bar ʿEḇrōyō wrote the *Mnōraṯ qūḏšē*, 'Candelabrum of the sanctuary', which again not only presented a systematic disposition of the theological teachings of the Syriac Orthodox Church, but also contains many remarks on philosophy, ethics, and the natural world (Takahashi 2005: 175–91).

The exegetical works of this period, the commentaries on biblical books and on the church fathers, although they have been widely read and utilised even to the present as a theological foundation, have nonetheless found a mixed reception in recent scholarship in comparison to the achievements of Late Antiquity. Bas ter Haar Romeny (2010) has called for a thorough review of the received lists of works by Baumstark, as philology has disclaimed a number of authors in recent years. Dionysius bar Ṣalīḇī, however, remains a prominent representative. He innovated exegetical writing by presenting factual and spiritual commentary in synoptic columns, thus enabling the reader to compare and to identify relations. He also aimed at comprehensiveness by abridging and structuring commentaries of the Syriac Orthodox tradition in one coherent work (only some of his commentaries are edited, e.g. Ryan 2004). It was also in the thirteenth century that Bar ʿEḇrōyō wrote his commentary on the bible (*Awṣar rōzē*, the 'Storehouse of mysteries'). From the Church of the East no systematic exegetical work is extant. Exegetical works were increasingly written in Arabic and not all of the known works have come down to us.

LAW BOOKS

Law is traditionally considered to be part of the history of Syriac literature. The main source of law was first of all early Greek legal material which remained of interest even after the denominational separation. Each church added new material, such as canons of synods, decisions and canons of patriarchs, or collections by specialists of law. The city, being the residence of the bishops, is the *Sitz im Leben* of legal texts. The bishops and the metropolitans practised law as judges in their communities, not only in ecclesiastical matters, but also in civil conflicts and even concerning crime as part of the communities' legal autonomy as *Dhimmis* (Kaufhold 1984). Today, historians increasingly use legal sources to gain insight into the social life of the communities (Simonsohn 2011; Weitz 2013; Weltecke 2013). Still, the validity of the extant legal norms as well as basic questions as to the relation between norm and reality or the practical function of each canon requires further research.

From the wealth of legal material written in our period, little has survived, although manuscripts containing law are continually being discovered (details in Kaufhold 2012). In this discipline, the authors of the Syrian churches often used Arabic: from the

Melkite and Maronite groups no Syriac material survived at all, in contrast to important collections that are extant in Arabic. Arabic texts were also produced by the Syriac Orthodox Church (Kaufhold 2012: 251, 254). Similarly, from the Church of the East several important collections in Arabic survive such as that by Bishop Eliyā of Nisibis or by the physician, secretary to the patriarch, and monk Ibn al-Ṭayyib (d. 1043). Arabic works and Arabic translations of legal collections (e.g. Pahlitzsch 2014) functioned as the medium for a lively inter-denominational exchange of law (Kaufhold 2012: 218) all over the Eastern Christian churches under Islamic rule and beyond, as dogmatical differences were less pertinent in this area.

In Syriac, fragments of legal material by the metropolitan Dionysius bar Ṣalībī and the lawbook by Bar ʿEḇrōyō survive from the Syriac Orthodox tradition. The extant canons by Dionysius bar Ṣalībī deal with penitential questions, with ritual matters like fasting or the Eucharist, with the conduct of the clergy and with regulations for the economical administration of monasteries and churches. These canons continued to be copied up to the seventeenth century and were also translated into Arabic (Kaufhold 2012: 250). Bar ʿEḇrōyō's lawbook written in the early years of his office as maphrian is the only comprehensive legal collection of the Syriac Orthodox tradition. The work consists of two parts. Part 1 (I–VIII) contains ecclesiastical law and profusely quotes ancient Greek and Syriac sources. Part 2 (IX–LX) deals with secular matters (civil and criminal law). Beside Christian traditions (also from the Church of the East), Bar ʿEḇrōyō makes ample and free use of Islamic sources for the latter, in particular the concise lawbook *Kitāb al-Wasīṭ* by Al-Ġazālī,[1] without identifying them (Weitz 2013; Takahashi 2015: 67). His lawbook was and still is in continual use by the Syriac Orthodox Church.

In the Eastern tradition, ʿAḇdīshōʿ bar Brīḵā's legal works in Syriac are extant. Both of his legal compendia, the earlier *Nomocanon*, 'Collection of Synodal Canons', and the *Ordo iudiciorum ecclesiasticorum*, 'Order of the Ecclesiastical Decisions', written 1314–5, were accepted by the Church of the East in the year 1318 as normative (Vosté 1940).[2] Concerning his conceptions of family law and the position of women, ʿAḇdīshōʿ bar Brīḵā was less dependent on Islamic traditions than was Bar ʿEḇrōyō (Weitz 2013: 414ff.). While he also included Muslim material, ʿAḇdīshōʿ rather relied on earlier compilations of his own tradition such as the legal works of Gabriel bar Baṣrā (fl. late 9th c.) or Eliyā of Nisibis (Kaufhold 2005: xiv). In the 'Order of the Ecclesiastical decisions', ʿAḇdīshōʿ identifies his Eastern Syrian sources. He also made use of the widely known *Nomocanon* by the Copt Al-Ṣafī ibn al-ʿAssāl (between 1253 and 1275), from which he translates passages verbatim, without identifying them (Kaufhold 1984).

Polemical attacks by Muslims and also by Jews against Christian law were mentioned by both Bar ʿEḇrōyō (*Chronicon*, ed. Bedjan 1932: 98; trans. Budge 1932: 92) and ʿAḇdīshōʿ bar Brīḵā (*Ordo iudiciorum*, ed. Vosté 1940: 24). Both wrote their books for practical use, but they also strove to produce something on an equal level with their competitors.

HISTORIOGRAPHY

The three extant monumental historical works in Syriac of the twelfth and thirteenth centuries all come from the Syriac Orthodox tradition: the chronicles of Michael the Great, the Anonymous Chronicle to 1234, and the chronicle by Bar ʿEḇrōyō. These works display a breadth of historical horizon probably not attained either before or after this period. They testify to individual and original decisions regarding form and scope, as well as active research into sources. The methodological skills of the three writers, especially those of Michael the Great, are outstanding within the chronicle-writing traditions of East and West. While Bar ʿEḇrōyō expressly intended his work to educate and to entertain, the other two were interested rather in historical knowledge as such. All three achieve a historical interpretation of Syriac Orthodox life and mishaps within the history of the world and, thus, a rational affirmation of their purpose.

The chronicles preserved verbatim insertions and excerpts from a number of important historical works from Late Antiquity to their own time that are no longer extant. They incorporate, for example, the church history of bishop John of Ephesus (507–586) (Ginkel 1995), the history of Theophilus of Edessa (695–785) (Hoyland 2011), the chronography of bishop Jacob of Edessa (d. 708), and the work of patriarch Dionysius of Tel-Maḥrē (773–845), who was the first Syriac historiographer to divide the Eusebian ecclesiastical history into a secular and an ecclesiastical part (Weltecke 2003a; Witakowski 2007; Hilkens 2014; Debié 2015). Their works must thus be seen as representatives of a lively historiographical tradition in Syriac that is now lost.

In historiography, too, Arabic had been for some time the language of choice for authors belonging to the Syrian churches. General historical works, lives, and local histories from the Melkite tradition were written in Arabic, parts of which are known but not extant (Graf 1944–53, II). The outstanding works of Arabic historiography from the Melkite church still known today (the chronicles by Agapius of Manbij, Eutychius of Alexandria, and Yaḥyā of Antioch), as well as of the Church of the East (the chronicle of Seert, *Kitāb al-Maǧal* 'The book of the Tower' by ʿAmr *ibn Mattā*, the chronicle by Eliyā of Nisibis), all date to the tenth and eleventh centuries (details in Graf II; Holmberg 1993). In view of the lively interest in universal chronicles and history writing in the Mongol Empire, the apparent lack of these in the thirteenth century comes as a surprise. Little to nothing is known about Maronite historical writing during the period, though it most likely existed in some form (Suermann 1998).

Patriarch Michael the Great (1126–1199) was one of the leading figures of the Syriac Orthodox reform movement (Weltecke 2003a, 2010 for general orientation; for details of the edition and translation, see bibliography). His office and his travels brought him into personal contact with Crusader princes, Latin patriarchs, the Seljuk sultan Qiliğ Arslān II (1155–1192), and various local Muslim rulers. During his office, he wrote his famous chronicle in twenty-one books, from the origin of the world to 1195. To the sources of his own tradition that he mentioned he added further material, of Melkite, Armenian, and Muslim origin, which is only partly identified today. For the structure of the chronicle, Michael blends both classical Eusebian genres, chronological tables and narrative ecclesiastical history. The historical material was originally organised into four columns, the first being designated as the 'succession' (*yubōlō*) of the patriarchs, the second as the 'succession of the kings', and the chronological canon as 'computation' or 'enumeration' (*menyōnō*) of the years. No title for the fourth column, containing information on other issues, is known. Michael inserted excursus, for example on the Council of Chalcedon (451) or the history of the Turks. Six appendices follow the text. The first is a directory of the kings and patriarchs mentioned. The second appendix is a treatise on the historical identity of the Syriac Orthodox Christians, who are connected to the Ancient Eastern empires and the Ancient Arameans. Michael intended his book for learned members of monasteries or clergy with a library close at hand. The Syriac text is not preserved in its entirety, and the layout of Michael's chronicle was distorted in the copies. The only extant sixteenth-century manuscript was the *Vorlage* for an Arabic translation. The chronicle was adapted to Armenian interests (1246 and 1247).

Sharing sources with Michael's chronicle but writing independently was the anonymous chronicler, who composed a world chronicle from the creation up to the 1240s, extant until 1234. In the year 1187, the chronicler became witness of the conquest of Jerusalem by Saladin. Later he joined the maphrian Gregorios Yaʿqōḇ (1189–1214). Probably a monk and a member of the clergy, the anonymous was yet more interested in the urban Arabic culture shared by Christians and Muslims in Mesopotamia than was Michael.

The anonymous followed the model set by the two-part history of Dionysius of Tel-Maḥrē, but he reversed Dionysius's order and included the origin and the early history of the world. His first section covers the creation of the universe to the reign of emperor Constantine. Afterwards the material is organised into an ecclesiastical part followed by a secular one that was written later. After its completion in 1203/1204, two continuations followed, which are mutilated at the end. The text is divided into short chapters with headings. For this writer, successions are not the backbone of his historical narrative. Instead he turns to tangible events, especially in the cities, with their Syriac Orthodox population and their worldly occupations. He also documents intellectual and cultural achievements and he, too, sees his readers as educated members of the clergy with access to books. The chronicle has lacunae throughout. The text was preserved in one fourteenth-century manuscript in Istanbul, the whereabouts of which are now unknown.

Bar ʿEḇrōyō also kept Dionysius of Tel-Maḥrē's two-part structure, but again made important alterations. The secular history is organised into eleven books, which are designated as 'successions' of empires, thus following Michael's model, who served as his major source. The ecclesiastical history is arranged into (part I) the succession of the Antiochean patriarchs and (part II) the succession of the maphrians. Into these he integrates the succession of the Armenian catholicoi and those of the Church of the East, thereby achieving the first comprehensive history of Christians in Mesopotamia. He is the only Syriac Orthodox historical writer (Ginkel 2008) who systematically integrated information on the Church of the East, for which he used the 'Book of the Tower' by Amr ibn Mattā and later material (Witakowski 2006). Bar ʿEḇrōyō also used Arabic and Persian narratives, for example the universal chronicle by Ibn Al-Aṯīr (1160–1233) and al-Juwainī (1028–1085) (Borbone 2009), as well as oral reports and anecdotes. He also exploited biographical catalogues (*ṭabaqāt*) of scholars (Todt 1988), recording scientific achievements as had the author of the anonymous chronicle to 1234. He wrote for readers or (lay) listeners and for popular education (*Chronicon*, ed. Bedjan, 457, 392).

The chronicle is extant in a number of manuscripts, which transmit the secular and the ecclesiastical part together, with later exceptions (Mazzola 2018). Several continuations up to fifteenth century were later collected and circulated with the extant copies. The much shorter Arabic version of his world chronicle, which he wrote afterwards, differs in the selection of sources. Whether the work was intended for Christian or Muslim readers is still controversial.

The genres of writing the three chroniclers used from their own period included universal chronicles, lives, local histories of cities or monasteries, lists of emperors and patriarchs, and reports of specific events. The works of three lost writers should be mentioned, which are known through the chronicle of Michael: metropolitan Basil of Edessa (d. 1169) wrote works on the history of Edessa, the conquest of the city by ʿImād ad-Dīn Zangī (1085–1146), and the subsequent massacres of the year 1144 (Hilkens 2014). Bishop Iwannīs of Kaisūm (d. 1171) probably wrote a history of his own time (Chabot 1899–1900: IV, 627; III, 256f.). Dionysius bar Ṣalībī composed a short history, the proem of which Michael copied. This proem documents that Dionysius had also planned a comprehensive universal chronicle featuring the tribulations of the Syriac Orthodox Church as a *memento* in which he wanted to combine ecclesiastical history and chronography. The work remained a project, but traces in Michael's chronicle indicate that Michael might have used the material for his own work (Chabot 1899–1900: IV, 627; III, 257). Besides these lost works, several shorter reports about contemporary events survived as colophons of manuscripts. Some of these are very important historical sources, such as two reports from twelfth-century Crusader Jerusalem (Palmer 1991, 1992), but yet cannot considered to be historical works in the strict sense.

From the Church of the East, however, a carefully composed historical report, a story (*tašʿīṯā*) survived: the extraordinary 'Story of Mār Yahḇallāhā and of Rabbān Ṣaumā', written between 1317 and 1319, which includes the only known Syriac travelogue (ed. Borbone 2000). Part I covers the journey of two Uigur monks from China to the West, the establishment of one of them as patriarch Yahḇallāhā III (1281–1317), and the mission to Europe of his companion and teacher, Rabbān Ṣaumā. Part II describes the later events during the life of patriarch Yahḇallāhā until his death, especially the persecution of the Christians during the Islamisation of the Mongol Khans, the torture of the patriarch, and the massacre of the Christians of Erbil. His successor Timotheus II (1318–1328), at the time metropolitan of Erbil, has been suggested as the author, who with this narrative demonstrated the universality of the Church of the East and the virtues of its leading hierarchs (Murre-van den Berg 2006; Borbone 2006).

Another work from the Church of the East should be referred to that represents an example of a genre unique in the entire Syriac tradition, namely ʿAḇdīshōʿ bar Brīḵā's *Mēmrā ḏ-Syāmē* 'The Metrical catalogue (of Syriac writers)', composed in *mēmrē* (1298), on all the divine books and ecclesiastical writers past and present. Apart from being a comprehensive index which became the foundation of the scientific history of Syriac literature, this *mēmrā* also defends the universality of the Church of the East by linking the Bible with the Church's battered present. Historiography, then, is a field in which the Syriac writers of the epoch attained by any standard an outstanding level of achievement.

CONCLUSION

The period of the Syriac renaissance was a decisive time in the history of the Syriac churches. Although a large part of the output of the period is no longer extant and much material is not edited, nonetheless there can be no doubt that the writers of that time did much more than compile and repeat. Within a world of potentially disadvantageous power structures, which was nevertheless their home, they wanted to develop spaces of autonomy as well as of participation and thus had to balance out separation and interaction, tradition, and innovation.

In some fields of Syriac literature the renovation of the language itself, its adaptation to the needs of the time, gained centre stage and was more important than to produce new content. This was especially the case in the fields of science and philosophy, in all their theoretical, practical, and natural aspects. Here, active participation in secular learning meant sharing the Arabic world of writing; and while the members of the Syrian churches were highly esteemed as professionals and learned specialists, too little of their work is extant to judge the remnants today. Other fields of writing offer a contrasting picture. In their struggle for religious and communal autonomy and self-organisation, the clerical lawyers of the Syrian Churches actively revised the traditional material and formulated norms according to the needs of the day. In theological poetry, grammar, and linguistics as well as historiography, the originality and individuality of the writers of the twelfth and thirteenth centuries set new standards, not only within their own culture, but also from a transcultural perspective. With them and because of them Syriac literature did not end in the fourteenth century, but was continued through the following centuries. Their striving for revival also became the model for modern movements, for example in the development of the Urmia literature, the school of Alqoš, and oral folktales and literature, which are based particularly on Classical Syriac literature (Mengozzi 2012; Murre-van den Berg 1998, 1999).

NOTES

1 For editions and online versions see www.ghazali.org/site/oeuvre-j.htm (seen 20/7/2017).
2 Since Kaufhold (2012), mention should be made that MS Mosul Chaldean Patriarchate 66 is available in print: www.lulu.com/shop/mar-audisho-bar-brikha/the-order-of-ecclesiastical-regulations/paperback/product-20201112.html (seen 25/07/2017).

BIBLIOGRAPHY

Primary Sources

Baumstark 1922, Barsoum 2012, The Comprehensive Bibliography of Syriac Christianity (www.csc.org.il/db/db.aspx?db=SB) and Syriaca.org (http://syriaca.org) should be always be consulted for comprehensive lists of writers and editions. This contribution does not include all the older editions.

ʿAḇdīshōʿ bar Brīḵā
Paradise of Eden
Pardaysā ḏa-ʿDen: d-sīm b-mēmrē tqīlay b-mušḥāṯā l-Mār ʿAbdīšōʿ Miṭrapōleyṭā ḏ-Ṣōbā wad-ʾArmanāyā. Ed. J. d-Bēt Qelayta. Urmia 1916; Mosul 1928; Chicago 1988.
A new edition with translation is in preparation by Helen Younansardaroud.
Marganita
Margānīṯā: ʿal šrārā da-ḵresṭyānuṯā. Ed. d-Bēt Qelayta, J. Mosul, 1924; 3rd ed. Chicago, 1989.
English translation: Appendix B in G. P. Badger. *The Nestorians and their Rituals*. London: Joseph Masters, 1852.
English translation: *The Book of Marganita the Pearl. on the Truth of Christianity*. Trans. Mar Eshai Shimun. Trichur, 1956; Chicago, 1988.

Dionysius bar Ṣalībī
Against the Melkites
A Treatise of Baṣalībi against the Melchites. Ed. and trans. A. Mingana. Woodbrooke Studies I, 1. Cambridge: W. Heffer, 1927.
Against the Armenians
The Work of Dionysius bar Ṣalībī Against the Armenians. Ed. and trans. A. Mingana. Woodbrooke Studies IV. Cambridge: W. Heffer, 1931.
Response to the Arabs
Dionysius bar Ṣalībī. A response to the Arabs. Ed. and trans. Joseph P. Amar. CSCO 614–615. Leuven: Peeters, 2005.
Psalms Commentary
Dionysius bar Salibi's Factual and Spiritual Commentary on Psalms 73–82. Ed. and trans. Steve Ryan. Cahiers de la Revue biblique 57. Paris: Gabalda, 2004.
Eliyā of Nisibis
Grammar
Turrāṣ mamllā suryāyā. A treatise on Syriac grammar. Ed. and trans. Richard J. H. Gottheil. Berlin et al., 1887. Reprinted Piscataway, NJ: Gorgias Press, 2003.
German translation: S. Weninger 1994 (see below).
Kitāb al-Burhān
German translation: *Des Metropoliten Elias von Nisibis Buch der Wahrheit des Glaubens*. Trans. Ludwig Horst. Colmar: Eugen Barth, 1886.
Gīwargīs Wardā
Pritula, A. *The Wardā: an East Syriac hymnological collection: study and critical edition*, Wiesbaden: Harrassowitz, 2015.
Gregorius Bar ʿEḇrōyō (Barhebraeus)
For detailed bibliographic information on all the works of Bar ʿEbrōyo, see Takahashi 2005.
Nomocanon
Nomocanon of Bar-Hebraeus. Ed. St. Ephrem der Syrer Monastery. Glane/Losser: Bar Hebraeus Verlag, 1986. [Earlier edition ed. Paul Bedjan. Harrassowitz: Paris, 1898].
Latin translation: Ecclesiae Antiochenae Syrorum Nomocanon a Gregorio Abulpharagio Bar-Hebraeo. Ed. and trans. J. A. Assemani, in: Angelo Mai, ed., *Scriptorum Veterum Nova Collectio*. Typ Collegii Urbani: Rome, 1838, vol. X, 2, 3–268, VII, 9.
Book of Splendors
La Livre des spendeurs. La grande grammaire de Grégoire Barhebraeus. Ed. Axel Moberg. Lund etc., 1922.
German translation: *Bar Hebraeus, Buch der Strahlen. Die grössere* Grammatik *des Barhebräus*. Ed. and trans. A. Moberg. Leipzig: Harrassowitz. Introduction and Part 2, 1907; Part 1 and Index, 1913.
Cream of Wisdom – the following parts have been published
Aristotelian meteorology in Syriac: Barhebraeus, Butyrum sapientiae, Books of Mineralogy and Meteorology. Ed. and trans. H. Takahashi. Aristoteles Semitico-latinus 15. Leiden: Brill, 2004.
A Syriac Encyclopaedia of Aristotelian Philosophy: Barhebraeus, 'Butyrum sapientiae', Books of Ethics, Economy and Politics. Ed. and trans. N. P. Joosse. Aristoteles Semitico-latinus 16. Leiden: Brill, 2004.
Aristotelian rhetoric in Syriac: Butyrum sapientiae, Book of rhetoric. Ed. and trans J. W. Watt. Aristoteles Semitico-latinus 18. Leiden: Brill, 2005.
Barhebraeus, Butyrum Sapientiae, Physics. Ed. and trans. Jens Ole Schmitt. Aristoteles Semitico-latinus. Leiden: Brill, 2017.
Chronicle
Bedjan, P. 1932, *Gregorii Barhebraei Chronicon Syriacum* Paris: Maisonneuve, 1890.

Eng. translation: *The Chronography of Gregory Abū'l Faraj, the son of Aaron, the Hebrew physician, commonly known as Bar Hebraeus, being the first part of his political history of the world.* Trans. E. A. Wallis Budge. London: Oxford University Press, 1932. Reprinted Piscataway, NJ: Gorgias Press, 2003, 2010.
Laughable Stories
The laughable stories collected by Mâr Gregory John Bar-Hebraeus, Maphrian of the East from A.D. 1264 to 1286. Ed. and trans. Ernest A. Wallis Budge. Semitic Text & Translation Series. London: Luzac & Co., 1897.
Khāmīs bar Qardāḥē
Khadbshaba, Sh. I., *Khamis bar Qardaḥe. Mimre w-mušḥātā.* Prisata da-Nṣibin 2. Nūhadrā: Iraq, 2002.
Michael the Great, Chronicle
Editons and French Translation: *Text and Translations of the Chronicle of Michael the Great.* 11 vols. Ed. G. Kiraz. Piscataway, NJ: Gorgias Press, 2009–.
Chronique de Michel le Syrien. Patriarche Jacobite d'Antioche 1166–1199. Ed. and trans. J. B. Chabot. Paris, 1899–.
The History of Mār Yahḇallāhā
Borbone, P. G. *Storia di Mar Yahballaha e di Rabban Sauma. Un orientale in Occidente ai tempi di Marco Polo.* Torino: S. Zamorani, 2000.

Secondary Literature

Baumstark 1922, the Comprehensive Bibliography of Syriac Christianity (www.csc.org.il/db/db.aspx?db=SB); Syriac Studies: A Classified Bibliography by Sebastian Brock (ongoing project since *Parole de l'Orient* 4 (1973) and Syriaca.org (http://syriaca.org) should be always be consulted for studies).

Arnason, J. 2004. Parallels and Divergences: Perspectives on the Early Second Millennium. *Medieval Encounters* 10(1–3), 13–40.
Badger, George. 1852. *The Nestorians and Their Rituals.* London: Joseph Masters.
Barsaum, Mor Ignatius Aphrem I. 1987. *Histoire des sciences et de la littérature syriaques.* Glane: Bar Hebraeus Verlag.
Eng. translation: Ignatius Aphram I Barsoum. *The Scattered Pearls: A History of Syriac Literature and Sciences.* Tr. Matti Moosa. Piscataway, NJ: Gorgias Press, 2011.
German translation: *Geschichte der syrischen Wissenschaften und Literatur.* Tr. Amill Gorgis und Georges Toro. Eichstätter Beiträge zum Christlichen Orient; Wiesbaden: Harrassowitz. 2012. [Note that the German translation is more reliable and more complete.]
Baumstark, A. 1922. *Geschichte der syrischen Literatur mit Ausschluss der christlich-palästinensischen Texte* Bonn: Marcus & Weber.
Bencheikh, J. E. 1978. Khamriyya. *In*: *Encyclopaedia of Islam.* Leiden: Brill, 4:998–1009.
Bertaina, D. 2011. Science, Syntax, and Superiority in Eleventh-Century Christian – Muslim Discussion: Elias of Nisibis on the Arabic and Syriac Languages. *Islam and Christian – Muslim Relations* 22(2), 197–207.
Bohas, G. 2005. *Les bgdkpt en Syriaque: selon Bar Zo'bī.* Éditions Amam-Cemaa; Amam-Cemaa: Toulouse.
Borbone, P. G. 2006. L'autore della Storia di Mar Yahballaha e di Rabban Sauma. *In*: P. G. Borbone, A. Mengozzi, and M. Tosco, ed., *Loquentes linguis: Studi linguistici e orientali in onore di Fabrizio A. Pennacchietti = Linguistic and Oriental Studies in Honour of Fabrizio A. Pennacchietti = Lingvistikaj kaj orientaj studoj honore al Fabrizio A. Pennacchietti.* Wiesbaden: Harrassowitz, 103–8.
———. 2009. Barhebraeus and Juwayni: A Syriac Chronicler and His Persian Source. *Acta Mongolica* 9, 147–68.

Brock, S. P. 1990. Syriac Manuscripts on the Black Mountain Near Antioch. *In*: R. Schulz and M. Görg, ed., *Lingua restituta orientalis: Festgabe für Julius Assfalg*. Ägypten und Altes Testament 20. Wiesbaden: Harrassowitz, 59–67.

Burnett, Charles. 1995. Magister Theodore, Frederick II's Philosopher. *In*: Centro italiano di studi sul basso Medioevo, ed., *Federico II e le nuove culture: Atti del XXXI Convegno storico internazionale, Todi, 9–12 ottobre 1994*. Spoleto: Centro Italiano di Studi sull'Alto Medioevo, 225–85.

Cardahi, J. 1875. *Liber thesauri de arte poetica Syrorum nec non de eorum poetarum vitis et carminibus*. Rome: Typographia Polyglotta, 107–113.

Chabot, J.-B. 1935. *Littérature syriaque*. Mayenne: Paris.

Daiber, H. 1985. Ein vergessener syrischer Text: Bar Zo'bi über die Teile der Philosophie. *OC* 69, 73–80.

Debié, M. 2015, *L'Écriture de L'Histoire en syriaque. Transmissions interculturelles et constructions identitaires entre Hellénisme et Islam*. Late Antique History and Religion 12. Leuven: Peeters.

Farina, Margherita. 2016. Barhebraeus' Metrical Grammar and Ms. BML Or. 298: Codicological and Linguistic Remarks. *Studi classici e orientali* 62, 345–60.

Furlani, Giuseppe. 1926–1927. La logica del Libro dei Dialoghi di Severo bar Shakkô. *Atti del Reale Istituto Veneto di Scienze, Lettere ed Arti* IX, 11(86:2), 289–348.

Ginkel, J. J. van. 1995. *John of Ephesus: A Monophysite Historian in Sixth-century Byzantium*. Phil. Dissertation. Groningen.

———. 2008. Aramaic Brothers or Heretics: The Image of the East Syrians in the Chronography of Michael the Great d. 1199. *The Harp* 23, 359–68.

Graf, G. 1944–1953. *Geschichte der christlichen arabischen Literatur*. 5 vols. Studi e testi. Città del Vaticano: Biblioteca apostolica vaticana.

Haar Romeny, Bas ter. 2010. The Contribution of Biblical Interpretation to the Syriac Renaissance. In Teule and Tauwinkel 2010, 206–21.

Haskins, Ch. H. 1927. *The Renaissance of the Twelfth Century*. Cambridge, MA: Harvard University Press.

Hilkens, A. 2014. *The Anonymous Syriac Chronicle Up to the Year 1234 and Its Sources*. PhD Dissertation. Universiteit Gent.

Holmberg, Bo. 1993. A Reconsideration of the Kitab al-mağdal. *PdO* 18, 255–73.

Hoyland, R. G. 2011, *Theophilus of Edessa's Chronicle and the Circulation of Historical Knowledge in Late Antiquity and Early Islam*. Translated Texts for Historians. Liverpool: Liverpool University Press.

Hugonnard-Roche, H. 1989. Notices sure Aristote. L'Organon. Tradition syriaque et arabe. *In*: R. Goulet, ed., *Dictionnaire des Philosophes Antiques*. Paris: CNRS Editions, 502–28.

———. 2008. L'œuvre logique de Barhebraeus. *PdO* 33, 129–43.

Immerzeel, M. 2004. Medieval Wall Paintings in Lebanon: Donors and Artists. *Chronos* 10, 7–47.

Kaufhold, H. 1984. Der Richter in den syrischen Rechtsquellen. Zum Einfluß islamischen Rechts auf die Christlich-Orientalische Rechtsliteratur. OC 68, 91–113.

———. 2005. Introduction. The Nomocanon of Metropolitan 'Abdīšō' of Nisibis. Ms 64 in the Collection of Trichur Thrissur, Metropolitan's Palace of the Church of the East. *In:* I. Perczel, ed., *The Nomocanon of Metropolitan Abdisho of Nisbis. A Facsimile Edition of MS 64 From the Collection of the Church of the East in Thrissur*. Piscataway, NJ: Gorgias Press, xi–xxiii.

———. 2012. Sources of Canon Law in the Eastern Churches. *In:* W. Hartmann and K. Pennington, ed., *The History of Byzantine and Eastern Canon Law to 1500*. Washington, DC: Catholic University of America Press, 215–342.

Kawerau, P. 1960. *Die jakobitische Kirche im Zeitalter der syrischen Renaissance. Idee und Wirklichkeit.* Berliner byzantinistische Arbeiten. Berlin: Akademie-Verlag.

Kedar, B. Z., and E. Kohlberg. 1995. The Intercultural Career of Theodore of Antioch. *The Mediterranean Historical Review* 10, 164–76.

Martin, J. P. P. 1879. *De la métrique chez les Syriens.* Abhandlungen für die Kunde des Morgenlandes 7,2. Leipzig: Brockhaus.

Marzolph, U. 1985. Die Quelle der Ergötzlichen Erzählungen des Bar Hebräus. *OC* 69, 81–125.

Mazzola, Marianna. 2018. The Textual Tradition of Bar Ebroyo's Chronicle: A Preliminary Study. *LM* 131, 73–100.

Mengozzi, A. 2002. *Israel of Alqosh and Joseph of Telkepe: A Story in a Truthful Language. Religious Poems in Vernacular Syriac (North Iraq, 17th Century).* CSCO 589/590. Lovanii: Peeters.

———. 2012. "That I Might Speak and the Ear Listen to Me!" On Genres in Traditional Modern Aramaic Literature. *JSS* 57, 321–46.

———. 2014. Persische Lyrik in syrischem Gewand: Vierzeiler aus dem Buch des Khamis bar Qardaḥe Ende 13. Jh. *In*: Martin Tamcke and Sven Grebenstein, ed., *Geschichte, Theologie und Kultur des syrischen Christentums: Beiträge zum 7. Deutschen Syrologie-Symposium.* Göttinger Orientforschungen, I. Reihe, Syriaca 46. Wiesbaden: Harrassowitz, 155–76.

Merx, A. 1889. *Historia artis grammaticae apud Syros.* Leipzig: Brockhaus. Eng. tr. by D. King forthcoming from Gorgias Press.

Mez, A. 1937. *The Renaissance of Islam.* Trans. from German by Kh. B. Salahuddin and D. S. Margoliouth. Patna: Jubilee Printing & Publishing House. German original 1922.

Murre-van den Berg, H. L. 1998. A Syrian Awakening. Alqosh and Urmia as Centres of Neo-Syriac Writing. *In:* René Lavenant, ed., *Symposium Syriacum VII.* OCA 256. Rome: Pontificio Istituto Orientale, 499–515.

———. 1999. *From a Spoken to a Written Language: The Introduction and Development of Literary Urmia Aramaic in the Nineteenth Century.* Leiden. Nederlands Instituut voor het Nabije Ooste.

———. 2006. The Church of the East in Mesopotamia in the Mongol Period. *In:* R. Malek, ed., *Jingjiao. The Church of the East in China and Central Asia.* Collectanea Serica. Sankt Augustin: Institut Monumenta Serica, 377–94.

Nicák, Maroš. 2016. *"Konversion" im Buch Wardā zur Bewältigung der Konversionsfrage in der Kirche des Ostens.* Göttinger Orientforschungen, I. Reihe, Syriaca 51. Wiesbaden: Harrassowitz.

Pahlitzsch, J. 2014. *Der arabische Procheiros Nomos. Untersuchung und Edition der Übersetzung eines byzantinischen Rechtstextes.* Frankfurt am Main: Löwenklau-Gesellschaft e.V.

Palmer, A. 1991. The History of the Syrian Orthodox in Jerusalem. *OC* 75, 16–43.

———. 1992. The History of the Syrian Orthodox in Jerusalem, Part Two: Queen Melisende and the Jacobite Estates. *OC* 76, 74–94.

Pinggéra, Karl. 2000. Christologischer Konsens und kirchliche Identität. Beobachtungen zum Werk des Gregor Bar Hebraeus. *Ostkirchliche Studien* 49, 3–30.

Pritula, Anton. 2014. Zwei Gedichte des Ḫāmīs bar Qardāḥē: Ein Hochgesang zu Ehren von Bar ʿEbrōyō und ein Wein-Gedicht für die Khan-Residenz. *In*: Martin Tamcke and Sven Grebenstein, ed., *Geschichte, Theologie und Kultur des syrischen Christentums: Beiträge zum 7. Deutschen Syrologie-Symposium.* Göttinger Orientforschungen, I. Reihe, Syriaca 46. Wiesbaden: Harrassowitz, 315–328.

Rabo, Gabriel. 2014. Dionysius Jakob Bar Salibi: Die Desiderata in der Handschriftenforschung zu seinem Werk. *In*: Dietmar W. Winkler, ed., *Syrische Studien: Beiträge zum 8. Deutschen Syrologie-Symposium in Salzburg.* Orientalia-patristica-oecumenica 10. Berlin: Lit, 119–27.

Rabo, Gabriel. 2015. Dionysius Jacob Bar Ṣalibi's Confession of the Syrian Orthodox Faith ܗܝܡܢܘܬܐ ܕܥܕܬܐ ܣܘܪܝܝܬܐ ܬܪܝܨܬ ܫܘܒܚܐ ܠܘܬ ܡܪܝ، ܕܝܘܢܘܣܝܘܣ ܝܥܩܘܒ ܒܪ ܨܠܝܒܝ. *Hekamtho, Syrian Orthodox Theological Journal* 1(1), 20–39.
Rubin, M. 1998. The Language of Creation or the Primordial Language: A Case of Cultural Polemics in Antiquity. *JJS* 49, 308–33.
Sachau, E. 1899. *Verzeichniss der syrischen Handschriften der Königlichen Bibliothek zu Berlin*. Berlin: A. Asher & Co.
Samir, S. Kh. 2005. Les Suryan et la civilisation arabo-musulmane: Conférence inaugurale. *PdO* 30, 31–61.
Scher, A. 1905. *Catalogue des manuscrits syriaques et arabes conservés dans la Bibliothèque Épiscopale de Séert Kurdistan*. Mossoul: Imprimerie des Pères dominicains.
Simonsohn, U. I. 2011, *A Common Justice: The Legal Allegiances of Christians and Jews Under Early Islam*. Philadelphia: Philadelphia University Press.
Sprengling, Martin. 1916. Severus bar Shakko's poetics, Part II. *The American Journal of Semitic Languages and Literatures* 32(4), 293–308.
Suermann, H. 1998. *Die Gründungsgeschichte der Maronitischen Kirche*. Orientalia biblica et christiana 10. Wiesbaden: Harrassowitz.
Takahashi, Hidemi. 2005. *Barhebraeus: A Bio-bibliography*. Piscataway, NJ: Gorgias Press.
———. 2006. Fakhr al-Dīn al-Rāzī, Qazwīnī and Bar Shakko. *The Harp* 19, 365–80.
———. 2010. Between Greek and Arabic: The Sciences in Syriac From Severus Sebokht to Barhebraeus. *In*: Haruo Kobayashi and Mizue Kato, ed., *Transmission of Sciences: Greek, Syriac, Arabic and Latin*. Tokyo: Organization for Islamic Area Studies, Waseda University, 16–39.
———. 2012. Edition of the Syriac Philosophical Works of Barhebraeus. With a Preliminary Report on the Edition of the 'Book of Heaven and the World' and the 'Book Generation and Corruption' of the 'Cream of Wisdom'. *In*: Aafke M. I. van Oppenraaij, ed., *The Letter Before the Spirit. The Importance of Text Editions for the Study of the Reception of Aristotle*. Aristoteles Semitico-Latinus 22. Leiden: Brill.
———. 2014a. L'astronomie syriaque à l'époque islamique. *In*: Émilie Villey, ed., *Les sciences en syriaque*. Études syriaques 11. Paris: Geuthner, 319–37.
———. 2014b. Syriac as a Vehicle in the Transmission of Knowledge Across Borders of Empires. *Horizons: Seoul Journal of Humanities* 5(1), 29–52.
———. 2015. The Influence of al-Ghazālī on the Juridical, Theological and Philosophical Works of Barhebraeus. *In:* G. Tamer and F. Griffel, ed., *Islam and Rationality: The Impact of al-Ghazālī. Papers Collected on His 900th Anniversary.* Leiden: Brill, 303–25.
Taylor, David G. K. 2010. Your Sweet Saliva Is the Living Wine: Drink, Desire, and Devotion in the Syriac Wine Songs of Khāmīs Bar Qardāhē. *In* Teule and Tauwinkel 2010, 31–52.
Teule, H. 2007a. Ishoʿyab bar Malkon's treatise on the veneration of the holy icons. *In:* Martin Tamcke, ed.,*Christians and Muslims in Dialogue in the Islamic Orient of the Middle Ages = Christlich-muslimische Gespräche im Mittelalter*. Beiruter Texte und Studien 117. Würzburg: Ergon-Verlag, 157–169.
———. 2007b. Jakob bar Šakko, the Book of Treasures and the Syrian Renaissance. *In:* J. P. Monferrer-Sala, ed., *Eastern Crosssroads: Essays on Medieval Christian Legacy*. Piscataway, NJ: Gorgias Press, 143–54.
Teule, H., and Tauwinkel, C. F. 2010. *The Syriac Renaissance*. Eastern Christian Studies 9. Leuven: Peeters.
Todt, S. R. 1988. Die syrische und die arabische Weltgeschichte des Bar Hebraeus – ein Vergleich. *Der Islam* 65, 60–80.
Volkmer, J. A. 2008. Review of Georges Bohas, Les bgdkpt en Syriaque: selon Bar Zoʿbî. *JSS* 53, 351–3.
Vosté, J. M. 1940. *Ordo iudiciorum ecclesiasticorum, ordinatus et compositus a Mar Abdišo*. Rome: Typis Poliglottis Vaticanis.

Watt, J. W. 2010. Graeco-Syriac Tradition and Arabic Philosophy in Bar Hebraeus. *In:* Teule and Tauwinkel 2010, 123–33.

Weitz, Lev E. 2013. *Syriac Christians in the Medieval Islamic World: Law, Family, and Society.* PhD Dissertation. Princeton University.

Weltecke, Dorothea. 2002. Überlegungen zu den Krisen der syrisch-orthodoxen Kirche im 12. Jahrhundert. *In:* Martin Tamcke, ed., *Syriaca: Zur Geschichte, Theologie, Liturgie und Gegenwartslage der syrischen Kirchen, 2. Deutsches Syrologen-Symposium.* Studien zur orientalischen Kirchengeschichte 17. Münster: Lit, 125–45.

———. 2003a. *Die "Beschreibung der Zeiten" von Mor Michael dem Großen (1126–1199): eine Studie zu ihrem historischen und historiographiegeschichtlichen Kontext.* CSCO 594. Louvain: Peeters.

———. 2003b. Die Konjunktion der Planeten im September 1186. Zum Ursprung einer globalen Katastrophenangst. *Saeculum* 54, 179–212.

———. 2008. 60 Years After Peter Kawerau. Remarks on the Social and Cultural History of Syriac-Orthodox Christians From the IIth to the XIIIth Century. *LM* 121(3–4), 311–35.

———. 2010. Michael the Great. *In:* Graeme Dunphy, ed., *Encyclopedia of the Medieval Chronicle* 2. Leiden, Brill, 1110–11.

———. 2013. Zum syrisch-orthodoxen Leben in der mittelalterlichen Stadt und zu den Hūddōyē dem Nomokanon des Bar ʿEbrōyō. *In:* P. Bruns and H. Luther, ed., *Orientalia Christiana. Festschrift für Hubert Kaufhold zum 70. Geburtstag.* Wiesbaden: Harrassowitz, 586–613; 678–81.

Weninger, S. 1994. Das 'Übersetzerbuch' des Elias von Nisibis 10./11. Jh. im Zusammenhang der syrischen und arabischen Lexikographie. *In:* W. Hüllen, ed., *The World in a List of Words.* Tübingen: Niemeyer, 55–66.

Winkler, D. W. 2003. *Ostsyrisches Christentum: Untersuchungen zu Christologie, Ekklesiologie und zu den ökumenischen Beziehungen der Assyrischen Kirche des Ostens.* Münster: Lit Verlag.

Winkler, D. W., and L. Tang. 2013. *From the Oxus River to the Chinese Shores: Studies on East Syriac Christianity in China and Central Asia.* Zürich-Berlin: Lit Verlag.

Witakowski, W. 2006. The Ecclesiastical Chronicle of Gregory Bar ʿEbroyo. *JCSSS* 6, 61–81.

———. 2007. Syriac Historiographical Sources. *In:* Mary Whitby, ed., *Byzantines and Crusaders in Non-Greek Sources 1025–1204.* Proceedings of the British Academy. Oxford: Oxford University Press.

Wright, W. 1894. *A Short History of Syriac Literature.* London: Adam and Charles Black.

Wright, W. and S. A. Cook. 1901. *A Catalogue of the Syriac Manuscripts Preserved in the Library of the University of Cambridge.* 2 vols. Cambridge: Cambridge University Press.

Younansardaroud, H. 2006. A List of the Known Manuscripts of the Syriac Maqāmāt of 'Abdīšōʿ bar Brīkā's (d. 1318): Paradise of Eden. *Journal of Assyrian Academic Studies* XX(1), 28–41.

CHAPTER THIRTY-FIVE

SYRIAC IN A DIVERSE MIDDLE EAST

From the Mongol Ilkhanate to Ottoman dominance, 1286–1517

Thomas A. Carlson

INTRODUCTION

The late mediaeval period is one of the least studied sectors of the Syriac world. Western overviews of Syriac literature become uncharacteristically terse in this period. Only Barsoum's *Scattered Pearls* (Barsoum 2003) might be said to devote considerable space to the era after Bar ʿEbroyo, but then only for the Syrian Orthodox. Coverage of the late mediaeval period in more recent overview histories of Syriac Christianity is similarly uneven. This neglect of late mediaeval Syriac Christians is consistent with a broader scholarly neglect of the regions which they inhabited in this period: between 1258 and 1501, Syria, south-eastern Anatolia, Mesopotamia, northern Iraq, and north-western Iran are all relatively lightly studied by Islamicists, and with a rare exception Armenologists move quickly from the study of the Armenian kingdom of Cilicia, which came under Mamluk domination by 1325 and ceased to exist in 1375, to the forced relocations of Armenians by the Safavid Shah ʿAbbas in 1604. To understand the place of Syriac in the polyglot and fragmented late mediaeval Middle East, it is necessary to bring it into perspective alongside these other, and also neglected, fields of inquiry.

Due to the difficulty of accessing reasonable summaries in any field of inquiry in the late mediaeval Middle East, this chapter will summarise the political history and the ecclesiastical history of this period. An important ongoing social process in the late mediaeval period was the Islamisation of the population, which remains poorly understood, but some tentative suggestions for the region inhabited by Syriac Christians are offered. The chapter then offers an overview of various late mediaeval Syriac authors, followed by a discussion of liturgical developments during this period.

POLITICAL HISTORY

At the death of Bar ʿEbroyo in 1286, the Mongol Ilkhans based in Iran claimed hegemony over every part of the Middle East where Syriac Christians were numerous, except the region of Syria which was under the control of the Mamluk sultanate of Egypt. After the Ottoman sultan Selim I conquered Mamluk Egypt in 1517 and his son Suleiman conquered Iraq in 1533, the Syriac world was again partitioned between only two powers, with most of it governed by the Ottomans but the eastern edges under Safavid control. The claim of hegemony can mask variations in local arrangements under broad imperial tents, of course, but in between these two end-points there was little pretence of regional unity, as the Syriac world was governed by many dynasties of smaller scope (Bosworth 1996). The proliferation of ruling dynasties in the late mediaeval Middle East was just one symptom of the broad social and political instability of the period. The Syriac Christians in Central Asia and southern India during this period, of course, dealt with dynasties outside the Middle East, either the failing Chaghatayid Mongol polity and its successors or the competing kingdoms of mediaeval Kerala.

The Mongol Ilkhan Arghun (r. 1284–1291) continued the policy of his father Abaqa (d. 1282) and grandfather Hülegü (d. 1265) of favouring non-Muslims in certain positions in government. The catholicos Yahballaha III of the Church of the East benefited from his patronage, and from that of his successor, his brother Gaykhatu (r. 1291–1295). After Gaykhatu's death, Baydu, another grandson of Hülegü, claimed the throne briefly before he was defeated by Arghun's son Ghazan (r. 1295–1304) in a civil war. The first eighteen months of Ghazan's reign saw the state-supported destruction of many non-Muslim religious buildings in the Ilkhanate, the execution or torture of a number of Christians, and large fines imposed on Christian patriarchs, until the death of Ghazan's kingmaker Nawruz, who was blamed for the disturbance. Thereafter Ghazan returned to the earlier Ilkhans' policies of patronage for the Christian clerical elites, now alongside increased patronage for Muslim religious leaders (especially Sufis). Ghazan invaded Mamluk-controlled Syria in 1299 for the first time since his grandfather Abaqa's death almost twenty years before, followed by invasions in 1301 and 1303, each time ending in either a Mongol withdrawal or defeat. Ghazan was succeeded by his brother Öljeitü Khudabanda (r. 1304–1316), who continued to pursue the possibility of a joint military action with Western Europeans, while he provided decreasing support for the Christian leadership and increased patronage particularly for Twelver Shiite scholars. He was succeeded by his young son Abu Saʿid, under the effective regency of the Mongol emir Choban, until the latter was killed by a vassal ruler at the Mongol Ilkhan's order in 1327. The Ilkhanate had made a formal peace treaty with the Mamluk Sultanate of Egypt in 1322, and Abu Saʿid died in 1335.

Until the death of Abu Saʿid the Mongol rulers largely managed to hold their vassals in check, so that the various dynasties served as governors and client kings rather than independent rulers. The civil war which followed Abu Saʿid's death without an obvious heir, however, quickly fragmented the Mongol state in the Middle East and opened the door for notable families to take power in their own name and establish ruling dynasties. The Chobanids controlled most of north-western Iran, around the Ilkhanid capital, until 1357. The Jalayirids, after briefly controlling the former Ilkhanid capital of Tabriz, settled in Baghdad except for brief exiles when Timur Lenk ('Tamerlane') twice captured the city, once in 1393 and once in 1401. The Artuqids had ruled Mardin before and under Mongol rule, and continued to do so after the end of the Ilkhanate until around 1409. A junior branch of the Ayyubid dynasty descended from Ṣalaḥ al-Din persisted in Ḥiṣn-Kayf (Ḥesno d-Kifo) until the 1460s. Kurdish dynasties ruled in Bitlis and Hakkari. A Türkmen confederation known as the Qaraqoyunlu ('Black Sheep' Türkmen) gained prominence first to the north-west of Lake Van, and then in and around Mosul, and finally in Tabriz and Baghdad itself, from which they ousted their Jalayirid lords in the first decade of the 1400s.

While some of these local rulers were wealthy enough to mint coins or merit mention in histories composed for distant Timurid, Mamluk, or Ottoman sultans, in many cases the primary evidence we have for the rapidly shifting political situation in this period is found in the colophons of Armenian manuscripts and in Armenian or Syriac chronicles produced under these various rulers, such as the anonymous continuations of the chronicles of Bar ʿEbroyo. Alongside these various local dynasties, the Mamluk rulers of Egypt often sought to extend their control of Syria into Anatolia or Mesopotamia, with their most lasting acquisition being the Armenian kingdom of Cilicia, which they finally abolished in 1375. In its place, the Ramaḍanoğulları family took over Cilicia, sometimes as a vassal of the Mamluks and later the Ottomans.

The multiple invasions of Timur Lenk (d. 1405) and his successors in Samarqand and Herat repeatedly displaced Iraqi dynasties momentarily, but rarely resulted in significant dynastic shifts. On the other hand, Timur's last Middle Eastern campaign did enable a new Türkmen confederation, the Aqqoyunlu ('White Sheep' Türkmen) to gain control of significant areas of upper Mesopotamia. The Aqqoyunlu eventually absorbed the lands of the Artuqids, the Ayyubids, and various Kurdish principalities, and even defeated the Qaraqoyunlu and the later Timurids to make a brief bid for universal Islamic sovereignty under Uzun Ḥasan (d. 1478). The breakdown of the Aqqoyunlu, partly as a result of Ottoman aggression, was completed by the young Safavid Shah Ismaʿil I (d. 1524), who took the capital of Tabriz in 1501 and destroyed the last remnants of the Aqqoyunlu by 1507. The defeat of Shah Ismaʿil I by the Ottoman sultan Selim I at Çaldıran in 1514 and Selim's subsequent conquest of the Mamluk sultanate of Cairo divided the Middle East into two, with the Ottomans wielding greater power. The Ottoman conquest of Baghdad in 1533 by Suleiman the Magnificent confirmed that most early modern Syriac Christians would be Ottoman subjects.

ECCLESIASTICAL HISTORY

The political fragmentation of the late mediaeval period left its mark on the ecclesiastical history of Syriac Christianity. At the death of the Syriac Orthodox patriarch Philoxenus I Nemrud in 1292, no fewer than three successors were elected in his place, one in Melitene, one in Sis in Cilicia, and one in Mardin. The one in Melitene turned out to be ephemeral, and the one in Sis relocated to Damascus, while the Mardin patriarchate remained in Dayr al-Zaʿfaran monastery outside the city. Another patriarchal line was inaugurated by Sobo for the Ṭur ʿAbdin region in 1364, reflecting the political division between the Artuqid emirate of Mardin, the Ayyubid emirate of Ḥiṣn-Kayf, and the control of Syria and Cilicia by the Mamluk Sultanate of Egypt. In 1445, Behnam Ḥedloyo, the patriarch of Mardin, travelled to Jerusalem and suppressed the Syriac Orthodox patriarchate in Damascus following the death of patriarch Shemʿun Manʿamoyo.

In the aftermath of the breakdown of Mongol power in 1335, the upper Iraqi hierarchy of both the Church of the East and the Syrian Orthodox became unstable, and Christians in Iraq spent years or even decades without a senior ranking churchman.

Catholicos Denḥa II (r. 1336–1381/2) lived in Karamlish in the Mosul plain, but the succession to the patriarchate after him is unclear. The traditional view of Shemʿon IV reigning for sixty-some years in the fifteenth century, from the 1430s to 1497, must be abandoned due to a single colophon from 1463 naming a catholicos Eliya. By the 1470s, a new patriarch named Shemʿon lived in Mosul, but he was buried in Rabban Hormizd monastery outside Alqosh, north of Mosul, in 1497. By 1500, an Eastern Syriac catholicos was living in a monastery outside Gazarta (Cizre) and was buried at Mar Awgen nearby, while his successor was buried at Mart Meskinta in Mosul in 1504. The radical changes of residence and uncertain succession indicate the instability of Christian ecclesiastical hierarchies in late mediaeval Iraq during the wars of the Türkmen confederations, as does the fact that there was no Syriac Orthodox maphrian in Iraq for at least sixty-five years out of the one hundred fifty following the end of Mongol rule, including during the quarter century between 1379 and 1404.

It is also during the late mediaeval period that some of the Syriac patriarchates experimented with hereditary successions, whereby a brother or a nephew would be elected following the death of the incumbent. This had earlier been an occasional practice among Armenians (e.g. Nerses Shnorhali, d. 1173), and one Syriac Orthodox critic of the practice blamed it on imitation of Armenians and Muslims (perhaps thinking of hereditary Sufi shaykhs). The Mardin line was the first Syriac patriarchate to adopt hereditary succession, in 1333, and even when the family controlling the office changed, the practice of patriarchal nepotism characterised this line down to at least the 1480s. By contrast, the Syriac Orthodox patriarchates of Syria and of Ṭur ʿAbdin do not seem to have practiced hereditary succession. It was apparently in the early 1480s that the Eastern Syriac catholicos designated a nephew as his successor, and the office of catholicos-patriarch of the Church of the East remained hereditary into the twentieth century. But it is important to note that the hereditary patriarchate was not a distinctive feature of the Church of the East when it was adopted.

During the late mediaeval period, monasticism also declined in the Syriac churches. No more than fifteen Syrian Orthodox monasteries are mentioned in the continuations of Bar ʿEbroyo's chronicle, and a similar number of Eastern Syriac monasteries are attested by manuscript colophons as operational between 1335 and 1517. Operational Syrian Orthodox monasteries centred, unsurprisingly, around Ṭur ʿAbdin, with outposts in Sis (Cilicia) and around Mosul. For the Church of the East, the plain from Mosul up to Alqosh contained the highest concentration of monasteries, followed by clusters around Nisibis, Gazarta (Cizre), and Erbil. With the decline of monasticism in the post-Mongol period, among the Church of the East a greater proportion of manuscripts than previously seem to have been copied by village or urban clergy than monks, before the monastic revival of the sixeenth and seventeenth centuries again reversed this trend (Wilmshurst 2000: 384–424; Murre-van den Berg 2015: 88–9).

The late mediaeval period is also when we have the most extensive evidence for branches of the Church of the East in Cyprus, in China, in Central Asia, and in India. Syriac Christians in Cyprus may have retreated there with Western Europeans at the end of the Crusader kingdoms and then the Armenian kingdom of Cilicia. In 1445, a group of 'Nestorians' on Cyprus entered an apparently ephemeral church union with Rome after the Council of Florence. Syriac manuscripts from near Dunhuang in western China attest Christianity there up to the fourteenth century, and the late thirteenth and fourteenth centuries yield the largest number of Turkic gravestones in

Syriac script from Kyrgyzstan and Russian Central Asia. The Christian 'King George' of the Öngüt is named in Chinese records and the letters of the Latin missionary John of Montecorvino, and other Christians in China were recorded as government officials. Christians in China disappear from Chinese imperial records after the rise of the Ming dynasty, although Matteo Ricci around 1600 still heard rumours of 'cross-worshippers' in remote villages. The Armenian historian T'ovma Mecop'ec'i dated the end of Central Asian Christianity in Samarqand to the 1420s, blaming a Nestorian priest for provoking a persecution under Timur Lenk's grandson Ulugh Beg. A manuscript copied in Kerala in 1301 testifies to the Syriac Christian presence along the Indian Ocean trade routes. Sources for Christianity in India are subsequently lacking until the end of the fifteenth century, when a document records a delegation of Christians from India to the catholicos of the Church of the East, who consecrated several bishops for them. The late Mongol period was perhaps the period of widest extent for Syriac ecclesiastical networks, but the post-Mongol transition saw the demise of those same networks outside of the arc from Lebanon to north-western Iran, with the exception of Christianity in Kerala.

ISLAMISATION

Between the Arab Conquests of the Fertile Crescent in the 600s and the Ottoman conquests of the 1500s, after which we begin to have tax census records, Islam went from being the religion of a tiny number of rulers over a large sedentary agricultural population to that of the majority of the people in most areas of the Syriac world. Correspondingly, in the same period, Christianity of a largely Syriac character shifted from being the religion of the majority of the population in Syria and much of Mesopotamia to being a distinct minority, with the exceptions of mountainous areas inhabited by Maronites and the Church of the East, and perhaps the Ṭur ʿAbdin region. Syriacists have typically left the study of Islamisation to Islamicists, who in turn have relied primarily upon literary texts authored by Islamic religious leaders with no interest in documenting the presence or persistence of non-Muslim groups, except to complain about them. The result is that what has been taken as the definitive study of Islamisation remains Richard Bulliet's (1979) *Conversion to Islam in the Medieval Period*. Bulliet estimated that the Islamisation of Syria and Iraq was 'substantially complete' by shortly after 1000. Unfortunately, Bulliet's methods consistently over-report the degree of Islamisation, and his avowedly tentative approach did not inspire imitators and correctors. By contrast, Dina Rizk Khoury's study of Ottoman Mosul (1997: 29) concluded on the basis of sixteenth-century tax census records that the population around Mosul remained 37% Christian in 1541.

A recent article (Carlson 2015) suggests on the basis of Arabic geographical works that large and central portions of the population of Syria, not including Mesopotamia, remained significantly Christian until the era of the Mamluk conquests of the last Crusader states in the late 1200s. But in the absence of population data, it is important to consider Islamisation not as an exclusively demographic trend, but instead as a multifaceted phenomenon incorporating sacred landscape, architecture, urban texture, legal regulations on non-Muslims (or the absence of such regulations), and the relationships between Muslim rulers and non-Muslim subjects.

The Islamisation of al-Jazira and Iraq remains to be studied in detail.

LINGUISTIC DIVERSITY

Although Syriac continued to be used as a literary and liturgical language, late mediaeval authors from Syriac denominations composed texts in Arabic less frequently than their earlier co-religionists. Bar ʿEbroyo had composed texts in both Syriac and Arabic, as did his junior contemporary ʿAbdishoʿ bar Brikha. But only one text is known to have been composed in Arabic by an Eastern Syriac author within several centuries after ʿAbdishoʿ, the *Kitāb asfār al-asrār* of Ṣaliba b. Yuḥanna al-Mawṣili, composed in the 1320s and 1330s perhaps on Cyprus. Arabic continued to be used by Syriac Orthodox authors slightly more than in the Church of the East, with a new *Kitāb uṣūl al-dīn* by the late fourteenth-century Daniel of Mardin. A very terse world chronology and a sermon delivered by Nuḥ Puniqoyo, during his tenure as maphrian, reveal that Arabic was used by Syriac Christians in Mosul, as do the Arabic glosses in Isḥaq Shbadnaya's largest poem, but very few Arabic texts exist from Syriac Christians in this period.

Other Middle Eastern languages were used in the context of the late mediaeval 'Syriac world', but did not provide a medium for literature to a significant degree. The late thirteenth-century author Khamis bar Qardaḥe composed a poem listing the dominical feasts with alternating stanzas in Syriac and a 'Mongol' language (Turkic in fact, with some Persian words), perhaps for catechetical purposes. The *History of Mar Yahballaha and Rabban Ṣawma* contains numerous Mongol, Turkic, and Persian words, some of which were likewise incorporated into the continuations of the chronicles of Bar ʿEbroyo. But no independent texts completely in Mongol or Turkic are known to have been composed by Syriac-speaking Christians in the period under discussion. Persian was reportedly the language of the lost travel diary of Rabban Ṣawma, the source for his journey in the *History of Mar Yahballaha and Rabban Ṣawma*, and a Persian Diatessaron with numerous Syriac loanwords was copied in the Crimea in 1374, probably for a merchant community there. We should presume that non-Syriac dialects of Aramaic were spoken by many 'Syriac' Christians, especially in the mountainous areas of Ṭur ʿAbdin and Hakkari, but they were not written until the Ottoman period.

In addition to this natural linguistic diversity, the poets of these communities flaunted their erudition by deploying Greek words, as well as by inventing Syriac neologisms. While it is true that the Syriac lexicon contains a very large number of Greek loanwords from Late Antiquity, these late mediaeval occurrences are sometimes inflected according to Greek morphology and not always attested earlier. It is in order to compensate for the difficulty of this vocabulary that several late mediaeval Syriac poems include marginal or interlinear glosses. Some of this knowledge of Greek may have come from the retinues of princesses of Trebizond who married Türkmen rulers in Amid (modern Diyarbakır) and Tabriz, although the extent of such retinues and their contacts with Syriac Christians remains unknown.

This situation of Syriac as the literary and liturgical language of the religious elite, but not the daily vernacular of common Christians or the political elite, is closely parallel to the role of classical Arabic among Middle Eastern Muslims. The Turko-Mongol political elite presumably spoke primarily Turkish, but Persian was used as their bureaucratic and literary language east and north of Arabia and Egyptian-controlled Syria. While from Iraq westward, excluding Anatolia and the mountainous areas of

Kurdistan, most areas used Arabic as their daily language, the spoken vernacular 'Middle Arabic' was a dialect distinct from the classical and Qur'anic Arabic used for Islamic religious texts and for the Muslim prayers.

SYRIAC LITERATURE

If Syriac continued to be the main language of literary composition, augmented by occasional works in Arabic, nevertheless it appears that on the whole less literature was composed during this period, especially after the breakdown of the Mongol Ilkhanate in 1335. More new Syriac literature survives from the last fifty years of Mongol rule than from the following two centuries. Murre-van den Berg (2015: 8) has pointed out for a later period that a dearth of new compositions is not a lack of a 'lively book culture', as scribes continued copying manuscripts. While it is plausible that some literature was composed which has been lost in the intervening centuries, the late mediaeval period in Syria, eastern Anatolia, Kurdistan, and Iraq was rather more politically unstable and militarily violent than the subsequent centuries under Ottoman rule, with a few exceptions among the latter. In this period, it was more challenging for authors to find the conditions for successful composition. More succeeded, however, than modern scholarship has taken much cognizance of, and in part the scholarly lack of awareness of later authors, at least from the Church of the East, is due to the first history of Syriac literature, the 'Catalogue of Ecclesiastical Books' by ʿAbdishoʿ bar Brikha, ending around 1300.

Later Mongol rule, 1286–1335

By far the most prolific author of this period, ʿAbdishoʿ bar Brikha (d. 1318) wrote works in several genres, both in Syriac and in Arabic. His 'Catalogue of Ecclesiastical Books' ended with a list of his own works, many of which have not survived, such as a commentary on the Old and New Testaments, a work on Greek philosophy, a refutation of heresies, a commentary on the Pseudo-Aristotelian letter to Alexander 'on the great skill' (i.e. alchemy, perhaps the work known in Arabic as the *Kitāb sirr al-asrār*), a lost Arabic *Book of Shāh Marwarīd* of unknown contents, and a book entitled *Catholicos* which is about *mdabbrānūthā*, an elastic term pertaining to God's theological economy or providential governance of the world, especially the incarnation of Christ. The title of *Shāh Marwarīd* means 'King Pearl' in Persian, and may have been taken from the 'Mongol' refrain of the bilingual Syriac-'Mongol' poem by Khamis bar Qardaḥe, in which that title describes Christ. Of his surviving works, the one preserved in the largest number of mediaeval manuscripts is his poetic compilation *The Paradise of Eden*, which demonstrated his virtuosity with the Syriac language and set the stage for subsequent Eastern Syriac poetry to require aids for reader comprehension. His *Book of the Pearl on the Truth of Christianity* provides the closest thing to a brief systematic theology in his tradition. His two works of canon law were declared to be normative for the Church of the East by the Synod of Timothy II in 1318, nine months before the author's death. Among shorter works, he composed an explanation of how to compute the liturgical calendar, a metrical commentary on an earlier poem by Shemʿon of Shanqlabad, and various liturgical *turgame*. In Arabic he also composed two distinct works on the basic principles of Christianity (*uṣūl al-dīn*), a sermon on the Trinity and Incarnation, a confession of faith, and a rhymed Arabic (*saj'*) translation of a Gospel lectionary with prologues for each gospel.

Perhaps the most extensively studied Syriac text from the fourteenth century is the *History of Mar Yahballaha and Rabban Ṣawma*. Transmitted anonymously, the text describes the birth and youth of Rabban Ṣawma and his student Rabban Marqos, the future catholicos Yahballaha III, two eastern Turkic[1] Christians in northern China in the mid-thirteenth century. The two decided to go to Jerusalem on pilgrimage, but they were prevented from achieving their goal by the Ilkhanate's war with Mamluk Egypt. Instead, Marqos was consecrated first a metropolitan, and then catholicos Yahballaha III upon the death of Denḥa I in 1281, while his teacher Rabban Ṣawma led a Mongol diplomatic mission to Byzantium, Rome, and France in 1287–1288. The account continues after Rabban Ṣawma's death in 1294 through Yahballaha's relationships with the various Ilkhans and the uneven but generally worsening situation for Christians under Ilkhanate rule. Murre-van den Berg (2006: 392–3) very plausibly suggested that the author is catholicos Timothy II.

Timothy II was the final patriarch of the Church of the East during the Mongol Ilkhanate. Canons survive from the synod following his enthronement in 1318. Other than the anonymous *History of Mar Yahballaha*, his only substantial known work is a commentary on the seven sacraments. While it agrees with 'Abdisho' bar Brikha's *Book of the Pearl* in listing seven sacraments, the two authors chose different sacraments to make up the number, indicating that the number seven was more significant than the precise canon of sacraments to the Church of the East at this time.

It is probably to the late thirteenth century that we should date one of the most prolific Eastern Syriac liturgical poets, Khamis bar Qardaḥe, a parish priest in Arbela (Erbil). The date is based on his widely transmitted correspondence with the Western Syriac author Daniel bar Ḥattab, which includes an answer by Bar 'Ebroyo as a senior authority. Khamis also expanded a poem by Bar 'Ebroyo on theology and perfection by inserting a couplet of his own in front of each couplet of the original, giving the result the new title *memrā zawgānāyā* ('double poem'). This poem was later expanded in the same way by Isho'yahb bar Mqaddam (see below) in 1452, by the Chaldean patriarch Joseph II in 1697, and by at least three later authors in the Eastern Syriac tradition, as recently as the twentieth century. A series of Syriac wine songs by Khamis have also been preserved. But Khamis is most known for his liturgical poetry, which came to constitute an additional service book of the Church of the East transmitted under his name. Later liturgical poems of the Church of the East, such as those of Isḥaq Shbadnaya (see below), were incorporated into this collection.

The important Arabic theological *Book of the Volumes of Secrets* (*Kitāb asfār al-asrār*) by the Eastern Syriac priest Ṣaliba b. Yuḥanna of Mosul was composed in 1332 (Gianazza 2017, 2018). Teule (2006: 236–7, 239, 245) suggests that the text may be intended to justify Eastern Syriac Christianity to the Latin Christians who ruled Cyprus. This work is an Arabic theological and historical compendium which defends Christianity against its detractors, demonstrates the primacy of the East over the West[2] in everything important for humanity and Christian faith, summarises the history of Christianity, and provides a categorisation of other religions. The work draws extensively from earlier authors in Arabic and Syriac.

Among the Syriac Orthodox, a greater number of authors are known due to Barsoum's *Scattered Pearls*, although in many cases their works consist of notes on other texts rather than stand-alone compositions, and none of these texts have received much study, if they have even been edited. Bar ʿEbroyo's brother and successor Barṣawmo al-Ṣafi (d. 1307/8) is credited with continuing both the secular and ecclesiastical chronicles of his predecessor, which were subsequently expanded further by other authors to the last years of the fifteenth century. Diosqoros Gabriel, the metropolitan of Gozarto d-Beth Qardu (Cizre), composed verse biographies of Bar ʿEbroyo and of his brother. Abu al-Ḥasan Ibn Maḥruma annotated Bar ʿEbroyo's *Book of the Dove* and composed notes, some quite lengthy, in refutation of the apology for Judaism penned by the philosopher Saʿd Ibn Kammuna (d. 1284). Yeshuʿ bar Kilo composed a brief manual of epistolography, while patriarch Badr Zakhe Bar Wahib of Mardin (d. 1333) penned a book each in Syriac and Arabic on the spiritual meaning of the letters of the Syriac alphabet, as well as a book of regulations for church prayers. Abu Naṣr of Barṭelle (d. after 1290) composed a verse *vita* of the monk Matthew after whom the monastery of Mor Matay was named. Yeshuʿ bar Khayrun (d. 1335) wrote comments on the lexicon of Bar Bahlul, as well as rules for priests and a few poems on various subjects, while his father Ṣlibo bar Khayrun (d. after 1340) compiled a calendar of saints. A scribe named ʿAbdallah of Barṭelle composed two historical notes on the Mongol ruler Ghazan Khan. In addition, Barsoum's *Scattered Pearls* mentions new liturgical texts composed by Abu Nasr of Barṭelle, Diosqoros of Gozarto, Thomas of Ḥaḥ, Badr Zakhe Bar Wahib, Cyril of Ḥaḥ (fl. 1333), Yeshuʿ bar Khayrun, and Ṣlibo bar Khayrun.

Baumstark (1922: 322–3) also mentions the Eastern Syriac authors of 'secular poetry', Rabban Quryaqos, Ḥalya Ṣaydaya, Yoḥannan b. Yakk, and Rabban Isḥaq, all of uncertain date and with evidently limited surviving works. Similarly uncertain is his inclusion of Abbot Brikhishoʿ bar Eshkaphe of Beth Qoqa, whose introduction to the compilation of the Ḥudra liturgical book 'must have belonged at the latest to the fourteenth century'. Two poems listing the catholicoi of the Church of the East, one putting 'Yawsep' after Yahballaha III as the episcopal name of Timothy II before his election, and the other ending with 'the deceased Timothy II', might also date from the final phase of Mongol rule,[3] as might the anonymous poems which typically accompany them in honour of Khudahwi and Sabrishoʿ of Beth Qoqa.

After Mongol rule, 1335–1517

The rest of the fourteenth century saw very little new literature. Among the Syriac Orthodox, patriarch Iwannis Ismaʿil of Mardin composed a *memrā* against 'adversaries of Lent' (HMML CFMM 144: 205–208). Daniel of Mardin (fl. 1382) wrote an Arabic exposition of Christianity, *Kitāb uṣūl al-dīn*, as well as a brief Syriac account of the tortures to which he was subjected by the Artuqid ruler when his Arabic apologetic text or a similar work by him fell into the hands of a leading Muslim *faqīh*. He evidently also prepared Arabic summaries of several works of Bar ʿEbroyo and annotations to the latter's works, mostly now lost. Manuscripts of the *Kitāb uṣūl al-dīn* confuse him with Bar ʿEbroyo's younger contemporary Daniel Ibn al-Ḥattab, who corresponded with Khamis bar Qardaḥe. Barsoum's *Scattered Pearls* also alludes to a short historical account of the Syriac Orthodox in Erzincan and the monastery of Mar Barṣawmo outside

Melitene, ascribed to an otherwise unknown fourteenth-century author named Abraham of Mardin, and to liturgical prayers ascribed to Metropolitan Abu al-Wafa of Ḥiṣn-Kayf, Metropolitan Dionysios Joseph bar Gharib of Amid, and patriarch Abraham bar Gharib (d. 1412). By contrast, with the possible exception of the undated Shemsha of Beth Ṣaydaye who wrote three *memrē* for Nativity, Epiphany, and the Finding of the Cross, the last of which appears in a fifteenth-century manuscript, no named authors are known from the Church of the East between the end of the Ilkhanate and the early fifteenth century.

The Middle Eastern conquests of Timur Lenk (d. 1405) provided a theme for two *memrē* by the Syriac Orthodox author Isha'ya of Beth Sbirino (d. 1425), and Barsoum referred to a poem by a priest named Sahdo from around the same time. The former author also composed an acrostic *sūgītho* on wine and a *memro* on Job and his wife (HMML CFMM 144: 202–205, 510–511). In the middle of the century, patriarch Behnam Ḥedloyo (d. 1454) made a selection from the psalm commentary of Daniel of Ṣalaḥ and authored various *memrē* on saints and repentance, while the maphrian Basilios Barṣawmo Ma'dani (d. 1455) abridged the scholia on the gospels by Dionysios Bar Ṣalibi and composed a few *memrē*. Liturgical texts during this period were authored by Isha'ya of Beth Sbirino, a priest named Shem'un of Amid (d. ca. 1450), patriarch Qawmo of Ṭur 'Abdin (d. 1454), Behnam Ḥedloyo, Basilios Barṣawmo Ma'dani, and Gharib Man'amoyo (d. after 1476).

New Syriac literature increased in the later fifteenth century. Patriarch 'Aziz bar Sobto of Ṭur 'Abdin (d. 1481) composed a work on spiritual visions entitled 'The Ascent of the Mind', a monastic work entitled 'The Path of Truth', and a treatise on the liturgy. In addition, at least six sermons from him have survived. A monk named Malke Saqo (d. 1490) composed at least two *memrē* on the Virgin Mary, while Yeshu' of Beth Sbirino (d. 1492) composed *memrē* on Mor Dodo and on penitence. Penitential *memrē* were likewise composed by patriarch Yuḥanon bar Shayallah of Mardin (d. 1493)[4] and Dawid Puniqoyo (d. ca. 1500), the latter of whom also authored a partial autobiography, a biography of Yuḥannan of Dalyatha, a psalm commentary, and various other poetic works, including a *memro* 'On the Afflictions of Exile' (Butts 2009). Patriarch Nuḥ Puniqoyo of Mardin (d. 1509) composed a substantial collection of short poems, a terse chronology in Arabic, and an Arabic homily against 'Nestorians', which he delivered in Mosul while still maphrian. Patriarch Mas'ud of Ṭur 'Abdin (d. 1512) composed a lengthy verse doctrinal survey entitled *The Spiritual Ship*, as well as five shorter *memrē*. It is in this period that the anonymous continuations of Bar 'Ebroyo's chronicles terminate. Barsoum suggested identifying the continuator as Addai of Beth Sbirino (d. after 1502). Other short historical works listed by Barsoum from this period include two contemporary biographies of patriarch Yuḥanon bar Shayallah (see Palmer 2007), a pilgrimage account by Sargis of Ḥaḥ (probably d. 1508) who likewise wrote a poem about Jerusalem, a brief biography of patriarch Mas'ud of Ṭur 'Abdin and two other short accounts by 'Aziz of Midyat (d. after 1510), an anonymous poem about an invasion of Ṭur 'Abdin in 1505, and an otherwise unidentified 'historical tract' attributed to patriarch Ya'qub I (d. 1517). Barsoum listed liturgical authors including Malke Saqo, Yeshu' of Beth Sbirino, Yuḥanon Giwargis of Beth Sbirino (d. 1495), Dawid Puniqoyo, Addai of Beth Sbirino, Sargis of Ḥaḥ, Mas'ud of Ṭur 'Abdin, and Grigorios Yawsef the Georgian (d. 1537).

Only a few authors from the Church of the East are known from the same period. The most prolific seems to have been Isḥaq Shbadnaya, sometimes named Asko or Eshbadnaya, who composed a long 'Poem on God's Economy (*mdabbrānūthā*) from 'In the Beginning' until Eternity', supplemented by a prose commentary largely drawn from earlier authors of his tradition, in somewhat over 100 folios, which is slowly being edited by the author of this chapter. His three shorter liturgical poems dated 1440 (one for the Fast of the Ninevites, one for St George, and one for the Finding of the Cross) were incorporated into the Khamis collection. Metropolitan Ishoʿyahb bar Mqaddam of Erbil composed a Syriac grammar in verse in 1444, as well as at least three liturgical poems (one commemorating St George, one commemorating Rabban Hormizd, and one for the Fast of the Ninevites).[5] He is also identified as the author of four funeral *madrāshē*, some riddles, and a further enlargement of the *memrā zawgānāyā* of Bar ʿEbroyo as expanded by Khamis bar Qardaḥe. Of uncertain date, Sargis bar Waḥle composed a long verse biography of Rabban Hormizd (7th cent.) largely rephrased from an earlier prose text, as well as a shorter verse biography of Mar Aḥa. In the first years of the sixteenth century, the prolific poet Ṣliba of Manṣuriyya composed poems about the difficult events of 1510–12, a martyr in 1523, Mart Shmuni and her sons, St George, the Cross, repentance, the Fast of the Ninevites, and Nestorius.

Historical texts are almost entirely lacking from the Church of the East in the fifteenth century. A brief chronology of human history survives from 1458 (HMML CCM 20: 235r-v), as well as an account of a delegation from the Christian community in Kerala to the catholicos of the Church of the East at the end of the fifteenth century, which resulted in the consecration of several bishops for India and the lands beyond. This account is preserved with a letter dated 1504 by one of the bishops sent out, in which the relationships of the Portuguese with local Indian rulers are described in some detail. One of the priests from India in the original delegation may also have been the priest Joseph 'the Indian' who travelled to Portugal, whose summary of Christian customs in Kerala was translated into several European languages (Vallavanthara 2010), at the beginning of a new period of deep engagement between the Syriac world and Latin Christendom.

LITURGY

If the late mediaeval period was productive of new liturgical texts, for the Church of the East and especially for the Syriac Orthodox, scholars have also noted certain disappearances from the Eastern Syriac liturgy during this period. The last known defence of icon veneration by an author from the Church of the East occurs in the *Kitāb asfār al-asrār* of Ṣaliba b. Yuḥanna in 1332, whereas by the time American missionaries arrived in the mountains of Kurdistan in the 1830s, they were persuaded that the 'Mountain Nestorians' had never used icons. It may be that the cost of replacing church movables, repeatedly plundered by passing Türkmen armies and occasional Kurdish bandits, became prohibitive during the late mediaeval period. It is probably in the early fifteenth century that the diptychs of the Church of the East ceased to be updated, and it is unclear whether they continued to be recited thereafter.[6] The architecture of churches may also have changed with the disappearance of the *bēma*, a platform in the centre of the sanctuary from which scripture lections were read. Taft (1968) demonstrated the presence of the *bêma* in older church architecture in Syria (see Chapter 28), and it had played an important role in the liturgy of the Church of the East, but what is evidently the last Eastern Syriac liturgical manuscript to mention that liturgical use is dated 1496 (Taft 1970: 32). The development of Syriac Orthodox liturgy during this same period has not been clarified, other than the composition of new texts mentioned by Barsoum, but it is certain that the liturgy of the 'Nestorians' of the Ottoman Empire had changed significantly from that attended by the Mongol Ilkhans three centuries earlier.

NOTES

1 Scholars have debated whether these two were Uyghur, as Bar ʿEbroyo asserted, or perhaps rather Öngüt.

2 These are the author's terms. It is perhaps important to remember that for Christians from Iraq, the 'West' includes all the lands presently or formerly belonging to the Roman Empire.

3 Baumstark (1922: 331) dates the former to the fifteenth century based on a reference to a reigning patriarch named Eliya, but the mention might have been a post-mediaeval scribal substitution of an earlier 'Mar So-and-so'.

4 Mingana (1933: 195) lists the author as 'Ignatius VII Ḥannanya bar Shilla'.

5 It is unknown on what basis Scher (1906: 30) asserted that he composed around forty *ʿonyatha*, although the manuscript Siirt (Scher) 54 and 55 each apparently contained at least ten otherwise unknown poems by Ishoʿyahb. Scher's reference to fifty letters might be a confusion with the earlier collection of catholicos Ishoʿyahb III, who was likewise metropolitan of Erbil before his election to the patriarchate.

6 Fiey (1963: 376) dated the diptychs to the reign of Denḥa II in the mid-fourteenth century, but all copies of the diptychs mention at least two successors of that catholicos.

BIBLIOGRAPHY

Barsoum, I. A. 2003. *The Scattered Pearls: A History of Syriac Literature and Sciences*. Trans. Matti Moosa. 2nd rev. ed. Piscataway, NJ: Gorgias.

Baumstark, A. 1922. *Geschichte der syrischen Literatur mit Ausschluss der christlich-palästinensischen Texte*. Bonn: Marcus und Weber.

Bosworth, C. E. 1996. *The New Islamic Dynasties: A Chronological and Genealogical Manual*. Enlarged and updated ed. New York: Columbia University.

Brock, S. P., A. M. Butts, G. A. Kiraz, and L. Van Rompay, ed. 2011. *Gorgias Encyclopedic Dictionary of the Syriac Heritage*. Piscataway, NJ: Gorgias Press.

Bulliet, R. W. 1979. *Conversion to Islam in the Medieval Period: An Essay in Quantitative History*. Cambridge, MA: Harvard University Press.

Butts, A. M. 2009. The Afflictions of Exile: A Syriac *Memrā* by David Puniqāyā. *Le Muséon* 122, 53–80.

Carlson, T. A. 2015. Contours of Conversion: The Geography of Islamisation in Syria, 600–1500. *Journal of the American Oriental Society* 135, 791–816.

———. 2018. *Christianity in Fifteenth-Century Iraq*. Cambridge Studies in Islamic Civilisation. Cambridge: Cambridge University Press.

Fiey, J. M. 1963. Diptyques nestoriens du XIVe siècle. *Analecta Bollandiana* 81, 371–413.

Gianazza, G. Trans. 2017. Ṣalībā ibn Yūḥannā al-Mawṣilī. I Libri dei Misteri. Patrimonio Culturale Arabo Cristiano 12. Canterano: Aracne.

———. 2018. Ed. Ṣalībā ibn Yūḥannā al-Mawṣilī. Asfār al-asrār. Vol. 1. Patrimoine Arabe Chrétien 33. Beirut: CEDRAC.

Khoury, D. R. 1997. *State and Provincial Society in the Ottoman Empire: Mosul, 1540–1834*. Cambridge Studies in Islamic Civilisation. Cambridge: Cambridge University Press.

Mingana, A. 1933. *Catalogue of the Mingana Collection of Manuscripts Now in the Possession of the Trustees of the Woodbrooke Settlement, Selly Oak, Birmingham*. Vol. 1. Cambridge: W. Heffer.

Murre-van den Berg, H. L. 2006. The Church of the East in Mesopotamia in the Mongol Period. *In:* Malek, R., and Hofrichter, P., ed., *Jingjiao: The Church of the East in China and Central Asia*. Sankt Augustin: Institut Monumenta Serica, 377–94.

———. 2015. *Scribes and Scriptures: The Church of the East in the Eastern Ottoman Provinces (1500–1800)*. Eastern Christian Studies 21. Leuven: Peeters.

Palmer, A. 2007. John Bar Šayallāh and the Syrian Orthodox Community under Aqquyunlu Rule in the Late Fifteenth Century. *In:* Tamcke, M., ed., *Christians and Muslims in Dialogue in the Islamic Orient of the Middle Ages*. Beiruter Texte und Studien 117. Beirut: Ergon, 187–205.

Scher, A. 1906. Étude supplémentaire sur les écrivains syriens orientaux. *Revue de l'Orient chrétien* 11, 1–33.

Taft, R. F. 1968. Some Notes on the Bema in the East and West Syrian Traditions. *OCP* 34, 326–59.

———. 1970. On the Use of the Bema in the East-Syrian Liturgy. *Eastern Churches Review* 3, 30–9.

Teule, H. G. B. 2006. A Theological Treatise by Išoʿyahb bar Malkon Preserved in the Theological Compendium *Asfār al-asrār*. *Journal of Eastern Christian Studies* 58, 235–52.

Vallavanthara, A. 2010. *India in 1500 AD: The Narratives of Joseph the Indian*. Piscataway, NJ: Gorgias.

Wilmshurst, D. 2000. *The Ecclesiastical Organisation of the Church of the East, 1318–1913*. CSCO 582; Subsidia 104. Leuven: Peeters.

———. 2011. *The Martyred Church: A History of the Church of the East*. London: East & West.

CHAPTER THIRTY-SIX

THE MARONITE CHURCH

Shafiq Abouzayd

THE MONASTIC FOUNDATION AND SPIRITUALITY

The word 'Maronite' points clearly to the monastic origin and identity of the Maronite Church, for the monks of *Beth Maroun* are the real founders of the Maronite Church and consequently have greatly shaped its personality throughout history. The Maronite Church claims to be named after a fourth/fifth-century hermit called Maron, whose life was briefly written by Theodoret of Cyrrhus in his *Historia Religiosa XVI*. The church also believes that the disciples of St Maron formed the great Maronite monastery, which was built in Syria II (Syria Secunda, or Syria Salutaris) in 452 by the Roman emperor Marcianus (451–457), according to the Arab historian Abu al'Fida (Naaman 2009: 1–19). It was called the monastery of *Beth Maroun* and its superior, Paul, who attended the Council of Constantinople in 536, signed the Decrees of the Council as the head of the whole monastic community in northern Syria. Yet the first historical report of the monastery of *Beth Maroun* appears in the *Chronicle* of Dionysius of Tal Mahre (d. 1199), who has left us with significant information about the early period of the Maronite Church (Chabot 1899: 4, 409–10).

The Maronite monks adopted the teaching of the Council of Chalcedon and fought for its implementation in their area of influence. As a result of their loyalty to the Chalcedonian faith, the Maronites were opposed by the miaphysites; and, according to a letter by the Maronite monks to Pope Hormisdas II in 517, the fratricidal fighting between the two sides was brutal. Around the beginning of the sixth century, the monastery of *Beth Maroun* was destroyed, either by an earthquake or by the miaphysites, but was rebuilt by emperor Justinian (527–565) (Naaman 2009: 132).

With the emigration of the Maronites to Mount Lebanon, the monks settled mainly in the Holy Valley (Qadisha), retaining their Syrian monastic spirituality and discipline. During the last decade of the seventeenth century, the Maronite patriarch, Istephan al-Duwaihi, decided to re-organise monastic life in the Maronite Church by introducing some discipline into its hierarchy as well as into the daily life of the monks (Nasser Gemayel 1991: 144). As a result, monasticism in the Maronite Church became institutionalised, and it borrowed some important rules from the

Figure 36.1 Deir Mar Elisha, Qadisha Valley

discipline and structure of the Western European monastic tradition in order to re-organise itself. Today the early Maronite rules of the enclosed monastic life are only followed by a minority; most Maronite monks and nuns are deeply involved in the various educational and spiritual activities of their communities.

The male monastic communities include the Lebanese Maronite Order, the Lebanese Mariamite Maronite Order (originally called the Aleppine Order), the Maronite Antonine Order, the Lebanese Maronite Missionaries, and the new Maronite Order of the Maronite dioceses in the United States, which follows the Maronite rules for enclosed monks (Al Manarah 1988).

The female monastic communities comprise the Lebanese Maronite Nuns, the Maronite Congregation of the Antonine nuns, the Maronite Visitandines, the Maronite Congregation of the Holy Family, the Maronite Congregation of St Theresa of the Child Jesus, the Missionaries of the Holy Sacrament, the Congregation of the Maronite nuns of Saint John of Ḥrache, and the Enclosed Maronite Nuns (Al Manarah 1990).

THE MARONITE PATRIARCHATE

Monothelitism and the foundation of the patriarchate

When the Roman emperor Heraclius came to power in 610, he attempted to unify his empire; part of this would involve trying to put an end to Christian divisions. After expelling the Persians between 622 and 628, he was attacked by the Arabs, who conquered Syria and Palestine between 635 and 640. After moving against them,

Heraclius published the *Ekthesis* in 638 in order to unify Christianity in the Eastern Roman Empire. The *Ekthesis* was the formula of monothelitism that consisted of the affirmation that the person of Jesus Christ, in spite of his dual nature as both man and God, had a single will, and it was considered at the time to be the dogma of the Byzantine patriarch as well as of Pope Honorius I. In 680, the Sixth Council, which was held at Constantinople, nevertheless condemned the *Ekthesis* and its monothelite teaching, but the Maronite community remained loyal to its tenets (Brock 1973a, b; Gribomont 1974; Dib 1971: 15–50).

Monothelitism triggered long-lasting hostility between the Maronites and Byzantium and caused a split within the Melkite Church; the Maronites decided in the last quarter of the seventh century to elect their own bishop, John-Maroun, patriarch of Antioch (Naaman and Gemayel 1992: 7, 34). Nonetheless, the Maronite self-determination angered the Byzantine emperor Justin, who launched a war in 694 to terminate the Maronite autonomy, in the course of which he destroyed the Maronite monastery in Apamea and killed hundreds of monks (Al-Masʿūdi 1839: 131–2). John-Maroun, however, fled with the remaining Maronite fighters to Tripoli, and then to Kfarḥai in northern Lebanon, where he established the seat of the Maronite patriarchate (Al-Duwaihi 1890: 79–80).

The Autonomous Maronite Church

The monastic community of Beth Maroun officially became a church when the Maronite patriarchate was instituted, as it possessed its own patriarch and had ecclesiastical autonomy. As a self-governing ecclesiastical body with its own apostolic roots and spirituality, the Antiochian Syrian Maronite Church has the full character of a church and merits the title, while at the same time being united to the Church of Rome, whose head is believed by the Maronites to be the successor of the Apostle Peter and the head of the universal church.

Owing to the Maronite-miaphysite struggle on the one hand and the monothelite theology of the Maronites (which caused a real conflict with Constantinople) on the other, the Maronite Church was cut off from its other Christian counterparts, and developed independently, with its own hierarchy. The destruction, for unknown reasons, of the Maronite monastery in northern Syria during the first half of the tenth century finally compelled the majority of the Maronite community to immigrate to Mount Lebanon in search of peace and freedom. Its isolation in the remote Lebanese mountains offered to the small Maronite flock wonderful protection from its hostile Christian surroundings.

THE MARONITE CHURCH'S SYRIAN/SYRIAC IDENTITY

The Maronite Church first developed in Syria, and consequently has a heritage of Syrian culture and liturgy. Although the Syriac language is the backbone of Maronite spirituality, it is important to note the distinction between the terms 'Syrian' (describing the culture) and 'Syriac' (specifically the language) when describing the character of Maronite spirituality, since its background also includes Syrian writers who wrote in Greek; thus it is better to use the term 'Syrian', rather than 'Syriac', since the term 'Syrian' includes the Greek elements of Syrian Antiochian Christianity.

MARONITE LITURGY

Origins

The Maronite liturgy has been a Syro-Antiochian liturgy since its beginning, but, like all Syro-Antiochian liturgies, it borrows some elements from the Jerusalemite liturgy, which are evident in its anaphora of St James. There is also another constituent of the Maronite liturgy, the Syriac liturgy of Edessa (Urha), which contributed to the Syriac identity of the Maronite Church. However, due to the scarcity of primary sources, it is quite difficult to define Maronite liturgy as it would have existed between the fifth and the tenth centuries. A deep study of Maronite books such as the anaphora 'šarar' and the 'šḥimto', however, shows that Maronite liturgy is quite close to that of the Antiochian-Jerusalemite communities. The manuscripts of the Maronite liturgy date to a period between the twelfth century and the sixteenth century, and the earliest manuscript of the Maronite mass is from 1454, with some pages from the twelfth century (Boutros Gemayel 1992: 9–10).

The Maronite liturgy has been reformed twice during its history. The first reform was launched by the graduates of the Maronite College of Rome, in particular by their most outstanding scholar, Istephān al-Duwaihi, who played a central role in updating and correcting the liturgical books. The second reform began after the Second Vatican Council, and the Maronite monks of the Holy Spirit University in Kaslik, Lebanon, were undoubtedly the driving force behind the new liturgical reform. The main purpose of the two instances of reform was the originality of the Maronite liturgy and its integrity within Syriac Christianity (Hage 1999: 45, 107–8).

The missal

The Maronite missal was first printed in Rome between 1592 and 1594, with some Latin influence on the text concerning the consecration of the bread and wine, and there is no doubt that the disciples of the Maronite College in Rome played a major role in the preparation of the manuscript for printing. The second edition of the Maronite missal appeared in 1716 and was bitterly criticised by Maronite scholars, having ended up being more Latinised than the first edition (*Book of Mass* 2005: 16).

There were many attempts to reform the Maronite missal and to bring it back to its sources, none of which survived beyond their initial stages (Nasser Gemayel 1991: 120–33). Vatican II finally opened the way to reform for all liturgies of the Roman Catholic Church, and after nineteen years of research (between 1963 and 1982), the final draft of the Maronite missal was accepted by the patriarchal synod and is now seen as an authentic Maronite missal (Boutros Gemayel 1992: 33). All its texts are translated into Arabic, the common language of the Maronites in the Middle East, and they are published alongside their original Syriac versions (*Book of Mass* 2005: 16).

The lectionary

The *riš qoryan* is the Maronite Syriac term for the lectionary (originally *fūroš qoryone*, or 'selected readings'), and there is no evidence at all that the Maronite Church had its own lectionary between the fifth and tenth centuries. It is assumed that the Maronites followed the practice of the Syro-Antiochian Church for Bible readings during Sunday mass and ecclesiastical feasts. Moreover, the daily mass in the Maronite Church did not exist before the eighteenth century, and thus there was no need for a weekly lectionary as it exists in its current form (Boutros Gemayel 2005: h; *Book of Mass*, 19).

The Maronite *riš qoryan* dates back to 1242 and contains 755 readings from the Old and New Testaments, but none from the Gospels. The Syriac texts were taken from the *Pešiṭta*, and the readings are designed to fit the different hours of the Maronite Divine Office throughout the liturgical year. It includes the readings for some ecclesiastical feasts and usually allocates three readings from the Old Testament and two readings from the New Testament for each day (Tabet 1988). During the first half of the second millennium, the readings of the Sunday mass came solely from the Gospels and the Epistles of St Paul, and the readings for morning prayer (ṣafro) came from the Old and New Testaments (Boutros Gemayel 2005: w). During the second half of the second millennium, the book of the Maronite mass was printed for the first time in 1592 with an annex of thirty readings in Syriac from the Gospels only for Sundays and main feasts. But, 103 readings instead of thirty were added to the second copy of the Maronite mass in 1716, the first seven readings from the Gospels were in Syriac and the rest in Arabic, and the readings from the Epistles of St Paul were in Syriac. Yet, the fourth edition of the Maronite missal appeared in 1816 with a new set of readings arranged by bishop Germanos Farhat, the Maronite bishop of Aleppo, who fixed the appropriate readings for the daily mass and feasts from the Gospels and the Epistles of St Paul for the whole liturgical year (Boutros Gemayel 2005: z). Finally, the current Maronite Lectionary was approved by the Maronite Synod during 2004, and it was printed in Lebanon in 2005 in two volumes, one for the Gospel readings and one for the rest of the New Testament.

The Divine Office

The Divine Office is called *šḥimto* in Syriac, meaning the common or ordinary daily office of the Maronite Church. The *šḥimto* is very similar to the Maronite *išḥim*, and the only difference between the two Syriac books is the Sunday office, which is included in the *šḥimto* but not in the *išḥim*. Yet, the common book of the *šḥimto*, which has been used by the Maronite monks and clergy for many centuries, constitutes only one part of the Maronite Divine Daily Office for the complete liturgical cycle. It was first printed in Syriac in 1624–5, in Rome, and reprinted many times in both Rome and Lebanon (Tabet 1991: h–n: Breydy 1971: IV).

The Maronite Lebanese Order launched its second initiative to reform the Maronite liturgical services with the permission of the Maronite patriarch, with the goal of translating all the Maronite Syriac liturgical books into Arabic. The order has printed the Office of the Holy Week, called *ḥash* (the passion of the Lord), which is its first ever translation into Arabic. This liturgy is followed by the office for the Christmas season, the office for the season of Epiphany, the office for Eastertide, and the office for Lent (see in the bibliography items: *Holy Week, Christmas Season, Epiphany Season, Easter Season, Great Lent Season*).

Al-Šarṭūniyyah

Al-Šarṭūniyyah (*Book of Ordinations*, from Gk *cheirotonia*; Syr *īyda syam*) contains the different ceremonies for the ordination of candidates for the service of the altar and the administration of the sacraments of the Church. The Maronite patriarch Istephān al-Duwaihi was the first Maronite scholar to gather the different manuscripts of *al-Šarṭūniyyah* in the Maronite tradition from 1296 onwards, in order to adopt the most complete one (Al-Shartūni 1902: 84–5). In 1734 he completed the final copy of *al-Šarṭūniyyah*, with an annex explaining the ambiguous points in each ceremony and the meaning of each ecclesiastical ordination (Nasser Gemayel 1991: 85–106, 115), and in 1756 the use of his *Šarṭūniyah* was established by the Maronite Synod (Al-Dfouni 1899: 640–51).

The rites of consecration and blessing

Patriarch Istephān al-Duwaihi collected all the Maronite rites of consecration and blessings together into two Syriac volumes. The first was called *Holy Consecrations (Šhareḥ al-takrīsāt al-moqaddasah)*, which gathered the Maronite ceremonies of the consecration of the church building and its altar, the rite of baptism, the consecration of the altar ṭablīt,[1] the consecration of the chalice and other items for holy communion, the consecration of liturgical vestments, the consecration of cemeteries, the consecration of icons and crosses, the consecration of the baptismal Myron and oil, the consecration of oil for the last sacrament, and the consecration of oil for the altar lamp (Al-Shartūni 1902). The second book was entitled *Al-Mota'ayyidāt* (*the Feasts for the whole Year*) and described many Maronite ceremonies, including the blessing of the Epiphany water, the consecration of the baptismal font, and Palm Sunday celebrations and blessings (Ḥarfouch 1903: 595–6).[2] Some of these ecclesiastical rites are translated into Arabic and published in the *Book of the Maronite Rites* (1984), which contains the 'Ceremony of the Blessing of Olive Branches for Palm Sunday', the 'Ceremony of the Washing of the Feet on Maundy Thursday', the 'Ceremony of the Adoration of the Holy Cross on Good Friday', the 'Prayer of Forgiveness on Great Saturday', and the 'Ceremony of Peace on Easter Sunday'.

In 1991, the book of the *Maronite Funerary Service* was published with a new Arabic translation alongside the Syriac text, and a selection of readings was taken from the 1266 Maronite manuscript for funerary services (Vatican Syriac 59), the *Funerary Service of Monks*. The manuscript for *The Rite of the Sacrament of Baptism and the Sacrament of Myron in Arabic* has been kept in the patriarchal library of Bkerke (Number 360) since 1411 (*Rite of Sacrament* 2003). *The Rite of Fiançaille and Crowning* (2004) is in Arabic, and is a rendering of the Maronite manuscripts Bkerke 20 (dated 1306), Bkerke 21 (dated 1606), and Vatican Syr. 52 of the sixteenth century). The Funerary Service of Nuns (2004) is the reprint of the 1898 Maronite Funerary Service for Virgins, but with a new Arabic translation alongside the Syriac text.

Liturgical music

The liturgical chants of the Maronite Church belong to the Syro-Antiochian liturgical tradition, and correspond closely to the chants of the Syriac (Syrian) Orthodox

Church, demonstrating that the Maronite chants cannot be traced back to Arab music or western Mediterranean music (Hage 1999: 10, 36–7). On the other hand, new research points to the Syrian pre-Christian origins of Maronite and Syriac Orthodox music; in particular, the solo melody of some Maronite liturgical texts confirms their pre-Christian origin (Breydy 1971: 36).

The Maronite chants were transmitted orally from one generation to another through the daily celebration of the Maronite liturgy, and liturgical reforms did not affect their authenticity (Hage 1999: 10, 15, 25–8, 39, 103; Hage 1987, 1990; Breydy 1979; *Book of Maronite Chants*). On the other hand, despite the existence of the archaic ekphonetic notation, which had been abandoned and lost by the eleventh century, a notation system for Maronite chanting was created just before the nineteenth century and was edited and completed in the second half of the twentieth century; consequently, Maronite Levantine melodies have been recorded using the Western musical system of notation (Hage 1999: 25, 30–3, 52–7). For more on Maronite chants, see Ashqar 1922, 1939; *Book of True Delight* 1928; Hage 1990/1, 1972–1991).

THE ROMAN CATHOLIC CHURCH AND THE MARONITE CHURCH

During the eleventh century, the Crusaders embarked upon their invasion of the Near East, and, on their arrival in northern Lebanon in 1099, the Franks received a warm welcome from the Maronites. William of Tyre, a contemporary, says in 1182 that 40,000 Maronites joined the Crusaders and gave up their monothelitism. History shows that not all Maronites welcomed the Franks; some Maronites from the high Lebanese mountains were quite hostile to the Maronite-Crusader alliance. This Maronite opposition did not stop the Maronite patriarch, Jeremiah al-ʿAmshiti (1199–1230), from making the first visit by a Maronite to Rome in 1213. He attended the opening sessions of the Lateran Council, and also received the Pallium of confirmation from the pope as a sign of formal Roman acceptance of his position as the head of the Maronite Church. After the death of al-ʿAmshiti, conflict among the Maronites surfaced again, and there is some evidence from the Maronite historian and poet, Jibrail al-Qilaʿi (ca. 1516) that the opposition group elected its own patriarch, Luke of Bnahran, who, together with his followers, fortified his position in Hadath near Bisharri. Nothing is known about Luke of Bnahran after 1283, but the work of the Arab historian Muhyi ad-Din Ibn ʿAbd az-Zahir (1223–1292) strengthens the belief that Luke of Bnahran was put to death with his followers by the Crusaders and their allies in 1283. Yet patriarch Istephān al-Duwaihi wrote in his book *Radd al-Toham wa al-Šobah* that Lūqa al-Bnahrani usurped the patriarchal seat after patriarch al-Ḥadšīti in 1282, who did not have the same faith as the Maronites and was not elected by the Maronite nation (Nasser Gemayel 1991; Salibi 1958; Abi-Aoun et al. 1994).

The alliance with Rome meant that the Maronite Church did not escape Latinisation, as the Latin Roman Church repeatedly tried to transform Maronite spirituality. The influence of Latinisation remained marginal until 1580, when Pope Gregory XIII ordered his legate, a Jesuit named John Baptist Eliano, to investigate the Maronite faith. Eliano destroyed many Maronite manuscripts, which were not in keeping with

Latin dogma and its distinctive ways of worship. Pope Gregory XIII found a more effective way to ensure the submission of the Maronite Church to the Latin Roman tradition: in 1584, he founded the Maronite College in Rome in order to educate the elite of the Maronite clergy in the spirit of the Roman Catholic tradition. This project was highly successful, and subsequent Maronite Councils merely endorsed decisions made by the Roman authorities. Another factor which contributed to the Latinisation of the Maronite Church was the establishment of both Roman Catholic missions, Jesuit and Franciscan, among the Maronites, and the consequent education of the elite of the Maronite community in the spirit of European Christianity (Moosa 1986: 217–78).

THE MARONITE CONTRIBUTION TO THE SYRIAC AND ARAB RENAISSANCES

The use of Arabic during the first half of the second millennium

It is striking that all Maronite non-liturgical literature is in Arabic, with the exception of one book by Theophilus of Edessa, which has been lost. Moreover, Arabic has been the dominant language of the Maronites since the beginning of the second millennium; two major documents of the eleventh century confirm that the Maronites were already Arabised and that Syriac was simply their liturgical language. The *Nomocanon of the Maronites* (*Kitāb al-Huda* or the *Book of Directions*) was originally written in Syriac by an unknown author and translated into Arabic by the Maronite bishop Dawood in 1059 for the use of the Maronite Church (Joubeir 1991), and the *Ten Chapters* was composed in 1089 in Arabic by the Maronite bishop Thomas of Kaphartab and addressed to John VI, the Melkite patriarch of Antioch, in defence of the Maronite faith (Soaiby 1985). In 1183, Jeremiah wrote a brief account of his election as a bishop and patriarch of the Maronite Church on the Syriac Gospel of Rabboula, in Arabic (Hayek 2009: 90–1).

Jibra'il ibn Buṭrus al-Liḥfidi, surnamed Ibn al-Qilaʿi, was born towards the middle of the fifteenth century in the village of Liḥfid near Jubayl (Biblos). He became a Franciscan and was sent to Rome in 1470 to study and take holy orders, and was thus the only educated Maronite in Europe in his day. While he was the superior of the Franciscans in Cyprus, he was chosen, in 1507, as Maronite bishop of Cyprus. He wrote his first book in Arabic, *Maroun aṭṭubāni* (the blessed Marun), extant only in manuscript form in the Vatican Library (Vat. Arab. 640, written in Karshuni in 1574), having never been published. In the first part of the book, he translated from Latin into Arabic the seven papal bulls which had been sent to the Maronite patriarchs since 1215. He wrote many books during his lifetime, and all his writings are in Arabic, but he shows an imperfect knowledge of the language, which recalls the Lebanese colloquial dialect of Mount Lebanon with its Syriac idioms and distinctive grammatical rules (Salibi 1991: 23–32; Douaihy 1993). Ibn al-Qilaʿi is well known for his *Zajaliyyāt*, or *Madāyiḥ*, which were written in the Lebanese vernacular using the Syriac metres of the Maronite Syriac melodies; a poetic art of the Lebanese dialect, which is used by many Lebanese poets even today (Boutros Gemayel 1982).

The Maronite College of Rome

The Maronite College of Rome was officially launched on 5 July 1584, with the primary aim of educating Maronites in the sciences of the Catholic Church. Of secondary concern was the need of the Roman Catholic Church for oriental Catholics in Rome to help with oriental languages, especially Arabic and Syriac. The Maronite College was an efficient instrument of the Catholic Church for keeping regular contact with the Christian East, and the college was administrated by Jesuits between 1584 and 1773.

The dissolution of the Jesuit Order by the pope in 1773 signalled the decline of the Maronite College in Rome, as the Vatican authority was unable to find a suitable alternative to the Jesuits to run (and fund) the college; neither was the Maronite patriarch successful in saving the college from total collapse. Yet the cultural achievements of its students contributed greatly to the Arab and Syriac renaissances in Europe and the Arab East. Moreover, Maronite scholars played a major role in the introduction of Arabic language and literature to the West, and thus encouraged Europeans to delve deeply into the history and culture of Arabic and Syriac civilisations, which brought to light the cultural wealth of the East (Nasser Gemayel 1984: 17–18, 33–43, 83–8; Daniel 1960: 295–6).

The Medici press

The Medicis founded the Oriental Press, also known as Typographia Medicea, in Tuscany in 1584. It was the only press in Europe that was able to print books in oriental languages. The Maronite Yaʿqūb Ibn Hilāl, whose Latin name was Jacobus Luna, and who was born in Lebanon in 1568, was among the first Maronites to study at the College of Rome. He began working at the Oriental Press in 1589 and composed the Syriac and Arabic typographic characters for the press between 1590 and 1594, enabling him to print the following books in Arabic: *Sacrosancta quattuor Iesu Christi D.N. Evangelia* (*The Four Gospels*) in 1590 (1,500 copies), followed by an Arabic and Latin edition in 1591 (3,500 copies;) *Alphabetum arabicum* (*The Arabic Alphabet*), in 1592; *Grammatica Arabica*(*Arabic Grammar*), known as *Agrumia*, of al-Sanhaji, in 1592; *Grammatica Arabica* (*Arabic Grammar*), known as *A*, of *al-Kaphia* of Ibn Hajeb, in 1592 (1,300 copies); *Geographia Nubiensis* (*Geography of Nubia*) of Al-Idrisi, in 1592, which was translated to Latin by the Maronite scholars Sionita and Hesronita in 1619; *Libri quinque canonis medicine,* (*Five Books of the Law of Medicine*) of Avicenna, in 1593 (1,700 copies); *Elementorum geometricorum libri tredecim . . . nunc primum arabice impressi, d'Euclidus* (The Book of Geometry of Euclid), 1594, translated from Greek by Nasir al-Din al-Tusi (3,000 copies); and *Missale Syriacum juxta ritum nationis Maronitarum* (*The Maronite Missal*) in 1592 and 1594. After his fruitful career at the Medici Oriental Press, Luna founded his own press in Rome, called 'Tipographia Linguarum Esternarum' (The press of foreign languages), which published five books, including *Liber ministri missae juxta ritum ecclesiae nationis Maronitarum* in 1596, which is the first impression of the *Maronite Diaconicon*; *Grammatica Syriaca, sive Chaldaïca* (*The Syriac Grammar*), by Ǧiriğis ʿAmīra, Romae, 1596 (Paris, BN, X. 1694; Sorbonne, L.P. os. 78); *Missale Syriacum juxta ritum ecclesiae nationis Maronitarum* (*The Maronite Missal*), 1608 (reprint) (Nasser Gemayel 1984: 74–6, 222–3).

The Maronite press in Rome

The Maronite press in Rome was established between 1614 and 1617 by a papal order, following the closure of the Vatican press in 1610. Many books were printed, including the following books by scholars of the Maronite College: Isḥāq al-Šedrāwī, surnamed Sciadrensis, *Syriacae lingue rudimentum, Romae, excudebat Stephanus Paulinus*, 1618 (Roma, BAV, R.G. Oriente, V 264) and *Grammatica Linguae Syriacae* (Paris, BN, X. 1697, & Par. Syr. 265); Victor Šalaq, surnamed Scialach, *Introductio ad grammaticam Arabicam*, Romae, apud Stephanum Paulinum, 1622 (Paris, BN, X 6405); *Totum arabicum alphabetum, ad unam tabellam cum suis vocalibus et signis, facilitatis causa, reductum*, Romae, apud Stephanum Paulinum, 1624 (Paris, BN, 8 X 21047); and Boutros al-Meṭūšī, surnamed Metoscita, *Institutiones linguae arabicae*, Romae, apud Stephanum Paulinum, 1624 (Graf, III, p. 336–337). But the most important work of the Maronite press is *The Syriac Maronite Šḥīm*, *The Officium simplex septem dierum hebdomadae*, printed in 1624 (Nasser Gemayel 1984: 77–80).

The scholars of the Maronite College

Ğibra'īl al-Ṣahyūnī, surnamed Sionita, was born in Ehden in north Lebanon in 1575, and was sent to Rome at a young age to study at the Maronite College. While in Rome, after finishing his studies, he taught Arabic and Syriac in Rome at La Sapienza University, before leaving for Venice at an unknown date to teach Arabic and Syriac. In Venice, he also composed an Arabic-Latin dictionary. In 1587, Henry III of France decided to establish a chair for the teaching of the Arabic language at the Collège Royal (later the Collège de France) in Paris, entitled 'Royal Professor for the Arabic language'. Several French scholars occupied this post, but their Arabic was either weak or non-existent. Ğibra'īl al-Ṣahyūnī was the first professor at the Collège Royal to have strong knowledge of Arabic, and was succeeded by Ibrahim al-Ḥāqilāni. Both men promoted deep study of the language and opened the way for French students to learn Arabic in France. In 1616, he published the *Kitāb fi ṣinā'at al-naḫawiyya* (*Grammatica Arabica Maronitarum*), in collaboration with Yuḫanna al-Ḥasrūni (Ḥesronita), which he used for his teaching at the Collège Royal, which surpassed the sixteenth-century Arabic Grammar by Guillaume Postel. Moreover, Sionita composed and translated many books, among them the translation from Arabic into Latin of the *Geographia Nubiensis*, which was re-published in Paris in 1619 in collaboration with Hesronita; the translation from Syriac into Latin of the poems of Barhebraeus (Paris 1628); and the translation of several books from Syriac and Arabic into Latin for the Polyglot Bible (Nasser Gemayel 1984: 218, 239, 308–34, 243).

Sarkis al-Ğamri, surnamed Sergius Gamareus or Gamerio and born in Ehden, Lebanon, and was an ancient student of the Maronite College in Rome and a Maronite priest. He took over the teaching post of Arabic at the Collège Royal after Ğibra'īl al-Ṣahyūnī in 1648, and immediately received the praise of the king of France for his services and his knowledge of many oriental languages: Arabic, Syriac, Turkish, and Hebrew, alongside Latin, French, and Italian (Nasser Gemayel 1984: 245–53).

Ǧirǧis ʿAmīrā was the first Maronite patriarch to be educated at the Maronite College of Rome. He was sent from Ehden to Rome in 1583 at a young age, and returned to Lebanon in 1595, after his graduation. He was elected a patriarch of the Maronite Church in 1634 and lived in the monastery of Qannūbīn. His most important work is his Syriac Grammar, which was printed in 1596 by the Maronite Jacob Luna (Ghaleb 1924: 341–50; Nasser Gemayel 1984: 343–5).

Naṣrallah Šalaq al-ʿAqūri, surnamed Victorius Cialac Accurensis, was born in ʿAqūra (Lebanon) around 1580, and he entered the Maronite College in Rome in 1584, where he graduated as a doctor in theology and philosophy. He composed, together with the Maronite scholar Al-Ṣahyūni, an Arab-Latin dictionary, which was revised by Jean-Baptiste Du Val. He also translated the *Doctrina Christiana* of Bellarmine from Latin into Arabic in collaboration with Al-Ṣahyūni, which was printed in 1613 and reprinted in 1847. Accurensis composed the *Introductio ad Grammaticam arabicam*, printed in 1622, and the *Totum arabicum alphabetum, ad unam tabellam cum suis vocalibus et segnis, facilitatis causa, reductum*, printed in 1624. From 1610, he was among the professors of the *Gymnasio Romano*, known as La Sapienza, for the teaching of Arabic and Syriac languages. He succeeded Marcus al-Duʿābili from Nisibis, known as Marco Dobelo, and his professorship lasted until 1631. He also taught Arabic and Syriac at the institute of St Pietro in Montorio to missionaries who intended to go to the Arab East. Accurensis replaced John-Baptist Raimondi as an ex-director of the Tipografia Medicea in Florence in 1617, and he occupied the post of *Interpreter* of oriental languages at the Holy Office in the Vatican. He died in Rome in 1635 (Yaʿqūb 2011: 27–32, 59–106; Nasser Gemayel 1984: 377–85; Diotallevi 1991).

Sarkis al-Rizzi, surnamed Sergius Risius, was born in Bqūfa near Ehden and went to Rome at a young age to study at the Maronite College. He was charged by the Propaganda Fide with examining the Syriac manuscripts of the Bible and comparing them with the Latin Vulgate translation. He also consulted the Arabic manuscripts of the Bible at the Vatican Library, and the results of his long research were published after his death in 1671 in a three-volume book entitled *Biblia sacra ad usum Ecclesiarum Orientalium, additis e regione Bibliis latinis Vulgatis*. Once his work was finished, he left the Vatican Library, but his post remained vacant until the nomination of another Maronite scholar, Ibrahīm al-Ḥaqilāni in 1660. He died in Rome in 1638 (Fahed 1982: 115–36; Nasser Gemayel 1984: 369–74).

Isḫāq al-Šedrāwī (Sciadrensis), originally from Ḥaṣrūn in north Lebanon, went to Rome in 1603 to study at the Maronite College. After the completion of his studies in 1618, he started teaching Syriac at the college and compiled a Syriac Grammar (*Syriacae Linguae Rudimentum*), which was printed in 1618 at the Maronite press in Rome, and reprinted in 1636 under the title *Grammatica Linguae Syriacae*. Isḫāq al-Šedrāwī was called by Cardinal Borromeo to teach Syriac and Arabic at the Academy of Milan, and he was also charged with organising and arranging the oriental manuscripts in the Cardinal's library. After Milan, Isaac Sciadrensis went to Florence and Pisa to teach oriental languages between 1636 and 1638. He died in Lebanon in 1663 (Nasser Gemayel 1984: 335–57, 365).

Ibrahim al-Ḥāqilāni, nicknamed Abrahami Ecchellensis, was born in Ḥāqil in Jubayl (Lebanon) on 18 February 1605 and entered the Maronite College of Rome in 1620. He was appointed an *Interpreter* at the Propaganda Fide in Rome, as well as a member of the Pontifical Biblical committee, and was the successor of Sarkis al-Rizzi in the editing of the Bible in Arabic. He was also entrusted with the teaching of Syriac and Arabic at La Sapienza University in Rome. Shortly after these appointments, he was called by Ferdinand II and Prince Leopold to Florence in order to examine the oriental manuscripts in the Pitti palace. In 1633, he went to Pisa to teach Arabic and Syriac. In 1640, he accepted an invitation to help with the Polyglot Bible in Paris, and he spent his time between August 1640 and December 1641 updating the translation work of Sionita and Ḥesronita. In 1646, during his stay in Paris, Ecchellensis published his liberal translation of the work of the Arab philosopher Burhān al-Dīn al-Zarnūji, which aimed to give a clear rendering of his thoughts rather than being a literal translation of his book. In 1647, he also translated a work by Abū-Bakr al-Suyūṭi on medicine and plants and gems from Arabic into Latin. His other work included (while in Paris) the translation into Latin of a Coptic book in Arabic, which contains a list of Egyptian khalifats and the Coptic patriarchs up to the thirteenth century, to which he added an annex about the history of the Arabs before Islam.

Ibrahim al-Ḥāqilāni returned to Rome after his career in the French capital and was appointed professor of oriental languages at the Gymnasio Romano (La Sapienza). He dedicated the rest of his time to writing his final books. He was also appointed by Pope Alexander VII as interpreter and head of oriental scribes in Rome. In 1643, during his teaching period in Rome, he translated the *Catalogue* of the Metropolitan ʿAbd Yeshūʿ Bar Brikha on the Syriac writers in the Levant, which was probably composed in 1298, from Syriac into Latin. Ecchellensis published his translation in 1653 in Rome, but the list was originally full of mistakes, and was subsequently corrected and published by the Maronite scholar Assemaʿāni in 1725. In 1628, He published (in Latin) his new book, *A Summary of the Principles of the Arabic Language*, and in 1633 he copied the *Introduction to the Logic of Avicenna*, which had been translated to Arabic by Gregorius Ibn al-ʿIbri (Gregorius Bar Hebraeus). In 1637, he copied the last three sections of Porphyry's *Isagoge*, which had been translated into Syriac by Athanasius of Balād, and in 1641 translated the *Summary of the Intentions of the Wisdom of Arab Philosophers* from Arabic into Latin. It was presented to Cardinal Richelieu, who invited Ecchellensis to come to Paris to help with the printing of the Polyglot Bible. He also translated the book of Ibn al-Rāheb, *Chronicon Orientale*, from Arabic into Latin. The Medici family in Tuscany boosted the intellectual work of Ecchellensis by giving significant help in printing his books; the Grand Duke Ferdinando II requested the translation from Arabic to Latin of the fifth, sixth, and seventh books of Apollonius of Perga, entitled the *Conics Book* of Abu al-Fateḫ, and it was translated with the help of the Italian mathematician Alfonso Borelli. Immediately after the completion of his translation of Apollonius of Perga, Ecchellensis proposed to Cardinal Capponi that he catalogue the Syriac and Arabic manuscripts at the Vatican Library, and on 21 May 1660 he was appointed the scriptor of the Vatican Library and began work on the first scientific catalogue of oriental manuscripts. The catalogue was left unfinished due to his death on 15 July 1664, but another Maronite, Fustus Naironus Banensis, continued the work, and it was completed by Assemani, who was undoubtedly the first scholar to compile a scientific catalogue of the oriental manuscripts in the Vatican Libray.

Ibrahim al-Ḥaqilāni also translated Archimedes's *Liber Assumptorum*, which was printed in 1661, from Arabic into Latin, and in 1662, the 'Rite of Confession' attributed to Dionysius Bar Ṣalibi from Syriac into Latin, and it was published by Leon Allatius (Ghaleb 1930: 186–93, 342–50; Nasser Gemayel 1984: 388–9, 396–7).

The parents of Merheğ al-Bāni were originally from the village of Bān in north Lebanon, and they emigrated to Rome in the early seventeenth century. Merheğ al-Bāni, nicknamed Faustus Naironus Banensi, was born in Rome in 1628 and was the brother-in-law of Ibrahim al-Ḥaqilāni. He was admitted at the Maronite College in 1638, and in 1664 took over the post of Abraham Ecchellensis in the teaching of oriental languages at La Sapienza. He wrote several books: one of them, in Latin, printed in 1694, is his defence of the Catholic faith, in which there is a good collection of important thoughts from oriental theologians and historians such as Athanasius, Eutychius, Barhebraeus, Jacob of Edessa (Jacob Baradeus or Yaʿqub Burdʿono), Elias of Nisibin, Dawood bar Boulos, Abu-Isḥaq ibn al-ʿAssāl, and the Canons of the Council of Nicaea in Arabic. Finally, Faustus Naironus Banensi was the second custodian of the Alexandrine Library in Rome, which was fused into the Urbanian Library, of which he became the first custodian (Nasser Gemayel 1984: 404–9, 481–2).

Boutros Dipy, a Maronite from Aleppo, was the last Maronite scholar to teach Arabic and Syriac at the Collège Royal. His teaching career began in October 1667 when he replaced Pierre Vattier, who had died on 7 April 1667. Boutros Dipy was also busy with the study of Arabic manuscripts in the Royal Libraries, where he spent thirty-nine years, becoming the Royal interpreter for oriental languages. Dipy was the author of several catalogues: *Catalogue des manuscrits arabes et persans de la Bibliothèque du Roi*, jointly with Mr Petis de la Croix, *Catalogue des manuscrits arabes de la Bibliothèque du Roi*, and *Catalogue des manuscrits turcs et persans de la Bibliothèque du Roi*. He died in France on 11 February 1709 (Nasser Gemayel 1984: 249–61, 290–1).

Istephān al-Duwaihi, or Stephanus Petrus Edenensis, was born on 2 August 1630 in Ehden and was sent when he was eleven years old to Rome to study at the Maronite College. He spent fourteen years in Rome studying theology, philosophy, logic, and languages such as Italian, Latin, Greek, Arabic, and Syriac. After his graduation, he went back to Lebanon to be ordained a priest by patriarch Yūḥanna al-Ṣifrāwi (1648–1656) on 25 March 1656. The Maronite Church at the time was very poor, scattered in the Levant, and run by eleven bishops, four of whom were students of the Maronite College in Rome. Al-Duwaihi wrote an account of the monastic life, arguing that it was disappearing because of the injustice of the political system and bad administration by certain monks. Moreover, the diocesan priests were mostly married and very poor, and only twenty of them studied in the Maronite College of Rome. Istephān al-Duwaihi was ordained the Maronite bishop of Cyprus on 8 July 1668, and he was elected the patriarch of the Maronite Church on 5 May 1670 and resided at the monastery of Qannūbin. Patriarch al-Duwaihi was interested in the educated Maronite clergy leading the Maronite Church into a new era and launched the first initiative in Lebanon to reform his Levantine Church. Consequently, most bishops ordained by al-Duwaihi were graduates of the Maronite College of Rome, and thus he hoped to establish the strong foundations of a new Maronite Church well rooted in its historical Levantine origins. Patriarch Istephān al-Duwaihi experienced a very unsettled life during his patriarchate: he was compelled to leave his residence in Qannūbin many times, because he was unable to pay his taxes to the Ottoman rulers, and was persecuted and chased by local governors. He fled to Kessrowan to enjoy the protection of the Maronite feudal family al-Khazen, whose area was within the Druze principality, and he went sometimes to the Shouf area protected by the Druze rulers. He died in Qannūbin on 3 May 1704. He was a very fruitful writer, who left many compositions behind him in Garshuni, some of which are still unpublished. The most important book he wrote was his *Tarīḫ al-Azminah* (*the History of the Times*), which undoubtedly made him the father of Lebanese history. Patriarch al-Duwaihi was very concerned with the Maronite liturgy, and he composed *Manārat al-Aqdās* to explain the Maronite liturgy and the meaning of each ceremony. He also composed a Syriac-Arabic dictionary, but the manuscript was lost. Al-Duwaihi also wrote many letters to different ecclesiastical and civil dignitaries, but most of them were addressed to Holy See in Rome (Nasser Gemayel 1992; Fahed 1983: V–XXIII).

Bouṭros Mubārak, nicknamed Ambarak or Pietro Benedetti or Petrus Benedictus, was born in 1663 in Baṭḥā near Ghosṭa in Kessrowan. He was sent to Rome on 10 November 1671 to study at the Maronite College and graduated in 1684. He returned in 1685 to be ordained a priest by patriarch al-Duwaihi, who charged him in 1691 with revising and correcting his books on the liturgy and history of the Maronite Church. Patriarch al-Duwaihi commissioned him to go back to Rome to solve some disputes with the Franciscans in the Holy Land, and once his mission was accomplished, he set off for Lebanon in 1693. On his way back, he went through Florence, and was asked by the Duke of Tuscany to put some order to the characters of six oriental languages in his Florentine press. In 1698, he was chosen by the duke as the chair of oriental languages to teach Syriac, Arabic, and Hebrew at the university of Pisa, while the Maronites Abraham Ecchellensis and Isaac Sciadrensis had taught only Syriac and Arabic before him. He remained in his post in Pisa until 1707, when he moved to Rome to become a Jesuit at the age of forty-four. After his novitiate in the Jesuit order, Petro Benedetti was chosen by Pope Clement XI to edit the sacred books in Greek. In 1725, he published his translation, from Arabic to Latin, of *The Life of St Alexus*; in 1727 he published his translation from Greek to Latin *The Greek Menology*; and in 1729 he published his translation from Syriac to Latin the *Acta Sanctorum* of Jacob of Sarug. But his major work was the editing of the translation of St Ephrem from Syriac to Latin, which had been partially done by previous Maronite scholars of the Maronite College and which he completed. He began in 1730, and published the first volume in 1737 and the second volume in 1740, but he was unable to finish the third volume, as he died in 1742 while he was still in the middle of his work (Nasser Gemayel 1984: 452–3, 522–6).

Elias Assemani was the son of the Maronite priest Yaʿqūb ʿAwwād from Ḥaṣrūn, and he studied at the Maronite College between 1685 and 1679. He was commissioned by Pope Clement XI to collect oriental manuscripts from Egypt, and he went there in 1707 and returned with forty manuscripts, although he was preceded in this by the Maronite monk Ğibraʿīl Ḥawwa, who was commissioned by Pope Clement XI in 1703 to meet the Coptic patriarch, and who, on his way back to Rome, brought with him a collection of rare oriental manuscripts (Nasser Gemayel 1984: 417–18).

Yūsuf Šemʿūn Assemʿāni, sometimes simply known as Assemani, was born in 1686 or 1687 in Ḥaṣrūn (north Lebanon), and in 1696 he was sent to Rome with another six

Maronites to study at the Maronite College. While a student, he was able to translate from Arabic into Latin and to compose academic manuals for the Syriac language, logic, and theology. At the end of his studies, he was chosen by Pope Clement XI to compile a catalogue of oriental manuscripts, and on 10 March 1710, he was named interpreter of Arabic and Syriac at the Vatican Library, i.e. the post of the *Scriptor Orientalis*, which was held before him by Ibrahim al-Ḥāqilāni. Assemani composed in Garshuni an *Introduction to Science, Logic and Dialectology* in 1710, and he graduated in the same year as a doctor in philosophy and theology. Shortly afterwards, he was named by the pope as an adviser for the new Vatican office to revise and correct the liturgical books of the oriental churches. Another book of Assemani came out in Garshuni in 1712 on the *Life of the Lord Christ*. In 1715, Pope Clement organised a third mission to collect manuscripts from the East, and he appointed Assemani to lead the new expedition, accompanied by the scribe of the Mission Fr Andrawos Iskandar, originally from Cyprus and a graduate of the Maronite College. He began his tour in Alexandria and moved to Cairo, and he visited most of the Coptic monasteries in Upper Egypt. Assemani bought back many rare manuscripts in Coptic and Arabic, despite the reservations and opposition of the Coptic monks, before going to Syria and Palestine in search of rare oriental manuscripts to enrich the Vatican Library. Assemani went back to Rome with a unique and very precious collection of rare oriental manuscripts in Arabic, Coptic, Syriac, Greek, Turkish, Armenian, and Persian. After his tour in the East, he started his major scientific catalogue in 1719, entitled the *Bibliotheca Orientalis Clementino-Vaticanus* of the oriental manuscripts in the Vatican Library, which was completed in 1728. His great success in the oriental collection earned him the privilege of becoming, in 1730, the second custodian of the Vatican Library, and in 1735, the pope named him a domestic prelate with the right to hold the dignitary alb and mitre. He was nominated the prefect or the custodian of the Vatican library in 1739, and he remained in this office until his death. Charles IV, then king of Sicily and later king of Spain, named him a historiographer of the kingdom of Naples in 1739, and in 1740, he was declared a Neapolitan citizen. In gratitude for his new honorary titles, he wrote two books on the history of Naples and Sicily, which were part of his six volumes on the writers of the history of Italy. Assemani was a very productive author, writing many books in Arabic, Latin, and Italian, although many of them were not printed. He edited the writings of Ephrem the Syrian in Greek and translated them into Latin. He also published five books on the sacred icons in the oriental churches, and he gathered all his knowledge about the history of Syria, Palestine, Phoenicia, Mesopotamia, Egypt, and Arabia in two books, which were destroyed by a fire while in manuscript form and therefore never printed. Assemani died on 13 January 1768, in Rome, and was undoubtedly the most famous student of the Maronite College of Rome; his fame and erudition are still very vivid among orientalists and researchers of mediaeval history (Nasser Gemayel 1984: 420–33, 489–507).

Stephanus ʿAwwād Al-Semʿāni, nicknamed Stephanus Evodius Assemanus, kept both names of his family, ʿAwwād from his father and Al-Assemʿāni from his mother, who was the sister of the famous Yūsuf. Both parents were originally from Ḥaṣrūn (north Lebanon), and their son Stephanus was born in 1709. Stephanus Evodius Assemanus was admitted at the Maronite College at the age of eleven on 16 November 1720. He decided to stay in Rome with his uncle Yūsuf after the completion of his studies in 1730. He became the scriptor for the Syriac and Arabic languages at the Vatican Library on 1 February 1731. Assemanus received an invitation from the duke of Florence, John Gaston, who needed him to organise the oriental collection of the Medici Library. In 1742 he published his famous catalogue *Bibliothecae Mediceae Laurentianae*, and completed the compilation of a catalogue of oriental manuscripts at the Palatina and Riccardiana Library, which is still an unpublished manuscript, in 1745. He engaged himself in a different literary work, the translation of St Ephrem's works into Latin, which had been started by another Maronite scholar Bouṭros Mubārak, who was not able to complete it during his own lifetime. Despite the aridity of the work, he was able to finish the first complete translation of St Ephrem in to Latin in 1746. He was then called back to Rome by Cardinal Flavio Chigi to catalogue the manuscripts of the Chigiana Library, which was finished in 1764. Another important work of Evodius Assemani was his translation, from Syriac to Latin, of the *Acta Sanctorum Martyrum Orientalium et Occidentalium*, which was brought to Rome by his uncle Yūsuf at the beginning of eighteenth century. Evodius Assemani did not merely translate the work, but he also made a scientific analysis of the date of composition and discussed its credibility and historical value. His translation was published in 1748, and it was translated into French in 1852. His literary activities stopped with the death of his famous uncle Yūsuf Šemʿūn Assemʿāni in 1768, who was his intellectual mentor and had been his coadjutor since 15 November 1766. We assume, however, that he continued as the scriptor for oriental manuscripts at the Vatican Library until his death on 24 November 1782 (Nasser Gemayel 1984: 435–40, 486–7).

Yūsuf-Louis al-Semʿāni, nicknamed Josepho Aloysio Assemani, was born in Ḥaṣrūn (north Lebanon) around 1710. His paternal uncle was the famous scholar Yūsuf Šemʿūn Assemʿāni, while his maternal cousin was Stephanus ʿAwwād Al-Assemʿāni. He studied at the Maronite College of Rome, and on 23 November 1737 began teaching Syriac at La Sapienza in Rome. He became a Jesuit in the early period of his teaching, following the examples of many Maronites in Rome, such as Ǧirǧis Ben Yammine, Bouṭros Mubārak, Mikhael al-Ǧazīri, and Boulos al-Haddār. He announced a series of fifteen books on *Codex liturgicus ecclesiae universae*, but only five volumes were printed. This was a unique collection to study the liturgies drawn from the oriental manuscripts of the Vatican Library. Thanks to his expertise in ecclesiastical liturgy, he was appointed in 1749 to teach oriental liturgy at La Sapienza, and he became a member of the Pontifical Academy. He also translated two books from Syriac to Latin: first *the Canonical Collection of 'Ebedješūʿ*, and then *the Nomocanon of Gregorius Abū al-Faraj*. His *Dissertation on the Sacred Rituals*, printed in 1757, was re-edited by Migne. He also composed a commentary on ten chapters from the Gospels in Arabic garshuni, but the manuscript was never published. A particularly important work is his *Commentary on the History and Chronology of the Chaldean and Nestorian Patriarchs*. Josepho Aloysio Assemani sent a report on 'Lingue arabice e siro caldaïca' on 20 May 1771 to the Propangada Fide to present the method of his teaching of Arabic and Syriac languages at the Urbanus College in Rome, and he mentioned in this report the manuals which were used to teach Arabic, those of Erpenius, Guadagnoli, Martelot, Obicini, and Pietro della Valle, and also the lexicons of Meninsky, Giggei, Golius, and Ǧermānos Farḥāt. The report also referred to the manuals used to teach Syriac, one by Ǧirǧis ʿAmīra to teach Syriac in Latin, one by Isḫāq al-Šedrāwī to teach Syriac in Syriac, one by Victorius Cialac Accurensis to teach Syriac in Arabic, and finally one by Abrahami Ecchellensis to teach Syriac in Arabic. We learn, in addition, that the Syriac and Arabic languages were taught at the Maronite College and La Sapienza. Josepho Aloysio Assemani died in Rome on 9 February 1782 (Nasser Gemayel 1984: 442–4, 508–13).

Maronite intellectual contribution after the College of Rome

The intellectual life of educated Maronite people was more intense during the nineteenth and twentieth centuries. First, the Maronites played a major role in the maintenance of the Arab language against the Turks, who imposed their language on all people in the Ottoman Empire. Even the Muslims in the Arab East neglected their own Arabic language, adopting Turkish instead (Moosa 1986: 37–8, 59–62). The Maronite Church Synod in 1736 ordered that Arabic be the official language of the Maronites and that it should be taught alongside Syriac, their liturgical language. Moreover, the Synod urged the Maronite clergy to create schools in every village and hamlet in order to educate all Maronite men and women, and that teaching should be conducted in Arabic, not in Turkish (Al-Majmaʿ Al-Loubnani 1900: 529–30, 535, 541, 546, 550–1). Therefore, the first pioneers of Arab unity in modern history were the Maronites, men such as Youssif Karam (1823–89), who launched the idea of an Arab confederation, and later Najib ʿAzuri, who specified in 1904 that the Arabs should be united in one nation against any foreign intervention (Aboumelhem 1998). Moreover, the Maronite educational system produced important Maronite writers and thinkers such as Boutros al-Bostani, Gibran Khalil Gibran, Maroun Abboud, Said ʿAkl, and others. However, the Maronite schools in Lebanon contributed greatly to the modern Arab renaissance, educating Christians and Muslims alike, and despite the atrocities of the late Lebanese civil war, many Maronite and Christian schools are still flourishing in Lebanon.

MODERN POLITICAL HISTORY

After the defeat of the Crusaders, the Maronites quickly forgot their internal dissensions and gathered themselves around their patriarch, who remained in union with Rome and maintained good relations with the Franks. It seems also that the hostile policy of the Mamluks towards those who collaborated with the Crusaders contributed greatly to Maronite unity, as well as their isolation in the Lebanese mountains. The Maronite Church suffered greatly during the nineteenth century under the Ottoman occupation of the Levant, and the civil wars between the Maronites and the Druzes in 1840–1845 and 1860 ended the autonomy of Lebanon and weakened Christianity in Lebanon and Syria. In spite of this, however, the long period of persecution ended with the creation of 'Greater Lebanon' in 1920 under the French mandate, and the new Lebanese state answered the expectations of the Maronites: a free country, independent from the Ottomans. On the other hand, the Maronites believe that their isolation in Mount Lebanon contributed greatly to their independent character as a Church and as a society, and their identity is consequently identified strongly with the identity of Lebanon. In fact, the Maronite Church has played a major role in the creation of modern Lebanon, and its followers have held some key positions in the modern Lebanese state (Dib 1971: 160–90).

NOTES

1 The ṭablīt in the Maronite church is the central piece of the altar, and it is an essential part of the altar for the celebration of the Eucharist. It is equivalent to the Byzantine endemousa (endemisi in Arabic pronunciation).

2 The Rites of Consecrations and Blessings was re-published by the Maronite bishop Boutros Shebli (1909).

BIBLIOGRAPHY

Non-authored books

Al-Majma ʿAl-Loubnani 1736 (Jounieh: Arz Print, 1900, reprinted 1986), 529–30, 535, 541, 546, 550–1 (Arabic).

Al-Manarah 29 (1988), 177–262.

Al-Manarah 31 (1990), 5–79.

Al-Ritab al-Marūniyyah (Kaslik, 1984).

The Book of the Maronite Chants According to the Rite of the Antiochian Syriac Maronite Church (Bkerke: Koreim Press Jounieh, 2008) (Arabic).

The Book of Mass, According to the Rite of the Antiochian Syriac Maronite Church (Bkereke, 2005), 16 (Arabic).

The Book of the True Delight in the Spiritual Chants (Kitab al-lazzah al-haqiqiyah fi al-taranim al-ruhiyah) (Beirut: Qozma Press, 1928).

The Christmas Season (Lebanon: Kaslik, 1977) (Arabic).

The Easter Season (Lebanon: Kaslik, 1977) introduction ṭ-y; (Arabic).

The Epiphany Season (Lebanon: Kaslik, 1978) (Arabic).

The Funerary Service of Monks (Kaslik, 2002) (Arabic & Syriac).

The Funerary Service of Nuns (Kaslik, 2004) (Arabic & Syriac).

The Great Lent Season (Lebanon: Kaslik, 1979) introduction l-m; (Arabic).

The Holy Week (Lebanon: Kaslik, 1976) (Arabic).

The Maronite Funerary Service (Kaslik, 1991) (Arabic & Syriac).

The Maronite Rites (Kaslik, 1984) (Arabic & Syriac).

The Rite of Fiançaille and Crowning According to the Rite of the Antiochian Syriac Maronite Church (Bkerke, 2004) (Arabic).

The Rite of the Sacrament of Baptism and the Sacrament of Myron According to the Rite of the Antiochian Syriac Maronite Church (Bkerke, 2003) (Arabic).

Secondary Literature

Abi-Aoun, B. et al. 1994. *Momies du Liban. Rapport préliminaire sur la découverte archéologique de ʿAṣi-l-Ḥadat*. Beirut: Edifra.

Aboumelhem, Ahmad. 1998. *Najib ʿAzuri: Yaqzat al-Ummah al-ʿArabiyyah*. Beirut, 1998.

Al-Dfouni, Boutros Shebli. 1899. Fi kitāb al-Šarṭūniyyah al-Marūniyah lilbatriark Istān al-Duwaihi. *Al-Mashreq* 2, 640–51.

Al-Duwaihi, Stefan. 1890. *Tarīḫ al-Ṭāifah al-Marouniyyah (The History of the Maronite Nation)*. Beirut: Shartouni edition.

Al-Masʿūdi. 1839. *Kitab al-Tanbih wa al-Ishraf*. Cairo.

Al-Shartūni, Rashid. 1902. *Shareh ritbat Al-Šarṭūniyyah al-Siryaniah*. Beirut.
Ashqar, P. 1922. *Musique orientale*. Lyon: F. Bellon.
———. 1939. *Mélodies liturgiques syro-maronites, recueillies et notées*. Jounieh.
Breydy, Michael. 1971. *Kult, Dichtung and Musik in Wochenbrebier der Syro-Maroniten*. Band II. Jounieh: Koreim Press.
———. 1979. *Kult, Dictung und Musik bei den Syro-Maroniten. Band III, Rishaiqole. Die Leitstrophen der Syro-aramäischen Litrugien. Repertorium und Kommentar*. Qobbayat, Libanon.
Brock, S. P. 1973a. An Early Syriac Life of Maximus the Confessor. *Analecta Bollondiana* 91, 299–346.
———. 1973b. A Syriac Fragment on the Sixth Council. *OC* 57, 63–71.
Chabot, J.-B. 1899. *Chronique de Michel le Syrien, patriarche jacobite d'Antioche (1166–1199)*. Paris: Ernest Leroux, 1899–1910. Reprinted Gorgias Press, 2009.
Daniel, N. 1960. *Islam and the West*. Edinburgh: Edinburgh University Press.
Dib, P. 1971. *History of the Maronite Church*. Beirut: Editions de la Sagesse.
Diotallevi, Alfredo. 1991. *L'Abate Victorio Scialac e il Collegio Maronita di Ravenna*. Occidente e Oriente cristiano 2. Bologna: Clueb.
Douaihy, Hector. 1993. *Un Théologien Maronite Gibra'il Ibn Al-Qala'i, Evêque et Moine Franciscain*. Kaslik: Université Saint-Esprit.
Fahed, Boutros. 1982. *The Maronite Patriarchs and Bishops During the Sixteenth Century*. Ashqūt/Lebanon (Arabic).
———. 1983. *Al-Baṭriark Istephān al-Duwaihi, Tārīḫ al-Azminah*. Beirut: Dar Laḥed (Arabic).
Gemayel, Boutros. 1982. *Zajaliyyat Jibra'il Ibn al-Qila'i*. Beirut: Dar Lahed (Arabic).
———. 1992. *The Maronite Missal*. Bkerke (Arabic).
———. 2005. Introduction. *In*: *The Gospel. The Lectionary for the Mass According to the Antiochian Syriac Maronite Church*. Bkerke (Arabic).
Gemayel, Nasser. 1984. *Les Échanges Culturels entre les Maronites et L'Europe, Du Collège Maronite de Rome (1584) au Collège de 'Ayn-Warqa (1789)*. Beyrouth.
———. 1991. *Al-Patriarch Istephān al-Duwaihi, Ḥayātoho wa Mu'allāfātoho*. Beirut.
Ghaleb, Boutros. 1924. Nawabeg al-madrassah al-marouniah: al-baṭriark Ǧirǧis 'Amīrā. *Al-Mashreq* 22, 341–50 (Arabic).
———. 1930. Ibrahim al-Ḥāqilāni (1594? – 1664). *Al-Mashreq* 28, 186–93, 342–50.
Gribomont, J. 1974. Documents sur les origines de l'Église Maronite. *PdO* 5:1, 95–132.
Hage, Louis, 1972–1991. *Le Chant de l'Église Maronite/Mouments du Chant Maronite*. 4 Volumes. Kaslik: Université Saint-Esprit.
———. 1987. *The Model Strophes and their Poetic Meters by the Maronite Patriarch Stephen Douayhi*. Kaslik: Université Saint-Esprit.
———. 1990/1. *Musique Maronite*. 7 volumes. Kaslik: Université Saint-Esprit.
———. 1999. *Précis de Chant Maronite*. Kaslik: Université Saint-Esprit.
Hage Soaiby, Philippe. 1985. *Le Monothélisme de Thomas Kaphartab dans ses "Dix Chapitres"*. Jounieh: Editions Apôtres.
Ḥarfouch, Ibrahīm. 1903. Athār al-Duwaihi fi Maktabat Marl Shallīṭa. *Al-Mashreq* 6, 595–6.
Hayek, Michel. 2009. *Writings in the History of the Maronite Church and Its Spirituality*. Hrajil/Lebanon (Arabic).
Joubeir, Antoine. 1991. *Kitab al-Huda, Essai*. 2nd edn. Kaslik/Liban.
Moosa, M. 1986. *The Maronites in History*. Syracuse: Syracuse University Press. Reprinted Piscataway, NJ: Gorgias Press, 2005.
Naaman, Paul. 2009. *The Maronites: The Origins of an Antiochene Church. A Historical and Geopgraphical Study of the Fifth to the Seventh Centuries*. Collegeville: Cistercian Publictions, Liturgical Press.
———, and Nasser Gemayel. 1992. *The 1300 Anniversary (686–1986) of the Foundation of the Maronite Patriarchate*. Kaslik: Holy Spirit University (Arabic).

Salibi, K. 1958. The Maronite Church in the Middle Ages and Its Union With Rome. *OC* 42, 92–104.
———. 1991. *Maronite Historians of Medieval Lebanon*. 2nd edn. Beirut: Naufal.
Shebli, Boutros. 1909. *Kitab Ritab wa 'Adāt ḥasab 'Adat al-Ṭa'ifah al-Marūniyyah*. 2nd edn. Beirut.
Suleiman, Mussa. 1986. *Al-Ḥarakah al-'Arabiyyah: al-Marḥalah al-Ula llinnahḍa al-'Arabiyyah al-Ḥadīthah 1908–1924*. Beirut: Dar al-Nahar llinnasher (Arabic).
Tabet, Jean. 1988. *Riš qoryan marouni qadim (1242 A.D.), Salamanca Manuscript 2647*. Kaslik (Arabic).
———. 1991. *Shimto. Daily Office*. Kaslik, Lebanon (Arabic).
Ya'qūb, Abdou Toufiq. 2011. *Al-'Allāmah Al-Ābbāti Naṣrallah Šalaq al-'Aqūri, 1564–1635, (Abbas Victorius Cialac Accurensis Maronita)*. Beirut: Dar Al-Farābi.

CHAPTER THIRTY-SEVEN

THE EARLY STUDY OF SYRIAC IN EUROPE

Robert J. Wilkinson

BEGINNINGS

The initial context of the study of Syriac in Europe was ecclesiastical, specifically explorations towards, or confirmations of, the union of the various Eastern churches with Rome. A delegation of Maronites attending the Fifth Lateran Council (1513–1515) brought native speakers to Rome who introduced the rudiments of their language and liturgy and copied a few scriptural manuscripts. Teseo Ambrogio (1469–1540) was the first to be taught the language and was asked to examine the Maronites' liturgy. He had hoped to publish a psalter in Syriac, but was frustrated by the Sack of Pavia in 1527. Thereafter in Reggio in 1529 he met Johann Albrecht Widmanstetter, travelling in the train of the emperor Charles V on his way to Bologna. Teseo apparently entrusted Widmanstetter with the task of carrying on his lonely attempts to print Syriac and gave him a Syriac Gospel book. In 1539, Teseo brought out his *Introduction to the Chaldean Language* in which he gives the first sketchy description of Syriac and its distinctive script, remarkably using moveable type (Nestle 1904). Cardinal Egidio da Viterbo (1469–1532), prince of the church, orientalist, and kabbalist was patron of the early encounters with the Maronites attending the Fifth Lateran Council. In addition, his book *On the Hebrew Letters* provided material for Teseo to ascribe a mystical significance to the Syriac alphabet (Copenhaver and Kokin 2014). The cardinal was thus initially responsible for imposing a mystical and Kabbalistic appreciation of Syriac in the first half of the sixteenth century (Wilkinson 2007a: 30–62).

THE FIRST EDITION OF THE SYRIAC NEW TESTAMENT, VIENNA 1555

The Maronite delegation was followed in 1549 by a scribe, Moses of Mardin, who was sent to Rome by the Syrian Orthodox patriarch of Antioch, possibly to pursue issues of church unity, but more particularly to arrange to meet the Eastern churches' perpetual shortage of scriptural and liturgical books by getting copies of the Syriac New Testament produced in quantity using the Western technique of moveable-type printing. In this he was surprisingly successful.

The first edition of the Syriac New Testament was printed in Vienna in 1555 (Figures 37.1–2). It was the product of Moses's cooperation with two Western scholars, J. A. Widmanstetter (to whom Teseo had entrusted a Gospel book) and Guillaume Postel (1510–1581) (Figure 37.3). Postel was a remarkable figure; a considerable scholar and linguist, he had knowledge of Teseo's Syriac type. But he was also a mystic, prophet, and kabbalist whose notions of his own messianic significance finally led to his confinement in a monastery as a madman. Moses was responsible for the delicacy of the script, which was based on his handwriting, and for the accuracy of the text.

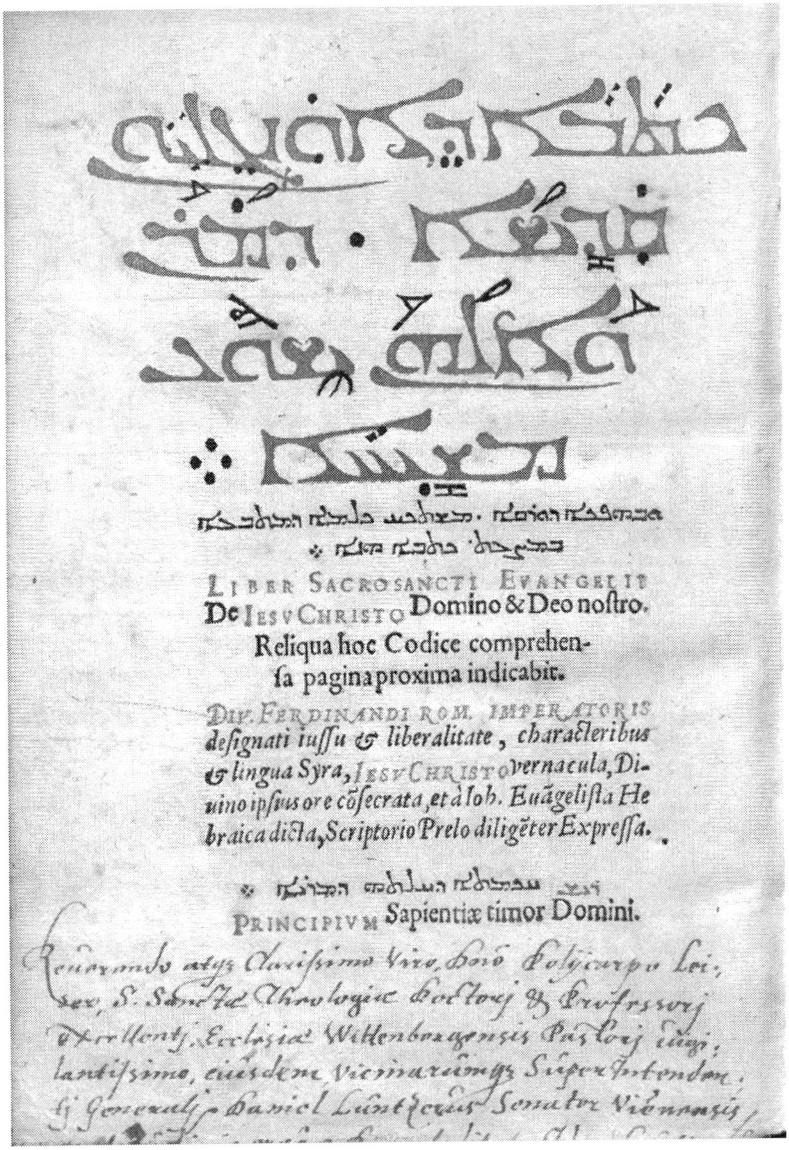
LIBER SACROSANCTI EVANGELII
De IESV CHRISTO Domino & Deo noſtro.
Reliqua hoc Codice comprehenſa pagina proxima indicabit.
DIVI FERDINANDI ROM. IMPERATORIS deſignati iuſſu & liberalitate, characteribus & lingua Syra, IESV CHRISTO vernacula, Diuino ipſius ore cõſecrata, et à Ioh. Euãgeliſta Hebraica dicta, Scriptorio Prelo diligẽter Expreſſa.
PRINCIPIVM Sapientiæ timor Domini.

Figure 37.1 Editio Princeps of the Syriac New Testament 1555

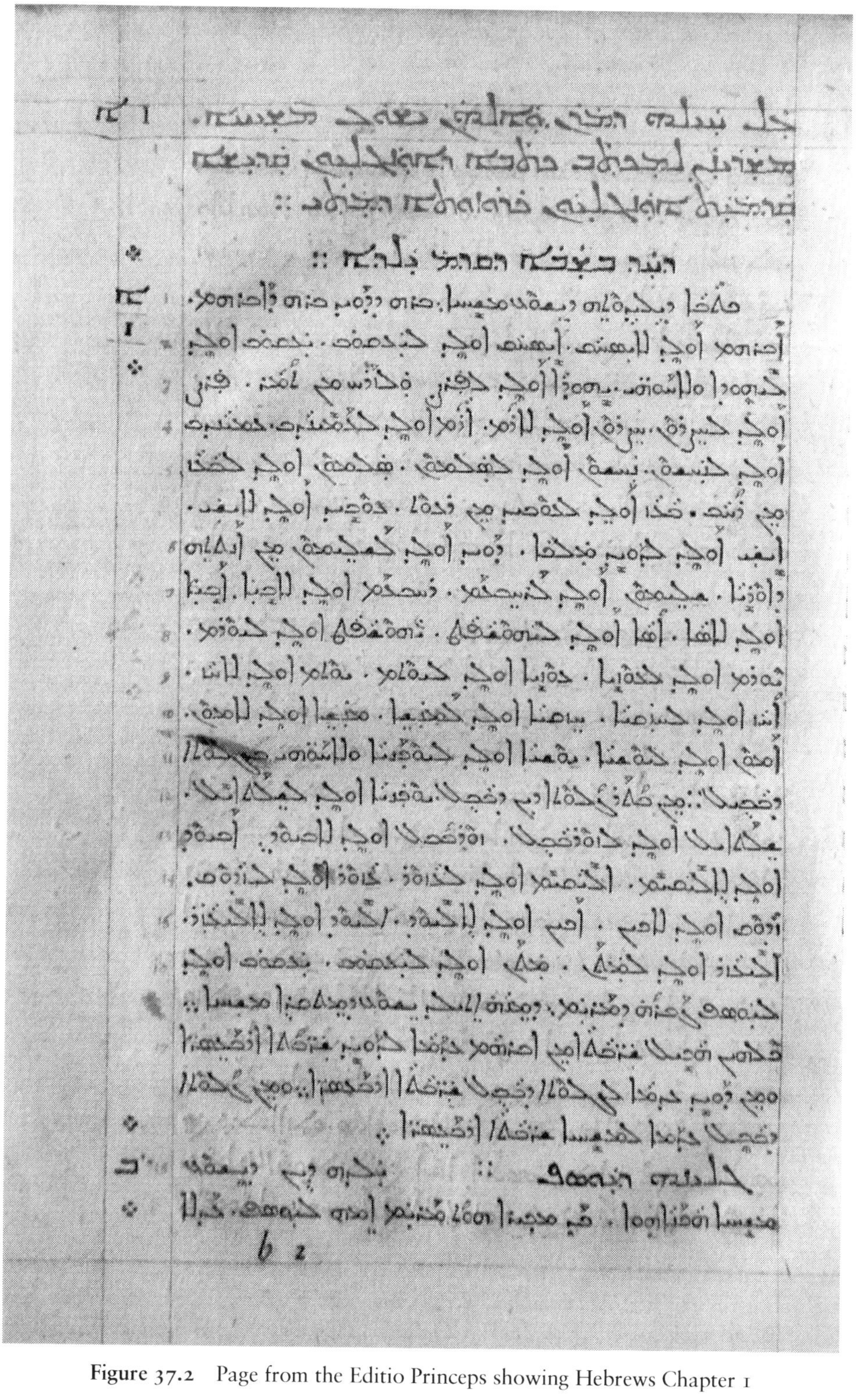

Figure 37.2 Page from the Editio Princeps showing Hebrews Chapter 1

Figure 37.3 Guillaume Postel

Postel's expertise lay behind the type. The book itself is a generally harmonious blend of features of an Eastern book (suitable for the purposes of the patriarch of Antioch) with features celebrating the Hapsburg Ferdinand I who was Widmanstetter's patron. It has, however, a remarkable plate showing a Kabbalistic Sephirotic Tree in relation with Christ on the Cross, which could have meant nothing to the patriarch, but which was evidently significant for the two Western scholars (Figure 37.4) (Wilkinson 2007a: xvi, 182–5).

The disposition to find mystical content in Syriac script and similar hidden secrets in Syriac was reinforced by the notion of the language entertained by the editors and by most of the early scholars studying Syriac. They generally believed that it was the vernacular language of Christ, his mother, and the apostles. This conviction led to Syriac for centuries being confused with Jewish Palestinian Aramaic and dated too early.

Figure 37.4 The Sephirotic Tree

The typographic achievements of the first edition were remarkable. It was no easy matter to cut the type, nor to cope with the ligatures which join the individual letters. Furthermore, Syriac takes vowel signs and other points both above and below the line. Teseo's initial successes with moveable type and Postel's growing expertise ensured the printing in Syriac type both of the first edition and also that of the subsequent Antwerp Polyglot Bible. However, the type was rare and difficult to cut. Many printers had to do without and used Hebrew letters instead. This was particularly the case with early Protestants (Coakley 2006: 29–39).

THE ANTWERP POLYGLOT BIBLE

The Antwerp Polyglot Bible (1568–1573) was a prestige project printed by Christopher Plantin in Antwerp which sought to surpass the Complutensian Polyglot Bible of half a century earlier. The patron was Philip II of Spain and the project was directed by Arias Montano. The Bible contains a Syriac New Testament in Syriac type produced with the cooperation of Postel and a vocalised Hebrew transcription by his pupil Guy Lefèvre de la Boderie, who also contributed a Lexicon with references to considerable Kabbalistic material. In part, the polyglot was the product of the Kabbalistic sympathies of Postel and Lefèvre de la Boderie (such sympathies may be found again the introduction to another edition of the New Testament by Lefèvre de la Boderie which appeared in Paris in 1584.) But what stands out is the contribution of the scholarly apparatus of the Bible made by Andreas Masius (1514–1573), a student of Moses of Mardin, who offered a lexicon (*Syrorum Peculium*) confined entirely to Syriac words from the New Testament and a few other texts he had to hand. He claimed in this work he had made a contribution to Hebrew lexicography, opening the possibility of an independent philological correction of the Jewish understanding of the Hebrew Bible upon which Christians were so unhappily dependant (Wilkinson 2007b: 78–81). His accompanying *Grammatica Linguae Syriacae* shows profound knowledge of the Hebrew grammarians and of Christian Aramaicists like Sebastian Münster (1489–1552) but also knowledge gained by direct contact with and interrogation of Moses of Mardin. The book exploits the Antwerp typographic mastery to present full paradigms of Syriac with accurate vocalisation. Masius's work is a significant milestone and became a model for subsequent Syriac grammars. Casper Waser (1565–1625) announced his debt to Masius on the title page of his1593 *Institutio Linguae Syriae ex optimis quibusque apud Syros scriptoribus, in primis Andrea Masio collecta* (Contini 1994: 22).

THE MARONITE COLLEGE

Relations with the Maronites were strengthened in the second half of the century by two missions of the Jesuit Giambattista Eliano the Younger. The result of his efforts was the founding of the Maronite College at Rome by Gregory XIII under Jesuit control (Raphael 1950: 11–69). The Maronites were allowed to celebrate their own liturgy and in May 1584 were given their own college which in time came to provide Syriac scholars the benefit of their own church but also stimulated Western interest in Syriac (Brock 1994: 97–8). The Maronite foundation would in time collect manuscripts, print works, and provide for scholars who took a significant role in the European Republic of Letters (Gemayel 1984). Other Eastern contacts were less successful. The Syriac Orthodox patriarch Ignatius Naʿmatallah visited Rome between 1577 and 1595, though any hope that he might facilitate the return of the miaphysites to union with Rome was ultimately disappointed. Nevertheless, Gregory appointed this learned scholar of medicine, mathematics, and astronomy to his Commission for the Reform of the Calendar. He was able to offer a different proposal for reform based on Eastern traditions (Wilkinson 2012: 63–71).

We owe much of our knowledge of Naʿmatallah's stay in Rome to the autobiography and notebooks of Cardinal Giulio Antonio Santoro, who was not only to concern himself with the patriarch but was also successful in attracting Robert Granjon, one of the greatest of all typographers, to Rome and into his entourage. Granjon was the man who had made possible Plantin's Antwerp Polyglot Bible for which he prepared the type after the model and direction provided by Postel. He would go on to develop the excellence of the Roman Stamperia Medicea Orientale (ca. 1590–1614) for which Na'matallah provided manuscripts (Farina 2012). Under Granjon's influence, Rome enjoyed a golden age of oriental printing, and oriental printing opened the gateway to the East. Much of this printing was done for the *Congregatio de Propaganda Fide*.

Several scholars of the Maronite College wrote Syriac Grammars and Lexicons. George Amira (ca. 1573–1644) wrote a Syriac-Latin lexicon for the college in 1619. Abraham Ecchellensis's Grammar appeared in 1628. The works of Sergius Risius (1635), Sciandrensis (1636), and Accurensis (1645) were intended primarily for native speakers. Amira's earlier Syriac Grammar of 1596 was the first scholarly Syriac Grammar to be edited by a Lebanese scholar and printed by a Lebanese printer (Figure 37.5). Amira also published the Maronite missal in 1594.

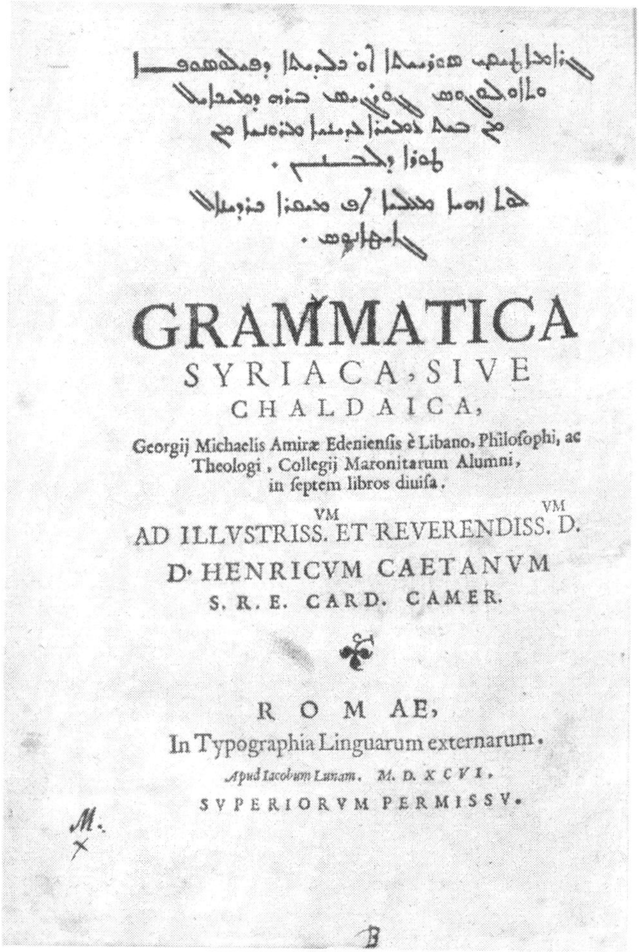
GRAMMATICA
SYRIACA, SIVE
CHALDAICA,
Georgij Michaelis Amiræ Edenienſis è Libano, Philoſophi, ac Theologi, Collegij Maronitarum Alumni, in ſeptem libros diuiſa.
AD ILLVSTRISS.VM ET REVERENDISS.VM D.
D. HENRICVM CAETANVM
S. R. E. CARD. CAMER.
ROMAE,
In Typographia Linguarum externarum.
Apud Iacobum Lunam. M. D. XCVI.
SVPERIORVM PERMISSV.

Figure 37.5 Amira's Grammar

THE PARIS POLYGLOT BIBLE

The Maronite Gabriel Sionita (1577–1648) was editor of a psalter printed in Paris in 1624–1625 and also of Barhebraeus's *Veteris philosophi Syri de sapientia divina poëma aenigmaticum* (1628). He was charged with the production of the Syriac and Arabic texts (complete with a Latin translation) for Le Jay's Paris Polyglot Bible. Sionita broke off his work abruptly at volume VII and declined to provide the material for the seven remaining volumes. The issue seems to have been financial and, after a trial before the Conseil d'État and internment in Vincennes, Sionita resumed his studies. Le Jay, however, was eager for a substitute should things go wrong again and sought a year's leave for another Maronite scholar Abraham Ecchellensis to join the project. He was required to review Sionita's work after his imprisonment and after five months of work declared the texts and translations sound.

It was in the Paris Polyglot that the complete text of the Syriac Bible – including the Old Testament – appeared for the first time. The Syriac text was based upon six or seven manuscripts, one of which Abraham Ecchellensis took to Paris in 1640. The New Testament text was that of the Antwerp Polyglot with De Dieu's text of the Syriac Apocalypse and his *Pericope Adulterae* and Pococke's four Syriac Letters (2 Peter, 2 & 3 John and Jude), for which see below. Sionita was responsible for the edition of the Syriac text and he translated it into Latin with the exception of Ruth, translated by Abraham Ecchellensis and Proverbs, Ecclesiates, Canticles, and Wisdom, translated by Joannes Hesronita.

The Paris Polyglot was a prestige project similar to the great Catholic polyglots of Alcalà and Antwerp. It facilitated a sustained comparison of the texts of the various biblical versions in different languages which was subsequently to become a standard activity of biblical scholars. Though academically soon replaced by the London Polyglot with its superior texts and apparatus, it nonetheless marked an achievement of both philology and printing. It was also the occasion for Syriac to establish itself as a scriptural language deserving of scholarly attention. And it was the occasion of bringing Maronite scholars to Paris. Abraham Ecchellensis, above all, took a conspicuous role in the European Commonwealth of Letters (Miller 2001a).

ABRAHAM ECCHELLENSIS

One of the most outstanding Maronite scholars in the West was Abraham Ecchellensis (1605–1664)(Heyberger 2010b) He succeeded in 1625 to the chair in Syriac and Arabic at the College of the Propaganda. He was corrector of the Maronite *Breviarium* (1624), and in 1628 he produced a popular Grammar *Linguae Syriacae sive Chaldaicae perbrevis Institutio* intended as a short Syriac introduction for Maronite beginners to sit alongside Amira's Grammar (which was perhaps a little less accessible, being in Latin) (Debié 2010).

After a period in the Lebanon and Italy, Urban VIII summoned Ecchellensis back to Rome to teach Arabic and Syriac at the Sapienza University and to assist in the Arabic translation of the Bible, which had been underway since the 1620s. It was a period of collaboration with Athanasius Kircher on his Coptic studies. The poems in Syriac and Arabic which Ecchellensis contributed to *Prodromos Copticus* in 1636 indicate their collegial relationship. In 1640 Ecchellensis was invited to Paris by Louis XIII and Richelieu to work on the Arabic of Le Jay's Polyglot.

In Rome, Ecchellensis was able to play a full part in the 'Republic of Letters' as Europe's leading oriental scholar with extensive connections across the continent(Heyberger 2010a). The context was controversial with confessional interests dividing scholars, but nonetheless the erudite elite of Europe were much taken with the Levant, the Near East, and their successive languages and civilisations. Kircher's engagement with Egypt was an example of this enthusiasm. There was a hunger for oriental documents – manuscripts, medals, inscriptions, coins – across Europe, and collections were formed in a context of national and confessional rivalry. Leiden possessed the largest Protestant collection of oriental manuscripts in Europe, and Pococke was building the collection in Oxford after his journey east. The largest Catholic collection was of course that of the Vatican library which had acquired oriental manuscripts from its inception (Wilkinson 2012: 56). In the seventeenth century, its collection was strengthened by manuscripts brought from the East by Leonardo Abel and Gianbattista Raimondi as well as those that arrived from Heidelberg in 1622. In the second part of the century, Colbert sought seriously to increase the Parisian holdings.

Peter Rietbergen described Abraham Ecchellensis as a mediator between the Mediterranean cultures of the seventeenth century, that is between Latin Christianity, oriental Christians, and Islam (Rietbergen 1989). Ecchellensis certainly moved Maronite Syriac out into the flow of European letters. In the context of European enthusiasm for the East, developing library resources and pedagogic tools made a substantial contribution of the identity of Syriac – with grammars, typography, a growing corpus of Scripture and a nascent awareness of literature and history. Ecchellensis also firmly identified the Maronites within the Catholic cause. The later Maronite dynasty of the Assemanis would continue this work of bringing Syriac scholarship to the European world.

There were other Roman scholars studying Syriac who were not Maronites. Giovan Battista Ferrari (1584–1655) was the Italian Jesuit professor of Hebrew and rhetoric at the Collegium Romanum. He brought out his lexicon, *Nomenclator Syriacus*, in Rome in 1622. Its main purpose was to explain words in the Syriac Bible, in which Ferrari was able to include several Old Testament books.He was able to boast of the help of his old student at the Roman College who subsequently became a professor of Syriac, the Maronite Isaac Sciadrensis and also his own Syriac teacher and colleague Peter Metoscita. A very different type of scholar was Tommaso Obicini da Novara (1585–1638), a Franciscan and a priest, one of the most distinguished Arabists of his day. His career illustrates the connection between mission to the eastern churches and the Orientalism sponsored by the Propaganda. In 1612 he became vicar to the custodian of the Holy Land and subsequently guardian of the Convent of Aleppo (1613–1620). During his time there, he became proficient in both Arabic and Syriac and was active in his attempts to reconcile the Syrian Christians to Rome. He was delegate of the Holy See at the synod held in Diyarbakir in 1616 and 1619 to consider union with the Eastern Syrian Church. He was elected custodian of the Holy Land in 1620 (Custode di Terra Santa e Commisario Apostolico per tutto l'Oriente) and moved to Jerusalem, before retiring to Rome to promote Arabic studies.

His 1636 *Thesaurus Arabo-Syro-Latinus* is a product of his personal learning and experience of Syriac in the Middle East. It is not focused upon the elucidation of the vocabulary of Scripture, but rather shows an engagement with the contemporary spoken language as means of daily communication in the East. There is no interest in historical or comparative grammar, nor any bookish reference to Hebrew. It is focused on contemporary spoken languages and their words used in practically determined semantic fields. Nevertheless it is not an original work but an expanded translation of a work of Elia bar Shinaya (Barsinaeus/Elias of Nisibis) who died in 1049. The book is arranged into tractates and then chapters of which each deals with a specific area of subject vocabulary. The list begins with names of God, includes parts of the body, religious sects and denominations, tools of trades, medical terms (after the Arabic alphabetical order), aqueducts, stars etc. Here is Syriac presented for the purposes of contemporary communication rather than for biblical philology.

PROTESTANT SCHOLARS

Most of the scholars of Syriac we have discussed so far were Catholics and knew each other at least by correspondence and often by cooperation. They were a small group but had had privileged access to Syriac native scholars and the texts they provided. The circumstances of early Protestant engagement with Syriac were very different from those of the Catholics. The Protestants were initially without Rome's ecclesiastical contacts in the East and consequently had no contact with native Syriac-speaking scholars and the precious manuscripts they brought to the West. Neither did they show interest in Christian Kabbalism. The first Catholic publications, particularly the 1555 first edition of the New Testament and the relevant volumes of the Antwerp Polyglot, were essential to them. Their motives were rather different too. Rather than the Catholic interest in reconciling the churches of the East, their focus was more upon the contribution of Syriac to Biblical studies. The Protestants also suffered early from a lack of type. They were reduced *faute de mieux* to using Hebrew type.

The first Protestant Syriac scholar was Emmanuel Tremellius (1510–1580), a Jew converted to Rome and then to the Reform who became professor of Hebrew at Heidelberg. His scholarly resources were a rigorous Jewish education and fifteen manuscripts in the Elector Palatine's Library, which Pfalzgraf Ottheinrich had acquired from an impecunious Postel. Amongst these was Vat. Sir. 16, the manuscript Tremellius used, together with Widmanstetter's first edition, to produce his own edition of the Syriac New Testament in Geneva in 1569. There was no Syriac type in Geneva at this time, and Tremellius was obliged to use Hebrew type (Figure 37.6).

Often bound with this New Testament is his grammar book of 1568, *Grammatica Chaldaea et Syra* in which, by using Widmanstetter's edition of 1555 and Vat. Sir. 16 as representatives of different stages of the later dialect of Syriac, he set about constructing a historical grammar of the development of Aramaic, upon which he based his understanding of Syriac. He had only Hebrew type, but he focused on the grammar of the whole of Aramaic, setting out vocalised paradigms after the manner of the great Hebrew grammarians, but morphological and other differences between earlier and later forms are given throughout and copiously referenced to occurrences in the Targums and the Syriac New Testament.

Tremellius's procedure with respect to the *editio princeps* was controversial. He held that in Vat. Sir. 16 he possessed an older text than the manuscripts to which Widmanstetter had access. Though the *editio princeps* was only partially vocalised and Vat. Sir. 16 not at all, Tremellius transcribed the text into Hebrew letters and then vocalised it in the light of the reconstruction of the history of Aramaic set out in his

~~105~~ 52 Pour l'hospital de Geneve

GRAMMATI-
CA CHALDAEA
ET SYRA,
JMMANVELIS TRE-
mellij, theologiæ doctoris et professoris
in schola Heidelbergensi.

Excudebat Henricus Stephanus,
M. D. LXIX.

Figure 37.6 Tremellius's Grammar

grammar and the assumption that the Syriac text came from early times: his older manuscript gave evidence of an older linguistic form of the text and that is what he was trying to restore. In short, he vocalised the text in what he considered the dialect appropriate to the time of its writing, *and not according to the barbarism of later vernacular Syriac*. This was a very specific aim: later Gabriel Sionita who was, of course, a native speaker would accuse Tremellius of 'Chaldeanising' the Syriac text in vocalising it, by which he meant correcting the vocalisation from that of the later dialect to that of the earlier. That, however, was exactly what Tremellius was consciously trying to do – to use an older manuscript to reconstruct the oldest possible form of a text he considered at least sub-Apostolic in date. It is clear that Tremellius had little interest in producing an edition for Eastern Christians in their own contemporary dialect. In fact, he went out of his way to prevent his edition being used in such a way, asking: Who would want a Demotic Demosthenes or an Italian Cicero? (Wilkinson 2007c).

Cornelius Bonaventura Bertramus (Bertram) was a Protestant student of the Parisian Scholars, Mercier and Caninius, who fled to Geneva to escape persecution, and there in 1574 he produced a comparative Hebrew and Aramaic Grammar: *Comparatio grammaticae hebraeae et aramaicae*. Like Tremellius, he had to make do with Hebrew type. What is of interest here is that beyond a comparison of Hebrew and Aramaic, we are offered a comparative account of Aramaic dialects which clearly isolates Syriac. The influence of Tremellius is clear. Bertram's remarks on Aramaic dialects are also notable inasmuch as he, quite exceptionally, does not confuse the later dialect of Syriac with the dialect spoken by Jesus.

John Gaspar Myricaeus (d. 1653), a German Swiss Reformed theologian and orientalist, in his two works, *The First Elements of the Syriac Language, the Vernacular of Jesus Christ* (1616) and *Two Books of Syro-Chaldaean Grammar* (1619), both printed in Geneva, stressed the double glory of Syriac as the language of Adam and of Christ (Amira had similarly considered Aramaic the language of Paradise.) The books use Johannes Richter's Wittenberg Serto type (Coakley 2006: 48–50).

ELIAS HUTTER

The last polyglot Bible of the sixteenth century to contain Syriac was not the product of a group of Catholic scholars, nor a Protestant project like the London Polyglot (Sporhan-Krempel and Wohnhass 1986). Rather it was the sole work of Elias Hutter (ca. 1553–1609) who studied oriental languages in Jena and was appointed professor of Hebrew at the University of Leipzig (1577–1579). He later taught and published in Nuremburg. Hutter can probably best be understood as an educational visionary and entrepreneur. One should not only read the Bible in different languages, he believed, but by understanding the principles of their construction, one will learn quickly to do so. The *Offentlich Außschreiben an allgemeine Christlische Obrigkeit* (Nuremburg 1602) gives an exposition of Hutter's notions of linguistic harmony. This is not just, as with others, a case of deriving Greek, Latin, and German (indeed all languages) from Hebrew. Rather, Hutter developed a morphological understanding of Hebrew (the isolation of the three radical letters which are the real bearers of meaning and the accidental letters which modify that meaning) to analyse the other languages. He demonstrates an organic similarity between the shape of their letters and postulates a common use of radical letters to claim that all became structurally transparent in the light of his analysis of Hebrew into radical and accidental letters(Arens 1955: 62).

Syriac appears in Hutter's Polyglot New Testament of 1599–1600, a handsomely printed Bible in twelve languages. It is given in Hebrew characters. Hutter appears to have little specific interest in Syriac other than as an early daughter of Hebrew and an illustration of his linguistic key, unfolding a structure in which the Holy Ghost had linked Hebrew to reality. We need not pursue Hutter further into the complexities of his mystical philosophy of language. He has no apparent interest in the Eastern Church, nor any interest in the differences in text and the minutiae of different vocalisations which would interest later Lutherans. Hutter was (alarmingly) content to add or subtract from those biblical texts he placed side-by-side in his Polyglot to make them concur, and was interested only in their proper structural analysis. His Syriac text is text-critically worthless.

OTHER LUTHERAN SCHOLARS – WITTENBERG

Other Lutheran scholars lacked the comprehensive and mystical insights of Hutter. What characterises them is a desire to develop what was available (often from the work of the Maronites); a thorough consolidation of understanding with attention paid to discrepancies in vocalisation and other details of previous grammars; an interest in establishing serviceable editions of the Scriptures; the production of helpful and accurate grammars for their students; and a desire to achieve a comparative context for the understanding of the languages. These scholars were generally careful philologists with a focus on biblical studies. Avid consumers of the earlier Catholic scholarship, they nonetheless worked to make it their own.

Increasingly we shall encounter comparative dictionaries and grammars – extending beyond merely the difference between Hebrew and Aramaic – which became increasingly popular. In the seventeenth century these tended to be called 'harmonic'. They are generally (but not all) less comprehensive and mystical than Hutter's and more straightforwardly empirical.

Valentin Schindler (1543–1604) was a Wittenberg Hebraist. With him we see a developing concern – evident already in Waser – to present grammar in a comparative context very much in parallel with the polyglot Bibles (in his case the Antwerp Polyglot). His *Lexicon Pentaglotton* was published posthumously in 1612. Here Schindler systematically developed his entries to display the similarities and filiation of Hebrew, Aramaic, and Arabic. He lists a root, gives information on its Hebrew meaning, and deals with words formed from it. He then does this for the Syriac and Arabic roots. As a model of a comparative lexicon, Schindler's work was influential and it remains, together with Hottinger (1661) and Castell (1669), one of only three comparative lexica of Semitic languages ever published.

Schindler was succeeded in 1592 by Laurentius Fabricius who taught Crinesius and Trost, who eventually succeeded his teacher in the Wittenberg chair of Hebrew in 1628. Like Crinesius, Trost gave serious attention to Syriac. Trost's pupil Andreas Sennert (1606–1689) worked in the Universities of Leipzig, Jena, Strasburg, and Leiden before returning to take the Hebrew chair at Wittenberg after Trost's successor, Jacob Weller. His career pathway passing through several universities of different Protestant confessions is illuminating. This was a subject with rare resources and few experts – one had to learn where one might. Increasingly these universities were developing formal teaching courses in Arabic, Aramaic, and Syriac. Jena began advertising Aramaic in 1601, though Wittenberg did not begin until 1632. Jena also offered the first formal course in Syriac in 1614. The following works we shall consider went some way to meet the demand for books suitable for these courses.

Christoph Crinesius's (1584–1629) Syriac Grammar, *Gymnasium Syriacum*, was printed in Wittenberg in 1611 and a *Lexicon Syriacum* followed in 1612. Crinesius repeated the lexical work of Masius and Guy Lefèvre de la Boderie essentially from the first edition of the New Testament and their other texts to produce an affordable dictionary in a convenient format for his students. Martin Trost (Trostius) (1588–1636) became professor of Hebrew at Wittenberg in 1629 in Fabricius's stead. Later he was to contribute to Walton's Polyglot Bible. In 1623, he brought out the largest Syriac Lexicon so far, his *Lexicon Syriacum*. He also published in 1621 the first Protestant edition of the Syriac New Testament to use Syriac characters (and the second after Tremellius). It was produced from previous printed editions and like Widmanstetter's edition omits the *Pericople adulterae* at John 8.1–11. The Richter Serto is used and vocalised. The editor relied upon his own careful analysis and consolidation rather than any new material or an authoritative teacher. Finally, Andreas Sennert (1606–1689), Trost's pupil, was in his turn professor of Hebrew at Wittenberg. His small quarto *Chaldaismus & Syriasmus* of 1651 displayed both languages together with Hebrew in a 'harmonic' grammar. Later in 1660, a more ambitious harmony of Aramaic in a growing network of Semitic languages was offered in his *Rabbinismus: h. e. Praecepta Targumico-Talmudico-Rabbinica*.

TÜBINGEN, JENA, ALTDOF, AND LEIPZIG

Wilhem Schickard (1592–1635) was appointed professor of Hebrew at the University of Tübingen in 1619(Ott 1995). He wrote a short harmonising work systematising the conjugations of five languages (Hebrew, Chaldean, Syriac, Arabic, and Ethiopic). He also left an unfinished Syriac grammar in manuscript written when he was a deacon in Nürtingen, which is now in the Universitätsbibliothek Freiburg. Their emphasis is upon comparison within an efficient pedagogic programme. A similar *Harmony* of Aramaic, Syriac, Arabic, and Ethiopic building upon Schickard's work was written by Johann Ernst Gerhard (1621–68), another Lutheran professor of theology at Jena. Gerhard was able to use Syriac (Arabic and a new Ethiopic) type. In 1649, Gerhard brought out another comparative work, his *Skiagraphia Linguae Syro-chaldaicae cum Analyseos Syriacae specimine*. Gerhard's own pupil Johann Michael Dilherr (1604–1669) in turn became professor of theology at Jena in 1640. His *Eclogae Sacrae Novi Testamenti, Syriacae, Graecae, Latinae* of 1637 was a selection of passages made from the whole New Testament. This was not just a matter of convenience: for reasons of rarity and cost, not every student could be expected to have even an edition of the Syriac New Testament. Other teachers would offer similar *excerpta*. Dilherr boldly ventured emendations to the newly available Syriac text of Jude (edited by Pococke, below). The work enjoys Syriac type (Richter's Serto). There are annotations on grammatical points and vocalisation: he discusses 'Chaldaeanising', the Eastern long /a/ and the Western long /o/. There is also consideration of others' errors: using *dagesh forte* as opposed to the use of Syriac *kuschoi* (seen as similar); gemination contrary to the practice of Amira and Sionita; shewas; silent letters (*alaph*) lost in pronunciation, and first person plural imperfects in /n/ rather than Syriac *yudh*. The work contains a *Censio in Scriptorem Tremellianum*. Dilherr makes reference (*z'l*) to Daniel Schwenterus (1585–1636), professor of sacred languages and professor of mathematics at Altdorf and his *Ventilatio Grammatica Gemina* of 1627. Schwenter addressed the vocalisation of the Syriac vowel sign *zqapha*, which he considered was pronounced /a/ (like a *Kametz Hebraeorum*) and not /o/. He also, like Dilherr, maintained that Syriac had no diphthongs.

J. A. Danzius (1654–1727) brought out his *Aditus Syriae reclusus, compendose ducens ad plenam linguae Syriacae Antiochenae seu Maronitae cognitionem* in Jena in 1689. In it, he argued that the language of the Maronites was not that of Christ, but rather that of Targums Jonathan and Onkelos. Hermann von der Hardt (1660–1746), professor of oriental languages at both Jena and Leipzig, was also given the chair of oriental languages in Helmstedt in 1690. His books of paradigms for his students, *Brevia atque Solida Syriacae Fundamenta* (1660) and *Elementa Syriaca in usum Auditorum suorum Helmestadi* (1694), have an evident didactic purpose but are less interesting than Hardt's attempt to derive not only Syriac but the other Semitic languages from Greek. This view received countenance from De Dieu and Hottinger. Finally, we may turn to Leipzig. Hieronymus Avianus, entertaining an interest in versification, produced a two-volume lexicon to facilitate the production of poetry. Words are listed by termination to facilitate the appreciation and composition of poetry which in these languages, rather than relying on quantity, uses rhythm, especially that of endings of words. There is sadly no Syriac type.

REFORMED SCHOLARS

The fruits of much of the developing Christian Aramaism were gathered in the works of solid textual scholarship exemplified for 135 years by the Buxtorfs – father, son, and grandson – with some sixty editions to their credit in Basel alone. The culmination of their work being perhaps the monumental *Lexicon Chaldaicum Talmudicum et Rabbinicum* (1639–40). J. Buxtorf *filius* (1599–1664) succeeded his father (1564–1629) as professor of Hebrew in Basel and became professor of theology in 1647.

J. Buxtorf *pater* had produced a Grammar of Aramaic and Syriac in Basel in 1615. He bewailed the lack of type in the Basel printing offices. His son produced his own Syriac Lexicon in 1622 with proper types.The Lexicon comprised Aramaic words from the Old Testament, the Targums, and the Syriac New Testament. He mentions Münster and Levita as predecessors. Buxtorf brought out his late father's Aramaic lexicon, the fruit of thirty years combined work, in 1639.

Other scholars maintained the distinguished standards that had been set. The Calvinist Louis De Dieu (1590–1642) studied at Leiden under Thomas Erpenius and Jacobus Golius before becoming regent of the Collège Wallon at Leiden. He brought out a Syriac edition of Revelation in 1627 which, together with Edward Pococke's Syriac edition of the Minor Catholic Epistles (2 Peter, 2–3 John, and Jude), was intended to complete the Syriac New Testament with the books absent from the ancient Peshiṭta. He published the first text of the *Pericope Adulterae* in 1631.His *Grammatica Linguarum Orientalium* of 1628displays together Hebrew, Chaldaean, and Syriac grammar.

Generally, he follows Buxtorf's vocalisation of Chaldaean, but is convinced that arbitrary European decisions rather than any rules of language are at work there. Buxtorf had done good work in emending Chaldaean vocalisings, but De Dieu felt there was a lot further to go in conforming the Chaldaean to the Syriac. Syriac grammar has surer rules than Chaldaean. He examines cases from Daniel correcting towards the Syriac. There is something of a new departure here. Jean Mercier had attempted to correct the Targums to Biblical Aramaic, and Tremellius had 'Chaldaeanised' the Syriac New Testament. Here De Dieu wishes to conform the Targums to Syriac! He expresses disagreement, however, with Erpenius on the writing of silent letters, having been advised by (reading) Gabriel Sionita,and he held that the stress (*tonus*) in Syriac generally falls on the penultimate syllable.

THE LONDON POLYGLOT BIBLE

Ten years after the Paris Polyglot, the printing of the London Polyglot, a peak of philological and typographical excellence, began (Miller 2001b; Schenker 2008: 781–4). It was principally the work of Brian Walton (1600?–1661), assisted by several other English scholars. The Syriac text was that of the Paris Polyglot, revised for the Old Testament by Walton with recourse to several manuscripts supplied by J. Ussher and E. Pococke (see Volume VI of 1657). In the New Testament, John 7:53–8:11 was printed from the manuscript of Ussher which De Dieu had previously used. Herbert Thorndyke (1598–1672), an orientalist and canon of Westminster Abbey,edited the Syriac portion. He was responsible for *Variantes in Syriaca versione Veteris Testamenti Lectiones e codicibus mss.* (also in Volume VI). John Viccars (1614–1660), by contrast from Oxford, also collaborated on the Polyglot. He produced a learned commentary on the Psalms, *Decapla in Psalmos: sive Commentarius ex decem linguis; viz. Hebr., Arab., Syriac., etc.*, which was published in 1639 and made use of manuscripts consulted in Paris and Rome. He shared with his brother Samuel the expense of new Arabic and Syriac types.

Christian Ravis (1613–1677) was an itinerant German orientalist and theologian, traveller, and manuscript collector. He played no part in the production of the Polyglot, yet produced the first English Grammar of Syriac, though setting the language in a rather unusual comparative context. His book, *A Generall Grammer for the Ebrew, Samaritan, Calde, Syriac, Arabic, and Ethiopic Tongue*, was published in London in 1648 and propounded his peculiar theory that these six languages are not merely related, but are in fact the same language (which may be called 'Arabic'). In spite of this, the *Discourse of the Orientall Tongues* printed in the *Grammer* is the first scholarly introduction to both Syriac and Arabic in English.

Far more substantial comparative work was done in the wake of the Polyglot project by Edmund Castell (1606–86), who had helped Walton and was appointed Professor of Arabic in Cambridge in 1666. His great work, the *Lexicon Heptaglotton Hebraicum, Chaldaicum, Syriacum, Samaritanum, Aethiopicum, Arabicum, et Persicum* (1669), took him eighteen years to complete, working (according to his own account) from sixteen to eighteen hours a day. He employed fourteen assistants on the project, and spent £12,000, ruining himself in the process, as there was little demand for his finished work.

The Syriac section was not the work of Castell but rather of William Beveridge (1638–1708), who had entered St John's College Cambridge in 1653 and in later life

(1704) became Bishop of St Asaph.Beveridge did his work badly.Perhaps he may be somewhat excused as at twenty years old he produced the first English Grammar solely of Syriac (though still, of course, in Latin). This appeared in 1658 in *De Linguarum Orientalium etc. praestantia et usu, cum Grammatica Syriaca* (London 1658, 1684). Thomas Roycroft, printer of the London Polyglot, used the Polyglot's type for Beveridge's *Grammatica Syriaca*.

The London Polyglot provided an enduring and definitive expression of seventeenth-century orientalism and biblical philology. It not only provided a complete Western canon of Scripture, particularly for Syriac, but also in supporting material gave scholarly definition to the languages involved. An *Introductio Ad Lectorem Linguarum Orientalium* (Roycroft, London 1655) provided a reading guide to the several scripts (pp. 39–55 for Syriac) and a *Praefatio* discussing the various languages. Walton's own *Dissertatio in qua de linguis orientalibus . . . disseritur* (1658) offers, for *lingua syriaca*, a compendious and authoritative statement subsequently widely cited. The comprehensive Prolegomena to the Polyglot deals with languages, scripts, editions, versions, and variant readings. Chapter 13, 'De Lingua Syriaca & Versionibus Syriacis', may be properly considered a full and authoritative statement of Syriac Studies to date. It thus marks the climax in our chosen period of Syriac's status as a learned biblical language, necessary for the study of the biblical text and enjoying edited texts, serviceable comparative and teaching grammars, and increasingly comprehensive lexicons.

NON-SCRIPTURAL BOOKS

The Syriac scholars of our period were very much busied by the establishment of the grammatical singularity of the language and the work of establishing editions of the biblical text. The progressive editing of the works of Syriac authors really got underway only towards the middle of the nineteenth century (Baumstark 1922: 3). Nonetheless, a beginning was made and two scholars of the Antwerp Polyglot may be considered to have attended the birth: Masius and Guy Lefèvre de la Boderie.

Masius published a Latin translation of Moses Bar Kepha's *De Paradiso* written ca. 850, from a text of Moses of Mardin (Wilkinson 2007a: 44). Masius was able to list the names of the authors Bar-Cepha mentioned. In 1572, Guy Lefèvre de la Boderie published *De Ritibus Baptismi*, a text and Latin translation of the Liturgy of Baptism and of the Eucharist attributed wrongly to Severus of Antioch (Wilkinson 2007b: 103–32). The *Dedicatoria Epistola* gives his motivation as confessional polemic and pedagogy. In 1653, Ecchellensis published in Rome a *Catalogue of Syriac Books* by ʿAbdishoʿ of Nisibis (d. 1318) taken from a manuscript found in Santa Croce in Gerusalemme near the Lateran and offering a native account of the corpus of Syriac literature. But in this case the motivation for the work was confessional controversy rather than the history of literature.

BIBLIOGRAPHY

Arens, H. 1955. *Sprachwissenschaft Der Gang ihrer Entwicklung von der Antike bis zur Gegenwart*. Freiburg/Munich: Verlag Karl Alber.

Baumstark, A. 1922. *Geschichte der syrischen Literatur*. Bonn: Weber.

Brock, S. P. 1994. The Development of Syriac Studies. *In*: K. J. Cathart, ed., *The Edward Hincks Bicentenary Lectures*. Dublin: University College, 94–113.

Castell, E. 1669. *Lexicon Heptaglotton, Hebraicum, Chaldaicum, Syriacum, Samaritanum, Aethiopicum, Arabicum, et Persicum*. London: Thomas Roycroft.

Coakley, J. F. 2006. *The Typography of Syriac a Historical Catalogue of Printing Types 1537–1958*. London: British Library.

Contini, R. 1994. Gli inizi della linguistica siriaca nell' "Europa rinascimentale". *RSO* 68, 15–30.

Copenhaver, B. and D. S. Kokin. 2014. Egidio da Viterbo's *Book on Hebrew Letters:* Christian Kabbalah in Papal Rome. *Renaissance Quarterly* 67/1, 1–42.

Debié, M. 2010. La grammaire syriaque d'Ecchellensis en contexte. *In*: B. Heyberger, ed., *Orientalisme, science et controverse: Abraham Ecchellensis (1605–1664)*. Turnhout: Brepols, 99–117.

Farina, M. 2012. La nascita della Tipografia Medicea: personaggi e idée. *In*: M. Farina and S. Fari, ed., *Le vie delle lettere La Typografia Medicea tra Roma e l'Oriente*. Florence: Mandragora, 43–72.

Gemayel, N. 1984. *Les échanges culturels entre les Maronites et l'Europe: du Collège maronite de Rome (1584) au Collège de 'Aya Warka (1789)*. Beirut: USEK.

Heyberger, B. 2010a. Abraham Ecchellensis dans la République des Lettres. *In:* B. Heyberger, ed., *Orientalisme, science et controverse: Abraham Ecchellensis (1605–1664)*. Turnout: Brepols, 9–51.

——— (ed.). 2010b. *Orientalisme, science et controverse: Abraham Ecchellensis (1605–1664)*. Turnout: Brepols.

Hottinger, J. H.1661. *Etymologicon orientale, sive Lexicon harmonicum heptaglotton*. Wilhelmi Ammonij & Wilhemi Serlini: Francofurti.

Hutter, E. 1602. *Offentlich Außschreiben an allgemeine Christlische Obrigkeit*. Nuremberg.

Kaufhold, H. 2010. Abraham Ecchellensis et le Catalogue des Livres de 'Abdisho Bar Brika. *In:* B. Heyberger, ed., *Orientalisme, science et controverse: Abraham Ecchellensis (1605–1664)*. Turnout: Brepols, 119–33.

Miller, P. N. 2001a. Making the Paris Polyglot Bible: Humanism and Orientalism in the Early Seventeenth Century. *In* H. Jaumann, ed., *Die europäische Gelehrtenrepublik im Zeitalter des Konfessionalismus*. Wiesbaden: Harrassowitz Verlag, 59–85.

———. 2001b. The 'Antiquarianization' of Biblical Scholarship and the London Polyglot Bible (1653–57). *Journal of the History of Ideas* 62/3, 463–82.

Nestle, E. 1904. Aus einem sprachwissenschaftichen Werk von 1539. *ZDMG* 58, 601–16.

Ott, C. 1995. Schickard als Orientalist – verkannter Genie oder interessierte Laie? *In:* F. Seck, ed., *Zum 400. Geburtstag von Wilhelm Schickard Zweite Tübinger Schickard Symposion*. Sigmaringen: Thorbecke, 117–30.

Raphael, P. 1950. *Le Rôle du Collège maronite romain dans L'Orientalisme aux XVIIe et XVIIIe siècles*. Beirut: Université Saint Joseph de Beyrouth.

Rietbergen, P. J. A. N. 1989. A Maronite Mediator Between Seventeenth-Century Mediterranean Cultures: Ibrahim al-Hakilani or Abraham Ecchellense (1605–1664): Between Christendom and Islam. *Lias* 16/1, 13–41.

Schenker, A. 2008. The Polyglot Bibles of Antwerp, Paris and London (1568–1658). *In:* M. Saebø, ed., *Hebrew Bible/Old Testament The History of its Interpretation II From the Renaissance to the Enlightenment*. Göttingen: Vandenhoeck & Ruprecht, 774–84.

Sporhan-Krempel, L. and T. Wohnhass. 1986. Elias Hutter in Nuremburg und seine Biblia in etlichen Sprachen. *Archiv für Geschichte des Buckwesens* 27, 157–62.

Wilkinson, R. J. 2007a. *Orientalism, Aramaic and Kabbalah in the Catholic Reformation: The First Printing of the Syriac New Testament*. Leiden: Brill.

———. 2007b. *The Kabbalistic Scholars of the Antwerp Polyglot Bible*. Leiden: Brill.

———. 2007c. Emanuel Tremellius' 1568 Edition of the Syriac New Testament. *JEH* 58/1, 9–25.
———. 2012. Syriac Studies in Rome in the Second Half of the Sixteenth Century. *JLARC* 6, 55–74.
———. 2016. Constructing Syriac in Latin – Establishing the Identity of Syriac in the West Over a Century and a Half (c.1550–c.1700): An Account of Grammatical and Extra-Linguistic Determinants. *Babelao (Bulletin de l'Académie belge pour l'étude des langues anciennes et orientales)* 5, 169–283.

CHAPTER THIRTY-EIGHT

SYRIAC IDENTITY IN THE MODERN ERA

Heleen Murre-van den Berg

INTRODUCTION

At the bethsuryoyo.com website, postcards are offered to commemorate the Syriac genocide of 1915. One of the cards carries the sentence 'Assyrian – Syriac – Chaldean – Aramean. United Even in Death. Sayfo 1915'. The text overlays a gruesome black-and-white picture of severed heads that are being pierced upon sticks, now lying on the ground. Along each of the four sticks, one of the four names has been printed.[1] The combination between remembering the Sayfo, as the genocide is usually called in Syriac Orthodox circles, and the multiplicity of voices that have a stake in this culture of remembrance could hardly have been expressed more graphically. However, the apparent need for such an over-explicit statement of inter-denominational unity indicates that such unity is not at all given and straightforward.

In the current essay, a brief overview of the history of the Syriac churches in the period since the Ottomans became the major power in the region in the early sixteenth century will serve to trace the history of these new ways of conceptualising what in this essay will be called the 'Syriac' communities. How did the two Syriac churches of the Middle East, the 'East Syriac' Assyrian Church of the East and the 'West Syriac' Syriac Orthodox Church, each split into two branches, a Catholic (Chaldean and Syriac Catholic) and a traditional one? What was the influence of the later Protestant missions that not only led to the emergence of Syriac and Assyrian Protestant churches but also contributed to a fundamental political and religious re-orientation of these communities? And when and how did this diversity of churches start to think of itself as one nation?[2]

Before starting our overview in the early sixteenth century, a few words on terminology are in place. Considering the thoroughly politicised nature of the identitarian discussions, it comes as no surprise that the names for the group as a whole as well as for its constituent parts are all contended. No nomenclature is universally agreed on, not in scholarly circles and not in the Syriac communities. In the current essay, I have chosen to use 'Syriac' as the epithet to refer to the group of churches and people identifying with these churches. This usage builds upon the earlier scholarly usage of 'West' and 'East' Syrian churches, with Syriac[3] referring to the

Classical Syriac language that plays a role in all of these churches and communities. These include the traditional Syriac Orthodox Church, the Assyrian Church of the East, and the Ancient Assyrian Church of the East, as well as the Catholic churches that derived from it: the Syriac Catholic Church and the Chaldean Church. It also includes the Protestant communities that continue to identify as part of the larger community, using the name 'Assyrian' or 'Syriac'. These Syriac churches are the major subject of this contribution. Note that the term 'Syriac' is often used in a wider sense to include the Maronite Church with its major base in Lebanon as well as the Syriac ('Thomas') churches of India. Most of the Indian churches have direct ecclesial links to the Syriac churches mentioned above; others, however, have become autocephalous or have united with Protestant churches. In varying degrees, they share the other Syriac churches' links with Syriac-language liturgy, Bible, and theological literature.

BACK ONTO THE WORLD STAGE: THE SYRIAC CHURCHES (1500–1800)

The period was characterised by a succession of rulers whose armies had little concern for local inhabitants, be they Muslim, Christian, or else. In addition, the bubonic plague wrought havoc, accompanied by widespread famines that resulted from a combination of climate change and war devastations. The dioceses in Central Asia disappeared, no regular connections between India and the Middle East were maintained, and church building and manuscript production in the heartlands were at low levels even if theological writing and thinking continued to be practiced.

Just before the Ottomans in the early sixteenth century conquered many of the regions that are the focus of our discussions, change had started to set in. In the late fifteenth century, Indian Christians from the Church of the East arrived in Gazarta Zabdayta (Cizre), where the patriarch of the Church of the East held his court. In all likelihood, it was the arrival of the Portuguese, impressing them with their military prowess in service of Christian colonialism, that encouraged these Christians to revive their own Christian networks. In turn, the Indian relations with Rome via the Portuguese and the Jesuit missionaries provided one of the incentives for Yuhannan Sulaqa, abbot of Rabban Hormizd, a monastery in North Mesopotamia, to seek help in Rome after he had challenged the patriarch of the Church of the East over a proposal for a successor from among his family. Sulaqa, provided with letters from the Jerusalem Franciscans, arrived in Rome in 1552. Early in 1553, he was consecrated by Pope Julius III as patriarch of the Catholic (later to be called 'Chaldean') Church of the East. While this first union between the Church of the East and Rome would not hold long, it inaugurated a period of intense and frequent contacts between the two churches; contacts that were initiated and maintained by the Syriac clergy as often as by Catholic missionaries.

A similar trajectory played out for the Syriac Orthodox Church. The first attempts at a union took place in 1551, and as with the developments in the Church of the East, it took until the late eighteenth century before a stable hierarchy was established. Like the Chaldean Church, the Syriac Catholic Church was strongest in urban contexts: in Mosul, Diyarbakir, and Mardin Syriac Catholic, Chaldean, and Catholic

Armenian communities were formed, whereas more extensive and long-term missionary presence and diplomatic protection made Aleppo into a major hub of Catholicism in the region. The majority of the Catholics in Aleppo belonged to the Maronite or Greek Catholic church, but Syriac Catholics and a small Chaldean community were also present.

In general, Ottoman courts (both locally and in Istanbul) tended to prevent all too easy transfer of churches and other possessions into the hands of the new Catholic churches. At the same time, however, they were not completely against such changes, and if there was sufficient support in the community for a separate hierarchy, they allowed its legalisation. In practice, these new communities often enjoyed much the same rights as the older Christian communities, building upon the rights of the 'people of the book' in Muslim societies. For communal leaders as much as for individual Christians, whether traditionally orthodox or Catholic, there were various recourses to justice, also outside the Christian communal patterns. Most important were the sharia courts, where also Christians and Jews could present their (civil and criminal) cases to a Muslim judge.

When looking at the Ottoman period from the perspective of the development of a new Syriac identity, three observations can be made. Firstly, contrary to expectation, the arrival of the Catholics did not necessarily lead to unbridgeable separations between the traditional and the Catholic parties. Both clergy and lay people would change sides fairly easy, and although the discussions were often fierce, the boundaries between the parties were fluid and kept moving. Given the fact that commitment to the Catholic cause often resulted from a mix of theological, familial, regional, and linguistic reasons, this is not surprising: their relative importance may easily change over time. Secondly, these fluid boundaries allowed the religious and societal modernisation that was introduced by the Catholic missionaries to permeate these Christian communities much further than the Catholic communities in the strict sense. Catholic influence in matters of popular devotion (think of new types of images, the rosary, and the introduction of new saints), the renewal of monastic life, and the importance of religious education of the clergy to better educate the lay believers became in this period part of the common heritage of the Middle Eastern world, of the traditionally orthodox as much as of the newly converted Catholics.

Thirdly, this period witnessed the emergence of a new understanding and appreciation of the Syriac literary heritage. While the majority of those within the Syriac communities may hardly have noticed their efforts, Maronite scholars such as Joseph Assemani, in cooperation with learned clergy from other Syriac churches as well as with European scholars, began to collect Syriac sources and treat these as a distinct heritage in need of collection, edition, translation and study. For the first time, *Bibliotheca Orientalis* brought together Syriac and related Arabic literature from the three major Syriac churches, Maronite, Syriac Orthodox and Church of the East, thus opening up this literature for scholars in West and East. By bringing together texts from all Syriac traditions into one (multi-volume) study, Assemani almost single-handedly created 'Syriac' literature. While this did not prevent later scholars from concentrating on the separate literary traditions, the awareness that 'Syriac literature' superseded these ecclesial boundaries had become part of the scholarly tradition.

NEW COMMUNAL IDENTITIES: THE BIRTH OF THE NATION (1800–1910)

Assemani's *Bibliotheca Orientalis* was one of the works that were studied by the early Protestant missionaries when they prepared for their activities among the East Syriac Christians of Iran. Works such as this made them aware of the fact that whatever the humble state of these Christians in the early nineteenth century might be, their ancestors' church had been much larger than its contemporary successor, with dioceses reaching into Persia, Central Asia, China, and India. It also made these American missionaries aware of the wealth of Syriac literature, leading them to cite early Syriac sources on schools and education in their newly founded missionary journal, *Zahrire d-Bahra* ('Rays of Light'), to publish translations of such texts in *Zahrire d-Bahra*, or to publish editions of texts in American scholarly journals.

After a preparatory period, Presbyterian missionaries of the American Board of Commissioners of Foreign Missions (ABCFM) started their mission in Urmia (in north-western Iran) officially in 1834. The station grew rapidly, with schools not only in Urmia but also in the mountain (Hakkari) districts, with a printing press from 1840 onwards, and with literature using a standardised form of vernacular Aramaic. One of the missions' major publishing projects was the translation and printing of the Bible in the vernacular, in parallel columns alongside an edition based on the early Classical Syriac translation, the Peshitta. The New Testament was published in 1846, the Old Testament in 1852. These activities all intended to contribute to the revival of the Syriac Christian community that the missionaries thought had lost much of its immediate connection to its spiritual sources because faith had become a matter of communal belonging rather than of personal faith. By stimulating Syriac Christians to read the Bible, the missionaries hoped to set them on a path of praying their own extempore prayers rather than the ritual prayers of the church, to examine their private conscience in order to acknowledge their sinfulness, and to experience divine forgiveness in a personal and highly emotional way. Incorporating Syriac Christians into this new spiritual world was also the larger aim of the schools, especially of the boarding schools for boys and girls where missionaries and pupils lived in close proximity.

Among the Syriac Orthodox Christians of Eastern Anatolia similar missionary activities were started, also by the ABCFM. In comparison to Urmia, the general reception was less enthusiastic, especially in hilly Ṭur ʿAbdin where the traditional church was strong. The work in Midyat led to the organisation of a small Protestant church, but no full Bible translation in the vernacular was produced, partly because the tradition of writing in Classical Syriac was considerably stronger here than it was among the Church of the East, and partly because Arabic was an important vernacular in the southern areas of this region. It was especially in the town of Harput, where the mission work was focused mostly on Armenians, that Syriac students were attracted to the schools and other activities of the missionaries. Students that were trained here influenced their families and friends in the wider Syriac Orthodox community, including Ṭur ʿAbdin.

As suggested by the missionaries' interest in the earlier glorious history of the Syriac Christians, the awakening the missionaries envisaged was to entail more than the revival of individual Christians. They hoped that individual spiritual awakening would lead to a communal awakening, transforming the traditional church into a reformed community that would start to missionise local Muslims and would venture out to Central Asia and China to convert the masses of Asia to Christianity. What actually happened was entirely different, though the impact was still substantial. In the 1860s, rather than transforming the church as a whole, the small Protestant community began to organise itself separately from the much larger traditional church. At the same time, new missions – Anglican, Catholic, and Lutheran – started their work in the Urmia region, each gaining their own supporters. In this increasingly religiously diverse context, the term 'Syriac' more and more explicitly became that of the group as a whole, the *mellat suryaya*, the 'Syriac nation' rather than the Church of the East, emphasising national unity over denominational difference.[4]

It is important to note that the increased use of such 'nationalist' terminology precedes the use of the term 'Assyrian'. This term starts being attested in *Zahrire de Bahra* in the 1880s and 1890s, building upon a complex interplay of the new historical sensitivity and appreciation of 'Classical' and pre-Christian history as introduced by the missionaries, the discovery of rich and impressive Assyrian remains in North Iraq in areas where East Syriac Christians lived, and the rediscovery of references in Syriac sources to the pre-Christian history of the Christians of the region. Its first usage, mostly in combination with *mellat*, seems largely parallel to 'Syriac', indicating the wider East Syriac community, separate from and transcending denominational differentiation. It took some time for this to become normative usage: even *Kokhwa* ('The Star'), the explicitly nationalist journal that was published from June 1906 onwards, carried the subtitle 'Journal of the Syriac nation' (*ruznama d-mellat suryayta*).

About the time when the term 'Assyrian' became wedded to explicit nationalist aims in Urmia in the early twentieth century, the term is also attested among Syriac Orthodox in Anatolia, especially in Harput. Though more research is needed, it is clear that 'Assyrian' in West Syriac contexts soon implied the unification of all Syriac Christians under a 'national', non-religious, banner. For some this included striving for a homeland and some measure of independence, for others identification with this particular national identity could be combined with integration into the pre-war empires and the nation-states that were to follow.

CLASHING NATIONALISMS AND THE SYRIACGENOCIDE (1910–1920)

Rather than this emerging Assyrian nationalism, however, it would be the clash of Turkish, Russian, and Armenian nationalisms that would provide the impetus to the largest genocide to date on the Syriac Christians, which took place mostly in 1915. Inspired by the separatist movements of the Greeks, Romanians, and Serbs, Armenian activists in Anatolia were envisioning a separation from the Ottoman Empire, perhaps with the help of Russia. Successive Ottoman administrations had tried to tie non-Muslims closer to the state by awarding equal rights regardless of religion to the non-Muslim communities, but failed to create a firm basis for inclusive Ottoman citizenship. While Christians were not satisfied with what the Ottomans offered, Muslims increasingly resented the growing public presence of Christians, even more so because the foreign powers kept pressuring the Ottoman administration for further reforms. This stimulated the emergence of a Turkish nationalism that excluded Arab and Kurdish Muslims as much as Armenians, Greeks, Serbs, Syriacs, and Jews.

The same factors that made Turkish nationalism triumph over Ottoman nationalism contributed to the genocidal politics of Turkey during the First World War. The Armenians were the first and primary victims of this, since they were perceived as allies of the Russians in the vulnerable eastern border zones. After some of the Armenians took up arms against the Turks to fight for Russia and their own independence, they were quickly cast as Turkey's major problem in the East. Given the lingering resentment against Christian progress over the last decades among Anatolian Kurdish populations, local troops needed little encouragement to engage in major operations against the Armenians, often including Syriacs among them. Starting in April 1915, upon orders from the centre, Armenian men were rounded up and killed, while their families were ordered to leave their homes and were marched out of their homelands. Many perished along the way to the Syrian desert, others were killed by marauding bands or by those that were supposed to protect them. Some survived the horrors, as wives and slaves in Muslim homes in Anatolia, as children in orphanages in Lebanon and Syria, and as refugees in Lebanon, Syria, Palestine, and Jordan. After the war, many migrated to the Americas, whereas others settled into new lives in the French and British Mandate areas.

The destruction of the Syriac communities in Anatolia was less systematic and complete than that of the Armenians. Sometimes local officers distinguished between the two communities, sparing the Syriacs, in other locations all Christians were killed indiscriminately. Most victims were from the Syriac Orthodox communities, but the Chaldean communities of Diyarbakir, Seert, and Mardin were also hit hard. As with the Armenians, those who survived the marches into Syria generally did not return but built up new lives elsewhere in the Middle East and in the Americas. The less systematic killing of the Syriac Christians as compared to the Armenians indicates that sometimes local circumstances mitigated the general anti-Christian sentiments. However, the great losses in the Diyarbakir province among all Christians (Chaldeans, Syriac Catholics, Syriac Orthodox, and Armenians) undeniably proves that securing the border region with Russia and Persia was far from being the only reason for expulsion and massacre.

The Assyrians in Hakkari and Iran were drawn into the war already in the autumn of 1914, when they refused to be drafted into the Ottoman army. Then, low-level violence against the Assyrians began, increasing after Turkish and Kurdish troops entered Iran early in 1915. They drove away the Russian troops, attacking and massacring Christian villages on the way. Most Christians from the Urmia and Salmas plains fled to Urmia, taking refuge in the Protestant and Catholic mission compounds. In May, the Assyrian patriarch declared war on Turkey and officially sided with the Allied forces, mostly the Russians and Armenians, later also the British. The Assyrian forces put up an extended fight against Turkish and Kurdish troops, holding parts of the mountains until early in 1918 though suffering many casualties, military and civilian. When the Russians retreated for the second time in the winter of 1917/1918, the situation quickly deteriorated for the Assyrians and Armenians and many again fled to the missionary compounds. In 1918, a large group sought British protection in a flight via Hamadan to the Baʿquba in Iraq.

The First World War thus heavily impacted the Syriac communities, resulting in the complete cleansing of Hakkari of Christians, in much reduced communities in

Ṭur ʿAbdin and the Urmia region, and in new or enlarged refugee communities in Iraq, Palestine, Lebanon, Syria, Georgia, Armenia, the Americas, and Europe. Only the communities of Syria and North Iraq, in cities like Aleppo, Homs, Mosul, and Alqosh, survived the war relatively unscathed. However, whether directly or indirectly affected by the war, for all Syriac Christians the first Middle Eastern genocide of the twentieth century cast a dark shade on whatever hopes there were for building modern states in which Christians and Muslims, Turks and Syriacs, and Arabs and Kurds could live together. This dark shadow of lingering Christian distrust of Muslims has played a role in societal and political decisions until the present day.

THE SYRIAC CONTRIBUTION TO THE MIDDLE EAST (1920–1970)

In the post-war states, Christians and Muslims shared a commitment to a form of secularism where religion, if not completely within the private, occupied more restricted roles in the public domain. This allowed Syriac Christians to participate in social and political life. In Turkey, the decimated Syriac Orthodox community led by patriarch Ignatius Eliyas III Shaker did not press for minority status, in contradistinction to the remaining Armenian and Greek Christians who were given special rights as to education in their own languages. However, patriarch Eliyas's loyalty did not protect him from government harassment, and in 1924/1925 he was forced to leave Turkey and settle the patriarchate in Homs, Syria. The remaining Syriac Orthodox managed to rebuild their community, but until today continue to suffer from harassment and restrictions in the field of language and education.

Syriac Orthodox in Lebanon, Syria, and Palestine generally kept a low profile and were able to profit from the relative stability in those countries. In Palestine, they kept aloof from the growing tension between Jewish Zionists and Arab-Palestinian nationalists, even if the latter included Christians of various denominations. This did not prevent the Syriac Christians from being affected by the war of 1948 and by the Israeli annexation of the Old City of Jerusalem in 1967, both of which impacted their neighbourhoods in Jerusalem. The latest threat is the increased isolation of the Bethlehem community, shut off from Jerusalem by the separation wall and the accompanying security measures. In Lebanon, the small Syriac Christian community was able to profit from the open atmosphere, both before and after independence. The Syriac Catholics made Sharfeh their headquarters, with the patriarch located alternatively in Sharfeh and Beirut. The Syriac Orthodox made Syria their home. Sizable communities of Syriac Orthodox had lived there already before the war, in and around the central city of Homs and in north-eastern Jazeera, in and around Hassake. After the war, the communities of Jazeera and Aleppo were enlarged by refugees from Ṭur ʿAbdin. In 1959, the patriarchate moved from Ḥoms to Damascus. In 1996, patriarch Ignatius Zakka I ʿIwas consecrated an impressive monastic complex in Maʿarat Saidnaya, where seminary training for Syriac Orthodox students from all over the world was to take place.

In Iraq, Chaldeans (who formed the majority of Iraq's Christians), Syriac Orthodox, Syriac Catholics, and part of the Assyrians chose a similar route of integration into the state, without special minority status. The Hakkari Assyrians in the Baʿquba camp, however, were not so easily co-opted. After their ancestral region became part of Turkey in 1923, preventing any resettlement there, they lobbied for semi-independence in North Iraq. The Iraqi state was not willing to accommodate them, fearing to upset the delicate power balance in the state with many religious and ethnic minorities living together. In addition, Assyrian support of the British, whose Mandate rule was coming to an end, was framed as disloyalty to the nascent Iraqi state. Though the small number of Assyrians did not pose any real threat, this framing set the stage for a massacre by army troops on disarmed men in Semele, in August 1933. Further massacres and looting in the region were tacitly supported by the army. The clash ended with the deportation of the young Assyrian patriarch Mar Shimun Eshai who, after a stay on Cyprus, settled in Chicago in 1940. His supporters were allowed to settle in the nearby Khabur region in Syria under French Mandate rule.

While the Semele incident showed how conflicting ideas about religious and nationalist communal identities could lead to violence, in general Christians did fairly well in the period between 1930 and 1970. Syriac Christians were politically active especially in Syria and Iraq, mostly in the socialist Baath party and in the communist parties. Christians often occupied important positions in journalism, public government, education, health care, and politics, even if almost never in the top positions. The major societal struggles were between the socialist and communist parties, and, especially in Iraq, between the Kurds and the central government. Christians were on all sides of these conflicts and seldom were targeted because of their Christianity. The period further saw increased urbanisation and the accompanying building of churches and educational institutes. Baghdad in particular welcomed a large Christian population which in majority belonged to one of the Syriac churches.

So far, the developmental lines of 'Syriac identity' of this period remain sketchy. In countries like Lebanon, Palestine, Syria, and Iraq, many Arabic-speaking Syriac Christians tended to identify with majority Arab identity. At the same time, others, also when Arabic was their main language, continued to see themselves as different from 'Arab' Christianity. For some, this difference was covered by the term 'Assyrian', which was in fairly common use, both in the Middle East and the diaspora, among West Syriac as well as among the East Syriac communities. While the use of this term for the Syriac Orthodox Church ('Assyrian' Orthodox Church) may have been motivated to avoid confusion with the Syrian Antiochian (Rum Orthodox) Church, it also implied acceptance of the wider Assyrian discourse, even if it did not carry the antagonistic nationalist overtones of today. In 1952, the Syriac Orthodox Church officially forbade the term, ending its use as loosely synonymous to 'Syriac' or 'Aramean'. Nevertheless, many individuals and churches continued to use the name, for social or political reasons. In 1950, a new nationalist party was established in Qamishli (Jazeera) Syria, the Assyrian Democratic Organization (ADO), with participants from the Syriac Orthodox, Assyrian, Protestant, and Catholic communities.

THE WEIGHT OF TRANSNATIONALISM (1970–2010)

The term Assyrian further politicised when in the 1970s diaspora communities gained political weight. Towards the end of the 1960s, migration of Syriac Christians accelerated. It started with the war between the Turkish state and the PKK (Kurdistan Workers' Party) which caught Syriac Christians in the middle. Already before the war broke out in full in the 1980s, some had settled as labour migrants to Europe in Germany, Sweden, and the Netherlands, easing the way for others to follow as asylum seekers when the situation in Ṭur ʿAbdin became increasingly dangerous. The first dioceses were instituted in north-western Europe in the early 1980s, adding a new destination to the earlier concentrations in the Arab Middle East, Caucasus/ Russia, North and South America, and Australia. By the early 1990s, the Syriac population of eastern Anatolia had shrunk to a couple of thousand people who feared Kurdish oppression as much as Turkish restrictions on their religious and cultural life. The communities in Europe and Australia received further Syriac Orthodox from the Jazeera region. While socio-economic motives played a role, some came as asylum seekers after participating in ADO that had joined the political opposition against Hafez al-Assad. The civil war in Lebanon (1975–1990) provided the impetus for yet another group of Syriac migrants.

Religion as a political factor had never really left the Middle East, but its return to the limelight is symbolised by the Islamic revolution in Iran of 1979. Though little of the revolutionary violence was specifically targeted at Christians, the upheaval provided another impetus for migration. Their numbers in the diaspora were augmented by Iraqi and Iranian Assyrians who fled the consequences of the Iran-Iraq War in the 1980s. In the final stages of this war, Iraq's brutal suppression of Kurdish political opposition also targeted Assyrian villages in North Iraq, whereas the occupation of Kuwait in 1990, the American military intervention of 1991, and the ensuing economic boycott made living conditions in Baghdad increasingly difficult. All of this encouraged Christians to leave the country. Soon after the US-led invasion of 2003, Iraq spiralled into a bloody civil strife during which Christians were among the express targets of the violence: churches, shops, and businesses were attacked, individuals were kidnapped for ransom, and women who were not properly veiled were threatened with acids. Many more Christians fled the country, or, if that was not possible, sought refuge in Iraqi Kurdistan that remained relatively stable. In 2014 and 2015, the rise of ISIS (Daesh) drove many more Syriac Christians from their homes, in Mosul and the Nineveh plains, in the Jazeera region and in Homs and its environs. For places like Mosul and Homs, this meant the end of long and stable periods of Christian presence, for the Jazeera region it meant the uprooting of Christians whose parents and grandparents had found refuge there after the horrors of the First World War.

The immediate result of all these migratory movements was the relative strengthening of Syriac communities outside the Middle East, and thus the increased weight of the diaspora vis-à-vis the remaining communities in the Middle East. While both nationalists and clerical leaders encouraged their flocks to remain in the region, many people chose what they thought would be best for their children, moving to countries with more educational and societal opportunities, leaving behind the societal discrimination and lingering fear that comes with being a Christian in a Muslim-dominated state. With the move to the West, however, came new fears and new types of discrimination: the fear of gradual assimilation of the community into mainstream culture, of becoming indistinguishable from the majority, while at the same time being discriminated against on grounds of name, accent, and appearance, as much as religion and culture. Much of what happened in the diaspora communities may be explained by the wish to counteract these two seemingly opposing fears of dissolution and discrimination.

The churches have invested enormous efforts in creating parishes and dioceses and in building churches and monasteries. In general, an ecclesial infrastructure has been successfully established, replicating the patterns of the homelands. The Syriac Orthodox have been active in the field of education, teaching Classical Syriac and sometimes the vernacular (earlier indicated as 'Ṭuroyo', now usually as 'Surayt'), and having recently (2015) inaugurated a programme of Syriac Theology at the Catholic Faculty of the University of Salzburg. In addition, all Syriac churches have been active in ecumenical dialogue, at the local and national levels in Councils of Churches, and with the Roman Catholic, other oriental and Eastern Orthodox Churches, especially via the Pro Oriente meetings in Vienna. Whereas community building and ecclesial modernisation have helped Syriac Christians to identify with their ecclesial communities, such activities also encourage denominalisation, in which Syriac churches adopt Western denominationalism without sufficiently addressing the differences between such denominations and Middle Eastern ethno-religious communities. Most importantly, this concerns the problem that in the West ecclesial affiliation is considered a matter of free individual choice, whereas in the Syriac churches it is also, and perhaps primarily, based on those familial and ethnic characteristics that most people consider an immutable given.

It is this tension that is being addressed by a plethora of cultural organisations and political parties. All of these attempt to build a secular ethnic identity, with or without nationalist aspirations, which fits the neat distinctions between religious and national identities that appear to be the norm in most Western societies. However, it becomes increasingly clear, in the Middle East, in Syriac communities, and in Western societies, that longstanding connections between religion and communal, 'ethnic' or 'national', identities are not so easily separated. This means not only that discrimination and exclusion form an intrinsic part of the diaspora experience, but also that 'unity' between the various Syriac parties is set up against the embodied communal experience of the separate churches with their own rites.

While the diaspora struggled with the demands of Western societies, the political developments in Iraq from the 1990s onwards posed a challenge to Assyrian political parties. First within the autonomous Kurdish region in the north and from 2003 also in the central government, Assyrian parties participated in the fast-moving political landscape. On the one hand, this provided as yet unprecedented possibilities for very tangible political influence, especially in the north, where Syriac Christians were able to build up a cultural and educational infrastructure, especially for teaching in and about Syriac. At the same time, the potential political gains also exacerbated existing rivalries, especially between the Assyrian and Chaldean factions, with some Chaldeans, particularly those in the central areas, tending to differentiate themselves from the Assyrian parties. Overall, and despite many difficulties, it is in Iraqi Kurdistan that something of an overarching Syriac identity has begun to take shape, in the midst of ongoing debate about its boundaries, cultural and linguistic characteristics, and political consequences.

CONCLUSIONS

In the midst of yet another phase of great uncertainty for the Syriac Christians, the first point to make in conclusion is that due to the small size of the communities,

Syriac Christians in the early modern and modern periods have always been to a great extent dependent on changing political circumstances. It is only through a careful analysis of these circumstances that one is able to understand the choices of earlier generations who were trying to carve out an existence for themselves amidst violence or at best a general indifference to their fate. It is these circumstances that have contributed to the emergence and current shape of something like a shared 'Syriac' identity, even if often other terms are used. This is most clearly the case for the history of genocide, expulsion, and marginalisation vis-à-vis a dominant Muslim majority. Much of modern Syriac identity is based on this shared history, committing Syriac Christians to their Christian identity more than anything else.

In the wider context of modernisation and secularisation, the appropriation of pre-Christian, 'secular' history was added to this, under the Assyrian, Aramean, or Chaldean flag. Underlying this is the growing awareness of a shared cultural history in the Syriac language, expressed in literary histories and an emphasis on language education. At the same time, despite more than a century of pan-Syriac activism, ecclesial boundaries remain of utmost importance. It is the church communities in which Syriac Christians are brought up which constitute the first circle of family and friends. Whatever social, cultural, and political reasons there may be for adding to this the layer an overarching Syriac ('Assyrian'/'Aramean') identity, for most people this addition would not elicit the same loyalties as the familial-regional-ecclesial basis of the church.

The future of the Syriac communities will largely depend upon how these conflicting tendencies develop, between church and pan-Syriac identities, between church and secular leadership, and between assimilation and isolation. Regardless of these varying circumstances, however, this overview also points to the enduring resilience of the Syriac communities, a resilience that will be able to survive and perhaps even flourish in the vibrant world of the transnational communities of homeland and diaspora.

NOTES

1 Assyrian Genocide of 1915 – Sayfo Remembrance Cards. Online at: www.bethsuryoyo.com/cards/Sayfo/Sayfo.html (last seen 19/08/18).

2 For this brief overview, article referencing has been kept to a minimum; for basic textbooks and a few specialised articles, the reader is referred to the bibliography at the end.

3 I follow the Syriac Orthodox Church that started to use Syriac rather than Syrian in English in its official name and its derivatives, in order to be able to distinguish between 'Syrian' as related to the nation-state of Syria, and 'Syriac' as related to the Syriac-heritage churches.

4 Alongside *mellat* (parallel to the Turkish term millet, from Arabic millā), also *ṭayepa* ('people' > ṭaʿifa) was used; for an extensive discussion of these and other terms (including their Classical Syriac parallels ʿamma (people) and umtha (nation) that became more popular over time), see Becker 2015, Atto 2011, and Jakob 2014.

BIBLIOGRAPHY

Assemani, J. S. 1725–8. *Bibliotheca Orientalis Clementino-Vaticana, in Qua Manuscriptos Codices Syriacos, Arabicos, Persicos, Turcicos. . . .* Rome: Ex typogr. congreg. de propaganda fidei.

Atto, Naures. 2011. *Hostages in the Homeland, Orphans in the Diaspora: Identity Discourses Among the Assyrian/Syriac Elites in the European Diaspora*. Leiden: University Press.
Bakker Kellogg, Sarah. 2015. Ritual Sounds, Political Echoes: Vocal Agency and the Sensory Cultures of Secularism in the Dutch Syriac Diaspora. *American Ethnologist* 42(3), 431–45.
Baum, Wilhelm and Dietmar W. Winkler. 2000. *Die Apostolische Kirche des Ostens: Geschichte der sogenannten Nestorianer*. Klagenfurt: Verlag Kitab.
Baumer, Christoph. 2006. *The Church of the East, An Illustrated History of Assyrian Christianity*. London/New York: I. B. Tauris.
Becker, Adam. 2015. *Revival and Awakening: Christian Mission, Orientalism, and the American Evangelical Roots of Assyrian Nationalism (1834–1906)*. Chicago: University Press.
Brock, S. P. and David G. K. Taylor. 2001. *The Hidden Pearl: The Heirs of the Ancient Aramaic Heritage*. Rome: Trans World Film Italia.
Butts, A. M., S. P. Brock, George Kiraz, and Lucas Van Rompay. 2011. *Gorgias Encyclopedic Dictionary of the Syriac Heritage*. Piscataway, NJ: Gorgias Press.
Donabed, Sargon George. 2015. *Reforging a Forgotten History: Iraq and the Assyrians in the Twentieth Century*. Edinburgh: University Press.
Gaunt, David. 2006. *Massacres, Resistance, Protectors: Muslim-Christian Relations in Eastern Anatolia During World War I*. Piscataway, NJ: Gorgias Press.
Hellot-Bellier, Florence. 2014. *Chroniques de massacres annoncés: Les Assyro-Chaldéens d'Iran en du Hakkari face aux ambitions des empires, 1896–1920*. Paris: Geuthner.
Jakob, Joachim. 2014. *Ostsyrische Christen und Kurden im Osmanischen Reich des 19. und frühen 20. Jahrhunderts*. Vienna: LIT Verlag.
Joseph, John. 1983. *Muslim-Christian Relations and Inter-Christian Rivalries in the Middle East: The Case of the Jacobites in an Age of Transition*. Albany: State University of New York Press.
———. 2000. *The Modern Assyrians of the Middle East: Encounters With Western Christian Missions, Archaeologists, and Colonial Powers*. SCM 26. Leiden: Brill.
Kaufhold, Hubert. 2012. Die Wissenschaft vom Christlichen Orient: Gedanken zur Geschichte und Zukunft des Faches. *In:* P. Bruns, ed., *Vom Euphrat an die Altmühl: Die Forschungsstelle Christlicher Orient an der Katholischen Universität Eichstätt-Ingolstadt*. Wiesbaden: Harrassowitz, 15–168.
Maggiolini, Paolo. 2012. Bringing Together Eastern Catholics Under a Common Civil Head: The Agreements Between the Syriac and Chaldean Patriarchs and the Civil Head of the Armenian Catholic Church in Constantinople 1833–1871. *JECS* 64, 253–85.
Murre-van den Berg, Heleen. 1999. *From a Spoken to a Written Language: The Introduction and Development of Literary Urmia Aramaic in the Nineteenth Century*. Publication of the "De Goeje Fund" 28. Leiden: Nederlands Instituut Voor Het Nabije Oosten.
———.2013a. A Center of Transnational Syriac Orthodoxy: St. Mark's Convent in Jerusalem. *Journal of Levantine Studies* 3(1), 61–83.
———. 2013b. Light From the East (1948–1954) and the De-Territorialization of the Assyrian Church of the East. *In:* W. Hofstee and A. van der Kooij, eds., *Religion Beyond Its Private Role in Modern Society*. Leiden: Brill, 115–34.
———. 2015a. Classical Syriac and the Syriac Churches: A Twentieth-Century History. *In:* M. Doerfler, E. Fiano, and K. Smith, ed., *Syriac Encounters: Papers From the Sixth North American Syriac Symposium, Duke University, 26–29 June 2011*. Eastern Christian Studies 20. Leuven: Peeters, 119–48.
———. 2015b. *Scribes and Scriptures: The Church of the East in the Eastern Ottoman Provinces (1500–1850)*. Eastern Christian Studies 21. Leuven: Peeters.
Omtzigt, P. H., M. K. Tozman, and A. Tyndall (eds.) 2012. *The Slow Disappearance of the Syriacs From Turkey and of the Grounds of the Mor Gabriel Monastery*. Berlin: LIT Verlag.
Sélis, Claude. 1988. *Les Syriens orthodoxes et catholiques*. Fils d'Abraham. Turnhout: Brepols.

Tamcke, Martin. 2009. *Die Christen vom Tur Abdin: Hinführung zur Syrisch-Orthodoxe Kirche*. Frankfurt: Lembeck.
Teule, Herman. 2008. *Les Assyro-Chaldéens. Chrétiens d'Irak, d'Iran et de Turquie*. Fils d'Abraham. Turnhout: Brepols.
Wilmshurst, David. 2000. *The Ecclesiastical Organisation of the Church of the East, 1318–1913*. CSCO 582, Subsidia 104. Leuven: Peeters.
———. 2011. *The Martyred Church: A History of the Church of the East*. London: East & West Publishing.

CHAPTER THIRTY-NINE

CHANGING DEMOGRAPHY
Christians in Iraq since 1991

Erica C. D. Hunter

Prior to 1991, Christians accounted for about nine percent of Iraq's population (twenty million). The largest Christian community was (and still is) that of Chaldæan Catholics, the Uniate branch of the Assyrian Church of the East. The Assyrian Church of the East, the Ancient Assyrian Church of the East, as well as the Syrian Orthodox Church and its Uniate counterpart, the Syrian Catholic Church, also have had a significant presence in Iraq. Small congregations are hosted by the Assyrian Evangelical Church (Presbyterian) and the Assyrian Pentecostal Church, as well as the Anglican Church (St George's in Baghdad). Irrespective of denomination, the Christians were an obedient minority – continuing a pattern that was already in evidence during Sassanid times – and maintained stable relations with the Ba'athist government. In fact, no other option was available to them, as loyalty was a prerequisite for survival. Under the presidency of Saddam Hussein, Christians were able to practice their faith freely and reached high places in the government: the former deputy prime minister, Tariq Aziz (baptismal name: Mikael Yohanna) came from a Chaldæan Catholic family in Mosul. Providing that Christians did not dissent from the Ba'athist party line, they were able to live a relatively affluent, largely middle-class way of life.

Since 1991, the profile of Christianity in Iraq has undergone a radical change. Numbers have plummeted to an estimated 300,000 persons, this being triggered by a variety of reasons: the stringency of the economic sanctions imposed on Iraq following the First Gulf War caused many people to leave, which they did if they were able; the Second Gulf War in 2003 and the subsequent aftermath that emerged in Iraq unleashed sectarian violence in which the Christian communities were enmeshed and dramatically impacted on communities in Baghdad and Basra, as well as in the northern cities of Mosul, Kirkuk, and the villages of the Nineveh plains where Christians had lived for centuries. The rapidly diminishing Christian population of Iraq has been counterbalanced by the growth of large diaspora communities, in other parts of the Middle East (notably Jordan and Syria) as well as in Europe, Australia, and North America. Whilst the demography of Christian settlement in Iraq has been severely curtailed by economic pressures, political turmoil, and Islamic terrorism, remnant communities still manage to cling on despite these challenges. Today the major cluster of Christians is in the northern region administered by the Kurdish

Regional Government (KRG), but there is also a small community in southern Iraq, principally in Basra.

2003 AND ITS AFTERMATH

The challenges faced by Iraqi citizens following 2003 have been formidable. All have suffered from the bombing and bloodshed, but the Christians have been disproportionally affected by the consequences of the aftermath that saw the wholesale breakdown of law and order. The Allies' dismantling of the Iraqi forces, which left thousands of able men armed and unemployed, led to an escalation of insecurity and violence that has had dramatic repercussions. In the post-war situation, the antagonism that was levelled against anyone thought to be aiding the occupying forces, most specifically the Americans, surpassed any notion of religious denomination. Muslims were targeted, but Christians were particularly singled out. Being proficient in English, some had acted as translators for the occupying forces. Furthermore, by virtue of the faith that they shared with the foreign forces occupying Iraq, Christians were often seen as 'collaborators'. Queries about loyalty and patriotism expanded to become a general attitude of opprobrium against 'Western influences' that were deemed to be anti-Islamic. Shops selling alcohol and even beauty salons were forced to close, often at gunpoint. Many of their proprietors were Christian. Doctors, academics, and other professionals who were suspected of having 'Western' inclinations were singled out and shot. Although these activities were not exclusively directed against the Christians, the communities who, since the mid-nineteenth century, had taken advantage of Western-style education and were at the forefront of professions, particularly medicine, suffered greatly. They were perceived to be wealthy and privileged and fell under the suspicion of colluding with the 'enemy'.

Fear and intimidation are constant companions for Christians in all walks of life. Between 2003 and 2016, more than two thousand Christians have been killed. Individuals have been shot on the spot after being identified as Christian upon being asked to produce their personal ID cards, which are issued by the General Directorate of Citizenship and are mandatory. These cards list the individual's religion, making it particularly easy to identify Christians. Whole areas have been ethnically cleansed of their Christian populations. In 2006, the predominantly Christian suburb of Dora in Baghdad (formerly known as the 'Vatican' of Baghdad, Figure 39.1) was almost entirely cleared of its Christian residents, with only about 150 remaining.[1] People would receive a letter informing them of indiscretions against Islam, requesting payment or conversion to Islam within twenty-four hours, upon pain of death. Families simply 'upped sticks' and fled. As the late Dr. Donny George, the erstwhile director of the Iraq Museum and director of Antiquities, who received such a threat, related, 'I wrote a letter of apology, and enclosed $1000 . . . I just turned the key on my flat and left everything as it was' (Bowder 2007). His situation is typical of that facing Christian families daily in what was an active campaign to expel them. After families fled their homes, Muslims would move in; some mullahs actively encouraged their congregations to do so. In October 2008, 12,000 Christian residents left Mosul due to a campaign of ethnic cleansing. Graffiti began appearing on walls telling them 'to leave or die'. Trucks, fitted with loudspeakers, drove through the streets requesting people to leave.[2] Gregorius III Laham, patriarch of the Greek Melkite Catholic

Figure 39.1 Easter Sunday breakfast at St George's Church, Dora, Baghdad

Source: Author

Church, estimates that between 17 February and 1 March 2010, 870 families, numbering around 4,400 persons, left Mosul because of confessional violence.[3] On 2 May 2010, a convoy of students from Qaraqosh, travelling by bus to the University of Mosul, was attacked by two car bombs. Four people were killed, 171 were injured.[4] Many of the young students sustained very grave wounds that required major plastic surgery. A previous attempt, on 19 April, was thwarted.

Clergy of all denominations have been threatened, and in some instances murdered. In August 2004, the erstwhile Chaldæan Catholic patriarch, Mar Emmanuel

Deli I, received a chilling, anonymous letter stating 'we will kill you' and accusing the church of colluding with the US-led coalition forces in Iraq (Rassam 2005: 188). An escalation of violence occurred after the publication by the Danish newspapers of the 'Muhammad' cartoons. Various religious personnel, including the Syrian Catholic bishop of Mosul, were kidnapped; most were released after the payment of ransom demands. Economics has played a major role in determining 'targets to abduct' since kidnapping is a lucrative business, but in some cases the driving force is Islamic extremism. In September 2006, Rev. Mundhir al-Dayr, a Protestant pastor, was seized in Mosul and killed. His abductors had demanded a massive ransom and also threatened to kill all Christians. A month later, the Syrian Orthodox priest, Father Paul Iskander from the Mar Ephrem church, Mosul, was taken; this was a direct response to the lecture on Islam and violence that Pope Benedict XVI had delivered to an academic audience at the University of Regensburg in Germany. Father Paul's kidnappers demanded that posters be displayed at thirty locations in and around Mosul, denouncing the papal speech. The fact that Fr. Paul belonged to the Syrian Orthodox church that has never had any union with Rome was immaterial to the militants. In accordance with their demands, posters were displayed at the designated spots and the ransom was paid to release Fr. Paul. All to no avail. His decapitated and dismembered body that bore the marks of torture was found dumped by the roadside.[5] In 2008, gunmen kidnapped the Chaldæan Catholic archbishop of Mosul, Paul Faraj Rahho, killing in the process his two bodyguards. His captors' demands included a ransom of three million dollars, that the *jizya* tax be paid to fund the *jihad*[6] and that Iraqi Christians form a militia to fight US forces. Monsignor Rahho, who may have died of natural causes (high blood pressure and diabetes), was buried in a shallow grave near Mosul. The Iraqi Criminal Court sentenced to death one of perpetrators of the kidnapping, Ahmed Ali Ahmed, an Al Qaida cell leader in Iraq, but the Chaldæan clergy requested that this be commuted to life imprisonment.[7]

Between 2004 and 2014, a total of sixty-four churches, forty in Baghdad, nineteen in Mosul, five in Kirkuk, have been attacked or bombed.[8] Multiple, coordinated attacks have often been levelled against these 'dens of evil, corruption immorality and evangelisation'. In January 2005, the residence of the Chaldæan Catholic bishop in Mosul was destroyed. In September 2006, St Mary's Cathedral, the home of Mar Addai II, patriarch of The Ancient Church of the East, was bombed. Located in the Riyadh district of Baghdad, the cathedral experienced dual bombings. A small device was followed, a few minutes later, by a car detonation carrying a large amount of explosives. The bombing was timed to take place as the worshippers were leaving the Sunday morning sermon.[9] Later that month a rocket attack was launched against the Chaldæan Catholic Church of the Holy Spirit in Mosul.[10] In April 2007, Islamic militants forcefully removed the cross from the churches of St John and St George in Dora, a month later the latter church was firebombed.[11] That same month Shiites occupied the Angel Raphael Convent in Dora, belonging to the Chaldæan Catholic sisters of the Sacred Heart, and turned it into a base for their military operations.[12] Violence escalated on 6 January 2008 (The Feast of Epiphany) when seven churches in Mosul and Baghdad, including the orphanage of the Chaldæan Catholic sisters, were bombed.[13] Three churches in Kirkuk were bombed three days later.[14] In July 2009, seven more churches in Baghdad were bombed; in November the Church of St Ephrem and the St Theresa Convent of Dominican Nuns were bombed and heavily damaged.[15] On Christmas Eve 2009, two churches in Mosul – the church of St George and the ancient church of St Thomas that is twelve hundred years old, were bombed.[16]

Many of the bombings were accompanied by loss of life, but the level of violence escalated to an unprecedented degree with the killings that took place at the 'Lady of Salvation' Church in Karrada, Baghdad, during Mass on Sunday 31 October 2010 on 'All Souls Day', when the dead are commemorated. Whether the ten insurgents deliberately selected this date is difficult to ascertain, but the targeting of a congregation in worship was singular: fifty-eight faithful, including a pregnant woman and a three-year-old boy, as well as two priests (Thahar Saadal and Wasim Sabih) were slaughtered; seventy-five other parishioners were wounded. Eighty percent of the parish had either died or been wounded. Father Nizaar Simaan summed up the situation in a sermon which he preached at the memorial mass held at the Syriac Catholic Mission in London: 'in what happened [in the Baghdad cathedral] we have seen evil at work in our world – real evil'.[17] October 31st has become a memorable date for Iraqi Christians in the same way that the 9/11 Twin Towers attacks has become indelibly engraved in the minds of the US public. A *tsunami* of fear has swept through the Christian communities – each being terrified of being the next target of Islamic fundamentalists.

The massacre at the 'Lady of Salvation' Church caused yet another exodus of Christians from Baghdad to safer environs. The patriarch of the Chaldæan Catholic Church, Louis Sako, has written about the situation facing the communities:

> [s]ince 2005, Christians have become a specific target. Conditions are deteriorating at an increasing and alarming pace . . . the real fact remains of kidnappings, ransom, torture and executions. The reasons for such attacks are various: not being Muslim, belonging to a Western religion, assimilation with the coalition forces, criminals looking for money, and the lack of an official position of Christians.
>
> (Sako 2009: ix)

The repercussions on Christian life in Iraq have been massive. Churches have reduced their activities to the minimum, although many clergy remain redoubtable in the face of grave peril. Imad Al Banna, the Chaldæan Catholic bishop of Basra, remained in his see through the very difficult years 2003–2008, continuing to minister to both Christians and Muslims alike.[18] However, many of the laity, due to the high levels of violence that they have experienced, have chosen to leave their Iraqi homeland in what patriarch Sako calls a 'mortal exodus' (Sako 2009, x). Between 2003 and 2009, numbers have plummeted with Christians now representing just three percent of the total population of Iraq. Most have left for the prospect of relative security elsewhere and believing that there is no future for them any more in Iraq. Of the 750,000 Iraqi refugees in Jordan and 1.2 million in Syria, a disproportionate number are Christian,[19] many having arrived in response to the violence that emerged in the lead-up to the elections in early 2010. Unlike Turkey, which has not participated in assisting Christian refugees (even though many families originate from its eastern territories), Jordan and Syria have traditionally welcomed large numbers of Iraqis. However, with the eruption of the civil war that erupted in Syria in 2010, many Christians now live in a state of limbo.

EVENTS AFTER 2014

The situation of Christians reached a new abyss with the arrival of Daʿesh Daʿesh (ISIS) in Mosul in early June 2014, which brought to an end the Christian occupation of this city that had spanned some sixteen hundred years. Militants identified homes belonging to Christians by spray-painting the Arabic letter Nun, an abbreviation for 'Nisrani/Nasareen' (Christian) on gateposts and exterior walls and declared that these houses were now the property of Daʿesh. The militants then decreed that all Christian citizens of Mosul had three options available to them. They could convert to Islam. If they did not choose to do so, they were required to pay the *Jizya* tax, a special tax for non-Muslims to be able to retain one's faith. If they did not choose either of these two options, they would be killed. The 'catch-22' was that the sum of money decreed by Daʿesh to pay the *Jizya* tax was so exorbitant that it was beyond the financial capacity of even the wealthiest families. The only other option available to Christians was to leave Mosul; the deadline being noon on Saturday, 19 July. Some Imams announced through loudspeakers that the Christians should leave or die.[20] Not unnaturally, Christians began to leave their homes in Mosul in droves, but were stripped of all their possessions at the checkpoints manned by Daʿesh militants. Even essential medicines were confiscated.

The atrocities experienced by the communities in Mosul in June were repeated in August 2014. Louis Sako, patriarch of the Chaldæan Catholic Church, has described how the militants attacked with mortars the villages of the plains of Nineveh on the nights of 6 and 7 August:

> The Christians, about one hundred thousand, horrified and panicked, fled their villages and houses with nothing but the clothes on their backs. An exodus, a real *via crucis*, Christians are walking on foot in Iraq's searing summer heat towards the Kurdish cities of Erbil, Dohuk and Soulaymiyia, the sick, the elderly, infants and pregnant women among them. They are facing a human catastrophe and risk a real genocide. They need water, food, shelter.[21]

The United Nations, the Iraqi government, and other international organisations have condemned outright many of these acts as crimes against humanity. Faced with the brutality of Daʿesh, many people had no option but to flee. The consequence was that the Christian population of Mosul and its surrounding villages has been so seriously depleted that senior Iraqi clergy fear that there will be no Christians left in the next five to ten years. Their ancient community will become extinct, as has happened to the once numerous Jewish population of Iraq.[22] Expelled from their homes by Daʿesh, Christians have come to the conclusion that there is no place for them (and other non-Muslim minorities) in an increasingly Islamicised Iraq. Many are very reticent about returning to their former homes since they fear for their security and safety. The levels of trust which once existed between Muslim and Christian neighbourhoods in Mosul have been eroded, and it is too premature to speculate as to whether the communities can co-exist in the future. With little hope of returning to their ancient homelands and re-establishing a secure and safe way of life, many Christians who have not been able to emigrate have settled principally in the Kurdish Regional Government (KRG)-administered region of northern Iraq and hope that a 'safe haven' might be established.

Christians in the KRG-administered region of northern Iraq

The KRG-administered region of northern Iraq has emerged as a major area of growth. Its capital city Erbil was already a diocese in the second century CE, but has experienced unprecedented numbers of Christians coming to settle in recent years. Many institutions have also relocated from Baghdad. The Pontifical Babel College for Philosophy and Theology, which was formerly in Baghdad, in the suburb of Dora, moved in January 2007 to the relative security of Ankawa in Erbil, Kurdistan.[23] Situated only a short drive from the capital city, Ankawa has seen a spectacular growth from a village to a thriving, bustling city with many churches. Ankawa has become a refuge for an estimated population of 40,000 Christians of various denominations, with between a third and a half of the people now resident there having arrived since 2003.[24] The KRG has been keen to promote its religious tolerance towards Christians and other minorities, thus reversing the exodus that took place in the early twentieth century when purges by the Ottoman Turks emptied the predominantly Christian villages of the Hakkari. The recent influx of Christians has given rise to a cultural resurgence, especially in the use of the vernacular Syriac language. Students are taught in Neo-Syriac. TV and radio stations, magazines, and newspapers have also burgeoned, all using Syriac over and above Arabic, encouraged by the KRG. The KRG has invested large sums of money into developing the Nineveh plains, a predominantly Christian enclave. However, as one young writer has commented, 'KRG officials are not angels, they are politicians, they do not do it because of the "black eyes" of Christians, they do it for votes and popularity' (Hunter 2014: 333, n.57). The Kurdish authorities have given support to the Christian population, but this must be measured in the context of the campaign for full and permanent independence. How the future will unfold for the place of the Christian communities within Kurdistan still remains to be seen.

The bulk of assistance to Christian internationally displaced persons (IDP) in Kurdistan comes from the churches, charities, and NGO organisations, notably Aid to the Church in Need, Iraqi Christians in Need (ICIN), Assyrian Church of the East Relief Organisation (ACERO), Misserio, and Caritas Iraq. These maintain a robust programme of support by providing shelter, education, and medical treatment as well as engaging in religious, social, and cultural activities, all of which form an important part of the communities' well-being. In 2015, funding from Aid to the Church in Need enabled the construction of the first school in Ankawa for IDP children, and more are planned.[25] Additional schools in Erbil are urgently needed, due to the massive influx from Al-Anbar and Salahaddin provinces, as well as the Nineveh plains, when people fled Daʿesh in 2014 adding to an already congested situation. In the northern city of Dohuk, ACERO established a school in 2013 and also has distributed shoes and financial aid to families (approx. 100,000 Iraqi dinars = $US 85 per family).[26] ICIN also financially underwrites medical clinics in Erbil, as well as emergency surgical treatment.[27] Despite these efforts, medical services are stretched to breaking point due to the sharp increase in psychological problems experienced by refugees and the sharp decrease in the distribution of medicine free of charge by the state.

Christians in Basra and southern Iraq

Another area of growth is in the far south of Iraq, at Basra and its surrounding regions. Although the number is far smaller than in the north, it is important to remember that Christians have lived in southern Iraq since the earliest centuries of the Christian era. Today the city of Basra hosts 350 families (including fifty refugee families who have fled Daʿesh), and there are smaller communities at the cities of Amara, Kut, and Nasiriyah in southern Iraq. The Chaldæan Catholics form the largest community and are under the leadership of Habib al-Naufaly, who was installed as archbishop of Basra in 2014. Archbishop Habib runs a full programme of worship, catechism classes, and other activities, including a kindergarten and computing classes. As well as establishing a library of 3,700 books and magazines in various languages, archbishop Habib has also been instrumental in creating a museum of religious artefacts that document the rich Christian presence over the centuries in Basra and southern Iraq.

Despite the vicissitudes that the city has experienced over the last few decades – the Iran-Iraq War, the Gulf Invasion in 1991, and the Allied Offensive in 2003 – the churches are still standing. Although six are redundant, many are still in use and are able to function openly. The largest and most significant church in Basra is the Virgin Mary Cathedral for Chaldæan Catholics that was begun in 1907. The St Thomas Chaldæan Church that was built in 1886 is the oldest and is distinguished by its Georgian-style windows. The church was functional until 2004, but a leaking roof meant that it could no longer be used for worship. This has recently been repaired and with some refurbishment, the church could return to usage, which the resident priest (Father Aram) would like to see come to fruition. A small, illustrated booklet recently produced by the Religions Heritage campaign, which details the religious institutions of Basra, has included all the churches in Basra, with brief details about their dates of construction and history.[28] Today, crosses juxtaposed with minarets dot the skyline of Basra. At night some of the crosses are illuminated, providing a very striking sight.

The number of Christian families still resident in Basra is a shadow of the former communities, but it is hoped that there may be an increase, especially since the Shia Muslims are now showing a 'new kindness' to Christians, having persecuted them during Iraq's recent civil war. According to archbishop Habib, the Shia have realised that the persecution of the Christians in the violence that erupted between 2004 and 2008 was ill founded. He actively participates in talks between Christian leaders, Arab tribal leaders, and Shia clerics that aim to encourage stability in the region between communities and to persuade Christians not to emigrate from this ancient bastion of Christianity. Efforts to reach out to the Shia, offering them pastoral care and also access to educational facilities, have met with some success. Archbishop Habib has said that Shia Iraqis often brought him crosses they had made, as gifts (Rouch 2016). This rapprochement is encouraging and, whilst in its tentative stages, might provide a paradigm for collaboration and consolidation between Christians and Muslims elsewhere in Iraq. Of course, there are many challenges still to overcome. Archbishop Habib stated in a recent interview in *The Tablet*, 'Christians in Basra continued to live in fear of the Shia militias active in the area, as the Iraqi Government was too divided to bring about peace and reconciliation' (Rouch 2016).

Cultural destruction by al Qaida and Da'esh

Da'esh has not been content to eradicate the living communities of the Christians but has also destroyed the physical symbols that stand as evocative reminders of the rich ethno-religious fabric of Iraq. The bombing and demolition of churches and monasteries, in keeping with the wider cultural destruction that Da'esh has perpetrated, goes hand-in-hand with their concept of expulsion of *al-jahiliyyah*,[29] to expunge all traces of 'undesirable, unethical' strands in the region. In doing so, Da'esh have merely stepped up the agenda that was already begun by Al Qaida terrorists in 2006. All denominations, both ancient apostolic and modern Western-oriented, have been targeted: Armenian Catholic, Armenian Orthodox, Syrian Orthodox, Syrian Catholic, Assyrian Church of the East, Anglican [St George's Baghdad], Seventh Day Adventist, Chaldæan Catholic. Following the arrival of Da'esh in Mosul in June 2014, all forty-five Christian religious institutions in Mosul have either been destroyed or used by militants for a variety of purposes, including as places of imprisonment. Some churches, including the Syrian Orthodox Cathedral in Mosul, have been converted into mosques. The net result is the complete stripping of the signs of centuries of Christian worship in the city, although prior to the arrival of Da'esh, churches had already been bombed. The tenth-century St George church was bombed on 23 December 2009. In March 2015, Da'esh attacked the church once again, using sledgehammers to smash crosses and icons. The iron cross was removed from the dome and replaced with the black flag of Da'esh.[30] The militants cheered as they threw the church bells to the ground. Such was the orgy of violence that not only the living but even the dead were targeted. Frenzied men wrenched crosses from graves. Da'esh militants also blew up *Al-Saa* ('the Clock') church that was paid for by Empress Eugenie and which was one of Mosul's most famous landmarks due to its imposing clocktower.[31]

Intent on wiping out the historic Christian footprint within Iraq, in July 2014 fighters from Da'esh stormed the fourth-century foundation, the Monastery of Mar Behnam and Sara, which is located south of Nimrud, expelling its monks. Unable to take any of the monastery's ancient relics or even their Bibles and other holy books, they left with just the clothes that they were wearing – and their faith. For some years it was not known whether the ancient manuscripts held by the monastery had been destroyed, although fortunately they had been digitised in a programme initiated by the Hill Museum and Manuscript Library (Minnesota, USA). In the recent return of the monastery to Syrian Catholic ownership, following the ousting of Da'esh from the region by Iraqi Armed Forces in November 2016, it is now known that the manuscripts have survived. Aware of the impending possibility of their destruction, the monks packed the manuscripts in iron chests and sealed them behind a wall where they remained undetected by the militants during their two-year occupation of the monastery.[32]

The recent liberation of the monastery from Da'esh has shown that much damage was done. A report on 19 March 2015 by Gianluca Mezzofiore in the *International Business Times* showed images of militants blowing up the tombs of the martyrs Behnam and his sister Sara, to whom the ancient monastery was dedicated.[33] However, substantial parts of the building are intact, albeit with Arabic graffiti sprayed on the walls proclaiming the militants' ethos. It is fortunate that some of the ancient thirteenth-century carved marble doorways have also survived, complete with proclamations of the Christian faith in estrangela Syriac (Figure 39.2). One can only presume that the Daʿesh fighters were ignorant and did not recognise that these mediaeval calligraphic treasures were actually inscriptions. The monastery also housed a unique bilingual Syriac-Uighur inscription, dating from the thirteenth-century Il-Khanate period when the Mongol rulers of Iraq were Uighur (Old Turkic) speakers. Outside of the Mongol homeland in Mongolia and western Turkestan, this inscription – which commemorated the gratitude of the monastery to the Mongol khans – was the most western example of the spread of Uighur and was singular, not just for Christianity or for Iraq, but for world heritage. Fortunately this priceless treasure appears to have survived with little damage.

Figure 39.2 Thirteenth century doorway, Mar Behnam monastery

Source: Author

Whither the future?

The events that have unfolded since 2003 have resuscitated the debate of an Assyrian enclave that was earnestly discussed at the beginning of the twentieth century. Opinions are divided; many Iraqi Christians remaining unconvinced by the prospect of long-term viability. On the other hand, the diaspora communities in the West have vigorously embraced various proposals. As might be expected there are many different ideas, ranging from

> support for total independence (which few seem to advocate) to an autonomous governorate in the Nineveh Plains area to the north and east of Mosul, attached either to the Baghdad adhministration or to the KRG. Others speak more vaguely of a 'safe haven' for the Assyrians and other Christians although this raises many questions about the defence of such a safe haven and its purpose.
>
> (Healey 2010: 52)

The 'safe haven' for Christians has received support from the Assyrian Democratic Movement that is represented in the Iraqi Parliament. There have been suggestions that the patriarchate of the Assyrian Church of the East might relocate from its base in the United States. This has yet to be realised, although the elevation in Erbil in November 2015 of Giwargis III, the erstwhile metropolitan of Baghdad and all Iraq, to be patriarch of the Assyrian Church of the East in Erbil has reiterated the church's Iraqi heritage and provides a powerful symbol anchoring the diaspora communities (now the second and third generation) to the land of their origins (Figure 39.3). The creation of a 'safe haven' represents a cherished hope for

Figure 39.3 Enthronement of Mar Giwargis III, patriarch of the Assyrian Church of the East, 2015

Source: Author

Figure 39.4 Easter celebrations at Qaraqoche (Baghdede) 1989

Source: Author

Christians of Iraqi origin, particularly of those expatriate generations who have lived in the cultural exile of the West. Whether the long-held desire for a homeland does translate into reality is at this stage uncertain. Whether the creation of a Christian enclave will ensure the survival of a religion that has contributed enormously to Iraq's rich history and culture also remains to be seen. Whether Christianity manages to remain in the land where it has been practised for nearly eighteen hundred years also remains to be seen. Despite the recent liberation of Qaraqoche from Daʿesh and the ongoing offensive by the Iraqi Army to remove the terrorist organisation from Mosul, there are still monumental challenges to be faced to provide security and a workable economy for the Christian communities. At present, the reality for Christians living in Iraq is still one of daily tension and terror. Hopefully they will remain resilient, summoning their courage and stoicism as they have been called upon to do so many times over the centuries. The cooperation and communication that is currently happening in Basra, building bridges between the Christian and Shia communities, might provide a glimmer of hope and a paradigm to implement for the future.

NOTES

1 http://dbpedia.org/page/Dora,_Baghdad
2 2008 attacks on Christians in Mosul. https://en.wikipedia.org/wiki/2008_attacks_on_Christians_in_Mosul
3 Patriarch Gregorios III appeal, "For Prayer and Forgiveness. For the Victims of Violence and Fanaticism in Iraq: Christians and Muslims Together for the Rejection of Violence and Fanaticism" 10/3/2010.
4 'Four Dead After Terrorist Attack Near Mosul Targets Buses of Christian Students' www.aina.org/news/20100504194249.pdf (posted 5/4/2010).
5 Personal communication to author by Eustathius Matta Roham, Metropolitan Jazirah and Euphrates, Hassake, Syria during his visit in November 2006 to London to deliver the Constantinople Lecture (St Paul's Cathedral, 23/11/2006) on behalf of the Anglican and Eastern Churches Association. Metropolitan Matta (Syrian Orthodox) was the superior of Fr. Paul.
6 The Jizya was a poll tax levied by Muslims on dhimmi communities for the privilege of practicing their faith – the concept being originally expressed in Qur'an 9:29.
7 'Iraq to Execute al Qaeda Leader in Bishop Murder' http://uk.reuters.com/article/idUKCOL85657520080518; 'Iraqi Bishops Oppose Execution of Prelate's Convicted Killer' *Catholic World News*, 20/5/2008.
8 'Church Bombings in Iraq Since 2004' www.aina.org/news/20080107163014.htm – updated to 2016.
9 Syndicated News, 'Assyrian Church bombed in Baghdad' 24/9/2006. www.aina.org.news/20060924135137.htm
10 Syndicated News, 'Second Attack in Three Days Against a Chaldean Church in Iraq' 26/9/2006. www.aina.org.news/20060926112353.htm
11 Aina News, 'Islamists Tear Down Crosses From Assyrian Churches' 14/4/2007. www.aina.org.news/20070414141226.htm; Aina News, 'Muslims Burn Assyrian Church in Baghdad' 18/5/2007. www.aina.org.news/20070518182239.htm
12 Syndicated News, 'Terrorists Sack and Occupy a Convent in Baghdad' 1/6/2007. www.aina.org.news/20070601151953.htm
13 Aina News, 'One Person Injured in Iraq Church Bombings' 6/1/2008. www.aina.org.news/20080106162040.htm
14 Syndicated News, 'Two More Churches Bombed in Iraq' 9/1/2008. www.aina.org.news/20080190856 42.htm
15 Syndicated News, 'Iraq Attacks Hit Christian Sites' 26/11/2009. www.aina.org.news/20091126150149.htm
16 As note 9 above. www.aina.org/news/20080107163014.htm
17 John Pontifex, 'Londoners Mourn Victims of Baghdad Massacre' *Catholic Herald*, (Monday 15/11/2010). www.catholicherald.co.uk/news/2010/11/15/londoners-mourn-victims-of-baghdad-massacre.
18 The Red Bull Report, 'Iraqi Priest Serves People of Basra' 17/7/2009. www.dma.state.mn.us/press_room/e-zine/red_bull_report/pdfs/090717_redbullreport.pdf
19 Aina News, 'Congresswoman Schakowsky Asks Clinton to Address Assyrian Crisis in Iraq' 10/8/2009. www.aina.org/news/20090810163037.pdf
20 Archbishop Athanasius Toma Daowd, Iraqi Christians in the United Kingdom. Press Release, 18 July 2014.
21 Chaldæan Patriarch's Appeal for Urgent Help S.O.S. (letter, 7th August 2014) quoted at https://rorate-caeli.blogspot.com/2014/07/nun-sign-of-genocide.html. See also www.bbc.com/news/world-middle-east-28381455.
22 A handful of Jews still live in Baghdad. In 2001, the author met the remaining community, numbering some fifty people, all of whom were elderly. There are no Jews left in Basra, a city which once hosted a thriving population.

23 US forces moved onto the site in April 2007 and used the seminary as a military base until November 2008. Whilst this may have had the intention of protecting the site and indeed great care was taken by the US military personnel to restore any damage that the site may have sustained, such actions actually placed the seminary at greater risk from Muslim insurgents. The library was sealed during the American occupation. Syndicated News, 'US Army Returns College in Baghdad to Chaldæan Catholic Church' 12/11/2008. www.aina.org/news/20081115004237.htm.

24 For further information on the settlement of displaced Christians in Erbil and other cities and towns of the KRG region, see 2011 Human Rights Report on Assyrians in Iraq: The Exodus from Iraq (Assyria Council of Europe, 2012), 5–6. www.aina.org/reports/acehrr2011.pdf.

25 Bashar Warda, *Christianity in Contemporary Iraq: Present Challenges and Future Expectations*. Talk at Heythrop College. University of London, 12 February 2015.

26 ACERO Newsletter (April 2014:1).

27 Private communication to author from ICIN (9 December 2016).

28 Edited by Bassam Al Alwachi under the supervision of the Antiquities Inspector of Basra region, Qahtan Al Abeed.

29 Ignorance, principally referring to the pre-Islamic days in Arabia.

30 Iraq: Isis blows up 10th century Assyrian Catholic monastery near Mosul. www.ibtimes.co.uk/iraq-isis-blows-10th-century-assyrian-catholic-monastery-near-mosul-1491281.

31 Richard Spencer, 'Islamic State Blows up Empress Eugenie's Clocktower Church in Mosul' *The Telegraph*, 25/4/2016. www.telegraph.co.uk/news/2016/04/25/islamic-state-blows-up-empress-eugenies-clock-church-in-mosul

32 Owen Jarus, 'Hundreds of Historic Texts Hidden in ISIS-occupied Monastery' *Live Science*, 16/12/2016. www.livescience.com/57240-historic-texts-hidden-isis-occupied-monastery.html#undefined.uxfs

33 Gianluca Mezzofiore, 'Isis Blows Up Famed 4th-century Mar Behnam Catholic Monastery in Iraq' *International Business Times*, 20/3/2015. www.ibtimes.co.uk/isis-blows-famed-4th-century-mar-behnam-catholic-monastery-iraq-1492703

BIBLIOGRAPHY

Bowder, Bill. 2007. Iraqi Christians May Never Return. Church Times, 26/1/2007. Online at https://www.churchtimes.co.uk/articles/2007/19-january/news/uk/iraqi-christians-may-never-return

Healey, John. 2010. The Church Across the Border. The Church of the East and Its Chaldean branch. *In*: A. O'Mahony and E. Loosley, ed. *Eastern Christianity in the Modern Middle East*. London: Routledge, 41–55.

Hunter, Erica C.D. 2014. Coping in Kurdistan: The Christian Diaspora in Religious Minorities. *In*: Kh. Omarkhali, ed. *Kurdistan: Beyond the Mainstream. Studies in Oriental Religions* 68. Wiesbaden: Harrassowitz, 321–38.

Rassam, Suha. 2005. *Christianity in Iraq: Its Origins and Development to the Present Day*. Leominster: Gracewing.

Rouch, Abigail Frymann. 2016. Shia Muslims in Basra turn to helping Christians. The Tablet 24.ix.2016.

Sako, Louis, 2009. Iraqi Christians should Remain in their land to uphold their millennial multi-heritage. In: Erica C.D. Hunter, ed. *The Christian Heritage of Iraq: Collected Papers from the Christianity in Iraq I-V Seminar Days*. Gorgias Eastern Christian Series 13. Piscataway, NJ: Gorgias Press, viii-x.

APPENDICES

APPENDIX I

THE PATRIARCHS OF THE CHURCH OF THE EAST

David Wilmshurst

The following list provides a convenient summary of the present state of knowledge of the patriarchal succession of the Church of the East. The list only contains the names of individuals who (a) actually existed and (b) are generally recognised as primates of the Church of the East. It does not include Saint Peter, who had no connection whatsoever with the Persian Church; nor the apostle Mar Addai, whose legend was invented between the third and sixth centuries; nor the second-century patriarchs Abris, Abraham, and Yaʿqob, who were invented in the ninth century; nor the third-century patriarchs Shahlufa and Aha d'Abuh, two historical bishops of Erbil who were retrospectively promoted. Neither does it include 'Denḥa III (1359–68)', invented by the priest Joseph Qellaita in the 1920s; nor 'Shemʿon VIII Denḥa (1551–8)', invented by Yoḥannan Sulaqa's supporters in 1552 to conceal the fact of their rebellion against the reigning patriarch Shemʿon VII Ishoʿyahb (1539–58); nor 'Eliya VI (1558–76)', whose existence is disproved by the epitaph of Eliya VII (1558–91). Augustine Hindi, the self-styled patriarch 'Joseph V' who administered the Amid patriarchate between 1802 and his death in 1827, does not strictly speaking qualify, as he was recognised by the Vatican merely as administrator of the Amid patriarchate and was never formally accorded the title of patriarch; but he is conventionally listed as a patriarch, and I have observed this convention.

There have been several counter-patriarchs in the history of the Church of the East, and several patriarchs whose reigns were later declared illegitimate. For simplicity's sake, I have listed them all as patriarchs, as they may well have enjoyed considerable support before their memory was vilified. Narsai and Elishaʿ (524–39) are therefore both listed as legitimate patriarchs, as are Farbokht (421), Yoḥannan the Leper (691–3), and Surin (753), despite their unsavoury posthumous reputations. The sixteenth-century patriarchs Shemʿon V (1497–1502) and Eliya V (1503–4) may have been counter-patriarchs, but there is so little evidence for their reigns that they have been given the benefit of the doubt. I was initially tempted to classify Yoḥannan Sulaqa (1553–5) as a counter-patriarch, but as his rebellion in 1552 was supported by most educated Nestorians, he has at least as reasonable a claim to legitimacy as Yoḥannan the Leper. On the same principle, I have recognised Thomas Darmo

(1968–9) and Addai II Giwargis (since 1972) as legitimate patriarchs, though I am conscious that their status is precarious and might well be subject to later review.

Although the reigns of most of the primates of the Church of the East can be accurately dated, several areas of uncertainty remain. The patriarchal succession in the second half of the fourth century was complicated by the continuing persecution of Christians in Persia during the decades that followed Shapur II's treaty with the Romans in 363, and the dates assigned to the reign of Tomarsa (388–95) may well need to be refined. The patriarchal succession in the fourteenth and fifteenth centuries is also unclear. It is not known when Timothy II (1318–ca. 1332) died. The forty-five year reign attributed to the patriarch Denḥa II (1336/7–1381/2), although unusually long, is not unparalleled (Timothy I reigned for forty-three years, and Shemʿon XXI Eshai for fifty-five years), and is supported by the evidence of manuscript colophons. I have postulated the existence of the patriarch 'Shemʿon III (ca. 1425–ca. 1450)' to avoid assigning an impossibly long reign to his successor Shemʿon IV Basidi (ca. 1450–1497), and to the best of my knowledge I am the first scholar to do so. My proposed reign dates for the patriarchs Shemʿon II (ca. 1385–ca. 1405), Eliya IV (ca. 1405–ca. 1425), Shemʿon III (ca. 1425–ca. 1450), and Shemʿon IV Basidi (ca. 1450–1497) match the evidence of a number of surviving manuscript colophons, but given the scarcity of information for this period can only be regarded as approximate. It is also unclear whether the reign dates assigned to the seventeenth- and eighteenth-century Kochanes patriarchs by the Anglican missionary William Ainger Wigram rest on reliable evidence. These conventional dates correlate with the evidence from the surviving correspondence of the Kochanes patriarchs with the Vatican, but may have been inferred by Wigram precisely on that basis. Unless and until better evidence turns up, they should be regarded as provisional. These and other problems are discussed more fully in the relevant chapters of this book.

Lists of the patriarchs of the Church of the East frequently attempt to assign a long string of patriarchs to a single patriarchal residence, such as Seleucia-Ctesiphon, Baghdad, Mosul, and Kochanes. I am wary of following suit, as the certainty suggested in such models is deceptive and tends to dissolve when the evidence is scrutinised more closely. Some patriarchs moved several times during their reigns, or had more than one residence, or preferred to remain in seclusion instead of governing the Church. The patriarch Denḥa I (1265–81), for example, resided for part of his reign in Erbil, then moved to Eshnuq. Yahballaha III (1281–1317) lived for much of his reign in the monastery of Saint John the Baptist in Maragha, but also visited Baghdad from time to time. It is fair to say that most of the predecessors of Ḥnanishoʿ II (773–80) resided in or near Seleucia-Ctesiphon, though there were important exceptions. The fifth-century patriarch Dadishoʿ (421–56) withdrew to Ḥirta during the later decades of his reign, and his example was followed a century later by Ishoʿyahb I (585–95). The patriarch Aba I (540–52) spent most of his patriarchate on the road, touring the far-flung dioceses of Persia and southern Iraq. The move from Seleucia-Ctesiphon to Baghdad was made by Ḥnanishoʿ II (773–80), not (as sometimes claimed) by his more glamorous successor Timothy I (780–823), and for the next five hundred years most (but not all) of the Nestorian patriarchs normally resided in Baghdad. The ʿAbbasid capital was moved temporarily to Samarra in the ninth century, and the Nestorian patriarch Sargis (860–72) resided in Samarra in preference to Baghdad. His predecessor Theodosius (853–8) may also have lived in Samarra during his final years, though he spent most of his reign in prison (probably, though not certainly, in Baghdad). The last Nestorian patriarch to reside habitually in Baghdad was Makkikha II (1257–65), who witnessed the city's sack by the Mongols in 1258.

For the next three centuries, the Nestorian patriarchs seem to have resided wherever they felt safest. Denḥa I (1265–81) is associated with Erbil and Eshnuq, Yahballaha III (1281–1317) with Maragha, Timothy II (1318–ca. 1332) with the monastery of Mar Mikha'il of Tar'il near Erbil, and Denḥa II (1336/7–1381/2) with the Mosul plain village of Karamlish. We do not know where the fifteenth-century Nestorian patriarchs lived, and attempts to place them either at Mosul or Alqosh seem little more than wishful thinking. Shem'on IV Basidi (ca. 1450–1497) was buried in the monastery of Rabban Hormizd near Alqosh, but did not necessarily live there during his reign. His immediate successors are associated with Gazarta, Mosul, and the monastery of Mar Awgin near Nisibis, not with Alqosh.

The tragic patriarchate of Yoḥannan Sulaqa (1553–5) was so brief that it would be eccentric to claim that he had a permanent residence. His successor 'Abdisho' IV Maron (1555–70) seems to have lived for much of his reign in the monastery of Mar Ya'qob the Recluse near Seert, and the third uniate patriarch Shem'on VIII Yahballaha may also have resided there. Shem'on IX Denḥa (1580–1600) is associated with the Salmas district. Shem'on X (1600–38) moved from Salmas to remote Kochanes, and as far as is known his successors all resided in Kochanes until 1915, though they also had 'patriarchal cells' elsewhere, notably in Urmia and Ashitha. The patriarchs of the Eliya line, the lineal successors of Shem'on VII Isho'yahb (1539–58), lived in the Mosul district, but it is not always clear where. They are variously recorded to have had residences in Mosul itself and in Alqosh, Telkepe, and Tel Isqof. They were nearly all buried in the monastery of Rabban Hormizd, but may not necessarily have resided there. Yoḥannan VIII Hormizd and most of the other nineteenth- and twentieth-century Chaldean patriarchs of Babylon normally divided their residence between Mosul and Baghdad. The present Chaldean patriarch, Emmanuel III Delly, resides in the village of Telkepe.

Attempts at neatness founder with the twentieth-century Assyrian patriarchs. The invalid Shem'on XX Paul (1918–20) resided for most of his brief patriarchate in the Jacobite monastery of Mar Mattai near Mosul. The much-travelled Shem'on XXI Eshai (1920–75) had several residences, in Iraq, Cyprus, and Europe, before he finally settled in Chicago. His successor Dinkha IV Ḥnanya, the present patriarch of the Assyrian Church of the East, also resides in Chicago, though if conditions are right he may one day return to Iraq and restore the patriarchate to its old home in Baghdad. Addai II Giwargis has resided in Baghdad throughout his patriarchate.

I am also wary of assigning religious labels to the patriarchs of the Church of the East. In the past, several patriarchs have been claimed as Catholics on little more evidence than a polite exchange of letters with the Vatican, and there has been a misleading tendency to assume that the 'union with Rome' meant as much to the Nestorian patriarchs as it did to the Vatican. I have honoured tradition to the extent of listing Yoḥannan Sulaqa and his three immediate successors as 'uniate patriarchs', but I am by no means sure that Shem'on VIII Yahballaha and Shem'on IX Denḥa were Catholics, although they obviously wanted the Vatican to assume that they were. I do not believe, on the basis of a close reading of their surviving correspondence, that any of the seventeenth- or eighteenth-century Mosul or Kochanes patriarchs were

Catholics. The death of ʿAbdishoʿ IV Maron (1555–70) effectively ended the 'union with Rome' for a century, before it was revived with the creation of the uniate Amid patriarchate in 1681. Joseph I (1681–93) and his four successors were, of course, devout Catholics. The Mosul patriarchate only became uniate in the early nineteenth century with the accession of Yoḥannan VIII Hormizd (1830–7), a bad patriarch but a good Catholic. All of his successors have also been Catholics.

The Bishops of Seleucia-Ctesiphon, ca. 280–399

Papa bar Aggai (ca. 280–329)
Shemʿon bar Sabbaʿe (329–44)
Shahdost (344–5)
Barbaʿshmin (345–6)
Vacant, 346–88
Tomarsa (388–95)
Qayyoma (395–9)

The Metropolitans of Seleucia-Ctesiphon, 399–421

Isaac (399–410)
Ahai (410–14)
Yahballaha I (415–20)
Maʿna (420)
Farbokht (421)

The Catholici of the Church of the East, 421–1558

Dadishoʿ (421–56)
Babowai (457–84)
Acacius/Aqaq (485–96)
Babai (497–502)
Shila (503–23)
Narsai (524–39)
Elishaʿ (524–39)
Paul (539)
Aba I (540–52)
Joseph (552–67)
Vacant, 567–70
Ezekiel (570–81)
Vacant, 581–5
Ishoʿyahb I of Arzun (585–95)
Sabrishoʿ I (596–604)
Gregory (605–8)
Vacant, 609–28
Ishoʿyahb II of Gdala (628–45)
Maremmeh (645–8)
Ishoʿyahb III of Adiabene (649–59)

Giwargis I (660–80)
Yoḥannan I bar Marta (681–3)
Ḥnanisho' I (686–98)
Yoḥannan the Leper (691–3)
Vacant, 698–714
Ṣliba-zkha (714–28)
Pethion (731–40)
Aba II (741–51)
Surin (753)
Ya'qob II (753–73)
Ḥnanisho' II (773–80)
Timothy I (780–823)
Isho' Bar Nun (823–8)
Giwargis II (828–31)
Sabrisho' II (831–5)
Abraham II (837–50)
Theodosius (853–8)
Sargis (860–72)
Vacant, 872–7
Enosh (877–84)
Yoḥannan II (884–92)
Yoḥannan III (893–9)
Yoḥannan IV (900–5)
Abraham III (906–37)
Emmanuel I (937–60)
Israel (961)
'Abdisho' I (963–86)
Mari bar Ṭuba (987–99)
Yoḥannan V (1000–11)
Yoḥannan VI (1012–20)
Isho'yahb IV (1020–5)
Eliya I (1028–49)
Yoḥannan VII bar Ṭarghal (1049–57)
Vacant, 1057–64
Sabrisho' III (1064–72)
'Abdisho' II ibn al-'Ārid (1074–90)
Makkikha I (1092–1110)
Eliya II (1111–32)
Bar Ṣawma (1134–6)
'Abdisho' III (1139–49)
Isho'yahb V ibn al-Hayik (1149–75)
Eliya III Abū Ḥālim (1176–90)
Yahballaha II (1190–1222)
Sabrisho' IV bar Qayyoma (1222–4)
Sabrisho' V (1226–56)
Makkikha II (1257–65)
Denḥa I (1265–81)

Yahballaha III (1281–1317)
Timothy II (1318–ca. 1332)
Denḥa II (1336/7–1381/2)
Shem'on II (ca. 1385–ca. 1405)
Eliya IV (ca. 1405–ca. 1425)
Shem'on III (ca. 1425–ca. 1450)
Shem'on IV Basidi (ca. 1450–1497)
Shem'on V (1497–1502)
Eliya V (1503–4)
Shem'on VI (1504–38)
Shem'on VII Isho'yahb (1539–58)

The Uniate Patriarchs, 1553–1600

Yoḥannan Sulaqa (1553–5)
'Abdisho' IV Maron (1555–70)
Shem'on VIII Yahballaha (1570–80)
Shem'on IX Denḥa (1580–1600)

The Mosul Patriarchs, 1558–1804

Eliya VII (1558–91)
Eliya VIII (1591–1617)
Eliya IX Shem'on (1617–60)
Eliya X Yoḥannan Marawgin (1660–1700)
Eliya XI Marawgin (1700–22)
Eliya XII Denḥa (1722–78)
Eliya XIII Isho'yahb (1778–1804)

The Amid Patriarchs, 1681–1827

Joseph I (1681–93)
Joseph II (1696–1713)
Joseph III (1713–57)
Joseph IV (1757–96).
Augustine Hindi (patriarchal administrator, 1802–27, self-styled patriarch 'Joseph V')

The Kochanes Patriarchs, 1600–1918

Shem'on X (1600–38)
Shem'on XI (1638–56)
Shem'on XII (1656–62)
Shem'on XIII Denḥa (1662–1700)
Shem'on XIV Shlemun (1700–40)
Shem'on XV Mikha'il Mukhtas (1740–80)
Shem'on XVI Yoḥannan (1780–1820)
Shem'on XVII Abraham (1820–61)

Shem'on XVIII Rubil (1861–1903)
Shem'on XIX Benjamin (1903–18)

The Patriarchs of the Assyrian Church of the East since 1920

Shem'on XX Paul (1918–20)
Shem'on XXI Eshai (1920–75)
Dinkha IV Hnanya (1976–2015)
Giwargis III (since 2015)

The Patriarchs of the Ancient Church of the East since 1968

Thomas Darmo (1968–9)
Addai II Giwargis (since 1972)

The Chaldean Patriarchs of Babylon since 1780

Yoḥannan VIII Hormizd (patriarchal administrator, 1780–1830; patriarch, 1830–7)
Nicholas I Za'ya (1840–7)
Joseph VI Audo (1848–79)
Eliya XII 'Abū-l Yūnan (1879–94)
'Abdisho' V Khayyāṭ (1895–9)
Emmanuel II Thomas (1900–47)
Joseph VII Ghanīma (1947–58)
Paul II Cheikho (1958–89)
Raphael I Bidawid (1989–2003)
Emmanuel III Delly (since 2003)

APPENDIX II

WEST SYRIAN PATRIARCHS AND MAPHRIANS

David Wilmshurst

The following list provides a convenient summary of the reign dates of the patriarchs and maphrians of the Jacobite Church up to the start of the fifteenth century. In most cases, these dates are uncontentious, and generally agree with those given in the *Gorgias Encyclopedic Dictionary of the Syriac Heritage* (*GEDSH*). In some cases, based on a close reading of the sources, I have modified the traditional dates by a year or two. For the purposes of this translation and the accompanying index, I have used the *GEDSH* dates for the reigns of the patriarchs Sargis of Tella (ca. 557–560), Paul of Beth Ukomo (564–81), and Peter III of Callinicus (581–91), but I am not entirely confident that they are correct. Certainty here may be elusive, as the dates found in the contemporary sources, particularly John of Ephesus, are vague and contradictory. Nevertheless, there are grounds for placing all three reigns earlier than *GEDSH* does. According to the *Chronicle of Zuqnin*, Sargis of Tella was patriarch as early as 544, and Paul of Beth Ukomo as early as 551.[1] There is also a plausible tradition that Paul was deposed in 578, not 581, and that Peter III of Callinicus was consecrated in the same year.[2] According to John of Ephesus, Paul of Beth Ukomo died in 580 or 581, two or three years after his own deposition and the death of Ya'qob Baradaeus in 578.[3]

The Syrian Orthodox patriarchs of Antioch to 1292

Severus (512–38)
Vacant, 538–ca. 544
Sargis of Tella (ca. 544–ca. 547)
Vacant, ca. 547–ca. 551
Paul of Beth Ukomo (ca. 551–578)
Vacant, 578–81
Peter III of Callinicus (581–91)
Julian II (591–94)
Athanasius I bar Gamolo (595–631)
Yoḥannon II (631–48)
Theodore (649–67)

Severus II bar Mashqo (668–80)
Vacant, 680–84
Athanasius II of Balad (684–87)
Julian III (687–708)
Eliya (709–23)
Athanasius III (724–40)
Iwannis I (740–54)
Isaac (755–56)
Athanasius Sandloyo (756–58)
Giwargis I (758–90)
Yoḥannon of Callinicus *intrusus* (758–62)
David of Dara *intrusus* (762–74)
Joseph (790–92)
Quriaqos (793–817)
Dionysius I of Tel-Maḥre (818–45)
Yoḥannon III (846–73)
Vacant, 874–78
Ignatius II (878–83)
Vacant, 883–87
Theodosius Romanus (887–96)
Vacant, 896–97
Dionysius II (897–909)
Yoḥannon IV (910–22)
Basil I (923–35)
Yoḥannon V (936–53)
Iwannis II (954–57)
Dionysius III (958–61)
Abraham I (962–63)
Yoḥannon VI Sarigta (965–85)
Athanasius IV Laʿzar (986–1003)
Yoḥannon VII bar ʿAbdon (1004–30)
Dionysius IV Ḥoye (1031–42)
Vacant, 1042–49
Yoḥannon bar ʿAbdun (1049–57)
Athanasius V Ḥoye (1058–64)
Yoḥannon VIII bar Shushan (1064–73)
Basil II (1074–75)
Yoḥannon IX ʿAbdon (1075–77)
Dionysius V Laʿzar (1077–78)
Vacant, 1078–86
Iwannis III (1086–88)
Dionysius VI Mark (1088–90)
Athanasius VI bar Khamoro (1090–1129)
Yoḥannon X Mawdyono (1130–37)
Athanasius VII bar Qeṭreh (1138–66)
Michael I the Syrian/the Great (1166–99)
Athanasius VIII (1199–1207)

Michael II (1207–15)
Yoḥannon XI (1208–20)
Vacant, 1220–22
Ignatius III David (1222–52)
Dionysius ʿAngur (1252–61)
Yoḥannon II bar Maʿdani (1252–63)
Ignatius IV Ishoʿ (1264–82)
Philoxenus Nemrud (1283–92)
Ignatius Constantine (1292–93)

The Eastern or Mardin patriarchs, 1293–1493

Ignatius V Bar Wahib (1293–1333)
Ignatius Ismaʿil (1333–65)
Ignatius Shahāb (1365–81)
Ignatius Abraham bar Gharīb (1381–1412)
Ignatius Behnam of Ḥadlī (1412–55)
Ignatius Khalaf of Maʿdan (1455–84)
Ignatius Yoḥannon bar Shayallāh (1484–93)

The Western or Sis Patriarchs, 1292–1445

Ignatius Michael (1292–1312)
Ignatius Michael II (1313–49)
Ignatius Philoxenus (1349–ca. 1360)
Basil Gabriel (1349–87)
Philoxenus the Scribe (1387–ca. 1421)
Basil Shemʿun of Beth Manʿem (ca. 1421–1445)

The Ṭur ʿAbdin patriarchs, 1364–1494

Ignatius Sobo of Ṣalaḥ (1364–89)
Ignatius Ishoʿ of Midyat (1389–1418)
Ignatius Masʿud of Ṣalaḥ (1418–20)
Ignatius Enoch of ʿAin Warda (1421–45)
Ignatius Qumo of Beth Sbirino (1446–55)
Ignatius Ishoʿ of ʿAin Warda (1455–60)
Ignatius Philoxenus ʿAziz Bar Sobto (1460–82)
Ignatius Sobo of Arbo (1482–89)
Ignatius Yoḥannon Qopar of ʿAin Warda (1489–93)
Ignatius Masʿud of Zaz (1493–94)

The Ṭur ʿAbdin patriarchs, 1515–1816

Ignatius Ishoʿ of Zaz (1515–24)
Ignatius Shemʿon of Hattakh (1524–51)
Ignatius Yaʿqob of Ḥesna d'Kifa (1551–71)

Vacant, 1571–84
Ignatius Sohdo of Midyat (1584–1621)
Vacant, 1621–ca. 1624
Ignatius Shemʿon (ca. 1624)
Vacant, ca. 1624–ca. 1628
Ignatius ʿAbdallah of Midyat (ca. 1628)
Vacant, ca. 1628–1674
Ignatius Ḥabib of Midyat (1674–1707)
Ignatius Denḥo of ʿArnas (1707–25)
Vacant, 1725–40
Ignatius Barṣawmo of Midyat (1740–91)
Ignatius Aḥo of Arbo (1791–1816)
Ignatius Ishaʿya of Arbo (1791–1816)
Severus Isaac of Azekh (1804–16)
Joseph of ʿArnas (1805–34)
Barṣawmo of Ḥbob (1816–39)
Mirza of Beth Sbirino (1816–42)
Gregory Zaitun Ghomo of Midyat (1821–44)
Severus ʿAbd al-Nur of Arbo (1834–39)

The Syrian Orthodox patriarchs, 1494–2016

Ignatius Nuḥ (1494–1509)
Ignatius Ishoʿ I (1509–19)
Ignatius Yaʿqob I (1510–19)
Ignatius David I (1519–21)
Ignatius ʿAbdullah I (1521–57)
Ignatius Niʿmatullah (1557–76)
Ignatius David Shah (1576–91)
Ignatius Pilate (1591–97)
Ignatius Peter Ḥadoyo (1598–1640)
Ignatius Shemʿon I (1640–53)
Ignatius Ishoʿ II Qamsho (1653–61)
Ignatius ʿAbd al-Masiḥ I (1662–86)
Ignatius Giwargis II (1687–1708)
Ignatius Isaac II (1709–22)
Ignatius Shukrallah II Saniʿa (1722–45)
Ignatius Giwargis III (1745–68)
Ignatius Giwargis IV (1768–81)
Ignatius Mattai Thaʿlab (1782–1819)
Ignatius Giwargis V Sayyar (1819–39)
Ignatius Eliya ʿAnkaz (1839–47)
Ignatius Yaʿqob II (1847–71)
Ignatius Peter VII (1872–94)
Ignatius ʿAbd al-Masih II (1894–1914)
Ignatius ʿAbdullah II Saṭṭūf (1914–17)
Ignatius Eliya Shakir (1917–33)

Ignatius Ephrem I Barsoum (1933–57)
Ignatius Ya‘qob III Severios (1957–80)
Ignatius Zakka I ‘Iwas (1980–2014)
Ignatius Ephrem II Karim (2014–)

The Syrian Orthodox grand metropolitans of the East, 559–1059

Aḥudemmeh (559–75)
Vacant, 575–78
Qamisho‘ (578–609)
Vacant, 609–14
Samuel (614–24)
Vacant, 624–29
Marutha (629–49)
Denḥo I (649–59)
Vacant, 659–69
Barisho‘ (669–83)
Abraham (ca. 684)
David (ca. 684–ca. 686)
Yoḥannon I Saba (686–88)
Denḥo II (688–727)
Paul (728–57)
Yoḥannon II Kionoyo (759–85)
Joseph (785–ca. 790)
Vacant, ca. 790–93
Sharbil (793–ca. 800)
Shem‘on (ca. 800–ca. 815)
Basil I (ca. 815–829)
Daniel (829–34)
Thomas (834–47)
Basil II (848–68)
Melchisedec (858–68)
Vacant, 869–72
Sargis (872–83)
Vacant, 883–87
Athanasius (887–903)
Vacant, 904–ca. 910
Thomas (910–11)
Denḥo III (913–33)
Vacant, 933–37
Basil III (937–61)
Quriaqos (962–80)
Yoḥannon III (981–88)
Vacant, 988–91
Ignatius bar Qiqi (991–1016)
Vacant, 1016–27
Athanasius II (1027–41)

Vacant, 1041–46
Basil IV (1046–69)
Vacant, 1069–75

The Syrian Orthodox maphrians of the East, 1075–1859

Yoḥannon IV Ṣaliba (1075–1106)
Vacant, 1106–12
Dionysius I Mushe (1112–42)
Ignatius II Laʿzar (1142–64)
Yoḥannon V (1164–88)
Dionysius bar Tammasiḥ (1189–90)
Gregory I Yaʿqob (1189–1214)
Ignatius III David (1215–22)
Dionysius II (1222–31)
Yoḥannon VI bar Maʿdani (1232–52)
Ignatius IV (1253–58)
Vacant, 1258–63
Gregory II Abu'lfaraj (Barhebraeus) (1264–86)
Vacant, 1286–88
Gregory III Barṣawmo (1288–1308)
Vacant, 1308–17
Gregory Mattai (1317–45)
Vacant, 1345–60
Gregory V Dioscorus (1360–61)
Vacant, 1361–64
Athanasius III Abraham (1364–79)
Vacant, 1379–1404
Basil Behnam of Ḥadlī (1404–12)
Vacant, 1412–15
Dioscorus II Behnam (1415–17)
Vacant, 1417–22
Basil Barṣawmo (1422–55)
Vacant, 1455–58
Cyril Joseph II (1458–ca. 1470)
Basil ʿAziz (1471–87)
Vacant, 1487–90
Basil Nuḥ (1490–94)
Vacant, 1494–96
Basil Abraham (1496–1507)
Basil Sulaiman (1509–18)
Basil Athanasius Ḥabib (1518–33)
Basil Eliya (1533–ca. 1554)
Basil Niʿmatallah (1555–57)
Basil ʿAbd al-Ghani (1557–75)
Basil Pilate (1575–91)
Eliya (ca. 1590)

Basil ʿAbd al-Ghani (1591–97)
Basil Peter Hadaya (1597–98)
Vacant, ca. 1598–ca. 1624
Basil Ishoʿ (ca. 1624–ca. 1646)
Basil Shemʿon (1635–39)
Basil Shukrallah I (1639–52)
Basil Behnam (1653–55)
Basil ʿAbd al-Masiḥ (1655–ca. 1658)
Basil Ḥabib (ca. 1658–ca. 1671)
Basil Yalda (ca. 1671–1683)
Basil Giwargis (1683–86)
Basil Isaac (1687–1709)
Basil ʿAzar (1709–13)
Basil Mattai (1713–27)
Basil Shemʿon (ca. 1727–ca. 1729)
Basil ʿAzar (1730–59)
Basil Giwargis (1760–68)
Vacant, 1768–1783
Basil Ṣliba (1783–90)
Basil Bishara (1790–1817)
Basil Yunan (ca. 1803–ca. 1809)
Basil Cyril (ca. 1803–ca. 1811)
Basil ʿAbd al-ʿAziz (ca. 1803)
Basil Mattai (1820–ca. 1825)
Basil Eliya Karmeh (1825–27)
Basil Eliya ʿAnkaz (1827–39)
Basil Behnam (1839–59)

The Syrian Orthodox maphrians of the East, from 1964

Basil Paul (1964–)

The Ṭur ʿAbdin maphrians, ca. 1479–1844

Basil (ca. 1479)
Basil Malke of Midyat (1495–1510)
Vacant, 1510–37
Basil Abraham (1537–43)
Vacant, 1543–55
Basil Shemʿon of Kfar Shamaʿ (1549–55)
Vacant, 1555–61
Basil Behnam of Kfarze (1561–62)
Vacant, 1562–1650
Basil Ḥabib Haddad of Midyat (1650–74)
Vacant, 1674–ca. 1688
Basil Laʿzar of Midyat (ca. 1688–ca. 1701)
Basil Shemʿon of Beth Manʿem (1710–40)

Basil Denḥo Baltaji of ʿArnas (1740–80)
Basil ʿAbdallah Yahya (1779–84)
Shemʿon of Bate (1786)
Ṣliba al-ʿAttar of Beth Sbirino (1779–1815)
Basil Barṣawmo of Enhel (1815–30)
Basil ʿAbd al-Ahad Kindo of Enhel (1821–44)

The patriarchs of the Syrian Catholic Church

Andrew Akhījān (1662–78)
Ignatius Peter Gregory (1678–1701)
Vacant, 1701–83
Ignatius Michael Jarweh (1782–1800)
Ignatius Michael IV Dāher (1802–10)
Ignatius Shemʿon Zora (1814–18)
Ignatius Peter Jarweh (1820–51)
Ignatius Anton I Samheri (1853–64)
Ignatius Philip ʿArkus (1866–74)
Ignatius Giwargis Shelḥot (1874–91)
Ignatius Behnam Benni (1893–97)
Ignatius Ephrem II Raḥmani (1898–1929)
Ignatius Gabriel I Tappuni (1929–68)
Ignatius Anṭun II Hayyek (1968–98)
Ignatius Mūsā I David (1998–2001)
Ignatius Peter VIII ʿAbdalaḥad (2001–8)
Ignatius Joseph III Yunan (since 2009)

NOTES

1 Chronicle of Zuqnin (ed. Harrak), 113–14 and 124.
2 Chronicle of Zuqnin (ed. Harrak), 137.
3 John of Ephesus, Ecclesiastical History, 3.4.58.

APPENDIX III

ONLINE RESOURCES FOR THE STUDY OF THE SYRIAC WORLD

Daniel King and David A. Michelson

It has become a truism to state that the Internet has revolutionised the way in which students and researchers are able to access materials within the field of Syriac studies (Michelson 2016, 64–65). Every year more and more material becomes available online. This is of undoubted benefit to the field and to all those concerned with it, although as always great care must be taken with all online material to ensure its quality and reliability. It ought further to be emphasised that particular resources (books, manuscripts, journals etc.) must never be privileged over others simply because they are more easily accessible. For further discussion of the issues, see Kristian S. Heal, "Corpora, elibraries and Databases: Locating Syriac Studies in the 21st century" (2012).

Digital resources are constantly changing, thus the list below will be obsolete almost immediately. Nevertheless, as of 2017, the following are among the most significant resources pertaining to the study of the Syriac World.

ACADEMIC RESOURCES DEDICATED TO SYRIAC STUDIES

Because Syriac studies is a relatively small and new academic field, there are only a handful of digital projects which are directly focused on the study of Syriac materials.

Beth Mardutho: The Syriac Institute www.bethmardutho.org

Beth Mardutho (*The House of Instruction*), founded by George A. Kiraz, was among the very first of scholarly organizations to begin to put Syriac academic resources online and to hold conferences on Syriac computing (what one might now call the intersection of Syriac studies and the digital humanities). In 1998, Beth Mardutho had the foresight to begin publishing an online open access journal, *Hugoye*, which is now the principal journal dedicated Syriac studies. In the same year, Beth Mardutho also began hosting an academic e-mail discussion group which 19 years later has grown to over 700 members and more than 7000 posts. More recently, Beth Mardutho has published a number of other resources online including *Meltho* – the standard set of Syriac unicode fonts bundled with the Windows operating system and available for free use in the Mac or Linux operating systems. Another resource is *eBeth Arké* – an open access digital library. Beth Mardutho has also released an open access electronic edition of the *Gorgias Encyclopedic Dictionary of the Syriac Heritage* (see below) formatted according to the widely-used standards of the Text Encoding Initiative (TEI) and incorporating the unique identifier (URI) numbering system designed by Syriaca.org.

The most notable online resource of Beth Mardutho is *SEDRA* (*Syriac Electronic Data Research Archive*) – a linguistic and literary database of the Syriac language and literature which features advanced morphological and lexical analysis tools (some lexica are open access and some require a subscription). The *SEDRA* site (http://sedra.bethmardutho.org/) has easy-to-use tools for parsing and defining Syriac text. SEDRA also features an API which allows any website to incorporate the SEDRA parsing and lookup tools into their own site automatically.

Syriaca.org: The Syriac Reference Portal www.syriaca.org

Syriaca.org is "a digital project for the study of Syriac literature, culture, and history" hosted by Vanderbilt University. It was founded by David A. Michelson and is currently directed by Daniel L. Schwartz. It was "conceived to produce tools and reference resources that will overcome some of the access and discovery problems which currently impede scholarly research on Syriac language, cultures, and history." The portal publishes a number of new resources, digital tools, and reference works which are the product of the latest scholarship. These include *The Syriac Gazetteer* – a dictionary of historical geography relating to the Syriac World, *The Syriac Biographical Dictionary* – with individual volumes devoted to Syriac authors and Syriac saints, and *A New Handbook of Syriac Literature* with descriptions of Syriac texts. Future development plans include *SPEAR: Syriac Persons Events and Relations* and a series of tools for the study of prosopography, historical events, manuscripts, and bibliography. All of Syriaca.org's resources are open access and available for free reuse under the Creative Commons licences. The full database can be downloaded in multiple formats including TEI XML and as linked data (RDF). Syriaca.org actively solicits proposals for new projects and also invites editorial collaboration from scholars in the field.

The main aim of Syriaca.org is to provide digital infrastructure for the creation of "Linked Open Data" to enable linking data and searching across various online projects in Syriac studies by assigning and ensuring editorial oversight for a system of unique identifiers for authors, texts, and other data similar to the way the identifier numbers have long been used in Greek studies (e.g. in the *Thesaurus Linguae Graecae*). These identifiers (URIs – uniform resource identifiers) are an emerging technology for linking resources in the field of Syriac studies and have even been incorporated into the "Index of Maps" for the present volume (see pages 824–834).

Syri.ac www.syri.ac

Syri.ac is a "comprehensive annotated bibliography of open-access resources related to the study of Syriac." It was developed by Jack Tannous (Princeton University),

Scott Johnson (University of Oklahoma), and Morgan Reed (Catholic University of America). Focusing on materials that are already freely available online and in the public domain, it constitutes an invaluable resource especially for accessing ancient Syriac texts. For example, the page on the poet Ephrem is an excellent place to navigate one's way through the various editions of his works. It is also the best available single website through which to find digitised versions of the numerous dictionaries, manuscript catalogues, and other print reference works now available through the internet (for example works in the public domain digitised by Google Books, The Hathi Trust, or The Internet Archive).

Syri.ac also houses a frequently-updated database of online manuscripts images (a rapidly growing area of enormous significance for the study of the Syriac world), an ongoing database of 'editions in progress', a collection of many further internet links, and substantial materials on Christian Arabic Studies. The project is open access (no subscription fee is required) and the editors state clearly and laudably their commitment to open scholarship: "We believe firmly that the free and open access of scholarly materials should be encouraged and will be a fundamental, non-negotiable cornerstone of future scholarship." No specific license terms are specified on the site and at present it is not possible to download the entire database.

e-GEDSH https://gedsh.bethmardutho.org/

e-GEDSH is the freely available online electronic edition of the *Gorgias Encyclopedic Dictionary of the Syriac Heritage*, a vital resource that has been available in print since 2011. The focus of GEDSH is on the Syriac Christian cultural tradition as it historically developed in the Syriac homelands of the Middle East, was carried on by a great number of religious communities of different backgrounds, and is still preserved, cherished, and studied by Syriac Christians today, in the Middle East, in India, and in the worldwide diaspora. Without excluding manifestations of Syriac Christianity in other languages and cultures, the primary focus is on the Classical Syriac expression of Syriac Christianity. The encyclopaedia contains numerous entries on many aspects of the Syriac heritage. The electronic edition is a model of digital scholarship. All entries can be downloaded in TEI XML and are clearly licensed under the Creative Commons CC-BY NC license. URIs from Syriaca.org allow entries from e-GEDSH to be integrated in other on-line projects.

Comprehensive Bibliography on Syriac Christianity www.csc.org.il/db/db.aspx?db=SB

Modelled on the decades-long work of Sebastian Brock to publish print bibliographies for Syriac studies, this database project was begun by Sergey Minov with the support of the Center for the Study of Christianity at the Hebrew University of Jerusalem. The open access project now offers more than 14,000 entries classified according to a subject taxonomy of several hundred terms. The aims of this database are to incorporate all the data that was previously being published in a multitude of printed bibliographies, to update this data regularly, and to maximise the benefits of searching online databases. This database is a crucial resource for scholars and researchers of the Syriac world and should be the starting point for any review of the literature in Syriac studies. The project is open access (no subscription fee is required), but license terms are not specified on the site. It is not possible to download the entire database.

The Digital Syriac Corpus www.syriaccorpus.org

The Digital Syriac Corpus is an open-access online repository of digitized Syriac texts. This project is the continuation of the Oxford-BYU Syriac Corpus (http://cpart.mi.byu.edu/home/sec), which was a collection of transcribed Syriac texts gathered by Kristian S. Heal (BYU) and David G. K. Taylor (Oxford). Under the editorial direction of James E. Walters (Rochester College), the Digital Syriac Corpus is in the process of converting these documents from word processor format into TEI/XML encoding, which allows for both advanced searching options across the corpus and easily shareable formatting in alignment with open-access commitments. All texts in the Digital Syriac Corpus are released under a Creative Commons license (CC-BY 4.0). Many of the texts in the corpus were transcribed from older print editions, but some have been transcribed directly from manuscripts. The Digital Syriac Corpus also accepts submissions of both transcribed texts and born-digital critical editions, which can be created using TEI/XML templates provided on the Corpus website. Texts in the Digital Syriac Corpus can be searched in a number of ways, and these searches can be limited or expanded by various facets. Ultimately, the aim of the Digital Syriac Corpus is two-fold: 1) to provide free and reliable access to Syriac texts of all time periods both for scholarly research purposes and for the benefit of Syriac heritage communities all over the world; and 2) to help preserve these texts for future generations through digital archiving. The project is a model of Syriac linked data integrated both with the SEDRA lexicon API and also with Syriaca.org URIS for authors and text titles. Published using the Srophé digital application developed by Syriaca.org, the contents of the Digital Syriac Corpus can be download easily as individual texts or as an entire corpus.

Canadian Centre for Epigraphic Documents www.epigraphy.ca

The Canadian Centre for Epigraphic Documents, hosted by the Department of Near and Middle Eastern Civilizations at the University of Toronto, has published four collections of Syriac epigraphy including the Amir Harrak Collection of Iraqi Syriac and Garshuni inscriptions, which it notes "is the largest collection of its type in the world." These inscriptions date from the 7th – 20th centuries CE and are documented in photographs taken from the 1930's to 2010. The project is open access (no subscription fee is required). The images are marked as copyright, and license terms are not specified on the site. It is not possible to download the entire database.

NISIBIN Research and Project Database https://nisibin-database.uni-frankfurt.de

NISIBIN is a newly created database curated by Ralph Barczok of the Research Centre for Aramaean Studies at the Goethe-Universität Frankfurt am Main. NISIBIN is a directory for tracking research projects, conference presentations, and workshops in Aramaean Studies and adjacent fields. Scholars are invited to submit descriptions of their research into the database using standardized keywords. The list of keywords is fully integrated with URIs from Syriaca.org's taxonomy and with entries from the Comprehensive Bibliography on Syriac Christianity. The database serves as a historical record of projects and conferences and allows users to search by author, keyword, and other filters. The project is open access (no subscription fee is required), but license terms are not specified on the site. It is not possible to download the entire database.

Dayr Mar Elian Archaeological Project (DMEAP) https://doi.org/10.5284/1000237

While there are few online archaeological materials concerning Syriac places, the DMEAP data repository is one of the more rich digital archives related to a single site from the Syriac World. The DMEAP project is the result of field work conducted by Prof. Emma Loosley (University of Exeter) at the monastery of Mar Elian in Syria. This online resource is of particular significance because the monastery was destroyed in 2015 as part of the conflict in the region. The DMEAP site follows the format of its host repository, The Archaeology Data Service (ADS) and includes an overview of the project, a gallery of images, metadata about the cultural heritage location, and usage statistics for the repository. The project is open access (no subscription fee is required). All data is copyrighted and no licenses are indicated which would allow permission to download or reuse the data.

Aramaic-Online Project (AOP) www.surayt.com

AOP is a joint project of the Freie Universität Berlin, University of Bergen, University of Cambridge, Leipzig University, and St Ephrem Syriac Orthodox Monastery to develop an online curriculum and language learning tools for Turoyo Aramaic, called Surayt. Sample materials have been released online in beta form in English and Surayt. The final site will be designed to be used in Arabic, Dutch, English, French, German, and Turkish and optimised for mobile devices. The project is open access (no subscription fee is required). The development version of the site indicates that Creative Commons licenses may apply, but license terms are not yet specified directly on the site and it is not yet possible to download the entire curriculum.

ACADEMIC RESOURCES GERMANE TO SYRIAC STUDIES

The general growth of digital humanities scholarship now means that there are also a number of online resources relevant to the Syriac World which are available as part of projects originating in neighbouring fields of study or with purviews broader than just Syriac studies. The list below is, by definition, not comprehensive.

Patrologia Orientalis Database (POD) www.brepolis.net

Since 1903, the *Patrologia Orientalis* series (originally titled *Patrologia Syriaca*) has published 234 texts and translations of Eastern Christian texts originally composed in Arabic, Armenian, Coptic, Ge'ez, Georgian, Greek, Slavonic, Syriac, and Latin. These texts are now available through *Brepolis*, the home of all online projects of Brepols Publishers and its partners. For the original language editions, at present, the site only allows one to access a PDF image of the printed page. The translations, however, are presented as a full text electronic corpus which can be searched by keyword and other filters through a multilingual interface in English, French, German, and Italian. Brepols indicates that this database will continue to grow as new fascicles are published in the *Patrologia Orientalis* series. This is a subscription service which is not open access. It is not possible to download the entire database. Older volumes of the *Patrologia Orientalis* may be in the public domain and are available elsewhere online.

Corpus Scriptorum Christianorum Orientalium (CSCO) www.peeters-leuven.be

Since 1903, the *CSCO* series has published over 600 volumes of texts and translations of Eastern Christian texts originally composed in Arabic, Armenian, Coptic, Ge'ez, Georgian, and Syriac. Approximately one third of the volumes are Syriac texts. Peeters Publishers (Leuven, Belgium), in partnership with the Oriental Institute of the Université catholique de Louvain (Louvain-la-Neuve, Belgium), has announce that they are preparing a digital version of the *CSCO*, which will be available online. The medium-term objective is to offer access to the Syriac texts of Ephrem, a corpus encompassing thirty-eight volumes of the series. A web-based interface is in development to allow scholars to explore both the Syriac texts and their German translations. This project paves the way for a wider one, aspiring to enlarge this first experience to the other volumes of the *CSCO*. This has been announced as a subscription service which may not be open access. Older volumes of the *CSCO* may be in the public domain and are available elsewhere online.

The Hill Museum & Manuscript Library (HMML) www.vhmml.org

HMML, a part of Saint John's University in Collegeville, Minnesota, hosts "the world's largest archive of manuscript photographs in both microfilm and digital format". Related to its core mission of preserving manuscript images, HMML also offers a number of online educational tools (*v*HMML) for the study of codicology and paleography. Manuscript cultures covered include Arabic, Armenian, Ge'ez, Latin, Syriac, and Persian. Different modules teach about scripts, transcribing of manuscripts, sample folia for teaching, a codicology lexicon, and secondary literature related to codicology. In addition, HMML's online catalogue offers access to a number of digitised Syriac manuscripts (see discussion below). *v*HMML contains both open access and copyrighted material and provides documentation regarding which materials are available for reuse under Creative Commons licenses. Registration is required for some features of the virtual reading room. The metadata is not available for bulk download but the source code is.

The Comprehensive Aramaic Lexicon (CAL) http://cal.huc.edu

Based at Hebrew Union College and founded by Stephen A. Kaufman, *CAL* is a database of the Aramaic texts in all dialects (Old Aramaic, Imperial Aramaic, Biblical Aramaic, Middle Aramaic, Palestinian Aramaic, Syriac, Babylonian Aramaic, Late Jewish Literary Aramaic) ranging from 9th Century BCE to the 13th Century CE. Texts were first encoded in the 1980s for this long running project which at present contains approximately 3 million lexically parsed words. Texts currently available include the Peshiṭta and Old Syriac Gospels as well as commentaries by Ephrem and Ishoʿdad, and a range of other early Syriac texts. *CAL* also offers digital tools for lexical and morphological analysis. The project is open access (no subscription fee is required), but license terms are not specified on the site and it is not possible to download the entire database.

The North Eastern Neo-Aramaic Database https://nena.ames.cam.ac.uk

The North Eastern Neo-Aramaic Database is hosted by the Faculty of Oriental Studies of Cambridge University under the direction of Geoffrey Khan. The purpose of the project is to document rapidly vanishing Neo-Aramaic dialects through survey questionnaires, dialect maps, audio recordings, images, and fieldwork. The results of the project are keyed to a map and list of dialects. The dialects included are from a variety of ethnic and religious communities including several who identify as Syriac in heritage. The project is partially open access (no subscription fee is required for some data). All materials are copyrighted and license terms are not specified. It is not possible to download the entire database.

Guide to Evagrius Ponticus http://evagriusponticus.net

Guide to Evagrius Ponticus is an open access, peer-reviewed publication edited by Joel Kalvesmaki of Dumbarton Oaks, Harvard University. The guide contains a variety of materials related to Evagrius Ponticus, an author whose corpus survives extensively (and for a few items exclusively) in Syriac. In addition to a *clavis* to the works of Evagrius with information about the Syriac corpus, the site includes an extensive bibliography and Zotero database. Future development of the site (already available online in a provisional form) includes a sophisticated database of aligned Greek and Syriac texts by Evagrius. The project is licensed under Creative Commons licenses and the texts and bibliography can also be downloaded in full through Github and Zotero libraries. This project is a model for future digital resources dedicated to the study of a single ancient author.

Clavis Historicorum Tardae Antiquitatis (CHTA) www.late-antique-historiography.ugent.be/database

CHTA is an inventory of all historiographical works from Late Antiquity (classified as the period 300–800 CE). The database publishes open-access catalogue-style descriptions of early mediaeval texts. The database covers texts in eleven mediaeval languages including Syriac and Aramaic. The CHTA database as a whole is edited by P. Van Nuffelen & L. Van Hoof at Ghent University. A subset of the database includes descriptions of 135 Syriac works collected and catalogued by Maria Conterno. Entries include titles in English and Syriac, dates of composition, notes on genre, and bibliography. The project is presently available online in a "preliminary" state and thus full documentation is not available for the project, but correspondence with the project team indicates that implementation of linked open data features is a part of future development.

The Goussen Library Collection http://digitale-sammlungen.ulb.uni-bonn.de/topic/view/16431

The Goussen Library Collection is hosted by the Universitäts- und Landesbibliothek Bonn which digitised over 1000 volumes primarily from the collection of Heinrich

Goussen (1863–1927). The Collection is focused on church history with attention to publications in Syriac, Coptic, Ethiopian, Arabic, Armenian, and Georgian. The digital collection aims to include all titles printed in these languages before 1800 and other rare items. Approximately 200 titles are included in the "Syrian group" of the digital library. For each title, high resolution scans are available (although not all are in colour). Its catalogue has metadata of very high quality which includes linked data with authority files from the Deutsche Nationalbibliothek as well as links to Wikipedia. Each record has a stable URN. Images can be downloaded individually as a .jpeg or .pdf or as an entire book. Metadata is encoded as a METS XML object available from an archival server using the Open Archives Initiative Protocol for Metadata Harvesting. Finally, all images are clearly marked as being in the public domain with a Creative Commons Public Domain Mark 1.0 International License.

Biblia Arabica Project http://biblia-arabica.com

The Biblia Arabica Project is a collaborative research project lead by scholars at three universities in Israel and Germany. The project is focused on the history of the Hebrew Bible and New Testament in Arabic translation from the 8th century CE onward. One strand of translation was from Syriac. The bibliographic portion of the project is being undertaken by Ronny Vollandt of the Ludwig-Maximilians-Universität. The resulting open access digital bibliography will be posted online under Creative Commons licenses and also available for download in full through Github libraries.

The Ancient World Online (AWOL) http://ancientworldonline.blogspot.com

AWOL is a project of Charles E. Jones, Tombros Librarian for Classics and Humanities at the Pattee Library, Penn State University. The primary aim of the resource is to notice and comment on open access material relating to the ancient world including Syriac studies. The site has won awards including the 2015 Archaeological Institute of America Award for Outstanding Work in Digital Archeology and the 2015 Digital Humanities Awards for "Best DH Blog Post or Series of Posts." It is a useful resource for discovering open access scholarship in Syriac studies or related fields. This open access site is licensed under a Creative Commons license and features RSS and other tools (AWOL index) for bulk download and automated query.

Trismegistos (TM) www.trismegistos.org

Trismegistos is a collection of databases focused on texts, collections, archives, people, places, and authors in the ancient western world, dated between roughly 800 BCE and 800 CE. The project is based at Katholieke Universiteit Leuven and originally focused on Egypt and thus contains some information related to the famous Syriac library at Dayr al-Suryan and Syriac manuscripts from Egypt. The project is now expanding beyond Egypt and aims to collect information about all texts from the ancient world in general. Similar to Syriaca.org the project has a core aim of providing stable identifiers for digital data. The project is open access (no subscription fee is required), but license terms are not specified on the site. It is not possible to download the entire database which resides in a MySQL instance.

A note on digitised manuscript collections

The digitisation of manuscripts is still a very new field, yet has advanced at a great pace over the last few years. The above-mentioned checklist of digitised manuscripts at *Syri.ac* provides the most comprehensive listings and entry-points for finding manuscripts that have been placed online. Because the number of libraries making their manuscript collections available online is constantly growing, it is not feasible to list them all here. Instead, it should be noted that the largest online collections of Syriac manuscripts to date are those of the Bibliotheca Apostolica Vaticana (www.mss.vatlib.it/guii/scan/link.jsp), and of the Hill Museum and Manuscript Library (www.hmml.org/). For the latter, Columba Stewart has untiringly been collecting digitisations from across the Near East, preserving precious collections many of which are under threat. Also of note is a project at Centre National de la Recherche Scientifique in Paris through the collaboration of André Binggeli, Françoise Briquel-Chatonnet, Muriel Debié and Alain Desreumaux. This project, *E-ktobe* (www.mss-syriaques.org), offers detailed palaeographical information and indexing of a number of manuscript collections in Europe and the Middle East. Future development of the *E-ktobe* project includes plans for integration and cross searching with the *Pinakes* database of Greek medieval manuscripts. This development phase includes plans for use of Syriaca.org URIs for cataloguing and making manuscript description data available in open access TEI XML format. Another collection of online manuscript images relevant to Syriac studies is the International Dunhuang Project (available through multiple partners including, http://idp.bl.uk/) which now includes several hundred Syriac texts.

Finally one exemplary model of an open access digital publication of a Syriac manuscript is the publication of the "Syriac Galen Palimpsest" (http://digitalgalen.net) by the Walters Art Museum and the University of Pennsylvania's *OPenn* digital repository. This resource provides open access images and high quality TEI XML metadata with Creative Commons licenses in a durable and easily downloadable digital format. It is hoped that future projects focused on a single manuscript will follow this model.

OTHER ONLINE RESOURCES

In addition to digital resources hosted by universities and research centres, there are any number of other resources online related to the Syriac World published by individuals or cultural heritage organizations. These cannot be all listed here, not least the numerous websites produced by the various ecclesiastical communities of the Syriac traditions. As an illustration of how useful academic resources for Syriac studies are also being published as part of personal online projects two representative examples are given below. Given the increasingly transitory nature of information posted to the internet, it is hoped that any resources of academic value will also be eventually archived by university libraries for preservation.

Roger Pearse's Pages www.tertullian.org/rpearse

Since 1999, Roger Pearse has combined his personal interests in computing and scholarship on early Christianity to build a useful if eclectic website. As part of this passion, he has even commissioned new scholarship including English translations. This site is relevant for Syriac studies because of several digitised editions of English translations of Syriac and Arabic texts and a few Syriac texts. The project is open access (no subscription fee is required), but license terms are not specified on the site although many texts are marked as being in the public domain. The simple HTML formatting makes it possible to download the entire database.

Dukhrana Biblical Research www.dukhrana.com

Dukhrana is a personal project of Lars J. Lindgren providing tools for the study of the Peshiṭta New Testament. Based on an earlier version of the *SEDRA* database published by Beth Mardutho, this site offers digitised versions of the Peshiṭta including transcriptions of a few manuscripts, a search function for some common Syriac dictionaries, a user-friendly grammatical analysis of the Syriac New Testament, translations of the Peshiṭta into different languages, and comparison with the Greek New Testament. The project is open access (no subscription fee is required). No license terms are specified on the site and some pages are copyrighted.

REFERENCES

Heal, Kristian S. 2012. "Corpora, elibraries and Databases: Locating Syriac Studies in the 21st century," *Hugoye: Journal of Syriac Studies* 15.1, 65–78. www.bethmardutho.org/index.php/hugoye/volume-index/505.html.

Michelson, David A. 2016. "Syriaca.Org as a Test Case for Digitally Re-Sorting the Ancient World." In *Ancient Worlds in Digital Culture*, edited by Claire Clivaz, Paul Dilley, and David Hamidović, 59–85. Leiden: Brill. http://hdl.handle.net/1803/8344.

INDEX OF MAPS

Prepared by William L. Potter and David A. Michelson

Note: This index lists the 909 places labelled on the maps in this volume (see pages xxxiv *ff.*). The corresponding map numbers are listed for each label as well as cross-references for when a related historical name has been used. To help the reader with disambiguation, each place name in the index is also identified according the URI identifier system used in *The Syriac Gazetteer* (http://syriaca.org/geo). Each URI can be resolved in the format http://syriaca.org/place/78, etc. The exact coordinates used to plot the maps are provided at these URIs.

ʿAbdasi (syriaca.org/place/4213), 8; *see also* Nahargur
Abila (syriaca.org/place/4355), 1, 4
Abivard (syriaca.org/place/4222), 9
Abr Shahr (syriaca.org/place/4220), 9, 10; *see also* Nishapur
Acre (syriaca.org/place/14), 2, 5; *see also* ʿAkka, Akko, Ptolemaïs
Aden (syriaca.org/place/4143), 6
Adharbayjan (syriaca.org/place/5), 2, 9
Adhorma (syriaca.org/place/4448), 14
Adiabene (syriaca.org/place/993), 1, 7, 14; *see also* Ḥadyab
Adulis (syriaca.org/place/4144), 6; *see also* Zula
Adummatu (syriaca.org/place/4001), 1; *see also* Dumatha
Adurbadagan (syriaca.org/place/798), 1; *see also* Ardabil
Aḥmadabad (syriaca.org/place/4335), 11
Ahvaz (syriaca.org/place/96), 2, 8, 9; *see also* Hormuz-Ardashir
Akhlat (syriaca.org/place/2312), 2, 7
Akhmim (syriaca.org/place/4169), 6; *see also* Panopolis
ʿAkka (syriaca.org/place/14), 2, 5; *see also* Acre, Akko, Ptolemaïs
ʿAkkaz Island (syriaca.org/place/4497), 6
Akko (syriaca.org/place/14), 1, 2, 5; *see also* Ptolemaïs, Acre, ʿAkka
Aksum (syriaca.org/place/4146), 6
Alangad (syriaca.org/place/4503), 13
Aleppo (syriaca.org/place/18), 1, 2, 3; *see also* Beroea
Alexandretta (syriaca.org/place/663), 2, 3; *see also* Iskenderun
Alexandria (syriaca.org/place/572), 5
Almaliq (syriaca.org/place/796), 10, 11
Alodia (syriaca.org/place/4540), 6
Alqosh (syriaca.org/place/19), 14
Altai Range (syriaca.org/place/4336), 11
Amaseia (syriaca.org/place/292), 1; *see also* Amasya
Amasya (syriaca.org/place/292), 2; *see also* Amaseia
ʿAmedia (syriaca.org/place/20), 14
Amida (syriaca.org/place/8), 1, 2, 7; *see also* Diyarbakir
Amman (syriaca.org/place/4061), 2, 5; *see also* Philadelphia
Amol (syriaca.org/place/4223), 9
Amu Darya River (syriaca.org/place/4224), 9, 10, 11; *see also* Oxus River
ʿAna (syriaca.org/place/429), 1, 2, 7
Anamur (syriaca.org/place/4003), 2; *see also* Anemurium
Anatolia (syriaca.org/place/504), 2, 3; *see also* Asia Minor
Anazarba (syriaca.org/place/9), 2, 3; *see also* ʿAyn Zarba
Anbar (syriaca.org/place/211), 2, 8; *see also* Piroz-Shapur
Ancyra (syriaca.org/place/494), 1; *see also* Ankara
Anemurium (syriaca.org/place/4003), 1, 3; *see also* Anamur
Angamaly (syriaca.org/place/666), 13, 12
Angkor (syriaca.org/place/4337), 11
Ani (syriaca.org/place/4005), 1, 2
Anjur (syriaca.org/place/4516), 12; *see also* Thozhiyur
Ankara (syriaca.org/place/494), 2; *see also* Ancyra
ʿAnkawa (syriaca.org/place/261), 14

Anti-Lebanon Mountains (syriaca.org/place/4524), 7
Antioch (syriaca.org/place/10), 1, 2, 3
Anuradhapura (syriaca.org/place/4521), 12
Apamea (syriaca.org/place/11), 1, 3
Aprah (syriaca.org/place/4226), 9, 10; *see also* Farah
Aq-Beshim (syriaca.org/place/4279), 10; *see also* Suyab
ʿAqaba (syriaca.org/place/4125), 5
Aqsu (syriaca.org/place/4281), 10, 11
Arabia (syriaca.org/place/716), 6, 9
Arabian Sea (syriaca.org/place/4338), 11
Aradin (syriaca.org/place/256), 14
Aral Sea (syriaca.org/place/4282), 10, 11
Araxes River (syriaca.org/place/4006), 1, 2, 7
Arbel (syriaca.org/place/13), 14; *see also* Arbela, Erbil
Arbela (syriaca.org/place/13), 1, 2, 7; *see also* Arbel, Erbil
Ardabil (syriaca.org/place/798), 1, 2, 9; *see also* Adurbadagan
Armenia (syriaca.org/place/576), 1, 2, 7, 9
ʿArqa (syriaca.org/place/432), 3, 4
Arsamosata (syriaca.org/place/286), 1, 2, 7; *see also* Shimshaṭ
Artaxata (syriaca.org/place/4007), 1
Arwad (syriaca.org/place/4062), 2, 3
Arzanene (syriaca.org/place/673), 14
Arzon (syriaca.org/place/285), 7; *see also* Arzun
Arzun (syriaca.org/place/285), 1, 2, 7, 14; *see also* Arzon
Ascalon (syriaca.org/place/674), 1, 2, 5
Ashtishat (syriaca.org/place/4008), 1, 7
Ashur (syriaca.org/place/4009), 1, 7, 8
Asia Minor (syriaca.org/place/504), 2, 3; *see also* Anatolia
Astarabad (syriaca.org/place/4228), 9
Aswan (syriaca.org/place/4178), 6; *see also* Syene
Atropatene (syriaca.org/place/4010), 1
ʿAynwardo (syriaca.org/place/29), 14
ʿAyn Zarba (syriaca.org/place/9), 2, 3; *see also* Anazarba
Azakh (syriaca.org/place/287), 14; *see also* Beth Zabdai

Baʿalbak (syriaca.org/place/577), 2, 4; *see also* Heliopolis
Babylon (syriaca.org/place/4011), 1, 8, 9
Bactria (syriaca.org/place/4229), 9, 10; *see also* Tokharistan
Badghis (syriaca.org/place/4231), 9, 10
Badlis (syriaca.org/place/2283), 2, 7, 14; *see also* Bitlis
Baghdad (syriaca.org/place/41), 2, 8, 9
Bahman-Ardashir (syriaca.org/place/4203), 8; *see also* Prat d-Maishan
Baku (syriaca.org/place/4063), 2, 9
Bala Murghab (syriaca.org/place/4258), 9, 10; *see also* Merv al-Rud
Balad (syriaca.org/place/42), 1, 2, 7, 14
Balasaghun (syriaca.org/place/4284), 10; *see also* Burana
Balikh River (syriaca.org/place/4183), 7
Balinea (syriaca.org/place/4101), 1, 3; *see also* Baniyas
Balkh (syriaca.org/place/4232), 9, 10, 11
Balkhash, Lake (syriaca.org/place/4303), 10, 11
Baniyas (syriaca.org/place/154), 2, 4, 5; *see also* Caesarea Philippi
Baniyas (syriaca.org/place/4101), 3; *see also* Balinea
Baʿquba (syriaca.org/place/4068), 2, 8
Bardhaʿa (syriaca.org/place/4064), 2
Barköl (syriaca.org/place/4339), 11; *see also* Ghinghintalas
Barṭelle (syriaca.org/place/260), 14
Barwari Bala (syriaca.org/place/254), 14
Bashawwat (syriaca.org/place/4110), 4
Başkale (syriaca.org/place/4449), 14
Baskinta (syriaca.org/place/4111), 4
(New) Baṣra (syriaca.org/place/4099), 8, 9; *see also* al-Ubulla
(Old) Baṣra (syriaca.org/place/4057), 2, 8, 9
Batnae (syriaca.org/place/48), 7; *see also* Serug
al-Bawazij (syriaca.org/place/806), 7, 8; *see also* Beth Waziq
Baxʿa (syriaca.org/place/4112), 4
Bay of Aden (syriaca.org/place/4149), 6
Bay of Bengal (syriaca.org/place/4341), 11, 12
Baylaqan (syriaca.org/place/4067), 2, 9; *see also* Paydangaran
Baysan (syriaca.org/place/180), 2, 5; *see also* Scythopolis
Baz (syriaca.org/place/734), 14
Bazyan (syriaca.org/place/4184), 7
Beijing (syriaca.org/place/2539), 11; *see also* Khanbaliq
Beirut (syriaca.org/place/46), 2, 4; *see also* Berytus
Beqaa Valley (syriaca.org/place/4113), 4
Beroea (syriaca.org/place/18), 1, 3; *see also* Aleppo
Berytus (syriaca.org/place/46), 1, 4; *see also* Beirut
Besh-Baliq (syriaca.org/place/4283), 10, 11
Betanure (syriaca.org/place/4451), 14
Beth ʿAbe (syriaca.org/place/223), 14
Beth Aramaye (syriaca.org/place/717), 1, 2, 8
Beth ʿArbaye (syriaca.org/place/31), 7
Beth Bgash (syriaca.org/place/580), 14
Beth Daraye (syriaca.org/place/4013), 1, 2, 8
Beth Daron (syriaca.org/place/2274), 8
Beth Dasen (syriaca.org/place/738), 14
Beth Garmai (syriaca.org/place/33), 1, 2, 7, 8
Beth Ḥuzaye (syriaca.org/place/34), 8; *see also* Elam, Khuzistan
Beth Kartwaye (syriaca.org/place/4464), 14
Beth Lapaṭ (syriaca.org/place/35), 1, 8; *see also* Gondeshapur, Jundishabur
Beth Lashpar (syriaca.org/place/220), 1, 7, 8; *see also* Ḥulwan

Beth Madaye (syriaca.org/place/4465), 8
Beth Mazunaye (syriaca.org/place/4477), 6
Beth Mihraqaye (syriaca.org/place/4466), 8
Beth Moksaye (syriaca.org/place/704), 7, 8
Beth Nuhadra (syriaca.org/place/36), 7, 14
Beth Parsaye (syriaca.org/place/84), 6, 9; *see also* Fars
Beth Qaṭraye (syriaca.org/place/37), 6
Beth Raziqaye (syriaca.org/place/38), 9; *see also* Rai
Beth Sbirino (syriaca.org/place/49), 14
Beth Waziq (syriaca.org/place/806), 7, 8; *see also* al-Bawazij
Beth Zabdai (syriaca.org/place/287), 1, 2, 7; *see also* Azakh
Beth Zabdai (region) (syriaca.org/place/39), 2
Bədyal (syriaca.org/place/4450), 14
Bian (syriaca.org/place/4342), 11; *see also* Kaifeng
Bijar (syriaca.org/place/4069), 2, 9
Bilbeis (syriaca.org/place/4126), 5
Bishapur (syriaca.org/place/4235), 9; *see also* Veh-Shapur
Bitlis (syriaca.org/place/2283), 14; *see also* Badlis
Biye (syriaca.org/place/4452), 14
Black Sea (syriaca.org/place/503), 1, 2
Bohtan (syriaca.org/place/583), 14
Bokan (syriaca.org/place/4185), 7, 9
Bombay (syriaca.org/place/4344), 11; *see also* Mumbai
Boṣra (syriaca.org/place/40), 1, 2, 5; *see also* Bostra
Bost (syriaca.org/place/4237), 9
Bostra (syriaca.org/place/40), 1, 5; *see also* Boṣra
Brahmaputra River (syriaca.org/place/4346), 11
Bügür (syriaca.org/place/4307), 10; *see also* Luntai
Bukhara (syriaca.org/place/4238), 9, 10, 11
Burana (syriaca.org/place/4284), 10; *see also* Balasaghun
Burma (syriaca.org/place/4347), 11
Byblos (syriaca.org/place/52), 1, 4; *see also* Jubayl
Caesarea (syriaca.org/place/60), 1; *see also* Kayseri
Caesarea Maritima (syriaca.org/place/53), 1, 5
Caesarea Philippi (syriaca.org/place/154), 1, 4, 5; *see also* Baniyas
Cairo (syriaca.org/place/521), 5
Calcutta (syriaca.org/place/4348), 11; *see also* Kolkata
Calicut (syriaca.org/place/4425), 12; *see also* Kozhikode
Calliana (syriaca.org/place/4371), 11; *see also* Kalyan
Callinicum (syriaca.org/place/109), 7; *see also* al-Raqqa
Camacha (syriaca.org/place/4014), 1; *see also* Kamacha, Kamakh
Cambodia (syriaca.org/place/4350), 11
Cane Emporium (syriaca.org/place/4171), 6; *see also* Qana᾿
Cappadocia (syriaca.org/place/54), 1
Cardamom Hills (syriaca.org/place/4523), 13
Carrhae (syriaca.org/place/216), 1, 7; *see also* Ḥarran
Caspian Sea (syriaca.org/place/61), 1, 2, 9
Castabala (syriaca.org/place/4023), 1, 3
Ceylon (syriaca.org/place/4427), 12; *see also* Sri Lanka
Chagan Nor (syriaca.org/place/4468), 11
Chalcis (syriaca.org/place/162), 1, 3; *see also* Qenneshrin
Challa (syriaca.org/place/4453), 14
Champa (syriaca.org/place/4351), 11
Chang Jiang River (syriaca.org/place/4545), 11; *see also* Yangtze River
Chang'an (syriaca.org/place/479), 11; *see also* Xi'an
Chendamangalam (syriaca.org/place/4504), 13; *see also* Chennamangalam
Chengdu (syriaca.org/place/4352), 11
Chennai (syriaca.org/place/1960), 11, 12; *see also* Madras, Mylapore, Parangi Malai
Chennamangalam (syriaca.org/place/4504), 13; *see also* Chendamangalam
Chifeng (syriaca.org/place/4353), 11
China (syriaca.org/place/472), 11
Chu River (syriaca.org/place/4286), 10, 11
Cilicia (syriaca.org/place/55), 1, 3
Circesium (syriaca.org/place/62), 1, 7; *see also* Qarqisiya᾿, Qarqisyun
Cizre (syriaca.org/place/88), 2, 14; *see also* Gazarta
Cochi (syriaca.org/place/507), 12, 13; *see also* Kochi
Commagene (syriaca.org/place/4015), 1, 7
Constantia (syriaca.org/place/4047), 1; *see also* Salamis
Constantina (syriaca.org/place/200), 1, 7; *see also* Tella
Coromandel Coast (syriaca.org/place/4429), 12
Cranganore (syriaca.org/place/4430), 12; *see also* Kodungallur
Ctesiphon (syriaca.org/place/58), 1, 8, 9
Cudi Daği (syriaca.org/place/637), 14
Cyprus (syriaca.org/place/714), 1, 2, 3
Cyrrhestica (syriaca.org/place/4103), 3
Cyrrhus (syriaca.org/place/65), 1, 3; *see also* Qurus

Dailam (syriaca.org/place/4239), 1, 2, 9
Damascus (syriaca.org/place/66), 1, 2, 4, 5
Damietta (syriaca.org/place/4127), 5
Daquqa (syriaca.org/place/812), 2, 7, 8
Dara (syriaca.org/place/67), 1, 7, 14
Darabgird (syriaca.org/place/4240), 9
Dasht-e Kavir (syriaca.org/place/4241), 9
Dasht-e Lut (syriaca.org/place/4242), 9
Dasqarta d-Malka (syriaca.org/place/4016), 1, 8
Datong (syriaca.org/place/4417), 11; *see also* Xijing
Daybul (syriaca.org/place/4243), 9, 11
Dayirin (syriaca.org/place/4150), 6, 9; *see also* Tarut
Dayr al-Suryan (syriaca.org/place/360), 5

Dayr al-Za'faran (syriaca.org/place/69), 14
Dayr Qannubin (syriaca.org/place/270), 4
Dead Sea (syriaca.org/place/4017), 5
Delhi (syriaca.org/place/4354), 11
Diamper (syriaca.org/place/4432), 13, 12; *see also* Udayamperur
Didao (syriaca.org/place/4469), 11; *see also* Lintao
Dinawar (syriaca.org/place/4070), 2, 8, 9
Diyala River (syriaca.org/place/4186), 1, 2, 7, 8
Diyana (syriaca.org/place/1169), 14
Diyarbakir (syriaca.org/place/8), 2, 7; *see also* Amida
Dobe (syriaca.org/place/4454), 14
Dohok (syriaca.org/place/76), 14; *see also* Dohuk
Dohuk (syriaca.org/place/76), 1, 2, 7; *see also* Dohok
(Old) Dongola (syriaca.org/place/4168), 6
Drangtse (syriaca.org/place/4287), 10; *see also* Tangtse
Dumatha (syriaca.org/place/4001), 1; *see also* Adummatu
Dunhuang (syriaca.org/place/4000), 11
Dura (syriaca.org/place/77), 1, 7; *see also* Europos
Dvin (syriaca.org/place/4018), 1, 2, 9

Echmiadzin (syriaca.org/place/4054), 2; *see also* Vagharshapat
Edappally (syriaca.org/place/4529), 13
Edessa (syriaca.org/place/78), 1, 2, 7
Egypt (syriaca.org/place/715), 5, 6
Ehden (syriaca.org/place/271), 4; *see also* Mar Sargis
Elam (syriaca.org/place/706), 1, 8; *see also* Beth Ḥuzaye, Khuzistan
Emei, Mount (syriaca.org/place/4479), 11
Emesa (syriaca.org/place/215), 1, 3; *see also* Ḥomṣ
Enaton (syriaca.org/place/473), 5
Epiphaneia (syriaca.org/place/91), 1, 3; *see also* Ḥama
Erbil (syriaca.org/place/13), 2, 7, 9; *see also* Arbel, Arbela
Erzincan (syriaca.org/place/284), 2, 7; *see also* Erznka
Erznka (syriaca.org/place/284), 1, 2, 7; *see also* Erzincan
Erzurum (syriaca.org/place/484), 2; *see also* Theodosiopolis
Eshnuq (syriaca.org/place/2301), 7, 14; *see also* Šəno
Estil (syriaca.org/place/4455), 14
Ethiopia (syriaca.org/place/4541), 6
Euphrates River (syriaca.org/place/82), 1, 2, 3, 7, 8, 9
Europos (syriaca.org/place/77), 1, 7; *see also* Dura

Failaka Island (syriaca.org/place/4471), 6
Farab (syriaca.org/place/4315), 10; *see also* Otrar
Farah (syriaca.org/place/4226), 9, 10; *see also* Aprah
Faras (syriaca.org/place/4153), 6
Fars (syriaca.org/place/84), 6, 9; *see also* Beth Parsaye
Fayyum, Lake (syriaca.org/place/4134), 5
Fengzhou (syriaca.org/place/4356), 11; *see also* Huhhot
Ferghana (syriaca.org/place/4358), 10, 11
Fushanj (syriaca.org/place/4261), 9, 10; *see also* Ghurian, Pushang

Gabala (syriaca.org/place/85), 3
Gadara (syriaca.org/place/4128), 5
Galatia (syriaca.org/place/4019), 1
Ganges River (syriaca.org/place/4472), 11
Ganzak (syriaca.org/place/4020), 1, 7, 9
Ganzhou (syriaca.org/place/4359), 11; *see also* Zhangye
Gaochang (syriaca.org/place/4319), 10; *see also* Qara Qocho
Gawar (syriaca.org/place/815), 14; *see also* Yüksekova
Gawilan (syriaca.org/place/247), 14
Gaza (syriaca.org/place/87), 1, 2, 5
Gazarta (syriaca.org/place/88), 1, 2, 7; *see also* Cizre
Gerasa (syriaca.org/place/4021), 1, 5
Germanicea (syriaca.org/place/89), 1, 3; *see also* Mar'ash
Ghazni (syriaca.org/place/4244), 9, 10
Ghinghintalas (syriaca.org/place/4339), 11; *see also* Barköl
Ghurian (syriaca.org/place/4261), 9, 10; *see also* Fushanj, Pushang
Gilan (syriaca.org/place/4022), 1, 2, 9
Gilgird (syriaca.org/place/4205), 8; *see also* Malviran
Gilgit (syriaca.org/place/4289), 10, 11
Goa (syriaca.org/place/822), 11
Gobi Desert (syriaca.org/place/4360), 11
Godavari River (syriaca.org/place/4361), 11
Golkonda (syriaca.org/place/4362), 11; *see also* Hyderabad
Gomel (syriaca.org/place/4187), 7, 14
Gondeshapur (syriaca.org/place/35), 1, 8; *see also* Beth Lapaṭ, Jundishabur
Gor (syriaca.org/place/4245), 9
Guangzhou (syriaca.org/place/4364), 11
Gulf of Mannar (syriaca.org/place/4434), 12
(Old) Gurgan (syriaca.org/place/4246), 9
Gurganj (syriaca.org/place/4298), 10; *see also* Konye-Urgench

Ḥadithat al-Furat (syriaca.org/place/4071), 2, 7
Ḥadyab (syriaca.org/place/993), 2, 7, 14; *see also* Adiabene
Hagar (syriaca.org/place/4155), 6
Ḥaḥ (syriaca.org/place/217), 14
Hailun (syriaca.org/place/4473), 11
Hainan (syriaca.org/place/4365), 11
Hakkari (syriaca.org/place/2310), 2, 7, 14; *see also* Julamerk
Ḥalabja (syriaca.org/place/4188), 7, 8
Ḥama (syriaca.org/place/91), 2, 3; *see also* Epiphaneia
Hamadan (syriaca.org/place/823), 1, 2, 8, 9
Hangzhou (syriaca.org/place/4380), 11; *see also* Lin'an

Hari Rud (syriaca.org/place/4247), 9, 10
Ḥarran (syriaca.org/place/216), 1, 2, 7; *see also* Carrhae
al-Ḥasake (syriaca.org/place/213), 7, 14
Hasankeyf (syriaca.org/place/92), 14; *see also* Ḥesna d-Kifa
Ḥaṭra (syriaca.org/place/93), 1, 7
Ḥaṭṭa (syriaca.org/place/4156), 6, 9; *see also* al-Qaṭif
Ḥdatta (syriaca.org/place/2096), 1, 2, 7, 14
Ḥebton (syriaca.org/place/2316), 14; *see also* Ḥnitha
Hejian (syriaca.org/place/4366), 11
Heliopolis (syriaca.org/place/577), 1, 4; *see also* Baʿalbak
Helmand River (syriaca.org/place/4248), 9
Herat (syriaca.org/place/523), 9, 10
Hertevin (syriaca.org/place/4456), 14
Ḥesna d-Kifa (syriaca.org/place/92), 2, 7, 14; *see also* Hasankeyf
Hierapolis (syriaca.org/place/122), 1, 3, 7; *see also* Mabbug, Manbij
al-Ḥijr (syriaca.org/place/4147), 6; *see also* Madaʾin Ṣaliḥ
Himalaya Range (syriaca.org/place/4290), 10, 11
Hindu Kush Range (syriaca.org/place/4367), 9, 10, 11
al-Hinna (syriaca.org/place/4474), 6
al-Ḥira (syriaca.org/place/219), 1, 8; *see also* Ḥirta
Ḥirta (syriaca.org/place/219), 1, 8; *see also* al-Ḥira
Ḥirta d-Ṭayyaye (syriaca.org/place/4026), 1, 5; *see also* al-Jabiya
Hit (syriaca.org/place/4072), 2, 8
Ḥnitha (syriaca.org/place/2316), 14; *see also* Ḥebton
Ḥomṣ (syriaca.org/place/215), 2, 3; *see also* Emesa
Hormuz (syriaca.org/place/4158), 6, 9
Hormuz-Ardashir (syriaca.org/place/96), 1, 8, 9; *see also* Ahvaz
Ḥrbath Glal (syriaca.org/place/4458), 7, 14
Hromkla (syriaca.org/place/97), 2, 3, 7; *see also* Qalʿa Rumayta
Huhhot (syriaca.org/place/4356), 11; *see also* Fengzhou
Ḥulwan (syriaca.org/place/220), 1, 2, 7, 8; *see also* Beth Lashpar
Hyderabad (syriaca.org/place/4362), 11; *see also* Golkonda

ʾIbb (syriaca.org/place/4496), 6
Iconium (syriaca.org/place/4024), 1
Ili River (syriaca.org/place/4291), 10, 11
India (syriaca.org/place/500), 11, 13, 12
Indian Ocean (syriaca.org/place/4159), 6, 13, 12
Indus River (syriaca.org/place/4249), 9, 10, 11
Iran (syriaca.org/place/4073), 2, 8, 9; *see also* Persia
Iraq (syriaca.org/place/98), 2, 8
Irrawaddy River (syriaca.org/place/4368), 11
Iskenderun (syriaca.org/place/663), 3; *see also* Alexandretta
Islamabad (syriaca.org/place/4292), 10, 11
Ispahan (syriaca.org/place/830), 9
Issyk Kul, Lake (syriaca.org/place/4476), 10
Iṣṭakhr (syriaca.org/place/4250), 9
Ivan-e Karkha (syriaca.org/place/656), 8; *see also* Karka d-Ledan
Izla, Mount (syriaca.org/place/100), 14

al-Jabiya (syriaca.org/place/4025), 1, 5; *see also* Ḥirta d-Ṭayyaye
Jaffa (syriaca.org/place/4074), 2, 5
Jaffna (syriaca.org/place/4435), 12; *see also* Yalpanam
Jam-Baliq (syriaca.org/place/4293), 10, 11
Janza (syriaca.org/place/4075), 2
al-Jawf (syriaca.org/place/4076), 2
Jaxartes River (syriaca.org/place/4406), 10, 11; *see also* Syr Darya River
Jazira (syriaca.org/place/321), 2, 7, 14
Jerusalem (syriaca.org/place/104), 1, 2, 5
Jiankang (syriaca.org/place/4369), 11; *see also* Nanjing
Jibal (syriaca.org/place/4077), 2
Jidda (syriaca.org/place/4526), 6
Jilu (syriaca.org/place/759), 14
Jiuquan (syriaca.org/place/4404), 11; *see also* Suzhou
Joppa (syriaca.org/place/4027), 1
Jordan (syriaca.org/place/4129), 5
Jordan River (syriaca.org/place/4114), 4, 5
Jubayl (syriaca.org/place/52), 2, 4; *see also* Byblos
Jubayl (syriaca.org/place/4485), 6; *see also* Ramat
Jubbʿadin (syriaca.org/place/4115), 4
Judean Desert (syriaca.org/place/4130), 5
Julamerk (syriaca.org/place/107), 7, 14; *see also* Hakkari
Jundishabur (syriaca.org/place/35), 2, 8; *see also* Beth Lapaṭ, Gondeshapur

Kabul (syriaca.org/place/4251), 9, 10, 11
Kadamattam (syriaca.org/place/4530), 13
Kaduthuruthy (syriaca.org/place/4510), 13, 12
Kaifeng (syriaca.org/place/4342), 11; *see also* Bian
Kalyan (syriaca.org/place/4371), 11; *see also* Calliana
Kamacha (syriaca.org/place/4014), 7; *see also* Camacha, Kamakh
Kamakh (syriaca.org/place/4014), 2, 7; *see also* Camacha, Kamacha
Kandanad (syriaca.org/place/448), 13
Kanjur (syriaca.org/place/4531), 13
Karachi (syriaca.org/place/4252), 9, 11
Karaj (syriaca.org/place/4253), 8, 9; *see also* Kuj, Rudavar
Karajigach (syriaca.org/place/4294), 10
Karakum Desert (syriaca.org/place/4255), 9, 10
Karemlesh (syriaca.org/place/110), 14
Karka d-Beth Slokh (syriaca.org/place/108), 1, 7; *see also* Kirkuk
Karka d-Ledan (syriaca.org/place/656), 8; *see also* Ivan-e Karkha
Karka d-Maishan (syriaca.org/place/4028), 1, 8, 9

Karka d-Piroz (syriaca.org/place/4191), 7, 8
Karkha River (syriaca.org/place/4534), 4, 7, 8
Kars (syriaca.org/place/4029), 1, 2
Karun River (syriaca.org/place/4208), 8
Kashan (syriaca.org/place/4268), 9; *see also* Qashan
Kashgar (syriaca.org/place/4295), 10, 11
Kashkar (syriaca.org/place/111), 1, 8, 9; *see also* Wasiṭ
Kaveri River (syriaca.org/place/4437), 12
Kayseri (syriaca.org/place/60), 2; *see also* Caesarea
Kellia (syriaca.org/place/4131), 5
Kerala (syriaca.org/place/602), 13, 12
Kerend (syriaca.org/place/4192), 7, 8
Khabur River (syriaca.org/place/114), 1, 2, 7, 14
Khanaqin (syriaca.org/place/4078), 2, 7, 8
Khanbaliq (syriaca.org/place/2539), 11; *see also* Beijing
Kharg Island (syriaca.org/place/4160), 6, 9
Khartoum (syriaca.org/place/4161), 6
Khiva (syriaca.org/place/4296), 10
Khorasan (syriaca.org/place/603), 9, 10
Khorramshahr (syriaca.org/place/4065), 2, 8; *see also* Muḥammara
Khotan (syriaca.org/place/4297), 10, 11
Khuzistan (syriaca.org/place/929), 2, 8; *see also* Beth Ḥuzaye, Elam
Khwarazm (syriaca.org/place/4475), 10
Kirkuk (syriaca.org/place/108), 2, 7; *see also* Karka d-Beth Slokh
Kirman (syriaca.org/place/4233), 9; *see also* Veh-Ardashir
Kirman (syriaca.org/place/4256), 9
Klysma (syriaca.org/place/4132), 5; *see also* Qulzum
Kochi (syriaca.org/place/507), 12, 13; *see also* Cochi
Kodungallur (syriaca.org/place/4430), 12; *see also* Cranganore
Kokhe (syriaca.org/place/475), 1, 8; *see also* Maḥoza, Veh-Ardashir
Kolkata (syriaca.org/place/4348), 11; *see also* Calcutta
Kollam (syriaca.org/place/4441), 12; *see also* Quilon
Konya (syriaca.org/place/440), 2
Konye-Urgench (syriaca.org/place/4298), 10; *see also* Gurganj
Korea (syriaca.org/place/4373), 11
Korla (syriaca.org/place/4300), 10
Kormakitis (syriaca.org/place/4104), 3; *see also* Kurmajit
Koshang (syriaca.org/place/4374), 11
Kothamangalam (syriaca.org/place/4509), 12
Kottayam (syriaca.org/place/1947), 13, 12
Koy Sanjak (syriaca.org/place/4459), 14
Kozhikode (syriaca.org/place/4425), 12; *see also* Calicut
Krishna River (syriaca.org/place/4375), 11
Krorain (syriaca.org/place/4305), 10, 11; *see also* Loulan
Kucha (syriaca.org/place/4301), 10, 11
Kufa (syriaca.org/place/4079), 2, 8
Kuj (syriaca.org/place/4253), 8, 9; *see also* Karaj, Rudavar
Kunlun Shan (syriaca.org/place/4376), 10, 11
Kunming (syriaca.org/place/4423), 11; *see also* Yunnanfu
Kura River (syriaca.org/place/4030), 1, 2
Kuravilangad (syriaca.org/place/4511), 13
Kurmajit (syriaca.org/place/4104), 3; *see also* Kormakitis
Kyzylkum Desert (syriaca.org/place/4302), 10, 11

Ladakh (syriaca.org/place/4377), 10, 11
Lahore (syriaca.org/place/4304), 10, 11
Laodicea (syriaca.org/place/118), 1, 3; *see also* Latakia
Larissa (syriaca.org/place/119), 3; *see also* Shayzar
Latakia (syriaca.org/place/118), 2, 3; *see also* Laodicea
Lebanon (syriaca.org/place/487), 2, 4
Lebanon, Mount (syriaca.org/place/4122), 4
Leontes River (syriaca.org/place/4532), 4; *see also* Litani River
Leontopolis (syriaca.org/place/4135), 5
Lhasa (syriaca.org/place/4378), 11
Liaoyang (syriaca.org/place/4379), 11
Lin'an (syriaca.org/place/4380), 11; *see also* Hangzhou
Linfen (syriaca.org/place/4483), 11; *see also* Pingyang
Lingwu (syriaca.org/place/4382), 11; *see also* Lingzhou
Lingzhou (syriaca.org/place/4382), 11; *see also* Lingwu
Lintao (syriaca.org/place/4469), 11; *see also* Didao
Litani River (syriaca.org/place/4532), 4; *see also* Leontes River
Loulan (syriaca.org/place/4305), 10, 11; *see also* Krorain
Luntai (syriaca.org/place/4307), 10; *see also* Bügür
Luntai (syriaca.org/place/4309), 10; *see also* Ürümchi
Luoyang (syriaca.org/place/2534), 11

Maʿaltha (syriaca.org/place/4457), 14
Maʿarrat Ṣaydnaya (syriaca.org/place/281), 4
Mabbug (syriaca.org/place/122), 1, 2, 3, 7; *see also* Hierapolis, Manbij
al-Madaʾin (syriaca.org/place/4058), 1, 2, 8; *see also* Maḥoze, Medinata
Madaʾin Ṣaliḥ (syriaca.org/place/4147), 6; *see also* al-Ḥijr
Madras (syriaca.org/place/1960), 11, 12; *see also* Chennai, Mylapore, Parangi Malai
Madurai (syriaca.org/place/4438), 12
Mahabad (syriaca.org/place/4086), 2; *see also* Sablagh
Maḥoza (syriaca.org/place/475), 1, 8; *see also* Kokhe, Veh-Ardashir
Maḥoza Ḥdatta (syriaca.org/place/4209), 8; *see also* Rumiyya, Veh-Antiokh-e Khosrow
Maḥoze (syriaca.org/place/4058), 1, 2, 8; *see also* al-Madaʾin, Medinata

Maipherqaṭ (syriaca.org/place/134), 1, 2, 7, 14; *see also* Martyropolis, Mayyafariqin, Silvan
Maishan (syriaca.org/place/123), 1, 8
Makran (syriaca.org/place/4257), 9
Makuria (syriaca.org/place/4538), 6
Malabar Coast (syriaca.org/place/461), 11, 12
Malaṭya (syriaca.org/place/136), 2, 7; *see also* Melitene
Malayattur (syriaca.org/place/4506), 13
Ma'lula (syriaca.org/place/279), 4
Malviran (syriaca.org/place/4205), 8; *see also* Gilgird
Manbij (syriaca.org/place/122), 2; *see also* Hierapolis, Mabbug
Mannanam (syriaca.org/place/4512), 13
Mansura (syriaca.org/place/4136), 5
Manṣuriyya (syriaca.org/place/1417), 14
Mantai (syriaca.org/place/4439), 12; *see also* Mantota
Mantota (syriaca.org/place/4439), 12; *see also* Mantai
Manzikert (syriaca.org/place/462), 1, 2, 7
Mar Abraham of Kashkar (syriaca.org/place/384), 7, 14
Mar Antonios (syriaca.org/place/4116), 4; *see also* Qozhaya
Mar Awgen (syriaca.org/place/339), 14
Mar Elian (syriaca.org/place/275), 4
Mar Elisha' (syriaca.org/place/4118), 4
Mar Isho' (syriaca.org/place/1664), 14; *see also* Rustaqa
Mar Matay (syriaca.org/place/227), 14
Mar Musa al-Ḥabashi (syriaca.org/place/228), 4
Mar Saba (syriaca.org/place/4137), 5
Mar Sargis (syriaca.org/place/271), 4; *see also* Ehden
Mar Sharbel (syriaca.org/place/4119), 4
Mar Ya'qub (syriaca.org/place/398), 7
Mar Yuḥanon Maron (syriaca.org/place/4120), 4
Mar'ash (syriaca.org/place/89), 2, 3; *see also* Germanicea
Maragha (syriaca.org/place/129), 2, 7, 9
Mardin (syriaca.org/place/130), 2, 7, 14
Marga (syriaca.org/place/457), 7, 14
Ma'rib (syriaca.org/place/4478), 6
Marqab (syriaca.org/place/273), 2, 3
Martyropolis (syriaca.org/place/134), 1, 7; *see also* Maipherqaṭ, Mayyafariqin, Silvan
Masabadan (syriaca.org/place/4212), 8
Mashmahig (syriaca.org/place/4162), 6; *see also* Samahij
Mawana (syriaca.org/place/1443), 14
Mayyafariqin (syriaca.org/place/134), 2, 7; *see also* Maipherqaṭ, Martyropolis, Silvan
Mecca (syriaca.org/place/4165), 6
Media (syriaca.org/place/4034), 1
Medina (syriaca.org/place/4166), 6
Medinata (syriaca.org/place/4058), 1, 2, 8; *see also* al-Mada'in, Maḥoze
Mediterranean Sea (syriaca.org/place/135), 1, 2, 3, 4, 5
Medyad (syriaca.org/place/137), 7, 14; *see also* Midyat
Mekong River (syriaca.org/place/4384), 11
Melitene (syriaca.org/place/136), 1, 7; *see also* Malaṭya
Memphis (syriaca.org/place/4138), 5
Merki (syriaca.org/place/4311), 10
Meroë (syriaca.org/place/4167), 6
Merv (syriaca.org/place/607), 9, 10
Merv al-Rud (syriaca.org/place/4258), 9, 10; *see also* Bala Murghab
Midyat (syriaca.org/place/137), 7, 14; *see also* Medyad
Mizdakhkan (syriaca.org/place/4312), 10
Mlaḥso (syriaca.org/place/4193), 7, 14
Mongolia (syriaca.org/place/4385), 11
Mopsuestia (syriaca.org/place/138), 3
Mosul (syriaca.org/place/139), 2, 7, 14
Muḥammara (syriaca.org/place/4065), 8; *see also* Khorramshahr
Mulamthuruthy (syriaca.org/place/4507), 13
Mumbai (syriaca.org/place/4344), 11; *see also* Bombay
Muqan (syriaca.org/place/4080), 2, 9
Muqaṭam Mountains (syriaca.org/place/4480), 5
Murghab River (syriaca.org/place/4260), 9, 10
Muttuchira (syriaca.org/place/4513), 13
Muziris (syriaca.org/place/4499), 13, 12; *see also* Pattanam
Mylapore (syriaca.org/place/1960), 11, 12; *see also* Chennai, Madras, Parangi Malai
Mysore (syriaca.org/place/4386), 11, 12; *see also* Mysuru
Mysuru (syriaca.org/place/4386), 11; *see also* Mysore

Nablus (syriaca.org/place/4139), 5; *see also* Neapolis, Shechem
Nahargur (syriaca.org/place/4213), 8; *see also* 'Abdasi
al-Nahrawan (syriaca.org/place/1560), 8
Najran (syriaca.org/place/464), 6
Nakhchivan (syriaca.org/place/4081), 2, 7, 9
Nakshab (syriaca.org/place/4265), 9, 10; *see also* Qarshi
Nanjing (syriaca.org/place/4369), 11; *see also* Jiankang
Narmada River (syriaca.org/place/4388), 11
Navekath (syriaca.org/place/4313), 10, 11
Neapolis (syriaca.org/place/4139), 5; *see also* Nablus, Shechem
Neocaesarea (syriaca.org/place/4035), 1
Nepal (syriaca.org/place/4389), 11
Nerwa (syriaca.org/place/4460), 14
Nicosia (syriaca.org/place/4082), 2, 3
Nifr (syriaca.org/place/4083), 2, 8

Nihawand (syriaca.org/place/4036), 1, 2, 8, 9
Niksar (syriaca.org/place/466), 2
al-Nil (syriaca.org/place/4201), 8
Nile River (syriaca.org/place/629), 5, 6
Nineveh (syriaca.org/place/144), 1, 7, 14
Ningxia (syriaca.org/place/4528), 11; *see also* Xingqing, Yinchuan
Nippur (syriaca.org/place/4037), 1
Nishapur (syriaca.org/place/4220), 9, 10; *see also* Abr Shahr
Nisibis (syriaca.org/place/142), 1, 2, 7, 14
Nitria (syriaca.org/place/4481), 5
Nobatia (syriaca.org/place/4537), 6
North Paravur (syriaca.org/place/4518), 13; *see also* Parur
Nubia (syriaca.org/place/4539), 6
al-Nuʿmaniyya (syriaca.org/place/4215), 8

Olan Süme (syriaca.org/place/4390), 11
Olba (syriaca.org/place/4038), 1, 3
Oman (syriaca.org/place/4542), 6
Orchoe (syriaca.org/place/4039), 1, 8; *see also* Uruk
Ordos (syriaca.org/place/4391), 11
Orontes River (syriaca.org/place/147), 4
Osh (syriaca.org/place/4314), 10
Osrhoene (syriaca.org/place/145), 7
Otrar (syriaca.org/place/4315), 10; *see also* Farab
Our Lady of Mayfuq (syriaca.org/place/4121), 4
Oxus River (syriaca.org/place/4224), 9, 10, 11; *see also* Amu Darya River

Pagan (syriaca.org/place/4392), 11
Palayur (syriaca.org/place/4514), 12; *see also* Palur
Palestine (syriaca.org/place/698), 1, 2, 5
Pallippuram (syriaca.org/place/4508), 13
Palmyra (syriaca.org/place/153), 1, 3, 7; *see also* Tadmur
Palur (syriaca.org/place/4514), 12; *see also* Palayur
Pamir (syriaca.org/place/4393), 10, 11
Panjikent (syriaca.org/place/4317), 10
Panopolis (syriaca.org/place/4169), 6; *see also* Akhmim
Paphus (syriaca.org/place/4042), 1, 3
Parangi Malai (syriaca.org/place/1960), 11; *see also* Chennai, Madras, Mylapore
Partaw (syriaca.org/place/4043), 1, 9
Parur (syriaca.org/place/4518), 13; *see also* North Paravur
Patna (syriaca.org/place/4394), 11
Pattanam (syriaca.org/place/4499), 13, 12; *see also* Muziris
Paydangaran (syriaca.org/place/4041), 1, 9; *see also* Baylaqan
Pegu (syriaca.org/place/4395), 11
Pelusium (syriaca.org/place/1473), 1, 5
Penek (syriaca.org/place/253), 7, 14
Periyar River (syriaca.org/place/4482), 13, 12
Persia (syriaca.org/place/526), 9; *see also* Iran
Persian Gulf (syriaca.org/place/156), 6, 9
Peshawar (syriaca.org/place/4318), 10, 11
Petra (syriaca.org/place/157), 1, 5; *see also* Wadi Musa
Philadelphia (syriaca.org/place/4044), 1, 5; *see also* Amman
Philippopolis (syriaca.org/place/158), 1, 5
Pingyang (syriaca.org/place/4483), 11; *see also* Linfen
Piroz-Shapur (syriaca.org/place/211), 1, 8; *see also* Anbar
Pontus (syriaca.org/place/633), 1
Prat d-Maishan (syriaca.org/place/4203), 1, 8; *see also* Bahman-Ardashir
Ptolemaïs (syriaca.org/place/14), 1, 5; *see also* Acre, ʿAkka, Akko
Pushang (syriaca.org/place/4261), 9, 10; *see also* Fushanj, Ghurian

Qadisha Valley (syriaca.org/place/4123), 4
Qaimar (syriaca.org/place/770), 14
Qalʿa Rumayta (syriaca.org/place/97), 3; *see also* Hromkla
Qalamun Mountains (syriaca.org/place/597), 4
Qalʿat Simʿan (syriaca.org/place/635), 3
Qamishli (syriaca.org/place/160), 14
Qamul (syriaca.org/place/4396), 11
Qanaʾ (syriaca.org/place/4171), 6; *see also* Cane Emporium
Qandahar (syriaca.org/place/4264), 9, 11
Qara (syriaca.org/place/161), 4
Qara Qocho (syriaca.org/place/4319), 10; *see also* Gaochang
Qara Qota (syriaca.org/place/4397), 11
Qaraqorum (syriaca.org/place/4398), 11
Qaraqosh (syriaca.org/place/262), 2, 7, 14
Qarashahr (syriaca.org/place/4321), 10, 11; *see also* Yanqi
Qardu (syriaca.org/place/2355), 14
Qarqisiyaʾ (syriaca.org/place/62), 2, 7; *see also* Circesium, Qarqisyun
Qarqisyun (syriaca.org/place/62), 1, 2, 7; *see also* Circesium, Qarqisiyaʾ
Qarshi (syriaca.org/place/4265), 9, 10; *see also* Nakshab
Qarta (syriaca.org/place/2356), 14
Qarṭmin (syriaca.org/place/226), 14
Qash (syriaca.org/place/4267), 9
Qashan (syriaca.org/place/4268), 9; *see also* Kashan
Qaṣr Ibn Hubayra (syriaca.org/place/4216), 8
Qaṣr Ibrim (syriaca.org/place/4153), 6
Qaṣr-e Shirin (syriaca.org/place/4194), 7, 8
al-Qaṭif (syriaca.org/place/4156), 6, 9; *see also* Ḥaṭṭa
Qayaliq (syriaca.org/place/4323), 10
Qenneshre (syriaca.org/place/162), 3, 7;
Qenneshrin (syriaca.org/place/230), 1, 2, 3; *see also* Chalcis
Qozhaya (syriaca.org/place/4116), 4; *see also* Mar Antonios
Quanzhou (syriaca.org/place/2535), 11
Quilon (syriaca.org/place/4441) 12; *see also* Kollam

Qulzum (syriaca.org/place/4132), 5; *see also* Klysma
Qum (syriaca.org/place/4217), 8, 9
Qurus (syriaca.org/place/65), 2, 3; *see also* Cyrrhus

Rabban Bar ʿEdta (syriaca.org/place/167), 14
Rabban Hormizd (syriaca.org/place/168), 14
Radhan (syriaca.org/place/4045), 1, 8
Rafaḥ (syriaca.org/place/4084), 2, 5; *see also* Raphia
Rai (syriaca.org/place/38), 9; *see also* Beth Raziqaye
Ram-Hormizd (syriaca.org/place/4218), 8
Ramapuram (syriaca.org/place/4522), 12
Ramat (syriaca.org/place/4485), 6; *see also* Jubayl
Raphia (syriaca.org/place/4046), 1, 5; *see also* Rafaḥ
al-Raqqa (syriaca.org/place/109), 2, 7; *see also* Callinicum
Rasht (syriaca.org/place/4270), 9
Red Sea (syriaca.org/place/4536), 6
Reṣafa (syriaca.org/place/165), 2, 7; *see also* Sergiopolis
Reshʿayna (syriaca.org/place/172), 1, 2, 7
Rev Ardashir (syriaca.org/place/4173), 6, 9
Rima (syriaca.org/place/4487), 8
Riyadh (syriaca.org/place/4174), 6
Rudavar (syriaca.org/place/4207), 8; *see also* Karaj, Kuj
Rumiyya (syriaca.org/place/4209), 1, 8; *see also* Maḥoza Ḥdatta, Veh-Antiokh-e Khosrow
Rustaqa (syriaca.org/place/1664), 14; *see also* Mar Ishoʿ
Ruwanduz (syriaca.org/place/4085), 2, 7, 14

Sablagh (syriaca.org/place/4195), 2, 7; *see also* Mahabad
Ṣadad (syriaca.org/place/276), 4
Sainqala (syriaca.org/place/4196), 7, 9
Ṣalaḥ (syriaca.org/place/2), 14
Salakh (syriaca.org/place/2362), 14
Salamas (syriaca.org/place/177), 14; *see also* Salmas
Salamis (syriaca.org/place/4047), 1, 3; *see also* Constantia
Salmas (syriaca.org/place/177), 2, 7; *see also* Salamas
Salween River (syriaca.org/place/4399), 11
Samahij (syriaca.org/place/4162), 6; *see also* Mashmahig
Samarqand (syriaca.org/place/865), 10, 11
Samarraʾ (syriaca.org/place/4087), 2, 7, 8
Šammәsdin (syriaca.org/place/778), 14
Samosata (syriaca.org/place/178), 1, 2, 7; *see also* Sumaysaṭ
Ṣanʿaʾ (syriaca.org/place/4175), 6
Sanandaj (syriaca.org/place/867), 2, 8, 9; *see also* Sehna
Saqqez (syriaca.org/place/4088), 2, 7, 9
Ṣarrin (syriaca.org/place/655), 3, 7
al-Ṣaymara (syriaca.org/place/4202), 2, 8
Scetis (http://syriaca.org/place/289), 5; *see also* Wadi Naṭrun
Scythopolis (syriaca.org/place/180), 1, 5; *see also* Baysan
Sebasteia (syriaca.org/place/4049), 1
Segestan (syriaca.org/place/409), 9; *see also* Sistan
Sehna (syriaca.org/place/867), 2, 8, 9; *see also* Sanandaj
Seleucia (syriaca.org/place/182), 1, 8
Seleucia Pieria (syriaca.org/place/183), 1, 3
Seleucia Tracheotis (syriaca.org/place/174), 1, 3; *see also* Silifke
Semele (syriaca.org/place/4461), 14
Semirechye (syriaca.org/place/4488), 10, 11; *see also* Yeti Su
Sergiopolis (syriaca.org/place/165), 1, 7; *see also* Reṣafa
Serug (syriaca.org/place/48), 7; *see also* Batnae
Sevan, Lake (syriaca.org/place/4031), 1, 2
Šәno (syriaca.org/place/2301), 7, 14; *see also* Eshnuq
Shahr-e Piroz (syriaca.org/place/4271), 9
Shahrqart (syriaca.org/place/2370), 7
Shahrzur (syriaca.org/place/2371), 1, 7, 8, 9
Shaki (syriaca.org/place/4090), 2
Shamakhi (syriaca.org/place/4091), 2
Shangdu (syriaca.org/place/4400), 11; *see also* Xanadu
Shangwan (syriaca.org/place/4415), 11; *see also* Xiapu
Shaqlawa (syriaca.org/place/4462), 14
Sharfeh (syriaca.org/place/232), 4
Shayzar (syriaca.org/place/4089), 2, 3; *see also* Larissa
Shechem (syriaca.org/place/4139), 5; *see also* Nablus, Neapolis
Shenna (syriaca.org/place/869), 2, 7, 8; *see also* Shenna d-Beth Raman, al-Sinn
Shenna d-Beth Raman (syriaca.org/place/869), 1; *see also* Shenna, al-Sinn
Shimshaṭ (syriaca.org/place/286), 2, 7; *see also* Arsamosata
Shiraz (syriaca.org/place/4272), 9
Shui Pang (syriaca.org/place/4467), 10
Shushtar (syriaca.org/place/4092), 2, 8, 9
Sidon (syriaca.org/place/187), 1, 2, 4, 5
Siirt (syriaca.org/place/188), 1, 2, 7, 14; *see also* Sirte
Silifke (syriaca.org/place/174), 2, 3; *see also* Seleucia Tracheotis
Silvan (syriaca.org/place/134), 14; *see also* Maipherqaṭ, Martyropolis, Mayyafariqin
Sinai Peninsula (syriaca.org/place/4142), 5
Singara (syriaca.org/place/184), 1; *see also* Sinjar
Sinjar (syriaca.org/place/184), 2, 7, 14; *see also* Singara
Sinjar, Mount (syriaca.org/place/524), 14
al-Sinn (syriaca.org/place/869), 2, 7, 8; *see also* Shenna, Shenna d-Beth Raman
Ṣir Bani Yas Island (syriaca.org/place/4490), 6
Siraf (syriaca.org/place/4176), 6, 9
Sirawan (syriaca.org/place/4050), 1, 8, 9
Sirte (syriaca.org/place/188), 7; *see also* Siirt
Sis (syriaca.org/place/190), 2, 3

Sistan (syriaca.org/place/409), 9; *see also* Segestan
Sivas (syriaca.org/place/4093), 2
Siverek (syriaca.org/place/4197), 7
Soba (syriaca.org/place/4177), 6
Socotra (syriaca.org/place/642), 6
Sogdiana (syriaca.org/place/4273), 9, 10; *see also* Transoxiana
Solduz (syriaca.org/place/4198), 7, 14
Soltania (syriaca.org/place/4094), 2, 9; *see also* Sulṭaniyya
South China Sea (syriaca.org/place/4402), 11
Sri Lanka (syriaca.org/place/4427), 12; *see also* Ceylon
St Catherine's Monastery (syriaca.org/place/368), 5, 6
Ṣuḥar (syriaca.org/place/4164), 6
Sulemaniyya (syriaca.org/place/4096), 2, 7
Sulṭaniyya (syriaca.org/place/4094), 2, 9; *see also* Soltania
Sum Huh Burd (syriaca.org/place/4403), 11
Sumatar Harabesi (syriaca.org/place/643), 7
Sumaysaṭ (syriaca.org/place/178), 2, 7; *see also* Samosata
Sura (syriaca.org/place/4199), 7
Surkhan Darya River (syriaca.org/place/4491), 10
Susa (syriaca.org/place/415), 1, 8, 9
Suyab (syriaca.org/place/4279), 10; *see also* Aq-Beshim
Suzhou (syriaca.org/place/4404), 11; *see also* Jiuquan
Syene (syriaca.org/place/4178), 6; *see also* Aswan
Syr Darya River (syriaca.org/place/4406), 10, 11; *see also* Jaxartes River
Syria (syriaca.org/place/486), 1, 2, 3, 4, 7
Syrian Desert (syriaca.org/place/4051), 1, 2, 3, 4, 7

Tabriz (syriaca.org/place/308), 1, 2, 7, 9
Tabuk (syriaca.org/place/4180), 6
Tadmur (syriaca.org/place/153), 2, 3, 7; *see also* Palmyra
Tagrit (syriaca.org/place/193), 1, 2, 7, 8
Taiwan (syriaca.org/place/4408), 11
Taklamakan Desert (syriaca.org/place/4324), 10, 11
Tal ʿAfar (syriaca.org/place/4463), 14
Talas (syriaca.org/place/4325), 10; *see also* Ṭaraz
Taleqan (syriaca.org/place/4274), 9
Talgar (syriaca.org/place/4327), 10
Ṭamanon (syriaca.org/place/2395), 14
Tambraparani River (syriaca.org/place/4492), 12
Tana (syriaca.org/place/4493), 11; *see also* Thane
Tangtse (syriaca.org/place/4287), 10; *see also* Drangtse
Tangut (syriaca.org/place/727), 11
Tanjore (syriaca.org/place/4443), 12; *see also* Thanjavur
Ṭaraz (syriaca.org/place/4325), 10; *see also* Talas
Tarim Basin (syriaca.org/place/4409), 10, 11
Tarim River (syriaca.org/place/4328), 10, 11
Tarsus (syriaca.org/place/196), 1, 2, 3
Ṭartuṣ (syriaca.org/place/4108), 3
Tarut (syriaca.org/place/4150), 6, 9; *see also* Dayirin
Tashkent (syriaca.org/place/4329), 10, 11
Tatʿev (syriaca.org/place/4097), 2, 7, 9
Tatta, Lake (syriaca.org/place/4032), 1; *see also* Tuz, Lake
Taurus Mountains (syriaca.org/place/4106), 3
Taymaʾ (syriaca.org/place/4181), 6
Tehran (syriaca.org/place/4275), 9
Tel Bashir (syriaca.org/place/4107), 2, 3, 7
Telkepe (syriaca.org/place/197), 14
Tell ʿAda (syriaca.org/place/233), 3
Tella (syriaca.org/place/200), 1, 7; *see also* Constantina
Tenduc (syriaca.org/place/4410), 11
Tergawar (syriaca.org/place/250), 14
Thaj (syriaca.org/place/4495), 6
Thane (syriaca.org/place/4493), 11; *see also* Tana
Thanjavur (syriaca.org/place/4443), 12; *see also* Tanjore
Thar Desert (syriaca.org/place/4411), 11
Thebes (syriaca.org/place/4182), 6
Thekkumkur (syriaca.org/place/4498), 13
Theodosiopolis (syriaca.org/place/484), 1; *see also* Erzurum
Thiruvalla (syriaca.org/place/4445), 12
Thiruvananthapuram (syriaca.org/place/4446), 12; *see also* Trivandrum
Thiruvithamcode (syriaca.org/place/4502), 12
Thozhiyur (syriaca.org/place/4516), 12; *see also* Anjur
Thrissur (syriaca.org/place/876), 12; *see also* Trichur
Tian Shan Mountains. (syriaca.org/place/4412), 10, 11
Tiberias (syriaca.org/place/201), 1, 2, 5
Tibet (syriaca.org/place/646), 10, 11
Tigris River (syriaca.org/place/202), 1, 2, 7, 8, 9, 14
Tikab (syriaca.org/place/4098), 2, 9
Ṭirhan (syriaca.org/place/789), 4, 7
Ṭiyari, Lower (syriaca.org/place/761), 14
Ṭiyari, Upper (syriaca.org/place/790), 14
Tokharistan (syriaca.org/place/4229), 9, 10; *see also* Bactria
Toru Aygyr (syriaca.org/place/4330), 10
Transoxiana (syriaca.org/place/4273), 10; *see also* Sogdiana
Travancore (syriaca.org/place/506), 12
Trebizond (syriaca.org/place/4052), 1, 2
Trichur (syriaca.org/place/876), 12; *see also* Thrissur
Tripoli (syriaca.org/place/203), 2, 3, 4; *see also* Tripolis
Tripolis (syriaca.org/place/203), 1; *see also* Tripoli
Trivandrum (syriaca.org/place/4446), 12; *see also* Thiruvananthapuram
Ṭur ʿAbdin (syriaca.org/place/221), 7, 14
Turfan (syriaca.org/place/478), 10, 11
Turkistan (syriaca.org/place/647), 10

Ṭus (syriaca.org/place/4276), 9, 10
Tuz, Lake (syriaca.org/place/4032), 2; *see also* Tatta, Lake
Txuma (syriaca.org/place/251), 14
Tyana (syriaca.org/place/4053), 1
Tyre (syriaca.org/place/195), 1, 2, 4, 5

al-Ubulla (syriaca.org/place/4100), 1, 2, 8; *see also* (New) Baṣra
Udayamperur (syriaca.org/place/4432), 13, 12; *see also* Diamper
Ujjain (syriaca.org/place/4413), 11
ʿUkbara (syriaca.org/place/4056), 1, 8
Ulaan Tolgoi (syriaca.org/place/4332), 10, 11
Urgut (syriaca.org/place/649), 10
Urmi (syriaca.org/place/206), 14; *see also* Urmia
Urmi, Lake (syriaca.org/place/116), 14; *see also* Urmia, Lake
Urmia (syriaca.org/place/206), 2, 7, 9; *see also* Urmi
Urmia, Lake (syriaca.org/place/116), 1, 2, 7, 9; *see also* Urmi, Lake
Uruk (syriaca.org/place/4039), 1, 8; *see also* Orchoe
Ürümchi (syriaca.org/place/4309), 10; *see also* Luntai
Uzgand (syriaca.org/place/4333), 10

Vadakkumkur (syriaca.org/place/4501), 13
Vagharshapat (syriaca.org/place/4054), 1; *see also* Echmiadzin
Van (syriaca.org/place/791), 1, 2, 7, 9, 14
Van, Lake (syriaca.org/place/117), 1, 2, 7, 9, 14
Varappuzha (syriaca.org/place/4532), 13; *see also* Verapoly
Veh-Antiokh-e Khosrow (syriaca.org/place/4209), 1, 8; *see also* Maḥoza Ḥdatta, Rumiyya
Veh-Ardashir (syriaca.org/place/475), 1, 8; *see also* Kokhe, Maḥoza
Veh-Ardashir (syriaca.org/place/4233), 9; *see also* Kirman
Veh-Shapur (syriaca.org/place/4235), 9; *see also* Bishapur
Verapoly (syriaca.org/place/4532), 13; *see also* Varappuzha
Vijaya (syriaca.org/place/4414), 11

Wadi Musa (syriaca.org/place/157), 2, 5; *see also* Petra
Wadi Naṭrun (http://syriaca.org/place/289), 5
Wasiṭ (syriaca.org/place/509), 2, 8, 9; *see also* Kashkar
Wondrous Mountain (syriaca.org/place/4109), 3

Xanadu (syriaca.org/place/4400), 11; *see also* Shangdu
Xi'an (syriaca.org/place/479), 11; *see also* Chang'an
Xiapu (syriaca.org/place/4415), 11; *see also* Shangwan
Xijing (syriaca.org/place/4417), 11; *see also* Datong
Xingqing (syriaca.org/place/4527), 11; *see also* Ningxia, Yinchuan
Xining (syriaca.org/place/4420), 11

Yalpanam (syriaca.org/place/4435), 12; *see also* Jaffna
Yangtze River (syriaca.org/place/4545), 11; *see also* Chang Jiang River
Yangzhou (syriaca.org/place/2536), 11
Yanqi (syriaca.org/place/4321), 10, 11; *see also* Qarashahr
Yanuḥ (syriaca.org/place/4124), 4
Yarkand (syriaca.org/place/4334), 10, 11
Yazd (syriaca.org/place/4277), 9
Yellow River (syriaca.org/place/4421), 11
Yellow Sea (syriaca.org/place/4422), 11
Yemen (syriaca.org/place/4543), 6
Yerevan (syriaca.org/place/817), 2
Yeti Su (syriaca.org/place/4488), 10, 11; *see also* Semirechye
Yinchuan (syriaca.org/place/4419), 11; *see also* Ningxia, Xingqing
Yüksekova (syriaca.org/place/815), 14; *see also* Gawar
Yunnanfu (syriaca.org/place/4423), 11; *see also* Kunming

Zab River, Great (syriaca.org/place/204), 1, 2, 7, 14
Zab River, Little (syriaca.org/place/121), 1, 2, 7
Zabdicene (syriaca.org/place/4520), 1; *see also* Beth Zabdai
Zabe (syriaca.org/place/4219), 8
Zagros Mountains (syriaca.org/place/4200), 7, 8
Zakho (syriaca.org/place/208), 14
Zarang (syriaca.org/place/4278), 9
Zaz (syriaca.org/place/538), 14
Zeugma (syriaca.org/place/209), 1, 3, 7
Zhangye (syriaca.org/place/4525), 11; *see also* Ganzhou
Zhenjiang (syriaca.org/place/2537), 11
Ẓufar (syriaca.org/place/4152), 6
Zula (syriaca.org/place/4144), 6; *see also* Adulis

SUBJECT INDEX

ʿAbbasid Caliphate 121–2, 125, 183–4, 192–4, 198–200, 236, 411–12, 416, 429, 433, 441, 571–2, 576–7, 588–90, 602, 633–4, 701
ʿAbdishoʿ bar Brikha of Nisibis 327, 331–2, 334, 414, 584, 586, 589, 602, 609, 626, 685, 699, 704–5, 707, 710–11, 723–5, 767
Abgar II, king of Edessa 12
Abgar V Ukama, king of Edessa 22, 72–7, 164–6, 214, 262, 406–7, 409–10, 415
Abgar VIII the Great, king of Edessa 12, 17, 63, 74, 77, 83
Abgar X, king of Edessa 13
Abraham Ecchellensis 741–4, 747, 757–9, 767
Abraham of Kashkar 89, 94, 97, 197, 358
Abraham of Nathpar 94, 358
accents 299, 302
Accurensis, Victorius Cialac 741, 747, 757
Achaemenid Aramaic 208–13, 215–16, 219, 224, 237
Acts of Mari 81, 83, 164, 343
Acts of Sharbel 76, 347
Acts of Shmona and Gurya 53, 76, 78, 347
Acts of Thomas 17, 91, 230, 233–4, 246, 296, 309, 313–14, 317, 342–3, 378, 656
Addai 17, 21–2, 48–51, 53, 59, 64, 72–7, 81, 83, 135, 150, 164, 180, 214, 323, 342–3, 347, 391, 393, 397, 402, 406–7, 409, 415, 417, 693, 727, 786, 799–801, 805
Adiabene 12, 73, 80–1, 100, 134, 196–7, 212, 219, 700
Afghanistan 33, 122, 125, 184, 583–5, 591
Agapius of Manbij 411, 415–16, 708
Aggai 73, 584, 802
Agnoetes 379, 387–8
Aḥiqar 363
Aḥudemmeh 332, 810
Akkadian 59, 206, 216, 222, 232, 285, 329
Aksenaia *see* Philoxenus of Mabbug
Aleppo 61, 70, 78, 128–9, 244, 246, 442, 491, 573, 735, 743, 759, 772, 776
Alexander of Aphrodisias 316, 422–4, 426, 428
alexandrian (theological party) 24, 109, 111, 299, 380–3, 387
Aluoben 586–7, 626, 629–30, 633
ambon 526–7, 542, 548
Amida *see* Diyarbakir
Amira, George 739, 741, 746–7, 757, 762, 765
amulets 448, 460
Anastasius, emperor 26, 39, 112, 385, 484, 489, 574–5
anatomy 448, 451, 453
anchoritism 88–95, 97, 193, 300, 356, 360, 371, 560–1, 636
Andreas Masius 235, 238, 756, 764, 767
Andrew of Samosata 381
Anglican Church 122, 132, 389, 391, 774, 783, 791, 800
anti-chalcedonians 25, 123, 378, 381, 383, 385–8
anti-Judaism 50, 149, 151
Antioch 12, 18–19, 22, 24–7, 29, 53, 68–70, 73–4, 77–9, 82, 93, 101, 108–12, 115, 120–1, 123–5, 128–9, 131, 167, 187–9, 209, 244, 246, 253, 256, 301–2, 328, 333, 346, 358, 370, 379, 381–5, 387–8, 392, 395, 397–401, 423, 427, 450, 461–2, 479, 483–4, 489–90, 516, 532, 539, 547–8, 559, 570, 572–4, 590, 689, 701–2, 708, 733, 738, 751, 754, 767, 806
Apamea 22, 29, 70, 253, 484, 519, 522, 526, 574–5, 733
Aphrahaṭ 21, 74, 78–9, 90, 135, 138, 151, 176, 230, 296–7, 299, 301, 310, 317–18, 356, 368, 378
apse 249, 468, 498, 506–11, 514, 519, 522, 532, 539, 547
Arabicisation 30, 183, 230, 232, 411, 738, 777
Aramaean 40, 157–9, 163–7, 205–7, 218, 709, 770, 777, 780
Ardashir 33, 36–7, 39–40, 140, 142–3
Aristotle 183–4, 199–200, 322, 387, 422–33, 441, 701–2
Armenia 12, 17–19, 22, 27–8, 34–5, 37–9, 41, 76, 80, 120, 123–4, 134, 136, 154, 163, 165–6, 180, 196, 252, 261, 273–4, 297, 306, 309–10, 313, 317, 320–1, 362–3, 382, 385–6, 391, 407, 451, 466, 585, 605–7, 612, 698,

700, 708–9, 718, 720–2, 745, 772, 774–6, 791
Arsacid 12, 33–4, 210, 219
asceticism 3, 6, 21, 24–5, 63, 78–9, 83, 88–96, 99, 101, 116, 125, 151–2, 196, 294, 309, 313–14, 317–18, 322–3, 341, 343–6, 348, 355–68, 370, 407–8, 560–4, 608, 704
Assemani, Elias 261, 742, 744
Assemani, J. S. 261, 332, 742, 744–7, 772
Assemani, S. E. 261, 340, 746
Assyrian Church of the East 106, 119–20, 122–3, 127, 164, 392, 689, 705, 770–1, 774–80, 783, 789, 791, 793, 795–6
astrology 62, 140–1, 220, 314, 411, 422, 445, 701
astronomy 30, 199, 314, 426, 636, 641–3, 670–1, 701, 756
Atargatis 49–52, 63, 74
Athanasius of Alexandria 107, 344, 398
Athanasius of Balad 30, 180, 423–4, 742
Avicenna (Ibn Sīnā) 430, 447, 590, 701–2, 739, 742
Ayyubids 576, 719–20

Babai of Nisibis 96, 330
Babai the Great 330, 358, 363–5, 369, 388–9
Bactria 36, 41, 95, 208, 583–90, 633–4
Baghdad 7, 30, 81, 121–3, 126, 128, 132, 175, 192–4, 198–200, 271, 335, 362, 377, 415, 417, 427–9, 432–3, 440–1, 449, 576, 578, 591, 603, 606, 609, 701, 719–20, 777–8, 783–7, 789, 791, 793, 795–6
Balai 78, 322, 327–8
baptisteries 20, 78, 479–80, 482–4, 495, 516, 542, 544–5, 547–8
Bar Bahlul 236, 450, 453, 726
Bardaiṣan 12, 21, 47, 50, 52, 62–3, 74, 77–8, 81, 140, 161, 166, 215, 246, 314–16, 319, 322–3, 378, 422, 430, 562, 584
Bar Hebraeus (Bar ʿEbroyo) 7, 191, 193, 231, 235–7, 259, 301, 304, 306, 327, 331, 358, 361, 363, 366, 370, 395, 399–401, 411, 417, 423, 429–30, 447–8, 567, 602–7, 645, 699, 701–9, 718, 720–1, 723, 725–9, 740, 742–3, 758
Barṣauma 38, 99, 126, 330
basilicas 489, 491, 495, 498, 501, 504, 508, 510–17, 522, 531, 533, 547–8
bêma 150, 483, 522–6, 529, 533, 535, 542, 544–5, 547–8, 728
Beth ʿArabaye 26, 80, 705
Beth ʿAramaye 99, 198–9
Beth Garmai 100, 192, 196, 417
Beth Huzaye 99, 192, 198
Beth Nuhadra 197
Beth Qaṭraye 101, 249
Bible 5, 18, 30, 50, 64, 69, 71, 75, 106, 112, 140–1, 157–8, 161, 164–5, 167–8, 188, 200, 207, 235, 246, 256, 261, 293–304, 309–12, 316–23, 329–31, 339–40, 342, 400–1, 407, 462, 468, 470, 556, 558–9, 561–3, 588–9, 591, 602, 612, 629, 683, 699, 703–4, 706, 710, 735, 740–2, 755–60, 762–4, 766–7, 771, 773, 791, 819, 821, 823; exegesis of 77, 147, 150–1, 175, 182, 214, 231, 297–9, 301–4, 306, 310, 317–18, 321–2, 328–9, 339, 344, 364, 381, 387, 451, 589, 663, 703, 705–6; *see also* translation
bilingualism 98, 162, 166, 183–4, 199, 213, 215–17, 230–1, 249, 261, 274, 279, 310, 424, 429, 438, 596, 599, 638–9, 700, 724, 792
biography 24, 89, 94–5, 98, 198, 238, 331–2, 350, 360, 414–15, 585, 709, 726–8, 815
Birecik Inscription 60, 211
Al-Birūnī 590
Bokhtīshū 196, 438; Ğibrīl 447, 449; Ğūrğīs 447, 449
Book of Governors (Thomas of Marga) 197, 199, 345, 562, 589, 626
Book of Medicines 440, 444, 448, 451
Book of Steps 74, 78, 100, 298, 310, 322–3, 356, 364, 368
Book of Treasures 706
breviary 400, 626, 758
Buddhism 35, 122, 590–1, 594, 602, 606, 608, 610, 613, 629, 633–4, 636, 641, 643, 653, 659, 665–7, 674
Byzantine Empire 19, 27–30, 40, 90–1, 97, 100, 113, 115–16, 124, 128, 175, 180–1, 184, 189, 193, 246, 252–3, 259, 270, 304, 322, 359, 367, 377, 391–3, 410, 412, 461, 466–7, 470–1, 489, 491, 532, 547, 568, 571, 576, 625, 725, 733

Carrhae 19–20, 26, 70, 74, 79
catenae 301, 303–4
Caucasus 38, 271–2, 274, 363, 466, 572, 585, 778
celibacy 63, 89, 91, 99, 196, 313, 318, 555
Chaldaean Catholics 119–20, 122, 126–8, 270, 341, 544, 680, 771, 785–8, 790–1, 795–6
chevet 498, 504, 506, 508, 511, 514–16, 519
China ch.32 *passim*, 7, 41, 119, 122, 196, 249–50, 449, 451, 586–8, 594, 602, 604–5, 607–10, 612–14, 722
Christianisation 11, 18, 21, 70, 73, 76, 136, 217, 541, 603, 605, 640
Christology 6, 22, 27, 95, 100, 107–11, 120–1, 123, 125, 182, 185, 301, 322, 345, 357–8, 366, 377–8, 380–5, 387–9, 391–2, 395–7, 408, 432, 470, 479
chronicles, general 17, 20, 26, 37, 70, 97, 100, 135, 139, 164–6, 175, 179, 183, 186, 195, 248, 293, 359, 409–12, 414–15, 449, 555, 661, 701, 707–8, 710, 720–1, 723, 726–7, 731; Chronicle of Edessa 17, 53, 73, 75, 409, 416; Chronicle of Michael the Syrian (*see* Michael the Syrian); Chronicle of Pseudo-Dionysius 64; Chronicle of Pseudo-Joshua 38, 409, 571, 575; Chronicle of Pseudo-Zachariah 408, 432, 441, 585; Chronicle of Se'ert 35–6, 97, 99, 142, 199, 413–17, 575, 585, 587, 663, 693, 708; Chronicle of Zuqnin 75, 167, 184, 410–12, 416, 569, 806
Chrysostom 69, 110, 301, 303, 380, 398, 479
Cochin 664, 688, 690–1
codicology 161, 363, 701, 780, 819

cœnobitism 21, 88, 96–100, 356
coins 11, 14, 33, 37–8, 49, 53, 58–9, 74, 179, 211, 244, 588, 606, 720, 759
colophons 175, 252–4, 256, 446, 463, 562, 656, 690, 710, 720–1, 800
commentaries 30, 158, 160, 165, 167, 294–7, 299–304, 306, 309–10, 319, 321–2, 331–2, 341, 358–9, 361, 363–4, 368–70, 394, 397, 400, 402, 423–6, 428–32, 441, 446–8, 556, 602, 701, 706, 724–5, 727–8, 746, 766, 819
Confucianism 610, 641
Constantine the Great, emperor 19, 21, 36, 49, 69, 76, 105–6, 108, 136–8, 146, 405–6, 408, 464, 489, 606, 709
Constantius II, emperor 20, 106, 409
conversion, religious: Chinese to Christianity 644; Christians to Islam 29, 125, 176, 181–3, 189–90, 192–3, 200, 272, 411, 439, 576, 585, 612, 722, 784, 788; conversion to Manichaeism 21–2, 310, 343; Himyarite conversion to Judaism 27; Indians to Christianity 313–14, 342; Jews to Christianity 24, 77, 153; pre-Christian local religions to Christianity 15, 22, 25, 35, 64, 68–9, 73–4, 76–7, 81–2, 91, 138, 213–14, 220, 346, 407; Turkic peoples to Christianity 122, 274, 587, 589, 602–6; Turkic peoples to Islam 605–6, 655, 661; Zoroastrians to Christianity 91, 137–42, 343, 348; Zoroastrians to Islam 360
Coptic and Copts 106, 108, 111, 120, 154, 234, 238, 253, 306, 313, 378, 469, 473, 478, 559, 602, 698, 707, 742, 744–5, 758, 818–19, 821
councils of the Church, general 22, 106–14, 121, 360, 378–9, 381–3, 385–6, 556, 738, 779; Council of Chalcedon (451) 22, 24–5, 100, 105–6, 108, 111–14, 120–1, 123–5, 299, 377–8, 381–3, 385, 395, 415, 463, 471, 708, 731; Council of Florence (1445) 126, 128, 721; Council of Nicaea (325) 69–71, 106, 108, 111, 319, 379, 381–3, 489, 743; Council of Trent (1545–63) 655, 680; Fifth Lateran Council (1513–17) 751; First Council of Constantinople (381) 70–1, 106, 111, 379–80, 383; First Council of Ephesus (431) 22, 106, 108–11, 121, 378–9, 381–3, 392; Fourth Lateran Council (1215) 126, 737; Second Council of Constantinople (553) 112–14, 299, 379, 386; Second Council of Ephesus (449) 22, 111, 382; Second Vatican Council (1962–5) 734; Third Council of Constantinople (680) 29, 125, 379, 386, 733; Third Lateran Council (1179) 128
Crusades 124, 126, 128, 193–4, 413, 449, 466, 468, 576, 698, 708, 710, 721–2, 737, 747
Ctesiphon 12, 27, 33, 40, 80, 147, 248, 413–14, 568
Cyril of Alexandria 21–2, 24, 108–11, 301, 378–80, 382–3, 385–7, 398
Cyrillona 322–3, 328

Dadisho' Qaṭraya 90, 95, 300, 355, 359, 362–3, 366, 369
Damascus 19, 28–9, 122, 125, 192, 196, 225, 248, 270, 415, 446–7, 495, 567, 589, 720, 776
Daniel of Ṣalaḥ 167, 301, 727
Deir al-Suryan 24–5, 429, 440, 473
Denkard 140, 452
deportations 18, 26–7, 30, 82–3, 120, 122, 128, 134, 243, 319, 449, 466, 570, 574–7, 590, 777
Diatessaron 17, 24, 73, 152, 294, 296–7, 317, 321–3, 392, 723
diglossia *see* bilingualism
Diocletian 19, 68, 106, 254, 310, 346–7, 575
Diodore of Tarsus 121, 316
Dionysius bar Ṣalibi 186–7, 304, 306, 361, 363, 370, 397–9, 401, 429, 701–2, 705–7, 710, 727, 743
disputations, religious 140, 182, 703, 706
dispute poetry 323, 329, 332, 344
Diyarbakir (Amida) 19, 21–2, 26, 28, 70, 79, 96, 98, 100, 126–7, 266, 302–3, 345, 392, 408–9, 562, 568–9, 571, 574–5, 723, 727, 759, 771, 775
doctors *see* physicians
dots *see* pointing, orthographical
Dunhuang 7, 594, 601–2, 626, 629, 634–5, 637, 640, 644–5, 721, 822
dyophysite 22, 107, 110, 121, 299, 357, 366, 378, 384, 395, 413

Eastern Aramaic 206–7, 212–13, 219–20, 246, 570
Edessa, general 1–4, 164–7, 180–1, 243–6, 313–14, 322, 356, 383, 391, 405, 409–14, 461–5, 491, 531–2, 547, 555, 567, 569, 571, 573, 575, 705; dialect of Aramaic and early script 16, 157, 16, 206–7, 210–11, 215–17, 220, 222, 224–7, 243, 243–6, 251, 254, 256, 342, 479, 483; Judaism in 50; liturgical tradition of 392, 400, 734; Roman-era kingdom and city of 11–22, 27–8, 47–54, 57–64, 70, 74, 209–12, 309, 461; School of the Persians (*see* schools, general); theological disputes in 381–4, 386, 391
Eliya bar Shinaya of Nisibis 100, 415–17, 700–1, 703, 707–8, 743, 760
'Enanisho' of Beth 'Abhe 197, 345, 358–9, 362, 365, 369
encratite 91
Ephrem the Syrian 6, 19–21, 74–8, 89, 93, 100, 137, 151, 161, 165–6, 176, 230, 236, 238, 294, 296–9, 301, 303–4, 310, 312–14, 316, 318–23, 327–30, 334–5, 343–4, 356, 361, 368, 378, 383, 400, 406–7, 409–10, 413–14, 416, 422, 439, 554, 556–60, 562, 744–6, 816, 818–19
estrangela script 17–18, 213, 216–17, 244, 254, 256–7, 462, 792
Ethiopia 27, 120, 205, 222, 355, 366, 377, 467, 575, 821
Ethiopic 26, 154, 222, 306, 313, 362, 366, 764, 766

eucharist 113, 115, 126, 180–1, 312, 365, 393, 395, 397, 400, 402, 558, 564, 572, 707, 748, 767
Eusebius of Caesarea 3, 17, 21, 72, 74–6, 91, 105–6, 108, 116, 136, 146, 163–7, 216, 227, 315–16, 323, 342, 347, 405–10, 412, 416–17, 484, 489, 584, 657, 690
Evagrius of Pontus 300, 357–61, 363–7, 369–71, 427, 820

al-Fārābī 430, 432–3
farming 7, 567–75, 577–8
Fenqitho 333, 342, 344
festivals 64, 139, 149–50, 186, 393, 554, 590
Flavian of Constantinople 109, 381–2
florilegia 362, 364, 385

Gabriel Sionita 758, 762, 766
Galen 199, 423, 428–9, 431–2, 440–2, 444, 446, 448–53
Galen Palimpsest 440, 450, 452–3, 822
Gannat Bussame 303, 602
garshuni 260–1, 669–70, 686, 689, 691–3, 738, 745–6, 817
al-Ġazzāli 361, 705, 707
genocide 8, 770, 774–6, 780, 788
George, bishop of the Arabs 30, 327, 330, 400, 423
Georgia 35, 38, 76, 154, 271, 273–4, 306, 363, 466, 473, 692, 698, 727, 776, 790, 818–19, 821
Gewargis Warda 303, 327, 332, 393, 451, 704, 796, 808
gnosticism 62, 69, 77, 215, 271, 359–61, 363
grammar, Syriac 154, 231, 235–6, 254, 260–1, 268, 304, 312, 331, 385, 442, 699–700, 702, 711, 728, 741, 757–60, 762–7
Gregory of Cyprus 358, 362, 365, 369–70
Gregory of Nazianzus 21, 333, 398, 431
Gregory of Nyssa 357, 360, 364, 366, 442
Gundeshapur (Jundishapur, Beth-Lapaṭ) 82, 98, 191, 199, 449, 570, 577

hagiography ch.20 *passim*, 6, 17, 70, 88–9, 91, 94, 98, 111, 115, 149, 152, 154, 167, 175, 322, 331, 339–50, 360, 407–8, 413, 415, 451, 556, 559–63, 604, 665
Ḥarqlean Translation 295–6, 304
Ḥarran (Carrhae) 19–20, 26, 51–2, 54, 57–9, 70, 72–4, 79, 109, 165, 464, 575–6
Hebrew 157, 165, 199, 205, 210, 215, 218, 222–3, 232, 243, 253, 274, 301, 444, 447, 657, 666, 668, 741, 744, 751, 755–6, 760, 762–3
Hebrew Bible, Syriac translations of 5, 17, 50, 161, 293, 311, 319, 339
Hellenism 4, 11, 13, 30, 61, 63, 411, 438–9, 462, 539
Ḥenana 300, 302, 379, 388–9
Henoticon 111, 115, 123, 383, 385
heresy and heretics 21, 28–9, 47, 68, 77, 83, 107–8, 110–11, 114–15, 130, 146–50, 179, 192, 298, 315–16, 319, 358, 366, 378, 381–2, 408–10, 412, 557, 562, 608, 683, 685, 724
hesychasm 95–6, 359, 366
Hierotheos, book of 358, 361, 370
Himyarites 27
Hindu 35, 544, 653, 656, 659–62, 665–7, 687
Hippocrates 442–3, 446–8, 451
al-Ḥira 26–7, 37, 248, 535, 538, 541, 548, 568
historiography ch.24 *passim*, 5, 88–9, 98, 115, 164, 219, 340, 405, 408, 453, 563, 708, 710–11, 820
homiletics 150, 296–7, 300, 321–2, 329–31, 339–41, 343, 363, 402, 556, 558–9
Ḥunayn ibn Isḥaq 199–200, 301, 427–8, 431–3, 439–40, 442–6, 448–9, 451–2
hymns *see* madrashe

Ibas of Edessa (Hiba) 22, 109, 111, 114, 121, 299, 322, 378–9, 382, 386
icons 75, 467, 705, 728, 736, 745, 791
Iḥidayutha 90–1, 318, 348, 636
Isaac of Antioch 53, 328
Isaac of Nineveh 95, 327–8, 355, 359, 361–6, 369, 371
Isaac Sciadrensis 741, 759
Isaiah, Abba 300, 357, 359, 363–4, 367–70
Isḥaq Shbadnaya 231, 301, 303, 306, 723, 725, 728
Isho' bar 'Ali 236, 238, 446
Isho' bar Nun 302, 360
Isho'dad of Merv 231, 302–4, 306, 589, 602, 629, 819
Isho'denaḥ 95, 97–9, 198, 360, 415, 417, 589
Isho'yabh I, catholicos 115, 585–6
Isho'yabh II, catholicos 330, 586–7
Isho'yabh III, catholicos 178–9, 192, 197, 379, 393–4, 586–7, 626, 729
Isis (Daesh) 349, 778, 788, 796
Islam, Syriac relations with ch.11, 38, 39 *passim*, 4, 6, 8, 29–30, 100, 122–5, 157–9, 168, 189–94, 200, 207, 218, 293, 367, 438–9, 447–9, 452–3, 588, 603–8, 705, 707, 710, 718, 722

Jacob Baradaeus 25, 100–1, 113–15, 123–4, 345, 377, 395, 743
Jacob bar Shakko 335, 430, 700–2, 706
Jacobites 24, 95, 106, 119, 124, 130–1, 270, 377–8, 395, 412–13, 590, 681–2, 689, 801, 806
Jacob of Edessa 30, 157–8, 167, 220, 230, 235, 237, 259, 295–6, 301, 303–4, 327–8, 330, 333, 395, 398–400, 423–4, 426, 708, 743
Jacob of Nisibis 20, 78, 317, 319, 406–7, 409, 414, 416
Jacob of Sarug 26, 48, 52, 78, 166–7, 176, 301, 304, 327–8, 330, 343, 379, 381, 383, 398, 400, 556–60, 562, 564, 744
jingjiao 625–9, 634–5
John Barbur 379, 386–7
John bar Penkaye 180, 359
John bar Zo'bi 235, 331, 429–30, 433, 700, 702
John Chrysostom 69, 110, 301, 303, 380, 398, 479
John of Apamea 165, 360
John of Dailam 98, 101, 183, 187
John of Dalyatha 95, 355, 360–6, 369
John of Dara 401
John of Ephesus 22, 27, 69, 92, 94, 96, 98, 100–1, 115–16, 160, 163, 167, 345, 350, 408–10, 412, 415, 417, 561, 563–4, 569, 575, 708, 806, 813
John of Tella 113, 115–16, 123, 163, 167, 345, 560

John Philoponus 379, 387, 425–8, 432
John Sulaqa 126–7, 680, 771, 799, 801, 804
John the Solitary 322, 357, 359–60, 363–4, 368
Joseph bar Malkon 235, 260, 700, 705
Joseph Ḥazzaya 95, 359–63, 366, 369, 371
Joseph Huzaya 235, 300
Judaism 3, 27, 50, 73, 77, 83, 146–8, 150, 164, 167, 179, 190, 268, 317, 591, 726; involvement in Christianisation of Edessa 27–30, 35, 50–1, 69, 73, 77; Jewish interaction with Syrian Christians ch.9 *passim*, 1, 3, 5, 107, 3–4, 206, 215, 224, 268–74, 293–7, 309–10, 317, 321, 329, 393, 660, 664, 666–7, 688–90, 754, 756, 760, 788, 796
Julian, emperor 20–1, 36, 47, 53, 57, 137, 319, 409
Julian of Halicarnassus (Julianists) 379, 385–6, 407, 416
Julian Romance 21, 164, 407–8, 415–16
Julian Saba 322, 344, 406–7, 409
Justinian, emperor 25–7, 39, 95, 100, 112–16, 123, 125, 386, 389, 409, 422, 489, 569, 731

Kabbalah 8, 751–2, 754, 756, 760
Kerala 132, 248–50, 253, 258, 261, 333, 544, 548, 568, 671, 675–6, 693, 719, 722, 728
Khamis bar Qardaḥe 327, 332, 334, 393, 703–4, 723–6, 728
Khorasan 33, 81, 83, 192, 198, 583–5, 587, 590, 602, 608, 640
Khosrow I Anushirwan, shah of Persia 27–9, 39, 136, 142, 441, 570, 575, 585
Khosrow II, shah of Persia 39–40, 115, 124, 136, 414, 574
al-Kindī 192, 433
Kirkuk 91, 248, 271, 783, 786
Kurdistan 122, 126, 197, 248, 250, 261, 271, 273–4, 277, 472, 545, 719–20, 724, 728, 775–9, 783, 788–9, 795

Lebanon 8, 125–6, 129, 249–50, 252, 261, 272, 467, 522, 526, 567, 577, 722, 731–5, 737–41, 743–8, 757–8, 771, 775–8
lectionaries 295, 400, 596, 602, 675, 725, 734–5
lexicography 236, 238, 304, 453, 700, 702, 756
liber graduum *see* Book of Steps
limestone massif 22, 244, 462, 477–9, 491, 493, 495, 504, 576
liturgies 6, 21, 47, 91, 98, 101, 119, 130–1, 142, 150, 161, 216, 253–4, 260, 273, 296, 303, 306, 312–13, 319, 322, 328–34, 339, 342–4, 364, 391–3, 398–402, 450, 466, 476, 479, 483–4, 491, 522, 535, 539, 548, 555–6, 558–64, 584, 595, 625, 635, 640, 654–5, 663, 675, 680, 683, 689, 699, 703, 718, 723–9, 734–8, 745–7, 751
loanwords 142, 152, 209, 213, 215, 219–20, 232, 236, 274–5, 278–9, 296, 654, 704, 723
logic 30, 183, 423–7, 430, 432–3, 590, 702, 742–3, 745
Longmen 629, 635
Luoyang pillar 250, 587, 626, 630–2

Mabbug/Mabbog (Hierapolis) 50–2, 63, 70, 74, 78, 160
Macarius 105, 116, 363, 365
madrashe 19–21, 137, 142, 190, 297–8, 303, 310–14, 316, 318–35, 339, 343–4, 391, 393, 400–1, 556–9, 564, 594, 663, 665, 703–4, 728
Malabar 119–20, 130, 132, 391, 653, 656–7, 659–61, 664–5, 667, 672, 675, 680, 688–90, 693
Malankara 119–20, 130–1, 391, 653, 655, 660–1, 664, 666, 683, 689, 691
Malayalam 261, 654–7, 663–70, 676, 680–2, 686, 689–93
Mandaeans and Mandaic 147, 150, 206, 224, 237, 270–4, 277, 285, 567, 570
Manichaeism 2, 19, 21, 76–7, 82, 91, 135, 310, 313, 319, 323, 343, 381, 591, 594, 634, 637
al-Manṣur 197, 411, 449, 454, 590
maphrian 25, 124, 260, 331, 400, 447, 587, 590, 699, 701, 707, 709, 721, 723, 727, 806, 811–12
Mappiḷḷa Christians 654, 660–1, 680, 683, 685, 690
Mar Aba 139–41, 303, 387, 392–4, 585, 676
Mara bar Sarapion 161, 219, 230, 431
Mar Behnam 98, 262, 348–9, 535, 791–2, 796
Marcion and Marcionitism 2, 77, 309, 314–16, 319, 322, 381
Mar Denḥa of India 675, 680–3, 692–3
Mardin 125, 127, 129, 266, 273, 400, 700, 719–21, 771, 775
Mari, Mar 80–1, 89, 135, 150, 198, 343, 391, 393, 397, 572
Mark the solitary 357, 364, 368, 371
Mar Matai, monastery 25, 100, 124, 412, 602, 700, 726, 801
Mar Musa al-Habashi, monastery 467, 469–71
Maron 92, 125, 731
Maronite Collegium Romanum 261, 734, 738–41, 743–7, 756–7, 759
Maronites ch.36 *passim*, 8, 29, 119–20, 125–6, 129, 179, 256, 261, 306, 328, 330, 335, 342, 344, 391, 397, 410–11, 559, 707–8, 722, 751, 756–9, 763, 765, 771–2
Mar Qardagh 143, 348, 451
martyrdom 17, 19, 27, 36, 53, 68–9, 76, 78, 82, 92, 95, 98, 130, 136–40, 143, 151, 153, 166, 253, 310, 313, 322, 340, 343, 346–8, 350, 400, 406, 409, 413, 416, 470, 491, 529, 547, 555, 559, 561, 610, 791
martyria 79, 98–9, 138, 465, 483, 495, 516–20, 522, 535, 537, 541, 545–8
martyrology 36, 76, 78, 82, 142, 175, 342
Martyropolis 26, 28, 70, 135, 392
masora 295, 304
mathematics 30, 199, 423, 425–7, 430, 432, 571, 701–2, 756
medicine ch.26 *passim*, 4–5, 30, 121, 142, 191, 199, 310, 312, 321, 359, 370, 423, 428–9, 590, 593, 641–4, 701, 739, 742, 756, 760, 784, 788–9

Melitene 259, 304, 400, 574, 720, 727
Melkite 29, 106, 113, 192–3, 251–3, 256, 328, 333–4, 366, 377, 400, 410, 415, 449, 583, 590, 608, 634, 707–8, 733, 738, 784
Merv 196, 439, 584–7, 589–90, 594, 602–4, 609
Messalianism 93, 356–7, 359–60, 366, 381
metaphysics 423–8, 430, 701–2
miaphysite 24–5, 27, 29–30, 39–40, 95, 99–100, 107, 111, 120, 123, 125, 162, 165–7, 180, 182, 190, 251, 301, 345–6, 355–7, 378, 386–9, 391, 395, 405, 407–10, 412, 415–16, 460, 479, 483–4, 689, 731, 756
Michael the Syrian (Michael the Great) 6, 64, 128–9, 158, 167, 175–6, 186–8, 222, 302, 331, 341, 405, 411, 567, 569, 603–4, 707–10, 764, 807–8, 813
migrations 125, 134, 270–1, 273, 415, 664, 775, 777–8
missions and missionaries 7, 69, 71, 76–8, 82, 89, 99–100, 122, 126–32, 195, 214, 217, 248, 270, 274, 313, 343, 355, 391, 406, 408, 451, 478, 567, 584, 587, 589, 603–4, 626, 637, 640, 643–4, 653–6, 661–2, 678, 680, 683, 688, 722, 728, 732, 738, 741, 756, 770–5, 800
monasteries 17, 21–2, 24–5, 27, 30, 36, 58, 79, 81, 88–100, 114, 124–7, 129, 175, 184–5, 193, 196–9, 214, 248–9, 251, 253–4, 256, 261–2, 295, 331, 344–6, 349, 358–60, 362, 370, 387, 393–4, 400, 410, 412, 414, 423–4, 440–1, 453, 462–3, 467–8, 470–1, 473, 484, 506, 516, 532, 535, 537, 539–41, 548, 561–2, 567, 576, 578, 589, 591, 602, 612, 626, 629–30, 632–3, 635–6, 642–3, 645, 667, 675, 688, 700, 707, 709–10, 720–1, 726, 731, 733, 741, 743, 745, 752, 771, 779, 791–2, 796, 800–1, 818
monasticism 3, 36, 88–9, 91–101, 125, 131, 143, 152–3, 193, 197–9, 247, 300, 310, 322, 344–7, 358–63, 366–7, 371, 392, 414–15, 431, 447, 451, 462, 471, 495, 514, 535, 539, 548, 554–6, 561–3, 576, 602, 721, 727, 731–3, 743, 772, 776
Mongolia and Mongols 41, 100, 122, 125–6, 192, 194, 196, 249–50, 303, 392, 447, 449, 545, 576, 583, 591, 594, 602–12, 614, 625, 637–8, 640–5, 698, 704, 708, 710, 718–26, 729, 792, 801
monoenergism 29, 124
monophysite *see* miaphysite
monotheletism 29, 124–5, 412, 732–3, 737
mosaics 12–15, 48–9, 59–64, 74, 79, 83, 211–12, 220, 225, 227, 244, 246, 248, 254, 309, 461–3, 465–6, 473
Moses bar Kepha 231, 304, 397, 401, 767
Moses of Mardin 235, 251, 261, 751, 756, 767
Mosul 25, 88, 98, 100, 124, 126–7, 191, 196–8, 248, 261–2, 269, 274, 331, 349, 361–2, 393–4, 400, 446, 467, 537–8, 548, 607, 700, 702, 704, 711, 720–3, 725, 727, 729, 771, 776, 778, 783–8, 791, 793–6, 800–2, 804
mysticism 6, 8, 93, 131, 298, 306, 332, 355–68, 370, 561, 665, 705, 751–2, 754, 763

Nabataean 12, 15, 53–4, 62, 210, 219, 224, 243, 258, 567, 570, 577
Narsai 73, 78, 99, 196, 299, 301, 327–9, 331, 378, 383, 558, 799, 802
Nayars 653–4, 660–1, 664
Nemesius of Edessa 442
Neo-aramaic ch.16 *passim*, 223, 225, 231, 789, 820
Neo-Chalcedonianism 29, 385, 388–9
Neoplatonism 422–3, 425–7, 430–1, 433, 441, 702
Nestorianism 38–9, 106, 110, 120–1, 130, 132, 192, 217, 249, 270, 377–80, 382–5, 391–2, 415, 529, 568, 576, 590, 594, 603–4, 608, 611–13, 641, 655, 666, 675, 680, 682, 685, 689, 721–2, 727–9, 799–801
Nestorius 22, 24, 109–10, 121, 360, 366, 369, 377–81, 383, 387, 389, 392–3, 685, 728
Nineveh 80, 165, 248, 269, 349, 401, 577, 778, 783, 788–9, 793
Nisibis 12–13, 18–21, 26, 28, 35–6, 70, 73–4, 77–83, 88, 92–3, 99, 121, 137, 147, 165, 191, 196, 198–9, 209, 230, 297, 299, 309, 318–19, 331, 347, 406–7, 413–14, 531, 575, 700, 721
non-Chalcedonian 22, 24, 107, 111–16, 162, 165–7, 395, 398, 468–71, 698, 705

Odes of Solomon 161, 215, 230, 236, 296, 309, 311–12, 317, 378
Önggüt 602, 605–6, 608–11, 638, 640–1, 643, 722, 729
Origen 295, 316, 365, 389, 432
Origenism 357
orthography 17, 208–9, 211–12, 216, 219–20, 227, 230, 235
Osrhoene 1, 11–12, 17–20, 26, 70, 91–2, 97, 119, 123, 134, 159, 162–3, 207–8, 210–13, 217, 219–20, 225, 243, 246, 248, 479, 491, 526
Ottoman Empire 122, 128–9, 251, 261, 577, 718–20, 722–4, 729, 744, 747, 770–2, 774–5, 789

Palmyra 12, 19, 47, 50, 52–4, 58–9, 62, 206–11, 213, 215, 219, 224, 243, 461–2, 464, 483, 495, 511–12, 522, 526, 532, 535
papacy 22, 25, 107–11, 113–14, 116, 123, 126–9, 131–2, 334, 382, 408, 431, 606–8, 678, 682, 731, 733, 737–40, 742, 744–5, 771, 786, 799–801
papyri 16–17, 64, 211, 224–5, 251, 333, 399, 655, 690
Parthians and Parthian Empire 12–14, 16, 18, 57, 59, 62, 64, 71, 74, 76, 81, 110, 134–5, 137, 143, 160, 216, 219, 270, 309, 572, 583
Paul of Aegina 442, 446–7
Paul of Callinicum 386
Paul the Persian 423
persecutions 19–20, 24, 28, 35–6, 68, 82, 94–5, 99, 106, 113–14, 121, 123–4, 126, 136–9, 151, 190–1, 193–4, 310–11, 340, 346–7, 361, 388, 408–9, 413, 416, 555, 561, 609, 657, 664, 710, 722, 744, 747, 762, 790, 800
Peshiṭta 17, 24, 50, 142, 218, 227, 232, 237, 293–6, 302, 304, 735, 765, 773

philosophy ch.25 *passim*, 4–5, 12, 63, 74, 77, 100, 121–2, 134, 166, 175, 183, 191, 199–200, 215, 217, 231, 309–10, 314–16, 322–3, 361, 365, 387, 440–1, 557, 584, 699–702, 704, 706, 711, 724, 726, 741–3, 745, 763
Philoxenus of Mabbug 27, 78, 112–13, 163, 166–7, 295, 356–7, 363, 370, 379, 381–4, 389, 397–8
phonetics 205, 209–10, 213, 216–17, 218
phonology 5, 206, 208, 222, 235, 258–60, 268, 275–6, 304, 700
physicians 28, 191–2, 199, 313, 321, 346, 397, 428, 432, 438–9, 441–2, 446–7, 449, 451–3, 642, 701–2, 707, 741, 745, 784
physics 199, 365, 423, 425–8, 430, 432, 701–2
physiology 359, 451
pilgrimage and pilgrims 6, 52, 74, 89, 93, 100, 198, 249, 313, 323, 344, 347, 466, 483, 491, 504, 510, 540–1, 547, 638, 645, 657–8, 725, 727
Plato 314–15, 364, 423, 425, 427, 431–2
Plotinus 365
poetry chs.18, 19 *passim*, 4, 6, 21, 77, 161, 215, 220, 230–1, 298, 339, 343–4, 383, 391, 451, 558–9, 655, 700, 703–4, 711, 723–6, 738; versification of 333, 335, 704, 765
pointing, orthographical 209, 213, 217, 235, 254, 258–61, 277–8, 299–300, 700, 724, 755, 764
polyglot bibles 261, 740, 742, 755–8, 762–4, 767
Porphyry 363, 423–4, 430, 432, 742
preaching 69, 73, 76, 93–4, 128, 300, 313–14, 342
pre-christian religions ch.3 *passim*, 1, 106, 211, 213, 243, 415, 737, 774, 780
Proba (philosopher) 423, 425
Proba (theologian) 379, 386–7
Procopius 27, 39, 571
Protestant 8, 146, 270, 378, 689, 755, 759–60, 762–4, 770–1, 773–5, 777, 786
psalms 34, 99, 142, 261, 295, 301, 304, 311, 333, 394–5, 557, 560, 562, 596, 599, 638, 727, 751, 758, 766
Pseudo-Dionysius the Areopagite 331, 357–60, 366, 368, 398, 423, 427, 432
Pythagoras 363, 432

Qaraqosh 269, 275–6, 279, 285, 785, 794
Qarṭamin 98, 345, 410, 576
Qenneshre, monastery 30, 400, 412, 423, 425–7
Qennesrin (Chalcis) 70, 100, 328
Qur'an 190, 660, 795
Qurillona *see* Cyrillona

Rabban Ṣawma 608–9, 637, 640, 710, 723, 725
rabbinics 1, 3–4, 146–9, 151–4, 573
Rabbula, bishop of Edessa 24, 63, 77, 83, 90, 97, 100, 121, 245, 294, 322, 346, 378–9, 381–2, 463–4, 555–6, 560, 564
al-Rāzī 439, 447–8, 453
renaissance, European 8, 199, 739
renaissance, Syriac 7, 125, 186, 231, 304, 331, 429–30, 447, 533, 698–701, 710
Reṣafa 115, 248, 466, 470, 483, 489, 510–11, 513, 516, 519, 522, 525–6
rhetoric 151, 230, 322, 330, 335, 344, 422, 426, 432, 702
Roman Catholic 120, 122, 124–5, 127, 361, 654, 687–9, 734, 737–9, 779

Sabians 272, 567, 570
Sabrisho' 95, 330, 802–3
Safavid 577, 718–20
Sahdona (Martyrius) 358–9, 363, 365, 369, 379, 389, 561
St. Thomas Christians 130–2, 544, 632, 654–6, 682–3, 685, 771
Samaritan, language 206, 224, 766
Şanliurfa *see* Edessa, general
Sanskrit 451, 453, 636, 654, 691
Sayfo *see* genocide
schools, general 22, 99, 110, 273, 331, 422, 424, 427–30, 439, 441, 444, 532, 560, 562, 711, 789; School of Nisibis 22, 99, 121, 300, 303, 355, 378–9, 388, 413, 441; School of the Persians in Edessa 22, 121, 299–303, 329, 378–9, 381, 383, 392, 413; School of Gundishapur 191, 199, 449, 577
Sergius Bahira 185
Severus of Antioch 24–5, 112–15, 123, 157, 167, 246, 299, 301–2, 330, 333, 379, 383, 385–7, 397–401, 483–4, 767, 806
Severus Sebokht 30, 423, 425–6
Shapur I, shah of Persia 15, 18–19, 33–5, 82, 134, 449, 570
Shapur II, shah of Persia 20–1, 35–7, 79, 82, 136–7, 297, 310, 319, 348, 574–5, 584, 800
Simeon bar Ṣabba'e 138, 310, 348
Simeon d-Taybouteh 95, 359, 447
Simeon of Beth Arsham 345, 379, 384
Simeon the Stylite 63, 92, 329, 344, 409–10, 416, 468, 484, 489, 504, 541, 563–4
Simeon the Younger 93, 516
Sogdiana and Sogdian 119, 142, 249, 363, 371, 584, 586–8, 590–1, 594–5, 598, 602, 604, 612, 625, 634–7
soghyatha 298, 329–30, 332, 334, 344, 391, 704, 727
solitary *see* anchoritism
spirituality 355, 357, 361, 365–6, 368, 371, 540, 731, 733, 737
Stephen bar Sudaili 358, 366, 370
stylites 63, 88, 92, 101, 468, 484, 516, 563
sun-deity 53–4
synods of the Syriac Churches 70, 93, 120–1, 135, 139, 141, 143, 195, 409, 413, 584–6, 707; Synod of Seleuceia-Ctesiphon (410) 80–2, 121, 135, 392, 584; Synod of 420 80–1, 584; Synod of 424 135, 138, 584; Synod of Bet Lapaṭ (484) 38, 99, 121, 135, 413; Synod of Seleuceia-Ctesiphon (486) 38, 121; Synod of Aba (544) 387; Synod of Joseph (554) 584; Synod of Isho'yabh I (585) 149, 387, 585; Synod of Sabrisho' (596) 387; Synod of Gregory (605) 40,

387; Synod of Ctesiphon (612) 121, 388; Synod of Timothy II (1318) 707, 725; Synod of Angalamy (1583) 683; Synod of Diamper (1599) 130, 683, 685, 687, 691, 693; Synod of Diarbekir (1616) 759; Synod of Maronite Church (1736) 747; Synod of the Assyrian Church (2001) 705; Syrian Catholic 119–20, 125, 128–9, 252, 261, 302, 333, 384, 391, 689, 783, 786, 791, 813
syrian ethnicity ch.10 *passim*
Syrian Orthodox 24–5, 27–30, 92, 95, 100, 106, 111, 113–16, 119–20, 123–5, 128–32, 158, 161–2, 164, 167–8, 207, 248–9, 251–2, 260–1, 270, 327–8, 330, 333–4, 341–2, 344–5, 391, 395–6, 399–402, 446–7, 449, 460, 467, 469–70, 473, 584, 587, 590, 602, 604, 608, 655, 662, 688–9, 718, 720–1, 751, 783, 786, 791, 795, 806, 809–12

Talmud 146–9, 151–4, 296, 568
Tang Dynasty, China 119, 249, 449, 588, 625–6, 629, 633–5, 637–8, 644
Tangut 122, 608–10, 641, 645
Targums 224, 293, 329, 760, 765–6
Tatian 24, 73, 91, 152, 294, 317, 378; *see also* Diatessaron
Teseo Ambrogio 751–2, 755
Thaddaeus *see* Addai
Themistius 388, 428, 431, 433
Theodore bar Koni 302, 423
Theodore of Antioch 701–2
Theodore of Merv 602
Theodore of Mopsuestia 24, 111, 114, 121, 140, 299–302, 329, 357, 378–81, 383–4, 386–7, 389, 393, 413
Theodoret of Cyrrhus 3, 91, 93, 97–8, 111, 114, 140, 162–3, 166, 301, 344, 381–2, 386, 405, 407, 479, 560, 731
Theodosius I, emperor 19, 106
Theodosius II, emperor 24, 26, 110–11, 381–2, 489
Theodosius of Alexandria 25, 388
Theophilus of Alexandria 107, 109–10, 380
Theophilus of Edessa 183, 411–12, 415–17, 427, 708, 738
Thomas, Apostle 72, 74–5, 130, 313–14, 342, 398, 626, 656–8, 662, 679, 690
Thomas of Ḥarqel 30, 295, 398
Thomas of Kana 661, 663–5, 667, 670–1, 691–2
Thomas of Marga 191, 196–7, 199, 345, 360, 415, 562, 589, 626
Timothy I, catholicos 122, 184–5, 192, 195–6, 200, 357, 360, 366, 424, 428, 432–3, 441, 449, 545, 585, 589–90, 609, 626, 634, 800, 803
Timothy II, catholicos 332, 724–6, 800–1, 804
Timurids 100, 583, 605, 613, 720
translation: ʿAbbasid era translation movement 121–2, 132, 175, 183–5, 191, 199–200, 236, 295, 411, 414, 427–9, 441–54; early translations from Greek 4–5, 17–18, 22, 24, 72, 76, 78, 106, 108, 110, 115, 121, 140, 215–16, 227, 230, 235, 299, 310, 323, 343–5, 357, 379, 387, 392, 397, 400, 407, 423–7, 431, 441–3, 567; later translations of the 7th–8th c. 30, 157, 167, 333, 399; New Testament 59, 157, 161, 214, 246, 293–6; Old Testament 17–18, 50, 161, 214–15, 227, 232, 246, 293–6; translations from Syriac to other languages 136, 142, 166, 179, 313, 315, 321, 362–3, 366–70, 577, 595, 663, 707, 734–6, 634, 655; translations in the later periods 334–6, 701–3, 738–46, 758, 760, 773
Trinity, doctrine of 107, 185, 319, 380, 384, 387, 395, 638, 704
Tritheism 379, 387–8
Ṭur ʿAbdin 70–1, 83, 95–6, 98, 100, 125, 248–50, 254, 345, 348, 361, 370, 400, 478, 526, 533, 547, 568, 573–4, 576, 720–3, 727, 773, 776, 778, 808, 812
Turfan 7, 142, 448, 451, 591, 594–600, 602, 608, 613–14, 637
Turkic tribes and language 26, 583, 586–8, 591, 594, 602–5, 607–13, 625, 637–8, 640–1, 644, 721, 723, 792
Ṭuroyo 266, 271–6, 278, 280, 282–3, 779, 818

Uighur 122, 126, 261, 451, 584, 591, 594, 598, 600, 602, 607–9, 611–12, 638–40, 710, 729, 792
Umayyad 179–85, 187, 190–2, 197–8, 248, 411, 570, 575–7, 588
Urfa *see* Edessa, general
Urḥay *see* Edessa, general
Urmia 225, 249, 572, 711, 773–6, 801
Uzbekistan 545, 583–5, 588, 591, 594

Van, lake 225, 269, 720
Vatican *see* papacy
vocalisation 58, 216–17, 235, 258–60, 302, 690, 756, 760, 762–6

Widmanstetter, Johann Albrecht 261, 751–2, 754, 760, 764

xenodocheion 24, 95, 100, 441, 449
Xi'an Stele 7, 586, 587–9, 625–36, 644

Yahballaha I, catholicos 26, 584, 608–10
Yahballaha III, catholicos 126, 198, 586, 606–10, 637–8, 640–1, 645, 705, 710, 719, 723, 725–6, 800–1
Yazdbozid 588, 626, 633, 635–6
Yazdgerd I, shah of Persia 37, 82, 121, 136, 142–3, 406, 413
Yazdgerd II, shah of Persia 26, 37–8, 82, 98, 136
Yazdgerd III, shah of Persia 40–1, 587, 633
Yuan Dynasty, China 605, 613–14, 625, 637–8, 640, 643–5

Zeno, emperor 22, 111, 121, 123, 299, 383
Zoroastrianism 3, 20, 30, 34–40, 77, 82, 91, 94, 99, 137–43, 150, 189–91, 217, 343, 347–8, 360, 407, 470, 591, 594, 602, 604, 634, 636, 653, 664, 666–8

Zeitfracht Medien GmbH
Ferdinand-Jühlke-Straße 7,
99095 - DE, Erfurt
produktsicherheit@zeitfracht.de

FSC
www.fsc.org
MIX
Papier | Fördert
gute Waldnutzung
FSC® C083411